From its very beginnings, psychoanalysis has had an uneasy, even mistrustful, relationship to philosophy. Recognizing that they are interested in many overlapping issues, practitioners of both disciplines are dubious of both the methods and the conclusions of the other; the result is that opportunities for cross-fertilization are easily overlooked. In this Handbook, Aner Govrin and Tair Caspi create a conversation that aims to capitalize on the potential for mutual enrichment that is possible when psychoanalysts and philosophers carefully and respectfully address shared concerns. The editors have assembled a distinguished group of authors; some are psychoanalysts, some philosophers, and many are both. The result is a collection that is sure to engage and inform readers interested in deepening their understanding of some of the most foundational themes of both psychoanalysis and philosophy.

Jay Greenberg, Ph.D., Training and Supervising Analyst, William Alanson White Institute, United States. Former editor of *The Psychoanalytic Quarterly* and recipient of the Mary S. Sigourney Award for Outstanding Achievement in Psychoanalysis, 2015

Freud always thought that psychoanalysis would take over from the philosophy of mind and make it redundant. He seems to have been wrong because Aner Govrin and Tair Caspi, the editors, have collected a significant team of contemporary philosophers from around the world who are still investigating just how the two disciplines compare, contrast, discount each other or can collaborate together. So, what has psychoanalysis done with philosophy and for philosophy, they ask; and also philosophy for psychoanalysis.

There is a landmark quality about this extensive compendium of these two overlapping and penetrating disciplines. These thirty-three Chapters pick out the interacting schools – both philosophical and psychoanalytic – and the multiple philosophical influences on our confusing dispersion of the psychoanalytic schools. This wide-ranging gathering of knowledgeable philosophers and psychoanalysts will tell us, and if they don't, then they give us much to think about for ourselves. It is for reference, frequent reference.

Bob Hinshelwood, Professor Emeritus, University of Essex, UK

Panoramic in scope and scholarly in execution, the Handbook edited by Aner Govrin and Tair Caspi brings together contributions from some of today's leading thinkers across both disciplines, including philosophically-engaged practising psychoanalysts, to present a stimulating overview of contemporary developments. What struck me most about this collection is the multiple ways in which the essays variously bring the old and the established into innovative dialogue with the new and the forward-looking. Traditional giants of philosophy and enduring philosophical themes are here cross-fertilized with traditional giants of post-Freudian and enduring psychoanalytic issues. What emerges is a series of fresh perspectives on important topics on the interface of both disciplines some of these perspectives unfolding in the light of contemporary movements and concerns. There are some real gems amongst these contributions, and I expect that different readers will be rewarded by finding their own different favourites.

I recommend this handbook as a valuable and thought-provoking collection giving a timely snapshot of forward-looking twenty-first-century thinking about the interface between psychoanalysis and philosophy. In my view it will stand the test of time as a significant contribution to demonstrating that psychoanalysis and philosophy simply cannot do without each other.'

Agnes Petocz, PhD, Senior Lecturer, Western Sydney University, Australia. Author of *Freud, Psychoanalysis and Symbolism* (CUP, 1999)

THE ROUTLEDGE INTERNATIONAL HANDBOOK OF PSYCHOANALYSIS AND PHILOSOPHY

The Routledge International Handbook of Psychoanalysis and Philosophy provides a rich panoramic view of what philosophy offers or disturbs in psychoanalysis and what it represents for psychoanalytic theory and practice. The 33 chapters present a broad range of interfaces and reciprocities between various aspects of psychoanalysis and philosophy. The Handbook demonstrates the vital connection between the two disciplines: psychoanalysis cannot make any practical sense if it is not entirely perceived within a philosophical context.

Written by a team of world-leading experts, including established scholars, psychoanalysts, and emerging talents, the Handbook investigates and discusses the psychoanalytic schools and their philosophical underpinning, as well as contemporary applied topics. Organized into five parts, this volume investigates and discusses how psychoanalysis stands in relation to leading philosophies such as Wittgenstein, Heidegger, Nietzsche, and Kant; philosophical perspectives on psychoanalytic schools such as Freud, Klein, Bion, Kohut, and Lacan; and how psychoanalysis addresses controversial topics in philosophy such as truth, language and symbolism, ethics, and theories of mind. The last part addresses contemporary applied subjects in psychoanalytic thought: colonialism, gender, race, and ecology.

This Handbook offers a novel and comprehensive outlook vital for scholars, philosophers, practicing psychoanalysts, and therapists alike. The book will serve as a source for courses in psychoanalysis, philosophy of science, epistemology, ethics, semiotics, cognitive science, consciousness, gender, race, post-colonialism theories, clinical theory, and Freud studies, both in universities and psychoanalytic training programs and institutes.

Aner Govrin, Ph.D., is a philosopher, clinical psychologist, and psychoanalyst. He is the Director of the doctoral track "Psychoanalysis and Hermeneutics" in the Hermeneutics and Cultural Studies program at Bar-Ilan University, Israel. In addition, he is a member of the Tel-Aviv Institute for Contemporary Psychoanalysis (TAICP). He is the editor of the Routledge Introductions to Contemporary Psychoanalysis series and the author of *Ethics and Attachment: How We Make Moral Judgments* (Routledge, 2015) and *Conservative and Radical Perspectives on Psychoanalytic Knowledge: The Fascinated and the Disenchanted* (Routledge, 2019).

Tair Caspi, Ph.D., is a senior clinical psychologist and lecturer in the doctoral program of Hermeneutics and Cultural Studies, Psychoanalysis and Hermeneutics track, Bar-Ilan University. She is also a staff member of the advanced program for psychoanalytic psychotherapy at Tel Aviv University. She is an associate editor of the Routledge Introductions to Contemporary Psychoanalysis series. She is the author of *Metaphors in Psychoanalysis: Reflecting on the Language of Klein, Winnicott, and Ogden* (Resling, 2020). Additionally, she has published several journal articles and book chapters on the intersection between psychoanalysis and the philosophy of language.

THE ROUTLEDGE INTERNATIONAL HANDBOOK SERIES

The Routledge International Handbook of Consumer Psychology
Edited by Cathrine V. Jansson-Boyd, Magdalena J. Zawisza

The Routledge International Handbook of Sandplay Therapy
Edited by Barbara A. Turner

The Routledge International Handbook of Sexual Addiction
Edited by Thaddeus Birchard and Joanna Benfield

The Routledge International Handbook of Forensic Psychology in Secure Settings
Edited by Jane L. Ireland, Carol A. Ireland, Martin Fisher, Neil Gredecki

The Routledge International Handbook of Critical Positive Psychology
Edited by Nicholas J. L. Brown, Tim Lomas, Francisco Jose Eiroa-Orosa

The Routledge International Handbook of Sexual Addiction
Edited by Thaddeus Birchard, Joanna Benfield

The Routledge International Handbook of Self-Control in Health and Well-Being
Edited by Denise de Ridder, Marieke Adriaanse, Kentaro Fujita

The Routledge International Handbook of Psychosocial Epidemiology
Edited by Mika Kivimaki, David G. Batty, Ichiro Kawachi, Andrew Steptoe

The Routledge International Handbook of Human Aggression
Current Issues and Perspectives
Edited by Jane L. Ireland, Philip Birch, Carol A. Ireland

The Routledge International Handbook of Jungian Film Studies
Edited by Luke Hockley

The Routledge International Handbook of Discrimination, Prejudice and Stereotyping
Edited by Cristian Tileagă, Martha Augoustinos and Kevin Durrheim

The Routledge Handbook of Public Health and the Community
Edited by Ben Y. F. Fon and Martin C. S. Wong

The Routledge International Handbook of Perinatal Mental Health Disorders
Edited by Amy Wenzel

The Routledge International Handbook of Community Psychology
Facing Global Crises with Hope
Edited by Carolyn Kagan, Jacqui Akhurst, Jaime Alfaro, Rebecca Lawthom, Michael Richards, and Alba Zambrano

The Routledge International Handbook of Morality, Cognition, and Emotion in China
Edited by Ryan Nichols

The Routledge International Handbook of Comparative Psychology
Edited by Todd M. Freeberg, Amanda R. Ridley and Patrizia d'Ettorre

The Routledge International Handbook of Neuroaesthetics
Edited by Martin Skov and Marcos Nadal

The Routledge International Handbook of Psychoanalysis and Philosophy
Edited by Aner Govrin and Tair Caspi

THE ROUTLEDGE INTERNATIONAL HANDBOOK OF PSYCHOANALYSIS AND PHILOSOPHY

Edited by Aner Govrin and Tair Caspi

Routledge
Taylor & Francis Group
LONDON AND NEW YORK

Cover image: Getty images

First published 2023
by Routledge
4 Park Square, Milton Park, Abingdon, Oxon OX14 4RN

and by Routledge
605 Third Avenue, New York, NY 10158

Routledge is an imprint of the Taylor & Francis Group, an informa business

British Library Cataloguing-in-Publication Data
A catalogue record for this book is available from the British Library

Library of Congress Cataloging-in-Publication Data
Names: Govrin, 'Aner, 1966- editor. | Caspi, Tair, editor.
Title: The Routledge international handbook of psychoanalysis and philosophy / edited by Aner Govrin and Tair Caspi.
Description: Abingdon, Oxon ; New York, NY : Routledge, 2023. | Series: Routledge international handbooks | Includes bibliographical references and index.
Identifiers: LCCN 2022021185 (print) | LCCN 2022021186 (ebook) | ISBN 9780367276454 (hardback) | ISBN 9781032365251 (paperback) | ISBN 9780429297076 (ebook)
Subjects: LCSH: Psychoanalysis and philosophy.
Classification: LCC BF175.4.P45 R695 2023 (print) | LCC BF175.4.P45 (ebook) | DDC 150.19/5—dc23/eng/20220614
LC record available at https://lccn.loc.gov/2022021185
LC ebook record available at https://lccn.loc.gov/2022021186

ISBN: 978-0-367-27645-4 (hbk)
ISBN: 978-1-032-36525-1 (pbk)
ISBN: 978-0-429-29707-6 (ebk)

DOI: 10.4324/9780429297076

Typeset in Bembo
by Apex CoVantage, LLC

CONTENTS

ACKNOWLEDGMENTS

We are very grateful to Tamas Pataki, an extraordinary colleague, friend, and mentor during this journey. We thank the former editors of this book, Susannah Frearson and Alexis O'Brien, and the current editor, Sarah Gore, for their generosity and patience. Finally, we are incredibly grateful to Ed Greenstein and Daniela Dueck, two directors of the Hermeneutics and Cultural Studies program at Bar-Ilan University, for their generous support in our project.

Aner Govrin and Tair Caspi

Our thanks to the following publishers for granting permission to reprint essays for this Handbook:

Cavell, M. (1996). *The Psychoanalytic Mind: From Freud to Philosophy*. Cambridge, MA: Harvard University Press.

Govrin, A. (2019). "Facts and sensibilities: What is a psychoanalytic innovation?" *Frontiers in Psychology, 10,* Article 1781.

Kirshner, L. (2017). *Intersubjectivity in psychoanalysis: A model for theory and practice*. pp. 9–37. Routledge/Taylor & Francis Group.

Loparic, Z. (2010). "From Freud to Winnicott: aspects of a paradigm change." In: Abram, J. (ed.). *Donald Winnicott Today*. pp. 113–156. London: Routledge.

Mills, J. (2000). "Hegel on projective identification: Implications for Klein, Bion, and Beyond." *Psychoanalytic Review*, 87(6):841–874.

Žižek, S. (2004). What can psychoanalysis tell us about cyberspace? *Psychoanalytic Review, 91*(6), 801–830.

FIGURES

CONTRIBUTORS

Adela Abella is a psychiatrist and psychoanalyst for children, adolescents, and adults, as well as a training member of the Swiss psychoanalytical society (SPPsa-SGPsa). She is a former president of the APRF (Association romande des psychanalystes en formation), the CPSR (Centre de psychanalyse de la Suisse Romande) and the ASUPEA (Association suisse pour la psychanalyse des enfants et adolescents). Previously, she was a member of the IPA Culture Committee. Currently, she is a member of the board of the IJP and a reviewer for the *Revista de Psicoanalisis* (Association psychanalytique de Madrid). Her papers focus mainly on the interface of psychoanalysis and the arts, and on interdisciplinary, child, and adolescent psychoanalysis.

Matthew C. Altman is a professor of philosophy at Central Washington University. He is the author of *A Companion to Kant's "Critique of Pure Reason"* (2008), *Kant and Applied Ethics* (2011), and *A Theory of Legal Punishment* (2021); coauthor of *The Fractured Self in Freud and German Philosophy* (2013); editor of *The Palgrave Handbook of German Idealism* (2014) and *The Palgrave Kant Handbook* (2017); and series editor of *Palgrave Handbooks in German Idealism* and *Palgrave Handbooks in the Philosophy of Law*. He has also published numerous articles on the history of philosophy, applied ethics, and the philosophy of law.

Dana Amir is a professor at Haifa University, a clinical psychologist, a supervising and training analyst at the Israel psychoanalytic society, head of the interdisciplinary doctoral program in psychoanalysis at Haifa University, and the editor of *Maarag* – the Israel Annual of Psychoanalysis (the Hebrew University). She is also a poetess and literature researcher. She is the author of seven poetry books and four psychoanalytic non-fiction books: *Cleft Tongue* (Karnac, 2014); *On the Lyricism of the Mind* (Routledge, 2016); *Bearing Witness to the Witness* (Routledge, 2018); and *Psychoanalysis on the Verge of Language: Clinical Cases on the Edge* (Routledge, in print). She is the winner of many prizes, including four international psychoanalytic awards: the Frances Tustin International Memorial Prize (2011); the IPA (International Psychoanalytic Association) Sacerdoti Prize (2013); the IPA Hayman Prize (2017); and the IFPE (International Forum of Psychoanalytic Education) Distinguished Psychoanalytic Educators Award (2017). In 2020, she won the Outstanding Senior Researcher Award of the University of Haifa.

Simon Boag is an associate professor in psychology at Macquarie University. He has published numerous articles on the philosophy of psychoanalysis and is the author of *Metapsychology and the Foundations of Psychoanalysis* (Routledge, 2017) and *Freudian Repression, the Unconscious, and the Dynamics of Inhibition* (Routledge, 2012). He has also co-edited volumes including *Psychoanalysis and Philosophy of Mind* (Routledge, 2015) and *Philosophy, Science, and Psychoanalysis* (Routledge, 2015).

Linda A. W. Brakel, M.D., is an adjunct associate professor in psychiatry and a faculty research associate in philosophy at the University of Michigan. She is a faculty member of the Michigan Psychoanalytic Institute and has practiced psychoanalysis for almost 40 years. Her empirical research has centered on the independent measure of primary process mentation. She has co-authored three volumes and authored/co-authored many articles. She is also the solo author of four books – these at the intersection of psychoanalytic theory and philosophy: *Philosophy, Psychoanalysis and the A-Rational Mind* (Oxford, 2009); *Unconscious Knowing and Other Essays in Psycho-Philosophical Analysis* (Oxford, 2010); *The Ontology of Psychology* (Routledge, 2013); and *Investigations Into the Trans Self and Moore's Paradox* (Palgrave, 2020)

Tair Caspi, Ph.D., is a senior clinical psychologist and lecturer in the doctoral program of Hermeneutics and Cultural Studies, Psychoanalysis and Hermeneutics track, Bar-Ilan University. She is also a staff member of the advanced program for psychoanalytic psychotherapy at Tel Aviv University. She is an associate editor of the Routledge Introductions to Contemporary Psychoanalysis series. Caspi has published several journal articles and book chapters on the intersection between psychoanalysis and philosophy of language. Caspi's monograph *Metaphors in Psychoanalysis: Reflecting on the Language of Klein, Winnicott, and Ogden* was published in 2020 by Resling Publishing, Israel.

Marcia Cavell received her Ph.D. in philosophy from Harvard University and has taught at several colleges and universities, including the University of California at Berkeley, the New School in New York City, and for the longest time at the State University of New York, College at Purchase, from which she is Professor Emeritus. She was also a special candidate at the Columbia Institute for Training and Research and a CORST graduate of the San Francisco Institute of Psychoanalysis. She is the author of numerous articles published in both philosophic and psychoanalytic journals, and of two books: *The Psychoanalytic Mind, from Freud to Philosophy* (Harvard University Press, 1993) and *Becoming a Subject, Reflections in Philosophy and Psychoanalysis* (Clarendon Press, 2006).

Graham S. Clarke, Ph.D., took a first degree in architecture at the Bartlett School of Architecture, UCL, and an MSc in the applications of computing at the University of North London, and he worked in computing for some years. Clarke started work at the University of Essex as a computer officer in the Department of Computer Science. He took an MSc in psychoanalytic studies at the Tavistock Clinic and later a Ph.D. on the work of Ronald Fairbairn in psychoanalytic studies at the University of Essex. Since 2005 he has been a visiting fellow in the Department of Psychosocial and Psychoanalytic Studies. Clarke has published a number of journal papers and two books on Fairbairn – *Personal Relations Theory* (Routledge, 2006) and *Thinking Through Fairbairn* (Routledge, 2018) – and has been lead editor on *Fairbairn and the Object Relations Tradition* (Karnac, 2014).

Joseph Dodds, Ph.D., is a psychoanalyst with the Czech Psychoanalytical Society (IPA); a chartered psychologist (CPsychol) of the British Psychological Society; a psychotherapist (UKCP,

CAP); a clinical Fellow of the International Neuropsychoanalysis Society; and a senior lecturer in psychology at the University of New York in Prague and the Anglo-American University. He is the author of the book *Psychoanalysis and Ecology at the Edge of Chaos: Complexity Theory, Deleuze/Guattari, and Psychoanalysis for a Climate in Crisis* (Routledge, 2011) and other papers on psychoanalytic approaches to art, film, neuroscience, society, and climate change.

Ed Erwin is a professor of philosophy at the University of Miami. He is the author of *A Final Accounting: Philosophical and Empirical Issues in Freudian Psychology* (MIT Press, 1996); *Philosophy and Psychotherapy: Razing the Troubles of the Brain* (Sage, 1997); *Behavior Therapy: Scientific, Philosophical and Moral Foundations* (2010); Cambridge University Press [first edition, 1978]; and the editor of *The Freud Encyclopedia: Theories, Therapy, and Culture* (Routledge, 2002).

Roger Frie is Professor of Education at Simon Fraser University; Affiliate Professor of Psychiatry at the University of British Columbia in Vancouver; and Faculty and Supervisor at the William Alanson White Institute of Psychiatry, Psychoanalysis, and Psychology and Associate Member of the Columbia University Seminar on Cultural Memory in New York. He is an academic historian and philosopher, as well as a psychoanalyst and psychologist in private practice. He has published numerous interdisciplinary books and is the author most recently of the award-winning book *Not in My Family: German Memory and Responsibility After the Holocaust* (Oxford University Press, 2017). He is an editorial board member of *Contemporary Psychoanalysis, Psychoanalytic Discourse*, and *Psychoanalytic Psychology* and is a former editor of *Psychoanalysis, Self and Context.*

Shai Frogel, Ph.D., is Associate Professor of philosophy, Kibbutzim College of Education and Tel Aviv University, as well as an interdisciplinary member of Tel Aviv Institute for Contemporary Psychoanalysis (TAICP). He is the author of the books *The Rhetoric of Philosophy, Rhetoric* (Hebrew), *Ethics: Spinoza and Nietzsche* (Hebrew), and *Philosophical Chats* (Hebrew). His recent papers include "Descartes: Truth and Self-Deception" (*Philosophy*); "Understanding Kant's Ethics" (*Essays in the Philosophy of Humanism*); "The Will to Truth, the Death Drive and the Will to Power" (*American Journal of Psychoanalysis*); and "Either Religion or Ethics" (*Kierkegaard and Issues in Contemporary Ethics*).

Stephen Frosh is a professor in the Department of Psychosocial Studies at Birkbeck, University of London. He was pro-vice-master of Birkbeck from 2003 to 2017. He has a background in academic and clinical psychology and was consultant clinical psychologist and latterly vice dean at the Tavistock Clinic, London, throughout the 1990s, specializing in family and individual psychotherapy with children and young people. He is a Fellow of the Academy of Social Sciences, an Academic Associate of the British Psychoanalytical Society, a Founding Member of the Association of Psychosocial Studies, and an Honorary Member of the Institute of Group Analysis. Frosh is the author of many books and papers on psychosocial studies and on psychoanalysis. His books include *Hauntings: Psychoanalysis and Ghostly Transmissions* (2013); *Feelings* (2011); *A Brief Introduction to Psychoanalytic Theory* (2012); *Psychoanalysis Outside the Clinic* (2010); *Hate and the Jewish Science: Anti-Semitism, Nazism and Psychoanalysis* (2005); *For and Against Psychoanalysis* (2006); *After Words* (2002); *The Politics of Psychoanalysis* (1999); *Sexual Difference* (1994); and *Identity Crisis* (1991). His most recent book is *Those Who Come After: Postmemory, Acknowledgement and Forgiveness*, published by Palgrave in 2019.

Aner Govrin, Ph.D., is a philosopher, clinical psychologist, and psychoanalyst. He is the Director of the doctoral track "Psychoanalysis and Hermeneutics" in the Hermeneutics and Cultural

Studies program at Bar-Ilan University, Israel. In addition, he is a member of the Tel-Aviv Institute for Contemporary Psychoanalysis (TAICP). He is the editor of two book series: Narkisus: Psychoanalysis, Philosophy and Society (Resling Publishing House, Hebrew) and Routledge Introductions to Contemporary Psychoanalysis. Among his books are *Ethics and Attachment: How We Make Moral Judgments* (Routledge, 2015) and *Conservative and Radical Perspectives on Psychoanalytic Knowledge: The Fascinated and the Disenchanted* (Routledge, 2019).

Jill Gentile, Ph.D., is a faculty member at the New York University postdoctoral program in psychotherapy and psychoanalysis. She is currently an associate editor for *Psychoanalytic Dialogues* and *Studies in Gender and Sexuality*, and is on the editorial boards of *Contemporary Psychoanalysis, Psychoanalysis, Self, and Context*, and (formerly) *Journal of the American Psychoanalytic Association*. She was awarded the 2017 Gradiva Award for her essay "What Is Special About Speech?" and the 2021 JAPA prize for "Time May Change Us: The Strange Temporalities, Novel Paradoxes, and Democratic Imaginaries of a Pandemic." Her book *Feminine Law: Freud, Free Speech, and the Voice of Desire*, with Michael Macrone (Karnac, 2016), explores psychoanalysis as a practice of emancipatory democracy through the lenses of freedom of speech and the feminine. She maintains a clinical practice in New York.

Uri Hadar is a professor of psychology at Tel Aviv University (emeritus) and the Ruppin Academic Center, where he was head of the MA program in clinical geropsychology. He studied for his Ph.D. at the University of London. His research fields include psychoanalysis, nonverbal communication, and the cerebral representation of natural language. He engaged in both empirical and theoretical research in these fields and has published widely on these issues. His three books discuss psychoanalytic psychotherapy from the perspective of integrating Lacanian and Relational approaches.

Charles Hanly is a psychoanalyst in private practice, a training analyst at the Toronto Institute of Psychoanalysis, and Professor Emeritus (philosophy) at the University of Toronto. Hanly is the author of four books and many theoretical and applied papers in journals and books. He served two terms (2009–2013) as president of the International Psychoanalytical Association.

Edward Harcourt is Professor and Fellow at Keble College Oxford since 2005; his research lies in moral psychology and on the boundaries between ethics and the philosophy of mind. He has published on topics including neo-Aristotelianism and child development; the ethical dimensions of psychoanalysis; love and the virtues; Nietzsche's ethics; the philosophy of mental health and mental illness; literature and philosophy; and Wittgenstein. From 2010 to 2015 he convened the *Meaning and Mindedness: Encounters Between Philosophy and Psychoanalysis* seminars at the Tavistock Clinic, London. He has been principal investigator of the AHRC network 'The Development of Character: Attachment Theory and the Moral Psychology of Vice and Virtue' and of the Wellcome ISSF project 'Therapeutic Conflicts: Co-producing Meaning in Mental Health'. He is a director of Mind, Value, and Mental Health: The Oxford Summer Schools in Philosophy and Psychiatry, and is currently on secondment to the UKRI Arts and Humanities Research Council as Director of Research, Strategy and Innovation.

Lewis Kirshner is a member of the Boston Psychoanalytic Institute and a training and supervising analyst. From 2014 to 2016 he served as clinical professor of psychiatry, Harvard Medical School. He is currently a corresponding member of the faculty. From 1998 to 2004 he was an affiliate professor in the Department of Clinical Psychology, Université Lyon 2, France. He is the author of three books: *Having a Life: Self Pathology After Lacan* (Routledge, 2004); *Between Winnicott and Lacan: A Clinical Encounter* (Routledge, 2012); and *Intersubjectivity in Psychoanalysis*

(Routledge, 2017). He has authored 30 peer-reviewed articles on intersubjectivity, the self, philosophic contributions, and semiotic approaches to psychoanalysis. He has also authored eight chapters in edited books.

Zeljko Loparic is an emeritus professor of philosophy at the University of Campinas (Unicamp), São Paulo. With Elsa Oliveira Dias, he founded the Brazilian Society of Winnicottian Psychoanalysis (2005). In 2013 he created the International Winnicott Association (IWA) and was elected its first president. The following year, he coordinated and taught the Sino-Brazilian Training Course on Winnicottian Psychoanalysis at the Huilongguan Psychiatric Hospital in Beijing. He is the founder of the Brazilian Institute of Winnicottian Psychoanalysis (2015), which in 2017 initiated a full four-year training course in Winnicottian psychoanalysis at the Beijing Mental Health Centre. His publications include the books (in Portuguese) *Heidegger Defendant* (1990), *Ethics and Finitude* (1995), *Heuristic Descartes* (1997), *Kant's Transcendental Semantics* (2000), *On Responsibility* (2003), *Heidegger* (2004), *Winnicott and Jung* (2014), as well as numerous papers in journals and collective volumes on general philosophy of science (Carnap, Kuhn), history of philosophy (Descartes, Kant, Heidegger), and philosophy and the history of psychoanalysis (Freud, Winnicott).

Jon Mills, PsyD, Ph.D., ABPP, is a philosopher, psychoanalyst, and clinical psychologist. He is on faculty, postgraduate programs in psychoanalysis and psychotherapy, Gordon F. Derner School of Psychology, Adelphi University; Emeritus Professor of Psychology and Psychoanalysis at Adler Graduate Professional School in Toronto; and runs a mental health corporation in Ontario. He is the recipient of numerous awards for his scholarship, including four Gradiva Awards. He is the author and editor of over 25 books in psychoanalysis, philosophy, psychology, and cultural studies, including *Debating Relational Psychoanalysis: Jon Mills and His Critics* (Routledge, 2020); *Inventing God* (Routledge, 2017); *Underworlds: Philosophies of the Unconscious From Psychoanalysis to Metaphysics* (Routledge, 2014); *Conundrums: A Critique of Contemporary Psychoanalysis* (Routledge, 2012); *Origins: On the Genesis of Psychic Reality* (McGill-Queens University Press, 2010); *Treating Attachment Pathology* (Rowman & Littlefield, 2005); *The Unconscious Abyss: Hegel's Anticipation of Psychoanalysis* (State University of New York Press, 2002); and *The Ontology of Prejudice* (Rodopi, 1997). In 2015 he was given the Otto Weininger Memorial Award for Lifetime Achievement by the Canadian Psychological Association.

Leonardo Niro, Ph.D., is a lecturer at the Department of Psychosocial and Psychoanalytic Studies, University of Essex, where he is Course Director of the MA in psychoanalytic studies and coordinator of the Research Group in History of Psychoanalysis. His research focuses on topics related to the history and philosophy of psychoanalysis and the psy-disciplines (psychology, psychiatry, psychotherapy, neuroscience). In his current work, he establishes historical and conceptual links between psychoanalysis and the biological sciences.

Georg Northoff is a philosopher, neuroscientist, and psychiatrist, holding degrees in all three disciplines. Originally from Germany, he is now working in Ottawa, where he holds a Canada Research Chair for Mind, Brain Imaging, and Neuroethics. His research focuses on the relationship between brain and mind in its various facets, including neuroscience, psychiatry, and philosophy. He is interested in discovering the neuronal mechanisms related to consciousness and self in both healthy subjects and psychiatric disorders like depression and schizophrenia. The question driving him is: why and how can our brain construct subjective phenomena like self, consciousness, emotions. He is one of the leading figures in linking philosophy and neuroscience, as well as the founder of non-reductive neurophilosophy. He authored more than 270 journal articles and 15 books which are translated into several languages, including *Neuro-philosophy and the Healthy Mind* (Norton, 2016), which is also translated into several languages including Italian (Cortina 2019).

Michael Oppenheim is a distinguished professor emeritus in the Department of Religions and Cultures at Concordia University, Montreal. His teaching and research are in the areas of modern Jewish philosophy, Judaism in the modern period, philosophy of religion, and psychology of religion. His most recent books are *Trust and Trauma: An Interdisciplinary Study in Human Nature* (Routledge, 2021) and *Contemporary Psychoanalysis and Modern Jewish Philosophy: Two Languages of Love* (Routledge, 2017).

Tamas Pataki, Ph.D., is honorary senior fellow with the School of Historical and Philosophical Studies, University of Melbourne. He is editor, with Michael P. Levine, of *Racism in Mind* (Cornell University Press) and the author of *Against Religion* (Scribe Publications), *Wish-fulfilment in Philosophy and Psychoanalysis* (Routledge), and several journal articles and book chapters on the philosophy of mind, action theory, and religion.

John Hanwell Riker, Ph.D., has been a professor of philosophy at Colorado College for over half a century, where he has been named professor of the year a record four times, advisor of the year a record three times, and the initial recipient of the award recognizing someone who most promotes diversity and inclusion on campus. He has written four books intersecting psychoanalysis and ethics, including the recent *Why It Is Good to Be Good: Ethics, Kohut's Self Psychology and Modern Society* and *Exploring the Life of the Soul: Philosophical Reflections on Psychoanalysis and Self Psychology*.

Jared Russell, Ph.D., is a psychoanalyst in private clinical practice in New York City. He is a Fellow of the International Psychoanalytic Association and a faculty member and clinical supervisor at several analytic training institutes. He is the author of *Nietzsche and the Clinic: Psychoanalysis, Philosophy, Metaphysics* (Routledge, 2016) and *Psychoanalysis and Deconstruction: Freud's Psychic Apparatus* (Routledge, 2019).

Michael Rustin is a professor of sociology at the University of East London, and a visiting professor at the Tavistock and Portman NHS Trust. He is an Associate of the British Psychoanalytical Society. He has published widely on the interrelations between psychoanalysis, culture, and society. His books include *The Good Society and the Inner World* (1991); *Narratives of Love and Loss: Studies in Modern Children's Fiction* (with Margaret Rustin, 1987 and 2001); *Mirror to Nature: Drama Psychoanalysis and Society* (with Margaret Rustin, 2002); *Reason and Unreason: Psychoanalysis, Science and Politics,* (2001); *The Inner World of Doctor Who* (with Iain McRury, 2014); *Social Defences Against Anxiety: Explorations in a Paradigm* (edited with David Armstrong, 2014); *Reading Klein* (with Margaret Rustin, 2017); *Researching the Unconscious* (2020); and *New Discoveries in Child Psychotherapy* (edited with Margaret Rustin, 2020).

Robert A. Segal is Sixth Century Chair in Religious Studies at the University of Aberdeen, Honorary Professor at the University of Essex, and Professorial Research Fellow at the University of Vienna. He writes and teaches on theories of myth and theories of religion and on Gnosticism. Among the books that he has written or edited are *The Poimandres as Myth* (Mouton de Gruyter, 1986); *Joseph Campbell* (1987, rev. Penguin 1990); *In Quest of the Hero* (Princeton, 1990); *Explaining and Interpreting Religion* (Peter Lang, 1992); *The Gnostic Jung* (Princeton and Blackwell, 1992); *The Myth and Ritual Theory* (Blackwell, 1998); *Jung on Mythology* (Princeton and Routledge, 1998); *Theorizing about Myth* (University of Massachusetts Press, 1999); *Hero Myths* (Blackwell, 2000); *Myth: A Very Short Introduction* (Oxford, 2004, rev. 2015); *Vocabulary for the Study of Religion* (3 vols., Brill, 2015); *Myth Analyzed* (Routledge, 2021); and *Wiley-Blackwell Companion to the Study of Religion* (2006, second ed. 2021).

Robert D. Stolorow is a Founding Faculty Member at the Institute of Contemporary Psychoanalysis, Los Angeles, and at the Institute for the Psychoanalytic Study of Subjectivity, New York. Absorbed for more than five decades in the project of rethinking psychoanalysis as a form of phenomenological inquiry, he is the author of *World, Affectivity, Trauma: Heidegger and Post-Cartesian Psychoanalysis* (Routledge, 2011) and *Trauma and Human Existence: Autobiographical, Psychoanalytic, and Philosophical Reflections* (Routledge, 2007), and is the coauthor of nine other books, including most recently *The Power of Phenomenology* (Routledge, 2018). He received his Ph.D. in clinical psychology from Harvard in 1970 and his Ph.D. in philosophy from the University of California, Riverside, in 2007.

Alfred I. Tauber, Professor of Philosophy, Emeritus, and Zoltan Kohn Professor of Medicine, Emeritus at Boston University, has published extensively on the theoretical development of immunology, contemporary science studies, and medical ethics. His philosophical critiques of psychoanalysis and Freud's contemporary significance include *Freud, the Reluctant Philosopher* (Princeton, 2010) and *Requiem for the Ego. Freud and the Origins of Postmodernism* (Stanford, 2013).

Shlomit Yadlin-Gadot, Ph.D., is a clinical psychologist and psychoanalyst at the Tel Aviv Institute of Contemporary Psychoanalysis (TAICP). She teaches and supervises in TAICP, in the General Humanities Studies and the Doctoral and Psychotherapy tracks in the School of Psychotherapy, Sackler School of Medicine, Tel-Aviv University. She writes and lectures on the interface of psychoanalysis, philosophy, and cultural studies. She is the author of the book *Truth Matters: Theory and Practice in Psychoanalysis* (Brill, 2016). She lives and practices in Ramat-Hasharon, Israel.

Slavoj Žižek, a Slovenian philosopher and cultural theorist, a researcher at the Department of Philosophy of the University of Ljubljana, Faculty of Arts, and international director of the Birkbeck Institute of Humanities of the University of London. He is also a Global Eminent Scholar at Kyung Hee University in Seoul and a Global Distinguished Professor of German at New York University. Among his publications are *Iraq: The Borrowed Kettle* (Verso, 2004); *Organs Without Bodies: On Deleuze and Consequences* (Routledge, 2003); *The Puppet and the Dwarf* (Routledge, 2003); *Did Somebody Say Totalitarianism? Five Essays on the (Mis)Use of a Notion* (Verso, 2001); *The Fright of Real Tears, Kieslowski and The Future* (Indiana University Press, 2001); *On Belief* (Routledge, 2001); *The Fragile Absolute, or Why the Christian Legacy Is Worth Fighting For* (Verso, 2000); *The Art of the Ridiculous Sublime, On David Lynch's Lost Highway* (Walter Chapin Center for the Humanities: University of Washington, 2000); *Contingency, Hegemony, Universality: Contemporary Dialogues on the Left* (with Judith Butler and Ernesto Laclau; Verso, 2000); *Enjoy Your Symptom! Jacques Lacan in Hollywood and Out* (2nd ed., Routledge, 2000); *The Ticklish Subject: The Absent Centre of Political Ontology* (Verso, 1999); *The Abyss of Freedom Ages of the World* (with F.W.J. von Schelling, University of Michigan Press, 1997); *The Plague of Fantasies* (Verso, 1997); *Gaze and Voice as Love Objects* (with Renata Salecl; Duke University Press, 1996); *The Indivisible Remainder: An Essay on Schelling and Related Matters* (Verso, 1996); *The Metastases of Enjoyment: Six Essays on Woman and Causality (Wo Es War)* (Verso, 1994); and *Mapping Ideology* (Verso, 1994).

INTRODUCTION

Aner Govrin

The *Routledge International Handbook of Psychoanalysis and Philosophy* is about what psychoanalysis has done to and with philosophy and what it has done for philosophy. It provides a rich panoramic view of what philosophy offers or disturbs psychoanalysis and what it represents for psychoanalytic theory and practice. The book's 33 chapters present a broad range of interfaces and reciprocities between various aspects of psychoanalysis and philosophy. It shows that psychoanalysis cannot make any practical sense if it is not entirely immersed with philosophy.

Among the issues it addresses are questions like: How do psychoanalysis and other philosophical systems such as Hegel's, Wittgenstein's, or Nietzsche's interrelate? What are the philosophical foundations of psychoanalytic schools? What kind of truth does psychoanalysis stand for? What are the ethical implications of psychoanalysis? What can psychoanalysis contribute to understanding social phenomena and the climate crisis?

In turning its attention to these subjects, this volume does not take one single approach. It wants to offer the reader an encounter with the wealth and complexity of the many interrelations between psychoanalysis and philosophy, and some of the fascinating questions this engagement produces. Included are chapters by some of today's leading scholars – professional philosophers and psychoanalysts – who are investigating topics like truth perception, epistemology, ethics, philosophy of science, colonialism, and feminism. While some chapters in this collection look at how philosophical theories have informed psychoanalysis, others, conversely, discuss the impact psychoanalysis has had on the various fields of philosophy. Some attempt to clarify the philosophical status of a key psychoanalytic concept. Others examine the epistemological underpinnings of psychoanalysis. Yet, others shed light on how psychoanalysis has contributed to certain social phenomena.

The reciprocities between theory and practice constitute a central motif throughout the book. Contributors, alongside philosophers, therefore also include practicing clinicians, some of whom identify with a specific approach; others take an interdisciplinary perspective, while others are mainly involved in research. What they all share is a powerfully interdisciplinary orientation.

Through this Handbook, we hope to demonstrate that psychoanalysis' engagement with philosophy is not merely technical, marginal, and narrow in scope: it is essential to all its most central tenets. Not only does psychoanalysis require an external worldview (Freud, 1933); it needs such a worldview in its profound sense to make claims about the world.

DOI: 10.4324/9780429297076-1

But before setting out on a brief description of the chapters, I will first take some time to dwell on the points of contact and difference between these two disciplines and draw a broad frame of reference to accompany the reading of this book.

Any thinking about the relations between psychoanalysis and philosophy involves clashing ideas, emotions, and associations. In this short introduction, I will try to discuss some pre-existing opinions that might get in the way of enriching our sensibilities to the profound affinities of these two disciplines. Taking into account the various branches of philosophy and the engagements between philosophy and other bodies of knowledge, we may want to think of these interrelations from two possible perspectives:

1 Psychoanalysis is an autonomous and separate science, and its relation with philosophy resembles the relations the latter entertains with other domains, like physics, chemistry, social science, or literary criticism.
2 Psychoanalysis is a branch of philosophy: each and every thought or statement it produces is replete with philosophical axioms; like other branches of philosophy, such as phenomenology, existentialism, or the complex philosophical theories of Hegel, Nietzsche, and others, it directs itself to such problems as the human mind, freedom of choice, motivation, ethics, consciousness, the unconscious, and so on.

I would like to suggest that neither of these possibilities as such is adequate and that a third possibility might be what we have to think of: while psychoanalysis and philosophy are essentially and mutually embedded, they exist, at the same time, somewhat apart. This is mainly due to how psychoanalysts' professional identities evolved and our mental inclination to discipline-based categorizations based on group identities.

In one view, indeed, philosophical discussions of any academic subject are an early phase in the scientific study of that subject. Philosophy by this approach features as a form of protoscience on the basis of which any science subsequently develops. Hence, William James defined philosophy as "a collective name for questions that have not yet been answered to the satisfaction of all by whom they have been asked" (1979/1911, 23). Elsewhere, James suggests how we may identify the point in a discipline's evolution when it becomes autonomous: "As fast as questions got accurately answered, the answers were called 'scientific,' and what men call 'philosophy' today is but the residuum of questions still unanswered" (James, 1979/1911, 12).

It is not hard to see that this type of phenomenon – consisting of an early and immature stage of fusion followed by development and a separation process in the direction of autonomy – never took place in the case of philosophy and psychoanalysis. Psychoanalysis was conceived as a scientific discipline in its own right from the outset and never saw itself as part of philosophy. There was, therefore, nothing to split off from. But, in addition to the fact that what we are looking at is not the regular evolution of a scientific discipline from its philosophical beginnings, there are also indications that psychoanalysis never attained this kind of autonomy. When clearly demarcated intellectual domains are properly separated, experts in both fields will accept and respect each other's authority. Philosophers, for instance, usually avoid solving problems in physics by using their own logical or other conceptual apparatus, ignoring the existence of experimental physics. Nor will physicists, from their side, trespass into philosophy without thoroughly informing themselves of the conceptual and methodological ABC of philosophy. Such boundaries and distinctions are also observed in the softer social sciences – sociology, anthropology, and social work.

Psychology became an autonomous science in the 19th century with the inception of psychological experiments. In time, cognition and memory moreover grew into key psychological domains. Once computer science began to produce knowledge about the structure of concepts or cognitive processes, philosophy lost some of its critical areas to the new science.

But psychoanalysis and philosophy find themselves on rather a different footing. Psychoanalysis never appropriated or took over any intellectual territory, ousting philosophy. There is a rich philosophical oeuvre addressing the emotions, personality, the structure of the mind, consciousness, and knowledge, which neither relies on psychoanalysis nor refers to it. The same goes for psychoanalysis, some of whose core issues like psychic conflict or sexual drives remain completely foreign to mainstream philosophy.

One reason why psychoanalysis was never recognized as an autonomous branch, or an independent science, was that the body of knowledge it generated was never granted scientific status. This is illustrated by the pointed criticism it received during a symposium organized by Sidney Hook in 1958 (Hook, 1959). Philosophers on this occasion made painstaking and systematic efforts to show that the claims of psychoanalysis could not be taken seriously and that it did not meet the minimal requirements for being, in the usual sense, a scientific theory. Freudian hypotheses were deemed too vague to be subjected to empirical testing, there were no criteria for evaluating evidence, and the therapeutic efficacy of the method was questionable.

In the wake of this symposium, the critique of psychoanalysis almost grew into a research domain in its own right within philosophy, with leading philosophers like Karl Popper and Adolf Grünbaum taking a prominent part. In the eyes of the philosophers, one of the greatest sins of psychoanalysis was that it lacked conceptual clarity and tightness. Often using the same philosophical terms for different concepts, or vice versa, as well as deploying a range of concepts that could only be validated within their own terms, psychoanalysis produced a virtual Babel. For Wittgenstein,

> psychoanalysis essentially imposes interpretations rather than unfolding them as it claims. According to Wittgenstein, a psychoanalytic interpretation essentially involves a mythlike (that is, predetermined) explanation imposed on a mental state that reduces it to something familiar and common. Nevertheless, the assent of the person involved is the criterion of correctness. There is a fundamental tension here, for once the mental state has been identified, its correct explanation would seem to be given by the mythology applied, yet the assent or nonassent of the patient is supposed to be dispositive. It would be fair to say of Wittgenstein, I think, that for him, psychoanalysis is a kind of crude religion, one that does not even realize that that is what it is.
>
> *(Levy, 1996, 2)*

But paradoxically, this lack of clarity in its conceptual make-up only serves to bolster the connection between psychoanalysis and philosophy further. After all, the thinking of many philosophers is hard to understand, vague, and open to interpretation. The very quality of psychoanalysis that received such opprobrium from (positivist) philosophers is what is a major similarity and connection between it and philosophy (those branches, that is, which the positivists shrugged off as metaphysics).

This leaves us with the second question: why is psychoanalysis not considered a branch of philosophy?

Any attempt to answer this question runs into even more obstacles. First, it is hard to find anything philosophy addresses – ontology, reality, the soul, consciousness, truth, logic, ethics, free will, causality, knowledge, cognition, and language – that does not directly communicate with core issues in psychoanalysis. The two disciplines discuss the same topics to subject them to rational investigation. Philosophers' own definitions of their discipline even tend to identify their main concerns as overlapping with those of psychoanalysis. Theodore Lipps, for example, argued in the first half of the 19th century that "logic is a psychological discipline, as certain as the cognition occurs only in the psyche, and the thinking, which completes itself in the cognition, is a psychical event" (Dale, 2006, 88).

Lipps believed that philosophy is psychology or the science of inner experience, so philosophy should be considered part of the natural sciences. Other, more conventional definitions that identify between philosophy and science (Descartes, Hobbes, and Bacon) indicate the near absolute identity between the two disciplines. The same can be observed for approaches like Hegel's that consider philosophy the "science of principles". Many philosophers, moreover, like Nietzsche, Schopenhauer, Spinoza, Hegel, Kant, Heidegger, Husserl, and Sartre, developed detailed theories of the psyche, covering all its functions: perception, memory, emotions, development, adults-children relations, the perception of time, consciousness of self and society, and so on. It is difficult to fully keep apart from their philosophical investigations of psychological theories of the human psyche and behavior. However, Freud made his name as a psychoanalyst, not as a philosopher like Nietzsche, Schopenhauer, or Heidegger.

One possible way of understanding this is in reference to the fact that these disciplines both have different aims and achieve them using different methods. Psychoanalysis, indeed, is not only about an account or mapping of the human mind or psyche but also offers a method that seeks to alleviate individual suffering. Freud's theory, and of every other psychoanalytical approach, is largely devoted to exactly that, psychoanalytic healing. But many philosophical doctrines too suggest ways to heal the psyche (Banicki, 2014; Carlisle & Ganeri, 2010; Peterman, 1992). Almost every philosopher brings together precisely these two pillars of psychoanalysis: a theory of the human psyche and a theory for the healing of that psyche, that is to say, a set of values and principles that hold out a more meaningful life (existentialism), or a more intensely lived life (Nietzsche), or again, a life guided by reason and the regulation of emotions (Spinoza, Kant).

To explain why psychoanalysis is not a branch of philosophy, we might have to consider their respective research methodologies.

Philosophy has traditionally employed specific methodologies, including the systematic use of counterexamples, precise definitions, and logical analysis of the validity of arguments.

While philosophy relies on these, we might suppose that psychoanalytic knowledge is based on Freud's and his followers' clinical observations. This criterion also soon proves to be more knotty than it seems. First, we know how much any observation is determined by the observer's point of view, feelings, and needs. Second, the psychologies of thinkers like Nietzsche, Schopenhauer, or Hegel, too, refer back to some research object, in an act which we may call "observation", even if this particular kind of observation does not take place in the clinic. Instead, it relies on empirical acquaintance with and perception of human beings, mainly themselves and people encountered. In this argument, every branch of "scientific" thinking is, in fact, philosophy.

Two additional explanations for the separate existence of the two disciplines appear more adequate. A discipline defines and demarcates itself once it outlines a domain within which it aims to exist and operate while simultaneously indicating the group(s) to which it does not belong. This act of mapping is crucial to the discipline's self definition and the way it is publicly perceived. Now, what does and does not belong in the province of the discipline is clearly staked out. Freud and his followers determined these domains.

The first stage of a positive affirmation of identity emerged when psychoanalysis presented itself, early on, as a medical profession. Freud and his followers created a firm professional identity for the psychoanalyst as both physician and scientist. At the same time – and this is the negative corollary of the process of identification – Freud himself sharply criticizes philosophy as such (1933), pointing out its failures and limitations. He affirms very clearly that psychoanalysis is a science. Philosophy, he argues, has not succeeded in giving an account of the human psyche. Psychoanalysis, which he emphatically identifies as a science, produces, by contrast, more adequate and valid theoretical directions.

We can look at how these two reasons fatefully shaped the relations between psychoanalysis and philosophy.

Even though at the start of his studies at age 17, Freud took his initial steps in the direction of philosophy, mainly through the work of Ludwig Feuerbach (Levitt & Turgeon, 2009) and Franz Brentano (Domenjo, 2000) (taking no fewer than five university courses with the latter), began his formal studies at the laboratory of Carl Claus (Cornejo, 2018), one of Darwin's most influential proponents in the German language. Freud's first empirical work involved the sex glands of the eel. This helped Freud develop the patient and accurate examination of a research object into the focused attention which he later brought to bear so effectively when listening to his patients. For the time being, Freud was clearly preparing himself to become a scientist doing laboratory experiments. Next, he moved on to Ernst Brücke, his great mentor, whose laboratory he worked in for six years. Peter Gay, his biographer, describes (1995) how happy Freud was when solving the mysteries of the nervous system – initially that of simple fish, and next of humans. He deeply enjoyed fulfilling his admired teacher's exacting expectations. In 1881, Freud left Brücke's laboratory to take up his medical studies. As part of these studies, he joined the staff of Vienna's General Hospital for three years. He experienced various medical fields, like surgery, internal medicine, psychiatry, dermatology, neurological diseases, and ophthalmology. Freud was clearly heading for a career in medicine rather than philosophy or the humanities. He considered himself a scientist and researcher whose job was to ground each assumption he made in proven evidence.

The fact that Freud departed from philosophy eventually greatly contributed to Freud's (and his followers') professional identity. For many years after Freud's death, this identity grew ever more solid and fixed. In the United States, psychoanalysis was regarded as a branch of medicine for decades. Consequently, training institutes refused to admit candidates without medical training, like psychologists or social workers. This limitation was only removed in the 1980s, in a step that required legal intervention. Starting in Freud's lifetime, the debate around this issue was long-standing in the psychoanalytic community. Interestingly, Freud was adamant about enrolling non–medically trained candidates (see his remarks in the paper on lay psychoanalysis on this). It was one of the very few issues on which many (especially American) psychoanalysts disagreed with Freud.

This identification between medicine and psychoanalysis gave psychoanalysis prestige and respectability, not only among the general public but more specifically in the medical establishment. It seems doubtful whether such a reception would have been possible if psychoanalysis had considered and presented itself as an offshoot of philosophy.

There are, by the way, some interesting cases of philosophers becoming psychiatrists, like Karl Jaspers (1883–1969) and Ludwig Binswanger (1881–1966). Both were major philosophers-psychiatrists affiliated with existentialism who developed their own theories, like psychoanalysis, including psychological theory and an account of the ethically good and meaningful life. However, despite their being influential philosophers, neither gave rise to a community of followers. That two leading philosophers should have emerged from psychiatry suggests nevertheless that if we want to know why psychoanalysis did not end up being considered a branch of philosophy, we should look for a socially contingent component rather than expect to find some inherent feature of psychoanalysis.

Freud flirted with philosophy throughout his life, which inspired much of his thought. However, once he became interested in being a medical doctor, he stayed clear from pure medical research. Still, his lack of taste for certain aspects of philosophy, mainly metaphysics, together with his great admiration for scientific positivism, did not allow him to cross the lines. Freud's ambivalence about the disciplinary relations between psychoanalysis and medicine is reflected in his contribution to a symposium dedicated to the subject (Gay, 1995, 490).

Freud's writings also illustrate that the broad imbrication between psychoanalysis and philosophy was on his mind. He, too, believed psychoanalysis to occupy a place within philosophy, though it was admittedly idiosyncratic. In an early letter to his friend Wilhelm Fliess, Freud admits to "secretly nurs[ing] the hope of arriving by the . . . circuitous route of medicine . . . at my own original, objective philosophy" (1896/1954). In 1925 he wrote how he viewed psychoanalysis as occupying an uneasy "middle position between medicine and philosophy" (1925, 217).

Freud's own trenchant criticism of philosophy is the other reason why psychoanalysis never evolved into a branch of philosophy. His efforts to keep the two disciplines separate were in fact substantial (Freud, 1933) (while, as we saw, he also was averse to identification with medicine). However, we must keep in mind that Freud's critique of philosophy aims more specifically at metaphysics.

Alfred I. Tauber (2010) argued that Freud rejected philosophy because of three weaknesses. First, philosophy represents comprehensive knowledge unresponsive to new empirical findings, which reduces it to an armchair theory. Moreover, philosophy is hermetic and limited. Finally, it unduly relies on non-scientific knowledge.

For Freud, psychoanalysis contrasts with philosophy in the narrow sense of metaphysics. He considers to dedicate itself, like religion, to offering humans the possibility to escape harsh and painful reality into illusion and soothing indifference. Like religion, metaphysics is the outcome of philosophers' desire to create a clean and coherent picture of the world that is far removed from a clear-eyed view of reality (Berthold-Bond, 1989). Psychoanalysis offers a more scientific and realistic perception of a life involving suffering, uncertainty, and the unknown. These are seen as phenomena to which human beings must reconcile themselves. Ironically, Freud's critique of metaphysics reproduces positivism's critique of psychoanalysis.

In "Inhibitions, Symptoms and Anxiety" (1926), Freud describes philosophers as in the business of "fabricating Weltanschauungen", driven by their inability "to make their journey through life without a Baedeker" or "Handbook of Life", which promises to give them answers to all of life's problems. The scathing satire continues to compare the philosopher to a traveler who "may sing aloud in the dark to deny his own fears" but who for all his singing "will not see an inch further beyond his nose" (96).

Freud was not alone in his critique of metaphysics – philosophers like Kant, Nietzsche, and Kierkegaard had also argued against it. Psychoanalytic theory is not a mere replacement of metaphysics; as for analytic philosophers, empiricism is a replacement, but a transformation and hence a recovery of it. Just as Kant did, Freud believes that metaphysical thinking is a natural human disposition. However, according to Berthold-Bond (1989), Freud seeks to account for this metaphysical disposition in terms of his remarkable theory of Freud's distinctive phylogenetic model of man's epistemological evolution. As such, metaphysics cannot simply be removed from the mental makeup of man but must be displaced, transferred, or sublimated into a different mode of knowledge.

We have seen how psychoanalysis cannot be regarded as autonomous and should, in many respects, be considered a branch of philosophy. Its historical development, however, problematizes this. We may compare these intricacies with the nature of family relations: one of the children (i.e., psychoanalysis) has chosen to turn away from the family (i.e., philosophy) in order to find a new family (in the shape of medical and biological science). Perceived as a foreign body and a stepchild, the child does not really fit in with his chosen family.

Yet, still. This comparison only serves us some of the ways. As we know, up until recently, many psychoanalysts liked to see themselves as scientists, much as Freud did. However, recently many wish to see their close connection to poetry. Ogden (1999), for example, describes the relationship between the way the analyst listens to a poem's language and the way the analyst and his patient speak with and listen to one another. Interestingly, it is most unusual to find an analyst that declares an affinity between his profession and philosophy. Psychoanalysts gain their reputation from clinical work or poetic language, not philosophical disputes about truth, free will, and the nature of consciousness.

Like medical doctors, psychoanalysts have patients who they receive in their clinics. The latter, like the former, see it as their task to alleviate patients' suffering and to practice; both have to be certified by the health authorities. While philosophers read, write, and debate, psychoanalysts treat patients (as well as read, write, and debate . . .).

This is the outcome of psychoanalysis leaving its original family, even though it never became fully part of its new family. Still, their strong ties endure.

A necessary and absolute interdependence can be said to exist between psychoanalysis and philosophy. Unable to generate a conceptual foundation of its own, psychoanalysis needs philosophy. When we discuss psychoanalysis, we cannot do it without reference to philosophy since virtually each and every sentence it has generated harks back to and is embedded in philosophy. Over and beyond serving as psychoanalysis' conceptual infrastructure and critically shaping its key assumptions, philosophy also seeps into psychoanalytic theory itself, becoming a constitutive factor.

One illustration of this is the crucial role of positivism in Freud's theory of development. The infant's main developmental achievement is the transition from the pleasure principle – absolute subjectivity – to the reality principle, which yields sensory-based understanding resulting from trial and error. Reality is distinct and separate from the subject. By contrast, theories like those of Winnicott or Kohut, who were not committed to positivism, generated a very different developmental model. Here the infant's most significant developmental achievements occur in a state of absolute subjectivity. The difference obviously has nothing to do with the infants – they stayed the same – but it involves changes in the theoretical, philosophical approach.

Having teased out and brought into view some of the family dynamics, historical and conceptual, between philosophy and psychoanalysis, by way of an introduction to and context for the following collection of chapters, it is high time to turn to these thought-provoking contributions themselves.

Structure of the Book

In the first part of this volume, "Philosophical Traditions and Psychoanalysis", relations and mutual influence between psychoanalysis and philosophers like Kant, Hegel, Nietzsche, and Wittgenstein come under discussion. The influence of psychoanalysis on philosophical traditions like phenomenology, hermeneutics, and positivism is examined. The fact that such a diversity of philosophical approaches has resonated or somehow chimed in with the psychoanalytic discourse testifies to the rich complexity and amplitude of psychoanalysis, though it would only be fair to remind that critics are bound to retort that this is nothing but evidence of its deep fragmentation.

In "Freud's Theory of Freedom: Between Kant's Faith and Schopenhauer's Pessimism," Matthew C. Altman argues that the work of the German Idealists, especially Kant and Schopenhauer, resonates with Sigmund Freud's theories regarding the limits of self-knowledge and the unconscious forces that motivate us. For all three thinkers, we can know ourselves in inner sense only as appearances, but while Schopenhauer and Freud believe that the complex feelings and associations that inform an individual's behavior can be discovered under specific conditions, Kant does not. On the other hand, Freud diverges significantly from Kant and Schopenhauer in developing an ideal of self-determination within a materialist framework: while Kant has practical faith in the possibility of autonomous self-determination and Schopenhauer's lack of belief in autonomy leads to a renunciation of the will, Freud shifts the debate in the direction of achieving limited autonomy. We make sense of ourselves by inserting our thoughts and behaviors into a conscious narrative, and the extent of our freedom is defined by our psychological health. Thus for Freud self-determination is a matter of degree – to what extent is the pursuit of our conscious aims disrupted by unconscious forces – rather than a matter of the absolute extrication of ourselves from a deterministic world, achieved either by means of pure practical reason (Kant) or by renouncing the drives that make us into who we are (Schopenhauer).

In "Hegel's Contributions to Psychoanalysis: Theory of Mind, Dialectics, and Projective Identification," Jon Mills posits that Hegel was the first philosopher to articulate the process of projective identification. He demonstrates how Hegel anticipated many key psychoanalytic insights which Freud formulated nearly 100 years later (Mills, 2000). Mills highlights the normative functions of projective identification and shows how it is an elemental ontological feature underlying all mental activity. Mills' appreciation of Hegel's logic of the dialectic explains why projective identification governs both unconscious and conscious life, a dynamic that brings Hegel into dialogue with Klein, Bion, and contemporary psychoanalytic thought.

In "Nietzsche, Psychoanalysis, Nihilism", Jared Russell discusses how the clinical practice of psychoanalysis can function as a countermeasure to the spread of nihilism and despair, which Nietzsche understood would increasingly come to define our age. Historically, the task of psychoanalysis has been conceived as an effort to decipher symbolic meaning. Nietzsche saw well in advance that the systemic pathologies of the coming era would crucially involve the destruction of symbolizing capacities with as a result the unleashing of destructive forces that would turn the world into a suicidal nightmare. Psychoanalysis can function as a response to this trajectory if it is reconceived as an effort to cultivate capacities for symbolization and to resist tendencies toward nihilistic abandon, which continue to invest in the general orientation of positivist science controlling the marketplace of current therapeutics. Russell gives special attention to the clinical implications of what the current psychoanalytic literature calls "concreteness" as an increasingly pervasive manifestation of psychopathology or nihilism in the 21st century.

In "Psychoanalysis Finds a Home: Emotional Phenomenology", Robert D. Stolorow traces the evolution of his conception of psychoanalysis from his and Atwood's early psychobiographical studies of the personal experiential origins of psychoanalytic theories to a vision of psychoanalysis as a form of phenomenological inquiry. Psychoanalysis investigates and illuminates the nature, origins, and therapeutic transformations of the principles that prereflectively organize emotional experience. Recognizing the centrality of emotional experience contextualizes the clinical phenomena of trauma and pathogenesis. The parts played by shattered metaphysical illusion and the absence of a relational context for holding emotional pain in the genesis of trauma are emphasized.

In "Bridging Philosophy and Psychoanalysis: A Hermeneutic Pathway Between the Disciplines", Roger Frie focuses on the intersection of philosophy and psychoanalysis and challenges common misconceptions about it. He challenges skepticism toward philosophy among mental health professionals in general and psychoanalysts in particular. Drawing on his experiences as an academic philosopher and practicing psychoanalyst, Frie shows how each discipline emerges from lived experience. The modern hermeneutic insight that human life is always already circumscribed by society, culture, and history in ways that are, in part, outside the reach of consciousness is evident in psychoanalytic approaches that pay particular attention to human situatedness. Drawing equally from philosophy and psychoanalysis, Frie lays out a hermeneutic perspective that presents human experience as inseparable from the social, cultural, and historical contexts in which it unfolds.

In "Wittgenstein: Disciple of Freud?", Edward Harcourt shows that although Wittgenstein's writings contain many discussions of psychoanalysis, his attitude toward Freud is hard to pin down. He describes himself as a "disciple of Freud" and condemns Freud's followers for leaving "an abominable mess". Is it possible cleanly to subtract what Wittgenstein criticized in Freud from what he admired? Some readers of Wittgenstein have thought so, extracting a purified version of Freud whose most salient feature is that psychoanalysis should be seen as an interpretative rather than a scientific enterprise, offering reasons for human thought and behavior rather than causes. Thus Wittgenstein's positive and negative attitudes to psychoanalysis are shared out neatly between Freud's bad theoretical account of what he was doing and his good first-order insights into the human mind. But is Wittgenstein's view of Freud that straightforward? And if it is, does it bring Freud so far down to earth that what we are left with is just common sense? Harcourt examines Wittgenstein's discussions of Freud, focusing especially on the explanation of dreams and jokes, and on the comparison between psychoanalysis and Wittgenstein's own philosophical method. He concludes that both psychoanalysis and Wittgenstein's attitude to it are more complicated than the purified version allows. But he also suggests that Wittgenstein's "Freudianism" goes beyond anything that finds expression in his strictly philosophical writings.

In "Freud and the Legacy of Sensory Physiology", Leonardo Niro explores how Freud imported – and extended – Helmholtz's theory of perception in developing his new psychology. Freud is often placed in a Kantian tradition via his engagement with authors such as Schopenhauer, Herbart, Lipps, Meynert, and, especially, the physiologists Hermann von Helmholtz, Emil du Bois Reymond, and Freud's mentor during his medical studies, Ernst Theodor Brücke. Niro argues that the physiologists' work on perception paved the way to an epistemology that would today be described as a type of epistemic structural realism, which, due to their influence, was also adopted (and again extended) by Freud. Niro then examines how the theories of perception proposed by Helmholtz and Freud are currently being recast under so-called predictive processing and embodied inference approaches in the neurosciences and philosophy of mind. The chapter concludes by schematically describing how the legacy of sensory physiology remained present (via Freud) in Kleinian psychoanalysis, and how this presents an isomorphism with predictive processing accounts of fantasy, dreaming, and primal forms of mental activity.

In "Trauma and Language", Dana Amir uses Roman Jakobson's accounts of metaphor and metonymy to understand the language of victims and perpetrators. Following both Jakobson's and Lacan's ideas, Amir suggests a distinction between a metaphoric and a metonymic mode of witnessing, and adds a psychotic mode which is completely outside the range stretching between the former two. First, Amir focuses on the language of the victim, tracing four modes of traumatic testimony, distinguished by the degree of psychic motility they enable. Next, she discusses the perpetrator's language, describing the phenomenon of "screen confessions": confessional texts produced by perpetrators, which subtly and unconsciously subvert themselves. Alluding to Freud's "screen memories", screen confessions refer to how memory is construed in language. Screen confessions thus do not omit the concrete facts, but their meaning. Distortion or error inheres in the syntax of the confession, which interferes with meaning even if all factual components are accurate and correct. The final section discusses the unbearable tension between the language of the victim and the language of the perpetrator, and their malignant interrelations.

In the second part of this collection, "Psychoanalytic Schools and Their Philosophical Perspectives", the influence of philosophical traditions on psychoanalysis – in Freud's time and later – takes center stage. Such influences are traced back in the output of, for instance, object relations, Fairbairn, Winnicott, self psychology, intersubjective psychotherapy, Lacan, and Jung.

In "Freud and the Unconscious", Marcia Cavell concentrates on Freud's theory of mind with its central concepts of the unconscious and repression. She posits that the Freudian unconscious is not to be confused with the mundane concept of the subconscious, which ordinarily refers to mental contents that are temporarily out of awareness but subject to voluntary control. Unconscious mental contents, by contrast, can only be retrieved under special circumstances, of which hypnosis, Freud's earliest therapeutic modality, is a prime example. Unconscious contents, which typically lead to self-deception and irrationality of various kinds, include desires, memories, intentions, wishes, and ideals. Cavell also addresses Freud's account of how, in part through repression, ideals and conscience are formed. In closing, she considers two of Freud's most trenchant critics, Adolf Grünbaum and Frederic Crews.

In "The Foundations of the Psychoanalytic Theories of Freud, Klein and Bion Compared", Michael Rustin considers the differences and continuities which characterized the development of psychoanalytic theory in the tradition initiated by Freud and subsequently developed by Klein and Bion. He describes the evolution of Freud's model of the mind. The first model is based on his early work as a neurologist, in which the accumulation and discharge of psychic energy is seen as its primary organizing force. The second model evolves with Freud's seminal paper "Mourning and Melancholia", in which a concept of the mind and its connection with others through processes of identification becomes central. Klein's model of the mind, as shaped by its relation to what she called objects, which were unavoidably at times both loved and hated, developed from this later phase of Freud's writing, many of whose presuppositions (e.g., the formative role of both love and hatred and of the life and death instincts), she continued to uphold. Next, Bion's work extended and deepened some of Klein's crucial insights. Bion's thinking contributes to the description of a third fundamental disposition, an innate desire for knowledge and understanding, in addition to the innate impulses to love and hate. Finally, Rustin discusses the contributions of psychoanalysts, including Ronald Britton, Michael Feldman, and John Steiner, who extended these ideas in their study of narcissistic or borderline states, and renewed the focus on the Oedipal situation in this tradition.

In "Fairbairn's 'Psychology of Dynamic Structure' and Philosophy", Graham S. Clarke shows how Ronald Fairbairn's psychology of dynamic structures relates to and evolves from several other Scottish thinkers' work, particularly Ian Suttie, John Macmurray, and Edward Glover. Clarke's rational reconstruction of Fairbairn's theory follows several changes in the model Fairbairn first put forward in 1944. In discussing the roots of Fairbairn's theory, Clarke refers to Andrew Pringle-Pattison, a British Idealist under whom Fairbairn studied at the University of Edinburgh in the early 20th century and whose work seems to have influenced Fairbairn's mature theory. He shows how personalism, critical realism, and Fairbairn's psychology of dynamic structure are fruitful conjunctions for further developing Fairbairn's theory.

In "From Freud to Winnicott: Aspects of Paradigm Change", Zeljko Loparic presents a unified view of Winnicott's contribution. He argues that Winnicott introduced revolutionary changes into psychoanalysis, and some other healthcare fields, and that these changes amount to a Kuhnian paradigm shift. Loparic gives an account of Kuhn's view of scientific revolutions and offers a reconstruction of Freud's Oedipal, triangular, or, as he terms it, the "Toddler-in-the-Mother's-Bed" paradigm. He then discusses Winnicott, and demonstrates how facing unsolvable problems (anomalies) in the Oedipal paradigm in the 1920s led him to initiate revolutionary research toward a more efficient framework. This resulted in Winnicott's dual, or "Baby-on-the-Mother's-Lap", paradigm. Loparic concludes with observations regarding Winnicott's heritage, teaching Winnicott and the future of psychoanalysis.

In "Kohut's Self Psychology, Ethics, and Modern Society", John Hanwell Riker describes how Heinz Kohut, in his work with narcissistic patients, discovered that the essential psychological task for humans is to develop a core nuclear self, rather than, as Freud held, achieving felicitous management of the drives. Kohut's largely unconscious nuclear self develops in the first half decade of life out of primary narcissism, and injuries to the self are the basis for most psychopathology. Riker shows how Kohut's theory of self integrates concepts from Plato, Aristotle, Nietzsche, and especially Hegel. Kohut's theory distinguishes itself in having an empirically based psycho/social theory of the development of the self, where self is differentiated from ego, and "selfobjects" (persons who perform self-functions when the self is unable to) play a primary role in its construction and ongoing viability. Riker suggests that Kohut's theory has profound implications for ethics. It offers a new vision for how best to live as a human being and gives a compelling argument for why, if we want to have solid and vibrant selves, we should strive to be ethical human beings.

In "What Is Intersubjectivity: From Phenomenology to Psychoanalysis," Lewis Kirshner introduces the concept of intersubjectivity by discussing its development in phenomenologic philosophy, infant research, neuroscience, and psychoanalysis. He argues for the necessity of a phenomenologic understanding of human behavior, especially in clinical work, to counter reductionist or objectifying approaches. While incorporating diverse models, intersubjective theory sees the origins and continuity of personal consciousness in the shared social world of language and relational codes and emphasizes the entanglement of individual personality in relationships from which it cannot be separated. The work of Heidegger, Husserl, Merleau-Ponty, Ricoeur, Sartre, and the contemporary scholars Gallagher and Zahavi illustrates this perspective. Lacan's reading of phenomenology and semiotics provided a bridge to psychoanalysis which remains relevant. Kirshner advocates the further integration of phenomenologic concepts of intersubjectivity into psychoanalytic training and practice.

In "Subject and Subjecthood: From Philosophy to Psychoanalysis", Uri Hadar posits a clear, though not self-evident, line of ideas leading from Descartes' thinking subject to Lacan's speaking being. Hadar draws this line via such phenomenological ideas as Hegel's self-consciousness, Marx's working being, Husserl's experiencing subject, and Freud's desiring subject. He examines the remarkable affinity between Husserl and Freud, arguing they were responsible for elevating subjecthood to its prime status in the human sciences. He reads Lacan's subject with reference to the notion of the subject in each of these thinkers and shows the continuities and ruptures marking the development of this phenomenological line of thought. Especially, he shows an affinity between Lacan's and Marx's subjects in terms of their foregrounding of action rather than interpretation. In addition, he discusses the prime role of the Hegelian idea of interdependence of Subject and Other, stressing the tension between the singularity of the Subject and the plurality of the Other. Finally, Hadar considers the manner in which the investigation of subjecthood may inform the rehabilitation of subjectivity in psychotherapy, where the particular practice of psychoanalysis unsettles the Marxist distinction between interpretation and action.

In "Is Jung a Philosopher of Religion as Well as a Psychologist of Religion?", Robert A. Segal asks if it is possible to be both a psychologist and a philosopher. Is it possible for a psychologist, or more generally a social scientist, to use social scientific findings to make philosophical claims? Specifically, is it possible for a social scientist to use social scientific findings to determine the existence of God? Similarly, is it possible for a social scientist to use social scientific findings to explain evil – not only evil done by human beings but also evil done to human beings? Did Jung profess to be only a psychologist or also a philosopher? If he professed to be both, did he enlist his psychological findings to make philosophical claims? Specifically, did he enlist his psychological findings either to determine the existence of God or to explain evil?

The third part of this volume, "Psychoanalysis, Epistemology, and Truth", brings together chapters that discuss various approaches to the concept of truth and the scientific status of psychoanalysis.

In "The Anxieties of Truth in Psychoanalytic and Philosophic Thought", Shlomit Yadlin-Gadot discusses the concept of truth in philosophic and psychoanalytic thought and its relation to psychic realities. Placed in a psychological framework, truth is redefined in terms of human experience, psychic structure, and mental dynamics. The notion of truth axes as organizational principles of the mind is introduced as the psychic source and reflection of paradigmatic, abstract conceptions of truth. Truth axes are related to basic human needs and anxieties, construals of reality and alternating self-states. This analysis gives rise to a post-postmodern view of truth, articulated in terms of finite, definable, non-contingent features of the psyche. It also emphasizes the ethical dimension involved in prioritization of truths in clinical practice.

In "Truth and Psychoanalysis", Charles Hanly discusses three criteria of truth: coherence, correspondence, and pragmatics. Hanly posits that coherence is neither a sufficient nor a necessary criterion of knowledge. Correspondence is the criterion Freud had in mind in his tally argument. A psychoanalytic interpretation is true if it tallies with what the patient is remembering or not remembering. Hanly argues that that correspondence is the necessary and sufficient core criterion of truth. As for pragmatism, he posits that it is necessary to differentiate scientific pragmatism from philosophical pragmatism. The pragmatism of psychoanalysis is scientific because it requires corresponding evidence that a beneficial change in a patient's functioning has been caused by the analyst's interpretations. Psychoanalysis as a therapeutic process is in part Socratic, except that intellectual self-knowledge is not an end in itself. The goal of clinical psychoanalysis, Hanly argues, is the improvements in psychic functioning that remembering and knowing bring about. He concludes that the scientific pragmatic test of psychoanalysis has an important place in estimating the truth of psychoanalytic knowledge.

In "Metaphors and the Question of Truth in Psychoanalytic Language", Tair Caspi explores the epistemological foundations of metaphors in psychoanalytic language and their relation to the concept of truth. Contrary to the Platonic, empiricist, and positivist perception of metaphor as a vibrant, suggestive configuration that diverts us away from the truth, Caspi posits that psychoanalytic metaphors hold power to reveal and conceptualize unconscious, innovative "metaphorical truths". It follows that psychoanalysis requires ample use of metaphors to provide detailed descriptions of human experiences, as well as of ineffable psychic processes. Drawing on post-positivist philosophers of language and science such as Boyd, Kuhn, and Lakoff and Johnson, Caspi shows that the elusiveness and ambiguity of psychoanalytic metaphors allow to depict multiple truths of the human mind. Finally, a combination of linguistic criteria is suggested to clarify the workings of successful, enduring metaphors in the psychoanalytic lexicon.

In "Facts and Sensibilities: What Is a Psychoanalytic Innovation?", Aner Govrin asks: Does psychoanalysis progress? And, if so, can we find regularities in the last decades of this progress? Moreover, what does progress mean? Does psychoanalysis progress by finding new "facts" about the mind (e.g., unconscious dynamics of borderline organization) or by changing its own ethics and epistemology? Govrin posits that the psychoanalytic community examines innovations in two ways: how well does the new development correspond to the field's ethical and epistemological requirements? And in case there is a contradiction between the two, another question arises: will the community drop the new development, or will it choose to alter its own ethical or epistemological requirements? Besides new discoveries concerning facts related to the psyche, psychoanalysts have during recent decades generated second-order innovations, which challenge epistemological and ethical assumptions. Three "sensibilities" emerged to join the canonical psychoanalytical thinking of the early and mid-20th century: the relational approach, infant research, and neuropsychoanalysis. They offer a new orientation for the psychoanalyst's attention and understanding based on existing psychoanalytic theory.

In "Psychoanalytic Evidence: The Old and the New", Ed Erwin analyzes and evaluates both early and recent psychoanalytic evidence. He starts by showing that from 1899, the year Freud's *The Interpretation of Dreams* was published, until 2000, most of the evidence for his theories and therapy came from clinical case studies. There were some experimental studies, but most psychoanalysts including Freud himself argued they were not needed. A shift occurred in the late 20th century, when leaders in the psychoanalytic community expressed severe dissatisfaction with exclusive reliance on a single case study approach. From then on, psychoanalysts began looking for new methodologies. One influential development, the Questionnaire Method, was pioneered by the American psychologist Martin Seligman (1995). Seligman's key idea was that in place of external controls typically used in scientific experiments, psychoanalysis could substitute "internal" controls. Besides Seligman's work, Erwin concludes, more and better experimental studies were done principally of short-term, psychoanalytically oriented psychotherapy alongside some experimental studies of long-term psychoanalysis. Perhaps the most significant new development has been the appeal to neuroscience to support Freud.

The fourth part of this volume, "Philosophical Debates", involves three domains: the self, rationality, and ethics.

In "The Psychoanalytic *das Ich*: Lost in Translation", Alfred I. Tauber asks: who is the psychoanalytic subject, and how should she be regarded? He discusses Freud's "das Ich" – "the I" – which is translated in English to "the ego," a semantic distortion introducing a host of philosophical issues. Tauber shows that ego refers to "the self," a construct subject to much debate and unresolved ambiguity in the western philosophical tradition. Freud avoids this imbroglio. Das Ich does not mean "ego" and, moreover, Freud does not use the word Selbst (self). Tauber posits that psychoanalytic theory, in its radical reconfiguration of the mental, eschews the metaphysics of Enlightenment notions of selfhood: a dominant consciousness with its conceits of reasoned deliberation is replaced with the hegemony of the unconscious. Accordingly, self-awareness in the Freudian construction can offer only limited insight into the repressive mechanisms employed to combat unconscious fantasy and desire. And, given the autonomy and dominance of das Es, das Ich – delimited in its rationality and understanding – is stripped of the free will underlying modernity's basic conception of personal identity. With the rejection of epistemological and moral autonomy, Freud joined 20th-century philosophers in dismissing modernity's attempts to define the self. Tauber shows how subjectivity, sui generis, in this reconfiguration of agency, remains Freud's abiding contribution.

In "Subjectivity in Philosophy, Psychoanalysis and Neuroscience: From World-Brain Relation Over Neuro-ecological Self to the Point of View", Georg Northoff defines a haunting problem in psychology and philosophy. Even though the search for the subjective nature of the self has a long tradition in philosophy, psychoanalysis, and more recently, also in neuroscience, the exact characterization of the subjective nature of self and how it, at the same time, is part of and fits into the seemingly objective world has remained elusive. Northoff pursues a non-reductive neurophilosophical approach by converging recent empirical data on self in neuroscience with philosophical-conceptual analysis of the notion of point of view. He shows how scale-free activity in world and brain – that is, activity extending across different time scales that exhibit temporal nestedness and long-range temporal correlation (LRTC) – are key in constituting the self. This is complemented by converging the scale-free and neuro-ecological nature of self and its basis in world-brain relations, with the conceptual notion of the point of view (PV). He postulates an ecological depth layer of PV that situates, constitutes, and emplaces the self within the world in an ontological way through scale-free activity featured by temporal nestedness and LRTC. He concludes that the basic subjectivity of self, as the key feature of the basis model of self-specificity, is scale-free, neuro-ecological, pre-phenomenal, and ontological. This distinguishes our notion of subjectivity from the more traditional and current views, where it is determined as scale variant, neuro-cognitive, objective, mental (or phenomenal), and epistemological. The convergence of world-brain relation, neuro-ecological self, and point of view allows for a novel determination of the subjectivity of self.

In "Psychoanalysis, Self-Deception, and the Problem of Teleology", Simon Boag examines repression and self-deception in light of the static and dynamic paradoxes of self-deception and the problem of knowing in order not to know. First, he addresses these logical paradoxes to clarify the actual issues and identify problematic strategies for explaining the harder cases of repression and self-deception. From this, strongly partitive accounts of the mind and the role of intentions and teleology in repression and self-deception are then addressed. The problem of teleology in functional accounts of repression is then discussed in the context of "betrayal blindness", as found within betrayal trauma theory. After demonstrating that teleology prevents such approaches from providing coherent theories of repression and self-deception, Boag develops a realist-relational view of mentality for addressing the logical difficulty with such positions. Finally, he proffers an alternative non-teleological account of betrayal blindness based on efficient causes in Freud's account of the "blindness of the seeing eye", which embraces an apparent paradox with respect to both knowing and not knowing the repressed simultaneously.

In "A-Rationality: The Views of Freud and Wittgenstein Explored", Linda A. W. Brakel discusses Freud's and Wittgenstein's respective notions of a-rationality, a contentful (representational) form of mentation. A-rational mentation is properly considered a mode of mentation distinct both from rationality and irrationality. Barkel finds similarities and differences in a-rationality for Freud and Wittgenstein. By 1900, Freud had observed two types of mental processes. Primary processes operate earlier in life, fuel impulses, and make connections based on associations and displacements rather than on any rational grounds or logical deliberations. Secondary processes are rationally based, reason responsive, and seem to predominate in conscious adult life. Freud, however, recognized that the primary processes are ubiquitous, unconsciously underpinning much of human behavior across many domains. Meanwhile, mid-century, Wittgenstein, in one of his final works, *On Certainty*, advanced what can be considered a radical view: He proposed that all of our grounded beliefs –moreover, our entire web of knowledge – rest on ungrounded, non-rational, undoubted, taken-for-granted assumptions. The ground of rationality is a-rational. Barkel also advances an evolutionary biological link, consistent with both thinkers, as a-rationality is rife in the non-human animal world.

In "Intersubjectivity and Responsibility in Relational Psychoanalysis and Modern Jewish Philosophy", Michael Oppenheim juxtaposes the work of Jessica Benjamin and Donna Orange, significant figures in the relational psychoanalysis movement, with the positions of the modern Jewish philosophers of encounter, Franz Rosenzweig, Martin Buber, and Emmanuel Levinas. His point of departure is the recent statement by David Goodman and Eric Severson that "Levinas claims that 'morality is not a branch of philosophy but first philosophy' and if he is right about this, might ethics also serve as a first psychology?" Two themes are prominent in this comparison: that relationships with others constitute the essence of human experience and that the issue of meaning is central to understanding both health and flourishing. A few of the complementary subjects highlighted by this multidisciplinary lens are the ethical precept of one's responsibility for others and the powers of speech. Finally, possible areas of cross-fertilization are identified.

In "Ethics of Discontent", Shai Frogel shows the connection between the ethical ideas of Spinoza and Nietzsche, the great precursors of modern secular ethics, and the ethical foundation of psychoanalysis. He calls this an ethics of discontent because psychoanalysis understands the good human life in terms of sublimation of existential discontents rather than in traditional terms of harmonic happiness. Spinoza explains moral values in psychological rather than religious terms and relates human good life to intellectual self-emancipation rather than religious faith, while Nietzsche declares the "death of God" and redefines human existence in psychological terms rather than metaphysical ones. Frogel's thesis is that Freud takes this psychological turn in human thought further and proposes new ethics that rejects religious and metaphysical ideas of salvation in the name of the reality principle, highlighting the conflictual existence of the modern individual. This ethics underlies psychoanalysis and grants its philosophical justification.

The fifth and final part of this volume, "Applied Subjects", examines how psychoanalysis serves as a research frame that enriches our understanding of both social and ecological phenomena.

In "What Can Psychoanalysis Tell Us About Cyberspace?", Slavoj Žižek shows how the media constantly bombard us with requests to choose, addressing us as subjects supposed to know what we really want (which book, what clothes, what TV program, what holiday destination, and so on; "press A, if you want this, press B, if you want that"). Žižek argues that at a more fundamental level, the new media radically deprive the subject of the knowledge of what he wants: they address a thoroughly malleable subject who constantly has to be told what he wants; that is, the very evocation of choice to be made performatively creates the need for the object of choice. Paraphrasing Hegel's dialectics of Master and Slave, Žižek posits that the main function of the Master is to tell the subject what he wants – the need for the Master arises in answer to the subject's confusion, insofar as he does not know what he wants. The suspension of the function of the (symbolic) Master is the crucial feature of the Real whose contours loom at the horizon of the cyberspace universe: the moment of implosion when humanity will reach the limit that cannot be crossed, the moment at which the coordinates of our societal life-world will dissolve.

In "Psychoanalysis, Race and Colonialism", Stephen Frosh shows how recent discussions of psychoanalysis' implication in discourses of race and practices of racialization have focused more on colonialism than on racism itself. This has led, Frosh explains, to some very productive work that locates psychoanalysis within the colonial project and explores the potential that psychoanalytic concepts have for critical analysis of that project. Much of this work has drawn on the writings (and figure) of Frantz Fanon, though there have also been major contributions from researchers on Indian and Latin American psychoanalysis. Frosh explores psychoanalysis' engagement with "race", racism, and colonialism from the point of view of the philosophy of psychoanalysis as (a) a body of developmental theory; (b) an individualizing practice; and (c) a potentially open discipline in relation to psychosocial formations of the subject. Frosh references Freud's anthropological writings but is concerned mainly with contemporary readings of psychoanalysis as a political philosophy that is implicated in the perpetuation of racist and colonialist ideas, yet also offers leverage in contesting these ideas. The author asks, to what extent can psychoanalysis become a "decolonizing" discipline, and what might need to happen for this to be achieved?

In "Narcissism in Religion," Tamas Pataki first posits that all religions have two highly variable poles or functions: on the one hand, explanation, prediction, and control and, on the other, communion, in which intimate relationship is sought with gods or spirits. Communion is the most prominent feature of contemporary monotheistic religions, and Pataki argues that the modes of achieving it are essentially the same as those available in human-to-human relationships, including narcissistic relationships. It follows that gods and spirits must be conceived in fundamentally anthropocentric terms, even if in some unfathomable respects they surpass the human. Pataki then sketches the psycho-historical evolution of the concept of a single, omnipotent, and caring god that made intense attachment, communion, and dependence possible. Of the many aspects of the peculiar relationship to an omnipotent and solicitous non-corporeal object, he highlights its identificatory and more broadly defensive uses (in the psychoanalytic sense) in sustaining the economy of narcissism. This leads to a discussion of deficiencies in the accounts of religiosity advanced in contemporary attachment theory and, finally, to a novel psychoanalytic account of the role of narcissistic processes in individual and group religious belief and behavior, especially their pernicious consequences.

In "The Missing Signifier and a Malfunctioning Paternal Law: On the Feminine Third as Vital Portal for Sexual Difference and Emancipatory Democracy", Jill Gentile calls psychoanalysis to revisit its treatment of the problem of sexual difference, which Luce Irigaray (some 40 years ago) characterized as "one of the major philosophical issues, if not the issue, of our age". Recent trends in Lacanian thinking suggest that it is not the phallic signifier but rather the missing signifier that has the latent power to open the gap of sexual difference. Gentile concludes that if we wish to render sexual difference a more robust and even revolutionary political force, signifying the feminine is required. Challenging the view that naming the missing signifier undermines its distinctive character, Gentile posits that the feminine signifier functions paradoxically, both enabling the ontological/structural crack of sexual difference (to which Lacanian theorists point) and granting the feminine (at least in part, but also, at last, in part) a symbolic foothold. She concludes that the commitment of psychoanalysis to signifying sexual difference is a necessary post-patriarchal intervention which enables a disruptive, decolonizing, and ultimately radically democratizing and contradictory telos of desire.

In "Ecopsychoanalysis and Climate Psychology", Joseph Dodds presents "ecopsychoanalysis" as a new transdisciplinary approach to thinking about the relationship between psychoanalysis, ecology, "the natural", and the problem of climate change. Although climate change is increasingly recognized as perhaps the single biggest threat our species faces, existing approaches largely constitute an "ecology without psychology". Dodds argues that psychoanalysis has a unique role to play with its emphasis on the unconscious dimensions of our mental and social lives. It is required to unmask the anxieties, deficits, conflicts, phantasies, and defenses crucial in understanding ecological crisis's human dimension and our civilization's highly ambivalent relation to the other-than-human world. With the new millennium, the awareness of the climate crisis brought a sense of urgency to psychoanalytic approaches to ecology with a cluster of important books and articles (Randall, 2005; Dodds, 2011, 2013; Weintrobe, 2012; Lertzman, 2015), an increasing interest in psychoanalytic organizations in this area, and the formation of the Climate Psychology Alliance, which attempts to create a community of psychoanalysts, psychotherapists, and psychologists working on issues of ecology and climate change.

In "The Evolution of Psychoanalytic Thinking About Aesthetics", Adela Abella differentiates three stages in the evolution of psychoanalytic thinking about aesthetics. Initially, attention was focused on the content of the work of art: following Freud's first hypothesis, artistic endeavor allows a return of the repressed through displacement and disguise. In this line of thought, art is aligned with dreams, neurotic symptoms, slips of the tongue, child's play, myths, and so on. The drawback of this model is that it cannot explain the special vigor of a literary masterpiece in comparison with a tabloid drawing on the same content. During the 1950s, Hanna Segal attempted to resolve this quandary, highlighting the impact of the formal presentation: like in tragedy, the beauty of a work of art allows the expression and the coming through of unbearable feelings and phantasies. However, this second model is of little use in approaching contemporary artistic trends which disregard formal beauty and perfection. Evoking some postmodern aspirations, recent psychoanalysts emphasize the multiple personal recreations of a work of art.

To explore their respective usefulness and limits, Abella applies these three models to one of the most frequent iconographies of Christian art: the Annunciation.

References

Banicki, K. (2014). Philosophy as Therapy: Towards a Conceptual Model. *Philosophical Papers* 43(1):7–31.

Berthold-Bond, D. (1989). Freud's Critique of Philosophy. *Metaphilosophy* 20(3/4):274–294.

Carlisle, C. & Ganeri, J. (Eds.) (2010). *Philosophy as Therapeia*. Cambridge: Cambridge University Press.

Cornejo, R. (2018). Origins of a Theory of Psychic Temporality in Freud: The Study of Eels and the Darwinist Influence of Carl Claus. *International Journal of Psychoanalysis* 99:450–467.

Dale, J. (2006). *Philosophy, Psychology, and Psychologism: Critical and Historical Readings on the Psychological Turn in Philosophy*. Dordrecht: Springer Science & Business Media, pp. 88, 89.

Dodds, J. (2011). *Psychoanalysis and Ecology at the Edge of Chaos: Complexity Theory, Deleuze/Guattari and Psychoanalysis for a Climate in Crisis*. London and New York: Routledge.

Dodds, J. (2013). Minding the Ecological Body: Neuropsychoanalysis and Ecopsychoanalysis. *Frontiers in Psychology*.

Domenjo, B. A. (2000). Thoughts on the Influence of Brentano and Comte on Freud's Work. *Psychoanalysis and History* 2:110–118.

Freud, S. (1896). *The Origins of Psychoanalysis: Letters to Wilhelm Fliess*, ed. Marie Bonaparte, Anna Freud, and Ernst Kris, tr. Eric Mosbacher and James Strachey. New York: Basic Books, 1954, letter 39, January 1, 1896, p. 141.

Freud, S. (1925). Resistances to Psycho-Analysis. In *SE*, Vol. 19.

Freud, S. (1926). Inhibitions, Symptoms and Anxiety. In *SE*, Vol. 20.

Freud, S. (1933). The Question of a Weltanschauung. In J. Strachey (Ed. & Trans.), *The Standard Edition of the Complete Psychological Works of Sigmund Freud* (Vol. 22, pp. 158–182). London: Hogarth Press.

Gay, P. (1995). *Freud: A Life for Our Time*. London: Papermac. ISBN 0-333-48638-2.

Hook, S. (Ed.) (1959). *Psychoanalysis, Scientific Method and Philosophy*. New York: New York University Press.

James, W. (1979). *Some Problems of Philosophy*, Vol. 7 of The Works of William James, ed. Frederick H. Burkhardt. Cambridge, MA: Harvard University Press (First published in 1911).

Lertzman, R. (2015). *Environmental Melancholia: Psychoanalytic Dimensions of Engagement*. London and New York: Routledge.

Levitt, C. & Turgeon, A. (2009). Sigmund Freud's Intensive Reading of Ludwig Feuerbach. *Canadian Journal of Psychoanalysis* 17:14–35.

Levy, D. (1996). *Freud Among the Philosophers: The Psychoanalytic Unconscious and Its Philosophical Critics*. New Haven & London: Yale University Press.

Mills, J. (2000). Hegel on Projective Identification: Implications for Klein, Bion, and Beyond. *Psychoanalytic Review* 87:841–874.

Ogden, T. H. (1999). 'The Music of What Happens' in Poetry and Psychoanalysis. *International Journal of Psychoanalysis* 80:979–994.

Peterman, J. F. (1992). *Philosophy as Therapy – An Interpretation and Defense of Wittgenstein's Later Philosophical Project*. SUNY Series in Philosophy and Psychotherapy. New York: Suny Press.

Randall, R. (2005). A New Climate for Psychotherapy? *Psychotherapy and Politics International* 3(3):165–179.

Seligman, M. (1995). The Effectiveness of Psychotherapy. The Consumer Reports Study. *American Psychologist* 50:965–974.

Tauber, A. I. (2010). *Freud, the Reluctant Philosopher*. Princeton: Princeton University Press. Kindle Edition.

Weintrobe, S. (2012). *Engaging with Climate Change: Psychoanalytic and Interdisciplinary Perspectives*. London and New York: Routledge.

PART I

Philosophical Traditions and Psychoanalysis

1

FREUD'S THEORY OF FREEDOM

Between Kant's Faith and Schopenhauer's Pessimism

Matthew C. Altman

Sigmund Freud has a complicated relationship with the history of philosophy, and with German Idealism in particular. He believes that philosophers have traditionally ignored or denied the existence of the unconscious (PT, 7:266; CP, 13:178; EI, 19:13; AS, 20:31), but he also compares the unconscious to Kant's thing in itself (UCS, 14:171).[1] He rejects metaphysics in favor of clinical observation and theoretical extrapolations from empirical psychology (PEL, 6:259), but Kant himself explains why metaphysics is impossible as a science (Kant 1998, A246–247/B303; Kant 2002, 4:315).[2] He claims that his later work regarding religion and the origins of civilization depends ultimately on patient observation rather than philosophical speculation (AS, 20:59), but he also acknowledges similarities between the death drive and Schopenhauer's claim that all life aims at death (AIL, 22:107). Freud is no idealist, but references to the German Idealists appear several times throughout his corpus, like symptoms of a half-acknowledged influence.

The affinities among Kant, Schopenhauer, and Freud are perhaps most apparent in their approaches to self-knowledge and the activity of judgment in making sense of ourselves. For all three of them, we can know ourselves in inner sense only as appearances, although Schopenhauer and Freud, unlike Kant, believe that unconscious forces can be discovered under specific conditions. Freud's most significant break with Kant and Schopenhauer is regarding his theory of freedom. While Kant has practical faith in the possibility of autonomous self-determination and Schopenhauer's lack of belief in autonomy leads to a renunciation of the will, Freud devises an ideal of self-determination within a materialist framework. For Freud, psychoanalysis can help us to overcome unconscious compulsions that disrupt our conscious lives. We become freer when we develop relatively healthy relationships with our drives, desires, and memories. To do this, we must integrate the content of our inner lives, which, although we cannot control its underlying forces, can be actively shaped by us in terms of its meaning. Drawing on Kant's insight into the discursivity of thinking, Freud develops a conception of human freedom that is more compelling than determinism and more appropriate to our materialistic worldview than either Kantian autonomy or Schopenhauerian renunciation.

Kant: The Limits of Cognition

According to Kant's transcendental idealism, we can know the world only as an appearance and never as a thing in itself (Kant 1998, A369). As finite beings, we perceive things in space and time, according to the pure forms of sensible intuition. We also make judgments about objects of

DOI: 10.4324/9780429297076-3

sensible intuition by using the pure concepts (or categories) of the understanding. The pure concepts, such as the concept of causality, are discursive rules that we use to think about objects, and they provide synthetic unity to the manifold of sensible intuition (Kant 1998, B128). Objective perception is called cognition (*Erkenntnis*), and it is a result of the activity of thinking applied to what is given to us passively through the senses (Kant 1998, B146, A320/B376–377). In other words, we synthesize various perceptions as objective unities that affect one another – for example, the sun warms the stone. Therefore, "the understanding is itself the source of the laws of nature," with nature understood as "the sum total of all appearances" (Kant 1998, A127, B163).

The fact that experience in general is subject to our epistemic conditions entails that knowledge of ourselves is also limited. When we introspect on the contents of our minds, our desires, volitions, and feelings occur in time. I may be hungry at one moment and angry at another, and then I try to eat so that I am not so cranky. I perceive these various mental events in time (I feel hunger and then I feel angry), and I think of them as causally related (my feeling of hunger makes me cranky). Thus, I know myself only through what Kant calls inner sense (*innere Sinn*; Kant 1998, A22–23/B37, B156). The objects of inner sense occur in time and time is a form of sensible intuition, so what we know about our own mental lives are mere appearances.

Although we can guess at what we are like apart from these epistemic conditions, our perceptions of what motivates us are necessarily limited. I may think that my eating is an uncomplicated response to being hungry, but it may (also) be motivated by complex feelings and associations that even I am unaware of, such as feelings of stress, anxiety, or an eating disorder. Kant says that even actions that seem morally praiseworthy (i.e., done for the sake of duty) may in fact be motivated by self-interest (i.e., merely in accordance with duty), but we can never know whether that is the case:

> It is indeed sometimes the case that with the keenest self-examination we find nothing besides the moral ground of duty that could have been powerful enough to move us to this or that good action and to so great a sacrifice; but from this it cannot be inferred with certainty that no covert impulse of self-love, under the mere pretense of that idea, was not actually the real determining cause of the will; for we like to flatter ourselves by falsely attributing to ourselves a nobler motive, whereas in fact we can never, even by the most strenuous self-examination, get entirely behind our covert incentives, since, when moral worth is at issue, what counts is not actions which one sees, but those inner principles of actions that one does not see.
>
> *(Kant 1996b, 4:407)*

We are used to the idea that our actions could be more selfish than we think they are. I may believe that I am acting beneficently, but someone could point out a pattern in my behavior that reveals my true intentions. Kant goes beyond this. Not only are our motives obscure, but this act of self-deception is not something that we could ever discover and correct. What seem like my actual motives, behind the self-deception, are also merely apparent motives. My real motives, whatever they are, are in principle introspectively unavailable. As Kant puts it, I cannot know the subjective principles of volition (or maxims) that govern particular actions (Kant 1996b, 4:400n), nor can I know the character (or supreme maxim) that informs my choice of particular maxims, whether it is good or evil (Kant 1996d, 6:30–32, 36–37). I am necessarily opaque to myself regarding even the most basic question of why I do what I do or whether I am a good or bad person.

Kant's analysis of the limits to self-knowledge is in contrast to Descartes's picture of the mind, according to which I am completely transparent to myself. For Descartes, there is nothing that

I know better than my own mind, both my existence as a thinking thing and the ideas that I can use to establish the veracity of the senses and the existence of an external world. For Kant, however, knowledge of the mind is of a piece with knowledge of the external world: both the mind and the world are perceived through the senses (inner and outer sense, respectively), both appear in time and are thought by means of the categories, and both are apprehended as mere appearances. I have access to my ideas and feelings in a way that you do not, but I can be just as wrong about who I am and my reasons for acting as I can be about other natural events.

Kant's alternative to Cartesian self-transparency does, however, allow for the possibility that there are reasons for my choices, not only causes. As a synthetic *a priori* concept, the category of causality governs the world of appearances. Every event has a cause, so even human actions are absolutely predictable in principle. Whatever I am apart from these epistemic conditions is unknown and unknowable. The limited scope of determinism means that free self-determination is possible, including acting purely for the sake of duty, when we consider things as they are apart from our epistemic conditions: as Kant famously writes, "I had to deny *knowledge* in order to make room for *faith*" (Kant 1998, Bxxx). The blow to our epistemic ambitions that rules out speculative metaphysics validates a sphere in which it is possible that we both choose among different options regardless of prior circumstances (negative freedom; Kant 1998, A555/B583; Kant 1996b, 4:446; Kant 1996a 5:33; Kant 1996c, 6:213–214) and act on a principle that we give to ourselves through pure practical reason (positive freedom; Kant 1996b, 4:446–447; Kant 1996a, 5:33; Kant 1996c, 6:213–214).

Although theoretical reason can establish the possibility of freedom, that we are in fact free is established on practical grounds. In the *Groundwork of the Metaphysics of Morals*, Kant appeals to the "idea of freedom": because we cannot avoid deliberating about our actions and acting under the assumption that our choices are free, we are constrained by the categorical imperative just as we would be if we knew that we were free (Kant 1996b, 4:448). And in the *Critique of Practical Reason*, Kant says that, when we reason about what to do, we have an immediate consciousness of moral constraint (the "ought") that confronts us as a "fact of reason." From the fact that we hold ourselves to account, it follows that we must really be free, because we can only be constrained to do the right thing if we are capable of choosing to do the right thing (Kant 1996a, 5:32). I have no knowledge of freedom (or whether I am free), but I am committed to freedom as a rationally justified object of practical faith.

Schopenhauer: Intellectually Intuiting the Will

Schopenhauer accepts Kant's distinction between appearances and the thing in itself, but he believes that it has very different implications for self-knowledge and human motivation. According to Schopenhauer, individual things are distinct because we perceive them in space and time – my body, for example, occupies this space at this time, as opposed to others. The *principium individuationis* (principle of individuation) thus gives us a false perception of what is in fact an undifferentiated unity that underlies all things (Schopenhauer 2010, 1:137–138, 152–153, 358, 392–393). The world is an illusion, which Schopenhauer, drawing on Indian philosophy, calls the "veil" or "web of *māyā*" (2010, 1:28, 38–39, 310, 378–379).

Although I am usually compelled by this view of the world, Schopenhauer says that I can become directly aware of the thing in itself through an acquaintance with my body. Despite Descartes's claim to the contrary, I am not *in* my body; I *am* my body. Yet the body can be experienced by me in two different ways. First, I perceive the body in space and time, like any other object. But I also perceive objects through the body. The body is both something that I know and that by virtue of which I am a knower. In addition, the body is not just another object in the world that affects and is affected by other things. When I do something, I act as a body; the body is what makes me capable of being an agent. Schopenhauer says that this "double cognition [*Erkenntnis*]" of myself is the key to understanding the thing in itself (2010, 1:128).

When I will something – not merely deliberating or wishing that something would happen – my willing is immediately expressed as an action. The willing does not occur at one point as the cause, and then the action follows as an effect. Rather,

> an act of the will and an act of the body . . . are one and the same thing, only given in two entirely different ways: in one case immediately and in the other case to the understanding in intuition [*Anschauung*]. An action of the body is nothing but an objectified act of will, i.e. an act of will that has entered intuition.
>
> *(Schopenhauer 2010, 1:124–125)*

We represent the will to ourselves as distinct things (separate objects in space and time), but the will as a thing in itself is an undifferentiated force that drives all change in the world of appearances, including human actions.

The "double cognition" of the body provides direct insight into the thing in itself. Schopenhauer criticizes Kant for only giving us "mediated, reflected cognition," while he appeals to "immediate and intuitive cognition" (Schopenhauer 2010, 1:481; see also 1:134; Schopenhauer 2018, 2:187–188). Through this subjective consciousness of the will, I can use "cognition of the Ideas to see through [*durchschauen*] the *principium individuationis*" and discover "the other side of the essence in itself of things" (Schopenhauer 2010, 1:327, 532). Although everyone is capable of intuiting the will as the thing in itself, it is an insight that not everyone achieves. The will hides itself from us, since we experience it mostly through the senses. The will to life (*Wille zum Leben*) distracts us with a constant stream of desires that need to be satisfied, including the instincts of self- and species-preservation: "Most people are pursued through life by wants that do not allow them space for reflection" (Schopenhauer 2010, 1:354; see also 1:301–303, 356–360; Schopenhauer 2018, 2:364–375). Our compassion for others reflects our awareness of our ultimate unity: you are only apparently distinct from me, and we are both only apparently distinct from other animals, trees, and rocks (Schopenhauer 2009, 200–201, 218, 255; Schopenhauer 2010, 1:402, 405; Schopenhauer 2018, 2:601–602).

Self-knowledge that breaks through the veil of *māyā* can be the first step in overcoming those desires and rejecting the world of appearances. Schopenhauer likens it – sometimes identifies it – as the achievement of enlightenment when the world becomes nothing and desires are overcome (2010, 1:417–418). Someone who accomplishes this is indifferent to the world. The ultimate ethical achievement is the renunciation and denial of the will.

Schopenhauer's rejection of Kant on self-transparency has dramatic implications for his supposedly Kantian practical philosophy. Kant is an epistemological pessimist in the sense that we are unknowable to ourselves, but a practical optimist regarding his faith in rational autonomy. Schopenhauer is optimistic about our ability to know our own motivations, but pessimistic about how the will is lived out – in a pointless striving coming ultimately to nothing. Since the thing in itself is the will and all apparent things are manifestations of the will, there is no personal moral responsibility. Like Kant, Schopenhauer claims that we use the *a priori* concept of causality when we make empirical judgments. So, human actions, like all other phenomenal events, are causally determined. While Kant believes that postulating an unknowable thing in itself "makes room for faith" in freedom, Schopenhauer claims that distinguishing the will from the world of appearances rules out the possibility of rational self-determination. Appearances are determined and, apart from the category of causality, the thing in itself is merely undetermined. Although it expresses itself to the senses in different forms, the arbitrariness of the will is consistent across all existing things: magnetism and crystal formation, the growing of grass, instinctual behavior in animals, and our seemingly self-determined moral actions (Schopenhauer 2010, 1:164–177). Self-reflection cannot fundamentally change our motivations, but only the direction of the will. Thus, while Kant claims that a consideration of things as they are apart from our ways of knowing allows us to traffic in the space of reasons, Schopenhauer claims that it precludes an appeal to reasons, either with regard to phenomena or noumena. The choice is between meaningless desire-satisfaction and the renunciation of the will, the latter of which would achieve nothingness. Schopenhauer shows what happens when transcendental idealism and its epistemic limitations come into contact with evolutionary theory, Eastern philosophy, and a disenchantment with the Enlightenment project: objective claims describe an illusory world, rational self-determination is impossible, and there is no meaning or purpose to existence.

Kant and Schopenhauer: Their Legacy for Freud

Several themes from Kant and Schopenhauer are important for understanding the legacy of German Idealism for Freud's psychoanalytic theory. First, the world that we inhabit is not passively perceived, as the empiricists would have it, but is the result of the activity of judgment in interpreting what we are given through the senses. Kant and Schopenhauer focus on the *a priori* concepts that any discursive thinker must use in order to make sense of the world, but later philosophers extend this idea to claim that we invest the world with different meaning and significance by means of language (Nietzsche and Derrida), shared forms of social understanding (Beauvoir and Merleau-Ponty), and our particular histories (Hegel and Gadamer).

Second, just as objective cognition is limited to appearances, self-knowledge is also limited. What I perceive of my inner life is situated in time, so I know myself in inner sense merely as an appearance, not as I am apart from my subjective conditions of knowing. Kant and Schopenhauer disagree, however, about whether this limitation can be overcome. For Kant, the limitation is absolute. I cannot even know what I am as a noumenon. The consciousness that allows appearances to be synthesized as a manifold (the "I think") is merely a formal condition for the possibility of experience (Kant 1998, A106–107, B131–132). Although I can postulate a soul on practical grounds and I can practically justify my commitment to rational self-determination, I cannot know theoretically whether a thinking thing is behind the activity of thinking or what reasons are behind my actions. By contrast, Schopenhauer claims that we are capable of intellectually intuiting the will, so I know that I and everything else that exists is driven by a blind, animalistic force that manifests itself in appearance as the will to life.

Third, their theories of freedom begin by acknowledging that all our actions are determined by events beyond our control – or, more properly, that our actions are nothing but natural events that are caused by other natural events. Both Kant and Schopenhauer are committed to complete causal determinism in the world of appearances, since the category of causality is a synthetic *a priori* concept that we use to make objective claims based on our perceptions. However, they disagree about what kind of freedom is possible apart from appearances. Kant believes that we can overcome our inclinations and act on the basis of a pure rational principle. Reasons and causes are different kinds of things. Schopenhauer believes that, since everything is the will, we are only capable of renunciation as an ideal, removing ourselves from the endless cycle of becoming and achieving nothingness, as in Hinduism. This is a kind of negative freedom only – a choice not to act – rather than Kant's faith in positive freedom.

Freud: Two Approaches to the Unconscious

Setting aside the biographical and historical question of whether Freud was directly influenced by Kant and Schopenhauer – little evidence suggests that he was – echoes of their work appear throughout his corpus nonetheless. Although Freud thinks of himself as an empirical scientist, he refuses the basic empiricist premise that the world comes to us through the senses without distortion. He believes that self-knowledge is limited and that insight into what motivates us is elusive but achievable under specific circumstances. Although these ideas are not new to him, he goes beyond Kant and Schopenhauer in developing a kind of freedom within our limitations. Unlike Kant, who says that we must act as if we are undetermined, and Schopenhauer, who says that the only true freedom is not willing, Freud explains how greater self-awareness of what drives us can allow us to live freely in a different sense: not getting beyond our basic drives (the life drive and the death drive), but having a healthy relationship with our psychical forces such that we can live without especially disruptive unconscious repetitions.

Kant's ideal is autonomous self-determination, which is not only the (negative) freedom to step back from our inclinations and choose but also the (positive) freedom to act purely for the sake of duty apart from any pathological desire. Schopenhauer claims that we are inescapably heteronomous in the sense that we are manifestations of a primordial will that appears spatiotemporally as the will to life, primarily the desire for sex (Schopenhauer 2018, 2:529–530). That will in no way belongs to us or is controlled by us as individual subjects. His pessimism is the result of a loss of the rational ideal: if we cannot autonomously govern our own actions, the only alternative is to deny the will. Freud gives us a third alternative. We are not purely rational, but that does not mean that we should simply resign ourselves to nothingness. We reconcile ourselves with our heteronomous impulses when we allow them to express themselves in healthier ways. This is not Kantian autonomy, since the person is not distancing themselves from their impulses. Rather, the impulses become part of who they are: the goal of analysis is "to subdue portions of his id which are uncontrolled – that is to say to include them in the synthesis of his ego [*sie in die Synthese des Ichs einzubeziehen*]" (ATI, 23:235). The first step in achieving this "synthesis" is developing a deeper kind of self-awareness through psychoanalysis.

With his conception of the unconscious, Freud imagines a permeable barrier to self-knowledge. Although we are often opaque to ourselves, the workings of the unconscious are available if it is approached in the right way. Thus, despite frequent comparisons between Kant's thing in itself and the Freudian unconscious (e.g., Bergoffen 1981, 160; Cavell 1987, 27), Freud's closer intellectual predecessor is Schopenhauer. Freud's drives and Schopenhauer's will are both primitive forces that get expressed in convoluted, indirect ways. For both of them, the unconscious is hidden, but it is open to scrutiny – though never fully transparent to consciousness. According to Freud, Kant is one of the philosophers for whom the "unconscious has been something mystical, something intangible and undemonstrable, whose relation to the mind has remained obscure" (CP, 13:178). By contrast, for Freud the unconscious is currently unknown but not unknowable.

The relationship between Kant's noumenal self and Freud's unconscious is complicated by their different epistemological and metaphysical commitments. Like Kant, Freud compares outer sense to inner sense: our perception of the world is like our perception of the mind. For Freud, this means that the unconscious is behind consciousness and is the cause of apparent symptoms, just as objects cause subjective perceptions. Although Kant sometimes talks about the thing in itself as a cause of sensible intuitions, and thus claims that its existence can be inferred on their basis (1998, A19/B33, A494/B522–523, A538/B566, 2002, 4:314–315), we can say nothing conceptually coherent about noumena. By contrast, Freud's rejection of idealism and embrace of empiricism and materialism means that the whole of the mind is just another object of scientific study.

For Kant, objective representations are perceptions that have been subjected to the forms of sensible intuition (space and time) and the categories. Kant thus makes a three-part distinction between perceptions (secondary qualities such as the color of a rainbow); objects that, according to transcendental idealism, are mere appearances (primary qualities such as the shape of the water droplets); and the thing in itself as the ground of appearances (Kant 1998, A45–46/B62–63). Within the mind as well, Kant distinguishes the desires and intentions I seem to have; the real psychological causes (desires, intentions, etc.) that, even though they may be "dark" or "obscure" (*dunkel*), are discoverable (Kant 2002, 4:307); and the mind as a thing in itself, which is unknowable in principle. By contrast, as an empiricist, Freud is only committed to a two-part distinction between perceptions and objects in outer sense, and between conscious inner perceptions and the "psychical reality" (or mental objects) behind conscious thinking:

> The unconscious is the true psychical reality; *in its innermost nature it is as much unknown to us as the reality of the external world, and it is as incompletely presented by the data of consciousness as is the external world by the communications of our sense organs.*
>
> (*ID*, 5:613)

Although we can be misled by the senses, a scientific investigation of the external world can reveal what it is like in itself, or the objective properties that, for the empiricist, constitute the world as it exists apart from our perceptions. Similarly, although we can be driven by unconscious forces, such as repressed traumas, the unconscious expresses itself through symptoms and dreams. The psychoanalyst can help the patient to discover the unconscious causes of these conscious experiences by means of empirically verifiable mental laws, such as the mechanism of repression and the mind's need to discharge its libidinal energy. Unconscious impulses are "inferred like some fact in the external world," and those facts (not a thing in itself) are all that stand behind the content of inner sense (AS, 20:32). According to the empiricist, we can infer the existence of water droplets from the appearance of the rainbow; and, according to Freud, we can infer the existence of unconscious traumas and anxieties from the appearance of symptoms. Thus, Freud says, "internal objects are less unknowable than the external world" (UCS, 14:171; see also CD, 21:69). Not everything is conscious, but everything is potentially available to be incorporated into consciousness. Freud's therapeutic method begins with the assumption that our motivations are not transparent to us but that they may be exposed through the process of psychoanalysis.

Freud claims that he can appeal to psychological laws to infer the existence of unconscious forces from apparent symptoms. This second-person perspective on the analysand is another of Freud's innovations. Like Descartes, both Kant and Schopenhauer believe that introspection is the most reliable road to self-knowledge, even if that self-knowledge is limited or ultimately ineffective. Kant says that even introspection falls short of knowledge of our true motives and of our status as free subjects, and Schopenhauer says that true self-knowledge is possible only if we get beyond thinking to a direct encounter with the will, which is beyond the self. As inscrutable as I am to myself, I am even more inscrutable to others. Freud's therapeutic practice inverts this: my motivations may be more accessible to others than they are to me. There is an interpersonal path to the unconscious, which displays patterns of meaning-making that are common to all of us. This means that other people can provide some insight into the unconscious that, although it is inaccessible to me, is not necessarily or universally hidden from consciousness, as it is for Kant. This introduces complications that Kant and Schopenhauer do not have to consider – such as the possibility of transference – but it also opens up the possibility of a therapeutic dialogue through which I can become aware of the meaning and significance of my own thinking and behavior, and then alter them. In this way, Freud's therapeutic ideal is a limited kind of freedom, one pervaded by heteronomy but not overwhelmed by it.

The availability of unconscious motivations marks Freud's turn away from Kant toward Schopenhauer. For Schopenhauer, although all of us are aware of the will through intellectual intuition, that the will as the thing in itself is understood only by a select few, namely artistic geniuses, ascetic saints, and some philosophers. For Freud, the unconscious is available to a select few well-trained observers, mainly psychotherapists, who can scientifically investigate the dynamics of an individual's mental life, armed with the psychological laws that Freud himself has discovered. Although their methods are different – intuition is immediate and direct, while empirical inferences are indirect – their aims and their conceptions of the unconscious are similar: the animalistic drives that motivate our behavior can be recognized and addressed, albeit in different ways.

The Purpose and Methods of Psychoanalysis

One of the central problems of psychoanalysis, especially in Freud's early work, is how to overcome repression. According to Freud, when a drive tries to express itself, the person may satisfy it in (more or less) healthy and socially acceptable ways, but some desires, feelings, and memories are "repudiated [*abgewiesenen*]" by the ego (IL, 16:350). When repressed, they must express their libidinal energy indirectly, and they repeat themselves as symptoms. When various symptom-formations become overly disruptive to one's normal life, then the person experiences neurosis, anxiety, hysteria, and so on. The person needs treatment so that they can become aware of what they have repressed and can expend the psychic energy more directly, through socially appropriate channels. This process makes sense – through psychoanalysis, we can understand how the mind functions – but it is not a rational response. That is, repressing the trauma does not accomplish the aim of undisturbed psychological functioning because what is repressed returns in the form of symptoms. To achieve some semblance of wholeness, we must work through the repression and recognize the source of these disruptions. Therapy assists us in the process of coming to terms our repressed desires – literally, bringing them to language, which requires the participation of others in our self-knowledge – and incorporating them into consciousness.

In order to bring these repressed desires and feelings to light, Freud (along with Josef Breuer) initially believes that the analyst can gain direct access to the unconscious by talking with the analysand, discovering points of resistance, and bringing repressed material into focus through hypnosis. By delving into the unconscious directly, the analyst can reconstruct for the analysand what is indirectly expressed through symptoms:

> As a rule it is necessary to hypnotize the patient and to arouse his memories under hypnosis of the time at which the symptom made its first appearance; when this has been done, it becomes possible to demonstrate the connection in the clearest and most convincing fashion.
>
> *(SH, 2:3)*

Once the repressed memory is discovered, then it is causally linked to the neurotic symptoms and their meaning becomes intelligible. With this early approach to the unconscious, Freud, like Schopenhauer, attempts to bypass the mind's discursive activity, which, for both of them, is prone to distorting reality: either by repeating a trauma in the form of seemingly unrelated symptoms (Freud) or by making us seem like separate individuals who are rationally self-determining (Schopenhauer). Hypnosis, like intellectual intuition, provides direct access to the unconscious motives of our conscious activity that are usually unavailable to us.

In his early work, Freud underestimates the active force of resistance that constantly preserves and shores up the repression, even as analysands are confronted with experiences that they themselves recall under hypnosis (HPM, 14:16). The effort to avoid trauma, like the instinct to self-preservation for Schopenhauer, is not easily overcome. The analysand cannot consciously accept the cause of a neurosis simply by being presented with an explanation discovered through hypnosis. The explanation seems foreign to the patient precisely because it is repressed: "The patient hears our message, but there is no response. He may think to himself: 'This is very interesting, but I feel no trace of it.' We have increased his knowledge, but altered nothing else in him" (ATI, 23:233). Repression forces the neurotogenic experience from consciousness through an act of resistance. The resistance continues even when the patient is told something about themselves that they did not know beforehand. Whether this is really "knowledge," as Freud claims, is debatable. The analysand cannot incorporate the repressed desires, feelings, or memories into their conscious understanding, such that they become part of the narrative they tell themselves about who they are.

In his mature work, Freud gives up on the fantasy of revealing the unconscious through hypnosis and adopts his method of the "talking cure": "the history of psycho-analysis proper . . . only begins with the new technique that dispenses with hypnosis" (HPM, 14:16). Freud realizes that, to help the analysand to work through the repressed trauma, it is not enough for the facts to be brought to light. Instead, the analysand must recognize the trauma, identify with the feelings that accompany it, represent it to consciousness, and actively incorporate it into their self-conception.

As I said earlier, Freud's unconscious is not Kant's thing in itself. For Freud, the contents of the unconscious can be made conscious and its mechanisms can be discovered empirically. But his turn away from hypnosis also represents a return to Kant in a very important sense. Kant's most significant insight is that thinking is judging. Cognition is not something that happens passively but is an act of claim-making. We know things only as they appear, including what I know of myself in inner sense, because we represent things to ourselves according to our subjective conditions of knowing. The self that I discover when I bring my "dark" thoughts to light is situated in time and interpreted by means of the categories. The objects of self-consciousness are the result of bringing the different parts of myself into relation with one another.

Similarly, for Freud, reestablishing an analysand's mental health depends on bringing traumatic ideas into proper relation with the person's internal narrative, so he begins with symptoms that are present to consciousness. When repressed experiences or libidinal desires have been disassociated from conscious ideas, symptoms express them in ways that the conscious subject cannot. For example, Emma's leg pains express self-reproach for coveting her sister's husband; her body enacts her self-reproach because she has repressed her feelings of guilt (SP, 1:353–356). Rather than illuminating the unconscious by bypassing repression and consciousness (through hypnosis), Freud studies the symptoms through which unconscious desires and traumas indirectly appear:

> When I set myself the task of bringing to light what human beings keep hidden within them, not by the compelling power of hypnosis, but by observing what they say and what they show, I thought the task was a harder one than it really is. He that has eyes to see and ears to hear may convince himself that no mortal can keep a secret. If his lips are silent, he chatters with his finger-tips; betrayal oozes out of him at every pore.

> And thus, the task of making conscious the most hidden recesses of the mind is one which it is quite possible to accomplish.
>
> (*CH, 7:77–78*)

The patient cannot accomplish "the task of making conscious" the repressed idea or emotion when they are presented with a story, even if it is true, that the analyst has discovered through hypnosis. Examining the patient's past through hypnosis is replaced by "*uninhibited association*," so that even the analysand can see how unconscious forces indirectly express themselves (SH, 2:11; see also CH, 7:12). The focus of treatment shifts from hypnosis to signs of the internal struggle that the patient can recognize, such as physical symptoms, verbal habits, or ideas to which they keep circling back during sessions with the therapist. The analyst serves as a kind of interpreter, noting the patient's stops and starts and directing them toward exploring these gaps. The patient can examine the symptoms, discover a common theme, make inferences about what is being repressed, and, eventually, recognize the source of psychic conflict. Analysis is the process of giving meaning to what had seemed meaningless.

Freud's Hermeneutic Turn

Freud's change of method is more consequential than it seems. They are not merely different approaches to treatment but presuppose fundamentally different conceptions of the person who is being treated. The focus on what is consciously available to the patient echoes an essentially Kantian idea: that what is perceived by the subject is not simply given but is conditioned by intellectual activity. The analyst attends to the analysand's observable behavior and communicable thoughts in order to deduce the activity that lies behind it. Freud attempts to change the way that patients relate to themselves. The goal of analysis shifts from the release of psychic energy (as a kind of mechanical process) to understanding one's active resistances so that the division between conscious and repressed thoughts can be overcome:

> the element of abreaction receded into the background and seemed to be replaced by the expenditure of work which the patient had to make in being obliged to overcome his criticism of his free associations, in accordance with the fundamental rule of psycho-analysis.
>
> (*RRW, 12:147*)

The "expenditure of work" in this case is the attempt to bring the patient's own thinking to bear on the unconscious trauma that resists acknowledgement. By being engaged more directly in the therapeutic process, the patient can, if the therapy succeeds, identify with the unconscious forces at work and bring them to consciousness – thus working through the trauma rather than repeating it in the form of symptoms.

In this sense, Freudian psychoanalysis is a hermeneutical practice: it is concerned with the construction of meaning by people who inhabit an interpersonal space of language. One sign of psychological disorder is the patient's construction of a separate system of meanings that conflict with the beliefs of her community (Ricoeur 1970, 366–367). Through the therapeutic process of free association, the meanings of the symptoms become apparent. The analysand comes to understand how their response to and interpretation of experiences and desires, rather than the experiences and desires themselves, have given rise to the trauma and the resulting symptoms. The event has to be invested with traumatic significance after the fact, which accounts for the latency period; it is not a foreign body that merely pierces the person's psychical skin (MM,

23:67–68). The therapeutic engagement with the patient's symptoms brings the neurosis and its causes into the sphere of language and interpretation, thus making it intelligible, rather than trying to get past that activity, by means of hypnosis, to some foreign body – the latter of which conceives of trauma as a thing in itself.

The method of hypnosis is meant to reveal the contents of someone's mind when introspection falls short. But Freud's later method emphasizes the dialogic engagement of the patient with themselves and of the therapist with the patient, such that meaning can be made of what has been hidden. Each individual has a conception of who they are and what they value. Through therapy, a person comes to terms with their unconscious experiences and desires so that they can either pursue what they value or can adjust what they value. For example, someone who has repressed their homosexual desires may, as a result of therapeutic self-examination, either accept that these are errant feelings of a straight person, with nothing to be ashamed of, or they may start down a long road of revising their conception of their own sexual identity. Freud emphasizes, to a greater extent than Kant or Schopenhauer, how deeply our relationships with others shape our psychological health. As a result, psychological health is inherently more fragile, but it is also amenable to positive intervention, such as therapy.

Hans-Georg Gadamer criticizes the Enlightenment desire to be radically purified of prejudice. Interpretation, including self-interpretation, is always partial (Gadamer 1989, 271–277). Since making, revising, and possibly remaking one's identity is an ongoing process, therapeutic intervention is not something that ends, even if a therapist is no longer involved. It is not that some discovery is made that completes the therapy, as in Freud's early work, when the results of hypnosis are presented to the patient. Analysis ends when the sessions stop, but the work of self-interpretation continues and is necessarily incomplete (ATI, 23:219–220).

Embodied Freedom

Freud was an avowed materialist and a believer in "complete psychical determinism" (PEL, 6:253). Our actions are the result of underlying psychic causes that, although they may be unknown to the analysand, can be discovered in the course of analysis, working backwards from their apparent effects. Slips of the tongue, dreams, and even free association are all "*determined by motives unknown to consciousness*" (PEL, 6:239). Even conscious action "receives its motivation from the other side, from the unconscious; and in this way determination in the psychical sphere is still carried out without any gap" (PEL, 6:254). There is no such thing as free, unmotivated will.

Despite Freud's explicit commitment to determinism, his psychoanalytic theory yields an account of human freedom – not, to be sure, as unmotivated or uncaused action, but a compatibilistic view that allows for more or less free activity even within a world of psychical laws and causally explicable behavior. Although we are subject to powerful, primitive drives and impulses, we can be free to the extent that are uncompelled by dynamically unconscious forces. That is, we become freer when we achieve a higher degree of psychological health.

Although the analysand is in a sense the victim of unconscious forces, in therapy they assume a kind of agency as something like a practical postulate. For Freud, there is no purely rational subject. Even normality is a fiction, something to strive after without ever definitively and permanently achieving it (ATI, 23:235). Therapy itself is infiltrated by unconscious fantasies and desires that often play themselves out in the form of transference onto the therapist and other forms of resistance. But the patient approaches the process as if they are capable of control – acting under the idea of freedom perhaps – so that they can do the interpretive work required of them. By taking themselves to be working through their own reactions and repressed ideas, they come closer to the ideal of self-possession, rather than being unknowingly dominated by "reminiscences," or symptoms of repressed memories and desires (SH, 2:7). They become freer, albeit as a conflict-ridden subject rather than a purely rational, noumenal being.

Freud's theory of freedom is, arguably, his most important advance over both Kant and Schopenhauer. Kant conceives of freedom in incompatibilistic terms: although we are determined as appearances, as things in themselves we are absolutely free to act, apart from any inclination, out of respect for the moral law. Schopenhauer argues that there is no pure practical reason, only the drive to self-preservation (the will to life). Knowledge and the intellect are purely instrumental, some of the tools by which we try to accomplish our self-interested aims more effectively. The only kind of freedom of which we are capable is the renunciation of the will. In other words, because we are incapable of absolute self-determination, there is no positive freedom, only freedom *from* the primal force underlying all things. For both Kant and Schopenhauer, then, the ideal of agency is absolute freedom: either we must act with the practical assumption that we are capable of such freedom (Kant), or we must give up on the idea and not will (Schopenhauer).

Freedom for the Freudian subject is finite and qualified, a limited kind of agency that is an alternative to both Kant's rational faith in autonomy and Schopenhauer's pessimism. The contents of the Freudian unconscious are foreign to consciousness insofar as they have been repressed. When symptoms are interpreted through the process of analysis, unconscious desires and memories are subject to conceptual transformation. They cease to be what they were: an obscure conglomeration of ideas, associations, and emotional charges. Instead, they come to make sense to us as they are situated in time and among other experiences, and they take on a conventional meaning. The symptoms become intelligible even though the repressive act is not justified on the basis of reasons. That is, we understand ourselves without rationalizing our protective but ultimately self-defeating attempt to avoid trauma.

Freud has fully absorbed Kant's lesson that nothing can be an experience for me unless I actively make sense of what I am given. My understanding of myself is built out of experiences, but experiences that I shape into a narrative of who I am. That narrative can be challenged – and one of the points of therapy is to challenge narratives that are not functioning well – but it has a certain weight or momentum that structures how I interpret new experiences.

Freud's case study involving Emma illustrates what this looks like in practice. Emma was anxious about going into shops alone, which she attributed to a memory of being laughed at by two shop assistants when she was twelve. According to Freud, this encounter caused Emma to have a "sexual release" because it reminded her of an earlier assault by another shopkeeper. Only after reaching puberty did she understand the sexual nature of the assault, resist the feelings of shame and desire, and repress the memory of it, expressing the trauma with agoraphobic symptoms (SP, 1:353–356). The association between the two memories is not rational, but the connection is intelligible: the shopkeepers in both cases laughed or smiled at her. When these experiences come out in analysis, Emma goes from having a bundle of anxious and confused feelings to something more conventional: being scared by others' sexual desire for her. The work of analysis in many ways attempts to support this interpretive work so that the subject comprehends how her behavior, dreams, and thoughts are the result of her particular psychological processes rather than simply being given to her by a mind-independent reality. And when the experience is known and interpreted, it ceases to be (as) disruptive of mental life.

Psychological disorders make a person unfree; they are imprisoned by their own compulsions. A key component of living freely is not being unknowingly dominated by reminiscences. Repression may result in disruptive symptoms, but drives can also be channeled into psychologically and socially valuable ends, and they can be expressed in more or less healthy ways. Freud's account of the psyche thus produces a modest optimism about our capacity to live happily:

> The programme of becoming happy, which the pleasure principle imposes on us, cannot be fulfilled; yet we must not – indeed, we cannot – give up our efforts to bring it nearer to fulfilment by some means or other. Very different paths may be taken in that direction, and we may give priority either to the positive aspect of the aim, that of gaining pleasure, or to its negative one, that of avoiding unpleasure. By none of these paths can we attain all that we desire. Happiness, in the reduced sense in which we recognize it as possible, is a problem of the economics of the individual's libido. There is no golden rule which applies to everyone; every man must find out for himself in what particular fashion he can be saved.
>
> *(CD, 21:83)*

We become happier when we figure out how best to manage our different and sometimes competing desires. As part of that goal, we achieve some level of freedom when we are not unknowingly dominated by repressed traumas and desires. We take possession of ourselves when those things are incorporated into our conscious narratives, and when our "efforts to bring [the pleasure principle] nearer to fulfilment" are not impeded by symptoms of repression.

This process is necessarily incomplete because any structure we achieve, any story we tell, will eventually be undermined and challenged by something else within our mental lives (ATI, 23:223). Our minds are inherently self-disrupting. As Jonathan Lear puts it, "the psychological achievements of maturity do tend to be somewhat fragile. There is always and everywhere the possibility of being overwhelmed" (2000, 110). Freedom is defined in terms of psychological health, and psychological health is a relative concept, depending on the level of disruption caused by behavioral or psychosomatic symptoms of repression (IL, 16:358). Our capacity for self-determination depends upon a kind of therapeutic negotiation between conscious narratives and unconscious pressures that motivate and destabilize those narratives.

Because of tensions within the individual psyche, and tensions between our personal desires and social expectations, we are left with a "reduced sense" of happiness and self-determination. Although Freud claims that psychoanalysis can illuminate our deep motives, he avoids the conclusion that we can achieve complete self-transparency. What is preconscious may be fully discovered – memories that are temporarily forgotten or unnoticed – but whatever populates the unconscious can only be revealed in part and in glimpses. The realistic goal for psychoanalysis is not to make patients absolutely free from repression, but to ensure that their repressed memories and emotions do not interfere too much in their everyday lives. In Freud's words, "the business of the analysis is to secure the best possible psychological conditions for the functions of the ego" (ATI, 23:250). We can live well, or well enough, as fractured selves.

Philosophers have struggled with how to understand Kant's theory of freedom, to make sense of how we can be both determined when our actions are considered theoretically (as causally determined objects of cognition) and free when our actions are considered practically (as the result of self-determined reasons). Freud's theory of freedom is at once simpler and more complex. Without two separate standpoints on human action, he does not need to explain the relationship between noumenal freedom and phenomenal determinism. The Freudian subject is at the intersection of two forces: the activity of interpretation and the passivity of the mind in encountering our drives. How we respond to our desires and our past is shaped by the fundamental drives that constitute the human being – the life drive and the death drive – but the drives themselves also affect us in idiosyncratic ways, depending on our particular act of interpretation – for example, when an event is responded to as a trauma and repressed. Emma's experience only becomes traumatic when she unconsciously invests it with meaning. The force of the given confronts the activity of interpretation, resulting in a theory of freedom that is more distinctively human, with our capacity both to transform the world through thinking and to be driven by animalistic motives, than either Kant's enlightenment ideal or Schopenhauer's pessimism.

Conclusion

Freud says that psychoanalysis "seeks to prove to the ego that it is not even master in its own house" (IL, 16:285). The conscious mind and seemingly self-directed activity are constantly at risk of being disrupted by forces that are beyond our rational control. Ironically, Freud draws on elements of German Idealism to develop a theory of materialistic, embodied freedom. Like Kant and Schopenhauer, Freud claims that we are not transparent to ourselves. However, echoing the Kantian idea that our experience is, in part, constructed by us, Freud shifts the meaning of what it is to achieve (partial) autonomy. We make sense of ourselves by situating our thoughts and behaviors into a conscious narrative, and the extent of our freedom is defined by our psychological health. It is a matter of degree – how much unconscious forces disrupt pursuit of our conscious aims – rather than an absolute removal of ourselves from a deterministic world, either through pure practical reason (Kant) or by renouncing the drives that make us into who we are (Schopenhauer). In rejecting both the Kantian fantasy of autonomy and the Schopenhauerian anxiety about determinism, Freud gives an account of limited, dialogic freedom within the therapeutic setting that reconciles us with the real condition of the human psyche.[3]

Notes

1 Works by Freud are cited parenthetically in the body of the text using the abbreviations listed below, followed by the volume and page numbers from the *Standard Edition* (Freud 1953–1974):

AIL: "Anxiety and Instinctual Life" (1933), 22:81–111
AS: *An Autobiographical Study* (1925), 20:1–74
ATI: "Analysis Terminable and Interminable" (1937), 23:209–253
CD: *Civilization and Its Discontents* (1930), 21:57–145
CH: "Fragment of an Analysis of a Case of Hysteria" (1905), 7:1–122
CP: *The Claims of Psycho-analysis to Scientific Interest* (1913), 13:163–190
EI: *The Ego and the Id* (1923), 19:1–66
HPM: "On the History of the Psycho-analytic Movement" (1914), 14:1–66
ID: *The Interpretation of Dreams* (1900), vols. 4–5
IL: *Introductory Lectures on Psycho-analysis* (1916–1917), vols. 15–16
MM: *Moses and Monotheism* (1939), 23:1–137
PEL: *The Psychopathology of Everyday Life* (1901), vol. 6
PT: "On Psychotherapy" (1905), 7:255–268
RRW: "Remembering, Repeating and Working-Through" (1914), 12:145–156
SH: *Studies on Hysteria* (with Josef Breuer) (1895), vol. 2
SP: *Project for a Scientific Psychology* (1950), 1:281–397
UCS: "The Unconscious" (1915), 14:159–215

2 As is customary in Kant scholarship, each parenthetical reference to Kant's writings gives the volume and page numbers of the Royal Prussian Academy edition (*Kants gesammelte Schriften*), which are included in the margins of the translations.

3 Some of the themes in this chapter are developed in more detail in Altman and Coe (2013). I am indebted to Cynthia Coe for helpful comments on an early draft.

References

Altman, M. C., and C. D. Coe. (2013). *The fractured self in Freud and German philosophy*. Palgrave Macmillan.

Bergoffen, D. B. (1981). Freud's philosophy. *Philosophy Today*, 25(2), 157–165.

Cavell, S. (1987). Psychoanalysis and cinema: The melodrama of the unknown woman. In J. H. Smith and W. Kerrigan (Eds.), *Images in our souls: Cavell, psychoanalysis, and cinema* (pp. 11–43). Johns Hopkins University Press.

Freud, S. (1953–1974). *The standard edition of the complete psychological works of Sigmund Freud*, 24 vols. (J. Strachey et al., Trans. and Ed.). Hogarth Press and Institute of Psychoanalysis.

Gadamer, H.-G. (1989). *Truth and method* (J. Weinsheimer and D. G. Marshall, Trans.). Rev. ed. Continuum (Original work published 1960).

Kant, I. (1996a). Critique of practical reason. In M. J. Gregor (Trans. and Ed.), *Practical philosophy* (pp. 137–271). Cambridge University Press (Original work published 1788).

———. (1996b). Groundwork of the metaphysics of morals. In M. J. Gregor (Trans. and Ed.), *Practical philosophy* (pp. 41–108). Cambridge University Press (Original work published 1785).

———. (1996c). The metaphysics of morals. In M. J. Gregor (Trans. and Ed.), *Practical philosophy* (pp. 363–602). Cambridge University Press (Original work published 1797).

———. (1996d). Religion within the boundaries of mere reason (G. di Giovanni, Trans.). In A. W. Wood and G. di Giovanni (Eds.), *Religion and rational theology* (pp. 55–215). Cambridge University Press (Original work published 1793).

———. (1998). *Critique of pure reason* (P. Guyer and A. W. Wood, Trans. and Eds.). Cambridge University Press (Original work published 1781 [A ed.] and 1787 [B ed.]).

———. (2002). Prolegomena to any future metaphysics that will be able to come forward as a science (G. Hatfield, Trans.). In H. Allison and P. Heath (Eds.), *Theoretical philosophy after 1781* (pp. 49–169). Cambridge University Press (Original work published 1783).

Lear, J. (2000). *Happiness, death, and the remainder of life*. Harvard University Press.

Ricoeur, P. (1970). *Freud and philosophy: An essay on interpretation* (D. Savage, Trans.). Yale University Press (Original work published 1965).

Schopenhauer, A. (2009). Prize essay on the basis of morals. In C. Janaway (Trans. and Ed.), *The two fundamental problems of ethics* (pp. 113–258). Cambridge University Press (Original work published 1840).

———. (2010). *The world as will and representation*, vol. 1 (J. Norman, A. Welchman, and C. Janaway, Trans. and Ed.). Cambridge University Press (Original work published 1818).

———. (2018). *The world as will and representation*, vol. 2 (J. Norman, A. Welchman, and C. Janaway, Trans. and Ed.). Cambridge University Press (Original work published 1844).

2

HEGEL'S CONTRIBUTIONS TO PSYCHOANALYSIS

Theory of Mind, Dialectics, and Projective Identification

Jon Mills

The psychic process known as "projective identification" has become a familiar tenet of psychoanalytic doctrine. The term was coined by Melanie Klein in 1946[1] where it was conceived as an aggressive discharge of certain portions of the ego *into* an external object, the aim of which is to dominate or consume certain aspects of the object's contents in order to make it part of the ego's own internal constitution. Not only has the introduction of this concept revolutionized Kleinian theory, further developments have paved the way toward its progressive application in understanding a number of mental processes, pathologies, and clinical encounters. To be sure, projective identification may be viewed in multiple fashions: (1) as a general process of mental activity, from unconscious structure to conscious thought, (2) as a defensive maneuver motivated by intrapsychic conflict, and (3) as an intersubjective dynamic affecting object relations, especially the process of therapy. But with a few noteworthy exceptions (see Bion, 1959), projective identification has been largely overlooked as a basic element of psychic organization.

Although largely unknown to psychoanalytic discourse, Hegel was the first philosopher to articulate the process of projective identification. In fact, Hegel anticipated many key psychoanalytic insights that Freud was to make more intelligible nearly one hundred years later (Mills, 1996, 2002). It is my intention throughout this chapter to highlight the normative functions of projective identification and show how it is an indispensable ontological feature underlying all mental activity. Through a proper appreciation of Hegel's logic of the dialectic, projective identification may be seen as the most elementary process that governs both unconscious and conscious life, a dynamic that brings Hegel into dialogue with Klein, Bion, and contemporary psychoanalytic thought.

Hegel's Logic of the Dialectic

Hegel's philosophy of mind or spirit (*Geist*) rests on a proper understanding of the ontology of the dialectic. Hegel refers to the unrest of *Aufhebung* – customarily translated as "sublation," a dialectical process continuously annulled, preserved, and transmuted. Hegel's use of *Aufhebung*, a term he borrowed from Schiller but also an ordinary German word, is to be distinguished from its purely negative function whereby there is a complete canceling or drowning of the

DOI: 10.4324/9780429297076-4

lower relation in the higher, to also encompass a preservative aspect. Unlike Fichte's meaning of the verb *aufheben*, defined as: to eliminate, annihilate, abolish, or destroy, Hegel's designation signifies a threefold activity by which mental operations at once cancel or annul opposition, preserve or retain it, and surpass or elevate its previous shape to a higher structure. This process of the dialectic underlies all operations of mind and is seen as the thrust behind world history and culture. It may be said that the dialectic is the *essence* of psychic life, for if it were to be removed, consciousness and unconscious structure would evaporate.

When psychoanalysis refers to dialectics, it often uses Fichte's threefold movement of thought in the form of thetic, analytic or antithetic, and synthetic judgments giving rise to the popularized (if not bastardized) phrase: thesis-antithesis-synthesis[2] – a process normally and inaccurately attributed to Hegel;[3] or it describes unresolvable contradictions or mutual oppositions that are analogous to Kant's antinomies or paralogisms of the self.[4] It is important to note that Hegel's dialectic is not the same as Kant's, who takes contradiction and conflict as signs of the breakdown of reason, nor is it Fichte's, who does not explicate the preservative function of the lower relation remaining embedded in the higher. Furthermore, when psychoanalysts and social scientists apply something like the Fichtean dialectic to their respective disciplines, the details of this process are omitted. The presumptive conclusion is that a synthesis cancels the previous moments and initiates a new moment that is once again opposed and reorganized. But the synthesis does not mean that all previous elements are preserved, or that psychic structure is elevated. In fact, this form of dialectic may lead to an infinite repetition of contradictions and conflict that meets with no resolve.

Hegel's dialectic essentially describes the process by which a mediated dynamic forms a new immediate. This process not only informs the basic structure of his *Logic* which may further be attributed to the general principle of *Aufhebung*, but this process also provides the logical basis to account for the role of negativity within a progressive unitary drive. The process by which mediation collapses into a new immediate provides us with the logical model for understanding the dynamics of projective identification. An architectonic process, spirit invigorates itself and breaths its own life as a self-determining generative activity that builds upon its successive phases and layers which form its appearances. Spirit educates itself as it passes through its various dialectical configurations ascending toward higher shapes of self-conscious awareness. What spirit takes to be truth in its earlier moment is realized to be merely one appearance among many appearances. It is not until the stage of Absolute Knowing as conceiving or conceptual understanding that spirit finally integrates its previous movements into a synthetic unity as a dynamic self-articulated complex whole.

Hegel's use of mediation within the movements of thought is properly advanced in the *Science of Logic* (1812) as well as the *Encyclopaedia Logic* (1817) which prefaces Hegel's anthropological and psychological treatment of spirit in the *Encyclopaedia of the Philosophical Sciences* (1817/1830). In the *Logic*,[5] thought initially encounters Being which moves into Nothing and then develops into Becoming, first as the "passing over" into nothing, second as the "vanishing" into being, and third as the "ceasing-to-be" or passing away of being and nothing into the "coming-to-be" of becoming. Becoming constitutes the mediated unity of "the unseparatedness of being and nothing" (*SL*, p. 105). Hegel shows how each mediation leads to a series of new immediates which pass over and cease to be as that which has passed over in its coming to be until these mediations collapse into the determinate being of *Dasein* – its new immediate. Being is a simple concept while Becoming is a highly dynamic and complex process. Similarly, *Dasein* or determinate being is a simple immediacy to begin with which gets increasingly more complicated as it transitions into Essence and Conceptual Understanding. It is in this early shift from becoming to determinate being that you have a genuine sublation, albeit as a new immediate, spirit has a new beginning.

In Hegel's treatment of consciousness as pure thought represented by the *Logic* (1812), as well as his treatment of history in the *Phenomenology of Spirit* (1807) and anthropology and psychology in the *Encyclopaedia* (1817/1830), spirit – whether it be the mind of each individual or the collective psyche of the human race – continues on this circular albeit progressive path conquering each opposition it encounters, elevating itself in the process. Each mediation leads to a new beginning, and spirit constantly finds itself confronting opposition and overcoming conflict as it is perennially engaged in the process of its own becoming. In the *Logic*, the whole process is what is important as reason is eventually able to understand its operations as pure self-consciousness; however, in its moments, each mediation begets a new starting point that continually re-institutes new obstacles and dialectical problems that need to be mediated, hence eliminated. But thought always devolves or collapses back into the immediate.

This dynamic is a fundamental structural constituent that offers systematic coherency to Hegel's overall philosophy of spirit which is furthermore germane to the specific issue at hand. The individual psyche – as well as culture itself – mediates opposition and conflict it generates from within its own evolutionary process and attempts to resolve earlier problems unto which new immediacy emerges. Mediation is therefore an activity performed from within the mind and between interpersonal forces that in turn make new experience possible. As we will see, projective identification becomes the basic structural process of dialectical progression that is responsible for the epigenesis of unconscious organization, consciousness, the ontology of the self, and civilization at large – a dynamic responsible for both maturation and psychic decay.

The Structure of Mind

Hegel's theory of mind is comprehensively outlined in the Philosophy of Spirit (*Philosophie des Geistes*) which is the third part of the *Encyclopaedia*.[6] Unbeknownst to psychoanalysis, Hegel provides one of the first theories of the unconscious. He gives most of his attention to the unconscious within the stage of presentation (*Vorstellung*) in the context of his psychology, thus belonging to the development of theoretical spirit. Here Hegel refers to a "nocturnal abyss within which a world of infinitely numerous images and presentations is preserved without being in consciousness" (*EG* § 453). Hegel explains that the nightlike abyss is a necessary presupposition for imagination and for higher forms of intelligence.[7] While these more complex forms of the psychological would not be possible without the preservation of images within the unconscious mind, the unconscious is given developmental priority in his anthropological treatment of the soul (*Seele*).

For Hegel, the unconscious soul is the birth of spirit which developmentally proceeds from its archaic structure to the higher order activities of consciousness and self-conscious rational life. Like Freud (1926a) who shows that the ego is a differentiated portion of the id,[8] the conscious ego is the modification and expression of unconscious activity. For Hegel, the soul is not an immaterial entity (*EG* § 389), but rather the embodiment of its original corporeality, the locus of natural desire (*Begierde*) or drive (*Trieb*).[9] As the general object of anthropology, Hegel traces the dialectical emergence of the feeling soul from the abyss of its indeterminations; at first unseparated from its immediate universal simplicity, it then divides and rouses itself from its mere inward implicitness to explicit determinate being-for-self. Through a series of internal divisions, external projections, and re-internalizations, the soul gradually emerges from its immediate physical sentience (*EG* § 391) to the life of feeling (*EG* § 403) to the actual ego of consciousness (*EG* § 411), which further becomes more refined and sophisticated through perceptual understanding, ethical self-consciousness, and rational judgment, the proper subject matter of the *Phenomenology*.

For Hegel, spirit begins, like ego development for Freud,[10] as an original undifferentiated unity that emerges from its immediate self-enclosed universality to its mediated determinate singularity. This is initiated through a dialectical process of internal division, self-externalization, and introjection as the reincorporation of its projected qualities back into its interior. Here lies the basic process of projective identification: unconscious spirit splits off certain aspects of its interior, externalizes its Self, and then reconstitutes itself by identifying with its own negated qualities which it re-gathers and assimilates back into its unconscious framework. Through the complexities of mediation and sublation, spirit achieves higher levels of unification until it arrives at a full integration of itself as a complex whole, uniting earlier finite shapes within its mature universality.

Negativity, aggressivity, and conflict are essential forces to the thrust of the dialectic, a process Klein emphasizes in her characterization of ego development. The sleep of spirit is an undifferentiated void with the inner ambience of violence. It experiences the primeval chaos of an intense longing to fill its empty simplicity, desire being its form and content, the desire to fill the *lack*. Through the drive toward self-differentiation, unconscious spirit defines itself as a determinate being for itself and thus effects the passage from the universal to the particular, from a unity which lacks difference to differentiated plurality and singularity. There is an antediluvian cycle of negativity that we may say belongs to the prehistory of conscious spirit, a circular motion of the drives that constitute the dialectic of desire. Awakening as sensation from its nocturnal slumber, the feeling soul remains the birthplace of what is the substance of the "heart," for the abyss is the midwife of mind.

The Dialectical Structure of the Unconscious

As we have seen, the dialectic informs both the inner organization and the content of the unconscious. It is the dialectic that provides the Self with intrapsychic structures and functional operations that can never be reduced or localized, only conceptualized as pure activity. This pure activity of the dialectic as Self is constantly evolving and redefining itself through such movement. The unconscious forms of spirit (initially as feeling soul and then as ego) are thereby necessarily organized around the dialectical activity of the abyss. These structural operations, however, are not mechanistic, reductionistic, or physical as in the natural science framework often attributed to traditional psychoanalysis.[11] They are mental, telic, and transcendental, always reshaping spirit's inner contours and the internalized representational world within the night of the mind. Therefore, as a general structure, the unconscious is *aufgehoben*.

For Hegel, the unconscious is pure *process*, a changing, flexible, and purposeful activity of becoming. As the very foundation, structure, and organizing principles of the unconscious are informed by the movement of the dialectic, the architecture of the abyss is continually being reshaped and exalted as each dialectical conflict is sublated by passing into a new form, that in turn restructures, reorganizes, and refurbishes the interior contours of the core self. Therefore, the structural foundations of the self are never static or inert, but always in dialectical movement – having its origin and source in the unconscious, revamping the texture in which spirit emanates. This self-generating dialectical movement of the unconscious is the evoking, responding, sustaining, and transcending matrix that is itself the very internal system of subjective spirit.

The concept of the self as subject in Hegel is of particular importance in understanding the unconscious nature of mind. Essentially, the stage-by-stage (phase) progression of the dialectic is expressed as an epigenetic theory of self-development. Through sublation, Hegel's notion of the self encompasses a movement in which the subject is opposed to an object and comes to find itself in the object. This is exemplified by Hegel's treatment of the master-slave dialectic outlined in the *Phenomenology*. During the dialectical movement of spirit, the subject recognizes or discovers itself in the object. This entails the mediation of its becoming other to itself, with the reflection into otherness returning back to itself. The process of the development of the self is, like the soul, a process of differentiation and integration. As seen in the *Logic*, Being is characterized by an undifferentiated matrix which undergoes differentiation in the dialectical process of Becoming that in turn integrates into its being that which it differentiated through its projection, reclaiming it and making it part of its internal structure.[12] This is the very fabric of projective identification. The outcome of the integration is once again differentiated then reintegrated; unification is always reunification. Therefore, spirit comes to be what it already is, the process of its own becoming.[13]

Interfaces With Klein

Klein's theory of splitting has revolutionized the way we understand ego development. For Klein, the ego exists at birth plagued by anxieties characteristic of psychosis which it attempts to fend off and control through the primary defense mechanisms of splitting, projection, and introjection giving rise to the paranoid-schizoid and depressive positions that mold object relations. While Klein refers to these defensive maneuvers as "mechanisms," they are not mechanistic. Ego activity is never fixed or static operations taking the forms of predetermined tropisms, rather psychic organization is the continuity of subjective temporal processes. It is more accurate to conceptualize these early mechanisms as defensive *process systems* comprised by the ego's intrapsychic relation to itself and its object environment, initially the maternal object. This makes ego development and object relations an intersubjective enterprise.

In her seminal essay, "Notes on Some Schizoid Mechanisms," Klein (1946) proclaims splitting as the original primordial defense, a process she started analyzing as early as 1929. Beset by the death drive (*Todestrieb*), the immature ego deflects the destructive impulse by turning it against the object accompanied by oral-sadistic attacks on the mother's body thus giving rise to persecutory anxiety. Splitting is the very first in a series of defenses that are never completely separate from one another, hence forming the dialectical cycle we have come to label as projective identification. While Klein cogently articulates the gradual evolution and strengthening of the ego, she concedes that "so far, we know nothing about the structure of the early ego" (p. 4). Here Hegel is instructive for contributing to psychoanalytic theory.

As previously outlined, Hegel traces the dialectic course of the soul as a sentient feeling entity – at first a prenatal agent – only to gradually acquire more personal unity and organization as ego. It is important to note that both Klein and Hegel use the same word *Ich* to designate the personal agency of the ego – at first an unconscious constellation that later makes consciousness possible. Klein says very little about the prehistory of the ego prior to birth, yet she is suggestive.

> The question arises whether some active splitting processes within the ego may not occur even at a very early age. As we assume, the early ego splits the object and the relation to it in an active way, and this may imply some active splitting of the ego itself.
>
> *(1946, p. 5)*

Klein is correct in showing that splitting is the ego's original defensive activity despite the fact that she omits explaining how the ego is formed in the first place. This is presumably due to her scientific attitude guided by empirical considerations, but by way of Hegel's speculative metaphysics, the logical progression of the dialectic clarifies this process. Through Hegel's logic, we can reasonably conclude that the ego exists prior to birth and is prepared by the unconscious activity of the soul lending increasing order to intrapsychic structure. Because the ego cannot simply materialize *ex nihilo*, it must emanate from a prior unconscious ground or abyss (*Ungrund*). The ego has a prenatal life which is developmentally prepared prior to conscious perception: unconscious experience precedes consciousness.

Not only does Hegel situate splitting at the inception of the soul's development, he demonstrates that splitting is the earliest activity of mind. Splitting becomes the prototype of mental process and remains a fundamental operation in the normative as well as the pathological functions of the psyche. The unconscious soul first undergoes an internal division or separation of its interior which it projects as an external object *within its own internality*, only to re-gather and again make it part of its inner constitution. This primary splitting activity is architectonic, thus forming the foundation for psychic growth. Since splitting is identified as the initial movement of the dialectic thus effecting its transition into mediatory relations, it becomes easy to see how splitting becomes the archetype of later ego activity which Klein emphasizes in her developmental framework. But unlike Klein (1946, 1955) who repeatedly tells us that the ego's first object is the mother's breast, it would follow that the ego's first object is itself – its own internality. Hegel does not contradict Klein's main theses, he only substantiates her theoretical innovations. The ego must first posit and set itself over its initial immediacy which it does through splitting.

In "Splitting of the Ego in the Process of Defence," a posthumously published unfinished paper, Freud (1940 [1938]) addresses the notion of disavowal and the "alteration of the ego" that goes beyond his earlier treatment of splitting in cases of psychoses (1924, *SE*, 19, pp. 152–153) and fetishism (1927, *SE*, 21, pp. 155–156) which is now included within his general theory of neurosis. Freud, as does Klein, generally sees the conceptualization of splitting as a defensive process that is usually confined to the domains of conflict, while Hegel's emphasis on the internal divisibility of the soul makes splitting a generic process that may be applied to any mediatory aspect of division and negation within the mind. But in *New Introductory Lectures*, Freud (1933) is clear that splitting is a general ego operation: "the ego can be split; it splits itself during a number of its functions – temporarily at least. Its parts can come together again afterwards" (*SE*, 22, p. 58). Freud also alludes to an innate and normative function of splitting as it is applied to the synthetic processes of the ego. He states: "The synthetic function of the ego, though it is of such extraordinary importance, is subject to particular conditions and is liable to a whole number of disturbances" (1940, *SE*, 23, p. 276). While Freud emphasized the synthetic functions of ego unification in several places before (see *SE*, 1926a, 20, pp. 97–100, 1926b, 20, p. 196, 1933, 22, p. 76), which had always been an implicit part of his theory, Hegel shows that splitting is a basic psychic operation that may take on more pathological configurations throughout development, such as in the cases of psychotic and schizoid disorders articulated by Klein and her followers, or in pathological narcissism and borderline personality, a topic that occupies much of the literature today (see Kernberg, 1975; Masterson, 1981).

For Hegel, the ego is unconsciously implicit within the sentient feeling soul and is already a prenatal form of self-awareness. Both a sensuous and cognizing agent, unconscious spirit intuits itself as an "intro-reflected" or pre-reflective, non-propositional self-conscious being – intro-reflection being the process of unconscious spirit's immediate self-awareness and self-identification. In Hegel's discussion of the ego's actual emergence from its natural embodiment as soul, the ego has to confront its corporeal confinement and inwardness. He states: "It is through this *intro-reflection* (*Reflexion-in-sich*) that spirit completes its liberation from the form of *being*, gives itself that of *essence*, and becomes *ego*" (*EG* § 412, *Zusätz*). In its alteration from mere immediacy to determinate mediate being, the soul *senses* its Self as an impression, already containing the rudiments of ego-awareness in its self-intuiting. In its ego explicitness, before the soul makes its final trajectory to consciousness, unconscious spirit has already undergone a splitting of its interior in manifold accounts by its own hands. In each incremental process of splitting that accompanies sublation there is an internal division, projection, and (re)introjection of its particularization back into its internality. Each introjective maneuver is a re-incorporation of its projected interior that takes place through an identification with its alienated shape(s) it takes to be an exterior object however possessing its internal qualities. Such projective identification may be said to be the truncated recognition the soul has with itself through the process of intro-reflection – itself a preliminary form of unconscious self-consciousness – only that the ego has undergone a splitting as an element of defense against its unconsciously perceived conflict which subsists due to the negative tension of the dialectic.

As noted, this continual process of internal separation, projection, and introjection as re-incorporation is the general structural operation of projective identification. The ego projects its internality as alienation, comes to recognize and identify with its alienated qualities, then takes hold of and repossesses its earlier disavowed shapes. It is through this continual elevating process that both the content and the developmental hierarchy of the mind becomes more complex and sophisticated. Unconscious spirt comes to take itself as its own object through intro-reflection once it projects its interior as its exterior then "reflects upon it, takes back into its internality the externality of nature, idealizes [or cognizes] nature" (*EG* § 384, *Zusätz*), and thus effects a transition back into reunification. Spirit is continually engaged in this dialectical process in all its shapes, however at this level in the soul's development, unconscious spirit displays an early form of self-recognition through its projective identification as mediated intro-reflection.

This model of unconscious self-consciousness as self-recognition becomes the logical template for Hegel's theory of self-consciousness outlined in the dialectic of desire and recognition advanced in the *Phenomenology* (§§ 166–230). Although Hegel discusses desire and recognition in his phenomenological treatment of self-consciousness, it is already prepared in the anthropology as an ontological feature of unconscious spirit. The soul is desirous – the abyss is unconsciously self-aware, with drive (*Trieb*) and intro-reflection providing the logical prototype for desire and self-consciousness to emerge in conscious life. While both Freud and Klein see the ego as a more modified portion of the id, Hegel more clearly shows that consciousness is the manifestation of unconscious structure.

But why would the unconscious ego *need* to split itself in the first place? Here Klein and Hegel are on the same page. The ego's original activity is one of negation: it defines itself in opposition to what it is not. Following Freud (1920), Klein speculates that splitting mechanisms arise in an effort to subvert the death drive which threatens the ego with internal destruction. Splitting is a defense against felt or perceived annihilation. As too for Hegel, unconscious spirit first encounters an inner negativity, aggressivity, or conflict that becomes the impetus for dialectical intervention. In fact, splitting itself is a violent cleaving operation that divides subject from object. For Klein, splitting disperses the destructive impulse, while for Hegel splitting is destructive – it destroys as it negates. But the destruction incurred by the canceling function of the dialectic is also preserved in the same moment as the ego sublates itself to a higher state. Splitting and projection highlight the negative side of the dialectic while introjection serves a synthetic function. The repetitive process of projective identification may be applied toward the general ascending thrust of sublation or succumb to contentious dichotomies that are mired in chaos. While the relationship between the death impulse and negation still remains equivocal, destruction is nevertheless a key element in the progressive unification of the ego.

In several works, Klein (1946, 1952) underscores the point that the ego has an orienting principle toward higher degrees of unification. Elsewhere she states: "Together with the urge to split there is from the beginning of life a drive towards integration" (1963, p. 300). This is the affirmative and ongoing drive of the ego that forms the edifice of the Hegelian dialectic, a proclivity that inevitably strives for wholeness to which Klein herself endorses. Hegel's emphasis on holism anticipates Klein's (1960) advocacy for a well-integrated personality, the goal of which is to master early developmental frictions that arise from persecutory anxiety and its vicissitudes.

But for Hegel and Klein, there is a dual tendency for both progression and regression, elevation and withdrawal back to previous points of fixation. As Klein (1946) puts it, "the early ego largely lacks cohesion, and a tendency towards integration alternates with a tendency towards disintegration, a falling into bits" (p. 4). Hegel refers to this disintegration as a fixation and/or regression to the form of feeling – the original self-enclosed simple unity of the feeling soul, a dynamic responsible for "madness" (see *EG* §§ 403–408).[14] Like Klein who stresses the primacy of developmentally working through the paranoid-schizoid and depressive positions, Hegel sees mental health as the ability to achieve holism through sublation: while feeling is never abandoned as such, it devolves into the higher instantiations of self-conscious rational thought. Even Klein (1963) herself says that "the urge towards integration, as well as the pain experienced in the process of integration, spring from internal sources which remain powerful throughout life" (p. 313). For Hegel, this would be tantamount to the labor of spirit, an arduous poignant crusade. If the subjective mind is not able to developmentally progress toward synthetic rational integration, then earlier primitive defensive constellations will persist unabated.

Bion on Thinking, Linking, and Phantasy

While Klein (1946) first defined projective identification as a defensive process expressed through splitting and schizoid mechanisms, she later (1957) suggested that envy was intimately imbedded in projective identification, a process by which the ego forces itself into the psychic reality of the other in order to destroy its coveted attributes. Shortly after this theoretical modification, Bion (1959) distinguished normal from pathological forms of projective identification which has further led revisionist Kleinians to articulate many distinct yet related modes of projective-identificatory processes (Hinshelwood, 1991).

Bion, himself analyzed by Klein, was the first psychoanalyst to recognize normative functions of projective identification imbedded in normal thought processes. Bion (1959, 1962a, 1962b) distinguished between two alternative aims of projective identification marked by difference in the degree of violence attached to the mechanism. The first, *evacuation*, is characterized by its forceful entry into an object, in phantasy, as a means of controlling painful mental states directed toward relief and often aimed toward intimidating or manipulating the object. This is a pathological manifestation of projective identification. The second, *communication*, is a more benign attempt to communicate a certain mental content by introducing into the object a specific state of mind, a function often seen in the process of *containing* – a process in which one person contains some part of another. This is a normative function. It may be argued that evacuation is itself a form of communication, thereby the distinction becomes blurred; but for our purposes, evacuation highlights the thrust, intensity, and urgency of the need to expel psychic content. In all likelihood, evacuation and communication operate in confluence separated only by their motives and force of violence enacted through projection.

In his influential essay, "Attacks on Linking," Bion (1959) presents his mature view of projective identification as a form of communication taking on both normal and abnormal valences. Drawing on Klein, pathological forms fall within a range of *excess*, such as the degree of aggressivity of splitting, hatred, intrusion, omnipotent control and fusion with the object, the amount of loss or defusion of the ego, and the specific awareness of destructive intent. Normal projective-identificatory processes, however, play an adaptive role in social reality and are ordinary operations of communication and empathy which furthermore transpire within the process of thinking itself.

Bion's (1957) model of thinking, linking, and phantasy is preliminarily addressed in his effort to differentiate psychotic from non-psychotic personalities with special emphasis on the awareness of psychic reality. For Bion (1954), drawing on Klein's (1930) and later Hanna Segal's (1957) work on symbol formation in the development of the early ego, the awareness of psychic reality is contingent upon the capacity for verbal thought derived from the depressive position; yet this process goes back even further. Linking – the capacity to form relations between objects or mental contents – serves a functional purpose, a process derived from the paranoid-schizoid position. Bion (1957, 1959) envisions psychotic organization to be largely plagued by violent attacks on the ego – particularly on the links between certain mental contents – and the awareness of inner reality itself. As a result, the schizophrenic lives in a fractured world of terror where mental links are "severed" or "never forged." Phantasy formation is fragmented, persecutory, and horrific. Attempts at linking conjunctions or making connections between objects are all but destroyed, and when minute links exist, they are impregnated with perversion and cruelty.

What is of importance in understanding the normative functions of projective identification is how Bion conceives of the phenomenology and evolution of thinking, a process that brings him in dialogue with Hegel. Bion (1957) informs us that "some kind of thought, related to what we should call ideographs and sight rather than to words and hearing exists at the outset," a capacity derived within the non-psychotic part of the embryonic psyche (p. 66). He continues to tell us that this crude level of thinking "depends on the capacity for balanced introjection and projection of objects and, *a fortiori*, on awareness of them" (p. 66). Ultimately for Bion, both pre-verbal and verbal thought necessarily requires an awareness of psychic reality.

Throughout the course of his theoretical contributions, Bion explicates three phases in the process of thinking. The first relies on the presumption of *a priori* knowledge whereby an innate *preconception* meets a *realization* in experience which results in a *conception*, the product of thought (Bion, 1959, 1962a). Bion's notion of preconceptions is similar to Segal's (1964) notion of unconscious phantasy used as a means of generating hypotheses for testing reality. A preconception may be understood as a predisposed intuition of and expectancy for an object, such as a breast, which "mates" with the realization of the actual object in experience, thus forming a conception.

The second phase depends on the infant's capacity to tolerate frustration. A positive conception is generated when a preconception meets with a satisfying realization. When a preconception encounters a negative realization – absence, frustration ensues. Klein shows that when the immature ego encounters absence, it experiences the presence of a bad object, or perhaps more appropriately, a bad self-object experience. Bion, however, extends this idea further and posits that the experience of absence is transformed into a thought. The notion of absence, lack, or nothingness is conceptually retained. Yet this process is contingent on the infant's ability to modulate frustration. If frustration tolerance is high, the generation of absence into a thought serves the dialectical function that presence is possible, viz. the absent object may appear or re-present itself at some later time in the future, such as the breast or bottle. For Hegel, affirmation and negation are dialectically conjoined, separated only by their moments. With application to Bion, nothing stands in opposition to being which, once realized, is expected to return. If the capacity to manage frustration is low, the experience of nothingness does not advance to the thought of an absent good object, but rather remains at the immediate level of the concrete bad object experienced in the moment which must be expelled through omnipotent evacuation.

Bion (1962a) believes that if this process becomes arrested, advances in symbol formation and thinking are deleteriously obstructed.

The third phase of thinking involves more advanced levels of projective identification which Bion (1962b) describes as the container-contained relationship. Here the infant has a sensory experience, feeling, or need which is perceived as bad which the infant wishes to banish. This type of projective identification evokes within the mother the same type of internal sensations experienced by the infant. If the mother is adequately well-balanced and capable of optimal responsiveness, what Bion calls *reverie*, she will be able to contain such feelings and transform them into acceptable forms which the infant can re-introject. Bion labels this process of transformation the *alpha-function*. In normal development, the container-contained relationship allows the infant to re-introject the transformed object into something tolerable which eventually results in internalizing the function itself. If successful, this process aids in the increased capacity to modulate frustration and developmentally strengthens the infant's cognitive capabilities to conceptualize and generate symbolic functions, which generally leads to the fortification of the ego. Not only does Bion breach the sharp schism between feeling and thought that has dogged philosophical rationalism, he shows how emotions are made meaningful within the broader conceptual processes of thinking (Spillius, 1988).

Hegel's Philosophical Psychology

Bion's theory of thinking is prefaced by Hegel's detailed analysis of the ontological processes of thought and the phenomenology of consciousness. In the *Science of Logic*, Hegel is concerned with articulating the ground, scope, and functional operations of thinking, reason, and the coming into being of pure self-consciousness, while the *Phenomenology of Spirit* comprehensively outlines the various appearances or shapes of individual and collective consciousness. Hegel's philosophical psychology is presented in his philosophy of subjective spirit outlined in the third division of his *Encyclopaedia*. Recall that Hegel discusses the role and function of the unconscious soul in the Anthropology which preludes the activities of conscious awareness. In the Psychology, he shows how the normative operations of thought, perception, attention, imagination, phantasy, memory, and concept formation are intimately associated with unconscious processes that are prepared by the soul or unconscious ego.

Subjective spirit expresses itself as cognition actively concerned with finding reason within itself (*EG* § 445). As the forms of theoretical spirit or intelligence unfold, the unconscious abyss is the primary domain of this activity. Hegel points out that intelligence follows a formal course of development to cognition beginning with (a) intuition or sensation of an immediate object (*EG* § 446), to (b) presentation (*EG* § 451) as a withdrawal into the unconscious from the relationship to the singularity of a presented object in consciousness and thus relating such object to a universal, leading to (c) thought (*EG* § 465) in which intelligence grasps the concrete universals of thinking and being as objectivity. In the stage of intuition as immediate cognizing, intelligence begins with the sensation of the immediate object, then alters itself by fixing attention on the object while differentiating itself from it, and then posits the material as external to itself which becomes intuition proper. The second main stage of intelligence as presentation is concerned with recollection, imagination, and memory, while the final stage in the unfolding of intelligence is thought which has its content in understanding, judgement, and reason.

By Hegelian standards, Bion's model of thinking appears rather simplistic; but in his defense, Bion (1962a) himself admits his theoretical system "differs from philosophical theory in that it is intended, like all psychoanalytical theories, for use . . . composed in terms of empirically verifiable data" (p. 306). However, Hegel is very clear that his speculative outlook is not at odds with empiricism, instead "experience" becomes the standpoint of "*speculative thinking*."[15] In the *Philosophy of Nature* he also states: "Not only must philosophy be in agreement with our empirical knowledge of Nature, but the *origin* and *formation* of the Philosophy of Nature presupposes and is conditioned by empirical . . . science."[16] Like Bion, Hegel is concerned with articulating the inner meaning and ontology of thinking that applies to both normal development and disease.

Bion's scheme is remarkably compatible with Hegel's on many levels emphasizing: (1) the awareness of inner reality, (2) the nature of pre-conceptual mental activity, and (3) the process of realization as conceptual thought. In our discussion of Hegel's theory of the soul, the unconscious ego attains for itself via *intro-reflection* a preliminary level of non-propositional, pre-reflective self-consciousness; that is, the nascent ego does not yet posit itself as a subject reflecting upon itself as an object, but rather is intuitively aware of its internal divisions and shapes that it sets over itself through its splitting activity. Such unconscious self-consciousness is the prototype for the process of consciousness. In fact, consciousness itself is a split off and projected instantiation of unconscious structure.

Unconscious intro-reflection corresponds to Bion's notion of innate *a priori* knowledge in the form of preconceptions, yet for Bion this gets explained through encounters with realized or non-realized objects resulting in positive (satisfying) or negative (frustrating, non-gratifying) conceptions. Hegel's epistemology derives from the logic of the dialectic, while Bion's is merely presupposed yet verified through the subjective encounter. In order for conceptualization to occur, certain mental pre-conditions or configurations must be thought to exist prior to experience which are mobilized from the beginning. Through the principle of sufficient reason, there must be a ground to psychic life that precedes conscious experience, and this assumption remains a cardinal pillar of psychoanalytic doctrine.

For Hegel, the process of conceiving or conceptual thought is a complex achievement, an activity attained very early from Bion's account. Bion's notion of preconceptions would be explained by Hegel as the implicit realization of ideas or the Concept (*Begriff*) within the deep internal abyss of spirit – a process fully actualized in Absolute Knowing. Put in more accessible language, the unconscious ego generates pre-conceptual, pre-linguistic ideas belonging to its innate natural constitution, what Klein and Bion would contend are drive derivatives. But Hegel also locates pre-conceptual mentation within the realm of unconscious feeling, a position closely allied with Bion's. Furthermore, both Hegel and Bion place primacy on the awareness of psychic reality – for Hegel, in the feeling soul, and for Bion, as a pre-condition for the process of thought and symbol formation to transpire. For both Hegel and Bion, awareness of inner reality is a necessary and universal condition for symbolization, phantasy, and language acquisition to occur.

Unconscious Intelligence

Hegel is very specific in tracing the intellectual development of the subjective mind, a process that has further implications for Bion and Klein. For Hegel, intelligence moves from sensation of its immediate material to attention, whereby it fixes the object as well as separates it from itself, to intuition as positing the object externally. At this point, the presentation of a certain object thrusts intelligence into its second main movement which has three corresponding substages: (a) recollection, (b) imagination, and (c) memory. Presentation (*Vorstellung*) is implicit within intuition because attention is paid to two moments, namely feeling and the attending act, whereby an object is isolated and related to externally. Attention now becomes introspective and must *re-collect* the content intuited within itself, "within its *own space* and its *own time*" (*EG* § 452). This content initially appears as an image (*Bild*) which is taken up by the ego and disassociated from its external context in which intuition had occurred. Abstracted from the concrete immediacy of intuition, the image becomes contingent or arbitrary and is but a fleeting moment since attention may focus on only one thing at a time.

Essentially, the ego internalizes its presented content by gathering up and separating the external image or impression and then making it part of its internal structure, but being only a transient impression it vanishes quickly from consciousness. "Intelligence is not, however, only the consciousness and the determinate being . . .; recollected within it, the image is no longer existent, but is preserved unconsciously" (*EG* § 453). Here Hegel points to the underworld of spirit; intelligence is *not only* consciousness but is a "nocturnal abyss (*nachtlichen Schacht*) within which a world of infinitely numerous images and presentations is preserved without being in consciousness." Hegel specifically equates "intelligence as this unconscious abyss," thus forming the domains of two fundamental realities, the world of the deep and the world of consciousness.

This is the first textual mention of the unconscious within the Psychology, § 453, thus pointing to its relationship with consciousness. Hegel explains how unconscious presentations are preserved within certain "fibers" and "localities" of the abyss, recalcitrant, as they were, to the tangibility of conscious processes, subsisting as intrinsically concrete yet simple universals. Intelligence has "imperfect control of the images slumbering within the abyss" that cannot be recalled at will (*EG* § 453, *Zusätz*). Hegel himself even concedes that we have no means of knowing the full extent of all that which lies within the unconscious, suggesting that there are certain elements to psychic life that may resist incorporation into the dialectic. "No one knows what an infinite host of images of the past slumbers within him. Although they certainly awaken by chance on various occasions, one cannot, – as it is said, – call them to mind" (*EG* § 453, *Zusätz*). This concession on Hegel's part points to the inner autonomy of unconscious processes and organizations, presumably belonging to the soul – the unconscious ego, and how, from the standpoint of consciousness, they share a divided existence within spirit. This suggests that there is always an element of "chance," as Hegel says, and contingency that spirit can never completely overcome.

Imagination

What is of particular interest here is Bion's theory of ideographs in relation to Hegel's theory of imagination and phantasy. Bion (1957) postulates that something analogous to ideographs and sight are formed in the pre-verbal ego, presumably as early as the paranoid-schizoid position if not from birth onward. This would collaborate Hegel's theory of imagination and particularly his notion of symbolization. As noted before, unconscious images are preserved within the abyss of the mind, and due to the negative character of the dialectic as well as early developmental contingencies that mold ego development and object relations, they can take on many persecutory qualities and valences that are in need of evacuation. To recall an image is to repeat or re-present an intuition, and this is why it is free of immediate intuition because it is "preserved unconsciously." We recognize in immediate perception images we have experienced before. While consciousness isolates a specific feature, it relates it to the universality of unconscious recollection. Representation is therefore the synthesized product of relating an immediate intuition to an unconscious universal which becomes an object for consciousness. It is in imagination, however, where the process of relating one representation to others is intellectually carried out.

For Hegel, imagination mediates between intuition and thought. In imagination, representations are related to one another in the flow of consciousness which becomes linked with other images, affects, and thoughts as they are generated and manipulated by the ego's activity. Retrieved from the abyss, they are now technically under the ego's control, but with qualifications. Imagination also assumes three forms or sub-stages, namely: (a) reproductive imagination,

(b) associative imagination, and (c) phantasy. First, representations are reproduced from the abyss but fall under the direction of the ego as "the issuing *forth* of images from the ego's own inwardness" which it now governs (*EG* § 455). The line of demarcation that divides the unconscious ego from the conscious ego is now breached: the ego vacillates between its unconscious and conscious counterparts.

Images are not only retrieved but issued forth from the ego itself, assuming that unconscious material is externalized into conscious apprehension, or as Hegel puts it, "excogitated . . . from the generality of the abyss." This process immediately initiates an association of variegated images and features that are related to further presentations which may be either abstract or concrete and varying in content and form, thereby the range of intellectual connections expands. However, if links are attacked, as Bion informs us, such connections would be attenuated. But normatively within this multiplicity of associations, the synthetic functions of intelligence are already operative as thought implicit within intelligence. Imagination in general determines images. As a formal activity, the reproduction of images occurs "*voluntarily*" (*EG* § 455, *Zusätz*); it does not require the aid of an immediate intuition to effect this process as in the case of recollection which is dependent upon the presence of an intuition. Distinguished from recollection, intelligence is now "self-activating."

Phantasy

Phantasy is the third movement of imagination where the ego fully manipulates its representations and images, drawing lines of interconnection where particulars are subsumed under universals and given the richer elaboration of symbols and signs which effect the ego's transition to memory, the third stage of presentation. Phantasy is a subjective bond the ego has with its contents, and with the introduction of symbolization, allegory, and sign, imagination gains increased synthetic mastery over its presentations that are imbued with "reason." Here the inwardness of intelligence "is *internally determined concrete subjectivity*, with *a capacity* of its own deriving" (*EG* § 456). Within fantasy, there is an imagined existence as hidden unconscious processes infiltrate the creative centers of subjectivity. This can be both monstrous and sublime.

While fantasy attains its most elaborate articulation in language and speech, it does not strictly require words in order to show itself. This may be achieved by the mind's manipulation of its own operations with respect to both content and cognitive functions, such as the confluence of certain feeling states attached to interrelated images. In fact, fantasy is the *a priori* condition for language, it is a pre-linguistic organization that precedes organized conceptual thought.[17] Here Hegel's position is Kleinian: phantasy precedes concept formation. While Klein, Bion, Segal, and others focus upon the content, motives, and qualitative attributes underlying the phenomenology of phantasy, Hegel clarifies the ontological processes that make phantasy possible.

Phantasy both symbolizes and engenders signs. Initially it subsumes singulars under a universal through symbolization, but because the immediate content is both a particularization and a universal, interpretation remains ambiguous. Phantasy becomes a central operation in unconscious production, a spewing forth of impulses and desires from the wishing well of the abyss. It may be suspended in space and time, conform to the abyss's will through regression or withdrawal irrespective of the ego's counter-intentions, and warp objective reality to the tone of the ego's own subjective caprice. This is why images may be either disturbing or pleasing. The "*symbolizing, allegorizing* or *poetical* power of the imagination" (*EG* § 456) is not confined to the mere subjective however, it may take an external objective referent as the embodiment of its creativity. This move constitutes "the phantasy of sign making" (*EG* § 457).

Through signification, intelligence is concerned with unifying the relations between determinate content and what it signifies universally. The synthesis of fantasy is the unity of the sign with the universal and its self-relation. Hegel states, "in phantasy intelligence has being, for the first time, not as an indeterminate abyss and universal, but as a singularity, i.e. as concrete subjectivity, in which the self-relation is determined in respect of being as well as universality" (*EG* § 457). This statement suggests that universality itself is a sort of abyss, in that all particularity is lost in it, whether this be the soul's initial immersion with and undifferentiation from nature or its subsumption in universal spirit. Such unification of the sign with universality is seen by spirit as its own activity that is internal and proper to it. Here intelligence gives itself being which is now within its own capacity to do. Not to be underestimated in its importance, the sign "adds proper intuitability" to images as an objective existent (*EG* § 457). While the symbol refers to the intuition of the content and its relation to its essence and Concept, the sign *designates* meaning in which the content of intuition becomes dissociated to what it signifies (*EG* § 458). In symbolic phantasy, intelligence pays attention to the given content of images, but in sign phantasy it replaces imagined universality with objective affirmation – the presented universal is liberated from the content of images. Hegel tells us:

> The *sign* is a certain immediate intuition, presenting a content which is wholly distinct from that which it has for itself; it is the *pyramid* in which the alien soul is ensconced and preserved.
>
> *(EG § 458).*

Hence intelligence proceeds from the pit to the pyramid, the soul sublated as intelligence gains more mastery over its self-designating operations. The content of intuition becomes "irrelevant" to what it signifies. Spirit may now focus on the signified universal rather than on the particular features of its intuited content. But before its final transition to memory, imagination must cancel its subjectivity, its internality, and give itself objective being. In this way it unifies "the universal and being, one's own and what is appropriated, inner and outer being, are given the completeness of a unit" (*EG* § 457). These operations belong to the mature liberated ego, a developmental progression from the primitive functions of unconscious phantasy guided by archaic forces.

Intelligence goes beyond the sign to understanding its meaning. With each new immediate intuition, intelligence moves from unconscious determinateness which transforms intuitions into images, images into representations, representations into associations, and is thus raised to the level of objective existence and self-determining being as sublatedness – a normative process conforming to the dialectic of projective identification. Intelligence is now presented (as presenting itself) with a "*tone*" from the unconscious soul "which intelligence furnishes from the anthropological resources of its own naturalness, the fulfillment of the expressiveness by which inwardness makes itself known" (*EG* § 459). Sound instantiates itself further in speech, and as the interrelations of words, in a system of language which endows the sensations, intuitions, and representations with a "second determinate being" that sublates the immediacy of the first. Spirit no longer needs the constant presence of external signs; when they vanish as ephemeral phenomena, intelligence draws upon its inner meaning and "inner symbolism" as it generates and relates to its own processes. Intelligence remains active, it confers meaning through sounds and words and as such becomes a sublated intuition for itself. Networks of meaningful relations are externalized as signs, and when they disappear the mind must reconstitute their significance through its own self-relating activity. Imagination first makes visible unconscious processes in the form of images, then manipulates their relations through phantasy, conferring symbolization and assigning meaning – the name, a word. When the name vanishes, imagination either must create a new name for its set of relations, or it must recollect a previous name and its meaning and attach it to new associations. This requires memory.

Intelligence has moved from its initial task of internalizing intuitions, to its externalization of the abyss through imagination, to which it takes its next shape as memory, the task of which is to integrate its previous two movements. While intelligence gains greater dynamic unity in verbal, reproductive, and mechanical memory, Hegel sees theoretical spirit through to its end, viz. to thought as understanding, judgement, and formal reason. Thought knows itself, it *re-cognizes* itself which achieves its fullest logical elaboration as pure thinking: thought thinking about itself and its operations. While these are the greater faculties of spirit, they need not concern us here. Bion's model of ideographs is given richer articulation by Hegel's analysis of imagination which has further implications for understanding unconscious phantasy.

We may say that the types of thoughts and conceptions Bion speaks of during the ego's early development of thinking, linking, and phantasy is not the type of conceptualizing belonging to formal intelligence or reason, but is instead associated to the *functions* objects serve. I believe the pre-verbal ego constructs meaning not through concepts or words, but through images, impressions, and/or sensory-tactile sensations that are internally processed in relation to a felt referent and related to objects encountered in phantasy, either real or imagined. Thought is originally the succession of sensory impressions imbued with emotional mediacy linked to functional meaning associated with objects of experience. What becomes encoded or imprinted on the psyche is the functional qualities, properties, attributes, and consequences of the presence and experience of objects. Under the influence of internal drives and their derivatives – such as wishes and their vicissitudes – the nascent ego constructs meaningful relations to objects through the functional attributions of phantasy which are subject to the anxieties and/or pleasure associated with its own internal impulses and subjectively perceived object attachments. Images and sensory experience related to objects are imbued with functional meaning, linked to associative affect or corresponding feeling states, recorded, and laid down as memory traces in the deep abyss of the unconscious which are called up when phantasy is mobilized.

We are justified, I believe, in further saying that the nascent ego performs such mediatory operations by attaching functional meaning to objects in the form of qualities and their related expectations which take on the signification of the affects evoked corresponding to gratifying or anxiety ridden associations. In effect, the ego assigns an object and the experience of such a task or job which is related to the quality and expectation it evokes, the represented meaning of which stands for the function the object serves. Thus, sensory impressions become the original contents for the earliest modes of thought, first having their origins in the prenatal activity of the unconscious mind where the embryonic ego senses its own internality along with the predisposed preconceptions belonging to its various constitutional pressures. In the beginning moments of conscious life, the ego forms meaningful associations to objects based on the functional qualities and evoked affective states mediated through phantasy, a process that becomes more robust during language acquisition and formal concept formation. What Hegel refers to as the function of symbols and signs, or what Bion calls ideographs, we may speculate occurs at the crudest level of conscious life if not before. While the incipient ego does not think in concepts or words, the experience of objects are dialectically mediated through projective identification in phantasy which signify various functional meanings. It is only when language is introduced that such mediatory relations acquire conceptual signification in the form of names and words.

We have seen the overwhelming presence and indispensable function of the nocturnal abyss throughout the stage of presentation, the necessary precondition for higher activities of mind to become manifest. Presentations are fleeting and much of memory fades, but it becomes imprinted within the soul and wells up from imagination. Hegel explains:

> The power of memory is replaced by an unchanging tableau of a series of images fixed in the imagination . . . Not only is spirit put to the torment of being pestered with a deranged subject matter, but whatever is learnt by rote in this manner is as a matter of course soon forgotten again. . . . What is mnemonically imprinted is as it were read off from the tableau of the imagination . . . and so really brought forth from within, rehearsed from the deep abyss of the ego.
>
> *(EG § 462)*

As Hegel reminds us once again, intelligence is unconsciously constituted as ego. There can be no doubt about the importance of imagination and its relation to the abyss; spirit is as much dependent on imagination – especially phantasy – as it is on reason. In fact, their relationship is so intimate that it leads Hegel to say, even with stipulations, that "phantasy is reason" (*EG* § 457). Imagination therefore becomes the locus of the powers of the mind.

Conclusion: Toward Process Psychology

Hegel's anticipation of Klein's and Bion's theories of projective identification as the process of the self returning to itself due to its own self-estrangement adds to our understanding of both the normative and pathological processes of mind. In health and illness the ego projects certain aspects of the self onto the object world, which it then identifies with and finally re-introjects back into the subject. In effect, the self rediscovers itself in the product of its own projection and then reintegrates itself within itself as reunification. This is the generic structural movement of the Hegelian dialectic, whereby internal division, external projection, and re-incorporation function as a mediating and sublating dynamic.

With the introduction of the Hegelian dialectic, psychoanalysis may enjoy new vistas and advances in theory, application, and technique (Mills, 2010). There is a preponderance of evidence in traditional and contemporary psychoanalytic theory to conclude that the mind in general and the unconscious in particular is dialectical both in its structural organization and its internal content.[18] In general, psychoanalysis would contend that the dialectical modes of *Geist* are themselves differentiated and modified forms of the mind maintained through ego mechanisms of intentionality and defense.[19] Klein herself, as well as all post-Kleinians, constantly refer to the dialectical forces of splitting accompanied by projection and introjection that are responsible for both good and bad self-object representations as well as the general division between the ego and the object and the internal polarities that maintain rigid antitheses struggling for reconciliation. Hegel's emphasis on psychic holism mirrors the general consensus among Kleinians that the ego strives for wholeness guided by an orienting principle aimed toward increased synthetic integration – the primary motive of sublation. This is simply the dialectic of desire, the internal thrust of spirit that yearns for self-completion.

While Klein discovered projective identification, which further led Bion to advance the distinction between its normal and pathological variants, Hegel was the first to articulate the formal structural processes of projective identification having its source and origins within the unconscious mind. Since Bion, a less pejorative attitude toward patients' use of projective identification has been adopted among clinicians, which has further initiated attempts to define different aspects and subtypes of this phenomena differentiated by form and motive – such as the degree of control over the object, the attributes acquired, the need to protect certain positive qualities or to avoid separation, their relation to splitting, the force of evacuation, communication, etc. – all subsumed under a general rubric (Spillius, 1988).

As we have seen, Hegel's philosophical depiction of projective identification has implications for understanding psychic structure, psychosis and schizoid mechanisms, linking, thinking, symbol formation, phantasy, and containers and change. More recently this concept has been given special attention in its relation to countertransference and empathy (see Ogden, 1982; Tansey & Burke, 1989). Generally we may say that within the context of therapy, the patient projects onto the therapist certain disavowed and repudiated internal contents which the therapist unconsciously identifies with, such as the behavioral fantasies, attributions, or personal qualities that are the objects of splitting, which the therapist then introjects as a function of his or her own ego, thus leading to conflicted inner states that the therapist must manage. If the therapist's countertransference reactions are too strong and/or remain unrecognized as the internalized projected attributions of the patient, s/he may potentially act out such negative states within the therapeutic encounter, thus potentially leading to further internal disruptions in both parties negatively affecting the intersubjective field. Seeing how such a process is dialectically informed may augur well for further advancements in theory and intervention.

Hegel's philosophy may be especially significant for the future of psychoanalysis. His logic of the dialectic adds systematic coherency and philosophical rigor to the theoretical speculations and empirical verity governing psychoanalytic investigation. For Hegel, psychic life is a burgeoning process of becoming: the reality of the inner world as well as that of nature and culture is a dialectical enterprise. If we are to espouse Hegel's great insight that reality – including every intellectual discipline – is about *process*, evolution, and change, then his implications for psychoanalysis may bring about a new relation between wisdom and science. Dialectical psychoanalysis becomes an auspicious sign for realizing the value of process psychology.

Notes

1 When Klein republished her 1946 paper, "Notes on Some Schizoid Mechanisms," in *Developments in Psycho-Analysis*, (London: Hogarth Press, 1952) she added the term 'projective identification' as a way of explaining the process of splitting in connection with projection and introjection (p. 300).

2 In his *Wissenschaftslehre* (§§ 1–3), Fichte discerns these three fundamental "principles" (*Grundsatz*) or transcendental acts of the mind. Cf. Johann Gottlieb Fichte (1794).

3 For example, see Donald Carveth's (1994) inaccurate assessment of Hegel's logic, p. 151.

4 Cf. Immanuel Kant (1781/1787), *Critique of Pure Reason*, Second Division: Transcendental Dialectic, Book II, Chapters I–II.

5 *Science of Logic*, trans. A.V. Miller (Atlantic Highlands, NJ: Humanities Press, 1812/1969). All references to Hegel's *Science of Logic* will refer to *SL* followed by the page number.

6 From the *Encyclopaedia*, M.J. Petry (Ed.), outlines Hegel's Philosophy of Spirit in *Hegel's Philosophy of Subjective Spirit, Vol.1: Introductions; Vol.2: Anthropology; and Vol.3: Phenomenology and Psychology*, (Dordrecht, Holland: D. Reidel Publishing Company, 1978). Petry's edition provides a photographic reproduction of Hegel's original text published in 1830 along with the Zusätze added by Boumann when the material was republished in 1845. Petry's edition also indicates variations between the 1927 and 1830 editions of the Encyclopaedia. His edition has several decisive advantages over A.V. Miller's edition of the *Philosophie des Geistes* translated as the *Philosophy of Mind*. In addition to having the original German text and his notations of the variations between the 1827 and 1830 editions, Petry also provides notes from the Griesheim and Kehler manuscripts. He further provides an accurate translation of the word "unconscious" (bewußtlos) whereas Miller refers to the "subconscious." For these reasons Petry's edition is a superior text to the Miller translation. For comparison, I have also examined Hegel's 1827–28 lectures on the *Philosophy of Spirit: Vorlesungen über die Philosophie des Geistes* (Hamburg: Felix Meiner, 1994). I have mainly relied on Petry's translation but provide my own in places that warrant changes. Hereafter, references to the *Philosophy of Spirit (Die Philosophie des Geistes)*, which is the third part of

Hegel's *Enzyklopädia*, will refer to EG followed by the section number. References to the Zusätze are identified as such.

7 Cf. Petry, *Hegel's Philosophy of Subjective Spirit*, Notes to Vol.3, p. 405.

8 Cf. *Inhibitions, Symptoms, and Anxiety, Standard Edition*, Vol. 20, p. 97. Hereafter all references to the *Standard Edition* will refer to *SE* followed by the volume and page number.

9 Compare to Freud, "The ego is first and foremost a bodily ego." *The Ego and the Id, SE*, 19, p. 26.

10 For both Hegel and Freud, the inchoate ego is originally encased in a unity and is therefore modally undifferentiated from external forces – the inner and outer are fused in a symbiotic organization. Freud informs us "originally the ego includes everything, later it separates off an external world from itself. Our present ego-feeling is, therefore, only a shrunken residue of a much more inclusive – indeed, an all embracing – feeling which corresponded to a more intimate bond between the ego and the world about it" (*Civilization and its Discontents*, 1930, *SE*, 21, p. 68). For Hegel, the natural soul moves from an undifferentiated unity to a differentiated determinate being; so too for Freud, ego boundaries gradually becomes more contrasted, constructed, and consolidated throughout its burgeoning activity. Freud notes that originally an infant is unable to distinguish between its own ego and the external world as the source of stimulation and sensation. But eventually the infant comes to discern its own internal sources of excitation, such as its bodily organs or somatic processes, from external sources of sensation, (e.g., mother's touch, breast, etc.), that become set apart and reintegrated within ego organization. It is not until this stage in ego formation that an object is set over against the ego as an existent entity that is outside of itself. Once the ego moves from primary to secondary narcissism, attachment to external cathected (love) objects form the initial dynamics of object relations and character development.

11 Freud is often misunderstood to be a reductive materialist, relying on his unofficial and immature views espoused in the *Project for a Scientific Psychology* (*SE*, Vol. 1, 1895, p. 295). Freud realized that he could never offer an adequate theory of mind solely from a neurophysiological account and by 1900 had officially abandoned his earlier materialistic visions for a psychological corpus (Cf. *The Interpretation of Dreams*, Vols. 4–5, 1900, p. 536).

12 This point has also been discussed by Jerome Levin (1992, p. 51).

13 In the *Phenomenology*, Hegel tells us: "As Subject . . . the True . . . is the process of its own becoming, the circle that presupposes its end as its goal, having its end also as its beginning; and only by being worked out to its end, is it actual" (*PS* § 18). Later he says, "The realized purpose, or the existent actuality, is movement and unfolded becoming . . .; the self is like that immediacy and simplicity of the beginning because it is the result, that which has returned into itself" (*PS* § 22). In the *Science of Logic*, Hegel further extends the development of the Self to that of the Concept: "The Concept, when it has developed into a *concrete existence* that is itself free, is none other than the *I* or pure self-consciousness" (*SL*, p. 583). For Hegel, the Self and the Concept are pure becoming: "The Idea is essentially *process*" (*Encyclopaedia Logic*, § 215).

14 Hegel offers a cursory description of thought disorder and insanity, however, a critical discussion of his contributions is beyond the scope of this immediate project. For a more detailed analysis of Hegel's theory of abnormal psychology, see Berthold-Bond (1995) and Mills (1996) for a review.

15 *Encyclopaedia Logic*, §§ 7–9.

16 *Philosophy of Nature*, § 246.

17 For Hegel, phantasy developmentally and temporally precedes language or linguistic acquisition. In his discussion in the *Encyclopaedia*, §§ 456–457, phantasy occurs before symbolization and signification and "derives from what is furnished by intuition." It is not until § 458 that he introduces language proper.

18 Freud's conceptualization of the unconscious is organized by the dialectical exchange of psychic forces that seek to maintain a homeostasis. Within all psychoanalytic disciplines since Freud, there appears to be a universal dialectical interplay between the subject and the object. Historically, the post-classical movement in psychoanalysis emphasized the role of the ego as agent of unconscious activity and focused on the ego's motives toward mastery and adaptation of inner forces via defensive construction and transcendence over instinctual demands. While the classical position emphasized the pleasure seeking aims of drives, object relations theories have emphasized the primacy of object relatedness as the central motive of unconscious activity oriented toward interpersonal involvement and relational attachment. Self psychology introduced the centrality of the self as agent motivated toward fulfilling "selfobject" needs of empathic attunement and validation from others, mirroring of self-worth, and the pursuit of idealized relationships all in the narcissistic service of the self. While the field of psychoanalysis has radically departed from Freud's metapsychology and presently focuses on relational theories, intersubjectivity, and contemporary selfobject theory, Freud's psychoanalytic theory remains subsumed as the

theoretical foundation of contemporary thought. However, whether unconscious motivation emanates from the influence of drives, the ego, object relations, or the self, all disciplines within the historical development of psychoanalysis observe the phenomenology of the dialectic. For a review see, Bacal and Newman (1990), Kohut (1984), and Mitchell (1988).

19 See Freud's discussion, *SE*, 19, p. 24; 20, p. 97; 22, pp. 75–76.

References

Bacal, Howard A. and Newman, Kenneth M. (1990). *Theories of Object Relations: Bridges to Self Psychology*. New York: Columbia University Press.

Berthhold-Bond, Daniel (1995). *Hegel's Theory of Madness*. Albany: SUNY Press.

Bion, W. R. (1954). Notes on the Theory of Schizophrenia. *International Journal of Psycho-Analysis*, 35: 113–118.

——— (1957). Differentiation of the Psychotic from the Non-Psychotic Personalities. In Spillius, E. B. (Ed.) *Melanie Klein Today: Developments in Theory and Practice. Volume 1: Mainly Theory*. London: Routledge, 1988: 61–78.

——— (1959). Attacks on Linking. In Spillius, E. B. (Ed.) *Melanie Klein Today: Developments in Theory and Practice. Volume 1: Mainly Theory*. London: Routledge, 1988: 87–101.

——— (1962a). A Theory of Thinking. In Spillius, E. B. (Ed.) *Melanie Klein Today: Developments in Theory and Practice. Volume 1: Mainly Theory*. London: Routledge, 1988: 178–186.

——— (1962b). *Learning from Experience*. London: Heinemann.

Carveth, Donald L. (1994). Selfobject and Intersubjective Theory: A Dialectical Critique. Part I: Monism, Dualism, Dialectic. *Canadian Journal of Psychoanalysis/Revue Canadienne de Psychanalyse*, 2 (2): 151–168.

Fichte, Johann Gottlieb (1794). Peter Heath's and John Lachs' (eds. & trans.). *The Science of Knowledge*. Cambridge: Cambridge University Press, 1970/1982.

Freud, Sigmund. (1886–1940). *The Standard Edition of the Complete Psychological Works of Sigmund Freud*, 24 Vols., James Strachey (Trans.). London: Hogarth Press.

——— (1895). Project for a Scientific Psychology. In *Standard Edition*, Vol. 1.

——— (1900). The Interpretation of Dreams. In *Standard Edition*, Vols. 4–5.

——— (1920). Beyond the Pleasure Principle. In *Standard Edition*, Vol. 18.

——— (1923). The Ego and the Id. In *Standard Edition*, Vol. 19.

——— (1924 [1923]). Neurosis and Psychosis. In *Standard Edition*, Vol. 19.

——— (1926a). Inhibitions, Symptoms and Anxiety. In *Standard Edition*, Vol. 20.

——— (1926b). The Question of Lay Analysis. In *Standard Edition*, Vol. 20.

——— (1927). Fetishism. In *Standard Edition*, Vol. 21.

——— (1930). Civilization and its Discontents. In *Standard Edition*, Vol. 21.

——— (1933 [1932]). New Introductory Lectures on Psycho-Analysis. In *Standard Edition*, Vol. 22.

——— (1940 [1938]). Splitting of the Ego in the Process of Defence. In *Standard Edition*, Vol. 23.

Hegel, G.W.F. (1807/1977). *Phenomenology of Spirit*, A. V. Miller (Trans.). Oxford: Oxford University Press.

——— (1812/1831/1969). *Science of Logic*, A. V. Miller (Trans.). London: George Allen & Unwin LTD.

——— (1817/1827/1830/1970). *Philosophy of Nature. Vol. 2 of the Encyclopaedia of the Philosophical Sciences*, A. V. Miller (Trans.). Oxford: Clarendon Press.

——— (1817/1827/1830/1971). *Philosophy of Mind. Vol.3 of the Encyclopaedia of the Philosophical Sciences*. William Wallace and A. V. Miller (Trans.). Oxford: Clarendon Press.

——— (1817/1827/1830/1991). *The Encyclopaedia Logic, Vol. 1 of the Encyclopaedia of the Philosophical Sciences*, T. F. Geraets, W. A. Suchting, and H. S. Harris (Trans.). Indianapolis: Hackett Publishing Company, Inc.

——— (1827–28/1994). *Vorlesungen über die Philosophie des Geistes*. Hamburg: Felix Meiner.

——— (1978). *Hegel's Philosophy of Subjective Spirit, Vol.1: Introductions, Vol.2: Anthropology, Vol.3: Phenomenology and Psychology*, M. J. Petry (Ed.). Dordrecht, Holland: D. Reidel Publishing Company.

Hinshelwood, R. D. (1991). *A Dictionary of Kleinian Thought*, 2nd ed. Northvale, NJ: Jason Aronson.

Kant, I. (1781/1787). *Critique of Pure Reason*, N. K. Smith (Trans.). New York: St Martin's Press, 1965.

Kernberg, Otto (1975). *Borderline Conditions and Pathological Narcissism*. New York: Jason Aronson.

Klein, Melanie. (1929). Personification in the Play of Children. In *Love, Guilt and Reparation and Other Works, 1921–1945*. London: Hogarth Press, 1981.

——— (1930). The Importance of Symbol Formation in the Development of the Ego. In *Love, Guilt and Reparation and Other Works, 1921–1945*. London: Hogarth Press, 1981.

——— (1946). Notes on Some Schizoid Mechanisms. *International Journal of Psycho-Analysis*, 27: 99–110; In *Envy and Gratitude and Other Works, 1946–1963*. London: Virago Press, 1988: 1–24.
——— (1952). The Mutual Influences in the Development of the Ego and Id. In *Envy and Gratitude and Other Works, 1946–1963*. London: Virago Press, 1988: 57–60.
——— (1955). On Identification. In *Envy and Gratitude and Other Works, 1946–1963*. London: Virago Press, 1988: 141–175.
——— (1957). Envy and Gratitude. In *Envy and Gratitude and Other Works, 1946–1963*. London: Virago Press, 1988: 176–235.
——— (1960). On Mental Health. In *Envy and Gratitude and Other Works, 1946–1963*. London: Virago Press, 1988: 268–274.
——— (1963). On the Sense of Loneliness. In *Envy and Gratitude and Other Works, 1946–1963*. London: Virago Press, 1988: 300–313.
Kohut, Heinz (1984). *How Does Analysis Cure?* A. Goldberg and P. Stepansky (Eds.). Chicago: University of Chicago Press.
Levin, Jerome D. (1992). *Theories of the Self.* Washington, DC: Hemisphere.
Masterson, James F. (1981). *The Narcissistic and Borderline Disorders*. New York: Brunner/Mazel.
Mills, Jon (1996). Hegel on the Unconscious Abyss: Implications for Psychoanalysis. *The Owl of Minerva*, 28 (1): 59–75.
——— (2002). *The Unconscious Abyss: Hegel's Anticipation of Psychoanalysis*. Albany, NY: SUNY Press.
——— (2010). *Origins: On the Genesis of Psychic Reality*. Montreal: McGill-Queens University Press.
Mitchell, Steven A. (1988). *Relational Concepts in Psychoanalysis: An Integration*. Cambridge, MA: Harvard University Press.
Ogden, Thomas G. (1982). *Projective Identification and Psychotherapeutic Technique*. New York: Jason Aronson.
Segal, Hanna (1957). Notes on Symbol Formation. *International Journal of Psycho-Analysis*, 38: 391–397.
——— (1964). Phantasy and Other Mental Processes. *International Journal of Psycho-Analysis*, 45: 191–194.
Spillius, E. B. (Ed.) (1988). *Melanie Klein Today: Developments in Theory and Practice. Volume 1: Mainly Theory*. London: Routledge.
Tansey, Michael J. and Burke, Walter F. (1989). *Understanding Countertransference: From Projective Identification to Empathy*. Hillsdale, NJ: Analytic Press.

3

NIETZSCHE, PSYCHOANALYSIS, NIHILISM

Jared Russell

When Nietzsche saw that bourgeois morality, as the secular articulation of monotheistic guilt having become an insistence at finding fault in the other for one's own weakness and suffering would give rise to a pervasive nihilism that would define our age to the point of consumption, he was warning us that the world was soon to become an unlivable, suicidal nightmare. Only the most deluded amongst us today – which is to say, and again as Nietzsche had predicted, the *vast majority of us* – would deny that he was correct in this pronouncement. We live in a world that has become unbearable, in which we are traumatically overstimulated to the point of exhaustion. The image of Nietzsche collapsing at the sight of a horse being beaten in Turin symbolizes what we are all living through at every moment of our contemporary lives – whether we know it or not – operating without any reliable sense that there is a sustainable future to come.

Any encounter between Nietzsche and psychoanalysis today must confront this trajectory towards individual and collective madness. Yet another scholarly appreciation of the occasional proximities of Nietzsche and Freud would be a merely academic exercise that would leave our dire circumstances unchanged. Nietzsche must instead be put rigorously into dialogue not only with psychoanalytic *theory* but with the everyday exigencies of psychoanalytic clinical *practice*. This is all the more so the case to the extent that the types of psychopathology that analysts encounter more and more these days approximate the forms of nihilistic abandon of which Nietzsche had forewarned.

What Nietzsche meant by nihilism must be articulated in terms of its current manifestations. With reference to the psychoanalytic clinic this can be achieved in relation to what the contemporary literature calls "concreteness." This increasingly pervasive clinical problem threatens the future not only of psychoanalysis as a therapeutic practice, but of the horizon of culture as such, in that it consists in a refusal to witness the *possibility* of symbolic meaning and therefore of what Nietzsche called the capacity for self-overcoming or *sublimation* – a term shared by Nietzsche and Freud.

Psychoanalytic thinking about concreteness has a great deal to add to a Nietzschean thinking about nihilism as the horizon of the world – which is a world increasingly without horizon – in which we are now living. At the same time, Nietzsche can help psychoanalysis understand that concreteness, as a form of positivistic fact-mindedness that refuses the possibility of difference in symbolic interpretation, is a pervasive form of contemporary cultural and political despair. It is to

DOI: 10.4324/9780429297076-5

this despair that both analysts and philosophers today must address themselves or risk becoming representatives of a perspective whose time is up.

Nihilism

Nietzsche foresaw thoroughly the age in which we live today, but his descriptions of this age need to be updated in contemporary terms. "Nihilism" can function as a reified concept, to the implications of which we are at risk of becoming immune. As Nietzsche anticipated, and as those who still promise socialist solutions refuse to acknowledge, the world today is one in which there is no possibility of formally situating oneself outside this trajectory in which we are all killing ourselves – with education that does not educate, with culture that does not cultivate, and with a form of politics that no longer resembles anything like politics at all. This is what Nietzsche called nihilism, for which he sought experimental procedures of life affirming resistance. This is the sickness of our age, of which our current economic, political, epidemiological and environmental crises are only secondary symptoms. Nihilism describes a world addicted to death.

"The nihilistic consequences of the ways of thinking in politics and economics," Nietzsche writes, "where all 'principles' are practically histrionic: the air of mediocrity, wretchedness, dishonesty, etc. Nationalism, Anarchism, etc." (1968, p. 8). Nationalism and anarchism, as presiding cultural and political manifestations of fundamentalism, reflect a degradation of the capacity of individuals to form principles, which is to say ideals – according to a process of *idealization* described by Freud (1914) – as the outcome of processes of sublimation that result in the conversion of the drives into desire. Desire projects future possibility as a horizon of achievement that the drives only recognize as a demand for immediate gratification. The bodily drives drive us forward, but it requires the sublimation of drives into desire as the production of meaning and value – which is to say, of a sense of the future as the ideal "object" of desire, no matter in which guise this future appears – to transform drives from something essentially predatory and stupid into something that pursues future possibility. This capacity is not on the order of object-seeking; it concerns not "object relations" but the relation to the time of the future. Sublimation involves the cultivation of object-seeking for the purpose of gratificatory exploitation into the temporal projection of an experience of self as something that can *become* over the *process* of time.

This capacity for transformation is the cultivation of experiences of value and meaning, which is why Nietzsche writes, "What does nihilism mean? *That the highest values devaluate themselves*" (1968, p. 9). For Nietzsche, there is no question of a post-modern or post-metaphysical age, but of a hyper-modern or hyper-metaphysical age that describes itself as "post-" only in the sense of that which can anticipate for itself no future. This is the age in which we have been living at least since the cultural upheavals of the 1960s during which ideologies of liberation began to proliferate as strategies for self-destructiveness in the guise of economic models of infinite sustainability.

Somewhere between 1893 and 1895 Nietzsche writes, "The entire idealism of mankind hitherto is on the point of changing suddenly into nihilism – into the belief in absolute *worth*lessness, i.e., *meaning*lessness" (1968, p. 331). Changing *suddenly* means in the absence of any dynamic historical or collective logic. This describes the moment at which fundamentalism becomes an organizing principle in the constitution of desire as desire for *nothingness*, which is to say the destruction of desire and the liberation of the drives as unsublimated consumer demand: "becoming aims at *nothing* and achieves *nothing*" (p. 12). This achievement of nothing is not a lack of achievement but rather an accomplished projection of nothingness as future horizon – what Nietzsche will call *active* nihilism, according to which, "Extreme positions are not succeeded by moderate ones but by extreme positions of the opposite kind" (p. 35). This ongoing amplification of extremes does not demonstrate a classical dialectical logic.

Nietzsche criticizes here the rational narrative of the Hegelian dialectic which insistently realizes neither freedom nor spirit (*Geist*) but only "the *deed of nihilism*, which is suicide" (p. 143). At the same time, for Nietzsche history is in no way in some state of decline (i.e., Spengler's "decline of the West") for which we should express reactionary nostalgia. To the contrary, autonomously programmed consumer markets to which we are now incessantly subjected indicate that history is ever more unstably "upwardly mobile" than could ever before have been imagined. Nietzsche described this mobility as increasingly non-dialectical, which is to say violently uncontrollable. As Adorno and Horkheimer put it: "The flood of precise information and brand-new amusements make people smarter and more stupid at once" (2002, p. xvii).

Hegel, in imitation of Rousseau, and in realizing that the theme of desire is what draws a line of convergence from Aristotle to Spinoza, articulates most insistently the concept of *progress* as the spirit that animates world history towards freedom. Hegel is the great thinker of historical progress as the world-historical figure of desire, as it would appear for Marx, who would project this emancipatory vision onto a materialist basis as a struggle for the rights of the worker as defined by his capacity to enjoy the products of his labor. Nothing in Marx or Hegel set them apart as anything but champions of what we now call neoliberalism.

Nietzsche objected to this vision entirely. What he called nihilism was not a loss of spirit but the tendency of spirit aggressively to despiritualize itself according to a non-dialectical logic that is again neither a regression nor a progression from idealism to materialism but a *devaluation* of the capacity to form conditions of desirability that encourages the predominance of drive-based immediacy and disorganization – metaphysics become nihilism. This regressive tendency, for Nietzsche, is the ontological principle of the "slave revolt in morality" which was originally realized in the appearance of Christianity as a form of "Platonism for the people" (2002, p. 4) and that engenders tendencies towards fundamentalism in their classically religious, political and contemporarily scientific (*qua* positivistic) forms:

> Given these two insights, that becoming has no goal and that underneath all becoming there is no grand unity in which the individual could immerse himself completely as in an element of supreme value, an escape remains: to pass sentence on this whole world of becoming as a deception and to invent a world beyond it, a *true* world.
>
> *(1968, p. 13)*

This gesture of escape transitions in the modern era via Kant from the Christian vision of eternal life to that of the objectively inaccessible thing-in-itself. What passes for science as a result becomes increasingly technocratic in being subordinated to instrumental ("evidence-based," "results-oriented") forms of understanding: "It is not the victory of science that distinguishes our nineteenth century, but the victory of scientific method over science" (1968, p. 261). Splitting understanding apart from meaning and value, science lends itself to nihilism, devolving into irrational strategies of control. As a result, younger generations inherit a world that celebrates stupidity as the ultimate form of rebellion (1997, p. 98).

Nietzsche's perspectivism is an effort to counter the prevailing positivism that is the spread of Platonic and Christian metaphysics defined by the injunction for individuals at ever more minute levels to interiorize guilt and tendencies toward self-hatred. This is not necessarily an affective self-hatred from which individuals suffer; it is an unconscious effort on the part of both individuals and collectives to render inner experience void and lacking in all individuation and autonomy. Positivism here is not merely an epistemological register. For Nietzsche, positivism reflects a fundamental commitment to arresting interpretive processes that might overturn any given state of affairs and open up underlying assumptions to radical questioning and revaluation. This is positivism's essentially nihilistic character, according to which democratically agreed upon "facts" become *truths* that are intended to pass judgment on how the world *ought to be.* In defiance, Nietzsche writes,

> Against positivism, which halts at phenomena – "There are only *facts*" – I would say: No, facts is precisely what there is not, only interpretations. We cannot establish any fact "in itself": perhaps it is folly to want to do such a thing.
>
> "Everything is subjective," you say; but even this is interpretation. The "subject" is not something given, it is something added and invented and projected behind what there is. – Finally, is it necessary to posit an interpreter behind the interpretation? Even this is invention, hypothesis.
>
> In so far as the word "knowledge" has any meaning, the world is knowable; but it is *interpretable* otherwise, it has no meaning behind it, but countless meanings. – "Perspectivism."
>
> *(1968, p. 267)*

For Nietzsche, facts are by definition interpretations, but not in any subjective sense. Interpretation is an activity carried out not by a self or subject but by a multiplicity of drives as an effort at producing value and meaning (even as the absence of all value and meaning). One does not, according to Nietzsche, interpret one's desire in the form of reflective self-interrogation (i.e., "What do I really want?"), rather desire is itself a capacity for interpretation that produces or develops an experience of world as desirable possibility. Where positivism assumes facts to be uninterpretable realities that reveal an objective dimension of truth that supersedes some distorted subjective position, this reflects the regression of a traditional or "strong" desire to interpret by engaging with the world to the level of the acceptance of fact as an indication of what the world merely *is* and as such *ought to be.* This is what Nietzsche called metaphysics:

> *The fiction of a world* that corresponds to our desires: psychological trick and interpretation with the aim of associating everything we honor and find pleasant with this true world.
>
> "Will to truth" at this stage is essentially an art of interpretation: which at least requires the power to interpret.
>
> This same species of man, grown one stage poorer, no longer possessing the strength to interpret, to create fictions, produces *nihilists.* A nihilist is a man who judges of the world as it is that it ought *not* to be, and of the world as it ought to be that it does not exist. According to this view, our existence (action, suffering, willing, feeling) has no meaning: the pathos of "in vain" is the nihilists' pathos – at the same time, as pathos, an inconsistency on the part of nihilists.
>
> *(1968, pp. 317–318)*

Nietzsche's understanding here of a systemically enforced destruction of the power to interpret, as a historical process of degeneration called nihilism, which again in no way constitutes a fall from some cultural or spiritual origin (whether "Greek" or otherwise), is the lever according to which thinking the relationship between Nietzsche and psychoanalysis today could result in something more than an academic exercise in scholarly prowess. What Nietzsche called philosophy anticipated Freud's move from a purely academic approach to the study of mind to an interpretive practice of difference, transformation and change.

Concreteness

Nietzsche considered himself first and foremost a psychologist because he understood that nihilism essentially, or rather originally (via Socrates) involved philosophy having become an effort to defend the status quo. With Socrates, philosophy became disingenuous critique by seeking after justice (*dikē*) in *justifications* of the world as it is:

> I try to understand from what partial and idiosyncratic states the Socratic problem derives; his equalization of reason = virtue = happiness. It was with this absurdity of a doctrine of identity that he fascinated: the philosophers of antiquity never again freed themselves from this fascination.
>
> *(1968, p. 237)*

Nietzsche fought insistently to counter the ironic spirit of Socratic commitments to uninterpretable, objective fact (*ti esti*). Anything that venerates immutable truths represents an attack on individuals capable of symbolizing singular, autonomous experience. This has nothing whatsoever to do with what has since been called "postmodernism," with which Nietzsche should not be associated. Instead, we should associate Nietzsche with a practice of *thinking beyond critique* (2002, p. 105) as the prerogative of "free spirits."

The psychoanalytic clinic, as an effort at cultivating a thinking beyond critique, is a clinic of interpretation. Freud's thinking evolved over the course of his career with respect to *what* analysts should interpret and *how* analysts should interpret, but the fact that interpretation can serve a therapeutic function was his core – perhaps his most radical – position. Clinicians today do not often enough reflect on this – on how and why interpretation can serve a therapeutic function. Doing so, and in a way that is informed by Nietzsche's understanding of what interpretation ultimately consists in, is crucial if there is to be a future for the psychoanalytic clinic and for the experience of symbolic literacy which concerns not *what* things mean but *that* things mean.

An emergent analytic literature today treats the problem of "concreteness." This describes a confounding clinical problem in which patients insistently seek out an interpretive therapeutic treatment but consistently refuse the possibility that experience might be interpretable. Concreteness – also known as *desymbolization* (Freedman and Lavender 2002) – refers to a state of mind dominated by literalness, precluding symbolization and serving as a more primitive means of managing psychic pain in response to the need for drive-based immediate gratification. In contrast,

> "symbolization" (or abstraction) refers to a process whereby we can meaningfully understand that an event can be looked at from a variety of perspectives. Symbolization makes it possible to look at thing in an "as if" way rather than as "true" or absolute.
>
> *(Frosch 2012, p. xx)*

The concrete patient is one for whom experience is as it immediately appears to be, for whom experience is dominated by positive facts to the exclusion of any possible difference or unforeseen possibility: something either *is* or *is not* true.

In "Use of the Analyst as a Fetish," Owen Renik (1992) evocatively describes the difficulties analysts encounter in working with these kinds of patients. He defers to Freud's treatment of fetishism in order to understand why these patients seem comfortable remaining in apparently stalemated analyses for years, even though it is clear both to the patient and to the analyst that nothing is actually occurring, that no progress is being made. Renik writes,

> By contrast with neurosis or psychosis, in fetishism, wishful fantasy is neither kept unconscious, nor does it entirely replace conscious objective perception. Rather, wishful fantasy is maintained alongside reality with equal conviction. There is a perpetual avoidance of clear thinking, so that the distinction between reality and fantasy is blurred and rendered inconclusive.
>
> *(Renik 1992, p. 549)*

Concrete patients use the treatment to act out fantasies for extensive periods of time, effectively conflating reality and fantasy: fantasy *is* reality, but not in such a way that compromises reality testing as in more classically recognizable forms of psychosis. For Nietzsche, this is metaphysics – idealism. What makes this conflation possible is the analyst's perceivable (fetishized) presence, from which the patient derives immense gratification, but in the absence of any real interest in the analyst's interventions or in their capacity to alter inner experience. All that matters is that the analyst is objectively perceived as *there* (as an equal), in such a way that reduces symbolic presence to immediate perception to the exclusion of any relation to an actual, individuated other.

Interpretation is an effort at making explicit or disclosing the possibility that something can also and at the same time indicate something else, beyond what is immediately, consciously apparent: something is both itself and something different, both identical to itself and differentiated from itself. When an analyst interprets, she is not explaining what something *really* means in an authoritarian manner; she is opening up the possibility that what something appears to mean on the immediate, conscious/perceptual surface *potentially* defers itself beyond itself, referring to something else that is both separate yet intrinsically connected. The concrete patient refuses this symbolic separation-connection in a gesture that is not a cognitive regression but an affective erasure of the boundary between fantasy and reality.

"Potentially" here is to be taken in Winnicott's (1970) sense of potential or transitional space. It is precisely this play-space – which is what the space of the analytic clinic attempts to make manifest – that concrete patients cannot tolerate. As Nietzsche well understood, interpretation is an intrinsically playful effort at entertaining the possibility that something can be both itself and other than itself, that identity is infused with difference. To open up recalcitrant psychic structures via interpretation is to introduce difference into the mind, and this differentiating function of interpretation is the basis for its therapeutic value. For some patients – or rather, for all patients, at least some of the time – this can be overwhelming, and not always for the reasons analysts typically think. Clinicians tend to think that when patients refuse symbolic meaning this has only to do with the *content* of their interpretations. Concrete patients instead refuse the interpretive *process* as such, because the differentiating function of interpretive separation-connection can be intrinsically anxiety provoking in precisely the way that Nietzsche had recognized in emphasizing the ways in which positivism, as a form of nihilism, defensively repudiates the reality of *becoming*.

The concrete patient manifests clinically what Nietzsche had called nihilism as the positivistic refusal of interpretation – the tendency to "halt at phenomena." For Nietzsche, the residue of interpretation that constitutes the general commitment of hyper-modern, positivistic science betrays itself as a "weak" incapacity to affirm the *play* of the world as chance, becoming and difference: "Logical world-denial and nihilation follow from the fact that we have to oppose non-being with being and the concept 'becoming' is denied. ('*Something*' becomes.)" (1968, p. 312). To the reign of positive fact in the era in which Christian or Socratic nihilism realizes itself as technological science, Nietzsche opposes gestures of affirmation of the interpretability of the world given that this names the irreducible and infinite reversibility of hierarchies of force. This is what Nietzsche describes as becoming, which is anxiety provoking to the extent that it provides for itself no guarantee or ultimate justification.

Passing sentence on the world, positing a "true" world – whether eternal or objective – in this way constitutes the basis for fundamentalism, positivism and instrumentalism as articulations of the nihilistic desert that the world today has become. The basis for this gesture can be thought psychoanalytically in terms of the concrete mindset that cannot witness the symbolic, differentiating aspect of all experience that makes meaning possible, and that must substitute for this knowable, unquestionable truths. Recall that, in contrast to concrete or desymbolizing defenses,

> "symbolization" (or abstraction) refers to a process whereby we can meaningfully understand that an event can be looked at *from a variety of perspectives*. Symbolization makes it possible to look at thing in an "as if" way *rather than as "true" or absolute.*
>
> *(Frosch 2012, p. xx; emphasis added)*

It is no accident that analysts often spontaneously lapse into this Nietzschean vocabulary when attempting to describe these phenomena. What threatens the future of our continued existence today issues from an unconscious effort to destroy symbolizing capacities and to insist – increasingly to the point of violence – on the absolute truth of any given position: "It is not doubt, it is *certainty* that drives people mad" (Nietzsche 2005, pp. 91–92). It is here, *with* Nietzsche, and as a *clinical* effort to resist and to overcome tendencies toward uninterpretable factical certainty, that psychoanalysis finds its contemporary political and social relevance.

Disintegration

At the opening of the Second Essay of the *Genealogy of Morals*, Nietzsche writes,

> To close the doors and windows of consciousness for a time; to remain undisturbed by the noise and struggle of our underworld of utility organs working with and against one another; a little quietness, a little *tabula rasa* of the consciousness, to make room for new things, above all for the nobler functions and functionaries, for regulation, foresight, pre-meditation. . . . The man in whom this apparatus of repression is damaged and ceases to function properly may be compared (and more than merely compared) with a dyspeptic – he cannot "have done" with anything.
>
> *(1967, pp. 57–58)*

Nietzsche repeatedly linked the breakdown of this apparatus (that of "active forgetfulness") to the advent of nihilism and weakness as what "cannot 'have done' with anything" in the generation of *ressentiment*. Overcome with *ressentiment*, such a will is as a result compromised in its capacity to project horizons of future possibility (i.e., "nobler functions . . . foresight"). This manifests historically in the disintegration of the relationships between the generations, which is to say in the destruction of care as investment in all processes of becoming mature (1997, pp. 97–98). Our contemporary world provides no shortage of opportunities for describing this breakdown.

In 1964 Winnicott published a little-known but remarkable fragment of a text titled "Youth Will Not Sleep" (collected in the volume *Deprivation and Delinquency*, 1990). The title referenced Shakespeare's *A Winter's Tale*, in which a shepherd laments,

> I would that there were no age between sixteen and twenty-three or that youth would sleep out the rest; for there is nothing in between but getting wenches with child, wrongdoing the ancientry, stealing, fighting.
>
> *(in Winnicott, 1990, p. 134)*

This is an expression of what Nietzsche called *ressentiment*.

Winnicott was at the time responding to the dilemma in which adults at the time found themselves hopelessly attempting to exercise control over the threat of youthful "hooliganism," which is not merely adolescent rebellion but the tendency of adolescents to gravitate towards group violence. He cites the Nazi regime's temporary yet extreme effectiveness in mobilizing this tendency by assigning "youth the role of superego to the community" (ibid.). The effectiveness of this gesture was to have induced the wished-for sleep not only in children but in adults themselves who were demanding that their children simply grow up so as not to be in need of parenting. Adolescent rebellion, for Winnicott, is the clearest indication that in human development "*a time factor is involved*." He was speaking out against those who wished to manage adolescent development by means of calculable techniques of immediate socialization.

Barely over a page in length and written for a popular audience, Winnicott's text pleads with adults intent on controlling the "antisocial" tendencies of youth to appreciate that such tendencies are in fact the motor of individuation itself. His key insight concerns the way in which adults who seek to suppress adolescent rebellion are in fact manifesting the very same demand for immediate change that motivates the as-yet-individuated adolescent's apparent will to violence: "Indeed, most of the loud-speaking comes from individuals who are unable to tolerate the idea of a solution in time instead of a solution through immediate action" (ibid.). Eliminating the time factor that sustains tradition by motivating the youthful demand for future justice, "loud-speaking" substitutes violence for justice by turning children prematurely into adults, depriving them of the *process* of becoming autonomous (cf. Nietzsche 1997, pp. 88–95).

Winnicott is closer to Nietzsche here than we might otherwise expect to find him. As a result, the text inadvertently makes an argument highly relevant to the age of contemporary media. In 1964 this was still called "publicity," referring to the industrial distribution of printed texts and not yet to the algorithmic "real-time" dissemination of digital images. What Plato had called the Republic (*res publica* – the shared thing) had always and from the outset been mediated by texts and images. A genuinely democratic community is always a republic of *letters*, as Kant had argued in his "What Is Enlightenment?" from 1784. Winnicott clearly grasps that there is no public without such publicity, and in fact this was always his position with regard to the function of transitional objects as what opens the child onto the cultural field at large. But his comments here reflect the status of a public that was already at the time being disrupted and de-constituted by its media, which is to say by the destruction of literacy:

> Publicity is given to every act of hooliganism because the public does not really want to hear or read about those teenage pursuits that are free from an antisocial bias. Moreover, when a miracle happens, like the Beatles, there are those adults who wince when they could sigh the sigh of relief – that is, if they were free from envy of the teenager in this teenage age.
>
> *(Winnicott 1990, p. 135)*

Citing a tabloid headline ("Rockers Held!"), Winnicott exposes the weakness of contemporary authority in which envy of youth motivates strategies for increasingly impoverished social and generational control. Almost sixty years later, we still have no vocabulary to describe this dynamic struggle. In the now massively publicized discourse of identity politics (Black, Queer, Latinx, etc.), no group has yet to adopt the signifier "Young." This is not an oversight.

Where Winnicott remains perhaps uncritically conservative in thinking the relationship between the generations is in his appeal to a framework that continues to oppose the "container" and the "contained." As clinically relevant as this framework may still be, Shakespeare's shepherd's wish – as an expression of envy or *ressentiment* having become generalized amongst all (parental) shepherds today – indicates that these concepts and their opposition have lost any meaningfulness at the social level. In Jonathan Crary's (2014) terms, this appears to the extent that the healthy adolescent refusal to be put to sleep now manifests as a relentless, 24/7 injunction to be *woke* – prematurely to have to become more adult than adults themselves.

Just as for Nietzsche in the passage from the *Genealogy of Morals* quoted above, at stake is a process of dehumanization that affects not only the memory but the ability of the human to articulate itself symbolically. In the second of his *Untimely Mediations* from 1874 ("On the Uses and Disadvantages of History for Life"), Nietzsche describes this degenerative process in which memory becomes a source of insufferable pain and the human as a result "envies the animal, who at once forgets and for whom every moment really. . . . Thus the animal lives *unhistorically*" (1997, p. 61). In contrast, "a living thing can be healthy, strong and fruitful only when bounded by a horizon; if it is incapable of drawing a horizon around itself, and at the same time too self-centered to enclose its own view within that of another, it will pine away slowly or hasten to its timely end" (p. 63). Unbounded by any temporal horizon as what emerges from the cultivation of symbolizing capacities, the spread of nihilism constitutes a regression to inhumanity.

To cite but a recent example of this desymbolizing dehumanization that results from the democratization of historical difference and hierarchy: on November 30, 2021, 15-year-old Ethan Crumbley murdered four of his classmates and wounded seven others in a high school shooting in Oxford, Michigan. According to authorities, the shooting "appeared random." That is, this child targeted no particular individuals, just the absence of any individuals to which he felt he could relate.

Earlier that day, Crumbley had been scheduled to meet with school officials to discuss his behavior on the previous day. By the time he arrived at this meeting, a teacher had raised concerns about drawings he had made which depicted a gun, a corpse and the words, "Blood everywhere" and "The thoughts won't stop. Help me." He was returned to class and soon after emerged from the school bathroom with a loaded semi-automatic weapon. Motivated by profound emotional desperation, Ethan Crumbley was subsequently charged by his county prosecutor as a terrorist for his desire to induce fear and panic in the community. One can only imagine the fear and panic that would lead a child to formulate such a desire in the first place.

In the ensuing days, the case took on an even more unprecedented political dimension when Crumbley's parents were themselves charged with abetting their son's crimes by failing to recognize and control the signs of massive adolescent distress. Text messages between Jennifer Crumbley and her son revealed that she had written, upon his having been called to the school principal's office, "LOL. I'm not mad at you. You have to learn not to get caught." Jennifer and James Crumbley were subsequently subject to a federal manhunt when they failed to appear in court for their arraignment. They were soon discovered hiding in a local commercial warehouse – like frightened children themselves.

Citing this incident is in no way intended to assert a decline in moral values evidenced by an increase in random acts of violence by children against other children today, which is again not how Nietzsche's account of the epochal realization of metaphysics should be read. Between 1964 and 2022, it is not a question of quantitatively increasing acts of violence by a quantitatively decreasing age limit of violent offenders. As Winnicott understood, it is a question of the disavowal of the temporality of human development (Nietzsche's becoming) that both separates and connects the generations, and that is being eroded today by the accelerating speed of our increasingly homogeneous, unmediated political community itself. It was this against which Zarathustra famously warned: "Deserts grow: woe to him who harbors deserts" (1961, p. 315).

This is what Jennifer Crumbley expressed when she did not say but texted to her child, "LOL." Whatever else she texted was already encapsulated in this confusion of intimacy with immediacy. That is, in the text message she sent to her troubled son – envying his youth, incapable of interpreting his experience and treating him as if he were an equal – Jennifer Crumbley demonstrated what it means to be what Winnicott called a "loud-speaking individual" (which is something other than an individual) without having uttered a single word. This was neither Jennifer's nor Ethan's fault any more than it was the fault of "rockers" in 1964 to have been publicly misrepresented as having been "held." Affirming the rights of youth not to be put to sleep in this late fragment, Winnicott warned at the same time against the possibility of an insufferable insomnia ("The thoughts won't stop") provoked by the absolute disintegration of all processes of individuation which Nietzsche understood as demanding of hierarchy, conflict and difference.

Resistance

In *Meaning and Melancholia: Life in the Age of Bewilderment*, Christopher Bollas (2018) addresses the psychopolitical dynamics of the twentieth century by describing how, the capacity to sense loss was annihilated by World War II and the development and deployment of the atomic bomb. In shock, loss gave way to a strangely deformed type of mourning, one that saturated the existentialist movement. Albert Camus stated the only real question remaining: should we commit suicide or not?

By the late twentieth century, this deformed response had morphed for millions into an unrecognized and unconscious state of melancholia: unresolved mourning shifted to despair, disorientation and anger (Bollas 2018, p. xxii).

Nihilism, which means that human beings "rather will *nothingness* than not will" (Nietzsche 1967, p. 97) is despair, disorientation and anger failing to recognize themselves for what they are. This failure and the violence it engenders are the result of breakdowns in the capacity to symbolize and to sublimate, which with each passing generation makes access to traditional ideals and practices and their overcoming increasingly unavailable. An encounter between psychoanalysis and Nietzsche's understanding of what interpretation as a thinking beyond critique intends to accomplish in the face of this manic abandon could articulate a new image of philosophy itself, in the service of "the true instinct for *healing*, which is the *human* instinct for weapons and war" (2005, p. 80; emphases modified). The war for our time, care and attention now being fought against us by algorithms that select and program our individuation for us will continue whether we choose to recognize this war or not.

From a Nietzschean perspective, efforts to import concepts from psychoanalytic theory into the critique of ideology entirely miss the point of what is most urgent today. What needs to be thought is rather how the clinical practice of psychoanalysis – as an effort at cultivating symbolizing capacities that are now being intentionally repudiated at a global scale – functions as a form of resistance to the destruction of those capacities that is everywhere being exploited by the pervasive digital desert of 24/7 consumer markets. A Nietzschean psychoanalysis would be one capable of registering that what is needed is not an effort to inject psychoanalytic insights into contemporary political theorizing or vice versa, but an effort to grasp how the individually disciplined work of clinical practice functions as an intrinsically politicized means of combatting the spread of nihilism, disorientation and despair. A Nietzschean psychoanalysis would be philosophy *weaponized.*

References

Adorno, T. and Horkheimer, M. (2002). *Dialectic of Enlightenment.* Trans. E. Jephcott. Stanford: Stanford University Press.

Bollas, C. (2018). *Meaning and Melancholia: Life in the Age of Bewilderment.* London: Routledge.

Crary, J. (2014). *24/7: Late Capitalism and the Ends of Sleep.* New York: Verso.

Freedman, N. and Lavender, J. (2002). "On Desymbolization." *Psychoanalysis and Contemporary Thought,* 25(2):165–199.

Freud, S. (1914). "On Narcissism." In *S.E.*, vol. XIV, 67–102.

Freud, S. (1915). "The Unconscious." In *S.E.*, vol. XIV, 159–215.

Frosch, A. (ed.) (2012). *Absolute Truth and Unbearable Psychic Pain: Psychoanalytic Perspectives on Concrete Experience.* London: Routledge.

Nietzsche, F. (1961). *Thus Spoke Zarathustra.* Trans. R. J. Hollingsdale. New York: Penguin Books.

Nietzsche, F. (1967). *On the Genealogy of Morals and Ecco Homo.* Ed. and Trans. W. Kaufman. New York: Vintage Books.

Nietzsche, F. (1968). *The Will to Power.* Ed. and Trans. W. Kaufman. New York: Vintage Books.

Nietzsche, F. (1997). *Untimely Meditations.* Trans. R. J. Hollingsdale. Ed. D. Breazale. Cambridge: Cambridge University Press.

Nietzsche, F. (2002). *Beyond Good and Evil.* Ed. and Trans. R. Horseman and J. Norman. Cambridge: Cambridge University Press.

Nietzsche, F. (2005). *The Anti-Christ, Ecco Homo, Twilight of the Idols.* Ed. and Trans. A. Ridley and J. Norman. Cambridge: Cambridge University Press.

Renik, O. (1992). "Use of the Analyst as a Fetish." *Psychoanalytic Quarterly,* 61:542–563.

Winnicott, D. W. (1970). *Playing and Reality.* New York: Routledge.

Winnicott, D. W. (1990). "Youth Will Not Sleep." In *Deprivation and Delinquency.* New York: Routledge, pp. 134–135.

4

PSYCHOANALYSIS FINDS A HOME

Emotional Phenomenology

Robert D. Stolorow

Phenomenology lets metaphysicians heal themselves.

Lee Braver (2012, p. 31)

Since its early beginnings, psychoanalysis has searched for a disciplinary identity in which to situate itself. Freud's (1895) "Project for a Scientific Psychology" embodied his early dream of finding a grounding for his clinical discoveries in the neuroscience of his day, a dream whose traces one can still detect in contemporary oxymoronic hybrids like *neuropsychoanalysis* and *neurophenomenology*. When many psychoanalysts fled the Holocaust by relocating to the United States, psychoanalysis became part of the psychiatric establishment there, and only physicians were admitted for training or membership at the institutes of the American Psychoanalytic Association. In the early 1980s, a group of psychologists sued the American Psychoanalytic Association for restraint of trade, and the organization reluctantly opened its gates to psychologists and, somewhat later, to practitioners from all of the mental health professions. What, then, became of psychoanalysis's disciplinary identity? The question became more and more complex, as institutes and organizations of varied theoretical orientations sprung up outside the jurisdiction of the American Psychoanalytic Association and in countries other than the United States. In this essay, my focus will be on how psychoanalysis's disciplinary identity evolved *for me*.

A pivotal work bringing some intelligibility to this complexity was George S. Klein's (1976) posthumously published *Psychoanalytic Theory: An Exploration of Essentials*. Klein claims that Freud's psychoanalytic theory actually amalgamates two theories – a metapsychology and a clinical theory – deriving from two different universes of discourse. Metapsychology deals with the material substrate of experience and is couched in the natural science framework of impersonal structures, forces, and energies. Clinical theory, by contrast, deals with intentionality and the unconscious meanings of personal experience, seen from the perspective of the individual's unique life history. Clinical psychoanalysis asks "why" questions and seeks answers in terms of personal reasons, purposes, and individual meanings. Metapsychology asks "how" questions and seeks answers in terms of the nonexperiential realm of impersonal mechanisms and causes. Klein sought to disentangle metapsychological and clinical concepts, expunging the former and retaining only the latter as the legitimate content of psychoanalytic theory. For Klein, the essential psychoanalytic enterprise involves the reading of disclaimed intentionality and the unlocking

DOI: 10.4324/9780429297076-6

of unconscious meanings from a person's experience, a task for which the concepts of the clinical theory, purged of metapsychological contaminants, are uniquely suited. Klein's proposal for a radical "theorectomy" for psychoanalysis has significantly influenced such contemporary thinkers as Merton Gill, Roy Schafer, and those, including myself, who have sought to rethink psychoanalysis as a form of phenomenological inquiry.

Expanding on Klein's distinction, I would characterize psychoanalytic clinical theory as a hermeneutic framework and psychoanalytic metapsychology as a form of metaphysics,[1] in that it postulates changeless realities and universal truths. This division is characteristic of all the major psychoanalytic theories – they are mixtures of hermeneutics and metaphysics. Hermeneutics embodies the tragic, in that human experiencing is finite, transient, context dependent, ever changing, and decaying. Metapsychology evades the tragic by means of metaphysical illusion. Hermeneutics/metapsychology is a trauma-driven binary insofar as finite human existing, stripped of sheltering illusions, is inherently traumatizing (Stolorow, 2011).

Freud's metapsychological vision of the mind significantly expanded the Cartesian mind – Descartes's (1641) "thinking thing" – to include a vast unconscious realm.

Nonetheless, the Freudian mind remained a Cartesian mind, a self-enclosed worldless subject or mental apparatus containing and working over mental contents and ontologically separated from its surround. Corresponding to its Cartesianism is traditional psychoanalysis's objectivist epistemology. One isolated mind, the analyst, is claimed to make objective observations and interpretations of another isolated mind, the patient.

Psychoanalytic Phenomenology

With what do I fill the gap in psychoanalytic theory left by the excision of Cartesian metaphysics? The answer to this question emerged over the course of my half-century-long collaboration with George Atwood (Stolorow & Atwood, 2018). The beginnings of our collaborative work consisted in a series of psychobiographical studies that we conducted in the early and mid-1970s of the personal, experiential origins of the theoretical systems of Freud, Jung, Wilhelm Reich, and Otto Rank, studies that formed the basis of our first book, *Faces in a Cloud: Subjectivity in Personality Theory* (Stolorow & Atwood, 1979), completed in 1976. From these studies we concluded that since psychological theories derive to a significant degree from the emotional concerns of their creators, what psychoanalysis needed was a theory of emotional experience itself – a unifying framework capable of accounting not only for the psychological phenomena that other theories address but also for the theories themselves.

In the last chapter of *Faces* we outlined a set of proposals for the creation of such a framework, which we called *psychoanalytic phenomenology*. Influenced by the work of George Klein (1976), we envisioned this framework as a depth psychology of personal experience, purified of the mechanistic reifications of Freudian metapsychology. Our framework took the experiential world of the individual as its central theoretical construct. We assumed no impersonal psychical agencies or motivational prime movers in order to explain the experiential world. Instead, we assumed that this world evolves organically from the person's encounter with the critical formative experiences that constitute his or her unique life history. Once established, it becomes discernible in the recurrent themes that characterize the person's experiences. Developmentally, recurring patterns of interaction within the developmental system give rise to principles (thematic patterns, meaning-structures, cognitive-affective schemas) that unconsciously organize subsequent emotional and relational experiences. Such organizing principles are unconscious, not in the sense of being repressed, but in being *prereflective*; they ordinarily do not enter the domain of reflective self-awareness. These relationally derived, prereflective organizing principles are the basic building blocks of personality development, and their totality constitutes one's character. Psychoanalytic therapy is a dialogical method for bringing this prereflective organizing activity into reflective self-awareness, particularly as it shows up within the therapeutic relationship. During the period when Atwood and I were writing the concluding chapter of *Faces*, we collaborated on an essay applying our phenomenological principles to the psychoanalytic situation and the therapeutic process (Stolorow, Atwood, & Ross, 1978). Psychoanalytic phenomenology entailed a set of interpretive principles for investigating the nature, origins, purposes, and transformations of the configurations of self and other pervading a person's experiential world. For us, psychoanalysis was becoming a form of philosophy – a form of phenomenological inquiry. Importantly, our dedication to illuminating personal phenomenology had led us from isolated mind to relational world.

Traditional Freudian theory is pervaded by the Cartesian "myth of the isolated mind"[2] (Stolorow & Atwood, 1992, chap. 1). Descartes's (1641) metaphysics bifurcated the experiential world into inner and outer regions, severed both mind from body and cognition from affect, reified and absolutized the resulting divisions, and pictured the mind as an objective entity that takes its place among other objects, a "thinking thing" that has an inside with contents and that looks out on an external world from which it is essentially estranged. The Freudian psyche is fundamentally a Cartesian mind in that it is a container of contents (instinctual energies, wishes, etc.), a thinking *thing* that, precisely because it is a thing, is ontologically decontextualized, fundamentally separated from its world. Our psychoanalytic phenomenology mends this Cartesian bifurcation, highlighting the context-embeddedness of the experiences it illuminates. Our dedication to illuminating personal phenomenology had led us inexorably from mind to world and thus from mental contents to relational contexts, from the intrapsychic to the intersubjective.[3] From our phenomenological perspective, all of the clinical phenomena with which psychoanalysis has been traditionally concerned became intelligible as taking form within systems of interacting, differently organized, mutually influencing experiential worlds. Phenomenology had led us inexorably to contextualism.

How and why did this inexorable movement from phenomenology to contextualism occur? The central reason, I have come to realize, is that a psychoanalytic phenomenology, as opposed to other forms of phenomenological inquiry, is always devoted to investigating affectivity – that is, worlds of emotional experience. During the period when Atwood and I were fleshing out our psychoanalytic phenomenology, I was working on an article with Daphne Socarides Stolorow (Socarides & Stolorow, 1984/85), in which we were suggesting that Heinz Kohut's central clinical contributions to the psychology of narcissism pertained essentially to affective experience. Furthermore, the experience of affect was grasped in this article as being inseparable from the contexts of attunement and malattunement in which it is felt. This understanding became seamlessly woven into the fabric of psychoanalytic phenomenology.

The shift in focus from the primacy of drive to the primacy of affectivity moves psychoanalysis toward a phenomenological contextualism and a central focus on dynamic intersubjective systems. Unlike drives, which are claimed to originate deep within the interior of a Cartesian isolated mind, affect – emotional experience – is something that from birth onward is co-constituted within ongoing relational systems. Therefore, locating affect at its center automatically entails a radical contextualization of virtually all aspects of human psychological life. For example, the focus on affect contextualizes the very boundary between conscious and unconscious. Unlike the Freudian repression barrier, viewed as a fixed intrapsychic structure within an isolated Cartesian container, the limiting horizons of emotional experiencing are conceptualized as emergent properties of ongoing dynamic intersubjective systems. Forming and evolving within a nexus of living systems, the horizons of experiencing are grasped as fluid and ever-shifting, products both of the person's unique intersubjective history and of what is or is not allowed to be felt within the intersubjective fields that constitute his or her current living.

A consistently phenomenological approach has also been especially fruitful in the effort to grasp the context-embeddedness of emotional trauma (Stolorow, 2007, 2011). From a phenomenological perspective, developmental trauma is viewed not as an instinctual flooding of an ill-equipped Cartesian container, as Freud (1926) would have it, but as an experience of unbearable affect. Furthermore, the intolerability of an affect state cannot be explained solely, or even primarily, on the basis of the quantity or intensity of the painful feelings evoked by an injurious event. Traumatic affect states can be grasped only in terms of the relational systems in which they are felt. Developmental trauma originates within a formative intersubjective context whose central feature is malattunement to painful affect – a breakdown of the child-caregiver interaffective system, leading to the child's loss of affect-integrating capacity and thereby to an unbearable, overwhelmed, disorganized state. Painful or frightening affect becomes traumatic when the context of emotional understanding – the relational home – that the child needs to assist in its tolerance and integration is profoundly absent. Such contexts of developmental trauma are where pathogenesis takes form, a claim that calls for a radical revision of the concept of psychiatric diagnoses. In work too voluminous to review here, Atwood and I have shown that the intersubjective context plays a constitutive role in all forms of pathogenesis and in all aspects of the psychoanalytic process. Emotional phenomenology and relationally always already form an indissoluble unity, because relationality is constitutive of emotional experience. As I will discuss below, this understanding holds enormous implications for the formulation of a therapeutic comportment.

Within academic philosophy, perhaps the most important challenge to Descartes's metaphysical dualism was mounted by Heidegger (1927). Heidegger sought to re-find the unity of our being, split asunder in the Cartesian bifurcations, by unveiling the constitutive structure of our existence as a primordial contextual whole – Being-in-the-world. In Heidegger's vision, our Being and our world in their indissoluble unity "primordially and constantly" (p. 65) contextualize one another; human Being is saturated with the world in which we dwell, and the world we inhabit is drenched in human meanings and purposes. In light of this fundamental contextualization, Heidegger's consideration of affectivity is especially noteworthy.

Heidegger's term for the existential ground of affectivity (feelings and moods) is *Befindlichkeit*, a characteristically cumbersome noun he invented to capture a basic dimension of human existence. Literally, the word might be translated as "how-one-finds-oneself-ness." As Gendlin (1988) has pointed out, Heidegger's word for the structure of affectivity denotes both how one feels and the situation within which one is feeling, a felt sense of oneself in a situation, prior to a Cartesian split between inside and outside. *Befindlichkeit* is disclosive of our always already having been delivered over to the situatedness in which we find ourselves.

Heidegger's claim that *Befindlichkeit* is equiprimordial with understanding (*Verstehen*) and discourse (*Rede*) as a mode of disclosing Being-in-the-world is a definitive answer to criticisms of his alleged neglect of the body in *Being and Time* (Aho, 2009). This is so because *Befindlichkeit* always shows up in lived experience in the form of a mood (*Stimmung*), and moods always include an experienced bodily component that is more or less integrated with language.

For Heidegger, *Befindlichkeit* – disclosive affectivity – is a mode of Being-in-the-world, profoundly embedded in constitutive context. His concept underscores the exquisite context-dependence and context-sensitivity of emotional experience – a context-embeddedness that takes on enormous importance in a phenomenological perspective like mine that locates affectivity at the motivational center of human psychological life.

Heidegger's Being and Time

In the year 2000, I undertook a yearlong study of Heidegger's (1927) magnum opus, *Being and Time*, a study that proved pivotal for me. *Being and Time* is an investigation of the meaning of Being (i.e., of the intelligibility of entities). Three aspects of Heidegger's investigation soon stood out for me as holding striking relevance for an evolving psychoanalytic phenomenology. First was his brilliant initial move in choosing the inquirer himself/herself as the entity to be interrogated as to its Being. Heidegger reasoned that, because an unarticulated, pre-philosophical understanding of our Being is constitutive of our kind of Being, we humans can investigate our own kind of Being by investigating our understanding (and lack of understanding) of that Being. Accordingly, the investigative method in *Being and Time* is a phenomenological one, aimed at illuminating the fundamental structures of our understanding of our Being. Just as *Faces in a Cloud* began with our investigations of the personal phenomenologies of psychoanalytic theorists *en route* to a recasting of psychoanalysis as a form of phenomenological inquiry, *Being and Time* begins with the phenomenology of the inquirer *en route* to a claim that ontology is possible only as phenomenology.

Second, Heidegger's ontological contextualism (which I discussed earlier) – his mending of the Cartesian subject/object split with the claim that our Being is always already a Being-in-the-world – immediately struck me as providing a solid philosophical grounding for our psychoanalytic contextualism, replacing the Cartesian isolated mind that undergirds Freudian theory.

Third, and even more important for me, when I read the passages in *Being and Time* devoted to Heidegger's existential analysis of *Angst*, I nearly fell off my chair! Both his phenomenological description and ontological account of *Angst* bore a remarkable resemblance to what I had concluded about the phenomenology and meaning of emotional trauma some two years earlier (Stolorow, 1999). In short, Heidegger's analysis of *Angst*, world-collapse, uncanniness, and thrownness into Being-toward-death provided me extraordinary philosophical tools for grasping the existential significance of emotional trauma. It was this discovery that motivated me to begin doctoral studies in philosophy and to write several articles, a dissertation, and two books (Stolorow, 2007, 2011) on Heidegger and what Atwood and I had come to call *post-Cartesian psychoanalysis*. My dual aim in this work has been to show both how Heidegger's existential philosophy enriches post-Cartesian psychoanalysis and how post-Cartesian psychoanalysis enriches Heidegger's existential philosophy.

Heidegger's existential analytic teaches that, contrary to the Freudian/Cartesian vision of a self-contained "mental apparatus," human existence is always already situated, intelligible only in terms of the world in which it is embedded. Context-dependence and death are two dimensions of human finitude that Heidegger has brought into bold relief, much to the benefit of clinical psychoanalytic work. Emotional trauma produces an affective state whose features bear a close similarity to the central elements in Heidegger's existential interpretation of anxiety – the world is stripped of its significance and of its "homeness" – and it accomplishes this by plunging the traumatized person into a form of authentic (i.e., non-evasively owned) Being-toward-death. Post-Cartesian psychoanalysis gives an account of the relational contexts that make it possible for one to dwell in and bear the traumatizing emotional impact of human finitude, thereby illuminating the rich relationality of authentic existing. From the encounter between Heidegger's existential philosophy and post-Cartesian psychoanalysis, both emerge enriched (Stolorow, 2013).

Crumbling Metaphysical Illusions

The first Western philosopher to examine systematically the relationship between the tragedy of human finitude and the ubiquity of metaphysical illusion was Wilhelm Dilthey (1910). As is elegantly reconstructed by de Mul (2004), Dilthey's life's work can be seen as an effort to replace the Kantian *a priori* – the timeless forms of perception and categories of cognition through which the world becomes intelligible to us – with "life categories" that are historically contingent and constituted over the course of a living historical process. There is a tragic dimension to Dilthey's historical consciousness, in that it brings out the "tragic contradiction between the philosophical desire for universal validity [the metaphysical impulse] and the realization of the fundamental finitude of every attempt to satisfy that desire" (de Mul, 2004, p. 154). Dilthey's recognition of this tragic contradiction leads him to elaborate a hermeneutic phenomenology of metaphysics. Dilthey's historical reconstruction of the development of metaphysics aims at no less than its "euthanasia." Although he holds that metaphysical desire is inherent to human nature, what he seeks to unmask are the illusions that this ubiquitous desire creates. Metaphysical illusion, according to Dilthey, transforms historically contingent nexuses of intelligibility – worldviews, as he eventually calls them – into timeless forms of reality. Anticipating Heidegger (1927), Dilthey holds that every worldview is grounded in a mood regarding the tragic realization of the finitude of life. The metaphysicalization of worldviews transforms the unbearable fragility and transience of all things human into an enduring, permanent, changeless reality, an illusory world of eternal truths. In permanentizing transience, language is employed to evade the traumatizing impact of human finitude.

The phenomenology of language investigates how the experience of language and its principles of organization play a constitutive, usually prereflective role in disclosing and opening up a world. Wittgenstein (1953), not often considered a phenomenologist, gives a brilliant account of how the constitutive power of language produces a "bewitchment of our intelligence" (sect. 109) through the creation of metaphysical illusion. He contrasts the meaning of a word found in its contexts of use with the projection of a picture:

> A picture is conjured up which seems to fix the sense *unambiguously*. The actual use, compared with that suggested by the picture, seems like something muddied.
>
> . . . . [T]he form of expression we use seems to have been designed for a god, who knows what we cannot know; he sees the whole of each of those infinite series and he sees into human consciousness.
>
> *(Wittgenstein, 1953, sect. 426)*

Wittgenstein is claiming here that when one projects a picture as the meaning of a word, it gives one the illusion of a God's-eye view of the word's referent as a thing-in-itself, an illusory clarity that one much prefers over the "muddied" view given in the understanding that the actual meaning of a word is to be found in its multiple and shifting contexts of use. When the illusory picture is then imagined as ultimately real, the word has become transformed into a metaphysical entity. In place of the "muddied" view given by contexts of use – finite, contingent, unstable, transient – one can imagine the clear outlines of an everlasting entity. Metaphysical illusion, mediated by reified pictures, replaces the finitude and transience of existence with a God's-eye view of an irreducibly absolute and eternally changeless reality (Stolorow & Atwood, 2018). A sense of the real is transformed into the *really real*. A bewitchment of intelligence by language is thereby accomplished!

In the absence of an understanding relational context that can hold and help integrate one's emotional reactions, the shattering of metaphysical illusion that has served to evade the avowal of human finitude can be severely traumatizing. This can be seen in instances of individual trauma, but also collective trauma and trauma of Apocalyptic proportions. I will discuss instances of each.

Love and Loss

With regard to individual trauma, it is likely that no one escapes the trauma of loss. Paradoxically, the philosopher who contributed more than any other to the formulation of relational or contextual ontology had almost nothing to say about love and loss in *Being and Time*. In my view, authentic Being-toward-death entails owning up not only to one's own finitude, but also to the finitude of all those we love. Hence, authentic Being-toward-death always includes Being-toward-loss as a central constituent. Just as, existentially, we are "always dying already" (Heidegger, 1927, p. 298), so too are we always already grieving. Death and loss are existentially equiprimordial. Existential anxiety anticipates both death and loss.

Love is a rich source of metaphysical illusion, which serves to eternalize the beloved. "I will love you forever," the lover feels – a feeling that immortalizes the beloved and the bond of love. When a beloved dies, the loss shatters this metaphysical illusion and destroys the world built around it. The impact of loss and grief on our emotional world was compellingly captured by Jacques Derrida (2001):

> [T]he world [is] suspended by some unique tear . . . reflecting disappearance itself: the world, the whole world, the world itself, for death takes from us not only some particular life within the world, some moment that belongs to us, but, each time, without limit, someone through whom the world, and first of all our own world, will have opened up. *(p. 107)*

Loss – especially traumatic or tragic loss – creates a dark region in our world that will always be there. A wave of profound sadness descends upon us whenever we step into that region of loss. There we are left adrift in a world hollowed out, emptied of light. It is a bleak region that can never be completely eradicated or cordoned off. The injunction to "let it go and move on" is thus an absurdity. There will always be retraumatizations that catapult us back into the darkness – the dark realm in which we need to be emotionally held so that the loss can be better borne and integrated.

Collective Trauma

Collective trauma is created when metaphysical illusions shared by a group of people – a nation, for example – are destroyed. A vivid example for Americans was the terrorist attack on the World Trade Center on September 11, 2001, which, by horrifyingly demonstrating that America can be assaulted on its native soil, shattered collective illusions of safety, inviolability, and grandiose invincibility – illusions that had long been mainstays of the American historical identity. In the wake of such shattering, Americans became much more susceptible to what I call *resurrective ideologies* that promised to restore the grandiose illusions that had been lost. It was in this context of collective trauma and resurrective ideology that Americans fell prey to the abuses of power of the Bush administration. Fueling and exploiting the dread of retraumatization, Bush et al. declared war on global terrorism and drew America into a grandiose, holy crusade that enabled Americans to feel delivered from trauma and called upon by the Lord to rid the world of evil.

Apocalyptic Trauma

I first experienced a whiff of Apocalyptic trauma nearly four decades ago when I took my young son to a planetarium show at the New York Museum of Natural History. In the course of the presentation, it was predicted that in a billion years the sun would become a red giant and completely engulf and destroy the solar system. This prospect filled me with intense horror. The sun's becoming an engulfing red giant represents not just the destruction of individual human beings but of human civilization itself. It also announces the shattering of metaphysical illusions of the permanence and indestructability of earth itself – illusions that are currently crumbling in the face of worsening climate change. The human way of being cannot survive the impending homelessness with which climate change threatens us, a prospect so horrifying that people turn away from it altogether, thereby evading the threat and abandoning the search for solutions.

Emotional Dwelling

The recurrence of emotional trauma is ensured by the finitude of our existence and the finitude of all those with whom we are deeply connected. Authentic temporality, insofar as it owns up to human finitude, is traumatic temporality. "Trauma recovery" is an oxymoron – human finitude with its traumatizing impact is not an illness from which one can recover. "Recovery" is a misnomer for the constitution of an expanded emotional world that coexists alongside the absence of the one that has been shattered by trauma. The expanded world and the absent shattered world may be more or less integrated or dissociated, depending on the degree to which the unbearable emotional pain evoked by the traumatic shattering has become integrated or remains dissociated defensively, which depends in turn on the extent to which such pain found a relational home in which it could be held.

It follows from the relational constitution of emotional trauma – individual, collective, or Apocalyptic – that one's therapeutic comportment to it will also be a relational one. How can a therapeutic relationship be constituted wherein the analyst can serve as a relational home for unbearable emotional pain and existential vulnerability? I have proposed an active, relationally engaged form of therapeutic comportment that I call *emotional dwelling*. In dwelling, one does not merely seek empathically to understand the other's emotional pain from the other's perspective. One does that, but much more. In dwelling, one leans into the other's emotional pain and participates in it, perhaps with the aid of one's own analogous experiences of pain. The language that one uses to address another's experience of emotional trauma meets the trauma head-on, articulating the unbearable and the unendurable, saying the unsayable, unmitigated by any efforts to soothe, comfort, encourage, or reassure – such efforts invariably being experienced by the other as a shunning or turning away from his or her traumatized state.

If we are to be an understanding relational home for a traumatized person, we must tolerate, even draw upon, our own existential vulnerabilities so that we can dwell unflinchingly with his or her unbearable and recurring emotional pain. When we dwell with and hold others' unendurable pain, their shattered emotional worlds are enabled to shine with a kind of sacredness that calls forth an understanding and caring engagement within which traumatized states can be gradually transformed into bearable and nameable painful feelings. Formerly dissociated emotional pain becomes seamlessly integrated with whom one experiences oneself as being. Psychoanalytic therapy is disclosed here as applied emotional phenomenology.

Notes

1 That Freud's metapsychological theory of instinctual drives is a form of metaphysics is explicitly reflected in some of his remarks (Freud, 1937) explicitly linking his theory to the metaphysical thinking of the philosopher of ancient Greece, Empedocles. In the history of philosophy, metaphysics – the search for a changeless ground of entities and processes – has taken many forms. The one that I find most enlightening is the one appearing in Wilhelm Dilthey's (1910) conception of "metaphysical illusion." According to Dilthey, metaphysics evades the tragedy of human finitude by transforming the unbearable

fragility and transience of all things human into an enduring, permanent, changeless reality, an illusory world of eternal truths. Metaphysical illusion, according to Dilthey, transforms historically contingent nexuses of intelligibility – *worldviews*, as he eventually calls them – into timeless forms of reality. The metaphysicalization of worldviews transforms the transience of existence into an enduring, permanent, changeless reality, an illusory world of eternal truths. Heidegger (1961) appears to make use of Dilthey's conception of metaphysical illusion (without citation) in his interpretation of Nietzsche's doctrine of eternal recurrence as an injection of permanence into impermanence, a "permanentizing of Becoming into presence" (p. 156). In this Age of Scientism, the brain itself acquires the status of a metaphysical entity, transforming the transience and context-dependence of experience into the relative solidity of the body.

2 This claim is often misunderstood as an attribution of social isolation to Freud and before him to Descartes. The isolation named in formulating a Cartesian myth of the isolated mind is not social; it is ontological. Cartesian minds, including the Freudian mind, are isolated ontologically – that is, in their intelligibility – from their context. The antithesis of ontological isolation is context-embeddedness.

3 Atwood and I coined the term *intersubjective perspective* in the context of examining the impact on the therapeutic process of conjunctions and disjunctions between the emotional worlds of patient and analyst. Our use of the term *intersubjective* has never presupposed the attainment of symbolic thought, of a concept of oneself as a subject, of intersubjective relatedness in Stern's (1985) sense, or of mutual recognition as described by Benjamin (1995). Nor have we confined our usage to the realm of unconscious nonverbal affective communication, as Ogden (1994) seems to do. We use *intersubjective* very broadly, to refer to any psychological field formed by interacting worlds of experience, at whatever developmental level those worlds may be organized. For us, *intersubjective* denotes neither a mode of experiencing nor a sharing of experience but the contextual precondition for having any experience at all. In our vision, intersubjective fields and experiential worlds are equiprimordial, mutually constituting one another in circular fashion.

References

Aho, K. (2009). *Heidegger's Neglect of the Body*. Albany, NY: SUNY Press.

Benjamin, J. (1995). *Like Subjects, Love Objects*. New Haven, CT: Yale University Press.

Braver, L. (2012). *Groundless Grounds: A Study of Wittgenstein and Heidegger*. Cambridge, MA: MIT Press.

de Mul, J. (2004). *The Tragedy of Finitude: Dilthey's Hermeneutics of Life*. New Haven, CT: Yale University Press.

Derrida, J. (2001). *The Work of Mourning*, ed. P.-A. Brault & M. Naas. Chicago: University of Chicago Press.

Descartes, R. (1641). *Meditations*. Buffalo, NY: Prometheus Books, 1989.

Dilthey, W. (1910). *Selected Works: Vol. 3. The Formation of the Historical World in the Human Sciences*. Princeton, NJ: Princeton University Press, 2002.

Freud, S. (1895). Project for a scientific psychology. In *Standard Edition*, 1. London: Hogarth Press, 1950.

Freud, S. (1926). Inhibitions, symptoms, and anxiety. In *Standard Edition*, 20:77–175. London: Hogarth Press, 1959.

Freud, S. (1937). Analysis terminable and interminable. In *Standard Edition*, 23:216–253. London: Hogarth Press, 1964.

Gendlin, E. T. (1988). *Befindlichkeit*: Heidegger and the philosophy of psychology. In *Heidegger and Psychology*, ed. K. Hoeller. Seattle, WA: Review of Existential Psychology & Psychiatry, pp. 43–71.

Heidegger, M. (1927). *Being and Time*, trans. J. Macquarrie & E. Robinson. New York: Harper & Row, 1962.

Heidegger, M. (1961). *Nietzsche: Vol. III. The Will to Power as Knowledge and as Metaphysics*, trans. J. Stambaugh, D. Krell, & F. Capuzzi. New York: Harper & Row, 1987.

Klein, G. S. (1976). *Psychoanalytic Theory: An Exploration of Essentials*. Madison, CT: International Universities Press.

Ogden, T. (1994). *Subjects of Analysis*. Northvale, NJ: Jason Aronson.

Socarides, D. D. & Stolorow, R. D. (1984/85). Affects and selfobjects. In *The Annual of Psychoanalysis*, vol. 12/13. Madison, CT: International Universities Press, pp. 105–119.

Stern, D. N. (1985). *The Interpersonal World of the Infant*. New York: Basic Books.

Stolorow, R. D. (1999). The phenomenology of trauma and the absolutisms of everyday life: A personal journey. *Psychoanalytic Psychology*, 16:464–468.

Stolorow, R. D. (2007). *Trauma and Human Existence: Autobiographical, Psychoanalytic, and Philosophical Reflections*. New York: Routledge.
Stolorow, R. D. (2011). *World, Affectivity, Trauma: Heidegger and Post-Cartesian Psychoanalysis*. New York: Routledge.
Stolorow, R. D. (2013). Heidegger and post-Cartesian psychoanalysis. In *The Bloomsbury Companion to Heidegger*, ed. F. Raffoul & E. Nelson. London: Bloomsbury Academic, pp. 451–458.
Stolorow, R. D. & Atwood, G. E. (1979). *Faces in a Cloud: Subjectivity in Personality Theory*. Northvale, NJ: Jason Aronson.
Stolorow, R. D. & Atwood, G. E. (1992). *Contexts of Being: The Intersubjective Foundations of Psychological Life*. Hillsdale, NJ: The Analytic Press.
Stolorow, R. D. & Atwood, G. E. (2018). *The Power of Phenomenology: Psychoanalytic and Philosophical Perspectives*. London & New York: Routledge.
Stolorow, R. D., Atwood, G. E., & Ross, J. M. (1978). The representational world in psychoanalytic therapy. *International Review of Psycho-Analysis*, 5:247–256.
Wittgenstein, L. (1953). *Philosophical Investigations*. Malden, MA: Blackwell Publishing.

5

BRIDGING PHILOSOPHY AND PSYCHOANALYSIS

A Hermeneutic Pathway Between the Disciplines

Roger Frie

If the question "Why consider philosophy?" is ever raised among a group of psychoanalysts, consternation usually results. Why even ask? Is the practice of psychoanalysis not light years away from what philosophers do? Many philosophers, conversely, have little time for the theoretical, let alone practical pursuits of psychoanalysis. The notion that the mind is opaque and that transparency of thought and action are mere illusion is anathema to many who practice philosophy, those who strive to achieve clarity and cohesion in carefully constructed arguments about the nature of knowledge, language, and truth.

The simple fact is that philosophy and psychoanalysis often make for strange bedfellows. On the one hand, philosophy might be described as an academic pursuit that cherishes the process of isolated self-reflection. On the other hand, psychoanalysis is an inherently social endeavor, dependent upon the insights achieved through the interaction between patient and analyst. Yet despite their differences, the intersection of philosophy and psychoanalysis can be traced back to the very beginning of Freud's project. Indeed, it is difficult to conceive of the unconscious without acknowledging the enigmatic perspectives of Friedrich Nietzsche. But the inclusion of Nietzsche in the pantheon of philosophers inevitably raises the question of "What constitutes philosophy?" Confusion and ambivalence abound, in large measure because philosophy and psychoanalysis are both rife with intradisciplinary tension. Competing schools offer their own definitions. Philosophy and psychoanalysis are also linked in another way. Both are under enormous pressure to demonstrate their relevance in an academic and professional environment that privileges STEM (science, technology, engineering, and mathematics) subjects, embraces the promise of evidence-based practice and increasingly neglects the role of the humanities for human understanding.

The objective of this chapter is to develop a pathway between philosophy and psychoanalysis, to overcome common misconceptions about their interaction, and above all, to challenge the skepticism towards philosophy that exists among mental health professionals in general, and psychoanalysts in particular. Having spent my career at the intersection of philosophy and psychoanalysis, I will reflect on some of my own experiences as a trained philosopher and a practicing psychoanalyst. Using a personal narrative in this way may strike some readers as usual, but as I hope to show, philosophy and psychoanalysis both grow out of our lived experience.

DOI: 10.4324/9780429297076-7

The chapter will proceed in stages. I will begin by drawing on my own path in order to consider the challenges posed by common disciplinary boundaries. I will trace the early cross-fertilization between philosophy and psychoanalysis to the development of a hermeneutic perspective that encompasses both fields. The notion that our lives are circumscribed by society, culture, and history has its roots in the ideas of Wilhelm Dilthey; its early psychoanalytic application in the work of Ludwig Binswanger; and its contemporary expression in Hans-Georg Gadamer and psychoanalytic approaches that emphasize the contexts of human understanding.

Journeying Across Disciplines

When asked by a psychoanalytic audience to explain the pertinence of philosophy, I reply that the answer is both simple and complex. I suggest that the psychoanalyst enters into a form of dialogue with the patient in an attempt to better understand the possibilities and constraints of what it means to be human in a world shaped by social interactions. I then suggest that the psychoanalyst is also inherently a philosopher, a statement that is usually met with a puzzled response. I go on to point out that in the broadest sense, psychoanalysis relies on a set of assumptions about how we relate to others and ourselves. These assumptions are shaped by implicit beliefs and values about the nature of human relating and what constitutes a life well lived. The assumptions we make are at once personal, professional, and cultural in scope. They guide the way psychoanalysts work, the questions they ask, and the answers they find in the interaction with their patients. In a similar sense, I suggest that philosophy is a discipline that seeks to understand and articulate the foundations of our personal and societal assumptions about the nature of experience. It is this process of "laying bare" or "disclosing" the assumptions that shape human understanding which, in my view, inherently connects psychoanalysis and philosophy.

My attempt to explain the pertinence of philosophy for psychoanalysis reveals my own beliefs about how each discipline functions, as well as my specific background and training. If the question were asked of someone else, they might offer a different answer based on the distinct disciplinary definitions in which they trained and which they hold dear. This is an important point because there is a host of competing disciplinary definitions about what constitutes "psychoanalysis" and "philosophy," none of which is wrong, and which, taken together, provide a measure of the sheer breadth of these fields.

The complexity I am describing also relates to professional practice and identities. Depending on the context in which I am asked to talk or write about philosophy, I might worry that what I have to say will be deemed insufficiently "philosophical." A similar argument could be made about psychoanalysis. If I am asked to speak with psychoanalysts whose approach is different from my own, I know in advance that their understanding of the clinical material I present may not only differ, but even clash with what I have to say. Given the variety of schools and perspectives that have historically sought to dominate each field, how do we even begin to define what constitutes psychoanalysis or philosophy?

To illustrate the challenges of defining psychoanalysis or philosophy within narrow disciplinary boundaries, I will draw on my own experience as a trained philosopher and practicing psychoanalyst. On the one hand, I have a doctorate in philosophy and have published numerous articles and books that are of a philosophical nature. On the other hand, I have always been attracted to thinkers who are at the periphery of the academic discipline, at least as it tends to be defined in the Anglo-American academic milieu. I recognized early on that my interest in questions of human experience did not fit neatly into the philosophical field known as "analytical philosophy." But I have also learned that any answer to the problem of "What is philosophy?" depends upon who is asked and who seeks to define it.

Philosophical thinking, like psychoanalytic practice, enables us to reflect on, understand, and potentially articulate the nature of our lived experience. By lived experience I include such topics as our emotional being, our intersubjective existence, our social interactions, and our development within culture. My university education, which I completed in England, provides an illustration of many branches of philosophy that attend to these areas of study. All of my degrees were completed in interdisciplinary departments. As an undergraduate student at the University of London, I read modern history and political theory. I then went up to Cambridge, where I completed two postgraduate degrees, the first in social and political theory and the second in the history and philosophy of science. While none of my degrees stems from a philosophy department as such, I was taught, supervised, and completed my postgraduate training as a philosopher. From England I moved to the United States and then eventually back to Canada, where I grew up. Over the past twenty-five years I have taught in a number of university faculties, but never, strictly speaking, in a department of philosophy. I began my academic career by teaching psychoanalytic theory in a history of science department in Cambridge, Massachusetts, and then taught in a number of interdisciplinary programs over the following decade. Following the completion of a second doctoral degree in clinical psychology and training in psychoanalysis, I spent a decade in a psychiatry department in New York City, where I was responsible for teaching courses grounded in the humanities: history, ethics, and above all, theories of mind. Today I live in Vancouver, where I teach in a faculty of education and a department of psychiatry, and all the while my work continues to be shaped by my philosophical interests.

After sharing this academic path, you might better understand why I sometimes feel like an "interloper," someone who practices philosophy but does not easily fit into the discipline as it is commonly understood. Similarly, while psychoanalysis was once represented in a broad array of university departments, it is increasingly unusual for university professors to be practicing psychoanalysts. My colleagues respect my work as a psychoanalyst, but most have little understanding of what I do, in large measure because there are so few psychoanalysts in the academic world today. When I reflect on my career path, I recognize that regardless of my academic affiliations, my scholarship has always existed at the intersection of philosophy and the psychoanalysis. I use my philosophical training to disclose the underlying ideas and values that guide the clinical disciplines in which I practice. This involves a kind of critical thinking, a willingness to ask questions that often go unasked.

When we engage in critical thinking, we may find that the models and techniques that guide our clinical discipline are based on a host of underlying assumptions: above all, on personal and cultural ideas and values that go unacknowledged. These ideas and values may be culturally specific, gendered, racialized, and historically specific. The role of a philosopher, or critical thinker, I believe, is to shed light on such ideas and values and, in the process, make them explicit. Once they become explicit, we can articulate their meaning and understand their impact. We can also begin to ask why we use particular models and techniques, and consider possibilities of change that attend to the broader moral good. The process of disclosure I am describing has many similarities to the psychoanalytic method. Psychoanalysts may work with their patients to formulate the emotional and interpersonal patterns that have hitherto remained implicit and unformulated.

Intellectual Tribalism

If philosophical and psychoanalytic pursuits intersect in the manner I have described, then we may wonder why these fields are so often seen as distant, if not opposed. This relates, I believe, to the challenges posed by a kind of "intellectual tribalism." I want to provide an example of what I mean by drawing on my own experience of postgraduate training in philosophy, which was in essence an apprenticeship in the philosophical profession. It is perhaps at this crucial, early career stage that the definition of what constitutes philosophy matters most because it shapes the boundaries within which intellectual research is pursued.

Today, if someone asks me what philosophy means, I usually respond with a question (I am, after all, a psychoanalyst!): "Whose philosophy?" My point is to raise awareness that there is no single agreed-upon definition of the field and that there is a host of different schools. Philosophy, as it is generally taught and practiced in Great Britain, pertains to the "analytical" tradition. In light of what I have said about my interdisciplinary interests, you might wonder why I chose to pursue postgraduate research at Cambridge. After all, the university has been known as the birthplace of the analytical philosophy. To make matters even more complicated, I became a member of Trinity College, which is a historical bastion of analytical philosophers. Among its former members, Trinity College counts a famous trio: Bertrand Russell (1872–1970), G. E. Moore (1873–1958) and Ludwig Wittgenstein (1889–1951).[1] And indeed, when I was a student there, I learned, like other budding philosophers, to acknowledge Wittgenstein's rooms whenever I passed by.

I wish I could say that I went up to Trinity solely because I wanted to study in the shadow of these great minds. My reasons were rather more mundane: as a wealthy college, Trinity was known to offer generous fellowships. There is also another, more important reason for choosing to study at Cambridge. It allowed someone like myself, with diverse interests, to pursue interdisciplinary scholarship. The only difficulty was that the kind of scholarship I had in mind could not be undertaken in the Department of Philosophy because there was little interest in, or representation of, continental European philosophy.

The tension around what constitutes "philosophy" was present in a host of ways, but I remember it most when it came to how the work of Ludwig Wittgenstein was discussed and taught at the time. Today, we know Wittgenstein as a renowned philosopher whose writings cover a range of philosophical perspectives, from his early *Tractatus Logico-Philosophicus* to his posthumously published *Philosophical Investigations*, in which he revisited and questioned some of his earlier ideas. Wittgenstein may have hailed from Austria, but I came to know that at Cambridge he became the quintessential analytical philosopher. This Wittgenstein seemed to have little interest in the "woolly" concerns of continental philosophy. Wittgenstein's (1921/2007) famous statement at the end of the *Tractatus*, "That which we cannot speak about we must pass over in silence," was not understood as an invitation to explore the realm of unspoken or unspeakable but as a directive to focus our philosophical investigations on the visible, on logic and language. Some topics merited philosophical study. Others did not.

The Wittgenstein I was introduced to was wedded to clear analytical thinking. Yet there were whispers of another Wittgenstein: the private side of a man who lived an anguished emotional life and filled a diary with reflections of a quasi-religious nature – of experience that is often beyond words. This was Wittgenstein the human being, who struggled with existential questions about life's meaning, human mortality, and spirituality. Wittgenstein recorded his thoughts in a series of diaries that have since been published. For my Cambridge philosophy colleagues, Wittgenstein, the man of emotional turmoil, was not considered to be an object of study. If you were interested in that kind of experience, you might read literature or theology, or if all else failed, continental philosophy. Or you could go further afield to the strangest of all disciplines, psychoanalysis. And of psychoanalysis, as some of analytical philosophers might remark, "we must pass over in silence."

Lest you think I am drawing a one-sided picture, let me provide another illustration. In 1992, as I was finishing my doctorate, a fierce debate broke out in Cambridge after it was proposed that the French philosopher, Jacques Derrida, be awarded a honorary doctorate. Many in Cambridge scoffed at Derrida because they felt his work did not meet the standards of rigorous scholarship and thus did constitute academic philosophy. Some went so far as to describe Derrida's writings as absurd. Because of the protests, the university was forced to put the matter to a faculty ballot. It was the first time this had occurred in over three decades. Despite the charges against him, Derrida's was ultimately awarded a honorary degree by a vote of 336 to 204. I fully admit to finding Derrida's work challenging, and at times I am not at all sure what he is trying to say. But Derrida is hardly the only philosopher whose work can be difficult to decipher! Above all, it is hard to question Derrida's status as a serious thinker given his centrality to theory of deconstructionism and critical theory more generally.

If you think that this kind of sectarian thinking should have no place in the academic pursuit of knowledge, you would be right. But institutions of learning, be they philosophical or psychoanalytical, are rife with these kinds of divisions. Years later, when I began to train as a psychoanalyst I was struck by the extent to which similar divisions colored the psychoanalytic profession. The history of psychoanalysis is full of intradisciplinary tension: political infighting and long-lasting feuds are legion. Different traditions of psychoanalytic theory and practice, often allied with specific institutes or umbrella organizations, have sought to maintain the belief that they embody the true version of profession (see Govrin, 2016). Fortunately, these tensions have begun to wane, even if the underlying differences have not. Psychoanalysts, especially in North America, have learned that they cannot afford to spend time fighting amongst themselves while the broader profession of mental health is increasingly critical of any kind of long-term or open-ended psychotherapy.

In similar fashion, we might observe that there is now an increasing number of philosophers who are bridging the gap between analytical and continental philosophy. Wittgenstein's diaries, for example, have become a source of fascination (cf. Nordmann, 2001; Sass, 2001). I am not suggesting that the divisions between analytical and continental philosophy have disappeared. Many university departments continue to define themselves along disciplinary lines. But there is nevertheless a greater willingness to explore the spaces between them. An example of this kind of scholarly exploration was a seminar that I had the good fortune of participating in. Led by the analytical philosopher Stanley Cavell, it considered the parallels between the work of Wittgenstein and Lacan. The discussions that followed bridged disciplines and multiple points of view. Yet within universities today, the distinctions between analytical and continental philosophy, and the comparative absence of psychoanalysis, continue to shape what kinds of questions are asked, what kind of scholarship is carried out, and ultimately, who is chosen to practice and represent the discipline at the academic level.

During my postgraduate studies, I struggled to align my interdisciplinary interests with the need to achieve the kind of university degree that might enable me to have an academic career. At Cambridge it was clear that anyone with a serious interest in European thinkers had to look beyond the philosophy department. Fortunately, I found my way to interdisciplinary programs where I was taught that philosophy is multifaceted and that critical thinking can provide the means to cross disciplinary boundaries. I was supervised in turn by the social theorist Anthony Giddens, the historian of psychoanalysis John Forrester, and the specialist in German Romantic philosophy and aesthetics Andrew Bowie. They all encouraged me to read widely and to pursue my fascination with the interaction of philosophy and psychoanalysis.

From Psychoanalysis to Hermeneutics

Like anyone who expresses an interest in psychoanalysis, I began by reading Freud's key works. Trained as a neurologist, Freud was a stalwart believer in late 19th-century naturalism, even as he engaged in increasingly speculative theorizing (Sulloway, 1979). The early Freud posited an unconscious realm of the mind as a repository of hidden truths, a distinct entity in the mind that consists of repressed sexual and aggressive impulses and is governed by dynamic forces. Within a short space of time, the unconscious became the focal point of the psychoanalytic method. In its early iterations, Freudian psychoanalysis was deceptively simple and straightforward: the psychoanalyst was like an archaeologist who would excavate and interpret the contents of the unconscious, giving rise to a process of working through that would enable the patient to master the intrusion of unconscious impulses into conscious life.

Given Freud's embrace of science, it is not altogether surprising that he had a tenuous relationship with philosophy. On the one hand, Freud recognized the relevance of the humanities, and especially the classics, for psychoanalysis. Indeed, it is quite impossible to imagine Freud's work without the classical Greek mythology in which it is steeped. On the other hand, Freud sought to maintain a safe distance from the field of philosophy. Yet closer inspection of his writings suggests that Freud returned time and again to philosophy's thematic concerns.

Freud recognized early on the way in which the philosophies of the 19th-century German thinkers Arthur Schopenhauer and Friedrich Nietzsche coincided with psychoanalysis. In fact, Nietzsche developed a concise formulation of the notion of repression well before Freud reached a similar conclusion. Freud acknowledged the philosopher's insights, writing that,

> But not one amongst all of us has succeeded in describing this phenomenon and its psychological reasons as exhaustively and at the same time as impressively as Nietzsche did in one of his aphorisms: "I have done that," says my memory. "I could not have done that," says my pride, and remains inexorable. Finally, my memory yields.
>
> *(Freud, 1901, p. 158)*

Freud is even quoted by his biographer, Ernest Jones (1967), as stating that Nietzsche "had a more penetrating knowledge of himself than any other man who ever lived or was ever likely to live" (p. 385). Coming from Freud, this was impressive praise indeed! Yet Freud the scientist held fast to the promise of a scientific psychology and was reluctant to share the limelight with a philosopher. He went on to make the dubious claim that he had not actually read Nietzsche while developing his own ideas on the unconscious.

Freud's ambivalent relationship to philosophy had a lasting impact, especially in North America. To this day, very few psychoanalytic training institutes assign any readings, let alone courses, in philosophy. Over time, the profession of psychoanalysis became more aligned with medicine, and the humanities were increasingly neglected, despite their essential place in Freud's work. Today, some of Freud's essential texts, above all *Civilization and Its Discontents*, are far more likely to be read in university humanities departments than in psychoanalytic institutes. Why? Because Freud's accounts of human nature, religion, and societal interaction are deemed too distant from the concerns of the practicing psychoanalyst. Yet the fact that psychoanalysts make assumptions about human nature and are shaped by their culture's values and societal norms is thereby neglected.

As a postgraduate student in philosophy, and later as a psychoanalytic trainee, I was fascinated by Freud's forays into theory-building. The parallels with contemporaneous continental philosophers seemed noteworthy. I was particularly struck by the work of hermeneutic philosophers who developed an alternative to the scientific naturalism so popular in Freud's day. I delved into the work of Wilhelm Dilthey (1833–1911), a German philosopher and psychologist, and one of the founders of modern hermeneutics. Dilthey is probably best known for distinguishing between the human sciences and the natural sciences. Whereas the primary task of the human sciences is the understanding of human and historical life, the main task of the natural sciences is to arrive at causal explanations. Dilthey (1894/1977) sought to formulate a descriptive psychology of understanding (*verstehen*) in response to the emerging positivistic paradigm in psychology. Dilthey proposed that psychologists use their everyday experience as a basis for interpreting and understanding psychological meaning. He argued that psychological phenomena not only require interpretation, but they are also constituted by human interpretive practices, thus giving rise to the field of modern hermeneutics – broadly speaking, the study of human understanding and interpretation.

Using Dilthey as a starting point, I want to briefly elaborate some of the main ideas of philosophical hermeneutics before returning to my aim of mapping out a pathway between philosophy and psychoanalysis. Dilthey's "descriptive psychology" began with the examination of the totality of life experience: the lived reality that precedes the distinctly Western, Cartesian separation between mind and body, self and world. Dilthey argued that it is only against this ever-present, mostly unarticulated background of their experience that humans are able to perceive and comprehend things, including themselves.

> We live in this atmosphere, it surrounds us constantly. We are immersed in it. We are at home everywhere in this historical and understood world; we understand the meaning and significance of it all; we ourselves are woven into the common sphere.
>
> *(Dilthey, 1976, p. 191)*

In other words, we can only understand the human being in the life-world in which he or she exists. From the viewpoint of hermeneutics, this means that understanding is itself generated by our social interactions and cultural contexts. If our aim is to make sense of the world as it is experienced by human beings, not by natural objects or internal drives, then any philosophy or psychology that does not account for our interactions and contexts is necessarily incomplete. The problem with reductive strategies of the kind also found in Freud was that they tended to distinguish psychological phenomena from their social and cultural surround.

Dilthey's hermeneutics was revised and expanded by Martin Heidegger (1889–1976). His philosophical project is complex, and I will only briefly sketch some of his early ideas. In *Being and Time*, Heidegger (1927/1962) engaged in an investigative method – what he called a "fundamental ontology" – into the nature of Being. Heidegger refers to the entity, or human being, that questions the meaning of Being as "Dasein." The term Dasein translates literally as "There-being," but the German term is usually retained because there is no equivalent translation that adequately conveys the notion that Dasein exists only by virtue of its "thereness," of always being located in a specific place and time. To put it very simply, I exist as Roger Frie by virtue of the interactions with my environment and the relationships I have with other people in the specific time and place in which I live. All of these things make me who I am.

Whereas much philosophy, particularly after René Descartes (1596–1650), perceived the mind and world as separate entities, Heidegger argues that being involved in the world is definitive; Dasein is neither autonomous nor self-contained, but must always be understood to exist as "being-in-the-world."[2] This implies that the person is not simply *of* a particular context, and this context does not *only* form the background for activity. Rather, the embeddedness of the person in his or her contexts is so profound as to render any absolute distinction of action from context nonsensical. We are "always and already in the world." In essence, we find ourselves "thrown" into a world we neither create nor control.

The state of "thrownness" is described by Hans-Georg Gadamer as our "situated" existence. Gadamer (1900–2002) was a student of Heidegger and sought to work out the conditions that make human understanding possible. It is Gadamer who is most closely associated with hermeneutics today. Drawing on Heidegger, Gadamer (1960/1991, p. 301) states:

> The very idea of a situation means that we are not standing outside it and hence are unable to have any objective knowledge of it. We always find ourselves within a situation, and throwing light on it is a task that is never entirely finished.
>
> *(p. 301)*

For Gadamer, it is necessary that we see beyond our immediate concerns to enter into a dialogue with voices from the past that form our current interpretations of life. This requires us to develop an awareness of the situation in which we find ourselves and be cognizant of our "horizon of understanding." Being thrown into the world implies that we exist in specific horizons of understanding that shape what we experience and the interpretations we make. A person who looks to the horizon is not limited by what is immediately in front of her. By responding to the contexts into which we are thrown, we can begin shaping our possibilities of understanding into knowledgeable lives.

From Hermeneutics Back to Psychoanalysis

Despite my fascination with these hermeneutic philosophers, it was the attempt to apply their insights to psychoanalysis that really caught my attention. I refer in particular to the interdisciplinary work of the Swiss psychiatrist, psychoanalyst and philosopher, Ludwig Binswanger (1881–1966). Today, the pairing of hermeneutic philosophy and psychoanalysis has become more accepted, thanks in no small part to Paul Ricoeur's pathbreaking book on the art of interpretation, titled *Freud and Philosophy* (1970). But Binswanger's attempt to traverse the distance between hermeneutic philosophy and psychoanalytic practice in the early 20th century was truly novel (Frie, 1997). Not only did he introduce a range of philosophical ideas to psychoanalysis, but he also developed a clinical perspective on intersubjectivity and empathy well before these terms entered into the general psychoanalytic vocabulary.

So why do we know so little about him? There are a number of reasons. Binswanger's early foray into philosophy was met with bewilderment by his fellow psychoanalysts, not least by Freud himself. And many English-speaking psychoanalysts remain unaware of the breadth of Binswanger's work because only select pieces have been translated, in large measure due to their philosophical nature. Binswanger developed a small but devoted following that was made up of a diverse group of clinicians and philosophers. He eventually became known to many English speakers not as a psychoanalyst *per se* but as the founder of existential analysis. Binswanger was humbled by this interest, but never fully identified with the existential approach popularized by Rollo May in *Existence: A New Dimension in Psychiatry and Psychology* (May, Angel & Ellenberger, 1958). It is worth noting that when May edited this well-known book with his colleagues, Ernest Angel and Henri F. Ellenberger, he was still a training and supervising psychoanalyst at the William Alanson White Institute of Psychiatry, Psychoanalysis, and Psychology in New York City. May's attraction to Binswanger's work can be read as an outgrowth of his psychoanalytic training in the ideas of Harry Stack Sullivan, Erich Fromm, Frieda Fromm-Reichman, and Clara Thompson, all founders of the W. A. White Institute. May was himself analyzed by Erich Fromm and therefore well attuned to the contextual perspective by the time he discovered Binswanger's work.

In order to understand Binswanger's appeal to May and other philosophically inclined neo-Freudian psychoanalysts, it is important to provide some further background. Binswanger first met Freud in 1907, when Binswanger accompanied Jung to visit Freud and his family at their home in Vienna. In contrast to the short-lived relationship between Freud and Jung, Freud and Binswanger maintained a lifelong friendship, despite their growing and significant differences (Fichtner, 1992). Binswanger was a generation younger than Freud and came from a family of prominent psychiatrists who ran the Bellevue Sanatorium in Switzerland. Binswanger took over the directorship from his father in 1910 and devoted much of his career to the integration of philosophy and psychoanalysis. Binswanger's interests in philosophy were reflected in his personal associations with major German philosophers of the period and Bellevue became a center for interdisciplinary learning. Prominent thinkers who visited included Edmund Husserl, Martin Heidegger, Martin Buber, Karl Löwith, Ernst Cassirer, Alexander Pfänder, and Max Scheler.

Early on Binswanger was attracted to Freud because of insights that psychoanalysis could provide into human behavior. But he was also critical of Freud's reductive theorizing and embrace of scientific naturalism. In contrast to Freud, Binswanger sought to understand and explain human beings in the totality of their existence, not as natural objects constructed from various parts. In his first book, *Introduction to the Problems of General Psychology* (1922), Binswanger points to Dilthey as "the first to demonstrate the way to a psychology of the person" (p. 247). Building on this hermeneutic impulse, Binswanger suggests that understanding is made possible to by the structural continuum of lived experience prior to any division between subject and object, mind and world.

In the preface to *Introduction to Problems of General Psychology*, Binswanger articulates the objective of his work: "to achieve clarity about the conceptual foundation of what the psychiatrist perceives, reflects on and does with respect to psychology and psychotherapy, at the bedside" (1922, p. v). For Binswanger, it is precisely the question of *how* we understand the other person that is of central importance to clinical practice. His search for direct, intersubjective understanding led him to Edmund Husserl's phenomenological method – a descriptive approach that seeks to allow phenomena to "express themselves." This is achieved through a process of bracketing our preformed judgements. Binswanger suggests that the psychoanalyst explore the patient's lived experience without imposing his or her theoretical model onto that experience, akin to what is commonly understood today when psychoanalysts speak of "holding their theories lightly."

In addition to drawing on the phenomenological method, Binswanger turned to the notion of empathy, which was developed by Robert Vischer in 1873 as a means for understanding art. In 1903, the German philosopher Theodor Lipps argued that empathy could also be used to achieve psychological understanding of another person. While the term appears in Freud's writing, beginning in 1905 with his work on *Jokes and Their Relation to the Unconscious*, Freud never developed empathy as a substantive clinical concept. Binswanger read Lipps's work on empathy in 1913 and saw the interpersonal potential of empathy for the clinical situation.[3]

Like his American contemporary, Harry Stack Sullivan, Binswanger also felt that Freud's psychoanalytic techniques were of limited use to patients who suffered from psychotic disturbances. Moreover, he had difficulty accepting Freud's tenet of emotional neutrality and anonymity. Binswanger believed that the use of phenomenological intuition and empathy might enable the clinician to achieve a holistic understanding of the patient. Following Heidegger, Binswanger maintained that it was essential that the person be understood in his or her totality, without reducing experience to causal explanations or theoretical constructs. Heidegger's conception of world – the matrix of relations in which we exist and discovers meaning – provided Binswanger with a conceptual tool for understanding and describing human experiences "in their full phenomenal content and context" (Binswanger, 1955, p. 264).[4]

As a clinician, Binswanger sought to understand his patients in terms of their world-designs: their experiential horizon of meaning and understanding. Binswanger's concept of "world-design" has much in common with Gadamer's more familiar concept of "horizon of understanding." Both refer to the possibilities and limitations of understanding that are tied to our particular situatedness, to how we exist in the world. For Binswanger, our existence in the world is captured by Heidegger's concept of "thrownness." Binswanger suggests that we are thrown into situations, and it is this state of "thrownness" that we are forced to come to terms with. Any attempt to understand ourselves as human beings must therefore begin by understanding the nature of our existence as "thrown."

There is one other aspect of Binswanger's theory that needs to be included. Binswanger suggests that our experiential worlds are fundamentally social in nature. He was critical of both Freud and Heidegger because he believed they neglected the role of other people in the achievement of understanding. Binswanger suggested that it is through our interaction with others that we are able to grasp meaning in our lives, and in this sense his clinical practice is indebted to Martin Buber (1878–1965) and his philosophy of dialogue. According to Binswanger, the therapeutic process is dependent upon the psychoanalyst's attitude of loving openness to the patient – what Buber referred to as the I-Thou (Buber, 1923/1970) – which allows an analysis to evolve in an atmosphere of uninterrupted, direct communication. As Binswanger puts it,

> This communication may in no way, as the orthodox psychoanalysts believe, be conceived as mere repetition, in the positive case as transference and countertransference, or in the negative case as resistance and counterresistance; much rather, the relationship of patient and doctor represents always also an independent communicative novelty, a new linking of fate, and namely not only regarding the patient-doctor relationship, but also and above all regarding the pure relationship of being-with in the meaning of a genuine "with-one-another."
>
> *(Binswanger, 1935/1994, p. 215)*

In this sense, we might say that Binswanger's account of the therapeutic process, and his emphasis on the "genuine 'with-one-another'" between doctor and patient, places him alongside such early critics of Freud's technique as Sándor Ferenczi and Sullivan, though there is no indication that they knew of one another or had prior contact.

A Hermeneutic Pathway

In the hermeneutic-psychoanalytic perspective I have outlined, our situatedness gives shape to our "horizon of understanding," a largely invisible backdrop of "preunderstanding" that enables us to navigate our way in the world. From a clinical perspective, the goal is to discover the nature of our situatedness, so that we can begin opening up a space for new and different ways of being and relating. Yet this is far from easy. Our world-horizons are limited, meaning that there is a boundary to what we know or understand at any point in time. As a result, there will always be experience that escapes our awareness. This points back to the nature of the unconscious. As the hermeneutic psychologist Philip Cushman suggests,

> The unconscious is not an interior thing, but part of the patient's social landscape that contains potential feelings, thoughts, and experiences that are not able to show up because they lie on the other side of the patient's horizon of understanding.
>
> *(Cushman, 1995, p. 307)*

After his philosophical turn, Binswanger began to conceptualize the unconscious differently than Freud. When *Introduction to the Problems of General Psychology* was published, it was met with consternation by Freud, who wrote to Binswanger: "What are you going to do about the unconscious, or rather, how will you manage without the unconscious? *Has the philosophical devil got you in its claws after all? Reassure me*" (Binswanger, 1957, p. 64; emphasis added). There was, in fact, little Binswanger (1957, p. 64) could do to "reassure" his old friend and colleague. Yet as Binswanger points out, he never actually did away with the unconscious, as Freud assumed. Instead, he began to conceptualize the unconscious process in a different way. As Binswanger says,

> I have never managed without the unconscious, either in psychotherapeutic practice, which is indeed impossible without using Freud's concept of the unconscious, or in theory. But after I turned to phenomenology and [Heidegger's] existential analysis, I conceived the unconscious in a different way. The problems it related became broader and deeper, as it became less and less defined as merely the opposite of the conscious.
>
> *(Binswanger, 1957, p. 64)*

In order to appreciate Binswanger's position on the unconscious, it will be helpful to return to Dilthey, who acknowledged that we can never fully know our own minds and that understanding is always limited. However, rather than posit a separate unconscious to explain this limitation, Dilthey proposes different levels of awareness. In a remarkably contemporary sounding statement, Dilthey (1989, p. 311) declares: "Psychic acts are conscious, but not attended to, noticed, or possessed in reflexive awareness." In other words, we may have conscious states that are not attentively or reflexively observed, just as we may be lost in consciousness without being necessarily unconscious. Dilthey is describing a process of "not knowing" that is commonly referred to today as "dissociation." Perhaps most significantly, Dilthey insists that all psychological experience be understood on a continuum, where no experience can be understood in isolation from the larger social context in which we exist. According to the Dilthey scholars, Makkreel and Rodi,

> By making reflexive awareness the background for the focusing efforts of attentiveness (*Aufmerksamkeit*) and introspection (*Selbstbeobachtung*), Dilthey accounts for the so-called dark regions within consciousness without positing a separate realm of the unconscious. Instead of appealing to an unconscious depth, which is a grand explanative hypothesis, Dilthey conceives the mysteries of consciousness in terms of an ever-widening context whose basic contours can be described. Consciousness is conceived as a continuum where no content can be understood in isolation from its larger context.
>
> *(Makkreel & Rodi, 1989, pp. 35–36)*

As human beings, our situatedness always makes us opaque to ourselves. We are always limited by where we are and what we know, so that it is never possible to have a "God's-eye" view of the world. For this reason, a suitably trained and sympathetic interpreter may discern what we mean better than we do ourselves. The approach I am describing here is not like the "hermeneutics of suspicion," practiced by Nietzsche in *The Genealogy of Morals*, or advanced by Freud in *The Interpretation of Dreams*. Nietzsche's and Freud's interpretive strategies were predicated on the idea of an unconscious censorship and a clear distinction between manifest and latent content. Increased understanding is not about overcoming censorship to reveal hidden truths. The metaphors that have been traditionally used to define the nature of psychological experience – deep, internal, private, inaccessible – though highly descriptive, neglect the social and cultural contexts of experience in which understanding is generated.

When viewed from a developmental lens, we might say that the patterns of social practice and emotional interaction between a child and its caregivers always unfold in specific cultural contexts and historical trajectories and give rise to horizons of understanding that shape subsequent emotional experiences. These meanings are communicated through social interaction and form "organizing principles." By organizing principles, I refer to implicit patterns of relating that are, in effect, unconscious – not in the sense of being repressed, but in the sense of being prereflective. Thus, for hermeneutic philosophers and psychoanalysts, "unconscious experience" refers to the prereflective dimension of experience that is generated and maintained in our interactions with other people.

The psychoanalytic method that I am describing is akin to the process of hermeneutic disclosure. It is not a linear movement from inner to outer, from a lack of awareness to articulated knowledge. Hermeneutic disclosure is not an archaeological excavation of ever-deeper layers of an unconscious mind. It is an exploration of our relational and experiential worlds. What is known or not known, what is sayable or unsayable, is product of the ongoing interpersonal fields in which we participate. The aim, in this sense, is to formulate patterns of relating that have hitherto remained unformulated, a point of view that is present in work of many relational psychoanalysts (cf. Stern, 1997).

What It Means to Converse

I want to conclude by returning to the problem I introduced at the start of this chapter. How do we navigate the divide across disciplines and between different modes of thinking and practice? (see Burston & Frie, 2006) I have suggested that there is much to be learned from hermeneutic philosophers and psychoanalysts. They tell us that understanding is a fundamentally social process that always runs up against uncertainty. This is particularly the case when engaging another person in dialogue. Knowledge gained through dialogue always involves "not knowing." To truly converse with another person is to enter into a conversation without knowing in advance where it will take us. In a particularly important passage, Gadamer states:

> A genuine conversation is never the one that we wanted to conduct. Rather, it is generally more correct to say that we fall into conversation, or even that we become involved in it. The way one word follows another, with the conversation taking its own twists and reaching its own conclusion, may well be conducted in some way, but the partners conversing are far less the leaders of it than the led. No one knows in advance what will "come out" of a conversation. Understanding, or its failure, is like an event that happens to us.
>
> *(Gadamer, 1960/1991, p. 383)*

Following Gadamer, we might say that it is precisely "not knowing," the recognition that experience consists of more than we can ever put into words or actions, which enables us to appreciate what it means to be human. Even if we think we already know, our engagement with the other person opens up new possibilities, new avenues of thinking, seeing, and feeling that may not have been available to us before. This process of understanding cannot happen if we shut down dialogue, insist on the correctness of our position, or engage the other person in order only to demonstrate the veracity of our point of view. It requires us to listen to what others have to teach us. This perspective is as relevant to the practice of psychoanalysis as it is to the interaction of different disciplines that are willing to speak with one another.

What might it mean to apply the Gadamerian conversation to the interaction between philosophy and psychoanalysis? Perhaps, philosophers and psychoanalysts can learn to move forward together, allowing themselves to be less the leaders than the led, trusting in the belief that an openness to what the other discipline has to offer will provide an opportunity to expand their horizons. By outlining a pathway between philosophy and psychoanalysis, this chapter has sought to contribute to an interdisciplinary conversation that looks to future possibilities.

Notes

1 Another Trinity philosopher was Alfred North Whitehead (1861–1947), though during his time at Trinity he was primarily known as a mathematician and collaborated with his former student, Betrand Russell, on *Pricipia Mathematica.* Whitehead became famous for his philosophical work after he joined the philosophy department at Harvard in 1924, where he wrote his well-known book *Process and Reality.*

2 According to Heidegger, "It is not the case that the human being 'is' and then has, by way of an extra, a relationship-of-Being toward the 'world' – a world with which he provides himself occasionally. Dasein is never 'proximally' an entity that is, so to speak, free of Being-in, but which sometimes has the inclination to take up a 'relationship' toward the world. Taking up relationships toward the world is possible only because Dasein as Being-in-the-world, is as it is" (1927/1962, p. 84).

3 It is worth noting that Binswanger's embrace of empathy took place some fifty years before Heinz Kohut first began to write about the importance of empathy in psychoanalysis. This is an example of the way in which divisions between different schools of thought often stand in the way of a free-flowing exchange of ideas. See also Susan Lanzoni's (2003) discussion of empathy in Binswanger's work.

4 Binswanger's (1942/1993) chief and still untranslated work, *Grundformen und Erkenntnis menschlichen Daseins*, published in 1942, can be read as a critique of the lack of an adequate social theory in *Being and Time*, and as a response to the unfolding horrors of the time. Binswanger's critical stance, in addition to his own Jewish heritage, places him outside of the Heidegger controversy. See Frie (1999, 2010) and Frie and Hoffmann (2002).

References

Binswanger, L. (1922). *Einführung in die allgemeine Probleme der Psychologie.* Berlin: Julius Springer-Verlag.

Binswanger, L. (1935/1994). *Ludwig Binswanger Ausgewählte Werke Band 3: Vorträge und Aufsätze* (M. Herzog, Ed.). Heidelberg: Asanger Verlag.

Binswanger, L. (1942/1993). Grundformen und Erkenntnis menschlichen Daseins. In M. Herzog & H. J. Braun (Eds.), *Ausgewählte Werke Band 2.* Heidelberg: Asanger Verlag.

Binswanger, L. (1949/1955). Die Bedeutung der Daseinsanalytik Martin Heideggers für das Selbstverständnis der Psychiatrie. In *Ausgewählte Vorträge und Aufsätze*, Bd. II. Bern: Francke Verlag.

Binswanger, L. (1957). *Sigmund Freud: Reminiscences of a Friendship* (N. Guterman, Trans.). New York, NY: Grune & Stratton.

Buber, M. (1923/1970). *I and Thou* (W. Kaufmann, Trans.). New York: Charles Scribner's Sons (Originally published in 1923).

Burston, D. & Frie, R. (2006). *Psychotherapy as a Human Science.* Pittsburgh, PA: Duquesne University Press.

Cushman, P. (1995). *Constructing the Self, Constructing America: A Cultural History of Psychotherapy.* Reading, MA: Addison-Wesley.

Dilthey, W. (1883/1989). Introduction to the human sciences. In R. A. Makkreel & F. Rodi (Eds.), *Wilhelm Dilthey: Selected Works*, Vol. 1 (pp. 27–240). Princeton: Princeton University Press.

Dilthey, W. (1894/1977). *Descriptive Psychology and Historical Understanding* (R. M. Zaner & K. L. Heiges, Trans.). The Hague: Martinus Nijhoff.

Dilthey, W. (1976). *W. Dilthey: Selected Writings* (H. P. Rickman, Ed. and Trans.). New York: HarperCollins.

Fichtner, G. (Ed.). (1992). *Sigmund Freud – Ludwig Binswanger. Briefwechsel, 1908–1938.* Frankfurt a. M.: Fischer.

Freud, S. (1901). On the psychopathology of everyday life. In J. Strachey (Ed. and Trans.), *The Standard Edition of the Complete Psychological Works of Sigmund Freud*, Vol. 6. London: Hogarth Press, 1953–74.

Frie, R. (1997). *Subjectivity and Intersubjectivity in Philosophy and Psychoanalysis: A Study of Sartre, Binswanger, Lacan, and Habermas*. Lanham, MD: Rowman and Littlefield.

Frie, R. (1999). Interpreting a misinterpretation: Ludwig Binswanger and Martin Heidegger. *Journal of the British Society for Phenomenology*, 29, 244–258.

Frie, R. (2010). A hermeneutics of exploration: The interpretive turn from Binswanger to Gadamer. *Journal of Theoretical and Philosophical Psychology*, 30, 79–93.

Frie, R. & Hoffmann, K. (2002). Bridging psychiatry, philosophy and politics: Binswanger, Heidegger and Antisemitism. *Journal of the British Society for Phenomenology*, 32, 231–240.

Gadamer, H.-G. (1960/1991). *Truth and Method* (J. Weinsheimer & D. G. Marshall, Trans.). New York: Crossroads (Originally published in 1960).

Govrin, A. (2016). *Conservative and Radical Perspectives on Psychoanalytic Knowledge: The Fascinated and the Disenchanted*. New York: Routledge.

Heidegger, M. (1927/1962). *Being and Time* (J. Macquarrie & E. Robinson, Trans.). Cambridge, MA: Blackwell (Original work published in 1927).

Jones, E. (1967). *Sigmund Freud: Life and Work Vol. 2*. London: Hogarth Press.

Lanzoni, S. (2003). An epistemology of the clinic: Ludwig Binswanger's phenomenology of the other. *Critical Inquiry*, 30, 160–186.

Lipps, T. (1903). *Leitfaden der Psychologie*. Leipzig: W. Engelmann.

Makkreel, R. A. & Rodi, F. (1989). Editors' introduction to volume 1. In R. A. Makkreel & F. Rodi (Eds. and Trans.), *Wilhelm Dilthey: Selected Works*, Vol. 1 (pp. 3–46). Princeton: Princeton University Press.

May, R., Angel, E., & Ellenberger, H. F. (Eds.). (1958). *Existence. A New Dimension in Psychiatry and Psychology*. New York: Basic Books.

Nordmann, A. (2001). The sleepy philosopher: How to read Wittgenstein's diaries. In J. C. Klagge (Ed.), *Wittgenstein: Biography and Philosophy* (pp. 156–175). Cambridge: Cambridge University Press.

Ricoeur, P. (1970). *Freud and Philosophy*. New Haven: Yale University Press.

Sass, L. (2001). Deep disquietudes: Reflections on Wittgenstein as antiphilosopher. In J. C. Klagge (Ed.), *Wittgenstein: Biography and Philosophy* (pp. 98–155). Cambridge: Cambridge University Press.

Stern, D. (1997). *Unformulated Experience: From Dissociation to Imagination in Psychoanalysis*. Hillsdale, NJ: The Analytic Press.

Sulloway, F. (1979). *Freud, Biologist of the Mind*. Cambridge, MA: Harvard University Press.

Wittgenstein, L. (1921/2007). *Tractatus Logico-Philosophicus*. New York: Cosimo.

6
WITTGENSTEIN
Disciple of Freud?

Edward Harcourt

In the mid-1940s, Wittgenstein described himself to Rush Rhees as 'a disciple of Freud' and 'a follower of Freud' (LC: 41). Wittgenstein was 'greatly impressed when he first read Freud' (Malcolm 1958/1984: 39); on first reading *The Interpretation of Dreams*, he thought, 'Here at last is a psychologist who has something to say' (Rhees 1984: 136). To Malcolm he praised Freud's 'extraordinary scientific achievement', and to Drury – several years after Freud's death – he said 'no one today can do psychoanalysis the way [Freud] did' (Rhees 1970: 154). Elsewhere, however, Wittgenstein was less enthusiastic. Freud's 'whole way of thinking wants combatting'; it requires 'a very strong and keen and persistent criticism to see through the mythology' (LC: 50); he offered 'fanciful pseudo-explanations' (CV: 62); 'unless you think *very* clearly psychoanalysis is a dangerous and a foul practice' (Majetschak 2008: 39); Freud's followers had made 'an abominable mess' (Moore 1954–55: 107 [20]). Is it possible cleanly to subtract what Wittgenstein criticized in Freud from what he admired or, as Rhees put it, 'to separate what is valuable in Freud' from what should be rejected? (LC 1966: 41; cf. DB: 16–17).[1]

I'm going to begin by briefly surveying Wittgenstein's connections with Freud. I shall then examine the comparison Wittgenstein – and some of his followers – drew between psychoanalysis and philosophy as Wittgenstein conceived it: to the extent that the comparison is illuminating, this would help explain at least Wittgenstein's admiration for Freud, if not his reservations. I then turn to the account of Wittgenstein's view of Freud that is probably most widely held by defenders of psychoanalysis. On this account, Freud misunderstood the nature of psychoanalysis, saying falsely that the unconscious is a scientific discovery and that psychoanalysis is a scientific enterprise; for what psychoanalysis *really* does is 'interpretation', or giving 'reasons' not 'causes'. Thus Wittgenstein's positive and negative attitudes to psychoanalysis are shared out neatly between Freud's bad philosophy – his theoretical account of what he was doing – and his good 'psychology' or, perhaps more aptly (since Wittgenstein often describes psychology as itself a science), his good first-order insights into the human mind. I'll argue that while this account has something going for it, it neither does full justice to Wittgenstein nor is independently fully credible. In order, therefore, to make full sense of Wittgenstein's complex attitude to Freud, we need to look elsewhere.

DOI: 10.4324/9780429297076-8

I

Although Freud went on producing new work until his death in 1939, the only works by Freud cited by Wittgenstein date from before the First World War: *The Interpretation of Dreams* (Freud 1953–66a/1900), *The Psychopathology of Everyday Life* (2002/1901) and *Jokes and Their Relation to the Unconscious* (1953–66b/1905), and (co-authored with Breuer) *Studies in Hysteria* (1953–66/1895). But Wittgenstein began to discuss psychoanalysis in his writing only around 1930 (Wittgenstein 2000 MS 109: 174). Was it only then that Wittgenstein read these works? We do not know, but the works of Freud he cites are of a much earlier date, and his discussions of them lack detail, so it is possible that Wittgenstein was relying on memories of reading done much longer ago. Be that as it may, Wittgenstein surely knew of psychoanalysis well before 1930. His family's library contained the Breuer and Freud volume, and the Wittgenstein siblings enjoyed swapping jokes with one another, influenced by Freud's 1905 book (Prokop 2003: 104). Wittgenstein's sister Margarete sent her teenage son Thomas for analysis with Freud, because he had a stammer (Prokop 2003: 202, 222), presumably between 1916 and the early 1920s given that the boy was born in 1906; Wittgenstein begins a discussion on the criteria for the truth of psychoanalytic interpretations in 1938 with the words 'suppose you were analyzed when you had a stammer' (LC: 25).

Whatever the truth as to when Wittgenstein first read Freud, indirect personal connections would have made psychoanalysis salient to his mind from the mid-1920s. A junior member of the Vienna Circle, Heinrich Neider, is on record as saying that 'numerous members of the Vienna Circle were in analysis' (Bouveresse 1995: 7), and this was certainly true of Schlick (Money-Kyrle 1979: 266); Wittgenstein's meetings with the Circle started in 1928. Frank Ramsey travelled to Austria in 1923, visiting Wittgenstein in Puchberg to question him about the *Tractatus* (Misak 2020: 140), and again in 1924, also to have analysis with Theodor Reik, an early follower of Freud (Forrester 2004: 11; Misak 2020 162); Ramsey then argued with Wittgenstein about Freud in England in 1925 (Forrester 2004: 17; Paul 2012). Psychoanalysis was in any case fashionable in the Cambridge circles to which Ramsey belonged (Misak 2020: 100), and with which Wittgenstein would come into contact when he returned to Cambridge in 1929. Wittgenstein's sister Margarete, who became interested in psychoanalysis apparently before Wittgenstein and remained in contact with him throughout his life, constitutes a third line of connection. Already in 1918, she complained – as Wittgenstein himself did later – about Freud's insistence on the sexual meaning of dreams ('pity he's so [. . .] one-track', Prokop 2003: 100).[2] She found *Civilization and Its Discontents* 'dreadfully bad' when it was published in 1930: as long as Freud confined himself to 'the bodily and the psychical', he got it 'about 90% right', but 'when he gets philosophical and deals with guilt, happiness and such, he comes out with unfortunate rubbish' (Prokop 2003: 202). Still, she entered analysis with Freud in 1937, and in 1938 helped to get permission for him to leave Austria for England, receiving an inscribed copy of *The Future of an Illusion* from Freud the day he left (Nedo & Ranchetti 1983: 301) and a letter from him from England (Subotincic 2000: 60). She also composed, apparently in the early 1940s, a 'psychoanalytical investigation' of the success of the Nazis (Prokop 2003: 245 n. 415), though it was never published.

II

At a certain stage of his philosophical development, Wittgenstein took very seriously the comparison between psychoanalysis and his own (or at least what he thought of as his own) method in philosophy. But how close is the comparison really, and why was Wittgenstein so interested in it?

Wittgenstein began explicitly comparing Freud's method and his own around 1930, when he started writing what became the Big Typescript, and this goes on till the writing down of TS 220, in 1937 or 1938 (Baker 2004a, 2004b; Majetschak 2008). The most developed versions of the comparison are in the Big Typescript itself (PO: 158–99) and in 'Dictation for Schlick' and 'Our Method', dictated to Waismann (Baker 2003: 1–83; 277–311). The comparison takes off from an idea which to my knowledge has no echo in Freud, that philosophical problems stem from false 'analogies' or 'pictures' suggested by language. Philosophical puzzlement is then said to be a cause of mental unease (Moore 1954–5: 114 [27]) – also presumably the state of anyone who goes in for psychoanalysis. Philosophy, like psychoanalysis, is said to cure this unease by bringing what is unconscious to consciousness ('[A] simile at work in the unconscious is made harmless by being articulated' [Baker 2003: 69; cf. Wittgenstein 2000, MS 109: 174; PO: 162–5 (409); PG: 381–2]); and, less frequently, to have to deal with resistances to giving up such analogies ('What has to be overcome is not a difficulty of the intellect but of the will', PO: 160–1 [407]). The success of this philosophical cure depends – as Wittgenstein sometimes said, the success of psychoanalytic interpretation (LC: 25, 44, 52) and therefore of psychoanalytic treatment – on the 'analysand's' assent to a 'diagnosis' (LC: 164–5 [410]; Baker 2004a: 159). Giving assent removes the destructive power of the analogy and brings about 'a new way of seeing things' (Baker 2004a: 158).

Freud would readily have acknowledged that psychoanalysis proceeds by making the unconscious conscious, and that the difficulties in doing so are due to resistances on the analysand's part (Majetschak 2008: 52). Other aspects of the comparison, by contrast, depend on Wittgenstein's own counter-Freudian understanding of what Freud was *really* doing, of which more later. But even if we grant all that, the comparison falters. As Baker has argued, while psychoanalysis addresses conflicts of 'conative or affective states', philosophy seems to address only conflicts 'in ways of seeing things', in people's 'prejudices or dogmas [which] clash with each other and creat[e] fogs of confusion', or between different things which – thanks to these dogmas – we feel driven to say; in psychoanalysis we are concerned with 'patterns of behaviour (e.g. manifestations of an Oedipus complex)', whereas in philosophy – seemingly – our concern is 'with patterns in the uses of our words' (Baker 2004a: 153, 159).

Alice Ambrose (who helped to transcribe the *Blue Book*), Morris Lazerowitz and their followers (Lazerowitz 1985; Ambrose 1966, 1972; Lazerowitz & Ambrose 1984; Kennick 1970) accept the limitations of the comparison as stated, but attempt to repair its limitations by adding in a third layer of the 'three-layer structure of a philosophical theory' (Ambrose 1972: 25) on Wittgenstein's behalf, suggesting moreover that Wittgenstein only failed to do so himself because he couldn't bear to (1972: 25). On their view (non-Wittgensteinian), philosophers mistakenly believe that their words are 'being used to express a theory' when they simply 'herald a redefinition' (Lazerowitz 1985: 209). This is close to Wittgenstein's *Blue Book* view of philosophical disagreements over solipsism or over the existence of an unconscious mind. *Part* of the Wittgensteinian philosopher's task is therefore to 'expose the verbal content behind the ontological façade' (Lazerowitz 1985: 209). But, Lazerowitz continues, it's *difficult* for philosophers to accept that their theories are 'mere linguistic contrivance[s]' (Lazerowitz 1985: 211), because these theories are held in place by 'unconscious ideas', which it is psychologically costly for the philosopher to give up (1985: 236–7). Thus in Lazerowitz's view philosophers cannot acknowledge that 'one cannot think of what does not exist' is a mere 'redefinition', because treating the claim as substantive serves to fend off anxiety. Why? Because the *unconscious* meaning of those words is that 'there is something [sc., the penis] . . . not possessed by some and whose loss is feared by others' and 'whose non-existence is too painful to be thought of' (i.e., is such that one 'cannot think' of it; 1985: 238). But Ambrose and Lazerowitz's 'completion' of Wittgenstein's method is a dead end. For one thing, solipsists and others usually offer arguments for their views and an explanation in terms of unconscious defences is only attractive to the extent that the argument is weak: if the argument is strong, a good explanation of why the solipsist thinks as he does is already available. But Ambrose and Lazerowitz's diagnoses apply to philosophical positions *per se*, independently of the arguments anyone offers for them.

Secondly, philosophical problems are usually addressed in a way that bypasses the 'sufferer's' personal life: we don't ask fellow philosophers about their dreams, their childhood (etc.) to help them out of a philosophical tangle, because it's not clear why doing so would make a difference; but this sort of question is essential in psychoanalysis. This is not to say that philosophical problem-solving isn't tailored to the philosopher concerned (Baker 2004a: 210): different people may need different approaches to help them get philosophically unstuck. But still, none of these different bits of tailoring need involve the examination of a philosopher's personal life. Of course, even if this investigation of the personal is usually missing from philosophy, perhaps it shouldn't be. But in fact it's precisely this kind of personalization that is *missing* from Ambrose and Lazerowitz's version of therapeutic philosophy: philosophical solipsism (for example) is at once a 'symptom', but – quite unlike a 'symptom' for the psychoanalyst – a symptom whose meaning we can determine without knowing anything much about the person whose symptom it is (Brearley 1984: 183).

Eugen Fischer's view (2004, 2012), while contrasting sharply with that of Ambrose et al., also takes the analogy between philosophy and psychological therapy very seriously. Like Baker, Fischer is clear that the conflicts philosophy deals with *aren't* emotional ones – Wittgensteinian 'drives to misunderstand' (Fischer 2004: 107) are 'diseases of the intellect' (CV 50); philosophical disquietude is sufficiently explained by the thought that mere platitudes get 'distorted' 'through inadvertent misinterpretation or mindless inference, in line with ideas [one] unreflectively rejects' (Fischer 2004: 112). So though Wittgenstein's philosophy is indeed therapeutic, the therapy to compare it with is not psychoanalysis but cognitive behavioural therapy (CBT), which proceeds by 'identifying and . . . breaking the relevant cognitive habits' (2004: 91).

Supposing for a moment that philosophical tangles are cognitive and not emotional, is there any point to the comparison between philosophy as Wittgenstein saw it and psychoanalysis? One could still say that a philosophical theory can be *like* 'a kind of neurotic symptom' (Lazerowitz 1985: 236–237; for a more nuanced version of the comparison, see Wisdom 1964: 181; Farrell 1946a, 1946b) without actually being one. But it would be a distant likeness: as Baker has argued, the comparison with psychoanalysis breaks down at just the point at which it might begin to be theoretically useful. Why then, would Wittgenstein insist on the comparison? The best we can say is that Wittgenstein made as much of the comparison as he did only because at the time he was writing, CBT – worlds away from psychoanalysis, on the spectrum of 'talking cures' – had not yet been invented. But since Wittgenstein could hardly have known that with the advent of CBT and other talking therapies psychoanalysis would one day be but a species of a larger genus, that explanation is unsatisfactory.

But are philosophical problems, for Wittgenstein, merely cognitive? To say so fails to do justice to Wittgenstein's assertion that philosophical problems are 'deep disquietudes' (PI: 111), still less – though such remarks are rare in Wittgenstein – to the idea that to solve philosophical problems we need to overcome resistances of the will (PO: 160–1 [407]). Wittgenstein's struggle with philosophical problems seemed to be all-consuming; the high colour of the language in which he speaks of them and their solution betrays the presence of powerful emotions (Lazerowitz & Ambrose 1984: 13). So it is not credible that he should have thought of them simply as intellectual problems, however troubling they too can be. Wittgenstein, in my view, saw philosophical puzzlement not as a neurotic symptom but as the token of his fallen state (cf. Kenny 1984; Forrester 2004: 17). So ridding himself of it was, for him, a way of transforming himself from the bad person he thought he was (FB: 61) into somebody 'decent', and it's this that explains the more than intellectual significance which philosophical puzzlement, and finding a way out of it, had for him.[3]

Does this view rehabilitate the comparison between philosophy and psychoanalysis? Partly, because psychoanalysis engages emotional and personal problems and so, on this view, does philosophy, so the view brings the two closer together than they are on either Baker's or Fischer's view but without the mistakes of Ambrose and Lazerowitz. But only partly. First, it would be controversial to claim that psychoanalysis aims at the moral improvement of the analysand (Hartmann 1960). Secondly, the rehabilitation depends on an understanding of the significance of philosophical puzzlement which, I've said, was Wittgenstein's but is certainly not mandatory: one could be as philosophically puzzled as Wittgenstein, and by the same questions, and yet *not* see that as a token of one's fallen state. We would thus have a partial explanation of Wittgenstein's claim that he was a 'disciple of Freud', but because it depends at a crucial point on something personal to Wittgenstein, the appeal of psychoanalysis cannot be expected to carry over to everyone who finds themselves philosophically puzzled.

III

I turn now to what one might call the 'bad philosopher, gifted *Menschenkenner*' account of Wittgenstein's view of Freud. This account has been developed very fully, though in each case differently, since Wittgenstein's time by philosophers such as Alisdair MacIntyre (2004) and Ilham Dilman (1983, 1984, 1988; cf. Allen 1997). The main sources of the account lie in Wittgenstein's objections to Freud, and these revolve mainly around the unconscious, and the partially overlapping topics of the interpretation of dreams and jokes, and of the nature of explanation in psychoanalysis. I address these in turn.

Wittgenstein's most extensive remarks about the unconscious occur in the *Blue Book* (BB: 23, 57; cf. AWL: 39ff.) Psychoanalytic talk of 'unconscious thoughts, acts of volition, etc.' is philosophically neutral, he says, since all that has happened is that a 'new notation' – that is, a new use of the words 'thought' and so on – has been introduced. Indeed this usage *couldn't* involve a mistake, since notations on their own do not *say* anything, and can 'at any time be retranslated into ordinary language' (BB 23). Thus, Wittgenstein argues, we could introduce the expression 'unconscious toothache'. But the phenomenon dressed up as unconscious toothache by the new notation – a toothache in a particular tooth that comes and goes, perhaps – is highly familiar (cf. PG: 48, 106, 181; PI: 149).

So why is psychoanalytic talk of the unconscious worthy of philosophical attention? The answer, at least in the *Blue Book*, is that the notation 'call[s] up new pictures and analogies' (BB: 23), so it is easy to think – falsely – that its use reports a new discovery. If we are unaware of what's going on, we will 'be misled into thinking that a stupendous discovery has been made', like 'the psychoanalysts [who] . . . were misled by their own way of expression into thinking that . . . they had, in a sense, discovered conscious thoughts which were unconscious' (BB: 57). Or, alternatively, we shall be 'tempted to deny the possibility' of unconscious thoughts (BB: 57; like those 'revolted' by 'the idea of there being' such things, *ibid.*). Either way, the objection is not to Freud's first-order claims but rather to his philosophical packaging of them: it's 'the hypothetical part of his theory, the [un]conscious, . . . which is not satisfactory' (AWL: 39; Cioffi 1998: 206) – a compressed phrase which surely means not that the hypothesis that there is an unconscious is false, but rather that the status of talk of the unconscious is not that of a hypothesis. The thought that it *is* a hypothesis either leads Freud to overstate (or misstate) his own claims or expose him to undeserved criticism.

Wittgenstein presses a related, but richer, set of philosophical objections to Freud in the context of his discussions of Freud on dreams and, to a lesser extent, jokes. According to Wittgenstein, Freud gets it wrong about the link between the criteria for the truth of psychoanalytic interpretations and the status of psychoanalysis as a kind of science. This objection, which extends beyond dreams and jokes to distinctively psychoanalytic claims to knowledge more generally, is summarized by Moore in his notes on Wittgenstein's 1932 lectures:

> [Psychoanalysis] does not enable you to discover the *cause* but only the *reason* of, e.g., laughter. . . . [P]sychoanalysis is successful only if the patient agrees to the explanation offered by the analyst, and . . . since this is so, what is being agreed to isn't a hypothesis.
>
> *(Moore 1954–55: 108 [21])*

Freud, in other words, claims that the criterion for the correctness of a psychoanalytic interpretation of a dream or joke is the analysand's assent (cf. Wittgenstein 1979: 39–40). But assent, Wittgenstein argues, could not be the criterion for the truth of a causal hypothesis. So it cannot in Wittgenstein's view also be the case – as Freud claims – that the interpretation is a hypothesis about the dream's (or the laughter's) unconscious causes.

Now there are many phenomena, dreams apparently included, where in Wittgenstein's view explanation does depend on assent, for example having something on the tip of one's tongue (the speaker's saying '"that's it!" . . . certifies the word as having been found' [CV: 68; cf. LC: 18]), or overruling another's claims about their feelings (2000: MS 110: 230). A third such type of explanation is what Wittgenstein calls 'aesthetic explanations', explanations which are not 'causal' but do 'what aesthetics does: puts two factors together'; and Wittgenstein sees some psychoanalytic explanations as of this kind (e.g., of jokes; AWL 39), and Freud's connection between the foetal position and sleep (AWL 39; cf. LW II: 86). Indeed it is even in order, in explanations where the analysand's assent is the criterion for correctness, to say that the explanation gives the analysand's unconscious state of mind (e.g., the unconscious reason for the joke), as long as we do not make the mistake of thinking that in so saying, we are saying something 'as to what was happening at the moment when he laughed' (Moore 1954–55: 108 [21]). Thus, so far at least, Wittgenstein's objection to Freud is very modest. Freud's explanations themselves are in order, as is his use of the word 'unconscious'. The problem lies only in his self-understanding. This self-understanding would fit a 'psychologist' (i.e., a kind of scientist) since 'in psychology' we are 'interested in causal connections' (AWL: 38). But Freud himself – had he only been able to see it – wasn't one.

This account of Wittgenstein's stance vis-à-vis Freud is of a piece with some of Wittgenstein's views on other matters (e.g., mathematics): in clearing away the self-misunderstandings of psychoanalysis, philosophy would be 'leaving [psychoanalysis] as it is' (PI 124). But the account is risky for someone trying to mount a philosophical defence of psychoanalysis. Some readers of this chapter will have made claims to the effect that some individual unconsciously felt such-and-such or acted out of an unconscious desire, only to be asked, 'but where is your evidence for the existence of an unconscious mind?' These challenges are an irritant, and if Wittgenstein's idea that psychoanalytic talk of the unconscious merely introduces a notational change puts them to an end, Wittgenstein will have done us a service. Nonetheless, if *all* psychoanalysis does is introduce a notational change – and a potentially misleading one at that – while the first-order 'insights' left over are only facts, such as that toothaches can come and go, that we knew all about anyway, it is not clear what's so great about it – or, therefore, why Wittgenstein would have described himself as a 'disciple of Freud'.

IV

There is more, however, to Wittgenstein's stance than this, for several reasons. First, Freud's scientistic self-misunderstanding has consequences: he doesn't stick to the limits of interpretation which the assent criterion imposes but corrects the patient if their explanation doesn't accord with his 'hypothesis'. This is a mistake he, as it were, would not have dared to make had he realized what he was doing. So the project of – as Dilman puts it – removing the 'philosophical froth' (Dilman 1983: 3) from the first-order substance of Freud's work has a real point to it, since it shows that without the 'froth', psychoanalytic practice would not be 'left as it is' but, on the contrary, improved. That point goes some way towards rescuing the account which locates all of Freud's mistakes (as Wittgenstein saw them) in his philosophy rather than in his first-order views. But the account is limited nonetheless, because Wittgenstein's negative commentary on psychoanalysis does not relate only to Freud's philosophical account of his first-order views but to those views themselves.

On dreams, Wittgenstein agreed with Freud – though of course also with a great many others (Freud 1953–66a/1900: 1–5) – that dreams seem to have something puzzling and in a special way interesting about them, so that we want an interpretation of them (LC 45; cf. CV 75, 79; LW II §§195–6).

But he thought Freud was wrong – and this is a first-order and not a philosophical objection – to claim that all dreams are wish-fulfilments (LC 42; CV 50; Rhees 1970: 154). Nor is it that all dreams – the 'bawdy' Wittgenstein hated (LC 24) – that they all have sexual meaning (LC 23–4, 47–8).[4] He also said that 'in Freudian analysis the dream is as it were dismantled. It loses its original sense *completely*', because it substitutes an interpretation for 'the dream story [which] . . . has its own charm, like a painting that attracts & inspires us' (CV 78–9).

Moreover, the (first-order) dream-explanations Freud offers are, in Wittgenstein's view, unreliable in a way that saying what was on the tip of one's tongue is not: *a propos* Freud's explanation of a patient's 'beautiful dream', Wittgenstein says 'this ugly explanation makes you say you really had these thoughts, whereas in any ordinary sense you really didn't' (LC 20). People are 'charmed' by the kind of interpretation Freud is prepared to recognize as correct, so they assent to it, but this complicating 'charm' is no part of the operation of the assent criterion *per se*. Whereas in saying what's on the tip of one's tongue one is free to answer without undue influence from elsewhere, in Freud assent is contaminated by the 'charm' of his various 'mythologies' which attract us overwhelmingly to certain kinds of explanation. As to what this 'charm' is, Wittgenstein makes various suggestions: the charm of the ugly (LC 23), the charm of 'origins' (LC 43) or the 'secret cellar' (LC 25), the 'new mythology'. Wittgenstein is at least as hostile to the particular mythology that Freud is (in Wittgenstein's view) merely campaigning for as he is to the fact that Freud misunderstands his activity as a kind of science.

V

I want to raise two more questions for the account of Wittgenstein on Freud that locates all the shortcomings in Freud's philosophy. The first is this: if psychoanalytic explanations are not 'hypotheses', does the account have a satisfactory view to offer of what they are instead? The second parallels the question I have already raised about the comparison between psychoanalysis and Wittgenstein's view of the correct method in philosophy: does what's left over when we subtract both the (allegedly) mistaken philosophy and what Wittgenstein found objectionable in Freud's first-order views help to explain why he said – even if this was not all he said – that he was a 'disciple of Freud'?

On the first question, Wittgenstein's assimilation of Freudian dream- or joke-interpretations to 'aesthetic investigations' needs to be handled with care. In such investigations, various things are 'laid alongside' the initial object of investigation. Whether that achieves anything depends on somebody's assent – but whose assent? Wittgenstein's idea is that if dream-interpretations were not contaminated by Freudian suggestion, it's the *analysand's* assent that would properly be decisive. But although you can 'make a person see what Brahms was driving at by showing him lots of different pieces by Brahms' (Moore 1954–55: 106 [19]), it is one's interlocutor's assent, not Brahms's, that's relevant to the success of this exercise in 'plac[ing] things side by side' (AWL 40). Moreover, if you fail to make your interlocutor 'see what you see', this is not proof that you didn't, after all, see anything, but simply 'an end of the discussion' (Moore 1954–55: 106 [19]; cf. LC 20–1). So if dream-interpretation were exactly like 'aesthetic investigation', Freud would be justified in ignoring the analysand's dissent in favour of his own interpretation even without the (in Wittgenstein's view false) assumption that psychoanalytic interpretations are 'hypotheses': we can't expect every two people to 'see' the same thing. This wouldn't matter if Wittgenstein's objection to Freud is just that Freud chooses objects of comparison which Wittgenstein finds distasteful. But if the objection is – as it seems to be – also methodological, comparing psychoanalytic interpretation with 'aesthetic investigation' (which puzzled Moore; Moore 1954–55: 105 [18]) does not help Wittgenstein to make good his case.

But is the analysand's assent really the criterion of correctness for explanations that refer to unconscious thoughts and feelings? The idea is supposedly central to Wittgenstein's rejection of the claim that psychoanalytic explanations are causal hypotheses, but is it true? Did even Wittgenstein think it was?

Consider Wittgenstein's discussion of unconscious motivation in the 'Lectures on Aesthetics':

> Suppose Taylor and I are walking along the river and Taylor stretches out his hand and pushes me in the river. When I ask why he did this he says: 'I was pointing out something to you', whereas the psycho-analyst says that Taylor subconsciously hated me. . . . When would we say that Taylor's explanation was correct? When he had never shown any unfriendly feelings, when a church-steeple and I were in his field of vision, and Taylor was known to be truthful. But, under the same circumstances, the psycho-analyst's explanation may also be correct. . . . The explanations could in a sense be contradictory and yet both be correct.
>
> *(LC 22–3)*

This is striking: the unconscious explanation 'may . . . be correct', and yet there is no mention of Taylor's assent. What's relevant to its correctness is a further fact, that 'the person pushed in had a similarity with the father of the other person' (LC 22–3; cf. RPP I §225). The explanatory model Wittgenstein has in mind here seems closer to 'aesthetic investigation' than to the analysand's-assent-as-criterion model: even if, absent one's interlocutor's assent, reason-giving is surely not simply at an end (because, for instance, further reasons might lie in general observations about the emotions to which human beings are subject), certainly the reasons in the Taylor case 'are in the nature of further descriptions' (Moore 1954–55: 106 [19]). So, how to reconcile Wittgenstein's treatment of 'unconscious motive' in the Taylor case with his treatment of dream-interpretations? Perhaps further facts about the analysand are relevant in the former case but not in the latter. But though this *might* be true of claims about what is on the tip of one's tongue, it is surely not so for dreams: a psychoanalyst (or indeed anyone else) may be familiar with details of the dreamer's preoccupations, and with more general facts about what people in the dreamer's predicament think or feel, which suggest interpretations of the dream which the dreamer may well not acknowledge.

Even by Wittgenstein's lights, then, assent is not the sole criterion for the correctness of a psychoanalytic explanation. It thus seems indeterminate, so far, whether psychoanalytic explanations are hypotheses or not. Is the explanation-as-hypothesis view excluded by the idea that interpretation is a matter of 'further description' (as it sometimes clearly is)? If 'further description' is just another species of 'aesthetic explanation' where failure to get the other to 'see what you see' is just 'an end' of the discussion (Moore 1954–55: 106 [19]), then yes. But if exchanges of reasons in the psychological case are not to be thought of in this 'no fact' way, why couldn't psychological explanations proceed by 'further description' precisely because adding further descriptions is a way, if not of establishing a particular causal hypothesis, at least of ruling out inadmissible ones?

Moreover, consider what Anscombe calls the phenomenon of 'mental causation' (Anscombe 1957; cf. Wittgenstein REF), that is, claims such as 'the spider made me jump', which can easily be reformulated in terms of the authority of assent. ('Was it the spider that made you jump?' 'Yes.') Such claims seemingly state a (mental) cause, but the reporter is authoritative about it. So even to the extent that assent *is* a criterion of correctness for psychoanalytic explanations (such as dream interpretations), it would seem that it does not rule out the causal character of the explanation. We might insist on a distinction between a causal *claim* (which is confined to a particular case) and a causal *hypothesis* (which perhaps relates an observed effect to a presumptive cause because like pairs of phenomena have been observed to be so related in the past). That's part of Anscombe's point in drawing attention to the phenomenon: we can know some causes without having to draw upon previously established correlations. But if the assent criterion helps to rule out a hypothetical model of explanation, it looks as if it doesn't on its own rule in an altogether non-causal one, or therefore the idea that psychoanalytic explanations 'give reasons' where this is meant to exclude anything causal.

But even if it did, if the Wittgensteinian reconstruction of psychoanalysis includes the thought that psychoanalysis consists *simply* of 'interpretation' or 'giving reasons', it doesn't stand up. Psychoanalytic discourse is highly various, and alongside its interpretations of dreams, utterances and so forth and philosophical (or 'metapsychological') components, it also includes a number of claims, both general and particular, about human beings and their behaviour. While statements in the first two categories are not, let us grant, hypothetical, statements in the third category clearly are. Many statements in this category made by Freud are false (e.g., that 'the mental apparatus endeavours to keep the quantity of excitation present in it as low as possible'; Freud 1953–66c: 9), but his successors have made considerable efforts to repair a problem (Lacewing 2018) which 'hermeneuticism' (Cioffi 1998: *passim*) pretends to magic away. No one-dimensional theory about psychoanalytic discourse, whether hermeneuticism or scientism, can be right (Farrell 1981).

The 'bad philosopher, good *Menschenkenner*' account therefore doesn't make a very convincing case either that particular psychoanalytic interpretations (e.g., dream interpretations) state 'reasons not causes' or for hermeneuticism generally, or indeed provide a convincing reconstruction of the complexity of Wittgenstein's own thinking on the subject.

VI

Now to the second of my two questions for the 'bad philosopher, good *Menschenkenner*' account. Wittgenstein can of course be positive about Freud's first-order views. According to the *Blue Book*, the psychoanalysts *did* discover something, though it wasn't the existence of the unconscious: 'new psychological reactions' (BB 57; Moore 1954–55: 102 [15]) and 'phenomena and connexions not previously known' (BB 57; Moore 1954–55: 102 [15]). Unlike the 'toothache' case, that is, there's something both non-trivial and (unlike the 'secret cellar' mythology) worthwhile, that's left over when one abstracts from the theoretically misleading way in which psychoanalysis presents it. Moreover, Wittgenstein does not seem always to have regarded the language of unconscious states of mind as a terminological innovation (and so *a fortiori* not as an innovation liable to be misunderstood as a discovery). In a typescript from 1946–7, he says that 'we' – not just 'the psychoanalysts' – would ('perhaps') say that a man who 'suddenly climbs on a chair and then gets down again' without being able to say why, though 'he reports having noticed this and that from the chair, and that it seems as if he climbed up in order to observe this', had 'acted with *unconscious* intention' (RPP I §225; cf. LC 22–3; PI II.xi: 217). And in a 1931 manuscript, Wittgenstein speaks, without a trace of scare quotes, about 'unconscious contempt' (Wittgenstein 2000, MS 155: 30V–31R).

All the same, unconscious explanations of behaviour by way of thoughts, emotions, intentions and the like are a commonplace, at least in imaginative literature way before Freud (and continue to be so now; Whyte 1978; Gödde 2010), and surely Wittgenstein could not have failed to be aware of this. Indeed, this type of explanation is exemplified by Wittgenstein's case of the man who 'suddenly climbs on a chair'. So while this case goes well beyond a set of trivialities on a par with toothaches that come and go, such cases surely cannot be the 'new psychological reactions' (etc.) which Freud is said to have discovered. But until we can identify those, we are left without an account of why Wittgenstein thought Freud was a gifted observer of his fellow human beings, rather than merely not an egregiously bad one.

In search of what Wittgenstein thought was both exciting and really new in Freud, I shall appeal to two types of consideration.

The first is that psychoanalysis deploys a variety of forms of explanation beyond the simple appeal to an unconscious intention, of which I shall mention three.

In the first kind of case, we form an intention to utter a sentence, weak-willedly fail to act on it (e.g., out of fear), but the sentence 'escapes us' nonetheless (Freud 2002: 87–88). Here, the intention needn't be unconscious: it's rather that intentions the agent had – indeed intentions he is fully able to avow – explain the action so well that we say the 'mistake' was an intentional action.

Two further explanatory roles for the unconscious are exemplified by Freud's case of a girl's obsessively arranging her bedding before she went to bed (Freud 1953–66b: 264–269). The arranging of the bedding itself is (consciously) intentional. But these intentions (e.g., to prevent the pillow from touching the headboard) do not fully explain the action, since – unlike, for example, kicking a stone or uncrossing one's legs – actions of this kind do not make sense without further reasons, and yet the girl was unable to articulate any such further reasons. Freud of course points us to unconscious further reasons: the girl's obsessive routine stopped her parents from going to bed, thereby stopping them from having sexual intercourse and thus from producing a sibling rival for her, an outcome she (unconsciously) very much did not want. But, as MacIntyre has stressed, this is not – like Wittgenstein's 'chair' case – a matter of the girl's acting for reasons albeit unconsciously, but of her 'acting *as if* unconsciously guided by reasons'. For here, 'the motives that control [her] behaviour' 'preclude [her] from acting as a practical reasoner does', since they preclude her from asking whether her reasons for action are *good* reasons (MacIntyre 2004: 25–26). But clearly, the girl could have stopped her parents from going to bed in many different ways, so we still lack an explanation for the details of the routine, about which the girl was inflexible. To take one such detail, the girl would fluff the eiderdown in such a way that it made a hump, then flatten it again. Freud argues that the girl was thereby intentionally abolishing of her mother's (imagined) pregnancy (1953–66b: 268). But it would not make all the difference needed even if the intention was conscious: compare the case where a parent cuts their leg and their child strokes it to 'make it better', which can be intentional on the part of the child even though it knows the stroking will have no healing effect. To see how abolishing the pregnancy is what the girl is intentionally doing, we need to see the relation between the action and the intention as mediated by the *symbolic* connection – which the girl also cannot articulate – between the hump in the eiderdown and pregnancy (Gardner 1993: 116).

These explanations all differ substantially from the explanatory pattern exemplified by Wittgenstein's 'chair' case, and whose availability we did not need psychoanalysis to grasp. Wittgenstein does not indeed observe these types of explanation himself, but were he to be aware of them, it would supply grounds for his claim that Freud had 'discovered new psychological reactions'.

The second type of consideration is, as with Wittgenstein's interest in the methodological comparison between philosophy and psychoanalysis, partly personal in character. There are passages in Wittgenstein's philosophical writings where psychoanalysis is simply assumed rather than discussed: the painter 'guided by forces in his unconscious' who produces a likeness of M when intending to draw N from memory (RPP I, §262), or the groundless and mistaken conviction that a city lies to the right rather than to the left, which one might try to explain 'as it were psychoanalytically' (PI II xi, p. 215). Wittgenstein also made extensive reference to Freudian 'phenomena and connexions' in his own non-philosophical writing (i.e., where the philosophical evaluation of Freud was not in question). In a 1930 diary entry, for example, commenting on his love of cinema, Wittgenstein compares films to dreams and says, without any attempt at justification, 'Freudian thoughts/methods can be applied to them directly' (DB 28–31). Wittgenstein's diaries frequently record dreams, some of them with interpretations (DB *passim*; FB: 181). He and his sister Margarete wrote to one another describing their dreams and offering interpretations of a psychoanalytical kind: that is, though the interpretations are not narrowly Freudian in suggesting a fantasized wish-fulfilment or sexual meaning, they show that Wittgenstein accepted that his dreams would express matters of personal importance that were on his mind at the time (e.g., racial identity, or his then intended wife Marguerite Respinger). Indeed, notwithstanding his philosophical strictures against psychoanalysis elsewhere, he seems absorbed by this activity of interpretation and more or less uncritical of its basis: getting the dream right is important, but the method pursued in so doing isn't scrutinized. In a 1948 letter to one of his sisters, and not in the context of any philosophical discussion of psychoanalysis, he offers a psychoanalytical interpretation of the fact that he couldn't get a Mendelssohn passage out of his mind (FB: 194; cf. RPP I §262; PI II.xi: 215):

> Es ist natürlich *sehr* schön, aber gewiss eine Musik die mir nicht sehr nahe geht; und sie entspricht nicht meiner Stimmung. Es muss also ausser-musikalische Gründe haben, dass sie mir so standig einfällt. Freud würde vielleicht sagen, und vielleicht mit recht, dass ich mir damit immer sagen will 'Ich bin ein Esel'; weil mir besonders oft der Teil durch den Kopf geht, in welchem der Esel schreit.
>
> *(FB 194)*[5]

Passages such as these show how far Wittgenstein internalized psychoanalytical ways of thinking, quite independently of his philosophical appraisal of Freud: applying psychoanalytical ideas to his own dreams or thoughts had become as it were second nature to him. I suggest that the evidence for his having found in Freud 'phenomena and connexions not previously known' rests as much on his non-philosophical deployment of psychoanalytic ideas as in the cogency of any philosophical reconstruction of Freud he offers. In his non-philosophical thinking, then, Wittgenstein was perhaps indeed a 'disciple of Freud'.

Notes

1 This paper is indebted to Harcourt (2017).
2 All translations from Prokop (2003) are mine, but thanks to my colleague Dieter Jaksch for help with the slang.
3 I develop this suggestion further in Harcourt (2012).
4 Cf. Wittgenstein's admiration for 'I will show you differences' from *King Lear* (Monk 1990: 537).
5 'Of course, It's *very* beautiful, but definitely a kind of music that doesn't touch me very closely; and it doesn't fit my mood. So, the fact that it comes so often into my head must have an extra-musical explanation. Freud would perhaps say – and perhaps rightly – that I'm trying to tell myself "I'm an ass", because the bit that comes into my head especially often is the one where the donkey brays.' (My translation.)

References

Works by Wittgenstein (Including Lecture Transcripts etc.), With Abbreviations

AWL Wittgenstein, Ludwig (1979). *Wittgenstein's Lectures, Cambridge 1932–35, From the Notes of A. Ambrose and M. MacDonald.* Ed. A. Ambrose. Oxford: Blackwell (MS 110: 230).

BB Wittgenstein, Ludwig (1958/1969). *The Blue and Brown Books [1933–1935].* Ed. R. Rhees. Second edition. Oxford: Blackwell.

CV Wittgenstein, Ludwig (1977/1998). *Culture and Value: A Selection from the Posthumous Remains.* Ed. G. H. von Wright in collaboration with H. Nyman. Revised edition of the text by A. Pichler. Trans. P. Winch. Oxford: Blackwell.

DB Wittgenstein, Ludwig (1999). *Denkbewegungen: Tagebücher 1930–1932, 1936–1937. [Movements of Thought: Notebooks 1930–1932, 1936–1937*]. Ed. I. Somavilla. Frankfurt: Fischer.

FB Wittgenstein, Ludwig (1996). *Familienbriefe. [Ludwig Wittgenstein: Family Letters].* Ed. B. McGuinness, M. C. Ascher, and O. Pfersmann. Vienna: Hölder-Pichler-Tempsky.

LC Wittgenstein, Ludwig (1966). *Lectures and Conversations on Aesthetics, Psychology and Religious Belief. [1938–1946].* Ed. C. Barrett. Oxford: Blackwell.

LW II Wittgenstein, Ludwig (1992). *Last Writings on the Philosophy of Psychology (Vol. 2). [1949–1951].* Ed. G. H. von Wright and H. Nyman. Trans. C. G. Luckhardt and M.A.E. Aue. Oxford: Blackwell.

PG Wittgenstein, Ludwig (1974). *Philosophical Grammar. [1932–1934].* Ed. R. Rhees. Trans. A.J.P. Kenny. Oxford: Blackwell.

PI Wittgenstein, Ludwig (1953/1958). *Philosophical Investigations. [1938–1945].* Ed. G.E.M. Anscombe and R. Rhees. Trans. G.E.M. Anscombe. Second edition. Oxford: Blackwell. References are to numbered sections of Part I (except for footnotes), and to pages of Part II.

PO Wittgenstein, Ludwig (1993). *Philosophical Occasions: 1912–1951.* Ed. J. Klagge and A. Nordmann. Indianapolis: Hackett. Unless otherwise specified, writings in this anthology are cited after the original paginations, which are given in brackets.

RPP I Wittgenstein, Ludwig (1980). *Remarks on the Philosophy of Psychology (Vol. 1). [1945–1947].* Ed. G.E.M. Anscombe and G. H. von Wright. Trans. G.E.M. Anscombe. Oxford: Blackwell. References Are to Numbered Sections.

Wittgenstein, Ludwig (2000). *Wittgenstein's Nachlass: The Bergen Electronic Edition.* Ed. the Wittgenstein Archives at the University of Bergen. Oxford: Oxford University Press.

Other Works

Allen, Richard (1997). Psychoanalysis after Wittgenstein. *Psychoanalysis and Contemporary Thought* 20:3, pp. 299–322.

Ambrose, Alice (1966). *Essays in Analysis*. London: George Allen and Unwin.

Ambrose, Alice (1972). Ludwig Wittgenstein: A Portrait. In A. Ambrose & M. Lazerowitz (eds.), *Ludwig Wittgenstein: Philosophy and Language*, pp. 13–25. London: George Allen & Unwin.

Anscombe, G.E.M. (1957). *Intention*. Oxford: Blackwell.

Baker, G. P. (ed.) (2003). *The Voices of Wittgenstein – The Vienna Circle, Ludwig Wittgenstein and Friedrich Waismann*. Trans. G. P. Baker et al. London: Routledge.

Baker, G. P. (2004a). 'Our' Method of Thinking about 'Thinking'. In K. J. Morris (ed.), *Wittgenstein's Method: Neglected Aspects*, pp. 144–178. Oxford: Blackwell.

Baker, G. P. (2004b). Wittgenstein's Method and Psychoanalysis. In K. J. Morris (ed.), *Wittgenstein's Method: Neglected Aspects*, pp. 205–222. Oxford: Blackwell.

Bouveresse, J. (1995). *Wittgenstein Reads Freud*. Trans. C. Cosman. Princeton, NJ: Princeton University Press.

Brearley, Michael (1984). Psycho-Analysis and Philosophy. In I. Dilman (ed.), *Philosophy and Life: Essays on John Wisdom*. The Hague: Nijhoff.

Cioffi, Frank (1998). Freud's 'Abominable Mess'. In F. Cioffi (ed.), *Wittgenstein on Freud and Frazer*, pp. 206–234. Cambridge: Cambridge University Press.

Dilman, Ilham (1983). *Freud and Human Nature*. Oxford: Blackwell.

Dilman, Ilham (1984). *Freud and the Mind*. Oxford: Blackwell.

Dilman, Ilham (1988). *Freud: Insight and Change*. Oxford: Blackwell.

Farrell, B. A. (1946a). An Appraisal of Therapeutic Positivism I. *Mind* 55:217, pp. 25–48.

Farrell, B. A. (1946b). An Appraisal of Therapeutic Positivism II. *Mind* 55:218, pp. 133–150.

Farrell, B. A. (1981). *The Standing of Psychoanalysis*. Oxford: Oxford University Press.

Fischer, Eugen (2004). A Cognitive Self-Therapy – *Philosophical Investigations* 138–197. In E. Ammereller & E. Fischer (eds.), *Wittgenstein at Work*, pp. 86–126. London and New York: Routledge.

Fischer, Eugen (2012). Through Pictures to Problems: Cognitive Epistemology and Therapeutic Philosophy. In C. Jäger & W. Loeffler (eds.), *Epistemology: Contexts, Values, Disagreement*, Proceedings of the 34th International Ludwig Wittgenstein Symposium, pp. 475–492. Frankfurt: Ontos.

Forrester, John (2004). Freud in Cambridge. *Critical Quarterly* 46:2, pp. 1–26.

Freud, Sigmund (1953–66a/1900). *The Standard Edition of the Psychological Works of Sigmund Freud, vols. IV–V: The Interpretation of Dreams*. Trans. James Strachey et al. London: Hogarth Press/Institute of Psychoanalysis.

Freud, Sigmund (1953–66b/1905). *The Standard Edition of the Psychological Works of Sigmund Freud, vol. VIII: Jokes and their Relation to the Unconscious*. Trans. James Strachey et al. London: Hogarth Press/Institute of Psychoanalysis.

Freud, Sigmund (1953–66c/1916–17). *The Standard Edition of the Psychological Works of Sigmund Freud, vols. XV–XVI: Introductory Lectures on Psycho-Analysis*. Trans. James Strachey et al. London: Hogarth Press/ Institute of Psychoanalysis.

Freud, Sigmund (1953–66d/1930). *The Standard Edition of the Psychological Works of Sigmund* and *Freud, vol. XXII: Civilization and Its Discontents*. Trans. James Strachey et al. London: Hogarth Press/Institute of Psychoanalysis.

Freud, Sigmund (2002/1901). *The Psychopathology of Everyday Life*. Trans. Anthea Bell. London: Penguin.

Freud, Sigmund, & Josef Breuer (1953–66/1895). *The Standard Edition of the Psychological Works of Sigmund and Freud, vol. II: Studies in Hysteria*. Trans. James Strachey et al. London: Hogarth Press/Institute of Psychoanalysis.

Gardner, S. (1993). *Irrationality and the Philosophy of Psychoanalysis*. Cambridge: Cambridge University Press.

Gödde, Günter (2010). Freud and 19th Century Philosophical Sources on the Unconscious. In A. Nichols & M. Liebscher (eds.), *Thinking the Unconscious*. Cambridge: Cambridge University Press.

Harcourt, Edward (2012). Wittgenstein, Ethics and Therapy. In C. Jäger & W. Loeffler (eds.), *Epistemology: Contexts, Values, Disagreement*, Proceedings of the 34th International Wittgenstein Symposium, pp. 523–534. Frankfurt: Ontos.

Harcourt, Edward (2017). Wittgenstein and Psychoanalysis. In H.-J. Glock & J. Hyman (eds.), *The Blackwell Companion to Wittgenstein*, pp. 651–666. Oxford: Wiley.

Hartmann, Heinz (1960). *Psychoanalysis and Moral Values*. New York: International Universities Press.

Kennick, William E. (1970). On Solipsism. In C. Hanly & M. Lazerowitz (eds.), *Psychoanalysis and Philosophy*. New York: International Universities Press.
Kenny, A.J.P. (1984). Wittgenstein on the Nature of Philosophy. In A.J.P. Kenny (ed.), *The Legacy of Wittgenstein*. Oxford: Blackwell.
Lacewing, Michael (2018). The Science of Psychoanalysis. *Philosophy, Psychiatry and Psychology* 25:2, pp. 95–111.
Lazerowitz, M. (1985). The Passing of an Illusion. In M. Lazerowitz & A. Ambrose (eds.), *Necessity & Language*, pp. 200–240. Beckenham: Croom Helm.
Lazerowitz, M., & A. Ambrose (1984). *Essays in the Unknown Wittgenstein*. Buffalo, NY: Prometheus Books.
MacIntyre, Alisdair (2004). *The Unconscious*, 2nd ed. London: Routledge.
Majetschak, Stefan (2008). Psychoanalyse der grammatischen Missdeutungen: über die Beziehung Ludwig Wittgensteins zum Werk Sigmund Freuds. [The Psychoanalysis of Grammatical Misconstructions: On Ludwig Wittgenstein's Relationship to the Work of Sigmund Freud]. In A. Pichler & H. Hrachovec (eds.), *Wittgenstein and the Philosophy of Information*, Proceedings of the 30th International Ludwig Wittgenstein Symposium 2007, vol. 1. Heusenstamm: Ontos.
Malcolm, Norman (1958/1984). *Wittgenstein – A Memoir*, 2nd ed. Oxford: Oxford University Press.
Misak, Cheryl (2020). *Frank Ramsey*. Oxford: Oxford University Press.
Money-Kyrle, Roger (1979). Looking Backwards – and Forwards. *International Review of Psycho-Analysis* 6, pp. 265–272.
Monk, Ray (1990). *Wittgenstein: The Duty of Genius*. London: Vintage.
Moore, G. E. (1954–55). Wittgenstein's Lectures in 1930–33. *Mind* 63, pp. 1–15 and pp. 289–316; 64, pp. 1–27 and 264.
Nedo, M., & M. Ranchetti (1983). *Wittgenstein: Sein Leben in Bildern und Texten*. [Wittgenstein: His Life in Images and Texts]. Frankfurt: Suhrkamp.
Paul, Margaret (2012). *Frank Ramsey: A Sister's Memoir*. Huntingdon: Smith Gordon.
Prokop, Ursula (2003). *Margaret Stonborough-Wittgenstein: Bauherrin, Intellektuelle, Mäzenin* [Margaret Stonborough-Wittgenstein: Construction Magnate, Intellectual, Patroness of the Arts]. Vienna/Cologne/Weimar: Böhlau Verlag.
Rhees, R. (1970). On Continuity: Wittgenstein's Ideas 1938. In R. Rhees (ed.), *Discussions of Wittgenstein*, pp. 104–157. London: Routledge and Kegan Paul.
Rhees, R. (ed.) (1984). *Recollections of Wittgenstein*. Oxford: Oxford University Press.
Subotincic, Natalja (2000). Interpretation of Rooms – Sigmund Freud, His Collection, the Rooms and His Patients. In L. Wells-Bowie & E. S. Cathey (eds.), *Proceedings of the 88th Association of Collegiate Schools of Architecture (ACSA) Annual Meeting: Heterotopolis, Immigration, Ethnicity, and the American City*, pp. 55–61. Los Angeles, CA: Association of Collegiate Schools of Architecture (ACSA) Press.
Whyte, L. L. (1978). *The Unconscious Before Freud*. London/New York: Julian Friedmann/St. Martins Press.
Wisdom, John (A.J.T.D.) (1964). Philosophy and Psycho-Analysis. In J. Wisdom (ed.), *Philosophy and Psychoanalysis*, pp. 169–181. Oxford: Blackwell.

7
FREUD AND THE LEGACY OF SENSORY PHYSIOLOGY

Leonardo Niro

Introduction

In the literature on the philosophical background of psychoanalysis, Freud is often placed in a Kantian tradition via his engagement with authors such as Schopenhauer, Herbart, Lipps, Meynert, and, especially, the physiologists Hermann von Helmholtz, Emil du Bois-Reymond, and Freud's mentor during his medical studies, Ernst Theodor Brücke. Freud spent some of his most formative years, from 1876–1882, daily working at the Institute of Physiology of the University of Vienna. There, as he memorably described, 'in Ernst Brücke's physiological laboratory, I found rest and full satisfaction – and men, too, whom I could respect and take as my models: the great Brücke himself, and his assistants, Sigmund Exner and Ernst Fleischl von Marxow' (Freud, 1925a, p. 8). After leaving the institute, Freud continued to engage with the work of the group, in particular that of Fleischl and Exner,[1] well into the late 1890s. In fact, the *Project for a Scientific Psychology*, from 1895, can be read as Freud's attempt at reformulating Exner's *Entwurf zu einer Physiologischen Erklärung der Psychischen Erscheinungen* (Project for a Physiological Explanation of Psychical Phenomena), published the year prior (Exner, 1894).

Brücke, along with his friend and colleague Emil du Bois-Reymond, was a founding member and one of the leading figures behind the Berlin Society of Physics (*Physikalische Gesellschaft zu Berlin*), whose wide impact in nineteenth-century science led to its achieving a mythical status in the history of science (Schreier et al., 1995; Fiedler, 1998; Wise, 2018). While the goal of the society was that of the 'promotion of the study of Physics in a broader sense' (*Urkunde der Physikalischen Gesellschaft*, 1845), thus counting among its members with physicists, chemists, mathematicians, and engineers, as well as doctors, du Bois-Reymond and Brücke's initial aim in starting the society had been to create a space to share their physiological research (Finkelstein, 2013). The physiological work of the group came to form a coherent research programme – which later scholars titled *organic physics* – that became the most influential approach to physiology in late nineteenth-century Germany. Many of the founders of psychology – William James, Wilhelm Wundt, Ivan Pavlov, Ernst Mach, and Ewald Hering, among others – had their work directly influenced by organic physics. This was also the case of Freud.

The impact of their research programme in Freud's theories has not yet been thoroughly investigated; Freudian scholars have so far almost exclusively explored its influence in the metapsychological models, in particular the dynamic and economic models (Bernfeld, 1944, 1949;

DOI: 10.4324/9780429297076-9

Amacher, 1965; Pribram and Gill, 1976; Sulloway, 1979; Anzieu, 1986). Such analyses have led some authors to argue that due to the "scientistic" influence of organic physics – something that would be, along that reading, extraneous to the psychoanalytic project itself – it had come time to abandon metapsychology altogether, thus paving the way to a purely hermeneutic psychoanalysis (Ricoeur, 1970; Gill and Holtzman, 1976; Habermas, 1987). Such a reading presents, in my view, a gross oversimplification. The legacy of organic physics runs deep, constituting a central element of the psychoanalytic theory of the mind. Although the focus here will be on the impact of their work in sensory physiology in Freud's theory of perception, this is by no means their only influence – these are multiple and cannot be summarised in a single chapter.

In what follows, I will explore how Freud imported – and extended – Helmholtz's theory of perception in developing his new psychology. Further, I will also argue that the organic physicists' work on perception paved the way to an epistemology that would today be described as a type of epistemic structural realism, which, due to their influence, was also adopted (and again extended) by Freud. Following this assessment, I will present how the theories of perception proposed by Helmholtz and Freud are currently being recast in similar formats under predictive processing and embodied inference approaches in the neurosciences and philosophy of mind, as well as evaluating its epistemological implications. I will complete the chapter by schematically describing how the legacy of organic physics remained present (via Freud) in the work of the Kleinian school of psychoanalysis, and how this presents an isomorphism with predicted processing accounts of fantasy, dreaming, and primal forms of mental activity.

"Operationalised Kant": Helmholtz on Perception

In his *Handbook of Human Physiology* (1834–1840), the anatomist and physiologist Johannes Peter Müller (1801–1858), mentor to Helmholtz, du Bois-Reymond, and Brücke (cf. Otis, 2007), outlined his *Doctrine of Specific Nerve Energy*. At its core, the doctrine holds that the different sensory organs are connected to the external world via five different types ("energies") of sensory nerves in the human nervous system, representing each of the five senses. A consequence of the doctrine is that the direct object of sensation is the activity of the sensory organs themselves rather than properties of the external world (Müller, 1838, p. 253ff.). According to the doctrine, it was not the type of external stimulation that produced the quality of the sensation; this was a product, instead, of the type of nerve receiving the stimulus. The doctrine is based in two key observations: first, that one uniform cause – for instance, the rays from the sun – will appear to us as either light or warmth depending not on any inherent property of the cause itself but exclusively on the organ it excites (i.e., the eyes or the skin). Reversibly, widely different causes of excitation to the same organ generate similar qualities of sensation (ibid., p. 89ff.). Whether the retina is excited by a light source, or electricity, or simply by manual pressure to the eyeball, the different causes will all be experienced subjectively as light. Müller's doctrine, in short, holds a double dissociation between the causes of sensory input and its sensory effects (cf. Isaac, 2019).

If we only have access to the activity of our sensory organs – the 'egocentric predicament' described by Ayer (1940) – a potential epistemic consequence is global scepticism along the lines of a type of subjective idealism, the doctrine that only minds and mental contents exist. While Kant's defence against subjective idealism had been to propose the transcendental origins of intuition, Helmholtz in turn would deny any innateness in perception.[2] Although he depicted his theory of perception as an extension of Müller's doctrine into the specific energies of each sensory modality, and in agreement with Kant's doctrine of the *a priori* origins of perceptual experience, he also contended that 'the reasons which allow us to conclude that the intuitive form of space is transcendental are not necessarily sufficient to prove at the same time that the axioms are also of transcendental origin' (Helmholtz, 1878/1968a, p. 218). As his experiments indicated, perception was thoroughly a learned psychological process[3] – in Helmholtz's "operationalised Kant" (Lenoir, 2006), the *a priori*s of intuition are empirically generated through the agent's active engagement with its sensory inputs. Although Helmholtz departed from Müller and more traditional Kantian perspectives in essential points,[4] rather than radically diverging from them, he portrayed his work as an update of their theories of perception in the light of recent findings in physiology, and his divergence can be seen as a form of overcoming the challenge of global scepticism (and thus, of restoring a form of realism) given the abandonment of transcendental philosophy.

Since his first writing on the subject of perception, his 1855 Kant memorial address *On Human Vision*, delivered shortly after arriving in Königsberg, Helmholtz presented his central question: 'How is it that we escape from the world of the sensations of our nervous system into the world of real things?' (Helmholtz, 1855/1903, p. 116). Throughout the following decades, he turned this epistemological question into a coherent research programme while formulating a distinct theory of perception – the empiricist theory – developed in several public lectures and, especially, in his deeply influential *On the Sensation of Tone* (1863) and the three-volume *Handbook of Physiological Optics* (1856–1867). In Helmholtz's mature version of the empiricist theory of perception, a perceptual image is nothing like a passive copy of external things; perceptions are, instead, purely symbolic representations, actively constructed by the mind for the practical purpose of gaining control of the external world.

Whereas Müller had argued for an interaction between innate physiological mechanisms together with psychological factors,[5] Helmholtz rejected that anything was given in the act of perception. For him, even the most simple and basic sensation (e.g., "red" or the note "C") required a great deal of learning and judgement. The position of Müller (and later, Ewald Hering) was a target of Helmholtz's criticism as he assumed nativism – the theory that concepts, mental capacities, and mental structures are innate rather than acquired – created an intractable barrier between objective and subjective realities, which remained independent but somehow causally related. Nativism, in Helmholtz's view, necessarily implied some form of pre-established harmony between external reality and the subjective reality of perception – a theory he considered incompatible with science. Moreover, his discovery of the speed of nerve transmission (Helmholtz, 1850), one of the greatest achievements of nineteenth-century physiology, had demonstrated that the velocity of transmission was much slower than previously assumed, so that perception could not be as immediate as Müller contended and the nativist theory implied.

In Helmholtz's constructivist theory, perception functioned through a slow process of learning by trial, error, and continuous repetition. Simple associations of physiological sensory stimuli (not yet the content of perception or having the quality of sensation) are progressively organised into a system of dispositions to act.[6] As these dispositions also become organised, they form unconscious inferences onto the causes of the sensorium. The act of perception is therefore the result of a complex psychological process of unconscious inference onto the causes of percepts, to which we never have direct access. Helmholtz repeatedly made use of the analogy of perception and the activity of the scientist, where the act of perception is understood as a continuous process of inductive inference – which, he argued, is equivalent to an 'unconscious conclusion' (Helmholtz, 1867/1962, p. 4).[7] Repeated experiences of a similar effect enable us to form inferences as to the possible causes of change. The inferences are signs (*Zeichen*), generated by our active engagement with the effects. Since the signs are generated by a sensory apparatus with specific qualities, as well as the history of our experience and engagement with reality, they are also imbued with the observer's inner qualities and education. This psychological inferential process, Helmholtz would say, constitutes not only the foundation of perception but is the 'basis which underlies all that truly can be called thinking' (Helmholtz, 1878/1968a, p. 220).

If we do not have direct access to the causes of sensation, which are instead actively organised and constructed by the subject, Helmholtz argued that we *project* the inner activities of the nervous system externally (i.e., into space) as they would have to be present in order to cause these activities. Considering that perceptions are the result of inductive conclusions, of the same type as a 'scientific experiment,' in order to determine the distal cause of sensation an agent needs to perform experiments to test its inferences. This is firstly achieved by varying its perspectives upon them – that is, through *movement*:

> each voluntary movement by which we change the appearance of objects must be regarded as an experiment, by which we test whether we have correctly interpreted the lawful behaviour of the phenomenon in question, i.e. its postulated existence in a definite spatial arrangement.
>
> *(Helmholtz, 1878/1968a, p. 223)*

Space is therefore an *a priori* form of perception, learned through our active engagement with the world. In the Helmholtz scheme, action takes centre stage. Every movement, starting with eye movements, is understood as a perceptual experiment by which the agent (unconsciously, automatically) test its sensory signs, thus reaching an 'unconscious conclusion' – the perceptual image itself – in a process similar to hypothesis testing in the sciences. One special activity the agent needs to learn is to distinguish between themselves and the environment around. Such a distinction, he argued, is also learned through such a process of active experimentation. Percepts that can be changed (e.g., when I move my field of vision away from a light source), provide indications that they belong externally and are projected spatially; unchangeable states (e.g., memories, intentions, desires, moods) cannot be projected in space, and the mind learns to consider them 'the world of internal perception, the world of consciousness of one's self' (ibid., p. 214).

Helmholtz is emphatic in arguing there can be no possible relation of identity between the symbols of perception and the things they are meant to represent:

> In my opinion, therefore, can be no possible sense in speaking of any other truth of our ideas except of a practical truth. Our ideas of things cannot be anything but symbols (*Symbole*), natural signs (*Zeichen*) for things which we learn how to use in order to regulate our movements and actions. Having learned correctly how to read those symbols, we are enabled by their help to adjust our actions so as to bring about the desired result; that is, so that the expected new sensations will arise.
>
> *(Helmholtz, 1856/1968c, p. 80)*

As Lenoir aptly explained, 'the task of this symbolic language was to represent the relationship *between* objects affecting one another and our sense organs. The *structure* of the relationship was the crucial aspect to be grasped in a representation' (Lenoir, 1990, p. 144). This is important for two keys reasons: first, because the symbolic language allows the different sensory modalities to be linked together in an act of synthesis; and secondly, because a copy-theory of representation would not guarantee that the mind grasped the relations between objects and sensations. Since for Helmholtz the purpose of a representation is not that of providing a perfect copy of reality but of guiding action, a 'good representation is a symbol useful for organising the practical activities in terms of which we interact with the external world through our senses' (ibid.).

Perceptions are thus symbols that help us predict the structural relations between objects, as well as between our bodies and the world around.

Helmholtz's final position on the problem first expressed in 1855, articulated in his lecture *Facts on Perception*, was to claim that

> even if our sensory perceptions in their quality are only signs, whose special nature depends entirely on our organisation, they must not be discarded as empty appearances; rather, they are signs for something, either existing or happening – and, what is most important – they can represent the laws governing this event for us.
>
> *(Helmholtz, 1878/1968a, p. 213)*

His answer is therefore a pragmatic one. Although we do not have direct access to the properties of external reality, we have access to the structural relations *between* such properties. He would also defend a similar view in respect to the relation between our scientific concepts and theories, and the natural phenomena they are meant to represent (Helmholtz, 1856). Helmholtz's epistemology, articulated together with his research in sensory physiology, suggests a position that in contemporary epistemology would be called epistemic structural realism – the view that structural relations between simple perceptual properties convey knowledge of structural features of reality.

First introduced by John Worrall (1989) as a means of combining the claims of scientific realism and anti-realism in physics, structural realism defends that we commit ourselves only to the structural content of our theories. The debate has spawned an extensive literature in which numerous varieties of structural realism are advocated (cf. Ladyman, 2014). Realism, the view that 'we ought to believe in the unobservable entities posited by our most successful scientific theories' (ibid.), is countered by the history of radical theory change in science. Anti-realism, on the other hand, is countered by the "no miracles" argument, according to which the successes of science would be miraculous if not at least approximately true descriptions of the world. Structural realism would in that sense provide the "best of both worlds" (Worrall, 1989), since it accepts the historical contingencies of scientific theories but maintains that there is still retention of structure across theory change. Ladyman (1998) further raised the question as to whether Worrall's structural realism is intended as a metaphysical or epistemological modification of standard scientific realism, thus raising the distinction between ontic and epistemic forms of structural realism. Interpretations of Helmholtz's epistemology range from idealism (Heidelberger, 1995) to realism (McDonald, 2002), but most scholars contend his theory of perception implied a type of epistemic structural realism (Moulines, 1981; Hatfield, 1990, 2018; Lenoir, 1990, 2006; Isaac, 2020).

Inference, Translation, and Synthesis: Freud's Theory of Perception

'If I could give a complete account of the psychological characteristics of perception [. . .], I should have described a new psychology,' said Freud to Fliess in 1896 (Freud, 1985, p. 208). Throughout the following years, Freud would articulate a cogent 'new psychology' that retained the core elements of Helmholtz's theory of perception – namely, that we only have direct access to the activities of our sensory organs, a constructivist model of the formation of perceptual images, and the central role of action in perception. Further, Freud would extend Helmholtz's empiricist theory in three main ways: first, by giving greater consideration to the role of the endogenous sources of motivation (wishes, desires) in the construction of the perceptual image; secondly, by extending Helmholtz's analysis of the outer senses into the world of the inner senses; and finally, by extending Helmholtz's structuralist epistemology of external reality to also encompass the internal perception of our mental and bodily states.

Even though Freud never studied under Helmholtz, it is clear that he must have been well acquainted with the physiologist's work on perception, not only through his reading of Helmholtz's 'Lectures'[8] but chiefly as a result of his time at the Institute of Physiology with Brücke and Exner – who had been a student of Helmholtz in Berlin in 1867–8 and who advocated a theory of perception along Helmholtzian lines in *Entwurf.* Brücke's work continued to be faithful to the organic physics programme while Freud was his student, as demonstrated by the content of his *Lectures on Physiology* (Brücke, 1876) and the theory of perception depicted there. Further, the work on perception by Helmholtz owed a great deal to Brücke's earlier studies on the structure of the eye and retina (Brücke, 1843, 1845b, 1845a, 1847b, 1847a), as well as to his treatise *On Subjective Colours* (Brücke, 1851; Kremer, 1994). In his recent and comprehensive account of the socio-cultural background of the development of the Berlin Society, Norton Wise made the case that their work was marked by the division of labour amongst its members (Wise, 2018, p. 234). Their research in sensory physiology provides one prominent example. We can therefore consider their views on perception as generally in agreement and forming a uniform project, where Brücke concentrated in describing the anatomy and physiology of the eyes, while Helmholtz provided both physiological experiments and the theoretical framework which was subsequently used by Brücke in his *Lectures*.

Despite his engagement with both philosophy and physiology, Freud was neither a philosopher nor a sensory physiologist. As such, he was never required to articulate a theory of perception with the same level of detail as did Helmholtz. However, the psychology developed in some of his key theoretical works allows us to outline some of his key assumptions, as well as their main influences. A mind that displays the capacity for phenomena – such as projection, transference, and defense mechanisms that greatly disturb perception – cannot be based on a sensualist theory of perception, according to which the qualities of sensations are derived from the external world; neither can it subscribe to a form of strict realism, whereby we would have access to faithful representations (copies) of reality. And considering the centrality Freud gave to the activity of reality-testing, subjective idealism as well as global scepticism are also not viable candidates. For Freud, perception is an active psychological process deeply shaped by our internal states, which, as will be argued, retains some form of indirect realism.

Although Helmholtz had partially discussed the role of the will in guiding perception (Helmholtz, 1894/1968b, p. 260), he never gave a systematic treatment to the role of internal motivation in his writings. Probably due to his reading of G. Fechner, he went as far as to argue that 'above all, it is pain that teaches us most impressively about the power of reality' (1878/1968a, p. 226), an assertion that greatly resembles how Freud would come to describe the activity of reality-testing. If perceptual images are, as we have seen, symbols imbued with the perceiver's inner qualities and education, whose purpose is of guiding action, one might assume that perceptual images would be at least partially determined by our endogenous needs since they provide the motivational factors for action itself. This constitutes Freud's fundamental extension of Helmholtz's theory of perception: a deeper consideration of the role of endogenous motivational factors in determining both the internal and external senses.[9] One could in fact read Freud's theorisation of the mind since the *Project for a Scientific Psychology* (Freud, 1895) as attempting to formulate a psychology that dealt with that central problem. Freud's core question there was of how the brain, shut inside the skull, is capable of learning both about external reality as about the internal demands of the body so that it can accomplish the task of meeting the bodily needs in the environment.

This question, I believe, remained structurally the same in his later works – how is an infant, prior to any experience, capable of learning about themselves and the world around so that it can satisfy its needs and desires? The answer he provided in the *Project* persisted largely unaltered.

In the *Project*, Freud described a 'primary brain' as the source of the primal form of mentality, the predecessor of the primary process type of thinking. He argued that because the primary brain is directly connected to the interior of the body and shut off from the external world, it should be understood as a 'sympathetic organ' – that is, as responsible for signalling the body's 'endogenous excitations' (ibid., p. 302).[10] Increases in excitation, Freud maintained, are subjectively experienced as painful or unpleasurable, while pleasurable sensations are the subjective side of a quantitative experience of its pacification. The pacification of the endogenous sources of excitations, in turn, can only be brought about by an 'alteration in the external world (supply of nourishment, proximity of the sexual object)', which requires a 'specific action', such as feeding or nurturing. At first, 'the human organism is incapable of bringing about the specific action. It takes place by extraneous help, when the attention of an experienced person is drawn to the child's state by discharge along the path of internal change' (ibid., p. 318). This constitutes the first 'experience of satisfaction' of the infant, who is now capable, via a 'basic law of association by simultaneity', of linking the endogenous excitation with the object that pacifies it. As the association is one of memory (i.e., the memory of the experience of satisfaction being contiguous with the experience of the specific action), when an increase in endogenous excitation occurs again, it triggers a wishful activation of memory traces, which in turn produces the 'same thing as a perception – namely a hallucination' (i.e., a fantasy of wish-fulfilment; ibid., p. 319).

From *The Interpretation of Dreams* (Freud, 1900) onwards, Freud would introduce one important change to his previous model, derived from his encounter with the work of philosopher T. Lipps (Freud, 1985, p. 325). Consciousness starts being treated as 'a sense organ' (*Sinnesorgan*) that receives stimuli from both the external world as from inside of the body itself (Freud, 1900, p. 574), which it translates into sensory qualities – in the *Project*, this function had been instead attributed to the neurons ω. Sensory perception henceforth becomes thus an exclusive attribute of consciousness, which in the topographical model is designated by a single rubric, the *Pcpt-Cs.* system. The qualities of sensation, along those lines, do not derive directly from the excitations themselves but are a characteristic of our physiological organisation and mental attributes, and our only means of access to the distal causes of perception (both internal and external) is through a process of *translation* of physiological excitations ("quantities") into psychological sensations ("qualities") – which are, by Freud's own definition, conscious. The activity of translation functions, much as in Helmholtz's theory of signs, through a psychological process of inference onto the causes of the sensory excitation:

> Every science is based on observations and experiences arrived at through the medium of our psychical apparatus. But since our science has as its subject that apparatus itself, the analogy ends here. We make our observations through the medium of the same perceptual apparatus, precisely with the help of the breaks in the sequence of 'psychical' events: we fill in what is omitted by making plausible *inferences* and *translating* it into conscious material. In this way *we construct, as it were, a sequence of conscious events complementary to the unconscious psychical processes.* The relative certainty of our psychical science is based on the *binding force of these inferences.* Anyone who enters deeply into our work will find that our technique holds its ground against any criticism.
>
> *(Freud, 1938, p. 159; emphasis added)*

If consciousness alone has access to the qualities of the senses, Freud would contend that both the external world and the internal states are in themselves unknowable:

> The unconscious is the true psychical reality; in its innermost nature it is as much unknown to us as the reality of the external world, and it is as incompletely presented by the data of consciousness as is the external world by the communications of our sense organs.
>
> *(Freud, 1900, p. 613)*

Freud, therefore, subscribed to the Kantian dissociation between noumena and phenomena, and in particular to Müller's and Helmholtz's "egocentric predicament" that we only have direct access to our sensory organs. On this, he famously stated:

> Just as Kant warned us not to overlook the fact that our perceptions are subjectively conditioned and must not be regarded as identical with what is perceived though unknowable, so psycho-analysis warns us not to equate perceptions by means of consciousness with the unconscious mental processes which are their object.
>
> *(Freud, 1915b, p. 171)*

Given its role of providing sensory qualities to both the outer and inner senses, Freud stated that the *Pcpt-Cs.* system must lie 'on the borderline between outside and inside', since the perceptual image it provides consists of a *synthesis* of 'perceptions of excitations coming from the external world and of feelings of pleasure and unpleasure which can only arise from within the mental apparatus' (Freud, 1920, p. 24). Consequently, consciousness functions as a mediator between the internal and external worlds, with the role of translating endogenous and exogenous stimuli into sensory qualities, thus forming a unified perceptual image that must be a synthesis of both if it is to meet its purpose of meeting internal demands externally.

Action in Perception, or How to Test Your Hallucination

Considering the picture above, we have a model whereby perception is understood as a thoroughly constructed capability. At first, consciousness translates endogenous excitations into sensations along the lines of the 'pleasure-unpleasure series'. As the infant gathers 'experiences of satisfaction', it progressively learns to synthesise the outer senses with the inner sense (Freud, 1911a, p. 220), which are not yet differentiated. Whenever endogenous excitation is again increased, the infant hallucinates the satisfaction of its needs as a means of temporarily meeting the demands; the experience of hallucinatory wish-fulfilment constitutes, Freud says, the 'first psychical activity of the infant' (Freud, 1900, p. 566). This model provides us with one main reason why Freud – who, as often noted by his biographers, was chiefly interested in formulating a general psychology, and only secondarily in understanding and treating psychopathology – gave such central importance to the phenomena of dreams and hallucinations: they are not only analogous to perception, or yet abnormal states of perception, but are rather its original template. A perceptual image is, along those lines, the result of a reality-tested hallucination, and dreams and hallucinations are, reversibly, perceptual images that didn't go through the process of reality-testing.

A question is therefore raised as to what the task of reality-testing (*Realitätsprüfung*) exactly consists of; Freud unfortunately never managed to present a sufficiently clear definition. Although the problem prefigured in his earlier works, the term itself was first introduced in *Formulations on the Two Principles of Mental Functioning* (1911a). It wasn't, however, until *A Metapsychological Supplement to the Theory of Dreams* (1917) that he would treat it more systematically. There, reality-testing is described as the mechanism whereby the infant learns to discriminate 'between what is internal and what is external' (ibid., p. 233). In *Negation* (1925b) and *An Outline of Psychoanalysis* (1938), on the other hand, Freud defined it as the mechanism of discrimination between vividly experienced ("cathected") memories and perceptions. Such a distinction constitutes, along the lines of the model above, a false dichotomy since an experienced memory is by definition conscious and an object of perception, while a perception is a mnemonic experience since the inferential process that generates the perceptual image depends on associations of past experiences. All that would be required for the pragmatic purpose of meeting internal demands in the external world is that impingements belonging internally and externally are sufficiently discriminated.

In either case, the means by which the infant learns to discriminate, Freud argued, is *action*.[11] Regarding the first differentiation, he said:

> The still helpless organism [acquires the] capacity for making a first orientation in the world by means of its perceptions, distinguishing 'external' and 'internal' according to their relation to its muscular action. *A perception which is made to disappear by an action is recognized as external*, as reality; *where such an action makes no difference, the perception originates within the subject's own body* – it is not real.
>
> (Freud, 1917, pp. 231–232; emphasis added)

Nearly paraphrasing Helmholtz, Freud contended it is muscular action that allows the infant to determine whether a sensation pertains to the inner or the outer world, which explains his later assertion that 'the ego is first and foremost a bodily ego' (Freud, 1923, p. 26) – something that had been germinating in his writings since the *Project* (cf. 1895, p. 331). Freud followed Helmholtz in arguing that percepts that can be changed are projected spatially, and extends the projection theory to percepts that cannot be altered – these, he claimed, are projected onto the body. The subjectively experienced body is the result of 'the projection of a surface' (Freud, 1923, p. 26) and something that, just like perception of external reality, is psychologically constructed. In short, the process of discriminating between the inner and outer worlds is something entirely learned, mediated by a psychological process of inference and projection (as well as translation into sensory qualities), and reality-tested via muscular action.

Freud also found in action and active exploration the means for discriminating between memories and perceptions. In *Interpretation of Dreams*, after discussing his theory of 'perceptual identity' – that is, the indiscriminateness between memory and perception in early mental life – he argued that since hallucinatory wish-fulfilment is insufficient as it only allows the infant to momentarily meet its demands, the task of lowering the endogenous sources of excitation becomes diverted to 'a second system, which is in control of voluntary movement – which for the first time makes use of movement for purposes remembered in advance' (Freud, 1900, p. 565). Freud maintained there that this experience constitutes, on the one hand, the origin of thinking while, on the other, it provides the mechanism for discrimination between memories and perceptions. Though he did not make it quite clear there how this is achieved, he would hint at it later in *Formulations*: 'the motor discharge was now employed in the appropriate alteration of reality; it was converted into action' (1911a, p. 221). Freud was here employing a similar strategy as previously: the act of discrimination between memories and perceptions is accomplished by changing our inner sense (i.e., by meeting a need and thus lowering excitation) through active exploration of the environment (i.e., by finding the object of pacification), something that cannot be achieved in a sustained manner through hallucinatory wish-fulfilment alone. Reality-testing is, in short, provided by action and active exploration, and they are, according to Freud, the mechanisms that allow the infant to overcome its "egocentric predicament".

Seeing Through Illusions: Distortions, Repression, and Motivated Misapprehension

Helmholtz devoted a substantial amount of his research and writing to describe the many ways human vision was less than perfect. Visual illusions, afterimages, spherical aberration of the eyeball, astigmatism, vitreous opacities, binocular rivalry, and the physiological blind spots generated by the head of the optic nerve in the retina were just some of the topics approached. In these phenomena, he saw examples of how perception's

> extraordinary value depends on the way in which we use it: its perfection is practical, not absolute, consisting not in avoidance of every error, but the fact that all its defects do not prevent its rendering the most important and varied services.
>
> *(Helmholtz, 1856/1968c, p. 80)*

Further, in visual illusions, he observed the mind's inferential process of perception at work, constructing visual images based on previous experiences, generating false conclusions to the causes of visual cues. For Freud, instead, by giving serious consideration to the role of endogenous motivation in the generation of perceptual images, distortions of perception were no longer simply the matter of the misinterpretation (or rather, mistranslation) of a "neutral" stimulus based on previous experience but indicated a *motivated* process of misapprehension. While for Helmholtz the formation of complete visual images despite the retinal blind spot revealed the operations, in psychoanalytic terminology, of the descriptive unconscious, Freud in turn believed that 'through the gap in the retina one could see deep into the unconscious' (Freud, 1930, p. 14) – that is, the dynamic and purposeful unconscious.

Since the *Project,* Freud had pointed out that 'the pathological mechanisms which are revealed in the most careful analysis in the psychoneuroses bear the greatest similarity to dream-processes' (Freud, 1895, p. 336). In his later works, he would describe a range of mental phenomena that do not go through reality-testing: dreams, psychotic hallucinations, neurotic symptoms, fantasising (the satisfaction of wishes in "day-dreaming" activities in waking life) and, most importantly, the unconscious contents of repression:

> The strangest characteristic of unconscious (repressed) processes, to which no investigator can become accustomed without the exercise of great self-discipline, is due to their entire disregard of reality-testing; they equate reality of thought with external actuality, and wishes with their fulfilment – with the event – just as happens automatically under the dominance of the ancient pleasure principle.
>
> *(Freud, 1911a, p. 225)*

Considering that in order for a sensory impingement to be perceived it must go through a process of translation into sensorial qualities, which are conscious by definition, Freud would argue that when an impingement is deemed intolerable to the individuals' morals and in sharp conflict with their expectations of themselves, the content is repressed (i.e., inhibited) and *projected* spatially as belonging externally. This process, first described as the psychological mechanism underlying paranoia (Freud, 1892, 1911b), was later extended as general defense mechanism characteristic of normal mental life (Freud, 1901, p. 255ff.). Because repressed unconscious contents cannot be directly perceived, they remain at an indiscriminate state since they cannot be reality-tested through action. As the internal contents are indiscriminate and still merged with the outer senses, the mind *purposefully* misattributes the origins of the causes of sensations as a means of avoiding unpleasurable experiences. Strictly speaking, as discussed above, projection itself is a psychological process underlying all perception, internal and external, while projection *as defense mechanism* is the act of motivated misattribution of perceptual contents. Similarly, the idea of transference – the act of misattributing perceptual contents and feelings from past experiences to present ones – is dependent on such a view of perception, whereby the contents of perception are psychologically constructed based on our history of interaction with the senses.

An analogous process of misattribution takes place at the origin of somatic disorders, says Freud – contents banned from conscious experience can also be projected onto the surface of the body:

> When one carries out the psycho-analysis of a hysterical woman patient whose complaint is manifested in attacks, one soon becomes convinced that these attacks are nothing else but *phantasies translated into the motor sphere, projected on to motility and portrayed in pantomime.* It is true that the phantasies are unconscious; but apart from this they are of the same nature as the phantasies which can be observed directly in day-dreams or which can be elicited by interpretation from dreams at night. [. . .] As a rule, owing to the influence of the censorship, the pantomimic portrayal of the phantasy has undergone distortions which are *completely analogous to the hallucinatory distortions of a dream*, so that both of them have, in the first resort, become unintelligible to the subject's own consciousness as well as to the observer's comprehension.
>
> *(Freud, 1909, p. 229; emphasis added)*

Whereas Helmholtz used the phenomena of visual illusions to make sense of the normal act of perception, Freud relied in acts of "'misknowledge" – in symptoms, parapraxes, dreams, and ordinary projections – to make sense of the ways in which misapprehension is motivated. Such acts provided access to both the motivations themselves and to the psychological processes underlying the formation of the misapprehended perceptual image. Through such means, an observer – an "interpreter of translations" – is able to trace back the inferences, thus bringing to light both the underlying mechanisms of how we obtain knowledge of ourselves and the world around, as well as how these may fail.

If Helmholtz contented that we do not have direct access to the properties of external reality but do have access to the structural relations *between* such properties, Freud defended a similar epistemological approach in regards to the unconscious structures underlying conscious experience. Such an inferential process from conscious to unconscious content, as he said, provided the only possible method for a proper psychological science: 'we construct, as it were, a sequence of conscious events complementary to the unconscious psychical processes. The relative certainty of our psychical science is based on the binding force of these inferences' (Freud, 1938, p. 159). This implies treating the unconscious contents *as if* they were carriers of sensorial qualities, thereby having access not to the unconscious processes themselves but to the structural relations *between* them. Such a methodological approach situates Freud's views within a form of epistemic structural realism, as applied to our inner senses.

Bursting Your Bubble: Predictive Processing and Embodied Inference

The view presented thus far brings Helmholtz's and Freud's theories in line with emergent trends in philosophy of mind and neuroscience that define the activity of agents (and in particular their brains) as one engaged in the task of prediction (Friston, 2010; Hohwy, 2013; Clark, 2016). According to the predictive processing (PP) framework, brains are biological systems that generate complex, self-organising hierarchies with the task of predicting their incoming sensory signals, where each level of the hierarchy statistically models the inputs from the level below all the way down to the sensory organs. Mismatches between the top-down predictive (Bayesian) models and bottom-up inputs are understood as "prediction-errors"; the brain, along those lines, is in charge of reducing prediction-error by either changing its models of the distal causes of sensation (perceptual inference and learning) or by performing actions to bring about sensory states in line with predictions (active inference; changing the world to fit the model; Friston et al., 2010). As Andy Clark noted, this is not so much a matter of predicting the future as that of 'trying to guess the present' by self-generating the sensory streams arriving from the world (Clark, 2017, p. 727).

Proponents of PP often cite Helmholtz as a precursor.[12] In machine learning, algorithms that operate by creating generative models of distal causes (also called "hidden states") are called *Helmholtz machines* (Dayan et al., 1995; Hinton and Dayan, 1996). Such proponents, however, disagree on its epistemological implications. The recent debate between philosophers Jakob Hohwy and Andy Clark provides a pertinent example. Hohwy contends that PP's inferential character implies a 'veil of uncertainty' between perception and reality, so that we should embrace some form of scepticism (Hohwy, 2013). Considering that PP entails acceptance of the argument from Müller's *Doctrine* for the double-dissociation between the causes of sensory input and its sensory effects, it 'tells us how neurocentric we should be: the mind begins where sensory input is delivered through exteroceptive, proprioceptive and interoceptive receptors and ends where proprioceptive predictions are delivered, mainly in the spinal cord' (Hohwy, 2016, p. 18).

Andy Clark, on the other hand, contends that the "neurocentric" character of PP is minimised by a deeper appreciation of the role of embodiment and enactment, thus proposing a similar pragmatic epistemology to the one offered by Helmholtz as a means of breaking with our sense boundaries. For Clark,

> predictive processing results in the creation and deployment of 'pragmatic action-oriented representations': inner states tailored to the production of good online control rather than aiming for rich reconstructive mirroring of some action-independent world. Neural processing thus delivers a grip upon a world of possibilities for action and intervention. Perception delivers a world parsed for action, while action harvests the perceptual flows that secure both epistemic and practical success.
>
> *(Clark, 2017, p. 748)*

In much the same line of argumentation, computational neuroscientist Karl Friston also suggests that PP implies a form of *embodied inference*, the 'notion that our interactions with the world are akin to sensory experiments, by which we confirm our hypothesis about its causal structure in an optimal and efficient fashion' (Friston, 2012), thus counterbalancing the potential scepticism from PP and bringing it closer to realism. Following Helmholtz, Friston demonstrated how the act of sensory active experimentation starts with eye movements (Friston et al., 2012). The process of minimising prediction error in this embodied and enactive framework is known as *active inference* (Friston et al., 2010).

A fuller appreciation of embodiment entails not only a consideration for the role played by action, but also to the one played by our bodily states in both interoception (the sense of the internal state of the body) and proprioception (sense of bodily movement and position). Following embodied inference, as Friston notes,

> not only does the agent embody the environment but the environment embodies the agent. This is true in the sense that the physical states of the agent (its internal milieu) are part of the environment. In other words, the statistical model entailed by each agent includes a model of itself as part of that environment.
>
> *(Friston, 2011, p. 89)*

In interoceptive active inference, the body itself is deemed an object of inference and is seen as constructed from inferential hierarchical models, with higher levels 'integrating interoceptive, proprioceptive and exteroceptive cues in formulating descending predictions' (Seth, 2013, p. 567) – that is, forming a synthesis of the senses in the unified perceptual image. Such an extension of PP into the body and its internal states displays an isomorphism with Freud's extension of Helmholtz as described above.[13]

Freud had also proposed that inferences of internal states provided the initial prototypes for perception, which was progressively synthesised with the outer senses via experiences of satisfaction, with whom they subsequently formed a relation of co-dependence. Similarly, Anil Seth contends that a model of *interoceptive inference* starts with 'a desired or inferred physiological state' (ibid., p. 568) for creating generative models of both exteroception and interoception, so that 'the close interplay between interoceptive and exteroceptive inference implies that emotional responses are inevitably shaped by cognitive and exteroceptive context, and that perceptual scenes that evoke interoceptive predictions will always be affectively coloured' (ibid., p. 571). Such a co-dependence between inferred internal states (emotions) and inferred external percepts would imply that perceptions are not only 'affectively coloured' but affectively constructed. As affective researcher Lisa Barrett argued, 'the brain's ability to see in the present incorporates a representation of the affective impact of those visual sensations in the past,' where 'personal relevance and salience are not computed after an object is already identified, but may be part of object perception itself' (Barrett and Bar, 2009).

The Phantastic Organ and Unconscious Phantasy

The narrative above leads us to the picture of the brain as a 'phantastic organ' (Friston et al., 2014), that is, a biological structure capable of generating mental images (from Greek *phantastikos* = able to create mental images) that inferentially explain the causes of its sensory impingements. Similar claims have been made by various other proponents of PP, such as Chris Frith ('our perception of the world is a fantasy that coincides with reality'; Frith, 2007, p. 111) and Anil Seth ('we're all hallucinating all of the time, and when we agree about our hallucinations, that's what we call reality'; Seth, 2017). Though such assertions are by no means equivalent, they all convey the view that perception, hallucination, and fantasy are a lot more intertwined than formerly conceived in traditional cognitive science accounts, and that they serve the function of providing hypotheses about the causes of sensory impingements – which, as we have seen, have the nature of 'pragmatic action-oriented representations' (Clark, 2017, p. 748) rather than realistic copies of reality. This brings their views not only close to those of Freud, but also to later conceptual developments in psychoanalysis in the notion of unconscious phantasy by Klein.

Melanie Klein was notoriously not a very methodical theoretician. For instance, she never formally defined unconscious phantasy, and the concept became the most contentious topic of the *Controversial Discussions* (King and Steiner, 1991, p. 242ff.). The task fell instead to her followers and colleagues, such as Susan Isaacs and Hannah Segal. In *The Nature and Function of Phantasy* (1948), Isaacs provided its most coherent formalisation. Phantasy there was defined as the mental representative of the drives, which were henceforth understood as the purely physiological, non-mental, primarily somatic impingements. As such, phantasies were conceived as the primary content of all mental processes, and the basis 'of all unconscious and conscious thought processes' (Isaacs in King and Steiner, 1991, p. 277). Further, Isaacs argued that a hallucination is 'either identical with phantasy or the pre-condition for it' (ibid., p. 278). Unconscious phantasy, along those lines, is a primal picture – mostly visual, but not only – representing the internal bodily states of the infant, which grants it access to its own internal states and the world at large. Progressively, according to this account, external objects also become "introjected" (i.e., internalised, or modelled in the form of internal objects) and are reversibly used by the infant to represent internal processes, with whom they form a relation of co-dependence. This matches closely to what Klein described when she said:

> In the process of acquiring knowledge, every new piece of experience has to be fitted into the patterns provided by the psychic reality which prevails at the time; whilst the psychic reality of the child is gradually influenced by every step in his progressive knowledge of external reality.
>
> *(Klein, 1940, p. 129)*

Hannah Segal, in turn, would extend this analysis by likening unconscious phantasy to a type of *hypothesis* about the causes of sensory impingement: 'I think that it is implicit in desire that it gives rise to a phantasy of its fulfillment. A phantasy is like a wishful hypothesis which is constantly matched with reality' (Segal, 1994, p. 399). The infant is therefore likened – much as in Helmholtz – to a scientist conducting perceptual experiments, testing its hypothesis of reality: 'I see the infant experimenting in preverbal phantasy and testing in external reality as a budding scientist, and a successful one' (ibid., p. 400). By reality-testing its hypothesis, the infant is thus capable of using symbols, since only after achieving discrimination between internal and external realities in the depressive position does the symbol become 'a representation of the object rather than being equated with the object' (Segal, 1981, p. 90). In short, unconscious phantasy came to be understood in the Kleinian tradition as type of innate hypothesis, in the form of a perceptual image, about the origin of sensory impingements which allows them to be reality-tested, thereby learning to discriminate not only between inner and outer worlds but also between things and symbols.[14]

Such a view shares a close parallel to Friston and Hobson's notion that the brain is 'genetically endowed with an innate virtual reality generator' (Hobson and Friston, 2014). Allan Hobson, dream researcher and notorious anti-Freudian (Hobson, 2011), had previously proposed his *protoconscious theory*, the theory that a form of primal consciousness (both developmentally as evolutionarily) provides mammals and birds with an innate virtual reality model of the world, whose working is most clearly revealed in dreams. REM sleep – the sleep phase when most dreaming, and also the longest and most structured dreaming, occurs – developmentally reaches its peak in the third trimester of gestation, and it is progressively supplanted by what Hobson called *secondary waking consciousness*, 'the awareness of the external world, our bodies and our selves (including the awareness of our awareness) that humans experience when awake' (Hobson, 2009). Similar mechanisms of primal consciousness underlie not only dreams but also psychedelic states and psychosis (Carhart-Harris, 2007; Carhart-Harris et al., 2012, 2014, 2016). The hyper-activation of the brainstem in REM sleep, combined with the 'active suppression of both external sensory input and motor output' (ibid.), indicates that its main purpose is one of homeostatic regulation, and that the form of mentality correlated with this state is highly affective in nature (cf. Solms, 2014) – much as in Freud's description of primary process thinking (or the role of the "primary brain" from the *Project*) and the function of dreaming, as well as in the Kleinian notion of unconscious phantasy.

By embedding this theory into a PP framework, the 'virtual reality generator' becomes conceptualised as an innate model of belief used to infer the causes of sensory impingement via active inference. Consciousness, along those lines, 'is an operation that produces beliefs and is therefore quintessentially inferential in nature' (Hobson and Friston, 2014, p. 17), whose origin is prior and independent of secondary waking consciousness, so that 'sleep is just a special instance of conscious processing that is untethered from the sensorium,' thus 'generating fictive sensations, using generative or virtual reality models' (ibid.). Following this view, *qualia* – the name contemporary philosophers gave to the "qualities" of consciousness that Freud discussed – are seen as 'probability distributions over the hidden causes of sensations' (ibid., p. 22) embedded in the hierarchical models of the brain and, like in Helmholtz, they are understood as "signs" constructed by the brain with the purpose of granting access to the structural relations between objects (including our own bodies) and our sense organs.

Conclusion

Much as in Plato's allegory of the cave, according to Helmholtz's theory of perception we are unable of directly perceiving reality, relying instead on "shadows" to infer the true nature of the external world. Unlike chained prisoners in a cave, however, we are capable of moving and actively experimenting with our sensations as a means of testing our inferences, thereby reaching a practical, action-oriented representation of reality. Freud accepts and extends this theory by arguing that similar processes of action-focused inference take place in the realm of the inner sense. It is through action that we "reality-test" our inferences, thus learning to discriminate what belongs internally to what belongs to the world outside. Further, since the inner and outer senses must go through a process of synthesis to form a unified perceptual image so as to satisfy its purpose of meeting the internal demands externally (and thus, staying alive), they mutually influence one another in a relation of co-dependence.

Contemporary PP approaches reach very similar conclusions. Our access to the world and ourselves takes place via 'pragmatic action-oriented representations' that infer the causes of the sensorium by actively generating models ("hypotheses") that predict its inputs, testing them against the actual sensory signals through action. If perceptions are thus seen as hypotheses tested in reality, a question is raised as to what the first (original) hypothesis consists of. Authors in the Kleinian tradition have called this primal hypothesis 'unconscious phantasy', while Hobson and Friston called it an innate 'virtual reality generator'. In both cases, the primal model of hidden states is said to be closely linked to REM sleep and dreaming. As Hopkins aptly summarised:

> On both accounts waking consciousness is underlain by an original imaginary (virtual reality/phantasy) process that later appears mainly in dreaming, and whose operation in waking is constrained by a model or system of representations of the causes of sensory impingement. On both, therefore, a central aspect of development consists in constructing the worldly model whose adherence to reality inhibits and overlays the imaginary process in waking.
>
> *(Hopkins, 2019, p. 383)*

Further, it was argued that the perspectives of Helmholtz and Freud implied a form of epistemic structural realism, the view that structural relations between simple perceptual properties convey knowledge of structural features of reality. In particular, it was contended that Freud extended Helmholtz's arguments for a structural epistemology of external perception towards the inner sense of our unconscious states. Such a perspective underlined not only their theories of perception but also their philosophies of science.

The legacy of sensory physiology, I have tried to show, runs deep and remains present in contemporary psychoanalysis, as exemplified in the Kleinian school. Understanding this intellectual influence is significant, as it allows us to place Freud's views within a certain philosophical tradition, originating in Kant and continued to this day. Such an approach also allows for an integration of different psychoanalytic theories to one another, as well as of psychoanalytic theory with theories derived from other sciences – including the neurosciences, the biological sciences, as well as phenomenology and psychiatric phenomenology, given the embodied and enactive implications of this theory of perception. This reading, most importantly, also avoids the difficulties implicit in views that attempt to exclude causal approaches in psychoanalysis, aiming to convert it exclusively into a hermeneutic discipline and thereby isolating psychoanalysis from its neighbouring sciences – ultimately, in my view, leading to its asphyxiation. Psychoanalysis was born as a *bridge* discipline, aiming to formulate a theory of mind that integrated the subjective and objective selves, the internal and external worlds, the mental and somatic, understanding and explanation, meanings and causes. Obliterating one of its margins not only renders the bridge irrelevant but destroys the foundation upon which the whole structure rests.

Acknowledgements

I would like to acknowledge Mark Solms, Matt ffytche, Bruno Rates, and Richard Simanke for the helpful comments to an earlier version of this chapter, as well as Jim Hopkins for the many conversations surrounding topics explored here.

Notes

1 Josef Breuer was also closely associated with the group, being an intimate friend and collaborator of both Fleischl and Exner. His training in physiology, however, took place under J. Oppolzer and E. Hering, who shared views on the nature and methodology of their science in many ways opposed to that of Brücke. Breuer's standing in relation to the organic physics programme, therefore, is a more complex one that was discussed in length by Hirschmüller (1989).

2 Though Kant never made the explicit statement that the *a priori* categories were innate, this was how it came to be interpreted by nineteenth-century German physiologists, who turned it into a research question on the origins of perception (cf. Hatfield, 1990; Turner, 1994).

3 The only exception, Helmholtz would argue, is the causal law; it is a requirement of the empiricist theory and something that could not be learned by experience (Helmholtz, 1878/1968a, p. 226). In Helmholtz's theory, the causal law functions as a "law of lawfulness", thus taking on the role that Kant ascribed to the transcendental.

Müller, in turn had already significantly diverged from Kant at points. These were analysed in greater detail by Lenoir (2018) and Isaac (2019).

4 Müller, in turn had already significantly diverged from Kant at points. These were analysed in greater detail by Lenoir (2018) and Isaac (2019).

5 Müller had, for instance, defended the theory that stereoscopic (binocular) vision was unified into a single perceptual image via anatomical tracts uniting each retinal point to the one in the opposite retina. Brücke's first publication, written shortly after starting work as his assistant, was a defence of Müller's theory of identity of retinal spots against Wheatstone's attack (Brücke, 1841). He would later follow Helmholtz in rejecting it (Brücke, 1876, p. 138ff.). For more on Brücke's work on physiological optics,

see Schickore (1999, 2007). For more on the nativism-empiricism debate, see Turner (1994) and Hatfield (1990).

6 One such example of a disposition: 'When those nervous mechanisms whose terminals lie on the right-hand portions of the retinas of the two eyes have been stimulated, our usual experience, repeated a million times through life, has been that a luminous object was over there in front of us on our left. We had to lift the hand toward the left to hide the light or to grasp the luminous object; or we had to move toward the left to get closer to it' (Helmholtz, 1855/1903, p. 26).

7 Helmholtz at points also states that the reverse is the case, that is, that the activity of the scientist is an extension of our natural capacity for perceptual learning: 'The same great importance which experiment has for the certainty of our scientific convictions, it has also for the unconscious inductions of the perceptions of our senses. It is only voluntarily by bringing our organs of sense in various relations to the objects that we learn to be sure as to our judgements of the causes of ours sensations. This kind of experimentation begins in the earliest youth and continues all through life without interruption' (Helmholtz, 1867/1962, pp. 30–31).

8 In his letters to his friend E. Silberstein, Freud remarks on his reading of Helmholtz's "Lectures" and his intention of spending the winter semester of 1875–76 in Berlin 'in order to attend the lectures of du Bois-Reymond, Helmholtz, and Virchow' (Freud, 1990) – which never occurred. He was probably referring here to Helmholtz's three-volume *Populäre Wissenschaftliche Vorträge*, published in 1871.

9 Which indicates the influence of yet another "philosopher-physiologist" highly influenced by Kant: Schopenhauer. His early work on the physiology of vision, the treatise *On Vision and Colours* (1816) shared many similarities with Helmholtz's; after reading *On Human Vision* (1855/1903), Schopenhauer in fact accused Helmholtz of plagiarism. The charge was dismissed by the latter, who attributed the similitude to their common Kantian influence (Cahan, 2018, p. 193ff.).

10 As I argued in a previous article (Niro, 2017), Freud's notion of a primary brain responsible for signalling endogenous excitations (i.e., the internal milieu) was derived from his anatomical studies of the spinal cord and medulla oblongata (Freud, 1882, 1884, 1886, 1888; Freud and Darkschewitsch, 1886; Freud and Ossipowit, 1886) conducted while an assistant at T. Meynert's psychiatric institute. The idea of a primal brain, both phylogenetically and ontogenetically, appears for the first time in his monograph *On Aphasias*, where he says: 'The whole organization of the brain seems to fall into two central apparatuses of which the cerebral cortex is the younger, while the older one is represented by the ganglia of the forebrain which have still maintained some of their phylogenetically old original functions' (Freud, 1891/1953, p. 49).

11 Freud had also previously articulated this argument in "Instincts and their Vicissitudes" (Freud, 1915a, p. 119).

12 Though this is true in some aspects, it is certainly not in others. Given its impact since the nineteenth century, a wide range of perception researchers, including more contemporary authors such as Richard Gregory (1974) and proponents of PP, have been highly influenced by Helmholtz's treatment of perception as an inferential process. Helmholtz, however, only rarely discussed the brain itself, and in his *Handbook* he squarely situated the study of perception as belonging to the domain of psychology (Helmholtz, 1867/1962, §26). In the physiology section of the book (volume II), his analysis did not go further than the retina and the optical nerves.

13 Although different in points, a more detailed consideration of the consilience between psychoanalytic and PP frameworks was provided by Hopkins (2012, 2016, 2018, 2019) and Solms (2014, 2019).

14 In a Helmholtzian terminology, what Segal calls a representation of a thing is already a symbol. What she calls a symbol, along those lines, would be a "symbol of a symbol".

References

Amacher, P. (1965) 'Freud's Neurological Education and its Influence on Psychoanalytic Theory', *Psychological Issues – Monograph 16*, IV(4).

Anzieu, D. (1986) *Freud's Self Analysis*. London: The Hogarth Press and the Institute of Psycho-Analysis.

Ayer, A. J. (1940) *The Foundations of Empirical Knowledge*. London: Macmillan and Co. Limited.

Barrett, L. F. and Bar, M. (2009) 'See It with Feeling: Affective Predictions During Object Perception', *Philosophical Transactions of the Royal Society B: Biological Sciences*. Royal Society, 364(1521), pp. 1325–1334. doi:10.1098/rstb.2008.0312.

Bernfeld, S. (1944) 'Freud's Earliest Theories and the School of Helmholtz', *Psychoanalytic Quarterly*, 13, pp. 341–362.

Bernfeld, S. (1949) 'Freud's Scientific Beginnings', *American Imago*, 6, pp. 163–196.

Brücke, E. W. von (1841) 'Ueber die stereoskopischen Erscheinungen und Wheatstone's Angriff auf die Lehre von den identischen Stellen der Netzhäute', in *Archiv für Anatomie, Physiologie und wissenschaftliche Medicin*.

Brücke, E. W. von (1843) 'Ueber den inneren Bau des Glaskörpers', in *Archiv für Anatomie, Physiologie und wissenschaftliche Medicin*, pp. 345–348.

Brücke, E. W. von (1845a) 'Anatomische Untersuchungen über die sogenannten leuchtenden Augen bei den Wirbelthieren', in *Archiv für Anatomie, Physiologie und wissenschaftliche Medicin*, pp. 387–406.

Brücke, E. W. von (1845b) 'Ueber das Verhalten der optischen Medien des Auges gegen Licht- und Wärmestrahlen', in *Archiv für Anatomie, Physiologie und wissenschaftliche Medicin*, pp. 262–276.

Brücke, E. W. von (1847a) *Anatomische Beschreibung des menschlichen Augapfels*. Berlin: G. Reimer.

Brücke, E. W. von (1847b) 'Ueber das Leuchten der menschlichen Augen', *Archiv für Anatomie, Physiologie und wissenschaftliche Medicin*, pp. 225–227.

Brücke, E. W. von (1851) 'Untersuchungen über subjective Farben', *Annalen der Physik und Chemie*. John Wiley & Sons, Ltd, 160(11), pp. 418–447. doi:10.1002/andp.18511601104.

Brücke, E. W. von (1876) *Vorlesungen über Physiologie; unter dessen Aufsicht nach stenographischen Aufzeichnungen herausgegeben. Zweite Band*. 2nd ed. Wien: Wilhelm Braumüller. doi:10.5962/bhl.title.44731.

Cahan, D. (2018) *Helmholtz: A Life in Science*. Chicago: The University of Chicago Press.

Carhart-Harris, R. L. (2007) 'Waves of the Unconscious: The Neurophysiology of Dreamlike Phenomena and Its Implications for the Psychodynamic Model of the Mind', *Neuro-Psychoanalysis*, 9(2), pp. 183–211.

Carhart-Harris, R. L., et al. (2012) 'Neural Correlates of the Psychedelic State as Determined by fMRI Studies with Psilocybin', *Proceedings of the National Academy of Sciences of the United States of America*. PNAS, 109(6), pp. 2138–2143. doi:10.1073/pnas.1119598109.

Carhart-Harris, R. L., et al. (2014) 'The Entropic Brain: A Theory of Conscious States Informed by Neuroimaging Research with Psychedelic Drugs', *Frontiers in Human Neuroscience*. Frontiers Media S. A., 8(1 Feb), p. 20. doi:10.3389/fnhum.2014.00020.

Carhart-Harris, R. L., et al. (2016) 'Neural Correlates of the LSD Experience Revealed by Multimodal Neuroimaging', *Proceedings of the National Academy of Sciences of the United States of America*. National Academy of Sciences, 113(17), pp. 4853–4858. doi:10.1073/pnas.1518377113.

Clark, A. (2016) *Surfing Uncertainty: Prediction, Action, and the Embodied Mind, Surfing Uncertainty*. Oxford: Oxford University Press. doi:10.1093/acprof:oso/9780190217013.003.0001.

Clark, A. (2017) 'Busting Out: Predictive Brains, Embodied Minds, and the Puzzle of the Evidentiary Veil', *Noûs*. Blackwell Publishing Ltd, 51(4), pp. 727–753. doi:10.1111/nous.12140.

Dayan, P., Geoffrey E. Hinton, Radford M. Neal, Richard S. Zemel (1995) 'The Helmholtz Machine', *Neural Computation*, 7(5), pp. 889–904.

Exner, S. (1894) *Entwurf zu einer Physiologischen Erklärung der Psychischen Erscheinungen*. Vienna: Franz Deuticke.

Fiedler, A. (1998) *Die Physikalische Gesellschaft zu Berlin: vom lokalen naturwissenschaftlichen Verein zur nationalen Deutschen Physikalischen Gesellschaft (1845–1900)*. Aachen: Shaker.

Finkelstein, G. (2013) *Emil du Bois-Reymond: Neuroscience, Self, and Society in Nineteenth-Century Germany*. Cambridge, MA: The MIT Press.

Freud, S. (1882) 'Über den Bau der Nervenfasern und Nervenzellen beim Flußkrebs', in *Sitzungsberichte der Mathematisch-Naturwissenschaftlichen Classe der Kaiserlichen Akademie der Wissenschaften*, III(LXXXV).

Freud, S. (1884) 'A New Histological Method for the Study of Nerve-tracts in the Brain and Spinal Chord', *Brain*. Oxford University Press, 7(1), pp. 86–88.

Freud, S. (1886) 'Über den Ursprung des Nervus acusticus', *Monatsschrift für Ohrenheilkunde*, 20, pp. 245–251, 277–282.

Freud, S. (1888) 'Gehirn. I. Anatomie des Gerhirns', in Villaret, A. (ed.) *Handwörterbuch der gesamten Medizin*. Stuttgart, pp. 684–691.

Freud, S. (1892) 'Draft H Paranoia from Extracts from the Fliess Papers', in *The Standard Edition of the Complete Psychological Works of Sigmund Freud*, Volume I, pp. 206–212.

Freud, S. (1895) 'Project for a Scientific Psychology', in *The Standard Edition of the Complete Psychological Works of Sigmund Freud*, Volume I, pp. 281–391.

Freud, S. (1900) 'The Interpretation of Dreams', in *The Standard Edition of the Complete Psychological Works of Sigmund Freud*, Volume IV, pp. ix–627.

Freud, S. (1901) 'The Psychopathology of Everyday Life', in *The Standard Edition of the Complete Psychological Works of Sigmund Freud*, Volume VI, pp. vii–296.

Freud, S. (1909) 'Some General Remarks on Hysterical Attacks', in *The Standard Edition of the Complete Psychological Works of Sigmund Freud*, Volume IX, pp. 227–234.

Freud, S. (1911a) 'Formulations on the Two Principles of Mental Functioning', in *The Standard Edition of the Complete Psychological Works of Sigmund Freud*, Volume XII, pp. 213–226.

Freud, S. (1911b) 'Psycho-Analytic Notes on an Autobiographical Account of a Case of Paranoia (Dementia Paranoides)', in *The Standard Edition of the Complete Psychological Works of Sigmund Freud*, Volume XII, pp. 1–82.

Freud, S. (1915a) 'Instincts and their Vicissitudes', in *The Standard Edition of the Complete Psychological Works of Sigmund Freud*, Volume XIV1, pp. 109–140.

Freud, S. (1915b) 'The Unconscious', in *The Standard Edition of the Complete Psychological Works of Sigmund Freud*, Volume XIV, pp. 159–215.

Freud, S. (1917) 'A Metapsychological Supplement to the Theory of Dreams', in *The Standard Edition of the Complete Psychological Works of Sigmund Freud*, Volume XIV, pp. 217–235.

Freud, S. (1920) 'Beyond the Pleasure Principle', in *The Standard Edition of the Complete Psychological Works of Sigmund Freud*, Volume XVIII, pp. 1–64.

Freud, S. (1923) 'The Ego and the Id', in *The Standard Edition of the Complete Psychological Works of Sigmund Freud*, Volume XIX, pp. 1–66.

Freud, S. (1925a) 'An Autobiographical Study', in *The Standard Edition of the Complete Psychological Works of Sigmund Freud*, Volume XX, pp. 1–74.

Freud, S. (1925b) 'Negation', in *The Standard Edition of the Complete Psychological Works of Sigmund Freud*, Volume XIX, pp. 235–239.

Freud, S. (1930) 'Letter from Sigmund Freud to Arnold Zweig, September 10, 1930', in *The International Psycho-Analytical Library*, pp. 13–15.

Freud, S. (1938) 'An Outline of Psycho-Analysis', in *The Standard Edition of the Complete Psychological Works of Sigmund Freud*, Volume XXIII, pp. 139–208.

Freud, S. (1953) *On Aphasia: A Critical Study*. New York: International Universities Press.

Freud, S. (1985) *The Complete Letters of Sigmund Freud to Wilhelm Fliess, 1887–1904*. Edited by J. M. Masson. Cambridge, MA: Harvard University Press.

Freud, S. (1990) *The Letters of Sigmund Freud to Eduard Silberstein 1871–1881*. Edited by W. Boehlich and A. J. Pomerans. Cambridge, MA: The Belknap Press of Harvard University Press.

Freud, S. and Darkschewitsch, L. O. (1886) 'Über die Beziehung des Strickkörpers zum Hinterstrang und Hinterstrangskern, nebst Bemerkungen über zwei Felder der Oblongata', *Neurologisches Zentralblatt*, 5, pp. 121–129.

Freud, S. and Ossipowit, D. L. (1886) 'Über die Beziehung des Strickkörpers zum Hinterstrang und Hinterstrangskern, nebst Bemerkungen über zwei Felder der Oblongata', *Neurologisches Zentralblatt*, 5.

Friston, K. J. (2010) 'The Free-energy Principle: A Unified Brain Theory?', *Nature Reviews. Neuroscience*, 11, pp. 127–138. doi:10.1038/nrn2787.

Friston, K. J. (2011) 'Embodied Inference: Or "I Think Therefore I Am, If I Am What I Think"', in Tschacher, W. and Bergomi, C. (eds.) *The Implications of Embodiment: Cognition and Communication*. Exeter: Imprint Academic, pp. 89–125.

Friston, K. J. (2012) 'Embodied Inference and Spatial Cognition', *Cognitive Processing – International Quarterly of Cognitive Science*, 13, pp. 171–177. doi:10.1007/s10339-012-0519-z.

Friston, K. J., et al. (2010) 'Action and Behavior: A Free-energy Formulation', *Biological Cybernetics*, 102(3), pp. 227–260. doi:10.1007/s00422-010-0364-z.

Friston, K. J., et al. (2012) 'Perceptions as Hypotheses: Saccades as Experiments', *Frontiers in Psychology*, 3(May), p. 151. doi:10.3389/fpsyg.2012.00151.

Friston, K. J., et al. (2014) 'Computational Psychiatry: The Brain as a Phantastic Organ', *The Lancet Psychiatry*. Elsevier Ltd, 1(2), pp. 148–158. doi:10.1016/S2215-0366(14)70275-5.

Frith, C. (2007) *Making up the Mind: How the Brain Creates Our Mental World*. Oxford: Blackwell Publishing.

Gill, M. M. and Holtzman, P. S. (eds) (1976) *Psychology versus Metapsychology: Psychoanalytic Essays in Memory of George S. Klein*. New York: International Universities Press.

Gregory, R. L. (1974) 'Perceptions as Hypotheses', in *Philosophy of Psychology*. London: Palgrave Macmillan, pp. 195–210. doi:10.1007/978-1-349-02110-9_9.

Habermas, J. (1987) *Knowledge and Human Interests*. Cambridge: Polity.

Hatfield, G. (1990) *The Natural and the Normative: Theories of Spatial Perception from Kant to Helmholtz*. Cambridge, MA: MIT Press.

Hatfield, G. (2018) 'Helmholtz and Philosophy: Science, Perception, and Metaphysics, with Variations on Some Fichtean Themes', *Journal for the History of Analytical Philosophy*. McMaster University Library Press, 6(3). doi:10.15173/jhap.v6i3.3431.

Heidelberger, M. (1995) 'Helmholtz als Philosoph', *Deutsche Zeitschrift für Philosophie*. De Gruyter, 43(5), pp. 835–844. doi:10.1524/dzph.1995.43.5.835.

Helmholtz, H. von (1850) 'Vorläufiger Bericht über die Fortpflanzungs-Geschwindigkeit der Nervenreizung', in *Archiv für Anatomie, Physiologie und wissenschaftliche Medicin*, pp. 71–73.

Helmholtz, H. von (1856) 'On the Interaction of Natural Forces', *The London, Edinburgh, and Dublin Philosophical Magazine and Journal of Science*, 11(75), p. Supplement.

Helmholtz, H. von (1863) *Die Lehre von den Tonempfindungen als physiologische Grundlage für die Theorie der Musik*. Braunschweig: Friedrich Vieweg und Sohn.

Helmholtz, H. von (1867) 'Handbuch der physiologischen Optik', in Karsten, G. (ed.) *Allgemeine Encyklopädie der Physik*. Leipzig: Voss.

Helmholtz, H. von (1855/1903) 'Ueber das Sehen des Menschen', in *Vorträge und Reden. Vol. II*. 5th ed. Leipzig: Friedrich Vieweg und Sohn, pp. 85–117.

Helmholtz, H. von (1962) *Helmholtz's Treatise on Physiological Optics (Volume III)*. 3rd ed. Edited by J.P.C. Southall. New York: Dover Publications.

Helmholtz, H. von (1878/1968a) 'The Facts of Perception', in Warren, R. M. and Warren, R. P. (eds.) *Helmholtz on Perception: Its Physiology and Development*. New York: John Wiley & Sons, pp. 205–246.

Helmholtz, H. von (1894/1968b) 'The Origin of the Correct Interpretation of our Sensory Impressions', in Warren, R. M. and Warren, R. P. (eds.) *Helmholtz on Perception: Its Physiology and Development*. New York: John Wiley & Sons, pp. 249–261.

Helmholtz, H. von (1968c) 'The Recent Progress in the Theory of Vision', in Warren, R. M. and Warren, R. P. (eds.) *Helmholtz on Perception: Its Physiology and Development*. New York: John Wiley & Sons, pp. 61–108.

Hinton, G. E. and Dayan, P. (1996) 'Varieties of Helmholtz Machine', *Neural Networks: The Official Journal of the International Neural Network Society*, 9(8), pp. 1385–1403.

Hirschmüller, A. (1989) *The Life and Work of Josef Breuer: Physiology and Psychoanalysis*. New York: New York University Press.

Hobson, J. A. (2009) 'REM Sleep and Dreaming: Towards a Theory of Protoconsciousness', *Nature Reviews: Neuroscience*, 10, pp. 803–814. doi:10.1038/nrn2716.

Hobson, J. A. (2011) *Dream Life: An Experimental Memoir*. Cambridge, MA: MIT Press.

Hobson, J. A. and Friston, K. J. (2014) 'Consciousness, Dreams, and Inference: The Cartesian Theatre Revisited', *Journal of Consciousness Studies: Controversies in Science & The Humanities*. Imprint Academic, 21(1/2), pp. 6–32.

Hohwy, J. (2013) *The Predictive Mind*. Oxford: Oxford University Press.

Hohwy, J. (2016) 'The Self-evidencing Brain', *Nous*. Blackwell Publishing Ltd, 50(2), pp. 259–285. doi:10.1111/nous.12062.

Hopkins, J. (2012) 'Psychoanalysis, Representation, and Neuroscience: The Freudian Unconscious and the Bayesian Brain', in Fotopoulou, A., Pfaff, D., and Conway, M. A. (eds) *From the Couch to the Lab: Trends in Psychodynamic Neuroscience*. Oxford: Oxford University Press, pp. 230–265.

Hopkins, J. (2016) 'Free Energy and Virtual Reality in Neuroscience and Psychoanalysis: A Complexity Theory of Dreaming and Mental Disorder', *Frontiers in Psychology*. Frontiers Media SA, 7, p. 922.

Hopkins, J. (2018) 'The Significance of Consilience: Psychoanalysis, Attachment, Neuroscience, and Evolution', in Brakel, L. and Talvete, V. (eds.) *Psychoanalysis and Philosophy of Mind: Unconscious Mentality in the 21st Century*. London: Karnac.

Hopkins, J. (2019) 'Psychoanalysis and Neuroscience', in Gipps, R.G.T. and Lacewing, M. (eds.) *The Oxford Handbook of Philosophy and Psychoanalysis*. Oxford: Oxford University Press, pp. 376–406. doi:10.1093/oxfordhb/9780198789703.013.24.

Isaac, A.M.C. (2019) 'Realism Without Tears I: Müller's Doctrine of Specific Nerve Energies', *Studies in History and Philosophy of Science Part A*. Elsevier Ltd, 78, pp. 83–92. doi:10.1016/j.shpsa.2019.01.002.

Isaac, A.M.C. (2020) 'Realism Without Tears II: The Structuralist Legacy of Sensory Physiology', *Studies in History and Philosophy of Science Part A*. Elsevier Ltd, 79, pp. 15–29. doi:10.1016/j.shpsa.2019.01.003.

Isaacs, S. (1948) 'The Nature and Function of Phantasy', *International Journal of Psycho-Analysis*, 29, pp. 73–94.

King, P. and Steiner, R. (1991) *The Freud–Klein Controversies 1941–45*. New Library. London: Routledge.

Klein, M. (1940) 'Mourning and its Relation to Manic-Depressive States', *International Journal of Psycho-Analysis*, 21, pp. 125–153.

Kremer, R. L. (1994) 'Innovation through Synthesis: Helmholtz and Color Research', in Cahan, D. (ed.) *Hermann von Helmholtz and the Foundations of Nineteenth-Century Science*. Berkeley, CA: University of California Press, pp. 205–258. doi:10.1525/9780520914094-011.

Ladyman, J. (1998) 'What is Structural Realism?', *Studies in History and Philosophy of Science Part A*. Elsevier Ltd, 29(3), pp. 409–424. doi:10.1016/S0039-3681(98)80129-5.

Ladyman, J. (2014) *Structural Realism, Stanford Encyclopedia of Philosophy*. Available at: https://plato.stanford.edu/entries/structural-realism/ (Accessed: 1 September 2020).

Lenoir, T. (1990) 'The Eye as Mathematician: Clinical Practice, Instrumentation, and Helmholtz's Construction of an Empiricist Theory of Vision', in Cahan, D. (ed.) *Hermann von Helmholtz and the Foundations of Nineteenth-Century Science*. Berkeley: University of California Press, pp. 109–153.

Lenoir, T. (2006) 'Operationalizing Kant: Manifolds, Models, and Mathematics in Helmholtz's Theories of Perception', in Friedman, M. and Nordmann, A. (eds.) *The Kantian Legacy in Nineteenth-Century Science*. Cambridge, MA: MIT Press, pp. 141–210.

Lenoir, T. (2018) 'Helmholtz, Müller und die Erziehung der Sinne', in Hagner, M. and Wahrig-Schmidt, B. (eds.) *Johannes Müller und die Philosophie*. Berlin, Boston: Akademie Verlag, pp. 207–222. doi:10.1515/9783050068794-013.

McDonald, P. J. (2002) 'Helmholtz's Methodology of Sensory Science, the Zeichentheorie, and Physical Models of Hearing Mechanisms', in *History of Philosophy of Science*. Dordrecht, Netherlands: Springer, pp. 159–183. doi:10.1007/978-94-017-1785-4_13.

Moulines, C.-U. (1981) 'Hermann Von Helmholtz: A Physiological Approach to the Theory of Knowledge', in *Epistemological and Social Problems of the Sciences in the Early Nineteenth Century*. Dordrecht, Netherlands: Springer, pp. 65–73. doi:10.1007/978-94-009-8414-1_5.

Müller, J. (1838) *Handbuch der Physiologie des Menschen für Vorlesungen V. II.* Koblenz: Verlag von J. Hoelscher.

Niro Nascimento, L. (2017) 'Evolution in the Brain, Evolution in the Mind: The Hierarchical Brain and the Interface between Psychoanalysis and Neuroscience', *Psychoanalysis and History*. Edinburgh University Press, 19(3), pp. 349–377.

Otis, L. (2007). *Müller's Lab*. Oxford: Oxford University Press.

Pribram, K. H. and Gill, M. M. (1976) *Freud's 'Project' Reassessed*. London: Hutchinson.

Ricoeur, P. (1970) *Freud and Philosophy. An Essay on Interpretation*. Edited by D. Savage. New Haven: Yale University Press.

Schickore, J. (1999) 'The Body's Eye and its Technical Externalisation. Ernst Wilhelm Brucke's Research on Vision, 1841–1847', *Technikgeschichte*, 66(4), pp. 337–348.

Schickore, J. (2007) *The Microscope and the Eye: A History of Reflections, 1740–1870*. Chicago: University of Chicago Press.

Schopenhauer, Arthur. (1816/1994) *On Vision and Colors,* Translated by E. F. J. Payne, Edited with an Introduction by David E. Cartwright, Berg Publishers.

Schreier, W., et al. (1995) 'Geschichte der Physikalischen Gesellschaft zu Berlin 1845–1900', *Physik Journal*. Wiley Verlag, 51(1).

Segal, H. (1981) *The Work of Hannah Segal: A Kleinian Approach to Clinical Practice*. New York: Aaron Johnson.

Segal, H. (1994) 'Phantasy and Reality', *International Journal of Psycho-Analysis*, 75, pp. 395–401.

Seth, A. K. (2013) 'Interoceptive Inference, Emotion, and the Embodied Self', *Trends in Cognitive Sciences*. Elsevier Ltd, 17(11), pp. 565–573. doi:10.1016/j.tics.2013.09.007.

Seth, A. K. (2017) *Your Brain Hallucinates Your Conscious Reality*. Available at: www.ted.com/talks/anil_seth_your_brain_hallucinates_your_conscious_reality?language=en.

Solms, M. (2014) 'A Neuropsychoanalytical Approach to the Hard Problem of Consciousness', *Journal of Integrative Neuroscience*, 13(2).

Solms, M. (2019) 'The Hard Problem of Consciousness and the Free Energy Principle', *Frontiers in Psychology*. Frontiers Media S.A., 9, p. 2714. doi:10.3389/fpsyg.2018.02714.

Sulloway, F. J. (1979) *Freud, Biologist of the Mind: Beyond the Psychoanalytic Legend*. Cambridge, MA: Harvard University Press.

Turner, R. S. (1994) *In the Eye's Mind: Vision and the Helmholtz-Hering Controversy*. Princeton, NJ: Princeton University Press.

'Urkunde der Physikalischen Gesellschaft. Wahl zum ordentl. Mitglied am 14. Januar 1845', SD 3k 1841 (3) Bl. 59; 'Entwurk der Satzung fuer die physikalische Gesellschaft mit Bitte um Genehmigung', 5 January 1845, GStA I/77 Tit. 662 Nr.2 Bl. 16v–20v. https://www.dpg-physik.de/veroeffentlichung/archiv/pix/Gruendung_2.jpg.

Wise, M. N. (2018) *Aesthetics, Industry, and Science: Hermann von Helmholtz and the Berlin Physical Society*. Chicago: University of Chicago Press.

Worrall, J. (1989) 'Structural Realism: The Best of Both Worlds?', *Dialectica*, 43(1–2), pp. 99–124. doi:10.1111/j.1746-8361.1989.tb00933.x.

8

TRAUMA AND LANGUAGE[1]

Dana Amir

The psychoanalytic literature on trauma refers extensively to the major role of the other in bearing witness to a trauma the victim often has not, and could not have, witnessed himself or herself. Authors from various theoretical fields (Laub and Auerhahn, 1993; Oliner, 1996) describe trauma as something that has taken place "over there, far away", an event that does not belong to the experiencing "I". Trauma, both collective and individual, is often conceptualized as an external event, detached from the narrator who experienced it. Survivors of trauma claim that they live in two worlds: the world of their traumatic memories (a kind of everlasting present) and the real world (the concrete present). Usually they neither wish nor are able to integrate these two worlds. As a result, the traumatic memory is preserved frozen and timeless, and psychic movement becomes automatic, aimless and senseless (Laub, 2005). At the heart of the traumatic experience there is an experience of excess that escapes representation and leaves a lacuna within consciousness (LaCapra, 2001). Caruth (1996, pp. 91–92) writes about the traumatic paradox in which the most direct contact with the violent event may occur only through the very inability to know it. Trauma is not only an experience, but also the failure to experience that experience: not merely the threat itself, but the fact that the threat was recognized as such only a moment too late. As it was not experienced in time, the event is condemned not to be fully known (Caruth, 1996, p. 62). As such, it returns to claim its presence, trying to cover an experiential void through compulsive repetition. Van der Kolk et al. (1996) argue that while terrifying events may be remembered extremely vividly, they may equally resist any kind of integration. These memories remain powerful but frozen, un-transformable by either circumstantial processes or the passing of time. They are subject to neither assimilation nor developmental change since they are not integrated into the associative network. As a result, they remain concealed, retaining their magnetic force in their detailed and contradictory clarity, in the condensed vagueness that envelopes them. Rather than undergoing the transformation that leads to a personal narrative, traumatic experiences are imprinted as primary impressions that do not receive verbal representation (ibid., pp. 282, 296). As Modell (2006) suggests, trauma tends to freeze the past and therefore deprives it of the plasticity it needs if it is to connect to the present (Modell, 2006; Stern, 2012). Memories of trauma are not only rigid and concrete, but unmentalized. As such, they remain "raw": neither adaptable nor generative (ibid.).

Dori Laub (2005), in a paper titled "Traumatic Shutdown of Narrative and Symbolization", quotes Moore (1999) who argued that the traumatized subject cannot know that the traumatic

DOI: 10.4324/9780429297076-10

event has taken place until an other supplies it with a narrative. A person can know his or her story only when he or she tells it to what Laub calls "the inner thou" (internal other). But since trauma critically injures both the internal and external other, namely the addressee of any dialogical relationship, it ruins the possibility of an empathic dyad in the inner representation of the world, leaving the subject with nobody to address, either inside or outside himself or herself.[2] This catastrophic loss of the good object compels the victim to internalize the only available object, the aggressor himself, as a malignant self-object (Kohut, 1971) with whom he or she identifies. Laub further argues that the fragmenting effects of the traumatic experience can be better understood if we postulate the presence of unbound, un-neutralized death instinct derivatives. Conscious memory is the first casualty of these unbound death instinct derivatives. Furthermore, erasure of traumatically lost objects and of the traumatic experience itself, may lead the survivor to complete oblivion, or to doubt the veracity and authenticity of his or her own experiences, compromising his or her entire sense of identity and continuity. Laub contends that it is the traumatic loss of the (internal) good object and the libidinal ties to it that releases the hitherto neutralized forces of the death instinct and intensifies the clinical manifestations of its derivatives. "In the absence of an internal responsive 'thou', there is no attachment to, nor cathexis of the object" (2005, pp. 316–317).

Shoshana Felman (1992) similarly reflects on Albert Camus's *The Plague* (1975):

> [The protagonist] has to learn on his body what a holocaust – a situation of "total condemnation" – is: [. . .] an experience that requires one to live through one's own death, and paradoxically, bear witness to that living through one's dying; a death experience which can be truly comprehended, witnessed only from inside (from inside the witness's own annihilation); a radical experience to which no outsider can be witness, but to which no witness can be, or remain, outsider.
>
> *(p. 109)*

Traumatic experiences often activate a psychic process of self-annihilation. Their acidity creates a type of psychic holes which absorb the unbearable traumatic substances along with the subject who contains them, to the point of a total collapse of inner barriers. This collapse of barriers leaves the subject imprisoned in a territory of *negative possession* (Amir, 2012, 2014, 2016a, 2018), where the traumatic contents are neither digested nor worked through. The only chance of recovery from this condition lies in the possibility to deposit the traumatic substances in another subject who cannot be annihilated by them. This is the core of bearing witness.

The Language of the Victim: The Metaphoric, the Metonymic and the Psychotic Modes of Witnessing

Metaphor and metonymy are two forms of semantic shift, that is, two modes of transition from one semantic field to another. Metaphor is the use of a word or an expression in a borrowed rather than in its simple, original sense, or the use of the characteristics of one concept in order to illuminate another. Metaphor is based on analogy, on a relationship of similarity between two semantic fields. The sentence "My love is a rose" does not imply that the rose itself is the beloved one but that something in the beloved's features resembles that of a rose. Metonymy, by contrast, is a figurative tool that illustrates something by replacing it with something else that is situated close to it in time or space, or that belongs in the same context. The result is not logical in the simple sense and can only be understood through the proximity between the two elements. This is how the expression "the White House" comes to stand for the notion of "the president's spokesperson". As opposed to metaphor, in metonymy there is no transfer of characteristics between the two elements (the president's spokesperson does not share features with the White House). The connection between them is associative only, in a way that allows us to perceive the one as representative of the other.

In his article "Two Aspects of Language and Two Types of Aphasic Disturbances" (1956), Roman Jakobson presents metaphor and metonymy as polar opposites rather than parts of the hierarchical order in which they are more commonly seen. He stresses the *similarity* that metaphor installs between its signifiers versus the *contiguity* typical of metonymy. Each of these modes of transposition, he argues, relies on different cognitive skills. While metaphor is based on the cognitive ability to convert, metonymy implies the ability to connect and contextualize, that is, the ability to create continuity and to identify something as part of – and following from – a context. Jakobson divides the aphasic patients with whom his article is concerned into patients who suffer from impaired identification of similarities and those whose ability to combine and contextualize is affected.

Lacan's (1958, 1977) distinction between metaphor and metonymy diverges from Jakobson's. Though, following the latter, he associates metaphor with the axis of linguistic selection and metonymy with that of combination, metaphor for him acts to constitute meaning while metonymy resists meaning: the metonymic drive is related to the desire to recover the lost "Real". Metaphor, by contrast, is associated with "the symptom", whose creation is a constructive process in which new meaning emerges. Metaphor therefore maintains analogous relations between its subjects, while in metonymy subjects entertain relations of contiguous association. Metaphor is related to the ability to take a distance, thereby enabling the discussion of something that belongs to one conceptual field in terms that belong to another. Metonymy, by contrast, constitutes relations of continuity, that is, relations that maintain no distance.

Following both Jakobson's and Lacan's ideas, I would like to suggest a distinction between a metaphoric and a metonymic mode of witnessing, further adding a psychotic mode (divided into two sub-modes) which is completely outside the range stretching between the former two.

The term "metaphoric mode of witnessing" refers to those parts of the testimonial narrative where there is a shift from the "first person" to the "third person" of experience, or from the *experiencing I* to the *reflective I*,[3] further enabling the shift from the "position of the victim" to the "position of the witness" (Amir, 2012, 2014, 2016a, 2018). The metaphoric mode, by its very nature, creates movement and is based on movement. Unlike the other three modes – the metaphoric mode struggles against traumatic stagnation through creating a three-dimensional space based on the shift from the first person to the third person and back. Its metaphoric quality lies therefore in the fact that it involves an act of representation and the creation of new meaning, producing an integrated narrative within which the traumatic events are not merely repeated but also undergo transformation.

As against the metaphoric mode, the metonymic mode of witnessing remains a "first person" mode of report. It produces a text that preserves and enacts the traumatic memories and the traumatic features, and is thus characterized by the same sense of isolation, fragmentation, disorientation and lack of coherence that are typical of the traumatic experience itself. In that sense, the metonymic mode illustrates the very materials to which it testifies. It is based on the compulsive repetition of the experience itself, in the absence of the ability to represent it or reflect on it. So while the metaphoric mode of witnessing enables the shift between the first and the third persons of experience, the metonymic mode is located in the first person mode of report. It uses no distancing, maintaining a living continuum with the traumatic memories and through it also with a sense of selfhood. The metonymic mode lacks any reflective aspect. It enacts the traumatic experience without transforming it, incorporating it without being capable of transcending it. In the metonymic mode of witnessing, any transcendence is experienced as a split between the person and his or her identity.

To these two modes, I would like to add what I refer to as "the psychotic mode of witnessing". This mode of witnessing attacks every possible link with the trauma, separating between the person and his or her memories, as well as between the person and his or her own sense of selfhood. This modality includes two sub-modalities, or two subcategories: "the *Muselmann*[4] subcategory" and "the excessive subcategory".

The *Muselmann* mode of witnessing has only rare narrative manifestations, since it essentially attacks both the ability to narrate and language itself. The post-Holocaust literature includes diverse expressions of this mode in the form of survivors' accounts, some of which appear in the form of a semi-psychotic type of discourse, both intra-psychic and inter-psychic, a discourse that annihilates any contact with the psychic reality and the pain it involves. This mode of witnessing is founded neither on the ability to shift between the first and the third person of experience (like in the metaphoric mode) nor on the capacity to stay exclusively in the first person of experience (like in the metonymic mode). In fact, it destroys both the first person and the third person, and thereby the very possibility of an experiencing subject. This testimonial mode joins the traumatic "Real" without being able to distance itself from it on the one hand, or to create a vital link with it on the other. When the dominant mode of testimony is the *Muselmann* mode, trauma turns into a *negative possession* (Amir, 2012, 2014, 2016a, 2018): a psychic condition that annihilates both the capacity to represent the traumatic event as well as the ability to preserve vital contact with it.

Primo Levi (1959) writes:

> All the *Mussulmanns* who finished in the gas chambers have the same story, or more exactly, have no story; [. . .] the divine spark dead within them, already too empty to really suffer. One hesitates to call them living: one hesitates to call their death death, in the face of which they have no fear, as they are too tired to understand. They crowd my memory with their faceless presences, and if I could enclose all the evil of our time in one image, I would choose this image which is familiar to me: an emaciated man, with head dropped and shoulders curved, on whose face and in whose eyes not a trace of a thought is to be seen.
>
> *(p. 103)*

In the *Muselmann* mode, trauma operates like an impoverishing, reductive, and sterilizing mechanism, turning the entire internal discourse into one that separates both between the subject and the traumatic object as well as between the subject and his own self. In this state, the subject can neither distance him or herself from the trauma – nor approach it. This form of survival is not that of the "living dead", but rather that of the "neither dead nor alive".

The excessive subcategory, by contrast, is a much more illusory one. Here the traumatic object becomes an addictive and gratifying object in its own right, one whose totality replaces the functional sense of being. In this mode of witnessing, traumatic excessiveness is available to consciousness neither by way of an elaborate link (as in the metaphoric mode) nor by way of repetition (as in the metonymic mode). Witnessing in this case involves the traumatic memory becoming a "saturated object" (Bion, 1962a, 1962b, 1959, 1970), an object that resists transformation and to which the obstinate adherence becomes malignant. The illusiveness characteristic of this mode is related to its deceptive combination of a highly developed rhetoric on the one hand and a massive "attack on linking" (Bion, 1959) on the other. Adherence to the excessiveness of suffering and the traumatic object's imperviousness to new meanings or any other processes of change turn traumatic repetition into "a thing in itself" (*das Ding*). As opposed to the *Muselmann* mode, which annihilates both the first person and the third person of report, the excessive mode creates a pseudo–first person, a pseudo–third person and a pseudo-movement between them.

Lacan (1958) discusses the formation of subjectivity as being based on an experience of lack. The subject, according to him, is constituted at the point in time when he or she enters the "Symbolic order" through the mother's interpretation of the Real. Along with the experience itself, the infant is given an interpretation that renders the experience meaningful by introducing it into the order of language. Experiences that are attributed to an "identical category" come together to form what the child experiences as that category: pain, tickling, cold, missing. There is, however, always a remainder or surplus that stays outside this junction. This surplus, lost in the process of symbolization and thus remaining outside the order of language, becomes the object of desire. Psychic motion is always directed towards this object of desire, and it is through this motion that the subject is constituted *qua* living subject. In contrast to the common concept of the satisfying object, Lacan introduces the lack of the object as constitutive to the creation of the subject in the first place. No psychic motion will ensue without the experience of lack (Amir, 2014, 2016a, 2018).

The excessive mode of witnessing creates, through the consummate totality of the traumatic object, an illusion of fusion without lack, fusion which allows a lingering in the Real at the cost of the formation of both subject and subjectivity. The deceptiveness of this mode of witnessing is related to its intensive linguistic nature: while the register of the Real precedes language and in many ways also opposes it, the overt manifestation of the excessive mode is not an absence of language. On the contrary, it often presents articulate and well-developed language, with a wealth of rhetorical features. But underneath the rhetorical surface, this is a language that attacks rather than produces linking; a saturated language, one that under the guise of "full testimony" presents what Cathy Caruth (1996) calls "empty grammar": a grammar that empties the event, thus does not allow for its subjects to undergo transformation. And so while the excessive mode might well be replete with metaphors, the metaphoric mode, as I will show, might in fact be comparatively minor and minimalistic. Rather than by the presence or absence of overt linguistic characteristics, like metaphors, these two modes are distinguished by means of whether they are employed to link or to split.

Every testimonial narrative constitutes a certain combination of these four modes, marking zones of psychic transformation versus zones of saturated thinking, zones of linking versus zones of compulsive repetition, zones in which testimony annihilates the witness versus zones in which it constitutes him or her as such.

Agamben (2002) writes:

> To bear witness is to place oneself in one's own language in the position of those who have lost it, to establish oneself in a living language as if it were dead, or in a dead language as if it were living. [. . .] What cannot be stated, what cannot be archived is the language in which the author succeeds in bearing witness to the incapacity to speak. In this language, a language that survives the subjects who spoke it coincides with a speaker who remains beyond it.
>
> *(pp. 161–162)*

Since every testimonial narrative is an intersection between "what cannot be stated" and what is actually spoken, every act of testimony is simultaneously a collapse and a formation of language: a collapse of language, since bearing witness to what cannot be testified renders testimony a meaningless event, or one that conveys "archival meaning" (Agamben, 2002) only; and a formation of language, since where language succeeds to speak not in spite of the lacuna but in its name, not beyond it but through it, it becomes a real event of testimony, one that constitutes the subject of witnessing as such.

In each of these testimonial modes, language collapses in a singular way.

The metonymic mode collapses into repetition, allowing no room for reflection. It creates an experiential continuity between subject and traumatic event, thereby preserving a psychic outline, but in fact remains trapped in this outline without the freedom to retrospectively reconstruct the traumatic memory.

The excessive mode collapses into rhetoric. Via linguistic excessiveness, it creates an artificial bridge over the traumatic lacuna, but this excessiveness does not create a vital link; rather it constitutes a hollow, addictive syntax which fixates the traumatic object at the center while pushing the reflective subject to the margins.

The *Muselmann* mode collapses into the traumatic abyss itself. Here is where testimony is at its fullest and emptiest simultaneously: one that is present only in the form of its absence.

The metaphoric mode collapses into language while also constituting language. To this Agamben alludes when he speaks of the ability to intersect what is said with what cannot be stated: the *Muselmann* with the survivor. This is the only mode that can contain the uncanny "background noise", which cannot be transformed, along with the "speaker who remains beyond it" (Agamben, p. 162). The movement between different states (the position of the victim and the position of the witness, the experiential I and the narrating I, the *heimlich* and the *unheimlich*) which the metaphoric mode enables, creates the necessary intersection of dead language with living language. Amos Goldberg (2012) writes that "trauma is directed opposite to the trajectory of a life story" (p. 102). One can therefore think of the metaphoric mode as the site of struggle between the formative power of the life story and the destructive power of the trauma, with the latter prevailing.

The Language of the Perpetrator: Screen Confessions and the "Newspeak"

The perfect crime, as Jean-François Lyotard (1989) claims, does not consist of killing the victim but rather of obtaining the silence of the witness, the deafness of the judges and the inconsistency of the testimony. If one neutralizes the addressor, the addressee and the significance of the testimony, the result is that there is no referent: no crime has been committed. When, in other words, the witness is blind, the judge is deaf and the testimony has lost coherence and meaning, the crime goes unregistered and hence allegedly never happened.

The present section focuses on the ways in which the perpetrator "erases the referent" by silencing her or his inner witness and inner judge, turning the entire testimonial text into a false representation of a coherent discourse that in fact undermines its own validity. This erasure, as will be shown, is achieved by the emergence of a double language, one marked by a dissociation between its explicit and its implicit meaning. While claiming to generate meaning and adhering to a chronological sequence, this language creates what George Orwell (1949) called *Newspeak*: a language that rewrites factual and emotional history alike. This Newspeak yields a phenomenon that I call *screen confessions* (Amir, 2017): voluntary confessional texts produced by perpetrators of their own free will, which share the main characteristic of subtly and unconsciously subverting themselves. The notion of screen confessions was chosen to allude to Freud's *screen memories* (1899). Unlike the notion of screen memory – which refers to the way in which a relatively marginal memory covers another emotionally charged one that cannot be remembered – the notion of screen confession refers not to memory itself, but to how it is construed in language. Omitted from this kind of confession are not the concrete facts, but their meaning. Distortion or error do not inhere in the factual details, but in the syntax that interferes in different ways with the original (true) utterance, taking away its meaning even if all of its components are accurate and correct.

This brings to mind Fromm's (1941/1994) notion of the social character. In his discussion of the ways in which a given culture or society mediates what can or cannot penetrate consciousness, Fromm discusses three such socially conditioned filters: language, logic and social taboos. In the case of language, Fromm points out that the ability of certain affective experiences to enter consciousness is dependent on the degree to which a particular language can accommodate the potential experience. The whole structure of language, its grammar, syntax and so on, acts as a kind of boundary for aspects of experience (Durkin, 2014; Fromm, 1941/1994). Thus, language colludes with cultural and social taboos by means of preserving the culture's "unspeakable" from being both thought and uttered.

Theodor Adorno (1951) writes:

> The leaders are generally oral character types[. . .] . The famous spell they exercise over their followers seems largely to depend on their orality: language itself, devoid of its rational significance, functions in a magical way and furthers those archaic regressions which reduce individuals into members of crowds.
>
> *(p. 132)*

What is this linguistic magic?

The perpetrator's language serves, in fact, as a *pseudo-language* (Amir, 2010, 2014): a language that produces a correct speech that lacks truthfulness. While being perfectly eloquent, it actually serves as a partition between the individual and her or his inner world, and eventually comes to hermetically insulate the person from the truth s/he cannot bear – instead of being the tool by means of which this truth can be thought and expressed.

The first thinker to discuss the perpetrator's unique (pseudo-)use of language was Hannah Arendt (1963), who focused on Eichmann's consistent use of stock phrases and self-invented clichés as well as his reliance on officialese (*Ámtssprache*) and the euphemistic *Sprachregelung*, all aimed at presenting his actions as marginal, on the one hand, and inevitable on the other – as part, that is, of a general mechanism that does not allow for the individual's responsibility for her or his actions. The accomplices in the plan to annihilate the Jews used a neutral verbal mode – "final solution", "mercy death", "euthanasia" and "special treatment" – instead of "extermination". This particular deployment of language, Arendt argues, played an important part in keeping the general public in the dark. But it also served, and not less importantly, to allow those who participated in the genocide to avoid confronting the clash between their current actions and their former moral norms (p. 86), enabling them in that way not to know their own deeds.

One can say that this deployment of language opens an abyss between signifier and signified. This abyss makes it possible to hygienically articulate unspeakable acts – but, over and beyond their being addressed in this way to the external audience, such a linguistic split also facilitates an internal split, within the speaker, between act and thought. Not only is the erasure of the link between signifier and signified thus made possible, but also the erasure of the link between the deliverer of the word and the word itself. Eventually, both the subject upon whom these acts are visited, as well as the subject who perpetrates them, are annihilated as subjects of language.

Arendt writes:

> Whether writing his memories in Argentina or in Jerusalem, whether speaking to the police examiner or to the court, what he [Eichmann] said was always the same,

> expressed in the same words. The longer one listened to him, the more obvious it became that his inability to speak was closely connected with an inability to *think*, namely, to think from the standpoint of somebody else. No communication was possible with him, not because he lied but because he was surrounded by the most reliable of all safeguards against the words and the presence of others, and hence against reality as such.
>
> *(p. 44)*

Elsewhere, Arendt quotes Eichmann commenting on himself: "Officialese is my only language" (pp. 43–44). Arendt made a brave and subversive effort, in many ways ahead of its time, to understand this singular "pathology" of the perpetrator's language. As she listened to this language, she noticed in it various forms of inversion. She described, for instance, the "trick" Himmler used to overcome the "animal compassion" every normal human being experiences in the face of physical suffering – a sensation that also visited Germans who witnessed their victims' pain:

> it consisted in turning these instincts around, as it were, in directing them towards the self. So that instead of saying: what horrible things I did to people!, the murderers would be able to say: what horrible things I had to watch in the pursuance of my duties, how heavily the task weighed upon my shoulders!
>
> *(p. 93)*

This inversion of positions is, indeed, one of the key "syntactic rules" of the perpetrator's language. Often in testimonies (e.g., those given to the South African Truth and Reconciliation Commission), the perpetrators consider themselves victims of the regime rather than responsible for it. Himmler's solution, however, represents a much higher level of sophistication. Here we have a linguistic solution that transforms the one who *causes* the suffering into *the object* of suffering, while completely dropping the actual object of suffering (i.e., the victim) from the entire syntactic structure. Now the perpetrator – who caused the suffering – occupies both ends of the statement, constituting both subject and object of the act. Where is the victim? In this scene, dominated throughout by the perpetrator, the victim has become a marginal figure, reduced to being the thing by means of which the perpetrator causes the suffering which he, due to his total commitment to his mission, has to endure (Amir, 2017).

The victim's elision from the syntactic structure is by no means accidental. Rather, it reflects the subtle and consistent ways by which the perpetrator's language eliminates the meaning of the very events it describes. However, it is not only the victim whom this language obscures. In the end, through a circular move, it makes the perpetrator himself or herself, *qua* speaking and thinking subject, superfluous. Himmler erases not merely his "animal feelings" toward his victims' suffering (as Arendt put it), but also his most vital feelings concerning himself – splitting, in Waintrater's (2015) words, the living I from the speaking I.

One telltale sign of perpetrators' language, evident across all types of testimony, whether of collective or of individual perpetrators (Dilmon, 2004, 2007), is the use of the grammatical passive form. The accounts of Nazi officers, for instance, show frequent use of passive rather than active constructions, evidencing frequent occurrences of "were shot" or "were forced" rather than "I shot" or "I forced". Unsurprisingly, the testimonies of those who refused orders are marked, in contrast, by the use of the first person singular and the active mode. This ostensibly negligible feature conveys the manner in which language is enlisted to hide and camouflage perpetrators' responsibility and the fact that they acted voluntarily – even where this language is deployed to reveal the truth.

Another characteristic of perpetrators' language is the constant creation of a false hierarchy of values, one in which a low moral value is featured to conceal the breach of a high moral value. One illustration of this false hierarchy can be found in a letter (quoted in its entirety in Daniel Goldhagen, 1996) by Captain Wolfgang Hoffmann, who was responsible for the slaughter of tens of thousands of Jews, but who protested indignantly against the claim that he or his men could have robbed Poles of food. This ostensibly marginal contradiction in fact discloses his way of construing the traumatic reality, a construal in which the amorality of the massacre is camouflaged by a pseudo-moral vigilance. In this manner, the commandment "Thou shalt not kill" is silenced not by denying the murderous acts themselves but by the vociferous defense of the precept "Thou shalt not steal", which thus comes to serve as a cover-up.

Many SS officers after World War II admitted that they were motivated by a feeling that, if they managed to overcome their repugnance toward their own actions, this would make them more faithful soldiers in the service of a greater power for the sake of which they must overcome their "human limitations". This is another linguistic circularity characteristic of perpetrators' speak: the expression "human limitations", which usually refers to a person's difficulty in restraining her or his hostile feelings and summoning the best of their humanity, is here transformed into a perception of human-ness itself as a limitation that prevents one, with its "inferior" and "animal-like" emotions such as compassion and remorse, to carry out the required actions against humanity. As defined by Bollas' (1992) paper on the fascist state of mind, "professionalism" is the ability to overcome human identifications, to go beyond any feelings of love or hatred, and to execute orders "hygienically" simply because they are orders.

An appalling illustration of this type of "professionalism" is Milgram's (1974) (in)famous experiment, which, portraying itself as concerning processes of learning, led participants to administer increasingly powerful electric shocks to members of the research team, presented as participants who seemed to give the wrong answers. Sixty-five percent of the participants administered the maximum – apparently lethal – electric shock. Many participants perspired, stuttered, trembled – indicating that they were not unaware of what they were doing and the possible consequences, yet they did as they were told. The operative instruction that caused them to push the button was "the experiment requires that you continue". These words, carefully chosen – rather than characterizing the task as one in which a singular subject is acting on another singular subject – frame the setting as one in which an object acts on behalf of the experiment on another object; they silence, at least as far as it concerns the "true participants" (the ones who administer the electric shocks), the two subjects involved in the situation. But something else, too, is happening here: the longer the chain of command, and the less significant the role of the person in this chain, the easier it is for this person to deny the overall meaning of the orders s/he obeys. As the chain grows longer, the details of the act it accomplishes grow vaguer, fuzzier and more incomprehensible. When all a person is required to do is push a button during a scientific experiment, s/he will not consider themselves the cause of another person's pain, a person who momentarily is also perceived as an object hooked up to the other end of an electric wire rather than a fellow human being, and who – like the one who pushes the button – is nothing but a component in an experiment, an object in the service of something larger: the research, the experiment, science itself.

Perpetrators' language's denial has countless forms and manifestations. One such manifestation can be found in the testimony of Albert Fisher, a staff member at Lublin during World War II. In his testimony, Fisher describes another staff member, Max Dietrich, who was known for his extreme cruelty towards the Jewish prisoners. His testimony, quoted in Goldhagen (1996), focuses on one incident where a prisoner was beaten by Dietrich until he lost consciousness. Dietrich then forced other prisoners to pour water on his face, and, when he woke up, forced him to eat his own feces. At this moment, Fisher states: "I left because it disgusted me". The testimonial text creates here an interesting, though almost invisible, ambiguity: it can be understood as a statement of disagreement with Dietrich's cruel actions, but it can also be received in its simple concreteness. Fischer did not turn away because his friend's cruelty disgusted him, but because the sight of the man eating his own feces made him sick. Thus, the overt declaration of "turning away", allegedly "taking a stand", may mask the possibility that what made him turn away was not his empathy towards the human prisoner but rather the opposite: his inability to bear this unbelievable horror-show of the prisoner's naked humanity (Amir, 2017).

Another kind of denial can be found in the transcripts of interviews by Claude Lanzmann with Benjamin Murmelstein[5] in the documentary "The Last of the Unjust" (2013), dealing with Jewish collaboration with the Nazis in World War II. At one moment Murmelstein recounts how Hans Guenther, the German ghetto commander, called him in and asked what he thought about the film made of Theresienstadt[6] after Murmelstein's renovations of the ghetto, a propaganda film which misleadingly presented the place as the Nazis' paradise for Jews. Murmelstein tells Guenther that he thinks the film is "terrible": "Though I can understand why it doesn't show decrepit old people with one foot in the grave, it's ridiculous to show a camp where people just sing, who would believe that?" This moment is fascinating in terms of how it works as a screen confession. Here Murmelstein can be seen to "switch sides", looking at things, that is, from the Nazis' point of view rather than that of the Jews. He understands that as the Nazis see it, the point is to create a credible presentation, not one that is too utopian and unrealistic. But this moment, when he comments "terrible", is ambiguous: from the Jews' point of view, the film is terrible because it presents a fake image that glosses over the horrors with which they live. From the perspective of the Nazis, however, the film is terrible not because it fails to capture reality but because it fails to achieve its purpose, that is, it fails to disguise that reality. While Murmelstein offers his answer to Guenther as proof of his "putting himself on the line by telling the truth", as he declares, the truth he presents here is not the one he pretends to present. Thus, when he declares "I did not collaborate with their comedy", he actually exposes his very collaboration with the tragedy (Amir, 2019b).

Efrat Even-Tzur and Uri Hadar (2017), following Lacan and Žižek, suggest a distinction between the identification of the perpetrator with a "living father" and his or her identification with a "dead father":

> The identification of an agent of Law [. . .] with a "Living Father" [. . .] expresses such a belligerent and tyrant subject position that it does not seek any legitimacy or justification of its authority. The father is "living" in a sense similar to the vitality of the tyrant father of the primeval tribe in "Totem and Taboo", who takes pleasure in his power to rule, intimidate and determine arbitrary rules that he is not subjected to personally. On the other hand, the identification of an agent of Law with a "Dead Father" is identification with a fair, equal law that does not represent personal interests and desires. The father is "dead" or "castrated" in the sense that he does not experience absolute *Jouissance* but is, too, restricted by the law (Lacan, 1959/2006, 1960/2006; Žižek, 1994, 1999).
>
> *(p. 5)*

Taking Even-Tzur and Hadar's ideas one step forward: the split between the "Living Father" and the "Dead Father", or between the sadistic and obedient, may occur not only *between* perpetrators (who may divide into those who identify with the "Living Father" and find a sadistic pleasure in their power versus those who perceive themselves as merely obedient and take no pleasure from it), but also *within* perpetrators. One may assume, therefore, that both modes of identification exist within every perpetrator with varying dominance, and that confessional texts of perpetrators may thereby expose not only their dominant mode of identification, but also the relation and interaction between the two modes.

The screen quality of the perpetrator's confession is thus associated with the fact that it has a twofold function: while the explicit act of confession restores the position of the "Dead Father" – who is restricted by the law – the implicit act of confession comes to camouflage the "Living Father" who takes pleasure from his power. While the explicit act aims to constitute the subject as a subject within language, its implicit counterpart erases the subject as a subject within language. In order to maintain this complex structure, the perpetrator must at one and the same time confess and subvert this confession. These dyads (the living Father vs. the dead Father; the speaker as a subject of language vs. the speaker as a subject erased by language; language as an act of linking vs. language as an attack on linking) can be seen to make up the entire "language rules" used by perpetrators of all kinds. For instance, the use of passive constructions along with the third person and first person plural, rather than active constructions and the first person singular, not only removes the speaker from the event s/he describes, but also aims to extend the splitting between the "dead Father" and the "living Father", thus keeping out of consciousness the pleasure that the use of the first person singular and the active constructions would reveal. The use of "we" distributes pleasure among the many, while the use of the passive helps speakers to place themselves in a masochistic position in order to mask their own sadism. The common displacement of the victim position from the victim to the victimizer serves the same purpose: as the victimizer shifts attention to the injustice of the law – what Kant and Arendt called "reflexive judgment" (i.e., responsibility for personal injustice and the personal regime or law that allowed one to act in this particular way) is set aside. The ambiguity and circularity of the perpetrator's language has a similar goal: taking the guise of logic and morality, they allow one to construct a false logical and moral hierarchy (Amir, 2017).

In his article "The Fascist State of Mind", Bollas (1992) argues that, in this mindset, the space previously taken up by a plurality of meanings in the symbolic order is colonized by slogans. As long as the internal regime was democratic, words and symbols were free to associate with other words and symbols. But when representation becomes obstructed, signifiers lose this freedom. The elimination of the symbolic and the pluralistic is the fascist regime's first act of murder: this is because the symbolic, always unbinding any fixed meaning and undermining any act of solidarity, is the true subversive element of thought. Arendt (1963) observes similar qualities in Eichmann's language: "He was genuinely incapable of uttering a single sentence that was not a cliché" (p. 44). A cliché is not merely a turn to the lowest common denominator, as is commonly assumed, but also comes to make thinking itself superfluous, fixating it as a field of saturated meanings (Bion, 1962a, 1962b). "Language can function as a living system of signs which grants meaning to the encounter between the internal world and reality", writes Roth (2017), "and it can also serve as a 'fossil' in and of itself – a 'dead' sign system, which 'points toward' but never establishes a 'link with' what is signified. In this case, the sign functions without its symbolic quality" (p. 186). Screen confessions are not only linguistic fossils, as Roth argues, but also take on a radioactive quality, as Gampel (1999, 2017) has put it. As such they have an impact that goes beyond the immediate to the intergenerational; they influence, over and beyond their "official" recipients, those who are their passive audience and who unwittingly absorb the radiation.

When the disease is the splitting of language, the one possible basis for recovery is to reclaim language. Such reclaiming, in the case of perpetrators' confessions, implies restoring the function of the inner witness, the function of the inner judge and the function of creating meaning so that the testimonial event will turn from a pseudo-performance into a vital event – one in which the subject, facing her or his concrete or imaginary victims, will be fully present.

The Intersection of the Language of the Victim and the Language of the Victimizer

Much like the language of the victim, the language of the victimizer is characterized by different modes of testimony. In victimizers' testimonies, whether voluntarily or forcibly delivered, one can notice metaphorical or transformative areas of testimony, that is, testimonial areas which create a vital link between the subject and the weight and meaning of his or her deeds. Other testimonial areas are characterized by a metonymic poetics, one in which the subject unconsciously repeats, within the testimonial text, the characteristics of the events to which he or she testifies. Within this category one can find, for instance, testimonial texts that empty out the human characteristics of both perpetrators and victims, thereby transforming both sides into objects rather than subjects. In the same manner, there are areas of false causality which justifies acts of violence. This false causality in fact repeats the very deceit it attests to, one in which the perpetrators commit violent acts that have no sensible justification – under the protection and screening mechanisms of legal and military rhetoric. Further metonymic characteristics of perpetrators' testimonies are the creation of a false moral hierarchy in which a low moral value is featured to conceal the breach of a higher moral value; the accompanying of the overt description of the concrete facts by all sorts of covert denial of their moral and emotional meaning; the displacement of the position of the victim to the perpetrator himself or herself; and, finally, various expressions of pseudo-regret and false gestures of contrition, producing an illusion of compassion in testimonies whose hidden agenda is to undo the evil rather than to recognize it (Amir, 2019b). These characteristics have one main thing in common: they metonymically enact, in the testimonial language itself, the contents to which this language testifies.

There is a mutual intersection of the language of the victim and the language of the perpetrator at the level of the excessive testimonial mode as well. While the excessive rhetoric of the victim creates a "hermetic narrative" (Amir, 2016b), one in which the audience constitutes in fact a captive, muted audience, convened for the purpose of passively validating the narrative merely by its presence – the excessive rhetoric of the perpetrator creates a false representation within which both the listener and the speaker are excluded as thinking subjects. Similarly to the way in which the victims' excessive testimonies poke a rhetoric wedge between the testifying subject and the trauma to which he or she testifies, perpetrators' screen testimonies poke a rhetoric wedge between them and their deeds to which they attest. The result is a sophisticated, meticulous and convincing narrative, based on what seems like a perfect logic, which actually excludes the speaker and the listener as subjects of thinking and language, "an event without a witness" (Felman and Laub, 1992) – one from which the most reliable witness, the speaker him or herself, is absent.

Contact with traumatic zones, on both sides of the barricade, tends to create a certain quality which I call the "malignant sublime". Immanuel Kant (1763–1764) demarcated the *beautiful* from the *sublime*. As a part of the natural world, *the beautiful* fulfills a clear purpose: it stimulates our power of judgment. *The sublime*, belonging in the metaphysical rather than the physical realm, namely in the domain of absolute rather than relative values, obviates our power of judgment. The notion of the "malignant sublime" refers to a tendency to confer "absolute value" on relative experiences. Where absolute values prevail, an autoimmune attack on thinking is triggered, perpetuating the status of the absolute victim and the absolute perpetrator rather than allowing both sides to transcend this repetitive scenario by recognizing the relativity of their positions and stands.

Aleksandar Hemon concludes his autobiographical essay titled "Pathologically Bilingual" with the following words:

> at a certain level, all literature is multilingual. In each literary text registers overlap, ambiguities and multiple possibilities abound. No language can have a single source. It is always a massively collective endeavor that does not stop at borders or walls. All languages overlap or spill into one another, just like people.[7]

This is exactly what transcending the state of the *malignant sublime* is about: to escape from the monolingual trap of "absolute value" into a state in which recognition of the overlapping regions of language replaces the oppressive walls that divide one language from another; in which linear directionality is replaced by a rhizomatic multiplicity (Deleuze and Guattari, 1972); in which different narratives are allowed to spill into one other without erasing each other; in which it is possible to declare that suffering, like literature, is always multilingual.

Notes

1 This chapter is based on a research supported by The Israel Science foundation (Grant no. 679/13,194/17).

2 Gerson (2009) refers to this as "the dead third": "The 'dead third' is conceptualized as the loss of a 'live third' upon whom the individual had previously relied, had entrusted with faith, and in relation to whom or which, had developed a sense of personal continuity and meaning. In this regard, the third [. . .] serves the elemental function of solidifying an individual's sense of person, place, and purpose. [. . .] Under such circumstances, the living thirds in which the person was nested now become a nest of dead thirds from which he or she cannot escape" (ibid., p. 1343).

3 I draw on Astrid Erll (2011b, see also 2011a in this context), for whom "the distinction between an 'experiencing I' and a 'narrating I' already rests on a (largely implicit) concept of memory", or in other words, on the idea that there is a difference between pre-narrative experience on the one hand, and, on the other, narrative memory which creates meaning retrospectively.

4 *Muselmann* (pl. *Muselmänner*, German for "Muslim") was a term used among captives of Nazi concentration camps to refer to those of their fellow captives who, suffering from a combination of starvation (known also as "hunger disease") and exhaustion, had become apathetically resigned to their impending death.

5 Benjamin Murmelstein functioned as head of Theresienstadt's Judenrat. The third and last incumbent, he kept the Theresienstadt concentration camp going until the very last days of the war.

6 Constructed in 1941, Theresienstadt concentration camp, also referred to as Theresienstadt ghetto, was a unique location, which the Nazis selected to serve as a showcase – a "model ghetto", as Eichmann called it. In fact, it functioned as a concentration camp from which Jews were transferred to Auschwitz.

7 http://www.specimen.press/articles/pathologically-bilingual/

References

Adorno, T. (1951). Freudian theory and the pattern of fascist propaganda. In: A. Arato and E. Gebhardt (eds.) *The Essential Frankfurt School Reader*. Oxford: Blackwell, Part 1: pp. 118–137.

Agamben, G. (2002). *Remnants of Auschwitz: The Witness and the Archive* (trans: D. Heller-Roazen). New York: Zone Books.

Amir, D. (2010). From mother tongue to language. *Psychoanalytic Review* 97(4): 651–672.

Amir, D. (2012). The inner witness. *International Journal of Psycho-Analysis* 93(4): 879–896.

Amir, D. (2014). *Cleft Tongue: The Language of Psychic Structures*. London: Karnac Books.

Amir, D. (2016a). When Language meets the Traumatic Lacuna: The Metaphoric, the Metonymic and the Psychotic modes of testimony. *Psychoanalytic Inquiry* 36(8): 620–632.

Amir, D. (2016b). Hermetic narratives and false analysis: A unique variant of the mechanism of identification with the aggressor. *Psychoanalytic Review* 103(4): 539–549.

Amir, D. (2017). Screen confessions: A current analysis of Nazi Perpetrators' "Newspeak". *Psychoanalysis, Culture & Society* 23 (1): 97–114.

Amir, D. (2018). *Bearing Witness to the Witness: A Psychoanalytic Perspective on Four Modes of Traumatic Testimony*. London and New York: Routledge.

Amir, D. (2019a). The bilingualism of the language of the victim and the language of the victimizer. *Psychoanalytic Dialogues* 29(3): 367–381.

Amir, D. (2019b). The last of the unjust: Test case of a screen confession. *The International Journal of Psychoanalysis* 101(3): 597–610.

Arendt, H. (1963). *A Report on the Banality of Evil*. New York: The Viking Press.

Bion, W. (1959). Attacks on linking. *International Journal of Psychoanalysis* 40: 308–315.

Bion, W. (1962a). *Learning from Experience*. New York: Basic Books.

Bion, W. (1962b). The psycho-analytic study of thinking. *International Journal of Psychoanalysis* 43: 306–310.

Bion, W. (1970). *Attention and Interpretation*. London: Tavistock.

Bollas, C. (1992). The fascist state of mind. In: *Being a Character: Psychoanalysis and Self Experience*. New York: Routledge, pp. 193–217.

Camus, A. (1975). The Plague (trans: Stuart Gilbert). New York: Random House.

Caruth, C. (1996). *Unclaimed Experience: Trauma Narrative and History*. Baltimore, MD: Johns Hopkins University Press.

Deleuze, G., and Guattari, F. ([1972] 2005). *Anti-Oedipus* (trans: R. Hurley, M. Seem, and H. R. Lane). Minneapolis: University of Minnesota Press.

Dilmon, R. (2004). *Linguistic Differences between Lie and Truth in Spoken Hebrew*. PhD thesis. Ramat Gan, Israel: Bar-Ilan University.

Dilmon, R. (2007). Fiction or fact? Comparing true and untrue anecdotes. *Hebrew Linguistics* 59: 23–42.

Durkin, K. (2014). *The Radical Humanism of Erich Fromm*. New York: Palgrave Macmillan.

Erll, A. (2011a). *Memory in Culture*. Basingstoke: Palgrave Macmillan.

Erll, A. (2011b). Travelling memory. *Parallax, Special Issue: Transcultural Memory* 17(4): 4–18.

Even-Tzur, E., and Hadar, U. (2017). Agents of the father's law in a society of brothers: A philosophic and psychoanalytic perspective on legitimate use of violence. *International Journal of Law and Psychiatry* 51: 22–32.

Felman, S. (1992). Camus' the plague, or a monument to witnessing. In: S. Felman and D. Laub (eds.) *Testimony: Crises of Witnessing in Literature, Psychoanalysis, and History*. New York: Routledge, pp. 93–119.

Felman, S., and Laub, D. (1992). *Testimony: Crises of Witnessing in Literature, Psychoanalysis, and History*. New York: Routledge.

Freud, S. ([1899] 1962). Screen memories. In: *Standard Edition 3*. London: Hogarth Press, pp. 299–322.

Fromm, E. ([1941]1994). *Escape From Freedom*. Henry Holt and Company. New York: Owl Books Edition.

Gampel, Y. (1999). Between the background of safety and the background of uncanny in the context of social violence. In: E. Bott Spillius (ed. in chief) *Psychoanalysis on the Move*. London: Routledge, pp. 59–74.

Gampel, Y. (2017). Evil. In: R. Lazar (ed.) *Talking about Evil*. London and New York: Routledge, pp. 1–16.

Gerson, S. (2009). When the third is dead: Memory, mourning, and witnessing in the aftermath of the holocaust. *International Journal of Psychoanalysis* 90: 1341–1357.

Goldberg, A. (2012). *Trauma in First Person*. O-Yehuda: Kinneret, Zmora-Bitan, Dvir Publishing House; Beer-Sheva: Heksherim Institute, Ben Gurion University of the Negev.

Goldhagen, D. (1996). *Hitler's Willing Executioners: Ordinary Germans and the Holocaust*. New York: Random House.

Hemon, A. (15.9.2016). Pathologically bilingual. *Specimen: The Babel Review of Translations*. www.specimen.press/articles/pathologically-bilingual.

Jakobson, R. (1956). Two aspects of language and two types of aphasic disturbances. *Fundamentals of Language* 55.

Kant, I. ([1763–64] 1960). *Observations on the Feeling of the Beautiful and the Sublime*. Oakland, CA: University of California.

Kohut, H. (1971). *The Analysis of the Self*. New York: International Universities Press.

Lacan, J. ([1959] 2006). On a question prior to any possible treatment of psychosis. In: *Écrits: The First Complete Edition in English* (trans: B. Fink). New York: W. W. Norton, pp. 445–488.

Lacan, J. ([1960] 2006). The subversion of the subject and the dialectic of desire in the Freudian unconscious. In: *Écrits: The First Complete Edition in English* (trans: B. Fink). New York: W. W. Norton.

Lacan, J. (1977). The function and field of speech and language in psychoanalysis. In: *Écrits ([1958] 2007)* (trans: A. Sheridan). New York: Norton, pp. 30–113.

LaCapra, D. (2001). *Writing History, Writing Trauma*. Baltimore, MD: Johns Hopkins University Press.
Laub, D. (2005). Traumatic shutdown of narrative and symbolization. *Contemporary Psychoanalysis* 41: 307–326.
Laub, D., & Auerhahn, N. (1993). Knowing and not knowing: Forms of traumatic memory. *International Journal of Psychoanalysis* 74: 287–302.
Levi, P. (1959). *If This Is a Man* (trans: S. Woolf). New York: The Orion Press.
Lyotard, J.-F. (1989). The differend: Phrases in dispute. In: *Theory and History of Literature*, Vol. 46 (trans: G. Van Den Abbeele). Minnesota: University of Minnesota Press.
Milgram, S. (1974). *Obedience to Authority: An Experimental View*. New York: Harper and Row.
Modell, A. (2006). *Imagination and the Meaningful Brain*. Cambridge, MA: MIT Press.
Moore, R. (1999). *The Creation of Reality in Psychoanalysis*. Hillsdale, NJ: The Analytic Press.
Oliner, M. (1996). External reality: The elusive dimensions of psychoanalysis. *Psychoanalytic Quarterly* 65: 267–300.
Orwell, G. (1949). *1984*. London: Secker and Warburg.
Roth, M. (2017). The restorative power of reading literature: From evil to dialectics. In: R. Lazar (ed.) *Talking about Evil*. London: Routledge, pp. 181–199.
Stern, D. B. (2012). Witnessing across time: Accessing the present from the past and the past from the present. *Psychoanalytic Quarterly* 81: 53–81.
Van der Kolk, B., McFarlane, A., & Weisaeth, L. (1996). *Traumatic Stress: The Effects of Overwhelming Experience on Mind, Body, and Society*. New York: The Guilford Press.
Waintrater, R. (2015). Body image and identity in victims of extreme violence. In: E. Sukhanova and H.-O. Tomashoff (eds.) *Body Image and Identity in Contemporary Society: Psychoanalytic, Social, Cultural and Aesthetic Perspectives*. London and New York: Routledge, pp. 49–55.
Žižek, S. (1994). *The Metastases of Enjoyment: Six Essays on Women and Causality*. London and New York: Verso.
Žižek, S. (1999). *The Ticklish Subject: The Absent Centre of Political Ontology*. London and New York: Verso.

PART II

Psychoanalytic Schools and Their Philosophical Perspectives

9

FREUD AND THE UNCONSCIOUS

Marcia Cavell

Born in Vienna, Sigmund Freud (1856–1939) created and developed psychoanalysis. Along with Karl Marx and Albert Einstein he is widely considered one of the most significant, if controversial, figures of the twentieth century. Richard Wollheim writes:

> Operating from a private medical practice in Vienna, which he maintained from Easter, 1886, until he was forced into exile in 1938, Sigmund Freud. . . revolutionized the thought, the lives, and the imagination of an age. He contradicted, and in some cases, he reversed, the prevailing opinions, of the learned as well as of the common people, on many of the issues of human existence and culture. . . . It would be hard to find in the history of ideas, even in the history of religion . . . someone whose influence was so immediate, so broad, and so deep.
>
> *(Wollheim. 1971, pp. ix–x)*

Freud's most significant contribution to philosophy, specifically the philosophy of mind, is the concept of the unconscious. The importance Freud assigned to it, with its essential tie to the concept of repression, is the central feature that differentiates psychoanalysis from other psychological theories. Freud sometimes said that poets and thinkers had long known of the unconscious but that it had been left to him to give a scientific account.

This essay will explore the unconscious and its subsidiary concepts in the chronological order in which Freud expounds them. The chronology cannot be strict, however, as the explorations overlap. At the end is a section on irrationality and self-deception which should be of particular interest to philosophers.

1 Beginnings

Freud began his professional life in neurology and pathological medicine. In the years 1886–1889, he went from Vienna to Paris where he worked under the famous physician Jean-Martin Charcot, who was treating patients suffering from hysteria, a condition that affected both mind and body but that had no known physiological cause.

Charcot believed that hysteria can arise from traumatic psychological events as well as from ones that are physical. He had discovered that the symptoms of hysteria, for example, vomiting,

DOI: 10.4324/9780429297076-12

or paralysis of a limb, or the "forgetting" of one's own language, could sometimes be relieved by the use of hypnosis, and conversely that hypnosis could produce the symptoms. Thus, it was clear that an idea (in the form of a command) could work outside of consciousness to motivate behavior. The investigation of traumatic hysteria clearly revealed cases in which a patient's behavior could not be explained without reference to certain ideas of which the patient had no awareness. Conversely, such behavior could be induced intentionally by hypnosis.

Freud's work under Charcot set him off on a new career, and it encouraged three insights that became the foundation of psychoanalysis. The first was that one could remove pathological symptoms through the use of words. – Later Freud would come to understand that these words needed to be said in the setting of a particular kind of relation between patient and therapist. – The second was that the symptoms too could be traced to ideas. And the last was that a theory of the mind could be formed that would validate the therapy. Thus, psychoanalysis has a triadic nature: it is at once a theory of the mind, a form of therapy, and a theory of the therapy, any one of which might be correct and the others false.

The therapy was at first hypnosis. This form of therapy was followed by another in which, again under hypnosis, the patient talks, giving the physician information relevant to her condition and thereby ridding herself of the symptom. Freud called this the "cathartic" method. Here is the beginning of Freud's use of free association, in which the fully conscious patient is encouraged to say whatever comes to her mind without censoring it.

Along with these changes in therapy came a change in diagnostic account, according to which the disorder might be traced to a childhood constellation of experiences and events. This led to the so-called "seduction theory" according to which the innocent child, typically between the ages of six to eight, had been seduced by an adult, usually a parent, an idea that is expressed in the famous phrase: "hysterics suffer mainly from reminiscence." Later Freud wrote to his friend and mentor, Wilhelm Fliess, of his growing disbelief in this theory, for one thing because of its improbability, and for another because he had become convinced of the role of wish and desire in much of human activity. Accordingly, he thought that the ideas that account for the symptoms are repressed representations of wish and desire, a phenomenon he would come to call (unconscious) "phantasy." (I use the traditional psychoanalytic spelling to distinguish this form of psychic activity from conscious fantasy or daydreaming.) Freud went on to claim that a phantasied seduction can play the same causal role in psychological development as a real seduction, an idea psychoanalysts refers to as "psychic reality."

Controversy has swirled around this change for years Some critics have scolded Freud for letting real seducers off the hook; others for finding seductions where they didn't exist (see Crews, 2017). Later Freud would find unconscious phantasy at work in normal activities such as jokes, dreams, and slips of the tongue (see "The Psychopathology of Everyday Life," *SE* 1901, 6).[1]

The role of desire in human activity led to a clarification in the concept of the unconscious and to the crucial concept of repression. Whereas at first Freud had thought that the difference between a conscious and an unconscious idea was merely a matter of strength, he came to realize that the ideas can be equally strong; in the revised theory an unconscious idea is accounted for by the mental force of repression, which expresses itself in therapy in the form of resistance. Through repression, the wish retains its power while the relevant ideas serve both to express and cover it. The concept of repression is what distinguishes Freud's idea of the unconscious from earlier articulations, of which there were many (see Ellenberger, 1981). For example, what I had for dinner last night might be unconscious merely in the sense that it is not presently in mind. – Freud calls this the "descriptive" unconscious. The phenomenon of resistance, however, points to a repressive force that is keeping the motivating ideas unconscious. This introduces the idea of the "dynamic" unconscious, and with it the concept of the unconscious as a system. The essential characteristics of the unconscious as a system (Freud calls it the *Ucs.*) are the following: a) its contents are representatives of the instincts; b) these contents are governed by "primary process," particularly condensation and displacement. Condensation can be seen in dream formation, where one thought or image can represent simultaneously multiple and even contrary ideas, as when a white camellia might stand both for purity and, via "la Dame aux Camellias," sexual license. In displacement, a significance which properly attaches to one idea is given to another. Primary process is used for the purpose of disguise in both symptom and dream formation. There it is the principal mechanism of what Freud calls "dream work." c) It is more specifically childhood wishes that become fixated in the unconscious.

2 *Project for a Scientific Psychology* (*SE* 1950/1895, 1)

The roots of Freud's concept of the unconscious lie first in his work with hysteria, as noted, and second in a physiological theory of the mind that he developed in a posthumously published work, *Project for a Scientific Psychology*. He never gave up hope that a theory could be found that reduces mind to physiology, though he admitted in his 1915 essay, "The Unconscious" (*SE* 14), that for now we have to be content with a mentalistic vocabulary.

In the "Project" Freud enunciates a principle of inertia as the law governing the functioning of the "psychic apparatus." This economic point of view, as he calls it, qualifies "everything having to do with the hypothesis that psychical processes consist in the circulation and distribution of energy (instinctual energy); psychological processes can be quantified" (Laplanche and Pontalis, 1973, p. 127). The energy is mobile, i.e. easily displaced from one idea to another. This notion allows Freud to say how a seemingly important event in one's life can be evoked with indifference, while a seemingly unimportant idea can be painful or exciting. "Mobility of cathexis," which is one of the characteristics of primary process, refers also to the fact that energy seeks discharge by the shortest route possible, thereby producing phantasies and dreams rather than genuine satisfactions in the external world.

The philosopher Richard Wollheim characterizes phantasy as an instance of

> iconic imagining, an activity or a state caused by a wish or desire in which we represent the world as it might be if the wish or desire were fulfilled. Desire characteristically expresses itself in imaginative acts which tend to leave the imaginer in a condition appropriate to what they represent. Angry and wishing to express one's anger in a violent form, one imagines doing so and feels to some extent gratified in the process.
>
> *(1984, p. 185)*

The economic point of view posits a difference between sensory neurones, which receive stimuli, and motor neurons, which contain energy that derives from stimuli. Tension is eradicated in the first place by motor activity, e.g. flight. What Freud calls "the constancy principle," which seeks to keep the energy in a system constant, would seem to reduce energy to zero, but for the fact that stimuli also derive from inside the organism, from instinct and appetite, which manifest themselves as need, desire and wish. Internal needs can be fully discharged only if the external world satisfies them. But wish, an embryonic form of desire, causes, like physical need, an increase in tension and may arise either from the memory of a wished-for object, or from an image invested with the intensity of a perception, the "hallucinatory wish-fulfillment" of *The Interpretation of Dreams* (*SE* 1900, 4 & 5). Thus, wish seeks satisfaction indifferently in the external and the internal worlds, primarily through phantasy. To protect itself from phantasy the organism must develop patience: discharge must wait for an indication of reality, which comes from consciousness. This is an aspect of what Freud calls "secondary process."

3 First Exploration of the Unconscious: *The Interpretation of Dreams* (*SE* 1900, 4 & 5)

Freud presents his first exploration of the unconscious in *The Interpretation of Dreams*. Note that interpretation is a form of explanation appropriate only to texts, doings, or utterances that are meaningful, meaningful not only to the interpreter but also to the author. Wet streets, thunder, a child's spotted skin, are meaningful to us. So, in a different sense are the words of a parrot. But since in none of these cases is there an agent who might mean something by them, interpretation in the sense used here is not in order. The idea that dreams can be interpreted implies, then, Freud's basic premise that dreams are not idle excrescences of sleep but mental events with meaning to the dreamer.

Freud writes: "The interpretation of dreams is the royal road to a knowledge of the unconscious" (*SE* 5, p. 608). In his view every dream represents a particular state of affairs as one wishes it were. Its content and its meaning are the fulfillment of a wish. But there are important qualifications: every dream is the (disguised) fulfillment of a (repressed, sexual, infantile) wish.

A wish-fulfillment must bring pleasure; but the question is, to whom? To the person who has the dream, of course. "But as we know, a dreamer's relation to his wishes is a quite peculiar one. He repudiates them and censors them – he has no liking for them. . . ." (pp. 215–216). Thus, in a sense there are two separate people combined in a dream, one of whom has the wish and the other who repudiates it. Note that this is a partial account of Freud's concept of what we call "the self" and of what the philosopher and the layman call self-deception. Freud sees painful dreams as wish-fulfillments of the super-ego, or conscience.

Freud's examination of dreams, the errors of everyday life, what his editors call "parapraxes" (*The Psychopathology of Everyday Life* [*SE* 1901, 6]) – for example, the misplacing or the losing of an object – symptoms, and jokes all reveal the activity of wish or impulse in activities that we do not ordinarily think of as motivated "acts." In Part I of *Introductory Lectures on Psycho-Analysis* (*SE* 1916–17, 15 & 16), Freud writes that very often where chance is thought to reign there is an intention. His favorite example: the President of the Lower House of the Austrian Parliament who wished to declare the meeting as open instead declared it closed.

In later works Freud refers to symbolism in dreams, the fact that certain basic thoughts find a regular form of expression; for example, parents may be represented by kings and queens, a penis by a stick or an umbrella.

Freud calls dreams "the guardians of sleep" in that they prevent the dreamer from being awakened by a need or a wish.

Dreams are similar to symptoms in that both are disguised fulfillments of repressed wishes. As an example of a symptom Freud describes a woman – he refers to her as "the table-cloth lady" – who, separated from her husband for several years, obsessionally runs into the room next to her bedroom many times during the day, takes up a particular position next to a table on which she pours ink, rings the bell for the maid, then runs back into the bedroom, behavior as unintelligible to the woman at first as it is to Freud (*Introductory Lectures on Psychoanalysis*, 1916–1917, *S.E.* 15). As the case unfolds her behavior is linked to her husband's impotence on their wedding night. Many times, he had run back into the bedroom to try again but without success. The next morning, he had said that he would feel ashamed in front of the maid when she made the bed and had poured red ink on the sheet. As Freud and his patient finally reconstruct her "reasoning" she is repeating this traumatic scene, only now the table represents the bed, and she is imagining it is stained, as ideally it would have been, with her blood. Her repetition is then a kind of imaginative correction of her husband's impotence. Freud writes: "So the obsessional action was saying: 'No, it's not true. He had no need to feel ashamed in front of the housemaid; he was not impotent. It represented this wish, in the manner of a dream, as fulfilled in the present-day action" (1916–1917, p. 263).

Freud's earlier view of symptoms was that they were memories of a traumatic event, but in his mature view, what makes an event traumatic is that it contains an unconscious conflicted wish or impulse.

Freud's analysis of jokes along the lines of the analysis of dreams is far more complex and I omit discussion of it here.

4 "Repression" (*SE* 1915, 15)

In "History of the Psycho-Analytic Movement" Freud calls "the theory of repression the corner-stone on which the whole structure of psychoanalysis rests" (*SE*. 14, 1914, p. 16). He remarks that repression had been mentioned before by others but that his theory is new, basically because it emerges, like all his theories, from the clinical data, particularly the phenomenon of resistance. This was covered over when therapy was based on hypnosis: repression is revealed only through free association.

In "Repression" Freud asks the obvious question of why an instinct should undergo repression in the first place. He answers that a necessary condition is that the instinct's attainment of its aim, which normally would yield pleasure, instead produces unpleasure. This happens when the instinct's satisfaction is incompatible with other needs and intentions. Thus conflict occurs at the most basic instinctual level. Repression does not happen once but requires continual pressure, or "after-pressure"; otherwise the repression would cease and a new act of repression would be required.

5 "The Unconscious" (*SE* 14, 1915)

Freud's editors call the essay "The Unconscious" the most important of his theoretical writings. He begins with a defense of the concept, arguing that the usual equation of the mental with consciousness is untenable. First of all, there are gaps in consciousness which need somehow to be filled in. Ideas come into our heads from we know not where. Then too, without another order of the mental than consciousness we cannot explain the origin and meaning of dreams and parapraxes, nor understand the clinical phenomena of hypnosis, including post-hypnotic suggestion. Freud interestingly argues that in explaining their behavior we attribute mental acts to other people which to us are unknown; we do no more in explaining our own. The implication is that as other people are to some extent strangers – the philosophical problem of other minds – so we are to some extent strangers to ourselves. Freud compared his position on this matter as akin to Kant's on our perception of the external world, that we know it only as subjectively conditioned. So we must not equate our perception of mental processes with the objects themselves. – Presumably Freud means "thoughts" when he speaks of the "perception of mental processes." Freud adds, however, that we can learn of our unconscious processes to a degree to which we cannot know of objects in the external world.

Freud next distinguishes three perspectives from which we can describe the unconscious: the *descriptive*, the *dynamic*, and the *economic*. The first, as noted above, refers to ideas that are merely latent and not systematically different from conscious processes, as are those which were repressed. An idea that is dynamically unconscious manifests itself in behavior. The dynamic sense will be clearer when we come to Freud's later work, *The Ego and the Id* of 1923. And the economic, has to do with the hypothesis that psychical processes can be quantified, that they consist in the circulation and distribution of instinctual energy; that is, the energy is capable of increase, decrease and equivalence. It is the economic point of view to which the concept *cathexis* belongs. In effect the concept does no more than express an analogy between psychical operations and the workings of a nervous system in terms of energy. For example, an idea is said to be cathected if it is emotionally charged.

In Freud's mature view, everything in the psychic history of an individual is originally unconscious. Only under the influence of the external world do some mental contents become preconscious, and then, if the occasion arises, conscious. As this process goes on, the unconscious is replenished by fresh contents that are taken in, found unsuitable and repressed, so that the unconscious falls into two parts: that which was present originally and that which was acquired in the course of the ego's development.

Freud introduces the concept of the unconscious as a system, which he italicises. Its characteristics are "*exemption from mutual contradiction, primary process* (*mobility of cathexis* [including condensation and displacement, as in '*The Interpretation of Dreams*'], *timelessness, and replacement of external by psychical reality*. . . ." ("The Unconscious," *SE* 15, p. 187). In mentalistic language this means, for example, that in a dream or represented as both alive and dead; someone who is long dead may be represented as alive.

6 *The Ego and the Id* (*SE* 1923, 19)

The final phase of Freud's thinking about the unconscious gives us the "structural" theory of the mind, which divides it into the ego, the id, and the super-ego. Here Freud answers the question implicit in his earlier theories, namely, what is it that does the repressing? We have the unconscious and the conscious, but which, if either, is the force that represses? Freud answers that it is the ego. Part of it is unconscious, but not repressed. Thus, all that is repressed is unconscious; but not all that is unconscious is repressed.

The Id ("das Es" or "the it") is primarily instinctual. Its contents are unconscious, a portion of them being hereditary and innate, a portion repressed and acquired. The id conflicts with the ego and the super-ego, which are derived from the id. The word that Freud's editors translate as "instinct" is "Trieb," which means also "drive," or "urge." He has in mind the physiological concept of the reflex arc according to which a stimulus from the outside is applied to living tissue, then discharged by action to the outside. For example: light falling on the eye is not itself such a stimulus, but it is when it irritates the eye, causing it to water or to blink.

An instinctual impulse, on the other hand, arises from within the organism. When the stimulus is from the outside it can be discharged by flight; but an instinct equals a need, which cannot be eradicated by flight but only by satisfaction, either from the outside or in an illusory manner by phantasy or dream. The efficacy of muscular activity is a basis for distinguishing outside from inside the organism.

Freud writes: "The nervous system is an apparatus which has the function of getting rid of stimuli which reach it, or of reducing them to the lowest possible level" (*SE* 1923, 19, s. p. 120). Freud refers to this as "the constancy principle." Later he will say rather that its function is to get rid of stimuli altogether, which he calls "the nirvana principle," colloquially known as "the death instinct."

Now it is necessary to back to go the beginning and ask what an instinct is. In "Instincts and Their Vicissitudes" (*SE* 1915, 14) Freud defines "instinct" as

> a concept on the frontier between the mental and the somatic . . . a psychical representative of the stimuli originating from within the organism and reaching the mind

> as a measure of the demand made upon the mind for work in consequence of its connection with the body.
>
> *(pp. 121–122)*

In "Beyond the Pleasure Principle" (*SE* 1920, 18, p. 34) he speaks of instincts as "at once the most important and the most obscure element of psychological research."

As Freud thus himself acknowledges, "instinct," like "cathexis," is an ambiguous concept. Just what is this frontier? Frontiers can be crossed. Presumably in this case the passage is just one way, from body to mind. But how does body cross the frontier to mind and in what sense? How else do mind and body engage upon this frontier? How does a psychical event come to "represent" an instinct?

Freud is clearly attempting to deal with the philosophical mind-body problem. Descartes set the problem for modern times with his famous "Cogito" argument: "I think (or I doubt), therefore I am." But the "I" whose existence can be known with certainty, for Descartes, is only the *thinking* or the mental I, not the bodily I, which if it exists, must be of a different substance from the mind. Descartes then has two problems: first, knowing that the body exists; and second, showing how these two radically different substances, mind and body, interact. His solution is to posit the pineal gland as the site at which the interaction takes place, a mysterious interaction that Descartes doesn't explore.

Freud doesn't have the first problem since for him the ego, the "I," is bodily from the start, developing as it does from the Id, which is primarily physical, or neurological. But he does have the second, the "frontier" issue, which he acknowledges is problematic.

One way of posing the problem would be to make it a developmental question, that is, to ask at what point in the development of the infant brain can we accredit it with concepts; or when does the language of mind, not merely body, become appropriate? And how do these languages mesh? I might note that consciousness has equally resisted definition by philosophers. Just what is consciousness? To what sort of creature can we attribute it, and at what point in its life?

Freud always held a dual instinct theory, though his ideas about what the two are changed over time; and he always held that they can come into conflict with each other. In his early writings the conflict is described as between the ego and sexuality, later called "libido," a somatic tension regarded as a chemical process. "Ego" remained undefined for much longer. The "ego instincts" were in his writings first identified with the self-preservative instincts, and later included the repressive function.

The turn to a second dual instinct theory comes in *Beyond the Pleasure Principle* (*SE*. 18, 1920) where they are conceptualized as the life instincts versus the death instincts, the second working toward an eradication of all stimuli.

Freud's editors translate Freud's "das Ich" – the "I" – by the Latinate "ego," unfortunately blurring Freud's ordinary concept of "the self," referring as it does first of all to a person's self as a whole (including one's own body, as distinct from the bodies of other people). As a sub-system of the psyche "das Ich" partly replaces the earlier concept of consciousness, though the ego is not sharply differentiated from the id; rather it is that part of the id which has been modified by perceptions from the external world. The ego tries to bring the influence of the external world on the id and substitute the reality principle for the pleasure principle, for the id is governed naturally by the drive for pleasure and freedom from pain, while the ego largely represents reason and common sense.

Another factor in the formation of the ego (here meaning the sense of self) is the body, which is visible like any other object in space; but in addition the body receives two types of sensation derived from touch, the passive sensations of being touched, and the feelings which come from active touching. The latter, we might say, provide an early sense of agency, as when the infant grasps the bottle. The ego, Freud writes, "is first and foremost a bodily ego" (p. 26). All this would be much clearer if Freud would show us how his descriptions apply to the child.

Freud's "I" also refers to a coherent organization of mental functions to which consciousness is attached and which includes reality-testing and censorship. It is also, as we saw earlier, the source of unconscious repression.

Freud begins his discussion of the super-ego (das Über-Ich) – which comprises conscience, morality, and the roots of religion and which is largely unconscious – by noting that both what is lowest and what is highest in the mind is unconscious; for the super-ego is derived from the ego but fueled by the id. What follows is a simplified version of Freud's account of the Oedipal Complex, which founds the super-ego. Freud models it on the boy. The complex refers to the fact that the boy's earliest attachment is to the mother, while his earliest identification is with the father. For a while these two relations proceed side by side, until the (sexual) attachment to the mother becomes intense. At this point the father is perceived as an obstacle and the boy harbors murderous wishes against him. His relation to the father is now ambivalent, which brings about a modification in the ego, the super-ego, that poses a critical force against it. The super-ego's relation to the ego is complex in a special way. It says to it not only "You must be like your father," but also "You may not be like your father" (in relation to your mother). Like conscience the super-ego is thus self-referential; it contains values, at first from the father, and from other figures in the environment as the child's life story proceeds; and is susceptible to guilt and self-punishment. The ego is essentially a representative of the external world. The super-ego is in large part a representative of the internal world, or the id.

The unconscious sense of guilt is revealed in therapy both by resistance, but more specifically by the interesting phenomenon that the patient responds to success in treatment with discontent. He gets worse, revealing an unconscious need for punishment, but he does not feel guilty.

7 Guilt and Morality

In his late work, *Civilization and Its Discontents* (1930 [1929] 21) Freud analyzes valuing and conscience in general as rooted in the Oedipal Complex. Here Freud may owe a debt to Nietzsche, whose work he had studied. In the beginning, Nietzsche suggests, the language of value was an invention of those in power, the warriors and priests who composed a single class. More or less synonymous with "noble," "good," "beautiful" and "strong," "good" was the Greek aristocracy's description of itself. There was no concept of "evil," and no self-hatred in the form of bad conscience. "Bad" simply discriminated the weaklings, the Other.

But as culture developed, the classes of warrior and priest diverged in such a way that the powerful warriors whom the priests now admired and envied, and so in a way loved, were reviled as sinners. Not only did the powerful, or formerly powerful, now think themselves "bad," but the priests, identifying with the warriors whom they desperately wanted to replace, thus seeing themselves in the warriors' eyes, despised what was "good" in themselves. Under the banner of Christian love, weakness sought to mortify strength and accepted, even glorified, its own humiliation. "In the earliest phase," Nietzsche writes,

> bad conscience is nothing other than the instinct of freedom forced to become latent, driven underground, and forced to vent its energy on itself. . . . The invention of guilt, which the Judeo-Christian tradition proclaims its greatest spiritual treasure, represents rather the ignoble triumph of repressed envy, resentment, and self-disgust.
>
> *(Nietzsche 1956, p. 220)*

In the climactic fifth chapter of *Civilization and Its Discontents* Freud says that the clue to man's discontent under the yoke of civilization is supplied by the command to love one's neighbor as oneself. "What could the source of such a strange and impossible demand be other than the need to counter an aggressive instinct so violent that it threatens to destroy both individual and society?" (p. 109). The unhappy solution, Freud contends, so far, a tenable but costly compromise in the war between Eros (sexuality and the life force) and Thanatos, is that aggression, in the form of guilt, is directed backward onto the self. Like Nietzsche, Freud sees the moral sense as the uneasy resolution in a dialectic between impotence and power, love and hate. In Freud's story the roles of strong and weak are played, of course, not by social classes but by parent and child. The dependent child rages against the powerful adult whom he would like to replace and whose retaliatory vengeance he fears. The child borrows the father's "You must not do x" (take your mother to bed) and makes it his own, deriving the strength for compliance from the combined motives of fear of the father and rage, whose target he has now become.

For both Freud and Nietzsche, the final outcome is the same: resentment and aggression, flourishing secretly in the dark of the mind behind a mask of love; self-hatred; repression and the creation of a mortal enemy within the self, in the shape for Freud of the superego. The Oedipal Complex is Freud's version of the Fall, for he thinks that moral values can bloom only in the opening of a fissure between child and father, self and self, a divide across which the Unconscious speaks in a strange language unintelligible to the conscious mind.

8 Reasons, Irrationality, and Self-Deception[2]

Freud's originality as an interpreter lies not in a brand-new model for explaining behavior but in the ingenuity with which he applies a familiar model, namely describing an action in terms of its reasons, that is, its intention, itself a composite of desire and the relevant beliefs. For example, Mary left the house in a rush because she thought it was on fire. In other words, Mary rushed out of the house (intentionally) because she thought there was a fire – the belief – and she didn't want to be burned – the desire. Where common sense is puzzled by seemingly incoherent utterances and behavior, Freud assumes that given the right circumstances, "nonsense" reveals sense; an apparently idle and "irrational" idea reveals a recognizable psychological attitude like belief or desire; an action which is apparently contrary to the agent's conscious reasons becomes intelligible in terms of reasons that are unconscious. Finally, thoughts may themselves have a structure resembling that of actions, as when a "memory" or a "forgetting" or an act of phantasizing is the product of desire.

But in novel ways, Freud extends and embroiders the familiar reasons-explanation model. Consider the seemingly incoherent behavior of the "table-cloth lady" cited above, the woman who runs into the neighboring room, spills ink on the table, rings the bell for the maid, then rushes back into the bedroom. We recall that Freud explains it in terms of the lady's wish to prove her husband's potency on their wedding night when he had thrown some red ink on the sheet to convince the maid that intercourse had taken place.

The problem with such explanations is that if what the woman did (as described by Freud) is an action, as fully intentional behavior, then it seems we must impute to her a particular desire to revise her wedding night, a particular belief that pouring ink on the table is a way of satisfying that desire, and some very general beliefs such as that the past can be redone. And that someone might have such beliefs and desires is not plausible.

Freud believes that the seeming problem only points to some needed qualifications in the reasons-explanation model. Where a piece of behavior crucially involves phantasy, the woman does not have such beliefs. Under the description "putting ink on the table" her behavior is an action and is fully intentional; but under a fuller description which makes reference to an anxious phantasy, "putting ink on the table as a way of imagining the past as undone," it is not. There is a wish, and an imagining in which the wish is fulfilled. An anxious wish causes a defensive activity in the absence of any instrumental belief. The structure of a phantasy is thus similar to that of a dream.

The wish that spurs anxiety is typically an anxious wish, or rather, a wish to escape an awareness of some sort that makes one anxious. The imaginative act is defensive and deceiving in nature: one imagines that the world is other than one knows, or could easily know, that it is, as in phantasy. It is, in short, the sort of imaginative act Freud links to repression.

Freud was working towards articulating a number of ideas that are new to philosophical psychology, the network of concepts which includes "phantasy," "repression" and "acting out," gathering together discoveries both about the use of the imagination in defense and about psychological time: the past is "remembered" in the light of phantasy, which may be taken for memory; the present is (unconsciously) seen, or rather enacted, as a repetition of the past. And the very fact of acting *as if* a certain story were true, itself begins in the mind of the agent to lend some credence to the idea that it is. Freud writes that "the patient does not *remember* anything of which he has forgotten and repressed but *acts* it out" (*SE* 1915, 1914, pp. 150–153). Repression allows the past to be remembered, but not *as* memory. This protects the table-cloth lady from the pain of realizing that as past there is nothing to be done about her husband's impotence; and it allows her to act as if the action might be redone.

I want now to discuss a crucial sense of irrationality that interests philosophers as well as Freud, namely self-deception, a phenomenon that is implicit in much that has already been said. The irrationality concerns a behavior or belief that is *internally* inconsistent, that is, inconsistent in the person's own terms, and thus paradoxical.

To elaborate the paradox, take the case of interpersonal deception. When John intends to deceive Mary, as distinct from merely saying something to her that is false but that he sincerely believes to be true, he intends Mary to be taken in by a belief he thinks is false. So, in the one-person case, John sets out to believe something that he knows he does not believe. The obvious problem is that this would seem to undermine the intention itself. For example, in the case of the table-cloth lady, the woman knows that the table is not the bed, that it was not blood on the bed, and so forth, but she intends to believe, and apparently does believe, what she knows is false.

Freud tries at first to resolve the paradox – though he doesn't describe it as such – by assigning deceiver and deceived to different systems, consciousness versus the unconscious, apparently preserving the duality but losing the concept of unity between deceiver and deceived. In a later refinement, however, the deceiver, that is, the ego as the source of repression, is itself described as unconscious. But in positing an unconscious repressing ego, unaware of its own act of repression, Freud reinstates the unity of deceiver and deceived now on the side of the unconscious. And it is just this unity, Sartre points out (1956), that drives the paradox. In the resolution I want to suggest on Freud's behalf, we preserve the model of mental partitioning in a way that doesn't merely give us names for old problems.

Let's begin by thinking of the mind as a network of interlocking beliefs, desires, memories and so on in which there may be sub-divisions that partly overlap with the whole. The philosopher Donald Davidson defends the following claims, all of which he contends are to be found in Freud.

First, the mind contains a number of semi-independent structures, these structures being characterized by mental attributes like thoughts, desires, and memories.

Second, parts of the mind are in important respects like people, not only in having (or consisting of) beliefs, wants, and other psychological traits, but in that these factors can combine, as in intentional action, to cause further events in the mind or outside of it.

Third, some of the dispositions, attitudes and events that characterize the various structures of the mind must be viewed on the model of physical dispositions and forces when they affect, or are affected by, other sub-structures in the mind" (192, pp. 290–291).

It is this last point, Davidson argues, which justifies Freud's use of metaphors from hydraulics and mechanics to describe certain kinds of psychological phenomena.

What, if anything, does this model explain? Have we, once again, simply given the problem of internal irrationality another name? No, in that the idea of semi-independent but overlapping structures within a single mind, a structure of mental states like belief, desire, and intention, keeps the notions of duality – or multiplicity – implicit in the idea of deception together with that of a single self, without paradox. Yes, in that Davidson does not enlighten us as to how the partitioning takes place.

To explore Freud's partitioning, let's take another famous case of his that Davidson also mentions, "The Rat-Man."

> One day, when he was out with her (his lady) in a boat and there was a stiff wind blowing, he was obliged to make her put on his cap, because a command had been formulated in his mind that *nothing must happen to her.* This was a kind of *obsession for protecting,* and it bore fruits besides this . . . On the day of her departure he knocked his foot against a stone lying in the road and removed the stone because the idea struck him that her carriage would be driving along the same road in a few hours' time and might come to grief against this stone. But a few moments later it occurred to him that this was absurd, and he was obliged to go back and replace the stone in its original position in the road.
>
> *(Freud, 1909, 10, pp. 189–190)*

The Rat-Man's narrative begins with a tale of dreadful punishment by which he is obsessed – rats boring into the victim's anus – and which he vividly imagines happening to his father and his lady. At first the obsession presents itself as "just a thought"; but the fact that his feelings about this thought are anxious fascination and guilt suggest that he is envisioning this torture as a violence or a punishment he would like to inflict on the two victims of the torture, and that for him it is as if the punishment he would like to inflict were about to come true. Freud links this incident of the stone in the road to others of the Rat-Man's obsessively violent thoughts, and to his bizarre compulsion to work until late at night, followed by his masturbating in front of a mirror. Freud analyzes the last compulsion as, in part, the acting out of a phantasy that the father he knows is dead is alive, and horrified by his son's defiantly exhibitionistic behavior.

What are the beliefs and desires in terms of which these phantasies are intelligible? None, on Freud's analysis, that are acknowledged or acknowledgeable by the Rat-Man's grown-up self. They include, among others, very early Oedipal feelings of hatred towards his father; perceptions of him as very powerful; a projection of his own anger onto the father, perhaps mis-perceived as anger toward the child; self-deceptive feelings of his own innocence, and so on.

In sum, the process of interpretation leads Freud from the episode in the park to a much earlier mental structure of beliefs and desires that are alien to the man's adult self, and that are the partial cause of his adult behavior. The structure is characterized as a whole by phantasy's confusion between past and present, between what is and what one wishes there were.

On Davidson's analysis the irrationality and the self-deceptions in the man's behavior with the stone enter at the point at which the man ignores the principle of rationality that Davidson calls "the principle of continence," which enjoins the mind to behave out of the most coherent structure of beliefs and desires, all things considered. Instead he acts out of irreconcilable motives that are explained by splits between different mental structures.

Freud's account, on the other hand, suggests that a split like the one Davidson describes – involving closely related beliefs, desires, memories, phantasies, anxieties, and so on – took place much earlier, creating a kind of psychological fault existing through time. Imagine now that the anxiety situation, in this case the full Oedipal Complex, is chronic. Thus, habits of mis-perception, dividing past from present, may begin to consolidate and settle.

We can now see how a mental sub-structure with some of the characteristics of primary process might begin to crystallize: timelessness, or impervience to the passage of time, exemption from mutual contradiction, replacement of eternal reality by internal reality (phantasy) – for example, the dead father is imagined as alive. Furthermore, more and more situations may come to remind the person of what he or she doesn't want to confront so that new thoughts are drawn into the archaic structure, itself seeded by repression.

Is this account vulnerable to Sartre's criticism, that the split between deceiver and deceived now occurs on one side, between repressor and repressed, thus ignoring the duality implicit in self-division? Not quite. Or if it is, the picture of the self that emerges is very different. The concepts of both the unconscious and repression call attention to ways in which the adult mind can be compromised by the childhood minds which inhabit it. And whereas often we can explain an action by staying fairly close to the agent's immediate beliefs and desires, neurotic actions typically will make sense only in a context that reaches further back into the agent's life. (The analysis of the table-cloth lady that Freud gives us does not go far enough to incorporate childhood states of mind.)

The concept of the unconscious in general calls attention to the way in which earlier mental states scarcely intelligible to the adult mind can be preserved, stunted and isolated. The adult uncovers her unconscious as she learns to hear the voice of the child she harbors.

Epilogue

As we have seen, the general idea of the unconscious is that the mind, or psyche, is split between parts of which it is unaware and a part of which it is. The splits are motivated by repression; and this mental force that causes and maintains the splits is also ordinarily unconscious. Human being is essentially a stranger to itself, and thorough self-knowledge is as impossible as our knowledge of other minds. The purpose of psychoanalytic therapy is to unite the self as much as possible, to replace the id by a largely conscious ego, and phantasy by "the reality principle." There is now *a* self, a being that is an agent, capable of genuine intentionality and of acting responsibly. Though some degree of self-estrangement will always remain.

Suggested Reading

The best introduction to Freud's work is Freud's own "Five Lectures on Psychoanalysis," based on his lectures at Clark University (*S.E.* 11, 1910).

Three standard biographies of Freud are: Gay, P. 1988. *Freud: A Life for our Time.* London: J. M. Dent & Sons. /Jones, E. 1955. *Sigmund Freud: Life and Work.* London and New York: Hogarth Press; and /Clark, R. W. 1980. *Freud, The Man and the Cause.* New York, Random House.

An excellent account of Freud's work, particularly its roots in biology, is Sulloway, F. 1977. *Freud, Biologist of the Mind: Beyond the Psychoanalytic Legend.* New York: Harvard University Press.

Two of the best-known critiques of Freud are Masson, J., 1985 (see below) / and Grünbaum, A. 1984. *The Foundations of Psychoanalysis: A Philosophical Critique*. Berkeley: University of California Press.

Some explorations of Freud from a philosophic point of view: Cavell, M. 1993. *The Psychoanalytic Mind: From Freud to Philosophy*. Cambridge, Mass. and London: Harvard University Press. / Cavell, M. 2006. *Becoming a Subject: Reflections in Philosophy and Psychoanalysis*. Oxford: Clarendon Press. / Wollheim, R. & Hopkins, J., eds. 1983. *Philosophical Essays on Freud*. Cambridge, England: Cambridge University Press. / Wollheim, R. 1971. (See below.)

Notes

1 All references to Freud are to the *Standard Edition of the Complete Psychological Works of Sigmund Freud*. 1966–1974. Trans. and ed. J. Strachey et al. London: Hogarth Press. This will be abbreviated throughout as *SE*, followed by date, volume, and page numbers.

2 For an extended discussion of these issues see 9 and 10 in Cavell, M., *The Psychoanalytic Mind, from Freud to Philosophy*, Cambridge, Harvard University Press, 1993.

References

Cavell, M. 1983. *The Psychoanalytic Mind, from Freud to Philosophy*. Cambridge: Harvard University Press.

Crews, F. 2017. *Freud, The Making of an Illusion*. New York: Metropolitan Books.

Davidson, D. 1982. "Paradoxes of Irrationality." *Philosophical Essays on Freud*. Ed. R. Wollheim and J. Hopkins. New York and Cambridge: Cambridge University Press.

Ellenberger, H. 1981. *The Discovery of the Unconscious: The History and Evolution of Dynamic Psychiatry*. New York: Basic Books.

Freud, S. 1909, "Notes upon a Case of Obsessional Neurosis." *S.E.* 10.

Freud, S, 1914. "Remembering, Repeating, and Working Through." *S.E.* 12.

Freud, S. 1916–1917. Introductory Lectures on Psychoanalysis. *S.E.* 15.

Laplanche & Pontalis. Tr. Nicholson-Smith, D. 1973. *The Language of Psychoanalysis*. New York and London: W. W. Norton & Company.

Masson, J. M. 1985. *The Assault on Truth: Freud's Suppression of the Seduction Theory*. New York: Penguin.

Nietzsche, F. 1956. "The Genealogy of Morals. *The Birth of Tragedy and The Genealogy of Morals*. Tr. Goffing, E. New York: Doubleday.

Sartre, J. P. 1956. *Being and Nothingness*. Trans. H. E. Barnes. New York: Philosophical Library.

Wollheim, R. 1971. *Sigmund Freud*. New York: Cambridge University Press.

10

THE FOUNDATIONS OF THE PSYCHOANALYTIC THEORIES OF FREUD, KLEIN AND BION COMPARED

Michael Rustin[1]

The paradigm of psychoanalysis, invented by Freud early in the twentieth century, has undergone considerable development and evolution since its beginnings. Some of this took place within Freud's own work, during his long lifetime. In this article, I am going to focus on psychoanalytic work which has taken place mainly in Britain, in a tradition which has emphasised its consistency and continuity with Freud's ideas while nevertheless making some significant new departures from them. This is the tradition whose foremost figures were Melanie Klein and Wilfred Bion, but which has been elaborated by a considerable circle of practising psychoanalysts influenced by and associated with them. The purpose of this chapter is to clarify the essential features of this field of work, taking note of its aspects of consistency with Freud's original insights, its divergences from Freud's initial assumptions, and its theoretical developments of these. We shall be defending the theoretical and clinical fertility of this tradition, and will seek to show how large and coherent its scope has become over the century or so of its existence, since Klein first began her development of Freud's ideas in the 1920s.

There have of course been several other significant and distinctive developments of Freud's original paradigm, each of them influenced by the cultural context in which they have occurred. We will here mention two in particular. The first is the tradition of "ego psychology" which developed from the 1930s onwards, mainly in the United States, but which gained its greatest influence after the Second World War.

This body of work, initially accomplished by exiles to America from Nazi Europe, remained attached to Anna Freud's conception of Freudian orthodoxy,[2] evolved in part in opposition to the theoretical and technical innovations proposed by Melanie Klein when she came to work in England, and by her followers there. The second is a different psychoanalytic tradition, which termed itself "relational psychoanalysis" (a founding text is Greenberg and Mitchell 1984). This emerged in the later decades of the twentieth century, in part in reaction to the domination of psychoanalysis in post-war America by the ego psychologists. There are some affinities between this relational tradition and the ideas of "object relations" which were developed in Britain, each arguing for a model of the mind centred less on its innate instinctual drives, and instead attaching greater importance to the self's formative relation to others. The primary "objects" of British object-relations theory are those to which the infant becomes related in early life, and

DOI: 10.4324/9780429297076-13

whose presence in the mind is therefore substantially unconscious. The main focus of "relational psychoanalysis" has by contrast been the "objects" whom individuals become identified with and related to not merely in infancy, but throughout their lives. "Relational psychoanalysis" has been a discourse through which psychoanalysts can take account of the many kinds of diversity and difference (e.g., of gendered, sexual, and ethnic identity) which exist in contemporary society, and through which such differences can be explored and negotiated in the contexts of psychoanalytic clinical work. This movement was in part a reaction to the normative assumptions concerning middle-class family life in America in the period of greatest influence of psychoanalysis, and to the undermining of these in a later period of cultural dissention, conflict and pluralism. Encountering these fields of cultural difference led relational psychoanalysts to repudiate some of the tacit assumptions of scientific objectivity and authority which had been Freud's aspiration for psychoanalysis, and to propose that in the psychoanalytic encounter analysts' own cultural and normative beliefs might need to be explored and made explicit. By contrast, the "object-relations" tradition has been much less interested than "relational psychoanalysis" in issues of cultural diversity and social conflict. It has correspondingly remained more committed to the specific focus of psychoanalysis on unconscious mental life, and to the idea that analysts can bring a distinctive kind of capability and even authority to this kind of understanding.

The third important development from Freud's foundational work which we wish to mention here is that which was created by Lacan in France (Roudinesco 1997). Lacan positioned this development against what he saw as the weakened recognition of the force of the unconscious in the ego psychologists' development of Freud's ideas in the United States. He recognised some affinity with Klein's committed attention to unconscious mental life, although their understanding of the nature of this was different. Lacan's primary interest was in the disruptive and challenging nature of desire and its transformations. He believed that the exploration of this in all its difficulties was the essential task of psychoanalysis. Language was the vital and unavoidable resource for conducting this exploration in analysis, as it revealed, concealed and misrepresented the vicissitudes of human desire, both in individuals' specific experience and in the larger symbolic structures whose effect was to define identities (e.g., of gender or race) within larger cultures. An idea of the ultimate "impossibility" of finding satisfaction of human desires, through a primordial experience of "lack", seems to characterise the Lacanian world-view. This perhaps corresponds to one latently anti-social current in French social thought, which has found expression in both its existentialist and revolutionary traditions. There is little space to be found within this conception of identity between extreme assertions of individual autonomy and a utopian concept of group harmony, as originally in Rousseau's idea of a "general will". As we will see, the Klein-Bion development of Freud's ideas has been more sympathetic to the idea that "good enough" solutions to the problems of human lives may be found, and that psychoanalysis can contribute to the project of finding them, both for individuals and in the larger context of culture and society.

We have suggested that all of these "post-Freudian" developments have been shaped by a particular societal and cultural context, including the specific "British" development we will be describing here.[3]

Freud[4]

Although in the writing of Freud's two most important successors in the tradition we are considering there are both developments of and differences with Freud, it is essential to see how many of the ideas which have come to constitute this tradition have their origin in Freud's own writing. This is the case even for ideas of, for example, our relations with internal objects and the place of the epistemophilic instinct, whose main development took place in his successors' work. In our section on Freud's ideas, we will summarise some key elements of Freud's paradigm and identify elements in his work which were the location of developments and of divergences.

The Unconscious

The most fundamental psychoanalytic idea, both in Freud's work and that of his successors, is that of the unconscious mind, and that of unconscious desires. Freud understood these to be both sexual and aggressive in nature, from this essential duality arising his conception of the life and the death instinct. From the idea of primary libidinal desires, and of its earliest object in the maternal figure, arose the central importance of the Oedipus complex in Freud's theory. The male infant's libidinal desire for its mother set up an unavoidable conflict with mother's sexual partner, father, for the sole possession of mother. Freud believed that male infants were obliged, if normal sexual development was to be achieved, to renounce their desire to possess mother, in rivalry with father, and that this developmental stage was normally achieved through the infant's becoming identified with father, and recognising that with maturity he would come to emulate father's role in his own generation. Freud's understanding of the early development of the female was much less secure than his understanding of the male child – he acknowledged his uncertainty about the psychology of the female. On the one hand, there was an element of symmetry in the experience of male and female infants, in so far as both of them were believed to form, and were then obliged to renounce, libidinal attachments to their opposite-sex parent. The process through which these desires and attachments were formed, and were then transcended by identification and through the sublimation and externalisation of desires, was often stressful. Freud located many developmental difficulties, and the origin of several psychopathologies in this early experience of the Oedipal situation. But on the other hand, Freud postulated a deep asymmetry in the psychological formation of males and females, believing that female infants believed themselves to be suffering from a deficiency in comparison with the male child – namely the absence of a penis. This necessarily implied that adult females suffer from this lack as well, thus instituting at the heart of Freud's psychoanalytic theory a postulate of female deficit and inferiority.

One of the most important evolutions in psychoanalytic theory after Freud was in the understanding of female development. Klein attended much more closely than Freud to the experiences of the first months of life, and to the early relations of mother and infant. She, and subsequently Bion, held that this relationship between mother and infant was formative for the development of the self, and that this was prior to Oedipal rivalry for libidinal possession of the parent, which was central to Freud's account of development. Klein did not discount or minimise the importance of Oedipal conflicts, holding instead that they emerged much earlier, in the first year of life, than Freud believed, even before the constituting of a desiring ego and the onset of repression. But there is a corresponding significant change in Klein's understanding of the Oedipal situation. In her view, the anxieties it gives rise to are not only concerned with libidinal desires and the fear of paternal retribution for these, expressed in Freud's view as "castration anxiety". Klein accepted, and found in her clinical work with young children, that such anxieties existed. But in her view, the issue for the infant was not merely that he could not be the sole possessor of his opposite-sex parent, but also involved anxieties about what the parents' sexual coupling might produce, in the form of new babies who threatened the displacement of the infant from its privilege of exclusive parental care and preoccupation. (Klein suggested that the experience of weaning induced this anxiety.) Thus, Klein's version of this early development story brings a partial shift of focus from experiences of libidinal desires and their prohibition, to anxieties about the security and care of the infant.[5] This is one aspect in a larger shift in this tradition from desires to relationships as central issues in psychoanalytical theory.

Transference

A second concept central to Freud's psychoanalytic theory is that of transference. Freud discovered the phenomenon of transference in his treatment of Dora, the human subject of his paper "Fragment of a Case of Hysteria – (Dora)" published in 1905, but based on work conducted five years earlier. Dora had consulted Freud after her father had become involved in an affair, and after the deceived husband, Herr K, had, it seemed, attempted to seduce Dora, who had been shocked and pushed him away. She was disturbed by the episode, and felt disgust whenever she was in male company. Freud came to understand the symptoms she revealed in her work with him as hysterical in nature, with underlying sexual meanings which involved multiple unconscious attractions to Herr K, to her father, and to her mother. Freud came to believe that this real attempt at seduction was so disturbing to his patient in part because it evoked an unconscious phantasy of childhood seduction by her father. Freud's discovery of transference came when he understood that it was because of Dora's transference to him that she had unexpectedly withdrawn from her analysis after only three months. Freud came to believe that if he had recognised her transference to him at the time, he might have been able to sustain the analysis.

The idea of the transference became, following Freud's discovery, one of the fundamental building blocks of psychoanalytic theory and method. However, its full development as a source of understanding of patients, and of the relationship between patients and analysts, came from Freud's successors. Freud for the most part saw himself as engaged in investigations of his patients' unconscious minds, undertaken from as detached and objective a position as he could find in relation to them. They would tell him what was in their minds, according to the desired but difficult-to-follow principle of free association, and he in the role of psychoanalyst would seek to unravel and to reveal to them the unconscious meaning of their desires. Freud did not work solely in the mode of an investigator of the meanings of the thoughts his patients disclosed to him through their dreams and associations. His writings sometimes show him to have been aware of the complexity of his patients' feelings for him, and of his feelings for them. But what is now called the "here and now" of the transference relationship was very different from Freud's own practice.

It was Sándor Ferenczi, among his close group of followers, who came to understand that the psychoanalyst should have an emotionally engaged and expressive relationship with his patients and who urged this on Freud. Ferenczi was also keenly aware of the intensity of the relationships which existed within Freud's own circle, and the jealousies and antipathies which they generated. However, Freud retained his preference to see himself in the role of an objective investigator of the new field of the unconscious (his own mind included), and this inhibited him from developing a fuller interest in the nature of the transference relationship as an essential resource of psychoanalytic understanding and change, as it became in the British object-relations tradition.

Melanie Klein, whose first analyst in Budapest was Ferenczi, and whose clinical approach was influenced by him (Likierman 2002), was one of those who developed the greater understanding of the centrality of the transference relationship to psychoanalytic practice, through her analytic treatment of young children from the early 1920s. She found in this work that the intensity of the transference of her patients to her, and the ways in which through this they gave expression to their inner world of phantasy, was unmistakable. Among young children, transferences of feeling between parental figures and other adults with whom they come into significant contact are quite normal – how often do small children find themselves even explicitly addressing their grandmothers or nursery teachers as "mummy" before recognising and correcting their mistakes. It was in 1934 that James Strachey, who was one of Klein's supporters in the British psychoanalytic movement (Alix and James Strachey in 1925 first invited Klein to lecture in London), gave in a classic paper what has become the canonical expression of the understanding of the role of the transference in making possible psychoanalytic understanding and change (Strachey 1934). Later, in the work of Paula Heimann (1950), then a member of Klein's close circle, came the recognition of the significance of the counter-transference – the nature and experience of the analyst's transference to her patient – as a further crucial development of the understanding of the significance of this relationship. This perspective became still broader and deeper in the work of the next generation of Kleinian analysts, for example in Betty Joseph's (1985) focus on the "total transference situation" – originally a concept of Klein's – as an essential technique of psychoanalytic inquiry and treatment.

The Theory of Drives and Freud's Individualism

Freud began his career as a neurologist whose initial interest was in the brain and the nervous system and in the biophysical origins of the functions of the mind. His development of a psychoanalytic perspective involved a shift from the functions of the brain to the phenomena of the mind.[6] These are parallel ontologies and fields of explanation which remain distinct and irreducible to one another even to this day. It is an aspiration of neuroscience to be able to explain the phenomena of the mind, and to be able to correct its pathologies by reference to the phenomena of the brain, with consciousness understood as an effect of physical and chemical processes. A great deal of progress has been made by neuroscientists in correlating events in these spheres, for example establishing a topography in which different functions of mind have been shown to be located in specific regions of the brain. A therapeutic ambition which follows from these investigations is to be able to influence mental states through interventions, principally pharmacological, which impact "directly" on brain functions. Considerable successes of this kind have been achieved, enabling different kinds of mental pathology – depressive and psychotic illnesses, for example – and their accompanying kinds of pain and distress to be alleviated. However, it is rare that such interventions achieve all of their purposes, and the idea that mental states should need to be regulated through dependence on drugs arouses disquiet. This is from the perspective that human beings should be self-determining through their capacity for understanding of themselves and for free choice. This resistance has roots in philosophical and cultural beliefs about how human lives should be lived, but it is also one shared in everyday life – most individuals would prefer not to be dependent on medically prescribed drugs for their well-being, at least for any length of time.

The model of the brain and its functions on which Freud's neurological work was based gave great importance to flows of energy, which were managed by the human organism to maintain a state of equilibrium. This model of the mind was influenced by the "psychological materialism" of the English empiricist philosophical tradition.[7] Thomas Hobbes in his *Leviathan* (1651) sought to understand the "laws of motion" governing human lives. (Newton stated the three universal laws of motion later in 1687 in his *Principia*.) Hobbes, and the utilitarian philosophers who followed him, understood the human mind as organised through its aversion to pain and its desire for pleasure. Pleasure was achieved through the satisfaction of appetites. Human beings were constructed in effect as desiring machines (Deleuze and Guattari 1977 [1972], 1987 [1980]). Modern times have made a great deal of this model, whose minds had the role of estimating how pleasures and pains could respectively be achieved and avoided.

In 1905, Freud followed *The Interpretation of Dreams* (1900) with *Three Essays on the Theory of Sexuality* (1905a) and *Fragment of a Case of Hysteria – [Dora]* (1905b). In the second of these works, Freud set out in a succinct way his "libido theory", analysing libidinal desires as the principal motivating force of the mind and differentiating between their impulses, objects and aims. This text integrates several fields of inquiry into a single psychological model of the mind, giving prominence to Freud's core conception of unconscious mental conflict but drawing on both Newtonian and Darwinian presuppositions. Darwin's theory of natural selection gave a scientific legitimacy to Freud's belief in the central role of sexuality in human life.

There is an affinity between the theory of libidinal desires seeking gratification and the utilitarian philosopher's model of pleasure-seeking as the fundamental human motivation. Freud's interest in utilitarian philosophy, and its probable implicit role in the framing of this thinking, is attested by the fact that he made his own translation of four works by John Stuart Mill. This framing of human motivation is inherently "individualistic" or self-regarding. Since fundamental desires and appetites arise from within the individual organism, there is the innate probability – indeed certainty – of conflict and competition between individuals for their satisfaction. The utilitarian tradition sought to elaborate regulatory norms and principles by which individuals might be persuaded in their own and others' interest to restrain their own appetites and allow a common human interest – "the greatest happiness of the greatest number" in Bentham's terms – to be served. They thus superimposed a moral principle onto their central theory of self-regarding motivation. (The superego had similar function in Freud's theory.) This "problem of order", as it came to be described later in influential sociological writing (Parsons 1937), is quite closely related to the problems of reconciling conflicting human desires and impulses which Freud had discussed in a somewhat pessimistic spirit in his *Civilization and Its Discontents* in 1930. In the second utilitarian generation, Mill – some of whose writing Freud translated into German – proposed a more complex idea of pleasures, differentiating between those of a higher and lower kind (Wollheim 1993, pp. 22–38) and creating philosophical space for the psychoanalytic idea of the sublimation of pleasure-seeking impulses into higher-order satisfactions.

Freud's first psychoanalytic theory of the mind came to be called the "topographical" model, postulating conscious, preconscious and unconscious levels of mental functioning. The unconscious, in Freud's account, arose from the repression of libidinal and aggressive desires within the Oedipal situation through the conflicts to which they gave rise with parental figures. Later, in Freud's subsequent "structural" theory of mind, in which a different tripartite structure of id, ego and superego had primacy, the unconscious was understood to be the location of desires themselves, in their original polymorphous and unregulated form. In Freud's psychoanalytic theory, this division of the mind, and the function of repression in bringing it about, was the (imperfect) solution to the "problem of order" to which his account of self-gratifying libidinal and aggressive desires at the core of human nature gave rise.

A further aspect of the "individualism" of Freud's foundational model of the mind was his belief that human lives began in a state of what came to be called "primary narcissism".[8] In the first instance, that is to say, human infants are without a conception of the existence of others, but they imagine or fantasise that their appetites are being satisfied by their own actions. Recognition of the existence of others, and of their entire dependence on them, comes at a later stage of development, according to Freud, who did not psychoanalyse children and gave little attention to the experiences of infants. Klein, who was herself a mother, and who psychoanalysed children from under three years of age onwards, took a different view. Her insistence that human beings were "object related" from the moment of birth – that is to say they had an innate awareness of the existence of the maternal breast – was perhaps the most fundamental of her disagreements with Freud, and it was foundational for the development of the object-relations tradition in psychoanalysis.

Freud seems to have been unaware of, or uninterested in, the parallel but diverging tradition of English empiricist philosophy which had a greater recognition of the innate "social" nature of humankind. This was set out in the philosophy of David Hume and Adam Smith, among others, in the more peaceful climate of eighteenth-century Scotland and England, which had succeeded the preceding period of religious and civil conflict. Its central idea was that human beings had an innate capacity for sympathy with one another's states of feeling and could be motivated by responses to others' sufferings and pleasures. Freud's focus on the aims and objects of desires, and on their inhibition and repression and its psychological consequences, led him to give little attention to affects – states of feeling (as distinct from the aims and objects of desire) – as constitutive of mental life.

Janet Sayers (1991) has argued that greater attention to states of feeling, including those involved in the sufferings of others, emerged with the participation of women analysts in the psychoanalytic movement (these included Helen Deutsch, Anna Freud, Karen Horney and Melanie Klein). Male analysts central to the development of the object-relations tradition, such as Bowlby, Winnicott and Bion, were also keenly interested in the role of mothers in human development, more than Freud had been. One can thus see the growth of object-relations psychoanalysis as the outcome of a partial "feminisation" of psychoanalysis.

Freud's work was, of course, shaped by influences other than the empiricism of the British empiricist/scientific tradition and its model of desires and energies seeking discharge. Carl Schorske (1980) refers to Freud's dual attachments to the "passion" of French and the "reason" of British culture, and we can add to this an affinity with an idealist tradition which gives central importance to the change which can arise from the understanding of meanings. While Freud saw the function of interpretation, so central to psychoanalysis, in part as the identification of mental chains of cause and effect, its role is just as much one of making connections in conceptual and emotional terms. (We can say in terms of Max Weber's *Methodology of the Social Sciences* [1949] at the level of meaning *and* cause.). This is fully evident in Freud's own writing – and is inherent in his appreciation and love of literature – even if its implications do not fully find their way into his scientific theory of the mind. Freud's later writing, notably *Mourning and Melancholia* (1917) and *Group Psychology and the Analysis of the Ego* (1921), gives emphasis to the role of identification with others in the formation of identity and was foundational for the conception, in the object-relations tradition, of a self that was more "social" in its essence than it had been in Freud's earlier writing. The full development of the idea of a personality or self that was formed by love and hatred of others, rather than mainly by a need or wish to gratify appetites through relations with them, came with work in the object-relations tradition.

Klein[9]

In her psychoanalytic treatment of children, from the early 1920s, Klein adopted Freud's own understanding of the personality as initially dominated by its bodily appetites and needs. Through her technique of play therapy and her interpretation of the meaning of patients' play with the toys she provided, she developed an understanding of infants' mental lives as dominated by intense preoccupation with mothers' bodies and with their physical interactions with them. Freud's postulated states of successive oral, anal and genital preoccupation provided a framework for her – a bodyscape – through which she inferred the infant's way of experiencing the main elements of its relationship with mother. She believed this relationship to be dominated by intense feelings of both love and hate, in which its bodily functions (feeding, biting, urinating, excreting) were made use of as forms of action and expression. As we have said, Klein believed that the Oedipal situation and the feelings aroused by it became part of the infant's mental world in the first year of life, and not after the age of three, related to the onset of repression, as Freud believed.

Thus, although we argue that Klein had a major role in recognising the importance of relationships between the self and its objects from the beginning of life and achieved a crucial understanding of the emergence of a form of love and care for another which were not merely an expression of libidinal desire, it is important to see what else is essential to her theory of development. What has remained contentious in Klein's theoretical system is the extent to which she recognises the power of destructive and aggressive feelings in early infantile experience. What was challenging in her therapeutic technique was the directness, even starkness, with which she sought to understand and interpret the phantasies about the bodies and body parts of infants and parents, and their interactions, giving a highly concrete dimension in her psychoanalytic work with children to some of Freud's beliefs about early development. She also took into her work with children his belief that interpretation, and the recognition of the transference relationship between patient and analyst, was the crucial therapeutic resource of psychoanalysis. This was contrary to the belief of Anna Freud that the transference and interpretation could only have an important role in child analysis once a sufficiently developed ego had developed, once the child became capable of establishing an emotionally intense relationship – a transference relationship – with someone outside of their immediate family,

We will be arguing that Klein's discoveries made possible a more "relational" conception of human life. But for a perspective to be "relational" does not imply that it is inherently benign, or that aggression and destructiveness becomes a significant issue only where nurturing and early development have failed in some way. Indeed, this issue of an innate potential for aggression has constituted an important line of division within the object-relations tradition.[10] The dualism of instincts and feelings that characterises Freud's way of thinking – between life and death instincts, and dispositions to love and hate – was fully endorsed by Klein. There are different interpretations of the meaning of the "death instinct" even within the Kleinian tradition – some seeing it as primary motivational force, others as a form of aggression turned on the self in response to terror and threats of annihilation. Nevertheless, a primordial dualism of dispositions to love and to hate, and the crucial significance of the balance that is achieved in the mind between these two kinds of impulses, is central to the Kleinian perspective.

The Psychoanalysis of Children

Klein's invention and development of her distinctive version of the psychoanalysis of children was in itself a major extension of the scope and value of the psychoanalytic project. It took place in the same period as the development of a somewhat different view of child analysis by Anna Freud and her colleagues, which was more educationally and environmentally focused than Klein's insistently psychoanalytic view. In an alliance that was at times somewhat tense, the two approaches led to a significant expansion of the psychoanalytic profession (whether under the designations of child analysts or psychoanalytic child psychotherapists) in work with children and families. In Britain, the field of child and adolescent psychotherapy has been able to achieve broader support from the public health system (the National Health Service) than has been generally the case for the psychoanalytic treatment of adults, who have been more often subject to stigma and neglect from society. A profession of psychoanalytically trained child psychotherapists has become well established in Britain, and its membership is now far larger than that of the British Psychoanalytical Society.[11] This has been an aspect of the development of the British welfare state which was distinctively oriented towards the needs of children, since in the post-war period they were believed to carry the promise of a better society.

We have noted how psychoanalysis became more focused on the experience of mothers and infants as a consequence of Klein's work and that of other women analysts. The intense passions of the mother-infant relationship brought emotions of both love and hatred into the centre of psychoanalytic awareness, in a register of feelings somewhat distinct from Freud's formulations of instinctual and libidinal desires. The latter arose from his focus on the Oedipal situation rather than from the earlier two-person relationship between mother and infant. One could say that the phenomena of affect, or feeling, gained their full place in the psychoanalytic discourse not in Freud's writing (which is still influenced by a neurologically derived focus on the discharge of energy) but when analysts gave full attention to mothers and babies, and indeed to children more generally. The experience of female analysts as themselves sometimes mothers was also significant in this development. It seems likely that the conflictual aspects of mother-infant relationships which feature in Klein's writing were in part a reflection of Klein's own maternal experience, which seems not to have been the easiest. In Freud's lifetime, and for some decades beyond, the intimate care of infants was not something with which fathers were usually deeply involved.

The differences between the Freudian and the Kleinian (and Winnicottian) eras of psychoanalysis are thus substantially shaped by cultural changes in Britain, to which issues of gender were central.

Klein's Theoretical Developments: The Paranoid-Schizoid and Depressive Positions

he greater "relational" focus of psychoanalysis in Britain emerges not only from the substantive extension of its practice into the sphere of childhood, but also through the theoretical and technical advances which accompanied this. The crucial step was Klein's recognition of what she termed the paranoid-schizoid and depressive positions as key moments in the development of infants (Klein 1940, 1946). She found it necessary to explain how it was that the most angry and hate-filled feelings of the infant were a normal element in its development, which did not usually give rise to disastrous breakdowns in relationships with parents. She came to believe that a "mechanism of defence" (to use Anna Freud's term) became operative earlier than the repression theorised by Freud, because at this early stage of development the ego or integrated self was not sufficiently well formed for repression to be possible. This defence was described by Klein as "splitting", the separation of the infant's feelings of love from those of hate, and the division in the infant's mind of its image of the loving, good mother from the hateful mother who sometimes left it in a painful state of need. (She had in mind the unavoidable normal moments of deprivation in every infant's life, not extreme conditions of neglect or abuse.) This paranoid-schizoid state enabled the infant to preserve an idea or image of a good mother even when it was also consumed by moments of hatred for her (which we may observe, for example, in states of screaming rage in infants). Klein believed that the paranoid-schizoid position was itself a necessary aspect of development. It was not merely a stage experienced and then surpassed, but remained a configuration of mind, capable of later reactivation especially in times of anxiety. It is important to see that Klein's focus on the unavoidable place of hatred and destructiveness in the mind (a reason for some to have rejected Klein's ideas) arises because of her desire to see how hateful impulses were usually successfully contained, in normal development, rather than how they were not. The early function of paranoid-schizoid splitting was to achieve this containment of hateful feelings and to keep feelings of love separate from them and their destructive and fragmenting effects on the growth of the mind.

Klein saw this paranoid-schizoid state being followed, during normal development, by a further stage, what she called the "depressive position". This emerges when the infant becomes capable of observing or imagining the harm that its aggression may be causing to mother. He becomes aware that his mother, as well as himself, can suffer pain, and that the "hated mother" is one and the same person as the beloved one. It is at this point that the infant comes to have feelings for mother's well-being, as well as his own. We can say that it is in this state of mind that the infant comes to feel love for his mother as an object of value in herself, and not merely as an object which is valued as the provider for its own needs. Klein went on to argue that the impulse to make reparation for the harm he may have done or wished for this mother arises from this "depressive" state of mind. Various kinds of reciprocity in the mother-infant relationship are linked to the infant's recognition of mother's own feelings. It is important to note that "depressive" in the Kleinian lexicon is not a synonym for "depression" or "depressed" (an easy elision of meanings), although states of despair and loss of capacity for love may come about where depressive pain and its attendant guilt is unbearably intense. Klein is here postulated an innate "moral" propensity, this being conceived not merely as the imposition of a prohibition by the superego but as a natural propensity for love and care of the other.[12]

Klein and her interpreters, such as Hanna Segal (1957), believed that the recognition that the infant's feelings of love and hatred were focused on the same maternal object, who was both loved and hated, was a crucial step in the integration of the personality, involving recognition of both the loving and hating aspects of the self. She and Klein believed that this integration was a precondition for the development of mind. Klein believed that the "depressive position" involved the capacity to bear mental pain arising from the suffering of the other and the feelings of guilt that might arise from this. One can see in these ideas Klein's response to Freud's *Mourning and Melancholia* (1917), where he described the complex feelings evoked by the loss of a loved object. These could include attacks on the object for its desertion, guilt for harm caused in fantasy to the object, and reparative desires to restore it. From the experience of mourning, the object's loss could be accepted and the self then become free to find new objects to love.

Klein's concepts of the paranoid-schizoid and depressive positions were her most important development of Freud's ideas. They encompass the recognition of a fully relational conception of human identity, which Freud's mostly individual-centred model of the mind did not achieve. Other formulations in Klein's work, from early on, can be seen to fill out her belief in the fundamental object-relatedness of human beings. For example, she disputed Freud's theory of "primary narcissism", arguing that relationship to an "object" was present in the infant's mind from birth. Klein wrote:

> The analysis of very young children has taught me that there is no instinctual urge, no anxiety situation, no mental process, which does not involve objects, external or internal; in other words, object-relations are at the centre of emotional life. Furthermore, love and hatred, phantasies, anxieties, and defences are also operative from the beginning and are ab initio indivisibly linked with object relations. This insight showed me many phenomena in a new light."
>
> *(Klein 1952, p. 53)*

Klein also asserted the existence of a primary "epistemophilic instinct" (taking up a suggestion in Freud's work; Klein 1930, 1931). This was an idea of an innate desire for knowledge (initially, she thought, directed towards mother and mother's body) which she thought was parallel in its importance to the primary impulses to love and hate. The idea of symbol formation and its relevance to development, which was further elaborated by Hanna Segal, followed from the recognition of the desire for understanding, and it became important to the psychoanalytic understanding of art and literature. The therapeutic possibility of interpretation and self-understanding depends on this capability in human subjects. Klein's idea of the epistemophilic instinct was further developed in Bion's work, giving rise to his investigation of the development of the mind and of the importance of space for thought and thus development in both individual lives and in society.

Wilfred Bion[13]

Klein had described in her writing the intense projections which occurred in infants' relationship to their mothers, principally identifying these by inference from the meaning of what she observes in the play of her child analytic patients.[14] She had developed a concept of projective identification, which she understood as the unconscious placing in the other of intolerable aspects of the self. Paula Heimann, in a crucial paper in 1950,[15] had explored the disturbing effect of such projections on herself as a psychoanalyst. She proposed that the analyst's responses to these (her "counter-transference") could be understood as unconscious communications from patients and be recognised as material for interpretation. Klein was sceptical of this extension of her idea, but the "countertransference" has nevertheless since become a widely used element in psychoanalytic practice.

Bion's distinctive interest was in the emotional and mental work which mothers undertook in their experience of receiving their infant's intense projections. He proposed that the mother's crucial role was to mentally "process" her infant's projective communications, recognise their meaning (e.g., the nature of the infant's suffering) and make this meaning accessible to her infant through her understanding, and in the care of the infant which was shaped by this. Bion termed this the relation of "container" (the maternal function) and "contained" (the chaotic impulses and desires which the infant was projecting). This mental function had various bodily equivalents (e.g., the relations in reality or phantasy of mouth and nipple). Bion remained committed to Freud's and Klein's understanding of infant development. He believed that the mother's function in containing the chaotic instinctual impulses of her infant was crucial to the development of the infant's mind, or "mental apparatus". Klein saw infant development as, in benign circumstances, achieving progression to a more or less integrated personality. However, Bion also gave attention to the more extreme outcomes that could occur, to the disintegrated states of mind which he observed in the psychotic patients work with whom he described in the seminal essays published as *Second Thoughts* (1967). He describes in this work his experience of the fragmented and hallucinatory minds of his patients, who had not been able to accomplish in their development the relatively well-ordered paranoid-schizoid forms of splitting theorised by Klein. The conjunction in Bion's work between the investigation of the mental states of infants and mothers, and those of patients suffering from psychotic disintegration, is a remarkable one.[16]

Understanding the mechanisms of splitting and of projective identification became essential in the extension of psychoanalytic practice to the treatment of more extreme (psychotic) forms of mental illness which Freud believed were beyond the capacity of psychoanalysts to treat. The recognition by analysts that the pain and distress which was inflicted on them by some patients could be understood as unconscious communications from them, or evacuations of states of mind intolerable to them, provided a means by which analysts could understand the extremity of their patients' states of mind, and the functions of "containment" in managing and treating them. This has been helpful in the understanding of clinical work with autistic and psychotic patients, and has been a significant although still limited advance in psychoanalytic practice.

Bion's contribution to psychoanalytic theory in this tradition gave great importance to thinking as a mental function. He understood this to be the central role of "containment", which he saw as a process of "thinking for" the infant before it was able to think for itself, but through this process enabling its own mental capacity. He also drew on Klein's idea of the epistemophilic instinct in giving this additional foundation for psychoanalytic thought. In his view, human nature was composed not only of the two essential instincts or drives first formulated by Freud (love and hate) but three: love, hate, and the desire for understanding or knowledge, which he formulated in an algebraic notation as L, H and K.

A focus on the existence or otherwise of the capacity for thought, K, or symbol formation in patients, has become an important resource for contemporary psychoanalysts in this tradition, enabling new discriminations to be made regarding where patients' (and analysts') principal difficulties may lie.[17] The idea that the presence or absence of "thinking space" may be an important indicator of institutional and societal health has also been an outcome of Bion's influence on psychoanalysis.[18]

I will conclude with a brief reference to one another contribution to this psychoanalytic tradition, which has further enlarged its scope of understanding. This is the work of John Steiner (1993), Ronald Britton (1998), Michael Feldman (2009) and Edna O'Shaughnessy (2014), which can be understood as a response by mainly male analysts to the somewhat female and maternal focus of Klein and her colleagues' work, but also to Bion's discoveries about the nature and importance of mental function. These analysts were responding to the emergence in their clinical practice of a previously unrecognised – perhaps less common – psychopathology, which they termed "narcissism". Herbert Rosenfeld's (1971) recognition that narcissism could take two somewhat different forms, one dominated by libidinal (self-loving) impulses and the other by destructive (other-hating) impulses, gave an important foundation to these ideas. Here were patients who seemed to lack fully "depressive" capabilities for attachment to or love for others, but who were not wholly in the grip of paranoid-schizoid states of mind. They seemed, as these analysts saw it, to exist in a kind of "borderline state" and to have developed what Steiner described as a pathological organisation of their personalities of a fairly stable and, within limits, serviceable kind. But they nevertheless existed in a kind of emotional limbo, aware of the limitations of their relationship with their objects.

These analysts developed the view that what had failed in the development of these patients was a resolution of their Oedipal experience (Britton et al. 1989). This failure manifested itself in the extreme intolerance, enacted within in the analytic situation, of any relationship other than one of exclusive possession of a single "object". Actual relationships were therefore liable to be wrecked by excessive and jealous claims on others and were feared and avoided for pain they brought. Britton proposed that inability to tolerate the existence of "third" or "multiple" objects inhibited the capacity to think or understand. In the psychoanalytic situation, Britton reported, even the patient's perception of the analyst's dialogue with themselves would be liable to evoke to evoke anger or despair.

These analysts' insistence on the recognition of the Oedipal situation and its primordial "facts of life" (Money-Kyrle 1968) represents on the one hand a return within the Kleinian tradition to one of Freud's most fundamental ideas. In the context of the earlier Kleinian focus on the earliest relationship between mothers and infants, it proposed the return of fathers to the centre of the narrative.[19]

I have shown in this chapter the important developments of Freud's original ideas which were achieved in the Klein-Bion version of the object-relations tradition. I have also argued that fundamental problems of human life, which Freud confronted in his work, have remained the central topics of psychoanalytic theory and practice. Neither an acceptable balance between the impulses to love and to hate, nor the capacity to resolve the dilemmas and conflicts of mental and social life through thinking and symbolic activity ("sublimation", as Freud termed it), can thus be achieved without difficulty. In this work, psychoanalysis continues to have a necessary place.

Notes

1 I am grateful to Margaret Rustin for her help with the preparation of this paper.

2 Makari's excellent history of psychoanalysis (2008) describes Anna Freud's *The Ego and the Mechanisms of Defence* (1936) as one of its central texts, together with the work of Heinz Hartmann (1939).

3 Another development in the United States, which preceded in the 1960s in Chicago that of relational psychology, is the "self-psychology" of Heinz Kohut, which was also a departure from classical Freudian ideas. It is not possible to discuss that development in this article.

4 Jean-Michel Quinodoz, *Reading Freud* (2005), provides an admirably clear and detailed exposition of Freud's writings.

5 Sarah Hrdy's work of evolutionary psychology, *Mother Nature* (1999), explored the origins in early hunter-gatherer societies for the realistic anxieties that infants might have that births of additional children might threaten them with abandonment given scarce resources in precarious environments. This provides an evolutionary and thus ultimately a genetic explanation for some of the infantile anxieties postulated by psychoanalysts. Jim Hopkins (2003) has written further on connections between evolutionary psychology and psychoanalytic theory.

6 Although Freud abandoned the approach of his *Project for a Scientific Psychology* (1895), the emergence of a field of neuropsychoanalysis has brought a return of interest to it. (See *Annals of the New York Academy of Sciences (1998),* DOI:10.1111/(ISSN)1749–6632.

7 A comparable influence on Freud's early thinking came from the Helmholtzian school of biophysics in Germany, of which one of Freud's teachers, Brücke, was a leading member. On this see Whitebrook (2020).

8 Freud wrote: "Recent investigations have directed our attention to a stage in the development of the libido which it passes through on the way from auto-erotism to object-love. This stage has been given the name of narcissism. What happens is this. There comes a time in the development of the individual at which he unifies his sexual instincts (which have hitherto been engaged in auto-erotic activities) in order to obtain a love-object; and he begins by taking himself, his own body, as a love-object and only subsequently proceeds from this to the choice of some person other than himself as his object" (Freud 1911, pp. 60–61). And earlier: "Narcissistic or ego-libido seems to be the great reservoir from which the object-cathexes are sent out and into which they are withdrawn once more; the narcissistic libidinal cathexis of the ego is the original state of things, realised in earliest childhood, and is merely covered by the later extrusions of libido, but in essentials persists behind them" (Freud 1905a, p. 219).

9 *Reading Klein* (2017), by Margaret and Michael Rustin, is an exposition of Klein's ideas and their development. The Melanie Klein Trust website (https://melanie-klein-trust.org.uk/) provides substantial material.

10 The existence of innate aggression is a principle axis of disagreement between the Kleinian and "Independent" components of the object-relations tradition in Britain, in which Winnicott is perhaps the most significant psychoanalyst for the Independents. This is not withstanding the fact that, for example, Winnicott's paper "Hate in the Counter-Transference" (1949) is highly esteemed across the entire object-relations tradition. However, the present chapter is wholly focussed on the Kleinian and post-Kleinian development, and it would require another article to explore the similarities and differences between the Kleinian and Independent traditions.

11 Closely linked with this profession, and with the influence of Kleinian ideas, has been the growth, on a worldwide basis, of the practice of psychoanalytic infant observation, as a method of experience-based psychoanalytical education, taking place outside the context of the clinic (Miller et al. 1989; Reid 1997; Briggs 2002).

12 There is a connection between the object-relations tradition and a more other-regarding aspect of Darwinian thinking than the "survival of the fittest". Animals and human beings frequently display strong attachments to their kin and are thus, within the limits of their own "kinds", capable of altruism and "sympathies". John Bowlby's attachment theory was strongly influenced by Darwinian ideas, and his

work and object-relations psychoanalysis have affinities in this respect. The problem for human societies is how social attachments can be extended beyond circumscribed social groups defined narrowly as "us" to human beings and species more broadly.

13 Donald Meltzer's *The Kleinian Development* (1978) reviews the work of Freud, Klein and Bion, although it discusses only *The Narrative of a Child Analysis* among Klein's works. *Bion Today* (2011) edited by Chris Mawson, contains informative essays on Bion.

14 The fullest description of these is given in her *Narrative of a Child Analysis* (1961), in which late in her career she wrote up in detail a child analytic case she had undertaken in 1941 at the time when her most original discoveries were being made.

15 Heinrich Racker (1953) in Buenos Aires set out a similar idea.

16 Margaret Rustin has conjectured that Bion's knowledge of the contemporaneous work of Esther Bick, the pioneer of psychoanalytic infant observation, may well have influenced his close attention to the experiences of infancy.

17 O'Shaughnessy (1981) has provided an exceptionally clear account of how Bion's notation of L, H and K can be made use of in psychoanalytic clinical practice.

18 I have focused on the many continuities between the work of Freud, Klein and Bion in their clinical context. There is an aspect of Bion's later writing which is more philosophical, even mystical, in character which is concerned with the unknowable – or "noumenal", in Kant's terms – which I have not considered. On this see his Californian interpreter, James Grotstein (2007).

19 My view, set out in Rustin (2019), is that virtually all the theoretical developments in this tradition have been achieved in this tradition through psychoanalysts' reflections on their experiences with patients in the consulting room. In this respect, I believe this tradition to have been empiricist in its commitment.

References

Annals of the New York Academy of Sciences (May 1998) *Neuroscience of the Mind on the Centennial of Freud's Project for a Scientific Psychology*, Volume 843, Issue 1, pp. 1–184.

Bion, W. R. (1967) *Second Thoughts: Selected Papers on Psychoanalysis*. London: Heinemann.

Briggs, A. (ed.) (2002) *Surviving Space: Papers on Infant Observation*. London: Karnac.

Britton, R. (1998) *Belief and Imagination: Explorations in Psychoanalysis*. London: Routledge.

Britton, R., Feldman, M., O'Shaughnessy, E., and Steiner, J. (1989) *The Oedipus Complex Today: Clinical Implications*. London: Routledge.

Deleuze, G. and Guattari, F. (1977) *Capitalism and Schizophrenia*. New York: Viking Press (Original was published on 1972, translated to English in 1977).

Deleuze, G. and Guattari, F. (1987) *A Thousand Plateaux*. Minneapolis: University of Minnesota Press (Original was published on 1980, translated to English in 1987).

Feldman, M. (2009) *Doubt, Conviction and the Analytic Process*. London: Routledge.

Freud, A. (1936) *The Ego and the Mechanisms of Defence*. London: Hogarth Press.

Freud, S. (1905a) Three Essays on the Theory of Sexuality. In *S.E.*, 7, pp. 123–243.

Freud, S. (1905b) Fragment of an Analysis of a Case of Hysteria (Dora). In *S.E.*, 7, pp. 1–122.

Freud, S. (1900) *The Interpretation of Dreams*, SE 4:1–338, SE 5:339–621.

Freud, S. (1911) Psychoanalytic Notes on an Autobiographical Account of a Case of Paranoia (Dementia Paranoides). In *S.E.*, 12, pp. 1–79.

Freud, S. (1917) Mourning and Melancholia. In *S.E.*, 14, pp. 237–258.

Freud, S. (1921) Group Psychology and the Analysis of the Ego. In *S.E.*, 18, pp. 63–143.

Freud, S. (1923) The Ego and the Id. In *S.E.*, 19, pp. 1–59.

Freud, S. (1930) Civilization and its Discontents. In *S.E.*, 21, pp. 57–145.

Greenberg, J. and Mitchell, S. (1984) *Object Relations in Psychoanalytical Theory*. Cambridge, MA: Harvard University Press.

Grotstein, J. S. (2007) *A Beam of Intense Darkness: Bion's Legacy to Psychoanalysis*. London: Karnac.

Hartmann, H. (1939) *Ego Psychology and the Problem of Adaptation*. New York: International Universities Press.

Heimann, P. (1950) On Countertransference. *International Journal of Psychoanalysis*. 31: 81–84.

Hobbes, T. (1651). *Leviathan, or the Matter, Forme, and Power of Common-Wealth Ecclesiastical and Civil*. London: Crooke, 1968.

Hopkins, J. (2003) Evolution, emotion and conflict. In Chung, M. and Feltham, C. (eds) *Psychoanalytic Knowledge and the Nature of the Mind*. Basingstoke: Palgrave Macmillan.

Hrdy, S. B. (1999) *Mother Nature: A History of Mothers, Infants, and Natural Selection*. New York: Pantheon.

Joseph, B. (1985) Transference: The Total Situation. *International Journal of Psychoanalysis*. 66: 447–454.
Klein, M. (1930) The importance of symbol formation in the development of the ego. In Klein, M. (ed) *Love, Guilt and Reparation and Other Works 1921–45*. London: Hogarth Press (1975a).
Klein, M. (1931) A contribution to the theory of intellectual inhibition. Reprinted in Klein (1975a) op. cit.
Klein, M. (1940) Mourning and its relation to manic-depressive states. Reprinted in Klein (1975a) op cit.
Klein, M. (1946) Notes on some schizoid mechanisms. Reprinted in *Envy and Gratitude and Other Works 1946–63*. London: Hogarth Press (1975b).
Klein, M. (1952) The origins of transference. Reprinted in *Envy and Gratitude and Other Works 1946–63*. London: Hogarth Press (1975b).
Klein, M. (1961) *Narrative of a Child Analysis*. London: Hogarth Press.
Likierman, M. (2002) *Melanie Klein: Her Work in Context*. London: Continuum Books.
Makari, G. (2008) *Revolution in Mind: The Creation of Psychoanalysis*. London: Duckworth Overlook.
Mawson, C. (ed) (2011) *Bion Today*. London: Routledge.
Meltzer, D. (1978) *The Kleinian Development*. Perthshire: Clunie Press.
Miller, L., Rustin, M. E., Rustin, M. J., and Shuttleworth, J. (eds) (1989) *Closely Observed Infants*. London: Duckworth.
Money-Kyrle, R. (1968) Cognitive Development. *International Journal of Psychoanalysis*. 49 (4): 691–698.
O'Shaughnessy, E. (1981) A Commemorative Essay on Bion's Theory of Thinking. *Journal of Child Psychotherapy*. 7 (1): 181–192.
O'Shaughnessy, E. (2014) *Inquiries in Psychoanalysis: Collected Papers of Edna O'Shaughnessy*. London: Routledge.
Parsons, T. (1937) *The Structure of Social Action*. Glencoe, IL: Free Press.
Quinodoz, J.-M. (2005) *Reading Freud*. London: Routledge.
Racker, H. (1953) A Contribution to the Problem of Counter-transference. *International Journal of Psychoanalysis*. 34 (4): 313–324.
Reid, S. (ed) (1997) *Developments in Infant Observation*. London: Routledge.
Rosenfeld, H. (1971) A Clinical Approach to the Psycho-analytical Theory of the Life and Death Instincts: An Investigation into the Aggressive Aspects of Narcissism. *International Journal of Psychoanalysis*. 52: 169–178.
Roudinesco, E. (1997) *Jacques Lacan*. Cambridge: Polity.
Rustin, M. E. and Rustin, M. J. (2017) *Reading Klein*. London: Routledge.
Rustin, M. J. (2019) *Researching the Unconscious: Principles of Psychoanalytic Method*. London: Routledge.
Sayers, J. (1991) *Mothering Psychoanalysis: Helene Deutsch, Karen Horney, Anna Freud and Melanie Klein*. London: Hamish Hamilton.
Schorske, C. (1980) *Fin-de-Siècle Vienna*. New York: Random House.
Segal, H. (1957) Notes on Symbol Formation. *International Journal of Psychoanalysis*. 38: 391–397.
Steiner, J. (1993) *Psychic Retreats*. London: Routledge.
Strachey, J. (1934) The Nature of the Therapeutic Action of Psycho-analysis. *International Journal of Psycho-Analysis*. 15: 127–159.
Weber, M. (1949) *Methodology of the Social Sciences*. Glencoe: IL: Free Press.
Whitebrook, J. (2020) *Freud: An Intellectual Biography*. Cambridge: Cambridge University Press.
Winnicott, D.W. (1949). Hate in the Countertransference. *International Journal of Psychoanalysis*. 30: 69–75.
Wollheim, R. (1993) *The Mind and Its Depths*. Cambridge, MA: Harvard University Press.

11

FAIRBAIRN'S "PSYCHOLOGY OF DYNAMIC STRUCTURE" AND PHILOSOPHY

Graham S. Clarke

Timely Meditation

It is inconceivable that my approach to this topic should not reflect in some way the circumstances during which it was written, by which I mean the coronavirus pandemic. The original aspect of Fairbairn's contribution lies in his recognition of, and insistence upon, the crucial importance of relationships and interdependencies for human beings. Consequently, his theory is more topical now than it ever was, since the dominance of neoliberalism, originated by Thatcher and Reagan – "there is no such thing as society" – leading to the enforced production of entrepreneurial selves (Foucault), has proven to be a manifest and deadly backwater in the face of a global pandemic and climate crisis, and antithetical to a global future, in which we all might thrive, in a flourishing biosphere.

Background

Fairbairn collected his most important papers together in a book, *Psychoanalytic Studies of the Personality* (1952), including the crucially significant set of papers in which his original theory was developed, written during and around the Second World War and published in the *International Journal of Psychoanalysis*. Fairbairn went on to produce a detailed application of his model to hysterical states (1954) and the consequences of his model for an understanding of the nature and aims of therapy (1958), from which his view of science is drawn. He also produced a number of synopses of his psychoanalytic theory of personality, or "psychology of dynamic structure", as he came to call it (1944, 1946, 1949, 1951a, 1954, 1955, 1963) earlier work towards which can be found in Birtles and Scharff (1994).

Fairbairn's model and thinking are rooted in Scottish thinking about personality and psychoanalysis, in part influenced by the lively debates during the late 19th and early 20th centuries between the absolute idealists and the personal idealists of the day (Mander, 2005) and earlier by approaches to the social during the Scottish Enlightenment (Clarke, 2008a). I have looked closely at Fairbairn's relationship with Macmurray (Clarke, 2006), Suttie (Clarke, 2011) and Glover (Clarke, 2018), and at a Fairbairnian explanation of DID/MPD (Finnegan and Clarke, 2014). I think that his turn towards a model-based form of explanation of psychoanalytic thinking (Fairbairn, 1944) may well have been influenced by Craik's introduction of mental models (Craik, 1943). Craik's work was later used by Bowlby to motivate the introduction of "internal working models of mother" into Bowlby's theory of attachment. These models and the ways

DOI: 10.4324/9780429297076-14

they are internalised and dynamically interact are consistent with Fairbairn's own earlier description of them (https://en.wikipedia.org/wiki/Internal_working_model_of_attachment).

There is a different provenance for Fairbairn's model, which has been explored, in part at least, by those scholars interested in identifying religious influences on his thinking (Kirkwood, 2012; Hoffmann, 2014; Symington, 2014) purporting to show the degree to which the whole of his theory was grounded in religion. The fundamental importance of relationships to Fairbairn's theory is the main support for this claim. But, the fact that we come to be who we are and continue to flourish, or not, among a community of others through our relationships with them, is not exclusively Christian and might be more generally described as our social nature and circumstances. Fairbairn did write about social groups and did think that his theory was applicable to groups (Fairbairn, 1935).[1]

Fairbairn's Model of Endopsychic Structure and His Psychology of Dynamic Structure

Fairbairn's own hopes, expressed at the end of his part I, chapter 5 on *Object Relationships and Dynamic Structures* (Fairbairn, 1952) are that his efforts will afford "some indication . . . of the process whereby a psychology of dynamic structure has developed out of a psychology of object-relationships" (ibid., p. 151). The following outline in my own words is closely based upon my understanding of his model as it is described in his various synopses.

1 We all start with a *pristine bodily self*, libidinally oriented towards a world which we trust to satisfy our needs.
2 We soon learn that there are unsatisfactory aspects to our relationship with the world and start to internalise our relations with our original object (pre-ambivalent) as a form of defence.
3 As we grow and develop teeth, we become ambivalent and can discriminate between those relationships that are satisfactory and those that are unsatisfactory, and we now differentiate them into good and bad relationships and internalise them as such.
4 To be able to control our responses to the world we differentiate between those relationships that are too exciting and those that are too rejecting and separate them off from those that are acceptable.
5 Different sets of object relationships form different structures – a *central self* from the acceptable relationships, a *libidinal self* from the too-exciting relationships and an *antilibidinal self* from the too-rejecting relationships.
6 We idealise some of the acceptable object relationships to form an *ideal self* which, along with the central self, we use to control the subsidiary libidinal and antilibidinal selves as they are activated by our experiences and their internal dynamics.
7 As we develop and experience more of the world, and our relationships with others become more complex, we don't just continue to internalise relationships with others into the central libidinal and antilibidinal selves but, using the *moral defence* we are able to bolster the ideal self by internalising good aspects of significant others' behaviour.
8 By the time we are expected to choose a gendered identity, our experience of our mothers and fathers, or male and female significant others, is sufficiently developed to have coloured our choices, and we decide for ourselves who we will identify with or in opposition to.
9 During the developmental process, some of the object relationships that we internalised and made important in our internal world will have turned out to be poor or unnecessary choices that we want to modify. At this time, what Fairbairn calls the *transitional techniques*, the equivalent in many ways to the neuroses – *hysteria, obsession, phobia* and *paranoia* – are brought into play defensively to alter the ways that we relate to and use objects.
10 In Fairbairn's account of the development of the personality, the final goal is that of *mature dependence*. This is achieved when all the repressed aspects of the endopsychic structure – the

unconscious libidinal and antilibidinal selves – have been worked through and there are only *preconscious* libidinal, antilibidinal and ideal selves available.

11 This working through of the subsidiary unconscious libidinal and antilibidinal selves and their transformation into preconscious libidinal and antilibidinal selves has important consequences for the ideal and central selves, which grow at the expense of the subsidiary selves.

12 Consequently, the ideal self will become more realistic depending upon the experience of the person, and the central self will behave realistically within that person's world view.

13 In contrast to the *initial pristine self*, with its ignorance of the world and its libidinal orientation, the *maturely dependent self* will be deeply knowledgeable of the world and capable of working positively and realistically within it. It will have control of its emotional responses to the world, which will be loving and giving whilst recognising the fundamental nature of aggression and the need for its being channeled productively.

14 A personality that is initially unitary but essentially needy, ignorant and vulnerable, becomes over time, through its relations with others in a social setting, an integrated personality that is worldly and loving. It takes the world in, learns from it and acts upon and/or within it, and in so doing transforms itself into a positive and unselfish contributor to the general good.

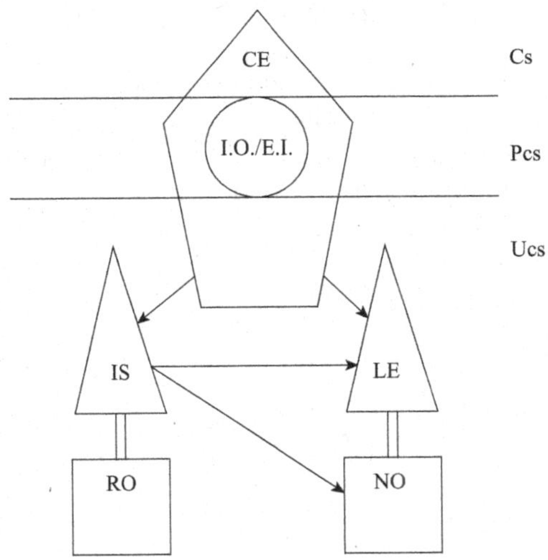

Figure 11.1 Based on Fairbairn's original 1944 diagram

The labels for the different dynamic endopsychic structures were later modified. In his 1954 paper on Hysterical States, Fairbairn introduces the Antilibidinal Ego and Object, and in the 1963 synopsis of his theory he uses the following:

In the Unconscious (Ucs) part of the mind:
The Internal Saboteur (IS) became the Antilibidinal Ego.
The Rejecting Object (RO) became the Antilibidinal Object.
The Libidinal Ego (LE) remains the same throughout.
The Needed Object (NO) becomes the Exciting Object (EO) in 1952 and then in later accounts the Libidinal Object (LO).

In the Preconscious (Pcs) part of the mind:

He places the Ideal Object (I.O.)/Ego Ideal (E.I.) in the Preconscious (Pcs) part of the Central Ego (CE) [Author's addition to original diagram based upon the 1952 text (Clarke, 2005).]

In the Conscious (Cs) part of the mind:

The Central Ego (CE) remains the same throughout.
The Central Ego or Self also contain Preconscious and Unconscious aspects which are part of the unrepressed, everyday, unconscious and preconscious, aspects of our internal world.

Fairbairn and Klein: Phantasy and Inner Reality

During the Second World War, when Fairbairn produced the papers developing his new model of inner reality, he made one contribution to the *Controversial Discussions* in 1942 (*From Instinct to Self* [*FITS*], vol. II, chap. 15), read in his absence by Glover, which represents his break with Kleinian thinking even if he had been hopeful of being accepted as a Kleinian.

> the explanatory concept of "phantasy" has now been rendered obsolete by the concepts of "psychic reality" and "internal objects" which the work of Mrs. Klein and her followers has done so much to develop . . . the time is now ripe for us to replace the concept of "phantasy" by a concept of "inner reality" peopled by the Ego and its internal objects. These internal objects should be regarded as having an organised structure, an identity of their own, and endopsychic existence and an activity as real within the inner world as those of any objects in the outer world.
>
> *(ibid., p. 294)*

In a 1942 letter to Marjorie Brierley, Fairbairn comments on his contribution, which was rejected by the Kleinians: "the Klein group disclaim any paternity – or should I say "maternity?" (ibid., p. 444). This sketches out the mature model of dynamic structure that appeared a year later in his paper on endopsychic structure. He also comments to Brierley that "The point of view I have developed is admittedly of Kleinian lineage, although privately I regard it as a definite advance beyond the Kleinian standpoint" (ibid.). Later in the same letter, in relation to his position within the British Psychoanalytic Society, he describes his theory as having fallen between two stools – the Kleinians and the (Anna) Freudians – "indeed between three, because I seem to have rather missed the boat as far as the Middle Group are concerned; and it is with the Middle Group that I should certainly align myself politically" (ibid.).

Fairbairn's View of Therapy

In his paper on the nature and aims of psychoanalytic treatment (1958), Fairbairn confesses that his own "chief conscious psycho-analytical interest . . . lies in promoting a more adequate formulation of psycho-analytical theory" (ibid., p. 78), and his hope is that such a reformulation "will have the effect of rendering the application of psycho-analytical theory a more effective therapeutic instrument" (ibid.). Fairbairn describes the therapeutic situation and the importance of the relationship with the therapist, to the outcome of the therapy.

> the disabilities from which the patient suffers represent the effects of unsatisfactory and unsatisfying object-relationships experienced in early life and perpetuated in an exaggerated form in inner reality; and . . . the actual relationship existing between the patient and the analyst as persons must be regarded as in itself constituting a therapeutic factor of prime importance. The existence of such a personal relationship in outer reality not only serves the function of providing a means of correcting the distorted relationships which prevail in inner reality and influence the reactions of the patient to outer objects, but provides the patient with an opportunity, denied to him in childhood, to undergo a process of emotional development in the setting of an actual relationship with a reliable and beneficent parental figure.
>
> *(ibid., p. 79)*

Fairbairn sees therapy as a synthetic rather than an analytic activity regarding the split inner world, carried out between two people, analyst and analysand.

> the chief aim of psycho-analytical treatment is to promote a maximum "synthesis" of the structures into which the original ego has been split, in the setting of a therapeutic relationship with the analyst. Involved in the achievement of this aim are two further aims, viz. (a) a maximum reduction of persisting infantile dependence, and (b) a maximum reduction of that hatred of the libidinal object which, according to my theory, is ultimately responsible for the original splitting of the ego.
>
> *(ibid., pp. 83–84)*

> the primary aim of psycho-analytical treatment is to effect a synthesis of the personality by reducing that triple splitting of the pristine ego which occurs to some degree in every individual . . . *the greatest of all sources of resistance – viz. the maintenance of the patient's internal world as a closed system . . . it becomes still another aim of psycho-analytical treatment to effect breaches of the closed system which constitutes the patient's inner world, and thus to make this world accessible to the influence of outer reality.*
>
> *(ibid.)*

> psycho-analytical treatment resolves itself into a struggle on the part of the patient to press-gang his relationship with the analyst into the closed system of the inner world through the agency of transference, and a determination on the part of the analyst to effect a breach in this closed system and to provide conditions under which, in the setting of a therapeutic relationship, the patient may be induced to accept the open system of outer reality.
>
> *(ibid., p. 92)*

The death instinct and the repetition compulsion are both regarded by Fairbairn as a consequence of attachment to bad objects which have been internalised and repressed (Fairbairn, 1952, p. 78). His conception of the death instinct is

> an obstinate tendency on the part of the patient undergoing psycho-analytical treatment to keep his aggression localized within the confines of the closed system of the inner world.
>
> *(Fairbairn, 1958, p. 92)*

Fairbairn gives an account of the structural conformations that underlie both neurosis and psychosis in chapter 2 of his book (1952):

> the essential difference between a psychoneurosis and a psychosis . . . in my opinion . . . is quite simple, viz. to the effect that, whereas the psychoneurotic tends to treat situations in outer reality as if they were situations in inner reality (i.e. in terms of transference), the psychotic tends to treat situations in inner reality as if they were situations in outer reality.
>
> *(Fairbairn, 1958, p. 85n)*

As far as the Oedipus situation is concerned, Fairbairn believes that this is important for therapy but not for theory, since he believes that the child "comes to equate one parental object with the exciting object, and the other with the rejecting object and by so doing *the child constitutes the Oedipus situation for himself*' (Fairbairn, 1952, p. 124) much earlier than the time the classical Oedipus conflict arises.

The Psychology of Dynamic Structure as an Explanatory System

Whether or not Fairbairn was influenced by Craik's (1943) idea of a mental model as explanation or not, since there were always Freud's structural and topographic models to legitimise a model-based approach, nevertheless he quite explicitly refers to his model as an explanatory system. Fairbairn argues that "the psychology of dynamic structure" he has developed

> provides a more satisfactory basis than does any other type of psychology for the explanation of group phenomena.
>
> *(Fairbairn, 1952, p. 128)*

He argues that his model has the requisite variety to explain a wider set of psychoanalytic principles than Freud's:

> from a topographic standpoint, Freud's theory only admits . . . three factors (id, ego and super-ego) in the production of the variety of clinical states . . . my theory admits of the operation of five factors (central ego, libidinal ego, internal saboteur, exciting object and rejecting object) – even when the super-ego as I conceive it is left out of account . . . of the three factors envisaged in Freud's theory, only two (the ego and the super-ego) are structures properly speaking – the third (viz. the id) being only a source of energy. The energy proceeding from the id is . . . conceived by Freud as assuming two forms – libido and aggression. Consequently, Freud's theory admits of the operation of two structural and two dynamic factors in all. Freud's two dynamic factors find a place . . . in my own theory; but . . . the number of the structural factors is not two, but five. Thus . . . my theory permits of a much greater range of permutations and combinations than does Freud's theory.
>
> *(ibid., pp. 128–129)*

And Freud's dualism is unduly limiting. According to Freud, the endopsychic drama largely resolves itself into a conflict between the ego in a libidinal capacity and the super-ego in an anti-libidinal capacity. The original dualism inherent in Freud's earliest views regarding repression thus remains substantially unaffected by his subsequent theory of mental structure, whereas Fairbairn's theory

> possesses all the features of an explanatory system enabling psychopathological and characterological phenomena of all kinds to be described in terms of the patterns assumed by a complex of relationships between a variety of structures . . . [and] . . . possesses the advantage of enabling psychopathological symptoms to be explained directly in terms of structural conformations, and thus of doing justice to the unquestionable fact that, so far from being independent phenomena, symptoms are but expressions of the personality as a whole.
>
> *(ibid., p. 129)*

Fairbairn is concerned with the mutability of his model from the topographic and the economic standpoints. Topographically it is relatively immutable:

> although I conceive it as one of the chief aims of psychoanalytical therapy to introduce some change into its topography by way of territorial adjustment.
>
> *(ibid., pp. 129–130)*

Fairbairn conceives it as among the most important functions of psychoanalytical therapy:

> (a) to reduce the split of the original ego by restoring to the central ego a maximum of the territories ceded to the libidinal ego and the internal saboteur, and (b) to bring the exciting object and the rejecting object so far as possible together within the sphere of influence of the central ego.
>
> *(ibid.)*

Economically, by contrast, the basic endopsychic situation is capable of very extensive modification and another of the chief aims of psychoanalytical therapy is to reduce to a minimum

> (a) the attachment of the subsidiary egos to their respective associated objects, (b) the aggression of the central ego towards the subsidiary egos and their objects, and (c) the aggression of the internal saboteur towards the libidinal ego and its object.
>
> *(ibid., p. 130)*

Fairbairn's Criticisms of Freud's Structural Model

At the beginning of his paper on psychoanalytic treatment (1958), Fairbairn gives a pithy statement of his object-relations theory, which is to

> replace Freud's description of the mental constitution in terms of the id, the ego and the superego. It has assumed the form of the description in terms of a libidinal ego, a central ego and an antilibidinal ego, together with their respective internal objects; and the basic endopsychic situation so constituted is conceived as resulting from the splitting of an original, inherent, unitary ego and of the object originally introjected by it.
>
> *(Fairbairn, 1958, p. 74)*

Fairbairn made many detailed investigations of aspects of Freud's psychoanalytic theory (1927, 1929a, 1929b, 1930, 1935, 1938a, 1938b, 1940, 1941, 1943a, 1943b, 1944), from which he developed his own model of personality. This is clearly parallel to Freud's structural model in some respects but is significantly different in terms of the scientific understanding of the physical and biological sciences that informed it.

Fairbairn's criticisms of Freud's model, which led to his proposing his own model, concerned advances in the understanding of the natural physical and biological world that had occurred since Freud developed his own ideas. The first objection was that in the modern scientific view energy and structure are inseparable:

> although Freud's whole system of thought was concerned with object-relationships, he adhered theoretically to the principle that libido is primarily pleasure-seeking, i.e. that it is directionless . . . I adhere to the principle that libido is primarily object-seeking, i.e. that it has direction . . . I regard aggression as having direction also, whereas . . . Freud regards aggression as . . . theoretically directionless. . . . Freud regards impulse (i.e. psychical energy) as theoretically distinct from structure, whereas I . . . adhere

> to the principle of dynamic structure . . . if we conceive of energy as inseparable from structure, then the only changes which are intelligible are changes in structural relationships and in relationships between structures; and such changes are essentially directional.
>
> *(Fairbairn, 1952, p. 126)*

Fairbairn's second significant objection relates to the biological understanding of organisms and the burgeoning systems approach to understanding living organisms:

> The conception of erotogenic zones is based upon an atomic or molecular conception of the organism. . . . Such atomism seems to me a legacy of the past quite alien to modern biological conceptions, in accordance with which the organism is regarded as functioning as a whole from the start . . . it is impossible to gain any adequate conception of the nature of an individual organism if it is considered apart from its relationships to its natural objects; for it is only in its relationships to these objects that its true nature is displayed.
>
> *(ibid., pp. 138–139)*

These two scientific and philosophical criticisms of Freud's structural model are explored at length and in detail in Fairbairn's most important paper, "Endopsychic Structure Considered in Terms of Object-Relationships" (1944) and in part one, chapter 5 of his book *Object-Relationships and Dynamic Structure* (1946). At the beginning of a detailed review of the process, whereby a "psychology of dynamic structure" has developed out of a psychology of object-relationships, he offers the following:

> the ultimate principle . . . may be formulated in the general proposition that libido is not primarily pleasure-seeking, but object-seeking. The clinical material on which this proposition is based may be summarized in the protesting cry of a patient to this effect – "You're always talking about my wanting this and that desire satisfied; but what I really want is a father."
>
> *(ibid., p. 137)*

Fairbairn and Pringle-Pattison

Fairbairn, as I have argued, was influenced by Andrew Pringle-Pattison, who produced a number of influential books on personality and idealist philosophy (1887, 1890, 1897) and was regarded as the pre-eminent British [*sic*] idealist at the turn of the century. The *Stanford Encyclopedia of Philosophy* argues that personalism as a distinct philosophy or world view "focusing on the full, accumulated import of the concept of the person" only emerged in the context of a broad critical reaction against what could be called *impersonalistic* philosophies, which came to dominate the Enlightenment and Romanticism in the form of rationalistic and romantic forms of pantheism and idealism, from Spinoza to Hegel. This modified idealistic, theistic personalism became decisive via its late German representative, Rudolph Hermann Lotze, not only for the American, idealistic personalism but also for the parallel, British idealistic personalism whose leading representative was Andrew Pringle-Pattison.

From the beginning, personalism proclaimed in its own way the communitarian values of solidarity and interrelation. In their insistence on inviolable dignity, personalists resisted a utilitarianism which would make one person merely "useful" for another. Whereas individualism tends to seek the self above all and often views others as means to one's own profit, personalism seeks to make of the self a gift to another (personalism's historical antecedents: https://plato.stanford.edu/entries/personalism/).

Pringle-Pattison taught Fairbairn during his undergraduate and postgraduate study in philosophy and divinity at Edinburgh University (1911–1915). Fairbairn also knew Pringle-Pattison, and Fairbairn's personal library, held by the National Library in Edinburgh (www.fairbairn.ac.uk), contains a book by Haldane (1921) that had been previously owned by Pringle-Pattison and contains a discussion of his later views on personality.

Mander, writing in 2005 of the philosophical landscape at the end of the First World War in Britain, says:

> For all its current empirical character British philosophy is not an unbroken lineage from the days of Bacon and Locke. From the second half of the nineteenth century into the early years of the twentieth the dominant school of philosophy in Britain was idealist; and this understood in a Kantian or Hegelian, not a Berkeleyan, way. The key figures from this period are T. H. Green, Edward and John Caird, and F. H. Bradley – all of whom put forward systems which were monistic as well as idealist. However, from an early date there existed also a rival school of Personal Idealists – for whom reality was best understood, not as a single spiritual structure, but as a plurality of distinct spirits. They included J.M.E. McTaggart, W. R. Sorley, J.J.C. Webb, Hastings Rashdall, and James Seth. Although this division between Absolute and Personal Idealism runs throughout these late nineteenth and early twentieth-century years, the 1918 Aristotelian Society symposium[2] is the only point at which we find a direct head-to-head debate between the two schools.
>
> *(Mander, 2005, p. 111)*

After a detailed look at the arguments presented by Bosanquet and Pringle-Pattison, Mander concludes that, at this point in the history of British philosophy, idealism was going out of vogue fast, and absolute versions were no better able to resist the ebbing fashion than personalist ones. The 1918 Aristotelian Society debate "summed up" rather than "inaugurated" a period of thought.

Whilst I think that there are parallels between Fairbairn's account of the development of the personality and Pringle-Pattison's historical and philosophical account as represented in his last *Gifford Lectures* (1922), I think that Pringle-Pattison's discussions of whether there is an enduring soul and what the nature of that might be have the most direct echoes in Fairbairn's account of the high point of his developmental schema, which goes from infantile dependence through a transitional phase to the achievement of mature dependence:

> mature dependence . . . is characterized . . . by a capacity on the part of a differentiated individual for co-operative relationships with differentiated objects. So far as the appropriate biological object is concerned, the relationship, is, of course, genital; but it is a relationship involving evenly matched giving and taking between two differentiated individuals who are mutually dependent, and between whom there is no disparity of dependence. Further, the relationship is characterized by an absence of primary identification and an absence of incorporation . . . never completely realized in practice, since there is no one whose libidinal development proceeds wholly without a hitch.
>
> *(ibid., p. 145)*

I suggest the Edinburgh *Gifford Lectures* of 1922, "The Idea of Immortality", could be the key to the philosophy behind the object relations theory of personality developed by Ronald Fairbairn, his "psychology of dynamic structure". As has been argued, Pringle-Pattison's twin enemies were English empiricism and the Anglo variant of Hegelianism. According to Pringle-Pattison, both manners of philosophy degraded the independence of the individual:

> Each self is a unique existence, which is perfectly impervious . . . to other selves – impervious in a fashion of which the impenetrability of matter is a faint analogue.
>
> *(Pringle-Pattison, 1887, p. 232)*

Pringle-Pattison's comments here stand in stark contrast to the British and American Hegelianism of the turn of the 20th century. He asserted that personality should not be merged into the absolute:

> We are anthropomorphic . . . to the inmost fibre of our thinking . . . Every category . . . every description of existence or relation, is necessarily a transcript from our own nature and our own experience . . . Everything, down to the atom, is constructed upon the scheme of the conscious self, with its *multiplicity of states and its central interpenetrating unity*. We cannot rid our thought of its inevitable presupposition.
>
> *(ibid., p. 113; emphasis added)*

In Alexander Broadie's discussion of Pringle-Pattison's view of the self in his *A History of Scottish Philosophy* (2009), he says:

> Pringle-Pattison's claim therefore is that *a self must be a self for itself, not just an object to another who is subject in relation to our self-as-object; a self must be conscious of itself as a subject in relation to something other*. . . . This implies not that we are divine but that we finite spirits are no less truly selves than God is a self, that we are neither an adjectival qualification nor an adverbial modification of him, and we are therefore, as Pringle-Pattison affirms, exclusively ourselves, where the exclusiveness is so exclusive that it excludes even God. Our exclusiveness cannot be overcome except by means of our annihilation – we would cease to be selves in ceasing to stand over against other selves. This is a deeply un-Hegelian picture driven partly by a deliverance of consciousness as endorsing an uncompromising, unsurmountable real plurality as contrasted with the Hegelian idea that the real is one. The outcome is a version of personal idealism or personalism. Pringle-Pattison was the first of the Scottish, indeed the British, idealists to provide a detailed statement of personalism, and many followed him.
>
> *(Broadie p. 321; emphasis added)*

Hallett (1933), Pringle-Pattison's assistant, suggests that in *The Idea of God in the Light of Recent Philosophy* (1917) and *The Idea of Immortality* (1922) may be found Pringle-Pattison's "mature and detailed philosophical system" (Hallett, p. 143). The following brief discussion of Pringle-Pattison's conclusions in his 1922 *Gifford Lectures* tries to show the parallels that I believe exist between Fairbairn's and Pringle-Pattison's view of a person:

In Pringle-Pattison's discussion of Cartesian theory, he says:

> If we start with the living body as the embodied soul, the problem of interaction ceases to exist, and laboured schemes of parallelism become unnecessary . . . [and] . . . we

> shall be on the way to a better understanding of the kind of unity which can really belong to soul or self.
>
> *(Pringle-Pattison, 1922, p. 92)*

While there are no direct discussions of embodiment per se in Fairbairn's work, Sutherland's comment that "[Fairbairn's] concept of a unified self that is an autonomous potential, at first, and which is then suffused with a sense of being a person in proportion as a mother's loving care is assimilated" (Sutherland, 1989, p. 169) does suggest this to me.

Pringle-Pattison discussion of parts and wholes might be profitably compared with Fairbairn's systemic view of organisms already cited above:

> The organism . . . is the first real whole, the first natural unity. It exhibits a *unity in multiplicity* far more impressive and far more important than the punctual unity of the hypothetical atom . . . in this unity and mutual implication of whole and parts we have the best analogue of the *kind* of unity which we may expect to find . . . in the self-conscious being.
>
> *(Pringle-Pattison, 1922, p. 93; emphasis added)*

This is a view which would seem to be consistent with Sutherland's assertion that

> having a self that is autonomous yet preserving its autonomy or identity by means of its matrix of relationships is the essential resource for effective enjoyable and satisfying living. . . . Fairbairn attributes all psychopathology to the splitting of the self in early experience.
>
> *(Sutherland, 1989, p. 169)*

Pringle-Pattison argues that Hume's criticism of a self, distinct from all its states and which remains the same through all their changes, is unanswerable,

> and his celebrated description of the mind as "nothing but a bundle or collection of different perceptions, which succeed each other with an inconceivable rapidity and are in perpetual flux and movement" is defective only because of the psychological atomism on which his whole theory is based.
>
> *(Pringle-Pattison, 1922, p. 96)*

Pringle-Pattison cites William James' dictum that "the passing thought is the only thinker" and argues that James overcomes Hume's atomism by the saying that "it is not to be taken . . . as a self-contained unit knowing only itself but as we really find it in life, appropriating to itself all the thoughts or states that went before" (ibid., pp. 97–98). He goes on to say, quoting Hume, that he cannot more properly compare the soul

> to anything than to a republic or commonwealth, in which several members are united by the reciprocal ties of government and subordination, and give rise to other persons, who propagate the same republic in the incessant changes of its parts . . . the idea of a system or of the *unity in multiplicity* which characterises a state or an organism supplies just what was lacking in his original account of the soul.
>
> *(ibid., p. 99; emphasis added)*

This I see as an approach that is closely related to Fairbairn's multiple-self model.

Pringle-Pattison discusses the soul as "the systematic unity of the conscious experiences of a particular individual centre – the individual centre being defined or determined at the outset by the bodily organism" (ibid., pp. 99–100), which I see as another way of describing Fairbairn's pristine self. Pringle-Pattison goes on to assert the essential nature of the subject:

> Modern psychology has sometimes boasted of being a psychology without a soul . . . but no psychology can dispense with the conception of a subject. We must recognize, as Stout puts it, that "there is a mind and not merely mental states or processes" . . . every conscious or mental state is the state or experience of a conscious individual. "The universal conscious fact is not 'feelings and thoughts exist', but 'I think' and 'I feel'".
>
> *(ibid., p. 101)*

Returning to the importance of embodiment, Pringle-Pattison maintains that

> if we must indulge our imagination with the picture of some bearer of the conscious life, let us be satisfied with the body, in which that life is certainly rooted in a very real sense . . . it remains for each of us, throughout life, the centre from which we speak and act and look out upon the universe.
>
> *(ibid., pp. 103–104)*

While there is no explicit mention of embodiment in Fairbairn, I have always thought that his underlying position is one where a primitive self, a body ego if you will, exists from the beginning – his so-called pristine ego – which is never thought about separately from the body. It is an implicitly realist acceptance of our embodiment.

Pringle-Pattison then raises and defends the fundamental importance of the personality, which is a view surely shared by Fairbairn:

> A man's self will then be for us the coherent mind and character which is the result of the discipline of time, not some substantial unit or identical subject in his body all along . . . where such an evolution has been achieved, the self-conscious life is the pre-eminent reality, which the body in its structure and organization exists to actualise . . . the concrete individual, can be adequately or properly described only in terms of personality or character – by reference to his dispositions and affections, his interests and ideals . . . man, as self-conscious, can distinguish himself even from his Maker, and set his own will against the divine.
>
> *(ibid., p. 105)*

With its own parallel to Fairbairn's conception of therapy, Pringle-Pattison stresses the importance of love:

> The highest conception we can form of perfect personality is Love, not in any shallow sentimental sense, but the self-giving Love which expends itself for others and lives in their joys and sorrows.
>
> *(ibid., p. 195)*

In a comment of direct relevance to the question of the development of mature dependence, Pringle-Pattison comments on the uniqueness of the personality:

> personality or selfhood . . . [cannot] . . . be conferred by another, it is emphatically something that must be won before there can be any question of its conservation. . . . If a man is no more than a loosely associated group of appetites and habits, the self as a moral unity has either flickered out or has never come into existence. To the constitution of such a real self, there must go some persistent purpose, or rather some coherent system of aims and ideals, and some glimpse at least, it would seem of the eternal values.
>
> *(ibid., p. 196)*

Pringle-Pattison's comments on the question of immortality suggests a more nuanced approach to mature dependence:

> there is no soul . . . except the unified personality built up by our own acts. . . . To assure people that, whatever they do, all will come right in the end is not an effective method of awakening them to the gravity of decisions here and now.
>
> *(ibid., p. 203)*

This suggests to me that Fairbairn's understanding of mature dependence is not in the realisation of a soul but the creation of a personality.

Other Potentially Relevant Philosophical Thinking That Might Be Compatible With Fairbairn's Theory

Since I have previously discussed the degree to which Fairbairn's theory and critical realism are compatible (2003, 2008b), I am sympathetic towards the critical realist personalism (CRP) of Christian Smith (2015) as a way of locating Fairbairn's model within contemporary debate. CRP's view of the person is totally consonant with Fairbairn's view, as this characterisation of a mature person from *To Flourish or Destruct* bear's witness:

> What is a person? By "person" I mean the particular kind of being that under proper conditions is capable of developing into . . . a conscious, reflexive, embodied, self-transcending centre of subjective experience, durable identity, moral commitment, and social communication who – as the efficient cause of his or her responsible actions and interactions – exercises complex capacities for agency and intersubjectivity in order to develop and sustain his or her own incommunicable self in loving relationships with other personal selves and with the nonpersonal world.
>
> *(ibid., p. 35)*

The places that Fairbairn's psychology of dynamic structure might engage with CRP are in the basic tenets of personalism:

> A moment's reflection by the (presumably sane) reader on their own subjective experience of personhood will validate this point about the person being and having a "centre of" coordinated awareness and activity. It is precisely the breakdown of such a "centre of" in the forms of multiple personality disorder, schizophrenia, and other psychotic thought and identity disorders that we judge that human personhood itself is being threatened by pathological person-damaging forces. The normally developed person, by contrast, operates primarily out of a deep, single, centred nucleus of being, self-governance and self-direction.
>
> *(ibid., p. 43)*

It was of course quite explicitly to understand and treat these "pathological person-damaging forces" that Fairbairn developed his psychology of dynamic structure. I think that it could be useful to look at CRP from the perspective of Fairbairn's psychology of dynamic structure to see if and how this model might help to clarify CRP's principles and how CRP might be modified to properly take account of the unconscious aspects of our lives, since it is not clear that "the normally developed person" is as unproblematic as is implied by the quotation.

Conclusion

My investigations into the philosophical underpinnings of Ronald Fairbairn's "psychology of dynamic structure" have led me towards "personalism" as a potential "deep structure" of his approach. This personalism – aspects of which I believe Fairbairn could have taken, consciously or unconsciously, from Pringle-Pattison – grew out of Pringle-Pattison's detailed study of classical and enlightenment thought (Aristotle, Hegel, and the Scottish Enlightenment), which Fairbairn originally encountered as an undergraduate and was a topic of detailed public discussion at the time Fairbairn was still developing his own ideas. This view of Fairbairn's theory throws some light on the many similarities between his approach and that of John Macmurray (1957, 1961), who also adopted a form of personalism. I think that a secular critical realist personalism might be the best candidate for the philosophical foundation of a thoroughgoing object-relations psychoanalysis of the sort Fairbairn developed, a psychology of dynamic structure, that might also help us to change the social order to embrace relationships and dependencies rather than seeing them as fatal flaws.

Acknowledgements

I would like to thank Tamas Pataki for reading and commenting on this chapter and making a number of very helpful suggestions on its structure and content.

Note

1 For a recent synoptic view of Fairbairn's work see Clarke and Scharff (2014).
2 'Do finite individuals possess a substantive or an adjectival mode of being?' *Proceedings of the Aristotelian Society*, 1917–18, 18, pp. 479–581.

References

Birtles, E. F., and Scharff, D. E. (Eds.) (1994) *From Instinct to Self: Selected Papers of W.R.D. Fairbairn, Volume II: Applications and Early Contributions*. Jason Aronson: Northvale, NJ.

Broadie, A. (2009) *A History of Scottish Philosophy*. Edinburgh University Press: Edinburgh.

Clarke, G. S. (2003, November) "Fairbairn and Macmurray: Psychoanalytic studies and critical realism". *Journal of Critical Realism*, 2(1).

Clarke, G. S. (2005) "The preconscious and psychic change in Fairbairn's model of Mind". *International Journal of Psychoanalysis*, 86(1): 61–77.

Clarke, G. S. (2006) *Personal Relations Theory: Fairbairn, Macmurray and Suttie*. Routledge: London.

Clarke, G. S. (2008a) "Notes on the origins of 'personal relations theory' in aspects of social thinking of the Scottish Enlightenment". *Psychoanalysis, Culture & Society*, 13: 325–334.

Clarke, G. S. (2008b) "The internal conversation: A personal relations theory perspective". *Journal of Critical Realism*, 7(1): 57–82.

Clarke, G. S. (2011, October) "Suttie's influence on Fairbairn's object relations theory". *Journal of the American Psychoanalytic Association*, 59(5): 939–960.

Clarke, G. S. (2018) *Thinking through Fairbairn*. Routledge: London.

Clarke, G. S., and Scharff, D. E. (Eds.) (2014) *Fairbairn and the Object Relations Tradition*. Karnac: London.

Craik, K. (1943) *The Nature of Explanation*. Cambridge University Press: Cambridge.

Fairbairn, W.R.D. (1927) "Notes on the religious phantasies of a female patient". In: *Psychoanalytic Studies of the Personality* (p. 183). Tavistock: London.

Fairbairn, W.R.D. (1935) "The sociological significance of communism considered in the light of psycho-analysis". In: *Psychoanalytic Studies of the Personality* (pp. 233–246). Tavistock: London, 1952.

Fairbairn, W.R.D. (1938a) "Prolegomena to a psychology of art". Ch. 23 in *From Instinct to Self Vol II* (1994) (Eds.) Scharff, D. E. and Fairbairn Birtles, E. Jason Aronson Inc: London.

Fairbairn, W.R.D. (1938b) "The ultimate basis of aesthetic experience". Ch. 24 in *From Instinct to Self Vol II* (1994) (Eds.) Scharff, D. E. and Fairbairn Birtles, E. Jason Aronson Inc: London.

Fairbairn, W.R.D. (1941). "A revised psychopathology of the psychoses and psychoneuroses". *International Journal of Psychoanalysis*, 22(3, 4): 250–279. In: *Psychoanalytic Studies of the Personality* (pp. 28–58). Tavistock: London, 1952.

Fairbairn, W.R.D. (1942) "Letter to Marjorie Brierley". In: *From Instinct to Self Vol II* (pp. 443–547) (1994) (Eds.) Scharff, D. E. and Fairbairn Birtles, E. Jason Aronson Inc: London

Fairbairn, W.R.D. (1944). "Endopsychic structure considered in terms of object relationships". *International Journal of Psychoanalysis*, 25: 70–92. In: *Psychoanalytic Studies of the Personality* (pp. 82–136). Tavistock: London,1952.

Fairbairn, W.R.D. (1946). "Object-relationships and dynamic structure". *International Journal of Psychoanalysis*, 27: 30–37. In: *Psychoanalytic Studies of the Personality* (pp. 137–151). Tavistock: London, 1952.

Fairbairn, W.R.D. (1949), "Steps in the Development of an Object-Relations Theory of the Personality (1949)". In: Part One, Ch.VI in *Psychoanalytic Studies of the Personality*. RKP: London.

Fairbairn, W.R.D. (1951a) "A synopsis of the development of the author's views regarding the structure of the personality (1951)". In: Part One, Ch. VII in *Psychoanalytical Studies of the Personality*. RKP: London.

Fairbairn, W.R.D. (1951b) "Phantasy and Inner reality". Ch. 15 in *From Instinct to Self Vol II* (1994) (Eds.) Scharff, D. E. and Fairbairn Birtles, E. Jason Aronson Inc: London.

Fairbairn, W.R.D. (1952) *Psychoanalytic Studies of the Personality*. RKP: London.

Fairbairn, W.R.D. (1954) "Observations on the nature of hysterical states". Ch. 1 in *From Instinct to Self Vol 1* (1994) (Eds.) Scharff, D. E. and Fairbairn Birtles, E. Jason Aronson Inc: London.

Fairbairn, W.R.D. (1955) "Observations in defence of the object-relations theory of the personality". Ch. 6 in *From Instinct to Self Vol 1* (1994) (Eds.) Scharff, D. E. and Fairbairn Birtles, E. Jason Aronson Inc: London.

Fairbairn, W.R.D. (1958) "On the nature and aims of psychoanalytic treatment". Ch. 4 in *From Instinct to Self Vol 1* (1994) (Eds.) Scharff, D. E. and Fairbairn Birtles, E. Jason Aronson Inc: London.

Fairbairn, W.R.D. (1963) "Synopsis of an object-relations theory of the personality". Ch. 9 in *From Instinct to Self Vol 1* (1994) (Eds.) Scharff, D. E. and Fairbairn Birtles, E. Jason Aronson Inc: London.

Finnegan, P. A. and Clarke, G. S. (2014) "Fairbairn and multiple personality". Ch. 16 in *Fairbairn and the Object Relations Tradition* (Eds.) Clarke, G. S. and Scharff, D. E. Karnac: London.

Haldane, J. S. (1921) *Mechanism, Life, and Personality: An Examination of the Mechanistic Theory of Life and Mind*. John Murray: London.

Hallett, H. F. (1933, April) Obituary. "Andrew Seth Pringle-Pattison, 1856–1931". *MIND*, XLII(166).

Hoffmann, M., and Hoffmann, L. (2014) "Religion in the life and work of W.R.D. Fairbairn". Ch. 6 in *Fairbairn and the Object Relations Tradition* (Eds.) Clarke, G. S. and Scharff, D. E. Karnac: London.

Kirkwood, C. (2012) *The Persons in Relation Perspective: In Counselling, Psychotherapy and Community Adult Learning*. Sense: Rotterdam, Boston, and Taipei.

Macmurray, J. (1957) *The Self as Agent*. Vol I. The Form of the Personal, Faber and Faber: London.

Macmurray, J. (1961) *Persons in Relation*. Vol II. The Form of the Personal, Faber and Faber: London.

Mander, W. J. (2005) "Life and finite individuality: The Bosanquet/Pringle-Pattison debate". *British Journal for the History of Philosophy*, 13(1): 111–130.

Pringle-Pattison, A. (1887) *Hegelianism and Personality*. William Blackwood and Sons: Edinburgh and London.

Pringle-Pattison, A. (1890) *Scottish Philosophy*. William Blackwood and Sons: Edinburgh and London.

Pringle-Pattison, A. (1897) *Man's Place in the Cosmos*. William Blackwood and Sons: Edinburgh and London.

Pringle-Pattison, A. (1917) *The Idea of God in the Light of Recent Philosophy. The Gifford Lectures Delivered in the University of Aberdeen in the Years 1912 and 1913*. Oxford University Press: London.

Pringle-Pattison, A. (1922) *The Idea of Immortality, The Gifford Lectures Delivered in the University of Edinburgh in the Year 1922*. Oxford University Press: London.
Smith, C. (2015) *To Flourish or Destruct: A Personalist Theory of Human Goods, Motivations, Failure, and Evil*. University of Chicago Press: London.
Sutherland, J. D. (1989) *Fairbairn's Journey into the Interior*. Free Association Books: London.
Symington, N. (2014) "Fairbairn, Suttie and Macmurray – An essay". Ch. 5 in *Fairbairn and the Object Relations Tradition* (Eds.) Clarke, G. S. and Scharff, D. E. Karnac: London.

12
FROM FREUD TO WINNICOTT
Aspects of Paradigm Change[1]

Zeljko Loparic

The main purpose of this chapter is to present a unified view on Winnicott's contribution to psychoanalysis. Although Winnicott is presently recognized as one of the great figures in the history of psychoanalysis it is evident that a *systematic* philological, historical and conceptual study of his writings are rare, in spite of some notable exceptions (see Abram, 2007, 2008; Davis and Wallbridge, 1981; Ogden, 1986; Phillips, 1988). Moreover, we are still waiting for the publication of Winnicott's *Collected Works*, and generally speaking, Winnicott research can hardly be compared with current Freudian scholarship. This situation is changing, particularly in Latin America, where Winnicott has become the most quoted psychoanalytic author after Freud (cf. Abadi and Outeiral, 1997). Unfortunately, citation does not necessarily mean that the work is truly studied and understood.

My emphasis in this chapter is on the *nature* of Winnicott's contribution rather than a focus on one or another of his many contributions to psychoanalysis. I aim to achieve this by *conceptual analysis* largely based on a study of the *historical development* of Winnicott's ideas. Winnicott himself recommended a historical approach to the understanding of his views on emotional development. In his posthumously published book *Human Nature*, after explaining some of his ideas on the imaginative elaboration of body functioning, he added:

> The reader must form a personal opinion of these matters, after *learning* what is *thought* as far as possible in the *historical manner*, which is the only way that the theory of any one moment [in personal development] becomes *intelligible* and *interesting*.
>
> *(Winnicott, 1988: 42; emphasis added)*

Here I suggest that 'interesting' means both personally appealing and theoretically important. Clearly this applies to any attempt to understand other parts of Winnicott's theory and indeed psychoanalysis in general:

> Readers of analytic literature may easily become impatient if they take some statement of analytic theory and treat it as if it were a final pronouncement, never to be modified. Psychoanalytic theory is all the time *developing*, and it must develop by *natural process* rather like the emotional condition of the human being that is under study.
>
> *(ibid., 46; emphasis added)*

DOI: 10.4324/9780429297076-15

It would be very tempting to try to develop this Winnicottian 'natural process' view of the origin of the scientific attitude and of the growth of scientific knowledge as Winnicott begins to do in the first chapter of *Human Nature*, but instead, I shall limit myself to apply an already existing model of natural growth of science expounded by Thomas S. Kuhn.[2]

There is one straightforward reason to appeal to Kuhn's theory in the present context: both Winnicott and Kuhn were strongly influenced by Darwin. Winnicott is indebted to Darwin for his view that 'living things could be studied scientifically, with the corollary that gaps in knowledge need not scare me' (Winnicott, 1996: 7). Kuhn, in turn, learned from the British biologist that the growth of science is a struggle between rival paradigms for survival in scientific communities. The aim of that struggle is not towards something like the final truth, but the temporarily greater problem-solving efficiency of scientific knowledge.[3] This shaky goal is achieved by dramatic changes in established scientific world-views or, more technically, by Gestalt switches in scientific paradigms commonly called 'scientific revolutions'.

Following Kuhn, I shall therefore be discussing the *paradigm switch* introduced by Winnicott into the psychoanalytic discipline. To present this with clarity, I shall start with an outline of Freud's paradigm that resulted from 'normal research' and show how it was the emergence of anomalies that subsequently brought about a crisis that triggered Winnicott's revolutionary research. My main thesis here is that Winnicott's research concluded by Winnicott introducing a new paradigm for psychoanalysis, that is, new guiding problems and a new conceptual framework that would enable him to solve the anomalies he discovered. My conclusion is that Winnicott was a revolutionary thinker and that he paved a new way for scientific research and practice in psychoanalysis. Furthermore, I aim to show how he achieved a great deal of such research, without ever intending that his alternative framework or his results were 'final pronouncements'.[4]

I am not the first one to speak of Winnicott's paradigm and several authors have used Kuhn to study of the history of psychoanalytic thought (Modell, 1968; Levenson, 1972; Lifton, 1976). Greenberg and Mitchell view the history of psychoanalysis as

> the dialectic between the original Freudian model,[5] which takes as its starting point the instinctual drives, and an alternative comprehensive model initiated in the work of Fairbairn and Sullivan, which evolves structure solely from the individual's relationships with other people.
>
> *(Greenberg and Mitchell, 1983: 2)*

The results reached by the latter two authors are, however, severely limited by the fact that they only considered the metaphysical component of psychoanalytic theory, which completely leaves aside concrete problem-solutions (i.e., the so-called exemplars'), which are the main components of Kuhn's model of analysis.

Kuhn's concept of the exemplar is applied by Judith Hughes, whose attempt is to depict 'the paradigms which constitute psychoanalytic theory' by describing the 'Freudian paradigms' and scrutinizing their 'transformation' in the work of Klein, Fairbairn and Winnicott (Hughes, 1989). To that end, she not only analyzes specific theoretical difficulties in paradigm formation but also pays attention to clinical issues and clinical practice, which forced the re-shaping of the psychoanalytic domain within the British Psychoanalytical Society. With Klein, she concentrates on the case of 'Richard', and with Winnicott, the case history titled *The Piggle*. 'The consulting room', writes Hughes, 'has, after all, provided the empirical base for the psychoanalytic enterprise, and nowhere has it been more apparent than in Britain' (Hughes, 1989: 176).

More recently, a view congenial with applying Kuhn's approach to the history of psychoanalysis, has been adopted by Joyce McDougall (1996: 226), and Jan Abram has referred to the Kuhn-based paradigm switch thesis as an arguable alternative interpretation of Winnicott's contribution to psychoanalysis (2008: 1205).[6]

In 1988, Adam Phillips approached Winnicott in a way which, although not presented in Kuhn's terms, uses a very similar language. Phillips admitted, without the ambiguities which spoil so many other accounts, that Winnicott introduced 'important innovations' in psychoanalytic practice and technique which represent – despite Winnicott's 'disingenuous' disguises – 'radical departures from Freud'. The main departure selected by Phillips consists in the observation that Winnicott 'would derive everything in his work, including a theory of the origins of scientific objectivity and a revision of psychoanalysis, from the *paradigm* of the developing mother-infant relationship' (1988: 5; emphasis added). For Winnicott, says Phillips, the mother-infant relationship was becoming 'the *primary model* for the psychoanalytic situation' and the main '*source of analogy* in his work' (1988: 87; emphasis added). Let me provide an example among many given by Phillips:

> But whereas for Freud psychoanalysis was essentially a 'talking cure', for Winnicott, the mother-infant relationship, in which communication was relatively non-verbal, had become the paradigm for the analytic process, and this changed the role of interpretation in psychoanalytic treatment.
>
> *(ibid., 1988: 138)*

Guided by the mother-baby paradigm, Winnicott was led to new questions and thus to new results. Examples of such questions 'rarely addressed in psychoanalytic theory' are the following: What do we depend on to make us feel alive or real? And: Where does our sense come from, when we have it, that our lives are worth living? Winnicott approached these issues, continues Phillips, by linking the 'observation of mothers and infants' with 'insights derived from psychoanalysis' (1988: 5–6). But it was not simply that. Winnicott also enriched psychoanalysis with essential *new insights* which turned out to be incompatible with those of Freud, since they were 'rarely linked by him [Winnicott] with the place of the erotic in adult life'. For Winnicott, the 'crux of psychoanalysis' was the 'infant's early dependent vulnerability' in a *two-person relationship* with the mother, not 'the Oedipus complex – a three-person relationship'. Whereas Freud, starting from the Oedipus situation, was interested 'in the adult's struggle with incompatible and unacceptable desires', which put in danger their 'possibilities for satisfaction', Winnicott, starting with the relationship of total dependence, treated these possibilities as 'part of a larger issue of the individual's possibilities for personal authenticity, what he [Winnicott] will call 'feeling real' (1988: 7). Working in that manner, and 'neglecting Freud's metapsychology' (1993: 43), Winnicott evolved, during the 1940s, 'a powerful rival developmental theory to those of both Freud and Klein' (1988: 97).

What have I to add to the above results? Firstly, a more systematic and precise account of the essential constitutive elements of Winnicott's paradigm and, secondly, a more detailed analysis of the process Winnicott went through in searching for these elements. To that end, I shall use, as previously stated, the word 'paradigm' not just in the common-sense meaning of a model, but in the more technical sense defined by Thomas Kuhn in the postscript of the second edition of his book *The Structure of Scientific Revolutions* (1970a). I shall also borrow Kuhn's general view on scientific research and on the growth of science.[7] In substance, I aim to produce a more accurate picture of Winnicott's procedures and contributions, which may serve as a blueprint for further research on his contribution, as well as help to avoid some not infrequent misunderstandings.[8]

Kuhn's View of Empirical Science

According to Kuhn, normal, everyday science is a *problem-solving activity* guided by a *paradigm*. Scientific problems resemble *puzzles* in so far as they are thought of as having an assured solution within the adopted theoretical framework (1970a: 37). Socially important problems become scientific only after they have been reduced to puzzles, their solution depending exclusively on the ingenuity of practitioners trained in a paradigm. Scientists do not intend, and even refuse, to cope with every problem. 'Scientism' – the idea that science can solve all questions that are important for human kind – is a peculiar philosophical stance on science and not at all part of what scientists actually are aiming at.

Paradigms, presupposed in scientific puzzle solving, are of two kinds. Firstly, there are *accepted examples* of actual scientific practice which provide '*models* from which spring particular coherent traditions of scientific research' (1970a: 10; emphasis added). In the postscript to the second edition of his book, Kuhn calls these accepted models 'exemplars', by which he means 'the concrete problem-solutions that students encounter from the start in their scientific education' (p. 187). Secondly, paradigms are 'conceptual, theoretical, instrumental and methodological *commitments* that guide the scientific research' (p. 42). In the postscript Kuhn offered a more detailed analysis of this second concept of paradigm and specified that its main components are guiding empirical generalizations,[9] ontological models of the subject matter, authorized heuristic procedures (preferred or permissible analogies and metaphors) and finally, values or norms which define scientific practice by specific groups and provide their members with a sense of community (1970a: 182–185). Exemplars and constellations of commitments, taken together, constitute the 'disciplinary matrix' of a scientific discipline.

Exemplars are the more important of the two. To start with, a science is not *learned* by becoming acquainted with verbal statements of laws or rules, but by being taught how to see new problems in the light of exemplars: 'That [scientific] sort of learning is not acquired by exclusively verbal means. Rather it comes as one is given words together with concrete examples of how they function in use, nature and words, learned together' (1970a: 191). By saying that we learn 'nature and words' together, Kuhn implies that scientific groups with different paradigms live, in some sense, in *different worlds* and that they use language in essentially different ways. This in turn accounts for the *incommensurability* of theoretical statements and the absence of supra-paradigmatic criteria of truth and interpretation. Indeed, in order to be able to interpret a statement we must first be able to see a case of it, and this requires a paradigm for observing the case. The verbal interpretation (being 'a deliberative process by which we choose among alternatives as we do not in perception itself') always comes second (p. 194). The knowledge that is learned from paradigmatic examples is not 'explicit' but rather 'tacit'.

The change of paradigms for seeing the world is initially also a tacit, unintentional and even unconscious process. It resembles Gestalt switches, which happen 'suddenly' and 'involuntarily', 'over which we have no control' (pp. 111 and 194). The central aspect of Gestalt switches which are at the 'heart of the revolutionary process' (p. 202) is 'that some of the similarity relations change' (p. 200), which again implies the changes in the use of language. Kuhn writes:

> Objects that were grouped in the same set before are grouped in different ones afterward and vice versa. [. . .] Since most objects within even the altered sets continue to be grouped together, the names of the sets are usually preserved. Nevertheless, even the transfer of a subset is ordinarily part of a critical change in the network relations among them. [. . .] Not surprisingly, therefore, when such re-distributions occur, two men whose discourse had previously proceeded with apparently full understanding

> may suddenly find themselves responding to the same stimulus with incompatible descriptions and generalizations.
>
> (Kuhn, 1970a: 200–201)

Differences in responses to the same stimuli do not only mean that our world-view has modified, they also reveal that the world itself has suffered a change. These disagreements cannot be eliminated 'simply by stipulating definitions for troublesome terms', nor can we resort to a 'neutral language', for no paradigm independent of language exists. A paradigm change is, therefore, necessarily followed by a 'communication breakdown'. In such cases, translation from one scientific idiom to the other is a resource of dialogue, but not of consensus; moreover, 'it is threatening and is entirely foreign to normal science' (p. 203). It is clear that holding different paradigms scientists usually disagree on at least three points: first, the list of problems that any candidate must be able to resolve in order to enter a paradigm; second, the list of criteria for acceptable solutions; third, the list of criteria for what exists, since, when a paradigm changes some things simply cease to exist and others start to exist. For instance, what was previously seen as a duck, was called, and has been a duck is now seen as, is called, and has become a rabbit (Winnicott, 1971: 111). Under such circumstances, the procedure of translating does not lead us very far, because, according to the context, being a duck might indeed have a very different meaning from being a rabbit.[10]

The other important point is that science does not make progress in solving problems by applying theories and rules, but by seeing new problem situations in the light of exemplars: 'Scientists solve puzzles', writes Kuhn, 'by modelling them on previous puzzle situations, often with minimal recourses to symbolic generalizations' (p. 190). That brings us back to the thesis that scientific knowledge is embedded in shared exemplars rather than in rules, laws or criteria of identification.

Guided by a way of seeing the world, scientists attempt 'to force nature into the pre-formed and relatively inflexible box which the paradigm supplies' (p. 24). Kuhn adds:

> No part of the aim of normal science is to call forth new sorts of phenomena; indeed those that will not fit the box are often not seen at all. Nor do scientists normally aim to invent new theories, and they are often intolerant of those invented by others. Instead, normal scientific research is directed to the articulation of those phenomena and theories that the paradigm already supplies.
>
> (Kuhn, 1970a: 24)

To summarize: in normal science, scientists restrict their efforts to solve three kinds of problem: to determine significant facts, to match facts with theory and to articulate existing theories (p. 34).

Why then, do paradigmatic changes occur at all? The answer is: when a *crisis* occurs, that is, 'a pronounced failure' of the old theory 'in the problem-solving activity' (ibid., pp. 74–75). Now, every paradigm is constantly confronted with anomalies, recalcitrant problems which should have been solved but were not. Usually, scientists leave such problems provisionally to the side and do not reject the paradigm because of this kind of failure. However, it also happens that some persistent anomalies may oblige a scientist to interrupt their normal research and pause over them, and reasons may vary. They may become concerned about the absence of guiding generalizations, or about the impossibility of solving a particularly important social problem or a problem felt to be significant for technical and technological reasons (p. 82). When anything like this happens, 'an anomaly comes to seem like more than just another puzzle of normal science', and the transition to crisis and to extraordinary science or to revolutionary research has begun. Kuhn describes the emergence of a crisis in the following way:

> More and more of the field's most eminent men devote more and more attention to it. If it still continues to resist, as it usually does not, many of them may come to view its resolution as *the* subject matter of their discipline. [. . .] An [. . .] important source of change is the divergent nature of the numerous partial solutions that concerted attention to the problem has made available. [. . .] Through this proliferation of divergent articulations (more and more frequently they will come to be described as *ad hoc* adjustments), the rules of normal science become increasingly blurred. Though there is still a paradigm, few practitioners prove to be entirely agreed about what it is. Even formerly standard solutions of solved questions are called in question.
>
> *(Kuhn, 1970a: 82–83)*

Finally, how are we to describe the progress achieved through scientific revolutions? The answer is that they will not be an approximation to the truth. Whereas normal science is cumulative, revolutions introduce new problem fields and incommensurable world-views. We have therefore to 'relinquish the notion, explicit or implicit, that changes in a paradigm carry scientists, and those who learn from them, closer and closer to the truth' (ibid., p. 170). Scientific growth is not a process of evolution in the direction of an ultimate goal at all. In what terms, then, can we speak about the progress of science? Let's take an analogy inspired by Darwin: just as the evolution of the species is a result of a natural selection of organisms 'more adapted' to the environment (and has no final goal set by God or by Nature), so the evolution of scientific theories are a product of 'the selection by conflict, within scientific communities, of the fittest way to practice future science' (ibid., 172). This evolution also has no final goal.

Not all sciences are *mature* enough to be able 'to work from a single paradigm or from a closely related set' (ibid., 162). This kind of maturity is rather rare. Even in highly developed sciences we encounter competing paradigms at any given time (ibid., 209). Moreover, one has to distinguish between scientific communities that have achieved the mature paradigm stage, from schools that are still in the 'pre-paradigm' period. During such a period, individuals may be said to practice science, but 'the results of their enterprise do not add up to science as we know it' (ibid., 163). Fact-gathering, for instance, may occur, 'but it is far more nearly at random than the one subsequent scientific development makes familiar' (ibid., 15). Some data may be obtained from observation, others from experiments and still others 'from established crafts like medicine', which is 'one readily accessible source of facts that could not have been casually discovered' (ibid., 15). When the 'fundamental tenets of a field are once more at issue' and 'doubts are continually expressed about the very possibility of continued progress if one or another of the opposed paradigms are adopted' – that is, during periods of revolution – scientific fact-gathering usually regresses to a situation very similar to the pre-paradigmatic one. Cumulative scientific progress seems both obvious and assured only during periods of normal science (ibid., 163).

Objections Against the Application of Kuhn's Theory to Review the History and Structure of Psychoanalysis

Before applying Kuhn's view of science and scientific progress to Winnicott's contribution to psychoanalysis, I shall briefly address two possible objections to a Kuhnian reading of psychoanalysis in general. In the first place, it might be said that Kuhn's view only applies to natural sciences and therefore not to psychoanalysis, which is a science of man. This way of reading Kuhn is not without difficulties. It is true that for Kuhn it remains an open question 'what parts of social science have yet acquired such fully-fledged paradigms at all' (ibid., 15). However, by saying this, Kuhn does not imply that there are no paradigm-like elements in social sciences. In fact, Kuhn observes:

> members of all scientific communities, including the schools of the 'pre-paradigm' period, share the sorts of elements which I have collectively labeled 'a paradigm'. What changes with the transition to maturity is not the presence of a paradigm but rather its nature. Only after that change is normal *puzzle* solving research possible.
>
> *(Kuhn, 1970a: 179)*

Nor are we prohibited to speak of progress in disciplines different from natural sciences, or even in areas very remote from empirical research, such as theology and philosophy: 'The theologian who articulates dogma or the philosopher who refines Kantian imperatives contributes to progress, if only that of the group that shares his premises' (ibid., 162). The real issue for Kuhn in discussing psychoanalysis and social sciences in general is the problem of transition from pre-scientific or pre-paradigmatic kinds of questions answering to the specifically scientific or paradigmatic way of problem-solving. This process can be studied in its own right, since it is constantly going on in several fields of Western culture. Current research 'in parts of philosophy, psychology, linguistics, and even art history' suggest, according to Kuhn, that these disciplines are looking for new paradigms (ibid., 121 and 162).

In the postscript of the second edition, Kuhn stresses once again that his main theses about the structure of science and of scientific revolutions are applicable to many other fields as well: 'To the extent that the book portrays scientific development as a succession of tradition-bound periods punctuated by non-cumulative breaks, its theses are undoubtedly of wide applicability' (ibid., 208). And he explains why it is so:

> But they should be [applicable], for they are borrowed from other fields. Historians of literature, of music, of the arts, of political development, and of many other human activities have long *described their subjects in the same way.* Periodization, in terms of revolutionary breaks in style, taste, and institutional structure, has been among their standard tools. If I have been original with respect to concepts like these, it has mainly been by applying them to the sciences, fields which had been widely thought to develop in a different way.
>
> *(ibid.; emphasis added)*

As Kuhn says earlier in the text (ibid., 92), it was indeed politics which provided him with the initial idea of revolution. What Kuhn did is nothing other than isolate features of problem-solving activity, 'none necessarily unique to science' (ibid., 209). This is why he cannot but agree with those who feel the need 'for comparative study of the corresponding communities in other fields'. The questions to be asked are:

> How does one select and how is one elected to membership in a particular community, scientific or not? What is the process and what are the stages of socialization to the group? What does the group collectively see as its goals; what deviations, individual or collective, will it tolerate; and how does it control the impermissible aberration? A fuller understanding of science will depend on answers to other sorts of questions as well, but there is no area in which more work is so badly needed.
>
> *(ibid., 209–210)*

Against my application of Kuhn's theory of scientific-problem solving to psychoanalysis it might be objected, in the second place, that Kuhn did not consider that psychoanalysis was a scientific activity at all, since, in an article written in 1970, he agreed with Karl Popper who wrote that psychoanalysis 'cannot *now* properly be labelled a "science"' (Kuhn, 1970b: 7; emphasis added).

A careful reading of Kuhn's article allows for several caveats to argue against this objection. To start with, the very phrasing of Kuhn's agreement with Popper indicates that it is restricted to the present, the implication being that though psychoanalysis is not a science *now*, there is no reason for thinking that it could not become a science in the future. There is thus nothing intrinsically non-scientific in the project of psychoanalytic research.

This reading is confirmed by Kuhn's comparison of 'contemporary [*sic*] psychoanalysis' with 'older medicine' and with crafts and practical arts in general, such as astrology as it was practiced in the more remote past by famous astronomers, including Ptolemy, Kepler and Tycho Brahe, and even with engineering and meteorology, as they were 'practiced a little more than a century ago'. Kuhn writes:

> In all these fields shared theory was adequate only to establish the plausibility of the discipline and to provide a rationale for the various craft-rules which governed practice. These rules had provided their use in the past, but no practitioner supposed they were sufficient to prevent recurrent failure.
>
> *(Kuhn, 1970b: 8)*

All mentioned crafts were constantly searching for a more stable and effective paradigm. Indeed, writes Kuhn:

> a more articulated theory and more powerful rules were desired, but it would have been absurd to abandon a plausible and badly needed discipline with a tradition of limited success because these desiderata were not yet at hand. In their absence, however, neither the astrologer nor the doctor could do research. Though they had rules to apply, they have no *puzzles* to solve and therefore no science to practice.
>
> *(ibid., p. 9)*

From this historical sketch, Kuhn extracts that the main consequence for psychoanalysis is that it is still unable to formulate puzzles of the kind which are currently being solved by normal science during normal research. The problem-situation of psychoanalysis is similar to that of medicine (engineering and meteorology in the recent past), and to that of astrology, in earlier periods of Western culture. If, *for that reason*, it may be said that psychoanalysis resembles astrology, this *does not* imply that it must have the same destiny and, that it cannot possibly come to formulate its own fully-fledged paradigms to solve puzzles.

Kuhn's article contains an important remark about the similarity between the behaviour of scientists in pre-paradigmatic and revolutionary periods and that of philosophers in general. Kuhn understands that 'the reasons for the choice between metaphysical systems', as described for instance by Popper, 'closely resemble' his own 'description of the reasons for choosing between scientific theories'. In other words, the main resemblance, between paradigms, consists in the fact that, in neither choice 'can testing play a quite decisive role' (ibid., p. 7): just as there are no second-level criteria for choosing between rival metaphysical systems, there are no meta-scientific criteria for choosing between sets of scientific test-criteria.[11] The difference between science and philosophy is thus not a matter of decision-procedures for networks of commitments. Rather, it is due to the capacity of science to produce exemplars, that is, commonly accepted solutions of shared empirical or factual problems. Whereas philosophers remain always, so to speak, in a pre-scientific stage and never 'come down' to 'normal science', scientists only go through this same kind of process in early phases of their disciplines or in periods of crisis. Since psychoanalysis is a new science, which is still trying to produce its full paradigmatic frame, it is only natural – and this seems to be the position of Kuhn – that it goes on making choices which are more like those which are currently practiced by philosophers, than like those which characterize mature sciences, and that therefore, it still lacks shared exemplars.

Now, Kuhn seems to be right as to the first point, but he is apparently wrong as to the second. It is simply not true that psychoanalysis does not have puzzles to solve. Psychoanalysis actually started (I shall come back to this point later on) by Freud's formulation of specific puzzles and by solving them in a way that he himself and the psychoanalytic community in general considered extraordinarily fruitful in current psychoanalytic research and practice. My difference with Kuhn here is not conceptual but factual, the implication being that Kuhn was simply not familiar enough with what was and what is going on in psychoanalysis.

I trust that the way is now free to start a description of the (natural) process by which Winnicott found his paradigm related to Kuhn's thesis. I shall proceed historically in the first place, by reconstructing the Freudian Oedipal, triangular, 'three-body' paradigm, whence Winnicott started from.[12] I shall then go on to examine the crisis that Winnicott fell into soon after he began his study of psychoanalysis. I shall suggest that this crisis was initially motivated by the result of Winnicott's observations of very early infantile psychic disturbances which seemed to go against the Freudian theory of sexuality (i.e., against the leading generalization of the Freudian paradigm). Secondly, Winnicott came to recognize that the problems of maladjusted children were not thought to be sexual and were, therefore, excluded from treatment by psychoanalysts; instead children were sent to institutions. Thirdly, related to the first two problems, the original Freudian setting showed up technical insufficiencies. In short, Winnicott's crisis was founded on all of the three main grounds stated and explained by Kuhn as the existence of a crisis.

Following the above suggestion, I continue to show how Winnicott tried to find his way out of the crisis by making an alliance with Melanie Klein, but that he gradually came to the conclusion that Klein, and others (including Fairbairn), offered no solution to the observed problem areas. Subsequently, I shall re-construct the main steps of Winnicott's own revolutionary research that led him to propose a new non-Oedipal, dual or 'two-body'[13] paradigm, based on the infant-mother dual relationship. According to my perspective, Winnicott's main contribution to psychoanalytic theory and practice is seen as an attempt to overcome his particular crisis with psychoanalytic theory by developing a new theoretical matrix for psychoanalysis as a whole that would be capable of solving the problems which had led him and others into a cul-de-sac. It should be added that his achievement did not lose anything of his predecessors' and contemporaries' achievements that he saw as important.

Freud's Oedipal Paradigm

What are the main exemplars that classical psychoanalysts encounter in their formation and apply in their clinical practice? In a paper delivered in 1913 to a broad scientific audience, Freud characterized psychoanalysis by showing how it proceeds in explaining slips and dreams. Dreams, in particular, are regarded 'as normal prototypes of all psychopathological structures'. Anyone who understands dreams 'can also grasp the psychical mechanism of the neuroses and psychoses' (Freud, 1953–74 13: 172).

In this statement, there is no special significance attributed to sexuality. Freud comes to that topic later on in the same paper, by saying that:

> at an early stage of its researches psychoanalysis was driven to the conclusion that nervous illnesses are an expression of disturbance of the *sexual function* and it was thus led to devote its attention to an investigation of that function – one which had been far too long neglected.
>
> *(Freud, 1953–74 13: 180; emphasis added)*

To that effect, it was necessary, in the first place, to develop the 'unduly restricted concept of sexuality, a development that was justified by reference to the behaviour of children'. Freud's *final formula* on the nature of neuroses was: 'The primary conflict which leads to neuroses is the one between the sexual instincts and those which maintain the ego' (ibid., p. 181).

The important question is: what was the *clinical material* regarding the primary conflict that this formula was related to? In Kuhn's terms, what were the concrete clinical problems that the theory of sexuality was supposed to make intelligible and to solve? The unequivocal answer is not just slips or dreams, but all problems that arise for the child from what Freud called the Oedipus complex. This is the meaning of Freud's later statement, found in a footnote added in 1920 to the fourth edition of *Three Essays on the Theory of Sexuality*:

> it has justly been said that the Oedipus complex is the nuclear complex of neuroses, and constitutes the essential part of their content. It represents the peak of infantile sexuality, which, through its after-effects, exercises a decisive influence on the sexuality of adults.
>
> *(Freud, 1953–74 7: 226n)*

> A close study of Freud's research on sexual development leads to the conclusion, firstly, that Freud's theory of sexuality started simultaneously with discoveries in the clinical material of work with hysterics alongside Freud's self-analysis. These discoveries led and illustrated the existence of the Oedipal constellation and the theory of infantile sexuality. Secondly, the theory developed mainly by recognizing, to an ever-increasing extent, the importance of the Oedipus complex as the *central phenomenon* of the sexual period of early childhood. [Quotation eliminated] In the same footnote that I have just quoted, Freud says: 'With the progress of psychoanalytic studies the importance of the Oedipus complex has become more and more clearly evident'. And he adds: 'Its recognition has become the *shibboleth* that distinguishes the adherents of psychoanalysis from its opponents'.
>
> *(Freud, 1953–74 7: 226n; emphasis added)*

By making a 'shibboleth of the Oedipus complex' (i.e., an 'identification sign'), Freud was specifying what Kuhn named the 'exemplar' that serves to establish the community of psychoanalysts. Freud's identity criterion for psychoanalysis is a problem-situation that, in his opinion, has been solved in an exemplary manner by the constellation of psychoanalytic theoretical commitments. Thus, the psychoanalytic theory of sexuality reinforced Freud's metapsychology. It was not long before Freudians started to use the Oedipus complex as a concrete rule for expelling dissident members. The example was provided by Freud's theoretical separation from Jung. It is important to observe in the specifics of that argument that Freud's only text in which he makes an attempt to prove the historical and material existence of the primal scene (i.e., the Oedipal situation) is 'The Wolf Man', which is a text directed explicitly to refute Jung's position.[14]

We have thus identified the main exemplar and the most important guiding generalization that constitutes a central part of the new 'constellation of commitments' by which Freud produced his revolution in the scientific research on sexuality and psycho-neuroses and created psychoanalysis, that is, the Oedipal conflict and its solution by means of the theory of sexuality.[15] In the constellation of commitments that constitute Freud's disciplinary matrix, there are three further elements that I wish to account for: his ontological model of man, his heuristic rules and his values. Very briefly, Freud's *ontology* includes a number of suppositions, more precisely, 'speculations' about psychic forces and energies as well as those of the innate constitution of the mental apparatus.[16] As to Freud's *methodology* and *heuristics*, they are based on the transference relationship, specific to psychoanalysis, combined with methods common to all scientific research: fact-gathering, formulation and testing of hypotheses (empirical generalizations). Freud also believed, as did all other members of the Helmholtz School of natural sciences, in some methodological tenets which, in essence, go back to Kant. Namely, that no empirical science can be complete without 'auxiliary constructions', and that all explanations have to be dynamic explanations based on quantifiable forces. Furthermore, in the case of human individuals, the interplay of forces takes place in an apparatus that is inherited and further developed. This methodological stance allowed for bold *speculations*, which for Freud were based on a vast range of metaphors, taken mainly from biology and from both psychological and philosophical theories of consciousness.[17]

Finally, there is a set of *values* contained explicitly or implicitly in the Freudian paradigm. Just as any other inquiry that is guided by the scientific method, psychoanalysis is a never-ending search for empirical truth about clinical phenomena. And, as in all other sciences, the results achieved by psychoanalysis are essentially revisable in the sense that there is no final truth, no absolute true belief, since in science we can have only provisional beliefs, subject to correction.[18] Although he assumes a positivistic view of science,[19] Freud is obliged to work with heuristic speculations which are metaphysical in character, and he proceeds thus as a Kantian. Nevertheless, psychoanalysis, as a science, remains different from philosophy – in so far as it does not offer a general and final world-view but rather a way of attempting, step by step, to enlarge objective knowledge – as distinct from the arts and, particularly, from religion. As to the social utility of psychoanalysis, it is concerned with relieving unpleasure and pain caused by an excessive repression of desire (i.e., by the censured libido).[20]

It was within this disciplinary matrix that Freud produced a *clinical psychology* and a *metapsychology.* The first is an empirical science that studies four main areas: sexuality, neuroses, psychic structures and social order. The second is a 'speculative superstructure' of the first. Whereas the theory of sexuality and other parts of clinical psychology may lay claims to empirical truth, metapsychological parts of psychoanalysis are introduced as mere *conventions.* For instance, instincts (*Triebe*) are conventions. Accordingly, metapsychology cannot be used as a *foundation* of clinical psychology, the only possible foundation of this kind of knowledge is clinical experience itself. Nevertheless, metapsychology was viewed by Freud as having great *heuristic value* through providing guidelines for empirical (clinical) research and schemes for organizing results already obtained. To that effect, metapsychological hypotheses and speculations must be *coherent* with clinical experience and with conscious experience in general, as well with each other.[21]

Freud's metapsychology is a vast and sophisticated speculation about an unconscious scene of mental life that is seen to be inhabited by entities analogous to conscious mental entities, for instance representations, impulses and desires. Mental processes that govern these entities – although they do not obey the same laws as those that govern conscious mental processes – are conceived as resulting from psychic forces that act in agreement with the principle of universal determinism. In that way, Freud transferred to the unconscious domain the general empirical, as well as metaphysical, properties of conscious states. Most of these elements, well known to the empirical psychology of his time,[22] are taken from the Kantian theory of subjectivity, which, as is well known to philosophers, was founded on a dynamic view of nature and included the two basic forces of attraction and repulsion, and a theory of psychic structure. The Freudian dualism of forces appears to be an adaptation of the Kantian metaphysical dualism, and the main elements of his psychic apparatus are the Kantian faculties, now called agencies or instances for the purpose of psychoanalytic research.[23] Influenced by his medical training, Freud *naturalized* all these ingredients of the unconscious and even tried to construct a *machine* capable of producing the same effects as those observed in clinical practice and everyday life. In the initial version of Freud's metapsychology the machine was a biological one (cf. the *Project of a Scientific Psychology*). In the later version, formulated around 1915, the prevailing metapsychological model of the human being is a psychological machine, which appears to be inherited from Leibniz, Kant and others. At that period, Freud was speaking exclusively of *psychic* forces and of the 'psychic apparatus'.

There are several reasons why Freud's metapsychological speculations have to be carefully distinguished from his exemplar (the Oedipus complex) and his guiding generalizations (which belong to the theory of sexuality and its extensions). Firstly, exemplars are different from other commitments and, furthermore, are by far the most important elements of a disciplinary matrix. Secondly, empirical commitments should not be mixed up with ontological ones. Thirdly, these differences are important for the understanding of the history of psychoanalysis. As we shall see later, Winnicott's crisis was not triggered, in the first place, by problems related to Freudian metapsychology, but rather because the Oedipus exemplar (and theory of sexuality) did not always assist with the clinical problems that he happened to find important in his paediatric and psychoanalytic practice.

Winnicott Crisis

The Oedipal paradigm proved itself extremely successful in dealing with a number of new problems, and the theory of sexuality served as the starting point for various extensions and applications of psychoanalysis. Firstly, and most significantly for psychoanalysis itself, it served to develop the theory of neuroses and of psychic disturbances in general (paranoia, homosexuality, fetishism). Secondly, it helped in elaborating the theory of psychic development and of the structure of the psychic apparatus. Thirdly, it served as a starting point in the theory of society, religion and morals. Let me note that Freud ventured a very bold assertion about morals, namely, that 'Kant's categorical imperative is the direct heir of the Oedipus complex' (Freud, 1953–74 19: 169), which implies that the very essence of traditional morality was a derivative of human sexual life.

But the Oedipal paradigm was also confronted very soon with serious anomalies. Freud himself found one of them: the early pre-Oedipal relation of female children with their mothers. Melanie Klein followed this up and made the case for the existence of anxieties earlier than the fully developed phallic or genital Oedipus complex.[24] In the 1940s, Fairbairn added a new criticism to the Oedipal paradigm and indeed to the whole of Freud's libido theory (Fairbairn, 1952).

However, according to my research, the first real challenge to Freud's Oedipal paradigm within psychoanalysis came from Winnicott. While still undergoing psychoanalytic training, Winnicott became 'astounded both by the insight psychoanalysis gave to the lives of children and by a *certain deficiency* in psychoanalytic theory' (Winnicott, 1965: 172). He describes this deficiency in the following way:

> At that time, in the 1920s, *everything had the Oedipus complex at its core.* The analysis of the psycho-neuroses led the analyst over and over again to the anxieties belonging to the instinctual life at the 4–5-year period in the child's relationship *to the two parents.* Earlier difficulties that came to light were treated in analyses as regressions to pre-genital fixation points, but the dynamics came from the conflict at the full-blown genital Oedipus complex of the toddler or late toddler age.
>
> *(ibid.; emphasis added)*

Winnicott makes the same point in a later autobiographical report about his learning process of psychoanalysis, phrased almost directly in Kuhnian terms:

> When I came to try and to learn what here was to be learned about psychoanalysis, I found that in those days we were being taught about everything in terms of the 2-, 3-, and 4-years-old Oedipus complex and regression from it.
>
> *(Winnicott, 1989: 574–575)*

While learning to see every psychic disturbance in the light of the Oedipus complex, Winnicott, who at the same time was a practising paediatrician, found himself in the following difficulty:

> Now, innumerable case histories showed me that the children who became disturbed, whether psycho-neurotic, psychotic, psycho-somatic or anti-social, showed difficulties in their emotional development in infancy, even as babies. [. . .] *Something was wrong somewhere.*
>
> *(Winnicott, 1965: 172; emphasis added)*

What is described here are the *clinical problems* that triggered Winnicott's *revolutionary research*, namely the disturbances which belong to the intended field of the Oedipal paradigm but which do not fit it. The Oedipal paradigm was not entirely wrong, it was even constantly confirmed, but it was insufficient; more precisely, it *could not do* all that Freud hoped it could do. Winnicott's first, and by far most important, difficulty with Freudian psychoanalysis was thus about its *shibboleth*, not about metapsychology. In Kuhn's terms, what happened to Winnicott during his learning process is that he found a serious *anomaly* in the framework of the paradigm he was trained in. What is more, he found an *entire field of problems* that resisted the 'classical' psychoanalytic understanding and treatment.

After having made this discovery, although may be not as a direct consequence of it, Winnicott was alone and found himself in between both the Anna Freudians and the Kleinian group post *Controversial Discussions*. In the 1920s and 1930s, he writes in 'D.W.W. on D.W.W.' (Winnicott, 1989) that the very existence of something like obsessional neurosis in a 16-month-old baby was simply denied as a fact. It was rebuffed with the objection: 'But this can't happen'. Winnicott comments:

> There wasn't an audience for that, because of the fact that to have an obsessional neurosis one would have to have had a regression from the difficulties of the Oedipal stage at 3. I know that I overdo the point but that was something that gave me a line. I thought to myself, I'm going to show that infants are very ill early, and *if the theory does not fit it, it's just got to adjust itself.* So that was that.
>
> *(Winnicott, 1989: 575; emphasis added)*

We have thus identified the exact point at which Winnicott started to depart from Freud and initiated his revolutionary research which, as I argue here, concluded by the substitution of Winnicott's new mother-baby or two-body paradigm instead of the original Freudian Oedipal or three-body paradigm.

The Attempt to Find a Solution in the 'Learning Area' of Melanie Klein

Winnicott's first move, however, was to try to save the Oedipal paradigm. From the mid-twenties onward he gave 'many tentative and frightened papers to his colleagues', in which he described samples of cases histories of emotionally ill babies 'that had to be reconciled somehow with the theory of the Oedipus complex as the point of origin of individual conflicts' (Winnicott, 1965: 172). Yet, Winnicott soon came to the conclusion that what he needed was a *psychology of the new born infant* which would *not* try to reduce all problems just to 'castration anxiety and the Oedipus complex' (Winnicott, 1958: 34, footnote 2). He felt 'that the psychology of the small child and of the infant is not so simple as it would at first seem to be, and that a quite complex mental structure may be allowed even in the new born infant' (Winnicott, 1958: 34, footnote 2). But Winnicott did not know where to look for such a psychology. He stood quite alone, and without a guiding paradigm.

It was an important moment in Winnicott's life when James Strachey, his analyst at that time, sent him to Melanie Klein, who was also trying to apply psychoanalysis to small children (Winnicott, 1965: 173). Winnicott took her a paper which presented an example of 'pre-Kleinian' child analysis which he realized on the basis of his own analysis with Strachey. 'This was difficult for me', remembers Winnicott, 'because overnight I had changed from being a pioneer into being a student with a pioneer teacher' (Winnicott, 1965: 173).

Winnicott discovered very soon, however, that the psychology of the newborn infant he was looking for could not be of the Kleinian type. In different writings, Winnicott spelled out his main reasons for rejecting the Kleinian line of approach (e.g., in Winnicott, 1965: 177). According to Klein, the relevant clinical material 'either has to do with the child's object relationships or with mechanisms of introjection and projection' (ibid., p. 174). These were 'deep' mechanisms but, Winnicott felt, not 'early' mechanisms. As he puts it in 1962, much of what Klein wrote in the last two decades of her fruitful work may have been 'spoiled' by her tendency to push unwarrantedly the age at which deeper mental mechanisms appear further and further back. According to Winnicott, Klein made mistakes because 'deeper in psychology does not always mean earlier'. Winnicott was convinced that 'when you are going back to the deepest things you won't get to the beginning' (1989: 581). For instance, the talion dread and splitting the object into 'good' and 'bad' are truly deep mechanisms. Yet, the capacity to use them is not established before the capacity of using projection and introjection mechanisms, and these capacities, in turn, are dependent upon *previous* good mothering which, by the way, is neither a mental mechanism nor a mental phenomenon at all. Moreover, Winnicott never accepted Klein's theory of the nature and aetiology of *psychosis*, formulated in terms of hereditary mental mechanisms and conflicting instincts.

Winnicott and Fairbairn

One might think that Winnicott should have felt himself closer to Fairbairn, who was also critical of the Oedipus paradigm. Indeed, in 1941, Fairbairn complained about the misconception of regarding 'the Oedipus situation as a psychological, in contrast to a sociological, phenomenon'

(Fairbairn, 1952: 36–37). In 1944, he declared that the Oedipus situation is not 'an explanatory concept' but rather a 'phenomenon to be explained' (ibid., p. 121).

These remarks seem to be compatible with Winnicott's findings. However, a closer examination of Fairbairn's position shows that this is not so. Fairbairn looked for causes of all pathological psychic conditions in disturbances of object relations (ibid., p. 82), in particular of relations with internalized objects. Schizoid disturbances, specifically, were thought of as results of the process of introjections. As such they were viewed not as primary processes but as a defence mechanism (Winnicott, 1989: 418). The question is: defence against what? Against ambiguity in object relations, which calls for the repression of the libido. The rationale for repression is not to be found in the (late) Freudian Oedipus situation, because the initial oedipal situation '*is not really an external situation at all, but an internal situation*'. The fundamental difference from Klein is that the situation is not built around the symbolic mental equation 'breast = penis' and the conflict between death and libido instincts, but '*around the figures of an internal exciting mother and an internal rejecting mother*'. (Fairbairn, 1952: 123–124). Fairbairn sums up his position in the following way:

> Thus, in my view, the *triangular situation* which provides the original conflict of the child is not the one constituted by three persons (the child, his mother and his father), but the one constituted essentially by the central ego, the exciting object and the rejecting object.
>
> *(Fairbairn, 1994, vol. I: 28; emphasis added)*

Fairbairn's aetiology of pathological conditions is thus still Oedipal, triangular, although the triangle is defined differently from Freud and Klein. It is no more the actually lived objective Oedipal situation, as it was originally in Freud, but an 'internalized' condition. Internalization implies the existence and the functioning of mental operations and mechanisms that Winnicott came to reject, as I said above, on the basis of his clinical observations.

In 1953, Winnicott wrote a devastating review of Fairbairn's 1952 book of articles. What were his main critical points? Firstly, that Fairbairn 'starts off with an infant that is a whole human being, one experiencing the relation to the breast as a separate object, an object that he has experienced and about which he has complicated ideas' (Winnicott, 1989: 416). Secondly, Winnicott criticizes Fairbairn's explanation of the disturbances found in individuals displaying schizoid features as a regressive phenomenon determined by unsatisfactory emotional relations with parents, without making clear whether 'the mother only "provokes the regression" to this early state or is the creator of it'. In other words, Fairbairn does not decide 'whether deprivation is the result of a deficiency in the mother's care or inevitable in childcare'. It is therefore very difficult 'to work out whether Fairbairn considers this maternal failure to be truly the mother's failure or the child's projection on her of his own fate' (Winnicott, 1989: 417–418). If the two are held to be the same on account of the imperfect maturity of all persons (including mothers), then it must be said that Fairbairn did not '*find the language* that covers both the normal and the abnormal' (ibid., p. 417; emphasis added). This faulty 'theoretical structure' spoils what can be learned from Fairbairn's valuable 'flashes of clinical insight'.

This is essentially the same objection Winnicott addressed to Klein, regarding the treating of early disturbances as internal mental problems without taking enough account of the actual mother-baby relationship dynamic. This difference is all-important because, in the second case, one is confronted with the additional task of defining the good-enough maternal care, whereas in the first case, no such question arises.[25]

Winnicott Revolutionary Research

Winnicott did not want to abandon the efficient problem-solving procedures of classical psychoanalysis, even though they were embedded in metapsychological postulates (psychic forces and mental mechanisms) which he rejected. We have seen him saying that the existence of the Oedipus complex was confirmed. He also recognized the Kleinian theory of the depressive position as important and empirically founded, in which he saw a dual and not, as Klein saw, a triangular situation.[26] On the other hand, he needed, as I have indicated, a new and more powerful procedure to solve clinical problems that have their origin in the very early actual mother-baby relationship. So, how did he get out of this predicament?

One important element of Winnicott's solution came from his study of the '*environment*.' Beginning in 1923 he became increasingly aware of the fact that there is a relationship between the environment and psychic disease, and, he says, this 'led to something in me' (Winnicott, 1989: 576). In the 1920s and 1930s, no analyst was interested in this problem. Winnicott was even deterred from doing this sort of research by his first analyst James Strachey (1923–33), who was a classical Freudian, and later on by Joan Riviere, his second analyst (1933–38). Riviere bluntly refused even to consider a planned paper of Winnicott's on the classification of environments. At that time, psychoanalysts, writes Winnicott, 'were the only people [. . .] who knew there was anything *but* the environment' (Winnicott, 1989: 577). Yet, Winnicott could not help but agree with those who were screaming out that a child might become ill by his father being drunk. Thus he was confronted with the following: 'How to get back to the environment without losing all that was gained by studying *inner factors*' (ibid. p. 577; emphasis added).

How did Winnicott solve this? He was helped very much by an accidental factor: the war, and probably also by Clare Britton, his future wife. By being involved in the evacuation operations of small children in the London area, Winnicott was obliged, 'at last', he writes, to treat abandoned and maladjusted children.[27] Until then, he avoided treating such cases, remaining in line with the official position that psychoanalysis has nothing to do with 'real' situations. This is how Winnicott came to the 'original idea' of the links between the 'anti-social tendency' and 'hope', which is one of the essential discoveries of his child psychology and 'extremely important' for his clinical practice. The idea was that 'the thing behind the anti-social tendency in any family, normal or not, is deprivation', and that hope has the unconscious meaning of 'trying to reach back over the deprivation area to the lost object' (ibid., p. 577).

Having discovered the connection between maturational processes and the facilitating environment, between *nature and nurture*, Winnicott found himself confronted with a new task, that is, of formulating 'a sort of a *theoretical basis* of environmental provision starting at the beginning with 100 percent adaptation and quickly lessening according to the ability of the child to make use of failure of adaptation' (ibid., p. 579; emphasis added). This task, in turn, required elaboration of 'dependence and adaptation theories' in a developmental and historical perspective (ibid., p. 579).

Winnicott's Exemplar: The Baby on the Mother's Lap

While working on the theory of the infant's relationship to, what he named, the 'environment', Winnicott came to two decisive results. Firstly, that it is 'impossible to talk about the individual without talking about the mother', because, speaking the language of late Winnicott, the mother 'is a subjective object [. . .] and therefore how the mother behaves is really part of the infant' (ibid., p. 580).[28] Secondly, that the initial mother-baby relationship is not a *triangular internal* (mental) relationship, but a very special kind of *dual external* (not mental) relationship. In 1958, Winnicott put this point in the following terms:

> Any attempt to describe the Oedipus complex in terms of two people must fail. Nevertheless *two-body relationships do exist*, and they belong to relatively earlier stages in the history of the individual. The original two-body relationship is that of the infant and the mother or mother-substitute, *before any property of the mother has been sorted out and moulded into the idea of a father.*
>
> *(Winnicott, 1965: 29–30; emphasis added)*

In the beginning the father, from the baby's point of view, may or may not have been a mother-substitute. If he has, he was not there *as father*, that is, as somebody endowed with properties or roles different from that of the mother. In the initial two-body relationship, the mother can be said to start off 'as a part object or as a conglomeration of part objects'. The same is true of her surrogates and thus of the father as the mother-substitute. Yet, 'at some time', the father does begin 'to be felt to be there in a different role'. The time comes at which the individual is likely to use the father for a very specific purpose, namely

> as a blueprint for his or her own integration when just becoming at times a unit. If the father is not there the baby must make the same development but more arduously, or using other fairly stable relationships, to a whole person.
>
> *(Winnicott, 1989: 243)*

This being so, the main *initial* role of the father with respect to the developing child who is no more a baby is not at all that of a partial object, but rather to 'be the first glimpse [. . .] of integration and of personal wholeness. In favourable cases, the father 'as father, not as a mother surrogate' starts off 'as whole person', 'as an integrate in the ego's organization and in the mental conceptualization of the baby' (ibid., p. 243). It is *only later* that he 'becomes endowed with a significant part object' (the penis), which then plays a very important role in the child's three-body relationships.

This conception of the initial dual mother-baby relationship allowed Winnicott to come to a clear-cut formulation of his paradigmatic problem. This is the point from whence he started, that is, that babies suffer from anxieties which are not to be conceived as products of putative innate mental forces and mechanisms, but as a consequence of an external factor, albeit psychic, the early maternal failure to provide a good enough environment.[29] In a late text, Winnicott wrote:

> To make progress towards a workable theory of psychosis, analysts must abandon the whole idea of schizophrenia and paranoia as seen in terms of regression from the Oedipus complex. The aetiology of these disorders takes us inevitably to stages that precede the three-body relationship. The strange corollary is that there is at the root of psychosis an external factor.
>
> *(ibid., p. 246)*

Winnicott ends this passage with a remark (probably aimed at the Kleinians) by noticing that it is 'difficult for psychoanalysts to admit this after all the work they have done drawing attention to the internal factors in examining the aetiology of psycho-neurosis'.

By turning to 'external factors' as the cause of psychotic illness, Winnicott reversed the then prevalent tendency in psychoanalytic theory to formulate clinical problems in terms of mental mechanisms and still more radically in terms of innate symbolic equations (e.g., breast = penis) or of Lacanian symbolic castration.[30] Psychosis became a 'natural' process, having its causes in actual external human relations, not in inner, or still less symbolic, relations and processes. In opposition to Freud, Winnicott did not define external relations as sexual, social or even as psychological, but rather as 'personal', based on special forms of mutuality and intimacy between mothers and their babies. Thus, he switched to his new dual paradigm or, as I propose to call it, 'baby-on-the-mother's-lap' paradigm.[31] From that new perspective of clinical experience, situations causing schizophrenia *cannot* be seen as triangular:

> Just as a study of *psycho-neurosis* leads the student to the Oedipus complex and to the triangular situations that reach their height in the child at the toddler age and again in adolescence, so the study of psychosis leads the research worker to the earliest stages of infant life. This implies the infant-mother relationship since no infant develops outside such a relationship. (It involves the idea of dependence prior to the establishment of the operation of mental mechanisms of projection and introjection).
>
> *(Winnicott, 1965: 131)*

What Winnicott is rejecting, in this and many other texts, is the very idea that early infantile schizophrenia and paranoia can have anything to do with triangular or three body relationships. The only facts, that can possibly be potential causes of psychic disturbances of the kind mentioned, are related to the not good enough early mother-infant relationship at a time when, for the baby, there is no awareness of father, and therefore, cannot be any third. This is why Winnicott states that schizophrenia is 'a sort of environmental deficiency disease' (Winnicott, 1958: 162).[32]

Here we come to the crux of the matter: the psychology of a newborn is essentially different from the psychology of adults and even from that of young children. Not only does the theory of sexuality not apply, but also the Freudian metapsychological approach cannot be incorporated. A baby's life and his 'unconsciousness', if there is something like that at all in a baby, cannot be described in terms of mental forces and processes. In particular, his *needs* have to be distinguished from desires, which are mental states, as well as from drives or instincts, which are putative or actual biological entities, with or without a mental, 'psychological' or conscious-like counterpart.

Such mental states and processes are not there at the beginning. An individual's life develops out of something else, namely, out of an early psycho-somatic partnership established by the imaginative elaboration of body functions, instincts, sensations and feelings, which requires maternal care in order to succeed. In Winnicott, the binomial *nature and nurture* has taken the place of the classical polarity between an instinct-driven subject and its objects.

Yet, in a way, Winnicott was going back to Freud, since he saw no meaning in talking about Oedipus in terms of partial and internal objects. In *Human Nature*, Winnicott treats Freud's Oedipus complex as part of the problem of 'management of the first triangular relationship, with the child power-driven by newly established instincts of genital quality characteristics of the 2–5 year period' (Winnicott, 1988: 49). Thus there is no substance in the frequently repeated statements that Winnicott is fleeing from the erotic into infancy (cf. Phillips, 1988: 152). Winnicott is not fleeing from anything; on the contrary, he is confronting the problem traditional psychoanalysis is trying to escape, namely the fact that Freud's theory of sexuality implied in the Oedipal situation does not account for disturbances which arise in the dyadic relationship between mothers and their babies. None of the later efforts to extend the Oedipal situation and sexual theory related to it (theories rejected by Freud himself, Otto Fenichel and Anna Freud, among others) produced the desired results. (Reason for not giving the reference: I am only explaining what Winnicott seems to imply, and the same point is made in the quotation which follows.) These extensions were *theoretically degenerative*, if not meaningless:

> I think something is *lost* is the term 'Oedipus complex' is applied to the earlier stages, in which there are only two persons involved and the third person or part object is internalized, a phenomenon of inner reality. I cannot see any value in the uses if the term 'Oedipus complex' where one or more of the trio is a part object. In the Oedipus complex, for me at least, each of the three of the triangle is a whole person, not only for the observer but also and *especially for the child*.
>
> *(Winnicott, 1988: 49)*

Winnicott did not just retain Freud's late Oedipus complex, he even developed it further, by introducing, for instance, a new explanation of the origin of the fear of castration. This fear, says Winnicott, 'becomes welcome as an alternative to the agony of impotence' which characterizes the *genital* phase of sexual development where 'the child's performance is deficient, and the child must wait (till puberty as we know) for the ability to act out the dream' of genital relation with the mother (ibid., p. 44). I want to emphasize that it is a serious (though widespread) error to think that Winnicott flees from sexuality to early infancy. What he demonstrably does is to place each of these developmental moments into the appropriate stage in the process of personal growth. Thus he makes it clear and precise how the environment impacts on the individual at each stage of early development (Winnicott, 1958).

Winnicott Main Guiding Generalization: The Theory of Maturational Processes

The guideline for Winnicott's treatment of psychosis is his theory of emotional or personal development:

> To examine the theory of schizophrenia one must have a working theory of the emotional growth of the personality. [. . .] What I must do is to assume the general theory of continuity, of an inborn tendency towards growth and personal evolution, and to the theory of mental illness as a hold up in development.
>
> *(Winnicott, 1989: 194)*

Here Winnicott is describing two things: his main scientific problem (infantile schizophrenia) and the theoretical tool he uses to solve it (his theory of maturational processes or personal growth). In the study of schizophrenia, this theory has the same paradigmatic role as that held by the theory of sexuality in the study and treatment of psycho-neuroses within Freud's three-body paradigm:

> Also, I can say that the statement of infantile and child development in terms of a progression of the erotogenic zone, that has served us well in our treatment of psycho-neurosis, is not useful in the context of schizophrenia as is the idea of a progression from dependence (at first near-absolute) towards independence.
>
> *(ibid., p. 194)*

Like Freud's theory of sexuality, Winnicott's theory of dependency (from dependence towards independence) is an empirical generalization and not a metapsychological speculation (Abram,

2007: 130–147). It was initially constituted from clinical material in relation to deprived children and developed by application to the study of two-body relationships.

The theory of emotional growth stands at the very centre of Winnicott's theoretical matrix and represents one of his main contributions to psychoanalysis. In almost every article, Winnicott consistently returns to the main problem of the 'treatment of psychiatrically ill children, and the construction of a better, more accurate and more serviceable theory of emotional development of the individual human being' (1986: 64).[33] Curiously enough, in the secondary literature, this theory as such has received little attention, being simply forgotten or viewed as trivial and reducible to psychoanalytic common sense.

Other Components of Winnicott's Paradigm

In order to complete this schematic re-construction of Winnicott's paradigm, I will now examine his ontological model of man, his heuristics and the values he stressed – items which, according to Kuhn, must be present in the disciplinary matrix of any science.

Firstly his *ontology*: Winnicott's theory of personal growth is based on a new view of the human being. Winnicott defines psychoanalysis (perhaps in an unexpected and seemingly old-fashioned way) as 'the study of human nature' (Winnicott, 1988: 1). What Winnicott has in mind is the assumption that 'fundamentally all individuals are essentially alike, and this in spite of the hereditary factors which make us what we are and make us individually distinct' (Winnicott, 1964: 232–233). At face value, this assumption seems to be more philosophical in kind than biological. This impression is strengthened by Winnicott's subsequent commentary:

> I mean, there are some features in human nature *that can be found in all infants*, and in all children, and in all people of whatever age, and a comprehensive statement of the development of the human personality from earliest infancy to adult independence would be applicable to all human beings whatever their sex, race, colour of skin, creed, or social setting. Appearances may vary, but there are common denominators in human affairs.
>
> *(ibid.: 233)*

The common denominators identified are of two kinds – structural and developmental. The structural are that, 'The needs of infants and small children are not variable; they are inherent and unalterable' (ibid., p. 179). This same thesis is expressed in the following way:

> The essential needs of the under-fives belong to the individuals concerned, and the basic principles do not change. This truth is applicable to human beings of the past, present, and future, anywhere in the world, and in any culture.
>
> *(ibid., p. 184)*

As to developmental common denominators, they are obviously the invariant features of human personal growth. There is a straight connection between the two kinds of denominators, since needs are essentially related to the tendency towards integration, that is, to growth.

It is no surprise that some commentators interpret Winnicott's concept of human nature as a return to essentialism.[34] But this point should not be overdone. Human nature is something which, in spite of being invariable, has a beginning, the only certain date of which is that of conception (Winnicott, 1988: 29). It is not easy to ascertain the correct meaning of what Winnicott is saying here. One possible interpretation is that human nature is not a Platonic essence but the invariant structure of a particular kind of *temporalization* which manifests itself as a human being, who, as Winnicott puts it, 'is a time sample of human nature', just that. Where does this process of being start from? The answer is that it starts from 'not being', 'from nowhere', 'from aloneness' (ibid., p. 131).[35] Next we may ask where does the process go? The answer is the same – to 'not being', to 'nowhere', to 'aloneness'. Winnicott states that 'The life of an individual is an interval between two states of unaliveness' (ibid., p. 132). The important thing to notice here is that these two states of unaliveness, which are the extreme points of the human life interval, belong to human nature and can even be experienced. 'The experience of the first awakening gives the human individual the idea that there is a peaceful state of unaliveness that can be peacefully reached by an extreme of regression' (ibid., p. 132). If this is so, then human nature is, in itself, the negation of any fixed essence. The only thing a human being can have (as a time sample of human nature) is his history, that occurs due to the tendency 'to begin to exist, to have experiences, to build a personal ego, to ride instincts, and [. . .] to have a self that can eventually even afford to sacrifice spontaneity, even to die' (Winnicott, 1958: 304). 'Natural death is the 'final seal of health"' (Winnicott, 1988: 12).

This is the main ontological hypothesis presented by Winnicott. Elsewhere, I have tried to show that Winnicott's argument is in close agreement with Heidegger's concept of the human being as happening-in-the-world of a being-to-death (Loparic, 1995, 1999b). Be that as it may, one thing is certain: there is a great difference between Winnicott's concept of human nature and Freud's naturalistic concept of the mental apparatus driven by instinctual forces. The latter concept, as I have said, is taken from modern empirical psychology and, in the last resort, from the modern philosophical concept of a naturalized subjectivity.

As to heuristics, Winnicott continues to accept the Freudian method of research, that is, the clinical setting and work in the transference. However, he modifies its meaning by allowing for the occurrence, in the clinical setting, of regression to dependence. Moreover, Winnicott does not allow for any kind of metapsychological speculation and prohibits going 'behind' phenomena by means of metaphors. His view of human nature is based on a very general hypothesis concerning the development of the human capacity to live an experience, rather than a metapsychological structure and functioning of something like a 'psychic apparatus'.

As to his values, they can be divided into the theoretically and practically significant. Theoretically, Winnicott sees psychoanalysis as a science, which has to test its hypotheses and to obey the verdict of observed facts.[36] As any science, psychoanalysis must be formulated so that it can be submitted to public discussion by psychoanalysts, by other scientists in the related fields (such as child psychiatry and paediatrics) and by the public in general. In so far as practical values are concerned, Winnicott takes into account unduly censured sexuality (Freud) and intrapsychic pain caused by internal conflicts (Klein, Fairbairn). Yet he thinks that by far the most severe suffering is that which arises from unmet needs that originate from the infant's predicament at the beginning of his life (i.e., the need for the continuity of being). Paradigmatic examples of this kind of pain are described as 'unthinkable agonies' – unthinkable, because they precede the time the baby is able to have any mental representation, and agonies, because they imply a lack of a good-enough holding environment in which there is a struggle for the continuity-of-being. These troubles are 'early' but not 'deep', because they originate in the two-body relationship, before the existence of any representation structure in the human baby (Winnicott, 1989: 581).

A Comparison Between the Paradigms of Freud and Winnicott

Both Freud and Winnicott agree that psychoanalysis is a science, not a craft, art, philosophy or religion.[37] Neither classifies it together with 'mixed disciplines', like astrology or alchemy.

Both conceive psychoanalysis as a problem-solving activity, guided by concrete clinical problem-situations and their solutions, completed by an additional theoretical framework. Whereas exemplary problem-solutions are considered to be beyond question in normal research, they are not viewed as having an unlimited heuristic power. Both thinkers concede that new exemplars might be needed to complete the psychoanalytic picture of psychic diseases and to promote further research.

However, Freud and Winnicott disagree as to which problems are exemplary for psychoanalytic research and as to what empirical generalizations are to be taken as guiding lines. Freud made normal psychoanalytical research possible by demonstrating, through his work with the hysteric, that all psychopathological situations relate to Oedipal conflicts and by interpreting this situation in terms of his theory of sexuality. Winnicott, beginning his study of psychoanalysis in the 1920s, found that he could not see things exclusively in that way. He concluded his work by viewing the mother-baby situation as exemplary, a result which in turn forced him to develop a theory of emotional growth, that is, of nature and nurture. This is, in essence, the paradigm change which accounts for the difference between the Freudian Oedipal, triangular or three-body psychoanalysis and Winnicott's mother-baby, dual or two-body psychoanalysis.

There are also radical differences with regard to theoretical commitments. Whereas Freud, following the Kantian tradition, admitted a number of speculative auxiliary suppositions that he used to formulate his metapsychology, Winnicott decidedly rejected such a mode of theorizing and limited his explanatory hypotheses to the experiences of persons in treatment, in particular babies and young children. Winnicott does not allow for the reduction of personal 'subjective' phenomena to apply to the point of view of the patients' consciousness nor, even less, to that of an observer. He wants it the other way round: to make sure that these points of view, though external to the phenomena themselves, capture the patient's way of being and experiencing, even if this patient is a newborn baby. This is not always possible. In such cases, the analyst must stop trying to know what is happening 'behind the scene', he must refrain from making metapsychology and from theorizing, which means in clinical terms that he must give up interpreting and even saying anything whatsoever.

Thus, both Freud and Winnicott set limits on our possibility of actually knowing 'unconscious phenomena'. But they deal with this fact differently. Freud permits himself to speculate, that is, to project to the unconscious the properties, the dynamics and the structures of conscious subjectivity. And on the contrary, Winnicott, based on his experience with mothers and their babies, understands that such a procedure is not legitimate, because it makes us think of babies as being adults and forget what happened during the process of emotional growth. Winnicott's baby is a human being, yes, but not the one who can be thought of in terms of conscious mental phenomena. Seen from the vantage point of Winnicott's theory of emotional growth, Freud's theoretical errors come from the incorrect view that what is beyond consciousness may be conceived of as being similar to consciousness, as 'un-conscious'. What, in babies, is beyond consciousness is not just primary processes, which have *nothing to do* with anything like conscious forces and mechanisms. The baby's experience of the continuity-of-being is something very different from any state of consciousness. Thus, the true *philosophical* difference between Freud and Winnicott is that whereas Freud still thinks in terms of the theory of subjectivity, initiated by the seventeenth-century philosophers and represented paradigmatically by Kant, Winnicott in contrast thinks of human beings in an entirely different theoretical key, which has much affinity to Heidegger's fundamental ontology, as presented in *Being and Time* (Heidegger, 1962).[38]

Notes

1 This is a revised version of "From Freud to Winnicott: Aspects of a Paradigm Change". In: Abram, J. (ed.). *Donald Winnicott Today*. New York: Routledge, 2013. This 2013 article is an updated and greatly enlarged version of my Madeleine Davis Memorial Lecture delivered at the Squiggle Foundation, London, under the title "Winnicott´s Paradigm", on July 1st, 2000.

2 As is well known, Kuhn himself leaned heavily on psychology and sociology (especially on L. Fleck's theory of scientific communities), as well as on some philosophical sources (Wittgenstein's philosophy of language), in framing his view of science and scientific research. It could be a rewarding exercise to re-examine an event to complete Kuhn's theory of science by taking into account Winnicott's views on the genesis and the function of intellectual and other mental processes in human life.

3 In 1990 Kuhn characterized his position as a 'sort of post-Darwinian Kantianism' (Kuhn, 1990: 12) For comments on the resemblance between Darwin's history of life and Kuhn's history of science, see Hodge and Radick (2009: 165–166 and 172).

4 Winnicott strongly criticized a similar claim of Riviere's as regards the Kleinian development of psychoanalysis (Winnicott, 1987: 35 and 97).

5 In this passage and elsewhere, Greenberg and Mitchell prefer, for reasons which are not quite clear to me, to use the later Kuhnian term 'model' instead of the original term 'paradigm.'

6 For other accounts of the development of Winnicott's ideas, see Greenberg and Mitchell (1983) and Jacobs (1995).

7 In 1989, Holton and his collaborators introduced the concept of 'solace paradigm' in an attempt to solve the problem of human need for 'consolation', particularly urgent in our epoch which is 'overwhelmingly nihilistic'. In this context, Winnicott's concept of the transitional object is treated as a 'very important sub-class of solacing objects' (Holton et al., 1988: 62), the elements of 'transitional relatedness' being 'no less ubiquitous in life than are elements of the Oedipus complex' (ibid., p. 88). Though I agree that Winnicott's transitional objects are an important component of his new paradigm and that this paradigm is no longer based on the Oedipus complex, I cannot follow Holton and his group in the attempt to embed this concept in the solace paradigm of their own, presented as an 'enlargement' of the scientific world-view by a 'multiperspective' strategy, which combines scientific, philosophical and even theological backgrounds. There is little doubt that philosophy and theology have been and continue to be influential in framing of the scientific world-views, but I cannot see any value, just as Freud and Winnicott did not, in mixing up science with these two disciplines. Holton's concept of paradigm does not square with what we know about paradigms in *scientific* disciplines but rather portrays what happens in philosophical and theological disputes about fundamentals.

8 Let me give an example. Dodi Goldman puts much emphasis, as many other commentators do, on the personal factors in Winnicott's procedures. For example, he writes: 'By temperament, Winnicott was more an innovator than a curator. He needed to seemingly destroy certain facets of psychoanalytic theory so as to re-create them in his own image. Only then could theory feel real to him' (Goldman, 1993: 132–133). And: 'Winnicott's original contributions to psychoanalytic theory are best understood, therefore, as efforts to re-create for himself, in a personal way, aspects of theory that he has imaginatively destroyed' (p. 133). As I see it, Winnicott did not 'destroy' psychoanalytic theory and practice driven by needs flowing from his temperament. He rather developed and modified it, in such a way, however, that 'bridges that lead from older theory to newer theory' are kept 'open' (Winnicott, 1989: 256) In some cases, this was done in order to increase the problem-solving capacity of psychoanalysis, in others to correct errors ('blunders') of Freud's. One of the reasons for my use of Kuhn's theory of paradigms is that it illustrates more accurately that the kind of move practiced by Winnicott is part of the common scientific practice and that Winnicott took Freud as approving and welcoming 'revolutionary' procedures in psychoanalysis.

9 Kuhn's term for this component is 'symbolic generalizations', which covers empirical laws and definitions of empirical phenomena.

10 See, for instance, the very special personal significance of the duck figure in the squiggle game of Winnicott with Iiro, as specified in Winnicott (1971), chap. 1, which would get completely lost if this figure were seen as a rabbit.

11 At this point Kuhn agrees entirely with Heidegger who denies that there are independent criteria for choosing between competing metaphysical systems (seeHeidegger, 1961, vol. 2: 258, 264 and 290).

12 This is an expression which Winnicott takes from J. Rickman, who introduced the distinction between 'two-body' and 'three-body' relationships (see Winnicott, 1965: 29). I wonder whether Rickman's usage was not inspired by classical mechanics' distinction between two- and three-particle problems.
13 See the previous note.
14 Freud's coolness towards Melanie Klein can be explained in the same way. Moreover, the essential points of the debate between Anna Freud and Melanie Klein can be summed up as turning around the question of how far back are we allowed to displace the Oedipal elements of the mental apparatus (see Phillips, 1988: 43).
15 Freud's theory of sexuality is a result of a continuous, both empirical and metapsychological research, which extended over decades. At the beginning, it paid much attention to the problem of perversions – since Freud was standing still under the influence of Krafft-Ebbing – and to the differences between adult and infantile sexuality, including puberty. Yet, with time, questions related directly and specifically to infantile sexuality became predominant. Some of this work appears in additions to later publications of *Three Essays*. Particularly noteworthy are sections 5 and 6 of the Second Essay, which deal with infantile sexual theories and phases of development of sexual organization (the erotogenic zones), as well as section 3 of the Third Essay, which deals with the libido theory. Among significant developments in sexual theory present in other writings of Freud's we can mention the theory of libidinal types and of female sexuality.
16 See Loparic (1999a).
17 The term 'speculation' is my translation of Freud's 'Spekulation', which is taken from Kantian philosophy and characterizes Freud's way of constructing his metapsychology. Metapsychology is the speculative part of his new science, parallel to the speculative part of physics, which includes expressions and terms like 'gravitational force', 'particle of matter', 'absolute space', 'infinitesimal', etc. One main trait of Freud's speculative concepts is that they are 'conventions' ('Konventionen'), to be used not for making statements about matters of fact, conscious or unconscious, but exclusively for heuristic (problem-solving) and merely expository purposes, being 'heuristic fictions' in the Kantian sense. I guess that on this point many British contemporary Freudians differ sharply from Freud (perhaps due to the British empiricist tradition and Winnicott's influence).
18 Winnicott thinks the same way, because he praises Freud's openness to criticism and his readiness to abandon his ideas, whereas he criticizes the dogmatism of Klein and the Kleinians as not scientific (see, e.g., Winnicott, 1989: 460).
19 In 1911, Freud signed, together with Einstein and several other first-rate scientists of the epoch, a manifesto in favor of the foundation of a 'Society for Positivistic Philosophy'. This document is now published in *Natureza humana,* vol. 2, n. 2, 2000.
20 Klein was concerned about 'psychic pain.' Winnicott, as we shall see, is concerned about real failures in human relations (which are not just 'social', but personal, at any stage of development).
21 A non-coherent theory is a false theory. Because *ex falso sequitur quodlibet*, inconsistency has to be avoided.
22 As we know, one of the sources used by Freud in elaborating his metapsychology was the 1897 article by Theodor Lipps, a philosopher of psychology, titled 'The Concept of the Unconscious in Psychology'.
23 As Heidegger noticed (1987: 220), Freud's id is a new scientific name for unconscious *sensibility* and passions, ego for unconscious *understanding*, and super-ego for unconscious *reason*, in particular, practical reason.
24 As we know, Freud was not very happy about the proposal made by Klein.
25 In 1953, Winnicott still thought that Fairbairn was trying to take his distance from Klein. In his autobiographical report of 1967 (1989, postscript), however, he admitted that Klein and Fairbairn had several important things in common, but that he 'could not see that for years and years' (1989: 579).
26 On Winnicott's interpretation of the depressive position as a two-body situation, see 1965: 22, 30 and 176.
27 It is interesting to note that World War I triggered a similar need for further articulation in classical psychoanalysis. The discovery of the 'war neuroses' opened the way to a series of clinical developments and to Freud's new addition to his metapsychology of the death instinct (Freud, 1953–74 18: 12).
28 The same is true of transitional phenomena and has, according to Winnicott, 'quite a lot of philosophical importance'. I have tried to spell out a possible philosophical meaning of the environment as a part of the individual by approximating this idea to Heidegger's concept of man as having the structure of 'being-in-the-world' (see Loparic, 1995).
29 It might not be beyond the point to notice that Peter Sloterdijk, a German philosopher influenced by Heidegger and interested in psychoanalytic theory, also defends in his recent writings (see, e.g., Sloterdijk, 1998) the thesis that our original relationship to the external world is dual, not triangular. However, he does not conceive this relationship as the one between the baby and his mother, obtaining

in the 'subjective' world, but as a pattern which is realized in couples found in very different fields of study, such as theology (relation between soul and God or the soul and the guardian angel) or adult sexuality.

30 This tendency started with Freud's rejection of this first seduction theory.

31 This image, obvious in itself, is based in particular on a particular remark of Winnicott's that the relation of a child to his mother must be such that he can feel comfortable 'on her lap' (1964: 133).

32 This argument is parallel to the one used by Winnicott in criticizing Klein's theory of envy. Envy cannot be attributed to a newborn baby because the word 'envy' refers to an attitude, something maintained over a period of time, and to several other mental states which imply 'a degree of ego organization in the subject which is not present at the beginning of life' (1989: 444).

33 A brief account of this theory can be found in Winnicott (1988: 8 and 101–102).

34 Phillips, for instance, says that Winnicott was a 'pragmatist with an essentialist theory'. (Phillips, 1988: 97).

35 Thus, not as in Freud, who states that the individual emerges from an inorganic state.

36 See Winnicott (1996).

37 This stance is taken by Winnicott in many texts; see Winnicott (1986: 13ff; 1996, chaps. 1 and 29).

38 This idea is developed in Loparic (1996, 2001).

References

Abadi, Sonia and Outeiral, José (eds.) 1997: *Donald Winnicott na América Latina*. Rio de Janeiro, Revinter.

Abram, Jan 2007: *The Language of Winnicott*. 2nd Ed. London, Karnac.

——— 2008: "Donald Woods Winnicott (1896–1971): A Brief Introduction", *International Journal of Psycho-Analysis*, 89, 1189–1217.

Davis, M. and Wallbridge, E. 1981: *Boudary and Space: An Introduction to the Work of D. W. Winnicott*. New York, Brunner/Mazel.

Fairbairn, W.R.D. 1952: *Psychoanalytic Studies of Personality*. London, Routledge.

——— 1994: *From Instinct to Self. Selected Papers of W.R.D. Fairbairn*. 2 vols. London, Jason Aronson.

Fleck, Ludvik 1980 [1935]: *Entstehung and Entwicklung einer wissenschaftlichen Tatsache*. Frankfurt a. M., Suhrkamp.

Freud, Sigmund 1953–74: *The Standard Edition of the Complete Psychological Works*. 24 vols. London, The Hogarth Press.

Goldman, Dodi 1993: *In the Search of the Real. The Origins and Originality of D. W. Winnicott*. London, J. Aronson.

Greenberg, Jay R. and Mitchell, Stephen A. 1983: *Object Relations in Psychoanalytic Theory*. Cambridge, MA, Harvard University Press.

Heidegger, Martin 1961: *Nietzsche*. 2 vols. Pfullingen, Neske.

——— 1962: *Being and Time*. New York, Hagerstown, San Francisco, London, Harper & Row, Publishers.

——— 1987: *Zollikoner Seminare*. Frankfurt a. M., Klostermann.

Hodge, Jonathan and Radick, Gregory (eds.) 2009: *The Cambridge Companion to Darwin*. Cambridge, Cambridge University Press.

Holton, Paul C., Gewirtz, Herbert and Kreutter, Karole J. (eds.) 1988: *The Solace Paradigm: An Eclectic Search for Psychological Immunity*. Madison, CT, International University Press.

Hughes, Judith M. 1989: *Reshaping Psychoanalytic Domain. The Work of Melanie Klein, W.R.D. Fairbairn, & D. W. Winnicott*. Berkeley, University of California Press.

Jacobs, Michael 1995: *D. W. Winnicott*. London, SAGE Publications.

Kuhn, Thomas S. 1970a: *The Structure of Scientific Revolutions*. Chicago, University of Chicago Press.

——— 1970b: "Logic of Discovery or Psychology of Research?", in Lakatos, Imre and Musgrave, Alan (eds.) *Criticism and the Growth of Knowledge*. London and New York, Cambridge University Press, pp. 1–23.

——— 1990: "The Road Since *Structure*", in *PSA 1990*, vol. 2, pp. 3–13.

Levenson, E. 1972: *The Fallacy of Understanding*. New York, Basic Books.

Lifton, R. 1976: "From Analysis to Formation: Toward a Shift in Psychoanalytic Paradigm", *Journal of the American Academy of Psychoanalysis*, vol. 4, pp. 65–94.

Loparic, Zeljko 1995: "Winnicott e o pensamento pós-metafísico", *Psicologia USP*, vol. 6, nr. 2, pp. 39–61.

——— 1996: "Winnicott: uma psicanálise não-edipiana", *Percurso*, vol. 9, nr. 17, pp. 41–47.

——— 1999a: "O conceito de *Trieb* na psicanálise e na filosofia alemã", in Machado (ed.) *Filosofia e Psicanálise: um diálogo*. Porto Alegre, EDIPUCRS.

——— 1999b: "Heidegger and Winnicott", *Natureza Humana*, vol. I, nr. 1, pp. 103–135.
——— 2001: "Além do inconsciente – sobre a desconstrução heideggeriana da psicanálise", *Natureza Humana*, vol. 3, nr. 1, pp. 91–120.
McDougall, Joyce 1996: *Éros aux mille et un visages*. Paris, Gallimard.
Modell, A. 1968: *Object love and reality*. New York, International Universities Press.
Ogden, T. H. 1986: *The Matrix of the Mind: Object Relations and the Psychoanalytic Dialogue*. Northvale, NJ: Aronson.
Phillips, Adam 1988: *Winnicott*. London, Fontana Press.
——— 1993: *On Kissing, Tickling and Being Bored*. London, Faber and Faber.
Pontalis, Jean-Baptiste 1977: *Entre le rêve et la douleur.* Paris, Gallimard.
Rycroft, Charles 1985: *Psycho-Analysis and Beyond*. London, Chatto and Windus.
Sloterdijk, Peter 1998: *Sphären I.* Frankfurt a. M., Suhrkamp.
Winnicott, D. W. 1958: *Through Paediatrics to Psychoanalysis: Collected Papers*. London, Karnac Books.
——— 1964: *The Child, the Family and the Outside World*. London, Penguin.
——— 1965: *Maturational Processes and Facilitating Environment*. London, The Hogarth Press.
——— 1971: *Therapeutic Consultations in Child Psychiatry*. London, The Hogarth Press.
——— 1986: *Home Is Where We Start From*. London, Penguin.
——— 1987: *The Spontaneous Gesture*. London, Harvard University Press.
——— 1988: *Human Nature*. London, Free Association Books.
——— 1989: *Psycho-Analytic Explorations*. London, Karnac Books.
——— 1996: *Thinking About Children*. London, Karnac Books.

13

KOHUT'S SELF PSYCHOLOGY, ETHICS, AND MODERN SOCIETY

John Hanwell Riker

In this chapter I describe in detail Heinz Kohut's concept of the self, as I think it is of profound importance for our philosophical understanding of human life and is little known in academic circles. I further want to show how it can offer modern persons a new concept of what it means to be an ethical subject, and, even more important, how it can offer us compelling reasons for why we would want to become ethical persons. I conclude by showing how Kohut's concept of the self can be used to critique modern society as one that undermines the possibility of persons developing selves while posing as that culture most supportive of individuated selves.

More than any other theorist, Heinz Kohut changed psychoanalysis in America. His emphasis on empathy as the critical factor in therapeutic action transformed clinical practice away from the cool distance of the classical scientific clinician towards a more humane responsiveness; and his refocusing of the major psychological task away from a management of the drives towards the development and sustenance of a nuclear self not only gave clinical work a wholly new focus but offered a novel way to think about our selves and how we go about living our lives. Indeed, his finding of a largely unconscious self (not a conscious ego) at the core of psychological life, along with his grasping of its importance and dynamics, offers philosophy groundbreaking ways to think about ethics and philosophical psychology. It can even provide a substantial non-religious, non-metaphysical answer to the question of why it is personally good to become an ethical person, a question that haunts modern life and which no other naturalistic philosophical psychology can answer as well. It further offers an in-depth psychological ground for critiquing the way modern culture is constructing human beings.

Kohut's concept of the self is not the same as Freud's concept of the ego, nor is it like Winnicott's self in that it is not an inborn kernel. It is profoundly at odds with the ideal of the autonomous individual that is so prevalent in modern society. It has deep reverberations with Plato's connection of the self to ideals, Nietzsche's connection of the self with creative agency, Emerson's notion that the self must be distinctively unique, and feminist theory's notion that we are formed by and exist through relationships. It reverberates with Hegel's notion that spirit is always in the process of developing because it harbors profound dialectical tensions between the ideals it can potentially become and the particular reality that actually is.

Despite these many intersections with philosophies of the self, Kohut is not a philosopher and does not address many of the traditional conceptual problems surrounding who and what we are as humans. He never delves into the ontological status of the self. He never tackles the question

DOI: 10.4324/9780429297076-16

of what constitutes the reality of the mind or how the mind is related to the body. He knows, being a psychoanalyst, that unconscious mentality can seep into the body and express meanings in somatic symptoms, but he never confronts the conceptual conundrums of this interaction. He also never deals with the question of what makes a person the same person over time (the question of personal identity), although he will say that having an intact self is crucial for having *the experience* of continuity through time and space. He thinks the self is crucial for developing a sense of agency but never enquires into the freedom/determinism problem or the problem of how to grasp the ontological possibility of agency.

What does concern Kohut is determining the kind of psyche that is best able to freely live a robust human life – a life that feels real, personal, vital, and meaningful. In short, the philosophic importance of Kohut lies in the application of his theory to ethics in the tradition of the Greek philosophers, who thought that those human beings who have the best arrangement of the parts of the soul are most capable of living the best of human lives. While the Greek philosophers – and western philosophers in general – proclaim that a soul in which reason directs the emotions and desires is the best kind of soul, Kohut's theory will offer a remarkable challenge to this model by displacing the rational ego from the center of psychological life and replacing it with an unconscious narcissistic self.

Kohut's Concept of the Self

Heinz Kohut (1913–1981) was a Viennese Jew who fled the Nazis soon after Freud in 1939, went to Chicago, and established himself as a celebrated classical psychoanalyst. However, in his work with the transferences of narcissistic patients (whom Freud had declared unanalyzable), he discovered that their pathology did not stem from repressed sexual or aggressive wishes but from injuries to a core self. In attempting to repair these injured selves, Kohut not only developed an original and complex theory of the self but also a compelling account of how selves develop, how this developmental process can be derailed, and how it can be repaired.

For Kohut, selves emerge out of primary narcissism through a process in which the infantile senses of perfection and grandiosity transform into organic ideals and ambitions (1966, 1971). Like Freud (1914), Kohut sees the baby as an unmitigated narcissist, for it acts as though it were the center of the world: perfect, great, and all-powerful. It does not recognize others as independent centers of perception and initiative but treats them as servants there to do its bidding. While for Freud primary narcissism must eventually be converted into object love, Kohut thinks that narcissistic libido has its own developmental trajectory and optimally transforms into a self during mid-childhood. The transformation of primary narcissism takes two distinct paths, each of which will precipitate into a prime sector of the self: (1) the infant's narcissistic feeling that it is perfect needs to convert into ideals; and (2) the narcissistic fantasy of greatness needs to transmute into a realistic, vitalized sense of agency anchored in positive self-esteem.

The transformation concerning perfection begins when the narcissistic baby suffers a trauma – its pleas for mommy to attend to its needs are not responded to in due time – and the baby realizes it is not only not the most powerful and perfect being in the world but is in actuality the most helpless. This helplessness causes the baby to feel an intolerable anxiety, which it calms by projecting its perfection onto its chief caretaker(s), idealizing them as gods whose primary mission is to care for the child. Security is now regained and the child will live within the projected glow of its parents' perfection for much of childhood and often for a lifetime.

As childhood progresses, the parents will inevitably fail to live up to the child's idealization. If their failures are minor and non-traumatic, the child will, over the next half decade, re-introject the sense of perfection back into itself, but now not as "I am perfect," for reality will not easily allow that, but as a nascent set of ideals – "I am not perfect but I have perfect ideals that I long to attain." These ideals typically first take the form of "I want to grow up to be just like mommy or daddy" and will later become connected to the child's unique individuality.

If this side of development goes well, the child will be granted one of the most significant blessings/difficulties of being human: the ability to be motivated by ideals that one loves as one once loved oneself and one's parents. It is the ability to be motivated by beloved ideals that gives life a sense of meaningfulness or purpose. In short, Kohut's theory explains one of the most difficult problems in philosophical psychology: how is it that we can be so moved by ideals that we will endanger our lives and forgo our sexuality in order to stay true to them? Kohut's finding the source of ideals in an original narcissistic sense of perfection, grasping a process by which perfection becomes projected into beloved parents and then re-introjected as an essential sector of one's self, is a unique and compelling way to explain not only how ideals come to be formed but also why we feel such a heightened sense of wellbeing when we realize them – for it takes us back to an original narcissistic state of perfection.[1]

The second path of development involves the child's narcissistic grandiosity transforming into a realistic and vitalized sense of agency by passing through a series of "optimally frustrating" events in which the child needs to expand its skills or abilities to successfully solve the tasks of the events, often internalizing characteristics of its caretakers to accomplish this expansion. (Kohut calls this process "transmuting internalization" to emphasize that the child does not have a wholescale appropriation of others but one that transforms their character into the child's own idiom.) Toilet training is the archetypal instance of an optimally frustrating event. Before toilet training, the little narcissist could spontaneously eliminate its waste whenever and wherever it felt like it, and the "servants" would come to clean it up; but now the child must monitor its body, gain control over muscles, and get to the potty seat in time. While it is a blow to one's grandiosity to submit to these new limitations, the child can feel narcissistically replenished if it succeeds in mastering this task. Rather than the child's feeling "I am great just because I am," it begins to feel "I am great because of what I have accomplished." While toilet training stands out as an Everest in childhood, minor "optimal frustrations" occur many times daily, from getting blocks to fit together, to putting on one's clothes, to crawling, then toddling, then walking, and so on. If all of these events go well, one falls in love with accomplishing, accepts the challenges of the world with an optimistic anticipation, gains positive self-esteem, and develops a vitalized reservoir of energy for engaging in the tasks of life. Kohut calls this side of the self "the pole of ambitions," pointing towards that part of the self that wants to perform and be recognized as special. As he says, this side of us does not want the world to admire our perfect ideals but wants it to admire "me."

This side of the self is what grounds agency. Note that it is not selves that have agency, but persons. A strong grandiose sector of the self provides the psychological wherewithal to grant a person a sturdy sense of being able to be an agent in the world. What interests Kohut is not the philosophical question of how to conceptualize a kind of agentic autonomous motivation but rather the question of why some people seem able to act vigorously in the world in pursuit of their values while others either can't or have a highly diminished capacity for action. His inquiries are meant to understand our lived experience of agency or lack thereof rather than solving a general metaphysical worry about how to conceptualize freedom.

As much as success in optimally frustrating experiences can help build self-esteem and a vitalized core of energy for engaging the world, it is not the major basis for building a sense of self; rather, the presence of empathic mirroring is.

Kohut called empathy "vicarious introspection" and said that it was a "sixth sense" in which one could experience the interior feelings of another person (1959). We are empathic with someone when we mirror the other's internal feelings without identifying with them. I sadly experience your sadness, but I am not actually sad – you are. Because empathy involves a subjective mirroring of another subject's subjectivity, it not only allows one to know what the other is feeling but accepts and affirms the feelings in its duplication of them. It is the one form of knowing another subject that does not reduce the subject to an object but confirms the subjectivity of the other in the mirroring subjectivity of oneself.

When researchers studied the responses of new mothers to their babies, they found that some mothers changed their facial expressions almost instantly to empathically mirror their babies' change of affect, while other mothers did not immediately respond to the babies' change of affect but kept a smiling face, seeming to demand that the baby be happy, too (Beebe and Lachmann 2014). When the investigators followed the children into adolescence, they found that the children of empathic mothers showed little to no psychopathology, while those of non-empathic mothers invariably exhibited psychopathology – often in severe forms. Empathy is the psychic protein out of which selves are built.

We are now ready to get a full picture of Kohut's concept of the self. The self comes into full actuality when the dynamic energy of the pole of ambitions is used for the realization of the self's ideals, and both relate to the idiosyncratic traits and abilities of the individual. It is the fusion of ideals and ambitions with these traits that makes them organic and singular rather than being a mere variation of codes ingested from society. Self ideals differ from ingested social ideals in a number of ways. When we are realizing ideals of the self, we feel vitalized and that what we are doing is meaningful; we lose track of time and do not become depleted but fill with a joyful satisfaction. Social ideals, on the other hand, usually feel like obligations and our accomplishing them often leaves us depleted or drained. Being motivated by social ideals is important, for we are embedded in social contexts, but they are what others want us to do, not what we love to do. Freud found that when the superego imposes socially ingested ideals on the ego, it does so with aggression and often a fear of guilt if we do not perform according to their standards. This dynamic is absent when we are being motivated by our self's ideals, for we love our self's ideals and reap joy when realizing them.

The self is dialectical in the tension generated between its ideals and ambitions, between what I might be and what I in fact am. Our ideals are values to be achieved; our grandiosity is the reality that we want admired. When ideals predominate over ambitions, we can glow with the perfection that they represent, but have little energy for actualizing them. When ambitions predominate, we have incredible energy for accomplishment and success, but it might mean very little as it is unattached to the self's ideals.

Since a central sector of the self is its organic ideals, the self is essentially a set of developmental possibilities for what the person could be. In short, the self is not a thing with a set identity; rather, it is a process that is always seeking to go beyond itself, to go beyond any finished set of accomplishments. It is Faustian in that its essence is to be striving; it is Nietzschean in that it is that which must constantly overcome itself; it is Platonic in that its seeking is not concerned with desire gratification but with the erotic realization of ideals. However, unlike Plato, these ideals are not abstract generalities but personal ideals that emerge out of one's singular being. In Christopher Bollas' words, the self is a destiny (2011).

But what is the self in and of itself? The self cannot simply be an amalgam of ideals and ambitions, because Kohut too often says that the self *has* ideals and ambitions. What is it that *has* ideals and ambitions?[2] Kohut does not answer this question, but says "we cannot, by introspection and empathy, penetrate to the self per se; only its introspectively or empathically perceived psychological manifestations are open to us" (1977, p. 311). While we cannot know what the self is in any ontological or phenomenological way – it simply does not appear nor is the kind of thing that could appear – we can offer a kind of operational definition by saying that the self is a system that performs vital functions within the psychic economy. The self helps regulate the affects, grants us a feeling of vitalized aliveness, generates a sense that one's life is meaningful, and provides a sense that one is a unified being. Most of all, having a coherent self at the core of experience makes us feel like ourselves! When our selves are not present, we often fall into doldrums with flat affects, get pulled here and there by peripheral desires and emotions, and wander through the tasks of life without much sense of purpose. With a well-developed ego we might be able to interact with the world well in terms achieving successes, but we cannot emotionally inhabit it in any depth without a well-formed self. In short, we can tell when our psyches have an intact self by attending to whether the functions it is supposed to perform are being adequately achieved.

We need to add a crucial piece to this picture of the self, namely, selfobjects. Kohut realized that in his developmental schema others played self-functions for children when they were unable to do so themselves. These "objects" were so important that Kohut termed them "selfobjects," for they literally were part of the self when they performed the functions that the self was unable to. Kohut held that we need selfobjects not just in early childhood before the self is fully developed, but for the entirety of our lives, for the grandiose sector of the self – the part that harbors our self-esteem – is fragile and always vulnerable to narcissistic blows and disappointments.

> Self psychology holds that self-selfobject relationships form the essence of psychological life from birth to death, that a move from dependence (symbiosis) to independence (autonomy) in the psychological sphere is no more possible, let alone desirable, than a corresponding move from a life dependent on oxygen to a life independent of it in the biological sphere.
>
> *(1985, p. 47)*

> Under normal circumstances, we all need a steady stream of self-confirmation.
>
> *(1987, p. 36)*

In short, Kohut has a double dialectical notion of the self. It not only is a tense amalgam of ideals and ambitions but is located both in the psyche of an individual and in a field of relationships with others. It is akin to subatomic matter being both a particle and a wave at the same time.[3] Often when our spouses or best friends are away, we can have trouble feeling and regulating our emotions and can walk through days without much sense of purpose or vitality. We are not atoms – discrete points of existence – but ecosystems profoundly and inherently interconnected with others. We are both unique selves and embedded in the contextualities of our relations with others (Coburn 2017; Riker 2017b).

Given that Kohut's notion of the self has a Hegelian kind of dialectical essence to it – it both is in itself and in another and must always being developing beyond itself, it staves off the postmodern criticism of theories that posit the self as having a set essence, for such theories privilege oneness over multiplicity, permanence over change, and structure over activity. In contrast, Kohut understands the self as both a singularity and a multiplicity, as both structural coherence and disruptive change, as both subjective activity and objective structure, as both individualized and contextualized.

In order to more fully grasp Kohut's notion of the self, we need to see its difference from the ego and the other centers of motivation within the psyche. Throughout his works Kohut implies a distinction between the ego and the self but never elaborates on the distinction; yet this distinction is crucial, for the ego and the self have different functions and aspirations. The ego is very much as Freud described it: a psychological agency whose functions are to negotiate the organism's relations to its social and natural environments and to establish coherence within the psyche (without which the ego cannot perform its primary task of environmental negotiation). While the ego is capable of performing unconscious activities, such as repression to keep itself coherent, its essence is to be the seat of consciousness/self-consciousness. It develops its powers primarily through education and learning (1923).

The self, on the other hand, is a largely unconscious psychological structure that contains the values and vitalizing energy which, when infusing the ego and our activities, make us feel most like ourselves, most alive, and most actualized. It develops early in life through selfobject relationships, transmuting internalizations, and optimally frustrating experiences. While both the ego and self are involved in establishing psychic coherence, they do it in radically different ways. The self generates coherence by being a fulcrum of value and vitality – a nuclear core around which other motivational structures can revolve. The ego uses rational structuring to organize conscious life and defense mechanisms such as dissociation, repression, and projection to keep traumatizing experiences and emotions from fragmenting the psyche (A. Freud 1936/1938).

Almost all of western philosophy has identified the self with the ego, and this identification has led to the dangerous idealization of the autonomous, masterful, power-seeking individual that has become so predominant in the capitalist world of today. It might be Kohut's greatest contribution to western thought that he located the self in the realm of unconscious subjectivity and found its needs and trajectories to be fundamentally different from those of the ego.[4]

To grasp the difference between the ego and the self, one can do a phenomenological experiment. Remember times when you simply weren't feeling like yourself, lost yourself in a toxic relationship, or found yourself in a job that just wasn't you, and compare these to experiences in which you felt "this is really me." In both kinds of experience there is an "I" (the ego) having the experiences, but in one kind of experience the self feels absent while in the other it is present. That is, the "I" is always sensed in experiencing, but not the self. Hence, these must be two different psychic agencies. One of the crucial maxims in philosophic literature is "to be true to one's self," a statement that makes no sense unless the self differs from the "I" and can either be denied or affirmed by that "I".

The tensions between the ego and the self are critical, and how we resolve them will determine to a significant extent our abilities to live robust human lives. The ego seeks power over both its inner and outer worlds, for such control optimizes the ability to successfully get the organism's needs met. The self, on the other hand, seeks to find ways to actualize its singular ideals, even if this seeking makes the organism's survival more precarious (e.g., the starving artist). The ego needs to formulate an identity (Erikson 1980) through which it can be recognized by society and which usually includes adopting a set of social roles; the self, on the other hand, often finds that accommodation to social structures destroys its singularity and vitality.

While the ego and self are psychological structures that often conflict with one another, their felicitous alliance is needed if a person is to have a robust life. The ego needs to be infused with the self in order for life to feel vital and meaningful; the self needs to be coupled with a well-educated ego to discover and gain admittance to those forms of social life in which it can best be realized. Self-realization that has no social recognition feels unreal and cannot be distinguished from fantasy; however, social success that has little relation to the unique self often feels empty, as when one chooses the wrong mate or career because of social pressures. In optimal cases, the self and ego are so fused that we cannot separate them and simply feel like ourselves most of the time.

There are two other important centers of motivation: the social unconscious (the superego) and the biological needs/pressures (the id). The social unconscious is our introjection of the codes and mores that infiltrate us and make us automatically members of a culture, sub-culture, and/or a society. The voice of the body tells us what we as mammals biologically need – food, sleep, warmth, exercise, sex, and so on.

It is persons who think, feel, experience, and act – not egos, selves, the social unconscious, or biological drives. And yet when we inquire into why persons are doing what they are – what motivates them – we enter a realm of murky subjectivity in which not only the voices of the self, ego, social unconscious, and id are clamoring, but also expectations from the past. The unconscious has memories, unconscious organizing principles, an unconscious way of experiencing, and these engage and complexify each of the motivational sectors of the psyche. In short, the voice of the self is only one of a number of voices in the psyche. The ego's voice, by necessity, is the loudest, followed by the voices of the social unconscious and the body. The voice of the self, in comparison, seems almost like an extravagance, but it is that voice which most mobilizes our sense of aliveness and meaningfulness. The absence of the self's voice can be caused either by its being drowned out by louder psychic voices or because the self has suffered serious injuries, in which case debilitating psychopathology materializes.

For Kohut, most psychopathology arises from injuries to the self, typically resulting from selfobject failures – failures of neglect or traumatic abuse. When selves are injured, there are a number of serious consequences. First, the development of the self is arrested and with it the possibility of attaining a mature sense of self and the ability to experience a rich emotional life. The core of the self that had been developed is cocooned behind a set of defenses that will not let it or its pain flow into conscious ego life. Second, narcissistic symptoms appear, and these typically include feelings of inner deadness and meaninglessness along with compensating defenses such as a heightened sense of greatness and manic energy – energy that can accomplish a great deal but which does not lead to a deep or lasting sense of self worth. Often addictions, along with an increase in entitled behaviors, attempt to fill in the hole where a self should be. Third, narcissistic rage erupts and will remain until the self is repaired and able to resume development. Narcissistic rage differs from anger in that it is unrelenting and seeks to destroy those who have injured the self or others who are connected to the victimizers through transference. Ordinary anger and aggression typically arise when others stand in our way and dissipate when the obstacle is removed; not so with narcissistic rage, which can fester for a lifetime and take revenge on innocent others who unfortunately get unconsciously connected to the original victimizer.

In short, persons with injured selves tend to be those who perpetrate unnecessary suffering in the world – sometimes on a grand political scale like Hitler, or in small soap-opera scenarios, such as couples endlessly nagging one another in an attempt to destroy each other's self-esteem. People with intact selves who are able to find activities and relationships in which the self can be affirmed are not those who bring misery to the world. It is persons with injured/unrealized selves filled with narcissistic rage who tend to be devastating for others. As Jonathan Lear says, "It is cruelty that breeds cruelty; and thus the possibility of a harmonious cruel soul, relatively free from inner conflict and sufficiently differentiated from the cruel environment, begins to look like science fiction" (1990, p. 189). This insight that there is a profound connection between the internal structure of one's psyche and the ability to be an ethical human being brings us to a discussion of the complex interrelations between a self psychological understanding of the psyche and ethics.

Kohut's Self Psychology and Ethics

Insofar as self psychology posits character traits crucial for living well, it can be used as the basis for a virtue ethics, in distinction from a de-ontological ethics concerned with adherence to rules or a consequentialist ethic concerned with the production of a general welfare. A virtue ethics based in self psychology can incorporate much of what is important in the other two ethical systems by showing that it is only a certain kind of human being – one not suffering from significant injuries to the self – who can understand that they are not above the rules and who can have a general empathic concern for others. If one has a coherent self and has developed the kind of character traits necessary to generate and sustain a matrix of selfobjects, they will be the kind of person who can abide by common rules, have a general compassion for fellow humans, and not have narcissistic rage festering in them that wants to destroy others.

If we think of ethical persons, as Aristotle did, as those who have developed the moral virtues – including becoming just, moderate, and generous – then we can see that from the viewpoint of self psychology it behooves us to become ethical human beings, for it is this kind of person who is best able to generate and maintain a matrix of selfobjects. In adulthood, one will not be able to live among selfobjects who can give genuine support to the self unless one is able to act in a reciprocal way by being a selfobject for them. Hence, one needs to develop character traits that allow one to participate in relationships with other human beings who can love and care for one. That is, one needs to be capable of friendship.

Aristotle claims that it is only persons who have developed the moral virtues who can be true friends with one another. The virtues are crucial for interacting with friends, for, as Aristotle says, few people will want to be friends with someone who is a bad person – someone they cannot trust or who will be deficient in some major way, such as being greedy or immoderate or unable to regulate their emotions and desires. For Aristotle, good human beings need friendships both as the primary arena in which to actualize their virtues and as the place where they are sustained by being mirrored by others who are like them. Kohut and Aristotle go hand in hand in saying that when one develops the predispositions of character that are best for one's own well-being, one also develops the kind of character that can best help others and sustain community.

The one Aristotelian virtue that Kohut emphasizes is courage, now re-defined as the ability to stay true to the self's ideals in situations in which we might suffer grievously if we do so, and gives the example of persons, such as Hans and Sophie Scholl, refusing to go along with the Nazis even though it cost them their lives (1985). Society is always pressuring us to conform to its values; courage is necessary to generate and sustain integrity around the self's ideals – to stay true to oneself.

The most important non-Aristotelian virtue that self psychology advocates is empathy, a trait that inclines us to understand others from inside their experience before arriving at judgments of them. In emphasizing the importance of empathy, self psychology both avoids Nietzsche's devastating criticism of morality as an objectifying, life-negating discourse and aligns itself with much of feminist ethics. Nietzsche exposes traditional morality and its tendency to judgmentalism as a discourse that negates individual spontaneity and attempts to control others by holding them accountable to moral standards – hence demanding that all persons fit a general type. Rather than approaching others with a set of moral categories by which to judge them, empathic persons seek to know what they are feeling and why. Their empathy affirms and validates who they are in their individuality rather than taking the moral position of superiority that judges them according to a general standard.

I believe that empathy is the essence of "care," the trait that many feminist ethicists proclaim to be the essence of moral life. Virginia Held defines care as "attending to and meeting the needs of the particular others for whom we take responsibility" (2006, p. 10). It is particular others that count in ethics, not some generalized other or universal law applicable to all human beings. The particular others emphasized in feminist ethics are, for the most part, those that self psychology would recognize as persons with whom we have some kind of selfobject relationships – children, parents, friends. While a number of their needs might be apparent without much attention – such as the needs for food and warmth in children – deeper emotional needs, especially the needs surrounding narcissistic equilibrium, are not knowable without empathy. Further, food and other objective supplies can be given in various ways, such as mechanically or resentfully, but it is only when they are given empathically that the full needs of the person are met. To care for others is, primarily, to empathically respond to their needs.

Feminist ethics also tends to emphasize that we are not autonomous atoms but exist in relationships, and without these relationships we could neither grow up nor flourish. An ethical way of life arises out of the complex set of personal interactions we engage in as we develop into adulthood. It is the quality of these exchanges that produces the ability to be an ethical person who can empathically care for the selves of others.

One might now ask how the claims of justice fit into this framework, for it appears that an ethics based in selfobject connections will breed favoritism rather than fairness, a quality many think to be the essence of ethics (Rawls 1971). In a self-psychological view of ethics, the concerns of justice are placed primarily in the development of a predisposition to be fair rather acting out of a rule-generating rational ego. Unless there is a predisposition to obey what one recognizes as the claims of justice, those claims will not generate just actions. Nevertheless, the actions required by empathic care and those required by a sense of justice can and do conflict. I agree with Virginia Held that we cannot construct a rule that tells us to always favor empathy over justice or vice versa, nor can we devise an algorithm for saying which takes precedence when. In the end we hope that our decisions are those that a person of practical wisdom would make.

The difference between a self-psychological virtue ethics and other virtue ethics is the recognition that an intact unconscious self needs to be the fulcrum of psychological experiencing rather than a conscious ego. Not only is this a new, more complex view of what it means to be an ethical person, but it is also a view in which the conflict between narcissism and altruism is resolved, for in becoming ethical persons who can care for others we become the kind of person who can best nourish our individual selves. In short, if we think of ethical persons as those who exhibit the moral virtues, care deeply for and respect others, and have a depth of empathy with which to interact with others, then we have the kind of person who is also most able to care for themselves, for they are the most able to generate and sustain a selfobject matrix.

But now let an egoistic interlocutor ask, "Why can't I be a good person to those close to me – my friends – and be unethical with those who are not my friends?" Why should one's ethical stance govern one's relation to all human beings rather than just one's selfobjects? The major problem that critics have found with virtue ethics is that character traits tend to be context dependent. We can be generous, kind, caring humans with one set of persons and brutish, domineering, and callous with others. It seems that we have the ability to turn the virtues on or off depending on context – witness numerous Nazis who were loving family members at home and brutal victimizers at work in the camps. Why be an ethical person all of the time in all contexts, even those in which there is no possibility of selfobject reciprocity?

The fundamental reason for always acting as an ethical person is that if one doesn't, they lose the centrality of the self and with it the integrity of the psyche (Riker 2017a; Summers 2013). Integrity involves being who you are regardless of situation. If one needs to be an empathic caring person to sustain the self, then one must keep that character in all situations, including those that threaten one. If one becomes opportunistic and shifts character, value, and personality depending on context, then the self is displaced as the fulcrum of psychic life by the ego, for it is the ego that controls the switching. The ego is, by nature, opportunistic, for it seeks power and success. The self, on the other hand, seeks to live in an empathic, caring world, and as such needs to dwell within an empathic, caring person. To ignore the self or displace it depending upon situation means that one loses integrity. Kohut himself makes this point:

> We may justifiably deplore . . . the actions and attitudes of those who quickly and opportunistically adjust their convictions under the influence of external pressures. In such individuals the nuclear self ceases to participate in the overt attitudes and actions and becomes progressively isolated and is finally repressed or disavowed. The psychological outcome, *which is unfortunately more or less characteristic of the psychological makeup of the majority of adults*, is a person who, despite his smoothly adaptive surface behavior, experiences a sense of inner shallowness and who gives to others an impression of artificiality.
>
> *(1985, p. 11; emphasis added)*

Although the ideals of the self will be particular for each person, part of those ideals must be to sustain an empathic, virtuous way of being in the world, for these values are crucial for dwelling within a selfobject matrix. To abandon these values is to abandon the self and lose it as the pole star around which the rest of the psyche revolves.

However, it is one thing to be predisposed to treat all humans with empathy and care and quite another to deliberately seek to interact with those who are other or different. Such engagement with otherness is challenging because, as self psychology has shown, we need mirroring more than any other psychological nutrition, and mirroring is best given by those who look and think like us. Not only does this mirroring enhance the grandiose sector of the self, but so does merging with a group formed around some essential sameness. Members of these selfsame groups find their grandiose selves sustained both through mirroring and by merging with the greatness of the group.

While belonging to selfsame groups might be necessary for sustaining the self, it has proved highly problematic, for it typically involves the abjection of others who are different. When this abjection occurs within systems of power, the dominant groups tend to enact systems of prejudice, discrimination, and violence against those seen as other: men have subjugated women, westerners non-westerners, whites blacks and other people of color, and so on, endlessly. These systems of injustice have caused much of the suffering that human beings have historically inflicted on one another and continue to be devastating sources of misery throughout the world.

Kohut's discovery that mirroring is crucial for psychological life seems to doom us to an interminable repetition of group aggression and structures of injustice; however, self psychology can also show why persons need to engage with otherness. To remain vital, the self needs to constantly develop, and it can do this only if it is open to otherness – other ideas, diverse kinds of people, other cultures, different ways of engaging the world, diverse values. If we remain cozily in our favorite groups and petrify others through stereotyping, prejudice, and unwarranted aggression, we petrify our selves. Either we develop the propensity for engaging with difference or our selves wither and die in patterns of stultifying repetition.

In sum, self psychology, more effectively than any other theory, allows us to grasp the psychological roots of our compulsive attachment to sameness but also offers the vision of a new way of constructing humans – as beings who need to generate an integral self that approaches all humans with empathy rather than judgment and aggression. But can modern society construct such persons?

Self Psychology and Modern Society

Modern western society, although it purports to support individual selves more than any other culture, in fact undermines them in many ways, three of which I want to highlight: (1) through the dominance of an ideal autonomous individuality; (2) by confusing ego identity with self structure; and (3) by the pervasive undermining of selfobject relationships in the home, friendships, and workplace.

First, behind much of the dynamism, inventiveness, and mobility of modern life stands the ideal of the self-sufficient individual – someone who does not rely on tradition, religion, or others and who makes their way in world through their own initiative and wits. The defining trait of American individualism is the ability to be independent – to not depend on others for material or emotional sustenance. While individuals can choose to be with others – can choose to have friendships or erotic relationships – they can do so as long as they do not become overly dependent on them. The value of independence is so dominant that it has the tendency to undermine the possibility of committed love relationships and close friendships. That is, this concept of the autonomous self-sufficient individual undermines the self in denying our critical need for selfobject relationships to sustain the self. This ideal of autonomous individualism must be implicated in the sad statistic that about 60% of Americans feel desperately lonely, often in states of anxiety and constant despair. One of our new important categories in measuring social health is deaths due to despair – deaths that come from suicide, alcohol addiction, and drug overdoses – many due in part, on my account, to the loss of a vital self at the core of experience. To be an autonomous individual is to be a lonely, isolated, unsupported person with an insufficient flow of psychological nourishment.

Second, to be someone in the modern world is to have a socioeconomic identity, and these identities are ranked in terms of status and power (Foucault 1979). The best kind of life is supposedly had by those who attain the most esteemed socioeconomic identities. Having an identity is not the same as having a self. For Erik Erikson, the task of constructing an identity comes in late adolescence/early adulthood when one establishes in a pre-conscious/conscious way how one wants to be seen and recognized by society (1980). This typically involves choosing important socioeconomic roles such as career, marriage, and family and then identifying oneself with these roles. The self, on the other hand, comes into existence in childhood and is largely formed in an unconscious way through important selfobject interactions.

In the most felicitous cases we will choose social identities through which to fulfill our self's ideals and ambitions. However, the self's values can be quite idiosyncratic and not those that grant social prestige. Insofar as identities are strongly associated with the ego rather than the self, they will tend to value those positions and roles which grant the most power to negotiate the social and natural environments – those that pay the most and/or provide the most status. Such beliefs often de-value the need for selfobjects and one's peculiar ways of being oneself. That is, we tend to encounter extraordinary pressures to conform to social ideals when constructing our identities and often lose our selves in this process. I am reminded of a survey Colorado College took of its incoming class several years ago in which 80% of the students said that they wanted to be either doctors or lawyers – the two most prestigious professions in today's world. The students did not inquire into who they were; they just accepted that if they could be anything, they would adopt the most esteemed identities.

Third, modern society undermines the development and conservation of selves by destabilizing selfobject relationships in families, friendships, and the workplace. Since it is common for both parents to have to work to sustain a household and their socioeconomic identities, modern homes are often lonely places with scarcely enough selfobject interactions with young children to help them develop selves. Daycare centers simply are unable to respond with the full gleam and adoring care that loving parents can. When parents do get home, they often find themselves so drained from work and commuting that they can't nourish one another, let alone their children. Since the grandiose sectors of their selves are undernourished, parents often overly pressure their children to be stars at school, thereby affirming social values of success over developing the idiosyncratic potentialities of their children.

Not only has the home become a deficient place for getting selfobject needs met, but so has the workplace, which is now an "objectified" space in which the subjective experience and needs of employees are hardly recognized or responded to. Corporations reduce workers at every level to the functions they perform and make them replaceable by others – including machines – who can do the functions better or at a lower cost. In these objectified conditions, warmth and affection – friendship – among fellow workers is highly problematic, and, hence, neither the modern home nor the workplace is an adequate environment for sustaining selfobject interactions.

The extraordinary degree of modern mobility also adds to the difficulty of establishing selfobject networks. Indeed, contemporary persons move so often that friends seem to be changed every few years. With this kind of mobility, one has only oneself to rely on for psychological wellbeing, as the world and one's relations shift with incredible frequency.

The ego can get along fine without selfobjects, but the self cannot. Without selfobject nourishment, selves do not achieve a robust presence in the experiences of modern people who, dominated by ego concerns, develop into "masterful, bounded, and empty persons" (Cushman 1995). They are masterfully disciplined and self-controlled so as to operate the machinery of modern economic society; isolated within the boundaries of their individuality, and empty because they do not have a core sense of self vitalizing their lives.

These are also the kind of people who harbor narcissistic injuries or depleted selves and as such tend to try to fill the void at the core of psychic life with incessant excitement or feeling high – often becoming addicted to alcohol, drugs, sex, shopping, gambling, food, video games, and so on. They tend either to want to be center stage or retreat into the background for fear that any kind of success might stimulate shameful infantile needs for narcissistic acclamation. They have trouble tolerating criticism, cut in lines without permission, and demand that you drive your car the speed they want to go.

They are also the kind of person who cheats (Riker 2010). As David Callahan shows in his *The Cheating Culture,* cheating infects almost every aspect of American life, from individuals cheating on income taxes and their resumes, to doctors pushing pills for drug companies, lawyers padding their bills, car mechanics doing unnecessary repairs, students cheating on tests and papers, companies – such as Enron and WorldCom – cooking their books, and spouses cheating on one another (2004). While cheating is not a horrific moral crime, such as the genocides of Hitler and Stalin, it is a practice that undermines personal, social, economic, and political life. It creates a culture in which no one can really trust anyone else, helping to create a world of loneliness and isolation.

Kohut attempted to show that narcissism is not necessarily bad – it is an essential part of being human. However, there is a mature narcissism that comes into being if the self has a felicitous development and a pathological narcissism that occurs when the developmental trajectory of the self gets derailed. For Kohut, mature narcissists are creative, humorous, and empathic. They accept their mortality and merge their selves' values with wider, more transcendent ideals (1966). They recognize, respect, and affirm the selves of others and are willing to empathically help those selves flourish, as they are willing to let others be part of their selves. They do not measure themselves by the standards of society but by organically developed values in which they ask of themselves whether they are being true to themselves.

It is this kind of person that Kohut would prefer to inhabit our modern culture rather than the masterful, bounded, empty immature narcissists that seem so prevalent these days, prevalent in part because of the culture's conceptual misunderstanding of what it means to be and have a self.

In sum, Kohutian self psychology has a great deal to offer not only to philosophy but the wider world. Its conception of the self as a largely unconscious psychological structure that differs from the ego, which is built through intensive selfobject responsiveness, harbors the core vitality and sense of meaningfulness in a person, and has a lifelong need to be in such profound relations with others that they constitute a part of their selves is an attempt to re-conceptualize some of the most profound presuppositions of the modern world. Without this re-conceptualization of the self, modernity will continue to drive us into lives of loneliness, anxiety, despair, and aggressive competitiveness and, because it has no genuine answer to the question of why one should become an ethical human being, it will be constantly undermined by cheating and other narcissistic behaviors. A competitive, disciplined, isolated, empty human being might be just the kind of person that capitalism needs to endlessly consume market goods and work feverishly for the wherewithal to keep consuming, but such persons are never deeply fulfilled, and their incessant overheated production and consumption has led the world to the brink of environmental disaster.

This is not to say that Kohut has the final take on the nature of the human psyche. As he himself says, "Ideals are guides, not gods. If they become gods, they stifle man's playful creativeness. They impede the future" (1977, p. 312). Theories, like persons, must keep evolving or they die.

Notes

1 Freud also recognized that the ego ideal is a transformation of narcissism (1914) but does not follow the transformation of perfection through the idealization of caretakers and then the re-integration from them. The ego ideal for Freud gets largely converted into the superego (1923) and tends to carry guilt with it, while for Kohut, the ideals of the self do not have the feeling of an imposition on the ego but provide a deep source of meaning for a person.

2 In my own attempt to think into this problem, I have proposed that *eros* as conceived by Plato in his *Symposium* and the later Freud might be what the self most basically is. See Riker, *Exploring the Life of the Soul* (2017a, chap. 4).

3 The metaphysical system best able to grasp how all entities exist both in themselves and in connectedness with others is that of Alfred North Whitehead. In particular, see his *Process and Reality* (1927).

4 This articulation of the difference between the ego and the self is at best a sketch. For a more robust description of their functions and differences and their relation to subjectivity, see Riker, *Why It Is Good to be Good* (2010, chap. 4) and Riker, *Exploring the Life of the Soul* (2017a, chap. 3).

References

Beebe, B. and Lachmann, F. 2014. *The origins of attachment: Infant research and adult treatment.* New York: Routledge.

Bollas, C. 2011. *The Christopher Bollas reader.* New York: Routledge.

Callahan, D. 2004. *The cheating culture.* New York: Harcourt.

Coburn, W. 2017. Commensurability and incommensurability of paradigms among theories and persons. *Psychoanalysis, Self, and Context,* 12: 163–172.

Cushman, P. 1995. *Constructing the self, constructing America: A cultural history of psychotherapy.* New York: Da Capo.

Erikson, E. 1980. *Identity and the life cycle.* New York: W. W. Norton.

Foucault, M. 1979. *Discipline and punish.* Tr. A. Sheridan. New York: Vintage Bks.

Freud, A. 1936/1938. *The ego and the mechanisms of defense.* New York: International Universities Press.

Freud, S. 1914. *On narcissism: An introduction.* In Standard edition of the collected works. Trs. & Ed. James Strachey et al., 14: 73–102. London: Hogarth Press. Hereafter: SE.

——— 1923. *The Ego and the Id.* SE 19: 1–66.
Held, V. 2006. *The ethics of care.* Oxford: Oxford University Press.
Kohut, H. 1959. Introspection, empathy, and psychoanalysis. *Journal of the American Psychoanalytic Ass*, 7: 459–483.
——— 1966. Forms and transformations of narcissism. *Journal of the American Psychoanalytic Ass*, 14: 243–272.
——— 1971. *The analysis of the self.* New York: International Universities Press.
——— 1977. *The restoration of the self.* New York: International Universities Press.
——— 1985. *Self psychology and the humanities.* Ed. C. Strozier. New York: W. W. Norton.
——— 1987. *The Kohut seminars on self psychology and psychotherapy with adolescents and young adults.* Ed. Miriam Elson. New York: W. W. Norton.
Lear, J. 1990. *Love and its place in nature.* New York: Farrar, Straus, and Giroux.
Rawls, J. 1971. *A theory of justice.* Cambridge, MA: Harvard University Press.
Riker, J. 2010. *Why It Is good to be good: Ethics, Kohut's self psychology, and modern society.* Lanham, MD: Jason Aronson.
——— 2017a. *Exploring the life of the soul: Philosophical reflections on psychoanalysis and self psychology.* Lanham, MD: Lexington Books.
——— 2017b. The dialectical core of self psychology. *Psychoanalysis, Self, and Context*, 12: 173–181.
Summers, F. 2013. *The psychoanalytic vision: The experiencing subject, transcendence, and the therapeutic process.* New York: Routledge.
Whitehead, A. 1927. *Process and reality.* New York: MacMillan.

14

WHAT IS INTERSUBJECTIVITY

From Phenomenology to Psychoanalysis[1]

Lewis Kirshner

Intersubjectivity as a concept cannot be precisely defined. It may be one of those words whose sense becomes clearer in the negative, like "empathy," to which it is related. Different disciplines with their own independent histories and literature have applied the term to deal with concerns specific to them. While originally a product of philosophy and a cornerstone of phenomenologic thought, perhaps most notably explored by Husserl, the concept of intersubjectivity was adopted by the pioneer infant researcher Colin Trevarthen in the form of "primary intersubjectivity" to characterize early mother-infant communications. It entered psychoanalysis through Jacques Lacan during his Hegelian period and was subsequently taken up independently by the Relational School in the United States. Rather rapidly, the use of the term spread through different psychoanalytic groups, even gaining a school of its own: the "intersubjective psychoanalysis" of Stolorow and colleagues, heavily influenced by Heidegger. Finally, the neurosciences have attempted to naturalize intersubjectivity through systematic research on brain mechanisms.

In this chapter, I summarize major issues in philosophical approaches to intersubjectivity, particularly their influence on psychoanalytic theories. Lacan remains a major figure in this cross-disciplinary dialogue, although, as will be discussed below, he early abandoned intersubjectivity as a central concept. While it is correct to say that the field of intersubjectivity deals with complex processes in the relationship between two persons or subjects, each school has its own vocabulary and set of assumptions, so that one cannot assume a common understanding at this point. The phenomenologists vary in the extent to which they accord priority to intersubjective processes in the formation of consciousness, and analysts also differ in role attributed to shared experiences between subjects. Findings from philosophy, neuroscience (mirror neurons, for example), and infant research expand our awareness of the complexity of human interaction, without reaching a synthesis. Moreover, the goal of establishing a basic definition of intersubjectivity by incorporating evidence from different sources assumes that such an entity exists as an object that can be studied. It is always useful to remind ourselves that concepts like intersubjectivity use highly abstract language to construct ways of speaking about personal interactions, not to identify an object independent of the words employed. They can expand our ways of looking at human behavior, but they do not define a natural entity.

More fundamentally, we may wonder why we are confronted with such profusion of uses and definitions of the word intersubjectivity. The basic reason lies within the term itself. That is, our interpretation of the concept depends on how we think about the nature of the human subject.

DOI: 10.4324/9780429297076-17

Of which subject is it a question? And this remains a real problem for psychoanalysis, which tolerates a wide discrepancy around how closely related terms like subject, subjectivity, and self are actually employed. On a broad scale, there remains a tension across psychoanalytic theories between the assumption of a field independent subject, with a discernable internal structure of unconscious fantasies or desires, and a field dependent, malleable subject with permeable boundaries, arising out of messages and contextual interplay between persons. The "naturalized" subject as a product of normal operations of the brain, as proposed by some neuroscience researchers, offers another model endorsed by many psychiatrists, and each holds different implications for defining psychopathology.

The Subject/the Self

A focus on human subjectivity in psychoanalytic practice, so prevalent today, has not always been obvious. Freud, in his pioneering explorations, sidestepped the thorny philosophical problem of subjectivity as irrelevant to psychoanalysis as a science. Through the greater part of the last century, his followers approached the psyche as a system dealing with the channeling and discharge of energies through a structural model of drives, conflicts, and defenses. The terms "subject" and "self" were not part of the major concepts of classic analysis. Instead, Freud tolerated the ambiguity of his term *Ich*, referring to the system ego, the self, and the speaking subject in different contexts (*Ich*, of course, literally meaning "I" in German). For him, raising the problematic of the subject belonged to purely philosophical speculation. He looked instead to a more scientific view of the conscious mind as the product of internal forces (with a presumed organic substrate), rather than the humanistic concept of the self as a product of symbolic social interaction. Over the past decades, however, analytic thinkers of different schools have emphasized the notions of an agentic self and a desiring subject as central objects of therapeutic concern.

Phenomenology

As traditionally defined, phenomenology refers to the branch of philosophy that studies experience from the standpoint of individual consciousness. Philosophers who pursue this discipline have been historically associated with the concept of intersubjectivity, especially as it relates to basic structures of conscious experience. Phenomenology takes the perspective of a subjective or first-person point of view on behavior, with its intrinsic "intentionality" (which means simply that experience always pertains to an external object in the world to which attention is directed). It then analyses the conditions for the manifestations of personal agency, for example, what kinds of properties of consciousness are necessarily involved in organizing actions, relationships with other subjects, and using language. Different philosophers like Husserl, Heidegger, and Sartre prioritize conscious experience in different ways, but all question the Freudian idea of a divided consciousness (with an active unconscious behind the scenes).

Phenomenology carries important implications for how analysts should approach and address patients in clinical practice. The growing assimilation of the phenomenologic tradition into contemporary psychoanalytic models represents in part a reaction to classic theories of an objectified mental apparatus and a medical stance that sees patients as clinical objects. The paradigm of subject-to-subject relations that emphasizes recognition of the other as a primary ethical obligation has rightly become an influential component of clinical thinking. Buber's elaboration of the "I-Thou" relationship, for example, speaks directly to the therapeutic encounter, as does the ethical stance of Levinas towards "the other." Strictly speaking, of course, both subject-to-object and subject-to-subject relations are "intersubjective" in that participants in each version are equally subjects. The phenomenologic use of the term focuses on the "second person" approach – an "I-you," subject-to-subject perspective. The "other" is a subject like oneself, not an object of knowledge. Rather than supporting a specific theory or school of psychoanalysis, intersubjectivity represents a vantage point, a conceptual frame, and a position to occupy.

For psychoanalysts, inviting first person accounts of experience, rather than undertaking an objectifying, "I-it" dialogue of inquiry, provides access to another person that would be otherwise unobtainable. When we ask the other to tell us about her experience or what she is seeking from therapy (saying "you"), we invite a direct address (from an "I") that speaks to us immediately and, at least for the time of the exchange, creates a relationship, an entanglement, which can de-center us from our usual postures. We don't know what the other will say, and the spontaneity can surprise and disturb. As Freud discovered, the unpredictable flow of speech provides unique access to the life of the subject. Although several ways of knowing another person, including different theories and applications of empirical knowledge, play their parts in a typical psychoanalysis, the intersubjective turn over the past 25 years has shifted the balance of clinical listening toward a dialogic register.

The Hegelian Influence

The philosopher G. F. Hegel's famous parable of the encounter between master and slave has frequently been interpreted as a metaphor for the development of individual self-consciousness and has served as a starting point for numerous philosophers, political scientists, and ethicists dealing with human relationships. In psychoanalysis, Lacan was the first to discuss this parable on several occasions in his early work. Among others, Jessica Benjamin and Arnold Modell have also explored its implications, emphasizing the subject's search (and need) for recognition from an intersubjective counterpart. Blunden (2005) comments that the dialectic of recognition portrayed in the parable is today by far the most famous passage of Hegel's works, despite the fact that it makes up just 19 of the 808 paragraphs of the *Phenomenology* and was never mentioned by Marx or Engels in their entire oeuvres!

Hegel's parable portrays an imaginary encounter between two consciously aware but reflectively unconscious subjects in what can be regarded as both a stage in the moral progress of humanity and a personal crisis in individual development. For each subject of the parable, the confrontation with the existence of the other is a mortal threat to his own self-definition. Hegel's original German phrase, *Herrschaft und Knechtschaft*, has been translated as Lordship and Bondage, which sets up a bipolarity of positions. The confrontation between the two consciousnesses inevitably produces a struggle for dominance, hence the terms master and slave, each subject seeking to impose its desire for an absolute confirmation of self on the other. Their contest takes the form of a "struggle to the death," since everything seems to be at stake. In brief, in Hegel's scenario one subject saves his life by surrendering to become the slave, but the master soon realizes that a slave cannot provide the freely given affirmation he seeks. Neither subject can yet grasp that self-affirmation requires a recognition by another subject belonging to a social reality of which they both are part. Hegel asserts: "Self-consciousness exists in and for itself when, and by the fact that, it so exists for another; that is, it exists only by being acknowledged" (Hegel, 1807, p. 111).

In taking the phenomenology of consciousness as his reference point, Hegel remained within the Cartesian tradition with its idealist orientation. Like Kant, he renounced the notion of an introjected self that views representations of the world from "inside," by proposing that the world as experienced is essentially constructed by an active consciousness. An important difference from Kant was his rejection of a transcendental self existing *a priori*. Instead, he proposed that self-consciousness – the experience of having a self – requires engagement with another subject. The self comes to be, as Ver Eecke (1983) summarizes, through an intersubjective relationship in which each subject must discover in another entity a quality of being it possesses itself but of which it is not yet aware (p. 121). The French scholar Jean Hippolyte (Wilden, 1968) interpreted Hegel's rather obscurely worded passages as an attempt to show that "self-formation is only conceivable through the mediation of alienation or estrangement. Self-formation is not to develop harmoniously as if by organic growth, but rather to become opposed to oneself through a splitting or separation" (p. 372). In other words, man splits himself into a subject, recognizing himself in another, and an object, viewed through the eyes of another. In the Marxist philosopher Kojève's interpretation of this process (Wilden, 1968), consciousness presses for a kind of absolute recognition from the other, a desire for the other to attribute "an absolute value to his free and historical individuality or to his personality" (p. 292). This dialectic involves a kind of mirroring process, a passage back and forth from self-objectification in the eyes of the other to self-aggrandizement in obliterating the separateness and freedom of the other subject.

The Hegelian themes of the subject's search for recognition, of a mirrored consciousness that founds the subject, of the always problematic encounter with the other, and of a mediating system that transcends both subjects have permeated philosophical and psychoanalytic thinking since his time. We might see Freud's own parable of the meeting with the first object, the *Nebenmench*, in his *Project for a Scientific Psychology* (1895) as a commentary on Hegel. Winnicott, however, was the first psychoanalyst to situate the encounter at the level of the newborn's relationship with its mother. Stepping away from the encapsulated, representational tradition of regarding the interpersonal dynamic as a matter of projections and introjections, Winnicott began his story with the mother-baby relationship. Rather than treating the infant as a separate subject with a painful form of primary consciousness as Sartre might have, he began with the inextricability of the dual relation. In his well-known paper on the mirror role of the mother (Winnicott, 1956), he discussed the self-formation of the infant within the matrix of affective exchanges communicated by facial expressions, so that when the child looks at the mother's face, it sees itself, while the mother's communication depends in turn on what she sees of herself reflected in the baby. Winnicott famously summarizes this phenomenon: "When I look I am seen, so I exist. I can now afford to look and see. I now look creatively and what I apperceive I also perceive" (p. 114). Here, he affirms that recognition by the other as a self – one might say, by the other's desire to receive an affirming response from one's own self – is more basic than drive or need satisfaction in promoting the active emergence of an infantile subject that can construct a perceptual world, not merely passively receive one.

The fundamental shift in perspective or paradigm brought about by Winnicott's views on the formation of the self has been recognized most consistently by Arnold Modell, whose summary of the matter is clearly a version of Hegel's dialectic:

> The psychology of the self is embedded in this fundamental dilemma, namely, that the sense of self needs to be affirmed by the other, and yet a response from the other that is non-confirming or unempathic can lead at best to a sense of depletion or at worst to the shattering of the self. This results in a defensive quest for an illusory self-sufficiency which is in conflict with the opposite wish to surrender the self to the other, to merge, to become enslaved.
>
> *(1984, p. 131)*

The notions of recognition or affirmation become quite complex in this formulation. How they are conceived will influence the analyst's therapeutic behavior. In a sense, she is no longer functioning to analyze the other but to engage with her.

Phenomenology and Intersubjectivity

The universal desire to gain recognition underlines the inseparability of intersubjectivity from the ancient philosophical question of what it means to be a subject among other subjects. The problem runs through the writings of the great phenomenologists – Hegel, Husserl, Heidegger, Sartre, and Merleau-Ponty – to name the most important. Merleau-Ponty asserted in his *Phenomenology of Perception* that we do not begin our lives immersed in a private self-consciousness encased somewhere inside the skull but in the experience of being with others. This undeniable truth about human life was richly developed by Husserl and Heidegger well before the beginning of infant research and psychoanalysis. *Subjectivity is inconceivable without intersubjectivity.*

The phenomenologists refer to two apparently contradictory intuitions that form our experience of the other. The other is immediately present to us in its expressive behavior, while at the same time it escapes our understanding in a fundamental way. The paradoxical familiarity and strangeness of the other has been addressed in different ways by philosophers (also by Freud in his *Project*, 1895). For Heidegger, the human subject, the *dasein*, belongs by essence and from its very beginnings to the social world, hence his term *mitsein*. The subject is in the *we* already, not alone in a precarious position confronting an unknown other. Husserl's position is similar; as subjects, we have implicit knowledge of the other. By contrast, for Sartre, it is only through the concrete encounter of the subject with *l'autrui*, the unknown other who can perceive me and objectify me, that I discover the intersubjectivity of my individual existence. Levinas holds a yet more radical position on the encounter; it is "the *absoluteness* of the other's alterity that Levinas draws from the face-to-face relation" (Berge, 2015, p. 3).

Phenomenologists agree, however, that the constitution of the subject is given (uniquely) in consciousness, not determined by extrinsic structures. In his version of existential psychoanalysis, Sartre (1943) emphasizes the absolute freedom of consciousness (the *pour-soi*, the for-itself) and the attempt to escape this lack of essence by becoming a reified "me" (an *en-soi*, the in-itself). This is the origin of his analysis of bad faith or inauthenticity, which concerns the fantasy of possessing a substantive identity that defines the self. Consciousness lacks the substance that the ego (the "me"), as a unity of states and actions, appears to possess. In this way, Sartre does not bypass the dilemma of the Hegelian encounter as an existential threat to the reified self unrelieved by a third.

Despite his rejection of the unconscious in mental life, Sartre's conception of the essentially empty "for-itself" (*le pour-soi*) in dialogue with a consciousness seeking to objectify itself as an "in-itself" (*le en-soi*) strikes a persuasive note. Attempting to define a durable identity and resisting threats to it from others (the Hegelian encounter) describes a familiar clinical situation, often explicit with so-called narcissistic personalities, but present in most people at times. Because we cannot circle around the "me" that we sense in ourselves, we are left with the inescapable problem of needing to turn to others to find out (or to have affirmed) what kind of "me" we are. "To really know oneself is inevitably to take toward oneself the point of view of others, that is to say, a point of view which is necessarily false," says Sartre (1936–37, p. 87). The mirrored self, he might argue against Kohut, is an alienated self, an object which the *pour-soi* must negate to achieve authenticity. Both he and Lacan cite Rimbaud's celebrated phrase "*Je est un autre*" ("I" is another), which points to the distance between the object-like ego (*le moi*) and the speaking subject (who says *je*). Possibly no other thinker has insisted as much as Sartre on the pain of empty human consciousness. He aphorizes that "the *pour-soi* is a hole in the heart of being" (p. 711).

Lacan praised his contemporary Sartre and shared (or possibly adopted) his position that the self is absent in the Real (as taught by Eastern religions as well), but he could not accept the rejection of a Freudian unconscious. "This philosophy," he says (Lacan, 1966, p. 96), remains within "the limits of a self-sufficiency of consciousness." He regards consciousness "as irredeemably limited . . . a principle, not only of idealization, but of *méconnaissance* (misrecognition)." "For us," he continues, "consciousness matters only in relation to what . . . I have tried to show you in the fiction of the incomplete text" (Lacan, 1964, pp. 82–83). With the master and slave struggle clearly in mind, he asserts that existentialism reduces the subject to a violent encounter of wills (1964, p. 8), an "active annihilation" of the other, the "Hegelian murder" (1966, p. 96).

To be fair, Sartre's position does not entail an observing self in the way Lacan portrays, but insists rather on an inherent subjectivity in every perception, without any act of reflection. Among contemporary phenomenologists, Zahavi (2006, 2011) has been a strong proponent of the Sartrean view that rejects any notion of a subject outside of consciousness (thus, one acting upon or structuring the form of consciousness). Consciousness, he summarizes, "is characterized by a fundamental selfness or selfhood precisely because of this pervasive self-givenness, self-intimation, or reflexivity" (Zahavi, 2011, p. 57). The experiential core self is "an integral part of the structure of phenomenal consciousness" (Gallagher and Zahavi, 2008, p. 227). In response to the question of whether an inner self exists independent of experience or represents only an imaginary conflation of ever-changing experiences, Zahavi (2011) proposes "a ubiquitous dimension of first personal self-givenness" (Zahavi, p. 59). In this way, he seems to avoid the either-or dilemma of an enduring inner self versus self as illusion (as in Hume's classic argument). Although the perhaps logical necessity for this concept of pre-reflexive self-givenness remains far from a Cartesian subjectivity, which, nonetheless, hovers uncomfortably in the background.

Zahavi's discussion does not refer to psychoanalysis,[2] but the issue of how the self is conceived has been a recurring one for many psychoanalysts (Kirshner, 1991; Mitchell, 1991; Modell, 1993; Zahavi, 2008).[3] Like the phenomenologists, Mitchell observes that "we generally spend most of our time being conscious, not self-conscious, being aware of ourselves as an ongoing process, without objectifying ourselves in an active effort to grasp or understand or communicate" (1991, p. 121). He, too, is wary of reifications of the self as an entity, which he finds in Self Psychology, emphasizing instead a view of self as relational, multiple, and discontinuous. In the end, however, discussing his patient "L." who presents with problems of identity and disavowed aspects of herself, Mitchell supports a multiplex analytic approach leading to an enlarged experience of self, including a dependable sense of the self "as functionally integral and continuous" (p. 139), which may carry echoes of the Freudian ego. Zahavi advocates a similar multidimensional view of the self: "We are dealing with a culturally, socially, and linguistically embedded self that is under constant construction" (2011, p. 71). But how phenomenology can deal with these omnipresent elements within the exclusive notion of a conscious, experiential self is not obvious. The notion of an embedded self suggests a permeable boundary with the external structures that govern its functioning and from which it cannot be extricated.

Many patients seek psychoanalytic therapies because of an uncertain sense of who they are and their place in relationships with others. Certainly in such cases, the different kinds of techniques that Mitchell summarizes (he describes examples derived from object relations, Self Psychology, and Relational models) will have clinical consequences for the outcome, but it may be unrealistic to expect an analyst to move flexibly across them. In particular, the aim of affirming or restoring an inner core of self as something to be found and recognized conflicts with using the intersubjective process to foster expanded versions of self. Likewise, pursuing unconscious fantasies disguised by conscious preoccupations may be incompatible with the affirmation and recognition Kohut promoted, as well as constituting a self to object (third person) method. For this reason, a "naive" phenomenological view of interactions offers a healthy antidote to theory-laden constructions about the supposed inner world of the analysand, as one finds in some Freudian and Kleinian methods of interpretation. If an analyst concentrates his attention on what may be going on inside his patient's mind, he may have difficulty balancing this effort with observation of his own participation in creating the content of their interaction.

Although phenomenology has been accused of being solipsistic, interested only in the mental life of the isolated subject (as perhaps Sartre might appear to exemplify), Gallagher and Zahavi (2008) have taken up the Husserlian case for the immediacy of intersubjective awareness of others. In his early work, Husserl struggled to make sense of the experiential phenomenon of empathy as a way of connecting the subject with others around him, not as unknown objects or adversaries but as co-participants in a shared world. Most commentators would agree that this project was not successful. Many later theorists both in psychology and philosophy have confronted the same problem (of the existence of other minds), and, it might be said, remain stuck in a tautological and tendentious use of empathy as a core intersubjective concept.

Gallagher and Zahavi (2008) criticize mentalization concepts, theory of mind (TOM) approaches, and the model of implicit simulation of others' mental states (ST) as unnecessary, overcomplicated explanations for how we acquire knowledge of other minds. Instead, they assert, others are known immediately and implicitly in awareness (Gallagher, 2008), a position consistent with their rejection of a determining unconscious behind experience. They follow Merleau-Ponty's view that our awareness of others' mental lives belongs to the ordinary context of bodily interactions. Similarly, the phenomenon of empathy does not consist in feeling one's way into another mind or an active process of trial identification, as Self Psychologists have proposed. Instead, knowing the other derives from an intrinsic "ability to access the life of the mind of others in their expressive behavior and meaningful action" (Gallagher and Zahavi, 2008, p. 213). Somewhat surprisingly, like many psychoanalytic authors, they support this conclusion by citing the neurologic research of Rizzolatti and Gallese on mirror neurons as demonstrating "an enactment of intersubjective perception" (p. 199). Others use this discovery to emphasize the "hard-wired" nature of intersubjectivity. This cross-disciplinary hypothesis has been deservedly critiqued as neglecting all the social and personal information necessary for accurate "interpretation" of the cortical discharges involved in the phenomenon of neural mirroring, but remains influential. Of course, the brain does not interpret. Meaning-making is a cognitive-emotional mental property of persons. The cognitive neuro-analyst N. Georgieff (personal communication) suggests that in many respects the brain as a whole has evolved as a mirroring organ, evolved to perceive and respond to the emotions and messages of others – an organ of intersubjectivity and empathic connection. Of course, this formulation is metaphoric.

Husserl in his late unpublished notebooks carried a phenomenologic explanation of intersubjectivity to the furthest extent, as Zahavi (2002) has argued. Rather than developing a secondary model of subjects interacting in a shared space, Husserl came to understand intersubjectivity as inseparable from and immediately given to subjective consciousness. For him, the inextricability of the subject from its social life world was fundamental. The infant "pre"-subject, he emphasized, is immersed from the beginning in objects, events, and actions presented by its culture. These experiences exist as public, not private perceptions of the world; they are shared with other subjects. Husserl described this as a form of transcendent intersubjectivity that provides the ground for the emergence of subjects within an intrinsically shared life world. In Zahavi's formulation (2002, p. 9), "a phenomenological analysis, insofar as it unveils the being-sense (*Seinssinn*) of the world as intersubjectively valid, leads to a disclosure of the transcendental relevance of foreign subjectivity and thus to an examination of transcendental intersubjectivity." In a Kantian sense, the intersubjective world exists a priori as the basis of subjective experience.

Gallagher and Zahavi (2008) additionally find support for their model of transcendent human interactions in Trevarthen's theory of primary intersubjectivity. Trevarthen (1998) observed that the interactions of babies and their caretakers are spontaneous and immediate, as though innate and unmediated. There seems to be no organized subject to subject relationship, which only comes later in development; from birth, the intersubjective connection appears primary. Following this pattern of early infancy, Gallagher and Zahavi insist, "others are not given primarily as objects, or as entities in need of explanation" (2008, p. 211). Rather, as Merleau-Ponty (1962) proposed, we make sense of the behavior of others because it is expressed by actions in contextualized situations. For example, we can see that someone is sad or angry by his facial expressions within a familiar social situation, and we understand her intention to carry out a specific act by reading posture and movement. Merleau-Ponty's radical behaviorism asserted that the human body is comparable to a work of art whose expression becomes indistinguishable from that which is expressed.

Gallagher (2012) puts the matter quite unequivocally. He argues against TOM and other cognitive models:

> "In most situations we are not trying to mind read the other person; we are not concerned about the other person's mental states, although such concerns may be motivated by relatively unusual behaviors, or by attempts to give reasons or justify actions reflectively. Even in response to questions about why someone is doing something (as opposed to simply what is happening), . . . narrative accounts in terms of actions often suffice"
>
> *(p 193).*

His discussion brings out the extent to which the extension of primary intersubjectivity beyond infant research relies upon a behavioral, phenomenological methodology. Yet Gallagher also acknowledges the presence of non-experiential determinants of subjectivity, citing Merleau-Ponty's comment that the infant is born into a "whirlwind of language" and Rakoczy et al.'s conclusion that the actions children learn "are not just individual, idiosyncratic behaviors, but cultural conventional forms of action. And many of these forms of action are rule-governed and normatively structured" (Gallagher, 2012, p. 192). There is a tension here between the sense of immediate immersion in intersubjectivity associated with Husserl and a form of social cognitive learning as the foundation for intersubjective consciousness. Does the incipient subject have to learn linguistic and cultural rules to make sense of what it experiences or does a more basic intersubjective function already form part of its primary experience? Such questions complicate any notion of implicit knowledge by direct perception that dispenses with a cognitive process like mentalization (a form of awareness of other minds) or social learning to make sense of experience (see Noë, 2007, for a balanced discussion of these issues). Here, a psychoanalyst might observe that the meaning of perceived behavior is more idiosyncratic than Gallagher suggests and that, in addition to their recognizable features, actions represent symbolically structured carriers of unconscious meaning that can powerfully influence the subject without his knowledge (the subject may not actually "feel" sad or angry). At least in the case of personally important behaviors and messages, meaning is complex and even enigmatic, as Laplanche (1987) has presented at length in his theory of the human anthropological situation. If Trevarthen and Gallagher are correct in positing a radical intersubjective perspective on immediately shared experience, does this transcendent/apriori level underpin the gradual development of understanding meaning? Could this level continue to influence subjective experience – in the analytic transference, for example? Current concepts of analytic field theory, notably in writings of Civitarese and Ferro, challenge the primacy of the separate subject in traditional psychoanalytic models and present an alternative clinical model based on an intersubjective immersion (see review by Katz, 2017). These authors base much of their thinking on Husserl's (and Heidegger's) writings. For Civitarese, a pre-subjective dimension of passivity, anonymity, and reciprocal interweaving plays a part in the unfolding of a shared intersubjective field. He and Ferro build on Bionian ideas to speak about a waking dream emerging from an undifferentiated unconscious level in the analytic session. The narrative derivatives of the waking dream thought are interwoven in the analytic dialogue, but also may appear in reveries, sensations, feelings, and forms of action representations, presumably in both parties. Bion derives a shared mental state from the unconscious capacity of human beings to immediately enter into resonance with each other, as Freud much earlier suggested. In Civitarese's field model, shared unconscious emotion occupies the heart of clinical work. It lies within the on-going weaving of individual subjectivities achieved through the moments of at-one-ment. Concepts like projective identification and the metabolization of unsymbolized elements in the analytic situation point in this direction.

There are, of course, many critics of intersubjective theories. Dennett (1991) for example, criticized Phenomenology because its explicitly first-person approach to behavior is incompatible with a scientific third-person approach. Phenomenologists might respond that natural science makes sense only as a human activity that presupposes the fundamental structures of a first-person perspective. Searle (2008) has questioned what he calls the "Phenomenological Illusion" of assuming that what is not phenomenologically present is not real and that what is phenomenologically present is in fact an adequate description of how things really are. The content of this debate holds relevance for theories of psychoanalytic practice influenced by intersubjectivity, which depend to a great extent on the existential validity of "here and now" interactions to achieve their goals.

Lavelle (2012) contested the theory of unmediated knowledge by direct perception on two grounds. First, he endorsed the "establishment view" in which "'Epistemic Seeing' just isn't possible without a process of inference" (p. 222). Although, as noted, phenomenologists like Gallagher sometimes refer to the operation of the mirror neuron system to answer this objection, it seems obvious that neuroscientific findings of brain mechanisms cannot dispense with a theory of inferential rules. Even if goals of actions are "mapped" by a mirror system in the premotor cortex, as Lavelle comments, "one must be able to explain how the . . . system organizes and accesses the relevant contextual information" (p. 225). Understanding the goals and motivations of most actions requires complex cognitive processes that depend on learning and previous experience. Second, he continues, "visual stimulus alone does not give the mirror neuron system sufficient material to ascertain an intention. The additional information required is not 'direct' visual information, but information about culture, context, and expectations" (p. 227). For psychoanalysis, the latter information (again pertaining to personally important situations like intimate relationships or questions of identity) depends on links to associative chains and images that are far from universal and for which the hypothesis of a dynamic personal unconscious has been a crucial aspect. The Civitarese version of field theory may suggest an effacement of this personal unconscious level of meaning.

Despite this cautionary note, it seems increasingly clear that the wider acceptance of phenomenologic models of intersubjectivity by psychoanalysts has opened the traditional clinical situation to a deeper and more spontaneous engagement. Mitchell's innovative ideas about expansion of self-knowledge through dialogue and relationship, as opposed to accurate formulation and interpretation, can be seen now as a turning point. Yet for cultural reasons, intersubjective philosophy continues to play a minor part in psychoanalytic training in comparison to theoretical approaches that remain "subject to object" in form. The intersubjective field may not account for the entirety of psychoanalytic process, but it sets the context and creates the possibilities for interaction from the beginning,

Lacan and Intersubjectivity

It was probably Jacques Lacan who introduced (or at least foregrounded) the concepts of the subject and intersubjectivity in psychoanalysis. He insisted that even for Freud the true object of psychoanalysis was the human subject. The patient on the couch, unlike the manifestation of a psychic apparatus that one might study objectively, embodies a subject who speaks, listens, and reacts. Lacan's rejection of biological explanations of subjectivity in favor of experiential presence were strongly influenced by his readings of phenomenology, which he frequently discussed in his early period. During his "Hegelian" phase, in fact, he taught that the subject seeks recognition from the Other as a fundamental desire.[4]

In Lacan's treatment of Hegel's master-slave parable, the crucial element in resolving the paradigmatic death struggle became the presence of "a third," which in his formulation meant the symbolic order of language and transpersonal rules for using signifiers in speech that govern all subjects. By sharing a symbolic matrix that founds their subjectivities, the dyadic (dialectical) confrontation between master and slave rises to another level subsuming both adversaries.

Lacan's initial conception of therapeutic action in psychoanalysis relied heavily on a transferential demand for recognition that is obliged to pass through speech. In bringing this demand to the surface, the analysand repeats the stages of his own history of becoming a subject. The Lacanian analyst does not bestow the desired recognition but supports the unfolding of the analysand's past and, like Winnicott, exposes the place where it became derailed (see Julien, 1981, for a discussion of the development of this aspect of Lacan's theory). The human desire to be affirmed by the other has implications for a theory of narcissism, and may represent one of the rare points of intersection between Kohut and Lacan. Both saw a mirroring process as intrinsic to the interpersonal encounter. That is, a subject wants to be seen for who she is, but this usually means confirmation of a preferred self-image or identity. How one appears to others represents a central narcissistic concern. For Lacan, however, "mirroring" describes a phase in the evolution of treatment that must be surpassed to avoid repetition of the dyadic (Hegelian) fantasies of dominance or omnipotence. Whether recognition and affirmation by the analyst represent a necessary step in resuming a developmental process, as Winnicott and Kohut believed, or instead lead only to consolidation of resistances in the ego, as Lacan contended, has divided analysts. But the oppositional aspect of these models may be only a historical fact. Many Lacanians now incorporate a Winnicottian approach to the mirror phase (Kirshner, 2014) and many relational analysts recognize that a symmetrical (mirroring) dyad can operate to block change (Aron, 1991, 1999). The themes of recognition and the importance of a third to avoid repetition became a cornerstone of Benjamin's work (2004). These technical issues deserve independent discussion.

Lacan's use of the Hegelian expression, Man's desire is the desire of the Other, may have subtly changed in its implications over time. The encounter between two subjects as the primal scene of intersubjective recognition, beginning with the infant's reciprocal exchanges with the mother, constitutes one approach (with which the author identifies). The Lacanian construction of *(m)Other* emphasized this developmental aspect of intersubjectivity by equating the Other with the actual mothering person. By contrast, his later turn to emphasizing a structural or logical relationship between a split or barred subject (one with an unconscious) and the Other (Lacan's abstract term representing the universal field of signifiers) led away from a relational, phenomenological view towards a more impersonal formulation of "man's desire." Lacan's rejection of intersubjectivity (summarized by Fink, 2007, pp. 148–149) derived from this perspective. "Is not intersubjectivity what is most foreign to the analytic encounter?" Lacan wrote (1960–61, p. 21).

In his early seminars, Lacan also spoke about another subject, the subject of the unconscious, a concept suggesting Freud's famous metaphor of the mind functioning as if two separate persons were vying for control, a conscious one with definite beliefs and values and an unconscious one pursuing a pleasure-seeking agenda. Later, however, Lacan came to redefine the Hegelian desire to be recognized as the pursuit of an unrealizable unconscious fantasy of wholeness. With his conception of the unsymbolized real, Lacan specified that the subject in question in psychoanalysis emerges as an effect of discourse, a subject constructed by signifiers that constantly fall short of closure. The division or split in this conception refers to the unbridgeable gap between a verbally represented but evanescent subject using a code of signifiers and the silent, unconscious, unrepresentable domain of "the real" of organic life. Behind the symbolic realm of speech and forever seeking expression lies an unconscious fantasy of oneness that drives human desire. Lacan's concept of the *objet petit a* as the undefinable missing link to the fantasized lost object became the new key to analytic action. Now absent is the former attention to recognition by the Other or m(other) as the desire of the subject.[5]

Lacan left intersubjectivity behind in favor of the linguistically determined subject, arising from and persisting only for the duration of a speech act, and deriving its transient identity from the chain of signifiers in play. Influenced by his readings of the linguists Benveniste, Jacobson, Peirce, and Saussure, he pursued a semiotic approach, teaching that the subject transforms itself along the moving chain of spoken words (signifiers), which constantly revises prior self-definitions. The familiar vacillating subject of post-modern philosophy exists only during the time of the words at its immediate disposal for expressing itself, to be modified continuously by further enunciations. Lacan assigned notions like the self, the ego, and ego identity to the imaginary register; they are impermanent images or fantasies that attempt to reify complex, ephemeral processes, not substantive entities. The illusory construction of self-consciousness, the imaginary object "me," does become tied to specific memories and cultural labels that provide points of reference, halting the constant slippage of meaning along the unending chain of words. Through these *pointes de capiton* (a kind of upholstery button), the signifiers "subject" or "self" accumulate links to signifieds that circulate in the social world. Signified meanings that attempt to define the self lack a precise content, as Sartre had emphasized, but can be socially shared, like Winnicott's transitional objects, both created and discovered. In this sense, words can support a representation of individuality endorsed by the culture. Subjects are structural products of the culture that creates them, a formulation that suggests a return to intersubjectivity in another form (the culture gives birth to a collection of speaking subjects).

The Lacanian subject in its semiotic version can be described as the product of an unconscious structure of signifiers that have been internalized as a dialogue bridging a primal moment of separation. Lacan's discussion of Freud's famous *fort-da* game portrays this developmental step. In his account of this game, Freud (1920) described an infant playing at throwing away and retrieving a spool while his mother has gone out. The child has substituted for the relation with his mother the German words *fort* and *da* ("gone" and "here"), the shared language of his world by which he can symbolically master her presence and absence. For Lacan, however, the element of mastery is of secondary importance:

> "This reel is not the mother reduced to a little ball by some magical game worthy of the Jivaros it is a small part of the subject that detaches itself from him while still remaining his, still retained. How can we fail to recognize here – from the very fact that this game is accompanied by one of the first oppositions to appear that it is in the object to which opposition is applied in the act, the reel, that we must designate the subject. It is the repetition of the mother's departure as cause of a *Spaltung* (splitting) in the subject"
>
> *(1964, pp. 62–63).*

Later, in fact, Freud observed the child turning to the mirror to play at his own imaginary disappearance, confirming that he has taken the perspective of the mother. In the child's solitude, Lacan proposed, his desire has become the desire of another, "of an alter ego who dominates him and of whom the object of desire" (i.e., what the mother desires) will be henceforth "his affliction" (*peine*) (1966, p. 203). She is elsewhere, wants something that is not him, and thereby evokes by this "want" the child's desire, born of separation.

In this little drama, the child's sense of being a member of a disrupted pair is expressed by the phonemic opposition of the sounds *fort* and *da*. Already the product of a physical separation, the incipient infantile subject is split again by language, which forces him to become what Lacan calls an incomplete text, struggling to express through signifiers his inexhaustible desire for wholeness and reunion with the mother. Zahavi surprisingly evokes similar terms in speaking of episodic memory as involving "some kind of doubling or fission; it does involve some degree of self-division, self-absence, and self-alienation" (2011, p. 74). Yet he does not modify his support for a pre-reflexive, unitary experience of selfhood (*ipseite*) by this admission. Sartre debunked the psychoanalytic concept of a divided self on logical and commonsense grounds by appealing to an intuitive experience of self-awareness and by his critique of the Freudian "homuncular" unconscious, whose intentions and desires imply a non-existent locus of decisions about repression or expression. In sum, Sartre argued, any border between consciousness and unconscious requires a monitor (like Freud's second locus of agency).

Lacan read in these positions a blindness to the overarching role of speech in human life. Speech provides the child's entry into the symbolic order through which it can reach the mother through the power of words, but this power belongs to a structure that preexists the child and mother and presents an impassable step away from the preverbal oneness (or its fantasy) it desires. Rather than emerging from a primordial intersubjective matrix that will found the subject, language cleaves the wholeness of the infantile real. The phonemes *fort* and *da* reported by Freud represent a prototypal structure of the symbolic order within which the subject fleetingly emerges as figure to ground. Lacan stated that this order is represented by the father (or, more precisely, by the name of the father – *le nom du pere* – as a third party), the one who disrupts the enclosed world of the dyad and to whom the mother goes when leaving the child.

By grounding both "self" and other within the third term of the symbolic order, Lacan attempted to bypass the problematic Hegelian encounter. For Hegel, resolution of the dual desire for recognition by the other depended on a dialectical unfolding of consciousness (of which the struggle of master and slave represents an early form). The system of language, however, lies outside the realm of conscious experience. More specifically, the child's identity as subject originates in the desires of the parents and the words they use to speak about and to him. Lacan depicted the construction of the subject in its formative encounter with others in his schema L, a quadrangle whose four corners represent the egos of the subject and the other and their dual unconsciouses, which he describes as a couple in their "reciprocal imaginary objectivization." By this model, he illustrates the attempt by the ego to confirm unity as a complete self, while by speaking the subject acknowledges the impossibility of such total affirmation, since language coming from the Other implies absence, the possibility of being thrown away like the reel. This "genetic moment," he writes, "is reproduced each time that the subject addresses himself to the Other as absolute, that is to say, as the Other who can nullify the subject himself" (1966, p. 67). This formulation carries a theological ring. Although Lacan refers to the position in the transference held by the analyst as Other, he does not consider this an intersubjective relationship (which he equates with a kind of co-presence). Speech never succeeds in presenting a whole self, but only reaffirms the structure of a primal splitting.

At the same time, by referring to "Being" as a property of the Real and thereby linked to the body, Lacan (1962–63) implied a uniqueness and continuity of subjective existence, albeit represented in a kaleidoscope of changing forms.[6] Perhaps he was influenced by Sartre and Heidegger in this respect. Speculations about "Being" seem reminiscent of Winnicott's conception of the "true self," for which he also employed the term "being" and which certainly antedates the development of any symbolic identity in words. Perhaps the two men shared the notion that a primal intuition of *being* as the living substrate of the subject underlies all the subsequently evolving selves of later interactions (see Eigen, 1981). This interpretation suggests a sense in which a transcendent experience of being precedes any apprehension of the existence of separate subjects. The developmental researcher Rochat (2009) has written of an intrinsic property of sentient "awareness" that is not yet "self-awareness," while the neuroscientist-analyst Solms (2013) argues that this basic awareness includes a capacity for emotional responsiveness as a common mammalian property, prior to any reflexive, intersubjective consciousness of self and other.

Lacan did not indicate a clear position on early subjective life. Although he saw the infantile pre-subject as living in the unsymbolized "real," he increasingly emphasized the overarching presence and function of the Other (the mother for all practical purposes) from the very beginning. To the extent that the originary being of the infant can be psychically represented in awareness, the Other necessarily exists as a background or pre-condition as something impinging on this awareness. Infant researchers would probably agree that becoming organized (psychically and neurocognitively) as a self-system depends on the presence of the mother. From this highly speculative perspective, emergence of a proto self in the field of the Other precedes development of a subject with another (as in Winnicott's "baby is always baby with mother" paradigm).

As Lacan moved towards a more abstract set of ideas about the real and desire, he attacked philosophers for assuming a complete subject who engages his peers in an endless quest for recognition following the Hegelian paradigm. He took the position that the premise of a unified subject, which he found in phenomenology, simply reified an imaginary construction. In his seminar on the transference (1954–55), Lacan pointed out that the analytic relationship lacks reciprocity and symmetry as a basic feature – that is, the two subjects are not interacting on the same plane. The analyst, he argued, does not occupy the place of another subject but of the Other. Yet, even accepting these qualifications, does the Lacanian analyst not consciously and unconsciously express signs like any subject, manifest in the flux of his language and gestures? The asymmetry in the transference would not then preclude (and may actually heighten) the influence of the analyst on the patient's subjective position within an intersubjective field.

Already in the 1930s the social psychologist G. H. Mead (1934) observed that the self takes its form within the context of current interpersonal relationships, and we can easily verify this dimension of subjectivity for ourselves. One feels almost imperceptibly or even enormously different in each encounter with another person, especially if magnified by imaginary fantasy. Harry Stack Sullivan (1953) elaborated Mead's observation in his theory of interpersonal psychoanalysis, countering the exclusively intrapsychic model of Ego Psychology. How to preserve the analytic focus on the individual subject while recognizing its dependency on a bi- or multipersonal field has become a problem for contemporary analytic theory. Lacan's increasingly abstract course away from intersubjectivity and the humanistic ethos of his beginnings removed him from this dialogue.

Intersubjectivity Without a Subject

Consistent with his emphasis on the interpersonal field, Sullivan (1953) did not have much use for the notion of an inner self, unlike Winnicott, Modell, or Kohut (in their varied ways). On this issue, he joins the diverse group of classic Freudians, ego psychologists, French structuralists, and the skeptical philosopher David Hume in relegating the concept of a discrete subject or coherent self – what Kohut called a psychic center of initiative – to a retrospective illusion of consciousness, a "ghost in the machine" (in Ryle's famous phrase). Perhaps the notion of a substantial self embodies the residue of a Western religious belief in an immortal soul. Yet something like this concept remains part of the thinking of many psychoanalysts who hold to the concept of an authentic or core self that needs to be affirmed or restored.[7]

If philosophy and neuroscience cannot find a justification for the notion of an interior agentic self, psychoanalysts must face the question suggested above: Is there a subject of intersubjectivity, a durable center of some kind that retains its singularity across varied contexts? If not, are we then left with a version of intersubjectivity that problematizes the discrete individual subject? To take the argument a step further, could what we call the subject merely represent the consequence of having a position in an intersubjective network, a node in the structure of human relationships as Lévi-Strauss or Foucault understood the term? The fact that many human beings have the capacity to narrate a reasonably integrated story of their selfhood may only reflect the social imperative to give a credible account of oneself or, perhaps, to internalize the assorted labels, categories, names, and relational positions that a person is allotted within a designated familial network as if they amount to an internal identity.[8]

With few exceptions, the absence of the subject except as a formal term of reference is typical for both psychiatry and the neurosciences. Of course, the term subject is applied to the object of research when neuroscientists study the brain with the fMRI or its equivalent to determine, for example, which cerebral centers function during an act of empathy. Yet the notion of a phenomenal subject is put aside during this activity, unless the researcher opens a conversation after the experiment is completed. For the physician, as well, the subject has a medico-legal status, but does not constitute the true object of clinical work, which operates on systems and diagnoses. Contemporary psychiatry similarly targets the symptoms or dysfunctions of a patient as more or less correctable malfunctions of the biological organism. The psychiatrist would like his patient to feel better and especially to function better, but the psychoanalytic (and phenomenologic) principle that a symptom in some ways best represents the singularity of the subject, that it constitutes a sign of a trouble touching the very being of the subject, is put aside. Increasingly, the modern psychiatrist treats the diagnosis, not the subject, and his evaluation consists of an algorithm that leads to identifying one or more disorders. Psychopharmacologic interventions take him inside the gears and switches of the nervous system, not the structures of personhood. Because of the necessary isolation of the chemistry of the brain for psychopharmacologic purposes, the subject of psychiatry has become more and more a montage or bricolage of independent functions and systems – hence the famous problem list.

The psychiatric approach is, in fact, a derivative of the scientific materialist position of the neurosciences. Neuroscience research documents the reality that impulses and transmissions in the brain never arrive at a central point of synthesis and decision; nor does "information" flow to an internal judge. The brain contains no executive center (no "ghost") to direct its operations. No one seems to be at home, even if some researchers anthropomorphize the results of their studies. As many philosophers of science have pointed out, the brain has no desires or motivations, doesn't send messages, and carries no burden of guilt (all are properties of persons). The vocabulary of subjectivity translates very poorly to the laboratory, which at best can discover the mechanisms or processes enabling these personal phenomena to occur. To talk about the subject from a scientific perspective amounts only to a way of speaking, a retrospective footnote, a familiar term evoked to reassure ourselves that the neurologic mechanisms producing our behavior have a transcendent feature and cannot be reduced to the operations of an automatic and impersonal machine.

We find ourselves here in a paradox. Certainly, the subject is not the ego, nor any conscious agent that emerges, in a more or less fleeting or stable manner, from our mental activity. On this point, traditional psychoanalysis and the neurosciences are in accord. Yet at the same time, human beings do have a sense of enjoying or bearing an enduring nature of self or, I prefer to say, of a subjective organization that represents who they are – what Winnicott saw as a private center of self that is nurtured and protected from impingement. Lacan's view of a unique residue of a primal fantasy of origin and the clinical goal of finding one's desire suggest this singularity. A psychology that dispensed with subjectivity, with the sense of a continuity of existence in time and a set of private feelings rooted in the past, would be absurd. Patients seek a personal psychoanalysis to understand their specific lives more fully and to become better able to pursue private desires. Yet entering an intimate relationship, with its implicit transitionality (in which it is not questioned whether perceptions are objective or subjective), immediately blurs the boundaries of the self. In psychoanalysis, we learn that our cherished individuality is interwoven with the voices and messages of others who seem to reincarnate themselves in internal conversations and our actual relationships. This raises the question of whether one must speak of multiple subjects – as in Proust's famous phrase, "I was not one man; I was a crowd of men" – or, perhaps, of different subjective positions or voices. The Proustian polyphony of the subject may the most important conclusion we can draw from Lacan's structural analysis. In the end, we are left with a version of the uncertainty principle: human subjectivity retains a continuity and identity, yet is protean and contextual. In the latter sense, it goes beyond the Sartrean pre-reflexive subject.

The Contributions of Paul Ricoeur

We should not leave this subject without appreciating the contributions of Ricoeur, who more than any other philosopher, has devoted large portions of his work to defining the nature of psychoanalysis as a discipline. His important notion of the co-existing principles of mechanism (causation) and meaning in psychoanalysis influenced Leavy and Modell in their pioneering reformulations. From his origins in phenomenology, through immersion in Freudian theory, then a lengthy period of association with Lacan, and finally with his rejection of the classic analytic paradigm in favor of Kohut's self psychology, Ricoeur has grappled with intersubjectivity as the fundamental human situation.

The theme of intersubjectivity," Ricoeur writes (1970),

> is undoubtedly where phenomenology and psychoanalysis come closest to being identified with each other, but also where they are seen to be most radically distinct . . . If the analytic relationship may be regarded as the privileged example of intersubjective relations . . . it is because the analytic dialogue brings to light . . . the demands in which desire ultimately consists.
>
> *(p. 406)*

As I understand him, the distinction turns on the emergence of unconscious desire in the transference, which he saw as requiring technical management. Yet unlike Freud, desire for Ricoeur transcends sexuality. Even in infant development, the desiring relationship with the father and the mother is carried by language,

> because the child is born into an environment of language, meaning and discourse. In this pre-constituted realm, the father and mother are not only the "beings" or

> "parents" that nourish him, but rather also bring him into the community of language, and therefore into the lifeworld.
>
> *(cited in Busacci, 2015, p. 17)*

"Lifeworld," of course, belongs to the vocabulary of Husserl.

Late in his career, as a professor at the University of Chicago, Ricoeur reviewed the limitations of Freud's isolated intrapsychic model of the mind and turned to Heinz Kohut for an alternative. In the concept of the selfobject, he found the inextricability of subject from other, the dependence of psychic life on interaction with other subjects. As with Husserl, empathy became for Ricoeur the privileged vehicle of contact between subjects. "This need for empathy distinguishes the relation between the self and its selfobjects from the relation between the ego and its love objects. Before being the key weapon of the psychoanalytic cure, empathy is the basic structure of the relation between self and selfobject" (Ricoeur, 1986, p. 440). While not explicit in Kohut, the selfobject (more realistically, we should use the plural form of selfobjects) represents a transitional area between the me and the not me. This interpretation returns Ricoeur closer to Husserlian intersubjectivity. Empathy for Kohut became the essential tool of the analyst, but, here, Ricoeur went further to address the apparent circularity of the empathic relation. With whom does one empathize? Does the structure of a relationship create its own other, a projection of the self, more than a product of primary intersubjectivity? If the analyst represents a selfobject in the transference, is this construction a dual creation of both parties? Like many psychoanalysts, Ricoeur looked to the therapeutic and educational course of professional training to ensure independence from the countertransference tendencies of an impinging analyst in the place of a selfobject. This argument, however, fails to acknowledge the traditional analyst's problematic position of supposed neutrality and self-knowledge.

The analogous question of recognition (who is to be recognized by whom) emerges again in the selfobject transference. In one of his most significant contributions, Ricoeur (2004) plumbed the historic and semantic meanings of the term recognition (*reconnaisance*) and its ethical quandaries. In the final part of this work, he addressed personal ethics in the manner of Levinas. "The withdrawal or refusal of . . . approbation," he stated, "touches everyone at the prejuridicial level of his or her being with others . . . Deprived . . . the person is as if nonexistent" (2004, p. 191). This "prejuridicial level" recalls Husserl's notion of transcendent intersubjectivity. Ricoeur goes on to examine the Hegelian dilemma of mutual need and struggle for recognition. Using the metaphor of the gift, he observes that Hegel's encounter implies the paradox of the "irreplaceable character of each of the partners in the exchange . . . different from any form of fusional union . . . a just distance is maintained" (p. 263). This indeed seems a paradoxical distance that both separates two subjects and entangles them in their mutual constitution.

The Neuroscience of Intersubjectivity

During the past decade, intersubjectivity has gained a new perspective through the research of cognitive social neuroscience, which studies the brain basis of second person interaction. This is a vast area of research, which ranges from efforts to find a biological substrate for the phenomenology of intersubjectivity to reductionistic attempts to dispense with such language. Review articles by Hart and Kujala (2000), Georgieff (2011), and Przyrembel et al. (2012) explore the scope of this work, usually without mentioning psychoanalysis. As Hart and Kujala summarize (p. 18), "The mind, with its many levels, is socially shaped and reconstructed dynamically by moment-to-moment interactions." The integrative volume *The Birth of Intersubjectivity* by Ammaniti and Gallese (2014) represents a rare exception in integrating developmental research and neuroscience with psychoanalysis. Yet, as Przyrembel et al. observe, different disciplines can use the same term in much different contexts. This difficulty is magnified when the kinds of abstractions employed in phenomenology and psychoanalytic theory are in question.

The approach of N. Georgieff (2011, 2013) builds on the author's collaborative research with the neuroscientist Marc Jeannerod in France to address issues of concern to psychoanalysts. For example, he applies neuro-cognitive theories of action to study desire and motivation. Here he contends that we can study operations in the brain that produce effects observed in psychoanalysis, without recourse to phenomenologic concepts like subjectivity or to psychological terms like a dynamic unconscious. This goal depends on finding common objects between disciplines. Georgieff (2011, 2013) and Jeannerod (2006, 2011) identify research on the generation of actions in the brain as providing such a shared object with the psychoanalytic concept of the drive (a force which pushes towards action). Similarly, conscious feelings of empathy and immediate recognition of motives can be studied as effects of mirroring operations of neural networks that produce them. "Social neuroscience," Georgieff writes (2011, p. 5), "focuses on the mechanisms through which a person's psychic activity can be occupied, induced, and modified by another psychic activity."

Studies of mechanisms like mirror neurons or pathways of action generation that underlie the phenomenology of intersubjectivity, Georgieff maintains, demonstrate a type of influence between the brain processes of two subjects, now susceptible to scientific explanation. Neuroscience, he claims, confirms Freud's observation that one unconscious can influence another unconscious and obviates subsequent attempts to explain this phenomenon by metapsychological theories. This formulation follows many scholars from other disciplines in attempting to resolve the old philosophical problem of the existence of other minds by recourse to the discovery of mirroring operations in the brain. Yet it reverses the phenomenologic argument about the immediacy of conscious perception by substituting an automatic, unconscious process. What Jeannerod (1997, 2011) terms "mental physiology" thereby seems to provide a biological basis for what phenomenologists have long characterized as an immediate knowledge of the other – a kind of hard-wired intersubjectivity that does not need to be constructed by any cognitive process (Brunet-Gouet and Jackson, 2013).[9]

As critiqued previously, however, this conclusion claims too much for mirroring systems. Leys (2010) notes the "fascination in the humanities and social sciences with the neurosciences resulting in an often naïve and uncritical borrowing from the work of scientists such as Antonio Damasio" (p. 666). She sees a widespread tendency to short-circuit cognitive and intentional explanations of action and behavior, which are held to be determined by "material-corporeal affective experience" (p. 682). At the very least, we could say that dispensing with mind (or subjective agency) as the basis of phenomenal experience runs contrary to ordinary human experience. Major areas of interest to the neurosciences like psychopathologies of self and other (Feinberg, 2010), empathy (Decety and Jackson, 2004), and communication of affect (Damasio, 1994, 2003) cannot be fully explained by the mirroring system but utilize several brain locations and functions. Psychiatric disorders like misperceptions of the identities of others or of the self in schizophrenia, for example, cannot be localized to specific brain regions any more than the concepts themselves can be precisely specified. How we then define and operationalize terms like self or identity for research purposes limits the conclusions we can draw. As Georgieff (2011) observes, the sub-personal level of cortical processes elucidated by research does not in any way eliminate the relevance of phenomenologic observations of subjective, purposive, and unconscious aspects of intersubjective relationships, which can be independently studied by psychological methods. Yet, although Georgieff and Jeannerod affirm the value of clinical observations for therapeutic purposes, they insist that psychoanalytic hypotheses carry no explanatory value for science.

Like other neuroscientific approaches, the attempt by Georgieff and Jeannerod to find common objects does not escape the problem of reduction of meaningful intersubjective behavior to brain processes that underlie them. Because there is no wizard behind the screen making decisions, no internal entity in the brain who chooses, the basic notion of a subject deciding what actions to take lacks meaning for them. Instead, the narrative of decision-making and the conscious sense of willing an event to happen come after (or during) its completion. "The role of consciousness should rather be to ensure the continuity of subjective experience across actions which are – by necessity – executed automatically," Jeannerod argues (2006, pp. 36–37). While the research strategy of searching for relevant pathways correlated with particular behaviors makes scientific sense, conceiving of the subject as a belated narrative remains problematic. Can the cognitive neuroscience of intersubjectivity truly dispense pragmatically with a form of dualism, at least one that accepts the need for two languages of causality and intention to understand human behavior? This represents a perennial dilemma for philosophy.

Empathy

The intersubjective concept of empathy exemplifies the necessity for retaining psychological and phenomenologic languages of explanation. Empathy has been taken up by several disciplines and studied in numerous ways, to which neuroscience makes its unique contribution, but research has not identified a specific "empathy system" (Decety, 2010). Przyrembel et al. conclude that neuronal networks or single cells exclusively tuned to process social interactions have not yet been found. They make the added point that no current social neuroscience paradigm demonstrates "a pattern of actions and reactions in which living and uncontrolled partners engage in behavior that leads to reciprocal impact on each other's behavior" (2012, p. 10). On the other hand, developmental research does focus on mutual interactions over time, confirming the delicate attempts at attunement between infants and mothers (Tronick, 2007). No one would argue that what goes on in this relationship can be explained by mirror systems or any other automatic process, although simultaneous events in the two brains can be studied.

As Ammaniti and Gallese conclude (2014), we cannot dispense with knowledge gained from multiple disciplines including psychoanalysis to understand what goes into everyday social interactions. Intersubjectivity is inherent in human life because we dwell in a social world that includes language, shared symbols, and communication of affects and cannot be isolated or separated from it. Our understanding of these basic phenomena draws from domains of cognitive, philosophical, psychodynamic, and neuroscientific research. Some, but not all aspects of human interaction, may depend on asubjective, non-cognitive physiologic processes, but, as Leys (2010) argues, eliminating meaning and intention represents a nihilistic move. Decety and Jackson (2004) take the position that empathy "is not something one needs to learn. Rather, the basic building blocks are hardwired in the brain and await development through interaction with others" (2004, p. 71). Yet they qualify this comment by subsequently remarking that "empathy is not a simple resonance of affect between the self and other. It involves an explicit representation of the subjectivity of the other" (p. 72). Moreover, they conclude surprisingly, "Empathy is a motivated process that more often than commonly believed is triggered voluntarily" (pp. 93–94). For these researchers, neuroscience does not justify removing the psychological language of personal beliefs and desires from our understanding of behavior. Yet a reductionistic preference for the hard data of brain studies has gained support both in the humanities (as Leys has observed) and in consciousness studies. In this regard, phenomenology has become an important resource for psychoanalysts.

Summary

The concepts of intersubjectivity and the self have deep historical roots in philosophy, perhaps most importantly in phenomenology. Consciousness of self grows out of an interpersonal world of other subjects, with whom a continuous exchange and mutual influence takes place from birth. The shared participation in this life world first addressed by the philosophy of Heidegger and Husserl has become part of our knowledge of human development. Both the primary intersubjectivity in infants inferred by Trevarthen and the transcendent intersubjectivity hypothesized by Husserl suggest an innate feature of our species. Somewhat belatedly, psychoanalysis, at first through the work of Lacan, adopted these ideas, albeit in a tentative way, as they challenged Freudian assumptions of an instinctually determined subject. The insights of phenomenology do not invoke a Cartesian dualism of mind and body so much as they address different levels of explanation, which carry their own independent validity.

The bipersonal emphasis of intersubjectivity (the second person perspective of subject speaking to subject) adds crucial information to third person knowledge about the other – like psychological tests or brain scans. Personal interactions cannot be reduced to an automatic set of responses based on identifiable neurological systems, although they obviously depend on neural processes. Moreover, the physiological events in the brain that cause behavior may be more intertwined with cultural and linguistic symbols than we can conceptualize at this point. Language and culture "program" and colonize the developing brain with signs that shape behavior. This alone reinforces our intuitive sense of belonging to an intersubjective world from which we cannot separate without losing parts of our selves. As Zahavi has observed, he "I" and the "we" remain necessarily intricated. *Homo sapiens* shares the evolutionary achievement of mirror neuron systems with other species but adds to this process the phenomenologic architecture of semiotic, mutually reflective, and affectively charged capabilities on which psychoanalysis depends.

Notes

1 This paper is a revised version of chapter 1, Intersubjectivity, in *Intersubjectivity in Psychoanalysis: A Model for Theory and Practice*. Lewis Kirshner. London: Routledge, 2017.

2 Zahavi's (2006) book, *Subjectivity and Selfhood: Investigating the First Person Perspective*, which deals with issues of self in philosophic discourse, was favorably reviewed by Stolorow (2008). Stolorow concludes, however, that "Zahavi does not consider the intersubjective contexts that promote or undermine the experience of mineness itself. That is the job of psychoanalysts" (p. 1042).

3 Arnold Modell may be the analyst who has most consistently probed the nature of self. Beginning with his adaptation of the theories of Winnicott and continuing through his studies of infant research and neuroscience, Modell has supported the concept of a paradoxical self, both ephemeral and enduring (see Kirshner, 2010).

4 This anamnestic model of psychoanalytic therapeutics bears similarities to Winnicott's ideas about the freezing of development and the manifestation of this sticking point in the transference. Lacan may have been influenced by his readings of Winnicott, but the apparent similarity of their initial approaches to repeating the history of the patient did not remain, as Lacan vehemently rejected a developmental model. Their relationship is explored in Kirshner, 2014.

5 Lacan spoke of this metaphor in his seminar on psychoses, 1955–56.

6 Mead's thinking about subjectivity and consciousness anticipated many subsequent contributions by philosophers and psychologists. His conception was intersubjective, linguistic, and symbolic. "The process by which the self arises is a social process which implies . . . the preexistence of the group" (1934, p. 164), and "there neither can be nor could have been any mind or thought without language" (p. 192).

7 For Hume (1787), identity is an illusory product of the mind's capacity to remember and to infer causes – "the chain of causes and effects which constitutes our self or person" (p. 262).

8 Ruti's study (2012), *The Singularity of Being: Lacan and the Immortal Within*, takes on this problem from a Lacanian direction. She writes that "singularity is less a nameable quality than an inscrutable intensity

of being that urges the subject to persist in its unending task of fashioning or reiterating a self that feels viscerally 'real,' (meaningful, compelling, or appropriate)" (p. 9).

9 Jeannerod (2011, p. 157) writes that each state of mind, desire, belief, preference, will, judgment, etc. corresponds to an experience that can be identified with a concept and studied empirically (the common object of cognitive and neuroscience). This step invites research into the mechanisms subjacent to such concepts.

References

Ammaniti, M., & Gallese, V. (2014). *The Birth of Intersubjectivity: Psychodynamics, Neurobiology, and the Self.* New York: W.W. Norton.

Aron, L. (1991). The patient's experience of the analyst's subjectivity. *Psychoanalytic Dialogues*, 1: 29–51.

Aron, L. (1999). Clinical choices and the relational matrix. *Psychoanalytic Dialogues*, 9: 1–29.

Benjamin, J. (2004). Beyond doer and done to, an intersubjective view of thirdness. *Psychoanalytic Quarterly*, 73: 5–46.

Berge, B. (2015). *Reading Levinas as a Husserlian Might Do.* www.academia.edu/17068668/

Blunden, A. (2005). *Hegel: The Subject as Self-consciousness.* http://home.mira.net/~andy/works/hegel-habitus.htm

Brunet-Gouet, É., & Jackson, P. (2013). Ce que l'imagerie cérébrale nous apprend sur l'intersubjectivité. In *Psychopathologie de l'intersubjectivité*, ed. N Georgieff, pp. 141–150. Paris: Elsevier Masson.

Busacci, V. (2015). Habermas and Ricoeur on recognition: Toward a new social humanism. *International Journal of Humanities and Social Science*, 5: 11–20.

Damasio, A. R. (1994). *Descartes' Error: Emotion, Reason and the Human Brain.* New York: Putnam.

Damasio, A. R. (2003). *Looking for Spinoza: Joy, Sorrow, and the Feeling Brain.* New York: Harvest Books/ Harcourt.

Decety, J. (2010). To what extent is the experience of empathy mediated by shared neural circuits? *Emotion Review*, 2: 204–207.

Decety, J. & Jackson, P. (2004). The functional architecture of human empathy. *Behavioral and Cognitive Neuroscience Reviews*, 3: 71–100.

Dennett, D. C. (1991). *Consciousness Explained.* Boston: Little Brown.

Eigen, M. (1981). The area of faith in Winnicott, Lacan and Bion. *International Journal of Psycho-Analysis*, 62: 413–433.

Feinberg, T. (2010). Pathologies of self. *Neuropsychoanalysis*, 12: 133–158.

Fink, B. (2007). *Fundamentals of Psychoanalytic Technique: A Lacanian Approach for Practitioners.* New York: Norton.

Freud, S. (1895). Project for a scientific psychology. In *The Standard Edition of the Complete Psychological Works of Sigmund Freud*, Volume I (1886–1899): Pre-Psycho-Analytic Publications and Unpublished Drafts, pp. 281–391. London: Hogarth Press.

Freud, S. (1920). Beyond the pleasure principle. In *The Standard Edition of the Complete Psychological Works of Sigmund Freud*, Volume XVIII (1920–1922): 1–64. London: Hogarth Press.

Gallagher, S. (2008). Direct perception in an intersubjective context. *Consciousness and Cognition*, 17: 535–543.

Gallagher, S. (2012). In defense of phenomenological approaches to social cognition: Interacting with the critics. *Review of Philosophy and Psychology*, 3: 187–212.

Gallagher, S., & Zahavi, D. (2008). *The Phenomenological Mind: An Introduction to Philosophy of Mind and Cognitive Science.* London: Routledge.

Georgieff, N. (2011). Psychoanalysis and social cognitive neuroscience: A new framework for a dialogue. *Journal of Physiology – Paris*, 105: 1–5.

Georgieff, N. (2013). Intersubjectivité et subjectivité en psychopathologie. In *Psychopathologie de l'intersubjectivité*, ed. N. Georgieff, pp. 3–18. Paris: Elsevier Masson.

Hart, R., & Kujala, M. (2000). Brain basis of human social interaction: from concepts to brain imaging. *Physiology Revues*, 89: 453–479.

Hegel, G. (1807). *The Phenomenology of Spirit*, trans. A. V. Miller. Oxford: Oxford University Press, 1977.

Hume, D. (1787). *A Treatise of Human Nature.* Oxford: Oxford University Press, 1978.

Jeannerod, M. (1997). *De la physiologie mentale. Histoire des relations entre psychologie et biologie.* Paris: Odile Jacob.

Jeannerod, M. (2006). Consciousness of action as embodied consciousness. In *Does Consciousness Cause Behavior*, ed. S. Pockett, W. Banks, & S. Gallagher, pp. 25–38. Cambridge, MA: MIT Press.

Jeannerod, M. (2011). *La Fabrique des Idees*. Paris: Odile Jacob.

Julien, P. (1981). *Jacques Lacan's Return to Freud: The Real, the Symbolic and the Imaginary*, trans. D. B. Simiu. New York: New York University Press, 1994.

Katz, S. M. (2017). Post-Bionian developments in psychoanalytic field theory: The contributions of Antonino Ferro and Giuseppe Civitarese. *Psychoanal Q*, 86(2): 451–462.

Kirshner, L. (1991). The concept of the self in psychoanalytic theory and its philosophical foundations. *Journal of the American Psychoanalytic Association*, 39: 157–183.

Kirshner, L. (2010). Paradoxes of the self: The contrapuntal style of Arnold Modell. *Journal of the American Psychoanalytic Association*, 58: 327–345.

Kirshner, L. (2014). Winnicott with Lacan. In *The Winnicott Tradition: Lines of Development Evolution of Theory and Practice over the Decades*, ed. M. Spelman & F. Thomson-Salo, pp. 85–96. London: Karnac Books.

Lacan, J. (1954–55). *The Seminar of Jacques Lacan, Book II, The Ego in Freud's Theory and in the Technique of Psychoanalysis*, ed. J.-A. Miller, trans. S. Tomaselli. Cambridge: Cambridge University Press, 1988.

Lacan, J. (1955–56). *The Seminar of Jacques Lacan, Book III, The Psychoses*, ed. J.-A. Miller, trans. R. Grigg. London: Routledge, 1993.

Lacan, J. (1960–61). *Le Seminaire, livre VIII, Le Transfert*, ed. J.-A. Miller. Paris: Éditions du Seuil, 1991.

Lacan, J. (1962–63). *Anxiety: The Seminar of Jacques Lacan*, Book X, trans. A. R. Price. London: Polity, 2014.

Lacan, J. (1964). *The Four Fundamental Concepts of Psychoanalysis*, ed. J.-A. Miller, trans. A. Sheridan. New York: Norton, 1978.

Lacan, J. (1966). *Écrits*, trans. B. Fink. New York: Norton, 2002.

Laplanche, J. (1987). *New Foundations in Psychoanalysis*, trans. D. Macey. Oxford: Blackwell.

Lavelle, J. S. (2012). Theory-theory and the direct perception of mental states. *Review of Philosophy and Psychology*, 2: 213–230.

Leys, R. (2010). Navigating the genealogies of trauma, guilt, and affect: An interview with Ruth Leys. *University of Toronto Quarterly*, 79: 656–679.

Mead, G. H. (1934). *Mind, Self, and Society, Volume 1*. Chicago: University of Chicago Press.

Merleau-Ponty, M. (1945), *The Phenomenology of Perception*, trans. C. Smith. London and New York: Routledge, 1962.

Mitchell, S. A. (1991). Contemporary perspectives on self: Toward an integration. *Psychoanalytic Dialogues*, 1: 121–147.

Modell, A. H. (1984). *Psychoanalysis in a New Context*. New York: International Universities Press.

Modell, A. H. (1993). *The Private Self*. Cambridge, MA: Harvard University Press.

Noë, A. (2007). The critique of pure phenomenology. *Phenomenology and Cognitive Science*, 6: 231–245.

Przyrembel, M., Smallwood, J., Pauen, M., & Singer, T. (2012). Illuminating the dark matter of social neuroscience: Considering the problem of social interaction from philosophical, psychological, and neuroscientific perspectives. *Frontiers in Human Neuroscience*, 6(190): 1–15.

Ricoeur, P. (1970). *Freud & Philosophy: An Essay on Interpretation*, trans. D. Savage. New Haven: Yale University Press.

Ricoeur, P. (1986). The self in psychoanalysis and in phenomenological philosophy. *Psychoanalytic Inquiry*, 6: 437–458.

Ricoeur, P. (2004). *The Course of Recognition*, trans. David Pellauer. Cambridge, MA: Harvard University Press, 2005; orig. *Parcours de la Reconnaissance*. Paris: Éditions Stock, 2004.

Rochat, P. (2009). *Others in Mind: Social Origins of Self-Consciousness*. New York: Cambridge University Press.

Ruti, M. (2012). *The Singularity of Being: Lacan and the Immortal Within*. New York: Fordham University Press.

Sartre, J. P. (1936–1937). *The Transcendence of the Ego*, trans. F. Williams & R. Kirkpatrick. New York: Octagon Books, 1972.

Sartre, J.-P. (1943). *L'être et le néant: Essai d'ontologie phénoménologique*. Paris: Gallimard.

Searle, J. (2008). The phenomenological illusion. In *Philosophy in a New Century*, pp. 107–136. Cambridge: Cambridge University Press.

Solms, M. (2013). The conscious id. *Neuropsychoanalysis*, 15: 5–19.

Sullivan, H. S. (1953). *The Interpersonal Theory of Psychiatry, Beginnings of the Self-System*. New York: W. W. Norton & Company, pp. 158–170.

Trevarthen, C. (1998). The concept and foundation of infant intersubjectivity. In *Intersubjective Communication and Emotion in Early Ontogeny*, ed. S. Braten. Cambridge, MA: Cambridge University Press.

Tronick, E. (2007). *The Neurobehavioral and Social-Emotional Development of Infants and Children*. New York: WW Norton &Co.

Ver Eecke, W. (1983). Hegel as Lacan's source for necessity in psychoanalytic theory. In *Interpreting Lacan*, ed. J. Smith & W. Kerrigan. New Haven: Yale University Press.

Wilden, A. (1968). Lacan and the discourse of the other. In *Speech and Language in Psychoanalysis*, pp. 159–311. Baltimore: Johns Hopkins University Press.

Winnicott, D. W. (1956). The mirror role of mother and family in child development. In *Playing and Reality*, pp. 111–118. New York: Basic Books, 1971.

Zahavi, D. (2002). Merleau-Ponty on Husserl: A reappraisal. In *Merleau-Ponty's Reading of Husserl*. ed. T. Toadvine & L. Embree, pp. 3–29. Dordrecht: Kluwer Academic Publishers.

Zahavi, D. (2006). *Subjectivity and Selfhood: Investigating the First-Person Perspective*. Cambridge, MA: MIT Press.

Zahavi, D. (2008). The experiential self: Objections and clarifications. In *Self, No Self? Perspectives from Analytical, Phenomenological, and Indian Traditions*, ed. M. Siderits, E. Thompson, & D. Zahavi, pp. 56–78. Oxford: Oxford University Press, 2011.

Zahavi, D. (2011). The experiential self: Objections and qualifications. In *Self, No Self? Perspectives from Analytical, Phenomenological, and Indian Traditions*, ed. M. Siderits, E. Thompson, & D. Zahavi, pp. 56–78. Oxford: Oxford University Press.

15

SUBJECT AND SUBJECTHOOD

From Philosophy to Psychoanalysis

Uri Hadar

Introduction

What does it mean to be a subject? What does it take to become one? Does subjecthood constitute a particular state of affairs, a particular kind of being, or is it an ethical value, or even an esthetic value? These questions, in different shapes and forms, have guided the philosophy of the mind ever since Descartes formulated a principle of subjectivity as constitutive of the human condition: "I think therefore I am". Here, human existence is defined as being a subject – not any objective being, not even as an object of knowledge, not a product of a cognizing mind, but rather an activity whose sole witness is the human individual. There is no need for an external consciousness to validate human existence, only the performance of an un-observable activity: thinking. This is where the modern subject has started a remarkable revolution in understanding the human condition (Ricoeur 1981).

Many were quick to notice the paradigm shift: from aspiring to establish universal principles for world and man, where truth and morality largely overlapped, philosophy turned towards the particularity of the human mind and the human condition, trying to investigate their particular forms and the manner in which these forms come into being. Leibnitz, Hume, Kant and Hegel (as well as many others) continued explicitly from the point with which Descartes had left us. They tried to understand the paradigm shift that subjectivity entails and explore its consequences. By and large, this line of investigation had to reach a psychology, had to reach the attempt to understand the minds of particular people, as opposed to general principles. But there was more than one way to connect modern (or modernistic) philosophy with the understanding of people in their particularity.

One way continued directly from modernistic philosophy, grounding it, on the one hand, in the materiality of human existence and, on the other hand, in the rigor of formal logic. This line of investigation came to be known as phenomenology, a term that, together with a few important other terms, must be credited to Edmund Husserl (1936/1970). Other major names in this line of investigation were, of course, Hegel, Marx, Heidegger and Sartre. The latter explicitly addressed continental psychoanalysis and, in that sense, offered a bridge between philosophy and psychology. Like Sartre (1943/1958), I believe that psychoanalysis generally and Freud particularly were part of this line of developing ideas.

Another way of connecting philosophy to psychology followed a more empiricist line of investigation and was mediated by American pragmatists such as Dewey and James (James 1907/1975). At the center of this line of investigation was the attempt to achieve certainty in a

DOI: 10.4324/9780429297076-18

domain that repeatedly frustrates certainty: abstract thought. And the method was to connect abstract entities with external referential fields. In the words of Bertrand Russell, rules (like those of logic and mathematics) are discovered, not constructed. This has generally been the way of analytic philosophy and empirical psychology (Russell 1965). I contend without arguing in any detail that subject and subjectivity were not a central theme in this line of thought, and therefore I do not discuss it at any length.

Freud had never referred to himself as a phenomenologist. Rather, he was compared to Nietzsche by Ernest Jones (Jones 1953), especially in Nietzsche's notion of resentiment as anticipatory of the discovery of the unconscious. Freud himself, apparently, denied borrowing from Nietzsche and avoided reading him. In the end, it was the seminal work of Paul Ricoeur (1970), *Freud and Philosophy*, that strongly tied up Freud with phenomenology generally and Nietzsche particularly. In that sense, my paper follows up on Ricoeur's ideas. Ricoeur also offers the link to Lacan, albeit in a not entirely benign manner. When *Freud and Philosophy* started to acquire acclaim in the 1970s, Lacan accused Ricoeur of indirect plagiarism. Clearly, Lacan thought that Ricoeur's portrayal was rather similar to his own conception of the related history of ideas.

Lacan is probably the first of the psychoanalysts who regarded the task of psychoanalysis as the investigation and facilitation of subjectivity (Lacan 1955/2006). Like Freud, he saw the dialectic of object relatedness as crucial here (although he preferred the Hegelian terminology of subject and other [rather than ego and object]). Yet, unlike Freud, he did not predicate subjectivity on a mental activity (desire or being conscious) but rather on an observable activity (speaking). In that sense, he aligned himself with Marx (1847/1955), who also anchored subjecthood in an observable activity (work) as against the mental anchorings of all others (Descartes included) in the phenomenological line of thinking. This made Lacan a 'political' theorist in the sense that action always lay a central axis for the workings of psychoanalysis, both psychologically and as a method of treatment. It so happened – and not by chance – that the Paris rebels of 1968, including his son-in-law (Jacques-Alain Miller), understood Lacan's theory as contributive to their struggle to change society.

In the present chapter, I investigate the different notions of subjecthood along the phenomenological line of thought. I analyze the various approaches to subjecthood in order to elucidate its many faces rather than to derive an ultimate truth (regarding subjecthood). In my discussions, Lacan often acts as a central axis not so much because I view his approach as correct, but rather in order to create a reference axis for the chapter as whole. It is relevant, though, that Lacan is probably the most 'philosophical' of all major psychoanalysts. Indeed, he has explicitly discussed psychoanalytic ideas in their relation to a host of philosophers such as Aristotle, Plato, Descartes, Kant, Hegel, Heidegger and Sartre.

In the next section I present the landmarks I chose for the discussion of subject and subjecthood through the work of Descartes, Hegel, Marx, Husserl, Freud, Lacan and Benjamin. I elaborate on the association between Marx and Lacan in their view of the subject as rooted in action, rather than interpretation. I then discuss the role of the Other in the constitution of subjectivity by comparing Lacan's and Hegel's views. My analysis then situates Husserl as the interface between philosophy and psychoanalysis in construing subjectivity as an epistemological cornerstone. I show the remarkable affinity between Husserl and Freud and present Lacan's contribution as a Husserlian re-interpretation of Freud. I then describe briefly the relational contribution to understanding the subject.

In the third section, I discuss selected issues in subjecthood in order to derive a general characterization of the issues involved. These include self consciousness (SC), splitting, intentional action, the incorporation of otherness and reflective continuity (identity). I dwell on the issue of splitting at some length in order to derive the various notions of unconscious processes and then discuss *action* as a feature that renders subjecthood a developmental process. I show that there is a structural-developmental coherence that (1) starts with a basic mental activity, leading to (2) the representation in SC and culminating in (3) intentional action. I then define identity as a structural similarity (homeomorphism) among these three constituents of subjecthood. The general characterization of subjecthood leads me to examine the special status of a social group when it incorporates subjecthood, and I link this form back to Marx's view of social change, as well as to Lacan's Other.

The fourth section discusses a number of issues in the linguistic use of the word 'subject' and the possible consequences they entail for the understanding of subjectivity. I show that subjecthood implies the centering of the subject within the field of SC (self consciousness). I then discuss splitting in the linguistic sense of a possible gap between the subject of the statement and the subject of enunciation (in first-person expressions). Finally, and most informatively, I examine the cases in which 'subject' appears in a passive form (being 'subject to' something).

I conclude by making some comments regarding the implications of my analysis for therapy, broadly defined as the facilitation of subjecthood by conversation. I show that this largely agreed-upon definition of the aim of analysis implies an ethical position, namely, the facilitation of attunement to otherness.

Approaches to Subjecthood

What was the revolutionary thing that Descartes (1644/2016) did in his *cogito*? What did he do to deserve being widely considered the father of philosophizing the modern subject? What he did was to show that, when a being capable of a certain distinct mental faculty exercises this faculty, (s)he creates a whole ontology that centers around this faculty. Exercising a faculty effectively defines modes of being. Over a certain set of faculties that are by and large mental, their related mode of being is what we regard as subjecthood. What we have here is a transition – a regress, really – from exercising a faculty to a mode of being. This general formula has remained the same in the centuries that have passed since Descartes. What changed among different thinkers is the faculty whose exercising is the one that creates subjecthood in humankind. I state this here quite succinctly, but the underlying drama is huge. None less than a rational mythology of how an abstract idea turns into the reality of being human. And all that in a short, aphoristic line: *cogito ergo sum* – well, of course, together with the explanation that followed.

Hegel (1807/1977) introduced a considerable change of perspective in arguing that subjecthood is not a solid state, not something that is delivered to man wholesale, but rather something that has an entire developmental itinerary. It starts with an idea that has a somewhat Platonic existence and hovers around the universe until it negates itself onto the realm of the objective, of *das Ding*, of being in itself. This then enters a developmental process in its own right, largely describable as the increase in complexity that is created by a series of small-scale 'negations' of the kind that characterizes life. The 'thing' dies and then lives again. Increases in complexity and then dies again, and so on. At a certain point, the increasing complexity acquires a critical level and performs a qualitative leap that provides it with the ability to reflect upon itself, to become self conscious. It is this ability that renders (wo)man a subject.

What is revolutionary in Hegel's formulation is not only the idea that subjecthood is anchored in a developmental process, but also, and not less so, the idea that this is a process of negation, in which something requires an *otherness* in order to develop into a subject. No being can become a subject from purely within itself without relating to something that is crucially other than itself, so much so that the meeting of this being with its other amounts to a process of negation. In Hegel's words, the subject may be seen as "self-consciousness (that) has equally superseded its externalization and objectivity too, and taken it back into itself so that it is in communion with itself in its otherness as such" (Hegel 1807/1977, p. 479). Otherness is at the heart of the subject. I shall dwell upon this matter in discussing Lacan's elaboration of Hegelian ideas.

The next turn of the key of ideas came fairly soon after that of Hegel's and, to a large extent, as an elaboration of it. I refer to Marx's anchoring of subjecthood in work (Marx 1847/1955). The notion of 'work' already appears in Hegel (1807/1977) in the form of what the slave (bondsman) must do to obtain the recognition of the master. Only the master's recognition offers the slave something of a subjecthood, and (s)he needs to work for this. Marx (1847/1955) has made this into the prime route to subjecthood for all people. For him, work acts as a universal vehicle of subjectification, although some of us (masters or capital owners) deprive the working persons of their subject positioning and take it for ourselves. In order for working people to reclaim their subjecthood, they need to resist the masters' robbery. This is an act of rebellion that operates as Marx's rendering of Hegel's 'negation'. But in Marx's rendering (Marx 1845/1969), negation cannot be exercised by an individual mind. Rather, it acts on a collective level and requires intentional collaboration. The reason for this dwells in the fact that the logic of wealth appropriation is a logic of social order and social structure. And these can be changed only by a collective effort. For Marx, then, being a subject requires a double articulation of the process of liberation: once in the form of work and once in the form of collective resistance. This double articulation appears as the layering of subjecthood between a primary, constituting activity ('thought', 'work', etc.) and a secondary, elaborative 'action'.

The double articulation of the process of liberation (which for Marx is effectively the process of subject positioning) appears in Lacan through the double articulation of the other. Lacan adopts Hegel's idea that no subjecthood can develop from within itself: it requires an otherness that dwells at the heart of subjecthood. For Lacan, this double articulation represents different (psycho)logical systems, one between subject and object (paradigmatically the mother, but also the subject and its mirror image) and one between subject and the collective (Other with a capital 'O' or the order of 'the name of the father'). I shall discuss this double articulation of otherness in both Lacan and Marx later in this chapter, but before doing so, I wish to present three more approaches to subjecthood: Husserl's, Freud's and Benjamin's.

For Husserl (1936/1970), subjecthood is rooted in *experience*, namely, in the ability to register mental states. Again, it is not easy to convey the extent to which this idea is revolutionary. Before Husserl, everybody tried to be objective in order to present something of a general truth. Generality was identified with objectivity. Husserl, to my knowledge, was the first to present a radically subjective state/act – experience – as the basis for both subject positioning and *knowledge*. Of course, experience acted as a cornerstone of subjecthood before Husserl, especially in the romantic tradition, where it was radically individualistic (Morrow 2011). Husserl, however, developed a whole algorithm of translating individual experience into a general truth. By articulating it, Husserl effectively overcame the age-old schism between individual and collective. Crudely put, the algorithm works in the following way: first there is an individual experience; for example, the view of an apple. In the beginning, the subject has no idea what the truth value of this experience might be: there may be an apple out there but then again, there might not. At this point, rather than setting about corroborating or refuting the reality of the apple experience, the subject *brackets* it as a possibility: maybe an apple and maybe not. Then somebody else comes over, and they have or have not the apple experience, and after a number of 'social' iterations of that kind a truth emerges. The experience of the apple is (or isn't) an apple. A transition has occurred from individual experience to an *intersubjective* truth. We see here the traces of Marx's double articulation: one individual, one collective – or rather, intersubjective. Husserl was the first to use this term. In predicating truth on a (inter)subjective principle, Husserl presented a whole logic of subjectivity that is not less rigorous than any other logic. He thus promoted another project originating in Hegel, namely, the derivation of a formal inferential system that is not based on consistency (the Aristotelian absence of contradiction) and therefore allows a logic of change (Husserl 1913/2006).

Now, Freud and Husserl worked largely in parallel to each other, historically speaking, and developed theories whose *machineries* were very different. Husserl's was a formal logic, while Freud's was a biology. And yet, as far as the structural properties of subjecthood are concerned, they were remarkably similar. This similarity emerges if we consider the structural model of ego,[1] id and superego in the following way. Id may be considered as an unexamined or unprocessed level of mental activity, largely parallel to Husserl's 'experience'. Superego may be considered as a set of formal principles that determines what is and what is not socially ('intersubjectively', in Husserl's terminology) acceptable. And ego is comparable to Husserl's bracketing, inasmuch as it originates in the effort to suspend the determination or satisfaction of id-based mental dynamisms ('drives'). Of course, Husserl was a logician and a philosopher, while Freud was a biologist (Sulloway 1979), but this disciplinary difference renders their affinity even more remarkable. Clearly, at the beginning of the 20th century, the phenomenological itinerary led to structurally similar conceptions of subjecthood, irrespective of disciplinary differences. On this analogy, if Husserl's subject is an experiencing being, Freud's subject is a *desiring* being. Note that I equate here 'drive' and 'desire', which is acceptable in Freud's thinking, but not in Lacan's. Putting aside, for the time being, this difference between a push-based concept (drive) and a pull-based concept (wish), we can say that the main difference between Husserl's subject and Freud's subject concerns restlessness. Husserl's subject is relatively tranquil, whilst Freud's is in a frenzy, endlessly conflicted.

The source of restlessness of the Freudian subject dwells in the idea that subjecthood is tied up with sexuality. This idea is almost totally new in thinking the subject, no one before Freud even considered this possibility. But for Freud the biologist of the mind (Sulloway 1979), being a subject, being aware of oneself and able to exercise choice, had to be tied up with a particular drive that affords it, namely, a drive in which plurality is inherent. And this drive could only be a sexual drive. No other basic need could entertain such a wide range of possible satisfactions, both in terms of object and in terms of process. This is why the multiplicity of forms – an intrinsic *perversion*, as Freud called it – was grasped as written into human sexuality (Freud 1933/1964). One may say, in Freud's spirit, that sexuality could be considered as the subjecthood drive.

Lacan started thinking about these matters when both Husserl and Freud were still alive, and he knew the work of both very well. In some sense, Lacan set out to contain both models of subjecthood in a unitary system of thought. For him, this was a matter of developing psychoanalysis in the direction of a formal system of thought, namely, a re-construction of Freud in the direction of Husserl. His subject therefore is driven by desire in relation to the specular other, the object. Here the subject acquires an identity on the basis of similarity operations. The subject's identity is shaped on the basis of similarity to an ideal other, a (m)other, an ideal(ized) mirror image. His consciousness, on the other hand, is based on the ability to create formal models of a world in which the subject is a member. It involves differentiations that repeatedly accommodate social structures of various kinds. This action-oriented subject, like Marx's, operates his or her constructions in relation to collective entities: an Other with a capital 'O'. Lacan could have used Freud's superego here, but he had a problem with both the term and the concept. The idealized form of the other is part of the specular logic, namely, part of object relatedness, rather than something that 'elevates' the ego but, like the superego, still bases itself on ego constructions (as the term 'superego' implies). Lacan's Other has a logic that is utterly of its own. Of course, it incorporates mental abilities – everything mental does – but it builds itself on abilities that are critically non-self and non-ego. It is not, in that sense, a 'superego', but rather a language. It has 'lexical' building blocks and 'grammatical' rules that can operate repeatedly to create increasingly complex structures. It is even essentially oppressive, like Marx's class structure. Yet, it is not primarily moralistic, not necessarily a code of conduct, just like you can't treat the rules of chess as a code of conduct (despite the fact that in order to play chess, you must operate according to the rules).

The last twist I wish to present in the subjecthood story is that of relationality, a twist that started in the 1980s and had been influenced by feminist theory. To fit in the phenomenological line that I present here, Jessica Benjamin is probably the most representative theorist in this regard, situating her arguments in the Hegelian context, albeit in a critical manner. According to Benjamin (1995), all approaches to subjecthood have assumed a complementary asymmetry between subject and other that largely conformed to the distinction between master and slave or, rather, between doer and done to. This has resulted in various forms of oppression, some explicit and some implicit. Probably the most subtle forms of oppression appear in intimate relationships, which often involve power struggles. In order to escape this logic of subordination, the subject must be able to grasp the other as subject as well. This involves egalitarian modes of being together and acting together in the different spheres of living, be they intimate, collegial, friendly or other. The assumption of complementary rather than egalitarian practices necessarily drives those involved to subject-object patterns of relationship, rather than the more symmetrical subject-subject relationship. Benjamin's analysis departs from the others I present here in predicating subjecthood not on a particular mode of action or a mental faculty, but rather on a mode of relatedness. Relationships do not act, like before, as merely a medium of practice or a medium of expression, but rather as the breeding ground of subjectivity. In Benjamin one becomes a subject by relating oneself to an other who has a say on who the subject is. The other becomes a subject herself. One needs the other as a subject in order to become a subject oneself.

Issues in Subjecthood

In this section I wish to briefly discuss a selected issues that act to differentiate among the different approaches to subjectivity and, through this, help us understand what it might imply. Its growth potential, I would say. This discussion does not aim to rigorously define elements of subjectivity that constitute a 'core' or an 'essence', but rather to underline possibilities. Since, in my view, clinical psychoanalysis aims to promote subjectivity, the patterns that I discuss here could serve to open a range of developmental possibilities rather than portray an ideal model. In the conclusion of this chapter, I offer a number of pointers in this direction.

The first issue I want to discuss is that of self consciousness (SC). My claim is that all phenomenological approaches assume SC as a core feature of subjecthood, even when it does not appear explicitly. Descartes, for example, speaks of the *cogito* as such, irrespective of reference, but the wider context is about the validity of the 'I' as a source of knowledge and, in that sense, constitutes an essentially reflexive act – an SC. This use of the first-person singular in Descartes's formulation is a feat in its own right. Mainstream philosophizing has not been using the first person in order to formulate universal truths, not even Saint Augustine, who is probably the first to grasp the psychological value of saying 'I' (Augustine 870/1933). It is, to a large extent, this epistemological choice to situate the first person at the center of philosophizing that won Descartes the accolades of originator of the modern subject.

In all of the reviewed thinkers, SC constitutes a crucial step in establishing the conditions for freedom and choice. One has to be able to consider possibilities while deferring action in order to make a choice. This is the basis for the most basic split that lies at the heart of subjecthood:

the split between two ontological kinds, one of which is relatively resistant to change and one that is relatively flexible and reproduces the first in a reduced form. Of course, since Descartes, it is easy to place the said split in body and mind respectively, but this distinction does not indicate clearly enough that the crucial step for the establishment of subjectivity is that in which the mind relates itself to the body, the same body in which it necessarily dwells. There is a complicated relationship here between mind and body and it takes the entanglements of Hegelian dialectics to reach a fair representation of this relation, but such a representation also implies a shift in the definition of the related kinds. First, in this era of neuro-monism, the mind-body distinction cannot be sustained, since all mental processes are believed to be served by neural processes (Churchland 1986). There is a homeomorphy between them, an equivalence of complexity. Second, bodily processes already involve our reflections upon them, and the two domains do not remain apart even on a purely phenomenological ground. Freud was crucial in clarifying these processes in much detail, showing, as he did, the rich and elaborate manner in which thoughts and other mental processes transform into closely related bodily processes (Freud & Breuer 1895/1955). By and large, then, SC cannot be predicated on the mind-body distinction but could still, following the linguistic turn in philosophy, be predicated upon the sense-reference distinction (Frege 1892/1980).

Here, one level of mental events, a 'high' level, forms itself in relation to the other, 'low' level. The high level is said to be a representation of the low level. Often, the field of reference is considered 'dumb', lacking in intelligence or flexibility. This does not mean that the field of reference is physical and not mental (as in the mind-body split). Rather, it entertains less degrees of freedom. In some versions, for example, the referential field consists of sense data, of perceptions, while the higher level consists of thoughts or cognitive maps. It is interesting in this respect to note Lacan's distinction between the Real and the Symbolic. Both are aspects of 'speech' as well as of 'language', but the first creates mental effects that do not involve conventional meanings, while the latter is based on social conventions, on meaning. On this account, the danger of the Symbolic is its rigidity, because it is inherently lacking of anything Real. The Real is precisely what is missing in the Symbolic. Only by repeated subversion of the Symbolic, of social and linguistic constructs, can there be a renewal of life forces (or death forces; for Lacan there is some equivalence here).

A closely related axis for splitting in the subject is between the process and the content of representation (or enunciation). This is usually articulated under the distinction between two kinds of subject positions: the subject of the *statement* and the subject of *enunciation*. Since the discussion of this line of splitting relies on linguistic-pragmatic considerations, I elaborate upon it in the section on linguistic extensions.

Another issue that emerges as central for the phenomenological approaches to subjecthood is the role of action, of being active, as going beyond mere SC towards changing reality at the level of the other, that is, not merely by undergoing thought processes. Of course, thinking is an activity in and of itself, but it does not, on the face of it, require any transcendence, any transformation into a mode or a kind that is external to the thinking process itself. Again, I am saying "on the face of it" as a tribute to neuro-monism, where thought processes always already involve the externality of neural processes (Churchland 1986). But by 'action' I mean an activity that has one leg in internal thought processes, yet it also has an externality that lends it to intersubjective elaboration. In that sense, action always has a social potential, even when its performance is wholly individual. This social potential constitutes its externality, that is, it is external inasmuch as it has a social potential and vice versa. In that sense, my angle here is fairly much in accord with that of the saying that started the serious consideration of action as a dimension of subjectivity, namely, Marx's 11th thesis on Feuerbach: "Philosophers have hitherto only interpreted the world in various ways; the point is to change it" (Marx 1845/1969). When we try to formalize this thesis in a principle of subjectivity, we must assume that thought processes are insufficient as a medium of subjecthood. We must engage a whole series of phenomena – notably motor phenomena – that pass into objects. In that sense, actions are transitive and, through this, can change the (physical and social) world.

The principle of action, as I may call it, incorporates the Hegelian developmental model, namely, the idea that subjecthood involves a series of 'negations' (transformations) of ontological kinds. It has a time course that starts with an objective process A (experience), leading to representation B that is related to A and in some important sense homeomorphic to it (knowledge), culminating in a process C that is the implementation of B and emanates from it (action). This implies that, for subjecthood to develop, there must be some coherence (which I call here 'homeomorphy') between processes A, B and C. If the representational reality B is totally discordant with the mental processes of A (experience), than something is wrong, there is some pathology of subjecthood. Similarly, if the set of (motor) consequences C is discordant with the set of representations B, something is similarly 'pathological'. Now, it is not easy to determine the precise nature of the required homeomorphy between A, B and C. This homeomorphy is an object of investigation in and of itself and enters the psychoanalytic realm under the heading of *identity*.

It is clear from the above formulations that logical and phenomenological (or psychoanalytic) identity are not the same thing. In logical identity, if A and B have the same identity, everything that holds for A also holds for B. Phenomenological identity, on the other hand, starts with the assumption that, despite their common identity, something crucial must be different between A and B. This principle is probably the distinguishing property of the logic of subjecthood, as against the logic of objecthood (classical logic) and has given rise to the most distinguishing claim of deconstruction (Derrida 1967/1976), but it appears already in Husserl (1936/1970). This raises the question as to what needs to remain the same in order for identity to be preserved at the level of the subject.

The easiest element of identity is the proper name. If a subject has a name that is unique to her, then on the face of it, this suffices for the maintenance of subject identity. Of course, this solution seems something of a bluff: the proper name is totally arbitrary, it can be this and it can be that, it possesses nothing of the intrinsic properties of the subject. Moreover, everything can have a proper name, even kinds that are utterly devoid of subjecthood. Nevertheless, the proper name is often the only common denominator among the different phases of subjecthood (experience, representation, action) and answers well to the global skepticism of the linguistic turn in philosophy (see the *Routledge Encyclopedia of Philosophy*: www.rep.routledge.com/articles/thematic/linguistic-turn/v-1). Yet, psychoanalysis aspires to do better than that.

In psychoanalysis, identity is formed by a certain set of 'I' functions that allows the subject to experience herself as the same over time. An important aspect of these functions concerns the defense mechanisms, namely, the manner in which the subject resists external influences and preserves cohesion. This is a very powerful distinctive feature of subject identity: the ability of a person to experience herself as one, and the various ways in which she defends herself against losing this experience. If we now assume the Lacanian perspective of the speaking being, then identity becomes the ability to say 'I am me' or 'I am myself' (Rozmarin 2009). It is important to stress here the difference between saying 'I', namely, being able to use the first person, and saying "I am myself": the former could be considered a mark of subjecthood (and it often acts in this manner for philosophers who exercise the linguistic perspective on ontology), yet it does not carry the full, three-phase characterization that I have formulated here. "I am myself", on the other hand, preserves the tightness of the linguistic turn, while also preserving the complexity of subjecthood, its objective facet.

Above I emphasized that the principle of action renders subjecthood a developmental process, an ontological kind that requires time and qualitative leaps ('negations') in order to establish itself. Now, the principle of action does more than that inasmuch as it also establishes subjecthood as a *social* phenomenon. This, of course, is inherent in Marx's ideas, but he approached it from the vantage point of social action, while I approach it from the vantage point of mental structure. It is therefore particularly significant that here too, action leads us from the individual to the social. It objectifies mental activity and may, in that sense, lead to the various forms of *alienation* (as Marx has shown extensively). At the same time it allows collective action to develop, simply because it makes subjectivity visible or graspable by the other. That means that subjecthood may establish itself on a social level as well as on the individual level. I want to stress that its social mode is not an external property, even though it encapsulate a principle of externality (action). Yet, it is inherent in the individual potential of subjecthood, even when it takes a logic of its own. Let me call the entity of social subjecthood a social group and denote it by SG.

Social Subjectivity

Ideally, we would like the SG to bear all the marks of individual subjecthood. For a start, we would want to be able to identify the 'mental' activity that defines the SG. Here is where Marx and Lacan become crucial. In individuals, the defining mental activity may be un-observable, but in SGs it may not. Of course, there are zeitgeists, unconscious motives, waves of social affects that are not initially observable, and these are in the nature of SGs, but the activity that defines the SG must be shared by its members and therefore be perceivable. Let us say that for an SG there is always some primary activity that is part of its *existence*, rather than being a part of its self consciousness (SC). For a factory it is the production activity, for a football team it is playing football, for a political group it is the conduction of political activities, etc. We shall see below how these defining activities differ from the kind of action that we consider the third phase of subjecthood. In fact, since in social subjecthood the constituting activity cannot be purely mental, its consideration may help us distinguish between levels of activity as they bear upon the constitution of subjecthood.

In addition to a defining activity, we would like to be able to identify in SG the developmental three-phase or three-level structure of individual subjecthood. The level of un-mediated existence is relatively guaranteed by the logic of representation. If the SG represents itself in any way, then this representation always already has an externality to which it refers. Thus, the SG always has members who are human beings who are related to each other in some stable way. These people and their relationships offer the unmediated, primary level of the SG. A member may be ill and not appear to an activity in which (s)he usually participates. This forms a primary event that may or may not be noted and communicated. In fact, the primariness of experience reflects in the fact that *some field of events (experience) is always richer than its representation*. This may effectively act as a definition of the primary experience. Thus, for example, an SG like a football club has members, players, fans, home ground, properties and so on, which form the externality in which the SG is grounded.

Then there is the manner in which SG represents itself. For the sake of simplicity, let me call this representation a 'manifesto'. Notice, however, that the most important component of the manifesto, in terms of subjecthood, is a set of rules that govern the SG (and effectively define it). For example, let us look at a particular factory as an SG. There are rules of working hours, pay, areas of specialization and so on that regulate the operation of the factory and act as a manifesto.

These rules, in and of themselves, effectively also act as an SC, namely, as a self consciousness. Of course, if there are also meetings of management, workers, auxiliary staff and so on, then these meetings augment SC – they make it richer. And if somebody decides to write the history of the factory, then this further enriches its SC. But the manifesto, in and of itself, suffices to create the level of SC that is necessary for social subjecthood. Finally, the level of action is defined by all planned or intended activity beyond the constituting activity. In the case of the factory, its very operation is part of its constituting activity and will not be considered part of its SC. In addition to this, there will also be the various meetings, development plans, social events and so on that form 'action' as an extension of the primary activity. By analogy to Marx's notion of praxis, one may say that the height of action dwells in *changing the manifesto*, but this is not a prerequisite for being an SG.

Now, SGs will typically also have an identity, marked by some proper term. The factory surely will have a name (like, "The Intel industries in Kiryat Gat"), and so would the association ("The Israel association for the advancement of women in politics") or the football club ("Maccabi Tel Aviv FC"). Again, for the sake of simplicity, we can assume that all SGs have proper names that effectively mark their subjecthood. There is a certain balancing act here between the total dependence on context of the first person 'I', as against the strong anchoring of the proper name, 'PN', in a unitary referential entity. The former indicates the structural property of being at the center of interest or the center of a semantic field (see below). These centers may vary among and within subjects. The latter refers to subjectivity on the whole, or rather, to the objective pole of subjecthood (see below). Being a subject involves the fluctuation between the range of possibilities that is open to subjecthood and the need to anchor it in a particular field of reference – the need to have an identity.

Linguistic Extensions

There are a few senses or usages of the word 'subject' that contribute significantly to the understanding of subjectivity. These senses could be derived from the philosophical literature, but the fact is that they have not been discussed in the way that other issues have been, or very partially so. Linguistic analysis, on the other hand, immediately brings out these senses and contributes significantly to the understanding of subjecthood. This chapter is dedicated to these senses.

The first sense I wish to discuss here usually refers to products of the human mind and specifies their primary theme. It is easiest to see this sense in linguistic objects such as sentences, passages, texts of various lengths and so on. Thus, at sentence level, we have the subject as a specific grammatical category, referring to the noun or the noun phrase on which the sentence focuses. In "the boy closed his eyes" the subject is 'the boy', in "the girl in the blue skirt fainted" the subject is 'the girl' and so on. By way of extension, we say that the subject of the book may be something like the civil war in the United States and so forth. This applies to other intentional entities such as films, exhibitions, a particular collection of artworks and so on. We can see that the term 'subject' in this usage applies to entities that indeed have a subject: they are products of intentional activity. I shall generally refer to such products of intentional activity as 'collections'. We can see that when 'subject' is used to denote 'a primary theme' (the subject of the specific collection), it is clearly related to the issue of subjectivity simply in the sense that 'collections' are always products of intentional activity.

By and large, the sense of 'a primary theme' means that the subject is always at the center of a particular semantic field, namely, his or her own conscious life. Subjecthood, in that sense, implies a whole semantic field, a whole consciousness, in which the subject forms the center. Note that this linguistic derivation is semantically fuller than the minimalistic position whereby subjecthood is empty: the ability to say 'I'. Here I claim that saying or thinking or feeling 'I' implies the existence of a whole semantic field, a consciousness, whose center resides in the particular first person (both singular and plural, as we have seen above). In my 2005 paper on gender (Hadar 2005), I suggested that the mathematical structure of the group encapsulates and specifies this sense of 'subject' (or property of subjecthood). There, the group is analogous to the present 'semantic field' or 'subjective consciousness'. Each group is associated with a certain operation ('mental activity' in the sense of the present chapter) and a particular element called 'the unit element', around which all other elements of the group are arranged. Specifically, it means that for each element in the group (or the subjective semantic field), there is another element such that the 'operation' on those two elements yields the 'unit' element (the subject). For example, as the subject of political ideas, the individual will tend to perceive the political field of ideas in a way that makes her the center. An extremist is always somebody else. Similarly, as a member of a family the subject will always feel that all other members are defined in their relation to her. To sum up, *subjecthood implies being at the center of a particular semantic field.* We can refer to this semantic field as the subjective consciousness. By 'subject' we usually refer to the 'center' (or unit element, in the language of group theory), but the whole semantic field, no matter how small, is a necessary property.

The second sense of subject I wish to mention here derives from the first and serves for defining the kind of splitting that subjecthood always entails. I refer here to the distinction between 'the subject of the statement' and 'the subject of enunciation'. For the speaker of a natural language (Greek, English, Hebrew, etc.), her propositional[2] speech always has a particular content that is marked by the primary theme. This is the subject of her statement. However, the basic tenet of the Cartesian split is that the act of stating (or 'thinking' in Cartesian terms) defines the speaker as a mode of being. This mode of being is what is linguistically referred to as 'the subject of enunciation'. Of course, it is easiest to distinguish between the two subjects in cases when they dissociate from each other. Thus, in the statement "I am dead", the subject of the statement is an 'I' who is said to be dead, but the speaker, who is the subject of enunciation, is very much alive. It is easy to see that the subject of enunciation is always the subject in the primary sense in which we discuss it in the present chapter, namely, the speaker. Yet, as I have shown above, the subject of the statement is also intimately tied up with subjecthood. The whole splitting issue, to my mind, presents itself best in this split between subjects, and this is also the sense that Lacan preferred in arguing that the (speaking) being is always split for subjecthood (Lacan 1960/2006). In fact, there is always a gap between the subject of the statement (the primary theme) and the subject of enunciation (the speaker), but in many cases it is hidden. For example, in statements in the first person ("I am tired") one assumes that the subject of the statement and the subject of enunciation are identical. Yet, they are not: the subject of the statement is only tired, while the subject of enunciation is many other things as well. For example, if a moment after uttering the statement the speaker experiences a threat to her life, then (s)he may immediately experience a wave of energy that is entirely absent from the statement.

The third sense of 'subject' that derives from its linguistic usages has so far been left entirely outside of my discussion, yet it is crucial for the understanding of subjectivity. Consider the meaning of 'subject' in such a sentence as "The man was subject to intense questioning". Here 'subject' refers to a passive position, while throughout my discussion so far I emphasized agency, namely, the state of being active in the realm of subjective consciousness. Nevertheless, one cannot be subject to something unless one is a subject. The stone cannot be subject to intense pressures (despite its similarity to "The man was subject to intense questioning"). In fact, the prize for being deprived of agency (in being subject to something) is a double subjecthood: the something to which one can be subject is always an intentional act of an agent. Subjecthood is represented in both the subject and the object of the sentence. Thus, one is never subject to bad weather, an avalanche or an earthquake. What one may be subject to has an agent, so subjecthood is represented in this inflection of subject in the usual sense of a freedom of choice. However, the choice is located in the other.

We can see the other-locatedness of the subject in this form in a slightly different semantic structure, as in "The contract was agreed, subject to approval by the board". Here, it seems, the only locus that entertains subject positioning is that of the other ('the board' in my example). This underlines domination by another subjectivity, but the grammatical subject here is non-human and non-living which, on a superficial level, seems to contradict the idea of double subjecthood (under duress). Still, in this usage, the grammatical subject, despite being non-human, carries subjecthood by virtue of being a product of intentional action (contract, agreement, law, and other entities that require approval, confirmation, validation and the like).

We see here two forms of being subject to something, one in which there are two entities with the potential for subject positioning ("The man was subject to intense questioning") and one in which the product of subject activity is in suspense ("The contract was agreed, subject to approval by the board"). In both instances, the subjugating act brackets the ability for subject positioning and, by doing so, reveals a fundamental feature of subjecthood. In the first instance, the something to which the subject is given is always negative. One is never subject to a birthday party or to winning the lottery. In my understanding, the negativity of what one may be subject to comes to mark its secondary locus as a subject position. In being subject to something, the situation preserves all the marks of subjecthood in an inverted form. In the second instance, the subjugating act suspends the subjecthood that is represented in the prime theme (the contract, agreement, etc.). In both instances, being subject to something is not a choice, but it still represents a feature that is crucial to subjecthood: one can be deprived of it. It is not something to which a person or some other intentional entity are doomed, like needing to breathe in order to live or like having a body. Subjecthood is something that one can be deprived of.

An extended sense of this kind of positioning is seen in 'subject' when it refers to a person who is under the jurisdiction of a king (or equivalent ruler). Here too, being a subject implies the passive position of being governed by a 'ruler' – namely, really, a set of rules originating in somebody else's will. In this sense, like everywhere else in the realm of the subject, the rules that govern the subject are the products of intentional activity. One is not the subject of a gravitational field (or another law of nature) but rather the subject of an intentional entity (usually the personal[3] authority behind a set of rules). It is precisely in that sense that I consider 'subject' here (as a juridical personal status, namely, the ruler's subject) as a linguistic and semantic extension of 'subject' as a descriptive status (subject to). In both, the locus of subjecthood is the other rather than the primary theme. The two senses, it seems, are closely related (see also https://english.stackexchange.com/questions/204691/subject-to-vs-subject-of-what-is-better-what-is-correct).

All in all, the variety of passive forms of 'subject' convey the idea that subjecthood takes place within a rule-governed system. There must be a rule system in order to create the possibility of subjecthood, and all subject positions are governed by one rule system or another. This idea is perfectly encapsulated in Lacan's Other, and the present discussion only serves as an explicit construal of this.

Conclusion

In this chapter I have undertaken to clarify the central issues involved in the definition and characterization of ideas regarding subjectivity and the related special ontological kind that we have come to call 'the subject'. I have sketched a very partial line of ideas along only one trajectory of thought: phenomenology. I do not make a global epistemological claim for this choice as against the trajectory that leads via analytic philosophy to experimental psychology. Rather, and this is somewhat of a linguistic irony, I made it primarily for the purpose of accommodating (psycho) analysis into my discussion. Truly enough, psychoanalysis centers around the issues of subject and subjectivity. Yet, some of the terms and ideas I have used here are gleaned from analytic philosophy (e.g., the term 'kind', as in 'ontological kind'; see Kendig 2016). Nevertheless, the gist of my argumentation (or even description) comes from the phenomenological line of thought. Now, if this is not an epistemological choice, what is it? I think that it is, to a large extent, an ethical choice. Ethical even in the sense of practical (as in Kant's [1788/2004] use of 'practical reason' as underlying ethics). Especially, if being a subject depends in a critical manner on incorporating otherness, as Levinas (2000) has argued, then this means that being a subject is not only a psychological achievement but rather, and perhaps more meaningfully, an ethical positioning. This idea offers a cornerstone for analytic psychotherapy (Hadar 2013). Psychotherapy, as an interface between the practical (social and personal function) and the ethical (incorporation of otherness), unsettles the distinction between action and interpretation. Action, in the present perspective, forms the advanced phase of subjecthood and builds upon the representation of self in SC. In analytic psychotherapy, interpretation does exactly that: it examines the experience of the subject and the SC to which it has given rise, with the aim of Improving cohesion between the two (ibid.). Moreover, it may be enunciated equally by either subject or other (the therapist) and thus incorporates otherness into subjecthood in perhaps the most radical possible way. The therapist's enunciations both emanate from within the realm of the subject and preserve their quality as 'other'. Here we may recall Lacan's definition of the unconscious as 'the discourse of the Other' (Lacan 1954/1991). A discourse that aims to unravel unintended messages incorporates the other in its very intention, in the very act of intending to do so, let alone when interpretation is enunciated in a clear and loud voice by either patient or therapist.

Notes

1 I use here the terminology of the Strachey translation of Freud, despite the fact that it is clearly a deficient translation, as Lacan (1954/1991) neatly showed.

2 Speech, of course, does not have to be propositional. People may speak by way of stammering, screaming at somebody, sighing, etc. In these cases, there is no 'subject of the statement' and therefore no clear splitting.

3 What distinguishes between a subject and a citizen is precisely this matter, that the ruler of the subject is a personal entity, while the ruler of the citizen is the state.

References

Augustine, Saint (870/1993). *Confessions*. Indianapolis: Hackett Publishing.

Benjamin, Jessica (1995). *Like Subjects, Love Objects*. New Haven: Yale University Press.

Churchland, Patricia (1986). *Neurophilosophy: Toward a Unified Science of the Mind-Brain*. Cambridge, MA: MIT Press.

Derrida, Jacques (1967/1976). *Of Grammatology*. Baltimore: Johns Hopkins University Press.

Descartes, Rene (1644/2016) *Principles of Philosophy*. Electronic edition by Dancing Unicorn Books.

Frege, Gottlob (1892/1980). On sense and reference. In P. Geach and M. Black (eds. and trans.), *Translations from the Philosophical Writings of Gottlob Frege*. Oxford: Blackwell.

Freud, Sigmund (1933/1964). New introductory lectures on psychoanalysis. In *The Standard Edition of the Complete Psychological Works of Sigmund Freud, Volume 22*, pp. 5–157. London: The Hogarth Press.

Freud, Sigmund & Breuer, Joseph (1895/1955). Studies in hysteria. In *The Standard Edition of the Complete Psychological Works of Sigmund Freud, Volume 2*. London: Hogarth Press.

Hadar, Uri (2005). Algebraic perspectives on the symbolic constitution of gender in Lacan. *Journal for Lacanian Studies*, 3: 48–66.

Hadar, Uri (2013). *Psychoanalysis and Social Involvement*. London: Palgrave.
Hegel, Georg Wilhelm Friedrich (1807/1977). *The Phenomenology of Spirit*, translated by A. V. Miller. Oxford: Oxford University Press.
Husserl, Edmund (1913/2006). *Logical Investigations*. Milton Park: Routledge.
Husserl, Edmund (1936/1970). *The Crisis of European Sciences and Transcendental Phenomenology: An Introduction to Phenomenological Philosophy*, translated by David Carr. Chicago: Northwestern University Press.
James, William (1907/1975). *Pragmatism: A New Name for some Old Ways of Thinking*. Cambridge, MA: Harvard University Press.
Jones, Ernest (1953). *The Life and Work of Sigmund Freud, Volume 1*. London: Basic Books.
Kant, Immanuel (1788/2004). *Critique of Practical Reason*, translated by Thomas K. Abbott, 1909. London and New York: Dover.
Kendig, Catherine (2016). *Natural Kinds and Classification in Scientific Practice*. New York: Routledge.
Lacan, Jacques (1954/1991). *The Seminar of Jacques Lacan, Book II: The Ego in Freud's Theory and in the Technique of Psychoanalysis*, translated by S. Tomaselli. New York: W. W. Norton.
Lacan, Jacques (1955/2006). Seminar on "The purloined letter". In *Écrits*, The first complete English edition, translated by Bruce Fink. New York: WW Norton, pp. 6–50.
Lacan, Jacques (1960/2006). Remarks on Daniel Lagache's presentation: "Psychoanalysis and personality structure". In *Écrits*, The first complete English edition, translated by Bruce Fink. New York: WW Norton, pp. 543–574.
Levinas, Emmanuel (2000). *Alterity and Transcendence*. New York: Columbia University Press.
Marx, Karl (1845/1969). *Theses on Feuerbach*, translated by W. Lough. London: Progress Publishers.
Marx, Karl (1847/1955). *The Poverty of Philosophy*. London: Progress Publishers.
Morrow, John (2011). Romanticism and political thought in the early 19th century. In Gareth Stedman Jones and Gregory Claeys (eds.), *The Cambridge History of Nineteenth-Century Political Thought*. Cambridge: Cambridge University Press, pp. 39–76.
Ricoeur, Paul (1970). *Freud and Philosophy: An Essay on Interpretation*. New Haven: Yale University Press.
Ricoeur, Paul (1981). *Hermeneutics and the Human Sciences: Essays on Language, Action and Interpretation*. Cambridge: Cambridge University Press.
Rozmarin, E. (2009). I am yourself: Subjectivity and the collective. *Psychoanalytic Dialogues*, 19(5): 604–616.
Russell, Bertrand (1965). *On the Philosophy of Science*, edited by Charles A. Fritz, Jr. Indianapolis: The Bobbs-Merrill Company.
Sartre, Jean-Paul (1943/1958). *Being and Nothingness: An Essay on Phenomenological Ontology*. London: Methuen.
Sulloway, Frank (1979). *Freud, Biologist of the Mind: Beyond the Psychoanalytic Legend*. Boston: Burnett Books.

16

IS JUNG A PHILOSOPHER OF RELIGION AS WELL AS A PSYCHOLOGIST OF RELIGION?

Robert A. Segal

Who would deny that a psychologist can also be a philosopher, or vice versa? Plato, conspicuously a philosopher, offers his own psychology, the best-known instance of which is his tripartite division of the soul, or the mind, in the *Republic*. More specifically, who would deny that a psychologist of religion can be also be a philosopher of religion, or vice versa? Plato is, if not quite a psychologist of religion, certainly a sociologist of religion. In the *Republic* he bemoans the bad example for citizens set by the immoral gods in Homer and Hesiod, and he proposes the bowdlerizing of both authors.

In modern times, the grandest example of someone operating as both psychologist of religion and philosopher of religion is William James, and most grandly in the same book: *The Varieties of Religious Experience* (1902). As a psychologist, James explains the origin and function of religion. He happens to focus less on the origin, which for him can be anything, than on the function, or effect. As a philosopher, he argues for the truth of religion, and he uses his psychological findings about the effect of religion to argue for the truth of religion.[1]

This chapter asks whether Jung is like James. There is one immediate difference. James was indisputably a professional philosopher of religion and a professional psychologist of religion. Jung was not a professional philosopher. Professionally, he was a sheer psychologist. Yet clearly he had a philosophy, and clearly his philosophy – which, rightly or wrongly, he attributed above all to Kant – influenced his psychology, not least his psychology of religion.

The question considered in this chapter is, however, the reverse. Did Jung's psychology of religion influence his philosophy of religion? Whether or not it did so, is his psychology relevant to the philosophy of religion?

Let me state upfront my view. I maintain that Jung did take a stand on the existence of God. He declared that God exists. Jung's stand did not, however, rest on his psychology. Jung rightly distinguished the domain of the psychology of religion from that of the philosophy of religion. Yet it is still possible, I maintain, to use psychology for philosophical ends. Jung was wrong to deny that the psychology of religion can bear on the issue of the existence of God.

Jung's refusal as psychologist to take a stand on the existence of God was typical of twentieth-century social scientists of religion, as typified by the celebrated sociologist Peter Berger. By contrast to Jung and Berger, earlier social scientists, notably James and Freud, sought to use their findings either to prove (James) or to disprove (Freud) the existence of God. Whether or

DOI: 10.4324/9780429297076-19

not their arguments are convincing, James and Freud were, I argue, entitled to make them. Jung drew too sharp a boundary between psychology and philosophy.

The Origin and Function of Religion

Psychology is one of the social sciences. The others are sociology, anthropology, politics, and economics. "Social science" is the counterpart to natural science, which social science usually, though not always, seeks to emulate. The "social" of social science does not mean the group rather than the individual. It means the distinctively human rather than the animal. Therefore social science can focus as readily on humans *qua* individuals as on humans *qua* members of a group. Sociology itself is divided into the variety, going back to Max Weber, that starts with the individual; and the variety, going back to Emile Durkheim, that starts with the group. To whatever extent Jungian psychology focuses on the individual, it still falls snugly within social science.

There is a long-standing divide among social scientists between those (the majority) for whom social science should emulate natural science and those (a minority) for whom social science should emulate the humanities. The term "social science" is used by both groups. The group that seeks to emulate the humanities often calls the social sciences the "human sciences" but still considers them sciences. The goal of the human sciences is typically said to be *interpretation* rather than *explanation*. Sometimes interpretation is associated with reasons, or intentions, and explanation associated with causes. Other times interpretation is associated with mental causes – but still causes – and explanation associated with physical causes.[2]

Jung seems unaffected by this debate as well. In regularly calling himself a "scientist," he seems to be aspiring to follow natural scientists. He seems to be seeking causes, but not thereby excluding either the intentional or the mental. I take Jung to be deeming himself a social scientist à la the natural sciences. I am claiming not that Jung succeeds in making his psychology as scientific as a natural science but only that he, just like Freud, usually aspires to do so.

When modeled on natural science, the social scientific study of religion concentrates on two questions: what is the origin and what is the function of religion? The question of origin starts at the point before religion exists and asks why religion arises. The answer is a need of some kind. What the need is varies from theory to theory and from social science to social science. The question of function starts with religion already present and asks why religion lasts. The answer is likewise a need, and it is the same need: whatever need accounts for the emergence of religion also accounts for the continuation of religion.

As a psychologist of religion, Jung, like James, professes to know the origin and function of religion. Unlike James, he gives equal weight to origin and to function. Like James, he focuses on experience rather than on belief, which for both is derivative from experience. By contrast, Freud concentrates on belief and practice.

As a psychologist, Jung seeks to explain why adherents have the experiences that they do. He does not question whether adherents genuinely believe in God, pray to God, or experience what they take to be God. Quite the opposite: he seeks to explain why they do so. His starting point is their convictions, which, far from denied, are the data to be explained. Denying them would leave him with nothing to psychologize.

The reality of the convictions of believers is the starting point for all social scientific theorists of religion. Freud, no less than Jung, is seeking to figure out why religion not merely exists but has the hold on humanity that it does. For him, the matter is especially pressing because he, unlike Jung, judges religion not only dysfunctional but also false. How humanity can remain swayed by beliefs so blatantly preposterous puzzles him. But then he is presupposing the truth of those beliefs for believers themselves.

The Truth of Religion

As a philosopher of religion, Jung would be evaluating the truth claims of religion. He would be seeking to determine whether the figure to whom they pray and sacrifice and dedicate themselves is real, not for them but in fact.

Jung can, of course, be a psychologist of religion in his day job and a philosopher of religion after hours. His philosophizing can operate independently of his psychologizing. The issue in this chapter is whether in his day job Jung is operating as a philosopher and in any event whether he, as a psychologist, is entitled to do so.[3]

Earlier Sociology of Science

One way to approach this issue is to take the case of another discipline and see how far the social sciences claim to go. The best case is that of natural science, and exactly because its truths seem immune to social scientific factors. The social science that has claimed to go the furthest in explaining natural science is not psychology but sociology.

Thomas Kuhn declares that "sociology of science, if it ever develops sufficiently to embrace the cognitive content of science together with its organizational structure," might "help to bridge the . . . gap" between history and philosophy (Kuhn, 1977, p. 13). By "history" Kuhn means origin. By "philosophy" he means truth claims.[4] Kuhn wants to bring sociology to bear on the content of science.

In Kuhn's day there existed a "Berlin Wall" between the sociological, or "external," history of science and the intellectual, or "internal," history. On the one hand, Kuhn explains, celebrated "internalists" such as Alexander Koyré

> have . . . usually minimized the importance of nonintellectual aspects of culture to the historical developments they consider. A few have acted as though the obtrusion of economic or institutional considerations into the history of science would be a denial of the integrity of science itself.
>
> *(Kuhn, 1977, p. 109)*

On the other hand equally celebrated "externalists" such as the sociologist Robert Merton considered the content of science inviolate. Merton famously argued (1970 [1938]) that ascetic Protestantism spurred the development of science in seventeenth-century England. More generally, he argued that the sociological norms of scientific behavior – "universalism, communism, disinterestedness, and organized scepticism" – account for consensus on the content of science (see Merton, 1973). Yet he never dared sociologize the content itself, on which he deferred to internalists.

Besides Merton, early sociologists of science included Karl Mannheim (1936, pp. 237–280), Bernard Barber (1952), and Joseph Ben-David (1971). One can go back to Durkheim (1965, pp. 486–487) and even Karl Marx, who believed firmly in the inviolability of natural science. Also included would be the philosopher of science Imre Lakatos (1978, especially pp. 102–138). Early externalists sociologized *scientists*. Since then, externalists have sociologized *science*.

Kuhn strives to bring the sociology and the content of science closer together. He makes external factors central to the *formation* of what he famously calls a scientific "paradigm," or research program. But he still considers external factors marginal to the *operation* of a paradigm once established:

> Early in the development of a new field . . . social needs and values are a major determinant of the problems on which its practitioners concentrate. . . . The practitioners

> of a mature science are men trained in a sophisticated body of traditional theory and of instrumental, mathematical, and verbal technique. . . . The problems on which such specialists work are no longer presented by the external society but by an internal challenge to increase the scope and precision of the fit between existing theory and nature.
>
> *(Kuhn, 1977, pp. 118–119)*

For Kuhn, not only "normal" science but even scientific "revolution" is internalist in nature.

Early sociologists of science, including Kuhn, distinguished rigidly between true or rational beliefs and false or irrational ones. The content of true or rational beliefs was to be explained internally, or intellectually. Sociological and other external, or nonintellectual, factors did not carry over from the holders of these beliefs to the beliefs themselves.[5] By contrast, external factors explained the content of false or irrational beliefs. The epitome of true or rational beliefs was scientific truths. The epitome of false or irrational beliefs was religious truths.

Early social scientists were applying what the philosopher of science Larry Laudan calls the "arationality assumption": "the claim that the sociology of knowledge may step in to explain beliefs if and only if those beliefs cannot be explained in terms of their rational merits" (Laudan, 1977, p. 202). One starts with an intellectual explanation of beliefs. Only when the intellectual explanation of beliefs proves inadequate does one turn to a sociological explanation. Hence Laudan's apt phrase "steps in."[6]

Earlier Sociology of Science Applied to Jung

If the arationality principle were to be applied to Jung, he would be permitted to explain psychologically all beliefs – once he had shown that they could not be explained merely rationally, which for him would roughly mean explained consciously. He would not be permitted to bypass conscious explanations and jump to unconscious ones.

To be sure, Jung would not be obliged to follow early sociologists of science and exclude scientific beliefs from psychological scrutiny. If he were to deem Gnosticism or at least alchemy proto-scientific, his psychologizing of either would not be improper – once he had established that their content could not be explained wholly intellectually.

But Jung does not operate this way. He does not first demonstrate the inadequacy of a sheer intellectual account either of Gnosticism, which I will be using as an example of what he does do, or of alchemy. Rather, he starts *by* psychologizing. If he is offering a psychological explanation *alongside* an intellectual one, he leaves unanswered the question of the relationship between them. If he is offering a psychological explanation *in place of* an intellectual one, he is presupposing the very relationship between them that he must first establish.

Recent Sociology of Science

The difference between recent and early sociologists of science can be put summarily: recent sociologists of science reject the arationality principle. They reject the divide between an intellectual approach to scientific beliefs and a sociological approach to religious beliefs. Notably, the Edinburgh "Strong Programme" of David Bloor (1991), Barry Barnes (1995), Steven Shapin (1994), and John Henry maintains that even scientific truths, which can still be true and rational, are held for sociological reasons. The nemesis of this school is Merton, whose refusal to sociologize the content of science makes for "weak" sociology, or the sociology of "error" – that is, the sociology of the content of only false or irrational beliefs. The Edinburgh school rejects the arationality principle in favor of the principle of "equivalence":

> Our equivalence postulate is that all beliefs are on a par with one another with respect to the causes of their credibility. It is not that all beliefs are equally true or equally false, but that regardless of truth and falsity the fact of their credibility is to be seen as equally problematic. The position we shall defend is that the incidence of all beliefs without exception calls for empirical investigation and must be accounted by finding the specific, local causes of this credibility. This means that regardless of whether the sociologist evaluates a belief as true or rational, or as false and irrational, he must search for the causes of its credibility.
>
> *(Barnes and Bloor, 1982, p. 23)*[7]

The principle of equivalence is also called the principle of "symmetry," and the arationality principle also gets called the "asymmetry" principle. It means equal treatment for all beliefs.

The Edinburgh school argues that intellectual justifications are insufficient, if not outright unnecessary, to explain the holding of scientific beliefs. The intellectual justifications given by scientists are transformed by this school into sociological imperatives, not least indoctrination and self-interest. Epistemology becomes sociology.[8]

Because even the most abstract intellectual justifications operate within what the Edinburgh school calls "social determinants," the justifications vary from culture to culture and from period to period. Insofar as the acceptance of truths is therefore dependent on what *counts* as evidence in a society, the Edinburgh school is relativistic. The school is not, however, relativistic over scientific truths themselves.

Other, still more radical sociologists are. Bruno Latour and Steven Woolgar (1979) and Harry Collins and Trevor Pinch (1982) contend that facts themselves are "socially constructed." The subtitle of Latour and Woolgar's *Laboratory Life* is *The Construction of Scientific Facts*, and the subtitle of Collins and Pinch's *Frames of Meaning* is *The Social Construction of Extraordinary Science*. What are now sociologized and relativized are not merely, as for the Edinburgh school, the justifications given for holding scientific beliefs but even the data on which those justifications rest. Long before Latour, Woolgar, Collins, and Pinch, the objectivity of scientific data had been challenged. No one today deems observations altogether free of "contamination" by theory. But Latour and company turn merely theory-laden observations into observations actually created by theory.

The Edinburgh school retains the distinction between observations and interpretations. But for it sheer observations do not yield science. A community determines what observations mean. Still, and contrary to Collins and others, observations themselves are not sociologically determined.[9]

The Edinburgh school retains the distinction between true or rational beliefs and false or irrational ones. The school distinguishes between the "credibility" of beliefs, which is its concern, and the "validity" of beliefs, which is the concern of philosophers and natural scientists. For all its radicalness, the school subscribes to the conventional view that the truth of a belief is separate from the origin of the belief.

Recent Sociology of Science Applied to Jung

If the symmetry principle were to be applied to Jung, he could be taken as doing psychologically what the Edinburgh school does sociologically. Rather than offering any argument, as the arationality principle of earlier sociologists of science would require, Jung would be seen as taking for granted that the holding of all beliefs – scientific, religious, and philosophical – is to be explained psychologically. Thus, in *Psychological Types* (1971) he would legitimately be continuing a tradition that he traces back to William James: attributing to personality type the kind of theory that one holds.

Typology would not, however, relativize the positions themselves, any more than sociology for the Edinburgh school would relativise scientific beliefs themselves. As an explanation, typology would be no less objective than class is for the Edinburgh school.[10]

How fully Jung could match up abstract positions in science, philosophy, or religion with personality type it is hard to see. This problem faces all those who try to correlate ideas with their holders. The more abstract ideas become, the less tethered to the character or status of their holders they seem.[11]

But is Jung actually prepared to go along with the symmetry principle of the Edinburgh school and psychologize the holding of scientific beliefs? For example, if he were to maintain that he espouses synchronicity at least partly because of his type, then he would be adhering scrupulously to the symmetry principle. But if he were to maintain that he espouses synchronicity because it is demonstrably true, then he would be doing what the Edinburgh school opposes: offering no cause for holding the position he does beyond the recognition of its truth. He would be doing psychologically what the Edinburgh school scorns doing sociologically.

Even if Jung could be taken as going as far as the Edinburgh school, he presumably could never be taken as going so far as Latour, Woolgar, Collins, and Pinch. To do so, he would have to be claiming that observations themselves are constructed – psychologically, not sociologically. By appeal to typology he would have to be claiming not merely that persons of different types *focus* on different aspects of the same thing but that they *see* different things. Freudians and Jungians would thus be seeing (or hearing) different things, not merely interpreting them differently. Critics of Freudian and Jungian psychology alike continually charge that the data on which the theories depend are concocted by the theories – the status of the theories themselves aside – but Freudians and Jungians themselves demur.[12]

The philosophy of science raises many questions about the status of scientific claims. Induction, verification, falsification, relativism, the theory-ladenness of observations, and the underdetermination of hypotheses by data are among the standard topics. But these topics are internalist. The issue at hand is externalist: do psychological and sociological factors bear on the truth of either scientific or religious claims?

Jung as Psychologist of Religion

Like Uriah Heep, Jung humbly maintains *ad infinitum* that he is only a psychologist of religion and not also a philosopher of religion. At the outset of the 1937 Terry Lectures, *Psychology and Religion*, he declares the following:

> Although I have often been called a philosopher, I am an empiricist and adhere as such to the phenomenological standpoint. . . . I approach psychological matters from a scientific and not from a philosophical standpoint. Inasmuch as religion has a very important psychological aspect, I deal with it from a purely empirical point of view, that is, I restrict myself to the observation of phenomena and I eschew any metaphysical or philosophical considerations.
>
> *(Jung, 1969b, pp. 5–6)*

Elsewhere he states more succinctly that ‘Psychological truth by no means excludes metaphysical truth, though psychology, as a science, has to hold aloof from all metaphysical assertions’ (Jung, 1967, p. 231).[13] Jung equates philosophy with metaphysics. Freud does the same.

In categorizing himself as a psychologist, a scientist, an empiricist, and a phenomenologist rather than a philosopher, a metaphysician, or a theologian, Jung is maintaining the traditional view that social scientific findings are irrelevant to the truth of religion. He can determine only why believers believe, not whether what they believe is true.

To take the case I know best, Gnosticism,[14] Jung asserts that ancient Gnosticism, together with alchemy, was a forerunner of his own psychology:

> The experiences of the alchemists were, in a sense, my experiences, and their world was my world. That was, of course, a momentous discovery: I had stumbled upon the historical counterpart of my psychology of the unconscious. The possibility of a comparison with alchemy, and the uninterrupted chain back to Gnosticism, gave substance to my psychology.
>
> *(Jung, 1963, p. 205)*

Gnosticism and alchemy were psychological enterprises in metaphysical garb.

Jung interprets Gnosticism and alchemy identically. The alchemical process of extracting gold from base metals is for him a continuation of the Gnostic process of liberating fallen sparks from matter. Psychologically, both processes represent a procession from sheer ego consciousness to the ego's rediscovery of the unconscious and reintegration with it to forge the self. In alchemy the progression is from base metals to the distillation of vapor out of them and the return of that vapor to the metals to form gold. In Gnosticism the progression is from the Gnostic's sheer bodily existence to the release of the immaterial spark within the Gnostic's body and the reunion of that spark with the godhead. In both cases the state most deeply sought lies within human beings – between the ego and the unconscious – rather than outside them – between the vapor and the metals or between the spark and the godhead.

Jung contends that in Gnosticism and alchemy the psychological state is projected onto the outside world in the form of physical and nonphysical entities. But he is not denying the reality of these entities for Gnostics and alchemists themselves. Rather, he is analyzing the belief in them.

Yet Jung is not doing what a doctor would ordinarily do in treating a headache: granting the reality of the headache in fact and simply accounting for it biochemically. As a mere psychologist, Jung is sidestepping the question of the reality of the entities in which Gnostics and alchemists believe and is limiting himself to the reality of the *belief* in them.

Only if Jung were denying the reality of the beliefs themselves would he be an "eliminativist." But he is not. He is rendering Gnostic deities and worlds the equivalent of UFOs: psychological phenomena, whether or not also real "out there."[15]

In "Gnostic Symbols of the Self," Jung psychologizes this religion as relentlessly as elsewhere he does every other one. For example, God symbolizes the ideal psychological state of wholeness, or selfhood: "these [Gnostic] symbols [of God] have the character of 'wholeness' and therefore presumably *mean* wholeness" (Jung, 1968, p. 194). Similarly, "the myth of the ignorant demiurge who imagined he was the highest divinity illustrates the perplexity of the ego when it can no longer hide from itself the knowledge that it has been dethroned by a supraordinate authority" (Jung, 1968, p. 189).

Jung contends that Gnostics not merely projected onto the world deities and worlds created out of their unconscious but also experienced those deities and worlds. But insofar as these entities were nonphysical, the choice between the position of the Edinburgh school on observations and that of Collins et al. does not apply.

As a psychologist, Jung is prepared not merely to identify the function of religion but also to evaluate the worthiness of the function and the effectiveness of religion in fulfilling it. He touts religion for offering perhaps the fullest means of encountering the unconscious short of analysis. Among religions, he favors Gnosticism over mainstream Christianity for offering entrée to more of the unconscious. Within Christianity he favors Roman Catholicism over mainstream Protestantism for doing the same.[16]

In assessing the effect of religion, Jung is no different from any other social scientist. Some social scientists like religion because they like its effect, whether on individuals or on a group. Other social scientists dislike religion because they dislike its effect. Freud hates religion because he judges it not only false but also harmful. Jung loves religion because he judges it exceedingly helpful, whether or not true.

Jung as Philosopher

Does Jung ever venture beyond the origin, function, and content of religion to the truth of religion? Does he ever argue that religion is true as well as functional? If so, does he enlist psychology to do so?

In, notably, the case of synchronicity, or the coincidence of our thoughts with the behavior of the world, Jung does not. Synchronicity refers to the coincidence itself, not to its cause, and the coincidence is an entirely empirical matter, not a metaphysical one (see Jung, 1969a, pp. 419–531). Synchronicity is the sheer parallel between us and the world. It is neither the collapse of the world into us, as in idealism, nor the projection of ourselves onto the world. If synchronicity were either, it would be just about us. Since synchronicity is about more than us, psychology cannot explain it. At most, psychology can register the human side of the coincidence. Because psychology is not about the world, it has no possible metaphysical ramifications.

By contrast, Jung's professions of religious belief are unabashedly metaphysical. For example, he thanks God daily for allowing him "to experience the reality of the *imago Dei* in me" (Jung, 1979, p. 209). In *Memories, Dreams, Reflections* he discloses that "From the beginning" he had a sense of a divinely bestowed destiny:

> Nobody could rob me of the conviction that it was enjoined upon me to do what God wanted and not what I wanted. . . . Often I had the feeling that in all decisive matters I was no longer among men, but was alone with God.
>
> *(Jung, 1963, p. 48)*

For God to have been present with Jung, God must, for him, exist.

Best known of Jung's religious pronouncements is his answer to the question whether he believes in God: "I know. I don't need to believe" (Jung, 1977, p. 428). What Jung means by knowing vis-à-vis believing is scarcely clear. What matters is that he nowhere adduces psychological support for his conviction, which thus comes from his moonlighting as a philosopher or theologian and not from his day job.

Explanation and Truth

The issues of function and truth seem distinct. Religion can be functional yet false or even true yet dysfunctional. To be functional, religion must only be *believed* true by believers. A belief believed true is no less efficacious when actually false than when true.

Whether *origin* and truth are distinct issues is a more complicated question. A naturalistic, or social scientific, account of the origin of a would-be experience of God would, if accepted, prove that God need not have caused the experience. But the account would not disprove the existence of God.

Many classical social scientists do assess the truth of religion, but not on the basis of the origin and function of religion. For example, Marx (see Marx and Engels, 1957) judges religion dysfunctional – not because it fails to accomplish its intended function but because the escapist and justificatory functions it does accomplish are more harmful than helpful. Religion would not, however, be escapist if Marx believed in the place of escape: heaven. Marx does, then, deem religion dysfunctional because false, but he does not deem religion false because dysfunctional. Someone else might invoke economic harm as an argument against the existence of either a just or a powerful God, in which case the dysfunctional effect of religion would argue for the falsity of religion. But Marx himself disbelieves in God of any kind and does so on philosophical rather than economic grounds.

For the Freud of *The Future of an Illusion* (1961), religion is, as for Marx, dysfunctional despite the fact that it accomplishes its intended function. Religion does transform an indifferent, even hostile outer world into a caring and fair one. But where for Marx religion is dysfunctional because the accomplishment of its function is harmful, for Freud religion is dysfunctional simply because the accomplishment of its function presupposes a false belief in a kind and just God. Like Marx, Freud disbelieves in God on grounds independent of its effect. By vaunting a benevolent God, religion does not, as for Marx, exacerbate human suffering. Rather, religion rationalizes it. Still, Freud, like Marx, contends that religion is dysfunctional because false: the comfort religion provides would be unobjectionable if Freud believed in God. But like Marx as well, he is not contending that religion is false because dysfunctional.

For the Freud of *Totem and Taboo* and to a lesser extent of *Moses and Monotheism*, religion is dysfunctional because, more straightforwardly, it fails to accomplish its intended function: alleviating guilt over past parricidal deeds or present parricidal urges. At the same time religion here is not even dysfunctional because false. While Freud here, too, scarcely believes in God, he objects to what believers do in the name of God: vainly attempt to repress irrepressible desires. That attempt would be no less vain and no less harmful if God did exist.

Among classical social scientists, the anthropologist J. G. Frazer (1922) least hesitates to pronounce religion dysfunctional because false. Certainly religion for him is not dysfunctional because of its intended function: providing food. Rather, religion is dysfunctional because it fails to deliver the goods, and it fails because God, whom believers either ask for food (religion) or compel to provide it (magic plus religion), does not exist. Frazer assumes not that believers thereby starve but that human efforts rather than divine ones secure food. Yet precisely because he judges religion dysfunctional because false, he cannot be judging religion false because dysfunctional.

By contrast to classical social scientists, most contemporary ones shun the issue of truth altogether, and do so on the same grounds as Jung: that the issue is beyond their social scientific ken. For example, the sociologist Peter Berger (1969), echoing Jung, rigidly separates a social scientific explanation of the origin and function of religion from any assessment of the truth of religion:

> [I]t is impossible within the frame of reference of scientific theorizing to make any affirmations, positive *or* negative, about the ultimate ontological status of this alleged reality. Within this frame of reference, the religious projections can be dealt with only as such, as products of human activity and human consciousness, and rigorous brackets have to be placed around the question as to whether these projections may not *also* . . . refer *to* something else than the human world in which they empirically originate. . . .

> In other words, every inquiry into religious matters that limits itself to the empirically available must necessarily be based on a "*methodological* atheism."
>
> *(Berger, 1969, p. 100)*[17]

By "atheism" Berger really means agnosticism, and elsewhere writes that "religiously speaking, sociology must always remain agnostic" (Berger and Kellner, 1981, p. 85).

More commonly, contemporary social scientists avoid the issue of origin altogether and focus entirely on function, which, they assume, has even less bearing on truth. One conspicuous exception is the anthropologist Mary Douglas, who on occasion uninhibitedly assesses the truth of the religious beliefs of at least alien cultures.[18] But an exception she is.

For Jung, religion provides a most effective, albeit unconscious, vehicle for encountering the unconscious. Religion is functional in all respects: it serves the function for which it was at least unconsciously intended; the function it serves is not just helpful but indispensable; and it is an exceedingly useful means of serving that function.

So insistent is Jung on the distinction between utility and truth that he refrains from broaching the question of truth with any patient for whom religion works. The efficacy of religion depends on the patient's believing religion true, not on its being true:

> I support the hypothesis of the practising Catholic while it works for him. In either case, I reinforce a means of defence against a grave risk, without asking the academic question whether the defence is an ultimate truth. I am glad when it works and so long as it works.
>
> *(Jung, 1969b, p. 45)*

A Link Between Explanation and Truth

Present-day social scientists like Jung are prepared to pronounce religion helpful or harmful, but rarely true or false. That determination they happily entrust to philosophers and theologians. They fear that their use of their social scientific findings to evaluate the truth claims of religion would commit either the genetic fallacy or what I call its functional counterpart: basing the truth or, more commonly, the falsity of religion on the effect of religion on adherents. Even if present-day social scientists do not base their stand on their social scientific findings, in which case they are immune to the charge, they are still wary of abandoning their familiar habitat.

By contrast, classical social scientists, despite their eagerness to break free of the philosophical roots of their disciplines, rarely hesitated to take a stand on the truth of religion. Yet ordinarily, they first declared religion true or, more typically, false on philosophical grounds and only then, as social scientists, sought to account for beliefs so obviously false. They did not use their accounts to evaluate the truth of religion.

But would they have committed either the genetic or the functional fallacy if they had done so? Seemingly, they would have, for a social scientific explanation of the origin or function of religious belief has no apparent bearing on the truth of the belief. Seemingly, a social scientific account cannot establish that religious belief is either true or false but at most only that a believer's own account of the origin and function of the believer's belief is.

Take, for example, Freud's explanation of religious belief in *The Future of an Illusion*. Freud argues that the helplessness which all humans experience in the face of an impersonal, arbitrary, and amoral world makes them long less for maternal love than for paternal security, for the protection that their fathers had provided during childhood. That longing impels most of them to project their fathers onto the world in the form of supreme deities. Religious belief thus originates in the human yearning to transform the harsh, adult world into the comforting one of childhood. For Freud, religious belief is illusory not in the sense of false, though false, or delusory, it also is, but in the sense of originating and functioning to fulfill a wish: the wish to make the world nicer than it is.[19]

Whether Freud's explanation of religious belief is true is not relevant here. What matters is whether Freud's explanation would refute the truth of religious belief if it were.

Whether Freud's explanation would refute a believer's own explanation of religious belief is likewise not relevant here. The fact that a believer would have misunderstood how the belief had been acquired would hardly seem to falsify the belief itself. To claim otherwise would seemingly be to commit the genetic fallacy. Similarly, the fact that a believer would have misunderstood the effect of a belief would hardly seem to falsify the belief itself. To claim otherwise would be to commit the functional fallacy.

Not only believers but also philosophers of religion invoke the genetic fallacy or, less often, the functional fallacy to dismiss the would-be encroachment of the social sciences on the truth of religious belief. Most famous is James' sneering objection to what he calls "medical materialism":

> Medical materialism seems indeed a good appellation for the too simple-minded system of thought which we are considering. Medical materialism finishes up Saint Paul by calling his vision on the road to Damascus a discharging lesion of the occipital cortex, he being an epileptic. It snuffs out Saint Teresa as an hysteric, Saint Francis of Assisi as an hereditary degenerate.
>
> *(James, 1936, p. 14)*

The fallacy is the refutation of a belief by the sheer appeal to the medical condition that supposedly produced it. James himself strives to link the mind to the body but opposes an appeal to sheer bodily origin to refute truth.

Undeniably, true as well as false beliefs of any kind can have a medical or noncognitive or irrational origin, so that the origin of a belief in no way dictates its falsity. Otherwise many beliefs true on all other grounds would thereby be false. That an unseemly origin would likely differ from a believer's own view of the origin of the belief is beside the point.

Not only philosophers but even social scientists themselves spurn the relevance of the social sciences to the truth of religious belief. Peter Berger asserts that "religion constitutes an immense projection of [wished for] human meanings into the empty vastness of the universe" yet adds the disavowal, already quoted in full, that "rigorous brackets have to be placed around the question as to whether these projections may not *also* . . . *refer to* something else than the human world in which they empirically originate" (Berger, 1969, p. 100). Similarly, Jung maintains that religious belief originates in the projection of archetypes onto the world yet, as also already quoted in full, scurries to "restrict" himself "to the observation of phenomena" and to "eschew any metaphysical or philosophical considerations" (Jung, 1969b, p. 6).

These statements sum up the conventional view of the relationship between the social sciences and religious belief. Origin and function are one thing; truth is something else. As self-evident as this view seems, it does not in actuality rule out the relevance of the social sciences to the truth of religious belief. The social sciences, I maintain, can challenge the truth of religious belief without committing either the genetic or the functional fallacy.[20]

A social scientific explanation, if accepted, renders the truth of religious belief not impossible but improbable. To maintain, as Freud, Berger, and Jung do, that religious belief originates in projection is to say that it originates in error, for to *project* God onto the world is by definition to ascribe to the world that which is in humans rather than in the world. To project something onto the world is to confuse what is in oneself – whether a wish, as for Freud and Berger, or an image, as for Jung – with what is in the world. To project is to project falsely.

In denying that their explanations of religious belief refute the truth of religious belief, Berger and Jung are denying that the objects of projections are necessarily nonexistent. Incontestably, they are correct. But even if the object of a projection can yet exist on its own, projection itself still constitutes error. To project God onto the world is not to discover God in the world but to impose God on the world. Should God turn out to exist after all, the projection would represent no insight on the believer's part. It would represent mere coincidence. The extraordinariness that the coincidence would represent is what, I suggest, challenges the truth of religious belief. Projection challenges the truth of religious belief not because projection refutes the truth of the belief but because a belief originating in projection is statistically unlikely to be true.

Freud most of all perceives this challenge. Like Jung and Berger, he recognizes the logical distinction between the origin of religious belief and the truth of religious belief. He thus acknowledges that "to assess the truth-value of religious doctrines does not lie within the scope of the present [social scientific] enquiry" (Freud, 1961, p. 33), which is concerned with only the origin of those doctrines. He distinguishes between the illusory status of religious belief, which refers to its origin, and its delusory status, which refers to its truth-value. Religious belief is for him delusory as well as illusory, but it is delusory on nonpsychological grounds.[21]

Unlike Jung and Berger, Freud recognizes a connection between the origin and the truth of religious belief. The mechanism on which he happens to focus is not, however, projection but wish fulfillment, and of its consequence for the truth of religious belief he writes:

> We know approximately at what periods and by what kind[s] of men religious doctrines were created. If in addition we discover the motives which led to this, our attitude to the problem of religion will undergo a marked displacement. We shall tell ourselves that it would be very nice if there were a God who created the world and was a benevolent Providence, and if there were a moral order in the universe and an after-life; but it is a very striking fact that all this is exactly as we are bound to wish it to be.
>
> *(Freud, 1961, p. 33)*

Assuming wish fulfillment as the origin of religious belief, Freud is observing how extraordinarily coincidental it would be if our wishes about the world, constituting as they do "the oldest, strongest and most urgent wishes of mankind" (Freud, 1961, p. 30), matched the world itself. Similarly, it would be extraordinarily coincidental if our projections onto the world, originating as they do in error, matched the world itself.

The challenge to religious belief does not stem from the origin of belief in human wishes. To argue otherwise would be to commit the genetic fallacy. Rather, the challenge stems from the rarity with which humanity's mildest, let alone fondest, wishes get fulfilled. A wish to believe that God exists does not *preclude* the existence of God, but it does make the existence of God improbable.

Not every social scientific explanation of religious belief, to be sure, involves either wish fulfillment or projection. But every one does involve a naturalistic rather than supernatural origin. A naturalistic cause reduces, or tends to reduce, the would-be supernatural effect to error. The error lies not in the postulation of a being who does not exist but in the postulation of a being on a basis, be it a wish or projection, which does not warrant the postulation. Should that being exist in fact, the postulation would, again, represent a remarkable coincidence. The unlikelihood of the coincidence constitutes the challenge.

Now Jung, more than Freud, may appreciate the fit between what is projected and onto what it is projected. A projection takes hold only where there is a match between the one and the other. A projection thus latches onto something that is really out there. One might therefore propose that for Jung, projection argues for, not against, the existence of God. But projection remains an addition to the object of projection and as an addition therefore constitutes error.

In sum, Jung the psychologist of religion, no less than Freud the psychologist of religion, can be enlisted as a philosopher of religion, even in the face of his aversion to any enlistment. The rigid contemporary divide between the psychological and the philosophical study of religion is surmountable.

Notes

1 On James' use of psychology to prove the reality of religious experience, see Segal (2005, pp. 124–128).
2 On the confusing terms *interpretation* and *explanation*, see Segal (1992a).
3 It is Freud more than Jung who has sometimes been taken to be a social scientist à la the human sciences. Jürgen Habermas and Paul Ricoeur are the most famous advocates of an interpretivist, or hermeneutical, rendition of Freud.
4 The title of the introduction to Kuhn's *The Structure of Scientific Revolutions* (1970) is "A Role for History." See also Kuhn, "The Relations Between the History and the Philosophy of Science" (1968/1976), "The History of Science" (1968), and "The Relations Between History and the History of Science" (1971), all published or republished in Kuhn (1977, pp. 3–20, 105–126, and 127–161).
5 Not all philosophers of science grant any room to external factors. Karl Popper is contemptuous of both sociological and psychological explanations of science: see Popper (1963, pp. 208–223; 1970, pp. 57–58).
6 See, similarly, Mannheim (1936, pp. 239–240).
7 On the rejection of the arationality principle by the Edinburgh school and others, see Laudan (1977, pp. 203–205).
8 Just as the Edinburgh school wants to make sociology, not philosophy, the heart of epistemology, so the American philosopher W.V.O. Quine wants to make psychology, not philosophy, the heart of epistemology. Quine enlists Skinnerian behaviorism, the then reigning academic psychology: see Quine (1960).
9 Against Collins' "methodological idealism," see Barnes, Bloor, and Henry (1996, pp. 14–15).
10 For a superb account of Jung's use of typology to circumvent relativism over truth, see Shamdasani (2003, pp. 50–83).
11 On the difficulty of correlating ideas with holders, see Laudan (1977, pp. 218–219, 221).
12 See, e.g., chapter 14 ofEagle (1984), which is titled "The Epistemic Status of Clinical Data."
13 Jung is continually exasperated by those who, like Martin Buber, accuse him of collapsing the metaphysical into the physical: see Jung (1963, p. 350, 1976, pp. 663–670).
14 The following discussion of Jung and Gnosticism comes from my introduction to Segal (1992b).
15 On Jung on UFOs, see Segal (2003).
16 On the psychological superiority of Gnosticism to mainstream Christianity, see the selections from Jung in Segal (1992b, pp. 119–136). On the psychological superiority of Roman Catholicism to mainstream Protestantism, see Jung (1969b, esp. pp. 21–22).
17 See also Berger (1969, pp. 88–89, 179–185, 1970, pp. 46–47); Berger and Kellner (1981, pp. 84–90). To be sure, in subsequent works Berger sometimes reverses himself and argues from the *supernatural* origin of religion to the *existence* of God: see Berger (1970, pp. 52–97, 1980, pp. 58–60, 114–142).
18 See Douglas (1975, pp. ix–xxi, 1979, pp. 177–187).
19 In contrast to both *Totem and Taboo* and *Moses and Monotheism, The Future of an Illusion* roots religion in a wish rather than in guilt, and the wish is neither sexual nor repressed. The explanation here of religion is akin to that of secular existentialists like Sartre and Camus. Religion is self-deception, or "bad faith."
20 The following argument first appeared in Segal (1980) and appears in revamped form in Segal (1989, pp. 75–86).
21 Freud judges religion delusory less in *The Future of an Illusion* than in *Civilization and Its Discontents*.

References

Barber, B. (1952). *Science and the social order.* New York: Free Press.

Barnes, B. (1995). *The elements of social theory.* Princeton, NJ: Princeton University Press.

Barnes, B., & Bloor, D. (1982). Relativism, rationalism and the sociology of knowledge. In M. Hollis & S. Lukes (Eds.), *Rationality and relativism*, pp. 21–47. Cambridge, MA: MIT Press.

Barnes, B., Bloor, D., & Henry, J. (1996). *Scientific knowledge.* Chicago: University of Chicago Press.

Ben-David, J. (1971). *The scientist's role in society.* Englewood Cliffs, NJ: Prentice-Hall.

Berger, P. L. (1969). *The sacred canopy.* Garden City, NY: Doubleday Anchor Books [originally published 1967].

——— (1970). *A rumor of angels.* Garden City, NY: Doubleday Anchor Books [originally published 1969].

——— (1980). *The heretical imperative.* Garden City, NY: Doubleday Anchor Books [original published 1979].

———, & Kellner, H. (1981). *Sociology reinterpreted.* Garden City, NY: Doubleday Anchor Books.

Bloor, D. (1991). *Knowledge and social imagery.* 2nd ed. Chicago: University of Chicago Press.

Collins, H. M., & Pinch, T. J. (1982). *Frames of meaning.* London: Routledge.

Douglas, M. (1975). *Implicit meanings.* London and Boston: Routledge & Kegan Paul.

——— (1979). World view and the core. In S. C. Brown (Ed.), *Philosophical disputes in the social sciences*, pp. 177–187. Sussex: Harvester Press; Atlantic Highlands, NJ: Humanities Press.

Durkheim, E. (1965). *The elementary forms of the religious life.* Trans. J. W. Swain. New York: Free Press [Originally published 1915].

Eagle, M. N. (1984). *Recent developments in psychoanalysis.* Cambridge, MA: Harvard University Press.

Frazer, J. G. (1922). *The golden bough.* Abridged ed. London: Macmillan.

Freud, S. (1961). *The future of an illusion.* Standard edition of the complete psychological works of Sigmund Freud, vol. 21, pp. 1–56. London: Hogarth Press and Institute of Psycho-Analysis.

James, W. (1936 [1902]). *The varieties of religious experience.* New York: Modern Library.

Jung, C. G. (1963). *Memories, dreams, reflections.* A. Jaffé (Ed.). Trans. R. & C. Winston. New York: Vintage Books.

——— (1967). *Symbols of transformation.* Collected works of C. G. Jung (CW), vol. 5 (2nd ed.). Princeton, NJ: Princeton University Press.

——— (1968). *Gnostic symbols of the self.* CW 9, part 2 (2nd ed.), pp. 184–221.

——— (1969a). *Synchronicity: An acausal connecting principle.* CW 8 (2nd ed.), pp. 417–519.

——— (1969b). *Psychology and religion.* CW 11 (2nd ed.), pp. 3–105.

——— (1971). *Psychological types.* CW 6. Princeton, NJ: Princeton University Press.

——— (1976). *The symbolic life.* CW 18. Princeton, NJ: Princeton University Press.

——— (1977). *C. G. Jung speaking.* W. McGuire & R. F. C. Hull (Eds.). Princeton, NJ: Princeton University Press.

——— (1979). *Word and image.* A. Jaffé (Ed.). Princeton, NJ: Princeton University Press.

Kuhn, T. S. (1970). *The structure of scientific revolutions* (2nd ed.). Chicago: University of Chicago Press.

——— (1977). *The essential tension.* Chicago: University of Chicago Press.

Lakatos, I. (1978). *The methodology of scientific research programmes.* J. Worrall & G. Currie (Eds.). Cambridge: Cambridge University Press.

Latour, B., & Woolgar, S. (1979). *Laboratory life.* London and Beverly Hills, CA: Sage.

Laudan, L. (1977). *Progress and its problems.* Berkeley: University of California Press.

Mannheim, K. (1936). *Ideology and utopia.* London: Routledge and Kegan Paul.

Marx, K., & Engels, F. (1957). *On religion.* Moscow: Foreign Languages Publishing.

Merton, R. K. (1970). *Science, technology and society in seventeenth-century England.* New York: Harper Torchbooks [originally published 1938].

——— (1973). The normative structure of science [1942]. In R. K. Merton, *The sociology of science*, pp. 267–278. Chicago: University of Chicago Press.

Popper, K. R. (1963). *The open society and its enemies* (4th ed.). 2 vols. New York: Harper Torchbooks [1st ed. 1945].

——— (1970). Normal science and its dangers. In I. Lakatos & A. Musgrave (Eds.), *Criticism and the growth of knowledge*, pp. 51–58. Cambridge: Cambridge University Press.

Quine, W. V. O. (1960). *Word and object.* Cambridge, MA: MIT Press.

Segal, R. A. (1980). The social sciences and the truth of religious belief. *Journal of the American Academy of Religion*, 48, 403–413.

——— (1989). *Religion and the social sciences.* Atlanta: Scholars Press.

——— (1992a). *Explaining and interpreting religion.* New York: Lang.

——— (Ed.) (1992b). *The Gnostic Jung*. Princeton, NJ: Princeton University Press; London: Routledge.
——— (2003). Jung on UFOs. In Christopher Partridge (Ed.), *UFO religions*, pp. 314–328. London and New York: Routledge.
——— (2005). James and Freud on mysticism. In Jeremy Carrette (Ed.), *William James and "The varieties of religious experience"*, pp. 124–132. London and New York: Routledge.
Shamdasani, S. (2003). *Jung and the making of modern psychology*. Cambridge: Cambridge University Press.
Shapin, S. (1994). *A social history of truth*. Chicago: University of Chicago Press.

PART III

Psychoanalysis, Epistemology, and Truth

17

THE ANXIETIES OF TRUTH IN PSYCHOANALYTIC AND PHILOSOPHIC THOUGHT

Shlomit Yadlin-Gadot

Introduction

Truth is a traditional age-old topic in philosophy, reflecting the major part it played throughout the history of the human subject. Wars have been fought trying to enforce different truths, gods have been created to articulate them, and particular lives have been formed and reformed in their light. It seems that what we know of truth in a definite manner is that it carries with it weight and sanctity that appertain to its function as a directive, a value or a point of reference. Yet, any and all attempts to define it belay these possibilities. Philosophical thought hasn't achieved a consensual definition of the concept and the various paradigmatic definitions available are riddled with methodological, logical and ethical challenges (Kunne 2003).

In psychoanalysis as in philosophy, truth was and remains a nodal concept. From its very inception, psychoanalysis has defined its essence in terms of the pursuit of truth (Freud 1933/1964). Freud, in his early work as a modernist, strove to establish psychoanalysis as a science in search of truth as constructed in the framework of a realistic epistemology. Truth was the goal of psychoanalysis, the analyst's gift to his patient, the therapeutic factor in clinical practice. Following Freud, however, an epistemological shift was gradually effected in psychoanalytic thought. The transition from a realistic epistemology to a subjective one was accompanied by the splintering of the 'one' realistic truth – the truth of correspondence – into a multiplicity of truths: Ideal, subjective, intersubjective, coherent and pragmatic truths, etc.

Truth remained the *raison d'être* of psychoanalysis (Hanly 1990), but its various definitions resulted in the formulation of different objectives and methodologies for clinical psychoanalysis. These different perspectives on truth, organized in distinct theoretical discourses, split the psychoanalytic society into diverse schools. The discussions among them are often accompanied by antagonism, rejectionist critiques and difficulties in mounting real dialogue (Summers 2008; Cavell 1983, 1998). In the traditional psychoanalytic discussions of epistemology, each school takes a position that attests to the 'correctness' of a particular epistemology, explains its advantages as a framework for psychoanalysis, while arguing that other epistemological approaches are erroneous and may even endanger psychoanalytic practice.

The view that I wish to develop here does not propose to choose between epistemologies, but rather continues a line of thought that seeks to create the theoretical space for multiple epistemologies and the practical space for multiple truths, recognized as inherent features of our

DOI: 10.4324/9780429297076-21

psychic function. Articulating a psychological definition of truth, I will depict truth as a psychic dynamic that functions in accord with the human need for certainty as it expresses itself across critical dimension of the subject's life.

The vantage point of this psychological account is the Kantian assumption that the mind-independent external reality around us is an incomprehensible one. We can know it only as it is mediated by fixed categories of consciousness that structure perceived phenomena in particular ways (Kant 1781/2013). Following this stage of perception, our experience is further organized by means of attention and symbolic paradigms (Neisser 1967, 1976; James 1890/2013; Kuhn 1962/1996; Gedo 1997). We mold and remold our realities in light and by means of different organizational principles, creating within them continuously, automatically and unconsciously Archimedean points of stability and certainty.

The history of Western philosophical thought has given rise to six paradigmatic notions of truth, truths that frequent our language and clinical experience, philosophical theory and psychoanalytic meta-theory. I will present each of these truths as reflecting an organizing principle in the psyche and as constituting its Archimedean point of certainty. In each person's psyche, these principles of organization function simultaneously, embodied in distinctive cognitive, experiential and emotional modes and rooted in basic human needs. I term these organizational principles '*truth axes*'. Their unique configuration is shaped by a singular developmental history which enhances certain truths, inhibits and forecloses others and, in that way, determines their interrelations. These truths sometimes overlap but are often incompatible with each other, generating tensions within the psyche and driving processes of repression and dissociation (Yadlin-Gadot 2016, 2017a, 2017b, 2019).

From this perspective, truth must be recognized not as an abstract construct, external to the subject, but also, and perhaps more importantly, as an inherent group of distinct and definable organizing principles of the psyche. These organizational principles, truth axes, define epistemic multiplicity as a main feature of subjectivity. They construct the various images of reality we inhabit and create the multidimensional experience we have of our world and of ourselves. Moreover, this formulation explains both the multiplicity of truths recognized in philosophic and psychoanalytic thought and truth's irretractability, even after the postmodern turn which, on the face of it, has given the concept a mortal blow.

In the first part of the present chapter I describe, in a nutshell, aspects of the discussion of truth in Western philosophy that lead to the concept's psychological definition. In the second part, I review the evolution of truth in psychoanalytic thought. In the third part, drawing on the psychoanalytic and philosophic discussions, I offer a definition of truth as an active principle of the mind, rooted in basic needs and driving processes of repression and dissociation.

Part 1: Situating Truth in a Psychological Framework

Intuitively, truth *should be* self-evident and One. Yet the tensions aroused by truth as a question were already evident in ancient Greek philosophy, with Plato's eternal and objective 'idea' (Plato 380 BC/1871) – I call this 'Ideal truth' – pitted against the subjectivism implied in Protagoras's dictum that "man is the measure of all things".[1] Aristotle's 'substances' (Aristotle 350 BC/1953) in the framework of realistic epistemology offered an alternative, sense-based, anchorage for objective truth that came to be called 'Correspondent truth'.

Kant and Hegel, introducing the ideas of phenomena and ongoing dialectic, challenged the possibility of an absolute truth. They paved the way to the *linguistic turn*, which positioned meaning, conceptual and symbolic schemes as prior to fact (Habermas 2003), thus further challenging our ability to know objective reality or even define its basic characteristics (Russell 1961).

And yet, the linguistic turn did not end in a stoic relinquishing of 'truth' as a basic constituent of the mind's work. Indeed, latter-day thinkers, for whom the linguistic turn was pivotal, *also continued to debate the concept of truth and show its complex nature in novel ways* (Rorty 1989). Even in the face of the wide range of epistemological, logical and ethical arguments, the quest for truth continued, defining and re-defining its status and method, taking into account its problematic nature and criticizing earlier arguments.

The vital continuing search for truth begs the question of its intractability. What drives this search? What are its origins? *The history of philosophical thought suggests that the answer to this question is clearly of a psychological nature*: human beings have a need for certainty, security, control and the elimination of doubt. Nietzsche's (1886/2009) critique of metaphysics is accepted as a prime modern origin of the line of thought that led to the dismantling of our naïve belief in metaphysics inasmuch as it aspires for absolute truth on the one hand and explores the immense human attachment to absolute truth on the other.

In Nietzsche's view, the quest for truth is driven by our fears. When we aim for objectivity, we buy ourselves stability and direction, but we sacrifice our integrity and the vitality of our thought (Nietzsche 1886/2009, cl. 10). The 'Will to Truth' is characteristic of a more general psychological tendency for self-deception. Man lacks the courage and integrity needed to contain his natural curiosity (ibid., cl. 227). Humanity, ever attached to a thoroughly flawed idea called 'truth', actively represses its creativity and life forces.

The American Pragmatic view, influenced by Nietzsche's thought, posited that the concern of truth was to advance the welfare of the individual. Thinkers such as Charles Sanders Peirce, William James, John Dewey and Richard Rorty saw truth as a means to an end of improving humanity's lot (James 1907/2004; Rorty 1989). On the other side of the ocean, Heidegger (1996) saw truth as reflecting man's need to control the world in general and death in particular. Levinas (1969) and Derrida (1978) both associated metaphysics with violence, seeing truth as a result and paradigmatic example of an illusory purity that man tried to place as a guarantee of his identity and superiority, with the result of a looming xenophobia. The postmodern critique was formulated: generalization, categorization and truth are forms of symbolic violence the subject imposes on the objects of her thought.

Notwithstanding the differences in content, all of the above views suggest that the pertinence of truth is of a psychological nature: Human beings have a need for certainty, constancy and mental control. Contrary to naïve intuition, and many philosophical positions, this implies that what *truth satisfies are not states of affairs, but rather states of mind*. If until now the search for truth involved three orders – reality, propositions and the constraints of human consciousness – we now add a fourth order: that of the psychological needs of the subject-as-thinker.

These needs preserve the concept of truth, allowing it to rise like a phoenix from the ashes of discarded modern thought, retaining its traditional definitions and granting it contemporary meanings. Alongside the two essentialist truths – the 'Ideal' truth and the truth of correspondence with reality ('Correspondent' truth), both of which claim the existence of an order independent of consciousness – four additional conceptions of truth, which, in Hempel's words, entailed an "essential softening of the truth" (Hempel 1935/1994), remain vital in philosophic thought. I refer to these conceptions as Coherent, Intersubjective, Pragmatic and Subjective-Existential truths. I present here briefly these paradigmatic notions of truth, for clarity denoting them with capital letters (Ideal, Correspondent, etc.).[2]

The Correspondent conception of truth, introduced by Aristotle (Aristotle 350 BC/1953), maintains that truth values are established by correspondence between a proposition and an external mind-independent fact. Correspondent truth is anchored in a realistic epistemology, which maintains that the world has a mind-independent existence that the subject is able to know by means of his senses (Hetherington 2012).

The Coherent conception of truth as, for example, in Spinoza's thinking (Spinoza 1677/1989), determines truth values by examining the compatibility of a belief with a whole system of beliefs. This truth is often associated with 'idealistic' epistemology that posits a single, abstract and unconditional principle, unknown in itself, yet determining the unity of the world (Hetherington 2012).

The Ideal conception of truth, as in Plato's thought (Plato 380 BC/1871), determines truth values by the compatibility between particular beliefs or empirically perceived cases and their corresponding eternal decrees or forms. It is situated in the realm of 'objective idealism' that claims the existence of a mind-independent order inaccessible to the senses and partially known by means of laborious mental processes (Russell 1961).

Subjective Idealism shares the premise of absolute and objective idealism, that all known reality resides within the mind. But whereas the latter assumes a principle external to the system that creates and unifies it, the former assumes the 'I' or the Ego as the constituting source of reality. Subjective and Intersubjective truths are embedded in the assumptions of subjective idealism (Orange et al. 1998).

The Subjective-Existential conception of truth, seeds of which can be found in the work of Kierkegaard, perceives truth as highly personal, embodying the subject's experienced authenticity. Here, experience is prior to any essence or generalization (Elleray 2007).

The Intersubjective conception of truth regards objectivity as established by interpersonal agreement, sometimes explicit, often implicit. This truth reflects the logic of intersubjective epistemologies, whereby the world achieves its true transcendence through the presence of a foreign subjectivity (Husserl 1983).

Pragmatic truth concerns the usefulness and practicality of an idea in the context of the believer's life. A true belief is one that has been proven valid by the compatibility between its predictions and its results. Here, truth is process based and tomorrow, today's truth may be no more than an opinion (James 1912/2010, 1907/2004).

Part 2: Epistemology and Truth in Psychoanalytic Theory and Discourse

Psychoanalysis joined truth's odyssey at it modern apex, and has maintained with it a complex relationship, characterized by frequent vicissitudes. Psychoanalysis was born into one truth, the scientific or the Correspondent theory of truth. For Freud this truth was there to anchor psychoanalysis' standing as a science and to supply a rationale for clinical psychotherapy. In *The Question of a Weltanschauung* (1933), upholding Aristotle's concept of truth, Freud leaves no doubt as to which path psychoanalysis should follow: "Scientific thinking['s]" he states, "endeavour is to arrive at correspondence with reality. . . . This correspondence with the real external world we call 'truth'" (Freud 1933, 169).[3] The separateness of the external and internal worlds has always been a cornerstone of the Freudian theory of pathology and development as in meta-theoretical assumptions. The Freudian infant gradually and painfully moves from an internal world of wish fulfilment to a frustrating grasp of external (yet sustaining) reality, transforming an early 'pleasure-ego' into a 'reality-ego' (Freud 1911). The areas where the delineation of external and internal fails are those of neurosis and psychosis, and it is there that the subject, due to lapses in reality testing, loses hold of his Correspondent truth and allows Subjective-Existential truths to prevail. The latter is based on correspondence to psychic reality and the former on correspondence to external reality.

In this view, truth that critically relies on internal reality is the hallmark of neurosis and needs to give way, by means of the analyst's interpretations, to Correspondent truth. The *analyst* remains able to differentiate between the external and the internal truths even when his patient cannot. In the form they take in the Realistic-Correspondent meta-theory, both truths (Correspondent and Subjective-Existential) *are found or revealed; they are neither constructed nor co-constructed.*

The Kleinian infant, like the Freudian one, begins life in a reality that is wholly phantasmatic and internal (Klein 1930, 1932). Gradually, through such mechanisms as splitting, projection, introjections and identification, the differentiation of internal and external worlds evolves. Klein's concept of 'position' implied the ability to move *in* and *out* of depressive reality-testing. Winnicott's move from the experiential realm of 'relating' to 'usage' (1969/1971) reflects the same sensibilities as regards the delineation of inner and outer realities. Yet, Winnicott is the first to define as an autonomous entity the transitional realm as that which stands *between* the inner and the outer realities (Winnicott 1951). Winnicott's third area of intermediateness collapses the internal-external/subject-object divide that is inherent in the notion of Correspondence.[4] In this sense he is effecting an epistemological shift, *but only within this third area of experience.* Outside of it, we may still make clear the differentiation of realistic epistemology between inner and outer, psychic and external reality.

Whereas Winnicott maintains the traditional dualism of world and self, *values begin a movement of reversal*, because the inner 'true' is valued more highly than before. The transitional realm is understood as the source of meaning, subjectivity and culture, and its constitution and analysis become the main focus and interest of psychoanalysis. Here, Winnicott distances himself from the classical notion of pre-existent truths and forms a new understanding of knowledge as a process of becoming. Freud wanted Ego where there was Id. Winnicott, endowing the Id with the respected adjective of 'true', offers it vindication. Winnicott's chaperoning of Subjective-Existential truth and the transitional realm he created might well have played a part in the gradual legitimation of idealistic trends in psychoanalysis.

Kohut's self-psychology positioned itself in a similar manner. The self-psychologist validates the patient's concept of reality even if it conflicts with the 'objective' reality the therapist is familiar with (Kohut 1984). The core area of psychoanalytic metapsychology occupies, for Kohut, an imaginary position inside the psychic organization of the individual, the position of an observer with whose insights the analyst vicariously identifies through the process of empathy. And yet, the point that remains valid in Kohut's thought, as in the thought of his predecessors, is that inner and outer realities may be delineated by the *analyst.* The analyst strives to fortify the patient's subjectivity and its truths, but he does this without losing the clarity of his hold on the distinction between psychical and material realities.[5]

The first radical shift in object relation theory from realism to idealism may be attributed to Bion, who delved deeply into issues of knowledge and truth. The following brief review will not do justice to his complex ideas, but may illustrate their part in effecting the idealistic shift. With the use of 'O' and 'K', respectively denoting truth and knowledge, Bion articulates his late theory of knowledge: "O . . . the ultimate reality, represented by terms such as absolute truth, the godhead, the infinite, the thing-in-itself . . . does not fall in the domain of knowledge or learning save incidentally; O can 'become', but it cannot be 'known'" (Bion 1970, 25). For Bion, there is no convergence between K and O. This is because K is basically sense-based, while O is not (Bion 1970, 87). Therefore, the psychoanalytic and the scientific truths (and realities) are fundamentally different from each other. Psychoanalysis must be "a science that is not restricted by its genesis in knowledge and sensuous background. It must be a science of at-one-ment" (ibid. 88).

Only by means of 'at-one-ment' may O be touched upon and approached. At-one-ment is a way of being or becoming which is not only different from knowledge, but is indeed, obstructed by it. Near-O states, predicated on the departure from K, involve risking the loss of both meaning and the continuity of consciousness. And yet, the event of 'Becoming O' gives rise to psychic change. The subject is forced first to abandon K, hitherto fundamental in his consciousness, and then to return to it in order to bind the inchoate experience (Bion 1965, 151). The transformation effected is an emotional learning that is always mediated in an intersubjective fashion, predicated on the interaction between container and contained that transforms the indigestible into the thinkable.

The relevant truth and reality for psychoanalysis (O in Bion's case) can be experienced but cannot be known. Here the downfall of realistic epistemology, which is predicated on the assumption of a knowable reality. The method and criterion of O's appropriation are completely subjective and experiential. Finally, accessing any knowledge involves an intersubjective event; therefore, knowledge is necessarily infused with subjectivity and validated by it. These formulations may be viewed as 'stepping stones' in the river of psychoanalytic thought, marking the gradual transition from realistic to idealistic epistemology.

From a different direction, and by reference to Coherent and Pragmatic truths, Spence and Schafer did their part in effecting the epistemic shift in psychoanalysis.[6] Spence extended the purview of the Pragmatic approach in psychoanalysis, claiming that practitioners place the individual subject at the center of the psychoanalytic world and, as such, his wellbeing forms the criteria for truth. Spence described the therapeutic efficacy of narrative (Coherent) and Pragmatic truths,[7] but objected to accepting them as adequate substitutions for historic (Correspondent) truth. He warns that "microstructure analysis . . . may be our only defense against the perils of narrative persuasion" (Spence 1983, 480) and advocates a return to the bedrock of realistic epistemology. In contradistinction, Schafer, basing his theory on these same Coherent and Pragmatic truths, demotes Correspondent truth from the privileged status Spence granted it. The basic assumption of what came to be called the 'Narrative Approach' is that people construct stories of their lives in order to better understand them. The narrative rendered is always provisional, admitting potential retellings: "This point of view does not deny truth. There is plenty of truth. It is just that truth comes in different versions. It always has. In this regard, the entire matter may be formulated as one of giving up denials" (Schafer 1996, 250).

Two epistemological shifts are here effected. Firstly, we part from the realm of realism and of biographical, Correspondent truth. Secondly, we relinquish monistic epistemologies in favour of parallel, potentially incongruent truths. Thus, Pragmatic, Subjective and Intersubjective epistemologies accept that several truths may be pertinent to a particular subject, when mental materials are contextualized in different areas and phases of a person's life. This means that psychic realities do not lend themselves to unitary formulation.

The narrative approach leans heavily on Coherent truth. Yet, in the psychoanalytic context, it carries also a significant element of intersubjectivity inasmuch as the analyst, even only in the role of supplying the context and the legitimation of the telling, plays a role in the constitution of the patient's narrative. Acknowledging the analyst's influence in the evolving truth, we draw closer to the basic premise of intersubjective epistemology: a person attains his sense of certainty about objective reality through the agency of an 'other'. According to this approach, the reality and truth that psychoanalysis achieves are mutually constructed through the organization of experience within an intersubjective field of reference (Stolorow et al. 2001). Here, observer and observed, analyst and analysand, are inextricably involved, mutually and reciprocally determining themselves and their reality (Stolorow and Atwood 1997).

Different versions of the psychoanalytic understanding of reality have developed under the heading of subjectivist and intersubjectivist approaches, the common factor among them being the disbelief in the existence of one well-circumscribed objective reality.[8] Here, the task of the analytic dialogue shifts from a classical concern with interpreting reality of any kind to an interest in the process by which analyst and patient create and shape an impact on the other through the play of mutual influences.

The Relations of Truth and Epistemology, Values and Multiplicity

Looked at from a psychoanalytic perspective, epistemology and truth are not one and the same, but they are interrelated. The former defines the process and premises whereby and according to which belief transforms into knowledge, while the latter refers to an adequate description of a particular state of affairs. Now, *each epistemology has a notion of truth that it naturally gives rise to.* Thus, realistic epistemology, as applies to Freud's unconscious, is the natural home of Correspondent truth. Objective idealism, in which Bion's O resides, retains the possibility of objective truth but recognizes that the road leading to it is imbued with experiential subjectivity and intersubjectivity. Subjective epistemology privileges subjectivity as a realm where beliefs are validated and therefore promotes a Subjective-Existential truth. In Intersubjective epistemology, intersubjectivity (as a principle of truth, culture or language) is a precondition for subjectivity and precedes it logically and epistemologically. Therefore, subjective truths will always be coloured by the intersubjective and, in a way, subordinated to it.

Each epistemology, alongside its privileged truth, *also accommodates other truths, but values them differently*. For example, Coherent truth is a pivotal and valid possibility in idealist epistemologies but, within a realistic perspective, it will be considered as narrative. Similarly, the experience of Correspondence for a subjective epistemologist is, of course, an illusion. This has important implications for psychoanalysis and for the general understanding of the subject in his relation to truth. Subjective truths have been given recognition from the early days of Freud, but they were regarded as neurotic symptoms: mental health was asymptotic to objective truth. By contrast, Kohut and Winnicott acknowledged Correspondent truth but *privileged* Subjective-Existential truth as expressing the core essence of being human, as well as the vehicle of personal development and of therapeutic effect. Spence acknowledged Pragmatic truth but warned of its destructive effect on clinical methodology and objectives. Epistemologies may *recognize* various truths, but they favour the truth that is primary to them.

Another way in which psychoanalytic theories incorporate different truths (and determine their value and function in psychic life) is by means of their anchoring in different psychic structures. In Freudian theory, for example, Intersubjective truth appears as constitutive of the superego because, as a personality structure, the superego embodies socialization, a function mediated by parental agents. Intersubjective truths, internalized as personality structures, are often depicted as being in conflict with other truths, internalized in different structures: Subjective-Existential truth, for example, is anchored in Freud's Id or Winnicott's True self. Freud privileges the vitality of Correspondence as expressed in reality testing (Freud 1923). Winnicott, of course, believing in the True self and its spontaneous, body-based creativity, might find the reign of Correspondence restrictive, rendering emotional life poorer (Winnicott 1960).

A similar picture can be observed regarding Ideal truths. In certain psychoanalytic theories of personality, the Ideal truth appears as a psychic structure such as Freud's ideal ego (Freud 1914, 93).[9] In Kohut and Wolf (1978) theory, the *ideal* appears in various forms, especially that part of the self that ties up meanings with motivational force. By and large, most psychoanalysts would agree that ideals are often experienced as truths by patients. However, differences abound regarding their therapeutic use by analysts. Kohut's belief that a life bereft of ideal truth is barren (ibid., 420) translates into the recommendation that analysts should offer themselves to their patients as ideal objects.[10] Kleinians, on the other hand, find fault in the acceptance of ideals as truth, suggesting the influence of splitting as a defence against aggression (Klein 1932). Benjamin contends that the analyst who poses *an* ideal or *as* an ideal might seriously compromises the inquiry of the patient's experiences of lack, weakness and damage (Benjamin 1994).

Similar considerations apply to the analytic use of the Coherent-narrative truth. Whereas for Schafer (1996) Coherent truth is a condition of communication and knowability and supplies solid structure for formulating and enhancing identity, Levenson (1988) and Laplanche (2008) speak of narrative structures as defensive by definition: they translate the inchoate mental richness of the unconscious into congealed ego language. Laplanche (ibid.) stresses the importance of de-translation as a processes that decomposes the coagulated truths of the ego and allows greater flexibility.

What is clear from these short illustrations is that different psychoanalytic schools acknowledge the different truths that both reflect and influence mental life. However, they ascribe their value differently, often as dictated by their epistemological convictions, and interpret differently the processes that are set in motion when pursuing a particular truth. From the vantage point of the Ideal truth, Pragmatic truth may seem inferior. The reverse may hold as well, when Ideal truths are understood as defence against action, freedom and personal responsibility.

As stated above, traditional psychoanalytic discussions of epistemology attest to the 'correctness' of a particular epistemology as a framework for psychoanalysis, while arguing that other epistemological approaches are erroneous and may even endanger psychoanalytic practice (a review of these detailed discussions may be found in Yadlin-Gadot 2016). Alongside this traditional approach, there is a line of work in psychoanalysis that may be identified as accepting the phenomenon of multiple epistemologies. Here, the plurality of epistemologies is grasped as an integral characteristic of mental life. The different images of reality that manifest themselves through the various epistemologies are seen as inherent to the interpretative construction of the world. Thus, no single structure renders other structures redundant, but rather relies on the way in which the other perspectives 'capture' different aspects of mental life (Schafer 1995; Rosegrant 2010: Schermer 2011). In these formulations, truth, indeed 'reality', are no longer conceived of as existing 'out there' in the world, but rather as constituted by our epistemic and symbolic construals of the world, construals motivated by the demands of the psyche. Here, the psychoanalytic subject, indeed psychoanalysis itself, exist in a realm of multiple truths

The co-existence of paradigmatic notions of truth are naturally and unfailingly present, not only in theory, but in the experiential life of the subject both outside and inside the clinic. Patients and therapists constantly use the concept of truth and its derivatives. Thus, we can easily imagine a patient saying: "I felt that something real was happening to me in therapy", which expresses a Subjective truth. Similarly, in saying "Nothing I can do about it . . . it's the truth", the patient expresses a sense of discontent in relation to considerations regarding the externality of Correspondent truth. Occasionally, a patient may pit one truth against another, as in "Perhaps it's right, but it's not my experience, to me it doesn't ring true". Here, a Correspondent truth is set against a Subjective truth. To further demonstrate the scope of possibilities here, consider a patient saying "That's true, but so what?" Here the patient agrees that the therapist's description of some situation or other matches reality, but for him the statement doesn't offer a way forward; it has no Pragmatic truth value. "I may be like that, but this is not how I want to be". Here the patient's Ideal truth comes injured from an attack set by the Correspondent truth. "My friends think it is best for me to leave the job, but as far as I'm concerned, it's a betrayal of my principles". The Intersubjective truth here clashes with the Ideal truth. Such statements, whose basis may be Intersubjective, Correspondent or Ideal, negotiate among themselves and express different positionings of the self. In each of them, the speaking subject aligns himself with one truth or another and this alignment effectively defines his self-positioning.

The therapist is attentive, even if not consciously, to various kinds of truth. While he listens, he automatically and unconsciously considers a number of possible meanings to what he hears: he examines what the patient is referring to in the world around him; at the same time, he scrutinizes the internal coherence of what is being said in relation to the speaker and in relation to what is understood to be his inner world. The therapist compares this inner world with the world as he experiences it and understands what he is being told according to the relevant social contexts. He hears the various elements of the evolving narrative and, of course, experiences the meaning of the verbal message in terms of the impact of what is being said and the intentions he thinks gave rise to it. This rapid, complex, unconscious action of the therapist reflects features of communication and of the human mind as depicted in the different truth notions. The multiplicity of 'truth' and 'reality', as it appears here, illustrates the fact that, rather than trying to decide between different notions of truth, we relate to them as different perspectives that organize elements of perception, emotion and thought in distinct and paradigmatic forms.

Part 3: Truth as Organizing Principles of Mind

The thesis I offer here accepts epistemic multiplicity as its point of departure, and explains its inevitability in psychic existence in terms of basic needs. Nietzsche underlined the interpretative role human needs carry in relation to our construals of reality, also stressing their potential tyranny: "It is our needs that interpret the world; our drives and their 'For' and 'Against'. Every drive is a kind of lust to rule; each one has its perspective that it would like to compel all the other drives to accept as a norm" (Nietzsche 1888/1968, cl. 481).

This point, whereby the world is construed in accordance with our needs, is a nodal one. We create the realities we need. But as we have various needs we form various images of reality in accordance with them. Thus, we remain with different realities and different truths. In addition, every need has a 'lust to rule'; it craves exclusivity and aspires to an unshifting image of reality, the comfort of a single truth. Nevertheless, all needs continue with their 'interpretations' of the world, creating images of reality and truth that do not necessarily overlap or cohere. Each image of reality captures a possible, yet incomplete, aspect of experience, its organic truth serving as a point of certainty within it.

The philosopher and psychoanalyst Fiumara described reality's constitution:

> speaking of reality. . . . we are not referring to the world in itself . . . but rather to the sort of reality which the individual laboriously carves out . . . a construct negotiated within the limits of what may be thought and done within his symbolic horizon. . . . Before we decide to inhabit a specific epistemology. . . . we may have gone through several epistemological migration.
>
> *(1992, 3, 8)*

My basic contention is that we do *not* decide in which epistemology to dwell. Rather, our basic psychological needs determine our multiple existence within several epistemologically defined realities. Different truths govern our lives: we are realistic inasmuch as our truth corresponds to what we perceive as facts. We hold Subjective truth in believing in what we feel. We accord with Intersubjective truths, be they myth or decrees, often unaware that they are rooted in interpersonal agreements. We consider and act upon our Ideal truths, grounded in our principles and ethics. Similarly, foreseeing practical implications of our decisions, we give prevalence to pragmatic truths. All serve as mental guidelines; all are experienced as truths. All may be traced to recurring philosophical arguments.

In this vein, I discuss the paradigmatic truths described as organizing principles of the mind that satisfy the psyche's need for stability and certainty across critical dimensions of the subject's life. I suggest that all these truths, in different forms and ratios, are present in the mental space of every person, answering to different needs and dimensions of living. Each truth functions as an *organizational principle of psyche that provides for a deep emotional need which motivates its formulation.* Let me briefly sketch these needs.

At the root of the *Correspondent truth* is the need to be in touch with external reality so as to enhance the chances of survival, through explaining, responding to and anticipating events that influence the exchanges between man and what is perceived as the mind-independent world around him.

At the root of the *Coherent truth* is the need for compatibility and harmony among a person's beliefs, expectations and behavioural tendencies. Coherence allows the smooth transition among the various activities that the subject is engaged with, as well as among different fields of knowledge and different experiences. This, in turn, allows the individual to create a sense of identity, continuity and regularity across time.

Man's need for perfection and completeness, for that which bestows guidance, meaning and validity to daily life and allows overcoming the repulsive, the abhorred and the arbitrary, is at the root of the *Ideal* truth. Ideal truths give man a sense of the eternal, of harmony and beauty on the macro level, serving as both directives and sources of motivation.

The *Subjective-Existential truth* arises in the subject's need to be loyal to *himself*, to be positioned at center stage as a criterion for planning his life and determining meaning without subordinating himself to a universal concept of subject or truth. This axis of truth also embodies acutely bodily sensitivity and experience.

The organization of experience in terms of future benefit is the basis for *Pragmatic truth.* This axis addresses the need to feel effective in one's ability to achieve one's goals in the world. It embodies active agency and overcomes the experience of helplessness and inevitability. It differentiates between forward and backward in a person's life and allows a sense of progress or regress as time goes by.

At the root of the *Intersubjective truth* is the profound need for a connection with those around us and a shared reality with them. This truth is predicated upon the representation of the psychoanalytic object and the ability of the subject to cohere with the inner dynamics of this representation. But the axis also generalizes the need for a singular object to the gratifying experience of belonging and cohering with a whole social field.

These *different* needs drive the creation of various images of the world, each related to a different experienced reality. The Correspondent truth axis creates a 'factual' reality enabling us to negotiate the mind-independent reality around us. In this reality we rely heavily on sense information, observe and try to master the realistic constraints in which we live our lives. The Coherent truth axis produces for us a cohesive and consistent reality at the level of both personal identity and perceived externality. This axis often functions to downplay the significance of facts and tendencies that do not cohere with one's core beliefs about self and world. The Ideal truth axis embodies a reality to which we aspire and in which we believe. It exists within us and at times outside of us. We move toward its realization in many things we do and find guidance within it. The Pragmatic truth axis creates an image of reality that accommodates our objectives and interests. Here, we may plan and decide in ways that determine what may best enhance our well-being. We exist within it as active, initiating agents. The Subjective-Existential truth axis produces a person's subjective-authentic image of reality, containing his private, often hidden truths; finally, the Intersubjective truth axis creates the reality we share with those around us.

Since truth axes differ in the needs to which they answer and the realities they create, they also differ in the relationships between need and reality, namely, in their world experience. Recurring patterns of world experience create different states of self in the form of balancing mechanisms (Bromberg 2009; Mitchell 1991; Rowan 2010). The various states of the self are not perceived here as sporadic, infinite or situational, which is the accepted position of many relational and post-modern writers (e.g., Bromberg 2009; Gubrium and Holstein 1994; Rowan 2010). Rather, the different self-states are understood as subject to general alignments that correspond to the different truth axes, alignments that are universal and may be defined and described. The vulnerable subjective self of inner truths, to which experiences of shame, exposure and fear of annihilation are linked, differs from the matter of fact, realistic self of the correspondent axis. The self of the intersubjective axis is the one supported by agreement of its community, or lost within it, the one experiencing anxieties of alienation and questions of belongingness. The self that scrutinizes itself against its ideals and senses either guilt or satisfaction is once again a self that differs from the pragmatic one that aims to calculate and understand the ways reality could benefit it.

The complex of epistemic assumption, characteristic self-state, image of reality and experienced truth form together a truth axis. In that sense, a truth axis is a multi-dimensional mental domain. The various truth axes exist in the psychic space of every person in different forms and degrees of dominance. Each person may have one or two dominant axes, whose relation to other axes may vary considerably. One person may be more responsive to ideals, while another responds to the people around him and allows them to determine his aspirations, fears and wishes. This person will probably experience a sense of belonging and creativity when he is part of an establishment, while another person will only experience self-worth when he is guided predominantly by his inner truths. Every organizing axis can have constructive or pathological expressions but, in both cases, the underlying logic of truth will be apparent. Of course, a person does not always respond to events with the same logic of truth. Different contexts arousing different needs may activate one or another of the axes at particular times. Usually, one lives according to directives of various different truth axes simultaneously. Life, as we experience it, eclipses any one register, and is perpetually given in multiple significations.

Conclusion and Clinical Implications

The thesis presented in this chapter touches on metaphysical, epistemological and metapsychological issues. Despite the seeming complexity of these issues, I have attempted to explicate what is, in fact, a common feature of the human mind: epistemic multiplicity, as given in the mental and emotional experiencing of several unrelenting and often conflicting truths. Presenting paradigmatic notions of truth formulated in philosophic thought, I have tried to illuminate that, in the domain of truth, as in other subject-relevant domains, the individual subject recapitulates the path of the historic subject. The abstract notions of truth formulated in philosophic thought reflect the particular subject's search for stability and constancy across the critical dimensions of her life. The differential motivations driving truth's psychic creation serve to explain truth's intractability on the one hand, and its multiplicity on the other.

I have shown that as clinicians, we are intuitively tuned to our patient's various truths, constantly listening to what hasn't been said alongside what *is* being said. We are attentive, even if not consciously, to *various kinds* of truth. While listening to the information we are given, we attune to accounts, variations and meanings that are present in different ways in the analytic space, tapping different levels of awareness. When an analyst's conscious observation is directed through the prism of a certain epistemology – be it subjective, realistic or intersubjective, presenting a specific understanding of a particular object of analysis – it seems safe to say that he, in tandem, intuitively considers the totality of possible epistemologies and evaluates them for compatibilities, overlaps, conflicts or tensions. This rapid, complex, unconscious action of the therapist reflects features of communication and of the human mind as depicted in the different truth notions. The concept of the truth axes is, in a way, a formalization and articulation of part of our intuitive movements as therapists and our intuitive understanding of the complexity of human experience.

From the perspective I present here, each psychoanalytic theory may be viewed as focused on one or two truths or epistemologies, creating a deep analysis of their evolution, from the level of need to the level of health, pathology and therapeutic objectives. From this vantage point, the different psychoanalytic theories are not seen as competing, but as creating a theoretic arc that parallels the epistemic multiplicity of the mind.

The various psychic truths arise from different needs and express their associated dreads and desires. Their differential sources guarantee that they often do not cohere. We often see our patients battling among their conflicting truths, baffled by the different ways in which they experience one single event. The therapeutic objective here is not necessarily to resolve conflicts. In analysis, we can help our patients understand and articulate the different realities they inhabit. While doing so, we will discover and articulate the tensions and the difficulties that arise from the different intersections, tensions, contradictions and incompatibilities among these realities.

We grant legitimacy to the various truths, admitting that life is too complex to be accounted for by one reality alone. We avoid re-traumatization of our patients who, in the past, may have had their Subjective-Existential truths banned, their actual experiences ignored, their Pragmatic truths dismissed on moral grounds, their Ideal truths scoffed at, and so on. We learn the Intersubjective truths that shaped our patients' sensibilities and probably co-construct with them some new ones. We may allow patients to know, acknowledge and articulate the multi-dimensionality of their living and its discontents. Thus, the patient can better inquire into the range of meanings and truths in his world by overcoming or circumventing the compulsion to determine particular meanings with which he identifies and which he may keep repeating.

Acknowledging that all truth axes express basic needs and are determined by them draws together the dimensions of the therapeutic and the ethic. The analyst is not expected to be neutral in his relation to the different languages, to equally identify with them or to be devoid of natural preferences and tendencies. His challenge consists in being aware of these tendencies and their significance (Hoffman 2009). Thus, the value-laden character of our practice and its prioritization of psychic needs are acknowledged. From this perspective, analytic work may be construed as creating a space that may contain various versions of world, self and experience, acknowledging and recognizing their validity, though they often do not cohere. At its best, this dialogue holds the potential of unravelling dynamics of dissociation and denial, allowing the experience of possibility and choice, in place of restriction and inevitability.

Notes

1 As quoted in Plato's 'Theaetetus', http://classics.mit.edu/Plato/theatu.html.

2 Four of these notions appear most frequently in contemporary theory, both philosophical and psychoanalytic. These are the Correspondent, Coherent, Intersubjective and Pragmatic notions of truth (Hanly 1990, 2001; Kunne 2003; Lynch 2001). To these I add one classical notion, the Ideal truth, presented already by Plato. This truth is often considered obsolete outside religious context, but I will illuminate its enduring relevance in psychoanalytic theory and practice. I add also the Subjective-Existential truth, which appears in explicit and implicit ways in psychoanalytic theory and practice, reflecting its immense influence on psychic life. A detailed account of the way these truths are delineated and placed

in theoretic dialectic with further definitions, including deflationary theories of truth, appears in Yadlin-Gadot (2016).

3 He repudiates 'the anarchist theory' which argues that the criterion for truth – correspondence with the external world – is absent in the psychoanalytic method. Freud criticizes such a view on the ground that "it breaks down with its first step into practical life" (Freud 1933, 175).

4 Winnicott's concept of *psyche-soma* echoes the same sensibilities. Whereas in binary ontology the psyche and soma fall into the respective categories of inner and outer, for Winnicott this division is a distortion, similar to the one eventuating in a dominant false self that takes over space and functions from the true self (Winnicott 1949).

5 I am presenting here my analysis of Kohut's epistemology. Others, such as Gedo, situate him in a phenomenological-subjective epistemology, stating that "Kohut (1977, 1984; Kohut and Wolf 1978) and his followers . . . have founded a school of psychoanalytic thought conforming to the principle that our theories should be as near to personal experience as possible. As a result, the propositions of self-psychology deal only with issues that can be articulated in the language of subjectivity" (Gedo 1997, 782). Fosshage also perceives Kohut as updating psychoanalytic epistemology by means of the method of observation he introduced into the clinic. Kohut (1982) recognized "the relativity of our perceptions of reality", "the framework of ordering concepts that shape our observations and explanations" (ibid. 400), and that "the field that is observed, of necessity, includes the observer" (Kohut 1984, 41). Deeming the patient's subjectivity the principal focus of the analytic endeavor, Kohut (1959, 1982) delineated how our method of observation relies on empathy and vicarious introspection, what he called the "empathic mode of observation", and designated it the method by which the field of psychoanalysis itself is defined (Kohut 1977; Fosshage 2011, 140). Thus, when all is filtered through the analyst's subjective processing, epistemology transforms into the subjective-phenomenal.

6 As with many contemporary ideas, both referenced Freud in the development of their thinking. In 1937 Freud's states that "an assured conviction of the truth of [the] construction . . . achieves the same therapeutic result as a recaptured memory" (Freud 1937, 265). Freud engages here two notions of truth: the Coherent truth, appertaining to the fit between a newly formed construction and earlier conceptions held by the patient ('assured conviction'); and the Pragmatic truth, in which the construction is examined according to its therapeutic consequences ('the same therapeutic results'). Freud forms here a new equation between the practical implications of a belief and its presumed objective truth-value.

7 Spence gives here a detailed definition of what he terms narrative truth and of its constitution: "To the extent that a narrative is persuasive and compelling, it acquires features of what might be called *narrative truth*. Goodness of fit seems particularly significant in bringing about this change. A particular clinical event – an association, for example, or a partly-recovered memory – may seem to clarify the unfolding account of the patient's life history so precisely that both patient and analyst come to the conclusion that it *must* be true . . . under these conditions, narrative fit is usually taken to be conclusive, and if a piece of the past completes the unfinished clinical picture in just the right way . . . then it acquires its own truth value and no further checking is necessary. Many of Freud's constructions seem to have followed this path. What was originally hypothetical and problematic, possessing no known truth value, turns out to bring together pieces of the patient's life story which, up to that point, had seemed disconnected and even contradictory. The construction that began as a contribution to the coherence of the narrative . . . gradually comes to acquire truth value in its own right and is assumed to satisfy the criteria of accuracy. . . . As soon as that step is taken, the *construction* becomes a *reconstruction* – a piece of the past that is taken to be as real as the name of the patient's father or the date of his birth" (Spence 1982, 181).

8 Constructivist (Hoffman 1991), Hermeneutic (Bouchard 1995) and Perspectival Realism (Orange 1992; Orange et al. 1998) are examples of approaches in psychoanalysis that contend that human behaviour is not determined by reality, which cannot be known and therefore cannot be posited as existing in relations of causality, but by the constructions of human beings. These approaches vary in the degree to which they retain vestiges of realism. For a detailed discussion of the variations among these approaches, see Yadlin-Gadot (2016).

9 In 'Group Psychology and the Analysis of the Ego' (1921), Freud again relates to the ego ideal as a configuration that is distinct from the ego and which enables the understanding of diverse phenomena in which the other is perceived as superior. This explains submission to hypnosis and to leadership, infatuation and admiration, etc., when according to Freud, the subject projects his ideal ego upon another person.

10 The possibility of mitigating a persecutory superego through identification with the analyst as a benign, tolerant, auxiliary superego function was stressed early on by Strachey (1934).

References

Aristotle (350 BC/1953). *Metaphysics, 4:1.* Translated by W. D. Ross. Accessed 23.7. 2019, source: http://classics.mit.edu/Aristotle/metaphysics.4.iv.html

Benjamin, Jessica (1994). "Commentary on Papers by Tansey, Davies, and Hirsch". *Psychoanal. Dial.*, 4:193–201.

Bion, Wilfred R. (1965). *Transformations.* London: Tavistock.

——— (1970). *Attention and Interpretation: A Scientific Approach to Insight in Psycho-Analysis and Groups.* London: Tavistock.

Bouchard, Marc-Andre (1995). "The Specificity of Hermeneutics in Psychoanalysis: Leaps on the Path from Construction to Recollection". *Int. J. Psycho-Anal.*, 76:533–546.

Bromberg, Philip M. (2009). "Truth, Human Relatedness, and the Analytic Process: An Interpersonal/Relational Perspective". *Int. J. Psycho-Anal.*, 90:347–361.

Cavell, M. (1983). *The Psychoanalytic Mind: From Freud to Philosophy.* Cambridge, MA: Harvard University Press.

——— (1998). "Triangulation, One's Own Mind and Objectivity". *Int. J. Psycho-Anal.*, 79:449–467.

Derrida, Jacques (1978). "Violence and Metaphysics". In *Writing and Difference.* Translated by A. Bass. London: Routledge & Kegan Paul.

Fiumara, Gemma Corradi (1992). *The Symbolic Function.* Oxford: Blackwell.

Elleray, Rebecca (2007). "Kierkegaard, Socrates and Existential Individuality". *Richmond J Philos.*, 16:1–12.

Fosshage, James L. (2011). "The Use and Impact of the Analyst's Subjectivity with Empathic and other Listening/Experiencing Perspectives". *Psychoanal. Q.*, 80:139–160.

Freud, Sigmund (1911). *Formulations on the Two Principles of Mental Functioning.* SE 12, 213–227.

——— (1914). *On Narcissism.* SE 14, 67–103.

——— (1921). *Group Psychology and the Analysis of the Ego.* SE 18, 69–143.

——— (1923). *The Ego and the Id.* SE 19, 3–48.

——— (1933). *The Question of a Weltanschauung.* SE 22, 158–184.

——— (1937). *Constructions in Analysis.* SE 23, 255–271.

——— (1953–1974). *The Standard Edition of the Complete Psychological Works of Sigmund Freud.* Edited and translated by J. Strachey. London: Hogarth Press (in text reference: SE).

Gedo, John E. (1997). "Reflections on Metapsychology, Theoretical Coherence, Hermeneutics, and Biology". *J. Amer. Psychoanal. Assn.*, 45:779–806.

Gubrium, Jaber F., and Holstein, James A. (1994). "Grounding the Postmodern Self". *Sociol Q.*, 35(4):685–703.

Habermas, Jürgen (2003). *Truth and Justification.* Translated by B. Fultner. Cambridge, MA: MIT Press.

Hanly, Charles (1990). "The Concept of Truth in Psychoanalysis". In Hanly, C. (ed.) *The Problem of Truth in Applied Psychoanalysis*, pp. 1–24. New York: Guilford.

——— (2001). "Critical Realism: Distinguishing the Psychological Subjectivity of the Analyst from Epistemological Subjectivism". *J. Amer. Psychoanal. Assn.*, 49:515–532.

Heidegger, Martin (1996). *Being and Time.* Translated by J. Stambough. Albany: State University of New-York Press.

Hempel, Carl G. (1935/1994). "On the Logical Positivists' Theory of Truth". In Horwich, P. (ed.) *Theories of Truth.* Cambridge: Cambridge University Press.

Hetherington, Stephen (2012). *Epistemology: The Key Thinkers.* New York: Continuum International Publishing Group.

Hoffman, Irwin Z. (1991). "Discussion: Toward a Social-Constructivist View of the Psychoanalytic Situation". *Psychoanal. Dial.*, 1:74–105.

——— (2009). "Therapeutic Passion in the Countertransference". *Psychoanal. Dial.*, 19:617–637.

Husserl, Edmund (1983). *Ideas Pertaining to a Pure Phenomenology and to a Phenomenological Philosophy.* Translated by F. Kersten. The Hague: Martinus Nijhoff.

James, William (1890/2013). *The Principles of Psychology.* eBooks@Adelaide. Accessed 5.8.2019, source: http://ebooks.adelaide.edu.au/j/james/william/principles/

——— (1907/2004). *Pragmatism: A New Name for Some Old Ways of Thinking.* Project Gutenberg EBook. Accessed 5.8.2019, source: www.gutenberg.org/catalog/world/readfile?fk_files=3440524

——— (1912/2010). *Essays in Radical Empiricism.* Project Gutenberg Ebook. Accessed 5.8.2019, source: www.gutenberg.org/files/32547/32547-h/32547-h.htm

Kant, Immanuel (1781/2013). "On External Objects". In *The Critique of Pure Reason.* Translated by J.M.D. Meiklejohn. Project Gutenberg EBook. Accessed 3.8.2019, source: www.gutenberg.org/files/4280/4280-h/4280-h.htm

Klein, Melanie (1930). "The Importance of Symbol Formation in the Development of the Ego". In Klein, M. (1964). *Contributions to Psychoanalysis, 1921–1945.* New York: McGraw-Hill.

——— (1932). "The Psychoanalysis of Children". In Klein, M. (1964). *Contributions to Psychoanalysis, 1921–1945.* New York: McGraw-Hill.

Kohut, Heinz (1959). "Introspection, Empathy, and Psychoanalysis". *J. Amer. Psychoanal. Assn.*, 7:459–483.

——— (1977). *The Restoration of the Self.* New York: International Universities Press.

——— (1982). "Introspection, Empathy, and the Semicircle of Mental Health". *Int. J. Psychoanal.*, 63:395–408.

——— (1984). *How Does Analysis Cure?* Edited by A. Goldberg and P. Stepansky. Chicago: University of Chicago Press.

Kohut, Heinz, and Wolf, Ernest (1978). "The Disorders of the Self and their Treatment: An Outline". *Int. J. Psychoanal.*, 59:413–425.

Kuhn, Thomas (1962/1996). *The Structure of Scientific Revolutions.* Chicago: University of Chicago Press.

Kunne, Wolfgang (2003). *Conceptions of Truth.* Oxford: Clarendon Press.

Laplanche, Jean (2008). "Narrativity and Hermeneutics: Some Propositions". *Psychoanal Q.*, 77:1016–1018.

Levenson, Edgar A. (1988). "The Pursuit of the Particular- On Psychoanalytic Inquiry". *Contemp. Psychoanal.*, 24:1–16.

Levinas, Emmanuel (1969). *Totality and Infinity: An Essay on Exteriority.* Translated by A. Lingis. Pittsburgh: Duquesne University Press.

Lynch, Michael P. (2001). *The Nature of Truth: Classic and Contemporary Perspectives.* Cambridge, MA: The MIT Press.

Mitchell, Stephen A. (1991). "Contemporary Perspectives on Self: Toward an Integration". *Psychoanal. Dial.*, 1:121–147.

Neisser, U. (1967). *Cognitive Psychology Englewood.* Cliffs, NJ: Prentice-Hall.

——— (1976). *Cognition and Reality.* San Francisco: W. H. Freeman and Co.

Nietzsche, Friedrich (1886/2009). *Beyond Good and Evil.* Translated by Zimmern H. Project Gutenberg EBook. Accessed 5.6.2019, source: www.gutenberg.org/files/4363/4363-h/4363-h.htm

——— (1888/1968). *The Will to Power.* Translated with commentary, W. Kaufmann. New York: Vintage Books.

Orange, Donna (1992). "Perspectival Realism and Social Constructivism: Commentary on Irwin Hoffman's 'Discussion: Toward a Social-Constructivist View of the Psychoanalytic Situation'". *Psychoanal. Dial.*, 2:561–565.

Orange, D. M., Stolorow, Robert D., and Atwood, George E. (1998). "Hermeneutics, Intersubjectivity Theory, and Psychoanalysis". *J. Amer. Psychoanal. Assn.*, 46:568–571.

Plato (380 BC/1871). *Republic.* Translated by B. Jowett. Accessed 23.7. 2019, source: http://classics.mit.edu/Plato/theatu.html. The Internet Classics Archive by Daniel C. Stevenson, Web Atomics.

Rorty, Richard (1989). *Contingency, Irony, and Solidarity.* Cambridge: Cambridge University Press.

Rosegrant, John (2010). "Three Psychoanalytic Realities". *Psychoanal. Psychol.*, 27:492–512.

Rowan, John (2010). *Personification: Using the Dialogical Self in Psychotherapy and Counselling.* London: Routledge.

Russell, Bertrand (1961). *History of Western Philosophy.* London: Routledge.

Schafer, Roy (1995). "In The Wake of Heinz Hartmann". *Int. J. Psycho-Anal.*, 76:223–235.

——— (1996). "Authority, Evidence, and Knowledge in the Psychoanalytic Relationship". *Psychoanal. Q.*, 65:236–253.

Schermer, Victor (2011). "Interpreting Psychoanalytic Interpretation: A Fourfold Perspective". *Psychoanal. Rev.*, 98:817–842.

Spence, Donald P. (1982). *Narrative Truth and Historical Truth: Meaning and Interpretation in Psychoanalysis.* New York: Norton and Co.

——— (1983). "Narrative Persuasion". *Psychoanal. Contemp. Thought*, 6:457–481.

Spinoza, Baruch (1677/1989). *Ethics.* Translated by A. Boyle, Introduction and Notes by G.H.R. Parkinson. London: Everyman Classics.

Stolorow, Robert D., and Atwood, George. (1997). "Deconstructing the Myth of the Neutral Analyst: An Alternative from Intersubjective Systems Theory". *Psychoanal. Q.*, 66:431–449.

Stolorow, Robert D., Orange, Donna, and Atwood, George. (2001). "Cartesian and Post-Cartesian Trends in Relational Psychoanalysis". *Psychoanal. Psychol.*, 18:468–484.

Strachey, J. (1934). "The Nature of the Therapeutic Action of Psycho-Analysis". *Int. J. Psycho-Anal.*, 15:127–159.

Summers, Frank. (2008). "Theoretical Insularity and the Crisis of Psychoanalysis". *J. Psychoanal. Psychology.*, 25:413–424.
Winnicott, Donald W. (1949). "Mind and its Relation to the Psyche-Soma". In Winnicott, D. W. (1975). *Through Pediatrics to Psychoanalysis*, pp. 245–255. London: Hogarth Press.
——— (1951). "Transitional Objects and Transitional Phenomena". In Winnicott, D. W. (1975). *Through Pediatrics to Psychoanalysis*, pp. 229–243. London: The Hogarth Press.
——— (1960). "Ego Distortion in Terms of True and False Self". In Winnicott, D. W. (1965). *The Maturational Processes and the Facilitating Environment: Studies in the Theory of Emotional Development*, pp. 140–153. London: The Hogarth Press.
——— (1969/1971). "The Use of an Object and Relating through Identifications". In Winnicott, D.W. (1971). *Playing and Reality*, pp. 86–94. London: Tavistock.
Yadlin-Gadot, Shlomit (2016). *Truth Matters: Theory and Practice in Psychoanalysis*. Leiden and Boston: Brill Publishers.
——— (2017a). "Truth Axes and the Transformation of Self". *Psychoanal. Rev.*, 104(2):163–201.
——— (2017b). "(Ef)facing Truth: Between Philosophy and Psychoanalysis". *J. Theor. Philos. Psychol.*, 37(1):1–20.
——— (2019). "Post-truth, Hegemonic Discourse and the Psychoanalytic Task of Decentering". *Psychoanal. Dialogues*, 29(2):172–188.

18
TRUTH AND PSYCHOANALYSIS

Charles Hanly[1]

Introduction

The sophist Protagorean idea that individuals "are the measure of all things" has had a resurgence, in recent decades, with the rise of "postmodern" thinking. The postmodern viewpoint has been defined as one of "incredulity toward metanarratives," favouring instead a multiplicity of "language games" and "clouds of sociality" (Lyotard, xxiv). Such a viewpoint has found support within psychoanalysis. Supporters maintain that there are no facts at all in clinical psychoanalysis to be shared by competent observers. Goldberg (1976) qualifies this generality by acknowledging that analysts of the same theoretical school are able to share clinical facts but clinicians of differing theoretical schools cannot. In what follows, I will consider this general and qualified claim in the context of three main philosophical theories of truth: the correspondence, coherence, and pragmatic theories. In the course of the discussion, we will see that this postmodern trend in psychoanalysis depends on claims about truth which lack plausibility.

Philosophical Theories of Truth

The Correspondence Theory

The correspondence theory of truth is for many people the most intuitively plausible theory (see Hanly, 1990, 2006, 2009). It states that truth consists of the degree of correspondence between an object and its description. It assumes that under normal conditions the human mind is able to gain knowledge of objects by means of observation and its experimental refinement. This observational knowledge can then be used to test interpretations, formulations, diagnoses and theories. The correspondence theory is implied with oblique eloquence in Galileo's "eppur si muove" (see Drake, 1978, pp. 356–357). Neither his official recantation of his astronomical discoveries, nor the majestic coherence of Ptolemaic astronomy, nor the obvious agreement of Ptolemaic theory with experience, nor the consensus of generations of scholars and ecclesiastical authorities, could alter the fact that Galileo's observations of the moon, planets, and sun had enabled him to describe much more accurately the nature of these objects and what was actually happening in nature with their states of motion and rest. This same view of truth and of science has been held by the great seminal scientists: Harvey, Newton, Darwin, Einstein, and Freud,

DOI: 10.4324/9780429297076-22

and by scientists generally. The school of thought in philosophy with which the correspondence concept of truth is associated is realism: critics of correspondence would say naïve realism; advocates would say critical realism.

The Coherence Theory

The next theory of truth to consider is the coherence theory (see Hanly, 1990, 2009). At least in its "strong" version advocated by some philosophers, the coherence theory lacks the intuitive plausibility of the correspondence theory. It pushes the limits of the ordinary ways in which we understand truth and reality. Putnam (1981) has articulated one such strong version of the coherence theory of truth. According to Putnam, the question "What objects does the world consist of?" only makes sense within a theory or description:

> Truth . . . is some sort of (idealized) rational acceptability – some sort of ideal coherence of beliefs with each other and with our experiences as those experiences are themselves represented in our belief system – and not correspondence with mind-independent or discourse-independent "states of affairs" (p. 47).

Thus on a strong version of the coherence theory, there may be more than one true description of the world. The correspondence theory allows for only one. In effect, the coherence theory abandons objects as they actually are as the ground of truths about objects for objects as they are constructed or constituted by the belief and theory investments that govern their observation and the way in which they are experienced by observers. The mind must, as a matter of psychological and epistemological inevitability, subject the objects which it seeks to know to the conditions under which it is able to know them. The original form of this idea is traceable to Kant (1781), although Kant believed himself to be a scientific realist. Among its modern adherents have been Bradley (1897), Merleau-Ponty (1945), Sartre (1943), Ricoeur (1970), Habermas (1971), and the philosophers of science Kuhn (1970), Feyerabend (1965), and Putnam (1981). The school of thought, in philosophy, to which the coherence theory belongs is idealism or rationalism (analyst readers who are not philosophically sophisticated are reminded that "rationalism" when used to denote a school of thought does not imply that the ideas of the school are always rational or that the ideas of the school of thought opposed to it, "empiricism," are irrational).

A key reason why strong coherentism lacks plausibility is that, just as arguments can be valid without being sound because the truth of the conclusions depends upon the truth of the premises, so a theory can be logically consistent without being true. We can see this by considering the case of Euclidean geometry. This is a mathematical system that is complete and completely coherent. For this reason, it escapes Gödel's theorem that the axioms of complex mathematical systems allow for the formulation of theorems that cannot be proven by the axioms and theorems that can be proven. Yet it turns out that Euclidean geometry does not describe the space of the universe. Physics has been able to identify facts that show this to be the case. The axioms of Euclidean geometry were believed to be self-evidently true. Plato, Descartes, and Leibniz considered them to be innate to the mind. Kant considered them to be *a priori* conditions of experience. Yet despite this self-evidence and coherence, and despite the fact that we actually do observe the world in a Euclidean fashion, these axioms have been shown by relativity physics to be approximations suitable only to regions of space smaller than the solar system and on relatively short distances on the earth's surface.

Another example of coherence without truth is found in the neuroses and psychoses. If coherence were a sufficient and adequate criterion of truth, it would follow that the loss of reality in neurosis and psychosis would necessarily involve incoherence, but it does not. Psychoanalysis is familiar, in the psychoses, with systems of belief, observation, and behaviour that are remarkable both for their coherence and for their detachment from reality. The following bit of case history is representative. A psychotic student in a university seminar experienced growing agitation when certain topics were under discussion while the sounds of shuffling feet around the table were accompanied by the sounds of streetcars passing under the windows. This agitation cohered perfectly with his belief that such conjunctions of sounds signaled the approach of evil forces at work in the student's Manichean cosmos. Coherent as well with his beliefs were the ritual pre-cautions he undertook to oppose the advance of those forces. Nowhere are the shortcomings of coherence as a sufficient criterion of truth more forcefully demonstrated than in our own field. Just as an argument may be valid and yet have a false conclusion, so a system of beliefs or a narrative may be coherent but false. The concept of coherence is not sufficient to bridge the gap between ideas and objects.

The Pragmatic Theory

The third theory of truth under consideration is pragmatism (see Hanly, 2006). William James (1907) was the founder along with Dewey (1918) and Peirce (1903) of pragmatism. James affirmed that to say of an idea, "it is true because it is useful," is identical with saying, "an idea works because it is true," by which he meant, "It corresponds with reality."

However, there is an ambiguity in James's use of the term "useful" that needs elucidation. The term "useful" may mean "can be used to engineer or otherwise bring about specific changes that would not occur without the use of the idea," or it may mean "psychologically beneficial" for the individual in the sense of having advantageous consequences for the individual who has the idea. I propose to refer to the former as "scientific pragmatism" and the latter as "philosophical pragmatism." Like the strong version of the coherence theory, there are compelling reasons to reject philosophical pragmatism.

The problem with philosophical pragmatism becomes clear when we consider James's application of this theory to religion. James claimed that if a hypothesis works satisfactorily in the broadest sense, then it is true. Therefore, if the belief that God exists works well for a believer, for example, if it enables him to respond to misfortune with fortitude, then the belief is true. But no such implication can be drawn; all that is established is that the belief in the truth of the idea is beneficial, and not that the belief is true. By parity of reasoning on the basis of James's conception of pragmatism, Agamemnon's belief in the goddess Artemis, to whom he ritually sacrificed his daughter Iphigenia, was true because a brisk offshore wind subsequently got up, which enabled his becalmed fleet to sail to Troy. But this reasoning no more establishes the existence of Artemis in the forests of Olympus than the utility of a belief in a Judaic-Christian god proves the existence of an infinite creator of the universe. The fact that a belief is good for one, that it is useful in the broadest sense, does not prove its truth, that is, that there is a reality corresponding to it.

Russell (1945) states the underlying difficulty with James's definition of pragmatism in a colorful and insightful way:

> the fallacies spring from an attempt to ignore all extra-human facts. Berkeleian idealism combined with skepticism causes him to substitute belief in God for God, and to

pretend that this will do just as well. But this is only a form of the subjectivist madness which is characteristic of most modern philosophy.

(pp. 772–773)

Drawing on Insights From Coherentism and Pragmatism

I have argued that the strong version of the coherence theory and the philosophical version of the pragmatic theory are both implausible. However, there are more plausible versions of coherentism and pragmatism which incorporate some of the insights of these theories without entailing their problematic consequences. Indeed, these more plausible versions of coherentism and pragmatism are compatible with the correspondence theory of truth. We can see this compatibility by considering Freud's own position on the development of a scientific theory such as psychoanalysis.

Coherentism

Freud employed a coherence criterion within the framework of his realist epistemology. He appreciated the extent to which any inquiry has to be guided by preliminary ideas. In this respect, Freud's grasp of epistemology was more realistic and empirical than that of Bacon (1620), the great founder of modern empiricism. But Freud also thought that these preliminary ideas can and must be continually criticized and made to reflect the facts of observation more accurately. From the need to have a theory that will enable us to make predictions about what we will observe in order to make systematic observations, it does not follow that these predictions must govern what we will find. The preliminary ideas Harvey had concerning the circulation of the blood did not add or subtract anything from his crucial measurement of the amount of blood pumped by the heart in a single pulse. Hawking's (1988) mathematical derivation which proves, on current thermodynamic and quantum assumptions, that black holes emit particles does not affect the observations that will now have to be made on cosmic radiation to test the empirical truth of this derivation.

Nowhere is the use of coherence more evident than in Freud's (1918) effort to prove the objective reality of the Wolf Man's primal scene. But even though his interpretation makes coherent sense of the details of the Wolf Man's infantile history and its connection with both his infantile and adult neuroses, Freud does not claim that he had succeeded in proving that the primal scene was an occurrence rather than a fantasy. A crucial fact concerning the Gruska scene (the boy's urination) could only be established inferentially. Similarly, Freud only claimed that his hypothesis in 'Totem and Taboo' was more plausible than existing theories and that it probably contained some measure of truth. He did not claim either that its coherence made it true or that such coherence constituted a limit beyond which knowledge could not reach.

Thus, Freud used coherence as a necessary but not a sufficient criterion of truth. He took correspondence to be necessary and sufficient. Freud used coherence as a formal, logical criterion and correspondence as a material, epistemological criterion. Indeed, correspondence is built into the foundations of psychoanalysis. It is part of the meaning of the reality principle.

Pragmatism

What I earlier called "scientific pragmatism," which employs a scientific definition of "useful," is consistent with correspondence. According to scientific pragmatism, a hypothesis is rendered pragmatically true if there can be derived from it a means of bringing about a change predicted by the hypothesis in some thing or event and if it can provide an explanation including the mechanism of its production. It is the fact that the change is predicted, explained, and brought about – and not whether the change is beneficial or adverse – that is the crucial validating element that provides pragmatic evidence of correspondence.

The amelioration of the human condition is one of the great benefits of science and technology, but it is the fact that the change was predicted, and not the benefit, that confirms the hypothesis. The truth of the hypothesis, in cases of immunity to otherwise malignant infections, that the injection of a small, controlled amount of a disease-causing virus will stimulate the production of antibodies that will then protect against future infections from the virus is confirmed by a change in the body – its future resistance to the disease on account of the antibodies caused by the immunizing injection. There can be no question about the human benefits of immunization, but it is the ability to use the scientific ideas to bring about this change (granted, a highly desirable one) that provides a pragmatic confirmation of the ideas of the immunization hypothesis.

We find that Freud relied on a scientifically pragmatic criterion of truth in his construction of psychoanalytic knowledge. A familiar example of his use of a pragmatic criterion is his far-reaching modification of his early seduction theory when he came upon hysterical neurosis in which the stable remission of symptoms predicted by his theory was not brought about by the clinical technique that, according to the theory, should have worked. According to the principles outlined above, (1) Freud's seduction hypothesis could explain the nature and origin of these neuroses by tracing them to their causal origins: repressed memories of having been sexually seduced in childhood were rendered traumatic by the onset of sexuality at puberty and caused sexuality to become symptomatic; (2) the method of cure specified by the theory would consist of a cathartic return of the affect-charged memories and, in so doing, disarm their interference with normal sexual development and activity; (3) the seduction hypothesis predicted that the affect-laden return of the memories of childhood seductions would cure the symptoms by allowing sexual activity to flourish; but (4) Freud discovered that, in some cases, the return to consciousness of childhood scenes of sexual seduction resulted in no symptom change or in only a temporary improvement. Freud concluded that the seduction theory, in the form in which he originally stated it, was false on the pragmatic grounds that it did not work in the way it would have to have worked if it were true in all cases of hysteria.

In order better to explain the clinical phenomena he was observing, he modified the theory by introducing, in addition to the accidents of childhood object relations, the influence of an inherited sexual instinct active from birth according to a genetic program of developmental stages or infantile sexuality. He correspondingly modified the cathartic method by recognizing transference and processes of repeating, remembering, and working through. The fact that these theoretical and technical changes worked better than the theory and clinical technique they replaced constituted a pragmatic confirmation of them, just as the failure of the seduction theory to work provided a pragmatic disconfirmation of it.

Truth and Subjectivism in Psychoanalysis

As mentioned at the outset, the postmodern viewpoint of "incredulity toward metanarratives" has found support within psychoanalysis. Supporters are inclined to claim that there are no facts at all in clinical psychoanalysis to be shared by competent observers. A prominent American analyst affirmed at an anniversary scientific meeting of the *International Journal* that "it is a fact, that there is no such thing as a clinical fact." These postmodern analysts end up rejecting the correspondence theory of truth and relying on the problematic claims of strong coherentism or philosophical pragmatism that we have just considered. Let us consider some examples of analysts who have come to understand psychoanalysis in a way that is compatible with such a postmodern framework.

Goldberg

We find Goldberg (1976; 1988) articulating a coherence theory. The philosophical idea that observations are theory-bound is used to explain differences in clinical observation:

> when two individuals with roughly similar neurophysiological equipment view the same thing or event and each see it differently, it is not necessarily true that one is incompetent or even wrong; rather it may be that they each observe with a different theory.
>
> *(Goldberg, 1976, p. 67)*

From this epistemological premise we can infer that shared coherent theories will produce clinical observations that will confirm the theories that constitute the observations but there are no perspectives and no facts that could adjudicate any alternative theory. This idea agrees with Putnam (1981) that there may be more than one true theory about the same thing because the observations that confirm theories are contaminated by the very theoretical concepts they confirm. As Putnam states it, 'the very (experiential) inputs upon which our knowledge is based are conceptually contaminated' (1981, p. 54).

Spence

Spence (1982a, 1982b), despite some ambiguity, comes down in favour of coherence as the criterion of truth in psychoanalysis when he claims that "the analyst functions more as a pattern-maker than a pattern-finder" and goes on to refer to analyses as "artistic masterpieces." This account agrees with the notion that a present intention or perception interprets the past – that there is no discrete, specific, particular past which continues to be what it was; there are only the diverse perspectives on the past brought about by the intentions inherent in current projects, moods, affects, attitudes, and theories.

However, Spence does not accurately represent the analytic process. The description above of the uncertainty of associations is tendentious and incomplete. Even when a patient is filling the hour with reports of manifest dream contents to the exclusion of associations, the details of the material are clear and determinate. There is nothing indefinite or elusive about it. Of course, it is unintelligible and uninterpretable in the absence of associations and transferences, but this fact has itself an obvious interpretation: the patient is anxiously clinging to the manifest dream content. This interpretation, properly timed and expressed and linked to the transference, will begin a process of change that will enable the patient to begin associating to his dreams. These associations will then also be determinate and discrete. If they are incomplete – as they are likely to be – it will be because further resistances are at work. If they become vague and uncertain, it is for the same reason. Vagueness and uncertainty are themselves determinate states of affairs that have an explanation. They are not characteristic qualities of mental contents and states as such. The same is true of fantasies, memories, character traits, and so on.

Pattern-making by the analyst is not required so long as resistances and defences are interpreted in such a way as to allow the intrinsic forces at work in the psychic life of the patient to make themselves known. These forces will determine the pattern as they will determine the transference. The forces in question are the drives, their vicissitudes, and their derivatives.

The ideas of pattern-making, of theory-bound observation, and the like are rationalizations for countertransferential resistance to the threats posed by the drives, that is, by the instinctual unconscious of the analyst. It is for this reason that psychoanalytic adherents of coherence have to find some way to banish the drives conceptually. Psychoanalytic theories that repudiate the drives are also likely to employ coherence as a concept of truth. Freud (1900) was certainly aware of the complexity of dreams and the extent to which they are representative of all mental phenomena; however, Freud (1905) also believed that the obscurities of a dream can be cleared up, that each manifest element can be traced along the paths of displacement and condensation from whence it came and that the meaning of the dream is to be found in the unconscious wishes of the dreamer. We are not always able to find the meaning, but it is there to be found, independently of any pattern-making activity on the part of the analyst.

The task of interpretation as Freud conceived it is to make the interpretation correspond with the operative unconscious wishes of the dreamer – wishes that have a definite nature of their own. (For an opposing view, see Viderman, 1970).

Relational Analysis

Relational analysts who reject outright any drive factors in neurosis are a third example of psychoanalysts whose views on psychoanalysis can be seen to fit all too easily within a postmodern framework. These comments apply to and are limited to Stolorow's idea of co-creation. There are relational analysts, such as Greenberg and Mitchell (1983), who seek a synthesis of drive and relational causalities. Stolorow and Atwood (1992) and some relational analysts are inclined towards the claim that, because analytic truths are co-created by the analytic dyad, there will not necessarily be facts about the patient in clinical psychoanalysis which would be available to any competent observer who is not part of the dyad. Stolorow maintains that the analyst and the analysand are inextricably related to the extent of being reciprocally determinative the one of the other. Hence, in analysis a patient's associations and transference do not, under any conditions, convey who and what the patient is but only who and what the patient is in relation to the analyst.

Such analysts criticize psychoanalytic realists for being absolutists because they claim to be able to know who the patient really is and to be able to know what motivates the patient better than the patient does himself. These psychoanalytic criticisms cohere with the philosophical criticism of the critical realist's advocacy of correspondence and advance the further implication that the realist not only logically introduces a deity into epistemology but is also self-deifying with claims of omniscience.

These criticisms and the philosophical ideas on which they are based have, no doubt, a certain merit. It is possible to use a conviction of correspondence to believe that, because one sees something in a certain way, it must be that way. It would be bad analytic technique to see, for example, a woman patient's recurrent complaints about male peers being privileged over her at her place of work as being necessarily complaints about not having a penis. What the motives are cannot be decided *a priori*; it would be a misuse of theory and inadequate technique to do so. The analyst would, in such a case, be prescribing the motive rather than discovering it. Her complaints could be realistic, and the psychoanalytic question would then have to do with the motives of her passivity in the face of mistreatment. Her complaints could be unrealistic and symptomatic, yet not motivated by penis envy. Her complaints could be realistic and also motivated by penis envy. An analyst who failed to be open to the possibilities would have failed to maintain evenly suspended attention; he would be simplistic and narrow in his grasp of psychoanalytic theory and technique, and, on the assumptions we have made, probably unconsciously hostile toward the patient.

Shortcomings of this kind occur, but it would be a mistake to define an idea or to repudiate it on the basis of its misuse. The situation is more complicated. Good technique would invite the analyst to discover the motives of his patient's complaining by facilitating and following her associations and transferences, and bid the analyst not to rely on his/her preferred ideas. The scientific, philosophical, and common-sense idea of correspondence does not include the idea that truths are easily come by or that success is guaranteed.

In psychoanalysis, through sympathetic identification clarified by countertransference awareness, this same self-critical capacity can facilitate our search after an understanding of our patients in their terms rather than our own. The complement of this self-critical receptive observation on the part of the analyst is the struggle for self-honesty in the analysand. The view that an analysis consists of a mutual construction by analyst and analysand of the analysand's life fails to do justice to this struggle. There are analysands who have been able to use the analytic process to discover more about themselves, to recover more of their past and find ways to reconcile themselves with it, than their analysts could comprehend. Fortunately for our profession and for our patients, the process that the analyst facilitates can yield for the analysand a degree of resolving self-knowledge and improved functioning that exceeds those of his analyst. There is a common human nature, although to be sure not in the form of an Aristotelian essence that exists in nature and awaits our better understanding. It is embodied in the lives lived by individuals. These individual lives are part of nature. They are there to be known, however difficult that may be. The self-honesty of an analysand in his realization that he feared his father because he wanted to murder him, or of an analysand in her realization that her frigidity and the pleasure she took in rape fantasies was caused by her wish to use intercourse to castrate the man, implies that these realizations correspond with real wishes that continue to influence the individual's life. Neither the pain of those realizations nor their beneficial effects of this self-knowledge can be accounted for by any other assumption. In the end, each person has only his own life to live, however shared with others.

At the core of the being of each person there is a solitude in which he is related to himself. Truth resides in this solitude to the extent that one can remember one's own past as it actually was. The ground of good analytic work in the analyst is his attitude of respect for this solitude.

The Importance of Truth in Clinical Psychoanalysis

A notion of truth that corresponds to reality is essential to psychoanalysis. Indeed, sometimes it is a matter of the utmost urgency to be able to ascertain what is true in reality. Consider, for instance, a situation I once experienced in treating one of my analysands. A borderline patient in his second year of analysis, a young professional man who had lost his first job on account of a pretentious insubordination out of envy, now a student in his professional field, came to his session beside himself with rage and threatening to kill an external examiner who had failed him. I quickly became aware of how badly I needed to be able to estimate, by the end of the session, his capacity to contain the rage that drove his wish to revenge the insult to his grandiosity and how much I needed to help him with this task during the session. The patient had, during periods of severe depression, told me of wanting to let the world know "that he was somebody" by committing a mass murder; he owned a substantial arsenal of guns and ammunition. I was painfully aware of how much I needed to know whether or not he was likely to carry out his threats and how difficult it would be to know. There were no self-evident certainties on which to rely, nor anything either absolutistic or naïve about my urgent search for understanding. I was alone with his urgent need for my help without having any clear idea of what might emerge that would make it possible for me to help him. I did not for a moment think that his enraged murderous threat was a co-creation of him by his analysis or that I had any interpretive access to it for that reason. And I was aware that I would not be able to know with the confidence I wanted to have how well my thinking about him corresponded with his reality and what confidence I could place in whatever interventions I could make before the end of the session. The crucial observation would be what would happen to his murderous rage; for that observation I had no alternative but to wait for what would unfold in the session. I had no acceptable choice but to give myself up to the task.

I concluded from his account of the damaging interview with the examining professor, punctuated and disorganized as it was by outpourings of vengeful rage and death threats, that there was some possibility that he had been neither passed nor failed but would be required to resubmit his work after dealing with criticisms. I was confident enough of this construction, despite the fear that it might be the product of my own wishful thinking, that I communicated it to him as something he might want to explore further. I was concerned about the risk if it should turn out not to be true. But at least it might buy time for further analytic work. I offered this reality testing in the context of interpreting to him the intensity of his rage in words that implicitly pointed to but did not explicitly mention the work of a phantasy of having been castrated. I had learned to link interpretations with tentative alternatives to his view of the reality of situations in which he found himself because of his difficulties with reality testing. Instead of interpreting his grandiosity or his castration anxiety directly, I interpreted his hurt pride (Ferenczi, 1952). These interpretations facilitated an encouraging sequence of associations toward the end of the session about his immigrant father, often the object of his derogating criticism, who he now acknowledged had had the "balls" to leave his homeland and try to make a go of it in a new country, even though it didn't work out very well for him. I hoped that he was letting me know that he too might have the balls to go back to his faculty and find out what really confronted him instead of carrying out his death threats. By the end of the session I observed a diminution in the frequency of his outbursts of indignant, narcissistic rage and sensed some reduction in their intensity. But he was by no means either calm or appeased. I was left with the anxiety-provoking question as to whether or not he could sustain this fragile improvement in self-mastery after the session.

I was confident enough of what I had seen and understood not to warn my colleague or inform the police because of my impression that my interpretations corresponded well enough to be heard and because they appeared to have had some, at least temporary, beneficial effect. I was not confident enough to sleep that night. Without more evidence that I could not have until the next few days, I was taking a risk. I believed that any other action on my part would very likely be ruinous to the analysis. He had previously gone through a period in which he believed that I was taping his sessions in order to inform the police. All of these perceptions, estimations, hopes, fears, and judgements were fallibly based on the evidence that became available during the session.

I was relieved and grateful for the efficacy of psychoanalytic interpretation, when my patient arrived the next morning and kept subsequent appointments with only rumblings of his rage and humiliation audible in his complaints of unfairness in a mood that was by no means calm but was sufficiently reconciled to his situation to abandon his threats of revenge and to get on with the tasks at hand. I was lucky that, as I had surmised, he had not been failed; there were some inadequacies in his work that required improvement for the examination to qualify him for his graduate degree. I could now be reasonably satisfied that the observations and the ideas that guided my actions corresponded well enough with the reality of my patient's psychic life to help him modify his narcissistic, violent rage. My satisfaction was chastened by my realization that I would probably have to become the object of my patient's murderous rage in the transference in order for it to be finally worked through (Hanly, 1998).

In my opinion, psychoanalysis works best when analysts employ all three criteria of truth according their strengths and limitations.

Note

1 I am grateful for the excellent editorial work Bradley Murray Ph.D. contributed to the preparation of this chapter.

References

Bradley, F. H. (1897). *Appearance and Reality*. London: Swan & Sonnenschein.

Dewey, J. (1918). *Logic: The Theory of Inquiry*. New York: Henry Holt.

Drake, S. (1978). *Galileo at Work: His Scientific Biography*. Chicago: University Chicago Press.

Ferenczi, S. (1913). Stages in the development of the sense of reality. In *First Contributions to Psycho-Analysis*. London: Hogarth Press, 1952, pp. 213–239.

Feyerabend, P. (1965). Problems of empiricism. In R. G. Colodny (Ed.), *Beyond the Edge of Certainty: Essays in Contemporary Science and Philosophy*. Englewood Cliffs, NJ: Prentice-Hall.

Freud, S. (1900). *The interpretation of dreams*. In *S.E.* 4. London: Hogarth Press.

Freud, S. (1905). Fragment of an analysis of a case of hysteria. In *S.E.* 7. London: Hogarth Press.

Freud, S. (1918). From the history of an infantile neurosis. In *S.E.* 17. London: Hogarth Press.

Goldberg, A. (1976). A discussion of the paper by C. Hanly and J. Masson, 'A critical examination of the new narcissism'. *The International Journal of Psychoanalysis*, *57*, 67–70.

Goldberg, A. (1988). *A Fresh Look at Psychoanalysis: The View from Self-Psychology*. Hillsdale: The Analytic Press.

Greenberg, J. and Mitchell, S. (1983). *Object Relations in Psychoanalytic Theory*. Cambridge, MA: Harvard University Press.

Habermas, J. (1971). *Knowledge and Human Interests* (J. J. Shapiro, Trans.). Boston: Beacon Press.

Hanly, C. (1990). The concept of truth in psychoanalysis. *International Journal of Psychoanalysis*, *71*, 375–383.

Hanly, C. (1998). Reflections on the analyst's self-disclosure. *Psychoanalytic Enquiry*, *18*, 550–565.

Hanly, C. (2006). Pragmatism, tradition and truth in psychoanalysis. *American Imago*, *63*, 261–282.

Hanly, C. (2009). On truth and clinical psychoanalysis. *International Journal of Psychoanalysis*, *90*, 363–373.

Hawking, S. (1988). *A Brief History of Time*. Toronto: Bantam Books.

James, W. (1907). *Pragmatism*. New York: Longmans.

Kant, I. (1950). *Immanuel Kant's Critique of Pure Reason* (N. K. Smith, Trans.). London: Macmillan (Original work published 1781).

Kuhn, T. S. (1970). *The Structure of Scientific Revolutions*. Second edition, Enlarged. Chicago: University Chicago Press.

Lyotard, J. F. (1979). *The Postmodern Condition: A Report on Knowledge* (G. Bennington and B. Massumi, Trans.). Manchester: Manchester University Press.

Merleau-Ponty, M. (1945). *Phenomenology of Perception* (C. Smith, Trans.). London: Routledge & Kegan Paul, 1962.

Peirce, C. (1903). *Complete Papers of Charles Sanders Peirce*. Vols. 1–8, Ed. C Hartshorne & P. Weiss. Cambridge, MA: Harvard University Press, 1966.

Putnam, H. (1981). *Reason, Truth and History*. Cambridge: Cambridge University Press.

Ricoeur, P. (1970). *Freud and Philosophy*. New Haven: Yale University Press.

Russell, B. (1945). *History of Western Philosophy*. London: Routledge, 1961.

Sartre, J.-P. (1943). *Being and Nothingness* (H. E. Barnes, Trans.). New York: Philosophical Library, 1956.

Spence, D. (1982a). *Narrative Truth and Historical Truth: Meaning and Interpretation in Psychoanalysis*. New York: W. W. Norton.

Spence, D. (1982b). Narrative truth and theoretical truth. *The Psychoanalytic Quarterly*, *51*, 43–69.

Stolorow, R. D. and Atwood, G. E. (1992). *Contexts of Being: The Intersubjective Foundations of Psychological Life*. Hillsdale, NJ: The Analytic Press.

Viderman, S. (1970). *La construction de l'espace analytique*. Paris: Denoel.

19

METAPHORS AND THE QUESTION OF TRUTH IN PSYCHOANALYTIC LANGUAGE

Tair Caspi[1]

Introduction

Philosophers have been engaged in a prolonged, controversial debate on the nature of scientific language (Bono, 1990; Hoffman, 1980). Leading trends of thought in western philosophy, such as empiricism and logical positivism, maintained that scientific language should be articulated with literal, univocal, precise, objective, factual terms (Hobbes, 1968 [1651]; Carnap, 1959). According to this view, whose roots can be traced back to Plato's ideas, using metaphors in argumentative philosophical discussions might mislead and lead us astray. However, a growing trend in contemporary metaphor research fiercely maintains that metaphors should not be excluded, as they hold an integral, essential function in scientific language and possess an open-ended quality that may actually contribute to the exploration of unknown domains (Boyd, 1993; Kuhn, 1993). Furthermore, it has been suggested that metaphors may even serve an explanatory function (Levy, 2020), which forms one of the main goals of scientific research.

The last decades have seen a growing interest in the status, legitimacy, place, and function of metaphors, as playing out in psychoanalytic language. The founders of psychoanalysis, Freud and later Klein, aspired to establish it as a scientific method and theory. In line with the prevailing positivist philosophy of that period, they conceived psychoanalytic concepts to reflect universal phenomenological facts and did not use the term 'metaphor' since metaphors were seen as mere fiction that might obscure the truth. Later, the founders of the following psychoanalytic theories, like Bion, Winnicott, Kohut, and others, strove to draw up universal truths that describe the human psyche. For them, the terms they coined introduced actual revelations that offered absolute truths rather than metaphors (Govrin, 2016). Many contemporary psychoanalysts, on the other hand, especially across the post-modern relational and intersubjective trends, believe that psychoanalytic concepts are actually alternating metaphors that do not represent ontological entities and objective facts (Ogden, 2001; Mitchel & Black, 1996). And indeed, explicit discussion of the concept of 'metaphor' is all but absent from classical psychoanalytic discourse but has found itself at home in contemporary postmodern psychoanalytic discourse. Contemporary metaphor research sees general agreement that psychoanalytic language tends to be metaphoric by essence but debates its merits and limitations in conceptualizing the human psyche (Borbely, 2011; Caspi, 2018; Enckell, 2002; Hopkins, 2000; Modell, 2003, 2009; Spence, 1987; Wallerstein, 2011; Wurmser, 2011).

DOI: 10.4324/9780429297076-23

This state of affairs raises serious epistemological worries. If psychoanalytic language indeed tends to use metaphors, can we rely on such knowledge that may be articulated in a vague and foggy manner? How can such fluid theoretical knowledge guide us during analytical work? Moreover, if psychoanalytic concepts are no more than alternating metaphors, as may follow from Nietzsche's (1954 [1873]) well-known definition of truth, what kind of stability, objectivity, and authority can be expected of psychoanalytic knowledge? It follows that the question at the heart of the present discussion is whether the metaphoric nature of psychoanalytic language is at odds with its ability to convey truth.

The discussion about metaphors and truth in psychoanalytic language involves three distinct polemics: the linguistic debate about metaphorical meaning and metaphorical truth; the philosophy of science controversy on metaphors' role and legitimacy in scientific language; and the psychoanalytic debate on metaphors' role and status in psychoanalytic language. Much has been written about each of the three, but surprisingly, their reciprocal links were largely overlooked. However, the mutual links between these debates hold immense importance because if psychoanalytic language is fundamentally metaphoric, as many contemporary psychoanalysts contend, and if there is an essential contradiction between metaphor and truth, it may then be inferred that the psychoanalytic body of knowledge lacks objectivity and stability. Such a radical conclusion, in effect, negates psychoanalysis as an investigative method, therapeutic method, and cohesive theory, and in my opinion it cannot be accepted.

I will argue that the view of metaphors in psychoanalytic lexicon as an unwelcome rhetorical configuration rests on a narrow reductionist view that sees metaphor as inevitably obscuring the truth. This earlier dismissive view of metaphors in psychoanalysis conceives truth solely according to the correspondence theory of truth. Contrary to this approach, a wider view that accepts the relevance and usefulness of multiple truth theories, such as correspondence, coherence, pragmatic, and so on, constitutes a much more apt and stable epistemological foundation for psychoanalytic language (Yadlin-Gadot, 2016). This kind of 'post-postmodern' epistemological infrastructure, which leaves room for multiple perspectives on truth while avoiding the relativism pitfall, may allow the innovative use of metaphors beyond clinical psychoanalysis, where it enjoys considerable general agreement. It may also allow the use of metaphors in the conceptual-theoretical dimension provided that we take into consideration their limitations.

As we shall see, contrary to the Platonic and empiricist perception of metaphor as a vibrant, suggestive configuration that diverts us away from the truth, theories that started developing in the latter half of the twentieth century pointed to metaphor's cognitive value and its power to expose truths that literal language cannot reveal (Black, 1962; Boyd, 1993; Hesse, 1966; Kuhn, 1993). Based on these post-positivist theories, my main argument goes that the metaphoric language of psychoanalysis holds the potential power to expose 'metaphorical truths' (as I later explain). Psychoanalysis requires the prolific use of metaphoric language in order to describe interpersonal and intersubjective unconscious and pre-verbal contents and processes. Such contents can often prove ineffable for literal language (Botella & Botella, 2005; Caspi, 2020; Frie, 1999). However, while formulating psychoanalytic theories, unlike in clinical work, the use of metaphors may hold limitations that should be taken into consideration. Theoretical metaphors may be vague and less accurate compared to literal speech; they do not lend themselves to empirical validation and hold potentially misleading persuasive power. Moreover, metaphors may lead to reification, the concretization of abstract concepts, which distorts meaning and causes conceptual blurriness (Wallerstein, 2006).

I will briefly discuss each polemic in the first three sections. In the fourth section, I will analyze the main issue of metaphors' relation to truth in psychoanalytic language. The final section will address the pros and cons of metaphors in theoretical psychoanalytic language. Finally, I will suggest a possible 'solution' to address the shortcomings involved in the use of metaphors in psychoanalytic conceptual language.

Metaphorical Meaning and Metaphorical Truth

'Metaphor' derives from Ancient Greek, with *meta* indicating 'above', 'over', or 'across', while *pherein* is 'to carry', combining to denote 'transference' or 'carrying over'. The trajectory of this sharing or transfer of meaning runs from a secondary subject – which linguists usually refer to as the vehicle – to a principal or primary subject, commonly referred to as 'the topic'. The shared ground of the metaphor includes those qualities of the topic and vehicle, which together form the essence of the figurative interpretation (Richards, 1936).

Philosophers of language have traditionally been interested in issues of meaning and truth, but until the mid-twentieth century, their main focus was literal language, while research into figurative language was largely confined to the peripheries of aesthetics and rhetoric (Stern, 2006). Vico (1999 [1725]) described metaphor as "being the most luminous, most necessary and most used" (p. 404). Nevertheless, "until Black's seminal paper 'Metaphor', metaphor had been largely ignored by analytic philosophy, largely due to the dominance of logical positivism during the preceding decades" (Reimer & Camp, 2006: 627). "Thinkers of those periods deemed metaphor cognitively insignificant, assuming as they did that, metaphors lacked the crucial criterion for meaningfulness: verification conditions" (Lycan, 2008: 177). According to Ayer (1946), the verification principle is a criterion of meaning which maintains that a sentence has literal meaning if the proposition it expresses is either analytic or empirically verifiable. Correspondence with reality, fact, or states of affairs is one possible answer – indeed the most plausible and common answer – to the question of how a sentence can be verified.

According to the correspondence theory of truth, "a belief, hypothesis, or idea is true to the extent that it corresponds with reality. The correspondence criterion of truth is a basic premise of common sense as well as of scientific and philosophical empiricism" (Hanly, 2009: 366). It follows, therefore, that logical positivists, too, viewed metaphorical speech as lacking cognitive content altogether because a metaphorical utterance has no reference in reality (Carnap, 1959; Stern, 2006). Metaphor, therefore, was dismissed as trivial to truth and knowledge and seen as a configuration that merely served to inspire feelings and images. However, with the publication of Black's interaction theory, arguing for metaphor's irreducible 'cognitive content', analytic philosophers began to turn their attention to metaphor. Black (1962) argued that metaphors were cognitively significant in ways that set them apart from the literal. Let us consider Black's example: "man is a wolf." He used it to clarify the metaphorical interaction mechanism whereby some features of the concept 'man' are transferred to the concept of 'wolf' and vice versa. In Black's words: "the wolf-metaphor suppresses some details, emphasizes others – in short, organizes our view of man" (p. 288). Taken literally, this utterance represents an absurdity because obviously, no man is a wolf. As metaphor cannot denote any real reference in the actual world, it falls short of the verification criterion. Nevertheless, I reckon that when using a metaphor, *one typically says something false in order to draw attention to something true.*

Since the mid-twentieth century, there has been an outpouring of scholarly papers on metaphors' workings and metaphorical meaning. Four main trends can be inspected in contemporary metaphor research (Reimer & Camp, 2006), but only one of them, represented by Donald Davidson and later by Richard Rorty, rejects the concept of metaphorical meaning and consequently metaphorical truth as well. The concept of 'metaphorical truth' means the truth of an utterance under its metaphorical interpretation (Stern, 2000: 351). The concept of 'metaphorical truth' does not mean that the truth of the sentence is metaphorical, but rather that the sentence, taken metaphorically, is true (Goodman, 1979).

Simile theories are the oldest, having their roots in the teachings of Aristotle. These theories hold that metaphor is an elliptically stated, figurative comparison or a simile. Aristotle suggested that metaphors were abbreviated similes of sorts. Accordingly, the truth of the metaphor is reduced to that of the simile (Fogelin, 2011). This theory attracted criticism, citing the fact that not all metaphors were translatable into simile form.

Following Black's interaction theory, the *semantic metaphor theories* trend (Beardsley, 1962; Boyd, 1993; Kittay, 1987; Kuhn, 1993; Richards, 1936) holds that metaphor results from the interaction of words brought together and acting on each other in the settings provided by particular utterances on particular concrete occasions. Accordingly, a metaphorical statement is an utterance in which some kind of tension is at play between the relevant ordinary meanings of its constituent words and phrases, a tension that is only relieved if one or more of these meanings change so as to be brought into harmony with the rest. The emergence of the cognitive sciences has led to the development of fertile theory within the semantic trend, referred to as conceptual metaphor theory (CMT). Lakoff and Johnson (1980, 1999), founders of CMT, argued that our conceptual world is mostly metaphoric because we operate, understand, think, and indeed live by metaphors. They posited that more than a mere speech configuration or linguistic ornament, metaphor is fundamental to language, thinking, and human experience. This theory holds metaphor to be the key to deep truths about the human conceptual system.

According to the semantic metaphor theories, the metaphorical truth involves the assignation of distinctively *metaphorical truth conditions* to sentences and distinctively metaphorical semantic values to some of the words and phrases that figure in these sentences. Therefore, metaphorical truth can be rehabilitated in the form of metaphorical propositional content (Hills, 2004). Further developments suggest a semantic metaphor theory that considers both its context dependence and literal dependence (Stern, 2008). According to Lakoff and Johnson (1999), metaphorical truth is embodied, as the mind is inherently embodied, rather than 'objectivist'. However, embodied truth, too, is not a purely subjective truth. We all hold pretty much the same embodied basic-level and spatial relations concepts, and therefore there will be an enormous range of shared 'truths'. Thus, the metaphorical concept 'containment' rests on the scheme of THE MIND IS A CONTAINER, which we universally perceive through embodied sensual knowledge.[2]

The *pragmatic theories* maintain that metaphors are a type of speaker meaning, in which a speaker says one thing in order to mean something else (Grice, 1975; Searle, 1993). Accordingly, metaphor's truth value is reduced to that of the proposition that the speaker intends to communicate. The pragmatic theories, unlike the semantic ones, place the context of use at the heart of metaphor's deciphering. Pragmatic criteria of truth differ from semantic truth conditions. Camp (2009) suggested that metaphor fosters insight by highlighting or foregrounding previously unconsidered meanings, a metaphorical quality that has great significance for the psychoanalytic endeavor. Concerning the present discussion, it is safe to conclude that all three metaphor research trends accept the concept of metaphorical truth, albeit defining it differently.[3]

The fourth trend of metaphor research – *the non-cognitivist theories* – posits that metaphors have no distinctive 'meaning' at all but simply cause certain distinctive effects among their hearers (Rorty, 1989). Donald Davidson (1978), the most prominent proponent of this perspective, has raised a very radical argument, whereby "metaphors mean what the words, in their most literal interpretation, mean, and nothing more" (p. 32). This argument can be seen as a direct extension of logical positivism's dismissive approach to metaphor. Davidson and Rorty agree that metaphors' effects are non-propositional but go on to conclude that metaphors have no distinctive meaning at all (other than literal meaning), on the grounds that the only genuine candidates for 'meaning' are truth-conditional, propositional contents. Put differently, Davidson denies metaphor a semantic dimension other than the one based on literal meanings. Davidson and Rorty do not question metaphor's effectiveness but deny its cognitive value, that metaphors can be understood or misunderstood, true or false.[4] This metaphor trend has been criticized on various grounds and is inconsistent with the intuition that metaphors are cognitively significant, understood or misunderstood; that metaphors figure in our reasoning and thought and can be true or false (Reimer & Camp, 2006).

I believe that metaphors run a gamut of roles in human thought and conceptualization and serve as powerful cognitive tools that allow us to enrich our communications and venture into new domains. This notion will be applied to the understanding of metaphors' workings in psychoanalysis in the following sections.

Metaphors in Science

Metaphors are used across scientific disciplines to formulate hypotheses, interpret scientific results, and propose new avenues of research. Metaphors provide scientists with ways to interpret, present, and manipulate data within particular scientific disciplines in interdisciplinary or extra-scientific contexts. Many contemporary philosophers of science and linguistics believe that metaphorical reasoning is an essential ingredient of doing science because the conceptual power of metaphors provides scientists with efficient, productive ways to interpret and explore natural phenomena and processes.

Nevertheless, as outlined before, metaphor was considered for centuries as no less than an enemy of truth exploration and was therefore excluded from philosophical and scientific discussions. Plato believed that figurative language could be used to distract from the truth due to its persuasive rhetorical power. Images were seen as inferior to truth and reality, as a precarious ground for argumentation and a mere secondary method of exploration. Therefore, one could not rely on metaphor when drawing inferences. Aristotle believed metaphors were appropriate for poetry but not as a reliable source of information (Johnson, 1981; Lloyd, 1996). Later, empiricists viewed metaphors as words employed not in their proper sense; their charm is likely to mislead. They believed that metaphors created an illusion and that relying on them led to absurd inferences. Therefore, metaphors were considered unsuitable for scientific deduction and the inquiry into truth (Hobbes, 1968 [1651]). During the scientific revolution, metaphors were perceived to "introduce inappropriate, not-literary meanings into science, contaminating [. . .] precise and stable meanings" (Bono, 1990: 62). As we have already seen, logical positivism and early analytic philosophy objected to the use of metaphoric language in scientific discourse and saw metaphors' role as an illustration, emphasis, or ornament.

Recent decades saw philosophers of science develop theories that elaborated on metaphor's unique contribution to scientific inquiry. Mary Hesse (1966) applied Black's theory to the philosophy of science, arguing that models, analogies, and metaphors were vital for scientific explanation and theorization. Metaphors and analogies are not appendices to theory, but rather essential to its development and expansion into new domains of phenomena. Metaphors could be used as means to drive scientific development of its previous course and onto a new one, using a combination of new terms in the language of a given theory or scientific discipline. The incorporation of metaphors into a theoretical system leads to a reorganization and results in a change to the present terms. Consequently, the models and analogies derived from these terms also undergo transformation. Hesse took a pioneering role in contributing to metaphor's renaissance against her predecessors.

Richard Boyd (1993) looked into the role played by metaphors in formulating scientific theories. He observed two types of metaphors: 'exegetical metaphors', which serve to teach and explain the theory and can be expressed with non-metaphorical means; and 'theory-constitutive metaphors', which create an "irreplaceable part of linguistic machinery of a scientific theory" and are essential in formulating new scientific theories (p. 486). These metaphors express insights that defy literal formulation, meaning that "their cognitive content cannot be made explicit" (p. 487). Constitutive metaphors allow to formulate a new terminology where no terms existed before. According to Boyd, theory-constitutive metaphors have an innovative potential power. They may contribute to science by allowing to develop new conceptual systems in an emerging field with no such system in place, an aspect that literal language cannot always provide.

Thomas Kuhn (1993) argued that scientific theories arranged the world at any given time by the period's state of knowledge. The 'world' is a set of congruencies shared by experience and language. The relations between language and the world are not defined once and for all; rather, they experience change. Our planet did not change its shape when they started referring to it as a 'sphere' or 'earth' in antiquity and medieval times; it was the scientific language that changed and shall continue to change. In this process, "metaphor plays an essential role in establishing links between scientific language and the world" (ibid., pp. 415–416). Kuhn suggested that a change of metaphor is also a change of worldviews. I believe that these theories can be usefully applied in the psychoanalytic discourse and help to establish the epistemological basis for metaphors' use in the psychoanalytic lexicon.

Metaphors in Psychoanalytic Language

The debate on metaphors' position in psychoanalytic language dates back to Freud, but it was only in the 1960s that it matured into a full-blown polemic. Freud and later on Klein insisted that the quest for truth was an inherent human tendency and a fundamental aim of the analytic treatment. Moreover, the quest for truth, according to the Kleinian perspective, is fundamental to human relatedness, especially deep intimate relationships (Roth, 2018). Freudian and Kleinian psychoanalysts are committed to a realist ontology and epistemology and accordingly, perceive truth in objective terms, separately from the observer's subjectivity (Bell, 2009). Accordingly, Freud, who found psychoanalysis' scientific status immensely important, believed that metaphors were replaceable and that scientific assumptions should be tentatively formulated (Freud, 1914: 77). He made ample use of metaphors and analogies such as 'the unconscious', 'repression', 'transference', and many other metaphoric concepts borrowed from a variety of semantic fields, including hydraulics, biology, mechanics, legal proceedings, archaeology, anthropology, mythology, history, classical, and popular literature (Brunner, 1995; Edelson, 1983; Hopkins, 2000; Wallerstein, 2011). Metaphors that draw on the fields of space and energy stand out, but Freud's repertoire of images spans an enormous range (Petrella, 2007). Many of these metaphors have entered common usage and come to constitute the terminology of psychoanalytic theory. According to Freud,

> In psychology, we can only describe things by the help of analogies. There is nothing peculiar in this; it is the case elsewhere as well. But we have constantly to keep changing these analogies, for none of them lasts long enough.
>
> *(Freud, 1926: 195)*

Thus, for example, the relations shared by ego and id were described as those shared by a horse and its rider. Later, this metaphor was replaced to describe the ego as 'poor' because "it serves three severe masters" (Freud, 1933: 77). Freud made liberal use of metaphors, as evidently emerges from his writings (Nash, 1962). In Freud's words:

> I see no necessity to apologize for the imperfections of this or of any similar imagery. [. . .] We are justified, in my view in giving free reign to our speculations so long as we retain the coolness of our judgment, and *do not mistake the scaffolding for the building.*
> *(Freud, 1900: 536; emphasis added)*

However, Freud's liberal use of metaphoric language in his theoretical conceptualizations, particularly in formulating the meta-psychology of his theory, attracted scathing criticism (Shafer, 1976; Spence, 1987). According to Nash (1962), Freud not only illustrated by metaphor; he also conceived in metaphor. He cited the anthropomorphic metaphors of Freud's later structural model as leading to confusion.[5] Hartmann (1959) posited that an occasional lack of caution in Freud's formulation of its propositions, coupled with his tendency to use striking metaphors, precipitated the accusation that psychoanalysis was anthropomorphizing its concepts. According to Hartmann, it is important to replace metaphors, as the use of metaphors may interfere with meaning. Hartmann further argued that the value of the metaphors employed by Freud should be weighed on the merit of each metaphor in itself by checking the analogy's compatibility with reviewable knowledge.[6]

Most of the commentators that have criticized metaphor's use in psychoanalytic language did not advocate the exclusion of metaphor per se but were critical of what may be described in cognitive metaphor theory terms as reckless metaphorical shifts, that is, the metaphorical mapping from the source domain into the target domain. For instance, Nagel (1959), an American philosopher of science, invested metaphors and analogies with great heuristic values. Nevertheless, he stressed that "in Freudian theory, metaphors are employed without even half-way *definite rules* for expanding them," and accordingly admitted metaphors such as "energy" or "level of excitation" had no specific content and could be filled in to suit one's fancy (p. 41; emphasis added). This may mislead and blur concepts' lines.

Indeed, the metaphorical shift may lead to concretization and reification, as evident in a literal reading of Klein's colorful descriptions of unconscious phantasy. In other psychoanalytic concepts, the metaphorical mapping may draw redundant features, which results in distortion of meaning. Thus, for instance, Freud's hydraulic and electrical metaphors created a misguided impression of scientific precision. I believe the criticism reviewed here can be addressed by the implementation of clear mapping criteria developed by cognitive sciences. The application of these criteria is intended to chart the proper metaphorical use as a possible 'solution' to the limitations inherent in metaphoric conceptualization. I will elaborate on this point in the final section.

From the 1970s onwards, the so-called metaphorical turn gradually gained traction in psychoanalytic discourse, while the voices of authors who endorsed the use of metaphors in psychoanalytic jargon became prominent. Accordingly, Wurmser (1977) fiercely contended in metaphors' defense, believing they should not be banished from psychoanalytic theory, as they were crucial in formulating and constituting it. According to him, "All science is the systematic use of metaphor. Its critical, self-conscious use as symbolic, not concrete, reality is an inevitable necessity of the scientific process" (p. 477). Wurmser argued that the criticism leveled at the use of metaphors in psychoanalysis drew on a radical empiricism philosophy, which erred to psychoanalysis. In the same vein, Wallerstein (1988) argued that metaphors were not problematic in clinical theory, as he found that they could be validated just like clinical facts; he was skeptical about the prospect of replacing metaphors from meta-theory. According to Wallerstein, the rhetorical voice was an essential part of psychoanalytic theory. He contended for the centrality of metaphors in it yet stressed the importance of making flexible use of metaphors and cautioned against conceptual blunders (Wallerstein, 2011).

The so-called metaphorical turn in psychoanalysis can be seen as part of the gradual epistemological transition. This process took place while psychoanalytic thought was gradually moving from a realistic epistemology, characteristic of Freud and Klein, to a subjective epistemology. Postmodern psychoanalysis stresses experiential, subjective, and pluralistic aspects of the self-concept rather than absolute objective truth. Postmodern psychoanalysis is largely predicated on a relativist epistemology, which posits pluralism and multiplicity of truths and language games, instead of the perception of a single, one-of-its-kind, objective truth (Mitchell, 1993; Ogden, 2016; Orange, 2003). Ogden (2001) argued that psychoanalytic concepts, including his own, constituted metaphors rather than absolute truths. He further argued that metaphors allowed access to the analysand's unconscious (Ogden, 1997).

I believe that metaphors are indispensable, both in clinical psychoanalysis and in theory formation, as we conceive and experience the world and ourselves through a complex system of conceptual metaphors. The dismissive attitude towards metaphors in psychoanalytic theory rests on a misguided assumption of an inevitable contradiction between metaphor and truth. In fact, metaphors in psychoanalytic conceptual language are by no means enemies of truth. Metaphors may reflect deep objective psychoanalytical facts and reveal unconscious truths, provided that their use is not reckless or reified and concretized.

Merits and Shortcomings of Metaphors in Psychoanalytic Language

In light of the three polemics outlined above, how can we understand metaphor's place and function in psychoanalytic language? From its inception, many of psychoanalysis' innovative concepts were constructed as metaphors. 'Transference', 'unconscious', 'superego', 'projection', and 'containment' are but some examples from the full gamut of psychoanalytical metaphors (Leary, 1990). In all of these examples, a metaphorical shift from the source domain into the target domain can be inspected. For example, the containment metaphor sees borrowed features originating in a concrete container (which may be strong, stable, little, etc.) into the mental sphere, where it describes the analyst's success or failure in tolerating the analysand powerful feelings, depending on the features of the analyst's mental container.

As we have seen, metaphors are not at all unique to psychoanalytic language, and in fact, scientific rhetoric is replete with metaphors even in hard sciences, with instances like 'light is a wave', 'electricity is a fluid', and many others. Hoffman (1980) shows that the best metaphors in science are those that spawn theoretical ponderings over many years, such as the metaphor of light as a 'wave' or a 'particle'. "In science," he writes, "one can latch upon a metaphor or intuitively appealing vision (e.g., waves) and ride the vision for years, or generations, trying to unpack its implications (e.g., Bohr equations, wave-particle dualities, etc.)" (p. 415).

However, within psychoanalytic language, metaphors stand out. Since psychoanalysis is concerned with the exploration of abstract psychical and intersubjective unconscious processes that are inaccessible to direct examination, psychoanalysis must rely on a wide range of metaphors and imagery in order to think, conceptualize and formulate the psychoanalytic glossary. Thus, metaphors in psychoanalysis are used to express deep, ineffable emotional truth and can serve to reveal the truth (Caspi, 2018; Frie, 1999).

Metaphor may serve as important cognitive tool that holds the potential power to explore uncharted domains. These tropes have an embodied, bodily experiential basis (Lakoff & Johnson, 1999), and therefore they may function as an important source of unconscious knowledge.

Metaphor may bridge between different aspects of the mind: Emotions and intellect, bodily physical sensations and 'high' cognitive properties, unconscious preverbal sensations and rational reasoning, primary processes, and secondary ones (Modell, 2003).

Metaphors hold profound merits not only in clinical psychoanalysis (Arlow, 1979; Ogden, 1997) but in theoretical conceptualization as well. The pictorial nature of many metaphors encourages imagining and enables the formulation of ineffable unconscious contents. The power of metaphor, according to Black (1993), lies in the prospect of reorganizing categories that concern the world. Thus, metaphors may innovatively reveal ideas and emotions. An apt and generative metaphor enables us to introduce questions that were unthinkable before this metaphor was formulated. And indeed, many psychoanalytic metaphorical concepts allow us to reveal pioneering contributions and facilitate the exploration of new psychoanalytic domains. For instance, the 'transitional space' metaphor, coined by Winnicott, allows to explore a previously uncharted human experience. In this sense, metaphors are associated with the recognition of new epistemic phenomena (see, Black, 1993). Other metaphorical concepts in psychoanalytic language are not brand new, and yet they manage to rearrange our knowledge afresh and thus may acquire a new fundamental and creative meaning. The 'unconscious' concept, for example, is no Freudian invention, since many philosophers were ahead of him in employing it; however, he instilled it with new, innovative meanings, which came to underpin his psychoanalysis.

Metaphors promote conceptual reasoning and even enable scientific explanations. Figurative language serves a significant role when it comes to expressing affects, especially deep unconscious contents that we deal with in psychoanalysis.

Psychoanalysis has developed a remarkably rich language, made of a complex network of theories and concepts that serve to describe the human mind. The extensive psychoanalytic lexicon comprises sub-lexicons that originated across different psychoanalytic schools: Freudian lexicon, Kleinian lexicon, Winnicottian lexicon, and so on (Govrin, 2016). I believe that the different psychoanalytic sub-lexicons rely on different epistemology and meta-psychology, which involve different conceptions of truth. The different epistemes of each sub-lexicon offer a changing array of metaphors. Nevertheless, variant epistemes may coexist rather than exclude one another during analysis, in a manner that leaves room for exploration and self-understanding.

Yadlin-Gadot (2016) defined six paradigmatic notions of truth: correspondence, ideal, subjective, intersubjective, coherence, and pragmatic. Each of the specified truths is embedded in certain epistemic premises. Thus, the correspondent truth reflects a realistic epistemology that allows the comparison of statements and facts. The ideal truth is embedded in an objective-idealistic epistemology that posits the existence of ideal, mind-independent forms. Subjective idealistic epistemology is based on subjective and intersubjective truths. Coherent truth exists in both objective and subjective idealistic epistemologies. The pragmatic truth exists within the experiential realm and the confines of perceived external reality.

It follows that metaphors in psychoanalytic lexicon reflect the multiple truths conceptions cohabiting our inner world and are apt for describing the dynamic nature of the world. Psychoanalytic discourse is based on multiple epistemologies within which each epistemology may allow us to determine whether a statement or belief is true or false (Yadlin-Gadot, 2017). This multiplicity encompasses the anchor of objective truth concept, which is essential in constituting meaning and establishing clear and sound psychoanalytic knowledge (Mills, 2014). The correspondence theory of truth is vital to assess metaphors that deal with the connection between internal and external reality. Thus, in order to evaluate the truthfulness of the metaphor of 'projection' in a specific clinical context, the analyst has to take into consideration the relation between the emotion expressed by the analysand and the reality 'out there'. On other occasions, the analyst may wonder whether what the analysand had just told him really occurred or did they hallucinate it. Or else, the analyst must take into his clinical consideration the question of whether a child has really been abused at home and whether it should be reported or are we dealing with a frightening unconscious phantasy. Without considering the objective reality, the analyst is unable to locate himself in the right position toward his patient's discourse, and in fact, the analyst may make serious mistakes.

Nevertheless, the correspondence theory of truth cannot in itself provide the sole appropriate epistemological basis for all psychoanalytic metaphors because many metaphorical concepts cannot be validated by this theory. For instance, in order to order to evaluate the truthfulness of a common metaphoric conceptualization such as 'the patient suffers from a lacuna in his superego', it is appropriate to use the coherence conception of truth. This truth notion determines truth-values by examining the compatibility of a given belief with a whole system of beliefs. Accordingly, there may be more than one true description of the world. The application of this truth conception to the above-mentioned example allows us to examine how the different parts of the superego of that patient relate one to another and whether they constitute a coherent and integrated system. When a patient talks about his obsessive ritual system, the main question is not whether it corresponds to reality. Obviously, the patient is very much aware of the fact that those rituals do not serve any kind of realistic defense against whatever frightens or bothers him. Actually, the practice of these rituals may cause the patient deep suffering. So, the relevant questions may be, what is the emotional defensive function of the rituals, is it effective in anxiety reduction, and if so, how does it enable this effect? Moreover, the analyst may wonder what place this symptom takes in relation to his introjected object relations and so forth. In order to consider these aspects, the coherence notion of truth is much more apt and effective.

To evaluate the metaphorical conceptualization of the 'subjugating third' – Thomas Ogden's term – one needs to resort to what Yadlin-Gadot has called the "intersubjective notion of truth." The 'subjugating third' is a specific form of projective identification in which "the individual subjectivities of analyst and analysand [. . .] are subsumed in (subjugated by) the newly created analytic third" (Ogden, 1994: 9). So, in order to assess whether the intersubjective analytical space has indeed collapsed, we need the intersubjective notion of truth. The subjective notion of truth is needed to assess the truthfulness of a patient's metaphor describing for example, "holes in his 'self' sense." In this example, what Spence (1982) has termed 'historical truth' is not appropriate. Rather, what he called 'narrative truth' can provide the relevant frame of reference to appreciate the patient's self-sense. The pragmatic notion of truth concerns the utility and practicality of an idea in the context of the believer's life. Thus, theory-constitutive metaphors are productive and useful (Bono, 1990; Boyd, 1993). For example, the metaphor 'transference' transcends paradigms, endures over time, and allows the steady creation and emanation of creative theoretical and clinical thought. This concept remains soundly in place despite the turnover of paradigms over more than a century since Freud first coined it.

I believe that metaphorically constructed psychoanalytical concepts may reflect deep unconscious metaphorical truths. Many metaphors of psychoanalytic theory, like 'unconscious', 'transitional space', 'projective identification', 'containment', and others, play a constitutive theoretical function (Boyd, 1993). They cannot be verified, but they may convey metaphorical truth that pertains to the deep unconscious contents and processes of the mind, contents that may be beyond the reach of literal language. Metaphorical truth is not about the language-world compatibility (correspondence of truth); rather, it should be understood in deeper, broader intersubjective terms. The metaphorical truth is not delivered once and for all. Rather, the truthfulness of metaphorical concepts is judged based on their coherence within the paradigm limits (Kuhn, 1993). Metaphorical truth, in my opinion, is a truth concept that is dependent on context and on the circumstances under which a metaphor is being used as can be inspected from the very brief clinical examples appearing above.

Nevertheless, we must also take into consideration the shortcomings of metaphor's use. Theoretical metaphors in psychoanalysis may be vague and less accurate compared with literal speech; they are inaccessible to empirical validation and possess a potentially misleading persuasive power. Metaphors may carry redundant borrowed features that are likely to give a wrong impression; that is, Freud's energetic and physiochemical metaphors that produce the illusion of scientific precision. Moreover, metaphors may lead to reification, concretization of abstract concepts (Wallerstein, 2006). Wittgenstein (1953) believed that words might bewitch our thoughts and that the picture held in a word could lead to concretization and essentialist thinking. This may hinder our understanding of the emotional truth during therapy. In Wittgenstein's words: "A picture held us captive. And we could not get outside it, for it lay in our language and language seemed to repeat it to us inexorably" (Wittgenstein, 1953: § 115).

I would like to suggest a framework for a possible 'solution' to the shortcomings of metaphors in the psychoanalytic lexicon by implementing several mapping principles. Gentner and Jeziorski (1993) have identified the mapping principles that informed analogies in contemporary western science. They argued that a scientific analogy demonstrates a specific manner of knowledge mapping from the source domain into the target domain. Accordingly, ideal contemporary scientific reasoning includes several mapping principles: (1) structural consistency in interpreting an analogy, that is, people seek to put the objects of the source domain in one-to-one correspondence with the objects of the target so as to obtain the maximal structural match; (2) relational focus, in which relational systems are preserved and object descriptions are disregarded; (3) systematicity of mapping; (4) no extraneous associations; only commonalities strengthen an analogy; (5) no mixed analogies; the relational network to be mapped should be contained within one base domain; when two bases are used, they each convey a coherent system; and (6) An analogy is not causation (ibid., pp. 448–451).

Let us now examine how one of the most fundamental metaphorical concepts of psychoanalysis – the unconscious – meets Gentner and Jeziorski's criteria. Freud's (1915) topographical model conceptualizes the parts of the mind in terms of a spatial metaphor, where the unconscious is the 'lower' part, with the preconscious placed 'above' it, while the conscious is 'placed' at the 'top', dwelling in daylight. Using an eye-opening metaphor, Freud poses a groundbreaking idea, whereby unconscious, wild, primeval ideas play a dominant role in managing the individual's mental life, to a large degree dictating their feelings and conscious, manifest behavior. The spatial metaphor allows Freud to offer a new understanding of mental processes in a palpable, experiential manner.

This well-known metaphor compares the structure of the psyche to an iceberg, demonstrating that just as it is only the tip that is visible, while the bulk lies hidden under the ocean surface, so do consciousness and the contents accessible to it constitute only a small part of man's inner world, while the unconscious contains the bulk of it.[7]

In Lakoff and Johnson's terms (1980), the spatial metaphor of the topographical model sees a twofold mapping. First, the spatial source domain 'up–down' maps the target domain of 'consciousness' based on the KNOWN IS UP; UNKNOWN IS DOWN scheme. The higher the psychic part is 'located' metaphorically, the higher the level of consciousness it signifies. At the same time, this conceptual metaphor maps the 'consciousness' concept with the concept of 'light'. The more lit (and higher) the psychic part, the more conscious it is based on the CONSCIOUSNESS IS ILLUMINATION scheme. The scheme that ties light and consciousness or reason runs deep into culture, and Freud employs it to clarify the map of the psyche.

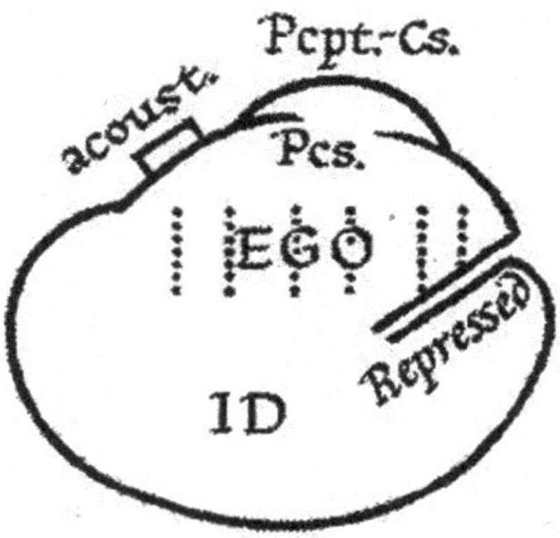

Figure 19.1 Freud's structural model of the mind (Freud, 1923: 24)

The unconscious concept relies on a clear, systematic, organized, and coherent mapping between the source domain 'up-down' and the target domain 'consciousness', in a manner that fits the perception of scientific analogy and meets Gentner and Jeziorski's criteria. This analogy carries no extraneous associations and does not inform causality between source and target domain. The same applies to the mapping between source domain 'light-dark' and target domain 'consciousness'.[8] The application of these principles may help to address the criticism leveled at metaphors' use in psychoanalytic lexicon, allowing them to offer a possible 'solution'.

Freud's concept of the unconscious works as a theory-constitutive metaphor (Boyd, 1993). It remained a fundamental concept to psychoanalytic thinking across different schools and therapeutics methods that were developed following Freud. Even after psychoanalysis had grown into a mature discipline, the unconscious concept remained in intensive, productive use.

I believe that the more successfully a metaphor meets the criteria of consistent systematic and coherent metaphorical mapping, the higher its chances of becoming a meaningful, useful, and stable concept that carries a sound metaphorical truth in psychoanalysis. Metaphors are no scaffolding that can be easily removed from the psychoanalytic language, as Freud believed (1900: 536). Rather, many metaphors form vital milestones in the constitution of psychoanalytic language. Furthermore, the psychoanalytic language in theory and practice rests on multiple truth conceptions embedded in the wide range of truth theories. It emerges from the present discussion that a seventh truth axis can be suggested as an addition to the paradigms outlined above (Yadlin-Gadot), that is, the metaphorical truth axis. As I have shown, metaphorical truth has unique qualities and is essential for deep analytical unconscious work. The metaphorical truth axis can compatibly co-exist with other truth axes. The rich psychoanalytic lexicon encompasses many metaphors, reflecting multiple truths perspectives, which are vital for the psychoanalytic endeavor.

Notes

1 I would like to thank Tamas Pataki for his illuminating comments and valuable suggestions.
2 Lakoff and Johnson (1980) write conceptual metaphors with capital letters to distinguish them from other kinds of metaphoric expressions. This term denotes the understanding of one idea, or conceptual domain, in terms of another.
3 Importantly, some pragmatic theories do not accept the concept of metaphorical truth, for example, the Relevant Theory of Deirdre Wilson and Dan Sperber.

4 Although Davidson (1978) denies the very motivation for other theories of metaphor and the problem of metaphorical truth of sentences, he nevertheless allows some kind of metaphorical truth (p. 39).
5 Anthropomorphization is a form of figurative language. It means to ascribe human form or attributes to an animal, plant, material object, etc.
6 According to Aristotle, analogies are metaphors of a kind; see *Poetics*, 1457b (in Aristotle, 1987).
7 Freud borrowed the iceberg metaphor from Gustav Fechner, professor of physics, philosophy, and medicine, who introduced an experimental approach to the study of the unconscious (Auchincloss, 2015: 43).
8 For further discussion on the analysis of the unconscious concepts with CMT principles, see Hopkins (2000).

References

Aristotle (1987). *The Poetics of Aristotle.* Halliwell S., translator and commentary. London: Duckworth.

Arlow, J. A. (1979). Metaphor and the psychoanalytic situation. *The Psychoanalytic Quarterly*, 48: 363–385.

Auchincloss, E. L. (2015). *The Psychoanalytic Model of the Mind.* Washington, DC and London: American Psychiatric Publishing.

Ayer, A. J. (1936). *Language, Truth and Logic.* New York: Oxford University Press, 1946.

Beardsley, M. (1962). The metaphorical twist. *Philosophy and Phenomenological Research*, 22(3): 293–307.

Bell, D. (2009). Is truth an illusion? Psychoanalysis and postmodernism. *International Journal of Psychoanalysis*, 90(2): 331–345.

Black, M. (1962). *Models and Metaphors.* Ithaca, NY: Cornell University Press.

Black, M. (1993). More about metaphor. In Ortony, A. (Ed.), *Metaphor and Thought*, 19–41. Cambridge: Cambridge University Press.

Bono, J. (1990). Science, discourse, and literature. The role/rule of metaphor in science. In Peterfreund, S. (Ed.), *Literature and Science. Theory and Practice*, 59–89. Boston: Northeastern University Press.

Borbely, A. F. (2011). Metaphor and metonymy as the basis of a new psychoanalytic language. *Psychoanalytic Inquiry*, 31(2): 159–171.

Botella, C. and Botella, S. (2005). *The Work of Psychic Figurability: Mental States without Representation.* New York: Routledge.

Boyd, R. (1993). Metaphor and theory change: What is 'metaphor' a metaphor for? In Ortony, A. (Ed.), *Metaphor and Thought*, 481–532. Cambridge: Cambridge University Press.

Brunner, J. (1995). *Freud and the Politics of Psychoanalysis.* Oxford: Blackwell Publishers.

Camp, E. (2009). Two varieties of literary imagination: Metaphor, fiction and thought experiments. *Midwest Studies in Philosophy*, 33: 107–130.

Carnap, R. (1959). Psychology in physical language. In Ayer, A. J. (Ed.), *Logical Positivism.* New York: Free Press.

Caspi, T. (2018). Towards psychoanalytic contribution to linguistic metaphor theory. *International Journal of Psychoanalysis*, 99: 1186–1211.

Caspi, T. (2020). *Metaphors in Psychoanalysis: Reflecting on the Language of Klein, Winnicott and Ogden.* Tel-Aviv: Resling Publishing (Hebrew).

Davidson, D. (1978). What metaphors mean. *Critical Inquiry*, 5: 31–47.

Edelson, J. T. (1983). Freud's use of metaphor. *Psychoanalytic Study of the Child*, 38: 17–59.

Enckell, H. (2002). *Metaphor and the Psychodynamic Functions of the Mind.* Doctoral dissertation. Kopio, Finland: Kuopion Yliopisto.

Fogelin, R. J. (2011). *Figuratively Speaking.* Oxford and New York: Oxford University Press.

Freud, S. (1900). *The Interpretation of Dreams*, SE 4:1–338, SE 5:339–621.

Freud, S. (1914). *On Narcissisms*, SE 14:73–102.

Freud, S. (1915). *The Unconscious*, SE 14:166–204.

Freud, S. (1923). *The Ego and the Id*, SE 19:3–66.

Freud, S. (1926). *The Question of Lay Analysis*, SE 20:177–258.

Freud, S. (1933). *New Introductory Lectures on Psycho-Analysis*, SE 22:3–158.

Freud, S. (1953–1974). *The Standard Edition of the Complete Psychological Works of Sigmund Freud.* J. Strachey, ed. and trans. London: Hogarth Press (in text reference: SE).

Frie, R. (1999). Psychoanalysis and the linguistic turn. *Contemporary Psychoanalysis*, 35(4): 673–697.

Gentner, D. and Jeziorski, M. (1993). The shift from metaphor to analogy in western science. In Ortony, A. (Ed.), *Metaphor and Thought*, 447–480. Cambridge: Cambridge University Press.

Goodman, N. (1979). Metaphor as moonlighting. *Critical Inquiry*, 6(1): 125–130.
Govrin, A. (2016). *Conservative and Radical Perspectives on Psychoanalytic Knowledge: The Fascinated and the Disenchanted*. New York: Routledge/Taylor and Francis Group.
Grice, P. (1975). Logic and conversation. In Cole, P. and Morgan, J. (Eds.), *Syntax and Semantics*, Vol. 3. New York: Academic Press.
Hanly, C. (2009). On truth and clinical psychoanalysis. *International Journal of Psychoanalysis*, 90(2): 363–373.
Hartmann, H. (1959). Psychoanalysis as a scientific theory. In Hook, S. (Ed.), *Psychoanalysis, Scientific Method and Philosophy*, 3–37. New York: NY University Press.
Hesse, M. (1966). The explanatory function of metaphor. In *Models and Analogies in Science*. Notre Dame, IN: University of Notre Dame Press.
Hills, D. (2004). *The Pleasure of Ulteriority: Four Essays on Verbal Metaphor*. Dissertation. Princeton: Princeton University Press.
Hobbes, T. (1651). *Leviathan, or the Matter, Forme, and Power of Common-Wealth Ecclesiastical and Civil*. London: Crooke, 1968.
Hoffman, R. R. (1980). Metaphor in science. In Honeck, R. P. and Hoffman, R. R. (Eds.), *Cognition and Figurative Language*, 393–423. Hillsdale, NJ: Lawrence Erlbaum Associates.
Hopkins, J. (2000). Psychoanalysis, metaphor, and the concept of the mind. In Levine, M. (Ed.), *The Analytic Freud*, 11–35. London: Routledge.
Johnson, M. (1981). *Philosophical Perspectives on Metaphor*. Minneapolis: University of Minneapolis Press.
Kittay, E. (1987). *Metaphor: Its Cognitive Force and Linguistic Structure*. Oxford: Oxford University Press.
Kuhn, T. S. (1993). Metaphor in science. In Ortony, A. (Ed.), *Metaphor and Thought*, 533–542. Cambridge: Cambridge University Press.
Lakoff, G. and Johnson, M. (1980). *Metaphors We Live By*. Chicago, IL: Chicago University Press.
Lakoff, G. and Johnson, M. (1999). *Philosophy in the Flesh: The Embodied Mind and its Challenge to Western Thought*. New York, NY: Basic Books.
Leary, D. E. (1990). Psyche's muse: The role of metaphor in the history of psychology. In Leary, D. E. (Ed.), *Metaphors in the History of Psychology*, 1–78. Cambridge: Cambridge University Press.
Levy, A. (2020). Metaphor and scientific explanation. In Levy, A. and Godfrey-Smith, P. (Eds.), *The Scientific Imagination: Perspectives from Philosophy and Psychology*. Oxford: Oxford University Press.
Lloyd, G. E. R. (1996). *Aristotelian Explorations*. Cambridge: Cambridge University Press.
Lycan, W. G. (2008). *Philosophy of Language: A Contemporary Introduction*. New York and London: Routledge.
Mills, J. (2014). Truth. *Journal of the American Psychoanalytic Association*, 62(2): 267–293.
Mitchell, S. A. (1993). *Hope and Dread in Psychoanalysis*. New York: Basic Books.
Mitchell, S. A. and Black, M. J. (1996). *Freud and Beyond: A History of Modern Psychoanalytic Thought*. New York: Basic Books.
Modell, A. H. (2003). *Imagination and the Meaningful Brain*. Cambridge, MA: The MIT Press.
Modell, A. H. (2009). Metaphor – the bridge between feelings and knowledge. *Psychoanalytic Inquiry*, 29: 6–11.
Nagel, E. (1959). Methodological issues in psychoanalytic theory. In Hook, S. (Ed.), *Psychoanalysis, Scientific Method and Philosophy*, 38–56. New York: NY University Press.
Nash, H. (1962). Freud and metaphor. *Archives of General Psychiatry*, 7: 25–29.
Nietzsche, F. W. (1873). On truth and lie in an extra-moral sense. In Kaufmann, W. (Ed.), *The Portable Nietzsche*, 42–47. New York: The Viking Press, 1954.
Ogden, T. H. (1994). *Subjects of Analysis*. Northvale, NJ and London: Jason Aronson.
Ogden, T. H. (1997). Reverie and metaphor: Some thoughts on how I work as a psychoanalyst. *International Journal of Psychoanalysis*, 78: 719–732.
Ogden, T. H. (2001). *Conversations at the Frontier of Dreaming*. Northvale, NJ: Aronson.
Ogden, T. H. (2016). On language and truth in psychoanalysis. *Psychoanalytic Quarterly*, 85(2): 411–426.
Orange, D. M. (2003). Why language matters to psychoanalysis. *Psychoanalytic Dialogues*, 13: 77–103.
Petrella, F. (2007). Freud's style terminology, metaphor and textual strategies in the works of Sigmund Freud. *The Italian Psychoanalytic Annual*, 1: 107–129.
Reimer, M. and Camp, E. (2006). Metaphor. In Lepore, E. and Smith, B. (Eds.), *The Oxford Handbook of Philosophy of Language*. Oxford: Oxford University Press.
Richards, I. A. (1936). *The Philosophy of Rhetoric*. Oxford: Oxford University Press.
Rorty, R. (1989). *Contingency, Irony, and Solidarity*. Cambridge: Cambridge University Press.
Roth, M. (2018). True love as the love of truth. *Psychoanalytic Perspective*, 15(2): 186–198.
Schafer, R. (1976). *A New Language for Psychoanalysis*. New Haven: Yale University Press.

Searle, J. R. (1993). Metaphor. In Ortony, A. (Ed.), *Metaphor and Thought*, 83–111. Cambridge: Cambridge University Press.

Spence, D. P. (1982). *Narrative Truth and Historical Truth: Meaning and Interpretation in Psychoanalysis*. New York: Norton.

Spence, D. P. (1987). *The Freudian Metaphor: Toward Paradigm Change in Psychoanalysis*. New York: Norton & Company.

Stern, J. (2000). *Metaphor in Context*. Cambridge, MA and London: The MIT Press.

Stern, J. (2006). Figurative language. In Devitt, M. and Hanley, R. (Eds.), *The Blackwell Guide to the Philosophy of Language*, pp. 168–185. Oxford: Blackwell Publishing Ltd.

Stern, J. (2008). Metaphor, semantics, and context. In Gibbs, R. (Ed.), *Metaphor and Thought*, 262–279. Cambridge: Cambridge University Press.

Vico, G. (1725). *The New Science*. Marsh, D., translator. London: Penguin, 1999.

Wallerstein, R. S. (1988). One psychoanalysis or many? *International Journal Psychoanalysis*, 69: 5–21.

Wallerstein, R. S. (2006). The relevance of Freud's psychoanalysis in the 21st century. *Psychoanalytic Psychology*, 23(2): 302–326.

Wallerstein, R. S. (2011). Metaphor in psychoanalysis: Bane or blessing? *Psychoanalytic Inquiry*, 31: 90–106.

Wittgenstein, L. (1953). *Philosophical Investigations*. Anscombe, G.E.M., Hacker, P.M.S., and Schulte, J. (Eds.). Oxford: Wiley Blackwell, 2009.

Wurmser, L. (1977). A defense of the use of metaphor in analytic theory formation. *Psychoanalytic Quarterly*, 46: 466–498.

Wurmser, L. (2011). Metaphor as conflict, conflict as metaphor. *Psychoanalytic Inquiry*, 31: 107–125.

Yadlin-Gadot, S. (2016). *Truth Matters: Theory and Practice in Psychoanalysis*. Leiden and Boston: Brill Publishers.

Yadlin-Gadot, S. (2017). On multiple epistemologies in theory and practice: A response to Jon Mills's "challenging relational psychoanalysis: A critique of postmodernism and analyst self-disclosure". *Psychoanalytic Perspectives*, 14: 341–345.

20

FACTS AND SENSIBILITIES

What Is a Psychoanalytic Innovation?

Aner Govrin

Psychoanalytic innovation is easy to recognize but difficult to define. There is a dearth of literature exploring the nature of innovation in our field. My main thesis is that psychoanalytic innovation can be of two types. Psychoanalytic innovation of the first order is about new discoveries concerning facts related to the psyche, development, transference relations, or psychopathology. It usually emerges as a development of insights from canonical psychoanalytic theory; offers an original explanation for a choice of empirical psychic phenomena hitherto unexamined; is perceived as creative and useful when it succeeds to reconceptualize the relations between the patient's past, unconscious dynamics, and the transference relations; often resembles poetic expression; and registers a truth we knew but did not yet put into words. When it is of the second order, psychoanalytic innovation challenges either methodological or philosophical assumptions held by psychoanalysis, without pretending to replace existing theories. It constitutes a "sensibility" that its adherents strive to incorporate into the existing corpus. I distinguish between two types of sensibilities: cultural-philosophical sensibility represented by the relational approach; and methodological sensibility represented by infant research, and neuropsychoanalysis. In the last part of the paper I analyze psychoanalytic progress pointing to its merits and shortcomings.

The Problem

Does psychoanalysis progress? And, if so, what does progress in our field mean? Can we find regularities in the last decades of this progress?

Understanding innovation in our field is challenging. On the one hand, psychoanalysis is in constant flux: Those who currently understand their patients according to Freud's original topographic and structural model are few and far between; members of the professional communities inspired by Klein or Kohut do not work in the same way as their predecessors. Even our understanding of fundamental psychoanalytic concepts such as the unconscious, interpretation, object relations, transference, and countertransference has grown extremely varied.

On the other hand, the past remains extremely influential: The twentieth century's grand theories are more dominant than any current development. No new school of thinking including a novel developmental theory, therapy, or psychopathology has emerged since the 1980s (for definition of a psychoanalytic school, see Govrin, 2006). Most current innovations are reinterpretations of old, canonical texts.

DOI: 10.4324/9780429297076-24

The most read and cited papers are by psychoanalysts who are no longer alive. Psychoanalysts representing different approaches continue to work in a way that does not stray far from Freud's method: together with the patient they create a narrative hinging on the latter's early development and transference relations. It is therefore practically impossible to distinguish between old and new.

First-Order and Second-Order Questions

We may subdivide the development of psychoanalysis after Freud into two periods. In the first four decades after Freud's death, there is a downpour of new and rich theories about the human psyche: Klein, Lacan, Winnicott, Bion, Mahler, Hartman, Kernberg, and others. We can call this the, second, "silver era" of psychoanalysis, coming after Freud's groundbreaking work. They focus on other psychic phenomena, have a different understanding of the transference relations, focus on other psychopathologies, and redraw the map of child development. They see themselves mainly as continuers, part of a line starting with Freud, rather than as revolutionaries, and they either compete with each other in terms of their adherence to Freud (Klein, Freud, Hartman) or work hard to show that they continue his theory in some way but differ in others (Kohut, Winnicott).

During this period, there is no declared change in philosophical and methodological assumptions. Clinical practice is revolutionary and seething with debate, but the methodological foundation stays as it was: it relies on clinical psychoanalytic observation in the development and construction of psychoanalytic theory. The prevailing truth is correspondence with reality, i.e., realism: The therapist is the authority; the distinction between subject and object remains in place; and developmental theories and psychic structures are considered mental realities rather than useful metaphors.

In this domain, debates are like those between scientists: Are the assumptions underlying the innovation valid or can they be refuted?

The arrival of postmodernism signals a breaking point and ushers in the third era. Self-psychology, in the 1980s, is the last major psychoanalytic school, or Grand theory, a mega narrative that encompass all mental phenomena.

From this point onward, there are two types of questions that analysts deal with: second and first order. The already existing schools of Lacan, Bion, Klein, and Winnicott continue to find explanations to first-order questions. They develop within the existing schools the meaning of psychic occurring such as envy, anxiety, sexuality, the unconscious, psychopathology, and transference phenomena (for a description of innovations of each school, see Govrin and Mills, 2019).

Second order claims are made about knowledge itself. If psychic phenomena involve first-order empirical questions about the substantive entities of the "mental", second-order questions concern the internal consistency, the methodology, or the epistemology on which first-order questions rely (Laudan, 1977). Why are there slips of the tongue is a first-order empirical question, the "fact" that it reveals an unconscious thought is a first-order explanation. However, what is the best way to validate our explanation about slips of tongue is a second order question. Note that the first-order question such as "why are there slips of the tongue?" is independent of its explanation. It does not need to be phrased in a psychoanalytic jargon. It is inseparable from Freud's repression theory, and therefore, it is not theory-laden. The importance of the difference between first-order questions and theories (explanations) which attempt to solve them will be elaborated later (see also Laudan, 1977, pp. 139–146).

During the last decade, a few psychoanalytic communities incorporate other fields of knowledge to create new sensibilities that deal with second-order questions. There are two kinds of sensibilities: Methodological sensibilities which are scientifically oriented and present a new source of information and methodology. Currently, there are at least two types of methodological sensibilities: Neuropsychoanalysis derives from brain research and infant research which incorporates finding from infant studies to the psychoanalytic encounter (mentalization-based therapy is also a methodological sensibility). The other type is a cultural-philosophical sensibility. It is influenced by changes in society, culture, and philosophy. It adapts psychoanalysis to the changing world. Since the 1990s, this sensibility can be observed in the relational approach, which was inspired by postmodernism, contemporary feminist thinking, and intersubjectivity. Neither of the three sensibilities are meant to be new psychoanalytic schools or alternative psychoanalytic theories. Nevertheless, they do want analysts to be sensitive to aspects of the psychoanalytic encounter that they argue were overlooked. Of the three sensibilities, the relational approach was the most influential with thousands of practitioners joining and establishing a worldwide organization that basically supported a transformation in how analysts perceive the analytic encounter and the analyst's subjectivity.

In this paper, I investigate innovations in first- and second-order questions. But let us begin with some preliminary remark.

I discuss psychoanalysis in general, even though it is far from being monolithic (English-speaking psychoanalysis is quite different from French or Latin-American psychoanalysis, not to speak about the variety of schools – Freudians, Lacanians, Millerians, Winnicottians, Kleinians, Jungians, etc.). But discussing the innovative aspects of each of these branches would require another paper. This paper does not present an historical description of innovations in psychoanalysis. Its focus is rather on particular revolutionary developments so as to illuminate what novelty in psychoanalysis involves.

Theoretical Innovations in Psychoanalysis

The Merriam-Webster dictionary offers two definitions for innovation: (1) the introduction of something new and (2) a new idea, method, or device.

For a theoretical innovation to be valuable, it can be expected to creatively improve something that already exists. I will therefore include this sense of usefulness in my notion of innovation, as well as a certain type of thinking outside the box.

How do psychoanalysts decide that something is innovative? Going by the above mentioned definition, psychoanalysts are not likely to agree what counts as innovative in their profession. When Klein presented her new ideas in the field of infant development at the London Institute of Psychoanalysis in the 1940s, she met with the opposition of Anna Freud and her colleagues who considered them as anything but an innovation: They saw them as a foreign body in psychoanalysis and did all they could to keep them out (King and Steiner, 1991). When Kohut introduced empathy as a central concept at a conference in the USA, some major establishment figures left the auditorium (Strozier, 2001). Both Klein and Kohut however created impressive and complex theories, which eventually changed psychoanalysis, and they have come to be seen as significant innovators.

While certain innovations were embraced by a majority of the psychoanalytic community, others were ignored and forgotten. Here are two examples.

First is Klein's concept of projective identification, which was developed by for instance Bion (1959) and Casement (1985).

It hits the psychoanalytic world like a meteor, leading to substantial changes in the perception of the psychoanalytic encounter. Projective identification prompted a wealth of publications and conferences elaborating it from various perspectives. Its brilliance lies in the same stroke of genius that produced Freud's notion of transference: Something hitherto regarded an obstacle to treatment transforms overnight into a resource, diagnostic as well as therapeutic. The notion of projective identification enables a new reading of therapeutic processes.

Second, there is innovative psychoanalytic knowledge that has not been well-received by the community, has been rejected and forgotten. An example is the fascinating experimental work of Silverman (Silverman, 1982, 1985) on subliminal psychodynamic activation. Through this method, Silverman attempted to identify the unconscious conflicts associated with specific symptomatic behaviors. Findings indicate that when participants are shown a subliminal message – "Mommy and I are one" – this leads to improved behavior and reduction of a variety of symptoms, from psychotic ones in schizophrenic patients, through nicotine addiction and academic underachievement all the way to phobias. The results of this research impressed psychoanalysts when they came out.

But in spite of its promising reception, the method was not eventually embraced by psychoanalysts and they did not seek to equip their clinics with a tachistoscope. No matter how innovative, subliminal psychodynamic activation never made it into psychoanalytic practice and fell into oblivion.

We may conclude that for an idea to be regarded as innovative, it takes a community to consider it as such. Truly innovative psychoanalysts never worked in isolation: their innovation was the product of an entire network. Obviously, it took genius and profound theoretical knowledge in order to invent notions like transitional object, schizoid-paranoid position, and reverie. But it was even more fundamentally necessary for there to be a tight network of psychoanalysts who were writing about the new conceptualization, elaborating it, employing it in the clinic, discussing it with their supervisees, and lecturing on it in psychoanalytic meetings.

This is why my preferred definition of psychoanalytic innovation crucially refers to the psychoanalytic community: Psychoanalytic innovation is a conceptualization found effective by the psychoanalytic community in yielding a new insight into psychoanalytic technique, clinical, or mental phenomena. An accepted innovation is where a psychoanalytic community finds something that so far eluded its understanding. This innovation must respect psychoanalytic specificity. It cannot be merely effective. Psychoanalysis, to begin with, is a special type of response to a special type of appeal. It rests on an ethics whose products are the results of the patient's psychic search into their self with as their main tool the therapeutic relationship and the centrality of the unconscious. Psychoanalysis aims not only to relieve suffering or to get rid of symptoms, it holds the fundamental principle of "Know Thyself" – a knowledge which every psychoanalytic approach conceptualizes in its own way.

Now, we are in a better position to understand why we do not find tachistoscopes in analysts' clinics, but we do find a preoccupation with projective identification, transitional objects, and self-object needs. Silverman's subliminal psychodynamic activation was not taken up in psychoanalysis precisely because it is very remote from the specificity of psychoanalysis: which aims to find where transference intersects with the patient's needs and conflicts. It is much closer to hypnosis and suggestion which impose conscious, explicit, and deliberate suggestion on the analysand. This is absolutely anti-psychoanalytical, "useful" as it may be. It is a short way to alleviate symptoms. It is not the psychoanalytic way.

Is Psychoanalysis Obsolete?

Critics of psychoanalysis argue that the discipline does not move with the times: psychoanalysts often refer to texts that were originally published a century, 80 or 50 years back. In this, they argue, psychoanalysis resembles religion, which refers to a static canon. This is factually undebatable. The Psychoanalytic Electronic Publishing (PEP) online archive comes up with two statistics: the most cited and most viewed articles. We may assume that most frequently read and cited articles reflect what is most influential among contemporary psychoanalysts, what has left most marks on the community, and the authors on whom psychoanalysts rely when they write their own papers. In PEP statistics for the past 5 years, the most frequently quoted article is by Klein, originally published in 1946: "Notes on Some Schizoid Mechanisms" (Klein, 1946). The list of the most frequently accessed articles is headed by an article by Winnicott from 1953: "Transitional Objects and Transitional Phenomena – A Study of the First Not-me Possession" (Winnicott, 1953).

Most papers on the list of the most popular articles were published between 1935 and 1992, and only two of them are from the early 2000s – Ogden and Benjamin. The majority of the best read psychoanalysts are no longer alive: Klein, Ferenczi, Bion, Rosenfeld, Winnicott, Strachey, and Joseph.

This state of affairs suggests two things: First, postmodernism's great insight about the nature of truth seems hardly to have penetrated the community. A huge proportion of the 30 most accessed and most cited papers are by authors who wrote before the advent of postmodernism (Winnicott, Klein, Joseph, Bick, Sandler, Kohut, Rosenfeld, and Heiman) and represent what relational psychotherapy has come to call a "one person psychology." This arguably signals a triumph of the old school over postmodern approaches.

Second, this list of dead authors might tempt one to draw the sad conclusion that psychoanalysis is grinding to a standstill; that the community goes on celebrating the achievements of the past; and that none of the articles written since have had a comparable impact to the cherished canonical texts written up to roughly the mid-1980s.[1]

As mentioned, critics of psychoanalysis comment negatively on its tendency to dwell on the past.

As Bornstein and Masling (1998) noted, "A geneticist of 1900 could not sustain a conversation with a contemporary geneticist, but Freud would have no trouble recognizing the psychoanalysis of 1997 or reading a modern psychoanalytic journal" (pp. xviii–xix).

According to Bornstein (2001), psychoanalysis lacks any innovative quality. Uncurious about the extra-analytical scientific world, and communicating only among each other, psychoanalysts do not expose themselves to alternative theories that might enrich their knowledge.

But this criticism mistakes the essence of psychoanalysis when it expects that, like scientific discovery, it will reveal new facts which then replace earlier, superannuated ones. It fails to bring into account that psychoanalysis is a language that deciphers meaning, yields insights about the psyche, insights that can be used again and again.

Psychoanalysis is more like philosophy and literature than like science. While scientific theories in use decades ago will have given way to more novel theories, philosophical theories going back to antiquity, for instance, still continue to inspire, drawing interest among contemporary philosophers. University departments of philosophy around the world teach ancient Greek philosophy all the way to the philosophy of the Modernity – Spinoza, Kant, Mill, Hume, Hegel, Nietzsche to mention but a few. These philosophers continue being read because the depth of their insights transcends historical periods, and their relevance does not diminish. If the type of statistics we found on PEP were to be done on periodicals in philosophy, they would also reveal a high percentage of quotations and viewings of no longer living authors.

The same goes for literature. Netz (2016) provides an illustration from the field of papyrology: In 1896, in Egypt, thousands of decaying papyrus scrolls were discovered. Scholars were excited: new texts and new books in the literature of ancient Greece were about to be discovered, they believed, and the study of Antiquity was about to undergo a great upheaval. Here and there, indeed, an ancient papyrus carrying a hitherto unknown text was found (a poem by Sappho, for instance). But such incidents were rare. By far, the most discovered scrolls were manuscripts of texts we already knew: the same Plato again, and the same Homer. The scholars' hope that our ancient forefathers knew other writers than the ones who were copied onto parchment in the Middle Ages proved vain. Monks in medieval Constantinople chose to copy the very same texts that had been copied on papyrus, in Egypt, a millennium earlier. It transpired that literary taste does not tend to change and renewal. Sophocles, Aeschylus, and Euripides were Athens' most popular playwrights even in their own life times. And they remained so for the next 2,500 years.

Conceptualizations concerning the psyche, likewise, do not lose their relevance rapidly. Truths of this type go on being discovered by one generation after another. This type of innovation might be captured by the notion of wisdom, which casts a new light on mental life. And much like in the case of philosophy, these ideas become the source of inspiration for new ideas, which in turn will multiply.

Analysts reread classical references and adapt Freudian or Kleinian or Winnicottian methods to contemporary clinical fields. Innovation comes through interpretive extension.

Three citations from a philosopher of science, a philosopher of aesthetics and a poet illustrate the connection between tradition and innovation in nonpsychoanalytic fields.

Kuhn writes on scientific revolution that it "requires a thoroughgoing commitment to the tradition" with which the fully successful innovator eventually breaks (Kuhn, 1977, p. 235).

Cavell, referring to art, also maintains that radical innovations occur in significant dialogue with the past. Here, he describes radical breaks in the music of twentieth century:

> "What looks like 'breaking with tradition' in the succession of art is not really that; or is that only after the fact, looking historically or critically; or is that only as a result not as motive: the unheard of appearance of the modern in art is an effort not to break, but to keep faith with tradition."
>
> *(Cavell, 1976, pp. 206–207)*

Eliot wrote: "The poem which is absolutely original is absolutely bad; it is, in the bad sense, 'subjective', with no relation to the world to which it appeals" (Pound, 1934, p. x).

Four Characteristics of Psychoanalytic Innovations of the First Order

Psychoanalytic innovation of the first order (new discoveries concerning facts) has four characteristics.

First, Most Innovations Concern New Psychic Dynamics Linking Between Transference, Psychopathology, and Infants' Mental Life

The 30 most cited and viewed papers written by Klein, Winnicott, Bion, and other prominent figures, the psychoanalytic canon, go on inspiring new work, and these prompt us to consider what it is about these inspirational sources that lead to innovative production.

While the innovative production represents different approaches (object relations, self-psychology, and relational psychotherapy), we can observe a common pattern: Almost without exception they tie together the three following domains: development, psychopathology, and therapy. Hardly, any one of them addresses only one of these topics in isolation. Psychoanalysts adhering to the various approaches find such narratives the most useful to their therapeutic work.

The specific psychoanalytic approach of the article in question does not seem to matter: Whether it is self-psychology, Klein, Winnicott, or Ferenczi, the patient's psychopathology appears in relation to the transference, and the transference is related to early interactions with the caregiver. Canonical articles, it appears, all present the regularities at work between these same components. So tightly interlinked are these three components, that it is enough to ask any psychoanalyst to describe the key stations in an infant's life to gain a revealing insight into his approach and the way he conceives of transference. And once we know how a psychoanalyst defines transference, we can tell with reasonable accuracy what her ideas about infant development are.

So, if a novel idea in psychoanalysis is to have an impact it should be tied to infantile mental life on the basis of both transference relations and mental distress and to the ability to give new meaning to transference relations on the basis of infantile mental life. Just as a problem in biology is solved in terms of biology not in those of chemistry a psychic fact is understood in this particular psychoanalytic way. This way of thinking has not altered since Freud and is in fact a variation on the transference neurosis, namely, the idea that the patient's early childhood conflicts resurface in the transference relationship with the psychoanalyst.

That innovations feed off the tradition does by no means reduce their creativity and contribution. Some innovators adhered faithfully to one theory, but were plentifully creative within that context, and their extension of it can be considered significant and very influential. This is the case for instance with Joseph's work on Klein, Ferro's on Bion, and Goldberg's on Kohut, to name just a few. Other authors do not follow one theoretician but refer playfully and creatively to the existing literature, dancing as it were between various theories, and leaving their personal marks in the creative links they forge, together with their own personal additions. Examples of this type of work are for instance by Bollas, Eigen, Phillips, and Milner.

New theoretical development can consist of illustrating an existing psychoanalytic conceptualization (through, for instance, a case study in which the concept is employed for clarification); extensions of a psychoanalytic conceptualization to new populations (e.g., applying self-psychological principles to issues concerning eating disorders); elaborating an existing conceptualization (e.g., manifestations of the female castration complex); discovery of an interesting therapeutic process and illustrating a clinical phenomenon by means of it; and in-depth discussion of the work of an important psychoanalyst, or exposition of a hitherto neglected text by her or him.

Second, Psychoanalytic Innovation Solves Empirical Problems

Psychoanalysis is a psychology. It addresses clinical phenomena, first-order facts, independent of theory: Patients suffering from hysterical symptoms visited Freud's clinic and he had no idea what might be wrong with them. Having identified hysteria as a clinical phenomenon, Freud was then able to discover the unconscious, the various other mental structures and eventually to develop his overarching theory.

The philosopher of science Laudan (1977) argues that science fundamentally aims at the solution of problems. He proposes that theories should be evaluated on the basis of how adequately they solve significant problems. It is much less relevant to ask whether they are "true," "corroborated," or "well-confirmed." He claims that one of the main kinds of problems scientific theories want to solve is empirical problem. An empirical problem, he argues, is "anything about the natural world which strikes us as odd or otherwise in need of explanation" (p. 15).

Empirical problems in psychoanalysis may be parapraxes, a 3-year old's fixation on her doll, intense, destructive jealousy, dreams. All these phenomena exist in the world as they are unrelated to psychoanalytic theory. In fact, human suffering in all its forms and variations constitutes an empirical problem, as well as the ways of treating it.

Some of the most interesting innovations in psychoanalysis have to do not just with solving empirical problems but discovering the problems in the first place. Many psychoanalytic phenomena had first to be recognized as empirical problems or felt to require explanation or clarification prior to these descriptions. Slips of the tongue were well known before Freud but were not considered to be a scientific or empirical problem. Another example is Winnicott's transitional object. The fact that a toddler clings to a teddy bear was well known before Winnicott gave it an explanation.

Often innovators focus on an existing (nonanalytic) phenomenon and show its relevance to psychoanalytic theory. Hence, I assume that psychoanalytic innovation will, more than anything, occur in the field of empirical problem solving. Regarding first-order questions, innovation means a new explanation ("solution") to psychic phenomenon ("empirical problem").

Psychoanalytic journals are simply bursting with such topics. Here are some examples: "The Role of the Nanny in Infant Observation" (Yakeley, 2017); "The Masculine Vaginal: Working With Queer Men's Embodiment at the Transgender Edge" (Hansbury, 2017); and "The Encounter Between Holocaust Survivors and Perpetrators" (Auerhahn and Laub, 2018).

Another type of problem that theory might address is conceptual in nature. Such problems emerge from the theory itself; they have no existence outside the theoretical field in which they arise. Here are some titles reflecting this:

> Projective Identification and Relatedness: A Kleinian Perspective (Roth, 2017); "Comparative Assessment of and Bion and Winnicott's Clinical Theories" (Aguayo and Lundgren, 2018); Truth Axes and the Transformation of Self (Yadlin-Gadot, 2017).

Third, Psychoanalytic Innovations Are Formulated Poetically

The new knowledge however is not communicated as if it was, say, medical knowledge. Often texts in this domain seem vague, open to interpretation, hard to understand, and more like poetry in their formulations.

In typical texts by Bion, Ogden, Winnicott, or Eigen, sentences are often ambiguous and labyrinthine, meaning is dense and layered, the opposite of the clear and simple style that scientists admire. Often the reader, in addition to gaining new knowledge or discovering an interesting solution, has an aesthetic experience which involves powerful emotional intensities. They seem to resonate deep layers with which the reader now makes contact for the first time. The echoes of the text, their links, the things they are attentive to, and all the others ways in which texts and objects can be tied, begin to struggle in the reader's or listener's mind with the semantic content (Scruton, 2015).

Canonical texts in this sense offer an enigmatic, complex phenomenon demanding explanation in its own right, like poetry. Most of the major psychoanalysts are rather gifted writers, and their texts may resemble literary prose or poetry more than properly scientific texts.

"As regards the beauty of Nature", writes Freud in On Transience (Freud, 1942/1915) when he was preoccupied with the losses of WWI, "each time it is destroyed by winter it comes again next year, so that in relation to the length of our lives it can in fact be regarded as eternal (Freud, 1942/1915). The beauty of the human form and face vanish forever in the course of our own lives, but their evanescence only lends them a fresh charm. A flower that blossoms only for a single night does not seem to us on that account less lovely" (pp. 304–305).

But psychoanalytic thinking is not poetry and the poet has somewhat different motivations from that of the analyst who uses words to describe the psyche, although the two may at times overlap.

Scruton (2015) thinks that the aim of a poem is not to convince readers of the correspondence of words to reality. Rather, its purpose is to facilitate readers to imagine the world as the poet depicts.

Now, although poetic truth of this kind is not alien to psychoanalytic writings it does seem to differ from it in some important sense. Think about the authors of psychoanalytic texts. They all want first and foremost to understand an unknown psychic fact (empirical problem). The innovative analyst has just met a patient. This patient suddenly behaves in a strange way. The analyst is puzzled. She feels that she cannot rely on current theories. She is holding a curious not-knowing position until she discovers an interesting innovative explanation. She knows that her description must correspond to the psychic reality "out there" in the transference relations and that she cannot imagine it or make it up like a poet. The truth value of her innovative explanation depends not merely on how successfully it conveys experience (although this too is very important, see next section) but on how adequate her description is in convincing the community that it corresponds to psychic reality.

She is fully committed to something to which the poet is only loosely committed, namely to understand what it was that happened there – both in the past and in the present.

Despite their differences psychoanalytic writing and poetic writing have much in common. When a psychic fact is put into words the effect is sometimes emotionally powerful. And so psychoanalytic thinking, when it works well, can form a genre in its own right representing psychic facts in a singular way through the symbolic. Often, psychoanalytic innovations will describe universal themes – but always in singular terms. It is exactly this combination between the universal and the singular that is so powerful.

Here, to illustrate, is a passage from Parsons, on creativity:

> If creativity is the discovery of what we had not thought of looking for, or the making of something which was, up till now, unimagined, it must call for a special sort of vulnerability. To open ourselves to the shock of creative discovery we must put ourselves at risk and be ready to give up, with no certainty about the future, ways of seeing which up till now have served us well.
>
> *(Parsons, 1990, p. 420)*

Parsons does not only present an answer to a question (What are the conditions under which creativity flourishes? Answer: The ability to take risks, to forfeit certainty, and in other words: to be vulnerable); his writing also includes a poetic element (the surprising and metaphoric association between creativity, the hitherto unthought – and, on the other hand, vulnerability; as well as the musical-rhythmic effect of the juxtaposition of creativity-discovery-vulnerability-certainty).

The solution or answer and its psychoanalytic textual form, the scientific element and the poetic, cannot be seen in isolation. The emotional, musical qualities of the language add validity to the conceptualization.

Parsons could have put the same idea in many different forms, some of them a lot more scientific and purely informative. But it is not clear whether it would have passed had he not used this poetic mode of expression.

All psychoanalytic writing displays this tension: Scientific writing aims at solving empirical problems. It is disciplined, clear-cut, and tells us how to think. It is systematic and aims at solving profound mysteries and riddles. Poetic writing is undisciplined, unpredictable, and full of subjectivity; but it is passionate and spontaneous, seeking, rather, what Bollas calls "psychic intensities" (Bollas, 1995, p. 60). We need both, as they seem to empower each other, creating a certain energy that outweighs their separate meaning and impact.

Fourth, Psychoanalytic Innovations Conceptualize What We Already Know

There is another sense in which innovation in science is unlike innovation in psychoanalysis. While new knowledge concerning a scientific problem reveals what we did not know earlier, psychoanalysis, like art, adds meaning to what we already knew. We can, in other words, regard psychoanalytic writing as a type of symbolic writing in so far as it takes an existing experience to which we had no verbal access and makes it accessible. Something we experienced without being aware acquires articulate meaning.

Both Meltzer and Bion emphasize that psychoanalysis has not discovered any new ideas about its subject, the human mind, and that it is unlikely to do so. But through the psychoanalytic method, old ideas can be rediscovered in a new context (Meltzer, 1983, p. 98).

And Freud writes:

> "I find myself for a moment in the interesting position of not knowing whether what I have to say should be regarded as something long familiar and obvious or as something entirely new and puzzling."
>
> *(Freud, 1940, p. 274)*

The truth of Winnicott's notion of transitional object as an object that is both real and also helps to maintain a connection to the absent mother is hence directly associated with the fact that a well-known and universal human experience here is formulated for the first time. When Klein spoke about manic defenses like contempt for the object and arrogance, she first put into words what we had known for a long time about our attitude to our closest objects. The psychic fact and the poetic are not two distinct modes of knowledge. The poetic supplies the esthetic experience to the real and rings with something of the mysterious truth we already knew.

While the clinical experience or phenomenon (envy, transitional object, slips of the tongue, castration experience) is what it is, in line with reality, its description can take many forms. This may be what characterizes psychoanalysis' epistemology. Psychoanalytic innovation, from this perspective, occurs when new facts concerning a psychic phenomenon come to light, but our ability to perceive them as correct is based on the fact that we were already familiar with them. The poetic language in which a new description of a clinical phenomenon is couched functions like a muscle that supports its approach to the truth: it elicits a powerful emotional engagement with the newly discovered facts. We have experienced this knowledge, but it was unconceptualized so far. For the discovered facts to ring true, the poetic quality of the text is crucial. Should facts about the mind be communicated in terse scientific language, the reader would be unable to connect with the actually lived experience.

Loewald thought that language "ties together human beings and self and object world, and it binds abstract thought with the bodily concreteness and power of life" (Loewald, 1978, p. 204). This is because language, in the form of the sounds of mother's speech, imbues the infant's lived experience from the beginning of life. The sounds of mother's speech are part of the infant's experience of interacting with the mother, and over time, those sounds become differentiated from other sensations of the lived world as a special kind of sound; these special sounds grow into words. But the sounds also remain connected in memory to the rest of experience and, for that reason, a powerful way to recall one's inner experience and communicate it to another. Indeed, the lived feeling that language can create is a reflection of its experiential nature. Although the semantic possibilities of words expand over development, they do not overtake the experiential possibilities. A word is always an experiential memory.

Sensibilities: Second-Order Innovations

I first encountered the word "sensibility" in an article by Stolorow et al. (2001), authors who took a central role in developing the intersubjective approach. Inspired by postmodernism, this theory claimed that in the therapeutic encounter, an intersubjective domain arises in which two partners mutually constitute each other. This co-creation – rather than the isolated mind of the patient – is the heart of the therapy. They call this theory a "sensibility" rather than a clinical theory: their work, they claim, is informed by the clinician's attitude and the ensuing process, rather than by any hard and fast procedure.

Psychoanalytic communities develop sensibilities when they turn outward: Methodological sensibilities absorb significant scientific changes (in brain science or in infant research); cultural-philosophical sensibilities incorporate changes in philosophy, culture, or society (e.g., constructivism, postmodernism, or feminism). Like a seismograph, they register these changes and bring them to bear in psychoanalysis. Introducing a foreign element to psychoanalytic discourse, texts of this kind are sometimes met with indifference or hostility. Studies based in brain or infant research seek to cast a different light on what exists, to change the approach to patients, rather than to change theoretical models. Both neuropsychoanalysis and infant research believe they are actually restoring something to psychoanalysis. Thus, infant researchers claim to only deepen analysts' knowledge of the nature of early development which is, after all, so central to their theory. Similarly, neuropsychoanalysts think their findings expand the analyst's therapeutic possibilities. They remind us that Freud himself was a neurologist and that he sought to integrate the study of the brain and psychoanalysis (Johnson and Flores Mosri, 2016).

The Relational Sensibility – Truth, Knowledge, and Politics

The implications of the relational approach for the psychoanalytic encounter are far reaching. It assumes that the analytic relationship is systematically mutual and two-directional throughout. The notion of the therapist as object of the patient's projected relations from the past is exchanged for one in which the therapist is a subject in the therapeutic relationship. Puget (2017) captures this difference in her use of "interference," a mutual process, with which she replaces "transference," which relies on notions of object-subject distinctness and wholeness.

The relational approach assumes that the therapist's personal involvement in the therapy is inevitable. It is a matter of mobilizing this involvement for the patient's benefit. Aron (1996) for instance argued that Freud's elimination of the "subjective factor" in the therapeutic situation has been a damaging omission. Freud's aim, in tune with the academic-scientific thinking of his times, was to achieve an objective science of the psyche. Postmodernism, as said, questioned this approach, by arguing that any theoretical model is historically and linguistically mediated. Thus, Hoffman (1998), a major proponent of the relational approach, argued that the patient's experience in the therapy and the way it is subsequently made sense of, are understandings that emerge in the course of the encounter, based on both therapist's and patient's personal histories and their typical modes of organization. It would be inappropriate to judge these construals as simply wrong or right, rather than to think of them as more or less applicable.

A similar shift also occurred on the epistemological plane, where the relational approach no longer assumes one monolithic truth, embodied in a grand theory. Instead, theories are seen as possibilities, narratives that help in framing the therapeutic relationship and the patient's psychic history and reality (Mills, 2005, 2017).

By redefining its boundaries of relevance, the relational approach has also come to include political issues that were outside the traditional scope of psychoanalysis. Clinical questions touching on gender and ethnicity are integral part of it, as well as for instance a critical attitude to the therapist's unconscious racism. Altman writes:

> "It should be taken for granted that none of us will be able to overcome our personal racist attitudes altogether. Thus, I am advocating that clinicians become familiar with their racism, not that they overcome their racist feelings and attitudes. The danger in implying that clinicians can and should overcome their racist feelings is that they will mistake their conscious goodwill and good intentions for a thoroughgoing nonracist attitude."
>
> *(Altman, 2000, p. 601)*

A Sensibility Related to Infant Observations

Innovation also occurs when psychoanalysts are powerfully attracted to an extra-analytic domain of knowledge which while relating directly to psychoanalytic theory uses a different language. This extraneous knowledge, they believe, has the potential to influence the conceptualization and understanding of the therapeutic situation, however, in this particular case, rather than by reference to the adult therapeutic situation, through the observation of real interactions between infants and their caregivers. Infant researchers consider the method whereby infant development is derived from the psychoanalysis of adults or older children as naive.

Fonagy writes:

> Melanie Klein's baby and Winnicott's baby were adultomorphic to a considerable degree. They seemed in some way put there to explain the conflicts and vicissitudes of the adult years rather than to genuinely map how the mind emerges from an early infant in many ways biologically and physically unprepared for the challenges of the external world. The infants of early psychoanalysis were retrofitted to the couch.
>
> *(Fonagy, 2014, p. xx)*

The infant in these studies is extremely unlike the one featuring in Freud, Klein, Bion, Winnicott, and Kohut (Seligman, 2018). Traditional psychoanalytic theories present a baby with a primitive psychic organization which develops into an adaptive organization. Initially, this baby's mental life is chaotic, unintegrated, and in conflict with the social world. Psychopathology is understood in terms of distortions in this process. The traces of psychosis or borderline personality can be discerned in early infancy.

Infant research has revealed a very different baby: This observed infant is not fundamentally disorganized, chaotic, or primitive, spending most of its time in a dream state or fearing persecution. Nor is it undifferentiated from its environment. From the very first moment, its life is organized around a relational matrix, which is continuously subject to reconstruction and change in line with experience (Stern, 1985). From day 1, the infant is already directed toward reality, influences and is influenced by its surroundings, is active and passive, dependent and independent, in possession of a variety of resources for organizing its behavior. One might have expected that anyone, once exposed to this research, would turn away from psychoanalysis – the chasm between these two conceptualizations is so enormous. But what actually happened was the opposite. The psychoanalytic infant research community, including researchers and practitioners who apply their insights in psychoanalytic psychotherapy, insists that its research is relevant to psychoanalysis and is bound to enrich it. They argue that their perspective is especially promising for work with adult patients who are more difficult to reach (Rustin, 2012).

In trying to understand the clinical distinction of this change in perspective, Stern observed that much of what occurs between people who are closely interacting involves an intersubjective consciousness. This implies that there is a realm of knowing that is implicit, outside awareness, and not requiring verbalization. The present moment, writes Stern (2004), rather than the past, becomes the focus. Stern (1985, 2004) extended this idea from everyday interaction to the patient/therapist encounter as crucial for an appreciation of how therapeutic change comes about. New ways of being and being with others are created through intersubjective processes of implicit relational knowing.

Rustin, who is identified with self-psychology, explains infant research's complementary role vis a vis existing psychoanalytic theories very well in her book *Infant Research and Neuroscience at Work in Psychotherapy* (Rustin, 2012).

Because new facts about human behavior emerge daily psychoanalysts need to integrate these facts into their practice. She writes "These theories, and their accompanying principles and techniques, inform everything that I do. Through immersing myself in infant research, I found a way to expand and update self-psychology in my clinical practice" (p. 171). She argues that infant research's focus on infant and caregiver relations underwrites Kohut's notion of empathic engagement. But it also contributes to self-psychology by demonstrating that "an interaction is always a bidirectional, co-constructed process, thereby bolstering my commitment to intersubjectivity as a two-person model of clinical practice" (p. 172). Infant research, for Rustin, is not a substitute for any of the traditional theories or techniques, but it holds out opportunities for knowledge and intervention: "[. . .] additional sources of fluidity and elasticity to the therapeutic relationship and clinical process" (pp. 172–173).

Infant research posited a challenge to psychoanalytic methodology. Green (2000), who was fiercely critical of infant research, noted that infant research deviates from psychoanalysis' investigation of the unconscious and the intrapsychic through the transference within the parameters set by the psychoanalytic setting. For analysts like him empirical researchers ignore the unconscious and change the psychoanalytic account into a theory of interpersonal relations.

Green even suggests that some researchers harbor sinister motivations, even those purporting to be acting in the interests of psychoanalysis: they want to get rid of psychoanalytic theories, in favor of a so-called scientific psychology, which is simpler, easier to teach, and more amenable to experimental studies. Green's fears were exaggerated. Infant researchers aspired to make analysts sensitive to empirical findings, not to replace existing theories.

A Sensibility Related to Neuropsychoanalysis

According to Johnson (2009), neuropsychoanalysis concerns the common ground between neuroscience and psychoanalysis. As said, neuropsychoanalysts claim that incorporating brain research into psychoanalysis is a continuation of Freud's project. The neuropsychoanalytic community is very active and vibrant. It has founded an organization for its members, a journal, an annual conference, and research study groups all over the world.

Kaplan-Solms and Solms (2000) described contemporary use of neuroscience in psychoanalysis: "The aim of a depth neuropsychology is not to replace our psychic model of the mind with a physical one. Rather, our aim is to supplement the traditional viewpoints of metapsychology with a new, "physical point of view. The aim is to gain an additional perspective on something that can never be known directly" (p. 251).

It is plausible to think that this was appealing for the Neuropsychoanalysis community. Psychodynamic concepts such as cathexis, dreams, self, and ego may now appear in new light if we can trace their neurological underpinning.

For example, Northoff (2012) regarding the "self" suggest that instead of searching for the self-region or self-network in the brain, it will be more productive to search for essential executive and operational regularities. The spatiotemporal structure of the resting state may present the basis for such regularities. If it is linked with the self or the ego, one would assume the organization of the resting state's spatiotemporal structure to somehow establish self-specific and thus to reveal the structure of the ego.

According to Yovell et al. (2015), for example, brain researchers discovered fear conditioning, a potent kind of implicit emotional learning. A person may have an extreme fear of a situation or another person without any explicit memory of why they have this fear. The corresponding implicit memory here is not repressed as classical psychoanalysis suggested. The authors argue that findings like this shed new light on a problem of traumatic memories that has haunted psychoanalysis from its first days. It explains why people who went through severe trauma were incapable to access direct memories of the traumatic events in spite of experiencing powerful, anxiety-inducing implicit memories.

Members of the neuropsychoanalysis community have published many other examples of how brain research can enrich and help analysts (Ruby, 2011; Giacolini and Sabatello, 2019; Iyengar et al., 2019). Some even have coined a new term "neuropsychoanalytic interpretation" (Johnson, 2009, p. 182).

Johnson, writes: "My definition of a 'neuropsychoanalytic' interpretation is a discussion of impingements on the patient's thinking that clearly had to do with known biological factors. These included drug dreams, craving, justifications of using (clearly influenced by craving such as, 'No one will know'), and telling her that craving would diminish with abstinence" (Johnson, 2009, p. 185).

In his case study he describes 28 "neuropsychoanalytic" interventions made in 60 h. These were the interpretations guided by his neurobiological knowledge regarding the patient's addiction to cocaine such as identifying long-lasting transformations in brain structure and function that affected "the ventral tegmental-nucleus accumbens shell/dopamine-glutamate/hippocampal-amygdalar-cingulate-frontal functioning. The foremost manifestation of this change is the drug dream" (p. 186).

The "neuropsychoanalytic interpretation" also helped to ease shame. Johnson's patient is enabled to understand that her behavior is not the outcome of some flaw in her personality.

He writes: "There is nothing remarkable or special about this treatment. It follows the ordinary psychoanalytic approach of having the patient free-associate and the analyst interpret. Comments about medication are required because they are part of the effort to facilitate her being sober" (p. 191).

According to Yovell et al. (2015), "psychoanalysis needs to be in a position to consider developments in science, even if it ends up dismissing some of them as irrelevant, due to the criteria and findings of its own epistemology" (p. 1528).

Like infant research and like the relational approach, neuropsychoanalysis challenges traditional psychoanalysis' epistemology and methodology.

Johnson and Flores Mosri write:

> "Neuropsychoanalysis is a twenty-first century development that has at its core the concept of dual aspect monism. Whether phenomena are evaluated empathically, or

through measurements and statistics, it introduces an artifact of perception. Empirical data is filtered through the means by which it is made. Therefore, we are in the delightful position of being able to make observations by psychoanalytic clinical means that can also, perhaps with some technical difficulties, be made with genetic testing, animal observation of homologous behaviors, fMRI scanning, or some other nomothetic approach."

(Johnson and Flores Mosri, 2016, pp. x)

Can Sensibilities Address First-Order Questions?

I have portrayed the relational approach as a sensibility that poses second-order questions regarding existing theories, while the latter in turn discovers first-order psychoanalytic facts. Most relational analysts do of course have a keen interest in "facts" and "empirical problems" (see Govrin, 2006). Ghent (1990) explores what patients need and how this need unfolds in therapy; Davies and Frawley (1992) discovered new facts regarding patients who suffered from sexual abuse and Stern discovered a new component of the unconscious which he called "unformulated experiences" (Stern, 1983). There is no hard, binary division between these orders of questions: it is rather a matter of a tension between facts and sensibilities, and this exists not only between different psychoanalytic communities but also within each psychoanalytic orientation and within analysts themselves. This also is true for infant research and neuropsychoanalysis. They too are interested in how new facts can change the clinical practice.

And yet, there is a difference between sensibilities and first-order psychoanalytic facts. Postmodernists, especially the USA relational group, select what they consider valuable in existing theories, extricate it from its positivist moorings, and insert it into an intersubjective and constructivist model. Likewise, findings from neuropsychoanalysis and infant research offer a new and additional perspective, specifically on nonverbal and nonconscious processes of clinical interaction. The newer perspectives have opened creative pathways for empathic immersion, interaction, clinical understanding, and intervention. As Rustin (2012) writes: "What I do offer is a way to use these research findings as another lens through which to view or think about some nonverbal, nonconscious aspects of clinical data and to tailor interventions so that they more effectively lead to therapeutic action. I view these concepts as additions that increase the possibilities for spontaneous and imaginative ways of working with patients" (p. 10).

Psychoanalytic sensibilities are an attempt to integrate new disciplines and world views into mainstream clinical practice. Psychoanalytic schools, by contrast, have more ambitiously presented fully-fledged alternatives to already existing schools and offered new psychic facts concerning the link between infancy, psychopathology, and transference.

Rather than posing themselves as alternatives to psychoanalytic theories sensibilities try to engage in a dialogue. In neuropsychoanalysis, conscious id is another good case in point. Solms cites evidence that the upper brainstem (together with associated limbic structures) performs the functions that Freud attributed to the id, while the cortex (and associated forebrain structures) performs the functions he attributed to the ego. This is a radical new fact. It reveals a stark contradiction between the current concepts of affective neuroscience and those of Freud. The realization that Freud's id is intrinsically conscious has implications for psychoanalysis, which Solms describes (for example, if the id is conscious what is unconscious is withdrawal of automatization processes).

Solms' paper is a wonderful dialogue between brain research and Freudian theory. Solms goes back and forth from Freud's writings to brain images and data to show where Freud was right and ahead of his time and where he erred. These illustrations show how neuropsychoanalysis and infant research mainly aim to shift the relations with the enduring metapsychology of psychoanalysis into something more workable.

Whereas psychoanalytic schools are all-encompassing and need no additions, the relational approach, infant research, and neuropsychoanalysis do not stand alone. They depend on a constant dialogue with psychoanalytic schools.

Does Psychoanalysis Make Progress?

Now, I want to return to the questions I posed in the beginning of this paper: Does psychoanalysis make progress?

Let us start with "first-order questions." If we accept Laudan's (1977) philosophy of science, we appraise a theory by one sole criterion: whether it provides acceptable answers to significant questions. According to Laudan, problem-solving activity has no direct connections with truth, but this does not deprive the problem-solving model of its explanatory force. Rationality, argues Laudan, consists in doing or believing things because we have good reasons for doing so. What counts as a sound reason for accepting a new explanation in psychoanalysis? How can we know if a suggested description of, say, the dynamic of analyst-patient relations is a sound one?

It is important to note that any assessment of the rationality of accepting a particular theory is relative: it is relative to other earlier and competing theories, and to prevailing views on methodology and in the case of psychoanalysis, it is relative to the therapist's own theoretical inclinations. So, a psychotherapist who prefers to base psychotherapeutic theory on evidence-based research will not find psychoanalytic solutions as effective. However, the solution can be satisfactory to a psychotherapist who perceives clinical observations and single case studies as valid sources of knowledge.

My own clinical experience demonstrates the power of psychoanalytic theory to solve puzzling empirical problems (see also Govrin, 2016). One of my patients, single and in his late thirties, presented significant progress. He had experienced years of harsh relations with people, periods of severe loneliness, and a lack of social relations. After several months in therapy, he seemed less guarded, his relations with his colleagues had improved, and for the first time, he had gained the approval of his directors. But the more he recovered, the more hostile he became to me and the more critical he grew of the therapy. He would joke at my lack of experience, mock my interventions, and complain about my inability to support him. When he was not in an aggressive mood, he would express his hopelessness feeling that I could not possibly help him. When he mentioned the improvements, he had made in his personal and professional life, he spoke with indifference, indicating that as far as he was concerned it had nothing to do with therapy. I was bewildered, ill at ease, and infuriated. It was odd: A person whose life had undoubtedly changed for the better because of therapy not only failed to acknowledge it as such but did everything he could to devaluate what had been attained. My patient's attitude toward me was a clinical/empirical fact. It was not a matter of interpretation. Many psychotherapists, working in different orientations, have reported similar reactions.

My Kleinian supervisor helped me understand my patient's inner dynamic and how it affected the transference relations. She explained how the Kleinian approach understands the phenomenon of the negative therapeutic reaction (NTR): Due to envy, which Klein maintained was the mental representation of the death instinct, the patient avoids any recognition of the goodness of the analyst so as to secure his omnipotent phantasy and deny his dependency. The libidinal force which directs him to love, show gratitude, and make amends – leading to a steady improvement of his condition – is overridden by envy, revenge, and contempt. My Kleinian supervisor added that the patient perceived "suffering" as the connection between us and could maintain contact with me only if he supposed we were both suffering.

I had no reason to doubt the accuracy of this "solution." It seemed right and appropriate to this regressive phenomenon.

The literature on NTR is simply enormous. Analysts from different orientations have tried to explain it starting from Freud in his Wolf Man case study. Because numerous analysts have shared their thoughts and clinical experience the community obviously knows more about NTR than it did 50 years ago. Of course, the problem-solving effectiveness of the theories that explain NTR is not scientifically experimentally backed. But if a community of psychotherapists dealing with first-order questions use a strong set of psychological theories which they believe to be essential to the understanding of psychopathology, then it is perfectly rational to assess innovations, that is, "solutions," in light of their capacity to be accommodated within that prior system of beliefs and assumptions. There is much more to say about the appraisal of effective "solutions" in psychoanalysis which is beyond the scope of this paper. This appraisal with its strange reliance on poetic style and the analysts' subjectivity might seem odd for an outsider. Still, the psyche is "odd" so it is likely that the explanations will match its awkwardness. As Lear (1998) wrote:

> "There is one way to refute psychoanalysis entirely: if from now on, every person would act rationally and clearly, it would be easy to dismiss psychoanalysis as idle chatter. However, since people often act in strange ways, causing pain to themselves and others, raising questions even among the players themselves, psychoanalysis will draw us to it."
>
> *(p. 25)*

Overall, I think that regarding first-order questions we are in a good position. NTR is just one example out of numerous "solutions" that psychoanalysts have found to puzzling psychic phenomena. Some of those problems (such as NTR) lack solutions from other nonpsychoanalytic theories (and other nonpsychoanalytic theories propose excellent solutions to other psychic first-order questions, though, I believe, in terms of scope, range and relevancy to human's life psychoanalysis outnumber other theories).

Concerning second-order questions we must distinguish between the cultural – philosophical sensibility of the relational approach and the methodological sensibilities of neuropsychoanalysis and infant research. The relational approach, even if one resists its worldview, is no doubt the most important recent innovation in psychoanalysis. It revolutionized psychoanalysis by embracing new approaches to knowledge which led to a novel perception of therapeutic relations.

The relational approach first refers, rather to a whole new worldview according to which therapy is a genuine relationship between two persons and not merely some one-way internal relations that belong exclusively to the intrapsychic life of the patient's mind (Davies, 1994, p. 168). The new worldview had important implications for analytic work (For example, how analysts work with enactments or the role of self-disclosure). As a result of this new worldview or, as I have been calling it, sensibility, analysts have changed how they think about their own subjectivity in the psychoanalytic encounter. This had put an end to therapists struggling to hide their personalities and blur their subjectivity in order to ensure patients' emotional issues would stay untouched by the countertransference. Of course, this has taken its toll in the form of an indifference to theory (Govrin, 2006) or excessive use of analyst self-disclosure (Mills, 2017).

The epistemology of methodological sensibilities is very unlike that of the cultural-philosophical sensibilities of the relational approach. In fact, by relying on scientific research the epistemology of both neuropsychoanalysis and infant research is strikingly similar to that of the "silver era" of psychoanalysis where realism and correspondence theory of truth prevailed. So, contrary to the revolutionary meta-psychology of the relational approach, methodological sensibilities offer a new source of knowledge with a traditional epistemology. They challenge psychoanalytic sources of knowledge by offering to extend these sources by relying on other fields of knowledge besides the clinical encounter.

I believe that their greatest challenge is addressing an external conceptual problem (Laudan, 1977, p. 50). External conceptual problems are generated by a theory when it conflicts with another theory or doctrine which its supporters believe to be rationally well founded. There is a difference between mainstream psychoanalysis and between infant research and neuropsychoanalysis. For example, many mainstream analysts still use the term symbiotic phase despite findings from infant research showing that the infant from the very beginning is aware that she is physically separate, conscious of her caregivers and continuously relating to her surroundings. In science the answer to a "tension" between a methodology and a scientific theory is in many cases reached by changing the scientific theory as to adjust it to the methodological standards. In other instances, it is the methodology itself which is transformed. Neither of this had happened in psychoanalysis because of infant research and neuropsychoanalysis.

As a result, infant research and neuropsychoanalysis have not so far prompted a paradigm shift in psychoanalysis. Perhaps this is because neuropsychoanalysis has not yet reached a point of development that obliges mainstream analysts to consider it a serious contributor. It did not lead mainstream analysts to think that the inconsistency and correspondence between methodological sensibilities are convincing enough probably because they speak different languages and methodologies.

To the credit of researchers from both infant research and neuropsychoanalysis, it must be said that they never thought that psychoanalysts should kneel before their own scientific findings because they are more grounded and evidence-based, nor have they expected analysts to abandon parts of mainstream psychoanalysis. I believe that psychoanalytic problem-solving effectiveness is improved by new insights from brain research and infant research through a process of inquiry, argument, and agreement within open-minded communities. And the reputation of psychoanalysis as a serious body of knowledge is enhanced if it can show that it is successful in incorporating current findings in science or at least conducts a healthy dialogue with these findings.

Conclusion

I have demonstrated that any attempt to outline innovations in psychoanalysis will have to tread a narrow, dialectic line between two opposing directions. On the one hand, we can point out a dynamic of change in therapeutic approaches, the rise and fall of theoretical models, and the development of new therapeutic understandings of numerous psychic phenomena such as transference and psychopathology. On the other, there is the fact that there has not been all that much change in the influence of main psychoanalytic theory (Freud, Bion, Klein, Winnicott, Kohut, and others).

In science, we witness the same duality (Laudan, 1977). Some philosophers of science emphasize the radical shifts in scientific thought. Others stress the outstanding continuities that mark its evolution. I think we can learn from Laudan's work on scientific progress and combine between the two perspectives within psychoanalysis when we think in terms of first and second order questions. Freud used a mechanistic-biological drive model to describe mental structures, object relations theories believe in self-object representations, whereas contemporary psychoanalysts perceive the analytic situation as shaped as a dynamic between two subjectivities. No doubt, this represents a movement of change in psychoanalysis. On the other hand, taking a "gradual" perspective, we may stress that psychoanalytic theory still champions Freud's original profound link between psychopathology, past experience, and transference. We still listen to our patients' unconscious, encourage them to free associate, interpret their dreams, consider unconscious transference dynamics as a decisive factor, and make the best interpretations that we think might help the patient to grow or improve his understanding of his inner motives.

The chief element of continuity in psychoanalysis (and in other sciences, see Laudan, 1977) is represented by the fundamental empirical problems or first-order questions. Ever since Freud every psychoanalytic school has addressed anxiety, psychosis, narcissism, perversions, regressions, dreams, and other psychic phenomena. Although the empirical problem domain varies (we see less hysterics and more personality disorders) as a result of cultural and social changes, psychic phenomena within the psychoanalytic encounter tend to endure.

Where radical shifts occur, it is not so much at the level of the formulation or identification of first-order problems as at the level of explanation or problem solution. There are, for example, radical differences between the way in which Kohut explains the parent-child relations and the way Freud did. But parent-child relations as such remain an essential problem for psychoanalysts. Of course, besides shared interest in the same psychic phenomena, there are often important common conceptualizations that persist through time (the central concept of transference, for example).

I assume this might seem strange to a contemporary relational analyst who perceives little if any contiguity between Freud's drive theory, with its quasi-mechanistic and biological language, and the relational approach. A postmodernist would moreover add that psychoanalytic theories also and nevertheless leave their imprint on the first-order questions too. Hence, if the relational approach differs from Freud's drive theory then all the terms within these theories must have different meanings.

However, even with using different epistemologies and methodologies, we still use different theories to explain the same problem (such as agoraphobia or psychosis) even when we describe the problem in different language.

In fact, I believe psychoanalysis' merit is exactly in its ability to find effective explanations to significant psychic phenomena and clinical facts which are different from the psychoanalytic theories which attempt to solve them.

Psychic phenomena are therefore the "engine" behind psychoanalytic progress. In fact, this was the reason psychoanalytic schools have emerged from the first place. Each school defined different set of clinical phenomena that previous theories either overlooked or proposed an unsatisfactory explanation. Self-psychology covered empathy in development and clinical encounter; Klein covered paranoia and destructiveness, Kernberg covered borderline patients; Sullivan the interpersonal cultural dimension and so on.

This merit compensates for a methodology that relies on a clinical observation and on subjective theorizing, which thought by many as "crippling epistemological defect uncharacteristic of other science in that its theories are not subject to verification but must rely upon the point of view and basic assumptions of groups of analysts (Hanly, 1983, p. 402). One promising solution of how we can test our subjective theories, at least in the clinical encounter, was proposed by Hinshelwood (2013) which offered a "testing process" (p. 130) between different psychoanalytic theories based on occurrences that happen before and after interpretation.

Further inquiry needs to find how we distinguish between far-fetched and appropriate therapeutic solutions. We need to consider psychoanalytic schools in terms of their weakness and strength in finding effective "solutions" to psychic phenomena. Such inquiry can guide us to use different theories for understanding different facts.

Note

1 It is worth mentioning that no article by Freud appears in the top 3 most accessed or quoted articles. However, since 2009 Freud appeared in the title of 8,161 papers (compared to Klein 569, Winnicott 416, Bion 411 and Mitchell 132).

References

Aguayo, J., and Lundgren, J. (2018). Introduction to a comparative assessment of W. R. Bion and D. W. Winnicott's clinical theories. *Br. J. Psychother.* 34, 194–197.

Altman, N. (2000). Black and white thinking. *Psychoanal. Dial.* 10, 589–605.

Aron, L. (1996). *A meeting of minds: mutuality in psychoanalysis.* Hillsdale, NJ: Analytic Press.

Auerhahn, N. C., and Laub, D. (2018). Against forgiving: the encounter that cannot happen between holocaust survivors and perpetrators. *Psychoanal. Q.* 87, 39–72.

Bion, W. R. (1959). Attacks on linking. *Int. J. Psychoanal.* 40, 308–315.

Bollas, C. (1995). *Cracking up: the work of unconscious experience.* New York, NY: Hill & Wang.

Bornstein, R. F. (2001). The impending death of psychoanalysis. *Psychoanal. Psychol.* 18, 3–20.

Bornstein, R. F., and Masling, J. M. (1998). Empirical investigations of events within the analytic hour. In *Empirical studies of the therapeutic hour.* eds. R. F. Bornstein and J. M. Masling. Washington, DC: American Psychological Association, xv–xxxiv.

Casement, P. (1985). *On learning from the patient.* London: Tavistock Publications.

Cavell, S. (1976). *Must we mean what we say?* Cambridge: Cambridge University Press.

Davies, J. M. (1994). Love in the afternoon: a relational reconsideration of desire and dread in the countertransference. *Psychoanal. Dial.* 4, 153–170.

Davies, J. M., and Frawley, M. G. (1992). Dissociative processes and transference-countertransference paradigms in the psychoanalytically oriented treatment of adult survivors of childhood sexual abuse. *Psychoanal. Dial.* 2, 5–36.

Fonagy, P. (2014). Introduction. In *Early parenting and prevention of disorder: psychoanalytic research at interdisciplinary frontiers.* eds. R. N. Emde and M. Leuzinger-Bohleber. London: Karnac.

Freud, S. (1940). *Splitting of the ego in the process of Defence.* Vol. 23. Standard Edn. London: Hogarth Press, 275–278.

Freud, S. (1942/1915). On transience. *Int. J. Psychoanal.* 23, 84–85.

Ghent, E. (1990). Masochism, submission, surrender – masochism as a perversion of surrender 1. *Contemp. Psychoanal.* 26, 108–136.

Giacolini, T., and Sabatello, U. (2019). Psychoanalysis and affective neuroscience. The motivational/emotional system of aggression in human relations. *Front. Psychol.* 9, 2475.

Govrin, A. (2006). The dilemma of contemporary psychoanalysis: toward a "knowing" post-postmodernism. *J. Am. Psychoanal. Assoc.* 54, 507–535.

Govrin, A. (2016). *Conservative and radical perspectives on psychoanalytic knowledge: the fascinated and the disenchanted.* New York, NY: Routledge/Taylor & Francis Group.

Govrin, A., and Mills, J. (eds.) (2019). *Innovations in psychoanalysis: originality, development and progress.* London: Routledge.

Green, A. (2000). Science and science fiction in infant research. In *Clinical and observational psychoanalytic research: roots of a controversy.* eds. J. Sandler, A.-M. Sandler, and R. Davies. Madison, CT: International Universities Press, 41–72.

Hanly, C. (1983). A problem of theory testing. *Int. Rev. Psychoanal.* 71, 375–383.

Hansbury, G. (2017). The masculine vaginal: working with queer men's embodiment at the transgender edge. *J. Am. Psychoanal. Assoc.* 65, 1009–1031.

Hinshelwood, R. D. (2013). *Research on the couch – single-case studies, subjectivity and psychoanalytic knowledge.* London: Routledge.

Hoffman, I. (1998). *Ritual and spontaneity in psychoanalytic process: a dialectical-constructivist Hillsdale.* New York, NJ: The Analytic Press.

Iyengar, U., Rajhans, P., Fonagy, P., Strathearn, L., and Kim, S. (2019). Unresolved trauma and reorganization in mothers: attachment and neuroscience perspectives. *Front. Psychol.* 10, 110.

Johnson, B. (2009). A "neuropsychoanalytic" treatment of a patient with cocaine dependence. *Neuropsychoanalysis.* 11, 181–196.

Johnson, B., and Flores Mosri, D. (2016). The neuropsychoanalytic approach: using neuroscience as the basic science of psychoanalysis. *Front. Psychol.* 7, 1459.

Kaplan-Solms, K., and Solms, M. (2000). *Clinical studies in neuro-psychoanalysis: introduction to a depth neuropsychology*. London: Karnac.
King, P., and R. Steiner (eds.) (1991). *The Freud-Klein controversies: 1941–45*. New York, NY: Tavistock/ Routledge.
Klein, M. (1946). Notes on some schizoid mechanisms. *Int. J. Psychoanal.* 27, 99–110.
Kuhn, T. (1977). *The essential tension – selected studies in scientific tradition and change*. Chicago: The University of Chicago Press.
Laudan, L. (1977). *Progress and its problems: towards a theory of scientific growth*. Berkeley, CA: University of California Press.
Lear, J. (1998). *Open minded: working out the logic of the soul*. Cambridge, MA: Harvard University Press.
Loewald, H. W. (1978). *Primary process, secondary process, and language. In papers on psychoanalysis*. Vol. 1980. New Haven: Yale University Press, 178–206.
Meltzer, D. (1983). *Dream-life. A re-examination of the psychoanalytical theory and technique*. London: Clinic Press, for the Roland Harris Trust Library.
Mills, J. (2005). A critique of relational psychoanalysis. *Psychoanal. Psychol.* 22, 155–188.
Mills, J. (2017). Challenging relational psychoanalysis: a critique of postmodernism and analyst self-disclosure. *Psychoanal. Perspect.* 14, 313–335.
Netz, R. (2016). Some reflections on the illusion of literary fame, Ho! *Lit. Mag.* 14, 191–203.
Northoff, G. (2012). Psychoanalysis and the brain – why did Freud abandon neuroscience? *Front. Psychol.* 3, 71
Parsons, M. (1990). Marion Milner's "answering activity" and the question of psychoanalytic creativity. *Int. Rev. Psychoanal.* 17, 413–424.
Pound, E. (1934). *Selected poems. Edited with an introduction by T. S. Eliot*. London: Faber & Faber Ltd.
Puget, J. (2017). Discussion of Dominique Scarfone's paper, "on 'that is not psychoanalysis': ethics as the main tool for psychoanalytic knowledge and discussion": terminable and interminable discussion. *Psychoanal. Dialogues*. 27, 401–405.
Roth, M. (2017). Projective identification and relatedness: a Kleinian perspective. *Psychoanal. Perspect.* 14, 350–355.
Ruby, P. M. (2011). Experimental research on dreaming: state of the art and neuropsychoanalytic perspectives. *Front. Psychol.* 2, 286.
Rustin, J. (2012). *Infant research & neuroscience at work in psychotherapy: expanding the clinical repertoire (Norton Professional Books)*: New York: W. W. Norton & Company Kindle Edition, 9.
Scruton, R. (2015). Poetry and truth, chapter 7. In *The philosophy of poetry*. ed. J. Gibsons. London: Oxford, 149–161.
Seligman, S. (2018). *Relationships in development – infancy, intersubjectivity and attachment*. London: Routledge.
Silverman, L. H. (1982). A comment on two subliminal psychodynamic activation studies. *J. Abnorm. Psychol.* 91, 126–130.
Silverman, L. H. (1985). Comments on three recent subliminal psychodynamic activation investigations. *J. Abnorm. Psychol.* 94, 640–643.
Stern, D. (1985). *The interpersonal world of the infant*. New York: Basic Books.
Stern, D. (2004). *The present moment in psychotherapy and everyday life*. New York: Basic Books.
Stern, D. B. (1983). Unformulated experience, from familiar chaos to creative disorder1. *Contemp. Psychoanal.* 19, 71–99.
Stolorow, R. D., Orange, D. M., and Atwood, G. E. (2001). Psychoanalysis—A contextual psychology: Essay in memory of Merton M. Gill. *Psychoanal. Rev.* 88(1), 15–28. https://doi.org/10.1521/prev.88.1.15.17545
Strozier, C. B. (2001). *Heinz Kohut: the making of a psychoanalyst*. New York: Farrar & Straus.
Winnicott, D. W. (1953). Transitional objects and transitional phenomena; a study of the first not-me possession. *Int. J. Psychoanal.* 34, 89–97.
Yadlin-Gadot, S. (2017). Truth axes and the transformation of self. *Psychoanal. Rev.* 104, 163–201.
Yakeley, J. (2017). Mind the baby: the role of the nanny in infant observation. *Int. J. Psychoanal.* 98, 1577–1595.
Yovell, Y., Solms, M., and Fotopoulou, A. (2015). The case for neuropsychoanalysis: why a dialogue with neuroscience is necessary but not sufficient for psychoanalysis. *Int. J. Psychoanal.* 96, 1515–1553.

21

PSYCHOANALYTIC EVIDENCE

The Old and the New

Ed Erwin

The old psychoanalytic evidence was amassed between 1900 and 2000. The new was published in this century.

We could ignore the older evidence, but many of the fundamental questions about how to interpret and weigh this evidence have not been answered to everyone's satisfaction. The issues that were raised in the last century will arise again in interpreting the new evidence.

The Old Evidence: Psychoanalytic Treatment

Establishing the effectiveness of a long-term therapy like psychoanalysis has long posed difficult problems. One is this: without random assignment to treatment and a placebo control, one cannot rule out spontaneous remission and placebo effects.

One might try to include a placebo control in outcome studies of psychoanalysis, but this is not easily done. It is one thing to compare a pill for depression to a sugar pill, quite a much harder thing to devise a placebo control for psychoanalysis. What would we provide to patients in the placebo group that would take the place of talking to the analyst, free association, and dream analysis?

Even if this conceptual problem were overcome, there would be a moral obstacle to giving a placebo treatment for two years or more to patients suffering from serious psychological problems such as clinical depression, agoraphobia, and severe anxiety.

Instead of relying on clinical trials, many psychoanalysts looked for alternatives. The American Psychoanalytic Association for a long time used base rates of improvement to show that psychoanalysis is effective in about two-thirds of all cases. Eysenck (1952) and Erwin (1980) showed that this way of proving effectiveness is too flawed to work.

Others resorted to philosophy arguing, as Thomas Kuhn (1970) had, that evidential standards need to be relativized to a paradigm. For behavior therapists, experimental evidence was a must on their standards, but were not needed in a psychoanalytic paradigm. On this issue, see Bachrach et al. (1991).

Seligman's Questionnaire Methodology

Many found more promising the effectiveness questionnaire methodology developed by the psychologist Martin Seligman. Seligman published his questionnaire in *Consumer Reports* (CR)

DOI: 10.4324/9780429297076-25

and reported on its findings in *American Psychologist* (1995). His conclusions were about psychotherapy in general, not psychoanalysis in particular, but others have applied his methodology to psychoanalysis (Freedman et al., 1999).

The idea that we can determine not only whether people undergoing psychotherapy improved after treatment, but also what caused the improvement by asking them for their opinions does not seem especially plausible. Seligman is aware of this fact. He agrees that credible alternatives to saying that the treatment worked need to be ruled out, but claims to have done this by using "internal controls" to discount rival hypotheses that say the beneficial effects were due to spontaneous remission or placebo factors.

The argument, roughly, is this: based on the CR figures, we can infer the following conclusions, which in turn can serve as internal controls: (l) longer duration of psychotherapy correlates with more improvement; (2) psychotherapy alone does just as well as psychotherapy plus drugs for all disorders, and given the history of placebo controls being inferior to drugs, one can infer that psychotherapy would have outperformed such controls had they been run; (3) marriage counselors treat the same sorts of problems as professional psychotherapists, but do significantly worse than psychotherapy professionals; and (4) family doctors also do significantly worse than mental health professionals when treatment continues beyond six months. The most likely explanation of these four facts, the argument continues, is that the psychotherapy received by respondents was generally effective, and the more of it the better; consequently, the CR study provides empirical validation of the effectiveness of psychotherapy as well as supporting longer term treatments.

How epistemically useful are Seligman's "internal controls"? The first correlation, between longer duration of treatment and effectiveness, cannot serve as a control for spontaneous remission. If a therapy is followed by spontaneous remission of symptoms, the longer the treatment, the greater the opportunity for spontaneous remission; so, even if factors outside the therapy setting were causing improvement, there would be more improvement with longer-term therapies.

The second internal control, that psychotherapy alone does just as well as psychotherapy plus drugs and that placebos are inferior to drugs, is also unsatisfactory.

First, in the treatment of depression, in two-thirds of all cases, placebos are not inferior to pharmaceutical treatments (Erwin, 1997). Second, some psychotherapies do better than others; see Dobson's (1989) reviews of meta-analyses showing the superiority of Beck's cognitive therapy for depression. Without knowing which kind of psychotherapy each respondent had received, we cannot know if they would have fared worse had they been given a placebo. Third, and most telling, without a placebo control, it cannot be inferred that any psychotherapy, including Beck's, is effective.

After criticisms were made of the Beck studies, the National Institute of Mental Health did a randomized controlled trial including a sugar pill as a placebo, Beck's psychotherapy and a second psychotherapy. Neither psychotherapy could beat the sugar pill, and neither did the standard pharmaceutical treatment also included in the study (Elkin et al., 1989). Contrary to what Seligman claims, we cannot reasonably infer that psychotherapy would have outperformed a placebo control in the CR study had one been included.

Seligman's (3) and (4) are also useless as internal controls. Conclusion (3) says that marriage counselors do significantly worse than psychotherapy professionals; and (4) says the same about family doctors who treat psychological problems when treatment continues beyond six months.

The evidence goes against both claims. In 41 of 42 studies comparing professional psychotherapists and paraprofessionals, the professional psychotherapists failed to outperform the paraprofessionals (Durlak, 1979). After reviewing improvements in the methodology of such studies and refinements in the evidence, Christensen and Jacobson (1994)) render the following verdict (p. 9): "Yet, whatever refinements are made, whatever studies are included or excluded, the results show either no difference between professionals and paraprofessionals, or, surprisingly, differences that favor paraprofessionals."

Finally, the results in the CR survey were not impressive. Only 13 percent of those receiving Seligman's survey responded. There is no way of knowing if the non-responders experienced far less improvement than those who responded. It should also be noted in passing that the spectacular results – 90 percent improvement – were arrived at by lumping together those reporting a great deal of improvement with those who judged that they had improved "somewhat" or a "lot." If one asks how many said that they had improved a great deal, the answer is: 54 percent, a percentage found in psychological studies of patients receiving no treatment at all.

In short, the CR survey provided evidence that a certain group undergoing psychotherapy were of the opinion that they had improved to some degree because of their therapy, but placebo factors or spontaneous remission were not ruled out as the cause of their perceived improvement.

Conclusion: Seligman's study did not provide evidence that psychotherapy of any form is effective for any clinical problem.

In a second study, a group of psychoanalysts, Freedman et al. (1999), followed up on the Seligman study. They claim that their study provides a replication of the CR finding that longer therapy tends to produce better results. For reasons I gave earlier, this was not demonstrated in the *Consumer Reports* study.

In their study, 99 outpatients attending the IPTAR clinic in New York City responded to the Consumer Reports questionnaire. On the basis of the patient responses, the authors claim to have demonstrated that as a result of receiving psychoanalysis, the quality of life of the patients who responded had been enhanced and, further, that duration and frequency of therapy contributed toward this end. The authors close with a bold declaration: "Our empirical findings, together with those in the evolving literature, establish this as a clinical fact" (Freedman et al., 1999, p. 770).

What were the findings that establish this clinical fact? Freedman et al. found an incremental gain in effectiveness scores from 6 months to over 24 months of treatment. Before concluding that the results support the Freedman et al. hypothesis, certain questions need to be answered.

First, how was the effectiveness score calculated? Following the practice of the original *Consumer Reports* Survey, it was composed of three factors: specific improvement with respect to the problems that led the respondent to therapy; satisfaction with the therapist's treatment; and global improvement, that is, how respondents felt at the initiation of treatment and how they felt after treatment had ended. Points were then assigned in each category depending on whether the respondent rated his or her improvement with respect to each condition as "a lot better," "somewhat better," and so forth.

The third factor, global improvement, is not a measure of specific improvement with respect to the problems that led the respondents to therapy. This factor measures how respondents felt at the time of the CR survey compared with how they felt when they began treatment. This does not tell us anything about diminishment of the problems that led them to seek treatment. There might have been a lot of improvement with respect to their marriage, their finances, their job prospects, or their physical health leading them to conclude that their lives were better, but little or no improvement on the problems that led them into therapy.

The second of the three factors, satisfaction with the therapist, also does not measure improvement in the patients' presenting problems.

Even if other factors are ignored, the results of the study were not encouraging. On the only factor that matters in assessing the effects of the treatment, symptomatic improvement, it failed to be significantly related to duration of treatment. Only liking the therapist's treatment was so correlated, and that could just as plausibly be interpreted as the reason for staying in treatment for a longer period rather than being an effect of longer treatment.

There are other problems with the study, some that are likely to reappear when the questionnaire method is used again. The authors label the therapy they studied "psychoanalytic psychotherapy," but this term is used to designate psychoanalytically oriented psychotherapy, which is not psychoanalysis.

The most significant problem, however, pertains to the authors' two central claims that (1) as a result of receiving psychoanalysis, the quality of life of the patients who responded had been enhanced, and (2) that duration and frequency of therapy contributed toward this end. Without controls for spontaneous remission or placebo factors, the authors provide no evidence that any improvement in quality of life was caused by psychoanalytic psychotherapy.

Seligman's questionnaire methodology has been used by others to study the effects of psychoanalysis (Sandell et al., 2000), but without success. This situation is not likely to improve for a simple philosophical reason.

If a placebo control is included in a study, we can rule out placebo effects if the treatment group did significantly better on the outcome measures than the placebo group. Internal controls cannot serve the same epistemic function; if they could, pharmaceutical companies paying for clinical trials could save millions of dollars by substituting internal controls for randomization, blinding, and placebo controls.

For researchers relying on internal controls only, the best they can do is to find significant correlations between certain factors, but without adequate external controls, they cannot establish the cause of the correlation. It could be accidental or due to a third variable. In a well-known case, a researcher concluded that he had found evidence that drinking a certain amount of coffee each day significantly increases the risk of pancreatic cancer, despite the fact that his study was not about coffee drinking. He had noticed that a subset of his subjects developed more pancreatic cancer than the others and they drank more coffee. His interpretation of his study results was later decisively discredited.

It is not logically impossible to establish causation relying on internal controls only, but to adopt this as a general strategy is to take another step backwards in trying to support psychoanalysis.

The Old Evidence: Psychoanalytic Theory

For almost a century, Freudians relied for supporting evidence on single case studies of patients treated by psychoanalysts. Many arguments were given to justify the case study method (for review, see Grünbaum, 1984). In the end, this type of evidence proved too weak to support any distinctively psychoanalytic theory (Grünbaum, 1984; Erwin, 1996).

Although Freud and most of his followers spurned the need for experimental studies, about 1500 were done (Kline, 1986, p. 205). They are reviewed, some favorably, by Fisher and Greenberg (1977, 1985) and Paul Kline (1981). Erwin (1996) argues that none of these studies provides empirical support for any distinctively Freudian theory. The failures to confirm are mainly due to methodological problems. These include (1) the failure to provide replications; (2) an overreliance on projective tests that have not been validated such as the Rorschach test and the Blacky cartoons; (3) the testing of hypotheses that were not distinctively Freudian; and (4) a failure to rule out credible rival explanations.

With a few exceptions, these failures to confirm are not evidence of falsity. Better studies or use of an entirely different sort of evidence such as evidence from neuropsychoanalysis (see the next section) might eventually confirm some major psychoanalytic theories.

The 21st-Century Evidence

In the present century, many psychoanalysts have rejected the traditional reliance on single case studies. Some have done experimental studies, the majority of which have been of short-term psychodynamic psychotherapy. Others have relied on evidence from neuropsychoanalysis.

The Fonagy Review

The Fonagy (2015) study provides a comprehensive review of the new outcome studies and meta-analyses of treatments for the major categories of mental health disorders. Fonagy concludes that the evidence generally but not invariably shows PDT (psychodynamic therapy) to be effective for depression, some anxiety disorders, eating disorders, and somatic disorders. The strongest evidence, Fonagy concludes, also supports long-term psychodynamic treatment of some personality disorders, particularly borderline personality disorder.

In his work, Fonagy encountered a philosophical problem due to the multiplication of therapies just as behavior therapists had when they stopped identifying a treatment as behavior therapy if it had a conditioning foundation (Erwin, 1978).

The same problem arises for psychodynamic psychotherapies. There are now more than 30 types based on different and sometimes conflicting psychological theories. Without being able to define "psychodynamic therapy," how does a reviewer of apparently favorable evidence know whether or not it supports the effectiveness of PDT?

As Fonagy points out, giving a definition of PDT has become more difficult in recent decades because of changes in PDT and cognitive behavior therapy leading to a blurring of the differences between the two.

He tries to get around this problem by adopting a "pragmatic" approach which uses "self-declared allegiance" as the guiding principle as to what constitutes PDT. However, this creates a problem for his entire review. Some therapists might see what they are practicing as cognitive behavior therapy, while others using essentially the same treatment may see it as psychodynamic therapy.

Without having any way of knowing whether or not a treatment described by someone as PDT truly is psychodynamic therapy, there is no way to separate studies of genuine psychodynamic therapy from masqueraders. Consequently, there is no way of knowing if any improvement found in the studies was due to psychodynamic therapy.

The Smit, Huibers, Ioannidis, Van Dyck, Tilburg, and Arntz (2012) review reports on a meta-analysis of randomized controlled trials of the effectiveness of long-term psychoanalytic psychotherapy (LTPP), which, again, is not psychoanalysis. The reviewers found that the recovery rate of various mental disorders was equal after LTPP or various control conditions including treatment as usual. They conclude that evidence for the effectiveness of LTPP was found to be limited and at best conflicting.

The review did not include randomized controlled studies of psychoanalysis because after an extensive search, the authors did not find any. This is the same situation that prevailed at the time of Erwin's (1996) review of outcome studies of psychoanalysis. There were no randomized controlled studies. On this issue, nothing has changed.

Psychoanalytic Theories and Therapy, and Neuropsychoanalysis

After decades of criticism of the case-study evidence for psychoanalytic theories and therapy (Grunbaum, 1984; Erwin, 1996), hope for support for psychoanalysis waned as the number of new patients entering psychoanalysis dropped to zero. The situation, however, has become more favorable largely due to recent work in neuropsychoanalysis.

Mark Solms, one of the leading proponents of neuropsychoanalysis, points out (Solms, 2004) that there are now interdisciplinary groups devoted to psychoanalysis and neuroscience in almost every major city in the world; that a new society has been formed, the International Neuro-Psychoanalysis Society, and that a journal, *Neuro-Psychoanalysis*, is now publishing papers on topics of common interest to psychoanalysts and neuro-scientists. There are also annual conferences on neuropsychoanalysis.

These events are consonant with, and likely reflect, developments in general psychology where there has been a trend towards neuroscience (see Satel and Lilienfeld, 2013). Despite these positive developments, some, most notably Blass and Carmeli (2007), have raised doubts about the entire neuropsychoanalytic enterprise.

The Blass and Carmeli Arguments

In a 2007 paper, Blass and Carmeli challenge the idea that neuroscientific findings are relevant and important for the development and justification of psychoanalytic theory and practice.

In a second paper (2015, p. 1155), Blass and Carmeli go far beyond their original point about the weakness of the neuropsychoanalytic arguments. They boldly claim that neuroscience has no contribution to make to psychoanalysis and it can never have any.

In their original paper, Blass and Carmeli examine arguments of neuropsychoanalysts in four areas. They argue that neuroscience has little or no relevance to psychoanalysis in any of these areas. Their arguments are important given the amount of attention paid to work in these areas, but they leave open the possibility that neuroscience will prove useful in areas they do not discuss. Consequently, the authors have not shown in their 2007 paper that neuroscience findings are never important and relevant to psychoanalysis.

Blass and Carmeli, however, have more general arguments, some of philosophical interest. One is worth quoting:

> Neuroscience can describe the neural networks underlying psychological phenomena, patterns, and tendencies, but these phenomena, patterns, and tendencies are recognized and their laws specified without any information regarding the neurons that function concomitantly. Only once these are recognized on the psychological level can neuroscience proceed with its description, but it does so without adding anything to the psychological knowledge already obtained.
>
> *(Blass and Carmeli, 2007, p. 10)*

This last sentence is crucial to their argument and should be challenged. Some psychoanalysts once tried to specify the causes of schizophrenia in terms of malfunctioning family relationships, but evidence of brain malfunctioning in schizophrenics was relevant to deciding whether their attempts would succeed. Studies of the brain made it likely that such attempts would fail. The neuroscience evidence was both relevant and important. The phenomenon of malfunctioning family relationships were recognized on the psychological level, but neuroscience added something important to the psychological knowledge, significant information about the causal role of these family relationships.

There is a point of logic here to be considered. A purely psychological theory that says nothing about neurons may by itself logically entail nothing about the brain; so, it might appear that neuroscience is irrelevant to a psychological theory's truth or justification. What this overlooks is that adding other premises to the propositions of the psychological theory may guarantee the relevance of neuroscience.

To take a controversial example, Freud's theory that dreams are instigated by repressed wishes says nothing about the brain, but we make neuroscience relevant if we combine his theory with the premises that (1) dreams are instigated by unconscious wishes only if higher-level motivational brain processes are responsible for the appearance of the dream; (2) that these higher-level processes cannot be responsible if all dreaming occurs only during REM sleep, assuming that REM processes are derived from automatic activity coming from the brain stem, and (3) in fact all dreaming occurs during REM sleep. This last premise was successfully challenged by work in neuroscience.

Blass and Carmeli have another argument, which they may consider their most important one. Psychoanalysis, they argue, is concerned with meanings as mental phenomena (2015, p. 2). Since it is a process and theory geared towards understanding the latent meanings and psychic truths determining the human psyche, neuroscientific findings are irrelevant to its aims and practices.

There is good reason to question this description of psychoanalysis.

In the 1970s, many psychoanalysts adopted a hermeneutical interpretation of psychoanalysis according to which clinical work does not consist of causal explanations but of ascriptions of meaning (Strenger, 2002). Jürgen Habermas, Paul Ricoeur, and many others said that the same about Freud's theory. The theory is concerned with ascriptions of and understanding meanings. It is not a theory about causation.

At first glance, there seems to be substance to the hermeneutical reading of Freud. Key Freudian hypotheses seem to be about meanings, the meaning of such items as neurotic symptoms, dreams, and slips of the tongue and pen.

In speaking of the meaning of behavior and mental states, the hermeneuticians were not talking about linguistic meaning, that is, meaning in the sense that words and sentences have meaning. If psychoanalytic theory were truly about linguistic meaning, neuroscience would likely not contribute anything to its understanding, but this reading of psychoanalysis would be utterly implausible. Freud's theories about dreams, the etiology and treatment of neuroses, and repression are not about the meaning of words. They are about dreams, treatments of neuroses, and repression.

Those favoring a hermeneutical reading of Freud generally were not talking about linguistic meaning (Ricoeur might be an exception). Their central claim was that psychoanalytic theory is not a causal theory. It is a theory that explains its phenomena in terms of meanings.

A good illustration is Freud's case of the woman obsessed with writing down the serial number of every one of her kronens, a unit of currency, before parting with it. Freud says that "in obsessive actions everything has its meaning and can be interpreted" (1907, SE 9: 122). This is clearly consistent with a hermeneutical approach.

What was the meaning of the woman's obsession? She became obsessed with writing down the serial numbers of her bank notes after her lover declared that he would never part with a 5-kronen note she had given him because it had passed through her hands. Because she had doubts about his intentions, she meant to challenge him later, but she realized that without knowing the serial number of the original note, she would have no way of knowing if the 5-kronen note he might show her was the original.

Freud comments that her doubt remained unresolved and it left her with the compulsion to write down the number of each banknote, by which it can be distinguished from all others. This, Freud claims, is the meaning of her obsessive actions. Yet, what did he mean in saying that her unresolved doubt left her with the compulsion except that it caused it? If the doubt had made no difference to the compulsion, there would have been no reason to single it out as the meaning of the compulsive behavior.

What this cases illustrates is that when Freudian theory talks about the latent meaning of a dream, the meaning of a neurosis or slip of the tongue, these hypotheses presuppose causal propositions either for their truth or proof. If we reinterpret Freudian theory so that all of the implicit and explicit causal hypotheses vanish, then what is left cannot explain the phenomena that Freud was trying to explain.

Some favoring a hermeneutical interpretation denied this. They claimed that what explains the phenomena is its meaning. Causality plays no role. Here they ran into a problem they were never able to resolve and which damned the entire phenomenological enterprise. When meanings are brought in to explain, as in the case of the obsessed woman, they either made a difference to the occurrence of the events or they did not. If they did not, they do not explain; if they did, they were causes. A cause is something that makes a difference to the occurrence of an event.

If psychoanalytic theory is a causal theory, then in this respect it is like any psychological theory that attempts to explain mental events or behavior. Some theories may dispense with talk of meanings and instead speak of cognitive dissonance, self-efficacy expectations, beliefs, desires, or latent feelings, but these superficial differences in terminology do not explain why neuroscience may be relevant to them but not to theories that speak of meanings. Until this is explained, Blass and Carmeli's claim that psychoanalysis is concerned with meanings as mental phenomena may be true but adds nothing to their earlier arguments.

The upshot of this discussion is that the relevance of neuroscience to psychoanalysis needs to be discussed on a case-by-case basis. Its relevance and importance cannot be ruled out *a priori.*

The Positive Case for Neuropsychoanalysis

Most of the arguments for neuropsychoanalysis' relevance to psychoanalysis are empirical, but philosophical issues also play a role.

One pertinent philosophical question is whether psychoanalysis and neuroscience study the same entity. Some neuropsychoanalysts who speak of the mind-brain appear to be saying "yes." They are the same entity. The mind is the brain.

This issue was debated for years in philosophy when the most dominant theory of mind was the identity theory, which says that the mind and brain are one and the same, or, as formulated by philosophers who denied mental entities, all mental states are brain states.

The identity theory was eventually rejected by most philosophers because of its inability to deal with several problems. One quite relevant to neuropsychoanalysis is that the theory has been impossible to prove.

Neuroscientists can correlate mental and brain states by asking subjects what is going through their mind at a given point of time, and then using functional magnetic resonance imaging (fMRI) to take pictures of the brain, but even if we had perfect correlations, these findings would be neutral between the theory, claiming there is only one thing and dualistic theories that say there are two. The correlational results would not support the identity theory or dualism.

One positive philosophical argument for neuropsychoanalysis concerns the mind's causal dependence on the brain. The argument goes like this. If all mental events are causally dependent upon neural events, then wherever there is a psychological cause of a behavior or mental event, there will be a preceding neural event causally sufficient for the event to be explained, thus rendering the appeal to the psychological cause superfluous.

Suppose a woman slaps a man because she believes he has grossly insulted her. If her belief plus certain other psychological conditions, such as the woman's desire to respond, are sufficient to explain the slapping, there will be a preceding brain event such that once it occurs, it necessitates the slapping. The reference to the belief and other psychological conditions can be skipped.

In general, wherever there is a causal sequence, N (neural event) → P (psychological event) → B (behavior), the middle link can be ignored. Since the occurrence of N is causally sufficient for B, the intervening psychological link is said to be not needed to explain or predict the behavior. All psychological explanations, then, can in principle be replaced by neuroscience explanations.

This "skipping a link" argument was used by B. F. Skinner (Erwin, 1996) and other psychologists. It is not a good argument. The dubious premise says that because the initial cause in the sequence necessitates the final result, the intervening link is not needed to explain the behavior. This is true of prediction but not explanation.

Making an insulting comment, on Skinner's view, is an environmental event, but how the target of the comment responds will depend on whether she interprets it as an insult. To leave out her belief about what was said about her, as Skinner recommends, is to fail to understand why the slap occurred. The same problem arises in using the skipping a link argument in neuroscience.

If the woman slapped the man because of what she believed, there will be a preceding neural event which in combination with other events is causally sufficient for the slapping, but the causal chain does not terminate with a brain event. The brain event in turn will be preceded by a biological-chemical event that is also causally sufficient for the neural event. If the skipping a link argument were sound, psychological explanations would be eliminable but so would all neuroscience explanations.

The Empirical Issues

Mark Solms, one of the leaders of the neuropsychoanalytic movement, claims that neuroscientists are uncovering proof for some of Freud's key theories, including his theories about unconscious motivation, repression, the pleasure principle, the idea that dreams have meaning, and the Id-Ego-Superego hypothesis. Before looking at the specific details of his arguments, some general problems with neuropsychoanalysis should be mentioned.

Small sample sizes: Neuropsychoanalytic studies generally suffer from small samples sizes as do most other neuroscience papers. In a 2014 paper titled "Power failure: Why small sample size undermines the reliability of neuroscience," Button et al. (2013) found that the average statistical power of studies in the neurosciences is very low primarily due to small sample sizes. The consequences of this include overestimates of effect size and low reproducibility of results.

In a follow-up study, Szucs and Ioannidis (2017) analyzed statistical information extracted from thousands of recent cognitive neuroscience and psychology research papers. They conclude that the statistical power to discover existing relationships in these fields has not improved during the past half century.

Solms' Arguments

One subject of interest to Solms has been the bearing of neuroscience on Freudian dream theory. In a section headed "Dreams Have Meaning," Solms points out that the dream theory was seemingly discredited with the discovery of a strong correlation between dreaming and REM sleep, but more recent work in neuroscience shows that dreaming and REM sleep are dissociable states, controlled by distinct mechanisms. In short, dreams also occur outside of REM sleep.

Although these findings answer a serious objection to Freud's dream theory, they do not show that dreams have meaning in the sense Freud intended. That dreams sometimes have meaning has been known for thousands of years; it is not peculiar to Freud, and it is widely accepted by many of Freud's critics (Hobson, 2004; Domhoff, 2004). What the critics question is whether dreams have the sort of hidden meaning postulated by Freud. It is important to note, then, that the assigning of meaning to dreams does not support anything specifically Freudian. In addition, the thesis that dreams have hidden meanings is not confirmed by evidence that dreaming occurs outside of REM sleep – removing one counterargument is not confirmation – and is not confirmed by any other evidence from neuroscience.

What parts of Freudian dream theory, then, are confirmed by recent neuroscientific work? Solms (2004) claims that contemporary knowledge of the dreaming brain is "broadly consistent" with Freudian theory, but he does not claim, and he would be wrong to claim, that any of the neuroscientific evidence confirms that dreams have hidden meanings, or that they require interpretation in therapy, or that dreams are wish fulfilments, or that dream censorship occurs, or that free association is useful in uncovering the hidden meaning of dreams.

It is possible that future neuroscientific research will support Freudian dream theory, but in considering this possibility, one needs to look at research already done in dream laboratories. The extensive evidence discussed by Domhoff (2004) makes it likely that central parts of the theory, including most of the theses mentioned above, are not just unfounded but false.

A second alleged success for neuropsychoanalysis is its proof for Freud's structural theory of the mind which postulates the Id, Ego, and Superego. In a paper providing this proof, Solms points out that the core brain stem and limbic system correspond roughly to the id; the ventral frontal system, the dorsal frontal region, and the posterior cortex amount to the ego and superego. But how does he know that any of these identities he postulates holds? There is an instinctual part of the brain, but without evidence that there is an unconscious mental agency or structure that has the basic properties that Freud attributes to the Id, such as being the source of much mental conflict and seeking its own gratification, why believe that the id is roughly identical to the parts of the brain Solms specifies?

Has Freud's theory of repression been vindicated? For doubts about Freud's repression theory, including doubts about its existence, see Erwin (1996, pp. 220–223). If Solms is right, neuroscience provides an effective answer to these doubts.

Solms (2004) discusses a 1994 study by Ramachandran of anosognosic patients who have damage to the right parietal region of the brain, making them unaware of certain gross physical defects such as paralysis of a limb. One such patient with a paralyzed left arm consistently denied that she had a problem. After Ramachandran artificially activated her right hemisphere, the woman suddenly became aware that her arm was paralyzed and that it had been paralyzed continuously since she suffered a stroke eight days earlier. Solms takes these facts as showing that the woman was capable of recognizing her physical deficits and that she had unconsciously registered her paralysis during the previous eight days. His interpretation, however, is open to challenge. Based on Ramachandran's description of what occurred, it is not clear that the woman unconsciously registered the fact of her disability at any time prior to having her right hemisphere artificially stimulated.

When the stimulation wore off, the woman once again believed her arm was normal and forgot that part of the earlier interview in which she acknowledged that the arm was paralyzed. Based on his observations, Ramachandran concludes that memories can be selectively repressed and that observing this patient convinced him of the reality of repression phenomena. It is not clear why this interpretation is mandated by his findings. The observed events could be interpreted as evidence of repression, but, they could equally well be explained by talking about brain deficits.

The brain impairment causes an incapacity to recognize the paralysis of the arm except when the parietal region is being artificially stimulated and it also causes an inability to remember being aware of the paralysis during the stimulation period; there is no storing of memories in the unconscious, and hence no Freudian repression.

A more recent study by Anna Berti and her colleagues (Berti et al., 2005) appears to support this alternative explanation. They compared the distribution of brain lesions in patients showing left spatial neglect, left hemiplegia, and anosognosia with patients showing neglect, left hemiplegia but not anosognosia. The authors found differences in brain lesions between two patients and concluded that anosognosia for hemiplegia is best explained by the involvement of motor and premotor areas. If this is correct, there is no need to bring in repression in such cases.

Even if the denial involved in anosognosia patients were motivated as opposed to being directly caused by specific brain lesions, there are findings that would raise questions about the postulation of repression. On Freud's theory of repression, repressed material is stored in the unconscious and can be returned to consciousness, but only if the anxiety associated with the repressed memory is removed. On this basis, one would predict that repressed memories would stay repressed without a removal of the anxiety and that the repression would not be lifted spontaneously. Yet studies of anosognosia find that it often does remit spontaneously. For example, in the study by Maeshima et al. (1997), anosognosia disappeared within three months in all cases (p. 696).

On another issue, Solms points out that major brain structures essential for forming conscious (explicit) memories are not functional during the first two years of life. Yet our infantile memories, despite not being consciously encoded, can affect adult feelings and behavior. This claim, however, is so general and vague that it says nothing which critics of Freud typically deny, nor does it warrant acceptance of any major thesis that is specifically Freudian.

On a final issue, Solms argues that if Freud was right about the operation of the pleasure principle, then damage to the inhibitory structures of the brain will release wishful, irrational modes of mental functioning; this prediction, he claims, has been confirmed. Patients suffering from Korsakoff's psychosis are unaware that they are amnesiac and fill in memory gaps with confabulations. Such patients, Solms continues, maintain false beliefs that are generated by the pleasure principle, but he cites no evidence that the ego or superego are involved. All that is claimed is that the patients, once their cognitive mechanisms are damaged as the result of brain lesions, construct confabulations to recast reality as they want it to be.

Some investigators interpret such confabulating activity in Freudian terms, but it is not clear what evidence justifies this interpretation. People often see the world the way they wish it to be; there is nothing new in saying this. The finding that victims of a certain type of brain disorder are not just randomly making up false beliefs about the world, but are constructing visions of the world as they wish it to be is interesting, but not specifically Freudian. What we are left with is: if Freud is right about the pleasure principle, then damage to a certain area of the brain will cause wishful irrational modes of thinking. The prediction is correct, but no evidence is provided that only Freudian theory makes this prediction.

Conclusion: I have pointed to problems with some of Solms' papers and to general problems with the neuropsychoanalytic literature including studies with small sample sizes; failures to rule out credible rivals to the hypothesis being tested; and the unargued identification of neural events or processes with mental events or processes postulated by Freud or other psychoanalysts. Some of these issues need to be resolved before neuropsychoanalysts can justifiably claim to have supported Freudian theory or any psychoanalytic theory. Yet without reviewing other papers by Solms and others working in this area, I am in no position to say that nothing done so far accomplishes this.

There was a low point for psychoanalysis in the last part of the 20th century when the traditional case method for obtaining evidence was discredited (Grunbaum, 1984; Erwin, 1996); when pharmaceutical and psychological alternatives to psychoanalytic treatment, such as cognitive behavior therapy, were being widely used; and when the rate of new patients entering psychoanalysis fell to zero. There was a lot of pessimism. Some predicted that psychoanalysis would never recover.

Things have changed. There are exciting things going on now in psychoanalytic research and not just in neuropsychoanalysis. Is Freud back? Solms says so (2004). Perhaps he is right, but given the serious defects in so many neuropsychoanalytic studies, more work will be needed before a confident answer can be given.

References

Bachrach, H., Galatzer-Levy, R., Skolnifkoff, A. and Waldron, S. (1991). On the efficacy of psychoanalysis. *Journal of the American Psychoanalytic Association*, 39:871–916.

Berti, A., Bottini, G., Gandola, M., Pia, M., Smania, N., Stracciari, A., Castiglioni, A., Vallar, G. and Paulesu, E. (2005). Shared cortical anatomy for motor awareness and motor control. *Science*, 309:488–491.

Blass, R. B. and Carmeli, Z. (2007). The case against neuropsychoanalysis. On fallacies underlying psychoanalysis' latest trend and its negative impact on psychoanalytic discourse. *International Journal of Psychoanalysis*, 88:1–15.

Blass, R. B. and Carmeli, Z. (2015). Further evidence for the case against neuropsychoanalysis: how Yovell, Solms, and Fotopoulou's response to our critique confirms the irrelevance and harmfulness to psychoanalysis of the contemporary neuroscientific trend. *International Journal of Psychoanalysis*, 96:1555–1173.

Button, K., Ioannidis, J., Mokrysz, C. and Nosek, B. (2013). Power failure: Why small sample size undermines the reliability of neuroscience. *Nature Reviews Neuroscience*, 14:365–376.

Christiansen, A. and Jacobson, N. (1994). Who (or what) can do psychotherapy: The status and challenge of nonprofessional therapies. *Psychological Science*, 5:8–14.

Dobson, K. S. (1989). A meta-analysis of the efficacy of cognitive therapy of depression. *Journal of Consulting and Clinical Psychology*, 57:414–419.

Domhoff, G. (2004). Why did empirical dream researchers reject Freud? A critique of historical claims by Mark Solms. *Dreaming*, 14(1):3–17.

Durlak, J. (1979). Comparative effectiveness of paraprofessional and professional helpers. *Psychological Bulletin*, 86(1):80–92.

Elkin, I., Shea, T., Watkins, J., Imber, S., Sotsky, S., Collins, J., Glass, D., Pilkonis, P., Leber, W., Docherty, J., Fiester, A. and Parloff, M. (1989). National Institute of Mental Health treatment of depression collaborative research program. *Archives of General Psychiatry*, 46:971–982.

Erwin, E. (1978). Spanish edition, ediciones piramide, 1985. In *Behavior Therapy: Scientific, Philosophical and Moral Foundations*. Cambridge: Cambridge University Press.

Erwin, E. (1980). Psychoanalytic therapy: The Eysenck argument. *American Psychologist*, 35(5):435–443.

Erwin, E. (1996). *A Final Accounting: Philosophical and Empirical Issues in Freudian Psychology*. Cambridge, MA: M.I.T. Press.

Erwin, E. (1997). *Philosophy and Psychotherapy*. London: Sage Publications.

Eysenck, H. J. (1952). The effects of psychotherapy: An evaluation. *Journal of Consulting Psychology*, 16:319–324.

Fisher, S. and Greenberg, R. (1977). *The Scientific Credibility of Freud's Theories and Therapy*. New York: Basic Books.

Fisher, S. and R. Greenberg. (1985). *The Scientific Credibility of Freud's Theories and Therapy.* New York: Columbia University Press.

Fonagy, P. (2015). The effectiveness of psychodynamic psychotherapies. *World Psychiatry*, 14:137–150.

Freedman, N., Hoffenberg, J., Vorus, N. and Frosch, A. (1999). The effectiveness of psychoanalytic psychotherapy: The role of treatment duration, frequency of sessions, and the therapeutic relationship. *Journal of the American Psychoanalytic Association*, 47:741–772.

Freud S. (1907). Obsessive actions and religious practices. In *SE* 9, edited by J. Strachey. London: The Hogarth Press, 1975.

Grünbaum, A. (1984). *The Foundations of Psychoanalysis: A Philosophical Critique.* (Pittsburgh Series in Philosophy and History of Science). Berkeley, CA: University of California Press.

Hobson, J. A. (2004). Freud returns? Like a bad dream. *Scientific American*, 290(5):89.

Kline, P. ([1972] 1981). *Fact and Fantasy in Freudian Theory*, 2nd ed. New York. Methuen.

Kline, P. (1986). Kline replies to Erwin. In *Hans Eysenck: Consensus and Controversy,* edited by S. Modgil and C. Modgil. London: Falmer Press.

Kuhn, T. (1970). *The Structure of Scientific Revolutions.* Chicago: University of Chicago Press.

Maeshima, S., Dohi, N., Funahashi, K., Nakai, Itakura, T. and Komai, N. (1997). Rehabilitation of patients with anosognosia for hemiplegia due to intracerebral haemorrhage. *Brain Injury*, 11:691–697.

Sandell, R., Blomberg, A. Lazar, Carlsson, J., Broberg, J. and Schubert, J. (2000). Varieties of long-term outcome among patients in psychoanalysis and long-term psychotherapy. A review of findings in the Stockholm Outcome of Psychoanalysis and Psychotherapy Project (STOPP). *International Journal of Psychoanalysis*, 81(5):921–942.

Satel, S. and Lilienfeld, S. (2013). *Brainwashed: The Seductive Appeal of Mindless Neuroscience.* New York: Basic Books.

Seligman, M. (1995). The effectiveness of psychotherapy. The Consumer Reports Study. *American Psychologist*, 50:965–974.

Smit, Y., Huibers, M., Ioannidis, J., van Dyck, R., van Tilburg, W. and Arntz, A. (2012). The effectiveness of long-term psychoanalytic psychotherapy: A meta-analysis of randomized controlled trials. *Clinical Psychology Review*, 32:81–92.

Solms, M. (2004). Freud returns. *Scientific American*, 290:82–88.

Strenger, C. (2002). Hermeneutics, and psychoanalysis. In *The Freud Encyclopedia: Theory, Therapy, and Culture*, edited by E. Erwin. New York and London: Routledge, pp. 256–257.

Szucs, D. and Ioannidis, J. (2017). Empirical assessment of published effect sizes and power in the recent cognitive neuroscience and psychology literature. *PLoS Biology*, 15(3):e2000797. doi:10.1371/journal.pbio.2000797.

PART IV

Philosophical Debates

22

THE PSYCHOANALYTIC *DAS ICH*

Lost in Translation

Alfred I. Tauber

The Problem

The English *Standard Edition* of Freud's works introduced translations that have purportedly altered basic understanding of psychoanalytic theory. Most prominent among the disputed meanings concerns the construal of Freud's use of '*das Ich*' – 'the I.' Some have maintained that translating 'the I' as 'the ego' introduces a semantic distortion with a host of issues embedding ambiguities in discerning Freud's intent and the development of his thought. The question is hardly trivial given that the very character of the psychoanalytic subject is at stake in this debate. So, when new English translations were prepared upon the *Standard Edition*'s copyright expiration in 1989, some of the translators made adjustments in answer to wide-ranging criticisms (Hawkins 2018).[1]

Although discussed earlier, the issue gained prominence in the 1980s as 'self psychology' emerged from 'ego psychology' and the orthodoxy of Freudian psychoanalysis underwent a major trial. The defense argued for the prior convention of 'ego' in the English translation of German that carries an implicit understanding: The Freudian subject is the individual who has the sense of experiencing his/her 'I-ness' (i.e., subjectivity; Solms 1999). Some have argued that Freud differentiates various meanings of the subject and much is inevitably lost in translation given the subtleties of his original style. In any case, irrespective of such concerns, the prevailing position argues that *ego* is capable of representing the different senses of the subject.[2] So, by common assent, given the strength of the *Standard Edition*'s use of the 'ego,' the issue is moot, for the English translation has assumed an authority freed from the German original (Ornston 1982; Wilson 1987).

In opposition, critics hold (noting Freud's meticulous use of language) that his word choice of 'das Ich' is deliberate. He might have used *ego*, inasmuch as it was introduced in the mid-19th century in psychology and was explicitly used in the literature on hysteria by the last decade (Clarke 1894, p. 130).[3] However, from his earliest clinical writings to his last summary statements, Freud conspicuously omits *ego* or *Selbst* (self) to designate the subject.[4] When *self* rarely appears in the English *Standard Edition*, it is misappropriated. Indeed, selfhood considered in any formal sense escaped Freud's interest. Instead of reference to a self or ego, he employed the pronominal – s/he, you, I. Accordingly, the counter-position argues that 'ego' (among other mis-translations) misconstrues and thus distorts Freud's intent despite

DOI: 10.4324/9780429297076-27

his approval of the term.[5] James Strachey, the principal translator and editor of the English *Standard Edition*, has been accused of obscuring Freud's humanism for a falsified scientism; by using Latinized terminology, strengthening the medical orientation and thus 'hardening' Freud's tentative prose into firm theoretical claims; and in too many instances employing idiosyncratic translations to support his own purposes, specifically, imposing his own interpretation of Freud's notion of conscious agency to serve as a foundation for a scientific-oriented psychoanalytic theory.

Although Strachey took responsibility for translating the so-called 'technical terms' and in regard to *das Ich*, he worked with the Glossary Committee led by Ernest Jones and Joan Riviere. They insisted on using 'ego' and 'id' instead of 'the I' and 'the It,' favored by James and Alix Strachey, John Rickman and Leonard Woolf. The exchange is noteworthy (as reported by Strachey to his wife):

> The little beast [Jones] . . . is really most irritating. . . . They want to call "das Es" "the Id." I said I thought everyone would say "the Yidd."
>
> So Jones said there was no such word in English: 'There's "Yiddish," you know. And in German "Jude." But there is no such word as "Yidd."'
>
> 'Pardon me, doctor. "Yidd" is a current slang word for a Jew.'
>
> 'Ah! A slang expression. It cannot be in very widespread use then.'
>
> Simply because that l.b. [little beast] hasn't ever heard of it.
>
> *(Ornston 1992).*[6]

And from that brief exchange, the entire matter was settled for better and for worse.

Of course, dissenters are substituting their own translations in the context of a complex agenda.[7] The dispute rests on a broader view of psychoanalysis that evolved as the post-Freudians asserted their own theoretical interests. *Ego* routinely appears later in the writings of the ego psychologists, who shifted from Freud's focus on the theory of the unconscious psyche to the psychological adjustments of the self-conscious subject of analysis.[8] With the introduction of Heinz Kohut's object relations theory in the 1970s, an explicit 'psychology of the self' was expounded. Although Kohut failed to provide a definition of the self that sat at the center of his theory (Kohut 1977, pp. 310–311), the ordinary meanings of *ego* and *self* became operative in the psychoanalytic literature as analysts turned to the broad concerns of development and adaptation of the individual.[9] And here we find the tension that lies at the base of the *das Ich*/ego controversy: Despite Freud skirting the psychology of what came to be called, 'the ego,' his followers could not relinquish the search for a latent conception of one's selfhood that lies at the base of his theory.[10]

The ready (and general) acceptance of *ego* for the knowing subject attests to its semantic and psychological standing. But it is inescapable that Freud himself consistently relinquished its use in his original writings and was satisfied with the implicit uses and meanings of *das Ich*. He says so himself: in 1926, Freud published a summary of psychoanalytic theory for a lay audience, *The Question of Lay Analysis*. There, he specifically addresses the use of *das Ich* (and *das Es* – the it) in contrast to 'choosing orotund Greek nouns' to describe the mind's functional domains (Freud 1926a, p. 195). He then affirms that :

> we take our stand upon the ground of popular wisdom and recognize in human beings a mental organization inserted between sensory stimuli and their perception of bodily needs on the one hand, and their motor actions on the other, and for a certain purpose negotiating between them. We call this organization the I. But this is nothing new; everybody assumes such an organization as long as they aren't philosophers, and some do even though they are philosophers
>
> *(Freud 1926b, p. 105).*

Freud goes on to explain that for his patients' sake, non-technical terms are being used, inasmuch as 'they need to understand our theories, and they are often very intelligent but not always highly educated' (ibid. p. 106).

Freud is undoubtedly correct in specifying that psychoanalysis is about elucidating 'mental organization,' for his *scientific* interest lies in dissecting the mind and discerning its functions. And with that theoretical focus, the subject *qua* the subjective becomes a secondary matter. Of course, *Dr. Freud*, the physician, was oriented by his patient's suffering and an implicit sense of I-ness the analysand experiences. Here, humanistic elements come into play. However, *Prof. Freud*, the scientist, develops his theory without confounding issues about consciousness and accompanying subjective states. And here we find the root of the terminology debate. In the space that opens between his scientific interests and the subjectivity of his patient, a gap appears, or perhaps a tension emerges. For Freud's interpretive method, the subjective serves primarily as the portal into the depths of the psyche. The subjective 'surface' would be pierced by an analysis to reveal the underbelly of feelings, self-awareness, and conflict. Later, the post-Freudians who practiced 'ego psychology' focused on the development and adjustment of this *experiential* I. Accordingly, in rescuing the subjective *me* from the objectified mental apparatus drawn from Freud's scientific presentation, the phenomenology of the personal gained prominence. And with this evolution of psychoanalytic practice, the embedded subjective/objective division was exposed to display the fundamental dispute about the character of the discipline.

A semantic distinction would have been useful to clarify the issues and refine the arguments of different orientations. Using the same terminology to capture two competing agendas obscures the underlying philosophical commitments of each point of view. Because Freud made no effort to eliminate the crossover of meanings that appear repeatedly in his writings, his readers must rely on the context of the discussion to discern his thought. The *Standard Edition* similarly made no effort to distinguish the various meanings of the subject by using *ego* in both contexts. This inattention leads to an intriguing philosophical issue, one that Freud scrupulously avoided, but nevertheless erupted in the *das Ich*/ego controversy: *Who* is the psychoanalytic subject, and how should she be regarded?

The Freudian Subject

The success of psychoanalysis depends on self-awareness in various contexts (traumatic memory, social interactions, self-appraisals, etc.). Indeed, the underlying premise that emotional recognition and rational insight leads to personal freedom makes self-consciousness the linchpin of psychological and existential health. Because Freud does not explicitly consider the character of self-consciousness – the 'relation of oneself to oneself' – he ironically left the introspective subject uncharacterized. Although he admits that self-consciousness is an 'accomplishment' of sorts (Tugendhat 1986, p. 127), Freud dismissed the need to probe the nature of consciousness and took it as given and thus assumed its immediacy – and reality. His interests lay elsewhere. As he explained in his *New Introductory Lectures*, 'There is no need to discuss what is to be called conscious: it is removed from all doubt' (Freud 1933, p. 70). And more specifically, Freud's critical evaluation of self-reflection remained peripheral to his theoretical interests. He accepted the analysand's memory (albeit screened, repressed and thus contorted), at least to the extent that it offered the basis for analysis.[11] For Freud, at least, remembrance *as given* – whether 'true' or not – was sufficient for his purposes. And, in bypassing self-consciousness as a warrant of interest, he abdicated efforts to seriously examine the modes of self-identification and self-reflection that define the analysand's *das Ich* or sense of self. This is an ironic move. After all, the analysand's subjectivity is the substrate for the work of psychoanalysis, but only in the aftermath of orthodox Freudianism did ego and self-psychologies directly address *me* as the object of clinical intervention.

In this regard, Freud remained the erstwhile scientist. In his mature thought, *das Ich* is characterized not by a sense of self, but as a locus of three functions: (1) a coherent organization of mental processes, (2) an assembly of defenses that mediate the competing demands of unconscious desire and social reality and (3) the construction of multiple identifications (Freud 1923).[12] This is a structural-functional psychological model that eschews, in its theoretical description, what may be captured as the sense of *me*. Simply, Freud's focus on the agency of the unconscious (the drives, primary processes) left the self-conscious subject in abeyance. Moreover, because the analysand only carries a phenomenological identity, unencumbered by implicit notions about personal identity, the schematized *ego* is a designation of a technical terminology with specific categorical meanings. As a neuro-anatomist, Freud followed the accepted paradigm of his era to present a model of the brain's structure-function relations, an erstwhile objective formulation far removed from the subjectivity of his patient. He would probe beneath the manifest person, the I of the self-aware, to describe the unconscious dynamics of the psyche in his quest for a science of the mind.

We may well ponder, again, *who* or *what* is *das Ich*? Freud was satisfied with the simple designation of 'I' – unencumbered with the diverse constructions associated with ego or self so dominant in the philosophy and psychology literatures. He held no commitment to some totality of personal identity, and thus he remained satisfied with a commonsensical notion of personhood. Taking this assumed position, he addressed his patient by the ordinary 'you,' 'he,' or 'she.' On this pragmatic view, the 'I' simply serves as a useful idiom to capture the voice of the interior. But what is the relation between such a conscious voice and the inexpressible, a-rational mental interior? Or in the specifics of psychoanalytic theory, where do repression and catharsis operate, and how are controls imposed?

On the one hand, psychoanalysis provides the self-aware subject a means of autonomous interpretation, where rationality confers (some limited) authority over inner drives and desires. Such a subject possesses the ability to survey objects of its own intention, which, in the case of Freudian psychoanalysis, is the intimate other – the unconscious. From that understanding, the analysand putatively obtains various degrees of freedom from the despotic a-rationality of libidinal drives. Here, the modernist model of an autonomous subject finds its full expression (Taylor 1989; Seigel 2005; Thiel 2014), and when placing Freud in this philosophical setting, we clearly see that he struggled to find an interpretive analytic for his new psychiatry of personal liberation. Committed to the ideals of reason's power, the perfection of humankind, and, from the vantage of a physician, the therapeutic promise of analysis, Freud embraced a meliorism moderated by a powerful ambivalence (Freud 1933, p. 171; Whitebook 1995; Tauber 2012).

On the other hand, that depiction is placed in opposition to the subject with no such authority and (unless enlightened) ignorant of those unconscious despotic forces. Acknowledging the limits of self-consciousness, the inability to 'reason' with the unconscious and the creation of psychic reality from the throes of unrequited desire, Freud portrayed the human subject much as Plato had in the *Phaedrus* (246a–254e) – like a charioteer holding in check two steeds, each vying to go his own way. The basic design of the psychoanalytic mind presents a reality organized by intentional desire (conscious and unconscious) mediated by a social-derived normative rationality. The line between fantasy and reality is no longer something like the difference between a mental event and a 'real' event in some simple sense. Moreover, reason plays only one part among other contributing faculties to create the mental world in which one lives. With the status of self-knowing precariously lodged between desire and the demands of reality, skepticism finds its home. What can one know about his or her very own desire and motivations that rationalize choice and action? Given this dichotomy, *Who am I?* demands complex consideration of how unconscious forces define *agency* (the forces driving choices and actions) and impact the self-knowing, conscious *subject* (Moran 1993).

The analysand is poised between scrutinizing her agency as some kind of 'other' and then turning self-consciously to reflect on her own subjectivity arising from those psychic depths. *Das Ich* is not coincident with the subject, and in fact it is precisely in the difference between the two that one begins to be able to discern the creation of a new conceptual entity: the psychoanalytic subject (Ogden 1992, p. 572).[13]

Freudian theory thus splits the knowing (conscious) *subject* from the *agent,* the locus of psychic determinative control of thought, words, and deeds (Moran 1993). This division highlights an unresolved dilemma of Freudian theory: *Who* is the true who – the voice of the self-conscious subject or the psychic apparatus? Freud answered, the unconscious was the 'true psychic reality' (Freud 1900, p. 5:613). By that, Groddeck fairly observed,

> I hold the view that man is animated by the Unknown, that there is within him an 'Es,' an 'It,' some wonderous force that directs both what he himself does, and what happens to him. The affirmation 'I live,' is only conditionally correct, it expresses on a small and superficial part of the fundamental principle, 'Man is lived by the It.'
>
> *(Groddeck 1976, Letter II)*[14]

Yet, the dynamics of exchange, the defenses, repression and all the other proposed mechanics makes the conscious self responsible for keeping the psychic house in order. However, psychoanalytic theory reverses the hierarchy of the mind. What seems rational control is but misplaced confidence where ignorance and fantasy rule.

While Freud recognized the necessity of a 'dialogue' of sorts between conscious mentation and unconscious drives, his theoretical concerns were focused upon the dynamics and effects of the latter (Ogden 1992). After all, the central tenet of psychoanalysis held that

> the unconscious is the true psychical reality; *in its inner most nature it is as much unknown to us as the reality of the external world, and it is incompletely presented by the data of consciousness as is the external world by its communications of our sense organs*
>
> *(Freud 1900, p. 613).*

This basic concept displaced consciousness and its attendant notions of the knowing agency as comprising *me* with revolutionary consequences: Freud repeatedly asserts that free will is an allusion, that humans are unconsciously directed by deterministic unconscious forces, and the 'true' *Ich* is *Es*.

So then, *who* is the das Ich Freud cites – Man or das Es? And more generally, is psychoanalysis about the conscious *I* or the unconscious *it*? When stated as an unadorned opposition, a synthesis beckons, for psychoanalysis does in fact regard the subject in both ways, but unresolved ambiguities accompany this division of the psyche. What is the role of conscious awareness within the context of unconscious psychic dynamics? How are arational forces linked to the self-reflective individual? How is rational insight transmuted into analytic cure? What, indeed, is the proper balance between the two domains of mental life, between erotic desire and social reality? (e.g., Horkheimer and Adorno [1947] 1993; Marcuse 1955; Brown 1959).

The basic schism of agency embedded in Freud's theory already appears clearly in *Interpretation of Dreams* (1900), where the psychic processes he described are 'devoid of a subject; they simply operate within the subject,' thus leaving an unaccounted gap between *das Ich* and the unconscious domain (Moran 1993. pp. 48–50). In his later writings, best developed in *The Ego and Id* (1923), Freud blurs the boundaries between the conscious and unconscious domains by placing *das Ich* straddling the boundaries and engaged in a repressed/repressing dynamic. And with *Civilization and Its Discontents* (1930), Freud makes one last stab at finding the missing connections between the conscious subject and the agency of the unconscious:

> Normally, there is nothing of which we are more certain than the feeling of our self [Selbst!], of our own ego [das Ich]. This ego [das Ich] appears to us as something autonomous and unitary, marked off distinctly from everything else. That such an appearance is deceptive, and that on the contrary the ego [das Ich] is continued inwards, without any sharp delimitation, into an unconscious mental entity which we designate as the id [Es] and for which it serves as a kind of façade – this was a discovery first made by psycho-analytic research, which should still have much more to tell us about the relation of the ego [das Ich] to the id [Es].
>
> *(Freud 1930, pp. 65–66)*

This passage reveals Freud's own appreciation of the split subject: The first two sentences assert the reality and immediacy of the sense of one own self, one's intimate subjectivity. He then shifts to objectifying this *I* in asserting the relationship of this conscious subjectivity with its unconscious components. Note, *das Ich* is used in both discourses – subjective and objective – and thus Freud embeds two meanings in the same terminology. When the analysand lies on the couch, the subjective 'I' becomes an object of analysis, an 'ego' defined by psychoanalytic theory. A distinguishing terminology would make these two points of view explicit and thereby clarify the character of the subject. And beyond the particularities of Freud's writings, the duality points to a larger philosophical conundrum opened for inspection.

A Philosophical Perspective

Reflexivity appeared as a way of self-understanding during the early modern period, which is hardly surprisingly considering the pre-occupation with optics on the one hand, and cognitive introspection on the other. 'Reflexive' as used to refer to 'thought as bending back upon itself' first appears in the 1640s, when theologians, philosophers and poets embarked on an introspective inquiry only to 'stop' at some point to re-direct consciousness into the world. And at the same time, 'conscious' as meaning 'inwardly sensible or aware' appears first in 1620, 'consciousness' or 'the state of being conscious' in 1678, and 'self-consciousness' or 'consciousness of one's thoughts, etc.' in 1690. In German the equivalent terms are found in the same period (Whyte 1978, pp. 42–43). Reflexivity formally enters the philosophical tradition with Descartes division of *res cogitans* and *res extensa*: In his scheme, the Latinized *ego* became the seat of the knowing agent and the epistemological base from which he launched the attack on skepticism. However, Descartes' self-assurance that he *knew* that he thought is insufficient to make the jump that the self-conscious subject has substantive knowledge of *what* that 'thinking thing' is, or as later critics maintained, whether such 'self-knowledge' is *knowledge* at all. Simply, Descartes did not prove or substantiate his claim beyond what he had already presupposed (Chiesa 2007, p. 15).

The basic problem, as first noted by Henry Jeanes (an obscure English minister, 1611–1662), is the infinite regress encoded in reflexivity, where 'the mind in its reflexive workings can proceed *in infinitum*' and, consequently, a definable bedrock of the ego's *is-ness* cannot be held as some object (Jeanes 1656, p. 42; quoted by *Oxford English Dictionary* vol. Q, 1971: 345).[15] This position was firmly established by Hume, who famously observed that instead of the Cartesian ego, he found a 'bundle . . . of different perceptions,' and opined that its handmaiden, consciousness, is only the piecemeal aggregate of those perceptions – fragmentary, often incoherent, frequently rationally disordered, and powerfully driven by the 'passions' (Hume 1978, p. 252).

Hume did not deny the sense of self, but he dismissed the notion of a self insofar as it is accessible through inner empirical experience (i.e., consisting only of perceptions). Simply, for him, it is an imaginary construct, a fiction that permits the sense of an integrated identity, which is conceived by the same criteria we organize the world at large.[16]

Kant agreed and formulated a 'solution' with wide-ranging import, a construction Freud closely followed. Kant's understanding of self-conscious awareness makes no claim about the functions of an ego – indeed, he does not postulate an ego as such (i.e., an entity) that performs this function. Instead, he was satisfied in establishing the necessary conditions for cognition that must cohere perceptual contents and thereby unify experience. He placed this synthesis as a necessary condition of all knowing and names that function of consciousness, the 'transcendental unity of apperception' (i.e., self-consciousness; Kant 1998, B138, p. 249; B140, p. 250).

> The consciousness of oneself in accordance with the determinations of our state in internal perception is merely empirical, forever variable; it can provide no standing or abiding self in this stream of inner appearances, and is customarily called inner sense or empirical apperception
>
> *(Kant 1998, A107, p. 232).*

As Béatrice Longuenesse explains,

> Kant does not think that from the pure consciousness of oneself expressed in 'I think,' or more precisely, 'I am thinking,' one can derive any knowledge of the nature of the referent of 'I.' Nevertheless, 'I think' entails, for Kant just as for Descartes, 'I exist.' And for Kant, the consciousness of thinking expressed in 'I think' is a consciousness of myself as an 'I, or he or it (the thing) that thinks,' namely, as an entity that thinks and is individuated, for itself, by its consciousness of thinking. Thus . . . according to Kant, using 'I' in 'I think' expresses the consciousness of oneself as a particular entity (oneself, the entity currently thinking, whatever that entity is). . . . [U]sing 'I' in 'I think' is premised on nothing but the consciousness of a mental activity one takes to be one's own in virtue of the fact that one takes oneself to be accountable for the correctness of its contents and their connections
>
> *(Longuenesse 2017, pp. 6–7).*

Freud had imbibed the Kantian ethers and as a university student studied this formulation. Indeed, whether consciously or not, the Kantian model of the mind was firmly implanted in his own education (Tauber 2010). However, whatever indebtedness Freud might have had, he scrupulously avoided acknowledging Kant in the attempt to purge the specter of philosophy in his efforts to establish psychoanalysis as a scientific endeavor. Yet, much suggests that Freud accepted the cardinal feature of the transcendental deduction and like Kant, deliberately avoided *ego* and its trappings. As G.E.M. Anscombe explained,

> the 'I' is not something that can be found as a mind or soul, a subject of consciousness, one among others; there is no such thing to be 'found' as the subject of consciousness in this sense. All that can be found is what consciousness is of, the contents of consciousness
>
> *(Anscombe 1959, p. 68).*

In other words, there is a language of thought, and 'I' is the formal point of reference for it; that is, *I* then becomes a subject in the language of thought, in a language that places a subject in relation to an object. And, by convention, the *I* may be split to become both the subject and the object of thought.[17]

The self-conscious first-person addresses 'my' inner state as in a third-person relationship, but always as an object lacking a defined 'thinghood.' So, when the *I* examines itself as both subject and object of its reflexivity, an endless recursion results (Tauber 2006). Because the representation of the Cartesian ego as a representation of itself is divided by its own self-consciousness, a gap appears between the "I' of the 'I think' and the 'I' of the 'I am,' which follows as a logical conclusion from the 'I think.' That is to say, either these two 'I's' are not the same thing or the second is already assumed in the positing of the first. Since 'I think' already entails the subject 'I,' the conclusion, 'I am' is strictly superfluous. Simply, the ego has been split and subjectivity swings between the self-consciousness of *I think* and the being of *I am*. And here are the origins of Wittgenstein's later critique (and those of many others) of the ego – subjectivity, agency, and the self – that are based on self-knowledge, introspection and self-consciousness as qualified *knowledge* (Wittgenstein 1960, p. 66; reviewed in Tauber 2013). Accordingly, a false object of scrutiny has been created from a reflexive construction. False in the sense that there is no object to 'see,' to 'know.' Thus, the entire notion of a core ego – a homunculus – residing at the seat of one's soul appears as an artifact of the human cognitive faculty.

Freud averted this result by finding an object at the core of the psyche, *das Es*, that the subject might examine, albeit indirectly. Through associations, transference and other modes of disclosure, unconscious dynamics are explained, not by self-reflection as traditionally understood but rather by an entirely new method of introspection. Accepting this basic psychoanalytic tenet, the predicate thinking that permeates Freud's theory escapes the reflexive regress by objectifying the unconscious and leaving the subjective *das Ich* as the scrutinizing subject. (Of course, the entire enterprise assumes that the Unconscious is, in fact, a suitable entity for objectification, a claim that has suffered grievous criticism.) In this sense, *ego* fulfills the requirements of Freud's objectifying epistemology and the terminology is consistent with its historical use in philosophy.

However, the Cartesian divide (where the faculty of reason and self-consciousness – *me* – is set in an autonomous realm against the other, *das Es*) could not be sustained. The ego proved to have its own unconscious domain, so the structural model's last iteration assigned the ego both conscious and unconscious characteristics (Freud 1923, p. 24). The second corruption of the insular ego was based on psychological considerations. Although Freud entrusted the analysand's rationality (albeit weak and fallible) to serve as a bulwark against unconscious forces, he also adamantly rejected the equation of mind with consciousness. He thus would dislodge 'the arrogance of consciousness' and asserted how 'it is essential to abandon the overvaluation of the property of being conscious before it becomes possible to form any correct view of the origin of what is mental' (Freud 1910, p. 39). And at the level of discourse where psychic data emerges and analysis begins, the standing of consciousness is unsteady in terms of the veracity of its conjured memory, the meaning of its associations, and the rational conclusions of its explanations. Simply, given the limits of the knowing conscious subject, analysis lacks a firm epistemological foundation and, correspondingly, no 'gold standard' of judgment. Accordingly, psychoanalysis is interpretation all the way down and thus open to severe criticism as a scientific enterprise. In this latter context much is at stake, for if autonomy has been so severely compromised, how can *I* function with the (albeit limited) authority Freud assigns *me*? Here, an unguarded theoretical flank has been exposed. Indeed, this assault on free will and self-knowledge became a critical factor in the ego's requiem during the postmodern appraisal of the subject (Tauber 2013).

An Accounting

Freud's choice of vocabulary, the unassuming *das Ich*, offers a deflationary portrait of the subject, one dramatically different from the Cartesian ego, who asserts his very existence based upon the certainty of his own thinking – a thinking *thing* (Descartes 1985, p. 127). In the psychoanalytic scenario, *das Ich* is *not* that sense of self. Indeed, the very notion of conscious certainty is an anathema to Freudian precepts.

Without defining the ego as some natural entity, suffice to accept that the mind integrates disparate forms of human consciousness as a fundamental condition of coherent human cognition. And by dispensing with 'a thinking thing' (an entity), Freud was satisfied with a structure for the 'coordinated organization of mental processes' (Freud 1923, p. 17; see Longuenesse 2017). In that depiction, he sought no further delineation of *das Ich* and left *me* in *the I*'s radical subjectivity of *my* self-consciousness. Indeed, the subjective ego never found its conceptual traction in Freud's oeuvre, and perhaps that is why Strachey accepted a vocabulary that would support a scientific orientation articulated with a specialized terminology.[18]

Who is the subject? remains an outstanding question (e.g. Borch-Jacobsen 1988; Lacan 1991; Ogden 1992; Moran 1993; Cavell 2006). *Das Ich* skirts the issue. Like Kant before him, Freud only sought to define the conditions from which the subject took form in actions and behavior (Longuenesse 2017), for he was not interested in issues framing personal identity or modeling conscious agency. As a psychologist focused on unconscious processes, the philosophical questions underlying conceptions of the self-aware subject were thereby eclipsed by other theoretical concerns. Indeed, the ego of Descartes' *Ego Cogito Cogitatum* is nowhere to be found in Freud's theory. He makes no inquiry.

> about the existential and thinking subject the question of the *I think, I am*. The *Cogito* does not and cannot figure in a topographic and economic theory of systems or agencies; it cannot possibly be objectified in a psychical locality or a role; it denotes something altogether different from what could be spelled out in a theory of instincts and their vicissitudes. Hence it is the very factor that escapes analytic conceptualization.
>
> *(Ricoeur 1970, p. 420)*

And here at the nexus of questions about the self-conscious ego, Freud employs *das Ich*, a nomenclature that makes no further *philosophical* claims about identity beyond standing for the analysand's own subjectivity and intellectual discernments. Instead, Freud remained satisfied with the voice of *the I*, whose associations, dreams and parapraxis offered an interpretive 'royal road' to the unconscious (Freud 1900, p. 608).

So why did Freud scrupulously avoid 'ego' in German and yet accept its use in the English *Standard Edition*? The simplest answer is that he was following precedent. Given his knowledge of German philosophy, he made a deliberate word choice that closely followed the semantic tradition of *das Ich* established by Kant and Fichte. That amorphous designation sufficed for his purposes.[19] Another possibility resides in an ambivalence about Freud's own overall goals. Jones insisted on the Latinized *ego* in orienting psychoanalysis as a scientific discipline. Freud aligned himself in that effort. However, beyond that aspiration, a humanistic agenda underlies Freud's thinking: psychoanalysis, putting aside Freud's theoretical concerns and postulated mechanisms, ultimately attempts to correct emotional suffering and dysfunction. Such an intervention requires a therapeutic effort that depicts the analysand as an autonomous agent (albeit compromised), who must exercise reason to achieve insight. Indeed, the entire enterprise resides in the analytic grounded in the circumspect freedom to understand deterministic forces at work in the psyche. This is the deepest stratum of Freud's meliorism and it grows from a long philosophical tradition based on Enlightenment ideals that assert the individual's autonomy, reason, and the authority of science. On this view, *ego* – at least as conceived in the modernist tradition – carries an understanding that (1) fulfills Freud's epistemological objectifying requirements (the Cartesian understanding of the ego 'seeing' the world and 'representing' what she sees [Tauber

2013)]) and (2) supports the moral ideals embraced by the therapeutic process based upon the Enlightenment ideal of autonomous self-knowledge (Schneewind 1998; Tauber 2010).

Perhaps these dual associations of *ego* account for the general appeal of the *Standard Edition*'s terminology. *Das Ich* offers no such connotations. By the mid-1920s, when the *Standard Edition* translations first appeared, Freud had completed the final iteration of his theory and increasingly applied his understanding to social matters. In this humanistic turn, accompanied with a more cautious view of the scientific standing of psychoanalysis, he might have been more inclined to endorse a more expansive approach to address the individual beyond the grasp of the scientific methods he held so dear (Freud 1920, p. 59). In fact, post-Freudians moved towards a larger construct of the individual and turned their attention to ego-based psychologies. With that shift, a firmer designation displaced the ambiguity of 'the I' with a new ego terminology that accommodated the effort to find developmental explanations for psychic dysfunctions and to better examine conscious processes linked to unconscious dynamics. And thus, *the ego* was ensconced as an effective idiom in the psychoanalytic literature, serving diverse theoretical and practical needs.

A third aspect of the *das Ich*/ego debate moves from the Freudian past to the contemporary assessments of the subject. Although dispute about the translation of *das Ich* had a long history (Loewenstein 1940, pp. 386–387; Hartmann 1958, p. 119; Hartmann 1964, p. 127; McIntosh 1986), the later polemics articulated a more general debate about the ways and means of the psychoanalytic endeavor. To fully analyze this argument requires a comprehensive review of the controversies about psychoanalytic agency over the past century, an inquiry stretching well beyond the confines of this discussion. However, such a study promises insight into the evolution of psychoanalytic theory and its wider influence on notions of selfhood, more generally. After all, the issues underlying the contested standings of *das Ich* versus *the ego* have not been put to rest as attested by the vast postmodern literature about subjectivity that has so dominated our own era. And Freud is a central voice in that discussion.

Given the autonomy and dominance of the unconscious, Freud's *das Ich* – delimited in its rationality and understanding – has conceded its free will, the underlying tenet of the Enlightenment's conception of agency. Accordingly, the authority of self-knowledge and rational deliberation guiding moral decision-making that grounds modernity's identification of the ego has been displaced for a more circumspect assessment. And as discussed, the epistemological status of the self-knowing ego has also been severely compromised. Freud thus served those postmodern attempts to decenter the subject and, in turn, this deconstruction has permeated psychoanalysis (e.g., Barratt 1993; Fairfield, Layton, and Stack 2002; Elliott and Spezzano 2019).

In this regard, the self-conscious, analytic ego has been subordinated to the unadorned voice of subjectivity in the rich development of Lacanian-oriented discourses (Lacan 1991, 2006; Fink 1995; Chiesa 2007; Neill 2011). In many respects, Lacan's slogan 'Back to Freud' may be viewed as an explicit returned to the 'voice' of *das Ich* without the trappings of a controlling ego. Ironically, by establishing the epistemological ambiguity of the ego, Freud perhaps inadvertently supported the 'egocide' refutations and the revisionist programs that followed (Rogozinski 2010, p. 5). How and why Anglo-American psychoanalysis followed a different theoretical trajectory that defended, even valorized the self-aware ego, must delve back into English philosophy, where a strong empiricist tradition supported the focus on the knowing-agent (Reé 2019). Following both arms of Freud's legacy, the translation dispute finds its wider significance and we may well ponder, on the one hand, how the supporting culture influences prevailing conceptions of the psychoanalytic subject, and on the other hand, how such an agent contributes to senses of the self in domains far removed from the psychoanalytic couch. The ramifications of how these fundamental questions are answered can hardly be overstated.

Acknowledgments

I am indebted to Béatrice Longuenesse and Gideon Freudenthal for their critical comments and editorial suggestions.

Notes

1 The Penguin translation, edited by Adam Phillips, set no standard editorial policy on the translation of technical terms, including das Ich and das Es ("id"). In this instance, Bance deliberately uses 'the I' for das Ich, and observes that "'the It' and 'the I' may seem strange at first, but my experience is that they read quite naturally after a while" (Bance 2002, p. xxviii), an impression categorically denied by others (Whiteside 2005, p. xxxii). So, while many of the Penguin series translators acknowledged the problem with the das Ich/ego conundrum and profess adherence to a more colloquial and accessible English to more closely approximate Freud's style, only a few chose to keep das Ich (Huish 2002) and the majority revert to *ego* because of its assumed standing in the psychoanalytic literature (Frankland 2005, p. xxii). Bilingual Freudian texts at www.freud2lacan.com/ allow direct comparison of the German original with the *Standard Edition*.

2 In reference to On narcissism (Freud 1914), "the term 'Das Ich' is used in three main senses: 1. The self: one's person as the intentional object of libidinal or self-preservative psychic investment. 2. The actual self: one's person as the actual object of investment, as distinct from the intentional object. In German this idea is conveyed by 'Das aktuelle Ich' or 'Das wirkliche Ich'. The distinction between the intentional and the actual self emerges very clearly in the German text, pp. 161–162. 3. The ego: the person as conscious subject or agent, in ordinary language usages which, however, sometimes suggest the theoretical idea of the system-structure ego. The German term is 'Das Subjekt-Ich' or 'Das Subjekt'" (McIntosh 1986, p. 441).

3 According to the *Oxford English Dictionary* ("Ego"), the use of *ego* in English psychology appeared by 1830: "In every act of consciousness we distinguish a self or ego" (*Edinburgh Review* 50:200, 1829; for general overview, see Smith, R. 1997)

4 Freud only used the word, *Selbst,* once in his writings (fourth paragraph of *Civilization and its Discontents* [1930]). He freely uses *das Ich* as opposed to *Selbst*, but the Freudian *das Ich* does not equate with 'the self,' although some commentators assume that an implicit understanding suffices (e.g. Dilman 1984, p. 106; McIntosh 1986).

5 "Freud never objected to the translation of das Ich as 'the ego'. When Chase translated the Clark University Lectures, under the direct supervision of Freud, as early as 1908, he used the term 'ego' where Freud had written das Ich. Perhaps this also explains why, when Freud wrote a letter in English to Jones on 18 February 1919, he himself used the term 'ego' in a place where he would almost certainly have used Ich in German. And for those who would retort that Freud was in no position to judge the appropriateness of an English term, we should remember Jones's and Riviere's assurances to the contrary: Jones declared that Freud 'had an excellent, rather literary command of [English]', and Riviere wrote that he had an 'amazing command of the English language . . . absolute mastery'. (Do not forget that Freud analysed Riviere, which gave her the closest possible opportunity to assess his grasp of the English language.)" (Solms 1999, p. 36.) For a review of how Strachey dealt with this issue (including comprehensive citations in which the translations are editorially defended), see Kernberg (1982).

6 How Freud's Jewish identity influenced the British translation, see Gilman (1991).

7 For critical appraisals see the entire issue of the *Journal of the Psychoanalytic Association*, Vol. 30 (1982; Hartmann 1964; La Planche and Pontalis 1973; Kernberg 1982; Bettelheim 1983; Meissner 1986; Steiner 1987; Gilman 1991). A useful exchange is found in Wilson's rebuttal of Ornston's criticism (Ornston 1982; Wilson 1987). The problem of translating Freud's writings into French is reviewed in Abensour (2014).

8 Note, Anna Freud, an early ego psychologist, followed the standard precedent: *Das Ich und die Abwehrmechanismen* (A. Freud 1936), which was translated as *The Ego and the Mechanisms of Defense* (A. Freud 1937). And a key theorist of ego psychology, Heinz Hartmann, in *Die Grundlagen der Psychoanalyse nach Sigmund Freud* (1927) also used *das Ich* instead of *ego*, as he did in his 1939 paper, Ich-psychologie und Anpassungsproblem. However, by the 1950s, writing in English, Hartmann would also employ *ego* for his original *das Ich*. Noteworthy in this terminology is a refinement of defining the subject. For him, the teleological task of an individual's psyche is to adapt to the environment, which required a new construct (and vocabulary) for psychoanalysis – the "autonomous ego" –

an inborn, biologically oriented mental apparatus that develops independently of the id (Hartmann 1958; Kobrin 1993).

9 In 1900, the year Freud published *Interpretation of Dreams*, Mary Calkins wrote a paper that would serve as the Ur-text of what she called, "self psychology" (Calkins 1930). The article defended her notions of a "personalist psychology" as opposed to "atomistic psychology" that "treat contents-of-consciousness as such . . . without reference to any self" (Calkins 1900, p. 490).

10 Various notions of selfhood implicitly reside in Freud's understanding of personal identity, a mosaic drawn from Spinoza, Kant, Schopenhauer, Kierkegaard, and Nietzsche (Tauber 2010).

11 The disputes centering on the interpretation of retrieved memory date from the earliest presentation of psychoanalysis and renewed in the 1990s during the "memory wars," when the métier of psychoanalysis again become the focus of controversy (Crews 1995, 2017; Loftus and Ketchum 1994; Shaw 2017).

12 I am indebted to Béatrice Longuenesse for noting the distinctive difference of das Ich as a "metapsychological" concept and the emphasis I place on the subjectivity of the *I* (private correspondence; see Longuenesse 2017). In regard to the various uses of das Ich Freud employs, she further notes that Freud left unresolved how the various notions of das Ich relate to one another, i.e., are these three different concepts or are they three different functions of one and the same structure?

13 Moran (1993) makes the same point by what she calls "structuring," in which structure and agency form an interdependent recursive process.

14 *Das Es* was coined by George Groddeck in 1923 and translated in English as "the It," a truly non-committal word choice that reflects the radical limits of characterizing the unconscious as an entity (Groddeck 1976). Here, he famously quipped, "Man is lived by the It" (Letter II).

15 The dilemma was clearly stated by Descartes' early critic, Pierre Gassendi in 1641:

> As far as your idea of yourself is concerned . . . far from having a clear and distinct idea of yourself you have no idea of yourself at all. This is because although you recognize that you are thinking, you still do not know what kind of thing you, who are thinking, are. . . . [Y]ou may be compared to a blind man, who on feeling heat and being told that it comes from the sun, thinks he has a clear and distinct idea of the sun in that, if anyone asks him what the sun is, he can reply: 'It is a heating thing.'
>
> [Y]ou say not only that you are a thinking thing but also that you are a thing which is unextended. I shall ignore the fact that this is asserted without proof, even though it is still a question, and simply ask you first of all: do you therefore have a clear and distinct idea of yourself? You say that you are not extended; that is, you say what you are not, not what you are. . . . is it not necessary to know the thing positively and, so to speak, affirmatively? (Gassendi 1984, pp. 234–235)

16 For Hume, a bundle of perceptions did not constitute a self, and because his self-consciousness comprises fleeting perceptions or thoughts, he "never can catch" *himself* "at any time without a perception, and never can observe any thing but the perception" (Hume 1978, p. 252). In other words, the 'me' of personal identity morphs from moment to moment and thus the 'I' is non-identical to itself. Absent an *entity*, there is "no owner" as such – experiences and perceptions exist without a discernable subject. In short, the self, originally conceived as a postulated homunculus (what Descartes called, the ego), lies beyond empirical characterization. This conclusion proves an insurmountable block to Hume's inquiry, for if the idea of the self is based on what introspection reveals, a "bundle of perceptions" – one thought or image jumping to another – seemingly without causal links, he could not establish the basis for integration of experience and thus he dismissed *the* self as an entity.

However, as pointed out by Udo Thiel, we should understand Hume's critique by his own limited criteria, namely, he is concerned only with what might be understood about the mind *empirically*. Accordingly, Hume is "concerned not with the mind's real nature but only with its introspectively accessible features" (Thiel 2014, p. 421). Thus the "bundle" observations do not address the mind's unknowable essence, but "only those features about which inner experience 'informs' us" (ibid. p. 422). Hume does not deny the existence of a persisting self beyond the perceptions, nor the inner sense of identity, just the empirical basis for such a sentiment. Kant, as mentioned, bypassed this problem by charting the conditions required for integrated experience and thus skirted the question of the self-as-entity altogether. Thiel's philosophical discussion of Hume's understanding of selfhood and its historical placement is highly insightful (pp. 383–430).

17 Anscombe builds from Wittgenstein understanding that the "self," while a useful linguistic tool, refers to a misleading metaphysical construction. In the World War I *Notebooks*, he mused, "The thinking subject

is surely mere illusion. But the willing subject exists. If the will did not exist, neither would there be that centre of the world, which we call the I. . . . The I, the I is what is deeply mysterious! The I is not an object" (Wittgenstein 1979, p. 80e).

Wittgenstein's discussion of the use of 'I' as subject and the use of 'I' as object (Wittgenstein 1960, p. 66) "insists that in its use "as subject," 'I' is not used to refer to myself as a particular person. Rather in its use "as subject" 'I' has no other function than to express the self-ascription of a subjective state (for instance tooth-ache, in: "I have a tooth-ache"), without any reference at all being made to a particular entity, distinguished from other entities in the world. In this respect, Wittgenstein provocatively maintained, saying "I have a tooth-ache" is no different than moaning" (Longuenesse, 2017, p. 2). Wittgenstein thus uses 'I' narrowly as a semantic expression of inner mental feelings or thoughts, and thereby avoids the self construed as an object, altogether (Shoemaker 2003, pp. 6–18). He came to this important distinction by following Hume's almost cursory, off-hand remark about grammar: "all the nice and subtile questions concerning personal identity can never possibly be decided, and are to be regarded rather as grammatical than as philosophical difficulties" (Hume, 1978, p. 262). The mistake is not philosophical (in traditional terms), but more basically an error in the use of language, a dominant theme of Wittgenstein's thought.

18 "What made the Strachey translation totally acceptable in the English-speaking world for over two decades is precisely what makes it problematic today. Strachey created the impression in the English-speaking world (with Freud's full support) that psychoanalysis was a scientific undertaking. And he created it through his invention of a specialized discourse for psychoanalysis" (Gilman 1991, p. 331).

19 Freud, despite his later aversion to philosophy, had sophisticated university training in the subject. His first courses were taken under the tutelage of Franz Brentano, and I have argued elsewhere that this intellectual relationship was instrumental in Freud's own approach in characterizing the mind (Tauber 2010, pp. 48–53). Freud was well acquainted with the German philosophical tradition that used das Ich in dealing with the issues of the knowing subject, Kant, most prominently (Tauber 2010). While Fichte based his entire philosophy on das Ich, with Hegel, Selbst makes its formal entry into the German canon. Of the vast literature see Ameriks and Sturma (1995), Klemm and Zoller (1997), Beiser (2002), Pinkard (2002).

References

Abensour, A. [2004] 2014. Es, Ich, Über-ich, *Dictionary of Untranslatables. A Philosophical Lexicon*, B. Cassin (ed.), Princeton: Princeton University Press, pp. 292–295.

Ameriks, K. and Sturma, D. (eds.) 1995. *The Modern Subject. Conceptions of the Self in Classical German Philosophy*, Albany: State University of New York Press.

Anscombe, G. E. M. 1959. *An Introduction to Wittgenstein's Tractatus*. Philadelphia: University of Pennsylvania Press.

Bance, A. 2002. Translator's Preface, *Wild Analysis*, London: Penguin Books.

Barratt, B. B. 1993. *Psychoanalysis and the Postmodern Impulse: Knowing and Being Since Freud's Psychology*, Baltimore: Johns Hopkins University Press.

Beiser, F. 2002. *German Idealism. The Struggle Against Subjectivism*, Cambridge: Harvard University Press.

Bettelheim, B. 1983. *Freud and Man's Soul*, New York: Knopf.

Borch-Jacobsen, M. 1988. *The Freudian Subject*, F. Roustang (trans.), Stanford: Stanford University Press.

Brown, N. O. 1959. *Life against Death: The Psychological Meaning of History*, Middletown, CT: Wesleyan University Press.

Calkins, M. W. 1900. Psychology as Science of Selves, *The Philosophical Review*, 9:490–501.

Calkins, M. W. 1930. Autobiography of Mary Whiton Calkins, *History of Psychology in Autobiography*, C. Murchison, Carl. (ed.), Vol. 1, pp. 31–61, Worcester, MA: Clark University Press. https://psychclassics.yorku.ca/Calkins/murchison.htm#f18

Cavell, M. 2006. *Becoming a Subject: Reflections on Philosophy and Psychoanalysis*, Oxford: Clarendon Press.

Chiesa, L. 2007. *Subjectivity and Otherness. A Philosophical Reading of Lacan*, p. 15. Cambridge, MA: MIT Press.

Clarke, J. M. 1894. Hysteria and Neurasthenia. I. Papers on the Theory of Hysteria and Neurasthenia, *Brain*, 17:120–145. https://doi-org.ezproxy.bu.edu/10.1093/brain/17.1.120

Crews, F. 1995. *The Memory Wars. Freud's Legacy in Dispute*, New York: New York Review of Books.

Crews, F. 2017. *Freud: The Making of an Illusion*, New York: Henry Holt.

Descartes, R. [1637] 1985. Discourse on Method, *The Philosophical Works of Descartes*, J. Cottingham, R. Stoothoff, and D. Murdoch (trans.), Vol. 1, Cambridge: Cambridge University Press.

Dilman, I. 1984. *Freud and the Mind*, Oxford: Blackwell.
Elliott, A. and Spezzano, C. (eds.) 2019. *Psychoanalysis at its Limits: Navigating the Postmodern Turn*, New York: Routledge.
Fairfield, S., Layton, L. and Stack, C. (eds.) 2002. *Bringing the Plague: Toward a Postmodern Psychoanalysis*, New York: Other Press.
Fink, B. 1995. *The Lacanian Subject: Between Language and Jouissance*. Princeton: Princeton University Press.
Frankland, G. 2005. Translator's Preface, *Sigmund Freud, The Unconscious*, London: Penguin Books, pp. xxi–xxvi.
Freud, A. 1936. *Das Ich und die Abwehrmechanisme*, Vienna: Internationaler Psychoanalytischer Verlag.
Freud, A. [1937] 1966. *The Ego and the Mechanisms of Defense*, C. Baines (trans.), New York: International Universities Press.
Freud, S. 1900. *Interpretation of Dreams*, *Standard Edition*, Vol. 4–5.
Freud, S. 1910. Five Lectures on Psycho-Analysis, *Standard Edition*, Vol. 11, pp. 3–55.
Freud, S. 1914. On Narcissism: An Introduction, *Standard Edition*, Vol. 14, 73–102.
Freud, S. 1920. Beyond the Pleasure Principle, *Standard Edition*, Vol. 18, pp. 7–64
Freud, S. 1923. *The Ego and the Id*, *Standard Edition*, Vol. 19, pp. 12–66.
Freud, S. 1926a. The Question of Lay Analysis, *Standard Edition*, Vol. 20, pp. 183–250.
Freud, S. 1926b. The Question of Lay Analysis, *Wild Analysis*, 2002, A. Bance (trans.), pp. 93–159, London: Penguin Books.
Freud, S. 1930. *Civilization and Its Discontents, Standard Edition*, Vol. 21. Bilingual Edition. www.freud2lacan.com/docs/Civilization and Its Discontents.pdf
Freud, S. 1933. *New Introductory Lectures on Psycho-Analysis*, *Standard Edition*, Vol. 22.
Gassendi, P. [1641] 1984. Fifth Set of Objections, *The Philosophical Works of Descartes*, J. Cottingham, R. Stoothoff, and D. Murdoch (trans.), Vol. 2, Cambridge: Cambridge University Press.
Gilman, S. L. 1991. Reading Freud in English: Problems, Paradoxes, and a Solution, *International Review of Psycho-Analysis*, 18:331–344, 339–340.
Groddeck, G. 1976. *The Book of the It*. New York: International Universities Press.
Hartmann, H. 1927. *Die Grundlagen der Psychoanalyse nach Sigmund Freud*, Leipzig: Georg Thieme Verlag.
Hartmann, H. 1939. Ich-Psychologie und Anpassungsproblem, *Internationale Zeitschrift für Psychoanalyse und Imago*, 24: 62–135.
Hartmann, H. [1939] 1964. Comments on the Psychoanalytic Theory of the Ego, *Essays on Ego Psychology*, pp. 113–141, New York: International Universities Press.
Hartmann, H. [1939] 1958. *Ego Psychology and the Problem of Adaptation*, D. Rapaport, (trans.), New York: International Universities Press.
Hawkins, S. 2018. Invisible Terminology, Visible Translations: The New Penguin Freud Translations and the Case against Standardized Terminology, *The Translator*, 24:233–248. https://doi.org/10.1080/13556509.2018.1503525
Horkheimer, M. and Adorno, T. W. [1947] 1993. *Dialectic of Enlightenment*, New York: Continuum.
Huish, L. A. 2002. *Sigmund Freud, the Wolfman and Other Cases*, London: Penguin Books.
Hume, D. [1739] 1978. *Treatise of Human Nature*, L. A. Selby-Bigge and P. H. Nidditch (eds.), Oxford: Oxford University Press.
Jeanes, H. 1656. *A Mixture of Scholastic Divinity*, Oxford: Printer to the University.
Kant, I. [1787] 1998. *Critique of Pure Reason*, P. Guyer and A. W. Wood (trans.), Cambridge: Cambridge University Press.
Kernberg, O. F. 1982. Self, Ego, Affects, and Drives, *Journal of the American Psychoanalytic Association*, 30:893–917.
Klemm, D. E. and Zoller, G. (eds.) 1997. *Figuring the Self. Subject, Absolute, and Others in Classical German Philosophy*, Albany: State University of New York Press.
Kobrin, N. 1993. Freud's Concept of Autonomy and Strachey's Translation: A Piece of the Puzzle of the Freudian Self, *Annual of Psychoanalysis*, 21:201–223.
Kohut, H. 1977. *The Restoration of the Self*, New York: International Universities Press.
Lacan, J. 1991. *The Ego in Freud's Theory and in the Technique of Psychoanalysis, 1954–1955. The Seminar of Jacques Lacan Book II*, J-A. Miller (ed.), S. Tomaselli (trans.). New York: W. W. Norton.
Lacan, J. 2006. *Écrits. The First Complete Edition in English*, B. Fink (trans.), New York: W. W. Norton.
La Planche, J. and Pontalis, J. B. 1973. *The Language of Psychoanalysis*, New York: Norton.
Loftus, E. and Ketchum, K. 1994. *The Myth of Repressed Memory. False Memories and Allegations of Sexual Abuse*, New York: St. Martin's Press.

Longuenesse, B. 2017. *I, Me, Mine. Back to Kant, and Back Again*, Oxford: Oxford University Press.
Loewenstein, R. 1940 The Vital or Somatic Instincts, *International Journal of Psycho-Analysis*, 21:377–400.
Marcuse, H. 1955. *Eros and Civilization: A Philosophical Inquiry into Freud*, Boston: Beacon Press.
McIntosh, D. 1986. The Ego and the Self in the Thought of Sigmund Freud, *International Journal of Psycho-Analysis*, 67:429–448.
Meissner, W. W. 1986. Can Psychoanalysis Find Its Self? *Journal of the American Psychoanalytic Association*, 34:379–400.
Moran, F. 1993. *Subject and Agency in Psychoanalysis*, New York: New York University Press.
Neill, C. 2011. *Lacanian Ethics and the Assumption of Subjectivity*. Houndmills, UK: Palgrave Macmillan.
Ogden, T. H. 1992. The Dialectically Constituted/Decentered Subject of Psychoanalysis. 1. The Freudian Subject, *International Journal of Psychoanalysis*, 73:517–526.
Ornston, D. G. 1982. Strachey's Influence: A Preliminary Report, *International Journal of Psycho-Analysis*, 63:409–426.
Ornston, D. G. 1992. Alternatives to a Standard Edition, *Translating Freud*, Ornston, D. G. (ed.), pp. 97–113, p. 108, New Haven: Yale University Press.
Pinkard, T. 2002. *German Philosophy 1760–1860: The Legacy of Idealism*, Cambridge: Cambridge University Press.
Reé, J. 2019. *Witcraft. The Invention of Philosophy in English*, New Have: Yale University Press.
Ricoeur, P. 1970 *Freud and Philosophy: An Essay on Interpretation*, D. Savage (trans.), New Haven: Yale University Press.
Rogozinski, J. 2010. *The Ego and the Flesh. An Introduction to Egoanalysis*, R. Vallier (trans.), Stanford: Stanford University Press.
Schneewind, J. B. 1998. *The Invention of Autonomy: A History of Modern Moral Philosophy*, Cambridge: Cambridge University Press.
Seigel, J. 2005. *The Idea of the Self. Thought and Experience in Western Europe Since the Seventeenth Century*, Cambridge: Cambridge University Press.
Shaw, J. 2017. *The Memory Illusion: Remembering, Forgetting, and the Science of False Memory*, New York: Random House.
Shoemaker, S. 2003. Self-Reference and Self-Awareness, *Identity, Cause, and Mind, Expanded Edition*, S. Shoemaker (ed.), pp. 6–18, Oxford: Oxford University Press.
Smith, R. 1997. *The Norton History of the Human Sciences*, New York: Norton.
Solms, M. 1999. Controversies in Freud translation, *Psychoanalysis and History*, 1:28–43.
Steiner, R. 1987. A World-Wide International Trademark of Genuineness? – Some Observations on the History of the English Translation of Sigmund Freud, Focusing Mainly on His Technical Terms, *International Review of Psycho-Analysis*, 14:33–102.
Tauber, A. I. 2006. The Reflexive Project: Reconstructing the Moral Agent, *History of the Human Sciences*, 18:49–75.
Tauber, A. I. 2010. *Freud, the Reluctant Philosopher*, Princeton: Princeton University Press.
Tauber, A. I. 2012. Freud's Social Theory: Modernist and Postmodernist Revisions, *History of the Human Sciences*, 25:41–70.
Tauber, A. I. 2013. *Requiem for the Ego. Freud and the Origins of Postmodernism*, Stanford: Stanford University Press.
Taylor, C. 1989. *Sources of the Self*, Cambridge: Harvard University Press.
Thiel, U. 2014. *The Early Modern Subject: Self-Consciousness and Personal Identity from Descartes to Hume*, Oxford: Oxford University Press.
Tugendhat, E. 1986. *Self-Consciousness and Self-Determination*, P. Stern (trans.), Cambridge: MIT Press.
Whitebook, J. 1995. *Perversion and Utopia. A Study in Psychoanalysis and Critical Theory*, Cambridge: MIT Press.
Whiteside, S. 2005. Translator's Preface, *Sigmund Freud On Murder, Mourning, and Melancholia*, pp. xxix–xxxiv, London: Penguin Books.
Whyte, L. L. 1978. *The Unconscious before Freud*, London: Julian Friedmann Publishers.
Wilson, E. 1987. Did Strachey Invent Freud? *International Review of Psycho-Analysis*, 14:299–315.
Wittgenstein, L. 1960. *The Blue and Brown Books. Preliminary Studies for the 'Philosophical Investigations'*, New York: Harper & Row.
Wittgenstein, L. 1979. *Notebooks 1914–1916*, 2nd ed., G. H. von Wright and G. E. M. Anscombe (eds.), G. E. M. Anscombe (trans.), Chicago: University of Chicago Press.

23

SUBJECTIVITY IN PHILOSOPHY, PSYCHOANALYSIS AND NEUROSCIENCE

Neuro-ecological Self and Its Point of View

Georg Northoff

Introduction

Concept of Self: Gap Between Philosophy and Neuroscience

What is the self? The concept of self has long been discussed in philosophy and psychoanalysis, more recently, in neuroscience. Since at least the beginning of modernity, the concept of self has been conceived to be the placeholder of the basic subjectivity of human man. This is also the role or place of the concept of self (or ego, using a yet different term) in psychoanalysis (Milrod 2002, 22–23; Solms 2015).

There is a gap between philosophy/psychoanalysis and neuroscience, though, as both are not talking about exactly the same kind of self. Philosophy focuses predominantly on the self as placeholder of subjectivity: why and how is it possible that there is something as subjective like the self in a seemingly purely objective world? In contrast, neuroscience, following the conceptual split of subjective ("I") versus objective self ("me"; James 1890; Northoff 2016), focuses more on the objective aspects of self (i.e., the objective self or the me), as those can be measured and observed (Sui and Humphreys 2015).

That leaves us with a gap between the subjectivity of self in philosophy/psychoanalysis and the objectivity of self in neuroscience. Closing this gap by introducing three key concepts – world-brain relation, neuro-ecological self, and point of view – is the goal of this chapter. This will allow taking into view how the self is intrinsically situated and embedded within the world, accounting for what philosophically has been described as "being in the world" (Heidegger 1927/2008; Gallagher and Daly 2018, 3n3).

Question, Aim, Argument, and Approach

How can we account for the subjectivity of self in neuroscientific terms without reducing or losing its essential subjectivity, as seems to be the case in current neuroscience? This is the key question guiding my chapter that, methodologically, relies on a non-reductive (rather than reductive) approach to neurophilosophy (Northoff 2014, 2018) and neuropsychoanalysis (Northoff 2011;

DOI: 10.4324/9780429297076-28

Boeker et al. 2019). My main aim is to converge the philosophical concept of point of view as placeholder of a most basic subjectivity (Nagel 1974) with recent neuroscientific results on how the self is shaped by its respective environmental context through the brain. This leads me to speak of a neuro-ecological self, which ultimately is based on what I described in recent work as world-brain relation (Northoff 2014, 2018).

My main argument is that such neuro-ecological self is based ontologically on a point of view (below for details) that, through world-brain relation, grounds the self in an intrinsically subjective (rather than objective) way in the world. The present characterization of the self as neuro-ecological and intrinsically subjective by a point of view is an elaboration of the basis model of self-specificity (BMSS) I postulated in 2016 (Northoff 2016). In a nutshell, the BMSS states that the self is a fundamental or basis function of the brain's spontaneous activity and its temporo-spatial structure rather than being primarily a higher-order cognitive function (Northoff 2016). Relying on both recent empirical evidence and conceptual determination of the point of view, I here extend the BMSS with regard to the spontaneous activity's neuro-ecological dimension and what that implies for the self and, specifically, its subjective nature.

While on the philosophical side, the present approach follows the recently developed concept of world-brain relation (Northoff 2018), which is here applied to the specific case of subjectivity and self. Specifically, I here aim to provide a neurophilosophical account of the self that conceives the brain at the junction of world, body, and brain (Gallagher and Daly 2018, 2n2) and can account for what philosophically has been described as "being in the world" (Heidegger 1927/2008; Gallagher and Daly 2018, 3n3). I briefly sketch in the conclusion how the convergence of the three key concepts of world-brain relation, neuro-ecological self, and point of view can address the question for subjectivity in philosophy and neuropsychoanalysis in a non-reductive neuroscientific way. Future work will be necessary to connect the three key concepts to the psychoanalytic (and neuropsychoanalytic) concepts and debates on the nature of self in a more detailed way.

Part I: The Neuro-ecological Self and Its World-Brain Relation

How is our self shaped by its environment? I here present three lines of empirical evidence for how the environment, through the brain, shapes the self; this, on a more conceptual level, leads me to speak of "world-brain relation" as the brain aligns its own activity to the world (Northoff 2014, 2016, 2018). The first line concerns the impact of early childhood traumatic experience on the self through the brain's resting state (i.e., its spontaneous activity).

The second line takes a more general view by showing how the brain's spontaneous activity continuously matches and compares its own temporo-spatial structure with the one of the environment in a way that extends beyond specific scales or ranges in time and space (i.e., scale-free), and how that shapes the self. Finally, the third line considers the phenomenological implications of the brain's alignment to the world (i.e., world-brain relation) by conceiving the experience of connectedness of the self to the world in hallucinogenic states and meditation.

The Neuro-ecological Self I: Traumatic Life Experience Shapes the Brain's Spontaneous Activity

We all experience adverse life events in both childhood and adulthood which shape our self. How can especially early traumatic childhood experiences shape our self in adulthood? Various brain imaging studies showed that early traumatic childhood experiences impact the spontaneous activity's temporo-spatial dynamics during adulthood. For instance, one fMRI study by Lu et al. (2017) demonstrated changes in both intra- and inter-regional synchronization (regional homogeneity, functional connectivity) in regions of the default-mode network (DMN) and salience network (SN; like the insula) in subjects suffering from early traumatic experiences. Somewhat analogous resting-state functional connectivity in insula and related regions of the salience network were also observed in another study by Gupta et al. (2017).

The impact of traumatic life experiences on the brain's spontaneous activity is further confirmed by various results in post-traumatic stress disorder (PTSD; Disner et al. 2018; Koch et al. 2016). One recent large-scale meta-analysis showed that here, too, regions of the DMN like the inferior parietal lobule (IPL) and the salience network such as the amygdala and the caudate exhibit decreased resting state activity; that is, intra-regional synchronization and neural variability in subjects suffering from PTSD (Disner et al. 2018). Focusing more on inter-regional (rather than intra-regional) changes (i.e., functional connectivity), a meta-analysis by Koch et al. (2016) observed dysbalance between decreased resting state functional connectivity in DMN and increased resting state functional connectivity in SN.

Yet other studies show how early traumatic experience do not only impact the resting state but that the latter, in turn, shapes the adult subject's task-related activity during for instance aversive stimuli. One fMRI study by Duncan et al. (2015) first measured entropy (i.e., the degree of disorder) in the resting state in adult subjects suffering from early traumatic childhood experiences. They observed that the degree of resting state entropy in a region of the DMN (anterior cingulate cortex) directly correlated with the degree of early life experience: the more subjects experience early traumatic experience, the higher their entropy (i.e., disorder) in resting state activity during adulthood (Duncan et al. 2015).

In a second step, the same study also investigated task-related activity applying an aversive stimulus (i.e., inducing pain by prick stimulus). They observed that subjects with high early traumatic experience exhibited reduced activity to the anticipation of aversive stimulus in specifically somatomotor cortex and insula which was directly related to (i.e., modulated by) increased entropy in DMN (i.e., anterior cingulate cortex).

The Neuro-ecological Self II: Traumatic Experiences Changes Brain and Self

Yet another study by Nakao et al. (2013), using near infrared spectroscopy (fNIRS) demonstrated that especially power in the very low infraslow frequency ranges (<0.04 Hz) was negatively related to early traumatic life experience in anterior DMN (i.e., medial prefrontal cortex): the higher the degree of early traumatic experiences, the less power in specifically infraslow frequency ranges in medial prefrontal cortex during adulthood.

They also included two tasks, one task involving the self (i.e., colour preference judgment) and one task not involving the self (i.e., colour similarity judgment). Interestingly, the degree of early traumatic life experience only correlated with infraslow frequency power in medial prefrontal cortex during the self-related task (i.e., colour preference judgment) but not the non-self task: the less infraslow frequency power and the more similar judgments during the colour preference task, the higher the degree of early traumatic experiences.

Together, these studies clearly demonstrate that early traumatic experience strongly shape both resting state and task-related activity during adulthood. This concerns those regions in the brain like the ones of the DMN (medial prefrontal cortex, anterior cingulate, posterior cingulate) and SN (insula, amygdala) that have been shown to be strongly involved in processing self-specificity (Qin and Northoff 2011; Qin et al. 2020).

We consequently can assume on solid empirical grounds that the self in adulthood is strongly shaped by its respective environmental context (i.e., the world) through the brain's spontaneous activity and its temporo-spatial dynamics in a long-term way, that is, across different time scales including short and long. Putting this in more conceptual terms, there is strong empirical support for (1) world-brain relation; (2) the world-brain relation shaping the self in a neuro-ecological way; and (3) such neuro-ecological shaping operating in a scale-free way across different time scales. We now need to better understand the scale-free nature of the self's neuro-ecological shaping – that shall be the focus in the next sections.

The Scale-Free Self I: Scale-Free Temporal Structure of the Brain's Spontaneous Activity

The brain's spontaneous neural activity can be characterized by different frequencies ranging from infraslow (0.01–0.1 Hz) over slow (0.1–1 Hz) and fast (1–40 Hz) to ultrafast (40–180 Hz) frequencies (Buzsaki 2006). Power is strongest in the infraslow range with decreasing degrees of power in slow, fast, and ultrafast ranges following power law distribution (see below for details; He 2014; He et al. 2010; Huang et al. 2016). Together, the different frequencies and their distinct degrees of power constitute a complex temporal structure in the brain's spontaneous activity which, in large parts, can be featured by the balance between slower (0.01 to 7 Hz) and faster (8 to 240 Hz) frequencies.

The relationship between slow and fast frequencies operates at different temporal (and spatial) scales and can therefore be characterized by what is described "scale-free dynamics" (He et al. 2010; He 2014; Linkenkaer-Hansen et al. 2001). Roughly, scale-free activity describes the fractal (i.e., self-similar) organisation and thus temporal nestedness in the relationship of the power between the different frequencies: the longer and more powerful slower frequencies nest and contain the shorter and less powerful faster frequencies – this amounts to long-range temporal correlation (LRTC) which operates across different time scales (i.e., frequencies; Northoff and Huang 2017; Linkenkaer-Hansen et al. 2001; He 2014; He et al. 2010).

The LRTC can be described as scale-free or scale-invariant which can be measured and expressed by $P \propto 1 / f^{\dagger}$ (where P is power, f is frequency, and β is the power-law exponent (PLE); He 2014). A high PLE value indicates relatively stronger power in slow frequencies and relatively less power in the faster ones, whereas the opposite is the case in a low PLE value. Alternative to the PLE that, operating in the frequency domain, accounts for the power relationship across the different frequencies, one can also probe the LRTC in the time domain by measuring the fluctuations in the amplitude of the oscillations using detrended fluctuation analysis (DFA; Linkenkaer-Hansen et al. 2001; He et al. 2010; Palva et al. 2013).

Independent of their differences (see below for more discussion), both PLE and DFA measure neural activity across different time scales and thus in a scale-free or scale-invariant activity. That makes possible to assess the degree to which past neuronal patterns to exert their influence on future dynamics and thus to account for LRTC (Linkenkaer-Hansen et al. 2001; Northoff and Huang 2017). High values in PLE/DFA indicate high degrees of LRTC with long stretches over which past, present, and future states correlate with each other – this reflects the relatively stronger impact of slower frequencies with their longer cycles. The opposite is the case in low PLE/DFA values, where only the most recent time intervals exert impact on present and future ones – this reflects the relatively stronger impact of faster frequencies with their short cycles.

The Scale-Free Self II: Temporal Nestedness and LRTC on Neuronal and Mental Levels

Recent studies showed that the brain's scale-free activity as measured with either PLE or DFA is related to mental features like self (Huang et al. 2016; Wolff et al. 2019; Scalabrini et al. 2017, 2019). These studies show that the degree of resting state PLE directly predicts the (1) degree of self-consciousness (Huang et al. 2016; Wolff et al. 2019), (2) task-related activity during self-specific stimuli (Scalabrini et al. 2019), and (3) the degree of temporal integration on a psychological level of self-specificity (Kolvoort et al. 2020). Hence, resting state scale-freeness seems to be central in mediating distinct components of self-specificity like self-consciousness, task-related activity, and temporal integration. Moreover, other studies demonstrated that scale-free activity is central in mediating other mental features like consciousness (Northoff and Huang 2017; Zhang et al. 2018) and mental abnormalities in psychiatric disorders like autism (Damiani et al. 2019) and schizophrenia (Northoff et al. 2020).

Taken together, these findings suggest that the brain's scale-free properties are central for mental features and thus, more generally, the mind including self and consciousness. Mental features like self and consciousness seem to operate across different time scales by integrating and nesting them within each other – one can speak of a scale-free self characterized by temporal nestedness and similarity across different time scales. Applying the above used terms, the self is scale-free and therefore featured by temporal nestedness and LRTCs on a mental level which seem to find their analogues on the neuronal level in the brain's spontaneous activity.

The Scale-Free Self III: Nature and World Exhibit Scale-Free Temporal Structure

What do brain, weather, seismic earth waves, and stock markets have in common? At first glance, you will say that they do not share anything. Brain is a gray matter consisting of a bunch of neurons. Nothing of that can be observed in the others. Hence, brain is brain. While brain is neither weather, seismic earth waves, or a stock market.

Despite these differences on the surface, they nevertheless share some similarity on a deeper level. They all fluctuate in their activity with these fluctuations exhibiting the same structure, that is, scale-free structure with temporal nestedness and LRTC. One of the most interesting appeals of scale-free activity is its universality. Scale-free activity is not only present in the brain but ubiquitous in nature, that is, it occurs in various systems like climate, whether, seismic earth waves, sandpiles, magnetic fields, stock markets, and so on (Cocchi et al. 2017; He et al. 2010). Basically, one can say that wherever it fluctuates in a seemingly irregular way, LRTC and scale-free activity may provide some structure to what appears to me mere noise and purely random. There is "structure to irregularity", and that seems to hold across different systems in nature – "structure to irregularity" seems to be a unifying principle and key feature of nature.

For instance, He et al. (2010) investigated in her paper not only the scale-free dynamics of the brain's neural activity and its nested frequencies using electrocorticography (ECoG). She also investigated time series of activities from spontaneous earth seismic waves (collected within a time span of four months, as relevant for predicting earthquakes) and fluctuations in the Dow Jones index indicating stock market fluctuations (collected within a time span of 80 years). Time series from both earth seismic waves and stock market fluctuations followed power-law distribution in their temporal power spectrum. Interestingly, their power-law exponent (1.99 for seismic waves and 1.95 for stock market) came close to the one of the brain's intrinsic activity as measured in ECoG during wakefulness (mean of 2.2 for <0.1 Hz). Most interestingly, the time series in both earth seismic waves and stock market fluctuations contained nested frequencies with higher frequency fluctuations nesting in lower frequency fluctuations, just like in the case of the brain's intrinsic activity.

The Scale-Free Self IV: Self Is Nested Within the World Through the Brain's LRTC

If both environment and brain exhibit scale-free structure, one would expect their interaction. Specifically, one would exhibit that the LRTC of the environmental structures are contained and nested within the ones of the brain's spontaneous activity – both ecological and neuronal LRTC would be assumed to match with each other. Such "complexity matching" (Borges et al. 2018) has indeed been shown in recent studies on language and music. Borges et al. (2018) demonstrated how the degree of scale-freeness in the brain in different frequency bands tracks and follows the variations in the scale-free envelope of speech and how their degree of correspondence impacts speech comprehension. Analogously, Teixeira Borges et al. (2019) show how the scale-free structure of brain and music adapts to each other with the brain's neural activity somewhat rescaling the musical structure – the degree of their mutual adaptation predicted the subjects' degree of pleasure during music listening.

Taken together, scale-free activity is not a unique feature of the brain but ubiquitous in nature (i.e., the world). That allows the brain to compare and match its own self-free nestedness and LRTC with the ones of its respective environment with the degree of their matching shaping mental features like perception. Unfortunately, no studies have yet been reported that investigate whether the degree of matching between world and brain LRTC is related to the self and how one perceives one's own self to be part of the world (i.e., ecological neuro-ecological self), as we say.

However, given the fact that the scale-freeness of the brain is directly related to the self (see above), one would assume that the self is connected and integrated within the world's scale-free structure through temporal nestedness and LRTC: like one smaller Russian doll is integrated within the next larger one and so forth and ultimately the most largest one, the self is integrated and nested within the brain which, in turn, is nested and integrated within the yet largest and most comprehensive temporal scale, the world. What connects the self through the brain to the world is its scale-freeness featured by temporal nestedness and LRTC.

Put into more conceptual terms, we can say that the (1) world-brain relation is scale-free characterized by temporal nestedness and LRTC such that the brain's smaller scale is nested and contained within the world's larger scale; (2) the scale-free nature of world-brain relation may be key in shaping and constituting the self; (3) the self is neuro-ecological and scale-free; and (4) the self intrinsically integrated within the world through the temporal nestedness and LRTC of world-brain relation.

Part II: Point of View Between World and Brain: Subjectivity in an Objective World

Point of View: Mental Surface Layer and Ecological Depth Layer

What is a point of view (PV)? The notion of PV is extensively used in literature and theatre with different persons or actors expressing different points of view on one and the same subject matter. Painting and photography rely on a slightly different notion of PV as providing access to events or objects and ultimately the world. The same applies to movies where the same event or object can be documented from different angles or PVs. Architecture and design provide yet another feature of PV as a multitude of perspectives can co-occur in a building like Gehry buildings (as the famous Guggenheim Museum in Bilbao).

Despite the extensive usage of PV in ordinary language and different disciplines, the concept of PV has rather been neglected in philosophy, as there is no established theory (see Campos and Gutierrez 2015, for a notable exception). Here I follow their account of PV although only to some degree. My main argument will be that the concept of PV can provide an intrinsic connection of world and self by providing the most basic and fundamental ground of subjectivity within the world.

According to Campos and Gutierrez, PV can be determined by two main features, reference to mental life including subject and access to something beyond itself (i.e., the world). Following their footpath, I will determine and rename these two features as deeper and surface layer of PV: the PV's reference to the subject and mental life is the surface layer of PV – I speak of a "mental surface layer". On the other hand, the PV's access to the world is primarily ecological and operates in the depth of the PV – I therefore speak of an "ecological depth layer".

The mental surface layer of PV refers to a subject with personal and mental features where it is manifest in terms like "opinion", "belief", "attitude", "feeling", "sentiments", "thoughts", "view", and so on of a particular subject or person (Campos and Gutierrez 2015, 2). Here PV is connected to the subject and its mental features in a necessary way:

> In that variety of uses, the notion of point of view may have two distinct meanings. In one of them, points of view are part of a mental life. They are connected to the mental life of some subjects with a personal character. In that sense, the expression "point of view" is interchangeable with words like "view", "opinion", "belief", "attitude", "feeling", "sentiment", "thought", etc. Points of view in that sense could not exist without a subject with quite a rich mental life.
>
> *(Campos and Gutierrez 2015, 2).*

In contrast, the ecological depth layer of PV is characterized by providing access to something that lies beyond the PV itself, namely the world – this pertains to what I describe as ecological depth layer of PV. Rather than on mental states within the subject itself (i.e., intra-subjectively), the focus is here on how the subject connects and relates to the world. Intra-subjectivity is replaced by inter-subjectivity, and isolation is replaced by relation:"

> There is another quite important meaning in the ordinary notion of point of view. In that second sense, points of view could exist without any actual subject exemplifying them. Here, points of view explicitly have a strong relational and modal, especially subjunctive, character. Points of view offer possibilities of having access to the world. They offer possibilities of seeing things (hearing them, touching them, etc.), possibilities of thinking about them (considering them, imagining them, etc.), and possibilities of valuing them (assessing them, pondering them, etc.).
>
> *(Campos and Gutierrez 2015, 3)*

Ecological Depth Layer of PV I: Relational Hub or Node

My main focus in this chapter is on the ecological depth layer of PV as it, as I argue, provides the ontological ground of subjectivity and ultimately also of the self, which is usually associated with the mental surface layer of PV. The key feature of the ecological depth layer of PV is its relational character as it relates and connects the self to and within the world. Relation means that the PV is connected and related to something beyond itself. Put into the context of ecological psychology, that "something beyond itself" is the world and specifically the environment that provides information. Such information includes natural, social, and cultural as well as descriptive and normative aspects (see below) – for the sake of simplicity, we will here lump them all together under the notion of ecological information understood in a broad way.

The ecological depth layer of PV shares ecological information with the world. That sharing is not total sharing though as the ecological depth layer of PV only offers the possibility of relating to certain kinds of ecological information of the world. For instance, the bat can access ultrasonar information in the world (Nagel 1974), which we as humans cannot do as related to distinct biophysical features based ultimately on different temporal and spatial scales or ranges. This leads us back to scale-free activity: the more different ranges or scales of time (and space) are covered by the ecological depth layer of its PV, the more extensively and better the self can relate to the world and its ecological information. We consequently assume that the ecological depth layer of PV is nested and contained within the world and its ecological information in a scale-free world.

Scale-free nesting of the ecological depth layer of PV within the world means that there are LRTC between world and self: the world's much longer timescales are correlated with the self's shorter time scales, as the former nest and contain the latter in a self-similar (or self-affine) way, just like the larger Russian doll contains the smaller ones. Accordingly, what empirically is described as scale-free activity featured by temporal nestedness and LRTC can now on the conceptual side be associated with the ecological depth layer of PV as the relational basis and fundament of the self.

We saw that the relation of self and scale-free activity is mediated by the brain's scale-free activity and how it relates to the world's scale-free (i.e., world-brain) relation. Putting all together, we now postulate that the ecological depth layer of PV is ontologically based on the world-brain relation through scale-free activity featured by temporal nestedness and LRTC: the more world and brain are temporally (and spatially) nested within each other exhibiting LRTC between them, the more the temporal (and spatial) range of the ecological depth layer of PV and ultimately its self can relate to and be extended towards and within the world. If, in contrast, the temporal range of the ecological depth layer of PV is more limited meaning low degrees of temporal nestedness and LRTC with the world, the more restricted and isolated the self will be in its relation to the world. We tentatively assume that the latter holds in case of a self suffering from early childhood trauma.

Campos and Gutierrez describe the PV is a "relational entity". However, the concept of entity means that something is somewhat clearly distinguished with clearly defined borders from that what surrounds it. That is not compatible with the intrinsically relational and scale-free nature of the ecological depth layer of PV though. Given the scale-free integration of the ecological depth layer of PV within the world and its scale-free features, one may better describe PV as "relational hub or node". Much like hubs or nodes are constituted by their relation or connectivity to the rest of the network, PV's are characterized by their relation or connection to the rest of the world's temporo-spatial networks. Taken as relational hub or node, the ecological depth layer of PV provides "structure to irregularity", namely it structures the world's various temporal scales for the self in such way that the latter can access the former (i.e., ecological information).

Ecological Depth Layer of PV II: Time as Intrinsic Rather Than as Add-On

What is a point of view? Traditionally, the point of view has been associated with a fixed entity like mental or physical substances or properties. Taken in such sense, the point of view is static and atemporal. That distinguishes the traditional concept of the point of view from our characterization of the ecological depth layer of PV that, rather than being static and fixed, is highly dynamic and flexible and therefore intrinsically temporal rather than atemporal.

Scale-free activity provides "structure to irregularity": even if, for instance, the activity of different regions or the power of single frequencies change in an irregular way, they can still maintain their overall structure. Hence, being susceptible to change as distinct from non-change, scale-free activity is neither purely irregular and 100% dynamic nor completely regular and 100% static – it operates beyond or, more precisely, on a continuum between the conceptual extremes of dynamic and static, flexible and fixed (see also Northoff and Tumati 2019).

This points a core feature of the ecological depth layer of PV, namely its intrinsically temporal nature as entailed by its scale-free features. That converges with Campos and Gutierrez (2015), who also characterize PV as intrinsically temporally.

> Let us say understand temporal points of view as follows: A temporal point of view is a point of view identifying some differences in non-conceptual contents (qualitative, phenomenal, experiential contents) as "changes" of content. The identification can be either conceptual or not conceptual. This is a very important point. Subjects without conceptual capacities could be capable of adopting temporal points of view. In any case, in a temporal point of view certain differences in non-conceptual content count as a "change": something future becoming present, or something present becoming past. The idea behind that characterisation of temporal points of view is very simple. Temporal points of view take some differences in the non-conceptual contents of experience as being temporal differences entailing a "change". This is the crucial point.
>
> *(Campos and Gutierrez 2015, 93)*

Where is the time of the ecological depth layer of PV coming from? We suppose that the intrinsically temporal nature of the ecological depth layer of PV is ultimately coming from and originates within the world itself (i.e., world-based time; Northoff and Chen 2019). By connecting and relating to the world in a scale-free way, the ecological depth layer of PV participates and integrates with the ongoing time of the world such that both share one and the same time in a scale-free way, that is, across their different ranges or scales of time. As its scale or range is much larger, the world's time nests and contains the time of the ecological depth layer of PV – the world emplaces PV within itself.

Interlude About World and PV: Emplacement World and Perspectival World

The intrinsically temporal and scale-free emplacement of the ecological depth layer of PV within the world specifies and converges well with the concept of "emplacement world" as proposed by Campos and Gutierrez (2015, 13–14, 40). They distinguish two concepts of world: "emplacement world" and "perspectival world". The emplacement world is the world within which PV is situated (i.e., emplaced), while the perspectival world is the one that one perceives and cognizes from a certain PV. Without going into much philosophical detail, I here use these two concepts of world to further characterize the two layers of PV.

The emplacement world reflects the deeper ecological layer of PV, it is the world within which PV is situated (i.e., emplaced), allowing its direct contact and relation with existence and reality of the world. PV is emplaced in the temporal (and spatial) structures and regularities of the world that signify the world prior to and independent of PV itself. Without going into full detail, we characterize the emplacement world as intrinsically temporal and scale-free between itself and its various parts like subjects or selves that, through temporal nestedness and LRTC, are nested and contained within the world in a temporal way. Taken in such sense, the concept of the emplacement world is an ontological concept as it refers to the existence and reality of the world as whole and its parts, like selves or subjects.

In contrast, the concept of perspectival world is primarily an epistemological (rather than ontological) concept as it refers to the surface cognitive layer of PV, that is, the world we as subjects perceive and cognize in a perspectival way in the terms of first-, second-, or third-person perspective (FPP, SPP, TPP). The self is typically associated with FPP, which is designated as subjective as distinguished from the more objective TPP. While not elaborating on this association, we here argue that all three perspectives characterize only the mental surface layer of PV but not the ecological depth layer of PV that remains pre-perspectival rather than being perspectival by itself. Let us illustrate that by the notion of pre-reflective self-consciousness as developed in phenomenology.

Ecological Depth Layer of PV III: Pre-perspectival and Pre-phenomenal

We experience our own self and the world in first-person perspective (FPP). FPP is conceived as the hallmark feature of both subjectivity and consciousness in phenomenology, as both are conjoint in what is described as pre-reflective self-consciousness (Zahavi 2005; Gallagher and Zahavi 2019). In a nutshell, pre-reflective self-consciousness describes the immediate and first-personal givenness of experiences that is always already there prior to and independent of any reflection, as in introspection, attention, or recognition. Even when I am conscious of an event or object in the world, I am already conscious of myself in the pre-reflective mode. Pre-reflective self-consciousness signifies the intrinsically subjective nature of consciousness featured by its first-person perspective and its phenomenal (rather than non-phenomenal) character.

How does pre-reflective self-consciousness stand in relation to PV? FPP is often equated with PV: the first-person perspective is supposed to be based on a specific point of view which marks FPP subjective, perspectival, and phenomenal. PV is taken here as intra-subjective, mental or phenomenal, and isolated. That pertains only to the mental surface layer of PV, whereas it does not apply to the ecological depth layer of PV that is inter-subjective, ecological, and relational. This is, for instance, reflected in the following quote by Thomas Nagel from his famous paper "What It Is Like to Be a Bat": "I am not advertising here to the alleged privacy of experience to its possessor. The point of view in question is not one accessible only to a single individual. Rather it is a type" (Nagel 1974, 441). (Note also that Nagel does not speak of FPP in this paper at all but only of a point of view that distinguishes bats' experience and subjectivity from the one of humans).

From that it follows that the ecological depth layer of PV can be characterized neither by FPP (nor by SPP and TPP, as those operate on the same level or layer as FPP) nor by pre-reflective self-consciousness. Characterizing the ecological depth layer of PV by FPP or pre-reflective self-consciousness would be to confuse the former with the mental (or phenomenal) surface layer of PV as their sufficient condition. We consequently need to characterize the ecological depth layer of PV in terms other than FPP (or SPP and TPP) and pre-reflective self-consciousness. At the same time, the ecological depth layer of PV must be somehow related to FPP and pre-reflective self-consciousness, as otherwise it could not serve as depth layer of PV but would remain unrelated to PV.

We propose that the ecological depth layer of PV can be conceived as "pre-perspectival" and "pre-phenomenal" (Northoff 2014, 2018) as it provides the necessary albeit non-sufficient condition of possible perspectives and phenomenality: rather than being actually perspectival and phenomenal by itself, the ecological depth layer of PV makes possible FPP and pre-reflective self-consciousness without actually realizing them yet as such. In other terms, the ecological depth layer of PV provides the ontological capacity or predisposition of perspectives and pre-reflective self-consciousness – it is an ontological predisposition of perspectives and pre-reflective self-consciousness that characterizes the mental surface layer of PV and its self (see Northoff 2018, chap. 10 for the concept of ontological predisposition).

In conclusion, we assume that the pre-perspectival and pre-phenomenal nature of the ecological depth layer of PV (as ontological predisposition of the perspectival and phenomenal nature of self) is based on its intrinsically temporal and scale-free nature that constitute its relation to and emplacement by the world (i.e., emplacement world). This marks the self as both neuro-ecological and pre-phenomenal, which first and foremost make possible the phenomenal, mental, and cognitive features of self as they can be associated with the mental surface layer of PV.

Conclusion

Subjectivity in Neuropsychoanalysis: Point of View and Psychoanalytic Concepts

One may now raise the question how the three key concepts – world-brain relation, neuro-ecological self, and point of view – stand in relation to psychoanalytic concepts of self and ego. Without being able to go into full detail, I make some hints in this direction.

The point of view is a temporo-spatial structure that, being intrinsically scale-free, operates across different spatial and temporal ranges or scales. That is exactly implied in Freud's original concept of the threefold structure of the ego that (as in id, ego, and super-ego) also operates in a scale-free way across different temporo-spatial scales. We may consequently want to extend the BMSS (Northoff 2016) in psychoanalytical terms, where id, ego, and super-ego can be conceived as distinct temporo-spatial layers that, as the Russian dolls or the different layers of an onion, are nested within each other. Future research may want to specify the temporo-spatial scales or ranges of id, ego, and super-ego on a psychological level and then associate them with corresponding scales on the neuronal level.

The point of view is based on continuous construction that, empirically, may be traced to the continuous relation of the brain's ongoing activity to the external environment's temporo-spatial scale-free structure. That very same relation of brain and environment has been described as self-related processing, as it constructs the self-specificity of otherwise non-self-specific events and objects (Northoff 2016). On the psychodynamic side, self-related processing may well correspond to what Winnicott 1975) described as "subjective relating" and Brockman (2002, 90) as "attachment" (see also Scalabrini et al. 2018) with the resulting self-specificity of particular events or objects corresponding to what Kohut described as "self-objects" (Kohut 1977; Northoff 2011).

Finally, as emphasized in psychoanalysis, the ego is threefold structure; similarly, the point of view is also determined by in a multi-layered way with deeper and surface layers that, as I assume, can be split into multiple layers in the future. Importantly, the distinct layers are nested within each other including showing LRTC. Analogously, one may assume that id, ego, and super-ego are all temporally nested within each other exhibiting LRTC which, for instance, would well explain the strong impact of the id on ego and super-ego. Due to its close neuro-ecological proximity to the environment with large extended temporo-spatial scales, one may not wonder that the id "knows more" (in an unconscious way) than both ego and super-ego which, being neuro-affective (Solms 2015) and neuro-cognitive, operate on more restricted temporo-spatial ranges than the Id.

References

Boeker H, Hartwich, Northoff G (2019) *Neuropsychodynamic psychiatry*. Springer Publisher, New York, Heidelberg.

Borges AFT, Giraud AL, Mansvelder HD, Linkenkaer-Hansen KJ (2018) Scale-free amplitude modulation of neuronal oscillations tracks comprehension of accelerated speech. *J. Neurosci.* 2018 Jan 17;38(3):710–722.

Brockman R (2002). Self, object, and neurobiology. *Neuropsychoanalysis*.4:87–99.

Buzsaki G (2006) *Rhythms of the brain*. Oxford University Press, New York, Oxford.

Campos M, Gutierrez A (2015) *Temporal points of view*. Springer Publisher, New York, Heidelberg.

Cocchi L, Gollo LL, Zalesky A, Breakspear M (2017) Criticality in the brain: A synthesis of neurobiology, models and cognition. *Prog Neurobiol.* 2017 Nov;158:132–152. doi: 10.1016/j.pneurobio.2017.07.002. Epub 2017 Jul 19.

Damiani S, Scalabrini A, Gomez-Pilar J, Brondino N, Northoff G (2019) Increased scale-free dynamics in salience network in adult high-functioning autism. *Neuroimage Clin.* 2019;21:101634. doi: 10.1016/j.nicl.2018.101634. Epub 2018 Dec 10.

Disner S, Marquardt CA, Mueller BA, Burton PC, Sponheim SR (2018) Spontaneous neural activity differences in posttraumatic stress disorder: A quantitative resting-state meta-analysis and fMRI validation. *Hum Brain Mapp.* 2018 Feb;39(2):837–850.

Duncan NW, Hayes DJ, Wiebking C, Tiret B, Pietruska K, Chen DQ, Rainville P, Marjańska M, Ayad O, Doyon J, Hodaie M, Northoff G (2015) Negative childhood experiences alter a prefrontal-insular-motor cortical network in healthy adults: A preliminary multimodal rsfMRI-fMRI-MRS-dMRI study. *Hum Brain Mapp.* 2015 Nov;36(11):4622–437. doi: 10.1002/hbm.22941. Epub 2015 Aug 19.

Gallagher S, Daly A (2018) Dynamical relations in the self-pattern. *Front Psychol.* 2018 May 11;9:664. doi: 10.3389/fpsyg.2018.00664. eCollection 2018.

Gallagher S, Zahavi D *Phenomenological approaches to self-consciousness*. The Stanford Encyclopedia of Philosophy (Summer 2019 Edition), Edward N. Zalta (ed.). URL = <https://plato.stanford.edu/archives/sum2019/entries/self-consciousness-phenomenological/>

Gupta A, Mayer EA, Acosta JR, Hamadani K, Torgerson C, van Horn JD, Chang L, Naliboff B, Tillisch K, Labus JS (2017) Early adverse life events are associated with altered brain network architecture in a sex- dependent manner. *Neurobiol Stress.* 2017 Feb 17;7:16–26. doi: 10.1016/j.ynstr.2017.02.003. eCollection 2017 Dec.

He BJ (2014) Robust, transient neural dynamics during conscious perception. *Trends Cogn Sci.* 2018 Jul;22(7):563–565. doi: 10.1016/j.tics.2018.04.005. Epub 2018 May 12.

He BJ, Zempel JM, Snyder AZ, Raichle ME (2010) The temporal structures and functional significance of scale-free brain activity. *Neuron.* 2010 May 13;66(3):353–369. doi: 10.1016/j.neuron.2010.04.020

Heidegger, Martin (1927/2008). *Being and time* (J. Macquarrie & E. Robinson, Trans.). Harper Perennial Modern Classics, New York.

Huang Z, Obara N, Davis HH 4th, Pokorny J, Northoff G (2016) The temporal structure of resting-state brain activity in the medial prefrontal cortex predicts self-consciousness. *Neuropsychologia.* 2016 Feb;82:161–170. doi: 10.1016/j.neuropsychologia.2016.01.025. Epub 2016 Jan 21. PMID: 26805557.

James W (1890) *Principles of psychology*. Harvard University Press.

Koch S, van Zuiden M, Nawijn L, Frijling JL, Veltman DJ, Olff M (2016) Aberrant resting-state brain activity in posttraumatic stress disorder: A meta-analysis and systematic review. *Depress Anxiety.* 2016 Jul;33(7):592–605.

Kohut H (1977) *The restoration of the self.* International Universities Press, New York.

Kolvoort IR, Wainio-Theberge S, Wolff A, Northoff G (2020) Temporal integration as "common currency" of brain and self-scale-free activity in resting-state EEG correlates with temporal delay effects on self-relatedness. *Hum Brain Mapp.* 2020 Jul 22;41(15):4355–4374. doi: 10.1002/hbm.25129.

Linkenkaer-Hansen K, Nikouline VV, Palva JM, Ilmoniemi RJ (2001) Long-range temporal correlations and scaling behavior in human brain oscillations. *J Neurosci.* 2001 Feb 15;21(4):1370–1377. doi: 10.1523/JNEUROSCI.21-04-01370.2001

Lu S, Weijia Gao, Zhaoguo Wei, Dandan Wang, ShaoHua Hu, Manli Huang, Yi Xu, Lingjiang Li (2017) Intrinsic brain abnormalities in young healthy adults with childhood trauma: A resting-state functional magnetic resonance imaging study of regional homogeneity and functional connectivity. *Aust N Z J Psychiatry.* 2017 Jun;51(6):614–623.

Milrod D (2002) The concept of self and self-representation. *Neuropsychoanalysis.* 4:7–23

Nagel T (1974) What is it like to be a bat? *Philos Rev.* 83(4).

Nakao T, Matsumoto T, Morita M, Shimizu D, Yoshimura S, Northoff G, Morinobu S, Okamoto Y, Yamawaki S (2013) The degree of early life stress predicts decreased medial prefrontal activations and the shift from internally to externally guided decision making: An exploratory NIRS study during resting state and self-oriented task. *Front Hum Neurosci*. 2013 Jul 3;7:339.

Northoff G (2011) *Neuropsychoanalysis in practice. Brain, self, and objects*. Oxford University Press, Oxford, New York.

Northoff G (2014) *Minding the brain. An introduction of philosophy and neuroscience*. Palgrave McMillan, New York, London.

Northoff G (2016) Is the self a higher-order or fundamental function of the brain? The "basis model of self-specificity" and its encoding by the brain's spontaneous activity. *Cogn Neurosci*. 2016 Jan–Oct;7(1–4): 203–222. doi: 10.1080/17588928.2015.1111868. Epub 2016 Feb 1.

Northoff G (2018) *The spontaneous brain. From the mind-body to the world-brain problem*. MIT Press, Cambridge/MA.

Northoff G, Chen K (2019) Levels of time in the Zhuangzi, A Leibnizian perspective. *Philos East West*. Oct 2019;69(4):1–20

Northoff G, Huang Z (2017) How do the brain's time and space mediate consciousness and its different dimensions? Temporo-spatial theory of consciousness (TTC). *Neurosci Biobehav Rev*. 2017 Sep;80:630–645. doi: 10.1016/j.neubiorev.2017.07.013. Epub 2017 Jul 28.

Northoff G, Sandsten KE, Nordgaard J, Kjaer TW, Parnas J (2020) The self and its prolonged intrinsic neural timescale in Schizophrenia. *Schizophr Bull*. 2020 Jul 2:sbaa083. doi: 10.1093/schbul/sbaa083. Online ahead of print.

Northoff G, Tumati S. (2019) "Average is good, extremes are bad" – Non-linear inverted U-shaped relationship between neural mechanisms and functionality of mental features. *Neurosci Biobehav Rev*. 2019 Sep;104:11–25. doi: 10.1016/j.neubiorev.2019.06.030. Epub 2019 Jun 25.

Palva JM, Zhigalov A, Hirvonen J, Korhonen O, Linkenkaer-Hansen K, Palva S. (2013) Neuronal long-range temporal correlations and avalanche dynamics are correlated with behavioral scaling laws. *Proc Natl Acad Sci USA*. 26;110(9):3585–3590.

Qin P, Northoff G (2011) How is our self related to midline regions and the default-mode network? *Neuroimage*. 2011 Aug 1;57(3):1221–1233. doi: 0.1016/j.neuroimage.2011.05.028. Epub 2011 May 15.

Qin P, Wang M, Northoff G (2020) Linking bodily, environmental and mental states in the self-A three-level model based on a meta-analysis. *Neurosci Biobehav Rev*. 2020 May 31;115:77–95. doi: 10.1016/j.neubiorev.2020.05.004. Online ahead of print.

Scalabrini A, Ebisch SJH, Huang Z, Di Plinio S, Perrucci MG, Romani GL, Mucci C, Northoff G (2019) Spontaneous brain activity predicts task-evoked activity during animate versus inanimate touch. *Cerebral Cortex*. 2019 Dec 17;29(11):4628–4645. doi: 10.1093/cercor/bhy340

Scalabrini A, Huang Z, Mucci C, Perrucci MG, Ferretti A, Fossati A, Romani GL, Northoff G, Ebisch SJH (2017) How spontaneous brain activity and narcissistic features shape social interaction. *Scientific Report*. 2017 Aug 30;7(1):9986. doi: 10.1038/s41598-017-10389-9.

Scalabrini A, Mucci C, Northoff G (2018) Is our self related to personality? A neuropsychodynamic model. *Front Hum Neurosci*. 2018 Oct 4;12:346. doi:10.3389/fnhum.2018.00346. eCollection 2018.

Solms M (2015) *The feeling brain. Selected papers on neuropsychoanalysis*. Routledge, London, New York.

Sui J, Humphreys GW (2015) The integrative self: How self-reference integrates perception and memory. *Trends Cogn Sci*. 2015 Dec;19(12):719–728. doi: 10.1016/j.tics.2015.08.015. Epub 2015 Oct 4.

Teixeira Borges AF, Irrmischer M, Brockmeier T, Smit DJA, Mansvelder HD, Linkenkaer-Hansen K (2019) Scaling behaviour in music and cortical dynamics interplay to mediate music listening pleasure. *Sci Rep*. 2019 Nov 27;9(1):17700. doi: 10.1038/s41598-019-54060-x

Winnicott D (1975) *Through pediatric to psychoanalysis*. Basic Books, New York.

Wolff A, Di Giovanni DA, Gómez-Pilar J, Nakao T, Huang Z, Longtin A, Northoff G (2019) The temporal signature of self: Temporal measures of resting-state EEG predict self-consciousness. *Hum Brain Mapp*. 2019 Feb 15;40(3):789–803. doi: 10.1002/hbm.24412. Epub 2018 Oct 4.

Zahavi D (2005) *Subjectivity and selfhood*. MIT Press, Cambridge/MA.

Zhang J, Huang Z, Chen Y, Zhang J, Ghinda D, Nikolova Y, Wu J, Xu J, Bai W, Mao Y, Yang Z, Duncan N, Qin P, Wang H, Chen B, Weng X, Northoff G (2018) Breakdown in the temporal and spatial organisation of spontaneous brain activity during general anesthesia. *Hum Brain Mapp*. 2018 May;39(5):2035–2046. doi: 10.1002/hbm.23984. Epub 2018 Jan 28.

24

PSYCHOANALYSIS, SELF-DECEPTION, AND THE PROBLEM OF TELEOLOGY

Simon Boag

Self-Deception and the Problem of the Dynamic Unconscious

The possibility of deceiving oneself provides an ongoing puzzle for both psychology and philosophy. Self-deception is construed variously but is typically modelled upon *interpersonal* deception (Baghramian & Nicholson, 2013; Van Leeuwen, 2013). With interpersonal deception, a person intentionally deceives another into believing that *p* while actually believing that not-*p* is the case. So applied to self-deception, the self-deceiver at once believes that *p* is false whilst deceiving himself or herself into believing that *p* is true. Two problems are associated with such self-deception: the so-called *static* and *dynamic* paradoxes (Mele, 1987). The static paradox entails the seeming impossibility of holding contradictory beliefs simultaneously (i.e., believing both *p* and not-*p*), whereas the dynamic paradox involves *intentionally* deceiving oneself, which is taken to be *prima facie* self-defeating.

Repression, the so-called "corner-stone on which the whole structure of psycho-analysis rests" (Freud, 1914, p. 16), is also comparable to self-deception. Simply put, "*the essence of repression lies simply in turning something away, and keeping it at a distance, from the conscious*" (Freud, 1915a, p. 147), and Freud, at times, compares repression to other- and self-deception:

> I must draw an analogy between the criminal and the hysteric. In both we are concerned with a secret, with something hidden. . . . In the case of the criminal it is a secret which he knows and hides from you, whereas in the case of the hysteric it is a secret which he himself does not know either, which is hidden even from himself.
>
> *(Freud, 1906, p. 108)*

With repression, not only do we commonly deceive ourselves, but such opacity is maintained by competing forces instigated by strong emotions and even unrelenting desires (Boag, 2012, 2017).

Explaining repression, however, involves addressing particular theoretical difficulties (Boag, 2012, 2017; Maze & Henry, 1996). Freud (1915a) notes that repression is not an event that simply occurs once but is instead an ongoing activity whereby an individual actively ignores the content of his or her own mind (Boag, 2012; Maze & Henry, 1996). As Freud writes:

> The process of repression is not to be regarded as an event which takes place *once*, the results of which are permanent, as when some living thing has been killed and from

DOI: 10.4324/9780429297076-29

> that time onward is dead; repression demands a persistent expenditure of force, and if this were to cease the success of the repression would be jeopardized, so that a fresh act of repression would be necessary. We may suppose that the repressed exercises a continuous pressure in the direction of the conscious, so that this pressure must be balanced by an unceasing counter-pressure.
>
> *(Freud, 1915, p. 151)*

The situation is further complicated, however, since the repressed target further acquires substitute aims in the form of phantasies (Freud, 1907),[1] which then attempt to force their way into both waking consciousness and dreams, requiring further acts of repression. Repression subsequently involves a two-stage operation whereby the objectionable impulse is initially prevented from entering consciousness ('primal repression'),[2] and thereafter the substitutive phantasies are targeted by 'repression proper' (*eigentliche Verdrängung*) or 'after-pressure' (*Nachdrängen*; Freud, 1915).[3]

As Maze and Henry (1996) point out, since the 'ego' is said to be both the repressing agency and the 'victim' of repression, then the ego must somehow continuously guard against intrusions of the repressed. Consequently, repression appears to be an impossible task since it appears to require the repressing subject (the ego) re-knowing the target in order not to know it. This paradoxical state of affairs is exemplified by the clinical phenomenon of resistance, an offshoot of repression. Resistance occurs when

> the desire to reveal one's unconscious feelings and thoughts to oneself and one's therapist is countered by an equally strong desire to keep those feelings and thoughts out of awareness and away from the therapist's attention. Thus every client struggles to reveal and to conceal, to express and repress.
>
> *(Auld, et al., 2005, p. 111)*

As such, with resistance, the person undergoing therapy both consciously attempts to discover what is unconscious, while simultaneously unconsciously resisting this. Such resistance is believed to be both a selective and discriminative process, actively opposing some, though not other, mental contents from becoming conscious (see Boag, 2012).

Such theoretical difficulties are not limited to repression and resistance and extend to other defensive processes. For example, Kernberg (1987) proposes that the defense of projective identification entails projecting "intolerable intrapsychic experiences" onto another person, not as a single act but as "a continuing effort to defend against the intolerable experience" (p. 796). The theoretical challenge here then is explaining how this ongoing response to the defended-against target occurs so as to externalise and manage the distress, while also explaining how the distressing event is defended against without being further recognised. Although a person might be able to turn their attention away from a distressing event once, an account is nevertheless required for explaining how the defense is maintained when evidence of the distressing target re-asserts itself or remains apparent.

Phenomena such as repression and resistance capture the essence and complexity of psychodynamic processes, and so explaining how these occur is an important challenge for psychoanalytic theory. The aim of the present chapter is to address the contributions of the philosophy of self-deception for understanding repression and defensive processes. To achieve this, the chapter first addresses the static and dynamic paradoxes of self-deception to both clarify where the actual problems lie and to identify problematic strategies for explaining the harder cases of self-deception. Strongly partitive accounts of the mind and the role of intentions and teleology in repression and self-deception are then discussed. The chapter then identifies problems with approaches proposing that self-deception and repression are both functional and have evolutionary adaptive benefits. The problem of teleology in functional accounts of repression is then discussed in the context of 'betrayal blindness' found within betrayal trauma theory. After demonstrating that teleology prevents such approaches from providing coherent theories of repression and self-deception, a realist-relational view of mentality is developed for addressing how repression and betrayal blindness can be maintained when evidence of the distressing target re-asserts itself or remains apparent. An alternative non-teleological account of betrayal blindness based on affects as efficient causes and Freud's account of the 'blindness of the seeing eye' is then put forward.

Clarifying the Paradoxes of Self-Deception

There are two paradoxes typically associated with self-deception: the static and dynamic paradoxes. The static paradox – where a person *S* both believes *p* and not-*p* simultaneously – is typically taken to the more difficult of the two paradoxes to address (Van Leeuwen, 2013). For some, holding contradictory beliefs "is thought to be an impossible state of mind" (Hohol & Urbańczyk, 2013, p. 221), while Baghramian and Nicholson (2013) write that this apparent logical contradiction "remains intuitively jarring if not absurd" (p. 1018). However, the problem of believing both *p* and not-*p* assumes rationality and transparency of mind and so is not as problematic as some might believe:[4] there is only an apparent paradox if the person is concurrently aware of holding contradictory beliefs. Put differently, if one considers the apparently infinite number of beliefs than any one person holds, and which, for the most part are rarely, if ever, reflected upon or brought to conscious attention, then there are infinitely numerous opportunities for holding contradictory beliefs. In some respects, this simply reflects a characteristic of Freud's system *Ucs.*, whereby incompatible beliefs can exist side by side without contradiction, and conscious recognition of such a contradiction is necessary for resolution (see Boag, 2015).

The dynamic paradox, on the other hand, pivots on the role of intentions, whereby *S* believes that *p* is the case but intends to falsely believe that not-*p*. The perceived problem here hinges upon the self-defeating nature of intentionally performing acts of self-deception. As Van Leeuwen (2013) writes,

> In order for A to deceive A, A must intend to cause false belief in A . . . but intentions are usually accessible to those who have them, so A would be aware that she intends to cause a false belief in herself; but being aware of this intention, it would be impossible for her to be fooled by it. So how is self-deception possible?
>
> (*p. 2*)

Again, however, there is an assumption of transparency, and so a psychodynamically oriented response might simply question the implicit Cartesian position here whereby the mind's acts are said to be transparent to itself. After all, it is not *a priori* obvious that it must be the case that any intention is automatically known. Nevertheless, intentionally deceiving oneself appears to be self-defeating if one is aware that one knows *p* but intends to believe not-*p*: "For if one were intentionally to decide to deceive oneself, to deny what one knows to be true, that would presuppose that one does already know what one knows to be true" (Neu, 1988, p. 81). Successful self-deception would then require preventing awareness of one's intention to self-deceive, threatening a regress of repressive-like acts to prevent awareness of each self-deceiving intention.

Strategies for Addressing the Paradoxes

One strategy for circumventing the static paradox involves partitioning the mind, either weakly or strongly (see Baghramian & Nicholson, 2013; Van Leeuwen, 2013). Weak partitioning separates conflicting beliefs by postulating "boundaries between parts of the mind . . . between any (obviously) conflicting beliefs" (Davidson, 1985, p. 147), such that a single person believes both *p* and not-*p* in different parts of the mind. Davidson (1998) recognises, however, that this approach is descriptive rather than explanatory, neither addressing how such splitting occurs in the first place nor how the splitting is maintained (cf. Heil, 1989).[5] Alternatively, if a single agent were to somehow initiate this division, along the lines of a "self-inflicted lobotomy" (Davidson, 1998, p. 8), then some account is required for explaining how this could intelligibly occur.

'Strongly' partitive accounts, on the other hand, propose that the mind is inhabited by a multiplicity of knowing subjects (Boag, 2005), and some view strong partitioning as a *sine qua non* of psychodynamic thinking (e.g., Lockie, 2003). Generally speaking, rather than attempting to understand how a single agent can simultaneously believe that *p* and believe that not-*p*, the contradictory beliefs are said to be held by different knowing subjects. Such strongly partitive approaches have a long history in psychoanalytic thinking, as is evident in Freud's censor of dreams (see Boag, 2012 for discussion). With such accounts, a censor stands between the unconscious content and the ego, allowing certain content to become conscious while repressing and distorting other content.

Strong partitioning has been criticised on logical grounds (e.g., Van Leeuwen, 2013) but on the position here, postulating multiple knowers provides no greater grounds for theoretical concern than compared to postulating a single knower (see Boag, 2005 for objections and responses). There are, nevertheless, several problems with postulating a censor for explaining repression and self-deception. As Sartre (1956) observes in his discussion of self-deception as 'bad faith' (*mauvaise foi*), any such censor must be an independent agency, discerning what shall and shall not become conscious.[6] Consider here, for instance, Lockie's (2003) claim that such censoring agents "have (partially successful) means of selectively concealing, revealing, and deceiving the other parts" (p. 128). If this is the case, then Gardner (1993) correctly concludes that the censoring agency "must have a greater capacity than any other part of the mind for (i) representing the contents of other mental parts, and (ii) controlling mental events" (p. 48). In other words, the censor must be a transcendental agency, superior to the conscious system, and capable of manipulating and distorting mental content to deceive the conscious system. At the same time, the only evidence for such a censor is the apparent censoring itself, and so any such agency appears to be an instance of reification and circular explanation whereby the supposed self-deceiving activity is reified into an agency performing that very same activity (Boag, 2012, 2017).

Intentions, the Censor, and Teleology

The role of the censor above draws attention to another problem relevant to explaining self-deception and repression. As outlined above, the censor appears to act intentionally, discriminating what may or may not pass into conscious awareness, *in order to* prevent the ego from coming to know the repressed. Lockie (2003), for instance, writes that the censor acts "to prevent the one part of the mind from fully realizing the desires of the other part of the mind. It *defends* the conscience from confronting these desires" (p. 130). Such accounts entail an apparent teleology whereby, broadly speaking, a *telos* ('end' or 'purpose') acts as a final cause constituting an explanation or partial explanation. Rather than repression being instigated by causal antecedents such as conflict and distress, the censor acts (or repressive processes occur) in order to prevent distress from occurring in the first place by keeping the conscious system ignorant.

Teleological approaches to repression are not limited to accounts proposing censors and notable examples of apparent teleology are found within the literature relating repression to 'evolutionary functions' (e.g., Slavin, 1985, 1990; Nesse, 1990, 2019). Here repression occurs to serve a purpose, rather than due to antecedent conditions such as anxiety: "[Repression occurs] because it allows people to deceive themselves about their true motives, and thus better deceive others as they unconsciously pursue these covert selfish motives" (Nesse, 1990, p. 273; cf. Slavin, 1990, p. 321). Thus, Nesse (2019) suggests that repression serves multiple purposes, including avoiding distress in the first place and fulfilling various desires and evolutionary goals:

> I suspect that keeping some desires out of consciousness is a major function of repression. We can only get a fraction of what we want. Gaps between what we have and what we want generate envy, anxiety, anger, and dissatisfaction. Keeping unsatisfiable desires out of consciousness not only avoids mental suffering, it also allows us to focus on projects that are possible, instead of ruminating about those that are not. More important, it allows us not only to appear to be, but also to be more moral than would be otherwise possible. Thanks to social selection, being good increases fitness. Repression makes it easier to appear good and to be good.
>
> *(Nesse, 2019, p. 194)*

Although whether or not such evolutionary accounts of repression explicitly subscribe to teleology remains to be seen, teleology is nevertheless at times unambiguously embraced as seen in Zepf's (2001) teleological reading of Freud: "Freud considers the engine of mental life to be not an efficient but a final cause" (p. 469). For Zepf, then, repression is not instigated by anxiety and distress, but instead occurs in order to avoid unpleasure, and so "the basis of the repression is seen to be not causal but a matter of intentionality" (p. 468). Consequently, if there are logical problems with teleological explanations, then such accounts cannot coherently explain how repression occurs.

The Problem With Teleological Accounts

There are many problems associated with teleology, including issues of vitalism, self-determinism, goal-directedness, and anthropomorphism (see Mayr, 1974). For instance, at face value, teleological explanations rest upon the premise that an end-state (an effect) is somehow causally efficacious (*S* does *A in order to bring about B*, where *B* is some future state of affairs). Obviously, it cannot literally be the case that future events – events that have not as yet occurred and may never occur – can act as the causes of events occurring presently (Mackay, 1996). In this respect, Mackay (1996) notes, "[t]eleological explanations breach the conditions for explanations; they treat the causes of current actions as goals, states which have not yet come about and indeed may never come about" (p. 10).

At the same time, humans do appear to act in a goal-directed manner, and so any explanation of human activity needs to satisfactorily address this. On the position here, any such explanation must be consistent with a deterministic account entailing mechanism and causal antecedents (i.e., efficient causality). The topic of causal explanation itself is of course complex (see Mackie, 1974), and the position advanced here proposes that rather than simply a cause-effect chain, causality is best understood as a dynamic network involving causes and effects occurring within a *causal field* ("a background against which the causing goes on" – Mackie, 1974, p. 63). On this view, all events arise out of causal antecedents and go on to cause other events, and in this respect, causality is a necessary condition for anything to exist. However, such an approach does not deny a role for human consciousness (e.g., forethought, planning) since such mental activities can operate as causal antecedents underlying apparent goal-directed activity (Maze, 1983; Michell, 1988). As such, the apparent teleology associated with 'reasons' can be accommodated within a natural science framework embracing efficient causality.

One perspective that addresses apparent goal-directedness in a manner consistent with efficient causality is a teleonomic approach (from Pittendrigh, 1958 in Thompson, 1987; Mayr, 1974). Teleonomic explanations are strictly causal and mechanistic: apparent goal-directed behaviour is initiated by mechanisms (or what Mayr [1974] broadly calls 'programs') such that any 'teleonomic' system, "living or mechanical, . . . is so constructed that, when activated in its environment of adaptedness, it achieves a predictable outcome" (Bowlby, 1969, p. 139). Taking into account feedback processes, one can attribute apparent goal-directedness to both living systems and machines (such as a guided missile), and thus making apparent goal-directedness consistent with a deterministic psychology (Bowlby, 1969). As argued elsewhere, Freud's general metapsychology explains apparent goal-directed human activity in such a teleonomic manner (Boag, 2017).

Mechanistic explanations themselves provide intelligibility for understanding how certain antecedent conditions give rise to certain effects (Maze, 1983).[7] One problem with teleological accounts of repression and self-deception, however, is that they are devoid of any coherent mechanism because they either propose effects as causes or require an unworkable account involving an intention to repress. Consider, for instance, Zepf's (2001) claim that "the basis of the repression is seen to be not causal but a matter of intentionality" (p. 468). If repression occurs in order to avoid unpleasure rather than being triggered by distress, as Zepf believes, then the person must somehow be able to predict that some occurrence *x* is likely to result in unpleasure, to thereby instigate repression. However, being able to predict that some occurrence *x* will incur unpleasure appears to be antithetical to the outcome of repression. That is, if we need to know *p* in order to intentionally repress *p*, then we have again the problem of knowing in order not to know, or we require some type of censoring agency to act on behalf of the ego. As such, the problem with teleological accounts of repression and self-deception is that, if anything, the *telos* is an effect to be explained and provides no coherent mechanism for how repression could occur: repression occurs either intentionally and so is either self-defeating or requires a problematic censor.

Betrayal Trauma and Teleological Accounts of Betrayal Blindness

Problems with explaining repression and self-deception teleologically are apparent in the explanation of betrayal blindness found in betrayal trauma theory (BTT). BTT proposes a form of self-deception occurring in the context of trauma (Birrel & Freyd, 2006; Freyd, et al., 2007; Freyd, 1994, 1996). Two factors conspire in facilitating this self-deception: young children are particularly vulnerable and dependent upon their caregivers for meeting both physical and emotional needs, while, at the same time, humans have evolved sensitivity to detecting instances of interpersonal betrayal via a 'cheater detector' mechanism (based on Cosmides, 1989). One such instance of betrayal involves a caregiver's physical, emotional, or sexual abuse. Ordinarily, detecting betrayal results in psychic pain, which in turn prompts avoidance of the perpetrator of betrayal. However, given that children are dependent upon their caregivers, detecting betrayal would be counterproductive to the child's survival. This conflict is resolved via 'knowledge isolation' or (betrayal blindness) whereby knowledge of the betrayal trauma is shut down, which prevents the psychic pain from occurring that would otherwise instigate the avoidance behaviour:

> If a child processed the betrayal in the normal way, he or she would be motivated to stop interacting with the betrayer. Instead, he or she essentially needs to ignore the betrayal. If the betrayer is a primary caregiver, it is especially essential that the child does not stop behaving in such a way that will inspire attachment. For the child to withdraw from a caregiver on which he or she is dependent would further threaten the child's life, both physically and mentally. Thus the trauma of child abuse by its very nature requires that information about the abuse be blocked from mental mechanisms that control attachment and attachment behaviour.
>
> *(Freyd, 1994, p. 312)*

As with self-deception, knowledge isolation involves keeping knowledge of betrayal "hidden from awareness" (DePrince, et al., 2012, p. 195) and so is comparable to repression or dissociation (Freyd, 1996, 1999; Freyd, et al., 2007).[8]

The Function of Betrayal Blindness

The link with childhood vulnerability and attachment means betrayal blindness serves a function: "Betrayal blindness may be the only mechanism by which children may seek out and accept emotional closeness from the same individual that is abusing them" (Freyd, et al., 2007, p. 298).[9] However, in contradistinction to accounts that explain repression in terms of distress, BTT explains betrayal blindness instead in terms of the 'social utility' of blocking out information that may interfere with attachment processes. As Freyd (1994) writes, "[b]etrayal trauma differs from the prevailing conception of traumatic adaptation in its emphasis on the social utility of forgetting abuse by caregivers, as opposed to the more standard emphases on trauma as overwhelming or unbearably painful" (p. 321).[10] As such, betrayal blindness is explained with respect to the purported effect: "children separate abuse experiences from memory and consciousness to maintain the attachment relationships with caregivers that they need to survive" (Goldsmith, et al., 2004, p. 454). So, rather than distressing affects acting as efficient causes that then instigate betrayal blindness, the motivation for betrayal blindness is viewed in terms of avoiding social conflict. The upshot then is that betrayal blindness is stated teleologically: "The theory argues that victims, perpetrators, and witnesses may display betrayal blindness in order to preserve relationships, institutions, and social systems upon which they depend" (Freyd, et al., 2007, p. 297). Consequently, explaining how betrayal blindness occurs requires an account of how someone can both detect betrayal and yet be able to intentionally keep this knowledge from awareness.

The Why and the How of Betrayal Blindness

BTT attempts to address the question of *why* traumatising events involving betrayal are more likely to be forgotten compared to non-betrayal traumatising events. As Freyd, et al. (2007) write, "Betrayal trauma theory . . . is, at its core, an attempt to account for why victims of abuse may appear to remain largely unaware of their abuse" (p. 297). However, addressing 'why' such abuse may be forgotten is not the same as stipulating *how* such forgetting could actually occur, especially in the face of chronic mistreatment. To address this, BTT embraces here the work by Anderson and colleagues to explain knowledge isolation in terms of active inhibition

(Anderson, 2001; Anderson & Green, 2001). Active inhibition involves suppression of a target and (at least initial) rehearsal of an alternative representation. Laboratory research indicates that suppressing memories under these circumstances makes the target memory less accessible to later recall. Applied to betrayal trauma, the abused child learns "to retrieve alternative diversionary thoughts in response to a reminder", which leads to subsequent betrayal blindness (Anderson & Huddleston, 2012, p. 67). Freyd et al. summarise:

> Active inhibition induces forgetting when a representation (Representation A) is associated with two or more other representations (B and C) and links to one of those representations (B) is rehearsed more frequently than the other (C). Under those conditions, Anderson and others have observed reduced recall for C. That is, the act of rehearsing A–B seems to actively inhibit C. Anderson (2001) has proposed that a parallel learning context exists for children in the untenable position of rehearsing very different associations regarding caretakers – e.g., parent–abuse (A–C) and parent–care (A–B). To the extent that many socio-cultural forces encourage practising the association parent–care and/or the child victim is motivated to rehearse the parent–care association, active inhibitory processes may decrease recall for parent–abuse information. Active inhibition provides a parsimonious explanation for how children exposed to repeated abuse could forget the event.
>
> *(Freyd, et al., 2007, p. 306)*

Consequently, when the child is being reminded of the betrayal (e.g., the parent-abuse association), the child rehearses (or reinterprets) a non-abuse parent association, which leads to memory of the abuse no longer being available for recall. This allows the abused child to suppress knowledge of the abuse despite constant reminders of it: "victims of abuse who are faced with inescapable reminders to an unwanted memory are forced into a situation of retraining their memory's response to the reminder, by selectively retrieving alternative thoughts and memories about the abuser" (Anderson & Huddleston, 2012, p. 67). The suppression is further reinforced given that there are also typically greater opportunities to retrieve non-traumatic knowledge over the life span compared to traumatic ones.

In due course, however, the retrieval suppression can occur independently of thought-substitution. Anderson and Green (2001) write:

> Our results imply that a process exists that impairs the retention of memories when they are deliberately kept out of consciousness. When people encounter a stimulus that is known to cue an unwanted memory, this process can be recruited to prevent awareness of the memory. The regulation of consciousness is accomplished by an inhibitory control mechanism that suppresses the unwanted memory itself . . . and not merely by the momentary filling of working memory with diversionary thoughts.
>
> *(p. 368)*

These authors liken this to a defensive or suppression mechanism postulated by Freud, leading to memories becoming relatively inaccessible: "if retrieving diversionary thoughts becomes habitual, inhibition may be sustained without any intention of avoiding the unwanted memory" (Anderson & Green, 2001, p. 368). Of course, however, if 'habit' simply means acting routinely and without apparent effort, then we require some kind of mechanism for knowing how this precisely occurs.

Can Selective Inhibitory Mechanisms Explain Betrayal Blindness?

Active inhibition and retrieval suppression seem, at first glance, particularly well-suited to explaining how long-term abuse and concomitant reminders are forgotten. The longer the abuse occurs, the increased likelihood then that it will be forgotten through repeated suppression: "Retrieval suppression seems more likely to contribute in cases where a person is forced to confront unwelcome reminders over a long time, and is motivated to control awareness" (Anderson & Huddleston, 2012, p. 110). Moreover, postulating a basic motivation to forget unpleasurable events is also not implausible (Anderson & Huddleston, 2012; Erdelyi, 2006). One question here, however, concerns what is meant by 'motivation'. Both BTT and Anderson and colleagues ascribe motivation to the teleological function that it serves, whereby the motive appears to be to avoid awareness of the abuse in order not to threaten the attachment relationship. For example, Anderson (2001) writes that "[i]n the case of betrayal trauma, traumatic memories intrude and must be suppressed to sustain behaviors and thoughts consistent with the goal of maintaining the current attachment relationships with the caregiver" (p. 204). In other words, the motivation behind betrayal blindness is stated in teleological and goal-directed terms.

By implication, then, these teleological motives appear to require the child anticipating the outcomes of detecting the betrayal and being able to segregate abuse from non-abuse information. Anderson and Huddleston (2012), say as much when they refer to the "motivated selective retrieval of non-abuse information" (p. 56), while Anderson (2001) writes that "[t]he ability to separate out abuse from non-abuse knowledge may thus allow the preservation of a necessary image or model of the parent" (p. 204). Thus, some explanation then is required for how a child *selectively* discriminates abuse from non-abuse despite constant reminders of it. As Anderson and Huddleston (2012) write: "victims of abuse who are faced with inescapable reminders to an unwanted memory are forced into a situation of retraining their memory's response to the reminder, by selectively retrieving alternative thoughts and memories about the abuser" (p. 67). In other words, explaining how betrayal blindness operates appears to necessitate some type of cognitive screening involved in selective retrieval of non-traumatic information. Consequently, betrayal blindness requires both anticipating the consequences of acknowledging betrayal and segregating knowledge in order to avoid acknowledging the betrayal.

As presented above, the child would need to detect the betrayal but also anticipate that recognising the betrayal would instigate withdrawing from the betraying caregiver and constitute a threat to survival. The child then also needs to be able to selectively retrieve non-traumatic knowledge while inhibiting knowledge of the trauma. If this is the case, then BTT's explanatory strategy entails either the problem of knowing in order not to know or deferring to a problematic censor that selectively retrieves non-traumatic knowledge in order to prevent traumatic memories from impeding attachment behaviours.

Is It Possible to Re-interpret Betrayal Blindness Non-teleologically?

The empirical findings associated with BTT indicate that the theory is contributing something valuable, and so one question then is whether the theory can be divested of teleology and made consistent with a natural science account entailing efficient causes. As will be demonstrated, it is possible to explain betrayal blindness in a mechanistic fashion, although there are some considerations to first address. To begin with, betrayal blindness and active inhibition must operate at the psychological level given that detecting betrayal requires a *judgement*, which cannot preclude both awareness and evaluation of target material (although this need not be conscious itself). In fact, 'betrayal', itself, is a complex social relationship between the betraying person (or institution, etc.) and the person (or group, etc.) betrayed. To say that *X* feels betrayed by *Y*, then, is to suggest that *X* expects *A* from *Y*, and yet *Y* does *B* (something harmful that opposes *A*). Moreover, to judge that one is being betrayed presumably involves a judgement that the betraying person's actions are intentional rather than accidental: *X* must judge that *Y* performs this opposing act deliberately, even if that may have not been actually so. As such, this judgement cannot be outsourced to some type of neural mechanism or cheater detection mechanism, even if, of course, neural mechanisms necessarily underlie betrayal blindness. Furthermore, any account must address how betrayal can be both somehow psychologically apprehended and yet not available for recall without either being self-defeating or requiring recourse to a censor. Last, according to BTT, knowledge of the abuse may remain isolated but is nevertheless potentially recoverable, especially once the situation of dependency ends. In such circumstances, strong feelings such as anger and rage might occur once the betrayal is acknowledged (Freyd, et al., 2007, p. 305). Any account of betrayal blindness thus must explain how knowledge is prevented while the threat based on dependency remains, but then be made available once the threat based on dependency recedes.

To begin with, if betrayal blindness occurs, it is not in order to do anything, but is instead presumably instigated by relevant causal antecedents. An obvious candidate here for triggering betrayal blindness would be affective states such as overwhelming distress. However, as discussed earlier, BTT appears to rule out betrayal blindness being instigated by distressing affects (Freyd, 1994). Nevertheless, distressing affects are at times implicated within the discussion. For example, Freyd, et al. (2007) describes a hypothetical example of a nephew sexually abused by a favourite uncle: the negative memories of the abuse compete with other positive memories, such as being taken to a ball game. In such circumstances, "[r]ecollection for the second event [the ballgame] is much more likely to be reinforced, whereas the abuse is likely to be accompanied by factors that inhibit recall, such as threats, denial, or pressure not to disclose" (pp. 454–455). As this quote indicates, the actual situation is far more complex that simply non-affective, intrapersonal active inhibition. For instance, 'threats' presumably exert their force via fear, and so this is not then motivation in the sense of serving a social function but rather fear of consequences of acknowledging the abuse. Thus, affective states such as fear are likely to be relevant to explaining betrayal blindness.

An Alternative Account of Self-Deception Betrayal Trauma

The aim of the present section is to propose a non-teleological account for explaining the self-deception and knowledge isolation in BTT in terms of distressing affects and defense. The aim here is simply to show, however, that it is logically possible to account for betrayal blindness in terms of efficient causes, rather than proving any specific theory correct. As noted earlier, one of the challenges with explaining betrayal blindness is addressing how the betrayal is not recognised in cases of chronic abuse. More specifically, we need to account for the more difficult cases whereby a cognitively intact person believes not-*p* despite all evidence to the contrary (Lockie, 2003). As Baghramian and Nicholson (2013) write, "[a] key feature of a self-deceptive belief is that is held 'in the teeth' of available evidence, where it does not seem plausible to blame the agent for intellectual sloppiness or other significant cognitive failures" (p. 1019). How does a person repeatedly confronted with betrayal then avoid recognising this as betrayal when all the evidence supports such a conclusion?

The approach here involves understanding betrayal blindness in terms of affective motivational states: distress and fear of anticipated consequences causes the child to anxiously deny the betrayal. The motivation here, though, is not in terms of an intention to produce self-deception: instead betrayal blindness, like repression, is comparable to a "flight reflex in the presence of painful stimuli" (Freud, 1901, p. 147). However, to avoid the difficulties associated with 'knowing in order not to know' and the problematic censor requires clarifying a theory of mind, and the position adopted here can be described as a relational-realist view of psychological processes (Boag, 2015, 2017). Brentano's Intentionality is a particularly useful starting point for discussing psychological processes since it is accepted by many as the defining criterion of mentality (e.g., Searle, 2004; Solms, 2013). Brentano (1874), believes that mental acts can be distinguished from physical processes by virtue of their Intentionality or their having a "direction toward an object" (p. 88), sometimes referred to as the *ofness* or *aboutness* of mental acts. One realist implication here is that cognition, then, is a particular *relation* between a cognising subject and an independent object term (Maze, 1983; Michell, 1988). Cognition here broadly refers to acts of *knowing*, such as believing, thinking, remembering, wishing, and desiring, whether they be veridical or non-veridical: "psychological processes are . . . typified by a kind of relation not to be found in merely physical interactions, and that is the relation of *knowing about* or *referring to*" (Maze, 1983, p. 83; cf. Maze & Henry, 1996, p. 1089). As a relation, any instance of knowing (where *S* knows *p*), involves (1) a *subject S* that knows something and (2) the something known (*p*). *S*'s knowing *p* is entailed by neither (1) nor (2) alone, and any account of cognition thus requires stipulating the subject term (the knower) and object term (the known) involved in the cognitive relation.

Although intentionality is helpful for understanding mentality, an apparent stumbling block arises with conceptualising 'unconscious mentality'.[11] Intentionality, by definition, appears to necessitate 'consciousness' (or awareness) of some state of affairs. Consequently, an unconscious mental process is sometimes taken to be a contradiction in terms since it entails a conscious process somehow existing without consciousness (Searle, 2004; Talvitie, 2009). The problem is only apparent, however, since there is an important but barely recognised distinction between 'knowing *x*' and 'knowing that you know *x*'. Having a belief, for instance, is a different state of affairs to knowing that you have a belief. On the relational-realist view, any mental act of knowing is not itself automatically known and requires a second mental act of reflection upon the first. A person *S* might believe *x* without knowing that *x* is believed (call this knowing relation *SRp*) and for *S* to come to know that *x* is believed (i.e., to become conscious of the belief) requires a *second mental act* such that *s/he knows that s/he knows SRp* (Maze, 1983; Michell, 1988; see also Boag, 2012, 2015, 2017). On the relational-realist view, then, an *unconscious mental act* is one whereby a person knows some state of affairs without at the same time knowing that that same state of affairs is known. Subsequently, we can make sense of what Freud means when he writes that "there are mental things in a man which he knows without knowing that he knows" (Freud, 1916–17, p. 101).[12] A person, for instance, could fear abandonment without knowing that abandonment is feared.

This distinction between 'knowing' and 'knowing that one knows' is not new and is found in various guises including Freud's descriptively preconscious and conscious process distinction, or the metapsychological cathexis and hyper-cathexis distinction (see Boag, 2017). More recently, the distinction is evident in the relationship between cognition and metacognition ('thinking about thinking'), 'primary' consciousness and a 'secondary reflective' consciousness (Brakel, 2013), and 'simple awareness' and 'reflexive awareness' (Solms & Turnbull, 2002). The point being made here is not to introduce new terminology, but rather simply to note the generally accepted distinction between a mental act of knowing something, and the logically independent mental act of knowing that knowing.

Accepting this distinction, Freud's 'descriptive unconscious' can be conceptualised in terms of presently unreflected upon mental acts, and whether these unconscious mental acts can be reflected upon or not distinguishes the dynamic unconscious from preconscious mental activity (Boag, 2012, 2017).[13] Adopting the realist-relational view of mentality thus allows conceptualising the dynamic unconscious not in terms of banishing the defended-against target into "the unconscious" (see Boag, 2015), but instead preventing secondary mental acts of reflection. Eagle (2000) proposes precisely this when he writes that "[t]he essence of repression lies in its interference with one's ability to reflect on one's mental state" (p. 173). A person may, for instance, hold certain desires or beliefs but be incapable of reflecting upon these due to intensely distressing affects (Boag, 2012). More specifically, then, repression could be explicable via unconsciously knowing the distressing event, but *without knowing (or acknowledging) that the distressing event is known* (Boag, 2012, 2015). Such interference may prevent reflection upon the whole target of repression, or upon various components, whereby the type of target may be miscategorised, or the object of the mental act may be misclassified, and so on (see Krickel, 2018; see also Suppes & Warren (1975) on varieties of defensive transformations).

The distinction between 'knowing' and 'knowing that one knows' is apparent in the example of Frank Fitzpatrick's recovered memories of childhood sexual abuse (cited by Freyd, 1999). Fitzpatrick had earlier forgotten and then later recalled abuse at the hands of Reverend James R. Porter. Freyd, citing a *New York Times* report (July 1992), writes:

> Mr. Fitzpatrick's retrieval of the repressed memories began, he said, when "I was feeling a great mental pain . . ." Mr. Fitzpatrick . . . slowly realized that the mental pain was due to a "betrayal of some kind," and remembered the sound of heavy breathing. "Then I realized I had been sexually abused by someone I loved," said Mr. Fitzpatrick.
>
> *(in Freyd, 1999, p. 5)*

On this account, we see that (1) Mr. Fitzpatrick first experienced a "great mental pain", without knowing the event that was the source of the pain; (2) before then connecting the mental pain with betrayal, before finally realising that (3) the "great mental pain" arose in response to being abused by someone he loved. If this account is temporally accurate, we have then a situation where at least on one occasion, Mr. Fitzpatrick appears to have known that he had been abused, which apparently instigated the mental pain, without knowing that he knew it. Put differently, Mr. Fitzpatrick unknowingly knew that he had been abused, before the betrayal blindness was finally lifted.

Such unconscious knowing may sound paradoxical, although ample evidence can be found in studies of subliminal perception and cases of both blindsight and anosognosia (Boag, 2020). In the context of defense, Freud refers to this apparent paradox as the 'blindness of the seeing eye'. As discussed elsewhere, this concept first appears in the *Studies on Hysteria* (Breuer & Freud, 1895), where Freud describes the wilful blindness displayed by Miss Lucy R. involving the apparent paradox of both knowing and not knowing some state of affairs simultaneously:

> I have never managed to give a better description than this of the strange state of mind in which one knows and does not know a thing at the same time. It is clearly impossible to understand it unless one has been in such a state oneself.
>
> *(Freud in Breuer & Freud, 1895, p. 117n)*

Freud views this self-deception as a defensive act:

> I myself have had a very remarkable experience of this sort, which is still clearly before me. If I try to recollect what went on in my mind at that time I can get

> hold of very little. What happened was that I saw something which did not fit in at all with my expectation; yet I did not allow what I saw to disturb my fixed plan in the least, though the perception should have put a stop to it, I was unconscious of any contradiction in this; nor was I aware of my feelings of repulsion, which must nevertheless undoubtedly have been responsible for the perception producing no psychical effect. I was afflicted by that blindness of the seeing eye which is so astonishing in the attitude of mothers to their daughters, husbands to their wives and rulers to their favourites.
>
> *(Freud in Breuer & Freud, 1895, p. 117n)*

Applying such unconscious knowing to betrayal blindness provides a means of conceptualising how someone could simultaneously know and not know betrayal: the betrayal is known but cannot be reflected upon and so cannot be acknowledged. The distress of abuse instigates an anxious denial which prevents the child from acknowledging the act as betrayal. The child thereafter thus knows the betrayal without knowing that the betrayal is known. As such, a child enduring chronic abuse could then repeatedly know that she or he is being abused but be incapable of reflecting upon or acknowledging that fact. Thus, it is logically possible to maintain relative ignorance in the face of evidence that would otherwise reveal itself as betrayal. As dependency recedes, the threat evaluation and consequent anxiety could then be tempered by modifying re-evaluations of the situation allowing the betrayal to be acknowledged. Such a state of affairs is presumably underpinned by specific neural activity (Boag, 2012), and further associated with various sensorimotor consequences including not acting upon recognition of the betrayal (see Bazan, 2012 for extensive theoretical discussion on this point). This position addresses the problem of knowing in order not to know because it is possible for one and the same person to know the betrayal but be prevented from reflecting upon this.

Conclusion

As this chapter demonstrates, it is possible to account for repression and more difficult cases of self-deception, such as betrayal blindness, in terms of efficient causes such as distress and a realist-relational view of mind. For betrayal blindness to occur in the face of chronic abuse, the betrayal can be known without a censoring agency there to protect the conscious system from the knowledge of the abuse. Instead, both repression and betrayal blindness could be motivated by a person anxiously denying that the offending target is known, which, mediated by neural inhibition, prevents both acknowledging the target and from acting upon it. As such, accounts of repression and self-deception can be consistent within a natural science framework and comprehensible in terms of natural defensive responses to painful stimuli, which situates these processes firmly within an evolutionary context. A child does not deny betrayal trauma for survival *per se*, although that may (or may not) be a consequence. Instead, humans have been shaped by evolutionary selective forces in such a way so that extreme distress prevents acknowledging certain situations, one consequence of which may have included survival. While the account above is speculative, avoiding teleological explanations and embracing efficient causality and mechanisms provides a logically coherent platform for understanding repression and self-deception. Acknowledging this has radical implications for psychological theory and addressing the complexities of the human mind.

Notes

1 "[Phantasies] are substitutes for and derivatives of repressed memories which a resistance will not allow to enter consciousness unaltered, but which can purchase the possibility of becoming conscious by taking account, by means of changes and distortions, of the resistance's censorship. When this compromise has been accomplished, the memories have turned into phantasies, which can easily be misunderstood by the conscious personality – that is, understood so as to fit in with the dominant psychical current" (Freud, 1907a, p. 58).

2 "We have reason to assume that there is a *primal repression*, a first phase of repression, which consists in the psychical (ideational) representative of the instinct being denied entrance into the conscious" (Freud, 1915d, p. 148). As argued elsewhere, however, there are theoretical difficulties with explaining such repression if the target is never in fact known (see Boag, 2012; Maze & Henry, 1996).

3 "The second stage of repression, *repression proper*, affects mental derivatives of the repressed representative, or such trains of thought as, originating elsewhere, have come into associative connection with it. On account of this association, these ideas experience the same fate as what was primally repressed. Repression proper, therefore, is actually an after-pressure" (Freud, 1915a, p. 148).

4 Heil (1989) writes: "If anything is obvious . . . it is that rationality is hardly universal: *all* of us fail to be rational some of the time, and *some* of us fail more often than is good for us" (p. 574).

5 Davidson acknowledges that this is a "highly abstract account . . . [and] never intended as a psychologically revealing explanation of the nature or aetiology of self-deception" (Davidson, 1998, pp. 8–9), and the model's "modest purpose was to remove, or at least mitigate, the features that at first make self-deception seem inconceivable" (Davidson, 1998, p. 9), namely how contradictory beliefs persist in one and the same subject so that one causes (without rationalising) the other.

6 Sartre's own analysis is problematic, however, because he believes that knowing involves 'knowing that knowing', and so the censoring agency must, he reasons, be cognisant of its own activity, and therefore be in 'bad faith' itself. However, his Cartesian perspective creates an *a priori* theoretical conflict *vis-à-vis* the psychoanalytic assertion of the existence of unconscious mental processes, and as many have pointed out (Lockie, 2003; Neu, 1988), the fact that the censoring agency may know its own activities does not succeed in undermining Freud's account since it is the conscious system that is being protected and not the censor.

7 A mechanism can be distributed across various contexts and settings, however, and need not be confined within any particular entity. The mechanism of 'natural selection,' for example, explains the continuity and discontinuity of species in terms of the interaction between properties and activities of biological organisms and environmental conditions across generations.

8 DePrince, et al. (2012) write that there are at least two forms of knowledge isolation: 'forgetting' or 'unawareness', which "describes situations in which abuse-related information is inaccessible to conscious recall" (p. 195). With such forgetting there is no recall of the event and essentially an absence of information. On the other hand, a person might also 'misremember' the abuse by reconstructing events as more positive or less negative than they actually were.

9 Betrayal trauma is not restricted to childhood abuse, however, and can be found occurring in adults in situations of dependence (Freyd, 1999).

10 Similarly, Freyd (1994) writes that "[t]he trauma of child abuse thus requires that information about the abuse be blocked from mental mechanisms that control attachment and attachment behavior. One does not need to posit any particular avoidance of psychic pain per se here; instead, what is of functional significance is the control of social behaviour" (p. 318).

11 It is also true that Brentano (1874) denied the existence of unconscious mental acts based on the assertion that mental acts were necessarily conscious. Brentano's position can be shown to be problematic (see Boag, 2015 for further discussion).

12 In all fairness to the various interpretations of what Freud means by the term 'unconscious', the viewpoint presented here is but one of many, and one can typically find support for one or another view based on Freud's inconsistent writing on the topic.

13 The discussion above requires a further word of clarification, however. None of this should be taken to mean that knowing is an all-or-nothing phenomena, since one can talk of levels or degrees of knowing (see Erdelyi, 2006). There are also, of course, nuances with respect to what is precisely the object of reflection (including sensory and emotional dimensions, for instance), as well as factors such as critical and uncritical assessment and so on (see Axelrod, 2012).

There is also a critical distinction between directly and indirectly knowing one's own mental acts. As Freud recognises, "[t]o have heard something and to have experienced something are in their psychological nature two quite different things, even though the content of both is the same" (Freud, 1915b, p. 176). That is, a person may be aware of holding a particular belief, say, via an analyst's interpretation, without being directly aware of the actual belief, or even while actively believing the opposite (see Finkelstein, 1999; see also Boag, 2010). In the former case, the person can be said to know the belief indirectly via the analyst's interpretation, in contrast to directly reflecting upon the belief.

References

Anderson, M. C. (2001). Active forgetting: Evidence for functional inhibition as a source of memory failure. *Journal of Aggression, Maltreatment & Trauma, 4*, 185–210.

Anderson, M. C., & Green, C. (2001). Suppressing unwanted memories by executive control. *Nature, 410*(6826), 366–369.

Anderson, M. C., & Huddleston, E. (2012). Towards a cognitive and neurobiological model of motivated forgetting. In R. F. Belli (Ed.), *True and false recovered memories* (pp. 53–120). New York, NY: Springer.

Auld, F., Hyman, M., & Rudinski, D. (2005). *Resolution of inner conflict: An introduction to psychoanalytic therapy*. Washington, DC: American Psychological Association.

Axelrod, S. D. (2012). "Self-awareness": At the interface of executive development and psychoanalytic therapy. *Psychoanalytic Inquiry, 32*, 340–357.

Baghramian, M., & Nicholson, A. (2013). The puzzle of self-deception. *Philosophy Compass, 8*, 1018–1029.

Bazan, A. (2012). From sensorimotor inhibition to Freudian repression: Insights from psychosis applied to neurosis. *Frontiers in Psychology, 3*, 1–19.

Birrell, P. J., & Freyd, J. J. (2006). Betrayal trauma: Relational models of harm and healing. *Journal of Trauma Practice, 5*, 49–63.

Boag, S. (2005). Addressing mental plurality: Justification, objections and logical requirements of strongly partitive accounts of mind. *Theory & Psychology, 15*, 747–767.

Boag, S. (2010). Repression, suppression, and conscious awareness. *Psychoanalytic Psychology, 27*, 164–181.

Boag, S. (2012). *Freudian repression, the unconscious, and the dynamics of inhibition*. London: Karnac.

Boag, S. (2015). In defence of unconscious mentality. In S. Boag, L.A.W. Brakel, & V. Talvitie (Eds.), *Psychoanalysis and philosophy of mind* (pp. 239–265). London: Karnac.

Boag, S. (2017). *Metapsychology and the foundations of psychoanalysis: Attachment, neuropsychoanalysis, and integration*. London: Routledge.

Boag, S. (2020). Reflective awareness, repression, and the cognitive unconscious. *Psychoanalytic Psychology, 37*, 18–27.

Bowlby, J. (1969). *Attachment and loss: Vol. 1: Attachment*. London: Hogarth.

Brakel, L.A.W. (2013). *The ontology of psychology*. New York: Routledge.

Brentano, F. (1874/1973). *Psychology from an empirical standpoint* (Translated by A. C. Rancurello, D. B. Terrell, & L. L. McAlister). London: Routledge & Kegan Paul.

Breuer, J., & Freud, S. (1895). *Studies on hysteria (1893–1895). S. E., 2*. London: Hogarth.

Cosmides, L. (1989). The logic of social exchange: Has natural selection shaped how humans reason? Studies with the Wason selection task. *Cognition, 31*(3), 187–276.

Davidson, D. (1985). Deception and division. In E. Lepore & B. P. Mclaughlin (eds), *Action and events: Perspectives on the philosophy of Donald Davidson* (pp. 138–148). Oxford: Basil Blackwell.

Davidson, D. (1998). Who is fooled? In J.-P. Dupuy (Ed.), *Self-deception and paradoxes of rationality* (pp. 1–18). Stanford, CA: CSLI Publications.

DePrince, A. P., Brown, L. S., Cheit, R. E., Freyd, J. J., Gold, S. N., Pezdek, K., & Quina, K. (2012). Motivated forgetting and misremembering: Perspectives from betrayal trauma theory. In R. F. Belli (Ed.), *True and false recovered memories* (pp. 193–242). New York, NY: Springer.

Eagle, M. (2000). Repression: Part II. *Psychoanalytic Review, 87*, 161–187.

Erdelyi, M. H. (2006). The unified theory of repression. *Behavioral and Brain Sciences, 29*, 499–551.

Finkelstein, D. H. (1999). On the distinction between conscious and unconscious states of mind. *American Philosophical Quarterly, 36*, 79–100.

Freud, S. (1901). *The psychopathology of everyday life. S. E., 6*. London: Hogarth.

Freud, S. (1906). Psycho-analysis and the establishment of the facts in legal proceedings. *S. E.*, 9: 97–114. London: Hogarth.

Freud, S (1907). Delusions and dreams in Jensen's *Gradiva. S. E.*, 9: 1–96. London: Hogarth.

Freud, S. (1914). On the history of the psycho-analytic movement. *S. E., 14*: 1–66. London: Hogarth.

Freud, S. (1915a). Repression. *S. E., 14*: 141–158. London: Hogarth.
Freud, S. (1915b). The Unconscious. *S. E.* 41: 159–215. London: Hogarth.
Freud, S. (1916–1917). *Introductory lectures on psycho-analysis. S. E., 15–16.* London: Hogarth.
Freyd, J. J. (1994). Betrayal trauma: Traumatic amnesia as an adaptive response to childhood abuse. *Ethics & Behavior, 4*, 307–329.
Freyd, J. J. (1996). *Betrayal trauma: The logic of forgetting childhood abuse.* Cambridge: Harvard University Press.
Freyd, J. J. (1999). Blind to betrayal: new perspectives on memory for trauma. *The Harvard Mental Health Letter, 15*, 4–6.
Freyd, J. J., DePrince, A. P., & Gleaves, D. H. (2007). The state of betrayal trauma theory: Reply to McNally – Conceptual issues, and future directions. *Memory, 15*, 295–311.
Gardner, S. (1993). *Irrationality and the philosophy of psychoanalysis.* Cambridge: Cambridge University Press.
Goldsmith, R. E., Barlow, M. R., & Freyd, J. J. (2004). Knowing and not knowing about trauma: Implications for therapy. *Psychotherapy: Theory, Research, Practice, Training, 41*, 448–463.
Heil, J. (1989). Minds divided. *Mind, 98*, 571–583.
Hohol, M., & Urbańczyk, P. (2013). Self-deception: Between philosophy and cognitive neuroscience. In J. Stelmach, B. Brożek, & Ł. Kurek (Eds.), *Philosophy in neuroscience* (pp. 219–253). Kraków: Copernicus Center Press.
Kernberg, O. F. (1987). Projection and projective identification: Developmental and clinical aspects. *Journal of the American Psychoanalytic Association, 35*, 795–819.
Krickel, B. (2018). Are the states underlying implicit biases unconscious? – A Neo-Freudian answer. *Philosophical Psychology, 31*, 1007–1026.
Lockie, R. (2003). Depth psychology and self-deception. *Philosophical Psychology, 16*, 127–148.
Mackay, N. (1996). The place of motivation in psychoanalysis. *Modern Psychoanalysis, 21*, 3–17.
Mackie, J. L. (1974). *The cement of the universe: A study of causation.* Oxford: Oxford University Press.
Mayr, E. (1974). Teleological and teleonomic, a new analysis. In R. S. Cohen & M. W. Wartofsky (Eds.), *Methodological and historical essays in the natural and social sciences* (pp. 91–117). Dordrecht: Springer.
Maze, J. R. (1983). *The meaning of behaviour.* London: Allen & Unwin.
Maze, J. R., & Henry, R. M. (1996). Problems in the concept of repression and proposals for their resolution. *International Journal of Psycho-analysis, 77*, 1085–1100.
Mele, A. R. (1987). Recent work on self-deception. *American Philosophical Quarterly, 24*, 1–17.
Michell, J. (1988). Maze's direct realism and the character of cognition. *Australian Journal of Psychology, 40*, 227–249.
Nesse, R. M. (1990). The evolutionary functions of repression and the ego defenses. *Journal of the American Academy of Psychoanalysis, 18*, 260–285.
Nesse, R. M. (2019). *Good reasons for bad feelings: Insights from the frontier of evolutionary psychiatry.* New York: Dutton.
Neu, J. (1988). Divided minds: Sartre's "bad faith" critique of Freud. *Review of Metaphysics, 42*, 79–101.
Sartre, J-.P. (1956). *Being and nothingness* (Translated by H. E. Barnes). New York: Philosophical Library.
Searle, J. R. (2004). *Mind: A brief introduction.* Oxford: Oxford University Press.
Slavin, M. O. (1985). The origins of psychic conflict and the adaptive function of repression: An evolutionary biological view. *Psychoanalysis & Contemporary Thought, 8*, 407–440.
Slavin, M. O. (1990). The dual meaning of repression and the adaptive design of the human psyche. *Journal of the American Academy of Psychoanalysis, 18*, 307–341.
Solms, M. (2013). The conscious id. *Neuropsychoanalysis, 15*, 5–19.
Solms, M., & Turnbull, O. (2002). *The brain and the inner world: An introduction to the neuroscience of subjective experience.* New York: Other Press.
Suppes, P., & Warren, H. (1975). On the generation and classification of defence mechanisms. *International Journal of Psycho-analysis, 56*, 405–414.
Talvitie, V. (2009). *Freudian unconscious and cognitive neuroscience: From unconscious fantasies to neural algorithms.* London: Karnac.
Thompson, N. S. (1987). The misappropriation of teleonomy. In P. P. G. Bateson & P. H. Klopfer (Eds.), *Perspectives in ethology* (pp. 259–274). Boston, MA: Springer.
Van Leeuwen, N. (2013). Self-deception. In H. LaFollette (Ed.), *The international encyclopedia of ethics* (pp. 4753–4762). Oxford: Wiley-Blackwell.
Zepf, S. (2001). Incentives for a reconsideration of the debate on metapsychology. *International Journal of Psychoanalysis, 82*, 463–482.

25

A-RATIONALITY

The Views of Freud and Wittgenstein Explored

Linda A. W. Brakel

Introduction

Humans prefer to think of themselves (ourselves) as rational. We look for reasons and then find them; but we also create them, rationalizing, sometimes with little evidence. As we will see below in discussing Freud's primary and secondary processes, the primary processes are the more basic, earlier form of mentation. Yet, the primary processes remain ever-present throughout adult human life. However, partly because they are a mode of a-rational rather than rational thinking, adult humans often automatically re-formulate primary process content into secondary process. A brief example most will have experienced involves normal persons and their dream reports. Dreams as they are dreamt frequently have sequences that demonstrate primary process content to the extent that they are not organized causally, not possible in the real world, phantasy driven, and hard to describe. When dreamers awaken and recount dreams, these primary process portions are almost necessarily described in secondary process terms, namely, noting that ordinary coherence is not present in the dream. (See Brakel, 2009, chap. 4 for more on this and related phenomena.)

Scientists and academics of all stripes are people too. When discussing a-rational mentation, particularly its utility in human and non-human animal life, terms suggesting some form of rationality, while omitting a-rationality, are often invoked. So, we have "bounded rationality" (Simon, 1956a); "ecological rationality" (Gigerenzer & Todd, 1999; Todd & Gigerenzer, 2000); "rationality1 vs. rationality2" (Evans & Over, 1996); and "biological rationality or b-rationality," defined by Kacelnik (2006, p. 87) as that in which "animals . . . behave as if they had been designed to surpass the fitness of their conspecifics." Kacelnik (p. 87) explains that in this way b-rationality is distinct from economic and/or philosophic/psychologic rationality. These latter have requirements, such as transitivity among choice preferences including consistency across contexts, "violated" routinely by animals exhibiting "b-rationality." One excellent anthology – *Rational Animals, Irrational Humans* (Hurley & Nudds, 2006) – by its very title summarizes and reinforces the notion that if mentation leads to pragmatic or adaptive results; that is, if it works, it must be some form of *rational*, even if it is descriptively a-rational.

In this chapter, I will take a different tack – exploring a-rationality as itself a contentful (representational) form of mentation. A-rationality, instantiated in a set of a-rational cognitive processes, is used sometimes to operate adaptively, sometimes problematically. But either way,

DOI: 10.4324/9780429297076-30

I shall argue that a-rational mentation is properly considered a mode of mentation distinct both from rationality and irrationality. I make this case discussing the views of Freud, then comparing and contrasting these with Wittgenstein's understanding of a-rational/non-rational grounds for rationality – both of these influential thinkers important contributors to our body of knowledge.

Freud and A-Rationality

Description of Primary Versus Secondary Processes

In his landmark book *The Interpretation of Dreams*, Freud (1900), consolidated earlier work[1] and added to it, outlining two different formal modes of mentation he had observed. The earlier, more basic type – prevalent in children, in the dreams and daydreams of normal adults, and in persons with neurotic problems, and/or those under stressful, intense situations – he termed the primary processes. He proposed that primary process–type mentation was unconsciously underlying much of adult human behavior, but that the more familiar secondary processes were operative in the conscious, rational operations of alert and wakeful adults.

The primary processes function prior to considerations of what is True and what is False. Therefore, they are properly considered a-rational rather than irrational in that they *lack*, rather than *violate*, the principles of everyday logic.[2] Primary processes operate such that opposites are not mutually exclusive, contradictions are tolerated, and evidence-based reality testing is not employed. Further, contextual time, both past and future, are not registered as such. Thus, under the sway of the primary processes one exists in what I've termed the "unexamined present" (Brakel, 2015, p. 131). Moreover, the primary processes employ associative rather than causally based connections. This has implications for categorizations – primary process–based categories are associative in that they are predicated on contiguity in time and space, displacements and condensations of contents, and small, superficial, even part-for-whole attribute similarities. Secondary process categorizations, in contrast, aim for similarities among category members based on more central, essential, rational etiologic features.[3]

Moreover, the primary processes are faster: closer to drives, instincts, and affects than are the secondary processes; the primary processes are impulse-linked, sometimes almost automatic, and in this way resemble the mentation of non-human animals.[4] This is quite different from the secondary processes in which tasks are more deliberative and require more psychological/mental work. Furthermore, the secondary processes are ever reality-testing, evaluating evidence, and striving for solutions (mostly) independent of emotions, sometimes even overriding very strong affects.

Finally, and of great importance for Freud, the primary processes – given their associative proclivities toward displacement, contiguity, and condensation of contentful elements – are regularly employed by persons for the purpose of disguising their unacceptable impulses and unfulfillable wishes. It is in this way – as neurotic and psychotic symptoms result from combining original impulses plus their disguises – that primary process a-rationality is used toward irrational and pathological ends. But note, the disguise function also occurs regularly, not irrationally but merely a-rationally, in normal healthy individuals; this in dreams, daydreams, and slips of the tongue. Here is one recent example from a daydream of mine, involving condensation, displacement, part for whole categorization, and associative contiguity. Since I have both a dear friend who studies wolf behavior, and a new acquaintance named Wolfgang, it is not surprising that today after getting an e-mail from my friend, but expecting a reply from my acquaintance, I found myself daydreaming about a pack (gang) of wolves.

Note just above, I indicated that the use of primary processes in order to disguise was of great importance to Freud. But, also note that I provided neither references nor examples. This omission owes to a reason I will own up to now. In the next two subsections of this chapter, I will first take up work that I have done over the last three decades to extend Freud's primary processes as *normal* a-rationality toward cognate fields in philosophy, psychology, and even biology. Then, in the second (and final) subsection on Freud's views on a-rationality, I will address a central Freudian theme that I have heretofore given short shrift. There, without abandoning my attempt to expand Freud's views within the context of the broader academic world, I will also provide examples and a few representative references demonstrating that with regard to the primary processes, psychopathology, no less (perhaps more) than a general theory of the human mind, was on Freud's mind, even if not on mine!

Extending Freud's A-Rational (Not Irrational) Primary Processes to Cognate Fields

Hoping to restore and secure the status of psychoanalysis in the academic world, I have, in multiple ways, attempted to demonstrate the relevance of Freud's account of a-rational primary processes to cognate fields. In this quest I have made much of two central ideas – that the primary processes are prior to considerations of True and False; and that primary process mentation is characterized by its associative nature.

Let me briefly recount the sorts of extensions I have found significant. First, in order to support the claim that there are testable aspects of psychoanalytic theory, we[5] performed a series of empirical experiments (referenced below in this paragraph) in which the prevalence of primary process a-rational categorization was compared with that of secondary process rational categorization. We indexed primary categorizations with attributional matches – i.e., categorization by simple, small, superficial similarity matches – while more essential, relational elements indexed the secondary process categorizations.[6] Following the work of cognitive psychologists, Medin, Goldstone, and Gentner (1990), we found that the a-rational type categorizations predominated in exactly the domains predicted by Freud: (1) in the similarity assessments made by young children (Brakel, Shevrin, & Villa, 2002); (2) when the stimuli were outside of consciousness (Brakel, Kleinsorge, Snodgrass, & Shevrin, 2000; Brakel, 2004); (3) when categorizations were performed by participants under stress (Brakel & Shevrin, 2005), and (4) by similarity assessments made by patients with serious psychiatric symptoms (Bazan, Van Draege, DeKrock, Geeradyn, Shevrin, & Brakel, 2013). The very disparateness of the several domains predicted does, along with the findings, further the credibility of Freud's view.

With these positive findings in hand, the next challenge was to investigate more fully the "prior-ness" of primary process from an evolutionary perspective.[7] Yes, the primary processes predominate in small children, and in non-conscious assessments, but are the cognitive operations in various non-human animals best characterized as associative, a-rational, primary process–like? If so, this would help establish that such mentation is evolutionarily adaptive.[8] With bird researchers we did gain positive evidence for attributional type categorization in a study on pigeons (Garlick, Gant, Brakel, & Blaisdell, 2011). And indeed, the phenomenon of imprinting (Lorenz, 1935) is predicated on a single attribute. Next, looking to field research studies across a variety of species,[9] animal researchers consistently found much behavior that was both a-rational and adaptive. Most notable were frequent "violations" of rational rules – specifically transitivity with consistency across contexts.[10] (For references to 18 of these studies, see Cutler & Brakel, 2014, pp. 792–809.)

Supplementing the animal a-rationality evidence, dual process theorists – most famously Tversky and Kahneman – provided a large body of empirical work supporting the notion of two types of mentation for humans too. (See Kahneman, Slovic, & Tversky, 1982; Tversky, 2004; Kahneman, 2011.) First, System One: a-rational in its operations without much regard for logical, rational norms, this earlier mode is tied to impulses and emotions, delivering associative, automatic responses. Then, the later developing System Two: characterized as rational, deliberative, and obeying rules of logic, one of System Two's roles is to inhibit System One responses. These two modes of mentation map very well onto Freud's primary and secondary responses, respectively.[11]

With this plethora of non-human animal findings, I felt able to posit that even a biological process as fundamental and widespread as conditioning could operate on the basis of primary process-like associative connections. Specifically, that attributional feature similarity, or contiguity in space or time between the unconditioned stimulus (US) and the conditioned stimulus (CS), could drive conditioned responses. (For details, see Brakel, 2013, chap. 1.) To demonstrate, let me offer a famous example. Pavlov's dogs salivated when presented with food, the unconditioned stimuli (US). When after a number of trials in which food (US) was paired contiguously in time or space with a bell, the conditioned stimuli (CS), Pavlov found that in subsequent trials the dogs salivated even when the bell (the CS) was presented alone!

From here the placebo effect can be similarly understood, in a-rational primary process terms. Following ameliorative responses to active medications (US), placebos delivered contiguously, especially those resembling the active medication in substance or context, constitute the conditioned stimuli (CS). When later, these placebos (CS) are delivered alone, they produce the conditioned placebo response. Positive transferences to healing clinicians also engender placebo effects, and are themselves based on primary process a-rational similarity categorizations (Brakel, 2010, chap 5).

Continuing the extension of Freud's views to cognate academic fields – now to philosophy of biology, and philosophy of mind – I devised a proper function account of the a-rational primary processes. Focusing on several primary process qualities – associative connections, subjective experience in the unexamined present, and actions predicated prior to considerations of Truth or Falsity – I made a case for a-rational mentation being determinatively contentful, but on a basis very different from the usual rational normativity. Clearly, *rational* normativity would not work for the a-rational! Instead, then, the proper function argument I advanced held that a-rationality's very particular non-rationalness promoted evolutionary fitness normativity, which in turn fixed determinate a-rational content. (Further explication will follow later in this chapter, but for a fuller account, see Brakel, 2002, 2009, chap. 5.)

Extending Freud's Primary Processes to Cognate Fields – A-Rationality to Irrationality

Although Freud acknowledges the existence of primary processes in normal waking life – obvious in jokes, and slips of the tongue; and ever-present in unconscious mentation undergirding all thought, thus central for transference-influenced life choices (e.g., picking a mate, finding a career) – by far, for Freud the use of a-rational primary processes in order to disguise is most important. Here are just a few of Freud's many comments to this effect. He says (1900, p. 515) of primary process–laden dream elements: "The modifications to which dreams are submitted . . . are associatively linked to the material which they replace." Then, not only in dreams, but significantly in psychiatric symptoms for which dreams are a model, Freud (1905, p. 171) states:

> Among displacements are to be counted . . . in particular the replacement of an important but objectionable element by one that is indifferent and appears innocent . . . something that seems like a very remote allusion to the other one – substitution by a piece of symbolism, or an analogy, or something small.

And in yet another passage he asserts (1900, p. 597):

> In hysteria . . . normal thoughts have been . . . transformed into symptoms by means of condensation and . . . by way of superficial associations and in disregard of contradictions . . . [demonstrating] the complete identity between the characteristic features of the dream-work and those of the psychical activity which issues in psychoneurotic symptoms.

To illustrate the a-rational primary processes at work in their disguise-agent role, producing a symptom that is irrational and yet quite understandable, I will present (again)[12] the case of Mrs. M. She arrived at the University of Michigan Psychiatric Emergency Service at age 55, presenting with an acute psychotic episode. This was a recurrence after decades of normal functioning, which included raising several children to adulthood. Just prior to this newest psychotic break, Mrs. M who had been suffering with abdominal pain, received terrible news – a diagnosis of a uterine malignancy with a grave prognosis, notwithstanding the surgery required. This background is essential to understand the contentful meaning of her hallucination/delusion: Mrs. M was forcefully trying to insert a hard plastic "Head and Shoulders" brand shampoo bottle into her vagina and yelling: "The head and shoulders are killing me." Clearly, her thought processes were idiosyncratic and associative, conflating aspects of normal vaginal childbirth – the decades-old pain, as well as the delivery of the babies' heads and shoulders – with her current cancer pain and the impending surgery. The conflation disguised the problem, had an obvious wishful element, and demonstrated many primary process features – condensation, reversal (she was inserting, not delivering), displacement, part-for-whole representation (the Head and Shoulders bottle standing for her newborns' heads and shoulders), and her experience taking place in the unexamined present.

Mrs. M's case proves instructive in another way; instrumental in relating Freud's understanding of a-rational primary processes to epistemological issues. First, let's examine Mrs. M's recovery from her psychiatric symptoms. This occurred within an hour after absorbing a sufficient dose of an anti-psychotic medication. Rapidly the associative contents that she had delusionally categorized as belonging together – the Head and Shoulders bottle with the emergence of the heads and shoulders of her newborns; the tumor-caused pain with childbirth pain; insertion into the vagina with birth from the vagina; the 1970s with the 1950s – she no longer put together at all. Instead, like her physicians, Mrs. M's mentation became ordinary, rational, and secondary process. She felt embarrassed about the shampoo bottle and realized that her pain was from the large tumor, not a pregnancy. Further she knew she was a 55-year-old woman, past pregnancy days, and that a difficult, frightening road lay ahead. Mrs. M also knew that she wished the upcoming surgery would be just like the happy occasions of giving birth.

Next, influenced by Mrs. M's dramatic recovery, my speculative leap: under Freud's assumption that the a-rational primary processes are developmentally prior to the rational secondary processes, I wondered if for all rational thinkers, an initial a-rational primary process stage of *putting things together, associatively, automatically*, and *idiosyncratically* necessarily precedes rational secondary process thought. Put in question form: is a-rational, associative thinking ontologically necessary for, and prior to, our normal epistemological functioning? There is some support for this idea from Kant. In the *Critique of Pure Reason*, Kant (1781/1787) sought an *a priori* principle, organizing the combination of part-representations and sensory perceptions so as to constitute (most basically) discrete objective objects. While associational law would be a natural candidate, Kant (1781, A121, p. 144) rejected this notion, contending that associations allowed representation to be placed "in any order . . . [which] would not lead to any determinate connection of them, but only to accidental collocations." But now, Kant, having dismissed the laws of association needed another organizing principle. He searched for "a relation [of representations etc.] which is *objectively valid*, and so distinguished from a relation of the same representations that would have only subjective validity – as when they are connected by the laws of association" (1787, B142, p. 159). Now of course for Kant, objective validity is not thing-in-itself objective validity, unknowable by human cognizers, but is instead the more modest species-wide, ordinary, consensually agreed upon objective validity of our ordinary world of objects, persons, and so on. Thus, Kant (1787, B142, p. 159) sought something quite like Freud's regular, secondary-process rationality for his *a priori* principle – one capable of producing a determinate organization of representations in which "they are combined in the object, no matter what the state of the subject might be." Without going more deeply into Kantian thought, I will simply aver that this reading of B142 suggests that subjects cannot bind things together as they are combined in the object without having had a *contrastive* ground that was an earlier, associative, subjective putting together. Mrs. M's case then, as she recovered, could be viewed as a striking analog to the necessary ontological priority of a-rational primary processes to any normal, ordinary, secondary process thinking, and thereby to any rational epistemological capacity.[13]

The idea that a-rational holdings are fundamental and prior to any systematic rationality, while quite different from the Freudian account, is central to views presented by Ludwig Wittgenstein in his seminal late work, *On Certainty*. Let us turn to consider Wittgenstein on a-rationality forthwith.

Wittgenstein and A-Rationality

Description of Wittgenstein's Views on the A-Rational Foundation of Rationality

Wittgenstein (1950/1969) makes clear in *On Certainty* that there can be no doubt that doubt itself, in fact the very capacity to doubt, must follow from assumptions[14] that are held/grasped, automatically, prior to considerations of doubt, truth, falsity – assumptions that are a-rational rather than rational. In perhaps the most famous example he explains (#125, pp. 18–19):

> If a blind man were to ask me "Have you got two hands?" I should not make sure by looking. If I were to have any doubt of it, then I don't know why I should trust my eyes. For why shouldn't I test my *eyes* by looking to find out whether I see my two hands? *What* is to be tested by *what*?

He goes on (#163, p. 24): "For whenever we test anything, we are already presupposing something that is not tested." And then continues (#166, p. 24): "The difficulty is to realize that groundlessness of our believing." Wittgenstein then adds (#205, p. 28): "If the true is what is grounded, then the ground is not *true*, nor yet false."

How do we know that these very groundings of "believing" are a-rational, and like Freud's primary processes, prior to considerations of Truth or Falsity? And, how do we know they are nonetheless foundational? Wittgenstein again invokes his "two hands" example. First, he states (#245–#246, p. 33):

> I could say: "That I have two hands is an irreversible belief." That would express the fact that I am not ready to let anything count as a disproof of this proposition. "Here I have arrived at a foundation of all my beliefs." "This position I will *hold*!"

With this, Wittgenstein has demonstrated that these grounds for belief are, like the primary processes, evidence insensitive and not responsive to reason.

Next, he addresses the foundational nature of these holdings (#247, p. 33): "What would it be like to doubt now whether I have two hands?. . . What would I believe if I didn't believe that? So far I have no system at all within which this doubt might exist." Wittgenstein continues (#248, p. 33): "I have arrived at the rock bottom of my convictions." And he elaborates (#250): "My having two hands is . . . as certain as anything that I could produce in evidence for it." And then Wittgenstein generalizes (#252): "But it isn't just that *I* believe in this way . . . every reasonable person does." Finally, he generalizes again, in a different and equally important direction (#253, p. 33): "At the foundation of well-founded-belief lies belief that is not well founded." Thus (#341, p. 44) "the *questions* that we raise and our *doubts* depend on the fact that some propositions are exempt from doubt, are as it were like hinges on which those turn."

Proceeding to discuss other foundational, non-rationally grounded, a-rational universally held "beliefs" (or "hinges," as he terms them), Wittgenstein asserts (#411, p. 52): "If I say '*we assume* that the earth has existed for many years past' (or something similar)[15] . . . it sounds strange that we should *assume* such a thing. But in the entire system of our language-games it belongs to the foundations." Later, regarding our language-game itself, Wittgenstein states unequivocally (#558, p. 73): "it is not based on grounds. It is not reasonable (or unreasonable). It is there – like our life." Action too would be at stake, as there are ungrounded a-rational hinges which "form the basis of action, and therefore, naturally of thought" (#411, p. 52). Continuing with the remarkable view that these a-rational hinges are necessary for action and indeed any rational thought at all, Wittgenstein asks the following two questions (#558, p. 73): "Wouldn't a mistake [about a hinge] topple all judgment with it? More: what could stand if that were to fall?"

Controversies About Wittgenstein's Views on the A-Rational Foundation of Rationality

Concisely summarizing what is uncontested, Duncan Pritchard notes that hinge commitments are "immune to rational doubt" (2018, p. 88). Moreover, given the centrality of these hinge holdings, Pritchard states Wittgenstein's radical view that "at the heart of our rational practices are essentially arational commitments" (2012, p. 225). Thus, while their a-rationality, and foundational importance is not at issue[16] there are several competing notions as to whether the hinge holdings are truly: (1) beliefs, (2) propositions, (3) contentful, or (4) epistemic in nature.

Pritchard, for example, over a series of articles (2012, 2018) considers the foundational hinges "commitments" rather than "beliefs." He finds them contentful, propositional, and non-epistemic, where epistemic pertains to knowledge-producing. Crispin Wright (2004a, 2004b), terming the hinge holdings "entitlements," puts forth their role as prudential and pragmatic in that they both allow inquiry and avoid cognitive collapse. He regards them as semi-epistemic, with some rational along with non-evidential warrant, so that they are "trusted as true." Also, for Wright these entitlements are propositional, and contentful, while not being "beliefs." Annalisa Coliva (2013) has a view, in contrast to all those above, which does question the hinges as foundational. For her, they not only provide the norms of judgment but are themselves also a sort of judgment, which renders them semi-epistemic contentful propositions that are nevertheless are not beliefs.

Daniele Moyal-Sharrock, in her several writings (2004, 2007, 2017) about Wittgenstein's *On Certainty*, returns us to the claim that the hinge certainties are foundational. Further, she considers them to be non-propositional, non-epistemic, and not contentful. For Moyal-Sharrock (2007, p. 81), they are not beliefs-proper, in which one holds "beliefs that X," but instead are "beliefs-in." The "beliefs-in" are described as a kind of know-how, one that is consistent with Wittgenstein's (1950/1969) comments on (1) the animal nature of our a-rational hinge assumptions[17] – "I want to conceive it as something that lies beyond being justified or unjustified . . . as something animal" (#359, p. 47) – and (2) with his take on know-how. For example, Wittgenstein (#534, p. 71) prefers that a child who masters a language-game be described as being "*able to do* certain things" over must "*know* certain things."

Moyal-Sharrock's account provides an important link to the next section, where I explore similarities (and differences) between Wittgenstein and Freud on their views on a-rationality. The issues of know-how activity as a type of knowledge, beliefs-proper versus other contentful attitudes, and animal a-rationality will be discussed.

Similarities (and Differences): Freud and Wittgenstein on A-Rationality

Know-How

With Wittgenstein's comment (#534, p. 71) cited above, he essentially asserts that hinge assumptions, enable one "*to do* certain things" rather than to "*know* certain things." Moreover, he describes (#510–#511, p. 67) his own experience of a hinge certainty in this way: "I don't think of past or future . . . It is just like directly taking hold of something . . . without having doubts . . . And yet this direct taking-hold corresponds to a *sureness*, not to a knowing." This amounts to a claim for know-how actions as prior to any rational beliefs, as well as to other types of knowledge. (And, as some have held, this might also point the way to the further claim that knowledge precedes belief and other cognitive attitudes, rather than the other way around.)[18] In any case, these sorts of know-how actions are enacted in the unexamined present, and they are prior to considerations of True or False – indeed, they are a-rational, measured not by Truth or Falsity, but only by whether they work or not. Freud's primary processes, too, are prior to considerations of Truth and Falsity, and are enacted in the unexamined present.

Non-human Animals

For both Freud and Wittgenstein, animals figure in their theorizing. The know-how connection leads Moyal-Sharrock (2016, p. 104) to characterize attitudes toward the hinge assumptions as "animal certainties," adding: "Wittgenstein is describing *what it is like* . . . to have an attitude of basic certainty – and the answer is that it is like a way of acting or know-how or reflex action." She continues: "Here, 'I have a body' is the expression of a non-propositional attitude; a way of acting *in the certainty of* having a body, acting embodied." For Freud, the instincts which fuel the primary processes are essentially animal instincts. He takes this up in several of his mid to later works – "The Resistance to Psycho-Analysis" (1924/1925, p. 218); "The Question of Lay Analysis" (1926, p. 208), "Moses and Monotheism" (1939, p. 100, pp. 132–133); and "An Outline of Psycho-Analysis" (1940, p. 147) – stressing that the barrier between humans and animals is not so great as some of the former would have it.

But at this point, the differences between Freud and Wittgenstein on non-human animals become more salient than any similarity. Whereas for Wittgenstein the "animal certainty" of the a-rational, not-doubted, not doubtable hinge assumptions, is central to the scaffolding of rational systemic thought itself; for Freud the animal-like, instinct-fueled primary processes, while necessary and prior to the secondary processes, need to be inhibited by these secondary processes. Why? Because Freud held that the instinct-led, drive-directed life would follow the pleasure principle, thereby ignoring reality, with the consequence of subjugating rationality to psychopathology.

Content

On the issue of a-rational attitudes[19] with or without content (i.e., representation), again Freud and Wittgenstein are both similar and different. As discussed briefly above, I have proposed a proper function case[20] in which Freudian primary process a-rational attitudes do have content – content that is fixed, not by rational normativity (which would obviously be a non-starter for a-rational attitudes), but instead by evolutionary selective fitness normativity, operative also in the non-human animal world. (See Brakel, 2002, 2009, chap. 5.) A quick example of my proper function argument: toads eat black bugs. If toads swallow black bugs and also black metal pellets reflexively and indiscriminately, a secondary process thinker might conclude that toads have a primary process category for "bug" that is too inclusive – a category a-rationally condensing bugs plus black pellets. But insofar as toads with this inclusive category do not suffer pre-reproductive-age death through metal pellet ingesting, and in fact eat more real bugs, thereby enhancing their selective fitness success over the toads with the more exclusive category, the pellets can be understood as mere misrepresentations of the fixed content "bug." With this move – finding fitness-based proper function for the a-rational primary process category, fixed determinate a-rational content can be established.

As for Wittgensteinian a-rational content, the picture seems mixed, partly depending on the particular hinge assumption. Those that are truly reflex-like, may be, as some of the philosophers above claim, without fixed content. And these may be the very most global of them. For example, Wittgenstein (#141, p. 21) states: "When we first begin to *believe* anything, what we believe is not a single proposition, it is a whole system." Yet, when Wittgenstein (#125, pp. 18–19), with hinge certainty, answers the blind man that yes, he, Wittgenstein has his two hands – this without checking – there is fixed content represented in the question and its answer.

Evidence Insensitive, Automatic, Associational

For Freud, a-rational mentation is described as thoroughly evidence insensitive. Wittgenstein's hinge certainties too do not admit of evidence, doubt, or skepticism – they are prior to considerations of True and False. The primary processes are evidence insensitive in that objective reality testing is absent. One can appreciate this in almost any hour of any psychoanalytic practice with any patient. Thus, a patient, a middle-aged professor, claims (and clings to the idea) that he is both unsuccessful and hated by his department – this despite recommendations for a promotion and an invitation to give an important lecture. While this might count as evidence to revise his belief were his attitude to be one of belief-proper, his attitude is not a belief-proper. It is instead what I've termed a "neurotic-belief." (See Brakel, 2001, 2009, chap. 7 for a fuller account.) Experienced and acted upon as beliefs-proper, neurotic-beliefs are different. They are hybrids – primary process phantasies employing psychic reality rather than reality-tested objective reality, yet disguised (to patient as well as analyst) as regular beliefs. Indeed, the professor-patient "explains" that the department chair really preferred another scholar for the talk, one who had just left for a better position. And, as for the promotion, it was done out of charity, and way overdue anyway.

The neurotic-belief is a primary process a-rational attitude in its associative and automatic character and in its evidence insensitivity. However, there are important differences with Wittgenstein's basic hinge assumptions. Though indeed automatic and beyond and prior to doubt, hinge holdings are not particularly associative. Further, whereas the Freudian primary process–laden neurotic-beliefs are part of psychopathology, the very opposite is true for the Wittgensteinian hinges – they allow and are necessary for the very system of rational thought we humans rely upon and prize.[21]

Family Resemblance and Evolution

Throughout this chapter, I've held that the a-rationality of Wittgenstein's foundational hinges is not particularly associational, unlike the largely associational primary processes of Freud. While this is the case, there is an important associational (and perhaps a-rational, or at least not fully rational) aspect of Wittgenstein's work that should not be overlooked – the Family Resemblance. Here is how Wittgenstein first put it in his *Blue Book* (1933–1934/1958, p. 17):

> We are inclined to think that there must be something in common to all games, say, and that this common property is the justification for applying the general term "game" to the various games; whereas games form a *family* the members of which have family likenesses. Some of them have the same nose, others the same eyebrows and others again the same way of walking; and these likenesses overlap.

In this early passage, one can appreciate, Wittgenstein's initial longing for a largely rational (in Freud's terms, secondary process) categorization. He would like to find something essentially linking all games, instead of the non-essential, primary process-like, superficial similarities of a nose here, an eyebrow there.

Elaborating the Family Resemblance idea in *Philosophical Investigations* (1953, #66, p. 31), Wittgenstein continues with games: "if you look at them you will not see something that is common to *all*, but similarities, relationships, and a whole series of them at that." He goes on, exclaiming (#66, p. 32) "but how many other characteristic features have disappeared! . . . we can see how similarities crop up and disappear. . . . And the result of this examination is: we see a complicated network of similarities overlapping and criss-crossing: sometimes overall similarities, sometimes similarities of detail." Wittgenstein famously then (#67, p. 32) "characterize[s] these similarities . . . [as] 'family resemblances'; for the various resemblances between members of a family: build, features, colour of eyes, gait, temperament, etc. etc. overlap and criss-cross."

What have we got then with Wittgenstein's Family Resemblance notion? An indication that certain natural categories are formed by individual members sharing different, but overlapping properties (or attributes); some quite superficial, none need shared by all, none necessary, and none essential. Let's see what happens when we play this out with a real and regular family, the Zekes. One can categorize the Zeke family members by associative similarities. But note, though Zeke Brothers A and B and Zeke Cousins G and H can indeed share the triangular family nose, Persons X and Y, unrelated to one another and to the Zekes, can also have this unusually shaped nose. Also, Cousins T and W can seem to have no obvious Zeke family traits and yet Zekes they are. So, we must conclude that successful categorization of Family Zeke by attribute association – an a-rational type process – is a rather iffy affair. Instead, one can more properly categorize the Zeke family, rationally. Family members all do share an essential legal or genetic tie, one directly linked and traceable to some Zeke or other, albeit not to one another and not to some original ur-Zeke progenitor. Thus, as Neil O'Hara (2019, personal communication) has astutely pointed out, a family (like the Zeke family) paradoxically does not conform to a Family Resemblance category.

Yet, there is something more to consider here. Recall that attribute matching (i.e., associative, a-rationally based similarity) often works toward evolutionary fitness success in the non-human-animal world. I discussed some examples of this briefly, earlier in the chapter – imprinting, conditioning, and bird similarity assessments. Now let us generalize and expand this. Take, for instance, flowers of a certain color (red) or shape (oval petals, arrowhead leaves). Birds, bees, and bugs are attracted differentially to flowers with these particular attributes. Why? Because bees, birds, and bugs who have interacted with flowers of a certain specific biological type have experienced enhanced selective fitness; *and* flowers of this certain specific biological type often, *but not always*, appear with that particular color or shape. For humans too, primary process–like a-rational categorizations can be and have been adaptive (evolutionarily) insofar as associative attributional feature similarities very often reflect more essential underlying commonalities. Thus, although young humans can mistakenly classify bats as birds, and whales as fish, most flying creatures that look like birds (or bats) are birds, and most swimming animals that look like fish (or whales) are fish.[22]

Fine for associative, a-rational, attribute matching, but we haven't addressed Family Resemblance categories. What about them, then? The flowers of a particular biological type don't make up that sort of Family Resemblance category; neither do the whales or the bats fit that sort of category. For that matter, the conjunctive categories – (1) flowers, whatever their biological type, as long as they are red with oval petals and arrowhead leaves; (2) birds plus bats; (3) fish plus whales – are also not Family Resemblance categories. Yes, games *do* make up a Family Resemblance category, and it is of interest to try to further understand what that means. In an essay on Wittgenstein's Family Resemblance idea, Bambrough (1960/1966, pp. 198–199) attempts to do just that:

> The nominalist says that games have nothing in common except that they are called games. The realist says that games must have something in common, and he means by this that they must have something in common other than that they are games. Wittgenstein says they [all] have nothing in common except that they *are* games.

On that basis, let me offer the following proposal. Freud's a-rational primary processes and Wittgenstein's foundational a-rational hinge assumptions constitute a Family Resemblance category. They have overlapping features in common, and equally important, criss-crossing differences. Starting with "what it feels like," the a-rationality of both is experientially similar – a felt automaticity. Relatedly, both have a link to non-human animals, and as well the evolutionary significance of that link. But despite these important similarities, there is a radical difference. In the Freudian version, humans acting on their primary process animal-like instincts often fall prey to severe individual psychopathology. Whereas in the Wittgensteinian version, persons *without* their animal-grasp on the foundational hinges would be quite insane. As a final criss-crossing, let's note that both Freud's primary processes and Wittgenstein's core hinges are evidence insensitive and prior to considerations of Truth and Falsity, but that this too plays out in a radically different way. Thus, without Wittgenstein's a-rational hinges, no rational systemic thinking could ever get off the ground; whereas operating with Freud's primary processes, alone and unchecked, rationality would be stranded on the runway.

If I have not made the case for the a-rationalities of Freud and Wittgenstein comprising a Family Resemblance category, let me at least close with something beyond contest – this from Yogi Berra, excellent New York Yankee catcher in the 1950s and '60s and practical philosopher/psychoanalyst before and thereafter. When asked if he found similarities between himself and his son, Dale, also a major league baseball player, Yogi replied: "Our similarities are different." And so, this is the case no less for a-rationality in the works of Sigmund Freud and Ludwig Wittgenstein.

Notes

1 See especially Freud (1895, pp. 324–327, 334–340, 357, 362), Freud (1893–1895, pp. 9, 15, 208–209, 214, 225, 239), and Freud (1896, pp. 198–199).
2 Ordinary rationality, in contrast, does not tolerate contradictions and is "reasonable" – predicated on reasons and reality testing, it is subject to change if evidence so warrants.
3 Transferences, ubiquitous in clinical psychoanalyses, form on the basis of a-rational primary process categorizations. In examining transferences, one can readily appreciate that experiences of "unexamined present" along with inessential associative feature matches serve to promote the transfer of feelings about one person inappropriately onto another.
4 See particularly Freud (1925, p. 218, 1926, p. 208), Freud (1939, pp. 97, 100, 132–3), and Freud (1940, p. 147).
5 "We" here refers to members of the Hunt Memorial Laboratory for the Study of Unconscious Processes in the Psychiatry Department at the University of Michigan.
6 These experiments were much aided by discussions with Douglas Medin and his writings on categorization. In particular, a work by Medin, Goldstone, and Gentner (1990) was instrumental.
7 Philosophical priority for a-rationality, both on Freud's account and that of Wittgenstein, will be taken up later in the chapter.
8 Mechanisms would include continued selective reproductive fitness for animals employing a-rational mentation as species branched off a common trunk, or parallel evolution of a-rational mentation in different branches.
9 Species studied include honeybees, pigeons, hummingbirds, starlings, gray jays, mice, and capuchin monkeys.
10 Note that the researchers did not describe the behavior as "primary process–like" or "a-rational," but instead "biologically rational." This exemplifies the tendency described above – tacitly concluding that anything pragmatically effective must be some form of "rational."
11 System One processes include (1) The overcounting of representability and availability. Thus, unusual and intense circumstances are viewed as more likely to occur, and represented with greater frequency than is accurate. (2) Recency and final effects (sometimes called framing) are more prominent. (3) Risk and loss aversion predominate over gain possibilities. (4) Transitivity is not respected. (5) Similarity can be based on inessential attributes. Interestingly, these System One operations can sometimes provide more effective outcomes than can System Two. (For the evolutionary advantage for humans see Gigerenzer & Todd [1999] and Todd & Gigerenzer [2000]).
12 For more on Mrs. M's case, and the Kantian-based speculations that follow, see Brakel (2009, pp. 44–49).
13 There is neuroscientific evidence for this view: Gerald Edelman (1987) explains that the world as first experienced is "unlabeled" (p. 7) and without "well arranged categories" (p. 24). As such, for many evolved organisms (including humans) "overall object distinction [is] not necessarily veridical" (p. 257).
14 The nature of what I'm calling "assumptions" is the subject of considerable debate. Are these holdings "propositions"? Are they "beliefs?" – Wittgenstein uses both of these terms frequently. He also speaks of "assumptions" (#411, p. 52) and "convictions" (#248, p. 33). These matters will be taken up below, along with another term Wittgenstein scholars use, "commitment" – this, as we discuss the related questions as to whether these holdings are contentful, and epistemic. Note that the term "hinge," introduced by Wittgenstein, seems acceptable to all, either as an adjective modifying one of the contested terms or as a freestanding noun.
15 Another example Wittgenstein offers (#479, p. 63): "Are we to say that the knowledge that there are physical objects comes very early or very late?"
16 More correctly, hinge commitments are most often regarded as foundational. For an exception, see the view of Coliva (2013) discussed briefly below.
17 It is not entirely clear that for Moyal-Sharrock these "beliefs-in" are without content. In a recent article (2019, p. 4, n. 5) she states: "I don't see 'content-involving cognition' as exclusive to humans." However, if Moyal-Sharrock regards "beliefs-in" as not "cognitive," then for her their status as not-contentful would remain.
18 For the philosophically radical idea that knowledge precedes belief, see Williamson (2000). See also Brakel (2010, chap. 1) for evidential support from psychoanalysis for the Williamson view.
19 I'm using the term "attitudes" as it has a broader compass than "proposition."
20 This proper function argument owes much to the work of Millikan (1993).

21 In between the Freudian and Wittgensteinian a-rational attitudes we have Gendler's aliefs (2008a, 2008b). These are belief-like attitudes, associative, automatic, and a-rational, and as such not evidence sensitive. They are developmentally and conceptually antecedent to beliefs-proper, and often tied to affect and action. However, unlike Wittgenstein's hinges, aliefs are in no way vital to ground rationality. And, unlike Freudian neurotic-beliefs, aliefs are not experienced as beliefs-proper, hence do not always lead to harmful neurotic actions. On balance, aliefs sometimes prove problematic, sometimes pragmatically good enough.

22 This idea was first imparted to me by Douglas Medin (personal communication) circa 2000.

References

Bambrough, R. (1960/1966). Universals and family resemblances. In *Wittgenstein: The Philosophical Investigations*. G. Pitcher (ed). Garden City, NY: Doubleday & Company.

Bazan, A., Van Draege, K., DeKrock, L., Geerardyn, P., Shevrin, H., & Brakel, L.A.W. (2013). Empirical evidence for primary process mentation in acute psychosis. *Psychoanalytic Psychology*. Vol. 30: pp. 57–74.

Brakel, L.A.W. (2001). Phantasies, neurotic-beliefs, and beliefs-proper. *American Journal of Psychoanalysis*. Vol. 61: pp. 363–389.

Brakel, L.A.W. (2002). Phantasy and wish: a proper function account of a-rational primary process mediated mentation. *The Australasian Journal of Philosophy*. Vol. 80: pp. 1–16.

Brakel, L.A.W. (2004). The psychoanalytic assumption of the primary process: Extra-psychoanalytic evidence and findings. *Journal of the American Psychoanalytic Association*. Vol. 52: pp. 1131–1161.

Brakel, L.A.W. (2009). *Philosophy, Psychology, and the A-Rational Mind*. Oxford: Oxford University Press.

Brakel, L.A.W. (2010). *Unconscious Knowing and Other Essays in Psycho-Philosophical Analysis*. Oxford: Oxford University Press.

Brakel, L.A.W. (2013). *The Ontology of Psychology: Questioning Foundations in the Philosophy of Mind*. New York: Routledge.

Brakel, L.A.W. (2015). Two fundamental problems for philosophical psychoanalysis. In *Philosophy, Science, and Psychoanalysis*. S. Boag, L.A.W. Brakel & V. Talvitie (eds). London: Karnac Books, pp. 119–143.

Brakel, L.A.W., Kleinsorge, S., Snodgrass, M., & Shevrin, H. (2000). The primary process and the unconscious: Experimental evidence supporting two psychoanalytic presuppositions. *International Journal of Psychoanalysis*. Vol. 81 (3): pp. 553–569.

Brakel, L.A.W., & Shevrin, H. (2005). Anxiety, attributional thinking and primary process. *International Journal of Psychoanalysis*. Vol. 86: pp. 1679–1693.

Brakel, L.A.W., Shevrin, H., & Villa, K. (2002). The priority of primary process categorizing: Experimental evidence supporting a psychoanalytic developmental hypothesis. *Journal of the American Psychoanalytic Association*. Vol. 50: pp. 483–505.

Coliva, A. (2013). Hinges and certainty. A precis of *Moore and Wittgenstein, Scepticism, Certainty and Common Sense*. *Philosophia*. Vol. 41: pp. 1–12.

Cutler, S., & Brakel, L.A.W. (2014). The Primary Process: a preliminary exploration of a-rational mentation from an evolutionary viewpoint. *Psychoanalytic Inquiry*. Vol. 34: pp. 792–809.

Edelman, G. (1987). *Neural Darwinism*. New York: Basic Books.

Evans, J., & Over, D. (1996) *Rationality and Reasoning*. London: Psychology Press.

Freud, S. (1893–1895). *Studies on Hysteria. Standard Edition 2*. J. Strachey (ed). London: Hogarth Press, 1955.

Freud, S. (1895/1950). Project for a scientific psychology. In *Standard Edition 1*. J. Strachey (ed). London: Hogarth Press, 1966.

Freud, S. (1896). The aetiology of hysteria. In *Standard Edition 3*. J. Strachey (ed). London: Hogarth Press, 1962.

Freud, S. (1900). *The Interpretation of Dreams. Standard Edition 4 & 5*. J. Strachey (ed). London: Hogarth Press, 1953.

Freud, S. (1905). *Jokes and Their Relation to the Unconscious. Standard Edition 8*. J. Strachey (ed). London: Hogarth Press, 1960.

Freud, S. (1924/1925). The resistances to psycho-analysis. In *Standard Edition 19*. J. Strachey (ed). London: Hogarth Press, 1961.

Freud, S. (1926). The question of lay analysis. In *Standard Edition 20*. J. Strachey (ed). London: Hogarth Press, 1959.

Freud, S. (1939). Moses and monotheism. In *Standard Edition 23*. J. Strachey (ed). London: Hogarth Press, 1964.

Freud, S. (1940). An outline of psycho-analysis. In *Standard Edition 19*. J. Strachey (ed). London: Hogarth Press, 1964.

Garlick, D., Gant, D., Brakel, L.A.W., & Blaisdell, A. (2011). Attributional and relational processing in pigeons. *Frontiers in Comparative Psychology*. Vol. 2: pp. 14–45.

Gendler, T. (2008a). Alief and belief. *Journal of Philosophy*. Vol. 105: pp. 634–663.

Gendler, T. (2008b). Alief in action (and reaction). *Mind and Language*. Vol. 23: pp. 552–585.

Gigerenzer, G., & Todd, P. (1999). Ecological rationality: the normative study of heuristics. In *Ecological Rationality: Intelligence in the World*. G. Gigerenzer & P. Todd, The ABC Research Group (eds.). New York: Oxford University Press, pp. 487–497.

Hurley, S., & Nudds, M. (2006) (eds.) *Rational Animals?*. Oxford: Oxford University Press.

Kacelnik, A. (2006). Meanings of rationality. In *Rational Animals?* S. Hurley & M. Nudds. (eds.). Oxford: Oxford University Press, pp. 87–106.

Kahneman, D. (2011). *Thinking, Fast and Slow*. New York: Farrar, Straus, & Giroux

Kahneman, D., Slovic, P., & Tversky, A. (eds.) (1982). *Judgement Under Uncertainty: Heuristics and Biases*. Cambridge: Cambridge University Press.

Kant, I. (1781/1787). *Critique of Pure Reason*. Trans. Norman Kemp Smith. New York: St. Matin's Press, 1965.

Lorenz, K. (1935). The companion in the bird's world. *J. fur Ornithologie*. Vol. 83: pp. 137–213; 289–413.

Medin, D., Goldstone, R., & Gentner, D. (1990). Similarity involving attributes and relations: Judgments of similarity and difference are not inverses. *Psychological Science*. Vol. 1: pp. 64–69.

Millikan, R. (1993). *White Queen Psychology and Other Essays for Alice*. Cambridge, MA: MIT Press.

Moyal-Sharrock, D. (2004). *Understanding Wittgenstein's On Certainty*. London: Palgrave Macmillan.

Moyal-Sharrock, D. (2007). Unravelling certainty. Chapter 5. In *Readings of Wittgenstein's On Certainty*. D. Moyal-Sharrock & W. Brenner (eds.). London: Palgrave Macmillan, pp. 76–98 [not sure of this last page.].

Moyal-Sharrock, D. (2016). The animal in epistemology. *International Journal for the Study of Skepticism*. Vol. 6: pp. 97–119.

Moyal-Sharrock, D. (2017). Wittgenstein on knowledge and certainty. Chapter 35. In *A Companion to Wittgenstein*. H-J. Glock & J. Hyman (eds.). First Edition. Hoboken, NJ: John Wiley & Sons, Ltd., pp. 547–562.

Moyal-Sharrock, D. (2019). From deed to word: gapless and kink-free enactivism. *Synthese*: pp. 1–20. https://doi.org/10.1007/s1129-019-02218-5.

Pritchard, D. (2012). Wittgenstein and the groundlessness of our believing. *Synthese*. Vol. 189: pp. 255–272.

Pritchard, D. (2018). Epistemic angst. *Philosophy and Phenomenological Research*. Vol. 96: pp. 70–90.

Simon, H. (1956a). Rational choice and the structure of environments. *Psychological Review*. Vol. 63: pp. 129–138.

Todd, P., & Gigerenzer, G. (2000). Precis of *Simple heuristics that make us smart*. *Behavioral and Brain Sciences*. Vol. 23: pp. 727–780.

Tversky, A. (2004). *Preference, Belief, and Similarity*. E. Shafir (ed.). Cambridge, MA: MIT Press.

Williamson, T. (2000). *Knowledge and Its Limits*. Oxford: Oxford University Press.

Wittgenstein, L. (1933–35/1958). *The Blue and Brown Books*. New York: Harper & Row Publishers.

Wittgenstein, L. (1950/1969). *On Certainty*. G.E.M. Anscombe & G. H. von Wright (eds.). Trans. G.E.M. Anscombe. New York, Evanston, San Francisco, London: Harper & Row Publishers.

Wittgenstein, L. (1953). *Philosophical Investigations*. Trans. G.E.M. Anscombe. New York: The Macmillan Company.

Wright, C. (2004a). Warrant for nothing (and foundations for free)? *Proceedings of the Aristotelian Society*. Vol. 78 (supplement): pp. 167–212.

Wright, C. (2004b). Wittgensteinian certainties. In *Wittgenstein and Scepticism*. D. McManus (ed.). London and New York: Routledge, pp. 22–55.

26

INTERSUBJECTIVITY AND RESPONSIBILITY IN RELATIONAL PSYCHOANALYSIS AND MODERN JEWISH PHILOSOPHY

Michael Oppenheim

At the beginning of the book *The Ethical Turn: Otherness and Subjectivity in Contemporary Psychoanalysis*, the editors David Goodman and Eric Severson (2016) write, "[Emmanuel] Levinas claims that 'morality is not a branch of philosophy but first philosophy' and if he is right about this, might ethics also serve as a first *psychology*?" (p. i). This chapter will explore two significant theorists, Jessica Benjamin and Donna M. Orange, representing the ethical turn within Relational Psychoanalysis.[1] It will also conduct a challenging dialogue with that stream of modern Jewish philosophy that includes the German and Israeli philosopher Martin Buber (1878–1965), the German philosopher Franz Rosenzweig (1886–1929), and the French philosopher Emmanuel Levinas (1905–1995), which has been described in terms of its ethics of moral perfectionism. "Moral perfectionists" believe that only by maintaining an "'impossible' [ethical] demand in view can one strive for 'one's unattained but attainable self'" (Putnam, 2008, p. 72). A few of the complementary issues to be pursued through this multidisciplinary lens are intersubjectivity, responsibility, meaning, and speech/language.

While a number of themes can be seen to coalesce in the emergence and prominence of ethics within the relational stream, two of these also connect this development with the three Jewish philosophers of encounter. The first is the tenet that relationships with others constitute the foundation of human growth and maturation, as well as of individual experience and self-understanding. Second is the view that human health, well-being, or flourishing, especially seen in terms of the problem of meaning,[2] needs to be addressed in the therapeutic context. The early, leading figure in Relational Psychoanalysis, Stephen A. Mitchell (2000), provides concise statements of these points, writing,

> Human minds are interactive phenomena; an individual human mind is an oxymoron; subjectivity always develops in the context of intersubjectivity.
>
> *(p. 57)*

> What the patient needs is not a rational reworking of unconscious infantile fantasies . . . [but] a revitalization and expansion of his own capacity to generate experience that

DOI: 10.4324/9780429297076-31

> feels real, meaningful, and valuable. (1993, p. 24). [Adding that] the term meaningful here refers to a sense of personal value, importance, and devotion.
>
> *(p. 234)*

Similarly, the notion of the interhuman, the life of persons with other persons, courses through all the works of the Jewish philosophers. Martin Buber's (1923/1970) famous book *I and Thou* highlights the insight that "I require a Thou to become, becoming I, I say Thou" (p. 62).[3] His discussion of meaning extends the treatment of interactions to include the divine, which is also a pervasive feature in the works of the other two Jewish philosophers. For Buber, the meeting or "association" with the divine "makes life heavier but heavy with meaning" (p. 158), something which must be put "to the proof in action" (p. 159).

The multidisciplinary approach utilized here is predicated on the understanding that in exploring our complex world, and in particular its human expanse, multiple cultural, disciplinary, and discursive approaches are required. This specific exposition should be taken as an invitation to even further cultural and disciplinary contributions, rather than being seen as somehow exhaustive. Accompanying this affirmation of the ultimate value of pluralistic avenues is the persistent rejection of all reductionist tendencies.

Relational Psychoanalysis

Relational Psychoanalysis is sometimes referred to as a psychoanalytic "school," but it is more accurately described as a convergence of interest and understanding by theorists and practitioners, that is, as a current or "tradition" (Mitchell & Aron, 1999, p. x).[4] Beginning in the 1980s and principally within the United States, it incorporates elements from many earlier post-Freudian streams, including Self-Psychology, Object Relations theory, and Interpersonal Psychoanalysis. It is also influenced by feminist psychoanalysis and several postmodern philosophical trends. Some theoretical and clinical features include the preeminent significance of the dynamics within the mother-infant dyad in the constitution of the self; the pervasiveness of conscious and unconscious, intersubjective and intrapersonal, intrapsychic/imaginary and external/realistic modes of relationality; the approach to analysis as a two-person encounter, characterized by both mutuality and asymmetry; and the wider view of psychoanalysis as a hermeneutical rather than scientific activity that offers a variety of narratives about the nature of the self and human experience.

The increasing prominence of ethics in relational presentations is not fortuitous. Goodman and Severson (2016) write,

> The *relational* turn surely laid the foundation for the ethical turn, but there is more to it than that. There are, no doubt, widely diverse entry points and angles from which to approach the turn to ethics within the psychoanalytic tradition.
>
> *(p. 4)*

They enumerate and describe three "cross-pollinating traditions": "attachment, mentalization, and evolutionary biology research," "scholarship related to critical theory and political positioning," and "phenomenological, hermeneutic, social constructionist, and dialogical literatures" (p. 4).

As indicated earlier, this chapter will pursue a more thematic orientation to possible "entry points" for the relational turn to ethics. In this context, intersubjectivity points to the ethical implications of the understanding that humans are inescapably immersed in a dialogical field of interconnection and interdependence, that individual action or inaction always has ethical ramifications. The subject of human health has a clinical and an existential axis. Responsibility to others is an inescapable feature in lives of meaning and purpose. These insights will be fleshed out and illustrated in the specific treatments that follow.

Jessica Benjamin and Donna Orange[5]

The writings of Jessica Benjamin, who was described decades ago as "one of the most profound psychoanalytic theoreticians of this generation" (Mitchell & Aron, 1999, p. 181), exemplifies many of the elements associated with the ethical turn in Relational Psychoanalysis. Her early trio of works, *The Bonds of Love* (1988), *Like Subjects, Love Objects* (1995), and *Shadow of the Other* (1998), advanced an understanding of intersubjectivity highlighting the concept of recognition. Benjamin (1998) describes intersubjectivity in terms of the relationship between one subject and an independent and outside other. In her words, "The problem of how we relate to the fact of the other's independent consciousness, a mind that is fundamentally like our own but unfathomably different and outside our control, has been a through line in my work" (p. xii). It is within the earliest dynamics with an outside other – usually the mother – that individual subjectivity develops, and ensuing relationships hopefully punctuate the path to some type of fullness and flourishing.

However, the path to this fullness is neither simple nor smooth. Benjamin (1999) finds that humans are riddled by two conflicting desires: "Our psychic makeup is such that we are torn between omnipotence, illusion of control, on the one hand, and the wish for contact with the different, the external, the not-me, on the other" (p. 202). Omnipotence points to the process whereby the ego seeks to master what is different, that is, outside of itself. The other is either fantasized as being totally subservient to the self's desire, or treated as a dangerous alien figure that must be destroyed. Still, as fundamentally social creatures, persons find pleasure in being with others and are excited by those who are different from themselves. In Benjamin's (1995) words, "We have a need for recognition and we have a capacity to recognize others in return, thus making mutual recognition possible" (p. 30). In this regard it is important to note that the basis for recognition is established because the other person can come to be experienced as someone similar to, rather than totally different from, the self.

Following her first major works, Benjamin introduces two new concepts, which are at the same time extensions of her earlier insights concerning intersubjectivity. These concern the relational drama of "doer and done to" and the transpersonal space beyond this struggle, defined as "the third." Doer and done to represents a complementary relation in which each side feels that it is being manipulated and dominated by the other. She explains, "It is as if the essence of complementary relations – the relation of twoness – is that there appear to be only two choices: either submission or resistance to the other's demand" (2012, p. 95). The concepts of the third and "thirdness" refer to an interactive space beyond the complementary dynamic. In a relation where the third is appreciated there is an openness to the other, a respect for difference, and a shared experience of recognition.[6] She writes, "The third appears only in the relationship of recognition, the space that mediates the two partners' viewpoints, preventing the collapse of tension" into the fruitless battle for domination (1999, p. 204).

Benjamin's increasing use and development of these ideas in the first two decades of this century also reflects her expanding focus on contemporary arenas of violence and collective trauma. In particular, she explores the psychic dynamics behind the failure of bystanders throughout the world to witness, acknowledge, and come to the aid of those who suffer from individual and collective violence; the propensity for victims to blame themselves and even to condemn themselves as guilty; and finally, the attitude of perpetrators of violence to see their targets as less than human, as disposable. Her answer, in summary, is that bystanders, victims, and perpetrators are pulled to respond to violence and trauma through the psychological process of splitting between the dishonorable, failed, and guilty, and the worthy, successful, and righteous – ultimately between "the discarded" and "the dignified" (2018, p. 226).

To explore the possibilities for a positive identification with those who suffer, and to block splitting between "those who may live and those who must die" (2018, p. 229), Benjamin introduces the concept of the "moral third" (p. 215). She identifies two facets of the "Moral Third," referring to both "the mental position," that is, specific ethical principles, and particular "interpersonal processes" (p. 225). In terms of the former, the moral third is defined as "the principle whereby we create relationships in accord with ethical values" (2012, p. 98). These values include commitments to a universal moral order or a "lawful caring world" (2018, p. 52), the dignity of all persons (p. 51), respect for human vulnerability (p. 90), responsibility for "fellow human beings" (p. 217), and the inclusiveness, interdependence, and union of the human community (p. 234).

The notion of lawfulness also spans the presentation of those interpersonal processes that manifest the moral third. Although the ideals apply equally to situations of collective trauma, the clinician's acts of equality, mutuality, asymmetry, responsibility, and surrender most prominently portray the intersubjective processes of the moral third. Equality and mutuality, or what Benjamin (2018) terms "a democratic or egalitarian view of the psychoanalytic process" (p. 42), highlight the importance of dialogue as a shared process and of two partners listening, learning, and developing together. The quality of asymmetry is most evident in the particular responsibilities that the therapist has. These include the honest acknowledgment that in the pursuit of the patient's health, the latter is brought to re-experience moments of violence, guilt, pain, and trauma. The psychoanalyst is also responsible for what Benjamin terms "surrender." She means by this that in the midst of a breakdown in the dialogue, it is the therapist's responsibility to acknowledge what is happening, and to confess their active part in the push and pull of blaming (p. 39).

A reference to an episode in the treatment of one of her patients encapsulates the deeply ethical dimension that Benjamin (2018) came to see in her work.

> I heard her [Jeannette] telling me that she needed me to embody *some* limit, some principle of right and wrong that I truly believed in, and that she could therefore believe in, too. This message from her was my first encounter in the context of violence with what I later came to formulate as the moral Third.
>
> *(p. 211)*

This vignette references equally the principles and intersubjective processes that constitute the moral third. Benjamin realized that a key to the recovery of her trauma victim was to introduce the "principle of right and wrong," the notion of lawfulness and of a transcendent moral order. However, this principle could not just be communicated; it had to be embodied, even created, through the intersubjective processes of responsibility, mutuality, asymmetry, humility, and surrender. As we have seen, Benjamin insists that this understanding of the moral third must also be transferred to the wider social scene of collective violence and genocide, where a commitment to the moral third constitutes the singular path to repair. In all, this ethical dimension of human relationships and human well-being, traditionally viewed as "outside the frame of . . . psychoanalysis" (p. 209), came to have a pivotal role in Benjamin's addressing traumatic suffering in both individual and collective life.[7]

Donna Orange's training, teaching, and clinical and scholarly work remarkably exemplify the integration of philosophy and psychoanalysis, as well as the ethical turn in both disciplines. After earning a doctorate in philosophy and teaching it at the college and university level, she earned a second doctorate in psychology and began a career, extending over three decades, of psychoanalytic practice and supervision. All of her writings are permeated with this dual-disciplinary approach, especially prominent in her 2010 book, *Thinking for Clinicians: Philosophical Resources for Contemporary Psychoanalysis and Humanistic Psychotherapies.*

Intersubjectivity, that relationship to others which constitutes the all-embracing atmosphere in all the periods of one's life, is the centerpiece of Orange's work. One source of this standpoint is the Boston Process Change Study Group, which explores the "minutiae of interaction, body language, gestural and facial expressive elements, vocal rhythms, tonal elements and timing" that transpire between mothers and infants (cited in Orange, 2011, p. 192). The more theoretical provenance is the collaboration between Robert D. Stolorow, George Atwood, and Orange that produced "intersubjective systems theory," which focused particularly on the analytic interaction. They suggest that "patient and analyst, like child and caregiver, form an inextricable psychological field or system outside of which no understanding is possible and from which no fully independent existence can be described" (Orange, 2011, p. 209). These key insights lead to her deeply ethical approach to the analytic encounter. Orange (2009) writes about being "drawn to dialogic theories and clinical attitudes that emphasize our responsibility to stretch empathically, to reach for contact, to understand, just as good enough parents do for many years, without expectation of any adequate recompense" (p. 235).

Orange (2011) describes her clinical attitude as the "hermeneutics of trust" (pp. 31–35), which she contrasts to Paul Ricoeur's famous depiction of the standpoint of the three masters of suspicion, Marx, Freud, and Nietzsche (pp. 26–31). In this vein Freud saw the psychoanalyst as an investigator or archeologist, who looked beneath the plain words and actions of the patient, beyond their defense and resistance, to uncover the hidden unconscious drives and motives. The hermeneutics of trust values the patient's reactions as genuine efforts to accommodate to traumatic situations of unbearable suffering. It is "an implicitly interpretive process of giving lived meaning and dignity to a shattered person's life by enabling integration of the pain and loss as opposed to dissociation or fragmentation" (2010, p. 116). This process thus necessarily upends the classical attitude of analytic neutrality and objectivity for one of empathy, compassion, the sharing of suffering, and the recognition of mutual vulnerability.

These features of the ethical approach to the patient are encapsulated in Orange's (2011) statement,

> Not only are we required to witness and to participate emotionally in the suffering of our patients, but, in addition, the process of understanding itself means that we place ourselves at risk and allow the other to make an impact on us.
>
> *(p. 23)*

Through experiencing and sharing the pain and suffering of their patients, what Orange terms "compassion," the analyst is able to arrive at an empathetic understanding of both the patient's situation and what is taking place between them in the give and take of therapy. The mutuality and equality of therapist and patient are highlighted here, as well as the ethical demand that the therapist open up to, or be vulnerable to, this suffering. In Orange's words, "This approach to clinical practice interprets from a point of view that assumes a common world, in which people live, suffer, play, and search for meaning together" (p. 38).

Orange (2011) is particularly perceptive in understanding the creative dynamics within the therapeutic process. While the tasks required of the therapist seem extreme, she recognizes that the shared process provides its own resources. In responding to the suffering of the other, one may be able to give – trust, peace, meaning – what was not actually possessed prior to the engagement: "Something happens to me in the face of the other's need so that my giving has the quality of participating" (p. 51).

The psychoanalytic engendered ethical commitment that Orange (2011) sees as required in analysis is equally applicable in addressing the wider world of conflict, humanitarian crises, and especially climate change. This note is championed in the "Afterword: The Next Step" in *The Suffering Stranger*:

> The implications of the book's thesis, that dialogic understanding, in a hermeneutic of trust, forms the hospitable response to the suffering stranger demanded by ethics of infinite responsibility, clearly extend beyond our "everyday clinical practice" into the larger worlds where suffering and injustice collide everyday.
>
> *(p. 237)*

Both the therapist and the humanitarian worker deal with trauma. In these cases, beyond their vocational positions, they and each of us are called as humans to respond to the call of the other. This response requires empathic understanding, compassionate witnessing, and responsible action to help alleviate injustices and suffering. Victims of violence cannot be left alone, or denied their basic dignity. Orange's 2017 book *Climate Crisis, Psychoanalysis, and Radical Ethics* focuses her ethical purview on the cause of climate justice in the name of our responsibility to the suffering stranger, that is, to the poor, exploited, and "dispensable" others, those struggling against historic and contemporary slavery, industrialization, and globalization. In her challenging words, "We need to see the naked faces of those suffering and dying from our carbon-drunk way of life, to make the links, to see their vulnerability as our responsibility, one we cannot pass on to others" (p. xv).

Last, there is one more facet to Orange's ethically infused psychoanalytic vision, which is the concern with human health, well-being, or flourishing. She recognizes that "psychoanalytic and psychotherapeutic work relies for their legitimacy and inspiration . . . on . . . accounts of the human good" (2010, p. 108). Taking responsibility for the plight of others is thus not only an obligation; it is a significant feature of the quest for "what constitutes the good life" for everyone (2011, p. 8). A life of meaning, what she takes as Levinas' notion of "ethical subjectivity" (2016, p. 50), arises through responsible witnessing and responding to the call of others, even though these calls never end and the requisite responses are never complete.

The Philosophers of Encounter: Martin Buber, Emmanuel Levinas, and Franz Rosenzweig

Martin Buber, whose name is synonymous with the term "dialogue," was already regarded as a significant European thinker at the beginning of the twentieth century. His book of 1923, *I and Thou*, is a philosophical and religious classic, as well as the cornerstone of all his multidisciplinary presentations that followed. The beginning of his essay "The History of the Dialogical Principle" features a statement emblematic of his understanding of what he had earlier termed the interhuman sphere – *das Zwischen-menschliche* (quoted in Mendes-Flohr, 2019, p. 50): "Through the fact that he enters into essential reciprocity, man becomes revealed as man . . . the saying of Thou by the I stands in the origin of all individual human becoming" (Buber, 1947/1965, p. 209).

The key to Buber's (1923/1970) *I and Thou* occurs early in the text: "There is no I as such but only the I of the basic word I–Thou and the I of the basic word I–It" (p. 54). The life of the individual cannot be understood isolated from the world and others. Persons are fundamentally relational and there are two basic types of relation. The I and It is the easiest to describe, and the most common in the everyday world. Here the individual stands back from a full encounter and turns to that other as an object for their design or use. This may include experiencing it as a scientific object to be manipulated, an artistic model to be reproduced through clay or pigment, or even as a friend with whom one meets in order to exchange information or close feelings. Buber does not condemn such relations as evil, but they do objectify the other and are limited by the programmed goal (pp. 54–59). Of the second type of relation Buber writes, "When I confront a human being as my Thou and speak the basic word I–Thou to him, then he is no thing among things nor does he consist of things" (p. 59). The relation of I and Thou requires both that the person strip off their partiality as a scientist, artist, or friend, as well as allows the encounter to be free of any predetermined design.

At its highest, life in the world is nourished by real encounters. In the relation between I and Thou, each of the partners turns with their "whole being" (Buber, 1923/1970, p. 54) to the other. There is both mutuality and reciprocity in these meetings. One person does not just give (information, love, etc.) and the other receive. Both are open to the possibility that something new might arise from the encounter, that is, they are open to being radically transformed. The individual is made through relationships with particular others, and thus all is not in one's own hands. In addition, since the life of dialogue only ends with death, this process neither has a last stage nor culminates in a finalized self-knowledge.

For Buber (1923/1970) there are three types of others, which he designates as the three "spheres in which the world of relation arises" (p. 56). There is life with nature, and life with the world of art (paintings, poems, sculptures, etc.). However, the paradigm of the I–Thou event is found in the life with other persons. Here the full mutuality of relation is evident, especially by way of the instrument of language. Through the mutuality of address and response the individual learns about the true nature of the self and the world. One realizes that the universe of things, experiences, causality, and necessity can be broken through by means of the life of dialogue. Each person has the possibility of raising themselves above egotist forces and truly caring and being responsible for others; this is expressed as: "Love is responsibility of an I for a Thou" (p. 66). The goal of living is not to annihilate the self but to live fully and freely with others in the human world.

Beyond the three spheres of relation is the encounter with God: "Extended, the lines of relationship intersect in the eternal Thou" (Buber, 1923/1970, p. 123). According to Buber, the life with other persons is, in particular, the preparation for the life with God. Even more than that, Buber holds that the life with other persons eventually points to a Power that is beyond the human. For Buber, the experience of revelation or the meeting with God has three aspects (pp. 157–160). First, one is aware that there is a Presence. Second, one grasps that life has meaning and purpose, even though no statement or dogma can contain this fundamental awareness. Third, one is directed from the relation to God back into the world. As Buber writes, "Man can do justice to the relation to God that has been given to him only by actualizing God in the world in accordance with his ability and the measure of each day, daily" (p. 163), and one must act through "the power of loving responsibility for the whole unexplorable course of the world" (p. 157). Among other things, this demands that one see the social world not as an illusion to be repudiated, but a dimension to be completed (pp. 156–157).

In Franz Rosenzweig's (1925/1999) essay "The New Thinking," which he allowed to be appended as the introduction to his earlier magnum opus *The Star of Redemption*, Rosenzweig represents himself as a "speech-thinker" (p. 87). It is in this vein that his relational understanding of life is expressed. Much as with Buber and the central roles given to dialogue and even the basic words "I and Thou" and "I and It," language and speech are the key to Rosenzweig's philosophical anthropology.

Rosenzweig (1925/1999) contrasts the "new thinking" and its "method of speech" revealing the relationality, temporality, and flow of life, with traditional philosophy's "method of thinking" and its elevation of the solitary individual and the quest for static essences (pp. 86–87). He writes,

> Speech is bound to time, nourished by time, [and] it neither can nor wants to abandon this ground of nourishment; it does not know beforehand where it will emerge; it lets itself be given its cues from others; it actually lives by another's life. . . . To need time means: not to be able to presuppose anything, to have to wait for everything; to be dependent on the other for what is ours.
>
> *(pp. 86–87)*

Rosenzweig is insistent on noting the place of temporality in human experience. Processes and developments have their stages and duration; they transpire in specific series over time. Providing a phenomenological approach to concrete living in the world, he offers as examples that one cannot just "begin a conversation with the end, or a war with a peace treaty . . . or life with death" (p. 83).

Rosenzweig uses the paradigm of speech or conversation to reveal the nature of the interhuman or intersubjective matrix in which persons live. In the back-and-forth of conversation, the physical boundaries between self and other, the whole idea of what is "ours" or what one takes as one's own thought is eclipsed. A word emerges out of the conversation – who remembers which person first spoke it? – and it turns the whole direction of what occurs afterwards. In responding to another's words, being cued by the other, one often introduces an idea that one did not have and could not have before.

The development of persons through encounters with others requires an openness, a willingness to address, to listen, and to be changed. Rosenzweig (1920/2005) understands that there is a fundamental obstacle to this, which he characterizes in *The Star of Redemption* as the fear of death. The traumatic awareness of the inevitability of death can easily become so intense that an individual is paralyzed, speechless, withdrawn into the self, and closed off from authentic relationships to others. Actually Rosenzweig sees this as the natural state of humans, for which "death has become the event that dominates . . . life" (p. 85). What alleviates this is Revelation. Revelation is a transformative meeting between God and the individual, which echoes in the ensuing relationships between persons.

Rosenzweig's (1920/2005) poetic treatment of Revelation draws upon the love sequence in the biblical text of the "Song of Songs" (pp. 213–219). The scene between an initiating lover and the receptive beloved, in harmony with traditional Jewish interpretations, is understood as describing the relationship between God and the individual or soul. God's call to the soul, expressed by the commandment to love God with all one's heart, is itself a manifestation of God's love. A trust in God and the world ensues and releases the individual from that earlier isolation, chained in by the fear of death. However, the empowering commandment to love God is quickly followed by a second commandment, which is to love the neighbor. "Only the soul loved by God can receive the commandment of neighborly love so far as to fulfill it" (p. 231). Guided by this obligation, the individual is directed into the world, where the initial divine love is spread from person to person. Rosenzweig captures this latter process under the term Redemption. In his words, "Where someone or something has become the neighbor of the soul, a part of the world becomes what it was not before: soul" (p. 252).

In less metaphoric language, Rosenzweig (1920/2005) is suggesting that there is a transformative function in the human concern for others, in love and in speech. In light of love's miraculous power, it draws upon a transcendent source.

> For it is not possible for love to be "purely human." When it begins to speak – and this it must do, for there exists no other utterance spoken besides itself than the language of love – so when love speaks, it is already changed into something superhuman; for the sensuous character of the word is full to the brim with its divine supra-sensuous meaning; like language itself love is at once sensible and supra-sensuous.
>
> *(p. 216)*

As an obligation, the turning to others is not just a feeling or a choice; it is an essential responsibility that gives meaning and direction to one's particular and unique path "into life" (p. 447).

Emmanuel Levinas offers a parallel philosophic version of *homo duplex*, that is, the twofold tension within the self, to Buber's I–Thou and I–It, and Rosenzweig's isolated self and transformed soul. Pieced together from his major philosophical works, *Totality and Infinity* and *Otherwise than Being or Beyond Essence*, Levinas sees a fundamental split between one's elemental egoism and that inescapable call of responsibility for the other.[8] He characterizes one polarity within the I as being essentially turned back upon itself or being self-absorbed. He writes in *Totality and Infinity* that "to be an I is . . . to have identity as one's content" (1961/1969, p. 36). This mode of existence is not innocent. Other persons are encountered, but only as objects, subject to my freedom and power (p. 84). The other is something to be dominated, possessed, or discarded, to be incorporated, surmounted, enveloped by my world – the same – or to be wiped out. Here freedom is arbitrary and unjustified, and beneath it lurks a murderous and violent self. This is the "I" of egoism, which Levinas does not hesitate to characterize from the point of view of ethics as "detestable" (p. 88).

While the self is ruled by its own self-interest, enjoyment, and happiness, it can also be pulled or inspired by a metaphysical desire for what is beyond itself. This desire is metaphysical in the sense that it is in a totally different plane than drives or needs which emerge from within oneself. In *Otherwise than Being* this dimension is discussed in terms of the way that subjectivity is an openness to the other: "Subjectivity . . . obligated with regard to the neighbor, is the breaking point where essence is exceeded by the infinite" (Levinas, 1974/1981, p. 12). The radical openness to the other, the inability to shut off the other's summons despite one's pretensions to autonomy and autocracy, is what Levinas designates as the I's "vulnerability" (p. 15).

For Levinas (1974/1981), egoism is not more "original" than love, the unconditioned desire for the other. This love for the other cannot be accounted for in history or biography. It affects the self as "an anachronous birth, prior to its own present, a non-beginning, an anarchy" (p. 139). Levinas means by this that the seizure by the other is structured into human existence and endures as the basis for subjectivity. The very "corporeality" of the human, the receptiveness of the skin or the breath taken into one's lungs, stand as bodily metaphors for this vulnerability of the I (pp. 51, 180–181).

The "face to face" relationship, particularly as depicted in *Totality and Infinity*, features that "dissymmetry" or asymmetry between the self and other/neighbor that characterizes authentic existence. In the encounter with the other the first impression upon the self is the forcefulness of a silent command: "you shall not commit murder" (Levinas, 1961/1969,

p. 262). This is correlative with the potential murderousness of one's freedom and power, and also the nakedness and defenselessness of the other's face. While a divine voice is not heard here, the command certainly represents a "clandestine dimension of the judgment of God," which has called the self to justify itself (p. 247). The other – or, in biblical language, the neighbor, poor, widow, orphan, and stranger – thus overturns my being-for-myself. They are experienced as both commanding and exposed, or in Levinas' vocabulary, in both the other's "height" and "destitution," as in "The transcendence of the other, which is his eminence, his height, his lordship, in its concrete meaning includes his destitution, his exile, and his rights as a stranger" (pp. 76–77).

Since the egoism of the self is so entrenched, the shattering of the individual's natural attitude must be extreme. The language Levinas (1974/1981) utilizes is violent: in order to achieve authentic subjectivity, the individual must be traumatized, hollowed out, inverted, extroverted, denucleated, even persecuted. In his words, "The subjectivity of the subject is persecution and martyrdom" (p. 146). The individual is made nothing less than a "substitute" or "hostage" to the other (p. 146). The most pervasive characteristic of that self given over to the other is responsibility (p. 15). The self, turned upon itself and de-legitimatized in its own eyes, subsequently becomes a responding, responsible being. The individual comes to recognize – to be obsessed with – an unrelenting responsibility, where one must answer with a biblical "here I am . . . for everything and for everyone" (p. 114). Importantly, not only is the self made responsible, but it is granted the powers to fulfill that which it is called upon to give.

Levinas' philosophical aversion to the self-constitution in the Cartesian *cogito ergo sum*, Spinoza's self-preservation or *conatus essendi*, and especially Heidegger's (1927/1962) "loyalty of existence to its own self" (p. 443), as the basis for a life of meaning and authenticity is palpable. In "Dialogue with Emmanuel Levinas," an interview first published in 1984, he writes,

> I am trying to show that man's ethical relation to the other is ultimately prior to his ontological relationship to himself (egology).
>
> *(1986, p. 21)*

> That is why I prefaced *Otherwise than Being or Beyond Essence* with Pascal's phrase, "'That is my place in the sun.' That is how the usurpation of the whole world began." Pascal makes the same point when he declares that "the self is hateful." Pascal's ethical sentiments here go against the ontological privileging of "the right to exist."
>
> *(p. 24)*

In all, Buber, Rosenzweig, and Levinas exemplify the commitment to ethics, which has been the hallmark of Jewish philosophy throughout its history.[9] They see this commitment as drawing upon a transcendent source, one which assigns the responsibility that must pervade every human relationship. In the afterword to *I and Thou*, Buber (1923/1970) unveils the "crucial vision" behind the work, which is "the close association of the relation to God with the relation to one's fellow-men" (p. 171). This sentiment is expressed by Rosenzweig (1920/2005) in his immediate juxtaposing of the two commandments: "Love for God must be externalized in love for the neighbor" (p. 230). For Levinas (1982/1985), in responding to the call of the other, the divine enters into language and experience: "I will say that the subject who says 'Here I am!' *testifies* to the Infinite. It is through this testimony . . . that the revelation of the Infinite occurs; . . . that the very glory of the infinite glorifies *itself*" (pp. 106–107).

Conclusion

As we have seen, the dual themes of intersubjectivity and ethics, so prominent in the works of Benjamin and Orange, are also central axes in the texts of Buber, Rosenzweig, and Levinas. Yet the treatment of the Jewish philosophers' works in the two psychoanalysts' writings could not be more divergent. Despite obvious similarities between the concept of the I–Thou relation and Benjamin's discussions of thirdness and the moral third, only in her latest text are there fleeting references to him (Benjamin 2018, pp. 10, 74).[10] Alternately, Benjamin's critical disagreement with Levinas is extensive and raises two issues. In essence, she insists that some identification with another, based upon similarity to the self, is an essential element in every relationship of dignity and value. Benjamin believes that this is impossible if the other person is viewed as totally other. In addition, she finds that Levinas' idea of "the essential, absolute and asymmetrical responsibility for the Other's suffering" controverts the significance that "the reciprocity of recognition and mutual knowing" has for both participants in the relationship (Benjamin 2018, p. 95).[11]

The philosophies of both Buber and Levinas play substantial roles in Orange's thinking and expositions. Appropriately, Buber is the first philosopher discussed in *Thinking for Clinicians*. Seeing herself as a dialogical analyst who shares with Buber the understanding that relatedness is the primary situation of humans, the philosophy of *I and Thou* is a continual resource for her (2009, pp. 234–235). Especially in the clinical context, Orange (2010) draws upon Buber's view of the mutuality of dialogue; the reaching over to experience the feelings, perceptions, and thinking of the other without erasing the particularity of both partners; and the confirming of the other in their present life as well as with a view toward the open potentialities that await in the future (pp. 24–30). Paramount in Orange's work is Levinas' notion of the infinite responsibility for the other; she recognizes in his philosophy the very essence of the ethical turn in psychoanalysis. This responsibility rests on allowing the traumatic suffering of the other to overwhelm the self's autonomy and sovereignty, and then, through responsive witnessing, refusing to be an accomplice in evil. While acknowledging that Levinas' ethical portrayal is radical and extreme, Orange (2016) argues that it is also necessary and empowering: "Though the ethic of responsibility – framed in response to extreme situations, and full of traumatic memory – often sounds extreme, it grounds itself in everyday proximity to those unexpected interpellations, situations that ethically call us out" (p. 30).

Of the three Jewish philosophers, only Buber offers detailed reflections on psychoanalysis.[12] For example, in a seminar on "The Unconscious" in 1957, he presents a view of the discipline, which anticipates major features within the contemporary relational stream. He writes,

> In the last ten years or so I have the impression of a certain change in psychotherapeutic practice in which more and more therapists are not so confident that this or that theory is right and have a more "musical," floating, relationship to their patient. The deciding reality is the therapist, not the methods. . . . He knows that at a certain moment the incomparable person of the patient stands before the incomparable person of the doctor . . . and accepts this unforeseeable thing that goes on between therapist and patient.
> *(1999, pp. 236–237)*

The quotation touches upon what is now seen as "two-person therapy," in the full intersubjective mode: that analysis is fundamentally about two persons in an encounter, that the analyst sees the other as a unique person and draws upon themselves as a person, that there are often "unforeseeable" events in the encounter that must be accepted and faced with little guidance from theory or technique.

In summation, this presentation examines the work of Benjamin and Orange as two examples of the ethical turn in Relational Psychoanalysis. For these psychoanalysts and the Jewish philosophers Buber, Rosenzweig, and Levinas, the prominence given to ethics is built upon an understanding of the primacy of intersubjectivity. The psychoanalysts explore two dimensions of this connection, the therapist's responsibility to the patient, and the notion of ethical witnessing to the other as a central element in the pursuit of health or authenticity, that is, in the constitution of a meaningful life. The Jewish philosophers emphasize the transcendent source or inspiration of the responsibility to the other through the divine commandment to love the neighbor.

There are many differences in the two approaches, most clearly seen in terms of the dynamics of the dialogue between therapist and patient in the psychoanalytic discussion, and the treatment of the divine as a transcendent dialogue partner in the philosophical exposition. There are also diverse emphases concerning the role of similarity and difference in genuine relationships. There is perhaps a heightened sensitivity, especially for Benjamin, to similarity and the clinical role of identification and empathy, while the Jewish philosophers emphasize the separation of or difference between the self and the other.[13] They are particularly apprehensive about the possible appropriation of the other, which Levinas (1961/1969) precludes through his notion of the "infinity" or absolute otherness of the neighbor and stranger.

Still, in light of the parallels between these discourses, it is not surprising that Levinas and, to a somewhat lesser extent, Buber, have had a strong impact on post-Freudian psychoanalysis.[14] Rosenzweig, admittedly offering a very challenging exposition, has been left behind. Yet, in light of the influence he personally had on Buber and his philosophy had on Levinas,[15] it is critical that his work be explored further.

Notes

1 Although there is a progressive, humanistic vision behind Freud's work, the classical model of clinical technique sanctions abstinence, neutrality, and objectivity. Psychoanalysts are seen as detached scientific observers, prohibited from becoming emotionally involved with the patient or providing encouragement, gratification, and suggestions. Their task is to provide "objective" interpretations. The psychoanalytic approach of Benjamin and Orange is representative of a significant change in this therapeutic dynamic, an "ethical turn."

2 A wider discussion of the concept of meaning in contemporary psychoanalytic literature is presented in the author's chapter "Revisiting an 'Illusion': On Meaning" (Oppenheim, 2017, pp. 135–167).

3 While Walter Kaufmann translates Buber's book title *Ich und Du* as *I and Thou*, he translates the German *Du* as "You" throughout the text of his translation. He explains this decision in his prologue to Buber's text (Buber, 1923/1970, pp. 14–15). However, I continue to use "Thou" rather than "You" when quoting from his translation.

4 See the treatment of the origins of the relational tradition (Mitchell & Aron, 1999, pp. x–xii).

5 For a wider treatment, see *The Ethical Turn in Psychoanalysis* (Goodman & Severson, 2016).

6 Samuel Gerson (2004) describes a variety of different uses of the term "the third" in the psychoanalytic literature (p. 65). All nine articles in this 2004 issue of *Psychoanalytic Quarterly* are dedicated to examining the history and concept of the third in psychoanalytic theory and practice.

7 Benjamin (1995) earlier argued that moral ideals, or what she called "normative ideals," were outside the parameters of psychoanalysis (pp. 20–21).

8 Some of this section is adapted from the author's earlier work (Oppenheim, 2017, pp. 27–29).

9 Steven S. Schwarzschild (1972) has explained the centrality of ethics throughout the history of Jewish philosophy: "The view held here . . . is that philosophy is Jewish by virtue of a transhistorical primacy of ethics" (p. 629).

10 See the author's chapter "Jessica Benjamin and [the Missing] Martin Buber: On Intersubjectivity" (Oppenheim, 2017, pp. 51–74).

11 This is also one of Benjamin's (2018) criticisms of Orange's use of Levinas (pp. 95–96).

12 Among Levinas' reflections on psychoanalysis, see (1981, p. 194, 2001, p. 118). Buber (1999) also joined in a long dialogue with the psychologist Carl Rogers (pp. 246–270).

13 There is a comparison of Benjamin's view of similarity and Buber's treatment of difference or separation as the primary foundation for authentic relationships in the author's *Contemporary Psychoanalysis and Modern Jewish Philosophy* (Oppenheim, 2017, pp. 59–60). This emphasis on respecting difference is also important for Rosenzweig and especially in Levinas' (1969) notion of "the infinite distance of the Stranger" or Other (p. 50).

14 See Henry Abramovich's (2015) "The Influence of Martin Buber's Philosophy of Dialogue on Psychotherapy." *The Ethical Turn* (Goodman & Severson, 2016) provides a good presentation of various aspects of Levinas' tremendous impact.

15 A treatment of Rosenzweig's relationship with and influence on Buber is presented in Mendes-Flohr's (2019) chapter "A Reverential Apikoros: Friendship with Rosenzweig" (pp. 132–162). Rosenzweig's impact on Levinas (1969) is signaled by the latter's early statement in *Totality and Infinity*, "We were impressed by the opposition to the idea of totality in Franz Rosenzweig's *Stern der Erlösung*, a work too often present in this book to be cited" (p. 28).

References

Abramovich, H. (2015). The influence of Martin Buber's philosophy of dialogue on psychotherapy. In P. Mendes-Flohr (Ed.), *Dialogue as a trans-disciplinary concept: Martin Buber's philosophy of dialogue and its contemporary reception* (pp. 169–182). Berlin: De Gruyter.

Benjamin, J. (1988). *The bonds of love: Psychoanalysis, feminism, and the problem of domination*. New York, NY: Pantheon Books.

Benjamin, J. (1995). *Like subjects, love objects: Essays on recognition and sexual difference*. New Haven, CT: Yale University Press.

Benjamin, J. (1998). *Shadow of the other: Intersubjectivity and gender in psychoanalysis*. New York, NY: Routledge.

Benjamin, J. (1999). Recognition and destruction: An outline of intersubjectivity. In S. A. Mitchell & L. Aron (Eds.), *Relational psychoanalysis: The emergence of a tradition* (pp. 181–210). Hillsdale, NJ: The Analytic Press.

Benjamin, J. (2012). Beyond doer and done to: An intersubjective view of thirdness. In L. Aron & A. Harris (Eds.), *Relational psychoanalysis vol. 4: Expansion of theory* (pp. 91–130). New York, NY: Routledge.

Benjamin, J. (2018). *Beyond doer and done to: Recognition theory, intersubjectivity and the third*. London, England: Routledge.

Buber, M. (1965). *Between man and man*. New York, NY: Collier Books (Original work published 1947).

Buber, M. (1970). *I and Thou* (W. Kaufmann, Trans.). New York, NY: Charles Scribner's Sons (Original work published 1923).

Buber, M. (1999). *Martin Buber on psychology and psychotherapy: Essays, letters, and dialogue* (Judith Buber Agassi, Ed.). Syracuse, NY: Syracuse University Press.

Gerson, S. (2004). The relational unconscious: A core element of intersubjectivity, thirdness, and clinical progress. *Psychoanalytic Quarterly*, 73.1, 63–98.

Goodman, D., & Severson, E., eds. (2016). *The ethical turn: Otherness and subjectivity in contemporary psychoanalysis*. New York, NY: Routledge.

Heidegger, M. (1962). *Being and time* (J. Macquarrie & E. Robinson, Trans.). New York, NY: Harper and Row Publishers (Original work published 1927).

Levinas, E. (1969). *Totality and infinity: An essay on exteriority* (A. Lingis, Trans.). Pittsburgh, PA: Duquesne University Press (Original work published 1961).

Levinas, E. (1981). *Otherwise than being or beyond essence* (A. Lingis, Trans.). The Hague, Netherlands: Martinus Nijhoff Publishers (Original work published 1974).

Levinas, E. (1985). Ethics and infinity: Conversations with Philippe Nemo (R. Cohen, Trans.). Pittsburgh, PA: Duquesne University Press (Original work published 1982).

Levinas, E. (1986). *Face to face with Levinas*. Albany, NY: State University of New York Press.

Levinas, E. (2001). *Is it righteous to be?: Interviews with Emmanuel Levinas*. Stanford, CA: Stanford University Press.

Mendes-Flohr, P. (2019). *Martin Buber: A life of faith and dissent*. New Haven, CT: Yale University Press.

Mitchell, S. A. (1993). *Hope and dread in psychoanalysis*. New York, NY: Basic Books.

Mitchell, S. A. (2000). *Relationality: From attachment to intersubjectivity*. Hillsdale, NJ: Analytic Press.

Mitchell, S. A., & Aron, L., eds. (1999). *Relational psychoanalysis*: The emergence of a tradition. Hillsdale, NJ: The Analytic Press.

Oppenheim, M. (2017). *Contemporary psychoanalysis and modern Jewish philosophy: Two languages of love*. London: Routledge.
Orange, D. M. (2009). Postscript: From postmodern skepticism to the search for psychoanalytic understanding. In R. Frie & D. Orange (Eds.), *Beyond postmodernism: New dimensions in clinical theory and practice* (pp. 231–235). New York, NY: Routledge.
Orange, D. M. (2010). *Thinking for clinicians: Philosophical resources for contemporary psychoanalysis and the humanistic psychotherapies*. New York, NY: Routledge.
Orange, D. M. (2011). *The suffering stranger: Hermeneutics for everyday clinical practice*. New York, NY: Routledge.
Orange, D. M. (2016). *Nourishing the inner life of clinicians and humanitarians: The ethical turn in psychoanalysis*. New York, NY: Routledge.
Orange, D. M. (2017). *Climate crisis, psychoanalysis, and radical ethics*. New York, NY: Routledge.
Putnam, H. (2008). *Jewish philosophy as a guide to life: Rosenzweig, Buber, Levinas, Wittgenstein*. Bloomington, IN: Indiana University Press.
Rosenzweig, F. (1999). The new thinking: A few supplementary remarks to the star (A. Udoff & B. E. Galli, Trans.). In A. Udoff & B. E. Galli (Eds.), *Franz Rosenzweig's "The new thinking"* (pp. 67–102). Syracuse, NY: Syracuse University Press. (Original work published 1925)
Rosenzweig, F. (2005). *The star of redemption* (B. Galli, Trans.). Madison, WI: Wisconsin University Press (Original work published 1920).
Schwarzschild, S. S. (1972). Modern Jewish philosophy. In A. A. Cohen & P. Mendes-Flohr (Eds.), *Contemporary Jewish religious thought: Original essays on critical concepts, movements, and beliefs* (pp. 629–634). New York, NY: The Free Press.

27
ETHICS OF DISCONTENT

Shai Frogel

This chapter analyzes the ethics of psychoanalysis. Ethics is not used here in the sense of morality or in the sense of an ethical code, as it is often used today, but in its original philosophical meaning of a stance regarding human good life. In the history of philosophy, two great works carry the title "Ethics" – those of Aristotle and Spinoza. Both works present a stance regarding human good life, which is based on their conception of the human psyche. The present chapter applies this conception of ethics in examining the ethics of psychoanalysis.

Freud made great efforts to convince his scientific colleagues that psychoanalysis is not an ethical stance but a science. However, in his essays on culture, he lays out a very clear ethical view maintaining that secular existence is superior to a religious one, using his psychological theory to justify this stance. Furthermore, as his thinking progresses, he puts increasing weight on the cultural aspect of the psyche, which obliges him to replace his earlier biological terms with ethical ones.

This line of thought links Freud and psychoanalysis with the development of modern secular ethics. Modern secular ethics begins with Spinoza's *Ethics*, where he explains our moral values in psychological terms rather than in religious ones and relates human good life to intellectual self-emancipation and not to religious faith. It continues with Nietzsche's declaration on the "death of God" and his redefinition of human existence in psychological terms rather than metaphysical ones. The claim in this paper is that Freud takes this psychological turn in human thought further and proposes a new ethics that rejects religious and metaphysical ideas of salvation in the name of the reality principle and highlights the conflictual existence of the modern individual. This ethics underlies psychoanalysis and grants its philosophical justification.

Ethics: The Question of Human Good Life

The purpose of philosophy, according to Socrates, is achieving a good life or "a good spirit" (*eudemonia*). He advises achieving this goal through a dialogue that allows the interlocutors to heal any contradictions they have in their souls for a better understanding of their existence.[1] This recognition is, according to this view, the origin of both virtue and happiness, since it allows for a life guided by the truth. Socrates does not label this practice ethics, but his philosophical activity actually outlines the meaning of this concept in traditional philosophy.

DOI: 10.4324/9780429297076-32

Aristotle's and Spinoza's "Ethics" follow Socrates' path; both introduce a practice of existential enhancement based on their psychological theory.[2] Freud did the same. I therefore propose understanding psychoanalysis as an ethical stance. Furthermore, similar to Socrates, Aristotle, and Spinoza, Freud probes the connection between human good life and morality. The Oedipus complex, an idea that Freud assumes to underlie both individual psychology and culture, illustrates this point well by linking together primary desires and basic cultural taboos. However, before delving deeper in a discussion of the ethics of psychoanalysis, further clarification of the philosophical concept of ethics is required.

Aristotle's *Ethics* begins with an unequivocal statement:

> Every craft and every inquiry, and similarly actions and choices, are thought to aim at some good; that is way the good has rightly been declared to be that at which all things aim.
>
> *(Aristotle, 2014, p. 215 [1094a])*

The concept of the good is central to ethical discussion. It is only natural therefore, that Aristotle begins his work by a logical elucidation of the concept. Logically, he argues, the concept of the good stands for accomplishing a certain purpose. To judge whether something is good or bad, one must therefore know its purpose. Since ethics deals with the question of a good human life, one must first ask what the purpose of human life is. Surprising as it may sound, Aristotle thinks that the answer to this question is simple and accepted by most humans:

> Verbally, pretty well everyone agrees; for both the general run of people and the refined say that it is happiness and assume that living well and faring well are the same thing as being happy.
>
> *(ibid., p. 218 [1095a])*

Aristotle uses this broad acceptation as the point of departure for his investigation.[3] After probing the true meaning of human happiness, he concludes that happiness means realizing one's virtue, since "every virtue both brings into good condition the thing of which it is the virtue and also makes it perform its task well" (ibid., p. 244 [1106a]). Aristotle emphasizes that "By human virtue we mean not that of the body but that of the soul; and happiness we call an activity of soul" (ibid., p. 235 [1102a]).

Therefore, he analyzes the human soul and concludes that there are two kinds of human virtue: intellectual and moral. The first is developed by learning and the second by habit. Aristotle's ethical discussion focuses on the second, given the practical rather than theoretical context of his discussion. In spite of that, he ends his discussion with the conclusion that "happiness, therefore, must be some form of contemplation" (ibid., p. 364 [1178b]). He explains this conclusion saying that contrary to our intellectual virtue, our moral virtue also involves emotions that partially depends on external circumstances. Aristotle acknowledges that living a purely contemplative life is impossible, since human existence is also physical and social. This recalls Socrates, who claims that human beings cannot be wise but mostly becoming "lovers of wisdom" (philosophers). In Aristotle's ethical view, then, a life of contemplation is an ideal rather than a realistic goal. Like a lighthouse, it should guide human existence.

Over 2,000 years after Aristotle, Spinoza defines the goal of his *Ethics* in the same way:

> I pass on now to explain those things which must necessarily follow from the essence of God or the Being eternal and infinite; not indeed to explain all these things, for we

> have demonstrated (Proposition 16, part I) that an infinitude of things must follow in an infinite number of ways – but to consider those things only which may conduct us as it were by the hand to the knowledge of the human mind and its highest happiness.
>
> *(Spinoza, 2001, p. 45)*

Spinoza's *Ethics* begins with an ontological proof of the immanent nature of reality. However, the above quotation, which is the short introduction to part two of his work, defines the purpose of the entire work: "knowledge of the human mind and its highest happiness" (ibid.). He argues that the intellect, being the essence of the human mind, is the source of both human morality and happiness. Morality, according to Spinoza, derives from our ability to universalize psychological affects through our intellect, and is a necessary condition for achieving superior human happiness, which he defines as *amor Dei intellectualis* (intellectual love of God). This concept of happiness could be interpreted as a modern articulation of the Socratic idea of philosophy (love of wisdom) and Aristotle's definition of happiness as a contemplative life. Yet, the intellect is not alone in the philosophers' definition of happiness. It is accompanied by the concept of desire (*philia/amor*), which is crucial in a discussion of the ethics of psychoanalysis. Spinoza, similar to Plato and Aristotle, sees ethical development as elevating human desire from its emotional state to an intellectual one.

Freud rejects the traditional philosophical view of a rational psyche, claiming that instincts and drives make the core of our psychological life and not the intellect. Our psyche, according to this view, has biological origins and is not metaphysical. Freud was not the first to express this view, but he was one of the first to formulate a systematic psychological theory based on this assumption. Psychoanalysis developed to be an original view of the human psyche. It rejects the old metaphysical views of philosophy and religion while also conflicting with the scientific psychology, which reduces human psychology to mere empirical facts. Freud's orientation in developing his theory of psychoanalysis was initially biological. Yet as his work progressed, he realized that the human psyche is as much a cultural phenomenon as a biological one. His conceptualizations of the Oedipus complex and the super-ego are genuine outcomes of this realization. It also made him introduce ethical terms into his psychoanalytic theory and discussing culture in his essays. In those essays, Freud explores the interrelations between culture and individual psychology but also the secular ethical ground of psychoanalysis. He claims that religious faith is a deeply illusion whose historical role has ended, and the time has come to overcome it. This idea links Freud and psychoanalysis with the emergent secular ethics in modern thought. The beginnings of this ethics are commonly thought to go back to Spinoza's *Ethics*, where he rejects the idea of a transcendent God and argues in favor of ethics based on human understanding and not on faith. Nietzsche's symbolic declaration on the "death of God" and his call for reevaluation of human values was another important philosophical milestone in the development of this ethics. Nietzsche recognized himself the similarity between Spinoza's central ideas and his, while Freud admitted that Nietzsche's ideas preceded his thought.[4] This historical and philosophical linkage is the subject of the next section, where I show how Spinoza's and Nietzsche's thought paved the way for the ethics of psychoanalysis.

Secular Ethics: From Ethical Psychology to Psychological Ethics

As shown in the first part of this chapter, ethics is concerned with human good life. Because monotheistic religion monopolized western culture, the origin and authority of ethics have related to the transcendent God. Morality and happiness have been regarded as the products of religious faith, and sinning as the cause of psychological distress. One might name this approach "ethical psychology", where the ethical outlook determines the psychological one. In this section, the central argument is that secular ethics has turned this perspective upside down by deriving human ethics from human psychology, creating a psychological ethics. The basic assumption underlying ethics of this kind is that investigation of the human psyche is a prerequisite in formulating an ethical outlook. In fact, this is how secular modern thinkers have revived Aristotle's approach to ethics. Freud's theory of psychoanalysis is part of the historical turn begun by Spinoza and brought significantly closer to psychoanalysis in Nietzsche's philosophy.

Spinoza: Immanent Ethics

Spinoza's immanent ontology and ethics were born from the modern spirit of the natural sciences. In his time, natural scientists began explaining natural phenomena by the laws of nature and not a transcendent cause. Indeed, these sciences secularized nature by disconnecting its laws from God. Spinoza's philosophy continued this revolution by giving it an ontological justification and by formulating an ethical view to suit it.

The first truth of Spinoza's philosophy is that reality is necessarily one whole and could not be otherwise since the idea of a transcendent reality (i.e., a reality beyond reality) is self-contradictory. By this, Spinoza excludes the possibility of a transcendent God, and maintains that the concepts of God and Nature refer to the same thing (*Deus sive Natura*), which is the only infinite reality. He rejects the old image of two worlds, heaven and earth, and replaces it by that of one world ruled by its own laws. This new ontology calls for formulating a new kind of ethics, based on the immanent nature of human beings and not on a transcendent authority.

Spinoza formulates a new ethics that is built on four central hypotheses which he validates in different parts of *Ethics*:

1 The intellect is the active aspect and essence of the human mind (Part II, under the title: "Nature and the Origin of the Mind").
2 The affects are the passive aspect and bondage of the human mind (Part III, under the title: "Origin and the Nature of Affects").
3 Morality is an outcome of the intellectualization of the affects (Part IV, under the title: "On Human Bondage").
4 Happiness means intellectual emancipation (Part V, under the title: "Of the Power of the Intellect").

Spinoza's ethics regards humans as rational beings whose existence is also determined by affects. This explains our need for moral concepts, which are intellectualizations of our feelings of joy and sorrow towards achieving happiness. In this process, the intellect releases the mind of the bondage of the affects and directs it towards self-emancipation. Moral concepts are, then, human inventions expressing human weakness and passivity (affects) but also power and activity (intellect). This explains Spinoza's definition of happiness as *amor dei intellectualis* (intellectual love of God), which stands for loving reality in its entirety as a consequence of intellectual emancipation. Despite mentioning God in the definition of happiness, this is secular ethics because God refers here to reality as a whole and not to a divine and transcendent authority. Underlying this ethics is human understanding rather than faith, and its purpose does not go beyond the actual life of human beings. As Spinoza puts it, "A free man thinks of nothing less than of death, and his wisdom is not a meditation upon death but upon life" (Spinoza, 2001, p. 212).

Spinoza brings ethics back from God's heaven to the actual human existence on earth. This signifies a psychological turn in the understanding of human ethics that originates from rejecting the transcendent world and the consequent need to formulate ethics in immanent terms. In formulating his ethics, Spinoza uses the psychological terms "affects" and "intellect" to argue that the shift from a life determined by affects to a life that is increasingly guided by the intellect enhances human existence. The intellect makes humans live up to their common essence, thus making a moral life possible. Morality, however, is not a purpose of itself but a means to achieving a better human existence. Since the intellect is the essence of the human mind, a full accomplishment of its potential is the only way to reach the most elevated state of human existence, which Spinoza names *amor dei intellectualis*. At this level of existence, the intellect alone determines one's desire (love), directing it towards the reality as a whole (God). By formulating his concept of happiness in terms of desire, Spinoza relates both to the ancient Greek idea of philosophy (love of wisdom) and to the new ethics of desire, psychoanalysis.[5]

Psychoanalysis does not share, however, Spinoza's metaphysical language and his belief that human beings are rational. The philosopher who takes the new secular view a step further towards psychoanalysis is Friedrich Nietzsche. To Spinoza's rejection of the transcendent God, Nietzsche adds the rejection of the metaphysical idea of human essence. Historical and biological forces determine individual human existence, he argues, and not a common essence, and this process is mostly unconscious. New ethics is therefore required that recognizes the individuality of each human being and is not based on the idea of a common good. "And how should there be a 'common good'!", he writes in *Beyond Good and Evil*. "The term contradicts itself: whatever can be common always has little value" (Nietzsche, 1989, p. 53). Nietzsche's philosophy replaces the abstractions of traditional philosophy, including Spinoza's, with the concrete life of the human individual. He does it by rejecting the idea of metaphysical truth, which he interprets as hostile to life, and therefore a bad foundation for human ethics. Instead, he proposes new ethics of life, which corresponds better to the view that human beings are organisms with a historical consciousness rather than metaphysical entities locked in physical bodies.

Nietzsche: Ethics of Life

"There are no moral phenomena at all", Nietzsche argues in his book *Beyond Good and Evil*, "but only a moral interpretation of phenomena" (ibid., p. 85). This statement is often mentioned to indicate Nietzsche's radical and even nihilistic thought. In the present context, however, it may serve to demonstrate a continuity between Spinoza's and Nietzsche's thought. Long before Nietzsche, Spinoza argued that morality is not embodied in the structure of the world but is a human invention based on an interpretation of the world from the human perspective. Yet there is a crucial difference between their approaches: while Spinoza argues for moral universalism based on a common human essence, Nietzsche argues for moral individualism based on human individuality. This difference represents a turn from the old concept of ethics of truth to the Nietzsche's new concept of ethics of life.

In his introduction to *Beyond Good and Evil*, Nietzsche accuses traditional religion and philosophy of planting wrong ideas in the minds of people. The most dangerous, he argues is "Plato's invention of the pure spirit and the good as such" (ibid., p. 2). He argues that such utopian ideas generate hostility towards actual life by judging it as poor, bad, and false. In his earlier book *The Gay Science*, he already suggested that these failed and dangerous ideas originate in the will to truth, which could be interpreted, he suggests, as a concealed will to death:

> Charitably interpreted, such a resolve might perhaps be a Quixotism, a minor slightly mad enthusiasm; but it might also be something more serious, namely, a principle that is hostile to life and destructive – "Will to truth" – that might be a concealed will to death.
>
> *(Nietzsche, 1974, p. 282)*

The interpretation of the will to truth as "a concealed will to death" indicates the general direction of Nietzsche's thought, particularly his ethical thought. He introduces an alternative to the ethics of truth, which puts at its center the actual life of the individual human being as an unavoidable conclusion from "the death of God."

Nietzsche's declaration on "the death of God" was first a sociological observation rather than a philosophical conclusion. It represented the historical fact that in the western culture of his time a growing number of people no longer believed in the existence of God. This crisis or "event", in his terms, sent him on a philosophical journey of examining the idea of truth and especially the human need for metaphysical truths. He concludes that the origin of our truths, especially metaphysical ones such as "the good in itself" or God, lies in our existential fears and weaknesses. These truths, he argues, are nothing more than existential supports that help us stabilize our fragile existence. He formulates this psychological idea in section 347 of *The Gay Science*, titled "Believers and Their Need to Believe":

> How much one needs a faith (*Glaube*) in order to flourish, how much that is "firm" and that one does not wish to be shaken because one clings to it, that is a measure of degree of one strength (or, to put the point more clearly, of one's weakness).
>
> *(ibid., p. 287)*

Nietzsche sees a direct connection between existential weakness and faith. This thought is not foreign to the monotheistic religions, which underscore the weakness of man to praise the power of God. However, Nietzsche's emphasis intends to undermine religion as such; religious truths that are rooted in human weakness are necessarily very doubtful. Furthermore, if they originate in our existential fears rather than in true understanding of the world, their acceptance involves self-deception, namely, a kind of wishful thinking. "The death of God", Nietzsche argues, can release us from this deceptive existence:

> Once a human being reaches the fundamental conviction that he must be commanded, he becomes "a believer". Conversely, one could conceive of such a pleasure and power of self-determination, such a freedom of the will that the spirit would take leave of all faith and every wish for certainty, being practiced in maintaining himself on insubstantial ropes and possibilities and dancing even near abysses. Such a spirit would be the free spirit par excellence.
>
> *(ibid., pp. 289–290)*

To Nietzsche, a non-religious existence is similar to dancing on a tightrope. In such an existence, he says, the individual overcomes the need for absolute certainty, which only metaphysical guarantees can satisfy, and is free from the chains of faith. The existence of that individual is less stable but more vital, as it is not curbed by eternal commandments. By rejecting the idea of eternal good and evil Nietzsche does not reject ethics itself, as the title of the book *Beyond Good and Evil* might imply. He clarifies this point in his next book *On the Genealogy of Morals: Beyond Good and Evil.* At least this does not mean "Beyond Good and Bad" (Nietzsche, 1989a, p. 55).

Nietzsche's ideas of "Slave morality" and "Master morality" may help clarify his new concept of ethics. "Slave morality" stands for ethics that originates in human fears and weaknesses, which is why Nietzsche's philosophy identifies it with the ethics of religion. Since this ethics is the product of a frightened consciousness, its concept of evil precedes the concept of good. Whatever threatens one's existence is defined as evil, and accordingly, whatever is able to rescue one from this threat is defined as good. The concept of evil is foreign to "Master morality" and is therefore useful in explaining the meaning of ethics that stands beyond good and evil. This ethics sees life as a broad expanse of opportunity and not as a threat, and its followers feel free to formulate their own ideals and define them as good. Accordingly, failing to realize these ideals stands for the bad in this ethics. Similar to Spinoza's ethics, and in contrast to "slave morality", the concept of good comes first in this ethics, and is defined by human power rather than by human fears. However, Spinoza sees our power in our common intellect and therefore argues for universal ethics, while Nietzsche sees it in the individuality of each human being, and therefore argues for individualistic ethics.

Ethical development, according to Nietzsche, can only occur if people succeed in overcoming the need for a common truth and live up to their individuality. The main ethical lesson Nietzsche derives from "the death of God" is that the claim for a cosmological moral order is nothing but an illusion. Enslaving our life to an illusion instead of living it as best we can is an ethical failure. This recognition increases the value of each individual's actual life. Life is no longer a pale or distorted mode of a pure or utopian idea but a unique mode of being. Nietzsche takes Spinoza's immanent ethics a step further. While Spinoza's ethics adopts the metaphysical idea of a common human essence, Nietzsche rejects this metaphysical remnant to underscore the individuality of each human being. However, it is possible to interpret Nietzsche's rejection of the metaphysical aspect of human's existence as an unavoidable outcome of Spinoza's ethics, where he discards God's heaven in favor of human earth. The epigraph Freud chose for his first book on psychoanalysis, *The Interpretation of Dreams*, implies that he followed this line of thought: "If I cannot bend the heavens above, I will move Hell" (*Flectere si nequeo superos, Acheronta movebo*; Freud, 1900). It symbolizes Freud's rejection of transcendent approaches to human life in favor of immanent ones. In his later essays dealing with culture, he explicitly continues Spinoza's and Nietzsche's line of thought by rejecting religious faith as an illusion and by seeing ethics as a human invention. His unique contribution to this modern approach to ethics is his original psychological theory, offering a systematic explanation for the origins of religious illusion and human values. At the core of this theory lies the claim that our civilized existence stems from repressed complexes and necessarily involves discontent. That is the reason for my referring to the ethics of psychoanalysis as the "ethics of discontent", a name that obviously echoes Freud's most important ethical essay, "Civilization and Its Discontents".

Freud: Ethics of Discontent

In his "Introduction Lectures on Psycho-Analysis", Freud links psychoanalysis with the process of scientific secularization of Man's self-perception:

> In the course of centuries, the *naïve* self-love of men has had to submit to two major blows at the hands of science. The first was when they learnt that our earth was not the center of the universe but only a tiny fragment of a cosmic system of scarcely imaginable vastness. This is associated in our minds with the name of Copernicus. [. . .] The second blow fell when biological research destroyed man's supposedly privileged place in creation and proved his descent from the animal kingdom and his ineradicable animal nature. This revaluation has been accomplished in our own days by Darwin, Wallace and their predecessors. [. . .] But human megalomania will have suffered its third and most wounding blow from the psychological research of the present time which seeks to prove to the ego that it is not even master in its own house, but must content itself with scanty information of what is going on unconsciously in its mind. We psycho-analysts were not the first and not the only ones to utter this call to introspection;

> but it seems to be our fate to give it its most forcible expression and to support it with empirical material which affects every individual.
>
> *(Freud, 1917, p. 285)*

To Freud, modern empirical science represents the reality principle: it takes humans away from their state of infantile phantasies and illusions and brings them down to the ground of reality by strictly adhering to knowledge based on empirical evidence.[6] This knowledge reveals that the world was not created for Man as the scriptures preach, but it is a boundless universe of which we are but "a tiny fragment" (ibid.). Our earth is not the center of the universe and we are not semi-divine creators but "descend from the animal kingdom" (ibid.). Psychoanalysis, Freud argues, follows this line of thought, substituting religious convictions with empirical recognitions. Furthermore, psychoanalysis' recognition is the most paralyzing, he claims, since it reveals that Man is "not even master in its own house" (ibid.). This is Freud's version of Nietzsche's declaration of "the death of God" that follows Spinoza's science-oriented spirit. Modern science, according to Freud, obliges human beings to cope with the shocking recognition that the universe has no father, a recognition which Nietzsche symbolically names "the death of God". Freud's psychological theory is rooted in this new recognition; as Lacan puts it: "The myth of the murder of the father is the myth of a time for which God is dead" (Lacan, 1992, p. 177). Freud, while fervently attempting to convince others that psychoanalysis is an empirical science and not an ethical stance, presents it explicitly as an ethical stance in his essays on culture. Psychoanalysis is a secular ethics that sees religious faith as an illusion that humans must overcome if they wish to have a better life. Unlike the metaphysical and religious ethics, this ethics does not revolve around salvation but around authenticity.[7] Ethics of this kind (e.g., Nietzsche's ethics) is not an ethics of harmony but of discontent.

The essay "Totem and Taboo" illustrates Freud's increasing attention to the cultural aspect of human psychology.[8] The essay is an attempt to bridge the gap between the end of the biological explanation of human evolution and the beginning of the anthropological one. Freud suggests that the psychoanalytical idea of the Oedipus complex can explain the birth of human civilization from human biology. We should assume, he claims, that human civilization began with the murder of a father that affected deeply the murderers, his sons. They consequently decided to bridle their biological drives by adopting the ideas of Totem (religion) and Taboo (morality). However, already in this essay he argues that the function of religion is merely emotional, whereas morality also has a practical facet (Freud, 1923, p. 15). In the essay "The Future of Illusion", Freud takes this argument a step further, claiming that religious faith is nothing but an illusion of a helpless mind. He concludes that the time has come in human history to replace the religious conception of life by a scientific one. The latter, he argues, does not promise salvation but is more realistic and thus enhances human existence. He elaborates on this ethical view in "Civilization and Its Discontents," which begins by dismissing religious or "oceanic" feeling as a mode of infantile regression. He argues that human existence would improve once the conflictual nature of the civilized psyche is acknowledged. Indeed, this conflictual psyche is the origin of psychological distress, but it is also the source of human achievements. Before delving deeper into "Civilization and Its Discontents", which stands at the focus of my discussion, let me clarify briefly Freud's rejection of religious faith in the essay "The Future of Illusion". This is a crucial step towards validating my argument that psychoanalysis is rooted in secular ethics.

"The Future of Illusion" ends with a very clear conclusion:

> Religion would thus be the universal obsessional neurosis of humanity; like the obsessional neurosis of children, it arose out of the Oedipus complex, out of the relation to

> the father. If this view is right, it is to be supposed that a turning-away from religion is bound to occur with the fatal inevitability of a process of growth, and that we find ourselves at this very juncture in the middle of that phase of development. Our behavior should therefore be modelled on that of a sensible teacher who does not oppose an impending new development but seeks to ease its path and mitigate the violence of its irruption.
>
> *(Freud, 1927, p. 42)*

The conclusion that "a turning away from religion is bound to occur" arises from Freud's psychological analysis of religious ideas. According to this analysis, they are illusions that have a very strong psychological effect. Their illusory nature and their psychological power are both explained by their origin in the most primitive fears of humanity, or, as Freud put it, "born from man's need to make his helplessness tolerable and built up from the material of memories of the helplessness of his own childhood and the childhood of the human race" (ibid., 17). The parallelism he established in "Totem and Taboo" between the development of a child and the development of civilization is used here to explain the extent to which we are trapped in religious ideas. Nietzsche names our difficulty to release ourselves from religious ideas "the shadows of God". He explains it in the fact that the idea of God has dominated western culture for centuries.[9] Freud's explanation is more systematic, going back to the beginnings of the civilized life of both infants and humanity. He bases his explanation on the capability of our psyche to turn anxiety into a defense mechanism by illusion. The fundamental expression of this capability is that the threatening father turns into an omnipotent protector by a process of idealization. Similarly, Freud argues, the adult human anthropomorphizes nature, turning it from an indifferent cruel entity into a protector. Illusions, Freud points out, are not necessarily false, but are always the result of our wishes and not of our understanding. That is why they teach us more about our subjective fears than about objective reality. According to Freud, the fact that religious ideas are illusions rooted in our basic existential fears explains their strong effect. He thinks, therefore, that a "sensible teacher" is required to release humans from this illusionary shield that protects them from their most primeval fears: "the time has probably come, as it does in an analytic treatment, for replacing the effects of repression by the results of the rational operation of the intellect" (ibid., p. 43).

Freud, much like Spinoza and Nietzsche, acknowledges the important psychological function of religious ideas, and like them thinks that the time has come to discard them. He is closer in spirit to the scientific stance of Spinoza's thought, but his conception of the human psyche is closer to Nietzsche's anti-metaphysical view. While urging to replace the religious view with a scientific one, he does not think in terms of metaphysical theory as Spinoza does, but in terms of biology and culture, like Nietzsche. He believes this change can help improve human life by making humans concentrate on their real life rather than enslave it to a protective illusion:

> By withdrawing their expectations from the other world and concentrating all their liberated energies into their life on earth, they will probably succeed in achieving a state of things in which life will become tolerable for everyone and civilization no longer oppressive to anyone.
>
> *(ibid., p. 49)*

In "Civilization and Its Discontents", Freud formulates the ethics of the new Man, who is no longer influenced by religious ideas. He argues that the life of such a person, although necessarily characterized by discontent, is more authentic and valuable, being guided by the reality principle. As he did in "The Future of Illusion", he presents it as a better alternative to religious existence, which he now rejects as a kind of psychosis. He criticizes religion ironically for pretending to explain the purpose of human life and suggests a less assuming point of departure for human ethics, one that is very similar to Aristotle's in his *Ethics*:

> We will therefore turn to the less ambitious question of what men themselves show by their behavior to be the purpose and intention of their lives. What do they demand of life and wish to achieve in it? The answer to this can hardly be in doubt. They strive after happiness; they want to become happy and to remain so.
>
> *(Freud, 1930, p. 75)*

Once free of a religious goal, the purpose of human ethics is human happiness. However, whereas a metaphysical view of human existence, such as that of Aristotle and Spinoza, interprets happiness as harmony, the anti-metaphysical view, such as that of Nietzsche and Freud, understands it as authenticity. Yet, Nietzsche, like other philosophers before him, thinks in ideal terms that lead him to formulate the new ethical ideal of the overman (*Übermensch*). Freud rejects this line of thought and criticizes Nietzsche's new ideal of being in his essay "Beyond the Pleasure Principle" directly:

> It may be difficult, too, for many of us, to abandon the belief that there is an instinct towards perfection at work in human beings, which has brought them to their present high level of intellectual achievement and ethical sublimation and which may be expected to watch over their development into supermen [*Übermensch* S.F]. I have no faith, however, in the existence of any such internal instinct and I cannot see how this benevolent illusion is to be preserved. The present development of human beings requires, as it seems to me, no different explanation from that of animals. What appears in a minority of human individuals as an untiring impulsion towards further perfection can easily be understood as a result of the instinctual repression upon which is based all that is most precious in human civilization.
>
> *(Freud, 1920, p. 42)*

Unlike the philosophers, Freud, as a scientist and therapist, thinks in terms of normal life and not an ideal one. Moreover, he interprets the ideal thinking and language of the philosophers as a defense mechanism, much like religious ideals. Although Freud is a great explorer of the productive function of phantasies and sublimations, he established his approach to human life on the reality principle. This is his point of departure as a physician and a positivist scientist, the *raison d'être* of his therapeutic method and the foundation of his ethical view. To Freud, the reality is that which positivist science considers as reality, namely, empirical facts.[10] Therefore, as the above quote indicates, he insists that any explanation of human life, its ethical goal, and its intellectual achievements should be restricted to biological instincts and their repression. This leads him to the theoretical idea of sublimation, which is a "certain kind of modification of the aim and change of the object, in which our social valuation is taken into account" (Freud 1933, p. 97). This psychological capability makes civilization possible and explains its achievements but bring discontent into the life of the civilized human being, since it requires struggling against the original biological instincts. In his essay "Civilization and Its Discontents", Freud explains the basic discontents that underlie the foundation of civilized life:

1 The pleasure principle determines the purpose of human life, although it can never be fully satisfied.

2 Sexual love works against the interests of civilization, and civilization devises restrictions to manage this love.
3 Civilization restricts the natural aggression of human beings.
4 Civilization is the source of the human sense of guilt.

According to Freud's biological approach, biology, rather than any metaphysical goal, determines the purpose of human life. The pleasure principle with which humans are born determines the life of each individual. It explains the direction life takes as earlier experiences of satisfactions and dissatisfactions shape mature choices. The most crucial point of this argument, however, is that while determining the purpose of human life, the pleasure principle can never be fully satisfied because the world around us acts against it. Humans are doomed to struggle to achieve an unattainable goal:

> We are threatened with suffering from three directions: from our own body, which is doomed to decay and dissolution and which cannot even do without pain and anxiety as warning signals; from the external world, which may rage against us with overwhelming and merciless forces of destruction; and finally from our relations to other men.
>
> *(Freud, 1930, p. 77)*

Our capability to satisfy the pleasure principle is very limited and more than anything else depends on good luck. For this reason, most human beings prefer, from the very early stages of their development, to avoid suffering than strive for ultimate pleasure. In psychoanalytical terms, this means transforming the pleasure principle into the reality principle, a transformation that produces discontent since it involves suspending and rejecting satisfactions. Yet it is crucial, according to Freud, for the development of each individual and the whole of civilization. This is the primary reason why Freud's ethical stance rejects ideas of eternal harmony as illusive and regressive.

We cannot completely avoid physical pain or pain caused by the external world, which is beyond our control. The question is why civilization, a human creation, brings discontent into our existence. Freud thinks that the primary cause for that is the cultivation of the original biological love. Our biology determines our first objects of love through the pleasure we derive from them regardless of the restrictions or taboos of civilization, which are foreign to biology. This explains why the Oedipus complex is so central to our psychological development, marking the transformation from sexual love to non-sexual or civilized love. In the civilization process, the sexual desire for the mother turns into love for the mother, and consequently into an ambivalent relation with the father. This primary sublimation, which bends biological desire to the laws of civilization, underlies the psychological development of every civilized human being. However, since the origin of every love is biological, it keeps undermining the civilized order and bringing discontent into the life of the civilized human being. Love, while being the source of the highest human satisfaction, is therefore also the source of discontent in human civilized life. This is the first answer to the question why civilization, which was created by humans for their own benefit, is also a source of psychological discontent. However, Freud does not use this insight to speak against civilization but against an ethical view based on love:

> According to one ethical view, whose deeper motivation will become clear to us presently, this readiness for a universal love of mankind and the world represents the highest standpoint which man can reach. Even at this early stage of the discussion, I

> should like to bring forward my two main objections to this view. A love that does not discriminate seems to me to forfeit a part of its own value, by doing an injustice to its object; and secondly, not all men are worthy of love.
>
> *(ibid., p. 102)*

Freud, a modern explorer of Eros, argues that ethics cannot and should not be based on the idea of universal love because the biological origin of love discriminates between objects, and therefore can never be authentically transformed into universal love. Ethics should not be based on universal love because its goal is achieving a better human life, which sometimes means hating those who deserve it. An ethical approach that castrates the highest human pleasure, which, according to Freud's theory, is also the criterion for our happiness, is wrong. True ethics should recognize that love discriminates between its objects and its formulation must take this into account. This is another example of Freud's rejection of ethics of harmony in favor of realistic ethics that is based on recognition of the conflictual nature of civilization and of each civilized human being. Freud admits that civilized life requires sublimating biological instincts but thinks it cannot and should not alienate them altogether. Therefore, discontent is a necessary part of ethical development, and any ethical approach that aims to annihilate discontent is, according to Freud, wrong and misleading.

While biology grants us love, it also breeds aggression, which means that the process of civilization requires the sublimation of aggression as well. This is another source of discontent for the civilized human: "If civilization imposes such great sacrifices not only on man's sexuality but on his aggressivity, we can understand better why it is hard for him to be happy in that civilization" (ibid., p. 115).

However, unlike love, which turns into a constitutive element of civilization by a process of sublimation, aggression is thoroughly destructive to civilization. Civilization, as the myth of "Totem and Taboo" tells, begins with an act of aggression against aggression and by giving up aggression. An aggressive father was murdered by the brothers who agreed after the murder to sacrifice aggression for a common social life. However, aggression is an expression of a primary drive, and eliminating it is impossible without eliminating life itself. It can only be civilized by sublimation, and like every sublimation, it is necessarily an insufficient substitute that generates discontent. The need to sublimate aggression is therefore another source of discontent for civilized Man. Moreover, the most effective way for civilization to cope with aggression, Freud argues, is by making us turn our aggression against ourselves. This gives rise to a sense of guilt, which Freud considers the most important issue in the evolution of civilization and the central origin of discontent in the life of civilized Man:

> In the first place, I suspect that the reader has the impression that our discussions on the sense of guilt disrupt the framework of this essay: that they take up too much space, so that the rest of its subject-matter, with which they are not always closely connected, is pushed to one side. This may have spoilt the structure of my paper; but it corresponds faithfully to my intention to represent the sense of guilt as the most important problem in the development of civilization and to show that the price we pay for our advance in civilization is a loss of happiness through the heightening of the sense of guilt.
>
> *(Freud, 1930, p. 134)*

Civilization was born, as explained in "Totem and Taboo", from the sense of guilt, the outcome of turning aggression from external objects to internal ones. However, the sense of guilt is also the source of morality, which Freud explain in his theory by the idea of the super-ego. This new psychological master, comprising internalized values, is a by-product of turning aggression inwards. One may regard it is an outcome of the primary trauma, where the fear of castration is so acute that it leads to self-castration. Once this happens, the inner world becomes as threatening as the external world, often even more so.[11]

Civilized life comes at the cost of discontent. The ethics of civilized human beings should therefore be grounded in this recognition. This ethics stands in contrast to metaphysical ethics, which promises salvation in the name of eternal truth. Freud rejects the idea of salvation by explaining it psychologically as an infantile phantasy or illusion. He formulates ethics derived from his psychological theory, calling upon humans to follow the reality principle and cope sincerely and pragmatically with their existence. It assumes that each human being is an individual with a different history, which makes it impossible and wrong to suggest a common prescription for a proper human existence. In Freud's view, human life is conflictual because the development of each individual and of humanity as a whole results from a sublimation of biological instincts, which necessarily produces discontent. The capability to cope well with this conflictual life without denying its conflictual nature or being defeated by it paves the way to morality and to the great achievements of human civilization. Freud therefore sees psychoanalysis as "inducing the patient to give up the repressions (using the word in the widest sense) belonging to his early development and to replace them by reactions of a sort that would correspond to a psychically mature condition" (Freud, 1937, p. 257). Freud, much like the thinkers of the enlightenment, understands human development in terms of maturation, represented in his theory by the reality principle. However, whereas the enlightenment scholars assume that man is a rational being, Freud assumes that the origin of psychological life is biological, and therefore irrational. In his view, maturity is not the end of conflictual life but its sublimation. Like Nietzsche's ethics, Freud's ethics is individualistic, but unlike Nietzsche's ethics, it is not reserved for outstanding people.

Conclusion

Psychoanalysis regards our psyche as a historical phenomenon originating in biology and shaped by culture. Accordingly, it interprets human existence in biological and cultural terms rather than religious ones. This makes it a secular ethical view, which has at its core the conflicts between the biological and cultural aspects of human existence. Its practice aims to enable living better with these conflicts rather than annihilating them, as the latter means annihilating psychological life.

Because it recognizes the historicity and individuality of human existence, psychoanalysis is not a moral doctrine that proposes definitive moral values. Paul Ricoeur rightly claims that it is unable to provide us with normative answers since it asks primary questions concerning the desires with which we approach concrete moral problems.[12] The priority that psychoanalysis gives to the concrete over the abstract brings it very close to Nietzsche's revaluation of values, giving priority to the concrete life of each individual over general and abstract truths. According to this psychological approach to morality, moral values are human inventions that should be constantly reexamined to prevent them from turning into psychological fixations.

Discontent, according to this view, is neither an ethical problem nor an indication of a moral sin. Discontent is a characteristic of a vital psychological life that might yield psychological distresses but is also the source of human achievements. According to this ethics, the purpose of human life and of psychotherapy is not reaching complete harmony. This is an illusionary goal that can only breed further frustration or psychological death. Like Nietzsche's ethics, it is an ethics of life, where moral values are tested in terms of life and death rather than of truth and falseness; whatever promotes life is good while whatever degenerates it is bad. Complete elimination of discontent, if at all possible, is a sign of death and not of a good life.

Regarded from this perspective, psychoanalysis is a major milestone in the development of secular ethics in western culture. The legacy of secular ethics, which originates in Greek philosophy and reemerges in the modern period in Spinoza's ethics, presents itself as an alternative to the mythical or religious type of ethics. Greek philosophy calls to replace the *mythos* by *logos*, and Spinoza revives this idea in modernity. Both, however, formulate their purpose, similar to the religious one, in terms of harmonic existence. Nietzsche and Freud reject the metaphysical idea of the psyche along with the prospect of harmonic existence.[13] In contrast to the metaphysical approaches, be they philosophical or religious, they explain psychological development as sublimation rather than purification. Accordingly, they offer an original view of ethics, which does not aim to eliminate existential discontent but reshape it into new forms of life.

Notes

1 In some cases, he argues that he practices it for the wellbeing of others, for example in "The Apology" (Plato, 2001); in other cases for his own wellbeing, for example in "Phaedo" (Plato, 2001a).

2 The paper refers to Aristotle's *Nicomachean Ethics*.

3 Freud begins his investigation in "Civilization and Its Discontents" with the same assumption, namely, that happiness is the purpose of human life (Freud, 1930, p. 76).

4 Nietzsche, in a postcard to Franz Overbeck, Sils-Maria, July 30, 1881:

> I am utterly amazed, utterly enchanted! I have a *precursor*, and what a precursor! I hardly knew Spinoza: that I should have turned to him just *now*, was inspired by "instinct." Not only is his over tendency like mine – namely to make all knowledge the *most powerful affect* – but in five main points of his doctrine I recognize myself; this most unusual and loneliest thinker is closest to me precisely in these matters: he denies the freedom of the will, teleology, the moral world-order, the unegoistic, and evil. Even though the divergencies are admittedly tremendous, they are due more to the difference in time, culture, and science. *In summa*: my lonesomeness, which, as on very high mountains, often made it hard for me to breathe and make my blood rush out, is now at least a twosomeness.
>
> (Nietzsche 1969, p. 177)

Freud on Nietzsche in "On the History of the Psycho-Analytic Movement":

> In later years, I have denied myself the very great pleasure of reading the works of Nietzsche, with the deliberate object of not being hampered in working out the impressions received in psycho-analysis by any sort of anticipatory ideas. I had therefore to be prepared – and I am so, gladly – to forgo all claims to priority in the many instances in which laborious psycho-analytic investigation can merely confirm the truths which the philosopher recognized by intuition.
>
> (Freud, 1914, pp. 15–16)

5 Accordingly, Paul Ricoeur compares psychoanalysis and Spinoza's *Ethics*:

> Thus, psychoanalysis would like to be, like Spinoza's *Ethics*, a reeducation of desire. It is this reeducation which it posits as the prior condition for all human reform, whether intellectual, political, or social.
>
> (Ricoeur, 1974, p. 194)

6 In light of this, it is ironic that the empirical sciences often dismiss psychoanalysis (see Popper, 1963).

7 Lacan claims that authenticity is one of the three basic ideals of psychoanalysis, the other two being human love and independence (1992, p. 9).

8 James Strachey emphasizes this fact in his editor's note to the standard edition of the essay "The Future of Illusion":

> In the "Postscript" which Freud added in 1935 to his *Autobiographical Study* he remarked on "a significant change" that had come about in his writings during the previous decade. "My

interest", he explained, "after making a long *détour* through the natural sciences, medicine and psychotherapy, returned to the cultural problems which had fascinated me long before, when I was a youth scarcely old enough for thinking" (*Standard Ed.*, 20, 72).

(Freud, 1927, p. 3)

9 Nietzsche (1974, p. 167).

10 Ludwig Wittgenstein expresses this idea explicitly in his *Tractatus Logico-Philosophicus*: "The world is a totality of facts, not of things" (Wittgenstein, 1971, p. 7).

11 Nietzsche also thinks that the major source of discontent in human life is a sense of guilt, but unlike Freud he claims that one should overcome it for a better life (Nietzsche, 1997, p. 36).

12 Ricoeur (1974, p. 194).

13 Nietzsche equates with irony Plato's ethics and Christianity: "Christianity is Platonism for 'the people'" (Nietzsche, 1989, p. 2).

References

Aristotle. (2014). *Nicomachean Ethics*. Translated by W. D. Ross. Princeton: Princeton University Press.

Freud, S. (1900). *The Interpretation of Dreams*. The Standard Edition of the Complete Psychological Works of Sigmund Freud, Volume IV. Translated by J. Strachey. London: The Hogarth Press and the Institute of Psycho-analysis.

Freud, S. (1914). "On the History of the Psycho-Analytic Movement" in *The Standard Edition of the Complete Psychological Works of Sigmund Freud, Volume XIV (1914–1916): On the History of the Psycho-Analytic Movement, Papers on Metapsychology and Other Works*. Translated and Edited by J. Strachey. London: The Hogarth Press and the Institute of Psycho-analysis, pp. 1–66.

Freud, S. (1917)." Introductory Lectures on Psycho-Analysis". *The Standard Edition of the Complete Psychological Works of Sigmund Freud*, Volume XVI (1916–1917): Introductory Lectures on Psycho-Analysis (Part III), 241–463.

Freud, S. (1920). "Beyond the Pleasure Principle" in *The Standard Edition of the Complete Psychological Works of Sigmund Freud, Volume XVIII (1920–1922): Beyond the Pleasure Principle, Group Psychology and Other Works*. Translated and Edited by J. Strachey. London: The Hogarth Press and the Institute of Psycho-analysis, pp. 1–64.

Freud, S. (1923). "The Ego and the Id" in *The Standard Edition of the Complete Psychological Works of Sigmund Freud, Volume XIX (1923–1925): The Ego and the Id and Other Works*. Translated and Edited by J. Strachey. London: The Hogarth Press and the Institute of Psycho-analysis, pp. 1–66.

Freud, S. (1927). "The Future of an Illusion" in *The Standard Edition of the Complete Psychological Works of Sigmund Freud, Volume XXI (1927–1931): The Future of an Illusion, Civilization and Its Discontents, and Other Works*. Translated and Edited by J. Strachey. London: The Hogarth Press and the Institute of Psycho-analysis, 1–56.

Freud, S. (1930). "Civilization and its Discontents" in *The Standard Edition of the Complete Psychological Works of Sigmund Freud, Volume XXI (1927–1931): The Future of an Illusion, Civilization and Its Discontents, and Other Works*. Translated and Edited by J. Strachey. London: The Hogarth Press and the Institute of Psycho-analysis 57–146.

Freud, S. (1933). "New Introductory Lectures On Psycho-Analysis". *The Standard Edition of the Complete Psychological Works of Sigmund Freud*, Volume XXII (1932–1936): New Introductory Lectures on Psycho-Analysis and Other Works, 1–182.

Freud, S. (1937). "Constructions in Analysis" in *The Standard Edition of the Complete Psychological Works of Sigmund Freud, Volume XXIII (1937–1939): Moses and Monotheism, An Outline of Psychoanalysis and Other Works*. Translated and Edited by J. Strachey. London: The Hogarth Press and the Institute of Psycho-analysis, pp. 255–270.

Lacan, Jacques. (1992). *The Ethics of Psychoanalysis (Seminar VII)*. Translated by Dennis Porter. New York: Norton & Company.

Nietzsche, Fredrich. (1974) [1882–3]. *The Gay Science*. Translated by Walter Kaufmann. NY: Vintage books.

Nietzsche, Fredrich. (1989) [1886]. *Beyond Good and Evil*. Translated by Walter Kaufmann. NY: Vintage books.

Nietzsche, Fredrich. (1989a) [1887]. *On the Genealogy of Morals*. Translated by Walter Kaufmann. NY: Vintage books.

Nietzsche, Fredrich. (1997) [1889]. *Twilight of the Idols.* Translated by Richard Polt. Indianapolis/ Cambridge: Hackett Publishing Company, Inc.

Nietzsche, Fredrich. (1969). *Selected letters of Friedrich Nietzsche.* Edited and translated by Christopher Middleton. Chicago: The University of Chicago Press.

Plato. (2001). "The Apology" in *Plato*, Vol I. Translated by Harold North Fowler. Cambridge, Massachusetts: Harvard University Press, pp. 61–145.

Plato. (2001a). "Phaedo" in *Plato*, Vol I. Translated by Harold North Fowler. Cambridge, MA: Harvard University Press, pp. 193–403.

Popper, Karl. (1963). "Science: Conjectures and Refutations" in *Conjectures and refutations.* London: Routledge & Kegan Paul, pp. 33–55.

Ricoeur, P. (1974). "Technique and Nontechnique in Interpretation" in *The conflict of interpretation: Essays in hermeneutics.* Translated by Peter McCormick. Evanston: Northwestern University press, pp. 177–195.

Spinoza, Benedict. (2001) [1677]. *Ethics.* Translated by W. H. White & A. H. Stirling. Ware: Wordsworth Editions Limited.

Wittgenstein, Ludwig. (1971) [1921]. *Tractatus Logico-Philosophicus.* Translated by D. F. Pears & B. F. McGuinness. London: Routledge & Kegan Paul.

PART V

Applied Subjects

28

WHAT CAN PSYCHOANALYSIS TELL US ABOUT CYBERSPACE?

Slavoj Žižek

The Informational Anorexia

Today, the media constantly bombard us with requests to choose, addressing us as subjects *supposed to know what we really want* (which book, clothes, TV program, place of holiday . . .) – "press A, if you want this, press B, if you want that," or, to quote the motto of the recent "reflective" TV publicity campaign for advertisement itself, "Advertisement – the right to choose." However, at a more fundamental level, the new media deprive the subject radically of the knowledge of what he wants: They address a thoroughly malleable subject who has constantly to be told what he wants, i.e., the very evocation of a choice to be made perform-atively creates the need for the object of choice. One should bear in mind here that the main function of the Master is to tell the subject what he wants – the need for the Master arises in answer to the subject's confusion, insofar as he does *not* know what he wants. What, then, happens in the situation of the decline of the Master, when the subject himself is constantly bombarded with the request to give a sign as to what he wants? The exact opposite of what one would expect: It is when there is no one here to tell you what you really want, when all the burden of the choice is on you, that the big Other dominates you completely, and the choice effectively disappears, i.e., is replaced by its mere semblance. One is tempted to paraphrase here Lacan's well-known reversal of Dostoyevski ("If there is no God, nothing is permitted at all"): If no forced choice confines the field of free choice, the very freedom of choice disappears.

This suspension of the function of the (symbolic) Master is the crucial feature of the Real whose contours loom at the horizon of the cyberspace universe: the moment of implosion when humanity will attend the limit impossible to transgress, the moment at which the coordinates of our societal life-world will be dissolved. At this moment, distances will be suspended (I will be able to communicate instantly through teleconferences with anywhere on the globe); all information, from texts to music to video, will be instantly available on my interface. However, the obverse of this suspension of the distance which separates me from a far-away foreigner is that, due to the gradual disappearance of contact with "real" bodily others, a neighbor will no longer be a neighbor, since he or she will be progressively replaced by a screen specter; the general availability will induce unbearable claustrophobia; the excess of choice will be experienced as the impossibility to choose; the universal direct participatory community will exclude all the more forcefully those who are prevented from participating in it. The vision of cyberspace

DOI: 10.4324/9780429297076-34

opening up a future of unending possibilities of limitless change, of new multiple sex organs, etc., etc., conceals its exact opposite: an unheard-of imposition of radical closure. This, then, is the Real awaiting us, and all endeavors to symbolize this real, from utopian (the New Age or "deconstructionist" celebrations of the liberating potentials of cyberspace), to the blackest dystopian ones (the prospect of the total control by a God-like computerized network . . .), are just this, i.e., so many attempts to avoid the true "end of history," the paradox of an infinity far more suffocating than any actual confinement. Is therefore one of the possible reactions to the excessive filling-in of the voids in cyberspace not the *informational anorexia,* the desperate refusal to accept informations?

Or, to put it in a different way, virtualization cancels the distance between a neighbor and a distant foreigner, insofar as it suspends the presence of the Other in the massive weight of the Real: neighbors and foreigners, all are equal in their spectral screen-presence. That is to say, why was the Christian injunction "love thy neighbor like thyself" so problematic for Freud? The proximity of the Other which makes a neighbor a neighbor is that of *jouissance:* When the presence of the Other becomes unbearable, suffocating, it means that we experience his or her mode of *jouissance* as too intrusive. And, what is the contemporary "postmodern" racism, if not a violent reaction to this virtualization of the Other, a return of the experience of the neighbor in his or her (or their) intolerable, traumatic *presence?* The feature which disturbs the racist in his Other (the way they laugh, the smell of their food . . .) is thus precisely the little piece of the real which bears witness to their presence beyond the symbolic order.

We are thus far from bemoaning the loss of the contact with a "real," flesh-and-blood other in cyberspace, in which all we encounter are digital phantoms: Our point is rather that cyberspace is *not spectral enough.* One of the tendencies in theorizing cyberspace is to conceive cybersex as the ultimate phenomenon in the chain whose key link is Kierkegaard, his relationship with Regina: In the same way Kierkegaard rejected the actual proximity of the Other (the beloved woman), and advocated loneliness as the only authentic mode of relating to a love object, cybersex also involves the nullification of the "real life" object, and draws erotic energy from this very nullification – the moment I encounter my cybersex partner(s) in real life is the moment of *desublimation,* the moment of the return to vulgar "reality." . . . Convincing as it may sound, this parallel is deeply misleading: The status of my cyberspace sexual partner is NOT that of Kierkegaard's Regina. Regina was the void at which Kierkegaard addressed his words, a kind of *"vacuole" weaved by the texture of his speech,* while my cyberspace sexual partner is, on the contrary, *overpresent,* bombarding me with the torrential flow of images and explicit statements of her (or his) most secret fantasies. Or, to put it in another way: Kierkegaard's Regina is the cut of the Real, the traumatic obstacle which again and again unsettles the smooth run of my self-satisfying erotic imagination, while cyberspace presents its exact opposite, a frictionless flow of images and messages – when I am immersed in it, I, as it were, return to a symbiotic relationship with an Other in which the deluge of semblances seems to abolish the dimension of the Real.

In a recent interview, Bill Gates celebrated cyberspace as opening up the prospect of what he called "friction-free capitalism" – this expression renders perfectly the social fantasy which underlies the ideology of cyberspace capitalism: the fantasy of a wholly transparent, ethereal medium of exchanges in which the last trace of material inertia vanishes. The crucial point not to be missed here is that the "friction" we get rid of in the fantasy of "friction-free capitalism," does not refer only to the reality of material obstacles which sustain any exchange process, but, above all, to the Real of the traumatic social antagonisms, power relations, etc., which brand the space of social exchange with a pathological twist. In his *Grundrisse* manuscript, Marx pointed out how the very material dispositive of a nineteenth-century industrial production site directly materializes the capitalist relationship of domination (the worker as a mere appendix subordinated to the machinery which is owned by the capitalist); *mutatis mutandis,* the same goes for cyberspace: In the social conditions of late capitalism, the very materiality of cyberspace automatically generates the illusory abstract space of "friction-free" exchange in which the particularity of the participants' social position is obliterated.

The easiest way to discern the set of social relations which overdetermine the mode of operation of cyberspace, is to focus on the predominant "spontaneous ideology of cyberspace," the so-called *cyberevolutionism* which relies on the notion of cyberspace (or the World Wide Web) as a selfevolving "natural" organism. Crucial is here the blurring of the distinction between "culture" and "nature": The obverse of the "naturalization of culture" (market, society, etc., as living organisms) is the "culturalization of nature" (life itself is conceived as a set of self-reproducing informations – "genes are memes"). This new notion of Life is thus neutral with respect to the distinction of natural and cultural or "artificial" processes – the Earth (as Gaia) as well as global market, they both appear as gigantic self-regulated living systems whose basic structure is defined in the terms of the process of coding and decoding, of passing informations, etc. The reference to the World Wide Web as a living organism is often evoked in contexts which may seem liberating: say, against the State censorship of Internet. However, this very demonization of State is thoroughly ambiguous, since it is predominantly appropriated by right-wing populist discourse and/or market liberalism: Its main targets are the state interventions which try to maintain a kind of minimal social balance and security – the title of Michael Rothschild's book (*Bioeconomics: The Inevitability of Capitalism*) is here indicative. So, while cyberspace ideologists can dream about the next step of evolution in which we will no longer be mechanically interacting "Cartesian" individuals, in which each "person" will cut his substantial link to his individual body and conceive itself as part of the new holistic Mind which lives and acts through him or her, what is obfuscated in such direct "naturalization" of the World Wide Web or market is the set of power relations – of political decisions, of institutional conditions – within which "organisms" like the Internet (or market or capitalism . . .) can only thrive.

What Can Meteorology Teach Us About Cyberspace?

In what, then, resides the key feature of *la coupure digitale*? Perhaps, the best way to approach it is via the gap which separates the modern universe of science from the traditional knowledge: For Lacan, modern science is *not* just another local narrative grounded in its specific pragmatic conditions, since it does relate to the (mathematical) Real beneath the symbolic universe. Let us recall the difference between the modern satellite meteorology and the traditional wisdom about weather, which "thinks locally." Modern meteorology assumes a kind of meta-language view on the entire atmosphere of the Earth as a global and self-enclosed mechanism, while the traditional meteorology involves a particular viewpoint within a finite horizon: Out of some Beyond which, by definition, remains beyond our grasp, clouds and winds arrive, and all one can do is formulate the rules of their emergence and disappearance in a series of "wisdoms" ("If it rains on the first of May, beware of the drought in August," etc.). The crucial point is that "meaning" can only emerge within such a finite horizon: The weather phenomena can be experienced and conceived as "meaningful" only insofar as there is a Beyond out of which these phenomena emerge following the laws which are not directly natural laws – the very lack of natural laws directly connecting actual weather here and the mysterious Beyond, sets in motion the search for "meaningful" coincidences and correlations. The paradox is that, although this traditional "closed" universe confronts us with unpredictable catastrophies which seem to emerge "out of nowhere," it nonetheless provides a sense of ontological "safety," of dwelling within a self-enclosed finite circle of meaning where things (natural phenomena) in a way "speak to us," address us.

This traditional closed universe is thus in a sense *more "open"* than the universe of science: It implies the gateway into the indefinite Beyond, while the direct global model of the modern science is effectively "closed," i.e., it allows for no Beyond. The universe of modern science, in its very "meaninglessness," involves the gesture of "going through fantasy," of abolishing the dark spot, the domain of the Unexplained which harbors fantasies and thus guarantees Meaning: Instead of it, we get the meaningless mechanism. This is why, for Heidegger, modern science stands for the metaphysical "danger": It poses a threat to the universe of meaning. There is no meaning without some dark spot, without some forbidden/impenetrable domain into which we project fantasies which guarantee our horizon of meaning. Perhaps, this very growing disenchantment of our actual social world accounts for the fascination exerted by cyberspace: It is as if, in it, we encounter again a Limit beyond which the mysterious domain of the fantasmatic Otherness opens up, as if the screen of the interface is today's version of the blank, of the unknown region in which we can locate our own Shangri-Las or the kingdoms of She.

Paradigmatic here are the last chapters of Edgar Allen Poe's "Narrative of A. Gordon Pym," which stage the fantasmatic scenario of passing the threshold into the pure Otherness of the Antarctic. The last human settlement prior to this threshold is a native village on an island with savages so black that even their teeth are black; significantly, what one encounters on this island is also the ultimate Signifier (a gigantic hieroglyph inscribed into the very shape of the mountain chain). Savage and corrupted as they are, the black men cannot be bribed into accompanying the white explorers further south: They are scared to death by the very notion of entering this prohibited domain. When the explorers finally enter this domain, the ice-cold polar snowscape gradually and mysteriously turns into its opposite, a domain of thick, warm and opaque whiteness . . . in short, the incestuous domain of primordial Milk. What we get here is another version of the kingdom of Tarzan or *She:* in Rider Haggard's *She,* Freud's notorious claim that feminine sexuality is a "dark continent" is realized in a literal way: she-who-must-be-obeyed, this Master beyond Law, the possessor of the Secret of Life itself, is a White Woman ruling in the midst of Africa, the dark continent. This figure of She, of a woman who exists (in the unexplored Beyond), is the necessary fantasmatic support of the patriarchal universe. With the advent of modern science, this Beyond is abolished, there is no longer a "dark continent" which generates a Secret – and, consequently, Meaning is also lost, since the field of Meaning is by definition sustained by an impenetrable dark spot in its very heart.

The very process of colonization thus produces the excess which resists it: Does the mystery of Shangri-La (or of Tarzan's kingdom, or of the kingdom of She or . . .) not reside precisely in the fact that we are dealing with the domain which *was not yet colonized,* with the imagined radical Otherness which forever eludes the colonizer's grasp? Here, however, we encounter another key paradox. This motif of *She* relies on one of the key mythical narratives of colonialism: After white explorers transgress a certain frontier which is taboo even for the most primitive and cruel aborigines and enter the very "heart of darkness," what they encounter there, in this purely fantasmatic Beyond, is again the rule of a mysterious White Man, the pre-Oedipal father, the absolute Master. The structure is here that of the Mobius strip – in the very heart of Otherness, we encounter the other side of the Same, of our own structure of masterhood. This figure of the white Master who rules in this fantasmatic domain of radical Otherness, is split into two opposites: either the horrifying embodiment of the "diabolical Evil" who knows the secret of *jouissance* and, consequently, terrorizes and tortures his subjects (from Conrad's *Heart of Darkness* and *Lord Jim* to the feminine version of it in Rider Haggard's *She*) or the saint who rules his kingdom as a benevolent theocratic despotism (Shangri-La in *Lost Horizon*). The point, of course, resides in the "speculative identity" of these two figures: The diabolically evil Master is "in himself or for us" *the same* as the saintly sage-ruler; their difference is purely formal – it concerns only the shift in the perspective of the observer. (Or, to put it in Schelling's [1946, p. 105] terms, the saintly wise ruler is in the mode of potentiality what the evil Master is in the mode of actuality, since "the same principle carries and holds us in its ineffectiveness which would consume and destroy us in its effectiveness.") What the hundreds-years-old monk who runs Shangri-La and Kurtz from *The Heart of Darkness* share, is that they both have cut their links with common human considerations and entered the domain "between the two deaths." As such, Kurtz is the Institution at its fantasmatic pure: His very excess merely realizes, brings to the end, the inherent logic of the Institution (the Company and its colonization of the wilderness of Congo). This inherent logic is concealed in the "normal" functioning of the Institution: The very figure which literally realizes the logic of the Institution is, in a properly Hegelian way, perceived as an unbearable excess which has to be finished off.

What, then, does all this tell us about cyberspace? Cyberspace, of course, is a thoroughly technological-scientific phenomenon, it develops the logic of modern meteorology to extreme: Not only is there no place for the fantasmatic screen in it, it even generates the screen itself by way of manipulating the Real of bytes. However, it is by no means accidental that *the modern science, inclusive of meteorology, inherently relies on the interface screen*: In the modern scientific approach, processes are *simulated* on the screen, from the models of atomic subparticles, through the radar images of clouds in weather reports, up to the fascinating pictures of the surface of Mars and other planets (which are all manipulated by computer procedures – added colorization, etc. – in order to enhance their effect). The outcome of the suspension of the dark spot of Beyond in the universe of modern science is thus that the "global reality" with no impenetrable dark spot is something accessible only on screen: The abolishment of the fantasmatic screen which served as the gateway into the Beyond, turns *the entire reality* into something which "exists only on screen," as a depthless surface. Or, to put it in ontological terms: The moment the function of the dark spot which maintains open the space for something for which there is no place in our reality is suspended, we lose our very "sense of reality."

The problem with today's social functioning of cyberspace is thus that it potentially fills in the gap, the distance between the subject's public symbolic identity and its fantasmatic background: Fantasies are more and more immediately externalized in the public symbolic space, the sphere of intimacy is more and more directly socialized. The inherent violence of cybersex does not reside in the potentially violent content of sexual fantasies played out on the screen, but in the very formal fact of seeing my innermost fantasies being directly imposed on me from without.

Oedipus or Anti-Oedipus?

So, again: How, then, does cyberspace affect the status of subjectivity? What are the consequences of cyberspace for Oedipus, i.e., for the mode of subjectivization that psychoanalysis conceptualized as the Oedipus complex and its dissolution? The fact that cyberspace involves the suspension of the symbolic function of the Master seems to confirm the predominant *doxa* according to which cyberspace explodes or at least potentially undermines the reign of Oedipus: It involves the "end of Oedipus," i.e., what occurs in it is the passage from the structure of symbolic castration (the intervention of the Third Agency which prohibits/disturbs the incestuous dyad and thus enables the subject's entry into the symbolic order), to some new post-Oedipal libidinal economy. Of course, the mode of perception of this "end of Oedipus" depends on the standpoint of the theoretician: First, there are those who see in it a dystopian prospect of individuals regressing to presymbolic psychotic immersion, of losing the symbolic distance which sustains the minimum of critical/reflective attitude (the idea that computer functions as a maternal Thing which "swallows" the subject who entertains toward it an attitude of incestuous fusion) – in short, today, in the digitalized universe of simulation, Imaginary overlaps with the Real, at the expense of the Symbolic (Jean Baudrillard, Paul Virilio).

This position is at its strongest when it insists on the difference between appearance and simulacrum: "Appearance" has nothing in common with the postmodern notion that we are entering the era of universalized simulacra in which reality itself becomes indistinguishable from its simulated double. The nostalgic longing for the authentic experience of being lost in the deluge of simulacra (detectable in Virilio), as well as the postmodern assertion of a Brave New World of universalized simulacra as the sign that we are finally getting rid of the metaphysical obsession with authentic Being (detectable in Vattimo) – they both miss the distinction between simulacrum and appearance: What gets lost in today's digital "plague of simulations" is not the firm, true, nonsimulated real, but *appearance itself.* So what is appearance? In a sentimental answer to a child asking him "How does God's face look?" a priest answered that, whenever the child encounters a human face irradiating benevolence and goodness, whomever this face belongs to, he gets a glimpse of His face. . . . The truth of this sentimental platitude is that the Suprasensible (God's face) is discernible as a momentary, fleeting appearance, a "grimace," of an earthly face. It is THIS dimension of "appearance" which transubstantiates a piece of reality into something which, for a brief moment, irradiates the suprasensible Eternity that is missing in the logic of simulacrum: in simulacrum which becomes indistinguishable from the real, everything is here and no other, transcendent dimension effectively "appears" in/through it. We are back at the Kantian problematic of the sublime: In Kant's famous reading of the enthusiasm evoked by the French Revolution in the enlightened public around Europe, the revolutionary events functioned as a sign through which the dimension of transphenomenal Freedom, of a free society, *appeared.* "Appearance" is thus not simply the domain of phenomena, but those "magic moments" in which the other, noumenal, dimension momentarily "appears" in ("shines through") some empirical/contingent phenomenon. Therein resides also the problem with cyberspace and virtual reality (VR): What VR threatens is NOT "reality" which is dissolved in the multiplicity of its simulacra, but, on the contrary, APPEARANCE itself. To put it in Lacanian terms: simulacrum is imaginary (illusion), while appearance is symbolic (fiction); when the specific dimension of symbolic appearance starts to disintegrate, imaginary and real become more and more indistinguishable. The key to today's universe of simulacra in which real is less and less distinguishable from its imaginary simulation resides in the re-treat of the "symbolic efficiency." This crucial distinction between simulacrum (overlapping with the real) and appearance is easily discernible in the domain of sexuality, as the distinction between pornography and seduction: Pornography "shows it all," "real sex," and for that very reason produces the mere simulacrum of sexuality, while the process of seduction consists entirely in the play of appearances, hints, and promises, and thereby evokes the elusive domain of the suprasensible sublime Thing.

On the other hand, there are those who emphasize the liberating potential of cyberspace: Cyberspace opens up the domain of shifting multiple sexual and social identities, potentially at least liberating us from the hold of the patriarchal Law; it, as it were, realizes in our everyday practical experience the "deconstruction" of old metaphysical binaries ("real Self" versus "artificial mask," etc.). In cyberspace, I am compelled to renounce any fixed symbolic identity, the legal/political fiction of a unique Self guaranteed by my place in the socio-symbolic structure – in short, according to this second version (Sandy Stone, Sherry Turkle), cyberspace announces the end of the Cartesian *cogito* as the unique "thinking substance." Of course, from this second point of view, the pessimist prophets of the psychotic "end of Oedipus" in the universe of simulacra simply betray their inability to imagine an alternative to Oedipus. What we have here is another version of the standard postmodern deconstructionist narrative according to which, in the bad old patriarchal order, the subject's sexual identity was predetermined by his or her place and/or role within the fixed symbolic Oedipal frame-work – the "big Other" took care of us and conferred on us the identity of either a "man" or a "woman," and the subject's ethical duty was limited to the effort to succeed in occupying the preordained symbolic place. (Homosexuality and other "perversions" were perceived as simply so many signs of the subject's *failure* to succeed in going through the Oedipal path and thus achieving "normal"/"mature" sexual identity.) Today, however, as Foucault allegedly demonstrated, the legal/prohibitive matrix of Power which underlies the Oedipal functioning of sexuality is in retreat, so that, instead of being interpellated to occupy a preordained place in the socio-symbolic order, the subject gained the freedom (or at least the promise, the prospect of freedom) to shift between different socio-symbolic sexual identities, to construct his Self as an aesthetic *oeuvre* – the motif at work from the late Foucault's notion of the "care of the Self" up to deconstructionist feminist emphasis on the social formation of gender. It is easy to perceive how the reference to cyberspace can provide an additional impetus to this ideology of aesthetic self-creation: Cyberspace delivers me from the vestiges of biological constraints and elevates my capacity to construct freely my Self, to let myself go to a multitude of shifting identities . . .

However, opposed to both versions of "cyberspace as the end of Oedipus" are some rare, but nonetheless penetrating theoreticians (see Flieger, 1997) who assert the continuity of cyberspace with the Oedipal mode of subjectivization: Cyberspace retains the fundamental Oedipal structure of an intervening Third Order which, in its very capacity of the agency of mediation/mediatization, sustains the subject's desire, while simultaneously acting as the agent of Prohibition which prevents its direct and full gratification – on account of this intervening Third, every partial gratification/satisfaction is marked by a fundamental "this is not THAT." The notion that cyberspace as the medium of hyperreality suspends the symbolic efficiency and brings about the false total transparency of the imaginary simulacra coinciding with the Real, while effectively expressing a certain "spontaneous ideology of cyberspace" (to paraphrase Althusser), dissimulates the actual functioning of cyberspace, which not only continues to rely on the elementary dispositif of the symbolic Law, but even renders it more palpable in our everyday experience. Suffice it to recall the conditions of our surfing along in the Internet or participating in a virtual community: First, there is the gap between the "subject of enunciation" (the anonymous X who does it, who speaks) and the "subject of the enunciated/of the statement" (the symbolic identity that I assume in cyberspace, and which can be and in a sense always is "invented" – the signifier which marks my identity in cyberspace is never directly "myself"); the same goes for the other side, for my partner(s) in cyberspace communication – here, the undecidability is radical, I can never be sure who they are: Are they "really" the way they describe themselves, is there a "real" person at all behind a screen-persona, is the screen-persona a mask for a multiplicity of persons, does the same "real" person possess and manipulate more screen-personas, or am I simply dealing with a digitalized entity which does not stand for any "real" person? In short, INTER-FACE means precisely that my relationship to the Other is never FACE-TO-FACE, that it is always mediat(iz)ed by the interposed digital machinery which stands for the Lacanian "big Other" as the anonymous symbolic order whose structure is that of a labyrinth: I "browse," I err around in this infinite space where messages circulate freely without fixed destination, while the Whole of it – this immense circuitry of "murmurs" – remains forever beyond the scope of my comprehension. (In this sense, one is tempted to propose the proto-Kantian notion of the "cyberspace Sublime" as the magnitude of messages and their circuits which even the greatest effort of my synthetic imagination cannot encompass/comprehend.) Furthermore, does the a priori possibility of viruses disintegrating the virtual universe not point toward the fact that, in the virtual universe also, there is no "Other of the Other," that this universe is a priori inconsistent, with no last guarantee of its coherent functioning? The conclusion thus seems to be that there IS a properly "symbolic" functioning of cyberspace: Cyberspace remains "Oedipal" in the sense that, in order to circulate freely in it, one must assume a fundamental prohibition and/or alienation – yes, in cyberspace, "you can be whatever you want," you're free to choose *a* symbolic identity (screen persona), but you must choose *one* which will always in a way betray you, which will never be fully adequate, you must accept to be represented in cyberspace by a signifying element which runs around in the circuitry as your stand-in. . . . Yes, in cyberspace, "everything is possible," but for the price of assuming a fundamental *impossibility*: You cannot circumvent the mediation of the interface, its "by-pass," which separates you (as the subject of enunciation) forever from your symbolic stand-in.

"L'autre n'existe pas" . . .

Our contention is that both these versions miss the point; they are either too strong (claiming that cyberspace involves a kind of psychotic suspension of the "big Other" *qua* the symbolic Law) or too weak (positing a direct continuation of Oedipus in cyberspace). The fact is that today, in a sense, "the big Other no longer exists" – however, in WHAT sense? In a way, with the big Other, it is the same as with God according to Lacan (it is not that God is dead today – God was dead from the very beginning, only that He didn't know it . . .): *It never existed in the first place,* i.e., the inexistence of the "big Other" is ultimately equivalent to the fact that the big Other is the *symbolic* order, the order of symbolic fictions which operate at a level different from direct material causality. (In this sense, the only subject for whom the big Other *does* exist is the psychotic, the one who attributes to words direct material efficiency.) In short, the "inexistence of the big Other" is strictly correlative to the notion of belief, of symbolic trust, credence, of taking what others' say "at their word's value."

In one of the Marx Brothers' films, Groucho, when caught in a lie, answers angrily: "Whom do you believe, your eyes or my words?" This apparently absurd logic renders perfectly the functioning of the symbolic order, in which the symbolic mask-mandate matters more than the direct reality of the individual who wears this mask and/or assumes this mandate. This functioning involves the structure of fetishist disavowal: "I know very well that things are the way I see them/that this person is a corrupted weakling/, but I nonetheless treat him respectfully, since he wears the insignia of a judge, so that when he speaks, it is the Law itself which speaks through him." So, in a way, I effectively believe his words, not my eyes, i.e., I believe in Another Space (the domain of pure symbolic authority) which matters more than the reality of its spokesmen. . . . The cynical reduction to reality thus falls short: When a judge speaks, there is in a way more truth in his words (the words of the Institution of law) than in the direct reality of the person of judge – if one limits oneself to what one sees, one simply misses the point. This paradox is what Lacan aims at with his "*les non-dupes errent*": Those who do not let themselves be caught in the symbolic deception/fiction and continue to believe their eyes are the ones who err most. . . . What a cynic who "believes only his eyes" misses is the efficiency of the symbolic fiction, the way this fiction structures our experience of reality. The same gap is at work our most intimate relationship to our neighbors: We behave AS IF we do not know that they also smell bad, secrete excrements, etc. – a minimum of idealization, of fetishizing disavowal, is the basis of our coexistence.

Today, with the new digitalized technologies enabling perfectly faked documentary images, not to mention virtual reality, the motto "Believe my words (argumentation), not the fascination of your eyes!" is more actual than ever. That is to say, the crucial point here is to keep in sight how the logic of "Whom do you believe, your eyes or my words?", i.e., of "I know well, but nonetheless . . ./I believe/," can function in two different ways, that of the symbolic *fiction* and that of the imaginary *simulacrum*. In the case of the efficient symbolic fiction of the judge wearing his insignia, "I know very well that this person is a corrupt weakling, but I nonetheless treat him as if/I believe that/the symbolic big Other speaks through him": I disavow what my eyes tell me and I choose to believe the symbolic fiction. In the case of the simulacrum of virtual reality, on the contrary, "I know very well that what I see is an illusion generated by the digital machinery, but I nonetheless accept to immerse myself in it, to behave as if I believe it" – here, I disavow what my (symbolic) knowledge tells me and I choose to believe my eyes only. . . .

This reversal signals the fact that, today, the big Other's in-existence has reached a much more radical dimension: What is more and more undermined is precisely this symbolic trust which persists against all skeptical data. Perhaps the most eye-catching facet of this new status of the "nonexistence of the big Other" is the sprouting of "committees" destined to decide upon the so-called ethical dilemmas which pop up when technological developments in an ever-increasing way affect our life-world: in medicine and biogenetics (at what point does an acceptable and even desirable genetic experiment or intervention turn into an unacceptable manipulation?), in the application of universal human rights (at what point does the protection of the victim's rights turn into an imposition of Western values?), in sexual mores (what is the proper, nonpatriarchal, procedure of seduction?), not to mention the obvious case of cyberspace (what is the status of sexual harassment in a virtual community? How does one distinguish here between "mere words" and "deeds"?). So, to resolve the deadlock, one convenes a committee to formulate, in an ultimately arbitrary way, the precise rules of conduct. . . . The work of these committees is caught in a symptomal vicious cycle: On the one hand, they try to legitimate their decisions in the most advanced scientific knowledge (which, in the case of abortion, tells us that a fetus does not yet possess self-awareness and experience pain; which, in the case of a mortally ill person, defines the threshold beyond which euthanasia is the only meaningful solution); on the other hand, they have to evoke some nonscientific ethical criterion in order to direct and posit a limitation to inherent scientific drive.

. . . et pourtant, il revient dans le reel

The first paradox of this retreat of the big Other is discernible in the so-called "culture of complaint," with its underlying logic of *ressentiment*: Far from cheerfully assuming the inexistence of the big Other, the subject blames the Other for its failure and/or impotence, as if *the Other is guilty for the fact that it doesn't exist*, i.e., as if impotence is no excuse – the big Other is responsible for the very fact that it wasn't able to do anything: The more the subject's structure is "narcissistic," the more he puts the blame on the big Other and thus asserts his dependence on it. The basic feature of the "culture of complaint" is thus a call, addressed at the big Other, to intervene and to set things straight (to recompense the damaged sexual or ethnic minority, etc.) – how, exactly, this to be done is again a matter of different ethico-legal "committees." Is thus the "culture of complaint" not today's version of hysteria, of the hysterical impossible demand addressed to the Other, a demand which effectively *wants to be rejected,* since the subject grounds his or her existence in his or her complaint – "I am insofar as I make the Other responsible and/or guilty for my misery"? The gap is here insurmountable between this logic of complaint and the true "radical" ("revolutionary") act which, instead of complaining to the Other and expecting it to act, i.e., displacing the need to act onto it, suspends the existing legal frame and *itself accomplishes the act*. . . . So what is wrong with the complaint of those who are really deprivileged?

The fact that, instead of undermining the position of the Other, they still address themselves to it: By way of translating their demand into the terms of legalistic complaint, they confirm the Other in its position in the very gesture of attacking it.

Furthermore, a wide scope of phenomena (the resurgent ethico/religious "fundamentalisms" which advocate a return to the Christian patriarchal division of sexual roles; the New Age massive resexualization of the universe, i.e., the return to pre-modern pagan sexualized cosmo-ontology; the growth of "conspiracy theories" as a form of popular "cognitive mapping") seem to counter this retreat of the big Other. It is all too simple to dismiss these phenomena as simply "regressive," as new modes of the "escape from freedom," as unfortunate "remainders of the past" which will disappear if we only continue to proceed even more resolutely on the deconstructionist path of historicization of every fixed identity, of unmasking the contingency of every naturalized self-image. These disturbing phenomena rather compel us to elaborate much more in detail the contours of the retreat of the big Other: The paradoxical result of this mutation in the "inexistence of the Other" – of the growing collapse of the symbolic efficiency – is precisely the *reemergence* of the different facets of *a big Other which exists effectively, in the Real,* not merely as a symbolic fiction.

The belief in the big Other which exists in the Real is, of course, the most succinct definition of paranoia; for that reason, two features which characterize today's ideological stance – cynical distance and full reliance on paranoiac fantasy – are strictly codependent: The typical subject today is the one who, while displaying cynical distrust of any public ideology, indulges without restraint in paranoiac fantasies about conspiracies, threats, and excessive forms of enjoyment of the Other. The distrust of the big Other (the order of symbolic fictions), the subject's refusal to "take it seriously," relies on the belief that there is an "Other of the Other," that a secret, invisible and all-powerful agent effectively "pulls the strings" and runs the show: Behind the visible, public Power, there is another obscene, invisible power structure. This other, hidden agent acts the part of the "Other of the Other" in the Lacanian sense, the part of the meta-guarantee of the consistency of the big Other (the symbolic order that regulates social life). It is here that we should look for the roots of the recent impasse of narrativization, i.e., of the motif of the "end of large narratives": In our era when – in politics and ideology as well as in literature and cinema – global, all-encompassing narratives ("the struggle of liberal democracy with totalitarianism," etc.) seem no longer possible, the only way to arrive at a kind of global "cognitive mapping" seems to be the paranoiac narrative of a "conspiracy theory" – not only for the right-wing populism and fundamentalism, but also for the liberal center (the "mystery" of Kennedy's assassination) and left-wing orientations (see the old obsession of the American Left with the notion that some mysterious government agency is experimenting with nerve gases that enable the Power to regulate the behavior of the population). The large majority of movies which, in the last two decades, were able to attract the public interest on account of their plot, not of the firecracking action, were different versions of conspiracy theory. And it is all too simplistic to dismiss conspiracy-narratives as the paranoiac proto-Fascist reaction of the infamous "middle classes" which feel threatened by the process of modernization: It would be much more productive to conceive "conspiracy theory" as a kind of floating signifier which, as we have just seen, can be appropriated by different political options, enabling them to obtain a minimal cognitive mapping.

This, then, is one version of the big Other which continues to exist in the wake of its alleged disappearance. Another version is operative in the guise of the New Age Jungian resexualization of the universe ("men are from Mars, women are from Venus"): According to it, there is an underlying, deeply anchored archetypal identity which provides a kind of safe haven in the flurry of contemporary confusion of roles and identities; from this perspective, the ultimate origin of today's crisis is not the difficulty in overcoming the tradition of fixed sexual roles, but the disturbed balance in the modern man who puts an excessive emphasis on the male-rational-conscious, etc., aspect, neglecting the feminine-compassionate, etc., aspect. Although this tendency shares with feminism the anti-Cartesian and antipatriarchal bias, it rewrites the feminist agenda into a reassertion of archetypal feminine roots repressed in our competitive male mechanistic universe. . . . Yet another version of the *real* Other is the figure of the father as sexual harasser of his young daughters, which stands in the very center of the so-called "false-memory syndrome": Here, also, the suspended father as the agent of symbolic authority, i.e., the embodiment of a symbolic fiction, "returns in the real." (What causes such controversy is the contention of those who advocate recovery of memories of childhood sexual abuses that sexual harassment by the father is not merely fantasized or, at least, an indissoluble mixture of fact and fantasy, but a plain fact, something that, in the majority of families, "really happened" in the daughter's childhood – an obstinacy comparable to Freud's no less obstinate insistence on the murder of the "primordial father" as a real event in the humanity's prehistory.) A further aspect of this "return in the real" of the father is undoubtedly the growing obsession of the popular pseudoscience with the mystery of the alleged Christ's tomb and/or progeny (from his alleged marriage with Mary Magdalene) which focuses on the region around Rennes-le-Château in the south of France, weaving into a large coherent narrative the Grail myth, Cathars, Templars, Freemasons, etc.: These narratives endeavor to supplant the diminishing power of the *symbolic fiction* of the Holy Ghost (the community of believers) with the *bodily Real* of Christ and his descendants.

The Digital Perversion

So, back to cyberspace: These complications seem to indicate how both standard reactions to cyberspace (cyberspace as involving a kind of break with the Oedipal symbolic Law; cyberspace as a continuation of Oedipus with other means) are deficient. There is, however, in the psychoanalytic clinic, a third, intermediary concept between these two extremes: that of *perversion*. The key point is clearly to delineate the specific intermediate status of perversion, in-between psychosis and neurosis, in-between the psychotic's foreclosure of the Law and the neurotic's integration into the Law. According to the standard view, the perverse scenario stages the "disavowal of castration": Perversion can be seen as a defense against the motif of "death and sexuality," against the threat of mortality as well as the contingent imposition of sexual difference – what the pervert enacts is a universe in which, as in cartoons, a human being can survive any catastrophe; in which adult sexuality is reduced to a childish game; in which one is not forced to die or to choose one of the two sexes. As such, the pervert's universe is the universe of pure symbolic order, of the signifier's game running its course, unencumbered by the Real of the human finitude.

In a first approach, it may seem that our experience of cyberspace fits perfectly this universe: Is cyberspace not also a universe unencumbered by the inertia of the Real, constrained only by its self-imposed rules? However, according to Lacan, what this standard notion of perversion leaves out of consideration, is the unique short circuit between Law and *jouissance* which characterizes the innermost structure of perversion: In contrast to the neurotic who acknowledges the Law in order occasionally to take enjoyment in its transgressions (masturbation, theft . . .), and thus obtains satisfaction by way of snatching back from the Other part of the stolen *jouissance,* the pervert directly elevates the enjoying big Other into the agency of Law. The pervert's aim is to *establish,* not to undermine, the Law: The proverbial male masochist elevates his partner, the Dominatrix, into the Law-giver whose orders are to be obeyed. A pervert fully acknowledges the obscene underside of the Law, since he gains satisfaction out of the very obscenity of the gesture of installing the rule of Law, i.e., of "castration." In the "normal" state of things, the symbolic Law prevents access to the (incestuous) object, and thus creates the desire for it; in perversion, *it is the object itself* (say, Domina in masochism), *which makes the law.* The theoretical concept of the masochist perversion touches here the common notion of a masochist who "enjoys being tortured by the Law": A masochist *locates enjoyment in the very agency of the Law which prohibits the access to enjoyment.* To put it in yet another way: In contrast to the "normal" subject, for whom the Law functions as the agency of prohibition which regulates (the access to the object of) his desire, for the pervert, *the object of his desire is Law itself* – the Law is the Ideal he is longing for, he wants to be fully acknowledged by the Law, integrated into its functioning. . . . The irony of this should not escape us: The pervert, this "transgressor" par excellence who purports to violate all the rules of "normal" and decent behavior, effectively longs for the very rule of Law.

So what is effectively at stake in perversion? There is an agency in New York called "Slaves are us," which provides people who are willing to clean your apartment for free, and want to be treated rudely by the lady of the house. The agency gets the cleaners through ads (whose motto is "Slavery is its own reward!"): Most of them are highly paid executives, doctors, and lawyers, who, when questioned about their motives, emphasize how they are sick of being in charge all the time – they immensely enjoy just being brutally ordered to do their job and shouted at, insofar as this is the only way open to them to gain access to Being. And the philosophical point not to be missed here is that masochism as the only access to Being is strictly correlative with the modern Kantian subjectivity, with the subject reduced to the empty point of self-relating negativity. The scope of the Kantian revolution can be discerned through an interesting detail from literary history: the sudden change in the perception of the theme of *double.* Till the end of eighteenth century, this theme mostly gave rise to comic plots (two brothers who look alike are seducing the same girl; Zeus seducing Amphitrion's faithful wife disguised as Amphitrion, so that, when Amphitrion unexpectedly returns home, he encounters *himself* leaving his bedroom; etc.); all of a sudden, however, in the historic moment which exactly fits the Kantian revolution, the topic of the double becomes associated with horror and anxiety – encountering one's double or being followed and persecuted by him is the ultimate experience of terror, it is something which shatters the very core of the subject's identity.

The horrifying aspect of the theme of the double thus has something to do with the emergence of the Kantian subject as pure transcendental apperception, as the substanceless void of self-consciousness which is *not* an object in reality. What the subject encounters in the guise of his double is himself *as object*, i.e., his own "impossible" objectal counterpoint. In the pre-Kantian space, this encounter was not traumatic, since the individual conceived himself as a positive entity, an object within the world. Another way to make the same point is to locate in my double, in the encountered object which "is" myself, the Lacanian *objet petit a*: What makes the double so uncanny, what distinguishes it from other inner-worldly objects, is not simply its resemblance to me, but the fact that he gives body to "that which is in myself more than myself," to the inaccessible/unfathomable object that "I am," i.e., to that which I forever *lack* in the reality of my self-experience. . . .

A feature which seems to confirm this hypothesis is the fact that the impact of cyberspace is strictly correlative to the changed status of sadomasochist bodily practices in our society. Let us explain this shift by way of addressing the standard criticism of psychoanalysis, according to which psychoanalytic interpretation reduces a work of art or a religious experience to a pathological perverse, neurotic, or even psychotic formation, to a sublimated expression of some unconscious impetus or conflict, etc. How does Lacan answer this criticism? By turning the terms of such "reductionist" interpretive procedure around: The problem, for him, is not to establish the pathological libidinal roots of a publicly acknowledged symbolic formation (religious vision, work of art, etc.), but the opposite, the question How is the public socio-symbolic space of the "big Other" structured so that an agent who undoubtedly displays the features of psycho-pathology acquires the status of a public person of great esteem? How is it – to take the classic case – that a woman with traits which, in an Oriental or so-called "primitive" culture, would cause her to be praised as a deep mystic visionary, is in our modern culture dismissed as the hysterical or even psychotic author of hallucinatory ramblings? How is it that a man who finds intense fulfilment in starving and whipping himself was in early Christianity hailed as an ascetic martyr, while today he appears to us as a masochistic pervert? Therein resided the wisdom of the Catholic Church: to allow a space within its institutionalized ranks for the exercise of the *jouissance feminine* irreducible to the paternal symbolic Law (nuns allowed to practice their mystical experiences). At a different level, the same goes for modern art: Say, how is it that today, a pervert ritual of piercing one's body, which even a decade ago would be dismissed as an abhorrent private monstrosity, can be staged in public and presented as an artistic performance? How is it that this is included into the "big Other"? Lacan's notion of perversion (the pervert ritual) as a process which, far from undermining the symbolic Law, rather stands for a desperate attempt of the subject to stage the scene of installing (setting up) the rule of the Law, of its inscription onto the human body, thus enables us to throw a new light on the recent artistic tendencies of masochist body performances – are they not an answer to the disintegration of the rule of Law, an attempt to restore the symbolic Prohibition? And, again, since the Law in its capacity of prohibiting direct ("incestuous") access to *jouissance* is getting more and more inoperative, the only remaining way to sustain the Law is to posit is as identical with the very Thing which embodies *jouissance*.

The Fantasy Which Cannot Be Subjectivized

How does all this concern cyberspace? It is often said that cyberspace opens up the domain to realize (to externalize, to stage) our innermost fantasies. Here, it is again crucial to bear in mind the key dimension of the notion of fantasy. Insofar as, according to Lacan, the subject of the signifier is the "barred," empty subject, *le manqué a etre*, lacking a support in the positive order of Being, what fantasy stages is precisely the subject's impossible Being lost on account of the subject's entry into the symbolic order. No wonder, then, that the fundamental fantasy is *passive*, "masochistic," reducing me to an object worked upon by others: It is as if only the experience of the utmost pain can guarantee to the subject the access to Being: *la douleur d'exister* means that I "am" only insofar I experience pain. At this point, a brief survey of post-Cartesian philosophy is very instructive: It was haunted by the vestiges of an Other Scene at which the subject – this free, active, self-positing agent – is reduced to an object of unbearable suffering or humiliation, deprived of the dignity of his freedom.

In "Le prix du progres," one of the fragments which conclude *The Dialectic of Enlightenment*, Adorno and Horkheimer quote the argumentation of the French nineteenth-century physiologist Pierre Flourens against medical anaesthesia with chloroform: Flourens claims that it can be proven how the anaesthetic works only on our memorial neuronal network – in short, while we are butchered alive on the operating table, we fully feel the terrible pain; the point is only that later, after the awakening, we do not remember it. . . . For Adorno and Horkheimer, this, of course, is the perfect metaphor of the fate of Reason based on the repression of nature in itself: His body, the part of nature in the subject, fully feels the pain, it is only that, on account of the repression, the subject does not remember it. Therein resides the perfect revenge of nature for our domination over it: unknowingly, we are our own greatest victims, butchering ourselves alive. Is it not also possible to read this as the perfect fantasy scenario of inter-passivity, of the Other Scene in which we pay the price for our active intervention into the world? A sadomasochist willingly assumes this suffering as the access to Being. Our second example: Kant, in a subchapter of his *Critique of Practical Reason* mysteriously titled "Of the Wise Adaptation of Man's

Cognitive Faculties to His Practical Vocation," answers the question of what would happen to us if we were to gain access to the noumenal domain, to Things in themselves:

> . . . instead of the conflict which now the moral disposition has to wage with inclinations and in which, after some defeats, moral strength of mind may be gradually won, God and eternity in their awful majesty would stand unceasingly before our eyes. Thus, most actions conforming to the law would be done from fear, few would be done from hope, none from duty. The moral worth of actions, on which alone the worth of the person and even of the world depends in the eyes of supreme wisdom, would not exist at all. The conduct of man, so long as his nature remained as it is now, would be changed into mere mechanism, where, as in a puppet show, everything would gesticulate well but no life would be found in the figures.
>
> *(Kant, 1956, pp. 152–153)*

No wonder that this vision of a man who, on account of his direct insight into the monstrosity of the divine being-in-itself, would turn into a lifeless puppet, provokes such an unease among the commentators of Kant (usually, it is either passed over in silence or dismissed as an uncanny, out-of-place foreign body): What Kant delivers in it is no less than what one is tempted to call *the Kantian fundamental fantasy*, the inter-passive Other Scene of freedom, of the spontaneous free agent, the Scene in which the free agent is turned into a lifeless puppet at the mercy of the perverse God. The lesson of it, of course, is that there is no active free agent without this fantasmatic support, without this Other Scene in which he is totally manipulated by the Other. In short, the Kantian prohibition of the direct access to the noumenal domain should be reformulated: What should remain inaccessible to us is not the noumenal Real, but our *fundamental fantasy* itself – the moment the subject comes too close to this fantasmatic kernel, it looses the consistency of his existence.

The ontological paradox, scandal even, of *fantasy* resides in the fact that it subverts the standard opposition of "subjective" and "objective": Of course, fantasy is by definition not "objective" (in the naive sense of "existing" independently of the subject's perceptions); however, it is also not "subjective" (in the sense of being reducible to the subject's consciously experienced intuitions). Fantasy rather belongs to the "bizarre category of the objectively subjective – the way things actually, objectively seem to you even if they don't seem that way to you" (Dennett, 1991, p. 132). (Dennett, of course, evokes this concept in a purely negative way, as a nonsensical *contradictio in adjecto*.) When for example, the subject actually experiences a series of fantasmatic formations which interrelate as so many permutations of each other, this series is never complete: It is always as if the actually experienced series presents so many variations of some underlying "fundamental" fantasy which is *never* actually experienced by the subject. (In Freud's "A Child Is Being Beaten," the two consciously experienced fantasies presuppose and thus relate to a third one, "My father is beating me," which was never actually experienced and can only be retroactively reconstructed as the presupposed reference of – or, in this case, the intermediate term between – the other two fantasies.) When, for example, we claim that someone who is consciously well disposed toward Jews, nonetheless harbors profound anti-Semitic prejudices he is not consciously aware of, do we not claim that (insofar as these prejudices do not render the way Jews really are, but the way they appear to him) *he is not aware how Jews really seem to him*? This brings us back to the mystery of "commodity fetishism": When a critical Marxist encounters a bourgeois subject immersed in commodity fetishism, the Marxist's reproach to him is not "Commodity may seem to you a magical object endowed with special powers, but it really is just a reified expression of relations between people"; the actual Marxist's reproach is rather "You may think that the commodity appears to you as a simple embodiment of social relations (that, for example, money is just a kind of voucher entitling you to a part of the social product), but *this is not how things really seem to you* – in your social reality, by means of your participation in social exchange, you bear witness to the uncanny fact that a commodity really appears to you as a magical object endowed with special powers." . . .

This is also one of the ways in which to specify the meaning of Lacan's assertion of the subject's constitutive "decenterment": Its point is not that my subjective experience is regulated by objective unconscious mechanisms which are "decentered" with regard to my self-experience and, as such, beyond my control (a point asserted by every materialist), but rather something much more unsettling – I am deprived of even my most intimate "subjective" experience, the way things "really seem to me," that of the fundamental fantasy which constitutes and guarantees the kernel of my being, since I can never consciously experience it and assume it. . . . According to the standard view, the dimension which is constitutive of subjectivity is that of the phenomenal (self) experience – I am a subject the moment I can say to myself: "No matter what unknown mechanism governs my acts, perceptions and thoughts, nobody can take from me what I see and feel now." Lacan turns around this standard view: The "subject of the signifier" emerges only when a key aspect of the subject's *phenomenal* (self) experience (his "fundamental fantasy"), becomes *inaccessible* to him, i.e., is "primordially repressed." At its most radical, the Unconscious is the *inaccessible phenomenon,* not the objective mechanism which regulates my phenomenal experience. So, in contrast to the commonplace, according to which we are dealing with a subject the moment an entity displays signs of "inner life," i.e., of a fantasmatic self-experience which cannot be reduced to external behavior, one should claim that what characterizes human subjectivity proper is rather the gap which separates the two, i.e., the fact that fantasy, at its most elementary, becomes inaccessible to the subject – it is this inaccessibility which makes the subject "empty" ($). We thus obtain a relationship which totally subverts the standard notion of the subject who directly experiences himself, his "inner states": an "impossible" relationship between the *empty, nonphenomenal subject* and the *phenomena which remain inaccessible to the subject.*

The Frog and the Bottle of Beer

Let us specify the status of these strange phenomena which cannot be subjectivized by a recent English publicity spot for a beer. Its first part stages the well-known fairy-tale anecdote: A girl walks along a stream, sees a frog, takes it gently into her lap, kisses it, and, of course, the ugly frog miraculously turns into a beautiful young man. However, the story isn't over yet: The young man casts a covetous glance at the girl, draws her toward himself, kisses her – and she turns into a bottle of beer which the man holds triumphantly in his hand. . . . For the woman, the point is that her love and affection (signaled by the kiss) turn a frog into a beautiful man, a full phallic presence (in Lacan's symbols, the big Phi); for the man, it is to reduce the woman to a partial object, the cause of his desire (in Lacan's symbols, the object small *a*). On account of this asymmetry, "there is no sexual relationship": We have either a woman with a frog or a man with a bottle of beer – what we can never obtain is the "natural" couple of the beautiful woman and man. . . . Why not? Because fantasmatic support of this "ideal couple" would have been the inconsistent figure of *a frog embracing a bottle of beer.* (Of course, the obvious feminist point would be that what women witness in their everyday love experience is rather the opposite passage: One kisses a beautiful young man and, after one gets too close to him, i.e., when it is already too late, one notices that he is effectively a frog . . .). This, then, opens up the possibility of undermining the hold a fantasy exerts over us through the very over identification with it, i.e., by way of *embracing simultaneously, within the same space, the multitude of inconsistent fantasmatic elements.* That is to say, each of the two subjects is involved in his or her own subjective fantasizing – the girl fantasizes about the frog who is really a young man, the man about the girl who is really a bottle of beer. What modern art and writing oppose to this is not objective reality but the "objectively subjective" underlying fantasy which the two subjects are never able to assume, something similar to a Magrittesque painting of a frog embracing a bottle of beer, with a title "A man and a woman" or "The ideal couple." (The association with the famous surrealist "dead donkey on a piano" is here fully justified, since surrealists also practiced a version of traversing the fantasy.) And is this not the ethical duty of today's artist – to confront us with the frog embracing the bottle of beer when we are daydreaming of embracing our beloved? In other words, to stage fantasies which are radically desubjectivized, which cannot ever be assumed by the subject?

This, then, is the point we were aiming at all along: Perhaps, cyberspace, with its capacity to externalize our innermost fantasies in all their inconsistency, opens up to the artistic practice a unique possibility to stage, to "act out," the fantasmatic support of our existence, up to the fundamental "sadomasochistic" fantasy which cannot ever be subjectivized. We are thus invited to risk the most radical experience imaginable: the encounter with our "noumenal Self," with the Other Scene which stages the foreclosed hard core of the subject's Being. Far from enslaving us to these fantasies and thus turning us into desubjectivized blind puppets, it enables us to treat them in a playful way and thus to adopt toward them a minimum of distance – in short, to achieve what Lacan calls *la traversee du fantasme*, "going-through, traversing the fantasy."

So let us conclude with a reference to the (in)famous last proposition of Wittgenstein's *Tractatus*: "*Wovon man nicht sprechen kann, davon muss man schweigen*." This proposition renders in the most succinct way possible the paradox of the Oedipal Law which prohibits something (incestuous fusion) that is already in itself impossible (and thereby gives rise to the hope that, if we remove or overcome the prohibition, the "impossible" incest will become possible). If we are effectively to move to a region "beyond Oedipus," Wittgenstein's proposition is to be rephrased into "*Wovon man nicht sprechen kann, davon muss man SCHREIBEN*." There is, of course, a long tradition of conceiving art as a mode or practice of writing which augurs that which "one cannot speak about," i.e., the utopian potential "repressed" by the existing socio-symbolic network of prohibitions. There is also a long tradition of using writing as a means to communicate a declaration of love too intimate and/or too painful to be directly asserted in a face-to-face speech act. Not only is the Internet widely used as a space for the amorous encounters of shy people; significantly, one of the anecdotes about Edison, the inventor of the telegraph, is that he himself used it to declare love and ask the hand of his secretary (being too shy to do it directly, by means of a spoken word). However, what we are aiming at is not this standard economy of using cyberspace as a place in which, since we are not directly engaged in it, i.e., since we maintain a distance toward it, we feel free to externalize and stage our innermost private fantasies. What we have in mind is a more radical level, the level which concerns our very fundamental fantasy as that "*wovon man nicht sprechen kann*": The subject is never able to assume his or her fundamental fantasy, to recognize himself or herself in it in a performance of a speech act; perhaps, cyberspace opens up a domain in which the subject can nonetheless externalize/stage his/her fundamental fantasy and thus gain a minimum of distance toward it. . . .

This, however, in no way entails that inducing us to "traverse the fantasy" is an automatic effect of our immersion into cyberspace. What one should do here is, rather, to accomplish a Hegelian reversal of epistemological obstacle into ontological deadlock: What if it is wrong and misleading to ask which of the four versions of the libidinal/symbolic economy of cyberspace that we outlined (psychotic suspension of the Oedipus; the continuation of the Oedipus with other means; the perverse staging of the Law; traversing the fantasy) is the "correct" one? What if these four versions are the four possibilities opened up by the cyberspace technology, so that, ultimately, the choice is ours? How will cyberspace affect us is not directly inscribed into its technological properties; it rather hinges on the network of socio-symbolic relations (of power and domination, etc.) which always-already overdetermine the way cyberspace affects us.

References

Dennett, Daniel C. (1991): *Consciousness Explained*, New York: Little, Brown.
Flieger, Jerry Aline. (1997, July): "Oedipus On-Line?" *Pretexts*, No. 1 / Vol. 6, pp. 81–94.
Kant, Immanuel. (1956): *Critique of Practical Reason*, New York: Macmillan.
Schelling, F.W.J. (1946): *Die Weltalter. Fragmente. In den Urfassungen von 1811 und 1813*, ed. Manfred Schroeter, Munich: Biederstein (reprint 1979).

29

PSYCHOANALYSIS, RACE AND COLONIALISM

Stephen Frosh

Colonialism and Psychoanalysis

Recent discussions of psychoanalysis' implication in discourses of 'race' and practices of racialisation have focused as much on colonialism as on racism itself. This has led to some very productive work that both locates psychoanalysis within the colonial project and explores the potential that psychoanalytic concepts have for critical analysis of that project. Much of this work has drawn on the writings (and figure) of Frantz Fanon (1952), though there have also been major contributions from researchers on psychoanalysis in the Global South and in postcolonial societies (Anderson et al, 2011). This work challenges the ethnocentrism of psychoanalysis as well as drawing attention to its colonial roots, which lie in tension with the anti-colonial and socially critical impulse given psychoanalysis by its Jewish origins and its resultant consciousness of antisemitism (Brickman, 2003; Frosh, 2013). Amongst the key issues here is whether the ambition of psychoanalysis to be a European science characterised by an Enlightenment vision of the virtues of rationality also positions it as colonial and racist in its attitudes towards the imagined non-European 'savage' or 'primitive' (Frosh, 2017). Brickman (2003) argues that the movement of savagery to embrace the indigenous African and Australian population was part of an effort by Freud to position Jewish identity as European, rather than as the 'other' to Europeanism assumed by Christian and now racial antisemitism – an enterprise characteristic of other secular intellectual Jews of the time. She comments (Brickman, 2003, p. 167), 'Categorized as a member of a primitive race, Freud repudiated primitivity, locating himself and his work within European civilization, with both its scientific and colonizing enterprises, and replacing the opposition of Aryan/Jew with the opposition of civilized/primitive.' This may indeed have been the case, but even if this argument is not completely convincing, it is undeniable that psychoanalysis invested in assumptions around cannibalism and primitivity that read disturbingly to postcolonial and decolonial eyes. Assuming an antagonism between irrationality and rationality that parallels the dimensions 'savage-civilised' and 'immature-mature', as well as – more ambiguously perhaps – 'unconscious-conscious', and freely deploying tropes of primitivity and cannibalism even to this day (Vyrgioti, 2018), psychoanalysis reproduces colonial fantasies.

In some places, this is not just an ideological issue but a very practical one, though it also has its ambiguities. For example, Anderson et al (2011, pp. 1–2) describe how psychoanalysis had quite specific colonial uses, yet also fed into some anti-colonial perspectives:

DOI: 10.4324/9780429297076-35

> From the 1920s, psychoanalysis was a mobile technology of both the late colonial state and anti-imperialism. Insights from psychoanalysis shaped European and North American ideas about the colonial world, the character and potential of 'native' cultures, and the anxieties and alienation of displaced white colonizers and sojourners. Moreover, intense and intimate engagement with empire came to shape the apparently generic psychoanalytic subjectivities that emerged in the twentieth century – whether European or non-European.

The papers in Anderson et al (2011) collectively demonstrate how the enterprise of psychoanalysis contributed to the perpetration of colonial power in the twentieth century, nominating certain subject populations as potentially analysable and hence 'civilised', which means convertible into Europeans or at least 'suitably modern subjects' (p. 8), and others as 'native' or indigenous, and hence on the subjugated, 'primitive' side of things. The regulatory or disciplinary functions of this are quite apparent: 'Psychoanalytic knowledge assisted in establishing a baseline for the native's personality, a critical dictum for the framing of colonial educational, judicial, and administrative policies in specific locales' (p. 8). Resonances of this can be seen in a different colonial environment, that of Brazil, in which psychoanalysis had a role to play as a mode of socialisation of a polity imagined to be uncontrollable in its forms of racial and sexual excess. As my Brazilian colleagues and I have described elsewhere (Rubin et al, 2016), the importation of psychoanalysis to Brazil happened early and was always ambiguously related to repressive policies (e.g., during the dictatorship of the late twentieth century) and to modernisation processes that were both emancipatory and controlling. Psychoanalysis became embroiled with the Brazilian League of Mental Hygiene, founded in 1923 as part of the project of sanitisation and hygienisation of the Brazilian population, based on eugenic theory and aligned with the tendency to biologise madness, race and cultural aspects of society. Even though some early psychiatrists in the League developed projects that went beyond the initial eugenic framework, the country's racial mixture was seen as a problem and as a cause of Brazilian 'backwardness' that had to be overcome (Russo, 2012). In this context, the psychiatrist Julio Porto-Carrero collaborated in the creation of the psychoanalytic clinic of the League. As Russo (2012) shows, his 'educational' intervention was based on two main aims arising from the psychoanalytic theory of sexuality, both of which can be read as normalising, albeit partly in tension with one another. One aim was to remove the taboo that surrounded sex, working towards a non-repressive morality; the second was to control and sublimate the sexual instincts towards more 'civilised' ends. Russo proposes that, although psychoanalytic practice first developed within the domain of hygiene projects, physicians like Porto-Carrero saw in its non-moralistic attitude a way to humanise the psychiatric movement. As such, it might be claimed to have had a *decolonising* effect in relation to psychiatry, whilst still being part of a project of normalisation based around colonial fantasies of race and 'miscegenation'. Cultural appropriations of psychoanalysis are also relevant here. For example, psychoanalysis had a notable presence in the art world and in debates surrounding the Week of Modern Art, held in São Paulo in 1922. Not only did several writers and painters enter into dialogue with psychoanalysis in their works, but the main document of modernism in the period, the *Manifesto Antropofagico*, written by Oswald de Andrade (1928), mentions Freud in the context of defending an original Brazilian identity free from repression and social restrictions. The social and cultural elites of the period also absorbed psychoanalysis in their search for modernity along European lines. On the other hand again, see-sawing between the different uses of psychoanalysis, the self-identity of Brazil as 'anthropophagous' explicitly relates to the idea of the colonised society as only developing through the materials it can ingest from the coloniser. Psychoanalysis is then one of those materials; and in being cannibalised in this way it is not destroyed, but rather consolidates from the inside a pattern of deference and control through identification and a kind of deathly possession.

This should not be pushed too far, however. From the start the situation was always ambiguous, as it had to be given the tension between psychoanalysis' universalising claims (the Oedipus complex assumed to exist everywhere, for example) and its rigorous focus on individuals' singular experiences; and also between the marginalising of 'savagery' to the 'primitive', racialised other and the revelation of exactly that savagery at the heart of the supposedly civilized European. Freud was certainly clear that barbarism could be found at home, not in his supposedly primitive Jewish 'heim' but in the antisemitic Christian society in which he lived and the pulse of which he took with unerring acuity. 'We must not forget,' Freud (1939, p. 91) wrote in the bitter times at the end of his life,

> that all those peoples who excel to-day in their hatred of Jews became Christians only in late historic times, often driven to it by bloody coercion. It might be said that they are all 'mis-baptized'. They have been left, under a thin veneer of Christianity, what their ancestors were, who worshipped a barbarous polytheism.

Even more incisively, the notion of a dynamic unconscious, expressive of a death drive as well as the loving bonds of Eros, does not suggest that the human condition is bounded by rationality even in its most civilised and scientifically non-illusory places, however much conversion of id into ego there might be. 'It is a work of culture,' writes Freud (1933, p. 80) about the triumph of egoic rationality over the id; but this is clearly also a fragile conquest, always set to fall apart under the continuing pressure of destructiveness and the drives – as indeed it did almost immediately after this Freudian hope was penned.

In addition, the decolonising possibilities of psychoanalysis were mined from early on and are not just the products of postcolonial thought, however important that might be (Greedharry, 2008). The founder of the Indian Psychoanalytic Society (incidentally, a remarkably early Society, begun in 1922), Girindrasekhar Bose, who dominated Indian psychoanalysis for most of his life, was clearly a highly educated, privileged colonial subject who made his living from the analysis of members of 'the British-educated urban elite whose professional life was interwoven with the interests of the colonial rulers' (Hartnack, 2011, p. 102). Nevertheless, he resisted much of Freud's ethnocentric thinking and associated himself strongly with the anticolonial movement; indeed, Hartnack notes (p. 109), 'His pronounced anticolonial attitudes were conformist within the circles to which he belonged.' More significantly perhaps, his psychoanalytic work was hybrid and critical in its use of Hindu ideas and its sensitivity to the specifics of his sociocultural milieu.

> Bose's creative efforts to integrate elements from European and Bengali Hindu psychological and psychoanalytic thought and practice were unprecedented in the field of academic psychology and psychiatry in colonial times and thus were groundbreaking. Instead of the binary concept of black skin – white mask that Fanon adhered to, Bose opted for interfaces (in the very sense of the word). His work was not limited by dichotomises but rather strove to establish connections.
>
> *(Hartnack, 2011, p. 109)*

Hartnack may be being unfair to Fanon in this quotation, because his supposedly 'binary' black-white conceptualisation of the colonial world contains within it a nuanced understanding of the multiple influences on the construction of black and white subjectivities and can be read as a polemical device to uncover the psychopolitical workings of racism that are harder to unpick through notions of hybridity. Nevertheless, noticing that the colonised users of psychoanalysis have not necessarily been anthropophagous – and indeed that when they have been so it has sometimes been in a spirit of irony – is an important step towards realising the potential of psychoanalysis itself for decolonising practice. One might indeed see this as part of the disruptive potential of psychoanalysis itself, something which, amongst others, Edward Said, no friend to colonialism, explicitly noted:

> Freud was an explorer of the mind, of course, but also, in the philosophical sense, an overturner and a re-mapper of accepted or settled geographies and genealogies. He thus lends himself especially to rereading in different contexts, since his work is all about how life history offers itself by recollection, research and reflection to endless structuring and restructuring, in both the individual and the collective sense. That we, different readers from different periods of history, with different cultural backgrounds, should continue to do this in our readings of Freud strikes me as nothing less than a vindication of his work's power to instigate new thought, as well as to illuminate situations that he himself might never have dreamed of.
>
> *(Said, 2003, p. 27)*

Said incorporates this generous reflection on Freud into his general argument for a 'contrapuntal' reading of great writers: critical and postcolonial, but also alert to how their thought is productive. The same might be said of psychoanalysis as a whole, or at least one hopes so. Of course, it has colonial origins and baggage; how could it not, given where and when it originated? More controversially, its institutions have often been places of conservatism and conformity, sometimes under the guise of psychoanalytic 'neutrality' (Frosh and Mandelbaum, 2017), and when they have branched out into social commentary it has not always been in the right direction – witness the attitudes towards homosexuality held by American psychoanalysts until late in the day in America, and still left unreconstructed in relation to the notion of 'perversion' by some contemporary Lacanians (Van Haute, 2016). Nevertheless, psychoanalysis also offers the most powerful vocabulary we have available for examining the 'psychic', or at least subjective, bases of colonial power and of racism; and in its history it has often promoted progressive thinking and practices that have counterbalanced its tendency towards conformism (Frosh, 2018). Despite its colonial roots, this is true of what it has offered postcolonial thought; equally, despite its inability to deal adequately with racism and antisemitism in its own ranks (Frosh, 2012; Winograd, 2014), it has demonstrated its potential as a source of contestation of racism. It is to this I now turn, asking, through the analysis of racism, to what extent can psychoanalysis become an anti-racist and 'decolonising' discipline, and what might need to happen for this to be achieved?

On Racism

Through its colonial enterprise, psychoanalysis has at times looked like a tool of racism, abbreviating its coverage of non-European psychology and more importantly asserting the domination of rationality over irrationality in a way that identifies the former with a more 'civilised' way of being and attributes the latter to a kind of atavism resonating with supposedly 'primitive' states of mind. However, largely because of its strong links with Jewish identity and hence psychoanalysts' shared experience of antisemitism – most egregiously of course during the Nazi era but not by any means confined to then – alertness to the irrationality of racism itself, the damage it does and the passion with which its adherents hold onto it has been a subtheme of much psychoanalytic thought. The issue to be considered here is whether there are 'philosophical' aspects of psychoanalysis that relate to these concerns and whether examining them can help move psychoanalysis from being an occasional and often backsliding, flawed fellow traveller of nonracism to a more active antiracist position. It is first, however, worth reminding ourselves of where an antiracist position has emerged. The critique of racism has mainly not been driven by a clinical drive towards understanding its effects in the consulting room, though this has become increasingly visible especially as analysts of colour have written or spoken about it (Winograd, 2014; White, 2002). Rather, it has usually come from social critics, philosophers and social theorists who have seen psychoanalysis as having something to contribute to the project of explaining and contesting the racist imaginary – the capacity of racism to maintain its hold over psychic processes, always seeming to return as the point of first contact when any kind of going gets tough. Antisemitism in contemporary Europe; anti-black racism in post-Obama America; Hindu-on-Muslim racism; extreme nationalism and xenophobia; post-Brexit racism; far-right racism and so on – the robustness of these phenomena is something that requires analysis, and critics have often deployed psychoanalytic ideas to help them in this. It needs to be added that this is not necessarily a reductive process in which the sociopolitical sources of racism are ignored, but a supplementary or complementary one in which the affective pull of racism is examined: why, when it is so destructive and so patently absurd, does racism *feel* so attractive, even so central, to the mental life of so many people? Even if we use the Marxist language of 'ideology' here, suggesting that we are dealing with the internalisation of socially produced canonical narratives and dominant discourses, what explains the hold such ideological tropes have over people, and what might make it possible to resist them? Psychoanalytically informed critics have come up with numerous answers to this, ranging from the work of the post-war *Studies in Prejudice* group of critical theorists (Adorno et al, 1950), through to contemporary Lacanians (Hook, 2018). For Adorno et al (1950), in their classic investigation of 'prejudice' informed by social psychology, critical theory and psychoanalysis, the source of this racist imaginary lay in a specific family scenario, in which an authoritarian father and the absence of affection produces a sado-masochistic personality structure unable to deal with the complexity of the world and insistent on the simplifying products of projection. This creates a persecutory environment full of hated beings, thus confirming the subject's vision of being ensnared in a dangerous situation in which the other has to be wiped out for the self to survive. In particular, *difference* cannot be tolerated because it always constitutes a threat. Racism is not a 'simple belief' and its irrationality is not solely in the area of its truth claims (though of course it is irrational in that sphere). It is precisely the *excessive* affect added to the systematically prejudiced ideology that makes for a racist imaginary in the sense of an all-encompassing fantasy. Adorno et al enunciate this in relation to the threat felt by the 'fascist character' when faced with difference, and there is a lot of other psychoanalytic evidence for this, as in Klaus Theweleit's (1977) famous investigation of the proto-fascists of Weimar Germany, which stressed the highly sexualised hatred these men had for women and the way this produced split fantasies of the 'Bolshevik' other, femininity ('pure' mothers and sisters versus the 'red woman') and of course Jews. Indeed, the general theme that racism becomes constituted through a projective process whereby the subject disowns aspects of the self which she or he then finds in the outside world and feels persecuted by – and consequently directs violent hatred towards – is rife in the literature. It has its limitations, as all simplifying explanations will have; but it conveys well the way in which a racist subject will both be drawn to and repelled by the object of hatred, and in spite of all evidence to the contrary, will hold a genuine conviction that its very existence is threatening.

Other examples of the application of psychoanalytic concepts to racism come from many sources. Those I have previously focused on (Frosh, 2006, 2013) have been the Kleinian theorisation of racism in relation to psychic processes of repudiation, splitting and projection, combined with social construction of abjected 'containers' for these projections (Rustin, 1991); the conceptualisation of anti-black racism in the context of the fantasised division 'bestiality/purity' produced by slavery (Kovel, 1995); Fanon's (1952) use of Lacanian psychoanalysis mixed with Sartrean existential analysis to examine the psychology of the colonial and of the colonised; and the idea that racism is fuelled by fantasies of 'theft of enjoyment' as understood by Lacanian and Žižekian theory (Hook, 2018; Dean, 2007). Without repeating too much of this material here, it is worth noting the overlaps and possible congruences of these somewhat different positions. For the Kleinian sociologist Michael Rustin, racism is built out of extreme defences against psychic fragmentation, defences which construct a paranoid world view that then reinforces the attack the racist psyche feels itself to be under. Intensely affectively charged beliefs about race, writes Rustin,

> are akin to psychotic states of mind. . . . The mechanisms of psychotic thought find in racial categorizations an ideal container. These mechanisms include the paranoid splitting of objects into the loved and hated, the suffusion of thinking processes by intense, unrecognized emotion, confusion between self and object due to the splitting of the self and massive projective identification, and hatred of reality and truth.
>
> *(Rustin, 1991, p. 62)*

The threat to the subject posed by fragmentary and vulnerable states of mind aggravated by social forces that undermine personal solidity and escalate hatred, are dealt with through projection of envy into the socially nominated other – the person of colour, the Jew, the immigrant, the religiously different. This makes it safer because it offers not just an *explanation* for one's own suffering ('they hate us and are persecuting us'), but because it confirms the state of mind that posits destructiveness as lying outside the subject and so defendable against. This is emotionally comforting even as it paradoxically stirs up feelings of paranoia and vulnerability, producing a vicious cycle built on a lie. Rustin (1991, p. 69) writes, 'The "lie" in this system of personality organisation becomes positively valued as carrying for the self an important aspect of its defence against weakness, loss or negative judgement.' Racism, socially structured though it may be, is consequently deeply invested in by the individual, distorting and disturbing relations with reality and with truth.

Although the specifics of the Kleinian vocabulary of projection, introjection and projective identification are not necessarily shared, the general perception that racism involves the use of socially nominated categories of derogated others as containers or channels for the socially produced vulnerabilities and hatreds of the subject is common to the positions listed above. For Kovel (1995), the sensuality forced out of the white American subject by capitalism and puritanism is projected into the black, who carries the legacy of 'bestial' fantasies produced by slavery. 'Could it be,' he asks (p. 212), reflecting on the historical development of white consciousness, 'that as the western mentality began to regard itself as homogeneous and purified – a *cogito* – it was also led to assign the negativity inherent in human existence to other peoples, thereby enmeshing them in the web of racism?' The vitality and diversity of the world becomes flattened and narrowed into a rigid mode of reasoning and a single narrative of experience; racism enters into the equation because irrationality and sensuality is defended against and located in the other – the one who, through exclusion and election as the 'alien', comes to embody the supposedly non-human. The implication here that racism is not just fuelled by hatred but also by *envy* – another important Kleinian idea – is not unfamiliar to readers of Fanon. It can be seen, for instance, in his comment that

> The white man is convinced that the Negro is a beast; if it is not the length of the penis, then it is the sexual potency that impresses him. Face to face with the man who

> is 'different from himself', he needs to defend himself. In other words, to personify the Other. The Other will become the mainstay of his preoccupation and his desires.
>
> *(Fanon, 1952, p. 170)*

Whilst the threat of the other is dominant in this quotation, the evocation of fantasies of 'sexual potency' reveals the ambivalent core of the racist imaginary: the other is hated for sure, but also envied for what he (in this case) embodies, and also possibly *desired*. The prevalence of so-called miscegenation in racist societies has many components, including the arrogance of power and the excitement of the prohibited, but it may also be connected at times and in part to a desire for the racialised other that is racist in itself. The recognition of ambivalence also fuels the contemporary Lacanian idea that racism revolves around a fantasy of the 'theft of enjoyment', which is to say that the other is imagined as being responsible for the lack in the subject, desired, envied and hated precisely because the other has what 'we' most want but can never (because subjectivity is constructed around lack) actually acquire. Derek Hook (2008) draws together some of these disparate threads by aligning Fanon and Žižek in their accounts of how racism gets 'under the skin'. Fanon's (1952) line of analysis emphasises the projection of the white's sexuality onto the black man, only for the white man to find it returning as envied aspects of his own disavowed sexual embodiment. Hook reads this in relation to the Lacanian idea of the surplus of enjoyment that is needed and yet is feared, because it locates the psychic life of the subject in the body and hence in what is 'bestial' and mortal. The consequence of this is that the racist subject is obsessed by a lack which she or he translates into a 'loss' – implying that it has been stolen by someone else, who now claims ownership of it. Hook (2008, p. 146) comments, 'We return thus to a familiar lesson in the psychoanalysis of racism: the "racial other" is needed, envied, desired far more than the racist subject can ever admit'.

The overlaps and connections between different psychoanalytic formulations of racism are instructive in revealing some core assumptions of the psychoanalytic approach. One is the notion of the outside other as a 'container' of some kind for inner turmoil. This does not necessarily resolve into a reductive account that implies that racism is psychologically produced, that it is for example a kind of attitudinal prejudice endemic to the human psychological condition (Frosh, 1989). Most of the ideas presented above are fully compatible with a notion of the inner turmoil that might be the source of the impassioned feelings of the racist being itself produced by the social forces that perpetuate racism. Even though this can be a truth quite hard to hold onto in the face of psychoanalysis' individualising tendencies, the most radical psychoanalytic theorists of racism were able to develop it out of their well-schooled critical (often Marxist) thinking. Ernst Simmel (1946), for instance, writing in the volume of essays that he edited out of a symposium on antisemitism organised by the San Francisco Psychoanalytic Society in 1944, makes the connection between modernity ('civilisation') and the canker that destroys it.

> Applying our method of psychoanalytic-dialectic thinking, we must infer not that antisemitism annihilates the achievements of civilization, but that the process of civilization itself *produces* antisemitism as a pathological symptom-formation, which in turn tends to destroy the soil from which it has grown. Antisemitism is a malignant growth on the body of civilization.
>
> *(p. 34)*

For Simmel, thinking back on the Nazi phenomenon, antisemitism is both a cancer and a mass psychosis, a 'social disease', despite the individuals concerned not being psychotic; or rather, it is the existence of this mass psychosis that *protects* antisemites from becoming psychotic themselves, because it contains their madness in the body of social norms. Although it is the case that there may be various neurotic processes at work, the individual antisemite is 'normal'. However, when this person joins a group the crowd dynamic takes over, distinguished particularly by 'unrestricted aggressive destructiveness under the spell of a delusion' (p. 39) – exactly the characteristic of psychosis. This further clarifies the comfortable way in which the antisemite can live with irrational beliefs:

> The antisemite believes in his false accusations against the Jews not in spite of, but *because* of their irrationality. For the ideational content of these accusations is a product of the primary process in his own unconscious and is conveyed to his conscious mind through the mediation of the mass-leader's suggestions.
>
> *(Simmel, 1946, pp. 51–52)*

As Otto Fenichel (1946, p. 20) noted in his contribution to Simmel's collection, 'Foreignness is the quality which the Jews and one's own instincts have in common'. The antisemite is attracted to 'irrational' beliefs precisely because they express the turmoil of a mind at war with itself and with the world, yet one that is structurally and socially weak, and needs the prop of the antisemitic society's containing madness to keep itself sane. And at the root of this turmoil, according to Simmel, is 'the process of civilization itself', suggesting that antisemitism is not something grafted onto modernity as an external force that disturbs what would otherwise be 'a culture of law, order and reason' but is expressive of the irrationality that lies within modernity itself, and is generated by it. This theme can also be found in some of Slavoj Žižek's writings, with unreason thought of not as a fundamental psychic structure, but one that is socially overdetermined.

> Is capitalism's hatred of the Jew not the hatred of its own innermost, essential feature? For this reason, it is not sufficient to point out how the racist's Other presents a threat to our own identity. We should rather invert this proposition: the fascinating image of the Other gives a body to our own innermost split, to what is 'in us more than ourselves' and thus prevents us achieving full identity with ourselves.
>
> *(Žižek, 1993, p. 206)*

Against the implication that it is the inner state of the subject that is primary in seeking out an external cause, Žižek (1997, p. 76) also gives us a more elaborated version of antisemitism in which it is produced by the structure of capitalism itself: 'social antagonism comes first, and the "Jew" merely gives body to this obstacle.' Culture's investment in this figure of the 'Jew' produces it as an element in the unconscious, and with it arises the widespreadness of antisemitism itself.

Psychoanalysis, then, has had something important to say about the way in which the racist imaginary works, basically interpreting it through various theoretical lenses as a process of libidinised investment in an ambivalent object that carries the weight of disowned and projected derogated or 'abjected' aspects of the psyche. Why these aspects are derogated and why these particular objects are chosen to contain them is a set of questions answered by more progressive theorists in social terms. The workings of a society constructed through colonialism, imperialism and racism are such as to leave its subjects alienated and vulnerable, in a state that both mobilises and makes unendurable rage-filled fantasies that have to be evacuated before they destroy the subject from the inside; and these same social processes elect various groups for historical reasons (Christian antisemitism, slavery, economic dispossession, imperialist self-justification) so that they are ripe for reception of the projected fantasies. This is why it does not matter if there really is 'a swarm of people coming across the Mediterranean', as a recent British Prime Minister claimed (BBC, 2015), any more than it matters if there are any Jews around; anti-migrant racism and antisemitism can still flourish, because they operate as phantasmagorical rather than reality-based processes. This theoretical contribution is a significant one in acting as a counterweight to the psychoanalytic tendency to individualise and subjectivise, hiding away both as a practice and a set of clinical ideas that have not spoken directly enough about racism. It also opposes the developmentalism of psychoanalysis that channels together colonial tropes about 'primitive versus civilised', associating the former especially with 'under-developed' modes of thought – Freud's (1913, p. 1) famous 'savages' whose 'mental life must have a peculiar interest for us if we are right in seeing in it a well-preserved picture of an early stage of our own development.' Racism has essentially nothing to do with the characteristics of the racialised other, though it might pick or invent some of those supposed characteristics as points to which racist fantasies can attach themselves (the claim to superiority as the 'chosen people' and the fact of male circumcision are two attributes of the Jews that Freud (1939) thought attracted antisemitic attention; supposed black 'physicality' might be a source of racist envy and assault, reducing black people to their bodies). Rather, racism is a product of racists, both as a society and in the space of the racist psyche; and psychoanalysis offers some useful tools to pick away at this in order to garner a fuller understanding.

Coda on Grievability

Taking this a little further, there is a contemporary move in both social theory and psychoanalysis that provides a slightly different lens on the processes that might comprehend and oppose racism. This starts from a perspective that Judith Butler has worked on over many years through her notion of 'precarity' that recognises how marginal and hence precarious some people – many groups of people – are made, particularly under conditions of racist and sexist exclusion (Butler, 2004). In the course of this, Butler has also developed a notion of 'grievability' which has now become central to much of her thinking, especially on resistance and nonviolence. Grievability distinguishes between lives worth preserving and others that are discardable; those lives that would be grieved if they were lost, and those that do not seem to count. Butler (2020, p. 17) is fierce on the implications and sources of this difference:

> They establish this inequality within a particular framework, but this inequality is historical and contested by competing frameworks. It says nothing about the intrinsic value of any life. Further, as we think about the prevailing and differential ways that populations are valued and disvalued, protected and abandoned, we come up against forms of power that establish the unequal worth of lives by establishing their unequal grievability.

Grievability is not in itself a statement about grief, but rather about mattering, in the sense of 'Black Lives Matter':

> To be grievable is to be interpellated in such a way that you know your life matters; that the loss of your life would matter; that your body is treated as one that should be able to live and thrive, whose precarity should be minimized, for which provisions for flourishing should be available.
>
> *(Butler, 2020, p. 59)*

Yet this is not so for all people, and the inequality in grievability – in the valuing of lives – is deeply racialised. Butler (2020) discusses this in detail in relation to the killing of black men in America, defined automatically within the racist phantasmagoria as posing a threat, even when running away; in the unreported and mislabelled deaths of black women ('overpoliced and underprotected' – p. 119); and in the contemporary European racism expressed in the willed deaths of 'thousands of migrants who have lost their lives in the Mediterranean', lives which are 'precisely lives that are not deemed worthy of safeguarding' (p. 120). She concludes,

> All of these forms of taking life or letting life die are not just concrete examples of how the metric of grievability works; they wield the power to determine and distribute the grievability and value of lives. These are the concrete operations of the metric itself, its technologies, its points of application. And in these instances, we see the convergence of the biopolitical logic of the historic-racial scheme with the phantasmagoric inversions that occlude the social bond: what may appear as an isolated act of violence or as the expression of an individual psychopathology shows itself to be part of a pattern, a punctual moment within *a reiterated practice* of violence.
>
> *(Butler, 2020, p. 121)*

The perceptions here are not peculiarly psychoanalytic ones, but Butler herself joins this recent extended statement about grievability to psychoanalysis, continuing a tradition of thought that is most apparent in *Giving an Account of Oneself* (Butler, 2005), which draws on psychoanalysis (especially the theories of Jean Laplanche) as part of a project of explicating ethical relationality. In *The Force of Nonviolence* (Butler, 2020) it is Freud and particularly Melanie Klein who have a more privileged position; the latter is used in an evocative portrait of vulnerability to understand how grievability might be part of a process of reparation for the damage that one has done to others and for the damage done to oneself. What is key here for Butler is the way in which reparation and the guilt that is associated with it function 'not only as a way of checking one's own destructiveness, but as a mechanism for safeguarding the life of the other, one that emerges from our own need and dependency, from a sense that this life is not a life without another life' (p. 93). What Butler points out about this is how reparation and guilt can be 'pre-emptive': how they can arise out of the wish *not to do* damage, or perhaps the knowledge that damage is very likely to be done, and then involve putting in place the conditions under which the life of the other – and hence one's own life – can be repaired, preserved and protected in the light of that future-and-past damage. And finally, Butler suggests a 'political principle' that arises from this perception, one that contains echoes of Levinas' (1991) use of the injunction against killing, what he calls (p. 104) 'A Thou-Shalt-not-Kill that can also be explicated much further: it is the fact that I cannot let the other die alone, it is like a calling out to me.' Butler's elaboration of this in the context of grievability is as follows:

> Perhaps the moral precept that prohibits killing has to be expanded to a political principle that seeks to safeguard lives through institutional and economic means, and to do so in a way that *fails* to distinguish between populations that are immanently grievable and those that are not.
>
> *(Butler, 2020, p. 100)*

The vulnerability one feels, the hurt that has been done to one – the conditions under which racism usually thrives, as it looks to project these hurts and vulnerabilities into their socially sanctioned derogated containers – can also be the basis for a philosophy of ethics that takes the grievability of others as foundational and so resists precisely that derogation, that disowning of precarity on which racist social forces feed.

I have offered this quite extended introduction to Butler's ideas in order to think about what psychoanalysis might say about a mode of engagement with others that acknowledges the systematic way in which racism damages lives. This is not to claim Butler totally for the regiments of psychoanalysts; but she nevertheless works in a tradition that draws creatively on psychoanalysis for insights both into psychological states (e.g., hurt and aggression as shared human conditions arising in response to dependency and vulnerability) and their intertwining with social conditions (subjectification in the context of precarity; melancholic formations of social coercion). In the material described here, there is a powerful acknowledgement of how lives are made to matter and not to matter, and how this construction of grievability is distributed on racialised grounds. Alongside this is the development of an argument for contestation of violence that is forged out of a psychoanalytic sensitivity to the conditions in which our vulnerabilities might become links with others rather than be translated into racist forms of repudiation. What psychoanalysis offers here is rather different from the descriptions of the phantasmatic enticements of racism described earlier. Instead, it suggests a set of ethical principles that could be brought to bear on racism through political action as well as social philosophy and social theory. It suggests that racialised forms of violence, so prevalent in so much of the world, can be interpreted through the lens of vulnerability and in this way can track the turning of the hurt received into the hurt inflicted. Without reducing the importance of understanding the centrality of social forces that intentionally cultivate this racism, the psychoanalytic insights that allow us to understand grievability as a potential opening out of relationality through turning back the temptation to project into others what we are afraid of in ourselves, is a compelling instance of how psychoanalysis might be drawn on to flesh out the affective domain that in its persecutory forms helps sustain racism. Our vulnerabilities make us sites for racist discarding of others and for the perpetuation of self-destructive inequalities and hatreds through this; the question is whether and how it might be possible to move from this enactive, reactive position to one in which pre-emptive work on reparative concern – 'safeguard[ing] lives through institutional and economic means' – becomes a primary, shared political concern, and one that does indeed not distinguish between different populations in terms of their racialised worth.

The focus on grievability here is part of a larger project that can be discerned within contemporary psychoanalysis, which is to articulate ways of relating that do not just *take account* of 'otherness' and relationships of sameness and difference, but that make these central to psychoanalytic concerns (Benjamin, 2018). In doing this, psychoanalysis needs to reflect back on its own practices of exclusion – class, sexuality and race have all featured in this over the years and continue to do so. The social theorists who have developed psychoanalytic accounts of racism have offered some persuasive portrayals of the workings of the racist imaginary; what Butler shows in her work on grievability is another side of this: how the temptation to racialise and exclude, to make lives ungrievable and to deny their mattering, is one that can be very easily mobilised in the service of the perpetuation of racist ideologies and practices. If, drawing especially on Freud and Klein, we might see this as an aspect of the death drive, exerting itself to preserve the subject by destroying the other, we might also hope that there is something still available from the opposing drive, Eros, in which the complexity and heterogeneity of life is welcomed. This might also mean that our awareness of the potential for doing damage that operates so strongly in our psyches and in our societies can be offset by reparative practices that understand how we are bound up with others. We do violence to ourselves when we do violence to them.

References

Adorno, T., Frenkel-Brunswik, E., Levinson, D. and Sandford, R. (1950) *The Authoritarian Personality*. New York: Norton.

Anderson, W., Jenson, D. and Keller, R. (2011) *Unconscious Dominions: Psychoanalysis, Colonial Trauma, and Global Sovereignties*. Durham: Duke University Press.

Andrade, O. (1928) Manifesto Antropofágico. *Revista de Antropofagia, 1*, 1.

BBC (2015) *David Cameron Criticised over Migrant 'Swarm' Language*. www.bbc.co.uk/news/uk-politics-33716501. Accessed 4 March 2020.

Benjamin, J. (2018) *Beyond Doer and Done to: Recognition Theory, Intersubjectivity and the Third*. London: Routledge.

Brickman, C. (2003) *Aboriginal Populations in the Mind*. New York: Columbia University Press.

Butler, J. (2004) *Precarious Life*. London: Verso.

Butler, J. (2005) *Giving an Account of Oneself*. New York: Fordham University Press.

Butler, J. (2020) *The Force of Nonviolence*. London: Verso.

Dean, J. (2007) Why Žižek for Political Theory? *International Journal of Žižek Studies, 1*, 18–32.

Fanon, F. (1952) *Black Skin, White Masks*. London: Pluto Press.

Fenichel, O. (1946), Elements of a Psychoanalytic Theory of Anti-Semitism. In E. Simmel (Ed), *Anti-Semitism: A Social Disease*. New York: International Universities Press.

Freud, S. (1913) Totem and Taboo. In *The Standard Edition of the Complete Psychological Works of Sigmund Freud, Volume XIII (1913–1914): Totem and Taboo and Other Works*, vii–162. London: Hogarth Press.

Freud, S. (1933) New Introductory Lectures On Psycho-Analysis. In *The Standard Edition of the Complete Psychological Works of Sigmund Freud, Volume XXII (1932–1936): New Introductory Lectures on Psycho-Analysis and Other Works*, 1–182. London: Hogarth Press.

Freud, S. (1939) Moses and Monotheism. In *The Standard Edition of the Complete Psychological Works of Sigmund Freud, Volume XXIII (1937–1939): Moses and Monotheism, An Outline of Psycho-Analysis and Other Works*, 1–138. London: Hogarth Press.

Frosh, S. (1989) *Psychoanalysis and Psychology*. London: Macmillan.

Frosh, S. (2006) *For and Against Psychoanalysis*. London: Routledge.

Frosh, S. (2012) The Re-Enactment of Denial. In A. Gulerce (Ed), *Re(Con)Figuring Psychoanalysis: Critical Juxtapositions of the Philosophical, the Sociohistorical and the Political*. London: Palgrave.

Frosh, S. (2013) Psychoanalysis, colonialism, racism. *Journal of Theoretical and Philosophical Psychology, 33*, 141–154.

Frosh, S. (2017) Primitivity and Violence: Traces of the Unconscious in Psychoanalysis. *Journal of Theoretical and Philosophical Psychology, 37*, 34–47.

Frosh, S. (2018) Psychoanalysis, Politics and Society: What Remains Radical in Psychoanalysis? In R. Gipps and M. Lacewing (Eds), *The Oxford Handbook of Philosophy and Psychoanalysis*. Oxford: Oxford University Press.

Frosh, S. and Mandelbaum, B. (2017) 'Like Kings in Their Kingdoms': Conservatism in Brazilian Psychoanalysis during the Dictatorship. *Political Psychology, 38*, 591–604.

Greedharry, A. (2008) *Postcolonial Theory and Psychoanalysis*. London: Palgrave.

Hartnack, C. (2011) Colonial Dominions and the Psychoanalytic Couch: Synergies of Freudian Theory with Bengali Hindu Thought and Practices in British India. In W. Anderson, D. Jenson and R. Keller (Eds), *Unconscious Dominions: Psychoanalysis, Colonial Trauma, and Global Sovereignties*. Durham: Duke University Press.

Hook, D. (2008) The 'Real' of Racializing Embodiment. *Journal of Community and Applied Social Psychology, 18*, 140–152.

Hook, D. (2018) Racism and *jouissance*: Evaluating the 'Racism as (the Theft of) Enjoyment' Hypothesis. *Psychoanalysis, Culture and Society, 23*, 244–266.

Kovel, J. (1995) On Racism and Psychoanalysis. In A. Elliott and S. Frosh (Eds), *Psychoanalysis in Contexts*. London: Routledge.

Levinas, E. (1991) *Entre Nous: On Thinking of the Other*. London: Athlone.

Rubin, A., Mandelbaum, B. and Frosh, S. (2016) 'No Memory, No Desire': Psychoanalysis in Brazil during Repressive Times. *Psychoanalysis and History, 18*, 93–118.

Russo, J. (2012) Brazilian Psychiatrists and Psychoanalysis at the Beginning of 20th Century: A Question for National Identity. *Psychoanalysis and History, 14*, 297–312.

Rustin, M. (1991) *The Good Society and the Inner World*. London: Verso.

Said, E. (2003) *Freud and the Non-European*. London: Verso.

Simmel, E. (1946) Anti-Semitism and Mass Psychopathology. In E. Simmel (Ed), *Anti-Semitism: A Social Disease*. New York: International Universities Press.
Theweleit, K. (1977) *Male Fantasies*. Cambridge: Polity, 1987.
Van Haute, P. (2016) Lacan Meets Freud? Patho-Analytic Reflections on the Status of the Perversions in Lacanian Metapsychology. *Studies in Gender and Sexuality*, *17*, 274–284.
Vyrgioti, M. (2018) *The Cannibal Trope: A Psychosocial Critique of Psychoanalysis' Colonial Fantasies*. Unpublished PhD thesis. Birkbeck, University of London.
White, K. P. (2002) Surviving Hating and Being Hated: Some Personal thoughts about Racism from a Psychoanalytic Perspective. *Contemporary Psychoanalysis*, 38 (3), 401–422.
Winograd, B. (2014) Black Psychoanalysts Speak. *PEP Video Grants*, 1 (1), 1.
Žižek, S. (1993) *Tarrying with the Negative*. Durham: Duke University Press.
Žižek, S. (1997) *The Plague of Fantasies*. London: Verso.

30
NARCISSISM IN RELIGION[1]

Tamas Pataki

Introduction

In his seminal work *Primitive Culture* (1873/2016), E. B. Tylor proposed a minimal definition of religion: the essence of religion, he said, is belief in spiritual beings. This doctrine Tylor named 'animism', and he maintained that it formed the core of the earliest religions and of all later ones. It has two parts:

> First concerning souls, second other spirits upward to the rank of powerful deities. Spiritual beings control events in the material world, man's life here and hereafter and have intercourse with men, receive pleasure and displeasure from their actions, and receive sooner or later active reverence and propitiation.
>
> *(I. 426–427)*

Many contemporary cognitive scientists and philosophers agree in seeing the essence of religion as belief, or at least as a disposition to believe, in spirits (e.g. Guthrie 1993, 2007; Barrett 2007; Whitehouse 2007; Bering 2011). But whereas they see this disposition as the product of various evolved cognitive modules, Tylor viewed the doctrine of spirits as involving a kind of hypothesis, an intellectual construction, that explained phenomena such as animacy, dreams, agency and causation, and several other mysteries of interest to our early ancestors. The nature of spirits (and souls) remains, of course, problematic.[2] Tylor's ethnographic data suggested that they were generally conceived by his 'savage philosophers' as 'thin unsubstantial human images, vapours, films or shadows', entities endowed with a 'misty and evanescent materiality' (I. 456). In many respects, spirits and souls are different from sticks and stones and human beings: they can be disembodied, travel swiftly from one place to another, or be at several places at the same time; they are often wiser and more powerful than humans, though occasionally more stupid: Agouti of the Kalapalo people of central Brazil is 'a sneak and a spy', and Jaguar is 'a violent bully who is easily deceived' (Bellah 2011, 136ff). They are, however, *always* anthropomorphic or person-like in key respects and possess human limitations; they may, for example, require a window or aperture to enter or leave a dwelling. The gods and spirits are highly diverse ontologically speaking; two illustrations must do for many. The *kwoth* of the Nuer people cannot be perceived by the senses and are indeterminate except in relation

DOI: 10.4324/9780429297076-36

to their effects. What a *kwoth* is like in itself the Nuer claim not to know: 'we are simple people, how can simple people know about such matters?' they say (Horton 1997, 24). On the other hand, some spirits are almost of the same order as human beings. The Kalabari of the Niger Delta recognize three categories of religious beings, the Deads (i.e. ancestor spirits), Village Gods and Water-People.

> the first two are seen as existing 'in spirit' only, while the last, like human beings, have both bodies and spirits: unlike Deads and Village Gods, they can be seen, heard, touched, and smelt by anyone who happens to cross their path in the rivers. They are not like the wind: they can be talked of inhabiting definite localities as the Deads and the Village Gods cannot. Many other gods of primitive peoples could be cited as resembling the Kalabari Water-People in their thorough-going materiality.
>
> *(Horton 1997, 25)*

Over the years the lucubrations of philosophers and theologians have introduced many more recherché conceptions of soul and spirit, gods and other non-natural beings, but it seems to me that the vast majority of religious people today still hold anthropomorphic conceptions of spiritual beings not very different from those of our ancestors and uncontaminated tribal religions. I will return to this issue presently.

Tylor was aware that his Intellectualist conception of religion as essentially an explanatory schema like science left out the emotional factors that so often – though by no means always – accompany religiosity: 'The intellectual rather than the emotional side of religion has here been kept in view', he writes. 'Even in the life of the rudest savage, religious belief is associated with intense emotion, with awful reverence, with agonizing terror, with rapt ecstasy when sense and thought utterly transcend the common level of daily life' (II. 359). Freud (1913) made an important advance along the lines of the Intellectualist hypothesis. The doctrine of spirits, he agreed with Tylor, was indeed a kind of hypothesis, a solution to a set of problems, but the problems were not only intellectual, as Tylor supposed, but emotional in character: how to explain the terror and ambivalence caused by the spirits of the recently departed. This work, unfortunately, had little lasting resonance among anthropologists.

The oversight was indirectly repaired by the anthropologist Robin Horton. Horton noted that the 'great value of Tylor's definition is that it leads us to compare interaction with religious objects and interaction with human beings' (1997, 26). Spirits and gods are like souls, anthropomorphic at least to that degree, and so it is inescapable that interactions with them should be modelled on human-to-human relations. To explain, predict and control the actions and intentions of gods and spirits, humans are compelled to use the same interpretative and practical devices that they use among themselves. In the effort to understand and predict supernatural behaviour beliefs, desires and intentions are attributed to the spirits; in the effort to control the spirits humans plead, pray, bargain, sacrifice, offer obedience and so forth, just as they do among themselves. This aspect or pole of religion Horton came to refer to as *explanation, prediction, control* (EPC, I shall say). But he identifies another aspect of religion, partly overlapping this transparently manipulative aspect, which is concerned with the emotional and intrinsic values of forming relationships with higher, wiser, more powerful beings. Horton refers to this as the *communion* (C) aspect of religion. On this view every human-to-god relationship can be placed on an EPC/C dimension of variability, and to the extent that one is emphasized, the other tends to be reduced (1997, 41). The Nupe people, for example, have 'religious systems characterized by an extreme emphasis on manipulating the gods as tools for the achievement of health, wealth and issue' (1997, 42). Interest in communion is scarcely present. Other societies, like our own, at least since about the 17th century when the scientific revolution began to erode the EPC credentials of religion among the educated, tend to emphasize sheer communion without (overtly) seeking other benefits. From these two aspects taken together it follows that 'religion can be looked upon as an extension of the field of people's social relationships beyond the confines of purely human society . . . with the exclusion of pets' (1997, 32). It can be noted that this view, arrived at from extensive ethnographic study, is entirely consonant with the kind of view that might be expected to spring from the various branches of psychoanalytic object relations theory, attachment theory and other lines of psychological investigation exploring religion through the lens of interpersonal relationships.

Horton did not attend to the C aspect of religion with the intensity he directed at EPC. However, he concludes that psychoanalytic investigation of communion is likely to be the most promising path to follow (1997, 369–372). In a book (Pataki 2007) published before I had encountered Horton's (or much other anthropological) work, I defined religions as attempts to extend unconscious interpersonal or object relations into a supernatural dimension. The definition seems consonant with Horton's conclusions. But whereas Horton, given his field-anthropological focus, elaborates on the overt similarities between human-to-human and human-to-god relationships, I focused (all too briefly) on the unconscious significance of these relationships. The reason is simple and material to what follows. Gods and spirits are not the kinds of entity one encounters in the normal run of things, not for most people anyway. However, it is clear that they *can* be objects of attachment and of intense emotion. This is a remarkable feature of humankind. We become emotionally attached to non-corporeal objects: angels, gods, fictional characters, ideologies and other abstract conceptions. But how is this incontestable circumstance possible? The matter doesn't strike most theorists as seriously problematic; for them it is 'just so' (e.g., Granqvist 2020, 39–46). My underlying thought, one that would perhaps be widely shared by psychodynamic thinkers and skeptics, was that in the human-to-god relationship there must be at deeper levels projections of the images or imagos of (corporeal) parental objects and of aspects of the self to which we are still attached – which are still unconsciously cathected. We can then go on to discuss two levels of engagement with religious objects. On one level, there is engagement with them *as objects defined by their culturally attributed characteristics*; on another level, as *representatives of internal objects or aspects of the self.* If that thought is true, then we should expect that attachment to religious objects, as well as providing social and religious identity, moral guidance and so forth, would also subserve many unconscious defensive functions – including the narcissistic defenses that appear so conspicuous in Abrahamic religions and, as we shall see, animate much of the intolerance and violence with which they are associated.

That is the broad context of what follows, but I need to make one last contextualizing remark. R. G. Collingwood said somewhere that the true study of psychology is history; and there are important seeds of truth in this remark. If we are to understand human psychology then surely we need to know what people in the past have believed, desired, achieved and endeavoured; as we need to know what cultures radically different from ours believe, desire, achieve and endeavour. If we are to understand religiosity, then we must appraise the full arc of it. Much of the contemporary philosophy and psychology of religion is confined to the study of contemporary monotheism. Given the empirical, not to say experimental, focus of the psychologists, and the religious commitments of many of the philosophers, this is understandable. But the result is distorted accounts of religiosity in general. By pegging out a vantage on a much larger field of religious expression, historically and culturally, I hope to avoid some of their limitations.

Anthropomorphism

Because I take it as a firm premise that the human-to-god relationship is modelled on the human-to-human relationship, I must insist (in the face of de-anthropomorphizing trends in some traditions; see below) on the essentially anthropomorphic character of gods and spirits. According to the Akkadian *Atrahasis*, before humankind there were only gods. Hence the gods had to do all the work of digging canals and building dikes. This led to a strike of the younger gods against their seniors, especially against Enlil the acting chief. Fortunately, the cunning god Enki found a solution to the troubles. Together with the mother Goddess, he created men to do all the toil the gods had been obliged to do: henceforth, 'they shall bear the burden'. But soon men became clamorous and disturbed the gods who decided to destroy them by sending a flood. Enki, however, ever resourceful and solicitous of men, directs the good man Atrahasis to build an ark. . . .

It is wrong to believe that this is poetic elaboration on a more abstract divine reality to which the ancients subscribed. In the forerunners to contemporary theistic traditions an almost iconic anthropomorphism prevailed. The Olympian deities 'are human almost to the last detail', says Burkert (2004, 183) and 'Ahura Mazda is a god in heaven, no doubt, but clearly conceived as a person in acting and reacting' (2004, 123). 'Mesopotamian religion was always strongly anthropomorphic', says Beaulieu (2007, 165). The expert conclusions could be multiplied. It is the same in traditional and tribal religions around the globe. Of African religions, Olupona writes:

> Stories across the continent depict the deities as anthropomorphic beings or impersonal spirits who share numerous characteristics with their human devotees. Gods and spirits are made in the image of humans. They speak, are heard, endure punishment, and attain rewards just like human beings.
>
> *(2014, 20–21)*

As we would expect the social and hierarchical arrangements of the gods of polytheistic pantheons are modelled on human arrangements: 'Divine constellations reflect the fundamental order and elementary structure of human society – husband and wife, brother and sister, mother and son, mother and daughter, father and son, . . . lover and beloved, lord and slave, hero and enemy and so on' (Assmann 2007, 19–20). Despite the redactions of many generations the old anthropomorphic God remains visible in the Old Testament. In the book of Job, God calls an assembly of his children, where Satan famously challenges Him. In Genesis 3:8, Adam and Eve hear the 'Lord God walking in the garden in the cool of the day', and later He (El) wrestles with Jacob. It appears that as late as the eighth century BCE, and probably much later, the goddess Asherah was worshipped as Yahweh's wife (Collins 2007, 182). Little changes in the Christian era or with the advent of Islam. As well as believing in a supreme anthropomorphic deity – albeit incorporeal, unchanging, omnipotent – primitive Christians also believed in a vast array of other spiritual anthropomorphic beings. Origen believed that the pagan gods were real, though he thought they were demons or fallen angels. Even the pagan Porphyry offered sacrifice to angels 'as a token of good will and gratitude', and presumably as a cheap hedge (Dodds 1965, 117–118).

I must add here that I do not for a moment wish to invidiously contrast these tales of anthropomorphic beings with a supposedly superior understanding of divinity today. On the contrary, I believe that the shift from the straightforward anthropomorphism of animism and polytheism with their predominantly EPC mode of relating – unimpressive as that may be – to a more abstract monotheism with its predominantly C form of relating is a regression, a slide towards more delusional modes of thought and feeling. In an extraordinary passage, David Hume asks:

> Where is the difficulty in conceiving that the powers or principles, whatever they were, which formed this visible world, men and animals, produced also a species of intelligent creatures, of more refined substance and greater authority than the rest? That these creatures may be capricious, revengeful, passionate, voluptuous is easily conceived. . . . And in short, the whole mythological system is so natural, that, in the vast variety of planets and worlds, contained in the universe, it seems more than probable, that, somewhere or other, it is really carried into execution.
>
> *(Hume 1757/1998, 151)*

The conception of such beings is arguably more defensible than the philosophically refined conceptions of Abrahamic deities.

To be sure, at least since Xenophanes philosophers, theologians and mystics have evolved conceptions of deity that purpose to avoid the inherent difficulties in the anthropomorphic notions. These conceptions belong in the dark province of philosophers of religion. Some reflective people may indeed entertain one or other of the abstruse conceptions, but there is little to suggest that it's more than a very few. The religiously sophisticated may discard the crude anthropomorphic notions of the 'simple' believer (Aquinas' term). But the vast majority who take a religious tradition seriously, perform its rituals, pray and seek communion with the deity, do not share the learned conceptions. Simple believers may not have expectations that prayers will be answered, sacrifices rewarded or sins punished, but they do expect to be heard, understood and considered by the deity. It is essential to any theistic religion that their god has intellection, emotion and agency and be capable of reciprocation. It is unsurprising, therefore, that in almost every significant historical expression of religion the gods, whatever other unfathomable characteristics they may have, manifest distinctly human traits.[3] That is the condition upon which the possibility of religiosity as communion rests. It is notable that the welfare states of advanced economies which, as we might say, provide a secure base and safe haven do not become objects of attachment and love (Granqvist 2020, chap. 11).

Monotheism as Progress Towards Personal Communion

The contemporary consensus among historians and archaeologists is that the biblical account of the origin of Israelite monotheism is insupportable (Dever 2006; Collins 2007). In all probability, the early Israelites crystallized from an indigenous Canaanite or West Semitic population, probably in the course of the 12th to 10th centuries BCE, and ancient Israelite religion is 'in the main an outgrowth of and part of Syro-Canaanite religion' (Wright 2007, 178). The details of its evolution are vague. In any case, by the end of the seventh century BCE Yahweh had acquired a following in elite circles in the southern Judean kingdom. At this point several dramatic political, historical and psychological developments rapidly converge. King Josiah's politically motivated suppression of Canaanite deities and his efforts to centralize the cult of Yahweh in Jerusalem were significant steps towards forging monotheism. The Babylonian exile following the destruction of the Jerusalem Temple exposed Judean intellectuals to the abstract conceptions of Persian religion and, very probably, to Mesopotamian and Egyptian literature. They were also confronted with the political and psychological trauma of the destruction of their nascent state, the subordination of their god and the humiliation of defeat and deracination. Whether it was the effectiveness of Josiah's brutal advocacy; or the collision between Israelite monolatry and the religious conceptions of older, more powerful polities; or, perhaps, the logic of humiliation and narcissistic rage;[4] or very likely the sum of these; it was on the return of some of the exiled elite to Jerusalem that a definitive monotheism was declared. Second Isaiah proclaims: 'There is no God but I'. The existence of other gods is denied, their worship is declared an abomination, and all religions but one are declared false and wicked. Israelite religion gave birth to a unique conception of a god that was revolutionary, complex and, in my view, baleful.

The advent of monotheism immensely complicated religious sensibility. Two of these complications are of particular significance. Monotheism opened the possibility of a more intimate and intense communion with the god. As Freud observed, 'Now that god was a single person, man's relation to him could recover the intimacy and intensity of the child's relation to his father' (1927, 19). Second, with the prospect of intimacy with an omnipotent god a new range of narcissistic relations was introduced. The relationship to a mostly caring, parent-like god becomes a major means of regulating distress and self-esteem. Before looking at these developments in more detail it is fascinating to observe their prefiguration in Egypt and Mesopotamia. A verse of the late third millennium BCE *Instruction for Merikare* (Assmann 2007, 22) goes:

> Humans are well cared for,
> the livestock of god:
> he made heaven and earth for their sake,
> he pushed the waters back
> and created the air so that their nostrils might live.
> His images are they, having come forth from his body.
> For their sake he rises to heaven;
> it is for them that he has made plants and animals,
> birds and fish,
> so that they might have food.
> If he killed his enemies and went against his children
> this was only because they thought of rebellion.
>
> For their sake he causes there to be light.
> To see them he travels [the heavens] . . .
> When they weep he hears . . .
> God knows every name.

Notice the contrast with *Atrahasis* where humans are created to serve the gods, to lift *their* burden. These verses, anticipating biblical cosmogenesis and anthropocentrism, present the novel idea that Creation is *for* humankind and fashioned for *its* needs – and, still more remarkably, because the gods *care*. The further idea of an unmediated *personal* and salvific relationship makes its appearance in Egypt during the second millennium BCE and even earlier at various times in Mesopotamia. Now each human being may have a personal god among the lesser gods who intercedes for them with greater gods. An Egyptian hymn from around the 1330s BCE illustrates the relationship (Bellah 2011, 245).

> You are Amun, lord of the silent,
> who comes at the call of the poor.
> I called you when I was in sorrow,
> and you came to save me.
> You gave breath to the one who was imprisoned,

and you saved me when I was in bonds.
You are Amun-Re, lord of Thebes,
you save the one in the netherworld.
You are the one who is gracious to the one who calls on him,
you are the one who comes from afar.

In Israel, in prophets such as Amos and Hosea, the human-to-god relationship undergoes a further transformation. It becomes libidinized or sexualized. God is not only a benign and loving lord, a shepherd to his flock, a deliverance from afar (the parent who comes to rescue the child). The familiar tropes are complemented with that of a betrayed, jealous and resentful God.

When Israel was a child, I loved him,
and out of Egypt I called my son.
The more I called him,
the more they went from me;
they kept sacrificing to the Baals
and burning incense to idols.
Yet it was I who taught Ephraim to walk,
I took them up in my arms;
but they did not know that I healed them.
I lead them with cords of compassion,
with bands of love . . .
and I bent down to them and fed them.
(Hosea 11 from Bellah 2011, 302)

We have arrived at an entirely new concept of a god intimately concerned with individual human needs and expecting in return, not cult, but love. The gods of polytheism occasionally intervened in human affairs but their solicitude for mortals was not unbounded. Reciprocally, although devout respect and fear featured, there was little in these religions which could be called 'love of god'. The author of the Aristotelian *Magna Moralia* wrote: 'It would be eccentric for anyone to claim that he loved Zeus'. Yahweh intervenes not occasionally but unceasingly. The other gods had domestic lives and cosmic responsibilities; human affairs were a distraction from these. Yahweh seems entirely invested in humankind and in their reciprocated love and loyalty. As the god becomes less anthropomorphic, shedding iconic form and human limitations, religion becomes more *anthropocentric*, a triumph of human narcissism. The human moves to the centre of the cosmos, the centre of God's attention and unwavering if severe love, just as God is idealized and abstracted beyond comprehension and the reach of envy.[5]

Monotheism decisively shifted the model of religion as principally providing EPC to its second pole, the model of communion. The residues of animism and polytheism such as attempts to influence the gods through prayer, sacrifice, magic (ritual) and so forth are not relinquished. But with biblical monotheism, the idea of communion with a single, personal, loving being graduates to the centre of religion. It is a costly graduation with two momentous consequences.

First, divine functions which had previously been distributed amongst the family of deities are invested in one all-powerful object of intense emotional attachment upon whom *everything* depends. No Enki can rescue humankind from the anger of Enlil. There is now nowhere to turn but God, and so to love 'the LORD your God with all your heart, and with all your soul, and with all your might' is the first principle of the new tradition. Where such personal attachment is profound failure to live up to divine demands is to risk abandonment. But dependence so complete engenders hatred and despondency, and since hatred of God must be repressed, it will tend to be either turned upon the self or projected. A pervasive sense of guilt and self-loathing was rare among pagans but becomes common in late Antiquity (Dodds 1965, 28; Brown 2018, chap. 4). Religious persecution unknown before monotheism becomes common as rain. Religious despair and persecution are for the first time engraved into humankinds' imaginary.

Second, idolatry, as paganism is now derided, is not only error; it is infidelity and immorality. The Egyptologist Jan Assmann (2007, 2010) has familiarized the notion of the *Mosaic distinction*. Revolutionary monotheism (as opposed to evolutionary monotheism, the final stage of polytheism) is 'based on the distinction between true and false gods, between one true god and the rest of forbidden, false, or non-existent gods' (Assmann 2007, 28). Polytheistic religions are concerned mainly with public actions such as the correct performance of rituals. Monotheism is concerned with orthodoxy, correct belief and sincerity of commitment. Monotheisms have in common an emphatic and exclusionary claim to revealed truth. The claim is not based on the evidence of the gods' activity in the world, as are the earlier religions, but on revelation. Natural evidence is disparaged as seduction 'luring people away from eternal truths into the traps and pitfalls of the false gods, that is, the world' (Assmann 2010, 29). From these claims to incontrovertible truth, the monotheisms draw their antagonistic energy.

For these religions and for these religions alone, the truth to be proclaimed comes with an enemy to be fought. Only they know of heretics and pagans, false doctrine, sects, superstition, idolatry, magic, ignorance, unbelief, heresy, and whatever other terms have been coined to designate what they denounce, persecute and proscribe as manifestations of untruth (Assmann 2010, 4).

Religious intolerance, hatred and violence enter a world that had been innocent of them: the hatred of the Elect directed at pagans, heretics, apostates and sexual non-conformists who threaten the Elect's certainties, and the retaliatory hatred of those who are excluded and maligned. To polytheists, monotheism's claim to exclusive truth and privilege was simply atheism, a contemptuous denial of *their* gods. These mutual hatreds have rippled through contending sects within the Abrahamic religions and between them, from antiquity to the present.[6] But hatred is not reserved only for the stranger or pagan but also for the Canaanite within. The mosaic distinction 'cuts right through the community and even through the individual heart, which now becomes the theatre of inner conflicts and religious dynamics. The concept of idolatry becomes psychologized and turned into a new concept of sin' (Assmann 2007, 30). A new avenue for self-hatred is also bequeathed to humankind.

Communion and Attachment

I have been sketching elements of the psycho-historical evolution of a concept of a god that made intense communion (or dependence or attachment) with the god possible. I have mostly used 'communion' to designate the relationship that evolved between human and god – in some parts of the globe and at least potentially – in preference to 'attachment' or 'dependence' because the word suggests a relationship that is intimate, open, sincere, but also conducive to merger or identification. The idea that the characteristics of the human-to-god relationship are based on human-to-human relationships is scarcely new. It is implicit in early Greek thinkers such as Euhemerus, and a version is elaborated by Feuerbach. Freud injected into this frame his novel developmental view: the relationship is shaped by and perpetuates that between young child and father.

> When the growing individual finds that he is destined to remain a child forever, that he can never do without protection against strange superior powers, he lends those powers

> the features belonging to the figure of his father; he creates for himself the gods whom he dreads, whom he seeks to propitiate, to whom he nevertheless entrusts his own protection. . . . The defence against childish helplessness is what lends its characteristic features to the adult's reaction to the helplessness which he has to acknowledge – a reaction which is precisely the formation of religion.
>
> *(1927, 20)*

Much of the subsequent psychoanalytically oriented work on religion, of attachment theory (Kirkpatrick 1999, 2005; Granqvist 2020), and other psychological approaches (such as terror management, coping theory) can be seen as elaborations of, or departures from, the ideas in this passage, with the role of the father replaced by mother or primary caregiver. On my reading, there is an ambiguity in the passage that points to a significant divergence between the psychoanalytic and other approaches. It is unclear in Freud whether it is unconscious infantile wishes for parental protection preserved in the unconscious, or the adult's quite realistic fears in a hostile world, that are being allayed in the relationship to God. The passage suggests an emphasis on allaying adult needs for protection, although these happen to have the same overall character as the child's. However, as I indicated in the introduction, the drift of psychoanalytic thought seems to be that supernatural figures unconsciously *represent* parental objects, and therefore relating to them symbolically or substitutively satisfies unconscious infantile wishes at the same time as adult dependent needs. Here the difference between psychoanalytic and attachment approaches becomes manifest. As Granqvist says: 'Unlike Freud . . . attachment scholars do not tend to view attachment behaviour in adults as manifestations of regression or unhealthy dependency' (2020, 88). Whether that dependency should be characterized as unhealthy is moot; but more to the point, attachment theorists don't see the earlier relationship as still alive in the later one, most psychoanalytic theorists do, I believe.

Attachment theorists recognize the many similarities between the infant's attachment behaviour and the religious adult's behaviour in relation to the noncorporeal attachment figure of God (e.g. Kirkpatrick 1999; Granqvist 2020). They are similar because the same motivational system, a primary attachment behavioural system, is active in both. The evidence for such a system is strong (Panksepp and Biven 2012; Granqvist 2020). It operates to secure proximity to a stronger, wiser attachment figure that functions as a safe haven and secure base when safety or emotional dysregulation are threatened. Some theorists also see it is as subserving 'mentalization', the capacity to understand others in terms of intentional states (Fonagy, Gergely and Target 2004; Hill 2010). There is an array of attachment outcomes along a secure/insecure spectrum. We need not go into details. In the case of religious objects extensive studies confirm that the vicissitudes of attachment history influence the person's representations – 'internal working models' (IWMs) – of God and other supernatural figures.[7] Broadly, people with secure attachment and with positive IWMs of themselves and others will tend to view God positively as a secure base and safe haven. People with insecure attachment, who are preoccupied/ambivalent or avoidant, are likely to have corresponding views of God as ambivalent or harsh. In his major work, Granqvist notes that these findings are borne out by cross-cultural studies: 'In cultures where parenting is typically harsh and rejecting, people tend to have corresponding representations of God or gods as wrathful and punitive. In contrast, in cultures where parenting is typically warm and accepting, people tend to have a corresponding representation of God or gods as loving and accepting' (2020, 139–140). But importantly, divine figures may become a surrogate for unsatisfactory attachment figures. Relations to God experienced as caring may compensate for insecure attachment and provide the kind of secure attachment relationship one never had with one's parents or other primary attachment figures. At the centre of this picture, then, are causal arrows from {benign or malign parenting} to {secure or insecure attachment} to {corresponding IWMs of parents and others} to {corresponding or compensatory IWMs of God}. Although the literature contains some additional vague references to the way in which adult 'religious standards' are configured on the basis of the standards of the attachment figures of childhood, there appears little discussion of the direct role of religious ideology, of the specific character and conceptions of a religion, in the formation of the child's and adult's IWMs of deity and their religious dispositions (but cf. Hill 2010). Consequently, the fundamental difficulty with the attachment theoretical study of religion is that although it captures some schematic elements of religious phenomenology it fails to capture many of its definitive features or content; a fact obliquely acknowledged, at least by Granqvist (2020, 267). I will now note some particular difficulties with the approach, with a view to exploring the richer defensive aspects, more specifically the narcissistic aspects, of religion.

As we have seen, for most of the historical record, not to say of prehistory, and in most regions of the world, religion did not have a prominent C or attachment aspect. Religious observance before and apart from monotheism is mostly at the pole of EPC. Love is often said to be central to most religious belief systems but this is simply not so. Rather it would seem, as Freud (1933, 165) obliquely observed, that only when a people lose confidence in their ability to influence the spirits do they abandon manipulation, the use of magic and imprecation,[8] and seek communion. Horton notes that many religions scarcely have a communion aspect at all but are marked by 'cool pragmatism' (Horton 1997, 373ff. for examples), a fact obviously inconvenient to the application of the attachment model. 'All vigorously flourishing religious traditions' Horton says, 'include a strong emphasis on explanation, prediction, and control of worldly events' because EPC is the basic sustainer of a religion's life, it creates a sense of the reality of its religious objects. Communion with a noncorporeal object involves a loss of a handle on reality, as rudimentary as that handle may be. The quest for communion is degenerative from the quest to control the material world and spirits.[9] The fact that historically EPC has been the dominant mode of religious expression is not only inconvenient to attachment research but raises the question what it is about humanity that has made – and arguably still makes – EPC, and not attachment, the default position.[10]

Again, to my knowledge the attachment studies direct limited attention to the influence of the *specifics* of religious doctrine on the religious development of the child. We know that the mind of the preschooler and early schoolchild is extremely receptive to religious and spiritual ideas and parents and teachers regard this period as particularly opportune for cultivating their brand of religious ideology and practice. The interaction between parent and child certainly shapes the child's IWMs of gods in significant ways, and the parent's religious beliefs (including their IWMs of God) may enter into that interaction. But the details of the religious ideology and practices to which the child is exposed, and the way these are *interpreted* by the child – interpretation that may depart markedly from the parent's beliefs – are also significant. Such details are treated as extrinsic to the main lines of attachment research.

Finally, religious profession and affiliation spreads over a broad spectrum. On one side of a mild centre are people whose adoption or profession of a religion has little psychological resonance. It may be a part of the 'social scene'; it may be habit. On the other side of the centre there may be very deep resonance indeed. Here are people referred to as fundamentalists, fanatics or religiose. They are the clamorous representatives of a larger group who are driven to religion by needs not well described as emerging from the correspondence or compensation pathways of the attachment crucible. The attachment orientated research, although focused on monotheism, scarcely touches on what in my view is most distinctive about it. At base, in the essential structure of its ideology and emotional impress, monotheism *is* fanatical.

Given the opportunity it quickly reverts to its principal tendencies: intolerance of difference, persecution, violence and hatred of mind when thought challenges its illusions. It has been so since antiquity and is evident today wherever religion has political influence: in Russia, Eastern Europe, Israel, many Muslim nations and the United States. Of course, many people, even those who know the historical record and acknowledge these tendencies, see them as incidental, as perversions of 'true religion'. My contention, foreshadowed above, is that these are *intrinsic* features of monotheism. That is not a proposition fully demonstrable here (Pataki 2010), but we can begin to see how it might be true by now examining further aspects of the role of narcissism in religion.

Narcissism and Identification

I want to briefly discuss a number of processes that in a loose sense could be called narcissistic defences because they are so intimately concerned with the economy of self-esteem and the reflexive modification of the self or self-image. Then I will relate these processes to religious development. My rather dogmatic account requires much in-filling, but its very sketchiness may perhaps render it uncontroversial from a range of psychodynamic perspectives. We do not need to be too specific about timing. It will be agreed that children of all ages wish to live in the circle of an omnibenevolent world and have available from early days the means of regulating their internal states and environment. Several are of particular significance in the maintenance of well-being and the development of the narcissistic economy. First there is the capacity to withdraw attention from, or to split off, bad or painful aspects of self and primary objects (mother) and to project (externalise) aspects of self into objects. A second involves introjecting (internalising) the good aspects of primary objects. The child can subsequently identify with objects introjectively (the object is in me, and I am like the object) or projectively (I am in the object, and it is like me).[11] These acts favourably alter the distribution of pleasure and pain in the child's world. The vehicle of some of these regulative mental acts is omnipotent (wish-fulfilling) phantasy: when some state of affairs is phantasised, it seems at the time to be real (Pataki 2014, 2019). The young child's mental life is under the sway of what Freud called 'the omnipotence of thought' and this experience of (quasi-)omnipotence combines with a number of incidental affirmations of it. The heightened experience of mastery when the child is beginning to walk and talk, and the new, exhilarating love affair with the world, augments it. Parents usually are still satisfying the infant's needs on demand and may be felt to be extensions of his will. The conjunction of these circumstances elates the infant and reinforces his sense of omnipotence and grandeur.[12] With the development of a mature ego or self – we do not need to be specific here – maintenance of the omnibenevolent world soon requires regard to the complex relations one has with oneself.

Two other factors tangential to the endeavour to maintain an omnibenevolent world, and a sense of omnipotent control over it, are of significance to the economy of narcissism. Early on, a child may insist on mother's presence and will do everything in his attachment repertoire to secure it. Disruption of the optimal ranges of attachment proximity and intimacy may create intolerable anxiety. Later, the child must *know* mother's whereabouts. This need to know may be deformed into a need to know everything which, under the impress of omnipotence and, later, the incorporation of the idealised omnipotent parent, may be transformed into the illusion of omniscience. The child may in phantasy become omniscient, or suffer desperately from the need to be so. It is remarkable that the attributes – omnipotence, omniscience and omnibenevolence – so necessary in the regulation of infantile narcissism and well-being, are precisely the key perfections attributed to God.

The second factor involved in the regulation of the narcissistic economy is the capacity for idealisation. Figures needed for protection and security are often idealised by having their 'bad' aspects stripped away, or split off, so as to not vitiate their goodness and obstruct the desired relation to them. Sometimes, as W.R.D. Fairbairn (1952) emphasised, the child in splitting the object takes its badness upon himself. This leads to guilt and shame and self-abasement. With these idealised images of himself and objects the child can in various degrees identify. Freud referred to the setting up of an 'ego-ideal' that is 'a substitute for the lost narcissism of his childhood in which he was his own ideal' – a kind of rescue operation for narcissism. But the child may also achieve idealisation of himself by identifying with his idealised parental objects. If he is like (or better) than his idealised objects, he too will be admirable and invincible; and, if not loved for his goodness and beauty, he will have the power at least to compel or extort love. Being able to idealise himself, the child now possesses another means to further idealise objects by projecting his own idealised conception of himself into them. The processes I have described are more or less normal developments. But in some circumstances identification with the idealised objects and idealised self-representations can lead to the creation of unconscious grandiose conceptions of the self that dominate the entire personality. One particularly malign outcome occurs when the self and object have been idealised for their aggression or destructiveness and the grandiose self that forms from the fusion of ideal self and idealised object is malignant and destructive (detailed discussion of these processes from different though converging perspectives may be found in Kohut 1968; Kernberg 1975; Klein 1975; Rosenfeld 1987).

It is difficult to sustain childhood narcissism. Parents become progressively uncompliant, and the child's expanded understanding soon discloses his real weakness and dependency. His maturing moral sense and love of others begin to render naked egotism unbearable. Various strategies are now available to keep a grip on his self-esteem and omnipotent control. He may consciously surrender much of his own narcissism but reinforce the idealisation of his objects and form a kind of hero-worshipping incorporative bond that delivers the narcissistic rewards of living in the orbit or radiance of the great and adored one. Or he can project his own idealised self-images into the parental figure, and then by re-identification restore what was earlier surrendered; unconsciously it then seems that he is the idealised incorporated figure or the one that he projectively lives in. These unconscious phantasies undergird and will decisively influence the adult's conscious beliefs, behaviour and sense of self.

I come at last to the interplay between the narcissistic economy and religious development, focusing in particular on the role of religious ideology. Religious instruction usually commences when the child is still under the sway of infantile narcissism, the capacity for distinguishing the real from the phantastic is not well established, and he is disposed to believe his parents unquestioningly. If ideas about supernatural figures are introduced to the child, he is likely to recapitulate in relation to them the strategies used earlier to regulate his self-esteem and sense of security. Religious teaching about God's omnipotence, omniscience and goodness are particularly fitted to re-invigorate narcissistic desires and to gratify them, for these are the very properties the child is striving more or less desperately to sustain or retrieve. So, for example, he may attempt to establish a relationship in phantasy with the ideal supernatural figures (as with a pop star or sporting hero) and bask in their radiance. Or the child may consciously surrender his self-love and then restore it in some measure by unconscious identification with God. In that way his self-love can be extended in loving God and in God's love for him.[13]

The sense of one's great goodness, importance and power is not easily surrendered. If it is forcefully extinguished with threats or punishment, or if parents are remote, the image of the self, fashioned on the images of parents and the child's own angry projections, may be angry and punitive, and the corresponding image of God is likely to be wrathful and vengeful. Children raised in a cold or crushing atmosphere – it is often part of religious upbringing to crush the child's 'willfulness' – are more likely to depend on supernatural substitutes to contain their narcissism, on the compensation model. Their self-esteem is likely to be precarious and sustainable only through unremitting efforts – prayer, sacrifice, self-abasement – to achieve emotional proximity to a remote God. If the child splits his self-conception, projects the good into the image of God and identifies with the bad, or if he has split the parental conception and projected the good into God and identified with the bad counterparts, then he is left with an unmoderated all-bad conception of himself. If, as is often the case, there arises a dominant identification with this bad self-image and the attachment to, and identification with, the idealised figure of God fails, then the expense of maintaining an image of an all-good, almighty God is to see oneself as sinful, weak and suppliant. Because of the close association between images of God and idealised parental and self images many people who have abandoned religion, may in later life return to it if, as in times of crisis, the lure of the omnipotent parental objects or of the ideal self become once again irresistible. Even when religious ideas are introduced later in life they may regressively reactivate the longing for the lost idealised objects. The point can be underscored: the object of longing is not just the parent who provides a secure base and safe haven, or the abstracted version of these; the longing is for the idealised parent and the lost ideal self.

These strategies can be repeated in relation to the religious group. The group may be idealised and identified with so that the greatness conferred on the group can be claimed for oneself. Identifying with a group – racial, religious, a football club – whose virtues are sublimed is a common way of elevating and sustaining self-esteem. The logic is simple: if the group is special, the members are special. This strategy also has the advantage of being able to diminish envy by appropriating the group's achievements. It also enhances one's power and scope for exercising it in the groups' superior ability to 'throw its weight around', an expression of narcissistic assertion. Consequently, religious group identity is prone to be an instrument of aggression that had to be suppressed in childhood. Becoming a member of the Elect is in itself a gratifying exclusionary process: being Elect means being one of the Few, not the Many. Consigning non-believers to hell is also gratifying, though not of the best elements in human nature. Proselytizing is a doubly rewarding act. Consciously, there is the pleasing knowledge of bestowing grace upon another; unconsciously, there is the narcissistic pleasure of stripping converts of their former identity and obliterating differences by aggressively incorporating them into the group. Compelling others to think and act as you do not only confirms faith and eliminates challenges to it, but it also nourishes grandiose self-conceptions by testifying to one's power. It affirms the special relationship or identification with an omnipotent God.

Finally, the unconscious need for omniscience that arises from the omnipotent denial of separation or abandonment forms a fateful combination with the revealed religion that knows no uncertainty or fallibility. Science and the humanities cannot provide certainties. Herein lays the great resource of the Holy Book. For people who may not know much, and don't care to know more, the Holy Book idealised provides all they need to know on all matters of importance. The word of God can be carried in the van to war, placed near head or heart or waved around in public demonstration of faith. Assiduously studying the word of God is unconsciously incorporating the mind of God: to thoroughly incorporate the mind of God is to be God. At a rally against COVID-19 restrictions, an American woman screamed, 'I don't need your science, I got my God', unknowingly echoing Tertullian 1800 years earlier: 'We have no need of curiosity after Jesus Christ, nor of research after the Gospel. When we believe, we desire to believe nothing more. For we believe this first, that there is nothing else that we should believe.' Reason threatens to subvert such grand presumption. So the eye is plucked out.

These then are some of the ways in which narcissism is intricated with religion in its broadly communion aspect. As noted, I have not attempted to discuss the important role of narcissism in relation to the EPC pole of religion, a matter for another occasion.

Notes

1 I would like to thank Agnes Petocz and Tair Caspi for their very helpful comments. The paper is greatly improved because of them.

2 That issue must be left largely indeterminate here; the various concepts of soul and spirit are vague, and modern concepts of the *material* and the *natural* don't always easily apply. I will generally use the phrase 'gods or spirits', or sometimes use the terms interchangeably where the sense is clear, to refer to the non-natural focal objects of religion. Roughly, gods are spirits who are worshipped. Some spirits, such as those of ancestors or dead kings, may be revered as objects of cult; others, such as the malicious spirits in the service of a hostile adjacent tribe, or the gods of Greece and Rome degraded into demons by the early Christians, may be greatly feared.

3 Xenophanes complained that men make the gods 'have clothing, voice and body just like them.' 'If cows and horses had hands', he said, 'they would draw their gods in the shape of cows and horses.' We do not know what Xenophanes thought the gods were like. I am of course glossing over vast tracts of mystical, apophatic, allegorizing and metaphysical de-anthropomorphizing over two millennia, but I deny that these efforts have altered the thought of the ordinary believer, nor of many of the learned. Moreover, if the psychoanalytic argument I develop below is sound, then it may be expected that even the most abstract conceptions of God are experienced unconsciously in a concrete manner, along the lines of parental introjects, and hence as at least partly anthropomorphic.

4 Robert Wright (2010) discusses the intense humiliation and resentment towards the oppressive regional powers expressed by the prophets of the time. 'In the end . . . the logic behind monotheism was pretty simple given the natural mindset of Israel's exilic intellectuals. Yahweh's honour, and Israel's pride, could be salvaged only by intellectual extremes. If the Babylonian conquest didn't signify Yahweh's disgrace, if Yahweh wasn't a weakling among the gods, then he must have orchestrated Israel's calamity – and orchestrating a calamity of that magnitude came close to implying the orchestration of history itself, which would leave little room if any for autonomy on the part of other gods' (180–81). 'Monotheism was amongst other things the ultimate revenge': the oppressors who tormented Israel are deprived of their gods and they must acknowledge Israel's superiority on both a political and theological plane (178).

5 In a private communication, Agnes Petocz has noted how the need to disguise God by abstraction becomes more urgent as religious need regresses to its *fons et origo* in the human need and helplessness of the child.

6 Gibbon (1776–1778/1993) is still the most vivid historian of the internecine massacres of antiquity. We require no illustration from the present.

7 Several writers of psychodynamic bent have arrived at similar conclusions in different theoretical frameworks (e.g., Meissner 1984; Faber 2004; Ostow 2007). Ostow argues that the covenantal relation to God 'provides both horizontal [to the group] and vertical [to God] attachment to a divine entity. I would guess' he continues, 'that this dual attachment provides the major motivation of religious affiliation' (84).

8 When, that is, in Freud's view, the omnipotence of thought subsides. The broad group of shamanistic religions may be viewed as an intermediate stage where the capacity for communion with the spirits, still directed more or less to manipulative ends, is invested in a single religious specialist (see Lewis 2003).

9 It appears to peak in times of social distress when ordinary human relations are disrupted. The search for communion seems to have arisen in Egypt and Mesopotamia during times of social dislocation. In Greece, eras of political and social discord gave rise to mystical movements in the sixth century BC (Pythagoras, Orphism); the aftermath of the Peloponnesian War (Plato); the first century BC (Posidonius, neo-Pythagorism); and the third century AD (Plotinus; Dodds 1965, *passim*). The misery of the third century provided the conditions for the rise of Christianity, when the urban centres of migration could no longer provide the security of family, lineage, clan and locality. People in a lonely and impersonal place were ready to accept 'a peculiarly intense parental relationship with a spiritual being – a relationship that had no real parallel in the locally based cults in their earlier lives' (Horton 1997, 374–375; see Brown 2018, 62ff).

10 The answer to this question would require a long excursion into our tendency to magical and omnipotent thought; certainly a matter intricated with narcissism, but not an aspect of narcissism I can address here.

11 Incorporative and identificatory processes in religious phenomenology in the ancient world and tribal religions are described *passim* in Dodds (1965), Lewis (2003), and Bellah (2011).

12 The *locus classicus* is Ferenczi (1913). The role of omnipotence in child development is influentially explored in D. W. Winnicott (1965, 1974).

13 Freud makes only passing remarks on narcissistic aspects of the relation to God. He notes that circumcised peoples feel exalted by it (1939, 29). This is explained in the Jewish context as a mark of specialness or choseness or at least equivalence with the Egyptians who practised it. He says that Moses inspired in the Jewish people the notion that they were God's chosen: 'they believe that they stand especially close to Him' (1939, 106). Mosaic religion increased Jewish self-esteem because (1) it allowed the people to take a share in the grandeur of the new idea of God, (2) it asserted that this people had been chosen by this great God and were destined to receive evidences of his special favour, and (3) it forced upon the people an advance in intellectuality (1939, 123). This last factor is explained as the consequence of a renunciation of instinct followed by superego approval. In relation to the first factor, Freud says that 'the pride in God's greatness fuses with the pride in being chosen by him' (1939, 112).

References

Assmann, Jan (2007) Monotheism and polytheism. In Johnston, Sarah Isles (ed) *Ancient Religions*. Cambridge MA: Harvard University Press.

Assmann, Jan (2010) *The Price of Monotheism*. Stanford: Stanford University Press.

Barrett, Justin L. (2007) Gods. In *Whitehouse and Laidlaw*.

Beaulieu, Paul-Alain (2007) Mesopotamia. In Johnston, Sarah Isles (ed) *Ancient Religions*. Cambridge MA: Harvard University Press.

Bellah, Robert N. (2011) *Religion in Human Evolution*. Cambridge, MA: Harvard University Press.

Bering, Jesse (2011) *The God Instinct*. London: Nicholas Brearley Publishing.

Brown, Peter (2018) *The World Of Late Antiquity*. London: Thames and Hudson.

Burkert, Walter (2004) *Babylon Memphis Persepolis: Eastern Contexts of Greek Culture*. Harvard MA: Harvard University Press.

Collins, John J. (2007) Israel. In Johnston, Sarah Isles (ed) *Ancient Religions*. Cambridge MA: Harvard University Press.

Dever, William G. (2006) *Who Were the Early Israelites and Where Did They Come From?* Grand Rapids: Wm. B. Eerdmans Publishing Co.

Dodds, E. R. (1965) *Pagan and Christian in an Age of Anxiety*. Cambridge: Cambridge University Press.

Faber, M. D. (2004) *The Psychological Roots of Religious Belief*. New York: Prometheus Books.

Fairbairn, W. R. D. (1952) *Psychoanalytic Studies of the Personality*. London: Routledge Kegan Paul.

Ferenczi, Sandor (1913) Stages in the development of a sense of reality. In *Sex in Psychoanalysis*. New York: Dover 1956.

Fonagy, Peter, György Gergely, Elliot L. Jurist, and Mary Target (eds.) (2004) *Affect Regulation, Mentalization, and the Development of the Self*. New York: Other Books.

Freud, Sigmund (1913) *Totem and Taboo*. SE XIII. London: Hogarth.

Freud, Sigmund (1927) *The Future of an Illusion*. SE XXI. London: Hogarth.

Freud, Sigmund (1933) *New Introductory Lectures*. SE XXII. London: Hogarth.

Freud, Sigmund (1939) *Moses and Monotheism*. SE XXIII. London: Hogarth.

Gibbon, Edward (1776–1788/1993) *The Decline and Fall of the Roman Empire*. New York: Alfred A. Knopf.

Granqvist, Pehr (2020) *Attachment in Religion and Spirituality*. New York: Guildford Press.

Guthrie, Stewart E. (1993) *Faces in the Clouds: A New Theory of Religion*. New York: Oxford University Press.

Guthrie, Stewart E. (2007) Anthropology and anthropomorphism in religion. In *Whitehouse and Laidlaw*.

Hill, David (2010) Fundamentalist faith states: Regulation theory as a framework for the psychology of religious fundamentalism. In Strozier, Charles B., Terman, David M. and Jones, James W. (eds) *The Fundamentalist Mindset*. Oxford: Oxford University Press.

Horton, Robin (1997) *Patterns of Thought in Africa and the West*. Cambridge: Cambridge University Press.

Hume, David (1757) The natural history of religion. In Antony Flew (ed) (1992) *Writings on Religion*. London: Open Court.

Kernberg, Otto (1975) *Borderline Conditions and Pathological Narcissism*. New York: Jacob Aronson.
Kirkpatrick, Lee A. (1999) Attachment and religious representations of behaviour. In Cassidy, J. and Shaver, P. R. (eds.) *Handbook of Attachment*. New York: Guildford Press.
Kirkpatrick, Lee A. (2005) *Attachment, Evolution, and the Psychology of Religion*. New York: Guilford Press.
Klein, Melanie (1975) *Envy and Gratitude*. London: Hogarth Press.
Kohut, Heinz (1968) The psychoanalytic treatment of narcissistic personality disorders. In Ornstein, Paul H. (ed) *The Search for the Self*. New York: International Universities Press 1978.
Lewis, I. M. (2003) *Ecstatic Religion: A Study of Shamanism and Spirit Possession*. London: Routledge.
Meissner, W. W. (1984) *Psychoanalysis and Religious Experience*. Ann Arbor: Yale University Press.
Olupona, Jacob K. (2014) *African Religions*. Oxford: Oxford University Press.
Ostow, Mortimer (2007) *Spirit, Mind and Brain*. New York: Columbia University Press.
Panksepp, Jaak, and Biven, Lucy (2012) *The Archaeology of Mind: Neuroevolutionary Origins of Human Emotions*. New York: W. W. Norton.
Pataki, Tamas (2007) *Against Religion*. Melbourne: Scribe.
Pataki, Tamas (2010) Religion and violence. In Bonett, W. (ed) *The Australian Book of Atheism*. Melbourne: Scribe.
Pataki, Tamas (2014) *Wish-fulfilment in Philosophy and Psychoanalysis*. New York: Routledge.
Pataki, Tamas (2019) Wish-fulfilment. In Gipps, Richard and Lacewing, Michael (eds.) *The Oxford Handbook of Philosophy and Psychoanalysis*. Oxford: Oxford University Press.
Rosenfeld, Herbert (1987) *Impasse and Interpretation*. London: Tavistock Publications.
Tylor, Edward B. (1873/2016) *Primitive Culture* (2 volumes). New York: Dover Publications.
Whitehouse, Harvey (2007) Towards and integration of ethnography, history and the cognitive science of religion. In *Whitehouse and Laidlaw*.
Whitehouse, Harvey, and Laidlaw James (eds) (2007) *Religion, Anthropology and Cognitive Science*. Durham, NC: Carolina Academic Press.
Winnicott, D. W. (1965) *The Maturational Processes and the Facilitating Environment*. London: Hogarth Press.
Winnicott, D. W. (1974) *Playing and Reality*. Harmondsworth: Pelican.
Wright, David P. (2007) Syria and Canaan. In Johnston, Sarah Isles (ed) *Ancient Religions*. Harvard, MA: Harvard University Press.
Wright, Robert (2010) *The Evolution of God*. New York: Little, Brown and Company.

31

THE MISSING SIGNIFIER AND A MALFUNCTIONING PATERNAL LAW

On the Feminine Third as Vital Portal for Sexual Difference and Emancipatory Democracy

Jill Gentile

> Sexual difference is probably the issue in our time which could be our "salvation" if we thought it through.
>
> *(Luce Irigaray, An Ethics of Sexual Difference, p. 5)*

Introduction

As early as 1892, Freud had speculated that "the essentially repressed element is always what is feminine" (p. 250), hinting at the close alliance between the feminine and the (traumatic) Real. Though he was unable to state the problem as directly as Lacan later would, he began to surmise that there wasn't a place, or proper signifier, for the woman in the psychical economy, nominating "passivity" as a (problematic) substitute. This solution, or impasse, has been subject to both a great deal of feminist and, particularly, Lacanian-inflected debate, and a certain dismissal or inattention among much of the rest of the field which has either accepted the lack of signification as valid, or simply doesn't contend with it. This missing conversation about a missing signifier, or "signifying minus," perpetually displaces and defers the field's own contestation with its "master discourses."[1]

Nevertheless, psychoanalysts of all persuasions concur that what eludes naming also eludes knowing, instead remaining inconceivable and linked to trauma, repression, and the unconscious. But how the feminine functions to sustain these links remains opaque, restricting both our theory and our praxis. Bear in mind, on this account, Freud's (1937) late conviction – rather equally presumed and contested – that the repudiation of the feminine functions as a bedrock principle for both sexes, against which psychoanalysis meets its limits and, we might say, ultimately stands defeated.

Psychoanalysis, on this account, has a great deal to gain, or so I imagine,[2] by naming a feminine signifier. But the choice to do so (and it is a choice) challenges our theoretical commitments to date, and our allegiances to the brilliance but also to the blindness of our patriarchal

DOI: 10.4324/9780429297076-37

forefathers. If psychoanalysis is to intervene at this time of global flirtation with autocracy, fascism, and pseudo-masculinist discourses, all of which reproduce misogyny, invidious hierarchies, and epochal social inequities, it must address what underlies these devastating effects. Whereas psychoanalysis has begun to grapple with its long disavowed racialized legacies, it must also contend with how it has underwritten misogyny into its theory by insisting upon a perpetual lack of representation and abjected status for the feminine.

Reading across psychoanalysis convinces me it is not equivocal in erasing what we might discern as the *feminine* – the paradoxical missing *sine qua non* of the symbolic order. This erasure in the signifying order functions structurally, I argue, as a proxy for other marginalized, excluded, colonized, racialized and "invisible" (notably, black) peoples, while also collapsing the gap that is constitutive of sexual difference, hence, difference itself. Thus, the field must wrestle with its continued complicity with a monosexual, masculinist symbolic economy, and with what it gains and with what (and whom) it sacrifices on the altar of its phallogocentric and phallophiliac order. My insistence is, of course, something of an ironic charge: Freud's point was that the formation of human subjectivity is coincident with the psychic acquisition of sexual difference but by placing his chips on the repudiation of the feminine and the acceptance of the castration complex, so that "difference" is constructed based, not on actuality, but on something imagined as "missing." Moreover, his complex and unwieldy argument, which locates asymmetry in the consequences of the encounter with sexual difference, has produced neither egalitarian nor inclusive effects, at least in part because it fails to articulate a law beyond, or asymmetrical to, paternal law, which thereby can enable the disruptive validity of any psychical constitution of (sexual) difference. If psychoanalysis is to fulfill its radical social and political offer, it must choose to be a theory and praxis not of the One, but also – as Luce Irigaray (1985, p. 26) compellingly framed it – of this sex which is not One. "She resists all adequate definition." *Other.*

Not the other of the same. Psychoanalytically speaking, we must embrace an economy of the non-self-identical. We must confront sexual difference, and we must grapple with how to signify it if we are to counter our shared vulnerability to repressive forces and commit ourselves to the creation of radically inclusive free speech spaces. This chapter, both an abridged and evolving, partly reconceived, analysis of what I've insistently elaborated at length elsewhere (Gentile, 2015a, b, 2016a, b, 2017, 2019, in press), locates itself within this forever displaced, elliptical, "forgotten" but urgently necessary conversation.

Tracing the Feminine and the Paradoxical Role of the Missing Signifier

Though Freud continually flirted with naming the feminine signifier (turning to dream symbols, proxies, and slang), the absence of a proper signifier for woman remains intriguingly unsettled. Not only was the feminine sex unacknowledged as valid, but its consequences for the turn to language were decisive. Only a phallic signifier was admitted into the symbolic order, relegating the feminine to a phenomenology of lack and inferiority insofar as she can't find Symbolic anchorage.

Both Freud and later Lacan, whose influence was especially profound on this point, have been indicted for injecting a misogynistic and patriarchal premise into psychoanalysis, with injurious effects most obviously for women. These indictments, it is countered, fail to recognize the rich complexity introduced, however paradoxically, by the enigmatic if absent feminine signifier which (at least in part) prompts and propels psychoanalysis's signifying mission. Paul Verhaeghe (1996) illuminatingly describes this mission as an hysterical, "drawn-out search for a signifier which simply wasn't there" (p. 63). Further, and not insignificantly, if paradoxically and insufficiently, the location of Woman in the Real (beyond the symbolic), per Lacan and as developed by in post-Lacanian thought, also offers her partial recuperation: a proximity to the sensuous textures of the maternal body, to truths and enigmas which elude symbolic capture, and offer possibilities beyond confinement within a categorical phallic identity.

At any rate, despite an implicit acknowledgement of the feminine's mobilizing force in free association, and an explicit pointing to "the gap" as the impossible of free association, Freud would never reconcile these notions, failing to recognize that the gap of free association was co-extensive with the truth-revealing, desire-inspiring action of the missing feminine gap (Gentile, 2015b, 2016a, b, c). Not to be rendered utterly mute, its enigmatic and relentless subterranean motions animated his otherwise phallocentric theorizing, which reveals a trail of signifiers orbiting around the female genital. Most famously, if also subject to psychoanalytic repression (mirroring his insights), he deciphered the uncanny (1919) as a revisitation of the female sexed body, the birth canal, a literal but also metonymic feminine gap, one we'd all encountered and known, *and* repressed, even as it antedates repression.[3] And the "missing" genital (1925) was credited with enough force to derail the child's, especially the boy's, reality-testing and to inspire infantile sexual theories.

Lacan's thought, preoccupied as it was in its earlier stages with his prioritization of the phallus, later returned to the uncanny effects issuing from Freud's. In this later turn, Lacan made a fuss over the missing signifier: the feminine sign was no mere omission. Its non-signification was the point; it pointed to the gap in the signifying order, to the contradiction, by means of the unconscious, in the structure of knowledge. Yet, even as the signification of the missing sign gains status, its feminine origins, it would seem, were siphoned off, abjected, repressed. The consequences became a two-sided coin: master signifier and missing signifier or "*objet petit a*."

Before turning to this elision of the feminine (which would later reassert itself in Lacan's conception of feminine jouissance), let me elaborate a bit on the reversal between his early and later thinking. Verhaeghe (1996, 2009) reminds us that Lacan's early thought, recognized as his return to Freud, involved the idea that human knowledge has a phallic underpinning because the unconscious is structured as a language, and there is only one signifier – the phallus – for both sexes. This signifier, the basis for the subject's division (from itself, and from a wordless, illimitable Real, from the body of the mother), creates differential effects for boys and girls who must rely on it in their quest to acquire a desire of their own. The castration fantasy (which interprets the girl's "lack" in phallic terms) tries to bridge the gap between what is "missing" and what is "seen," between the Real and the Symbolic. Lacan posits that by means of the father's symbolic function, *The-Name-of-the-Father*, the child becomes accountable to language and subject to law prohibiting incest, thereby setting a limit to the dual unity of mother-child. Lacking a proper signifier for femininity and because of her vulnerability to hysteria owing to its repression, the girl faces a more significant challenge than does the boy because she too must rely on the phallic signifier to locate her desire.

Lacan's later thought, however, marks something of a reversal because, at this stage, he came to more fully contemplate incompleteness of the Symbolic order, its structural gap or contradiction. This would have consequences for his conception of the father's symbolic function. A shift in emphasis revealed the master signifier "phallus" as figuring an illusory completeness, in effect signifying the contradiction: the totality of the symbolic order and its impossibility and lack. Hence, the *Name-of-the-Father* becomes the agent of *symbolic castration*; the phallus/master signifier functioning in effect as its own ironic critique of phallogocentrism.

With this revision, philosopher Alenka Zupančič (2017) explains, the missing signifier or, alternately, the "signifying minus," gains a new status. Whereas, initially, Lacan had credited the phallic signifier with inaugurating "the entire human 'dialectics,' and its contradictions," now it is "an *absence* at the very heart of this presence, namely, a gap that appears together with the signifying order, as built into it" (2017, p. 47). Zupančič's emphasizes how this shift powerfully reframes the stakes, by revealing the revolutionary character – of the missing signifier:

> Human (hi)story begins not with the very emergence of the signifier, but with *one signifier "gone missing."* We could indeed say that nature is already full of signifiers . . . and that at some point one signifier "falls out," goes missing. . . . This temporal way of putting it ("gone missing") is an expression of what would be better formulated as the signifying structure emerging not simply without one signifier, but rather *with-without* one signifier – since this "hole" has consequences, and determines what gets structured around it.

Andre Green (1997, p. 1081) arrives at a not dissimilar conviction. Noting that Bion, Winnicott, and Lacan each "use[s] absence as a precondition for [Freud's conception of] representation," he mused: "all these absences can be condensed in the idea of a gap. But that gap, instead of referring to a simple void or to something which is missing, becomes the substrate for what is real. Winnicott says the only real thing is the gap."

The paradoxical signifying function of the gap remains obscured but also freshly illuminated in the later Lacan. Sexual difference, sex, and the unconscious (the lack built into the structure of knowledge) are "absolutely, and irreducibly, linked" to this gap in the signifying order, "and not something beyond or outside this order" (Zupančič, 2017, p. 46). Lacanian theorist Joan Copjec (2016, p. 108) is similarly forceful on this point, indicting psychoanalysis's turn to gender theory as a means of neutering itself by exchanging sex with gender, a move which masks the "irreducible antagonism" constitutive of sex and the sexed subject (who is never at one with herself). But there is a further consensus: feminist philosopher Elizabeth Grosz (1994, p. 209), for example, too recognizes the gap's intimate co-implication with sexual difference: "sexual difference is the horizon that cannot appear in its own terms, but is implied."

Honoring Grosz's "horizon" – or Irigaray's "interval" or Zupančič's (2017, p. 44) "crack in being" – would enable feminism as an emancipatory, even "explosive" political movement, countering the patriarchal elimination, exclusion, and repression not only of this or that identity group, but of the antagonism of sexual difference itself (Zupančič, pp. 36–37). Put differently, in Irigarayan terms, patriarchy's move is to sustain "*the sexual indifference* that subtends it" (Irigaray, 1977, p. 72) and to render invisible the feminine's "disruptive excess" (p. 78). Consequently, as Irigaray would directly assert (1984, p. 5): "Sexual difference is one of the major philosophical issues, if not the issue, of our age."

Irigaray's ardent proclamation remains valid, perhaps not just for her age, or our age, but for any age. Zupančič's intervention, by rescuing the latent power of Lacan's missing signifier, reinvigorates and joins Irigaray's quest. Yet, it seems to me that the intransigence of patriarchy issues to us a further challenge: if we wish to render sexual difference a more robust political force, signifying the missing signifier – a contradictory and, on first impression, a possibly misguided quest – is required. Specifically, signifying the missing signifier would be to recognize its feminine dimension, thereby joining the missing signifier with sexual difference. This pursuit would *enable* the ontological crack of sexual difference (Zupančič's mission) by pointing to the infinity of missing signs – while also granting the feminine (at least in part) a symbolic foothold.

As I will describe more fully below, my claim is that the feminine functions paradoxically, as both missing/absent and present. It lies at the cusp where the unsignifiable Real meets the symbolic, figuring a "space between" wherein novel signs and replenishing drive energies cross a porous border, enabling symbolic freedom. By recognizing the gap of the feminine—i.e., the vaginal—as coextensive with the gap of the signifying order, the gap *of sexual difference* is constituted, rendered usable. As such, signifying the feminine gap may help us to reclaim and revivify the social and political (dis)order. Let's explore this proposal more fully below.

To Name or Not to Name?

Commenting on Lacan's treatment of sexual difference and his acknowledgment, beyond the phallic order, of a feminine sexuality, a "supplementary jouissance" that "escapes his linguistic model," Dana Birksted-Breen (1983, p. 493), writing some forty years ago, identified "the problem which has dominated the psychoanalytic debate on feminine sexuality to date: how to hold on to Freud's most radical insight that sexual difference is a symbolic construct; how to retrieve femininity from a total subordination to the effects of that construction."

As we have seen, these "pressing" concerns have been recently gaining renewed consideration. The missing signifier, per Freud and Lacan, remains *unnamed*, subordinated. Further, if we follow Zupančič's thesis, the fact that it is *unsignified* (and in contradiction to the phallic signifier) is precisely what enables the crack in being constitutive of subjectivity and of sexual difference. Thus, naming would install it in the Symbolic order and render it subject to patriarchal exclusions. The idea of naming the missing signifier would seem to violate the entirety of its function, actually negating its radical social potential.

Notwithstanding these wise and cautionary notes, the political force of the feminine is urgently needed to counter the contemporary rise of brute, antidemocratic, masculinist movements. Might it not be, actually, that what mitigates the disruptive effects of the "crack in being" is, as Irigaray (1985, p. 260) observed, that "[w]omen's genitals are simply absent, masked, sewn back up inside their 'crack'"? If so, any risks attendant to naming the feminine signifier are worth taking[4]. Moreover, failing to do so serves patriarchy's ends – by not only abetting the degradation of the feminine and other marginalized peoples, but by obscuring the very social antagonism or gap itself. Further, it may be possible and not simply theoretically naïve to name the signifier *and* to retain an intricate and valid theory. A quixotic quest perhaps. But I suggest that the risks of undermining the gap (by means of its naming) are substantially mitigated by its paradoxical status and specificity of the feminine signifier.

To explore this conjecture, let's return to Irigaray's groundbreaking contributions in greater detail. Irigaray mounted a passionate and often scathing critique of Freud's (1931, 1933) bequest of a phallic representational economy which effectively colonized the girl's memory and desire. Male "desire – discourse – law" (Irigaray, 1974, p. 53) would be not only propped up by the girl or woman but the sole means by which she constituted herself. Irigaray proposed a symbolic intervention: "two lips" to figure the carnality, indeterminancy, liminality, of the feminine ("She is neither one nor two"; Irigaray, 1985, p. 26). Though Irigaray's two lips, both vaginal and of the mouth, has been subject to essentialist critique, I'm persuaded by Diana Fuss,[5] who argued that the two lips are "neither literal nor metaphoric but metonymic," and that moreover they "operate as metaphor for metonymy" – for the perpetual contiguity and liminality of the feminine. Fuss enables us to read (by means of Bianchi, 2014, p. 105) Irigaray's two lips as contravening any false coherence or facile symmetry between feminine and phallic signifiers.[6]

Whereas Freud's and Lacan's masculinist economy immobilizes the feminine as reproduction of the same, Irigarary's feminine "must be deciphered as inter-dict; within the signs or between them, between the realized meanings, between the lines" (1974, p. 22). This figuration of an "interval," or space between, enables displacement to exceed fixed place, and for what Emma Bianchi (2014) discerns as the aleatory, restless motions of the non-unitary feminine (who was, for Irigaray [1977, p. 38] "indefinitely other in herself") to emerge as a subterranean, antipatriarchal political force.

Irigaray's non-unitary feminine finds resonance in Julia Kristeva's theorizing of maternal heterogeneity and alterity, which precedes and disrupts an identitarian symbolic. Per Kristeva, who too has recently insisted on the priority of sexual difference for displacing patriarchy (Kristeva, 2019), sensations and motions of a maternal *chora* or *semiotic*, an "infolding" of body and language (Ziarek, 1992, p. 93), remain forever resistant to symbolic inscription. Kristeva's "abject" is infused with this feminine liminality, coming to signify "what is on the border [but] what *doesn't respect borders*. It is "ambiguous," "in between" (Oliver, 1993, p. 56, citing Kristeva, 1980a, p. 4). By means of this liminality and disruptive abjection, Kristeva (2019) conjures an antipatriarchal and antihegemonic "detotalizing open structure of the feminine."

Joining these interventions, I have suggested that psychoanalysis recognize the proliferation of spatializing metaphors within its discourse as insistent manifestations of the deferred search for a feminine signifier (Gentile, 2015b, 2016a). Such metaphors, once perceived, are hiding in plain sight. Further, by figuring the *betweenness of* symbolic and enigmatic dimensions, these spatializing metaphors enable psychoanalysis's unwritten *feminine law* (etched in the Real) and its vital function in both shepherding the diasporic migration of novel elements and vibrational drive energies across the threshold of the Real, and in enshrining ambiguity and heterogeneity in the symbolic order. Put differently, feminine law functions to sustain a vitalizing *precolonized* lawful space (or spacetime) of *no* rule – perhaps what Jean-Luc Nancy (1988, p. 145) refers to as a "spacing essence of freedom." Contra Freud's pessimistic rock of castration, feminine law enables us to discern psychoanalysis's paradoxical *spatializing "bedrock."*

More specifically yet, I've nominated the *vaginal* (inclusive, as well, of the *vulva*) as the "proper" feminine signifier. Naming the vaginal, beyond mere sexed body part, rescues the feminine genital from the plight of nonrepresentation, aiding the enfranchisement of all (gendered and sexed) subjects in the (otherwise, exclusively phallic) symbolic order, but it does so mischievously, because it insinuates its contradictory (both of the Real and symbolic) non-unitary status, ever-partially into the Symbolic realm, thereby anchoring sexual difference as a +/− symbolic-and-not (contradictory) construction. In turn, the vaginal preserves, or assists in the labor, by which an irreducible gap comes into being. This double-sidedness (a Vaginal signifier that is both of and beyond the symbolic, with a foothold in the Real) enables a migrancy of drive energies that perpetually elude and exceed patriarchal surveillance, while also enriching and antagonizing the symbolic-phallic economy.

To put this differently, the feminine signifier functions metaphorically, opening symbolic spaces for representation, mediation, inclusivity, and difference, while gesturing towards what lies beneath the radar of the symbolic, at the limits of repression *and* prior to it. By means of a vaginal signifier, the symbolic intervenes in – and is disrupted by – a liminal traumatic Real but also by the unassimilable, untranslatable excesses of that Real, perhaps the force of a disruptive and surprisingly democratizing telos of eros (Gentile, 2016a, 2019).

As the precedent and asymmetrical counterpart to the phallic signifier, the vaginal aids the latter's function in the constitution of subjectivity for all subjects, regardless of sex or gender. Functioning uncannily, it sets up the conditions for dismantling a false binary, while instantiating a certain parity, which enables the pursuit of an egalitarian social order for differently situated, singular, sexed subjects, insofar as we now have two sexed signifiers, one which operates strictly in the symbolic plane, whereas the other functions *between* the symbolic and the Real. Taken together, they open up the possibilities for third, contradictory, nonbinary choices and effects.

It should also be noted that, per Lacan, the phallic signifier has an exceptional status – it is the sole signifier to escape lack insofar as it appropriates the missing signifier (the feminine depends upon the phallic signifier for symbolic anchorage). We might, however, ascribe a corollary exceptional status to the vaginal signifier. Because it figures the gap (and hence, of sexual difference), it also bridges that gap, operating *both* as metaphor and metonymy, signified and "missing." The remainder, the infinite "totality" of missing signifiers, or signifying minuses, retain their dispossession – lest the symbolic intervenes, and/or lest they migrate, and are grasped, possessed, named. In this way, the feminine signifier traffics in, and points to, an heterogeneous, ineluctable unconscious.

In effect, the phallic is to paternal law as the vaginal is to feminine law.

The Redistribution of Signifying Effects

I next explore the signifying impact that naming of the sexed feminine might have for the symbolic world and social discourse.

But first, let's consider the impact of Lacan's later interventions in which the missing signifier gains new status for the once imperious phallus. Though, intuitively, we might anticipate that it has now suffered a loss of some signifying privilege, what is revealed is that, as the (sole) phallic signifier (the missing signifier is, after all, missing), it has now amassed a more expansive purview. Whereas earlier, it had signified the totality of the symbolic order, (as if that were not sufficient!), Lacan now emphasizes the phallus's *posturing* as the master signifier, insofar as it not only signifies *completeness* but also *lack* (which would seem the domain of the missing signifier but for its reliance on the phallic signifier for its constitution), and hence, also *difference* (implying phallic or non-phallic), and *desire* (which finds its origin in the subject's symbolic castration, i.e., reliance on the phallic signifier in the acquisition of language). From there, Lacan posits that, insofar as there is no other than the phallus (p. 157), the phallus (as symbolic Name-of-the-Father) is the founding exception of the symbolic order, essentially transcending its function as a signifier (subject to division/lack), because it instead grounds the Other (the locus of all signifiers). Hence, the phallus becomes the basis of *law* and *the foundational signifier* of the entire symbolic order. Completion, lack, castration, difference, law, desire, and the opening of the entire symbolic order: the phallic has been tasked with some heavy lifting to do.[7]

How might signifying the feminine contravene the signifying burden of the phallus? First, we can surmise that because what is "missing" gains signifying "presence," it emerges as a promising candidate to signify *lack* and Real (not symbolic) castration. What's more, as the marker of Freud's uncanny, it would seem as well to stake a legitimate claim as the signifier of *difference*, to which the phallus, by means of its appropriative, hegemonizing impulse can only aspire with hypocrisy and cynicism. And because the vaginal both marks the origins of human life itself and signifies the signifying gap itself – and so, it would seem, births the signifying order – it (again intuitively) recommends itself as standing for the primal conditions of human subjectivity, just as it existed before human subjectivity. As such, we might add that insofar as the signifying gap is governed by the spatializing (non)essence of feminine law, it also figures "space," a space(time) which births *desire* and its unpredictable, pluri-temporal trajectory and opening to *futurity*.

My point is not to create parallel "monopolies" for feminine and masculine signifiers but to recognize that each sexed signifier stakes legitimate signifying claims, thereby prompting further questions of their shared, if asymmetrical, *and not completely arbitrary*, roles in figuring sexual difference. Further, to refuse signification of the feminine, at least from a psychoanalytic perspective that is not One but multiple, not only creates a monopolistic phallocratic symbolic economy but requires considerable mental and semiological gymnastics to fulfill all that Lacan asks the phallic signifier to carry. The labor of the feminine has always been underappreciated, of course, and that this would be the case with respect to its signifying labor is unsurprising and very much to my point. If we wish to make an emancipatory – and ethical – political intervention, the matter of signifying that which currently is rendered invisible (and which reveals otherwise obscured social contradiction) would seem compelling and urgent. Only then can we contend with the troubling yet potentially transformative effects that issue from the Real by means of a paradoxical signifier, heterogeneous to paternal law, insofar as it is subject, at least in part, to an/*other*, feminine, law which, *when honored*, disrupts the assimilative and appropriative inclinations of a patriarchal symbolic. Instead, the signification of the feminine – beyond grounding all subjects in shared reality insofar as, in fact, there is nothing missing in the real (body) – also functions as a vital portal (by instantiating the "missing signifier" into, or on the cusp, of the signifying order) by means of which radically inclusive free speech and democratized spaces for the movement of desire's heterogeneity come into being, themselves forever disrupted by *s/excessive* unconscious elements.

A Malfunctioning Paternal Metaphor: The Necessity of the Feminine Third

Insofar as the feminine signifier promises a gap, it dislocates an hegemonizing patriarchy, prefiguring the contradictory thirdness, hence sexual difference – a function which Lacan ascribes to the phallic signifier which subordinates that, for Freud, difference was inaugurated by the unrepresentable, uncanny feminine. Further, beyond the province of the phallus, the feminine signifier orients the subject to a contradictory, unassimilable dimension of psychical life that points to the unconscious and its disjunctive, untranslatable excesses.

Charles Saunders Peirce (1891/1992) introduced the concept of thirdness, situating semiosis beyond action-reaction pairing ("secondness") in a realm of shared or consensual reality. It is psychoanalysis's distinctive addition, now axiomatic, to name the father, or the paternal metaphor, as the signifier of this symbolic third. Rigorous challenges to a too facile coherence between thirdness and paternal law (e.g., Benjamin, 1995; Kristeva, 1980b, 1984), reinforced by substantial evidence for (triadic) intersubjectivity in the early mother-infant dyad (Muller, 1996, Winnicott, 1971), have not dismantled adherence to this seamless equation: The father's role, as (not necessarily gendered)[8] signifier of a third or "Other," in enabling the child's "early triangulation" and separation process (Abelin, 1975), reverberates across contemporary theorizing, usually, though not always, credited to Lacan's innovations (Barratt, 2015; Birksted-Breen, 1996, 2016; Britton, 1989; Diamond, 2017; Green, 2004; Greenspan, 1982; McDougall, 1989; Ogden, 1989, 2004; Perelberg, 2013), amounting to as near a consensus as just about any psychoanalytic concept that one might *name*.

This axiom finds its roots in Freud's fanciful mytho-historical treatise, *Totem and Taboo* (1912–13), which conjured notions of a primal horde riven by incestuous murderous and sexual impulses who committed parricide. Though Freud, it seems, conceived of this primal parricide as a real historical event, he posited (by means of the conjecture of Lamarckian inheritance) that it yielded a dead but now symbolic father whose function served to regulate incest, expiate guilt, and enable the survival of lawful sociality and cultural achievement.

Lacan (1966, 1977; and as traced by Verhaeghe, 2009) would both reproduce Freud's preoccupation, and extend the father's symbolic function, most notably through his innovation of the paternal metaphor – the father's "no" or prohibition of a lawless, unmediated) maternal-child duality. As we have already discussed, the child's subsequent "castration" upon entry to language thereby structures his relationship to symbolic, cultural reality. And though certainly psychoanalysis's patriarchal foundations have been amply critiqued (Benjamin, 1988; Butler, 1990), we have yet to adequately challenge the persistent and prevailing conundrum: "what is called 'civilization' balances tenuously on the shoulders of its patricidal-filicidal discontents" (Barratt, 2015, p. 354, mining Freud). If so, we might again, or once more, ask what remains obscured in the rush to instantiate the indestructible symbolic father. If so-called paternal/symbolic law is our antidote to patriarchy's antidemocratic force, why is it so utterly failing the culture?

Patriarchy, as several recent analyses posit (see, e.g., Gilligan and Snider, 2018), trades on binaries and hierarchies. It refuses to concede to loss, including those that inaugurate a valid paternal symbolic function. Beyond pointing to the insidious persistence of patriarchy's ways (and its alliance with a rapacious capitalism), this suggests that there is something undertheorized in the paternal function. Most obviously, it would seem, that there is something of a masculinist mythology at play. A vitally needed (transitional) third, along with missing signifier which (in part) sources it, and which has, too, "gone missing."[9]

That missing third, I suggest in the spirit of what philosopher Chiara Bottici (2014, 2021) calls "imaginal feminism," is the *feminine third*, a necessary but discontinuous conduit between patriarchy and a paternal function. A strong precedent for this vision is found in Kristeva's maternal semiotic (see Oliver, 1991), which, by insinuating drive energies heterogeneous to language and a paradoxical logic (of love and alterity) into it, prefigured the paternal symbolic. Taking a further step in this direction, we can add that the figuration of a feminine third is installed via the ever–partial symbolic anchorage of the feminine signifier. Without it, a third contradictory "space between" is annulled, exiling *otherness*, ablating sexual difference.

To put it straightforwardly, paternal law, absent a feminine metaphor, cannot redeem patriarchy because though it postulates a triadic operation, its actual structure remains strictly of the imaginary: self-identical and masculinist. As per Irigaray's (1974, p. 26) charge, sexual difference remains "a derivation of the problematics of sameness." The realm of the father, minus that of the feminine, can't sustain the dialectics of the uncanny contradiction of sexual difference. Left to its own masculinist devices, it can't instantiate sexual difference because it excludes and precludes what (and who) is heterogeneous and discontinuous (with the same).

Our psychoanalytic faith in (the idea of) the father as the sole signifier of triadic relations amounts to an unrecognized psychoanalytic mythologem that abets patriarchy by means of its phallogocentrism. It amounts to a form of collusion with social hegemony at best, and a form of psychoanalytic gaslighting, at worst. But as Andre Green (2004, pp. 128–129) perceptively observes,

> In thirdness, there is always one term that is disturbing by virtue of being undesirable or unwanted, or one missing term that changes the triangular structure to form a pair. . . . But this dualism at the start includes thirdness by inference (the two terms and their relationship as the third one). So it is in life, just as in thought.

Restoring that "missing term" (beyond mere inference) may help to counter patriarchal exemptions and create reparative, democratizing, desperately needed imaginal possibilities for an ailing, suffering, even withering world. If we conceive of a lawful, if uncanny, sexed third as both an aspect of the shared reality of the dyad and that stands apart from it, the vital bridging function of the vaginal signifier becomes perceptible. When destroyed or misrecognized, it is not just the feminine gap and its ethical valence that go missing; the paternal metaphor also atrophies and malfunctions. This eventuates in real castrative effects (in which actual impotence and fantasied omnipotence are two sides of a coin), derailing "successful" symbolic castration (surrender to language and lawful limit). A properly functioning paternal law depends upon a *dispossession* – a surrender to its asymmetrical, spatializing counterpart: feminine law.

Juliet Mitchell (2009, p. xiv) intriguingly observes that "psychoanalysis, like biology, find that it is death that is brought into play with the advent of sexual reproduction. There is no death with asexual reproduction such as cloning." There can be no paternal law or symbolic father if there is no dead father. Death requires sexual difference. Sexual difference requires a signifying gap, a *feminine* interval, between what can be birthed symbolically and what can't be.

Repetition With a Feminine Difference

Lacanian psychoanalyst Mladen Dolar (2016, p. 35) explicitly takes up the persistent charges of phallocentrism in psychoanalysis, asserting that it is precisely the naming or signification of the phallus, per Lacan, which paradoxically dethrones it, "setting the limit to phallocentrism." In turn, the problem of sexual difference, "a difference irreducible to any usual difference" is revealed, thereby enabling an approach to the antihegemonic terrain of sexuality and the unconscious.

Dolar, fascinatingly, tugs on the metaphor for psychoanalysis bequeathed to us by Anna O: "chimney-sweeping." Chimney-sweeping, he says, breaks apart the "balanced match" – say between the masculine and the feminine – by means of "the quirky phallic addition" (p. 33), which exposes "a rupture of meaning" (namely, the unconscious), and hence, "aims at the elaboration of sexuality that would escape the phallocentric logic" (p. 36).

Similarly, Joan Copjec (2016, p. 132), drawing from Lacan's (1999, p. 9) claim that "nothing is more compact than a fault," speculates that compactness is a "space of impossibility, the impossibility of union or encounter, *and at the same time* a space where something out of the ordinary happens: an eruption of jouissance." She, like Dolar, reaches for a metaphor, "that compact space in which lovers, the sexes, . . . 'hold each other tight'" (p. 134), to describe what lies beyond metaphor, beyond place, beyond time ('in futurity'), a coming, a feminine jouissance.

Alenka Zupančič, closes her challenging text, *What Is Sex?* (which though I have mined and perhaps creatively misread in this chapter for my own purposes bears repeated readings to appreciate its nuance and complexity), referring to Freud's (1900, p. 525) navel as the site of what remains unknown, and which, for Zupančič, registers the ontological crack, the gap in being.

It would seem that we might dare to interpret each of these theorists as reaching to represent not only what eludes signification but the feminine dimension of this loss. We might, just might, dare to signify, contra phallic readings, Dolar's chimney sweeping, Copjec's compact space of impossibility and jouissance, and ultimately, per Zupančič, Freud's navel, as displacements for another, primordial, missing feminine signifier, that however lost "forever" can nonetheless, in part, if only in part, be retrieved through its inscription, by naming it.

Patriarchy might just die. A valid symbolic paternal law, beyond an economy of One, might be born. If so, it would mean surrender to feminine law, and to its *space between* traumatic loss and rebirth: the feminine gap and the dis/ordering impossibility of unconscious life.

Notes

1 I use his term 'master discourse' to signal both the hysterical (per Lacan) aspect of this writing (to challenge the master discourse, to expose its lack, if also the impossibility of this quest). But, more colloquially, my goal is to insist that we must *unsettle* colonizing theoretical impositions in order to produce unsettling vitalizing, anti-patriarchal effects.

2 Naming what has insistently remained unnamed perhaps risks an operation of the Imaginary and thereby reproduce patriarchal effects, but because of the feminine's proximity to the real, its naming may produce real and necessary effects.

3 Zupančič, by contrast, refutes the signifier's very repression: "This is not a repressed signifier, but a signifier whose non-being is the only thing that makes repression possible, and structurally precedes it" (p. 126), that is, as the crack or non-being that inspires the "existence" of the unconscious ("as the non-existence of the Other inscribed in the Other)" (p. 53). We might wonder whether we have in mind two different signifiers or, as framed by Dolar (2016, p. 31), "two kinds of difference: the signifying

difference, the pure difference that all signification is based on, and on the other hand the sexual difference, which seems to be the most obvious natural difference, providing a model for all others." It would seem to me that, practically and theoretically, the feminine signifier bridges the gap between what is repressed and what is missing. It itself is both, and points to both.

4 It would seem that the recent devastation of abortion rights have reinforced the palpable need for the vaginal signifier/ symbolic, without which the vagina remains cordoned off to a mere (too easily colonized) body part.

5 Diana Fuss (1989, pp. 68, 69).

6 It is worth noting that the vaginal's (Irigarayan) "two lips" – per "the etymology of lip (*labi*), to slip or fall, to slide from meaning to meaning, to be *labile*" (Bianchi, 2014, p. 103) recalls once more the gap of free association which, in the German *freier Einfall* – "free irruption", denoted a "a spontaneous and coincidental *falling out* into the open" (Mahony, 1979, p. 21).

7 We might wonder if psychoanalysis' investment in degrading the feminine doesn't only function to mask castration fears but also to stoke them and thus, also, "toxic" masculinity.

8 See, e.g., Davies and Eagle (2013) who address the conflation of the paternal function with the role of the father.

9 As cited earlier, Zupančič (2017, p. 47). As she notes, her phrasing suggests a temporal dimension of the missing signifier ('gone missing') to mark its function in the constitution of subjectivity.

References

Abelin, E. (1975). Some further observations and comments on the earliest role of the father. *The International Journal of Psychoanalysis, 56*: 293–302.

Barratt, B. B. (2015). Fathering and the consolidation of masculinity: Notes on the paternal function in Andrey Zvyagintsev's *The Return. Psychoanalytic Review, 102*: 347–364.

Benjamin, J. (1988). *The Bonds of Love: Psychoanalysis, Feminism, and the Problem of Domination*. New York, NY: Pantheon.

Benjamin, J. (1995). *Like Subjects, Love Objects: Essays on Recognition and Sexual Difference*. New Haven, CT: Yale University Press.

Bianchi, E. (2014). *The Feminine Symptom: Aleatory Matter in the Aristotelian Cosmos*. New York, NY: Fordham University Press.

Birksted-Breen, D. (1983). Feminine sexuality. Jacques Lacan and the École Freudienne: Edited by Juliet Mitchell and Jacqueline Rose. London: Macmillan. 1982. Pp. 187. *International Journal of Psychoanalysis, 64*: 490–493.

Birksted-Breen, D. (1996). Phallus, penis and mental space. *International Journal of Psycho-Analysis*, 77: 649–657.

Birksted-Breen, D. (2016). Bi-ocularity, the functioning mind of the psychoanalyst. *International Journal of Psycho-Analysis, 97*: 25–40.

Bottici, C. (2014). *Imaginal Politics: Images beyond Imagination and the Imaginary*. New Directions in Critical Theory Book 15. New York, NY: Columbia University Press.

Bottici, C. (2021). *Feminist Mythologies*. New York, NY: Bloomsbury Press.

Britton, R. (1989). The missing link: Parental sexuality in the Oedipus complex. In R. Britton, M. Feldman, & E. O'Shaughnessy (Eds.), *The Oedipus Complex Today: Clinical Implications*. London: Karnac Books, pp. 83–101.

Butler, J. (1990), Gender trouble, feminist theory, and psychoanalytic discourse. In L. J. Nicholson (Ed.), *Feminism/ Postmodernism*. New York, NY: Routledge, pp. 324–340.

Copjec, J. (2016). The sexual compact. In A. Cerda-Rueda (Ed.), *Sex and Nothing*. London: Karnac, pp. 107–138.

Davies, N. & Eagle, G. (2013). Conceptualizing the paternal function: Maleness, masculinity, or thirdness? *Contemporary Psychoanalysis, 49*: 559–585.

Diamond, M. J. (2017). The missing father function in psychoanalytic theory and technique: The analyst's internal couple and maturing intimacy. *Psychoanalytic Quarterly, 86*(4): 861–887.

Dolar, M. (2016). Officers, maids, and chimneysweepers. In A. Cerda-Rueda (Ed.), *Sex and Nothing*. London: Karnac Books, pp, 19–36.

Freud, S. (1892). Draft M**3** [Notes II] from Extract from the Fliess Papers. *S.E., I* (1886–1899): Pre-Psycho-Analytic Publications and Unpublished Drafts: 250–253.

Freud, S. (1900). *The Interpretation of Dreams. S.E., IV*: ix–627

Freud, S. (1912–1913). *Totem and Taboo. S.E., 13*: 1–161.

Freud, S. (1919). The uncanny. *S.E., 17*: 219–256.

Freud, S. (1925). Some psychical consequences of the anatomical distinction between the sexes. *S.E., 19*: 248–258.

Freud, S. (1931). Female sexuality. *S.E., 21*: 221–244.

Freud, S. (1933). *New Introductory Lectures on Psycho-Analysis. S.E., 22.*

Freud, S. (1937). Analysis terminable and interminable. *S.E., 23*: 211–253.

Fuss, D. (1989). *Essentially Speaking: Luce Irigaray's Language of Essence. Hypatia, 3*: 62–80.

Gentile, J. (2015a). Parrhesia, Phaedra, and the polis: Anticipating psychoanalytic free association as democratic practice. *Psychoanalytic Quarterly, 84*: 589–624.

Gentile, J. (2015b). On having no thoughts: Free association and feminine space. *Psychoanalytic Perspectives, 12*, 227–251.

Gentile, J. (2016a). *Feminine Law: Freud, Free Speech, and the Voice of Desire*, with M. Macrone. London: Karnac Books.

Gentile, J. (2016b). On spatial metaphors and free association: Phallic fantasy and vaginal primacy. *Contemporary Psychoanalysis, 52*: 21–50.

Gentile, J. (2016c). Naming the vagina, naming the woman. *Division/ Review, 14*(Spring).

Gentile, J. (2017). Tugging at the umbilical cord: Birtherism, nativism, and the plotline of Trump's delivery. *Contemporary Psychoanalysis, 53*(4): 489–504.

Gentile, J. (2019). *Feminine revolt: Signs at the edge of the uncanny strange(r).* Keynote address, The Kristeva Circle: Trajectories of Psychoanalysis, Emory University, Atlanta, October 5.

Gentile, J. (in press). The democratic significance of anatomical difference. In J. Petrucelli, S. Schoen, & N Snider (Eds.), *Patriarchy and its Discontents.* New York, NY: Routledge.

Gilligan, C. & Snider, N. (2018). *Why Does Patriarchy Persist?* Cambridge, UK: Polity Press.

Green, A. (1997). The intuition of the negative in *playing and reality. International Journal of Psycho-Analysis, 78*: 1071–1084.

Green, A. (2004). Thirdness and psychoanalytic concepts. *Psychoanalytic Quarterly, 73*: 99–135.

Greenspan, S. (1982). The second other. In S. Cath, A. Gurwitt, & J. Ross (Eds.), *Father and Child: Developmental and Clinical Perspectives.* Boston: Little, Brown, pp. 123–139.

Grosz, E. (1994). *Volatile Bodies: Toward a Corporeal Feminism.* Bloomington, IL: Indiana University Press.

Irigaray, L. (1977). *This Sex Which Is Not One*, trans. C. Porter & C. Burke. Ithaca, NY: Cornell University Press, 1985.

Irigaray, L. (1984). *An Ethics of Sexual Difference*, trans. C. Burke & G. Gill. Ithaca, NY: Cornell University Press, 1993.

Irigaray, L. (1974). *Speculum of the Other Woman*, trans. G Gill. Ithaca, NY: Cornell University Press, 1985.

Kristeva, J (1980a). *Pouvoirs de l'horreur.* Paris: Seuil. [*Powers of Horror*, trans. L. Roudiez]. NY: Columbia University Press, 1982.

Kristeva, J. (1980b). *Desire in Language*, ed. L. Roudiez. NY: Columbia University Press.

Kristeva, J. (1984). *Revolution in Poetic Language*, trans. M. Waller. New York, NY: Columbia University Press.

Kristeva, J. (2019). *Prelude to an ethics of the feminine.* IPA keynote address, London, July 25.

Lacan, J. (1964–1980). *Feminine sexuality: Jacques Lacan and the École Freudienne*, eds. J. Mitchell & J. Ros; trans. J. Rose. New York, NY: Norton, 1983.

Lacan, J. (1966). *Écrits.* Paris: Seuil [*Écrits: The First Complete Edition in English*, trans. B. Fink. New York, NY: Norton].

Lacan, J. (1977). Subversion of the subject and dialectic of desire in the Freudian unconscious. In A. Sheridan (Trans.), Ecrits*: A Selection.* London, England: Tavistock, pp. 292–325 (Original work published 1966).

Lacan, J. (1999). *The Seminar of Jacques Lacan.* Book XVII. Encore. New York: W.W. Norton & Company.

Mahony, P. (1979). The boundaries of free association. *Psychoanalysis and Contemporary Thought, 2*: 151–198.

McDougall, J. (1989). The dead father. *International Journal of Psycho-Analysis, 70*: 205–220.

Mitchell, J. (2009). Foreward. In P. Verhaeghe (Ed.), *New Studies of Old Villains.* New York: Other Press, pp. vii–xiv.

Muller, J.P. (1996). *Beyond the Psychoanalytic Dyad: Developmental Semiotics in Freud, Peirce, and Lacan.* New York, NY: Routledge.

Nancy, J.-L. (1988). *The Experience of Freedom.* B. McDonald (trans.). Stanford, CA: Stanford University Press, 1993.

Ogden, T. (2004). The analytic third: Implications for psychoanalytic theory and technique. *Psychoanalytic Quarterly*, *73*: 167–195.

Ogden, T.H. (1989). *The Primitive Edge of Experience*. Northvale, NJ: Jason Aronson.

Oliver, K. (1991). Review: Kristeva's imaginary father and the crisis in the paternal function. *Diacritics*, *21*(2/3, A Feminist Miscellany (Summer – Autumn)): 43–63.

Peirce, C.S. (1891). The architecture of theories. In N. Houser & C. Kloesel (Eds.), *The Essential Peirce: Selected Philosophical Writings* (Vol. 1). Bloomington, IN: Indiana University Press, 1992, pp. 285–297.

Perelberg, R. (2013). Paternal function and thirdness in psychoanalysis and legend: Has the future been foretold? *Psychoanalytic Quarterly*, *82*: 557–585.

Verhaeghe, P. (1996). *Does the Woman Exist: From Freud's Hysteric to Lacan's Feminine*, ed. M. du Ry (2nd ed.). London, England: Rebus Press.

Verhaeghe, P. (2009) *New Studies of Old Villains: A Radical Reconsideration of the Oedipus Complex*. New York, NY: Other Press.

Winnicott, D.W. (1971). *Playing and Reality*. London: Tavistock.

Ziarek, E. (1992). At the limits of discourse: Heterogeneity, alterity, and the maternal body in Kristeva's thought. *Hypatia, 7, Philosophy and Language*: 91–108.

Zupančič, A. (2017). *What Is Sex*? Cambridge, MA: MIT Press.

32

ECOPSYCHOANALYSIS AND CLIMATE PSYCHOLOGY

Joseph Dodds

Introduction

Climate change and the ecological crisis in general are increasingly recognized as perhaps the single biggest threat to have faced our species, but existing approaches largely constitute an 'ecology without psychology'. Psychoanalysis has a unique role to play with its emphasis on the unconscious dimensions of our mental and social lives, and is required to unmask the anxieties, deficits, conflicts, phantasies and defences crucial in understanding the human dimension of the ecological crisis, and to our civilization's highly ambivalent relation to the nonhuman world. Psychoanalysis has long explored the connection between psyche and world, beginning with Sigmund Freud's writings on nature and civilization and also the early case histories where the 'animal' is omnipresent. However, psychoanalysis has remained largely a 'psychology without ecology', mostly limited to explorations of the 'environment' of the family. This is now thankfully beginning to change, and the time for opening out psychoanalytic theory into a more fully eco-psycho-social perspective is ripe. Ecopsychology has emerged to deal with this blind spot, but it runs the risk of idealizing and mystifying 'Nature', a danger Lacanian and postmodern approaches aim to deconstruct through an 'ecology without nature'. Taken too far, the latter leads to nature dissolving entirely into the human, all too human, realm of the signifier.

This chapters gives an overview of the development of *ecopsychoanalysis*, a new transdisciplinary approach to thinking about the relationship between psychoanalysis, ecology, 'the natural' and the problem of climate change, as well as viral pandemics such as COVID-19. It draws on a range of fields including, psychoanalysis, psychology, ecology, philosophy, science, complexity theory, aesthetics and the humanities. To do this, it is important to identify the different developmental lines and research traditions out of which ecopsychoanalysis is emerging. These include psychoanalysis first and foremost, but also ecopsychology (Roszak 1992; Roszak *et al.* 1995; Buzzel & Chalquist 2009; Rust 2008; Rust & Totton 2012; Winter & Koger 2004) and ecological thinking more generally; cybernetics and systems theory beginning with Gregory Bateson (2000, 2002); complexity theory and nonlinear dynamics; philosophical approaches to nature from deep ecology to post-nature and the new materialisms; postmodern and posthuman understandings of animality, human and nonhuman (Derrida 2008; Dodds 2012b, 2020a); the work of the Climate Psychology Alliance (Hoggett 2019); and the geophilosophy of Deleuze and Guattari (2003).

DOI: 10.4324/9780429297076-38

While some psychoanalysts after Freud were interested in a limited sense with our relation to the nonhuman world (such as Winnicott's transitional object), this trend was not really developed before the work of Harold Searles in the 1960s and 1970s with his writings on the nonhuman environment (1960) and the environmental crisis (1972). Searles' writings still constitute some of the clearest in psychoanalytic thought on our relation to nature, although unfortunately they remained largely ignored in the following decades. With the new millennium, the awareness of the climate crisis brought a sense of urgency to psychoanalytic approaches to ecology with a cluster of important books and articles (Randall 2005; Dodds 2011, 2013; Weintrobe 2012; Lertzman 2015; Hoggett 2019), an increasing interest in psychoanalytic organisations in this area, and the formation of the Climate Psychology Alliance, which attempts to create a community of psychoanalysts, psychotherapists and psychologists working on issues of ecology and climate change.

The climate crisis is also a crisis of theory. Academia has divided human thought into a schizoid fragmented space, but climate change (and global pandemics) forces us to think transversally, about a world of unpredictable, multiple-level, highly complex, nonlinear interlocking systems. There is therefore a need for a way of thinking able to integrate the disparate strands of analysis, related to what Bion (1984) calls the work of linking, connected with the alpha function and the dreamwork. Bion describes building links between mental objects, and the attack on linking characteristic of psychosis. When 'alpha-function' is compromised, we are left with undigested fragments of experience: 'beta-elements' incapable of being woven into the tapestry of our psychic landscapes. We require a means of linking diverse elements together without losing their specificity, able to connect our minds to what Searles (1960, 1972) referred to as the 'non-human environment', both synchronically (webs of interactions at a given moment in time) and diachronically (e.g., the interactions over evolutionary deep time). In his book *Chaosmosis*, Guattari (1995, 91) called for a generalized science of ecosystems or 'ecosophy', a generalized mechanics with "resonances, alliances and feedback loops between various regimes, signifying and non-signifying, human and non-human, natural and cultural, material and representational." Dodds (2011), argues that there is as much a need to bring nonlinear and ecological thinking into psychoanalysis as for a psychoanalytic approach to ecology, taking seriously the possibility of thinking in terms of what Guattari (2000) called in his final book, *The Three Ecologies*: the ecologies of mind, nature and society.

Scientists estimate that human demand may "have exceeded the biosphere's regenerative capacity since the 1980s" and already reached 120% by 1999, and this demand is still rapidly increasing (Wackernagel *et al.* 2002, 926; Norgaard & Randers 2002). Whether we make the conscious choice to live sustainably or not, this must come to an end one way or another. Science has grown up largely working with the concept of linear systems, but it is increasingly apparent that linear relationships represent merely a special minority case in an otherwise fairly non-linear world. *Attractors* are points towards which a system tends to converge. Wherever you place a marble in a washbasin, the marble will roll toward the 'plug hole attractor'. Any variation in starting point within the *basin of attraction* is cancelled out by the powerful pull of the attractor. Within limits, as our body or global climate temperature increases, negative feedback processes act to draw the system back to a more central point, the *point attractor* (other more complex attractors include 'periodic' attractors and 'strange' or 'chaotic' attractors). However, when the marble is moved to the edge of the basin, the slightest movement or air vibration can move it either back into the basin (of attraction) or into a completely different attractor (falling out and rolling on the floor). At these *bifurcation* points, non-linearities rule as the slightest difference in starting conditions or tiniest fluctuation causes a radical shift, a *phase transition* to a new attractor or set of attractors.

Scientists suggest our climate may be approaching several such tipping points (Sawaya 2010), or has begun to cross them, with potentially lethal *positive feedback* processes no longer capable of being damped out (involving social and psychological systems, as well as ecological, climatological and geological ones). A nonlinear perspective is crucial not only for climate science but for the psychology of climate change. Our familiar ways of thinking assume a linear relationship between CO_2 emissions and a warming, that there will always be time later to turn it around. This is a failure in our mental ecology which leads, via pathological forms of social ecology, into potential catastrophic collapses of natural ecology.

Psychoanalysis and Climate Change

Freud (1927) claimed civilization arose to defend us against nature, but that the aim of achieving total control over either our inner nature or the outer world was a dangerous illusion to defend against feelings of helplessness and fear in the face of the awesome power of mother nature, of acknowledging dependency on this largest of 'holding environments', the ultimate 'environment mother' (Winnicott 1987). Freud's 'eternal adversaries', Eros and Thanatos, are unfortunately unlikely partners in their destructive effects on nature. The 'nirvana principle's' desire for non-existence/annihilation can be seen in our virtual indifference towards the world's sixth great mass extinction and in the attraction of apocalyptic rhetoric for the environmental movement (Hoggett 2011) and recent 'eco-disaster' films. For Žižek (2007) "'The world without us' is . . . fantasy at its purest: witnessing the Earth itself retaining its pre-castrated state of innocence, before we humans spoiled it with our hubris". Eros, through over-consumption and overpopulation, also works towards the potential collapse of the biosphere (Bigda-Peyton 2004). However, in the form of 'biophilia' (Wilson 2003), Eros can work to reinvigorate our love of nature, which may help us turn back from the brink.

To explore climate denial further, we can turn to a joke Freud (1905, 62) used to illustrate the logic of the unconscious (Freud 1911; Matte-Blanco 1998). When a man is told he should replace a pot he borrowed and returned damaged, he refuses, claiming (1) I returned it undamaged; (2) the hole was there when you gave it to me; or (3) I never borrowed it! These mutually contradictory answers alert us to unconscious processes united by the motivation to remove the blame and prevent need for action, and correspond well with arguments against action on climate change.

1 *There's nothing wrong with the climate kettle* (here climate change is seen paranoiacally as a conspiracy to destroy our freedom or instead of capitalists trying to stop poor countries developing). Alternatively, 'the evidence is not conclusive', which involves playing Russian roulette with the entire planet.
2 *There was a hole in the planet when you gave it to me* (not caused by humans, or caused by other humans – either way, not-me, not my problem). However, unconscious deflection of guilt does nothing to stop the disastrous consequences of climate change, so we would still need to take urgent action. One psychoanalytically interesting conclusion is at times people can fear guilt more than their own, or everyone's, destruction.
3 *There is nothing we can do about it,* also found in burnt-out environmentalists filled with feelings of despair and disempowerment, allowing us to give up thinking.

The different arguments relate to defences against specific anxieties. *Its not happening* involves more psychotic defences against paranoid-schizoid anxiety (extinction, annihilation). *Its not our/my fault* involves neurotic defences against depressive anxiety (difficulty in acknowledging human culpability and guilt). *There's nothing I/we can do about it* is closest to recognising the problem but without realistic reparative possibilities the individual is stuck with the despair and pain of the depressive position without hope. As Searles (1972, 366) put it, "instead of feeling isolated within emotional depression, one feels at one with everyone . . . in a 'realistically' doomed world." Such defence mechanisms need to be understood not only individually, but as involving unconscious alliances (Kaes 2007) created socially, through small interactions at all levels giving rise to *social phantasy systems* (Jaques 1955). In complexity theory this is an example of *self-organization*, where lower levels interact to form higher-level structures embodying emergent properties which then feed back to lower levels in a process of ongoing recursivity.

Object Relations and Ecological Relations

Object relations, emphasising the self as constituted in and through relational webs, moves psychoanalysis in an ecological direction. Development involves moving from 'absolute dependence' to 'mature dependence' (Fairbairn 1992), suggesting a vision for a more mature culture, with self and society seen as inextricable from its relations to other beings, to ecological webs, and to the Earth. For Searles (1972, 368) "an ecologically healthy relatedness to our nonhuman environment is essential to the development and maintenance of our sense of being human", which has become "so undermined, disrupted, and distorted, concomitant with the ecological deterioration, that it is inordinately difficult for us to integrate the feeling experiences, including the losses, inescapable to any full-fledged human living".

Traditionally, psychoanalysts would analyse environmental concern as reflecting 'deeper' feelings relating to human 'objects', but human conflict could equally be a displacement from anxiety concerning the environment. If we broaden Winnicott's 'holding environment' to include the holding environment of the Earth, we can understand how the enormity of the crisis can threaten psychological disintegration and collapse. Furthermore, not only is environmentally damaging behaviour a form of addiction (e.g., consumer items functioning as Kohutian selfobjects to shore up a fragile self; Kohut 1985; Winnicott 1999, 1987), but addictions can also arise to deal with anxiety concerning our damaged world (Bodnar 2008; Dodds 2021). Psychoanalysts need to recognise engagement with ecology is not only for 'applied' psychoanalysis but is crucial to its core clinical domain.

The phrase 'Mother Earth' suggests our experience with the planet relates to our experience with our (m)other. Not only feelings of love and being held, but phantasies of an infinitely giving Earth-breast we feel entitled to suck on with ever-increasing intensity without limit. Unable to tolerate weaning, our response to ecological crisis includes rage, envy and destructiveness, including spoiling and omnipotent attacks on the earth-breast. Meltzer's (1967) 'toilet-breast' concept is useful here. Psychologically the breast is not only a provider of nutrition but a place where we expel unbearable states of mind.

Various developmental levels may intersect with our problematic relationship with nature (Randall 2005). The apocalyptic threat of climate change may evoke the extremely primitive persecutory anxieties of Klein's paranoid-schizoid position, leading to omnipotent defences to protect against feelings of helpless and fragmentation (Jordan 2009). The paranoia surrounding climate change allows the "bad sadistic enemy" to be fought against "not in the solitary isolation of the unconscious inner world, but in co-operation with comrades-in-arms in real life" (Jaques 1955, 483). Searles (1972) points out that ironically there is now a certain objectivity to schizophrenic 'end of the world' fantasies. This can lead many to intuitively feel ecological warnings are 'crazy' and we shouldn't listen to them, partly out of fear of contamination because they touch a 'crazy' part of all of us.

At the phallic-Oedipal level, Searles (1972, 364) identifies phantasies of eliminating Oedipal rivals (including future generations) and the 'moralistic' tone of much ecological writing involving projecting Oedipal guilt, accusing us of raping mother earth. In addition, through relentless advertising, possessions such as cars have become symbols of (male) genital achievement, and initiatives to reduce car use can feel like castration (Randall 2005). The ecological version of Klein's (1987) depressive position involves mourning for environmental destruction, guilt for the damage done, a growing awareness the lifestyles and civilization we are so proud of are causing such damage to planetary ecosystems, and a reparative drive to restore, repair and recreate the lost and damaged world (internal and external).

The environmental crisis forces us to face the traumatic aspects of transience, that nothing is permanent. Drawing on Freud's (1916) concept of anticipatory mourning, we might expect individuals and societies to adopt positions of consciously not caring about the environment or even our species survival, or becoming actively destructive and self-destructive, as a defence against the mourning yet to come. Alternatively, we may engage in a premature anticipatory mourning, falling into a despair preventing the very action which might avoid the feared loss, while there is still time. Freud (1916, 306) urges us to face with honesty and courage the fact that

> [a] time may indeed come when the pictures and statues which we admire to-day will crumble to dust, or a race of men may follow us who no longer understand the works of our poets and thinkers, or a geological epoch may even arrive when all animate life upon the earth ceases.

Randall (2009) argues that loss is central to our response to climate change, as which is processed through two parallel narratives, one about the *problems* of climate change (where loss features terrifyingly but located to a future or a place far from contemporary Western audiences) and the other about *solutions* to climate change in which loss is excised. This split narrative allows an inner split avoiding the required work of mourning and grief.

In the face of the enormous pain and fear the ecological crisis evokes, there is a need to find effective means of reparation, to restore and recreate the damaged world, inside and out. Without hope that meaningful, as opposed to manic, reparation is possible, there is only the choice between denial, madness and despair. As psychoanalysis opens itself up to a greater awareness of the web of life, the object-related self and the narcissistic self need to be viewed as developing alongside the ecological self.

Biophilia and Biophobia

While ecopsychology in its classic form is in danger of creating a new religion, there is much of value within the tradition, so we shall see what symbioses can occur in this ecology of ideas. Where Freud saw the oceanic feeling as "something like the restoration of the limitless narcissism", Roszak (in Roszak et al. 1995, 12) instead sees it as reclaiming the repressed of the ecological unconscious. This is connected to what the zoologist E.O Wilson calls 'biophilia': "the innately emotional affiliation of human beings to other living organisms" (Kellert & Wilson 1993), a consequence of our long evolution and adaptation to the natural world and for Wilson (2003, 137) a crucial force in countering the biodiversity crisis. Wilson's biophilia is something that can be learned, encouraged and developed, especially during the crucial stages of child development of such interest to psychoanalysts. He goes on to describe the stages of the acquisition of biophilia which can be interestingly compared to Freud's work on children's relations with animals (Genosko 1993; Dodds 2012b). Although Wilson does not say this, in some ways we could describe our culture as remaining stuck within the first stage of the development of biophilia.

> The critical states in the acquiring of biophilia have been worked out by psychologists during studies of childhood mental development. Under the age of six, children tend to be egocentric, self-serving, and domineering in their responses to animals and nature. They are also most prone to be uncaring or fearful of the natural world and of all but a few familiar animals. Between six and nine, children become interested in wild creatures for the first time, and aware that animals can suffer pain and distress. From nine to twelve their knowledge and interest in the natural world rises sharply, and between thirteen and seventeen they readily acquire moral feeling toward animal welfare and species conservation.
>
> *(Wilson 2003, 137–138)*

The secret places of childhood (Sobel 2001), such as hedges, nearby woods and streams, abandoned buildings, connect us to place, and help in our psychological development, "if played out in natural environments, they also bring us close to the earth and nature in ways that can engender a lifelong love of both". However, if we accept that biophilia is an innate tendency in human nature, we must also accept the possibility, or even the likelihood, that 'biophobia' is just as natural. This is a subject that ecopsychologists are often often conspicuously absent in addressing. This deep acceptance of the ambiguity of our relationship with nature found in Wilson, is something perhaps Freud would have appreciated. As Wilson (2003, 141) writes "the reverse side of nature's green-and-gold is the black-and-scarlet of disease and death", something the coronavirus pandemic is reminding us all too clearly. Biophilia and biophobia can be understood as the ecopsychological equivalent of Freud's (1920) Eros and Thanatos.

Ecopsychology, Ecotherapy and Health

Ecopsychologists have been interested in studying the psychological impacts of life in an age of ecological crisis. Heinberg (2009, 198) suggests that in this context we need also to consider the idea of *eco-grief*, the feelings of loss connected to ecological devastation and the threatened loss of a whole way of life, which one way or another is about to come to an end, in what he calls *pre-traumatic stress disorder*, related in many ways to Freud's (1916) anticipatory mourning. He suggests a psychological approach using the stages of grief described in the Kübler-Ross (1973, 2005) model (denial, anger, bargaining, depression, acceptance) to understand where we are as a society and as individuals. From this perspective, different types of interventions might be more or less "effective for helping people accept our situation, depending on their current stage of adjustment" (Heinberg 2009, 198). He suggests, however, that the classic stages are not enough, because beyond acceptance there needs to be action, not only due to the ecological urgency, but because accepting "the reality all too often leads to depression and despair".

Although Santostefano (2008) cautions us against a naïve version of ecopsychology that assumes nature automatically generates a sense of well-being and improvements in physical and mental health, there does seem to be an increasing amount of empirical evidence to support the contention that nature heals (e.g., Buzzell & Chalquist 2009; MIND 2007). Researchers from the VU University Medical Centre in Amsterdam recently conducted a large study of 350,000 people showing that living near green spaces had substantial physical and mental health benefits (BBC 2009). The greatest benefits were for those living less than a kilometre away and the largest positive impacts were on anxiety disorders and depression. Living near green areas reduced depression rates by 21% for children under 12. Physical disorders, such as heart disease, diabetes, stomach and respiratory infections, and neck, shoulder, back, wrist and hand complaints, also showed substantial improvements. In addition, research by Ulrich (1984) has shown that the view from a hospital window (whether natural or concrete) has a significant and measurable effect on the speed and completeness of a patient's recovery (Ulrich 1984; Verderber & Reuman 1987), and that pets have significant impacts on physical and mental health. For more information on the health effects of pets and natural environments, see Ulrich (1991, 1999, 2000), Ulrich *et al.* (1993), Ulrich *et al.* (1991), Kellert and Wilson (1993), Frumkin (2001) and Frumkin and Louv (2007).

This has led a number of therapists, including those coming from traditional psychoanalytic backgrounds, to explore the possibility of 'ecotherapy', which covers a wide variety of approaches, including taking psychotherapy outside the traditional consulting room into the outdoors (Buzzell 2009; Rust 2020). Jordan and Marshall (2010, 345) explore the various complex clinical factors involved in such a shift, in particular focusing on its impact on boundaries and the therapeutic frame (as both emotional and geographical space) from a relational perspective. Here, the "relational encounter within the dynamic nature of the natural world can provide rich opportunities for a new experiencing with immediacy for both therapist and client, all of which can be fed in to the therapeutic process" (Jordan & Marshall 2010, 349). Moving outdoors may also enhance mutuality (not identical with equality), given that the space within which therapy occurs is not owned by the therapist, and the process of choosing different terrain can become more a co-created ongoing experience within the therapeutic relationship. Placing therapy outdoors results in the normal static 'backdrop' of therapy becoming "a living presence . . . [where] therapist and client are constantly aware of (both consciously and unconsciously), and responding to, the presence of this vibrant living third in the dynamic" (Jordan & Marshall 2010, 353–354). For a Jungian ecopsychoanalytic approach to ecotherapy, see Rust (2020).

Dark Ecology: Ecology Without Nature?

In contrast with the call for reconnection at the heart of ecopsychological theory and practice, Morton's (2007) plea for an 'ecology without nature' uses ecocriticism to deconstruct the ecological imaginary, helping us become more aware of how we use 'nature' psychologically in ways which get in the way of genuine environmental practice. For Žižek, our very idea of 'Nature' is a problem:

> there is no big Other (self-contained symbolic order as the ultimate guarantee of Meaning); there is also no Nature *qua* balanced order of self-reproduction whose homeostasis is disturbed . . . by imbalanced human interventions . . . what we need is ecology without nature: the ultimate obstacle to protecting nature is the very notion of nature we rely on.

In our era of global warming, weather (as background) no longer exists, it now becomes a mere cipher for that threatening hyper-object we call 'climate'. Without background the foreground also disappears, and rather than retreating into comforting fantasies of 'Hobbit-like' Heideggerian 'life-worlds', Morton encourages us to embrace *dark ecology* involving a 'melancholic ethics' (see also Dodds 2012a).

However, there is a danger ecocritique can remove a primary motivation of the environmental movement. Discourses of 'nature no longer existing' may feed into psychological defences by arguing that as 'nature' is already so altered by human activity that 'wilderness' doesn't really exist, there is no reason to protect a nature which has no substance. In addition, this approach can lose sight of the fact that the ecological crisis ultimately reaches beyond any linguistic constructions, and is not itself a 'text' which can be 'deconstructed', but a 'Real' beyond language, traumatically rupturing the Symbolic order. Deconstructive approaches also have difficulty in giving ontological space to nature and the material as anything other than an effect of language, or its negation as the 'Real'.

With their mixed semiotics, Herzogenrath (2009, 3) claims a Deleuzo-Guattarian ecology "allows for the incorporation of the workings of the 'repressed' of representation . . . of the 'real', of 'nature'". According to Bonta and Protevi (2004, 4), Deleuze and Guattari's engagement with complexity theory "helps break free of the postmodernist trap by rethinking sense and reference", shattering "postmodernist equations of signs with signifiers", such that "at critical thresholds . . . physical and biological systems can be said to 'sense' the differences in their environment that trigger self-organizing processes". A nonlinear reading of Deleuze and Guattari offers not with a flight into eco-mysticism, or a naïve positivist reductionism, or even a postmodernist plays of signifiers, but an 'intelligent materialism', a 'geophilosophy'.

Complexity, Chaos and Self Organization

Complexity and chaos theories have strong implications for psychoanalysis (Piers *et al.* 2007) and have "changed the basic concept of the human mind itself" (Guastello 2004, 4), providing a new way of thinking about the three ecologies. Concepts such as 'phase space' embody complex relationships and dynamic processes of change, providing what Deleuze and Guattari call an 'abstract machine', embodying a structural pattern of relationships in many separate heterogeneous domains. For Deleuze and Guattari (2003, 514),

> every abstract machine is linked to other abstract machines, not only because they are inseparably political, economic, scientific, artistic, ecological, cosmic – perceptive, affective, active, thinking, physical, and semiotic – but because their various types are as intertwined as their operations are convergent.

Self Organization (SO), deriving partly from for example studies of social insects, occurs when global patterns *emerge* from interactions among lower-level components rather than being imposed from outside the system, or any type of 'leader'. For Palombo (1999, 24), SO is "the most significant missing ingredient in psychoanalytic theory", showing how small pieces of insight self-organise into ever larger structures. This abstract machine embodies a structural pattern of relationships occurring in many separate registers, including the psychological, ecological and social. Gordon (1999), for example, suggests a similar pattern can be found behind "molecular interactions within a living cell, the unfolding pattern of cells and tissues in an embryo, and the activity of the neurons that produce the mind." Any complex system can be viewed as a *morphogenetic cascade,* which can include flows from all registers. Thus we can see how the scientific apparatus of complexity theory, along with the philosophical perspective of Deleuze and Guattari can help to provide a meta-perspective from which to connect the various levels of mind, brain, society, ecology and climate, which this chapter argues is necessary to allow joined-up thinking on the topic of climate change and the psychological dimensions of the ecological crisis.

Climate change is sometimes referred to as 'climate chaos' because of the increasingly unpredictable nature of natural systems. A nonlinear perspective is thus crucial for climate science, but it also provides ways of engaging with the crisis on the social and psychological levels. *Chaos theory* shows us paradoxically that chaos is far from the opposite of order and structure. Chaos is a feature of all nonlinear systems, which show us that traditional linear approaches to scientific analysis only describe a special case situation within a larger non-linear world. Chaos is essential for SO as the latter involves the amplification through positive feedback of fluctuations created by phenomena such as "random walks, errors, random task-switching" (Bonabeau *et al.* 1999, 10). The fact that ants regularly get lost used to puzzle scientists who wondered why this 'inefficiency' wasn't eliminated by evolution, but lost foragers can sometimes find new food sources, and therefore randomness enhances the creativity of a system or what Bateson (2000) calls its *ecological flexibility*. This is true in psychological, social, biological and even non-living systems.

Similarly, and counterintuitively, studies of electroencepalograms, electrocardiograms and other biorhythmic measurements show *healthy* rhythms have greater turbulence or irregularity (complexity), whereas "unhealthy systems gravitate toward periodic and simplistic output" (Guastello 2004). Chaos also plays a crucial role in brain dynamics (Grigsby & Stevens 2000). Kelso's (1995, 26) work suggests that the brain

> is a self-organizing, pattern-forming system that operates close to instability points, thereby allowing it to switch flexibly and spontaneously from one coherent state to another . . . by living near criticality, the brain is able to anticipate the future, not simply react to the present.

This can be understood as a dynamic interplay between Deleuze and Guattari's (2003) deterritorialization/territorialization systems in constant flux.

We can also see examples from birds of what Deleuze and Guattari (2003) call the territorializing effects of the familiar. Sole and Goodwin (2000, 138) explain how "chaotic [brain] dynamics . . . represented the normal state when the animal was attentive" but that "these attractors underwent dramatic changes when some familiar odor was introduced", resulting in much more ordered neural fluctuation. The spatiotemporal pattern "exhibited a well-defined stable structure . . . characteristic for the specific odor". On the emotional level, Jaak Panksepp (2004), argues that the basic emotion systems in the mammalian brain form *attractor landscapes* involving vast assemblages of neurones operating at far-from-equilibrium states. Paradoxically, the nonlinear processes of chaos give rise to stability by allowing the system to creatively adapt to environmental change, something increasingly urgent in our current crisis.

We can understand more fully the function of chaos through its border with more stable states, a region called the *edge of chaos.* Living systems attempt to balance themselves on the fractal borderzone between stability and instability which provides maximum ecological flexibility, producing the *dissipative system* of life. Dissipative systems are open systems in constant reciprocal interaction with and adaptation to their environments and exist at *far-from-equilibrium* conditions where they can maintain themselves within a dynamically ordered structure. This is a fundamental challenge to long-held Western philosophical and scientific views on the relation between order and chaos, as order arises from chaos in a specific scientific sense. This principle can be seen as valid in all three of Guattari's three ecologies of mind, society and nature and has been applied to phenomena as far apart as organizational behavior (Dooley 1997) and communication dynamics within families (Pincus 2001). As Guastello (2004, 6) writes, "The general principle is that the organism is a complex adaptive system, and that the turbulence or complexity in its behavior allows for the broadest range of adaptive responses". With chaos, biology becomes no longer the 'bedrock' on top of which separate psychological and social worlds form, because the brain is itself formed through nonlinear interactions with the world (Edelman 2006).

In the clinical domain, Busch (2007, 429) describes pathological infantile attractors as "*black holes in psychological space*, sucking in everything in that comes near its orbit, remaining outside of awareness and thus unable to be modified by other structures." Psychoanalysis can be understood as a *coevolutionary system* (Palombo 1999), a 'destabilization' of such attractors in psychic space, changing point and periodic attractors to chaotic attractors. While most change is confined to the local level and absorbed by wider psychic defences, as the system reaches *self-organized criticality* (Bak 1994) the tiniest local shift can precipitate cascades of disorder through the entire system. Such models of dynamic change are also crucial for understanding the psychological and social shifts in human responses to ecological crisis. In social ecology and group analysis, Stacey (2003, 2006) argues that Bion's (1961) work group and basic assumption groups interact to create regions of stability and disintegration, with potentially creative fractal regions of bounded instability at the edge of chaos between them. Nonlinear fractal geometry undermines any clear line between inside and outside, providing new ways to think about the individual and group in terms of multidimensional fractal borderzones. Similarly, Jaques' (1955) social phantasy systems can be understood as emerging through the self-organization of individual defences, with global patterns feeding back to effect lower levels recursively.

Ecopsychoanalysis, Geophilosphy and Dynamics of Change

For an example of a nonlinear social phantasy ecosystem in climate change, we can turn to Randall's (2005) discussion of the non-active majority that projects environmental concern onto activists functioning as containers for the split-off collective environmental superego. A nonlinear, social systems perspective lets us explore the affective feedback loops carried around the circuit with complex social and psychological effects, as projective and introjective identifications, splittings and scapegoating, reverberate back and forth in new iterations as the system moves forward in time, as other individuals and groups get drawn in, either damping the mad oscillations (Bion 1961) or getting swept up in nonlinear amplification effects. Randal (2005, 176–177) suggests that as collective guilt becomes more shared, it can be "managed in more creative ways", becoming "less persecutory and destructive", where projections are reduced and a larger non-psychotic space created for reparative action. This embodies a system of multistability, with complex movements between basins of attraction as internal objects and affects flow through the network, with major shifts between states, sometimes after long periods when the system seems stuck despite the best efforts to destabilize it by pushing it towards a bifurcation.

We can see our current period as showing disorder and instability in some areas, while seeming stuck and frozen in others. The first can feel frightening, the latter deadening and demoralizing (Marks-Tarlow 2008). Periods of instability are "natural and necessary stages on the path toward greater self-organization" (Eidelson 1997, 68) but with no guarantee that what emerges will be more adaptive. What this research shows is that in a highly complex and interconnected system, relatively small changes of one parameter can have unpredictable (and disastrous) effects on the whole. This has important implications for the effect of climate change on the social, psychological, climate and ecological systems. This can bring a complexity-based approach to Jared Diamond's (2006) research on the collapse of civilizations, and the important roles he uncovered for systemic social interconnectivity, environmental damage and climate change. Crucially for us, many of these societies entered the period of collapse shortly after reaching to their apogee of power and wealth. Climate change appears to have played an important part in the rise and fall of many previous civilizations (Buntgen *et al.* 2011). We do not yet know whether our own civilization will share the fate of many that have gone before, but we would do well to grasp the complex nonlinear effects involved.

The task for change, whether in psychoanalytic clinical practice or social or ecological systems, then becomes experimental, including the search for 'lever points' to open up the possibilities of more radical transformation. As Deleuze and Guattari (2003, 161) write:

> This is how it should be done: Lodge yourself on a stratum, experiment with the opportunities it offers, find an advantageous place on it, find potential movements of deterritorialization, possible lines of flight, experience them, produce flow conjunctions here and there, try out continuums of intensities segment by segment. . . . It is through a meticulous relation with the strata that one succeeds in freeing lines of flight.

Psychoanalytic approaches to ecology have useful practical as well as theoretical applications to a range of fields. Renee Lertzman has been engaging in a fascinating range of psychoanalytically informed research and engagement with industry, organisations and the public. In her book *Environmental Melancholia* (Lertzman 2015) she utilized Dialogic Relational Interviewing to conduct in-depth interviews with people in Green Bay, Wisconsin, to explore their own relationship to nature and their immediate environment, their thoughts about the industry the town relied on, among other questions. She concluded that much of the public dismissed as either apathetic or actively hostile to green concerns are actually deeply connected to and affected by their relation to nature, but that its partly the way such questions are framed that prevents their engagement. Similarly, George Marshall (2015) has been engaging with different organisations and groups and explored the way framing the problem can appeal to differing political and social identities, something Paul Hoggett relates to differing 'subject-positions' and the role of affect. Rosemary Randall on the other hand through the 'carbon conversations' project and other means seeks to apply psychoanalytic and group analytic methods to understanding and working through barriers to change. Finally, in Dodds (2019a) we can see an engagement between ecopsychoanalytic concerns with older pioneering psychoanalytic approaches to the social world (e.g., Fenichel) and developments in the artistic field with combined works with artists to create joint artistic (sculpture, painting, photography) and textual reactions to the contemporary world (Dodds 2019b, 2019c).

Deleuzo-Guattarian philosophy is one of becoming rather than being (DeLanda 2005). Everything, from mountains to bodies to languages, represents structures produced by a temporary slowing down of the vast flow of becoming. Deleuze and Guattari create a vision of a world, according to DeLanda (2006), where "geology, biology, and linguistics are not seen as three separate spheres" but as "coexisting and interacting flows" where "one stratum can serve directly as a substratum for another". As Deleuze and Guattari (2003, 69) put it, "a semiotic fragment rubs shoulders with a chemical interaction, an electron crashes into a language". Deleuze and Guattari follow Bateson towards an ecology of mind leading to new ways of understanding subjectivity, where fallacies in the ecology of ideas have direct and catastrophic results on the social and ecological registers such that "there is an ecology of bad ideas, just as there is an ecology of weeds" (Bateson 2000, 492).

In our current ecological crisis, achieving the necessary ecological flexibility to survive requires a fundamental re-examination of the basic coordinates of our lives. As with the fitness landscape of evolutionary theory, deformed and morphed with each shift in the environment, or the patient stuck on a local optimum, unable or unwilling to cross the threshold to a more adaptive peak, entire species and civilizations have in the past found themselves in dangerous dead ends; including those within the ecology of mind, ways of thinking and being that become pathological if they fail to evolve along with the constantly shifting relations in the constitution of natural and social ecosystems. The contribution of psychoanalysis is to help us overcome such errors of thought through investigating their unconscious roots.

Animality and Virality

Dodds (2012b, 2020a) explores the idea of the animal from an ecopsychoanalytic perspective. The animal has long been a symbol of human psyche and culture, from fairy tales to horror films, Oedipal pets to animal phobias, scapegoating and large-group symbols, philosophy to ideology and myth. Drawing on Deleuze and Guattari (2003), three animal-types (Oedipal, mythic and wild) are identified, and these are placed within Guattari's 'three ecologies' of mind, society and nature, seen as in constant, complex nonlinear interaction with one another. The nonhuman animal extends back to the origin of psychoanalysis (e.g. Freud 1909) with Freud's clinical writings on the rat man, the wolf man, and Little Hans' horses, as well as his cultural writings on the origin of religion and civilization. In both, animal phobias and totems involve displacement of Oedipal anxiety onto the animal substitute. Animal symbols also function in the social ecology of groups (Volkan 2000; Dodds 2012b) as both totemic large-group symbols (British Lion) and 'suitable reservoirs' for archaic aspects of self to 'dehumanize' the enemy during scapegoating and intergroup violence (rat, cockroach). However, prior to humans being forced to take on animal characteristics (dehumanization), first the animal must take on rejected and projected human attributes (deanimalization), with genocidal and ecocidal violence on both sides of the border.

Ecopsychoanalysis interest in the nonhuman-human connection has also been applied to the complex way societies and psyches have responded to the coronavirus pandemic. The resulting anxiety, defence, conflict, effects on clinical practice, facing the possibilities of extinction and death can be fruitfully compared and contrasted with similar responses and reactions to climate change. In "Elemental Catastrophe: Ecopsychoanalysis and the Viral Uncanny of Covid-19", Dodds (2020a) suggests that the virus exists in the uncanny space between life and death, and through anxiety and denials it forces us to become aware in a very literal way of the vast connections between mind, nature, society, ecology and economy. These are no longer abstract but more directly experienced. The viral uncanny may be productive as well as terrible, by calling into question traditional binaries, breaking down old assemblages and building new alliances. This turbulent period may perhaps offer what Morton (2010) calls the 'ontological upgrade' required for this human story to continue into the future. The dangers of COVID-19 are all too real and need to be struggled against, but at the same time they have led to more carbon reductions than all the global summits put together, providing a chance to pause and rethink. The fixed certainties forming the unchangeable background of our societies and economies have proven more mutable than we imagined, giving rise to tremendous anxiety but also a fragile hope, as new forms of connections become possible, putting the world into a chaotic flux without any guarantee of where it will lead.

To conclude, ecopsychoanalysis is an emerging transdisciplinary approach, positioning psychoanalysis and human experience in a wider ecological space with relevance to clinical practice, as well as applications outside the clinic, and helping to understand the complex and sometimes chaotic world we live in.

References

Bak, P. (1994) Self-organized criticality: A holistic view of nature. In Cowan, G., Pines, D., & Meltzer, D. (eds.), *Santa Fe Institute Studies in the Sciences of Complexity, Proceedings Volume XIX. Complexity: Metaphors, Models, and Reality* (pp. 477–496). Addison Wesley.

Bateson, G. (2000) *Steps Towards an Ecology of Mind.* University of Chicago Press.
———. (2002) *Mind and Nature: A Necessary Unity.* Hampton Press.
BBC. (2009) *Green Spaces 'Improve Health'.* Available from: http://news.bbc.co.uk/2/hi/8307024.stm
Bigda-Peyton, F. (2004) When drives are dangerous: Drive theory and resource over-consumption. *Modern Psychoanalysis.* 29:251–270.
Bion, W. (1961) *Experiences in Groups and Other Papers.* Tavistock.
———. (1984) *Second Thoughts: Selected Papers on Psychoanalysis.* Karnac.
Bodnar, S. (2008) Wasted and bombed: Clinical enactments of a changing relationship to the earth. *Psychoanalytic Dialogues.* 18:484–512.
Bonabeau, E., Dorigo, M., & Theraulaz, G. (1999) *Swarm Intelligence: From Natural To Artificial Systems.* Oxford University Press.
Bonta, M., & Protevi, J. (2004) *Deleuze and Geophilosophy: A Guide and Glossary.* Edinburgh University Press.
Buntgen, U. et al. (2011, 4 February) 2500 years of European climate variability and human susceptibility. *Science.* 331(6017):578–582. Available from: www.sciencemag.org/content/331/6017/578.short?rss=1&ssource=mfr
Busch, F. (2007) 'I noticed': The emergence of self-observation in relationship to pathological attractor sites. *The International Journal of Psychoanalysis.* 88:423–441.
Buzzell, L., & Chalquist, C. (eds.) (2009) *Ecotherapy: Healing with Nature in Mind.* Sierra Club.
DeLanda. (2005) *A Thousand Years of Nonlinear History.* Swerve.
———. (2006) *A New Philosophy of Society: Assemblage Theory and Social Complexity.* Continuum.
Deleuze, G., & Guattari, F. (2003) *A Thousand Plateaus: Capitalism and Schizophrenia.* University of Minnesota Press.
Derrida, J. (2008) *The Animal That Therefore I Am.* Fordham University Press.
Diamond, J. (2006) *Collapse: How Societies Choose to Fail or Survive.* Penguin.
Dodds, J. (2011) *Psychoanalysis and Ecology at the Edge of Chaos: Complexity Theory, Deleuze/Guattari and Psychoanalysis for a Climate in Crisis.* Hove: Routledge.
———. (2012a) The ecology of phantasy. In Rust, M-J., & Totton, N. (eds.) (2011), *Vital Signs: Psychological Responses to Ecological Crisis.* Karnac.
———. (2012b) Animal totems and taboos: An ecopsychoanalytic perspective. *PsyArt Journal for the Psychological Study of the Arts.*
———. (2013, 25 March) Minding the ecological body: Neuropsychoanalysis and ecopsychoanalysis. *Frontiers in Psychology.*
———. (2019a) Otto Fenichel and ecopsychoanalysis in the anthropocene. *Psychoanalytic Perspectives.* 16(2):195–207.
———. (2019b) Between art, mind and nature, ecopsychoanalytic reflections on Jaro Varga's '*We don't know that we know*'. Exhibition Text, Huntkastner, Prague.
———. (2019c, 24 May) Feeling the future, finding our place in the world: Ecopsychoanalytic reflections on 'Future Perfect' by Taiyo Onorato and Nico. Krebs. Exhibition Text, Sies + Höke, Düsseldorf.
———. (2020a) Elemental catastrophe: Ecopsychoanalysis and the viral uncanny of COVID-19. *Stillpoint Magazine.* Available from: www.researchgate.net/publication/340870723_Elemental_Catastrophe_Ecopsychoanalysis_and_the_Viral_Uncanny_of_COVID-19
———. (2020b) Future perfect. *Foam Magazine #57: In Limbo*:265–280. EAN 8710966455234-00057. ISSN 0966-5551.
———. (2021) The psychology of climate anxiety. *BJPsych Bulletin.* 45:222–226, doi:10.1192/bjb.2021.18.
Dooley, K. (1997) A complex adaptive systems model of organization change. *Nonlinear Dynamics, Psychology, and Life Sciences.* 1:69–97.
Edelman, G. (2006) *Second Nature: Brain Science and Human Knowledge.* Yale University.
Eidelson, R. (1997, March) *Complex adaptive systems in the behavioral and social sciences. J. Review of General Psychology.* 1(1):42–71.
Fairbairn, R. (1992) *Psychoanalytic Studies of the Personality.* Routledge.
Freud, S. (1905) Jokes and their Relation to the Unconscious. *SE*: VIII, 1–247.
———. (1909) Analysis of a phobia in a five-year-old boy. *Pelican Freud Library*, Vol. 8. 1977.
———. (1911) Formulations on the two principles of mental functioning. *SE*:XII, 213–226.
———. (1916) On transience. *SE*:XIV, 303–307.
———. (1920) Beyond the pleasure principle. *SE*:XVIII, 7–66.
———. (1927) The future of an illusion. *SE*:XXI:1–56.

Frumkin, H. (2001) Beyond toxicity: The greening of environmental health. *American Journal of Preventive Medicine*. 20:234–240.

Frumkin, H., & Louv, R. (2007) The powerful link between conserving land and preserving health. *Land Trust Alliance Special Anniversary Report 2007*. Available from: https://www.atsdr.cdc.gov/emes/training/page6003.html

Genosko, G. (1993) Freud's bestiary: How does psychoanalysis treat animals? *Psychoanalytic Review*. 80:603–632.

Gordon, D. (1999) *Ants and Work: How an Insect Society Is Organized*. Springer-Verlag.

Grigsby, J., & Stevens, D. (2000) *Neurodynamics of Personality*. Guilford Press.

Guastello, S. (2004) Progress in applied nonlinear dynamics. *Nonlinear Dynamics, Psychology and Life Sciences*. 8(1):1–15.

Guattari, F. (1995) *Chaosmosis: An Ethico-Aesthetic Paradigm*. Indiana University Press.

———. (2000) *The Three Ecologies*. Athlone.

Heinberg, R. (2009) The psychology of peak oil and climate change. In Buzzell, L. & Chalquist, C. (eds.), *Ecotherapy: Healing with Nature in Mind*. Sierra Club Books.

Herzogenrath, B. (ed.) (2009) *Deleuze/Guattari & Ecology*. Palgrave Macmillan.

Hoggett, P. (2011, September) Climate change and the apocalyptic imagination. *Psychoanalysis Culture & Society*. 16(3).

———. (2019) *Climate Psychology: On Indifference to Disaster*. Palgrave.

Jaques, E. (1955) Social systems as a defence against persecutory and depressive anxiety. In Klein, M. et al. (eds.), *New Directions in Psychoanalysis*, pp. 478–498. Karnac.

Jordan, M. (2009) Nature and self: An ambivalent attachment? *Ecopsychology*. 1(1):26–41.

Jordan, M., & Marshall, H. (2010) Taking counselling and psychotherapy outside: Destruction or enrichment of the therapeutic frame? *European Journal of Psychotherapy & Counselling*. 12(4):345–359.

Kaes, R. (2007) *Linking, Alliances, and Shared Space: Groups and the Psychoanalyst*. IPA Publications.

Kellert, S., & Wilson, E. (eds.) (1993) *The Biophilia Hypothesis*. Island Press.

Kelso, J. (1995) *Dynamic Patterns: The Self-Organization of Brain and Behavior*. MIT.

Klein, M. (1987) *The Selected Melanie Klein*. Edited by Juliet Mitchell. Free Press.

Kohut, H. (1985) *The Analysis of the Self*. International Universities Press.

Kübler-Ross, E. (1973) *On Death and Dying*. Routledge.

———. (2005) *On Grief and Grieving: Finding the Meaning of Grief Through the Five Stages of Loss*. Simon & Schuster Ltd.

Lertzman, R. (2015) *Environmental Melancholia: Psychoanalytic Dimensions of Engagement*. Routledge.

Marks-Tarlow, T. (2008) *Psyche's Veil: Psychotherapy, Fractals and Complexity*. Routledge.

Marshall, G. (2015) *Don't Even Think About It: Why Our Brains Are Wired to Ignore Climate Change*. Bloomsbury.

Matte-Blanco, I. (1998) *The Unconscious as Infinite Sets: As Essay in Biologic*. Karnac.

Meltzer, D. (1967) *Psychoanalytical Process*. Clunie.

MIND. (2007) *Ecotherapy: The Green Agenda for Mental Health*. MIND.

Morton, T. (2007) *Ecology Without Nature: Rethinking Environmental Aesthetics*. Harvard University Press.

———. (2010) *The Ecological Thought*. Harvard University Press.

Norgaard, R., & Randers, J. (2002, 9 July) Tracking the ecological overshoot of the human economy. *Proceedings of the National Academy of Sciences*:9266–9271.

Panksepp, J. (2004) *Affective Neuroscience: The Foundations of Human and Animal Emotions*. Oxford University Press.

Palombo, S. (2007) Complexity theory as the parent science of psychoanalysis. In Piers, C., Muller, P., & Brent, J. (eds.), *Self-Organizing Complexity in Psychological Systems*. Jason Aronson.

———. (1999) *The Emergent Ego: Complexity and Coevolution in the Psychoanalytic Process*. International University Press.

Piers, C., Muller, P., & Brent, J. (eds.) (2007) *Self-Organizing Complexity in Psychological Systems*. Jason Aronson.

Pincus, D. (2001) A framework and methodology for the study of nonlinear, self-organizing family systems. *Nonlinear Dynamics, Psychology, and Life Sciences*. 5:139–173.

Randall, R. (2005) A new climate for psychotherapy? *Psychotherapy and Politics International*. 3(3):165–179.

———. (2009) Loss and climate change: The cost of parallel narratives. *Ecopsychology*. 1(3).

Roszak, T. (1992) *The Voice of the Earth*. Phanes Press.

Roszak, T., Gomes, M., & Kanner, A. (eds.) (1995) *Ecopsychology: Restoring the Earth, Healting the Mind*. Sierra.

Rust, M-J. (2008) Climate on the couch: Unconscious processes in relation to our environmental crisis. *Psychotherapy and Politics International*. 6(3):157–170.

———. (2020) *Towards an Ecotherapy*. Confer Books.

Rust, M-J., & Totton, N. (2012) *Vital Sign: Psychological Responses to Ecological*. Routledge.

Santostefano, S. (2008) The sense of self inside and environments outside: How the two grow together and become one in healthy psychological development. *Psychoanalytic Dialogues*. 18:513–535.

Sawaya, R. (2010) *The Runaway Effects That Could Accelerate Global Warming*. Available from: http://climate-change.suite101.com/article.cfm/positive_feedback_mechanisms_and_climate_change

Searles, H. (1960) *The Nonhuman Environment in Normal Development and in Schizophrenia*. IUP.

———. (1972) Unconscious processes in relation to the environmental crisis. *Psychological Review*. 59:361–374.

Sobel, D. (2001) *Children's Special Places: Exploring the Role of Forts, Dens, and Bush Houses in Middle Childhood*. (The Child in the City Series). Wayne State University Press.

Sole, R., & Goodwin, B (2000) *Signs of Life: How Complexity Pervades Biology*. Basic Books.

Stacey, R. (2003) *Complexity and Group Processes: A Radically Social Understanding of Individuals*. Brunner-Routledge.

———. (2006) Complexity at the edge of the basic-assumption group. In Gould, L., Stapley, R., & Stein, M. (eds.), *The Systems Psychodynamics of Organizations: Integrating Group Relations, Psychoanalytic, and Open Systems Perspectives* (pp. 91–114). Karnac.

Ulrich, R. (1984) View through a window may influence recovery from surgery. *Science*. 224(4647):420–421.

———. (1991) Effects of health facility interior design on wellness: Theory and recent scientific research. *Journal of Health Care Design*. 3:97–109.

———. (1999) Effects of gardens on health outcomes: Theory and research. In Marcus, C., & Barnes, M. (eds.), *Healing Gardens: Therapeutic Benefits and Design Recommendations* (pp. 27–86). John Wiley.

———. (2000) Environmental research and critical care. In Hamilton, D. K. (ed.), *ICU 2010: Design for the Future* (pp. 195–207). Center for Innovation in Health Facilities.

Ulrich, R., Lunden, O., & Eltinge, J. (1993) Effects of exposure to nature and abstract pictures on patients recovering from heart surgery. Paper presented at the 33rd Meetings of the Society for Psychophysiological Research, Rottach-Egern, Germany. Abstract published in *Psychophysiology*. 30(Supplement 1):7.

Ulrich, R., Simons, R., Losito, B., Fiorito, E., Miles, M., & Zelson, M. (1991) Stress recovery during exposure to natural and urban environments. *Journal of Environmental Psychology*. 11(3):201–230.

Verderber, S., & Reuman, D. (1987) Windows, views, and health status in hospital therapeutic environments. *The Journal of Architectural and Planning Research*. 4(2):120–133.

Volkan, V. (2000) *Animals as Large-group Symbols*. Available from: www.academia.edu/25208096/ANIMALS_AS_LARGE_GROUP_SYMBOLS

Wackernagel, M., Schulz, N. B., Deumling, D., Linares, A., Jenkins, M., Kapos, V., Monfreda, C., Loh, J., Myers, N., Norgard, R., Randers, J., & Monfreda, C. (2002) Tracking the ecological overshoot of the human economy. *Proceedings of the National Academy of Sciences*. 99:9266–9271.

Weintrobe, S. (2012) *Engaging with Climate Change: Psychoanalytic and Interdisciplinary Perspectives*. Routledge.

Wilson, E. O. (2003) *The Future of Life*. Abacus.

Winnicott, D. (1999) *Playing and Reality*. Routledge.

———. (1987) *Through Pediatrics to Psychoanalysis: Collected Papers*. Karnac.

Winter, D., & Koger, S. (2004) *The Psychology of Environmental Problems*. Lawrence Erlbaum Associates.

Žižek, S. (2007) *Censorship today: Violence, or ecology as a new opium for the masses*. Available from: www.lacan.com/zizecology1.htm

33

THE EVOLUTION OF PSYCHOANALYTIC THINKING ABOUT AESTHETICS

Adela Abella

We can describe three stages in the evolution of psychoanalytical thinking on aesthetics, which are intimately connected with the evolution of the discipline. Thus, tracing these three stages not only provides tools for approaching a work of art: it also allows us to take a look at the history of ideas in psychoanalysis. Indeed, these three stages are not neatly delineated, and we often find premises of subsequent models or remnants of preceding ones. Nevertheless, three globally distinct approaches can be identified, which will be described here.

The first stage is represented by the founder of psychoanalysis, Sigmund Freud (1856–1939). Freud defended a vision of art that is essentially optimistic and positive. The accent is placed on the libidinal/sexual aspects, on the quest for pleasure, beauty and omnipotence. In this line, Freud states that art is "almost always harmless and beneficent; it does not seek to be anything but an illusion", unlike religion which is also an illusion but more powerful and therefore more dangerous (1933).[1]

From the very beginning of his work Freud showed a deep interest in artistic activity, mainly literary pieces. Thus, in 1906 he devoted a long study to a novel written in 1903 by W. Jensen, the *Gradiva* (Freud, 1907), which provided a timely occasion to illustrate, and indirectly validate, his first model of the mind.

Briefly summed up, Freud's first model, the dream's model,[2] runs like this: it often happens that a wish, typically of a sexual nature, cannot be acknowledged because of a number of reasons. It can be frustrated by reality, forbidden by an internal moral ban, it can threaten the subject's security, and so on. The wish will therefore be pushed away into the unconscious. However, the repressed wish will not remain quietly secluded in the depths of the mind. On the contrary, it will push back towards the conscious in search of fulfilment. The solution will be found through a compromise where both the wish and the moral ban (or the dictates of reality or the life-preserving aim) will find a certain satisfaction. This is achieved by a series of disguise mechanisms, namely *displacement* (often working through metonymy: the accent is moved from the original representation to a more insignificant one which is connected by continuity, e.g., to drink a glass – the glass pointing to its content); *condensation* (several associative chains converge on a point [e.g., in neologisms such as this one offered by one of my patients: shocked by the ethical fault of a psychotherapist who had invited her patient to a painting's exhibition, he said "psychotherapute" instead of psychotherapist]); *symbolism* (one representation replaces another on the basis of a metaphorical dimension, which implies an association by similarity, for example, a lion can

DOI: 10.4324/9780429297076-39

stand for hunger); *conditions of representability* (given that dreams often use visual images, a thought must generally be capable of being translated into a visual representation); and, finally, *secondary revision* (whose function is to create an appearance of narrative coherence: "fill(ing) up the gaps in the dream-structure with shreds and patches", as Freud says (Freud, 1900).[3]

In artistic activity, disguise takes the form of sublimation: the forbidden wish will find its way out by sticking to a socially valued aim, such as artistic activity. Being compensated and laundered by its marriage to a highly prized enterprise, the public will find a reassuring outlet to the expression of forbidden desires through identification with the artist: *what I am not allowed to do, I can do through an activity as noble as art.* In fact, in this light the artist's specific merit is the capacity to express universal wishes. Thus, through art, the artist – and the public, vicariously – secure psychic gratifications that are unavailable in daily life.

In Jensen's novel, a young archaeologist, Arnold, conceals/expresses his unacknowledged love for Zoe, under the disguise of a series of dreams and delirious ideas. The various vagaries and turns of the novel allowed Freud to show how a repressed wish finds its way to the conscious mind thanks to a number of camouflages. In the following years Freud will show how his dreams model could be extended to very different phenomena: not only neurotic symptoms but also daydreams, children's play, slips of the tongue, myths, and so on. All of them allow the satisfaction of forbidden desires and needs, be it at an individual or a group level.

How can the unconscious repressed wish be deciphered? In a book written four years later, Freud makes an attempt to link Leonard da Vinci's work to what is known of his childhood (Freud, 1910). Freud aims to search for the infantile wish running through Leonardo's works and attitude towards art. Confronted by the scarcity of data at his disposal, Freud describes his method: it is possible to grasp small and apparently trivial details which unveil hidden motivations, such as, in the case of Leonardo, his ledgers for the expenses of his mother's burial. This "method of inquiry . . . closely related to the technique of psychoanalysis" is clearly described a year later in one of Freud's major applications of psychoanalysis to a non-clinical field: anthropology. While trying to find the unconscious meaning of totems and taboos,[4] Freud restates that it is possible to "divine secret and concealed things from despised or unnoticed features, from the rubbish-heap, as it were, of our observations" (1913). Thus, when looking at a work of art we should look carefully at small, incongruent details, which are the pointers towards repressed conflicting meanings.

This approach has proved useful for the understanding of a number of literary and visual art works,[5] but it has an important drawback. If we posit that the essence of artistic pleasure lies in the disguised satisfaction of a certain fantasy, a thorny question arises: how can we understand the different effect of a cheap novelette and a *chef d'oeuvre*? If only or mainly the unconscious content is relevant, both of them should touch us in a similar way.

The second stage of psychoanalytic thinking resolved this quandary thanks to the work of Hanna Segal.

Hanna Segal (1918–2011), a Polish native who worked mainly in London, belongs to an influential group inside the second psychoanalytic generation: the Kleinian group.[6] Drawing on her work with small and very disturbed children, Melanie Klein (1952) proposed a particular view of mental functioning. In a nutshell, at the very beginning the baby has good pleasurable experiences, which she attributes to a "good object", and painful ones which she understands as linked to a "bad object". She loves the first and hates the second. This is called the *paranoid-schizoid* position. With the passage of time and thanks to her cognitive development the baby comes to realise that the good object she loves and needs and the bad object she wants to annihilate are one and the same. Klein called this constellation the *depressive position*. In fact, this problematical situation is a source of distress, but it opens up an avenue towards a substantial leap in the baby's development. She feels sadness at the idea of losing the good object and experiences guilt at the idea of having attacked it and, therefore, of being responsible for its loss. The resolution is found through reparation: the baby will do her best to undo the harm she has done by taking care of the damaged object. It is important to note that these two positions persist all through our lives, in a different ratio and intensity, often alternating in various forms of oscillation: this persistence allows this model to be applied to a number of phenomena, including art.

In short, H. Segal (1952, 1991a, 1991b) brings three main developments to Freud's work on art. First, if Freud suggested sublimation as the basic mechanism of the work of art, Segal proposes to consider it under the prism of reparation. Second, while Freud insisted on the libidinal and positive aspects of art, Segal points out the centrality of aggression. Third, where Freud concentrated on the content of the artistic work, Segal highlights its dialectic relation with the formal aspect. Let's see how these three elements are interrelated in Segal's work.

Freud had related art to the attempt to escape a frustrating reality to the image of dreams or symptoms. Segal, on the contrary, understands artistic activity as an attempt to reparation in the context of the depressive position. For Segal, the creative stimulus is linked to the individual's need to overcome the overwhelming feelings of guilt and despair aroused by her fantasied attacks on her good objects. The individual may feel that she not only attacked the good object (the breast, the mother) in her childhood but that, throughout her life, she has attacked, destroyed and therefore lost other good objects. Art allows us to repair these losses: "all creation is really a re-creation of a once loved and once whole, but now lost and ruined object, a ruined internal world and self" (p. 199). This recreation is done through the formation of symbols. Therefore, its consequence is not only that the individual can mourn what she has destroyed or lost but also that, through this work of mourning, her internal world is enriched. The result of this process is twofold: on the outside a new reality is created in the form of a work of art, while on the inside the ego is enriched and revitalized.

An important contribution of Segal concerns the question of the artist's relationship with reality. In Kleinian theory, the result of the depressive position is precisely the achievement of a deeper contact with reality: the individual no longer sees only the good or the bad side of the object, but both of them together. Unlike Freud who had compared the artist to the daydreamer's attempts to escape from reality, Segal suggests that the artist needs an "extremely high reality sense" on two levels: on the one hand, she needs to be in contact with her internal world and, on the other hand, she needs the mastery of the technical means that allow her to reach technical perfection: "The real artist, being aware of his internal world which he must express, and of the external materials with which he works, can in all consciousness use the material to express the phantasy" (Segal,1952, p. 203).

This deeper contact with reality allows the artist to express not only his loving and caring aspects but also his aggressiveness. In fact, for Segal, ugliness, violence or destruction are integral parts of the work of art. The dynamic interplay between ugliness, in its broadest sense, and beauty opens up to two interrelated processes: on the one hand, this dynamic is the vehicle of integration between good and evil; on the other hand, it gives a particular strength to the work of art.

Another important feature of Segal's thinking concerns the basic mechanism involved in artistic creativity, and in the public's reception of a work of art, which is no longer sublimation but reparation.[7] The best example, she suggests, is Greek tragedy, where an abject crime is committed, so to speak, "innocently", by the force of destiny. The horror of the content and the depressive fantasies that it arouses are compensated for and repaired by the unity, the equilibrium and the formal beauty of the piece. Thus, the charming formal aspects allow the pain aroused by the content to be lived through and overcome. In this conception, and unlike Freud, what matters is not only the content conveyed by the work of art. On the contrary, it is the dialectical interaction between content and formal aspects that is fundamental. This allows us to resolve one of the weak points of the model proposed by Freud, which was not useful in order to distinguish a two-penny novel from a masterpiece on the same subject. Both, Segal says, can express the same fantasy, but the masterpiece owes its capacity for deep impact to the reparative value of formal beauty.

Last but not least, Segal agrees with Freud on an important point: for both of them, the aesthetic pleasure in the public stems from identification with the unconscious ideas and feelings expressed by the artist – be it the disguised satisfaction of a repressed wish (Freud) or the reparation of the fantasized destruction of good objects (Segal). As we will see, this view is at odds with the aspirations of an important group of contemporary artists.

Indeed, Segal's model struggles when confronted with contemporary art, where neither beauty nor identification of the viewer with the artist is a fundamental requirement. Given that the contemporary artistic scene is characterized by multiplicity and eclecticism, with no hegemonic ideology nor doctrinal or formal unity, it is difficult to generalize. However, a frequent goal in present-day artistic endeavour is to provide the spectator not so much a finished work of art but an artistic experience where he can feel and think in a new and personal way. The title of the 2008 Venice Biennale – "*Pensa con I sensi, senti con la mente*" (Think with the senses, feel with the mind)[8] – deftly conveys this aspiration.

In the wake of the postmodern claim for the variety of different legitimate views on a given issue, the questioning about the author's conscious or unconscious intentions has evolved to the questioning of the viewer's contribution. What matters is not what the author had in mind but what the beholder or the reader does with what is offered to her. There is not one pre-existing legitimate understanding of a work of art – the artist's – but a multiplicity of personal recreations by the public, recreations which can overstep and even contradict the author's conscious original intention.

In fact, since the last third of the twentieth century, reception theories in art history have highlighted the active role of the viewer, his capacity to appropriate and re-create a work of art. In doing so, the viewer modifies both the piece of art and herself. Therefore, the artistic domain becomes an area of self-transformation: if you see, feel and think something in a new and highly personal way, this experience may transform your way of relating to yourself and to the world.

One of the first artists who placed the accent on the way the viewer recreates the work of art was French artist Marcel Duchamp (1887–1968), considered by art critic P. Cabanne as "The greatest socio-cultural disturbance of the (XX) century". Duchamp justifies his famous maxim "It is the spectators who make the pictures" as follows: a work of art is "a product of two poles – there's the pole of the one who makes the work, and the pole of the one who looks at it. I give the latter as much importance as the one who makes it". For Duchamp, the artist's role is only that of a "medium" who is denied "the state of consciousness on the aesthetic plane about what he is doing or why he is doing it". The spectator, by "refining", "deciphering and interpreting its inner qualifications adds his contribution to the creative process" (Abella, 2007). Briefly summed up, this line of thought does not only suggest the unavoidable existence of different perceptions of an already finished work of art: the point is that, drawing on the artist's proposition, a series of different *recreations* of the work will be produced: some more interesting, some deeper, some superficial or irrelevant, but all of them legitimate. It is not a question of simple perception by the viewer but a real process of recreation.

A second important aspect of Duchamp's aesthetic credo is his refusal of beauty. Despising the "agreeable" and "attractive" paintings, the "appeal to the senses" as a lowly, animal-like pleasure, Duchamp opposes a dematerialized form of art: art must be cerebral and pure, the creative act is an act of thought; what matters is the idea. There must not only be "an impression, a pleasure. There must be a direction, a meaning, . . . painting . . . should have to do with the grey matter, with our urge for understanding" (Duchamp, 1973, p. 136).

In order to approach these trends of contemporary art, psychoanalysis needed to refine its theory of the conditions for creativity as well as its theory of thinking. Two English psychoanalysts have made major contributions in this respect. The first one, D. W. Winnicott (1971), proposed to consider the realm of culture as an "intermediate area" allowing the encounter between the "inside" and the "outside" of the individual. In this intermediate area, we can bring into play our illusions of omnipotence and, therefore, our creativity.

However, it is maybe W. R. Bion (1897–1979), the analyst whose thinking is more useful in considering reception theories. He did not contribute much to art in a direct way, but his ideas meet some of the concerns of reception theorists (Abella, 2012).

Bion developed certain ideas of Freud and Klein in radically new and sometimes startling ways and has been criticized for what appear to be esoteric and mystical trends.[9]

The traditional psychoanalytical hypothesis concerning the origin of verbal thought linked it to absence: we need the word *table* to refer to it in *its absence*. Bion adds a fundamental aspect: for this process to take place, it has to occur within a relationship with the mother or other privileged partner (Bion,1962a, 1962b). Briefly summed up: when the baby goes through an intense experience, raw sensual impressions, "indigestible facts" of a non-verbal nature are produced in its mind: Bion calls them *beta-elements*: the mother, thanks to her ability to *reverie*, can take in her mind these raw elements, she can contain and elaborate them and, then, return them back to the baby in the form of *alpha-elements*. These alpha elements, for example visual and auditory images, are the building blocks for the construction of thought. Let's take a baby that cries disconsolately. His mother comes, takes him in her arms, contains his despair and calms him down by saying, for example: "You thought mom would never come back". From the repetition of such experiences, the child will build the representation of "mom", "come back" and "never". Even if in this precise situation the mother's hypothesis was false (the child was crying because he was hungry or had been bitten by a mosquito) the child would incorporate the mother's procedure, that is, her capacity of *reverie*: taking in raw experiences, detoxifying them and transforming them into something thinkable. Instead of a distressing experience, a word.

Bion stresses the importance of the development of new thinking, putting forward an attitude of "negative capacity",[10] which opens up the individual to whatever a new experience might present to him. This attitude is conveyed by his famous maxim "without memory or desire". For Bion, psychoanalysis is not a business of working with the past. Its aim is not that the analyst might provide her patient with an unknown truth but, on the contrary, analysis should allow the analysand to find new, deeper and more meaningful truths, through joint work with her analyst. Therefore, the psychoanalytical encounter might rather be compared to mental fitness training, allowing the development of mental muscles. A good analysis should open up an avenue for looking afresh into the world and into oneself and, therefore, allow a process of self-transformation.

In which way may these ideas be useful for the understanding of contemporary art? In my opinion, they allow to explore the way in which artistic activity, either in the artist or in the public, allows to develop one's own creativity, pave the way for new representations of the world and of oneself and, therefore, favour a process of self-transformation.

We have seen three different approaches to art from a psychoanalytical point of view. We will now apply these three models to one of the most frequent iconographies of Christian art, the Annunciations, with the aim of exploring their respective usefulness and limits.

The Annunciations

By the term *Annunciations*, we refer to a set of religious representations in pictorial, mainly European art, ranging from before the fourth century to the present day. They depict the very moment when the angel Gabriel announces to Mary, a young virginal girl of modest circumstances, that she will bear and give birth to the son of God.

The first representation of an annunciation is found in Priscilla's catacomb in Rome and is dated from the late third century: Mary is on a throne, addressed by a wingless angel (there is, however some dispute concerning its reference to the Annunciation: it might refer also to the Visitation, where Mary, pregnant with Christ, visits her cousin Elisabeth, pregnant with John the Baptist). Up to the 12th century, this theme will be mostly represented in Eastern Mediterranean byzantine and orthodox art, often in a hieratic, conventional and scarcely emotional form.

The peak of the representations of the Annunciation will be reached in medieval and Renaissance Catholic Europe. (The Reformation put an end to plastic representations of sacred characters. It also brought about the destruction of a number of preceding works on this subject.) Thus, within the Catholic area, many great occidental painters have produced beautiful and impressive versions of this theme, with an increasingly naturalistic and emotional stance: Fra Angelico, Fra Bartolomeo, Botticelli, E. Burne-Jones, Caravaggio, Crivelli, Donatello (a sculpture, this time), Giotto, Goya, van Eyck, Piero della Francesca, Pilippo Lippi, El Greco, Leonardo da Vinci, Lorenzetti, Martini and Memmi, Murillo, Piero, Poussin, Rossetti, Tiziano, Uccello, van der Weyden, and so on, to which must be added a great number of pictures, drawings, low reliefs and altarpieces made by unknown painters and sculptors.

What Do Annunciations Speak About? Key Representations of the Feminine

The religious theme being central, we may say that they convey also key representations on femininity and maternity.

Two sorts of women are most often depicted in Christian European artistic production: on the one hand, the tempting, corrupting and sexualised female, whose paradigm is Eve. Two famous representatives of this evil image are Delilah and Salome. On the other hand, the Virgin Mary stands for the pure, idealised and beautiful version of femininity. In between the two, we find the more complex images of those heroic women who draw on their carnal sinful charms in order to deceive and aggressively defeat the enemies of their people. This is the case of Judith, treacherously but heroically beheading Holofernes, who is peacefully sleeping after making love. It is not difficult to feel, behind the idealizing stance of such a heroine, a deep typical fantasy: the fright and horror towards the castrating woman that may hide behind the loving one.

The Annunciations belong to the second series of these classical themes, that is, the pure idealized femininity, and is one of the most frequent topics in Christian iconography. This fantasy – a woman being mother to a god without a sexual exchange with a man – has been identified in some ancient cultures such as those of India or Egypt: their function is to highlight the extraordinary magical character of an outstanding individual (a king, a saviour, a hero), announced from the moment of his/her birth. The same theme is found in Greek mythology but with a different focus: Zeus impregnates Danaë, shut by her father in an inaccessible bronze chamber, through a golden rain which breaks through the only opening of her prison. In the Danaë myth, the meaningful point is that Zeus acts out of sexual desire. At first glance, the Annunciations' narrative explicitly links with the Indian and Egyptian tradition: it highlights a noble, pure and asexual conception. So, to say, at a manifest level it stands in clear opposition to the sexual desire conveyed by the Danaë legend. We will see later that, at a latent level, a sexual content is also conveyed by the annunciations, which seeps through some iconographic elements. I will come back to this.

Iconographic Elements

Each artist has produced a particular, original work which reflects the times they lived in with their ideological, religious and artistic concerns, as well as the artist's idiosyncratic personality. Several elements are, however, customary and, as was usual in old times, there is a profusion of symbols familiar to the painter, the sponsor and the public. The main characters are the couple formed by the Virgin Mary and Angel Gabriel. Mary is alone, be it in a palace, a church, in her garden or her bedroom, reading a book (supposedly a prayer book, possibly Isaiah's prophesy concerning the miraculous conception of the Messiah told in the Bible).

Angel Gabriel, depicted as a young man, addresses Mary, who reacts either with a gesture of surprise/awe/refusal or with humble acceptance. There are two main variations: sometimes an authoritative, bold Gabriel addresses a shy, disconcerted Mary; at other times a respectful Gabriel pays tribute to a queenly Mary. The scene is often of an intimate conversation which may be reminiscent of scenes of courtly love, that is a sublimated non-sexual love between a knight and his lady which nevertheless remains of a worldly, human and non-celestial, nature.

The impregnation by God the father is symbolised through a dove which stands for the Holy Spirit, through some rays coming from the heavens or from God the Father himself who is portrayed as a bearded old figure. Some elements with a phallic resonance often stand in between Mary and Gabriel: either some irises or a crystal vase with flowers which traditionally refer to purity and virginity or a column which symbolizes, amongst other things, the Christ or the Church.

During the 19th and 20th centuries, the interest in this topic decreases. We still find some quite classical representations (Burne-Jones, Rossetti) with a secular and human accent. More contemporary art often takes a deconstructive, critical stance far removed from religious concerns. These 20th-century Annunciations are depicted following the different trends in today's pictorial arts, often with a de-idealised, critical ironic and out-crying flavour. Some examples will suffice: Francis Bacon (*Painting 1946*) has produced a terrible and provoking canvas in which we see a monster dressed in black with a white collar, holding a yellow flower in the left hand, covered with an umbrella which is also black. Behind, a bovine carcass whose abdomen is cut open shows the empty hollow of the belly. His second version of *Painting 1946*, dated 1971, follows the same scheme and provides a similarly highly shocking representation. Gwynn Goodner (Figure 33.1) offers a dramatic expressionist version where a winged angel whispers in the ears of a sexualised breasted/wombed Mary: these two artists convey a shocking and violent emotional atmosphere in complete contrast to the peaceful and beautiful standards.

Nando Caballero (Figure 33.2) depicts a bottle of Coca-Cola and a glass traversed by a set of light rays, maybe representing the consumerist bible of our times; a similar suggestion might be carried by Gottfried Helnwein (Figure 33.3), where a girl sitting on the edge of her bed seems to be mesmerized by a very classical angel coming out of a TV set.

Figure 33.1 Gwynn Goodner, *The Annunciation* (1990). Oil on canvas.
Source: With kind permission of the artist.

Figure 33.2 Nando Caballero, *La anunciación 2* (2020). Obra digital.
Source: With kind permission of the artist.

Figure 33.3 Gottfried Helnwein, *Annunciation* (1993). Mixed media (oil and acrylic on canvas), 176 cm × 121 cm.

Source: With kind permission of the artist.

Using Freud, Segal and Bion for the Understanding of the Annunciations

What can we say from a psychoanalytical point of view? Freud's model is useful to tackle a first question: how have both the artist and her public tried to deal with such an extraordinary topic, that is, conception without the participation of a man? Incredulity and distrust run through the Annunciations since the very beginning. In the Evangelist Luke's description of this scene, Mary expresses her surprise at the unbelievable announcement made by the angel: "How will this be, since I know no man?" Despite the limitations of physiological knowledge in olden times and the weight of religious beliefs, the fact is that, even in Luke's narrative, this statement is hard to believe (an angel will have to visit Joseph in order to explain to him the situation). Still more important, the annunciations express a rejection of sexuality, the body being considered, in a Neoplatonic way, as a poor, sinful coffin imprisoning the pure longing-for-God soul. Therefore, it not only entails a denial of everyday experience, but it stands against the acceptance of sexuality – a fact heavy with consequences for each beholder. It is as if the text suggested: "If a holy woman can do without sexuality when making the baby God, then he/she who wants to be near God should be able to do without sexuality in his/her everyday life". How can the painter, and his public, internally deal with such a radical refusal of sexuality?

As I perceive it, this conflict infiltrates the pictorial expression in such a way that both aspects – the repressed and the defence against it – are represented. There are a number of iconographic elements which might convey not only the customary symbolic meaning socially accepted (the iris for purity, etc.) but which could act as a vehicle for the return of the repressed. As Freud had described, the sexuality so totally denied in this scene pierces its way back through a series of various subtle displacements and disguises. Let us consider some of them.

Mary and Gabriel are both handsome young people, often beautifully dressed, who meet in Mary's rooms. The atmosphere is of an intimate exchange. In some images of the Annunciation, for instance those painted by Fra Angelico, there is a blissful atmosphere of calm acceptance, trust and hope. However, this peaceful mood is not the only one: it follows a first movement which is described in Luke's Gospel as a moment of surprise. A number of painters have depicted this initial spontaneous reaction of Mary in terms of bewilderment, fear, refusal or withdrawal.[11] In the oriental Byzantine tradition (Armenian Gospel) we find a narrative which is still more transparent.[12]

In this version, Gabriel comes to Mary twice: the first time Mary is getting some water from a well when an invisible angel greets her. Fearing a devil's stratagem, she flees in horror and prays in these terms: "God of Israel, do not give me over to the temptations of the enemy and the ambushes of the seducer: but deliver me from the traps and the cunning of the hunter". The rest of the Armenian Gospel (chap. 4) is similar to Luke's except that the impregnation is made through the ear (we might say, through the Word, which is another traditional name for God). Thus, Mary's first reaction is that of a young girl fearing seductive, deceiving and aggressive pressure. In other words, the annunciation may be understood as conveying different layers, one of them being the traditional culturally determined woman's fear of a man's violent seduction.

At this point we can consider the distance between Mary and Gabriel. In some cases, the painter takes pains to neatly separate both of them: a wall, a column, a path sets Gabriel at a respectful, cautious distance. At other times, both characters are in a close relation, which in some cases looks like a delightful, mystical dance.[13] This close interaction between two beautiful young persons, which evokes earthly love, is suggested by a number of pictures in which the painter shows Mary's bed, sometimes seen through a half-open door; at other times in the very same room.[14] Caravaggio is even more explicit: a number of art critics have suggested that the angel's finger points critically to the unmade bed behind Mary.

Even the symbolic items intended to signify purity and the strictly spiritual intervention of God, may be seen as carrying another repressed and disguised meaning. Thus, the iris classically stands for purity but its position, between the two young persons, its long stalk setting off towards the Virgin, might suggest other more physical purposes.[15]

The same might be said about the impregnating ray descending from God onto the Virgin. This golden ray is reminiscent of Danaë's golden rain streaming from Zeus to the end of achieving a sexual relation.[16] It is difficult to fathom to what extent this topic was known to the painters of the Annunciation, but a present-day beholder may be drawn to think that this common iconographic element (a ray coming from God down to Mary) conveys a common fantasy, explicit for Rubens and just underlying for the Annunciation painters.

Thus, the images of the Annunciation might convey a set of different meanings. At a manifest level, they may give expression to the Christian anti-sexual narrative concerning the mystery of the conception of the Son of God, where two distinct worlds, the celestial and the human, come together. However, at a deeper, latent level, they may be seen as portraying a sexual encounter between a woman and a man, a relationship which is sometimes pure, trustful and tender; at other times passionate and dreadful; and sometimes also aggressively seductive and deceiving.

The majority of psychoanalysts would accept the application of Freud's ideas to the Annunciations as described up to this point. What can we say about Hanna Segal's contribution? She posited the reparative role of a work of art, in the sense that formal beauty and equilibrium may compensate the anxiety and discomfort aroused by a given issue. Can we identify any source of anxiety in the Annunciation's narrative?

It is difficult to ascertain the thoughts and feelings of medieval and Renaissance viewers confronted with pious images. Nevertheless, we can guess at some probable sources of uneasiness linked to this particular topic. The first one draws on the disturbing fact that for any Christian viewer, the end of the story was already known: the announced baby came to the world with the specific mission of a dreadful death on a cross in order to pay for the salvation of the believers. Mary's gesture of surprise/awe/refusal fits then a double meaning: at an apparent level, it signifies the surprise of a modest girl learning that she will give birth to God. On a more profound level, it conveys the understandable fearful retreat in front of such a terrible fate, a retreat which we can expect at least in the viewer. Another possible source of anxiety is the condemnation of sexual pleasure entailed in this narrative. Virginity is presented as the sacred, pure way which should be imitated by any good Christian, therefore confronting each viewer with the sinfulness of bodily pleasures.

Segal suggests the need of the presence, in the work of art, of death/destruction/ugliness and, simultaneously, of life/creativity/beauty. On a narrative level, portraying the announcement of the birth of a baby that we know will die on the cross carries a tragic undertone similar to that described by Segal in the Greek classics: happiness is confronted to sorrow, hope to despair, birth to extinction. When considering the formal aspect, the underlying unconscious anxieties (both those arousing from the foretold tragic ending and from the rejection of sexuality) are counterbalanced by the beauty of the formal treatment of the picture together with the climate of blissful serenity and harmony. When looking at these pictures we know they speak of a distressing and tragic story, but we are soothed and enchanted by the beauty and the formal perfection of their representations. The dialectic opposition between a disquieting content and its beautiful presentation gives the Annunciation a powerful magnetism which is absent in cheap representations of the same theme.

Moreover, considering the different thematic and formal layers of these works, assigning them the main intention of escaping from frustration seems partial and unconvincing. Following Segal, we might think that the artist is particularly in touch with his own ambivalences (between his love and his destructiveness) and that he manages to communicate them to his viewers. Contemplating an Annunciation could thus allow us to elaborate our own personal conflicts, feel both our aggression and our love, alleviate our feelings of guilt and, identified with the creativity of the artist, revitalize and repair what we feel we have destroyed and lost.

The anxiety aroused by the Annunciation's narrative is more manifest in 20th-century paintings. To what extent are Freud's and Segal's models helpful for the understanding of contemporary art, and, importantly, of the way in which contemporary viewers look at art? It is widely accepted that artistic endeavour both gives expression and contributes to the transformation of social constructs. We may say that the artist expresses a personal version of some fantasies which pertain to, and are shared by, her social group. Thus, looking attentively at pictorial works of art may illuminate the conscious and unconscious meanings, fantasies and feelings that the fact of being a woman carries in a given cultural tradition. However, concerning specifically the Annunciations, we might think that the social implicit assumptions about a woman's role conveyed by these pictures are so distant from our present world that they have become silent for us.

This distance towards this ancient tale was particularly conspicuous in a seminar given to a group of young psychiatrists and psychologists, mainly women, who were usually sensitive, intelligent and eager to engage in discussion. Having invited them to associate on several pictures of the Annunciation, I was surprised by the cold, heavy silence that followed. Finally, one of them said: "I might surely appreciate these pictures if I was informed about their artistic value, but they say nothing to me. I don't understand why you chose them. I cannot identify with a young girl who renounces a sexual life because she is asked to. There is an unbearable submission in it". Another young woman added: "And where is Joseph when something so important is happening to both of them? Guys are often like that; they manage to not be there at the crucial moments".

I was fascinated at this passionate and resentful response which was at the same time admirably fresh and creative. I suggest that their vindictive, angry reaction showed they had felt touched by being reminded of a social role that was unacceptable, and even menacing, for present-day women. Their illuminative reaction may be better understood through reception theories: what matters is not so much what a picture is offering but what the beholder can do with it. Confronted with the Annunciation pictures these young psychologists were able to grasp not the art historians' learned truth or the seminar director's version but their own personal recreation.

I suggest that these young women lived and recreated the very classical Annunciations in terms of their own feelings and expectations regarding sexuality, their relationship with others or what it means for them to be a woman. They put in words their revolt towards the submissive role traditionally given to women as well as some (probably) more personal experiences related to the behaviour of men. They expressed their rejection of an unacceptable submission, strong feelings of abandonment and misunderstanding (firstly with regard to the seminar director, whose intentions they could not understand, and then concerning "guys who manage to not be there"), as well as a willingness to collaborate and grow if the interlocutor was willing to help them. Viewed through Bion's theories, the participants to this seminar were able, in the context of a training activity, to explore their own feelings and thoughts, to exercise their mental musculature and, eventually, to achieve self-transformation and growth. Through these old pictures they transformed what we might call beta-elements (the cold, angry retreat of the beginning) into thoughts and feelings that could be expressed verbally. We can also think that all this mental work was made possible by the space of *reverie* allowed by the containing capacity of the group (had they been alone, these young women would have probably simply ignored what were for them incomprehensible and irritating pictures from a forgone past).

An Exercise in Personal Appropriation

The multiplicity and variety of the personal creative appropriations of a work of art can be exemplified by a particular reading, which will allow us to appreciate some values defended by contemporary psychoanalysis which are akin to the idea of fostering a personal creative appropriation of cultural products.

A very common iconographical feature in the Annunciations concerns a central aspect of femininity: at the Angel's arrival, Mary is by herself, most often reading, in what we can describe as an internal dialogue with herself through a book. Mary is turned towards her inner world, concentrating on the ideas and feelings aroused by the book. She is not busy doing important things: on the contrary, we could say she is in a position of (apparent) passivity and open receptivity. She can therefore listen attentively to the Angel's words and go through an intense emotional experience. Different painters convey the variety of feelings this experience arouses in her: surprise, incredulity, distrust, fear, awe, rejection and, after some internal work, understanding, trust and acceptance.

Bion insisted on the importance of a negative capacity[17] both for the analysts and the patients, and in recent years French psychoanalysis has pointed out the value of an attitude of passivity for mental health: being able to receive, to wait, to differ; having the capacity of listening both to others and to oneself; feeling one's own reactions to what is happening outside and inside. This passivity is only apparent, in the sense that it supposes a great deal of internal work. Moreover, it is the precondition for the establishment of relationships with others. The intense, intimate exchanges between Mary and the Angel may be used as a figuration of this capacity to listen both to oneself and to others and to engage in a meaningful interaction.

In our culture the masculine has usually been identified with action, courage, fighting and involvement with the exterior, whereas the feminine is more associated with reflection, acceptance of passivity, patience and the pre-eminence of internal life. Nowadays we tend to understand these two sets of attitudes as belonging to both genders. Nevertheless, the so-called feminine attitudes do not have presently a good press. Some trends of our present world favour competition, consumerism, perpetual change, multiple ephemeral/virtual relationships, lack of engagement and frenetic excitement, which are at odds with these "feminine", passive, receptive capacities. Therefore, one of the contributions of psychoanalysis to our present world might be the insistence on the value and the necessity of respect for a space where different forms of passivity and receptivity may flourish, and this for everybody and at each period of life: childhood, adolescence, active adult life and old age.

Moreover, those attitudes classically seen as feminine and exemplified by the Annunciations, that is, a disposition to listen, feel and think, the capacity to turn inwards, as well an aptitude to a healthy passivity, are those needed for psychoanalytical work, both for the patient and for the analyst. Contemporary psychoanalysis highlights the importance that the analyst listens not only to her patient but to herself during the process of listening. The analyst should sometimes restrain the ("masculine") activity of interpreting and give way to a ("feminine") receptive listening. The basic idea is that this listening may allow the analyst to feel/think or figure out that which the patient cannot feel/think or figure out by herself. This mental attitude of the analyst is intended to attain archaic levels of the mind, where experiences have been poorly or not at all symbolised and which remain as non-verbal inscriptions or as voids of representation. From this point of view, psychoanalysis aims not only at a certain degree of archaeological recovery of the repressed or the split off but also at a process of transformation and of constructing anew: the construction of new understandings of one's life, the integration of what was rejected and the construction of a mind more able to deal with the struggles and the joys of life. Thus, the Annunciations might prove useful as an image of a double endeavour: on the one hand, work to deal with conflicts, through the iconographic tension between repression and the returns of the repressed; on the other hand, work to give birth to new personal discoveries about oneself, represented by the exchanges between Mary and the Angel.

To sum up, the Annunciation, in its two fundamental meanings as repression of sexuality and acceptance of receptivity, might speak differently to present-day viewers. As the reaction of the young women in my seminar shows, the manifest level – implying a refusal of sexuality and a conception of femininity as necessarily submissive – scarcely speaks to our present secular occidental world, where a high level of sexual freedom is usual and where women increasingly have parity with men. The submissive position of Mary is at odds with the aspirations and behaviour of many women and many men. Thus, the Annunciations convey a certain Christian or social ideology, linked to a given historical and geographical context, to which we might be partially alien. However, it also carries a set of values, beliefs and attitudes which are urgently needed in present times and particularly with reference to psychoanalysis. The importance of listening to oneself and to others, of taking the time to think and to feel as well as the vital need of a space of silence, emptiness and quietness might be the greatest contribution of this ancient religious theme to our present secular world.

Conclusions

I have tried to describe in broad lines three psychoanalytical models that can be useful in approaching works of art. All three have some points in common and some particular characteristics that differentiate from, and sometimes oppose, the others. We could compare them to tinted lenses used to observe reality. Assuming that there is no understanding of reality independent of the theoretical apparatus with which it is observed (the entirely transparent lens does not exist), these models are different vertices from which a certain object is looked at. Thus, the fact that a certain narrative allows escaping the frustration of reality (Freud's point of view which underscores the content) is not contradictory with the specificity and expressive force of a particular work (which was attributed by Segal to the fact that its beauty may compensate the tragic blackness of the subject); neither of these avenues is contradictory with the existence of different personal recreations (following Bion's description of the search for new meanings and personal truths).

In other words, it may happen that different people, or the same person at different times, may use a work of art in a particular way: at one time, the aim (conscious or unconscious) will be to escape frustration, for example through identification with the modest young woman who will be the mother of God. At other times, we might live out and repair the anxieties and powerful raw emotions linked to life, sexuality and death – that is, our feelings of loss, guilt and hope – through the aesthetic pleasure aroused by the beauty of the work. At still other times, we may be able to reflect on or feel previously unknown aspects of ourselves and, therefore, achieve personal growth.

In any case, Freud, Segal and Bion, while thinking along different avenues, would agree on the value of art for mental health and personal transformation, that is, on art's caring, revitalizing and enriching value for the mind

Notes

1 For a discussion of Freud's thinking on issues like the value of art and the roots of creativity, see Abella (2007, 2010, 2016).

2 Later on, Freud proposed a second model, the structural model, in terms of id, ego and superego.

3 These defence mechanisms are fully described in chapter 6 of Freud's 1900 *The Interpretation of Dreams*. This classic book is an excellent introduction to Freud's dreams model.

4 A non-practising Jew, Freud was deeply interested in the origin of religions. In his book *Totem and Taboo*, he attempts to explore this question drawing on the work of some famous ethnologists of his time, Frazer and Wundt. The book was much criticised already at the moment of its publication: Freud was accused of having misinterpreted the ethnological facts and posited undue generalisations. To many present-day psychoanalysts, its main interest lies in the development of a series of constructs like animism, magical and omnipotent thinking, as well as its contributions to the theory of the Oedipal complex, such as ambivalence or unconscious guilt.

5 Freud's main approach to art, that is, the one centred in his dreams model (forbidden desire > repression > return of the repressed under the form of symptoms, dreams, jokes, etc.) has been further developed by an American psychoanalyst, Ernst Kris (1952), who collaborated with art historian Ernst Gombrich. Kris partly took inspiration from Freud's 1905 *Jokes and Their Relation to the Unconscious*, a pleasurable and easy-reading illustration of his dreams model. Freud's work on jokes, slips of the tongue and parapraxes (actions motivated by unconscious intentions) was also influential on the work of philosopher Richard Wollheim (1987), who suggested that paintings can be analysed as parapraxes.

6 Two excellent introductory books to Kleinian thought are Hinselwood R. H. (1989) and Bott et al. (2011).

7 It should be noted that the mechanisms of sublimation and reparation have a basic kernel in common. According to Segal, both imply a process of renunciation: in sublimation the giving up of an instinctual satisfaction, in reparation the loss of an object. Thus, both rest on a mourning process and both lead to the formation of symbols (Segal, 1952, p. 202).

8 This apparent paradox – thinking with the senses, feeling with the mind – is not really one in psychoanalytic thought. Thus, Melanie Klein proposed the concept of "memories in feelings", pointing out that preverbal records can resurface in the individual in the form of feelings. The intimate link between thought and feeling also appears in the notion of insight: for an insight to have a therapeutic effect, the cognitive content (*I have experienced this*) must be accompanied by the associated emotion (*and I felt that*). When the association between the cognitive representation and the deep corresponding emotion does not occur, we witness either emotional rationalization or catharsis. Both of them lack the capacity to durably transform the mind.

9 Bion's writtings are often difficult to read. There are many good introductions to his work, such as the one by G. Bléandonu (1990).

10 An expression taken from the poet John Keats.

11 See Guido da Siena or Sandro Botticelli.

12 This version is also contained in *The Golden Legend* (*Legenda aurea* or *Legenda sanctorum*), a collection of the lives of saints compiled around the year 1260 by Jacobus de Voragine, archbishop of Genes, that was widely read in late medieval Europe.

13 See, e.g., Ludovico Carracci 1603–04 or the several Annunciations painted by El Greco.

14 See Filippo Lippi 1440, Gentile da Fabriano, Jacobo Bellini, J. Tintoretto, J. Provoost, V. Carpaccio, Leonardo da Vinci or Caravaggio.

15 See Simone Martini and Lippo Memmi, Filippo Lippi c. 1443 or L. Carracci 1585.

16 Peter Paul Rubens, *Danaë and the Shower of Gold*, 1577–1640.

17 Taking the expression from Keats, Bion refers to an attitude of "being open to whatever new might arise in the session", that is, with "no memory, no desire and no understanding". For a detailed discussion of this concept, see Abella (2012).

References

Abella, A. (2007). Marcel Duchamp: On the fruitful use of narcissism and destructiveness in contemporary art. *Int. J. Psycho-Anal.* 88(4): 1039–1059.

Abella, A. (2010). Contemporary art and Hanna Segal's thinking on Aesthetics. *Int. J. Psycho-Anal.* 91(1): 163–181.

Abella, A. (2012): John Cage and W. R. Bion: An exercise in interdisciplinary dialogue. *Int. J. Psychoanal.* 93(3): 473–487.

Abella, A. (2016). *Psychoanalysis and the arts: The slippery ground of applied analysis. Psychoanal.* Q. 2016(1): 89–120.

Bion, W. R. (1962a). A theory of thinking, Int J. Psycho-anal, Vol. 43. Reprinted in *Second Thoughts,* (1967)

Bion, W. R. (1962b). *Learning from experience.* London: William Heinemann (reprinted London: Karnac Books).

Bléandonu, G. (1900). *Wilfred Bion. His life and works (1897–1979).* London: Free Associations, 1994.

Bott, E., Milton, J., Garvey, P., Couve, C., Steiner, D. (2011). *The new dictionary of Kleinian thought.* London: Routledge.

Duchamp, M. (1973). *The essential writings of Marcel Duchamp: The salt seller,* marchand, du sel, Sanouillet, M., Peterson, E., editors, p. 196. New York, NY: Oxford University Press.

Freud, S. (1900). *The interpretation of dreams,* SE, IV–V.

Freud, S. (1905). *Jokes and their relation to the unconscious,* SE, VIII.

Freud, S. (1907 (6)). *Delusions and dreams in Jensen's Gradiva,* SE IX, 3–93.

Freud, S. (1910). *Leonardo da Vinci and a memory of his childhood,* SE XI, 57–135.

Freud, S. (1913(12)). *Totem and taboo,* SE XIII, 1–162.

Freud, S. (1933). *New introductory lectures on psycho-analysis.* Standard Edition 22, pp. 5–182.

Hinselwood, R.D. (1989). *Dictionary of kleinian thought.* London: Free Association books.

Klein, M. (1952). Some theoretical conclusions regarding the emotional life of the infant. In: M. Klein, P. Heimann, S. Isaacs and J. Rivière, editors, *Developments in psychoanalysis*, pp. 198–236. London and New York: Hogarth Press.
Kris, E. (1952). *Psychoanalitic explorations on art.* New York, NY: International Universities Press.
Segal, H. (1952). A psycho-analytical approach to aesthetics. *Int. J. Psycho-Anal.* 33: 196–207.
Segal, H. (1991a). Art and the depressive position. In: *Dream, phantasy and art.* New York, NY: Routledge.
Segal, H. (1991b). Imagination, play and art. In: *Dream, phantasy and art.* New York, NY: Routledge.
Winnicott, D. (1971). Creativity and its origins. In: *Playing and reality*, pp. 65–85. London: Tavistock.
Wollheim, R. (1987). *Painting as an art.* Princeton: Princeton University Press.

INDEX

Note: Page numbers in *italic* indicate a figure on the corresponding page.